CORIOLIS

14455 North Hayden, Suite 220 • Scottsdale, Arizona 85260

Dear Reader:

Coriolis Technology Press was founded to create a very elite group of books: the ones you keep closest to your machine. Sure, everyone would like to have the Library of Congress at arm's reach, but in the real world, you have to choose the books you rely on every day *very* carefully.

To win a place for our books on that coveted shelf beside your PC, we guarantee several important qualities in every book we publish. These qualities are:

- *Technical accuracy*—It's no good if it doesn't work. Every Coriolis Technology Press book is reviewed by technical experts in the topic field, and is sent through several editing and proofreading passes in order to create the piece of work you now hold in your hands.

- *Innovative editorial design*—We've put years of research and refinement into the ways we present information in our books. Our books' editorial approach is uniquely designed to reflect the way people learn new technologies and search for solutions to technology problems.

- *Practical focus*—We put only pertinent information into our books and avoid any fluff. Every fact included between these two covers must serve the mission of the book as a whole.

- *Accessibility*—The information in a book is worthless unless you can find it quickly when you need it. We put a lot of effort into our indexes, and heavily cross-reference our chapters, to make it easy for you to move right to the information you need.

Here at The Coriolis Group we have been publishing and packaging books, technical journals, and training materials since 1989. We're programmers and authors ourselves, and we take an ongoing active role in defining what we publish and how we publish it. We have put a lot of thought into our books; please write to us at **ctp@coriolis.com** and let us know what you think. We hope that you're happy with the book in your hands, and that in the future, when you reach for software development and networking information, you'll turn to one of our books first.

Keith Weiskamp
President and Publisher

Jeff Duntemann
VP and Editorial Director

Look For These Other Books From The Coriolis Group:

Access 2000 Programming Blue Book

Access 2000 Client/Server Gold Book

Visual Basic 6 Programming Blue Book

Visual Basic 6 Black Book

Visual Basic 6 Core Language Little Black Book

Visual Basic 6 Object-Oriented Programming Gold Book

Visual Basic 6 Client/Server Programming Gold Book

Visual C++ 6 Programming Blue Book

To Brett: You are the light of my life; thank you so much for being my love, my wife, my partner. I love you always.

—Lars Klander

This book is dedicated to every user who ever dreamed of smart applications, to every manager who ever wished for prescience, to every developer who just wants to hear those two simple words "Works great!", and to all the great sci-fi writers who envisioned what could be many years ago.

—Dave Mercer

❧

About The Authors

Lars Klander, MCSE, MCSD, MCT, is the author or co-author of over half-a-dozen books, including *1001 Visual Basic Programmer's Tips*, and the winner of the 1997 *Visual Basic Programmer's Journal* Reader's Choice award. A professional network security consultant and Microsoft Certified Trainer, Klander has written on a wide variety of programming and network security topics, ranging from books about C/C++ programming to books about creating speech applications. Klander has been a professional author and trainer for several years and a computer professional for over 15 years. You can reach him at **lklander@lvcablemodem.com**.

Dave Mercer is a veteran database user, having worked in an industrial facility for over 20 years. From 1981, when Dave first used an Apple computer to solve a production problem, he became convinced that there must be a better way. He now uses Microsoft Access to design database solutions from his desktop for himself and others, both professionally and for fun. Dave recently wrote another book for The Coriolis Group called *MOUS Access 97 Exam Cram*. He is certified as an Access 97 Expert. Dave operates AFC Computer Services in Spring Valley, California, where he lives with his wife, JoAnn, and his cat, Taffy. You'll find him researching and designing databases in his office, or teaching at the local community college. You can reach him at **mercer@e4free.com**.

Acknowledgments

In publishing, like any other business, you learn quickly that the people around you can make you look good or they can make you look bad. While Dave's and my names are the only ones that appear on the front of the book, it takes a lot of people to put together all the text that makes up something of this size. While the number of contributors is too great to mention, I would like to thank several people who played key roles in the finishing of this book. First and foremost, Ann Waggoner Aken, the project editor for the book, is always a joy to work with and yet still manages to juggle more projects simultaneously than a circus full of clowns. Meg Turecek and Jon Gabriel, the production coordinators, and their team of layout professionals managed to take my chicken-scratch drawings and make them look good (no mean task) while still laying out a beautiful book. Robert Clarfield, the CD-ROM developer, and Diane Enger, the marketing specialist, helped put together crucial add-ons for the book, including all the CD-ROM contents and the back cover.

But the real kudos go to our editors. Our two copy editors, Bonnie Smith and Judy Flynn, who slaved over chapter after chapter to help ensure that every sentence in every paragraph made sense and was readable. Just as marvelous was our technical editor, Amy Sticksel, who saved me many instances of "egg-on-the-face" in making sure that all the code in the book was perfect, and worked as advertised—and didn't balk to suggest an alternate method where appropriate.

Last but not least, Stephanie Wall, the acquisitions editor for the project, and David Fugate, our agent, put us all together, and helped keep us both (or at least me) in dog kibble while the project was being completed.

—Lars Klander

My heartfelt thanks to Lars Klander, Ann Waggoner Aken, Stephanie Wall, Meg Turecek, Jon Gabriel, Robert Clarfield, Jody Winkler, and David Fugate for all their hard work making this book a reality, and for their patience when things got rough. Much appreciation is also due William Reschke, Robert Siciliani, and Dennis Araujo for their inspiring leadership and wholesale commitment to constant improvement and excellence in business. Finally, my warmest thanks and gratitude to my wife and family, JoAnn, Mike, and Charlene, whose total support made all the difference.

—Dave Mercer

Foreword

When I was first asked to write a foreword to a text on databases, I wondered what I might say that would be helpful to those few souls who even bother to read forewords. I certainly had no ambitions to deal with the technical issues of database development. The various text authors are the experts in that area. I then abandoned several philosophical approaches that endorsed decisions based on real data as more ethical and effective than decisions made with little or no objective data. I finally came back to the idea that this text is primarily intended for people who are developing databases. Since I am often accused of being data-driven to a fault, I decided to share with the reader what I believe a customer should reasonably expect from a database developer. From my perspective, there are four elements a database developer needs to accomplish in order to provide a good product for a potential consumer of data:

- Find out what questions the customer wants to answer.

- Determine what data is required to answer the questions.

- Simplify the data collection process.

- Automate the report generation function of the database.

My first point is that database developers need to work with database users to determine the complete range of questions to be answered. My experience is that many people initially ask for data in order to answer one particular question. For example, as a facilities manager, I want to know the number of planned maintenance hours for the equipment I am responsible for maintaining. The question is straightforward and the approach seems simple. All that is necessary is to examine each maintenance plan and add up the planned maintenance hours to arrive at a total. But, as it turns out, as soon as I know the total number of hours, I want to know how many of those hours required electricians as opposed to mechanics. Then I want to know how many hours I need to expend in a particular month. My point is that the database developer should understand that data is likely to beget requests for more data. How well the developer anticipates the need for associated data affects the customer's perception of the competency of the database developer and the usefulness of the database.

The second element requires the database developer to interact with people who have specific knowledge in the topic area. To extend the example from the preceding paragraph, the database developer needs to talk with experienced maintenance personnel to find out what particular information is important in determining the maintenance requirements for industrial equipment. Some obvious items might include lubrication requirements or routine replacement of filters. My point is that database developers are unlikely to be, and do not need to be, expert in a particular field in order to construct a very effective database. What is important is that database developers do not presume they have complete knowledge of what data is required to answer the user's questions.

The developer's ability to simplify data collection, the third element, is critical to the customer's decision to use databases. Data collection can be time consuming and expensive. No user wants to pay for data more than once. The database may provide a single slice in time, or the data may be continuously collected and analyzed. In either case, both the required data sources and the specific data must be clearly identified to whoever is going to gather the data. A system for continuous data collection requires significant attention to accuracy and cost.

After investing the time and resources to develop a database, the customer needs to generate reports, the fourth important element in database development. The report is the end product the customer uses to make decisions. Too often, as a customer, I've had to engage specialists in order to generate reports from the database that I already financed. A report function that allows the customer to personally generate tailored reports is an absolute requirement. After all, neither the customer nor the developer can anticipate all the reports that are potentially available from a well-developed database.

Finally, I am convinced there are two primary reasons that decisions are made without data. The first is that many of your potential customers have no idea how to gather the necessary data. The second reason is that many decision makers perceive the cost of data collection to be unacceptable. I believe that database developers who pay attention to the four elements I discussed and the expert guidance provided in this text will find an increasing number of enthusiastic customers for their work.

Respectfully,
Robert Siciliani, Ed.D.
Director, Industrial Planning

Contents At A Glance

Table Of Contents

Part II
Database Fundamentals

Part III
Modern Database Implementation

Part IV
Microsoft Access 2000 Overview

Part V
Microsoft Access 2000 Usage

Part VI
Database Application Design Reference

Part VII
Microsoft Access 2000 GUI And VBA Programming Reference

Chapter 25
Creating Forms And Reports **763**

Chapter 26
Creating Macros And Modules **803**

Part VIII
Microsoft Access 2000 And Client-Server Development

Introduction

This book is about power, the growing power of databases, computers, and networks to slash costs and dramatically increase effectiveness of communications and management. Databases touch everyone's lives in some way or another, and a clear understanding of what works and what doesn't puts that power within reach.

This book is aimed at *everyone* who must participate in a database project to ensure success: database designers, end users, database administrators, senior managers, front-line managers, as well as those who must wear all these hats at once.

- For experienced database designers and administrators, this book contains complete coverage of Microsoft Access 2000 in easy-to-understand (and use) examples, with plenty of reusable code and screen shots.

- For managers and end users, this book contains plain-English explanations of how databases are constructed, what the limitations are, and a broad, exciting view of the potential.

- For those who must act as designer, manager, and user, this book takes you from the most basic fundamentals to the most advanced programming steps, without requiring a degree in computer science.

In every sense of the word, this book is a practical, day-to-day guide for people involved in building database solutions. Not only does it guide you through the phases of successful database projects (large and small) and the pitfalls that have ruined some, it teaches you the language and terminology used on all sides as you go: project management, process reengineering, relational models, programming fundamentals, and so on. The emphasis throughout the book is on enhancing communications, because clear and timely communication is the primary attribute of a successful database solution.

Communication takes work. Everyone must be working from the same playbook for a database application to be effective and achieve widespread use. Traditionally, databases have been designed by computer scientists far removed from the day-to-day activities of work. A team of systems analysts would show up one day, gather what information they could about a process, then spend a year or two in the ivory tower building the application. The application would be instituted, workers trained to fill out the forms, and the reports would print, all according to the now-dated but assuredly very accurate specifications. For some applications, this system worked quite well, but for others it failed miserably. Where failure occurred, the primary cause was rapid change: changes in processes, requirements, business conditions, even changes in computer literacy. Today, because change is constant and the pace of change continues to accelerate, only excellent communication among everyone involved can overcome the swirling confusion born of change.

This book gives everyone the playbook that they need to achieve these implementation goals. It takes the best of all traditional methodologies for rebuilding an organization's processes *and* for developing and constructing database solutions, explains them concisely, and blends them together into a powerful toolkit for building effective applications in a rapidly changing environment. The power of Microsoft Access 2000 combined with the proven methods outlined in this book increase the probability that your database application, no matter the size, will "work" from all perspectives.

For the managing members of the team, the book helps you create a plan for effective and consistent implementation of your applications, whether destined for internal use throughout the enterprise or for public consumption. For those responsible for the creation of the implementation—the developers, power users, and users who will interact with the application on a regular basis—this book teaches you everything you need to know about making the application not only perform its tasks, but perform them well.

No matter what environment you are developing for—from standalone databases at workstations to databases that will serve intranet and Internet users—this book teaches you how to address development issues in that environment and make sure your product not only works, but shines. Real-world examples, step-by-step explanations, and thousands of lines of program code all work together to ensure that you have all the tools you need to be successful.

Contents Of This Book

This book is divided into 8 parts, intended to guide you through the steps of database development with Access from beginning to end. Part I, "Fundamentals Of Information," contains three chapters that consider the nature of information and how information relates to the design of databases. The three chapters in the section, Chapter 1, "Foundations For Database Construction," Chapter 2, "The Nature Of Information," and Chapter 3, "Data Organization," guide you through the principles of information theory and the ways in which data is organized. Each chapter provides you with important information that you must understand to master effective techniques of database design.

Part II, "Database Fundamentals," takes the information theory that you learned about in the first three chapters and brings it to the level of database design theory and principles. Chapter 4, "Relational Databases," introduces you to the principles of database design when working with relational databases like Access 2000. Chapter 5, "Database Structures," looks at the overall theory of database design and reviews the principles of relational database design that you learned in Chapter 4. Chapter 6, "Advanced Database Systems," considers the nature of advanced database architectures and the networks required to support them. By the time you finish Part II, you will have a solid knowledge base for database design—not only with Access, but with any relational database product.

Part III, "Modern Database Implementation," moves on to some of the specific types of database uses in business today. Chapter 7, "Data Warehousing," covers the construction of data warehouses in depth. Chapter 8, "Applications and Operating Systems," covers practical application and operating systems (OS) issues, namely, how to decide whether to buy or make apps and OSs, and how to find and use them if you do decide to buy. Chapter 9, "Marketing," discusses the important considerations for you to keep in mind when preparing to distribute your Access products. From identifying your target market to measuring and adjusting your market strategy, effective marketing techniques can make a product successful or, if implemented poorly, can ensure it never sells a copy.

Part IV, "Microsoft Access 2000 Overview," contains four chapters that address the specific improvements and changes to Access 2000, and the specific purposes for which Microsoft designed the Access 2000 product. Chapter 10, "Access 2000 Technologies," gives you a broad overview of some of the many component technologies that Access uses to simplify user access. Chapter 11, "New Features And Trends In Access 2000," considers some of the directions in which Microsoft has moved the Access product, including a discussion of the new Jet 4 engine and new integration with Microsoft's BackOffice products, specifically SQL Server. Chapter 12, "Access Purchasing And Installation," discusses such important implementation issues as who needs Access installations and what level they need, what the different types of Microsoft Office suites are, and specific installation concerns to keep in mind when purchasing the new Access 2000 product. Chapter 13, "Access 2000 Distribution And Training," addresses specific issues related to the deployment of the Access program in your enterprise. It also discusses built-in training support in the Access product and issues to consider when determining how and who to train.

Part V, "Microsoft Access 2000 Usage," contains three chapters, each of which considers a general category of the target market for the Access product and how to design databases for that market. Chapter 14, "Access For Personal And Small Office/Home Office Use," addresses common uses of Access at home and in the small office setting. It discusses both common situations in which you might use Access databases and ways in which to create those databases. Chapter 15, "Using Access In A Corporate Environment," addresses common techniques for Access deployment within companies. It also contains your first introduction to the new Access

Data Projects (ADPs) and their use as a SQL Server database front-end. Chapter 16, "Using Access For Scientific And Medical Purposes," considers common methods and implementations for Access in the scientific and medical communities. It also provides an introduction to the use of Access's graphing capabilities and presents useful information in both types of deployment environments.

Part VI, "Database Application Design Reference," moves on to the creation of databases in Access 2000. The five chapters in this section provide you with a method that you can use to define and create databases to meet any need. Chapter 17, "Problem Definition And Design Planning," discusses the specific steps you should take in planning the design of a database to solve a particular problem and walks you through an extended example of these crucial steps in the design process. Chapter 18, "Planning And Design," moves on to the specific discussion of designing a database in accordance with the design planning that you performed in Chapter 17. Chapter 19, "Database Construction," shows you how to take an actual design diagram and convert it into table and database definitions in Access. Chapter 20, "Implementation—Beta Testing And Bug Checking," moves on to the testing and implementation phases of application design, including discussions of the testing process you should use and more. Chapter 21, "Completing The Implementation," discusses post-release improvements you can make to the application, including optimization, compacting, and repair of the database, as well as using the Access-provided tools to analyze and improve performance of your application.

Part VII, "Microsoft Access 2000 GUI And VBA Programming Reference," covers the low-level, "nuts and bolts" of Access 2000 programming. The chapters take you from the initial creation of a database and its component tables through advanced programming with ActiveX Data Objects (ADO), Data Access Objects (DAO), and database management and security. Chapter 22, "Installation, Setup, And Configuration," discusses the installation specifics of the Access product, including the options you have during setup. It also introduces you to some of the specifics of Access database design—both for the standalone and the client-server environment. Chapter 23, "Developing Tables And Relationships," introduces you to the specifics of table creation and relationship definition, the core of database design. Chapter 24, "Creating Queries," takes you into the heart of relational database work, by teaching you how to create the different types of queries that lie at the heart of SQL's power. Chapter 25, "Creating Forms And Reports," teaches you the knowledge you need to create user interfaces and design effective reports that output data in the most usable form. Chapter 26, "Creating Macros And Modules," explains Access's macro language and introduces you to modules, which will contain Visual Basic for Applications code—code which will, in turn, unlock significant additional power for your database applications. Chapter 27, "Using Modules And Visual Basic For Applications," builds on the knowledge you gained in Chapter 26 to teach you what you need to know about writing VBA programs to "power-up" your Access applications. Chapter 28, "Working With DAO And ADO," introduces you to the database objects that VBA lets you use to manipulate Access, SQL Server, Oracle, and other ODBC- and OLE DB-compliant databases. Chapter 29, "Using Class Modules With Access," describes some basics of object-oriented programming and how you can use VBA class modules to implement custom objects within your Access 2000 applications. Chapter 30, "Advanced Database Design Techniques," shows you how to take advantage of VBA and Access's built-in features to make your applications more professional. It also focuses in-depth on the administration of security within your Access database.

Part VIII, "Microsoft Access 2000 And Client-Server Development," contains five chapters that teach you about client-server programming with Access 2000 and different server-based database products, as well as how to create World Wide Web front-ends for Access or server databases. Chapter 31, "Client-Server Programming With Access 2000," introduces you to SQL Server and working with back-end products from Access. It also covers, in detail, important conceptual information about client-server design that is applicable to any back-end. Chapter 31 also introduces you to the Microsoft SQL Developer Engine (MSDE), a local implementation of SQL Server that you can use to design SQL Server databases on your development machine. Chapter 32, "Using Oracle And Access For Client-Server," teaches you the fundamental concepts of Oracle database design and the differences in development between Access front-ends for SQL Server and Oracle. Chapter 33, "Advanced Client-Server Techniques," takes the knowledge from Chapters 31 and 32 and sends it to the next level with important information about topics such as triggers and stored procedures, transaction processing, Access Data Projects (ADPs), and more. Chapter 34, "Web Front-End Development," moves to the largest client-server environment in the world—the Internet. It covers historically proven and commonly used techniques for exposing databases through HTML pages. Chapter 35, "Using Data Access Pages For Web Front Ends," moves on to Microsoft's proprietary Access front-end technology, Data Access Pages (DAPs), which let you develop highly customized, highly responsive front ends for your Access databases, all from within the Access Interactive Development Environment (IDE).

In addition to a complete index, the book also contains an appendix of additional resources. From the first 9 chapters that step you through the fundamentals of database design and relate them to good programming practice and business process reengineering, to the next 26 chapters that cover every detail about how Access 2000 works (including how it interacts with the Web and mainframe databases), the purpose of this book is to build a common ground on which all people, from the novice user to the most sophisticated IT developer, can work together. Remember, people in organizations today recognize how important it is to make the powerful software tools on their desktops useful, and they need a tool like this book to make it happen.

Part I

Fundamentals Of Information

Chapter 1

Foundations For
Database Construction

In Depth

Prerequisites To Database Design

This chapter introduces the concepts of systems analysis, process engineering, and project management as central to any systematic effort to produce a successful database solution. We lay out the ground rules for everyone involved, expose the misperceptions and pitfalls common to most database projects, and offer a conceptual framework for building successful solutions. We call this new paradigm *Knowledge Design* (KD).

Everyone is a knowledge worker or should be. If your job is so repetitious that no thought is required, sooner or later someone will automate it. If thought is required, you're processing data into information and making decisions, which means automation can probably assist. Not all tasks can or should be automated, but the list is growing rapidly as technology prices fall and performance increases. The question is: When is a database solution appropriate?

Why Build A Database Solution?

A database is nothing more than a collection of data stored in an organized manner. The object of constructing any database should be to provide information to some user. Of course, the basic difference between data and information (taught in all introductory computer courses) is that data has no inherent meaning, while information has meaning to someone.

Long before computers and database software arrived on the scene, people were accumulating data and turning it into information. It's such a common activity that we may not even realize we're doing it. That's why it's so easy to jump to the conclusion that a database is required to solve a problem without carefully evaluating other alternatives first.

It's comical to review some failed database projects because simpler, cheaper, and much more effective solutions were available but never considered. So start by pushing computers and databases completely out of your mind, and examine the situation as objectively as possible. Process engineering, for example, looks at the processes any solution must support.

Process Engineering (Or Reengineering)

Individuals and organizations conduct many activities each day, generically called "living" or "doing business." Each of these activities is performed for a reason (goal, objective), perhaps several reasons. When the activities are designed to achieve a business goal, they're usually referred to as processes.

Effective processes achieve goals with the correct amount of resources, at the right time, and with acceptable quality. Unfortunately, effective processes (and ineffective ones as well) tend to become habits, and habits tend to persist long after they've become ineffective or even counterproductive. Process engineering or reengineering attempts to rebuild or reshape inefficient processes so they're once again effective or to eliminate obsolete processes altogether. Of course rebuilding processes implies change, and change is often frightening.

Change

Process engineering is associated with many negative terms: rightsizing (really a euphemism for downsizing), reengineering, efficiency experts, labor standards, and so on. As anyone who's been through it will tell you, fear and loathing are the ordinary reactions to the news that your processes will be reengineered.

Change is the culprit. We work hard to learn our jobs, to establish relations with those we work with, to gain a feeling of competence. Then some hotshot with no understanding of actual working conditions comes along to tell us how to do it better. And what's our reward? We may be laid off, forced to do more work for less pay, or worst of all, we may have to start all over to relearn our jobs. Who needs it?

On top of all that, management sends us to change management seminars, where we're told that significant change in our lives (like "rightsizing") may cause serious illness or even death because of the stresses involved. No wonder change is perceived as the equivalent of a death sentence!

Like it or not, though, rapid change is the one constant of life near the millenium. People and organizations that learn to cope with change and become more effective succeed; those who don't fade or fail. And like it or not, computer and database literacy has become just as fundamental to coping with the stresses of change as reading the newspaper and exercising daily.

Knowledge is power, and knowledge of the processes governing your situation coupled with knowledge of how computers and databases affect it can put you in the driver's seat. You can lead change, instead of being driven by it. You can become the changer, instead of the changee. As the old saying goes, if you can't beat them, join them (preferably as the leader).

Process Engineering

Process engineering views all work-related activities performed by organizations (and individuals) as goal-oriented processes. In addition, because change is constant and rapid, processes must be improved frequently to remain effective and efficient.

Phase 1—Understanding The Mission

The first step in understanding your situation is looking at the processes involved, and every employee should be involved. Do you remember Quality Circles (QC), Process Action Teams (PAT), Total Quality Management (TQM)? Rather than just another management fad to please the board of directors, these were fundamental instructions about how to objectively define the processes by which products are produced. Each new iteration may have a new name, but they all refer to some form of process engineering or Business Process Reengineering (BPR).

It starts with the fundamental culture and the goals of the organization you work within. Does your company or your business have a mission statement? If not, take a few minutes and jot down some of the things you know you're striving for. To tell whether your project is successful, you must measure the before and after (whatever that might be), and you need a starting point as a reference from which to measure (like the equator or the North Pole to measure longitude and latitude). That starting point is the organization's mission.

Phase 2—Process Analysis

From the overall goals of the organization (and the processes that directly support them), goals, objectives, and processes are defined more and more specifically in terms of cost, schedule, and quality until your specific processes are mapped and measured. Formally, this step is called the inventory of core processes.

For example, perhaps you must produce design drawings of mechanical components for a product your company makes. You must meet certain drawing standards (quality), you have a deadline to meet (schedule), and your boss expects you to get the job done with a reasonable expenditure of effort (cost).

Others affect your work as well. Before you can begin, the specifications for the component must be outlined (and hopefully you participate in this process). Perhaps you have a draftsman who turns your sketches into a Computer-Aided Design (CAD) drawing. You must communicate with the production folks to ensure that your design can be manufactured in the real world. And you depend upon the IT folks to support your efforts to manage your work efficiently using automated tools.

A process model diagram can be helpful to definitively quantify the processes you use and to determine how they interact with others in your company (or

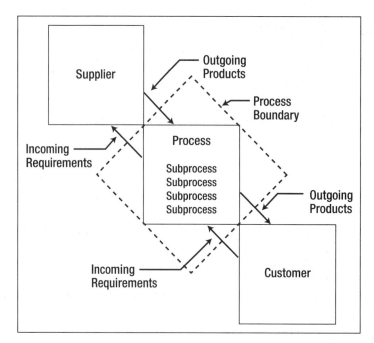

Figure 1.1   Process model diagram.

perhaps outside your company). It can be as simple as Figure 1.1. The boundaries of your process and the inputs from your suppliers, the outputs to your customers (and the feedback from both), should all be shown.

Later on, you'll make work-flow or process-flow diagrams. These will depict the events that cause you to begin producing your products and the steps you use during the process, including decision points and places where you depend on someone else to complete an action before you can proceed.

As you map each process that contributes to the mission of your organization, you must measure it in terms of effectiveness and efficiency. These two words have been so overused that their meaning may be unclear, so here are the definitions:

- *Effectiveness* measures how closely the process comes to achieving the desired result

- *Efficiency* measures wasted resources (time, money, and so on) within a process.

Phase 3—Process Improvement

When you have a clear picture of the current process, you can choose an improvement approach. The primary process improvement approaches are:

- Continuous improvement
- Benchmarking
- Reengineering

Continuous improvement works by carefully measuring the outputs of the current process to see if the process is stable and to see what the deficiencies are, identifying the root causes of any deficiencies, making relatively small changes, then measuring again to determine whether improvement has occurred. It's appropriate when the process isn't so far out of line that dramatic improvements need to be made immediately.

Benchmarking works by examining the best practices in the industry then attempting to emulate them. It's riskier and more painful (in terms of change) and it requires more resources than continuous improvement, but bigger gains can be expected. It's appropriate when competitors are threatening.

Reengineering works by completely rebuilding old processes or creating entirely new processes. It's risky, expensive, and painful (changes of this magnitude can be hard), but the payoffs are correspondingly large (assuming the effort doesn't fail). It's appropriate when immediate action is required, and it's best employed when a new branch, division, or subsidiary is being created (a clean slate for a clean start).

Phase 4—Implementation

Implementation implies that all planning has been completed and that the time is right for executing the plan. Preparing a timetable for execution and measuring progress against the timetable is an effective implementation method (we'll discuss this method more in the "Project Management" section).

Following implementation, the results should be measured and reviewed. Understanding the "lessons learned" is the first step toward increasing the probability of success on future projects.

Systems Analysis

Regardless of what you name the effort (TQM, QC, BPR, and so on), process improvement is essential for survival. Fortunately, process engineering works quite well with systems analysis; in fact, it's very effective to use the two techniques together.

Systems analysis is the formal name for the set of tools used by IT personnel to define problems and determine alternative solutions for automated information systems development. Systems analysis is the first phase of three in creating a new automated system:

- Systems analysis

- Systems design

- Systems implementation

Systems analysis focuses on breaking down complex systems into their constituent parts, rebuilding or replacing parts as necessary, then rebuilding the (presumably more effective) whole. Although systems analysis is used to analyze manual, partially manual and partially automated, and totally automated systems, it's ordinarily used with the intent to produce a mostly automated solution.

The conceptual framework of systems analysis rests on the assumption that a system (or subsystem) can be improved/automated by mapping its existing condition (including processes and the data input/outputs supporting them), evaluating what is found, proposing and selecting alternatives, and recommending a strategy for redesign.

Generally, systems analysis is performed by someone (called a systems analyst) other than the users, following a well-defined methodology aimed at uncovering business processes, business rules, level of automation, current (legacy) technologies in place, and the goals or products of the processes. The systems analyst may have many years of experience and training and may play detective, reporter, interviewer, investigator, evaluator, and other similar roles during the analysis.

Formal automated information systems development usually follows a step-by-step procedure:

- Project initiation

- Analysis

- Alternative development

- Design and testing

- Implementation

- Review

Although systems analysts will be involved in all phases of development, their primary concern is the analysis and alternative development phases. Analysis itself can be broken down into the following steps:

- Functional analysis

- Process analysis

- Activity analysis

- Data analysis

- Validation

- Alternatives development

Function, process, and task may seem to be similar terms, but in the context of systems analysis, they have different meanings. A task may be as simple as making one change to a product, while a process is a series of tasks for producing a particular outcome or product (but not necessarily a complete product). A function, on the other hand, refers to a set of processes that result in one or more complete products.

Keep in mind that, for this book, we define products to include internal and external products and services, meaning that broad functions, such as management of the accounting department, are products just as much as sales reports or manufactured items. Although this may seem unwieldy at first, it's very convenient because of the ease with which we can evaluate the costs and benefits of each function, process, or task.

Business functions can be categorized into line and staff functions, as well as competency and product team functions (depending upon the organizational responsibility matrix used). Further breakdown will identify the subfunctions that higher level functions depend upon for success. You'll know you've reached process analysis when complete products aren't generated.

Typically, organizational charts are used as a starting point for functional analysis, and function or responsibility documents, plus interviews, provide the remaining data. The resources consumed to perform a function are of primary interest to the analyst:

- Employee data
  - Number
  - Turnover rates
  - Training requirements
  - Perceived problems
- Location and size of facility
- Technologies deployed
- Documents used
  - Electronic
  - Paper
- Data storage requirements
- Mission
- Goals of the function

The purpose of business function analysis is to build a model of each of the major functions sustaining the continuing operations of the business. A graphic diagram using flowchart symbols is frequently the product of functional analysis (see Figure 1.2). The model should show the organizational units, the functions each one is responsible for, and their relationships to each other. In addition, the model should show the flow of information, control, and materials between functions/units, as well as serve as the foundation for process and task analysis.

Process And Task (Activity) Analysis

Process analysis is much like function analysis, except that it focuses on smaller, more well-defined objectives that are ordinarily limited in scope to one part of the organization (although processes may be related to other processes within the business). Task analysis is similar as well, focusing on the individual tasks making up the processes.

Business processes are performed sequentially or in parallel; may be manual, semiautomated, or entirely automated; and can be carried out by one or more people or by machine. Systems analysts gather most of the information concerning processes via interview, using the functional analysis as the starting point to identify supporting processes and the process analysis to identify tasks.

Like the functional analysis, process and task analysis asks who the users are and how, why, and what they do. Specifics about the technologies they use to accomplish their tasks are also helpful, including the hardware at their workstation, the applications they use, and the data they manipulate.

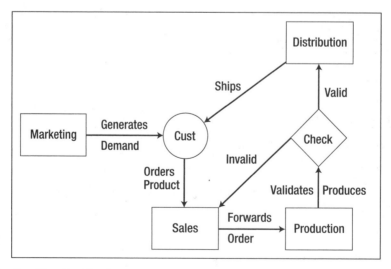

Figure 1.2   Function flowchart.

The purpose of process and task analysis, like functional analysis, is to build models of the actions and tasks making up the tasks and processes that in turn support the functions of the business/organization. Flowchart diagrams (see Figure 1.3) depict the various tasks, actions, decision points, and the relationships between them. The documentation accompanying the model should clearly define the inputs and outputs (and the required quality of both), as well as the events triggering the process or task and the time frame during which they occur.

In practice, task analysis is the lowest order of analysis and as such forms the basis for automated data processing. Each item of data must be identified, as well as the events generating the data and the impact the data has on subsequent tasks and processes.

Data Analysis

Data analysis occurs after the preceding analysis steps are complete. It focuses specifically on modeling the data that's gathered or generated during the functions, processes, and tasks performed and the data events, data triggers, transactions, and data carriers (forms and reports) that make up the overall data, information, and corporate knowledge/memory base of the business.

Problem identification is a key component in all these analytical steps. The analyst should always note any areas that obviously can be improved, are redundant, unproductive or outright useless, or don't achieve the desired result. This data is very helpful during the development of alternatives later on.

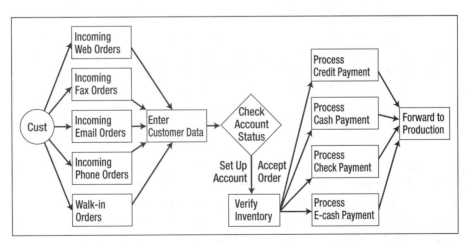

Figure 1.3   Process flowchart.

Validation

Validation is an attempt to verify the accuracy and consistency of the analytical models developed and in some cases the usefulness of the functions, processes, and tasks identified. Because complex organizations result in multiple models, these models may be cross-referenced both to their own documentation and to each other. The analyst will be looking for poorly documented processes; unterminated, mismatched, or mixed functions; orphan data; and diagrammatically inconsistent techniques.

Validation may be accomplished using some or all of the following methodologies:

- *Walk-through*—Essentially, this is a meeting of all interested parties (including the original analysts) to review the models and documentation and determine whether anything has been missed, improperly identified, or misunderstood.

- *Input/output validation*—This is a tracing process that follows each input or output from beginning to end, verifying each transformation along the way. It can be performed from either end; that is, you can go from input to output or vice versa.

- *Data source-to-use validation*—Similar to input/output validation, this variation attempts to confirm the requirement for each piece of data, as well as whether the data is useful as acquired, verified appropriately, accurate, available everywhere needed, saved as necessary, deleted when no longer needed, and properly documented and categorized during its time in the system.

- *Consistency analysis*—This form of validation looks at the tasks, processes, and functions themselves for inconsistencies. Poorly documented processes, poor or nonexistent connections between processes (where they should exist), responsibility without authority, mismatch between processes and job description, mismatch between functions and charter, and availability of proper data resources (at the proper time) are all examined.

- *Level-to-level consistency*—If the original analysis was performed in levels by different teams, a level-to-level analysis may be required to verify that there is correspondence (or at least no conflict) between the levels.

- *Carrier-to-data consistency*—The forms (paper and electronic data carriers) used to record and transmit data events are examined to confirm the accuracy, timeliness, and utility of data as it flows through the organization.

- *Process-to-process consistency*—The individual processes are examined for time constraints and proper documentation.

- *Zero-based analysis*—This technique is used when a completely new set of tasks, processes, or functions is required. As the name implies, it's a start-from-zero or start-from-scratch approach.

- *Data event analysis*—This analytical method views the business from the perspective of data events, assuming that all business activities are triggered by data events or transactions. It concentrates on data activity flows, examining what must be known about the event, whether that knowledge can be validated, what should be done with the resulting data, and where/how the data should be stored.

- *Methods and procedures analysis*—The focus here is to identify any manual portions of functions, processes, and tasks and relate them to the automated portions. It coincides with the analytical methods used during process engineering.

- *General-to-specific analysis*—This is a method of arranging the other validation techniques from the general to the specific, with the idea that starting with an overall view of the entire organization makes subsequent analysis of more detailed functions, process, and tasks easier.

Typically, users may be asked to assist in the validation process, and the analysts performing the validation may not be those who built the models. This ensures that the models represent the perceptions of the users and not the biases of the original systems analysts.

Alternatives Development

The final phase of systems analysis, alternatives (proposal) development, sifts through all known information about the current (existing, legacy) systems, all information available about new processes and the technologies to support them, then deduces problem areas and potential solutions. In this context, the term *problem* can mean a deficiency as well as erroneous conditions. For example, if using a new technology will result in lower costs, this would correct a deficiency in the current system (high cost of operations) rather than a problem in the strictest sense (such as incorrect processing of paychecks).

All the associated costs, benefits, risks, and resources required for each solution must be assessed then compared to the primary alternative, that is, doing nothing. Considering how painful, costly, and risky change can be, the "doing nothing" alternative should always be carefully checked.

Many of the same analytical techniques used to validate existing processes can be used to evaluate alternative processes. Whenever multiple processes must be changed, the interaction between the alternatives must be evaluated as well. Prioritizing the problems, ranking the alternatives for each problem, and assessing the dependencies between alternative solutions for different problems is a vital step in the development of workable alternatives.

The Systems Analysis Paradigm

Systems analysis is predicated on the belief that organizations (and individuals) process data to produce information then use that information to complete their work and accomplish their goals. Another part of that belief is that better information leads to more effective processes and a more successful organization.

So assuming little changes between the time a systems analysis project begins and the time it's completed, the product should be a set of proposed alternatives that will support the needs of the business into the foreseeable future. Hopefully, the new processes and automation (when implemented) will make the business, as a whole, more effective and less costly while enhancing the quality of work life. But effecting change can be a daunting task in itself, so tools have been developed to assist in the venture. One of the most effective is Project Management (PM).

Project Management

A very useful tool for analyzing, improving, and managing processes is Project Management (PM). It's also very useful for systems analysis itself. Project management is the measurement of resources (costs) required, assigned to the parallel or sequential steps to build a quality product in a reasonable time. It's another way of defining cost, schedule, and quality for management purposes.

Planning A Project

The time frame during which the project must be produced is depicted on a Gantt chart and the estimated length of each step is applied as a lengthwise bar (see Figure 1.4). Each bar is a task that's assigned resources (resources meaning the time of a skilled technician or artisan, time on a particular machine or in a certain facility, and so on). The bars are then ordered over time based on when tasks must be done, and in what sequence.

Some tasks can be performed in parallel, while others must be performed sequentially. Mapping the relationships and dependencies results in a Project Evaluation and Review Technique (PERT) or Critical Path Method (CPM) chart (see Figure 1.5). The critical path of a project is the series of tasks that must be performed sequentially and for which no slack time exists. Any delays along the critical path become delays to the entire project.

Assigning resources results in bar charts of resource usage versus availability over time (see Figure 1.6). These tools give the planner the ability to clearly see where available resources conflict with the needs of the project and where to adjust accordingly.

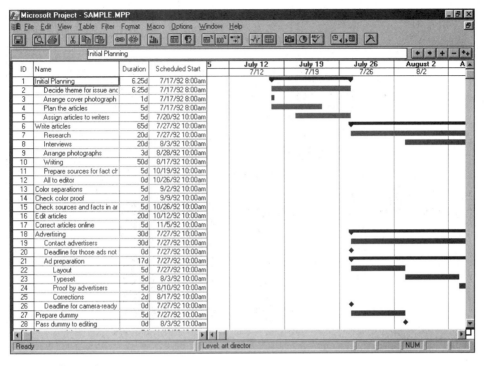

Figure 1.4   Gantt chart.

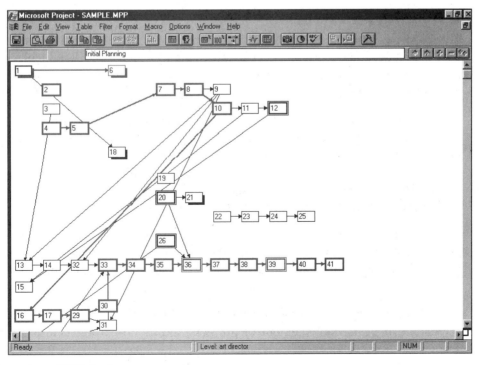

Figure 1.5   PERT chart.

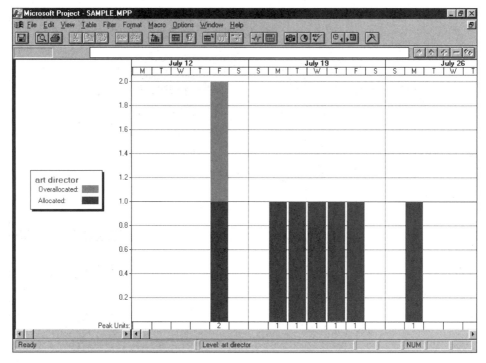

Figure 1.6   Resource bar chart.

Executing A Project

The initial plan should be completed before the project starts, so estimates of the cost, schedule, and quality of the plan can be made. When execution begins, the plan becomes a working model, allowing actual task completions and costs to be compared with the plan.

For instance, suppose a project is 10 percent of the way along its timeline. You would expect that all tasks scheduled for completion by now would be fully expended (or under) and fully complete. But measurement reveals that expenditures are running 5 percent over while the tasks are only 75 percent complete. Obviously the project is in trouble, but you still have a chance to get the project back on track because you're so close to the start.

Variations (over schedule and over budget) caught early on can be dealt with more effectively than those noticed near the project's conclusion. Moreover, problems are cheaper to fix early in the game. Problems noticed later may not be fixable at all.

The Department of Defense uses a system called Cost/Schedule Status Reporting (C/SSR) to plan the management of projects and monitor their health during execution. In the final analysis, C/SSR is really just common sense. C/SSR asks the questions: "What are you going to do?" and "Did you do what you promised, when you promised, and for how much you promised?"

The Project Management Paradigm

Typically, project management is used in situations where the product attributes are already fairly well defined (and by product, we're talking about services as well). There are plenty of software packages available (Microsoft Project, for one) that assist in the following processes:

- Defining projects in terms of tasks and resources.

- Assigning a work breakdown structure (WBS).

- Generating Gantt, PERT/CPM, and resource charts.

- Adjusting the schedule to level resource requirements.

Measuring Progress According To C/SSR

Just about any process can be viewed as a project, the benefit of which is the focus on resource consumption over time. Although PM makes a great tool for planning because it lends itself to "what-if" analysis, it performs less well under dynamic conditions.

Executing a plan requires accurate input of initial conditions (completeness of all current projects, estimated workload of projects that share resources, and so on) before starting, as well as constant updates of actual expenditures and completions. Missing any of this data can produce unreliable data, making correction decisions suspect. As complexity rises, processing and reporting must also improve for PM to remain a valuable execution tool. Fortunately, that's exactly what is happening in automation technology today.

Preimplementation Requirements

Success starts with planning, well before implementation. No matter which technique (or blend of techniques) you use to identify candidates for improvement/automation, you must pay attention to the following considerations:

- *The mission and culture of the organization and its capacity for change—* The mission statement should be very concise, clearly pointing toward the desired direction of the organization, and consistent with its culture (and vice versa). Change should be recognized as constant and something to be turned to advantage through leadership. These values should be reflected in a willingness to participate in the change process at all levels of the organization and a view of change as everyone's responsibility.

- *The political, regulatory, economic, and social environment the organization lives in*—No organization lives in a vacuum, and there may be external reasons why some changes cannot be tolerated, even if they would produce quantifiable benefits. Political whim, unusual economic conditions, dated government-industry regulations, and social dictums may prevent change/ improvement from successful execution or lead to other more serious problems.

- *Customers and competitors, both external and internal*—Organizations spend a surprising amount of time signaling their intentions to each other, and unintentional signals may provoke unwanted responses from competitors. The same is true at the individual level and true regarding customer's perceptions. You must carefully evaluate expected responses from both customers and competitors before implementing process changes because, as the saying goes, "sometimes it's better to let sleeping dogs lie."

- *Past, present, and future changes in technology*—Although the entire business landscape changes before our eyes (and the pace of change accelerates), the technologies (and user's perceptions about them) change as well. You must constantly ask yourself, will this project (and solution) make sense in one year? Chances are, in one year cost/performance ratios for computer technology will have greatly improved. At the same time, you can't let this become an excuse for inaction. Yes, you're right. Your job is now much more difficult.

- *Thorough descriptions of existing processes/technologies and their interrelations*—Incomplete or inaccurate process models can lead to errors, costs, and delays that you simply can't afford. Although mistakes can be tolerated in some situations, there's no foolproof way to make sure you only make these kinds of errors. No one is perfect, but extra time spent verifying the accuracy of the initial analysis up front is sure to pay big dividends down the road.

- *Elegant and comprehensive solution architecture*—Imagine designing a house by cutting and pasting pictures of everything you like from architectural magazines. No matter how hard you would try, it wouldn't look good. There'd be obvious inconsistencies at the surface level, and deep down inside there'd likely be major structural defects. Good design means compromises early on, restricting you to one or another set of viable alternatives within each previous compromise. But the result is a well-designed, consistent whole that performs the functions it was designed for superbly. It usually looks very nice on the surface as well.

- *Clear, concise functional and performance specifications*—It does no good to design processes that perform the wrong functions extremely well or that perform the right functions poorly. Clearly stating the desired functions and required performance will have the immediate effect of pushing technology capabilities to the forefront. You'll know right away if what you want done can be achieved for the price you want to pay. The second effect will be to make it easier for everyone else involved in the project to understand what must happen. Never assume specifications that are clear to you will be clear to everyone else. Always pass the specifications around a few times to be sure.

Design Considerations

The design of an improved process directly impacts the design of automated systems encompassed by it. How and when data is gathered; where it comes from and in what form; how it's processed and by whom; where, how securely, and for how long it's stored; when, how, and to whom it's available are all questions that deserve a well-designed solution. Because modern database tools make Rapid Application Development (RAD) easy and most hardware is (or easily can be) networked, a distributed network of small applications filling specific functions may be best. Keep in mind that a group of small applications working together is not the same thing as a distributed database or application; these terms imply a much more sophisticated and complex system.

The advantages of many small applications are numerous. The cost to document, develop, test, debug, implement, and maintain miniapps is smaller because they are less complex individually. Training costs are reduced for the same reason. They can even be implemented more easily because they may follow existing processes more closely at first. And the failure of one doesn't bring the whole project to a halt. It's our version of the old KISS principle, "Keep It Simple/Small."

Avoid the trap of using "the obvious solution" because if it's that obvious it's probably unnecessary or already obsolete. Sometimes a simple logbook can satisfy the requirements of a process much more effectively than a small database, even though the data dies there. Often a simple PC-based application can do the work that could only be done on a mainframe application a few years back. Remember, every extra bit of data collected, every extra function designed in, every extra step in the process adds to cost and complexity and eats valuable time (development, maintenance, and production time). If the justification is unclear, set it aside and examine what would happen without it.

Good design should make it easy to detect errors when they occur (and they will occur). And good design should also lend itself to modification during the construction and testing phases because changes will be made.

Finally, always consider Commercial Off-The-Shelf (COTS) solutions, as long as they're compatible (preferably platform-independent rather than wholly proprietary). COTS applications have the advantage of spreading development costs over many users, and the characteristics and costs are frequently known and well documented. Comparing them to your performance specifications should be fairly straightforward as well.

Performance Specifications

Performance specifications are the benchmarks by which you measure the success of a project, and for automated systems, they should provide understandable metrics for the performance of the final system. The specs should show how

- The applications fit into the proposed processes.
- What the inputs (data elements) and outputs are.
- How they are related within the applications (and the tables they reside in).
- What processing will take place in response to what events.
- The forms and reports making up the Graphical User Interface (GUI).

The specs should stand on their own. Anyone should be able to read them and understand the intent clearly if not the technical meaning of every word. That means using English plain enough for everyone, not computer science jargon. The reasons for specifying storage sizes, processing speeds, certain types of hardware and software, and so on should be explained in terms of costs, benefits, and risks, not just listed like so many items in a purchase order.

Construction Techniques

A variety of formal methodologies exist for constructing software solutions to perceived business and organizational problems (or requirements). Because there are so many types of situations, so many types of construction techniques, and so many types of solutions, it can be bewildering to simply get started. Add in the rapid change in business situations and in construction techniques and solutions and you may be unable to hit your target with any traditional methods. Things just won't sit still, but there's a way to manage under these circumstances.

Programmers tend to like things to be well organized, straightforward, and static. The problem needs to be defined, a solution decided upon, and the finished product implemented. Folks working at the operational level tend to do whatever works because they have a job to do. Managers want accurate and timely organizational information nicely summarized, so they can easily detect deviations from the norm that may require action on their part. Senior managers want strategic information comparing the results and position of the company or organization with competitors or with economic conditions in general.

Traditional systems design methodologies, by their nature, imply a separation of analysis, design, and implementation from the day-to-day, operational, and strategic functions of the company. It's as though only the systems analysts and designers can understand the intricacies of data flow and information management, even though they give lip service to the concept of asking the users—Subject Matter Experts (SMEs)—what's required.

This frequently leads to an us-versus-them perception and from there to poor prospects for system success. Analysts visit to gather data, head back to the ivory tower to do their analysis and evaluation in private, then display their brilliant solution, expecting everyone to jump on board in delight. Users are left out of the process, and by the time the system finds its way to them, conditions have changed so much that it's inefficient or useless. Then the analysts hear that tired refrain "It doesn't work." But there is a better way.

The Knowledge Design Paradigm

The formal term for this new approach is Knowledge Design. What does it mean? It includes the best of process engineering, systems analysis, and project management concepts, with the recognition that change is constant but the value of knowledge is paramount and actually increases with change.

Data is all around us, ready to be sampled. Information is essentially summarized data, meaningful to some, meaningless to others. Knowledge is power because it implies not just data and information but the wisdom to use them effectively to accomplish goals within the context of a constantly changing environment. Knowledge Design is the practical implementation of the methodologies to build systems that produce knowledge.

KD is based on the following principles:

- Success occurs when users have and use knowledge-generating processes.
- Users will do whatever it takes to successfully execute processes if they perceive a correlation between process success and their own success.
- The job of management (in this arena) is to illustrate the connection between the two.
- The job of the IT department (in this arena) is to support users while managing IT resources.

Mission-Critical Applications

The current paradigm for applications development is that management needs central control of mission-critical applications, the IT department is responsible for building and maintaining mission-critical applications, and users will use what management and IT dictate. (And by the way, please try to get some use out of that expensive desktop or laptop we bought you last year, would you.)

But in fact, no matter what the size or mission of the organization, the accurate, efficient, and secure generation, communication, and storage of information are constants. Some knowledge-producing applications (termed mission-critical) have a wide-ranging and immediate impact on operations, while disruption to others will merely result in a slow death. The term *mission-critical* is actually misleading; assuming all your processes are required for the ultimate success of the organization (and if not, why are they being performed?), every application is mission-critical.

Making Knowledge Design Work

If you accept that every application is (or should be eliminated if it's not) mission-critical, and you accept that only users can execute processes successfully, then how do you achieve this elusive and magical condition?

Management must educate users about factors affecting their processes, the inevitability of constant change and process improvement, and the alignment of the organization's and the user's goals. Management must also specify the minimum knowledge requirements (quality, timeliness, storage, and security of data) for mission-critical applications without mandating the specific technologies to be used.

The IT department must educate users about the technologies available to successfully execute their processes and how to select technologies that fit within the organization's overall IT strategy. The IT department itself has no knowledge requirements other than what is required to support users (including management) and should not allow itself to be drawn into a role of "owning" even mission-critical systems or functions.

Users must decide individually and/or collectively (depending upon the range of the application/process in question) what technologies will provide the most successful solution, given management's constraints. Users must be prepared to live or die by their decisions.

If management and the IT department have done their jobs properly, users will not only design the most cost-effective and efficient knowledge solutions to support their processes and functions (and compromise with other users as necessary), they will "leap tall buildings in a single bound" to ensure success. That's the power of ownership!

The User (Customer) Is King

The primary assumption that differentiates KD from previous analytical approaches is that only the user has the expertise to accomplish his or her job effectively, and the user must also have the ability to design (or at least conceptualize) systems that are appropriate for the task at hand.

The user must have a clear understanding of the processes (and data requirements) the job entails, the products that must be produced, and how these products and processes fit into their organizations and the outside world. The user must also be familiar with current information systems technology and must be able to devise (or at least be aware of the capabilities and limitations of) the systems that can support these processes and products.

Designers and analysts, are you skeptical? Think about this. Your users may easily have better computers and more capable software and Internet access on their home computers than they do at work, and many of them are becoming very adept at creating and implementing their own solutions. Contrary to popular opinion, this is not a problem, it's an opportunity. As a matter of fact, if you put this initiative to work it can make your job much easier and more rewarding.

So where does that leave you as IT folks? In the very position you want to be in, a supporting role. Rather than trying to build and enforce massive systems, you train, you consult, you explain. You're at your best when you help design, build, maintain, and improve systems according to the desires of the folks who need them.

The way to accomplish this is through training, and lots of it. No job is immune from the impact of computer technology, and no one can be called literate (these days) if he or she doesn't know how to use computers, office applications, and the Internet. It's like not knowing how to read, do arithmetic, drive a car, or use the telephone. It's simply that fundamental.

Fortunately, people are catching on. It's a short leap to merge process engineering (the end user side), systems analysis (the IT side), and project management (the management side) into a cohesive set of skills that all employees master. The job of the IT department becomes that of facilitator and consultant, providing the tools, training, and technical expertise to allow the rest of the organization to thrive, and building and maintaining the IT and communications infrastructure everyone depends upon.

Managers should build specifications from the top down, not systems. Your employees are pretty familiar with computer technology now, and they want to be successful. They're already using whatever technologies are available to do their jobs better. Rather than tell them what technologies to use, tell them the results you expect. Enforce the production of knowledge rather than the use of a particular piece of hardware or software.

Users, where do you stand? If you understand your position, you know that you must cooperate with other parts of the company on mission-critical and core infrastructure applications. You know that you're in a better position than anyone else to figure out what technologies are appropriate for your unique processes. You know that the IT department can help you implement these technologies effectively. And you know that you must achieve management's knowledge specifications, whatever process or solution you choose.

It's a brave new world full of opportunities and pitfalls. Climb on board, learn everything you can, and take a leadership position. It may be stressful, painful, and scary, but there's simply no turning back. And who knows? Once you get used to it, you may find it very rewarding and fulfilling.

Immediate Solutions

The following guide outlines process engineering, systems analysis, and project management techniques within the context of Knowledge Design (KD). Think of KD as simply a refocusing of your current skills, with the goal of making them more effective. Many of these techniques are already in use, and it doesn't take much to put a new spin on them.

Problem Identification

The first step in building new processes and automated solutions is recognizing that a problem exists. *Problem* in this context actually means problem or deficiency, so identification can occur as a result of actively looking for areas that can stand improvement, not just waiting for someone to voice a complaint.

Suppose you manage the IT department for a distribution company. Orders vary throughout the year, product mix changes, and so occasionally do product handling requirements. These variations and changes affect the company's core processes (inventory management, shipping and receiving, and so on) and the information driving decisions.

Rather than sending your analysts out to build a new system each time a change occurs, you decide to set a policy encouraging user participation. This policy will actively solicit suggestions about problems and potential solutions from every employee, educate users about IT's role and responsibilities, and begin breaking down resistance to change by making the user a key player.

Step 1—Creating a Formal Policy

A formal means of generating solution development requests should be in place. A written policy/procedure for identifying problem areas and initiating a response, with continuous updates to the workforce in general, can be very helpful in gathering data about potential problems, as well as educating everyone about how to proceed.

Therefore, a good first step is to write a policy document. Perhaps it would read something like this:

Purpose. The purpose of this document is to formalize policy and procedure for initiating and implementing information technology solutions within XYZ company. This policy will remain in effect until the next revision or cancellation.

Scope. This policy covers all IT solutions for all divisions of XYZ company, including computer, network, telephony, and communications and display hardware and software (both off-the-shelf, proprietary, and custom applications) for identification, design, test, implementation, maintenance, and improvement.

Background. XYZ company has a robust and customer-service oriented IT department. To serve our internal and external customers most effectively, the IT department recognizes the following:

- Customers know their rapidly changing needs best.
- Customers need the best possible information and support to make effective IT solution decisions for themselves.
- The IT department exists to provide the best possible information and communications infrastructure support to our internal and external customers.

Policy. IT solutions can be initiated by any internal or external customer or the IT department in response to:

- Process improvement efforts
- Changing customer needs
- Changing business conditions
- Deficiencies in the current solutions
- Problems with the current solutions

Internal and external customers should designate a representative to collect and communicate IT solution proposals to the IT department. The department can then assist in:

- Developing proposals
- Prioritizing proposals appropriately
- Finding the best technology (price/performance, life cycle) to meet the need
- Integrating the solution with current business processes (automated or manual)
- Training users
- Educating stakeholders
- Implementing, maintaining, and improving the solution

IT will also participate in all process improvement and reengineering efforts, identifying areas ripe for automation (or the elimination of automation or entire processes) as XYZ company responds to changes in the marketplace. Proposals generated within IT will follow the same procedure for evaluation as solutions generated elsewhere.

Step 2—Defining The Roles Of IT, Management, And Users

If you're a member of the IT department, you know how enticing new technologies are. Your company can gain maximum benefits from investments in new technology by following a disciplined approach such as Knowledge Design. In addition, it's helpful in gaining the confidence and participation of users, especially in terms of perceived equity.

By taking an active role in all process improvement efforts, the IT department guarantees that appropriate IT solutions occur everywhere they should, and, by the same token, don't appear in places they shouldn't.

Educate IT employees about their role by:

• Writing memos

• Conducting internal training

• Communicating directly to them

Ensure they understand their role as consultants and trainers to users. Train them to look at users as customers, and remind them that "the customer is always right." When your customers are educated sufficiently, they'll understand the constraints you work under and the constraints of the technology available. Consequently, they'll tend to ask for things that are possible, reasonable, and cost-effective (rather than impossible, unreasonable, and exorbitant).

If you're a member of management or an end user, an approach such as this beckons you to join in and play a part in accelerating your company along the path toward a leaner and more competitive organization. By offering you a chance to lead rather than follow, your IT department is ensuring that the eventual solutions work as planned because you are the "master of your domain."

Managers, it's your job to bring employees into the solution process. You should:

• Listen carefully to their concerns. Studies show that in any organization, 90 percent of the employees want to succeed.

• Convey to them how their success is related to the company's success.

End users, your role is to:

• Learn as much as you can about the direction in which your company is heading.

• Understand your role in the larger picture and the processes that affect your job. Technology won't replace you unless you let it. Knowing how to use technology will make you more valuable and strengthen your position.

- Take the lead.
- Make suggestions for improvement.
- Spend time on the process improvement teams if possible.

Evaluating Environment And Scope

Senior managers evaluate the environment the company lives in all the time (or they should). Making this part of overall company strategy and disseminating this practice to every level of the organization is the key to successful process improvement.

Suppose you manage a factory producing plastic models. Some are painted and some use specialized plastics, and maintenance of the extrusion machinery is a big job. Materials handling is a major portion of the job, and hazardous waste disposal is a core process.

As a first-line supervisor, you must ensure Materials Safety Data Sheets (MSDS) are posted, up-to-date, and accurate, and you must track hazardous materials usage and hazardous waste generated in your shop. You're considering creating a database just for your shop, but you're not sure how it would connect to the company-wide database application IT has already built or how the changing environmental regulations would apply.

Step 1—Stay Current

Before starting to build a new system to make your job easier, be aware of the conditions under which your company operates, both externally and internally. In fact, everyone in the company should have an understanding of the regulatory environment and community concerns, especially if you work with or produce hazardous materials and hazardous waste.

A good first step in educating every level of the company about the environment (the business environment, not just local environmental regulations) is through company news, whether it's a monthly hard-copy release or a daily email. Over a period of time, everyone from the file clerks to the senior scientists will become aware of the issues facing the company. Include:

- The company's efforts to improve processes
- The technologies being considered
- An offer to examine proposals from any quarter

As awareness builds throughout your organization, a steady stream of suggestions will appear.

Step 2—Examine All Factors Affecting The Process

Take a step-by-step approach to evaluating opportunities and threats, followed by simple discussion and subjective judgments. Ultimately, the importance placed on any particular subject will be decided on a human basis, and no one can perfectly predict the future. But a disciplined approach and hard facts shine light much more clearly than biases and technological dreams.

To sift through the issues surrounding any process, start by classifying according to two criteria:

- *Environmental factors*—Regulation, competition, market forces, company culture, and so on
- *Process scope*—Task, process, procedure, function, and the interrelations with other activities

Step 3—Gauge The Impact Of These Factors On The Process

A full-scale process improvement effort or systems analysis isn't necessary at this point. The purpose of this exercise is to find out where the process lies in the grand scheme of things. Ask yourself these questions:

- Does the process have a major impact on employees in general (such as changes in the way paychecks are processed or in staffing levels in certain areas)?
- Does the process meet all regulatory tests?
- Does the process generate extra information that may come back to haunt you later?

Unadvisable Policies

In the case of environmental compliance, you may have no choice. But in other cases, it may be in your best interest to do less. For example, several years ago a large online service instituted a policy of screening postings to its forums, purportedly to protect younger members. A court later found it liable when several damaging messages were discovered in one of its forums but found other online services (who had no such editorial policy in effect but who also had damaging messages) not liable.

In terms of process scope, ask yourself these questions:

- Is the process self-contained (limited to one person, such as a repetitive task)?
- Does the process affect many different processes, or does it change the security posture of the organization?

- Is the process something that can conceivably be accomplished by users themselves (assuming they are computer literate) with only limited assistance?
- If the process can be done by users, should it be?

This simple set of guidelines should be on everyone's mind because ideas occur in the strangest places and at the strangest times. A user who understands the business environment, technology, and processes involved in his or her job is more likely to initiate appropriate proposals and discard useless or counterproductive ones.

Understanding the total environment in which you work and how other processes and information systems may be affected (or may affect you) if changes are made is an important part of the development of any new solution.

Generating Potential Solutions

Solutions differ from proposals in that proposals generally attempt to address problems, while solutions offer specific actions designed to solve these problems (buying new technology, installing software, changing a process or procedure, and so on).

Suppose you're an end user in the customer service department of a company. You know the company needs a good answering system because you deal with it every day. Manually answering each call and manually monitoring people on hold just doesn't cut it anymore.

You want to make your job easier and the customers happier, so you make a proposal. Your typical proposal may read "Improve response times to customer service requests." This proposal addresses the problem of slow response times but doesn't offer a solution. A typical solution for this example might read "Install an automated answering system to take and forward calls to cut response time to three minutes or less."

Step 1—Brainstorming

To generate solution ideas, start with a clean slate and an open mind in an atmosphere where all ideas can flow freely. The eventual end users should generate all solution ideas, disregarding cost or other impacts, because often ideas that can't be carried out will lead to other ideas that are possible.

As a member of the IT department, it's your job to explain to users that their solutions must go through a rigorous process of elimination at several levels before any one may be adopted. At this early stage, ideas are like flowers; they all look pretty, but most will die off in a few days.

Keep in mind that many users, especially in larger organizations that have been around for a few years, are familiar with the principles of Quality Circles, Total Quality Management, and Continuous Improvement. They've probably learned traditional "brainstorming" principles, and it shouldn't be too hard to promote the kind of free and open exchange of ideas that leads to innovative "thinking out of the box" solutions.

Step 2—The Process Of Elimination

Part of the analysis of any potential solution is the quantification of four basic resources: materials, machinery, manpower, and methods. These actually stand for all the resources that must be applied to produce the desired result using the proposed process.

Several days after the freewheeling, thinking-out-of-the-box session, ask the same group of folks to quantify resources required for all the proposals in these terms. Some ideas will quickly be eliminated because it will be obvious to everyone concerned that they have no hope of success. The other ideas will remain but will now be ready for formal process engineering and systems analysis.

The great benefit of this approach is that the users will eliminate their own ideas and will likely support whatever approach is chosen because it's *their* idea. Still, success is not automatic. It depends greatly on user perceptions. Take the time to educate users as to the constraints IT operates under, and make sure to listen very carefully to their concerns.

Process Engineering And Formal Systems Analysis

By now you certainly understand that process engineering (or reengineering) and systems analysis are very similar methods for achieving much the same thing; the primary difference conceptually is that systems analysis leans toward automated solutions.

In our opinion, formal systems analysis is a subset of the process engineering paradigm in which your whole organization should be steeped (see Figure 1.7). At the same time, virtually all processes can benefit from automation, so the two disciplines should be pursued hand in hand.

If you've followed the steps for generating potential solutions, you should have a set of alternatives that are innovative but within the range of possibility. Now's

```
┌─────────────────────────────────────────────────────────┐
│              Organizational Survival Strategies           │
│                                                           │
│                   Process Engineering                     │
│  ┌─────────────────────────┬─────────────────────────┐  │
│  │     Reshape Culture      │     Analyze Processes     │  │
│  │                          │                           │  │
│  │   1. Form policy         │   1. Analyze processes    │  │
│  │   2. Educate             │   2. Identify problems    │  │
│  │   3. Manage change       │   3. Generate proposals   │  │
│  │                          │   4. Select solutions     │  │
│  │                          │                           │  │
│  │                          │     Systems Analysis      │  │
│  │                          │     Techniques Used       │  │
│  ├─────────────────────────┼─────────────────────────┤  │
│  │    Improve Processes     │     Measure/Maintain      │  │
│  │                          │                           │  │
│  │   1. Design improvements │   1. Measure performance  │  │
│  │   2. Implement           │   2. Survey customers     │  │
│  │                          │   3. Debug processes      │  │
│  │                          │                           │  │
│  │     Systems Analysis     │     Systems Analysis      │  │
│  │     Techniques Used      │     Techniques Used       │  │
│  └─────────────────────────┴─────────────────────────┘  │
└─────────────────────────────────────────────────────────┘
```

Figure 1.7   Diagram of process engineering and systems analysis.

the time to formally examine the processes/systems in question using process engineering and systems analysis concepts.

Step 1—Blending Process Engineering And Systems Analysis

Problems and potential solutions can be broadly categorized into two major areas:

- Infrastructure that affects the entire organization

- Solutions to specific, process-related problems or deficiencies

IT has the responsibility to ensure that the organization has the appropriate technology infrastructure within budget and mission constraints. For example, the IT department must plan for and implement networking and network security. The juggling act here is to build and control an infrastructure that facilitates rather than stifles user requirements.

Simultaneously, users must want the technology before they'll willingly use it. Education and a policy of encouraging innovation at the user level can make this happen.

We've progressed through the steps used to identify problems and generate potential solutions. Notice that the IT department has essentially been on the sidelines while users were encouraged to initiate proposals. Actually, IT has spent its efforts educating users about technology and the potential for improvements, and the users are now clamoring for IT services. The infrastructure is in place for improvements to happen successfully.

Step 2—Formally Selecting A Solution From The Alternatives

Now we need to select the best solution from the alternatives. We'll start by using both systems analysis and process engineering techniques to define the particulars of a proposal in terms of process data inputs and outputs as follows:

- Document existing functions, processes, and data inputs/outputs.

- Develop models depicting each of the alternative solutions:

  - Clearly describe the required functions.

  - List the data gathered to support the functions.

  - Note the processes that are initiated in response to the input data.

  - Include output data that's the result of the completion of processes.

  - Show the products flowing from the processes.

  - Include product quality and performance specifications in your model.

- Measure current process performance in terms of efficiency, effectiveness, and customer satisfaction. Differentiate between:

  - Measures of the resources consumed during a process.

  - The effectiveness of the process for producing products (or outcomes) in the required amounts and with the quality specified.

  - The satisfaction customers perceive from these products.

  - Model proposed solutions in the same terms.

- Examine the costs, benefits, and risks associated with new processes/systems during each stage of the project:

  - Design.

  - Implementation.

  - Maintenance.

- Select the alternative that best fits the costs, benefits, and risks your organization prefers. Knowing the mission and culture of your organization can assist in the selection process. Make sure to get approval not only from the official chain of command but also from those who have to implement and use the new process.

- Use validation techniques to assure that the selected model is workable. Build a data dictionary of the selected proposal. A data dictionary formally compiles and documents analytical information about the selected proposal. By the way, the term data dictionary in this context means a complete record of all data collected and generated for the proposal, not the much more specific data dictionary developed for the database itself.

Process Performance Measurement

Processes should be measured for their efficiency, that is, the cost of resources consumed to produce a given amount of output. Outputs (products) should be measured in terms of effectiveness, meaning the amount and the quality of the product. Outcomes (customer satisfaction) can only be measured after the products have been delivered and only from the standpoint of the customer using the products. It's entirely possible that product effectiveness and user satisfaction can be increased with more, less, or an equivalent amount of resources used; essentially, there's no linear relationship between resources consumed and the effectiveness of the final output.

Step 1—Taking Direct And Indirect Measures

Although direct benefits of a modified process (lower costs) are most easily quantified, indirect benefits can have as much or more impact on the bottom line. Performance measurement typically seeks to identify changes affecting four key groups:

- Customers care about:
  - Product utility
  - Satisfaction
- Shareholders want:
  - Lower costs
  - Greater profits
  - Higher market share
  - Less waste
- Employees look for:
  - Job satisfaction
  - Quality of work life
- The surrounding community wants:
  - Regulatory compliance
  - Good neighbor policies
  - A healthy tax base

Using these types of measures assures that the functions of existing processes are understood and that new processes won't be developed in a vacuum.

Within these four dimensions, costs are key criteria by which process changes are evaluated. For instance, if spending a little more will result in a product of much greater customer satisfaction, is it worthwhile? A value judgment to be sure, but there are clearly limits to how much more we can spend, regardless of the customer satisfaction we'd like to achieve.

Step 2—Measuring Process Capability And Variability

Controlling costs starts with determining process capability and decreasing process variation. Measuring process capability (the actual ability of the process to produce at a given level) points out discrepancies between specifications and processes that are not a defect of the current process but are, instead, attributes of it.

As for process variation, the preferred method of measurement has been given the name "six-sigma" (by Motorola, a winner of the United States Malcolm Baldrige National Quality Award). The six-sigma goal refers to the measurement of product variation in terms of the number of product defects falling outside a range of standard deviations. Measuring the current process in these terms lays the groundwork for improving the process later.

Measuring other less easily quantified elements of each dimension above is a more subjective exercise but still can be approached with consistency, so any improvements can be detected. For example, if customers are concerned about the image of a certain product, surveys to measure the perceived image before and after a change of materials (going from solid gold to gold-plated, for instance) can measure these attitudes. Many kinds of indirect costs and benefits can be measured consistently this way.

The Three Types Of Process Improvement

Once an alternative is chosen, it must be evaluated based on the degree of change needed to work out the proper implementation methods. The three kinds of process improvement are:

- Continuous improvement
- Benchmarking
- Reengineering

If the alternative chosen equates to a complete reengineering of the process, great care must be taken with regard to the impact of new processes on people as well as on other processes within the company.

In this particular case, you must choose which of the three to pursue, so we've labeled them Steps A, B, and C rather than 1, 2, and 3.

Step A—Continuous Improvement

Continuous improvement should be chosen when there's simply a need to improve overall efficiency in response to changing requirements and a changing business environment. It's the least painful of all improvement efforts and helps keep the organization lean and trim, kind of like taking a daily vitamin or exercising regularly.

A six-step approach is common:

1. Define the requirements of internal or external customers.
2. Measure current process performance.
3. Analyze the process.
4. Develop and select alternatives for improvement.
5. Implement the selected alternative.
6. Measure again, then maintain or improve by repeating this cycle.

This method is sometimes referred to more simply as the Plan-Do-Check-Act cycle.

Step B—Process Benchmarking

If you're familiar with reverse engineering, you have an understanding of where process benchmarking originated. Reverse engineering is the practice of purchasing competitor's products, disassembling them, then analyzing them to find out how they achieved a particular performance or set of features.

Process benchmarking attempts to do the same thing with competitor's processes. If your competitor answers all customer complaints within two days (versus your 12) you need to find out why, then meet or beat that figure to stay competitive (if customer complaint response time is important to your customers).

Benchmarks are the standards by which process and product performance can be judged across an entire industry. After all, whatever ultimate product customers might want to buy in the future, their only choices are what's currently on the market and these products are all made by you and your competitors. Theoretically, if you can beat your competitor's products attribute for attribute (and marketing and advertising educates your customers about this fact), you should become the market leader. Benchmarking is more expensive and more painful, and it should be used only when competitors are threatening in some way. Process benchmarking can be performed with the following steps:

1. Determine which outcome (product or service) can benefit most from benchmarking.

2. Determine whose processes or products to emulate.

3. Collect data about these processes or products.

4. Determine the performance gaps between your current processes and those you wish to emulate.

5. Determine the differences that create the gaps.

6. Forecast future performance (and gaps) if current industry trends continue.

7. Establish goals and develop improvement alternatives.

8. Implement, monitor, and recalibrate benchmarks.

Process benchmarking is much like continuous improvement, but it uses other processes (internal and external) as guideposts to improvement.

Step C—Reengineering

Reengineering is quite painful and costly, and should be used when new products or services are introduced. And it's most easily done when new companies, divisions, branches, and so on are set up. In one sense, reengineering is fun because you essentially throw out the old methods and start from scratch, but it can be extremely stressful as well. Carefully consider the costs, benefits, and risks whenever reengineering is proposed.

Reengineering projects can be categorized according to three types:

- *Fundamental*—All parts of the existing process are examined for improvement opportunities, in effect rebuilding the process from the ground up.

- *Radical*—The entire existing process is scrapped, and a new process is built.

- *Dramatic*— The goal is to build a new process that superlatively outperforms the old process so that an entirely new and dramatically more efficient and effective process takes its place.

Common Failure Factors

Because reengineering projects have experienced such a high failure rate (and keep in mind that automation projects, such as the implementation of a new database application, tend to involve fairly radical process reengineering), studies have been done to find out what factors are common in failed projects:

- *Resistance to change*—A cultural issue that could be resolved or mitigated with education.

- *Limitations of the current systems*—There may be no way to measure this, so the company is "flying blind."

- *Lack of management consensus*—Everyone knows change is required, but no two ideas coincide.

- *Lack of senior management support*— No one is willing to risk championing the ideas.

- *Unrealistic expectations*—Seen as a quick fix or cure-all.

- *Lack of cross-functional expertise applied*—IT (or some other department) "goes it alone."

It goes without saying that the best new processes simply "won't work" if the essentials are not in place. Getting the entire company to understand what it's doing and where it's at, plus recognizing the fundamental need for frequent change, should be the first order of business before attempting any change.

Critical Success Factors

Studies have identified the factors (called critical success factors) that are common to successful reengineering projects:

- Use of a project management approach
- Senior management commitment
- Culture accepting of change
- Undeniable call to action
- Early project success
- Information systems
- Speed
- Experience

Using PM techniques is fundamental to the other success factors because PM lays out the particulars of the project in a way most people can understand. Commitment of senior management, speed, and the integration of educational efforts all benefit from PM. The call to action should be apparent to everyone if the culture fosters clear communications to all employees, and this has the added benefit of gradually modifying the organizational culture (as we mentioned previously).

Early project success is harder to define, but it basically means "picking your battles." Choose processes early on in which the chances for success are high. If these efforts fail, distance them from the primary efforts. Reengineering team members will pick up valuable experience for later, major, and highly-visible reengineering efforts.

Finally, good information systems may already be producing the majority of data needed to measure accurately, and without them, you'll have no way of knowing whether you're proceeding along the desired path or veering off into uncharted territory. If they aren't already in place, create and test them before embarking on a reengineering project.

The process of conducting a reengineering effort is very similar to continuous improvement and benchmarking. Reengineering seeks to:

- Establish the groundwork for the project to succeed and initiate the educational and information systems required.
- Identify candidates for reengineering (problem identification).
- Launch the reengineering project with the support of upper management and an experienced cross-functional team.
- Propose, develop, and select alternatives.
- Implement and test (or measure) the new processes.
- Evaluate the outcomes and maintain and improve the processes.

Reengineering is best done swiftly—like pulling off a Band-Aid. Projects that go on too long without results are more likely to fail, even if they technically meet their specifications.

Project Management

Project management software packages are ubiquitous, and they all tend to have the same functions and features. Just about any package you pull off the shelf will do an adequate job, so pick one and learn to use it comfortably. It'll be a mainstay in the toolkit you bring to your job.

You've probably guessed by now that we favor a rational, data-driven approach to designing and implementing database solutions. Other than the simple one- or two-hour custom database developed to solve a one-time problem for an individual, with little impact on any other part of the company, database projects deserve deliberate project management, not a slap-it-together-and-let's-see-if-it-works approach.

Step 1—Communicating The Benefits Of PM

If you're a member of the IT department, you're fully aware of the necessity for a careful, deliberate stance when designing and implementing solutions, and you've probably seen the wreckage of poorly planned, user-generated systems that stretched well beyond the capabilities of the would-be designer. Remember that for every sloppy mess, users also created many working (if badly constructed) tools that made their jobs much easier than before. They're looking to you for guidance and leadership; it's up to you to educate and consult with them about how to do it properly. Focus their efforts; don't discourage them.

If you're a manager or end user, you must train yourself to give database projects the same thorough attention you give to the rest of your work. Any process could have profound influence on other parts of the organization, and you must review the consequences carefully before rushing to improve your processes. The more you learn about how processes and automation work, the more effective you are.

Project management is a useful tool not only for planning and executing database projects; it comes in handy when evaluating the impact of new processes on existing processes. Although it may not be practical to use project management techniques on a day-to-day basis for the normal work in your organization, planning new processes using project management can identify constraints and help highlight workaround strategies well in advance of production problems.

The bottom line is that your first step must be to ensure everyone involved is on board with the PM philosophy and understands clearly how it will benefit them and the project as a whole.

Step 2—Breaking The Project Into Measurable Tasks

Project management starts by defining:

- The steps that must be executed

- The resources required for these steps

- The order in which they must be performed

- The dependencies between them

You must define tasks at a manageable level, meaning:

- *Measurable*—In labor hours, time, and quality

- *Distinct*—Easy to tell when it's complete

For example, suppose you have a programming effort that takes three months and absorbs $2 million in resources. You'd want to break the effort into smaller tasks, perhaps one or two weeks in length, and define them by intermediate completion points (milestones). You must balance the desire to measure progress frequently (and thereby make the project easier to manage) with the administrative overhead and inevitable employee grumbling that constant progress checking requires.

Step 3—Assigning Resources To The Tasks

Labor is the most common resource assigned to tasks, but a great many other resources may also make up the mix for any given task. Specialized facilities, equipment, materials, and other significant resources should be considered. Most PM packages allow you to assign resources directly to a task (when you enter data for each task). You can set limits on the amount of resources that can be absorbed as the program calculates the resources required to meet the schedule, or the schedule required to cope with a given amount of resources.

Step 4—Building A Work Breakdown Structure

Some PM packages will automatically build a WBS for you based on the tasks and breakdown you supply, and some even let you change the type and numbering of WBS assigned. In any case, it's easy to perform and easy to use. Just keep in mind that the WBS is not necessarily the same as the tasks (and their sequence) because some tasks may be split into many different parts of the project, while in the WBS they're rolled up into one line item. For example, quality review may have only one WBS line item, but the actual reviews may occur many times during the course of the project.

A typical WBS will look something like this:

1.0 - Problem identification

    1.1 - Gather input from users

    1.2 - Identify problem areas

2.0 - Generate potential solutions

    2.1 - Brainstorm solutions

    2.2 - Quantify solutions

3.0 - Begin process/systems analysis

    3.1 - Process Engineering

    3.2 - Systems Analysis

Step 5—Generating Gantt, PERT, And CPM Charts

The PM package you use should make it easy to generate Gantt and PERT/CPM charts from the data you've entered, and you should be able to print them easily as well. They can come in handy for explaining the tasks and resources to those who do the work before they buy into the model.

When you enter tasks into a PM package, you're given the opportunity to link tasks together in sequence or series. Some tasks will be linked Start to Start, some Start to Finish, some Start to a percentage complete of another task. These linkages allow the program to calculate the earliest possible finish time, as well as the *critical path* (the sequence of tasks that has no slack time, also referred to as "the long pole in the tent").

Slack Time

Slack time is a big concern for everyone involved. It's the amount of time between the end of one task and the start of the next. A well-designed project will build in some slack time because it's a very unusual project that doesn't use more time per task than planned. In fact, you can consider slack time the same way you consider management reserve (the portion of the budget set aside for unexpected expenses). The project manager should monitor, allocate, and distribute slack time, not the leader of the task during which it happens to occur.

Nonlinear Relationship Between Resources Applied And Work Accomplished

Overloading tasks with resources is another major concern. Just because 5 people can accomplish a job in 3 days doesn't necessarily mean 10 people can accomplish the same job in 1.5 days. Although this is common sense, PM programs can easily lull you into false assumptions like this because modifying assigned resources and recalculating is so easy.

What actually happens during production is that people rush to meet the deadlines imposed and quality suffers. As you know, it's best to keep quality high throughout a project, because fixing things later, if possible at all, always comes at a higher price. It's best to pay attention to the concerns of those who must actually perform the work to schedule.

Step 6—Adjusting Project Constraints

Once you set your initial conditions for the project, you can perform "what-if" scenarios to determine the overall impact the project (as planned) will have on resources and schedules. You may have to reset the timing and resources consumed for tasks if the initial conditions don't match resources or time actually available.

Each time you make changes to the project to alleviate an overallocation of resources or an overschedule condition, you may cause problems elsewhere within the project. Generally, you can set the program to constrain one or the other, but not both. Sometimes you have no choice but to perform multiple passes to identify the best places to make changes, particularly if you must use judgment rather than hard data.

And don't forget, you may not have the luxury of integrating the planned new project with all the other projects (or processes) currently underway in your plant. It's always best to check with the folks who'll be doing the work so they can make reasonable estimates of the impact changes will have on current work and what they can actually perform to.

Step 7—Executing, Measuring, And Readjusting

When it's time to implement, the PM package makes it easy by allowing data entry of actual expenditures and completions versus the current date. If possible, connect the PM package to actual expenditure and completion data streams for automated updates. Reconcile any differences between the progress shown in the PM package and other expenditure measurement systems.

Variations in planned versus actual (time and money) expenditures are measured according to the following:

- *Planned expenditures/schedule*—The amount of money budgeted for work to be performed over time. On a chart, a line going from left to right depicts money on the Y axis and time on the X axis. The line reflects the planned resources consumed over the planned schedule as the planned work for each task is accomplished.

- *Actual work completed*—The amount of work completed by a given point in time.

- *Actual expenditures/schedule*—The amount of money actually spent by a given point in time.

The difference or variation between actual work completed and planned expenditures/schedule tells you whether you're ahead of or behind schedule. The difference between actual expenditures/schedule and planned expenditures/schedule tells you whether you're over or under budget.

Your PM program should tell you the percentage over or under schedule/cost both for the individual tasks and as a percentage of the project as a whole. The program should generate charts showing the entire project with the planned and actual performance to date, and you should make this data available (on some level) to everyone working on the project.

Completed Work Not Credited

Keep in mind that expenditures occur continuously, but credit for work completed may occur only at certain intervals, so it's possible to get a misleading picture of performance using these measures. Always check to verify actual progress before taking someone to task. Ideally, the leaders doing the work will also be using the tools and will inform you of any delays or problems rather than you calling them on the carpet.

Over-And-Above Work

When unplanned work occurs, it's called *over-and-above work*, because it's be-yond the scope of the original plan. You must find a way to translate necessarily vague estimates and unexpected new work back into the project. Continuing to manage using PM means a replanning effort that incorporates the new work into the original project.

Step 8—Blending Project Management Into The Toolkit

One of the critical success factors for reengineering projects is effective project management. Building a new process using a database application almost always involves some of the failure factors associated with reengineering. Some of the critical subfactors of using project management techniques are:

- *Effective use of teams*—Integrate the efforts required by each member and differentiate between tasks best accomplished by an individual and those requiring group collaboration. If the team is a "democracy," an odd number of members or a "tie-breaking vote" by the chairperson can make disputes easier to resolve.

- *Commitment of resources*—Upper managers need to be committed enough to share their valuable resources, and the people involved must demonstrate a personal commitment to accomplishing the team's goals.

- *Clarity of scope and purpose*—A clear purpose and a well-defined scope are essential to gaining commitment. The team's first tasks should be to:
  - Define the charter of the team
  - Define the expected products of the effort
  - Define how and when these products are going to be presented
  - Agree on a decision-making process

- *Effective and timely communications*—Communication must be:
  - Frequent
  - Directed to the proper stakeholders
  - Accurate from the beginning of the project until well after implementation
  - Managed by one person, preferably the chairperson

- *Realistic planning and schedules*—Projects always take longer than ex-pected and cost more. Incorporate this reality into the plan. One person should manage the schedule and ensure that everyone is apprised of changes in a timely manner.

Learning to use PM effectively is a process in itself and shouldn't be taken lightly. Spend the time and effort (and the training dollars) to do it well.

Chapter 2

The Nature Of Information

In Depth

This chapter provides an overview of our current understanding of data, information, and knowledge and how they relate to one another. We attempt to build the logical foundations for all subsequent manipulations of data within the processes supported by our eventual applications, Microsoft Access and Visual Basic for Applications (VBA).

Understanding the nature of information is necessary for effective application design and construction, and we shouldn't take it for granted. Although we won't delve into every complex aspect of data and information theory, we'll raise and carefully examine the significant issues. We want to lead you, the reader, to a fundamental understanding of how to accomplish the most basic objective of any application, a design that generates knowledge.

Information theory examines both the circumstances under which data is perceived as information and the mathematical conditions prerequisite for transmission of data. For example, the perception of data as information may not be shared by everyone who happens to be in the same situation because they each have unique notions of what makes data valuable. In the mathematical realm, however, when certain conditions (regarding transmission quality and the ability of data to represent information) are present, data can be transmitted at a certain rate.

Knowledge, of course, is very different from data or even information. As we alluded to in Chapter 1, data is equivalent to measurements, information is measurements processed, while knowledge is information combined with the recognition that action is called for. Let me give you my favorite example of the difference.

Say you're driving a car. You're doing 65 miles per hour (MPH) and the road is wet. If you could see the signals being sent to your speedometer, they wouldn't tell you anything. They're just data, a series of measurements. But your speedometer processes them and reads out something you can understand, 65 MPH. Not only is this information (processed measurements), but it's presented to you in a way that makes it easy for you to process further (because you have analog gauges, not digital readouts).

However, until you recognize that it's dangerous to be going 65 MPH on a wet road and you slow down, knowledge hasn't been generated. As a (hopefully) reasonably intelligent driver, you could use your experience (knowledge of similar situations) and slow down for yourself. If your car included a sophisticated expert system, it might automatically sense traction fading and issue a warning that you should slow down because an accident is likely. The expert system would be a knowledge-generating system (an automatic braking system [ABS] is a crude example).

Nearly as important as understanding data, information, and the production of knowledge is understanding the hardware that collects, transmits, processes, and stores it. Devices and associated technologies are constantly being invented, deployed, and discarded. Communications between devices are often complex or impossible, and the issues raised constantly change. Standards seem to solve the problems in some cases, but the standards themselves change frequently as well. Poor hardware choices or a lack of foresight have hobbled the efforts of many companies (and their Information Technology [IT] departments). This chapter provides some insight into the characteristics possessed by different technologies and how they might affect your data now and in the future.

Traditional information systems concentrate on producing information, resulting in information overload. It's now apparent that too much information can be as bad as or worse than too little. Building systems that filter unneeded information, present useful information in an easily digested format, and even take automatic action when appropriate is the objective of this book, and the foundations for doing these things are the subject of this chapter.

The Definition Of Data

There's no shortage of data. It exists everywhere around us. The photons (light) your eyes collect, the compression waves (sound) your ears hear, the pressure you feel in your posterior when you sit down, all contain data. Every form of energy expressed in our universe contains data. Generally, living things capture and process information to serve their purposes (this is one of the characteristics that mark the distinction between life forms and nonliving elements of our universe).

To make use of data, it must be captured and processed into information. Data that isn't digitized between transmission, capture, processing, or output is called analog data. For instance, when we read a book, we resolve the images on the page and translate them into words, phrases, and paragraphs. Our brains process the information into something we find useful or interesting (usually). Although we may read numbers and letters (in addition to viewing many other kinds of things), this process is still analog because the data was never digitized.

The distinction between analog and digital data is often illustrated with an example using audio wave forms. When someone plays a musical note on an instrument, it produces a wave form with smoothly curving lines (see Figure 2.1). The data inherent in the wave form is said to be analog because it changes smoothly over time and is never converted from or to numerical values during the transmission process. Although the initial signal may be pure, analog transmission and reception methods unavoidably lose signal quality because of mechanical imperfections.

When data is digitized at some point during the process, it's called digital data. One fundamental attribute of data used by computers is that it's digital, rather than analog. Digital data is created when some aspect of our universe is sampled using some kind of sensing or input method. Utilizing our audio example, the wave form is sampled (meaning a numerical value is assigned) at discrete intervals (see Figure 2.2), approximating the analog signal digitally. Digitization of analog data, by its nature, discards some of the data in the original source. However, sampling, interpolation, and error correction techniques make digitized capture and reproduction of signals superior to analog methods, in most cases.

Another benefit of digitization is the ability to store and output captured data precisely, without further degradation, as well as the ability to perform processing functions not possible with purely analog systems. Not only can signals be reproduced with a fidelity beyond the capacity of humans to discern, but the signals can be enhanced or modified with a few mouse clicks to become entirely new signals not found in the real world.

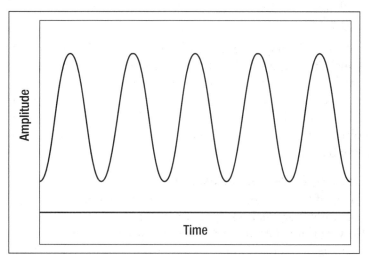

Figure 2.1 An audio wave form.

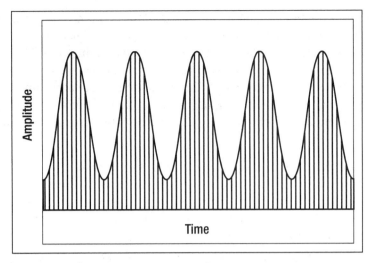

Figure 2.2   An audio wave form undergoing sampling.

Sampled data is recorded as numerical values, using a special numbering system that lends itself to processing by computers. Computers, as we all know, love numbers.

Numbering Systems

By now, it's fairly well known that computers use the binary (base 2) numbering system to store and process data. One unit of data in base 2 is called a *bit*, and by convention, 8 bits equals one *byte*. A byte has 256 possible values (2 to the 8th power), and bytes are often used to represent 256 characters—letters, numbers, special characters, and so on.

The advantage of the base-2 numbering system is that it contains only two digits, zero and one. This corresponds nicely to easily detected values in electrical circuits, *on* and *off*. Of course, any other values can be represented by assembling the digits of the binary numbering system into larger and larger blocks. For instance, the number 12 in our familiar base-10 (decimal) numbering system is equivalent to 1100 in base 2. And the number 100 in base 2 is equivalent to the number 4 in base 10.

Measurements, Units, And Dimensions

A single piece of data is defined as a measurement, sometimes called a data point. It could be a number, such as 4, or a letter, such as C, or something else altogether. However, for data to have meaning, it must include some indication of what it's a measurement of and the units used. For instance, the number 72 by itself, though constituting a valid data point, has no meaning until we declare that it's a *measure of height, in inches.* Furthermore, outside the context of a thing being measured, the data point, 72" high, has no informative value. It's meaningful data, but without context, it informs us of nothing.

In the previous example, 72 is the value of the data point. Inches are the units of the data point, and height is the dimension of the data point. If we were to store this data in a database about professional athletes, perhaps there would be a table containing data related to the athletes, and perhaps there would be a field named Height in Inches. The data value, 72, could be stored in this field, and the field name would give us the units and dimension of the data, while the Athlete Name field would tell us who the measurement applies to.

Although it may not be intuitive, we can think of all data as measurements. The first name of an athlete is a data point constituting a measurement of the name value from the domain of all possible first names. The first name can be thought of as a unit (although these units are not ordinal) and the dimension is full names. And by the way, an athlete's name is made up of text characters, so it falls into the text data type.

Data Types

Essentially, data values can assume any form. They can be numerical, text, dates, binary data, and so on. Although all digital data is sampled and stored as binary numerical values, the various types of data take on many forms, each with its own unique storage and processing requirements. Placing logical limitations on data by assigning a data type makes storage and processing easier and less prone to error. For instance, assigning a data type of string with a limitation to four characters tells the processor that this particular data must never exceed four characters, cannot be processed with arithmetical operators, and should not be mistaken for a date. Storage requirements are fixed, and data falling out of range or attempts at processing with forbidden operators result in error conditions. There are several data types we can use.

The Boolean Data Type

The simplest data type used is the Boolean (or logical) data type. In Microsoft Access, it's stored using two bytes, but it can be represented with just one bit, a single zero or one for False or True. For any condition or question with only two possible states, the logical data type is useful. Sometimes a series of Yes/No tests is preferable to a single, more complex evaluation, and in these cases, the logical data type comes in handy as well.

The Integer Data Type

Integers, of course, are whole numbers that may be operated upon with arithmetical operators. Some of the many variations on the Integer data type include: signed and unsigned, 8-bit, 16-bit, 32-bit, and so on. The range depends upon the number of bits available. For instance, with 8 bits, the range spans 256 values, while 32 bits allows 4,294,967,296 values. When the values are signed, half of them fall below zero and half above, while unsigned values are all positive (starting with zero, not one). Access (and VBA) use the Byte, Integer, and Long data types to represent whole numbers.

Integer values are commonly used as numbers, but a useful programming construct assigns integers to specific constants thereby allowing nonnumeric values to be evaluated. For instance, perhaps there are seven colors to choose from when buying a car. If each color is assigned a number (an enumerated list) using the Byte or Integer data types, programming, storage, and evaluation of the data are simplified.

Floating-Point Data Types

Floating-point data types, as the name implies, contain numbers with a decimal point. As with Integer data types, their range is determined by the number of bits available, and they allow positive and negative values. Single, Double, and Decimal data types are used in Access and VBA, and they range from an extremely minute fraction above or below zero to numbers so immense they are difficult to comprehend in any realistic way. The Single and Double data types use exponents to represent some values, while the Decimal data type uses straight numerical values.

In Microsoft Access, floating-point numbers can also be contained in the Currency and Variant data types (in fact, the Decimal datatype is a subtype of the Variant data type). The Currency data type uses what are called scaled integers to avoid rounding errors that can occur with ordinary floating-point values.

Rounding errors are caused by the fact that the precision of floating-point values in ordinary data types is limited by the size or accuracy of the number that may be represented. In many cases, the limits don't cause difficulty, but where the limits introduce significant error, some other solution must be used. Scaled integers eliminate rounding errors by multiplying numbers containing decimal places by powers of 10 until the decimal places (and potential errors) are gone. The caveat here is that scaled integer data types have their own range of values and are limited to four decimal places. Dates are numbers of a sort, but have their own data type.

Date Data Type

Like numbers, dates and times are used throughout our world to measure our passage through the fourth dimension. Unlike numbers, conversions between years, months, days, hours, minutes, and seconds are not straightforward, and because of leap seconds and leap years, accurate conversions depend on starting and ending points.

A special data type called Date is used to represent and store date and time values in Access and VBA. Dates are stored internally as 8-byte floating-point numbers. The value to the left of the decimal point equals the number of days since December 30, 1899, while the value on the right is a decimal fraction of a day (12:00 noon being 0.5000 days, and so on).

Storing date and time values as floating-point numbers has the advantage of allowing arithmetical calculations to be performed on them (handy if you want to add nonstandard time periods). Access and VBA also contain additional built-in functions for handling leap years and conversions from a variety of traditional date formats. Sometimes dates are inserted as strings, but most programs can translate strings into dates accurately.

String Data Types

Strings are useful for storing the vast majority of individual data items we encounter: names, addresses, phone numbers, ID numbers, people, places, things, and the adjectives used to describe their qualities. Strings are simply characters strung in a row, like beads on a string.

Strings are sequences of characters with no formal numerical value. Although they sometimes can look exactly like numbers to us, they can't be manipulated with arithmetical operators. For instance, the strings "4" and "four" have the same meaning and can't be added to each other. Likewise, the strings "Dave" and "JoAnn" can't be added arithmetically. However, string data can be concatenated (one appended to the other) so that, for example, the strings "data" and "type" become "datatype".

In Microsoft Access and VBA, strings can be either of variable length or fixed length, with a storage requirement slightly more than the string length and a range from 1 to nearly 2 billion bytes. Each byte can represent one of 256 characters; the first 128 correspond to the ASCII character set, and the second 128 are used for special characters.

Object Data Types

Object data types are pointers to objects, programming constructs that have properties you may manipulate. For instance, you may wish to reference and modify the properties of a spreadsheet programmatically. Access and VBA support the Object data type (four bits in size), allowing you to set the variable as a reference to the spreadsheet. Through the pointer, you can modify the properties of the spreadsheet.

Variant Data Type

The Variant data type is specific to Microsoft Access and VBA (although similar constructs appear in other programming languages and applications). It doesn't have a fixed type until it assumes a value, then it becomes the appropriate data type. It can contain the Empty and Null values, as well as changing data type as required. It's quite useful but should be avoided if possible (data type conversion errors are common when the Variant data type is used).

Custom Data Types

Assigning a name to a data type creates a custom data type. These are called user-defined data types in Access and VBA, and they can include one or more of the data types supported. Although defining a custom data type with a single type of variable is useful in some circumstances, it's more common to assign multiple data types to a custom data type. Because a user-defined data type with multiple data types included is actually a data structure, we'll cover it in the next section.

Data Structures

Now that you're familiar with basic data types, we can examine how these types can be used as building blocks for *data structures*. Data structures include user-defined data types, arrays, records, and other techniques for associating items of data. Their purpose is to make handling blocks of related data easier, and they do this by reducing the amount of work (or code) it takes to effect actions upon them. In a sense, the fields, records, and tables in a database are data structures because they define a relationship between the various items of data contained in them.

User-Defined Data Types

VBA allows you to write a statement defining a data structure that contains one or more data types, the user-defined data type. You might be wondering why this is necessary considering that this data can be stored in separate data types in a straightforward way. The answer is that setting a special data type for commonly used data makes it easier to manipulate the data programmatically. Passing a set of variables to a procedure can be done with one variable (as a user-defined data type), rather than several individual variables. Also, you can use the user-defined data type to build simple record structures within your VBA code.

Arrays

Arrays are indexed data structures that hold several data items in a single variable. Arrays are used when your data can be related by integers. The index can be a sequence of numbers or simply ordinal values, such as the year or the quarter (see Figure 2.3). Arrays can have more than one index or dimension but are ordinarily kept to just one or two; otherwise they can be difficult to visualize and to use properly. Arrays make the programmer's life much easier by allowing particular items to be accessed by their reference in the index. That makes it easier to concentrate on the real questions, like the fundamental properties of the data.

Index 1

Index 2	Stocks	Bonds	CDs	Gold
Q1	65	25	7	3
Q2	60	25	12	3
Q3	25	60	10	5
Q4	20	65	5	10

Year-To-Year Percentage Of Holdings

Figure 2.3 Data in an array.

Fundamental Data Properties

The circumstances under which data is collected say much about what the data means and how useful it is for any given situation. It's worth noting that the better data is documented, the more likely it will be useful for some purpose or another. Data collected in medical records often proves valuable to researchers years later as they struggle to understand epidemics or the cause of a drug's side effects.

On the other hand, each piece of information relating to data collected is an additional cost in terms of storage and manipulation. Some data may never be useful, at least not to you. Making sure you have at least enough data to serve your immediate purposes (as well as your anticipated needs) is your first priority. If you can then spare the time, effort, and storage space to accumulate additional data that may be pertinent, by all means, do so. Knowing which data is necessary and which data is just nice to have is a matter of categorizing the data according to the processes it supports.

Categorizing Data

Data can be categorized or classified by almost any characteristic, but obviously your first objective is to identify those categories that are of fundamental importance to your organization. A good place to start is with the mission statement. Just like the processes that support the mission, the data and information that support the processes are derived from the mission, and the relative importance of any given data is a direct function of the importance of the process it supports. Highly important data (and the applications that process it) are often termed *mission-critical.*

Even though the argument could be made that all data must be mission-critical (otherwise, why is it being collected at all?) the fact is that organizations may collect huge amounts of data that aren't critical and may even be frivolous, useless, or possibly harmful. We've listed some kinds of data collected by organizations in their common order of importance:

- Financial and accounting data; employees expect accurate paychecks, and shareholders abhor "restated" financial results.

- Customer and supplier records, along with the orders of each.

- Trade secrets such as product plans, manufacturing data, and research for existing or new products.

- Employee data, including personal data, assignments, and accomplishments.

- Current sales and marketing data, including trends in the marketplace.

As an example of data that may only weakly serve a stated company mission, consider the unofficial company bulletin board. Organizations routinely set up and maintain them and allow employees to post messages to them (either online or physically), and, yet, it's likely that no one could point to an improvement in the bottom line as a result of one. You could say they improve morale, but proving it would be difficult. Nevertheless, you'd probably hear plenty of complaints if you removed it.

Perhaps the best way to understand data is to remember that the importance of a particular piece of data (and the situation in which it's provided) varies according to the person making use of it. This is the relative value of data, and it changes unpredictably in many cases.

Relative Value Of Data

The value of a particular piece of data is in the eye of the beholder, and because organizations are made up of multiple individuals (as well as outside stakeholders), many opinions are usually available. Though it might seem straightforward to assume that a process requires a piece of data based on the systems analysis, if a person is involved, that person might decide otherwise. People tend to use judgment and experience rather than data for the simple reason that it's easier. In fact, people will argue endlessly about how their judgment is better than recently collected facts, and they seem to delight in "proving the machine wrong." It's human nature, and you'd better get used to it.

The point here is that although you can design a logically coherent system that takes all data into account and makes decisions based on the facts, people don't necessarily follow the same logic. They will frequently tell you to change the design to give them just the data they want in the format they want. Although it may result in a less than perfect system, your best bet is to make people happy. Just be sure to politely inform them (don't be patronizing), and if they become aware of their deficiency later, you can always provide the additional data. Chances are things are going to change anyway, and as they learn the system, they'll soon be asking you to make the changes you would have made in the first place.

The way data is displayed also affects its perceived value. As we began to discuss in the opening paragraphs, digital data (numbers) has far less meaning for human beings than analog-style data, even when exactly the same data is displayed. In the search for knowledge, anything that gives an indication of the whole situation rather than just a seemingly random data point is more helpful.

Many factors influence whether or not data is perceived as useful and meaningful to humans. Because human perception is the object of the data display, all the usual human failings come into play. Education, social background, habit, alertness, and so forth all play a role in beneficial data display. But there are some things designers can do to improve the situation across the board:

- Provide enough information to make the display interesting but not so much that the user is overwhelmed by information.

- Display the information to the user in familiar ways.

- Display information that's related to other information in a way that illustrates the relationship, if possible. For instance, when using charts and graphs, show limits or thresholds.

- Display information in pictures when practical. As the saying goes, a picture's worth a thousand words.

- Make it easy to navigate the information. Use a standard interface (one of the greatest things the Web is doing for us is training everyone to use a common interface).

- Involve as many of the senses as is practical in the display of information.
  Use color, sound, different sized fonts, anything that draws attention to
  relevant information.

Intelligent display of information makes all the difference in today's attention-
driven economy. With so many influences competing for our limited attention,
even seemingly mundane applications need to "toot their own horn," so to speak.
And because things change so rapidly, we need our information-producing devices to go out of their way to make us aware of it.

Change

Change, of course, is the one constant. In fact, the very definition of time is the
change we perceive. But the passage of time is only one type of change. Things
can change proximity (move in three dimensions), and the characteristics of things
can change. People can become taller, die, get sick, go bald, earn degrees, get
married, and so on. Buildings can be constructed, remodeled, added to, demol-
ished, sold, and the occupants of a building (as well as the use to which it's put)
can change. Even totally nonphysical things can change. Markets can shrink and
grow and be created by nothing more than perception. Sometimes people who
are stingy can have an epiphany and become generous (like Scrooge). All of these
changes can affect the value of data from one instant to the next.

Not only is change a constant, the fact is, change is accelerating. As advances in
communications, computational ability, and the innovation process change, everything about the technological landscape, markets, governments, and businesses
changes as well, and the changes feed upon themselves. The pace of change today will be considered mellow 20 years from now.

Because change is so common and so constantly accelerating, a significant portion of the data collected concerns changes to things that are being tracked. This
data is a good source of information about the importance of other data and also
provides the foundation for much of the process improvement we spoke of in
Chapter 1. Of course, it won't do much good to collect such data unless you've
made provisions for storing it in an accessible format.

Data Storage, Networking, And Processing

This section offers a brief overview of storage, networking, and processing architectures. Chapter 7 covers these subjects in much more detail and illustrates the
connection between architecture and database system solutions. So let's start at
the beginning, when data is initially acquired.

Sampling data requires a sensor that can convert the incoming signal into measurements. Immediately following the sampling there must be some means of
storing and/or transmitting the data, to further either storage or processing or

both. Data can be stored in ways limited only by your imagination, but as a practical matter, the key considerations are size, cost, and access speed.

Size, cost, and access speed are related. The larger the size (or weight) of a storage medium, the more it's likely to cost, either to purchase or to use. Lower cost may make it more practical to use less efficient media. Access speed is affected (generically across devices) by your ability to retrieve data in a sequential or random fashion—sequential retrieval being slower—and by the type of retrieval technology. And faster access speeds mean lower retrieval times (and, therefore, less time waiting) and greater effectiveness of the medium. There are quite a few methods that can be used to store data, but not all of them are viable.

Storage Media

Paper can be used to store digital data (remember punch cards?). Poke some holes in various locations in a card, and read these holes with a mechanical reader. But paper storage is large by today's standards, so the cost per data unit stored is high. Accessing the data is slow and cumbersome as well, and paper tends to degrade fairly rapidly.

Magnetic media are commonly used for data storage: cassette tapes, floppy disks, hard disks, and so on. Depending on the type of device, storage density, and retrieval methods, magnetic media can be among the most effective methods for storing data. Magnetic media are predicted to have useful lifetimes on the order of 30 years but shouldn't be considered reliable beyond three to seven years, particularly if subjected to a less than pristine environment.

Optical media such as compact disks (CDs) and digital video disks (DVDs) are close to magnetic media in storage densities, retrieval speeds, and cost and have the added benefit of lasting far longer under the same conditions. Both magnetic and optical media use sequential and random access retrieval methods, but some come much closer to electronic random access speeds.

Random access media (such as the RAM in your computer) store data as electrical charges on silicon chips. The data can be accessed directly using its address on the chip, and retrieval speeds are limited by the clock speed at which the computer system's data bus operates (or, more generally, by the speed of conduction for the material). Random access media are higher in cost but much faster at retrieving data, although they eventually burn out (they're electrical components). Also, many forms of electronic memory can't store data without the power being on.

Storage Formats

Are you familiar with Notepad, the basic text editor that comes with Windows? You can use it to perform very simple ASCII text editing functions, meaning you can type characters, edit them, copy and paste them, delete them, and save them as a file.

If you open a document created in Microsoft Word using Notepad, you'll notice thousands of extra characters in addition to the text that you entered in your Word document. These are formatting characters that Word uses to perform its word-processing magic. If you open an image file (try the CompuServe Graphics Interchange Format, GIF) you'll notice mostly funny computer characters rather than anything remotely intelligible.

The point, of course, is that these file types are full of data but not much information. The ability to generate information resides just as much in the application program that created (or can display) a certain file format as it does in the file of data. As new applications and file types are created, the data in older files becomes harder to use. Eventually, if the computer hardware and applications used to make a file can't be found, the data may lose its value entirely. In a similar fashion, data files originating in different applications may not be compatible. Incompatible or outdated formats can make it impossible to use some data, or they add tremendously to processing overhead. That's where processing technologies come into play.

Processing Technologies

File types and storage media are only one part of the equation. Databases are frequently too large to entirely read into RAM, and, therefore, only portions are selected and processed at any given time. The sequencing, ordering, and indexing of physical data on the disk plays an important role in determining retrieval and processing throughput.

Physically, a file on a disk contains data stored as records, each consisting of a sequence of bits. For example, the values for name, social security number, and phone number may be stored as a sequence of bits (according to the data type for each field) separated by separator characters (see Figure 2.4). On a disk, data is recorded in fixed-size *blocks* specified by the operating system. If the block size is larger than the record size, a single block may hold many records. If the opposite is true, a single record may span several blocks.

Because records may be of fixed or variable length, depending upon the data types and data stored, it's possible to waste a significant amount of disk space (and slow down retrieval) because the starting and ending points of the data don't match their corresponding points on the blocks. If records are of fixed length and smaller than block size, an unspanned record organization can be used, simplifying record processing because each record starts at a known point in the block. For records that are larger than block size or are variable in length, a spanned

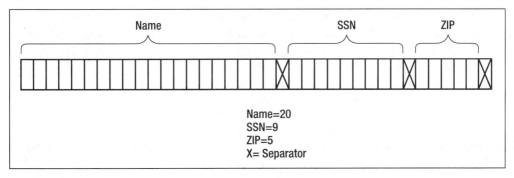

Figure 2.4   Illustrated data.

organization is used. In any case, the physical organization of records and the order in which they are stored has a significant effect on processing throughput, particularly searches.

Searching Records For Data Values

To review or process data, the data must be located and read into memory. *Retrieval* operations find data, while *update* operations make changes to it. Retrieval operations include:

- *Find*—Locates the first record in which the search condition is true.

- *Find Next*—Locates the next record in which the search condition is true.

Update operations include:

- *Insert*—Inserts a new record into the file.

- *Modify*—Changes some field value of the current record.

- *Delete*—Deletes the current record data and removes the record from existence.

Retrieval operations support update operations by finding the appropriate record according to specific *search conditions*. Search conditions can be very simple or extremely complex, but they have a common trait. Complex searches are composed of multiple simple searches. Suppose you want to find every employee named Jones making over $100,000, for example. Records would be searched for every instance of the data value "Jones" (at the location of the Last Name field), and the resulting record set would be searched for salary values higher than "100,000" (at the location of the Salary field).

Because the speed with which records can be processed depends on the speed with which they can be found, database researchers are constantly working to devise more efficient data storage methods that lend themselves to more efficient data *access methods*.

To illustrate this concept, imagine storing a new record in a file. If you just write the data for the new record at the end of the file, no other processing is required and you have a very efficient record insertion method. However, chances are good that the data in the files will be totally unordered, which means that finding a particular piece of data involves searching every record. Called a *linear search*, this is the slowest possible access method.

In addition, deleting records leaves empty, unused space within the file, wasting space and slowing retrieval speeds. To alleviate this condition, databases should be compacted or reorganized on a regular basis. Reorganization physically reorders the data to remove wasted space. To improve access speed even more, an index can be created.

Indexes

Encyclopedias and dictionaries are in alphabetical order for a reason: if you know the order, it's much easier to quickly locate data. But records could be ordered according to any of the fields, depending upon the data you need. Indexes solve this problem. They're a separate set of data that contains pointers to the actual location of the real data. Relational databases make use of a key field, automatically indexing and physically ordering records by this field. Other fields can also be indexed. Of course, the drawback is that two operations are required to update data, one to update the real data and one to update the index.

Several well-known types of indexes (primary, secondary, B-tree, B+tree, and so on) and a variety of algorithms exist for accessing data within them most quickly, but they're beyond the scope of this book. Please see the appendix of additional resources for further reading if you're so inclined. The important point is that differences in indexing strategy can impact your processing requirements.

Processor Strategies

In the early days of computing, most processing occurred sequentially, meaning step number two couldn't occur until the results of step number one were available. Technologists focused on increasing the power of single processors by packing ever more transistors on a silicon chip, increasing the instructions per cycle, and accelerating the clock speed.

But even in the early days, engineers realized that some problems lent themselves to distributed processing, and many of the technologies we take for granted today have their roots in the early research. Computer networks such as local area networks (LAN), wide area networks (WAN), the client-server environment, and improved processing architectures such as reduced instruction set computing (RISC), symmetric multiprocessing (SMP), and massively parallel processor (MPP) were developed to share processing resources and are now commonplace.

RISC is a successor to complex instruction set computing (CISC). Simply put, a smaller, less complex instruction set can be processed more quickly (on a computer chip optimized for this type of architecture) than a larger, more complex instruction set. Intel CPUs use a CISC design (x86 Pentium), but are due to introduce RISC designs by late 1999. PowerPC and Alpha CPUs already use RISC designs.

Another innovation that increases RISC speeds is *superscalar* design (see Figure 2.5). Superscalar means floating point operations are performed in parallel. *Pipelining* is another form of parallel processing, although both superscalar and pipelining, in this context, refer to processing functions taking place on a single chip, they shouldn't be confused with multiprocessor designs.

Multiprocessor computers contain several processors linked together. Intel's recent CPU offerings are designed to function well together, and more software applications are being designed or revised for multiple processors. Multiple processors gain processing speed by sharing the workload of any given problem among themselves, but poorly structured hardware or improperly designed software can actually reduce performance. In addition, the gains are nonlinear because of extra processing overhead with each processor added.

Another way to take advantage of multiple processors is to connect many computers together in *clusters* (see Figure 2.6). Because each computer may only be active for a portion of the central processing unit's (CPU) available cycles,

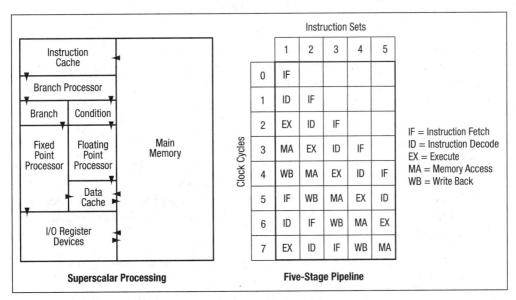

Figure 2.5   Superscalar and pipelining processor architectures.

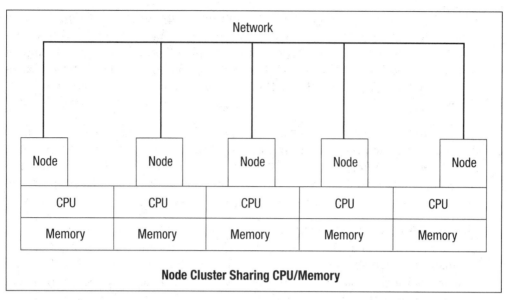

Figure 2.6   Cluster architecture.

workload sharing permits the system, as a whole, to get more work done in less time. Clustered systems lend themselves to processing across networks and are especially useful for distributed databases. Of course, even the best CPU or cluster must employ the right operating system to gain an advantage.

Operating Systems

Although Microsoft Access runs on Windows 95/98 and Windows NT, many other operating systems run mainframes, workstations, Apple computers, and other specialized systems. A quick search on the Web produced the following list of operating systems (some of which may not even technically qualify as operating systems, but you can bet some technophile somewhere is using them):

MaxFrame, VMS, TOPS-10, TOPS-20, Solaris, SunOS, MS-DOS, Ultrix/OSF1/Digital Unix, DG/UX, HP-UX, Dynix, ESIX, CTIX, Coherent, SCO, XENIX, UNICOS, MVS, VM, CMS, NOS, NOS/VE, AOS, AOS/VS, CP/M, IOS, Atari TOS, QNX, Apple OS, Magic Cap, MIMIX, Free|Net|OpenBSD386, BSDI, Linux, VENIX EDS, OS/400, OS/9, OS/2, IRIX, AmigaDOS, GCOS, MPE, MPE/IX, VS, UnixWare, NetWare, Windows 3.1x, Windows NT, Windows 95, Windows 98, Plan 9, Oberon, Amoeba, NEXTSTEP, and Mach

The major operating systems in use today are Unix and Windows variations, and they tend to be classified by the number of bits they process simultaneously, as well as by their file organization concepts and their networking capabilities. Multiple user, server, or enterprise editions tend to cost more, and although some

Unix variations are free, the support will end up costing just about as much. Most companies buy proprietary operating systems for the express purpose of having someone to call if problems arise, but because software interfaces (called drivers) must be created for every piece of hardware attached to a computer or network, plenty of gray areas still exist for software makers to hide in.

For example, suppose you buy a new brand name plotter to work with your big brand computer-aided drafting application, both of which need to run over your major manufacturer operating system. You set up the plotter and software according to the installation procedures provided, but it doesn't work. You call the application software maker, and they claim the operating system is at fault. You call the operating system maker, and they claim the driver is faulty. You call the plotter maker, and they claim their plotter works fine with other software.

Now take the same problem and multiply it one hundred times over the network of an ordinary corporation. No wonder network administrators are paid well. They need the money for the hair transplants they'll need after they've ripped out all their existing hair trying to solve network *interoperability* problems.

Networking Technologies

Networks of computers are ubiquitous (as is the word *ubiquitous*, I'm afraid) today, and they extend the power of computers in unprecedented ways. The melding of computers and communications increases our ability to collect, transmit, and process data into information beyond simply speeding things up. In the same way that each computer has an operating system to coordinate the functions of its hardware parts, a network of computers has a *network operating system* (NOS) coordinating communications among connected computers, printers, file servers, and so on. This section gives a brief overview of networking fundamentals. It isn't intended to make you a networking expert, but it should give you some insight into how networks operate, the common terminology, and the role networks play in your system. As mentioned, Chapter 7 gives a more complete analysis of the connection between networking and database systems.

Transmission of data among computers on a network is accomplished using various *transmission protocols*. Protocols define the coding and functions used to transmit data between computers and devices on networks and the Internet. At the macro level, networking can be split into two parts: the physical and the logical. The physical part is the actual hardware and electrical signals that transmit data. The logical part is the coding of the signals. How they interact is the subject of the open systems interconnection (OSI) model.

The OSI model (see Figure 2.7) was devised to offer a standard concept by which software and hardware manufacturers could organize their products so

Application	Layer 7
Presentation	Layer 6
Session	Layer 5
Transport	Layer 4
Network	Layer 3
Data Link	Layer 2
Physical	Layer 1

Figure 2.7   The OSI model.

that there would be at least the possibility of *interoperability* and *interconnectivity*. Interconnectivity refers to the ability of nodes on a network to exchange signals (Layer 1), while interoperability refers to the ability of nodes on a network to understand the signals being sent (layers 2 through 7). Nodes on a network may have limited interoperability if they can understand signals at some but not all of the layers, but true interoperability means full understanding across all layers.

Creating, updating, and maintaining transmission protocols is the job of a variety of organizations, such as the International Organization for Standardization (ISO), the Institute of Electrical and Electronics Engineers (IEEE), and, for Internet protocols, the World Wide Web Consortium (W3C). The OSI model splits the network into the following seven layers:

- *Physical*—The physical layer transmits and receives data at the most basic level. It consists of the wiring or cabling, the components that are used to connect a computer's network interface card (NIC) to the cabling, the signaling used to transmit and receive data, and the capability to sense and correct errors. The protocols supported are ISO 2110, IEEE 802, and IEEE 802.2.

- *Data link layer*—The data link layer, which logically sits atop the physical layer, synchronizes data transmission and provides frame-level error control and recovery. This layer performs frame formatting and the cyclic redundancy check (CRC). It uses Ethernet and Token Ring access methods, and supplies addressing at the physical layer for transmitted frames. Supported protocols are:

  - Serial Line Internet Protocol (SLIP)

  - Compressed Serial Line Internet Protocol (CSLIP)

- Point-to-Point Protocol (PPP)
- Maximum Transmission Unit (MTU)

- *Network layer*—The network layer manages message forwarding among computers. This layer forwards data in the most economical path (logically and physically), based on network information, and allows data to flow over other networks via routers (routers are defined at this layer as well). Supported protocols are:

  - Internet Protocol (IP)
  - Address Resolution Protocol (ARP)
  - Reverse Address Recognition Protocol (RARP)
  - Internet Control Message Protocol (ICMP)
  - Routing Information Protocol (RIP)
  - Open Shortest Path First (OSPF)
  - Border Gateway Protocol (BGP)
  - Internet Group Membership Protocol (IGMP)

- *Transport layer*—The transport layer is used for reliable end-to-end transmission of data, ensuring that data is sent quickly, error-free, and in the correct order. (Although data packets may be received out of order, this layer provides the ordering information to reassemble the data correctly.) Supported protocols are:

  - Transmission Control Protocol (TCP)
  - User Datagram Protocol (UDP)

- *Session layer*—The session layer provides a communications link for devices or computers on the network. It establishes the connection, maintains it while in use, and terminates the connection when transmission is complete. In doing so, it translates name-to-station addresses.

- *Presentation layer*—The presentation layer is used to translate the data to and from transmission formats into a format that can be used by an application, as well as enabling data encryption.

- *Application layer*—The application layer allows applications to run across the network. These applications include email, file transfer, remote management, and so on.

In addition to standard networking protocols, proprietary protocols are in use. Major networking software and hardware companies originally developed their own protocols for their clients, but as systems grew more interconnected, the need for translation increased. For example, Cisco Systems is a dominant supplier of hardware that forms the infrastructure of many networks. According to

Cisco's router configuration manual, Cisco networking hardware (routers, gateways, and bridges) supports AppleTalk, Apollo Domain, Banyan Vines, CHAOSnet, IP, ISO Connectionless Network Services (CLNS), Novell IPX, Phase IV DECnet, Xerox's PARC Universal Protocol (PUP), and Xerox Network Services (XNS).

For transmission purposes, data is often broken into chunks called packets. Each packet is sent across the network, and the original data set is reassembled at the other end. To illustrate how one of the logical layers formats data, examine Internet Protocol version 4 (IPv4). An IPv4 packet header (see Figure 2.8) contains the following data bits:

- Version, 4 bits
- Header length, 4 bits
- Type of service, 8 bits
- Total length of packet, 16 bits
- Identifier, 16 bits
- Flags, 3 bits
- Fragment offset, 13 bits
- Time to live, 8 bits
- Protocol, 8 bits
- Header checksum, 16 bits
- Source address, 32 bits
- Destination address, 32 bits

Only after this header data is the actual transmitted data included. Note the amount of overhead (160 bits) required for each packet just so the network can accomplish its transmission function. And note that various types of networks use different packet structures and have differing bandwidth specifications as well.

Network Topology And Bandwidth

Another consideration when building (or examining) a networking structure is the *topology* of the network. Note that, in many cases, the network is already in place, and you'll be limited in the amount of new hardware/software you can add

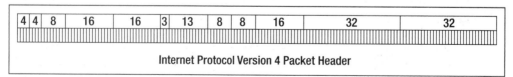

| 4 | 4 | 8 | 16 | 16 | 3 | 13 | 8 | 8 | 16 | 32 | 32 |

Internet Protocol Version 4 Packet Header

Figure 2.8   Illustrated IPv4 packet header.

(mainly by budget and the need to standardize with legacy systems). Network topology is the physical method by which computers and other network resources are connected and the strategy used to communicate among network nodes.

On LANs, some networks are connected in a daisy chain, meaning one system connects directly to the next, and the next, and the next, until the circle is closed. Other networks all connect to a central hub that resembles a star pattern (see Figure 2.9). Some wiring schemes allow for simultaneous sending and receiving of transmissions (full-duplex), while others may only send or receive at any given moment (half-duplex). Because all network devices can't send and receive at the same time and because each machine is only interested in messages addressed to itself, messaging schemes are also required. Token Ring schemes pass a token from node to node, and only the node possessing the token can "speak." As you can imagine, the topology and communications scheme used can limit data transfer speeds dramatically.

Another limitation on data transfer speeds is bandwidth. Bandwidth is related to information theory in that information theory forms the mathematical basis for determining the bandwidth available in a given connection. Bandwidth is defined as the amount of data that can be reliably transmitted in a time period (10 million bits per second, for instance). Bandwidth depends on the media used, the signaling methods, and the amount of noise (signal-to-noise ratio). A good illustration of bandwidth considerations is the analog modem.

Analog modems are used to transmit digital data over analog phone lines, using sensors at either end that differentiate between rapidly pulsed analog tones. The first modems developed had low bandwidth (I remember when 300 bits per second was common). As signaling methodologies and sensing hardware improved, transmission rates went up, until today we have modems that transmit 33,600 bits

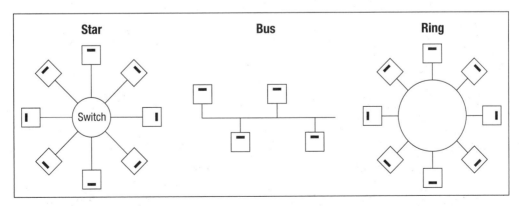

Figure 2.9   Common network topologies.

per second. The amount of noise present in analog phone lines and equipment limits further bandwidth improvement, but, as usual, computer and communications scientists have found some loopholes. The recent development of 56Kbps (56,000 bits per second) modems using analog phone lines takes advantage of the fact that many lines are digital at least part of the way. This means losses to noise are reduced, and higher bandwidths are possible (although, if you have a 56Kbps modem, you know that you never actually reach a full 56Kbps).

All the capture, storage, transmission, and processing technologies we've discussed so far are based on traditional silicon chips. They process data by relaying signals via electrical connections between the transistors etched into them and between themselves and supporting chip sets. In the future, wholly new technologies may change everything about how processing works.

Processors Of The Future

Work is ongoing to develop processors that communicate internally and externally with light rather than electricity, called (appropriately enough) optical computing. Other scientists are using the very stuff of life, deoxyribonucleic acid (DNA), to perform calculations, although in a much different manner than we're accustomed. And physicists are hard at work trying to create a quantum computer that can instantaneously give results to the most complex problems.

Even though about once a year a news story breaks foretelling the end of improvements in computing speed (supposedly due to reaching the physical limits of materials used to manufacture processors), computer researchers always seem to find a way to overcome the barriers. Chances are good that Moore's law (a doubling of computing speed with a corresponding halving of the price every 18 months) will continue to hold true for the foreseeable future.

Immediate Solutions

This section provides step-by-step instructions for identifying and using the correct data types and structures, as well as evaluating the worth of data as circumstances and the data itself change over time. Chapters 6 and 7 provide additional information along these lines, resulting in a data warehouse solution.

Identifying Sources And Types Of Data

Information (or knowledge design) systems begin with data, either imported, collected during use, or both. Therefore, the first step in building a functioning system is to recognize the kind of data available. As an example, we'll use a fictitious company that constructs animated forensic simulations for clients in the scientific, manufacturing, advertising, and legal arenas. Our company will be called Visualysis, to emphasize the visual nature of the finished products.

Step 1—Differentiating Between Internal Data And Product Data

First to be addressed is data concerning the company itself. Financial and accounting data, employee data, customers, orders, and suppliers must all be collected and stored in a relatively fixed (but scalable) system. On the other hand, data for each project may be all over the map. One client might want an accident reconstructed, meaning witness interviews must be correlated. Another might want the inner workings of a manufacturing process simulated for troubleshooting purposes. Project data forms the basis for the products the company produces, and each project may require a different and unique solution for capture, transmission, processing, and storage.

The source of internal company data is usually manual data entry (we'll discuss manual and automatic data capture and entry in Chapter 3), so let's turn our attention to the unusual data sources Visualysis must reckon with. Entering the name of a new employee or giving someone a raise is as simple as typing on a keyboard, so the sampling technique is pretty low-tech. But if accurate visualization of a scene requires motion capture or audio recording, that's a whole different story. This type of data is specific to projects.

Step 2—Determining Data Sampling Parameters

Simulating the motion of people is frequently the goal of computer animators, but it can be very difficult to achieve realistic motion patterns by programming alone. Motion capture techniques allow three-dimensional motion to be digitized, typically the motion of actors or of objects whose motion is not mechanical (and therefore not easily simulated). Motion capture systems use transmitters and sensors to track the location of points at key spots (on an actor's body, for instance) over time.

Because the system captures data in four dimensions, the data stream contains location data, time data, and point identification (ID) data. There is also some overhead data purely for processing purposes. The accuracy of the resulting data depends upon the specifications of the system in use, and the ability to derive fluid, lifelike motion to apply to animations depends on the sampling rate.

Step 3—Determining Units Of Measure And Dimension

Sampling rate is ordinarily limited by the quality of the equipment used to do the sampling. Higher quality equipment or instrumentation will have a lower signal-to-noise ratio and will usually have a complementary ability to achieve higher sampling rates. For our motion-capture example, a higher sampling rate equates to more raw data. In this case, a higher sampling rate relates to the units we're measuring.

For Visualysis motion-capture projects, location and time are the dimensions being measured, but the units of measure may vary. For example, time may be measured as seconds, milliseconds, microseconds, and so on. Distance may be measured using the English system or the metric system. And the points may be numbered or use a combination of letters and numbers to identify the specific grouping they're associated with (e-l for left elbow, for instance). Once the data source, type of data, and parameters have been established, the process of assigning data types can begin.

Assigning Data Types

Microsoft Access has quite a few data types we can choose from. They're assigned when tables are constructed, but the process involves more than just assigning a data type. For instance, a string data type can be set to a specific number of characters, and it can become a primary key or have an index set for it. Numeric data can be formatted using several common formats, and a special data type (Autonumber) will automatically increment a counter for each new record (very useful for assigning new primary key values).

The data type most of us are familiar with is text, called *string* data in the computer world. When we think of data in a database, we commonly assume it's text data. Names, addresses, phone numbers, zip codes, and myriad other things and adjectives describing them are text data. Common text is fairly easy to assign a data type to. It's the special characters and text masquerading as numbers that need to be watched out for.

Step 1—Determining String Data Parameters

String data can be anything from a single character to encyclopedias full of text, but string data is commonly limited to less than 100 characters. String data can also be identified by the lack of numeric operations that might be performed on it. For instance, although you might decide to segregate address or apartment numbers in a separate field of their own, apart from street names, you would never add two street numbers together or subtract one from another.

For the Visualysis internal company data, most string fields will be 20 to 50 characters in length. A field will contain a few short string codes associated with lookup tables, such as state of residence, educational level, and so forth. Regarding codes, avoid short codes except where they're easily recognizable (such as state codes in the U.S.). Although it may require a little more processing and storage cost, the improved readability, reduced conversion, and easier data entry make the trade-off worthwhile.

Step 2—Assigning Numeric Data Types

For computer purposes, numbers share the common trait that they can be manipulated using arithmetical operators. This is their primary distinguishing characteristic. For Visualysis, internal company data—things like cash flows, employee statistics, inventory numbers, sales figures, and so on—will be assigned Numeric data types (although some will use the Currency data type).

Visualysis motion-capture projects, on the other hand, collect quantities of raw data that consists of numerical values representing physical measurements. These data values will ordinarily be stored in proprietary database formats attached to special application programs that capture, convert, and merge the data with other programs that are used to create animations. Unless the data is extracted to support some explicit company process, chances are good the data will never see the light of day. It'll probably be stored after use as an object and simply pointed to with any applications we might create in Access.

Step 3—Using Dates And Times

For a company like Visualysis, dates and times play an important role not only in defining the beginning of things (employee start dates, project start dates, and so forth) but also elapsed time and transaction sequence. For example, rolling up quarterly results implies that we know the start and end of each quarter. By the same token, warranty periods extend from the start date for a certain period (elapsed time). And a customer contact database should show contacts in sequence by date and probably time as well.

Numbers and dates/times interact frequently in most databases because dates are stored as numbers that can be operated upon with built-in functions. These functions allow calculations such as elapsed time, identification of specific days in a week, and so on. Careful assignment and conversion between the two makes for smooth database operation.

Dates can be entered in just about any typically used form, such as 1/14/99, January 14, 1999, and so forth. Numbers affecting dates will frequently be generated programmatically. For example, some Visualysis projects are billed by the hour. When an engineer begins work he or she scans the bar code on the project folder to register the start time. Later, the engineer scans the bar code again to register the end time. The system calculates the number of hundredths of an hour worked, multiplies that by the hourly rate for the engineer (plus the standard company overhead rate), then converts the final figure to currency for inclusion in the billing portion of the database.

Step 4—Pointers And Objects

Large strings of text, streams of digital data, programmatically accessible objects (such as documents and spreadsheets), image files, and so forth are all examples of data that would be assigned some kind of object pointer. These data types generally reside in a separate area on disk, while the pointer to them is stored as part of the database itself.

Identifying Object or Pointer data types is sometimes a matter of judgment. You could assign the String data type to a large text string, but that may not be practical if you intend to create an index on that field.

Sampled data, such as motion capture or audio encoding, is a suitable candidate for the Object data type because it's unlikely to be searched or indexed, other than for its location.

A good rule of thumb for Object or Pointer data types is that you intend to operate upon them as a whole. For example, suppose the Visualysis creates employee records in a database. The employee phone number may be changed to incorporate a new area code, but the employee picture would only be removed and replaced when updated.

Step 5—Arrays And Other Data Structures

Arrays and custom data types are commonly used when programming database applications (or applications in general). Typically, these structures aren't assigned when building a database directly, but because they're used programmatically, it's worthwhile to note them when you find candidates.

Categorizing And Prioritizing Data

Properly categorizing and prioritizing data logically organizes data sources and types into a structure that lends itself to consistent and well-managed decision-making about the eventual database solution. Until you know *why* you're collecting data, it makes little sense to think about *how* you'll collect data or what you'll do with it afterward.

As in any business, Visualysis's main purpose is to stay in business. To do that, it needs internal company data about its finances, employees, customers, orders, and projects. These kinds of data are its top priority, and perhaps we should call them mission-critical. But even within this data, some kinds are more important than others.

Step 1—Listing All Top Priority Data

This is a good point. In the system design process, include users and managers again. Hold a meeting, and starting from scratch, make a list of all data the company must have to accomplish its mission and goals. During the systems analysis phase (discussed in Chapter 1), the mission of the company and the processes to support the mission should have been spelled out in detail. Compare the list just created with the results of the systems analysis for any discrepancies. It's better to catch them now rather than further along.

Step 2—Assigning Subpriorities

Highly personal employee data, trade secrets, financial plans, and the like must be treated with greater concern than ordinary data, simply because loss or corruption of this data may endanger the company immediately. It's a question of risk management, and priorities must be assigned accordingly.

Evaluate the risks associated with the production, safekeeping, and potential loss of data in each data category, then apply a subpriority to it. This prioritization scheme not only serves as a guidepost to appropriate solution expenditures, it also comes in handy when you're working on the security system.

Step 3—Identifying Probable Change

Data may change over time, not only in the data values themselves, but in its size, attributes tracked, and importance to the mission and goals of the company. Some changes can take you by surprise, but some are likely and can be anticipated and planned for.

For every data element, the systems analysis should show a link to a process or task supported by it. Each process, over time, will either continue to support other processes (and perhaps supply other data elements), decline in importance (and possibly even vanish), or (possibly) increase in importance.

For example, Visualysis intends to go public at some point. When the time approaches, financial data will probably be the most important data the company has. Financial data should then be accorded the highest priority of all important data in the company. New security measures may be warranted, better production and transmission methods may be put in place, and, of course, no Year 2000 difficulties should be acceptable.

Planning for potential change involves forecasting along several lines. Ask yourself the following questions:

- Will the data domain change?

- Will the data type change?

- Will the process supported decline, maintain, or increase in importance or frequency?

- Are there other uses to which the data could eventually be put, particularly if the data is merged with other data or accumulated?

- Is the value of the data dependent upon other data?

- Is the value of the data dependent upon some external influence?

Changes in the data and its value should be monitored and accomplished on the same regular schedule as process improvements for the company to remain competitive. Human beings have a tendency to keep useless things around because "someday we'll need that." In truth, we're wrong quite a bit more often than we're right in that regard, but only an objective risk analysis can give us the guidance we need.

Data Transmission Strategies Development

You might remember a time when most data stayed on a single computer, and data communications really wasn't involved. Even the early telephone systems relied heavily on analog transmission of electrical signals across a switching system. Today, much of the telephone system is digital, and just about any location in the world has access (or soon will) to the Internet. For a price, you can connect by telephone, satellite, or radio. It would seem that the solution is to use the Internet or a LAN for just about all transmissions. But there are so many choices, optimized in so many ways, that for any given requirement, the best solution isn't necessarily the seemingly obvious one.

Step 1—Defining Transmission Requirements

Transmission requirements include speed, cleanliness (signal-to-noise ratio), security, and format, all of which may affect the specific requirements for sending and receiving equipment and media. Depending upon the strategy selected, the format of the data and the conversions it undergoes, and the speed and reliability with which it's transmitted, the security of the data may be affected (and the process may not even be the same from packet to packet!).

Step 2—Selecting Transmission Hardware And Protocols

The person entering new employee data into the database may be doing so on a personal computer connected to the database server via coaxial cable (to the hub) and fiber optic cable between locations on the company campus. In this situation, the hardware is relatively straightforward and protocols are dictated by your choice of NOS.

Using the Visualysis motion-capture project as an example, motion-capture data is collected from sensors at the mo-cap studio, accumulated in a PC in a proprietary program, and delivered to the company using a variety of means. Maybe the technician will compress the data and store it on a floppy disk or Zip drive as a file, or perhaps it'll be transmitted via modem or Integrated Services Digital Network (ISDN) adapter across the Internet. If the company has a WAN, it may be transmitted in a proprietary format using a wireless technique.

TCP/IP is the protocol set used to transmit data over the Internet, and its reliability is suspect. Moreover, because packets are transmitted (sent to the nearest node, copied, and forwarded until they reach their destination address or die), anyone along the way can intercept, read, copy, and disrupt communications. If the data is highly important and especially if it's sensitive, encryption protocols at both ends may be necessary.

Step 3—Determining Network Topology

Chances are good that the network topology you'll use has already been determined, but if you have the chance to make a change or lead the way to a new structure, you need to consider how topology will affect your users' abilities to access the data and information they need to perform their functions. Choose a network topology that offers the speed, reliability, and cost that fit the applications and processes that must be supported.

Quantifying Data Storage Requirements

Static data (data that changes relatively infrequently or not at all) may only require a very small storage space. However, it's important to distinguish between data that's truly static and data that just appears static. For instance, an employee record will probably remain about the same size over the years, with perhaps a little growth for a few more attributes over time. But the total size of employee records taken together may increase dramatically in a high-growth company.

Transaction data can also grow by leaps and bounds, even though each individual transaction record shouldn't change at all. And tables of summary calculations, particularly where many variables are measured in relation to one another, can grow out of all proportion to the data they provide.

Step 1—Determining The Nature Of The Data

Evaluate the size in bits of each data element and the overhead associated with the format in which the data will be kept. Depending upon processing requirements, it may be practical to store data in a compressed form.

Step 2—Determining Storage Categories

Some data needs to be immediately available, some data can be kept on disk, and some data can be kept in storage offline. Data that needs to be immediately available is limited by the amount of RAM connected to the processor on the database server. Data that can be stored on disk might be stored on a single drive, on several drives, or on a redundant array of independent disks (RAID). And data that can be kept in long-term archives might be stored on tapes or optical disks in a vault, restored from backup only in emergency situations.

Access speeds are the criteria by which various media are judged. For instance, RAM has access speeds in the range of five to ten nanoseconds, while hard disk drives are orders of magnitude slower (seven to fifteen milliseconds), and tape or optical disk storage is much slower still.

Step 3—Evaluating Cost Per Data Unit Stored

Security and useful life are important considerations in choosing a data storage solution, but cost is the primary factor. Cost per megabyte is the typical measure used to compare devices and media, and removable media have the advantage of infinite scalability at lower price, although depending upon the situation, there may be a performance hit.

Total cost of ownership (the cost to purchase, install, maintain, upgrade, and support hardware over its expected life) is more of a forecast than hard figures. Benchmarking purchase costs and comparing them to previous ownership costs may be the easiest and most accurate method for comparing various brands and technologies. For instance, RAM prices have fallen below $1 per megabyte, hard disk drives have fallen below 5¢ per megabyte, and other devices and media are also very low in price.

Choosing Processing Hardware

Processing hardware includes central processing units (CPUs), supporting chipsets, data busses, graphics and audio circuitry, and input-output (I/O) controller circuitry. For some solutions, the hardware will all be resident on a single machine, while for other solutions, the hardware will be distributed among many machines.

Data capture devices may preprocess data before sending it along, and transmission devices may perform further processing before it arrives at its final destination. Processing hardware decisions must be made with raw data, preprocessing, and transmission processing requirements in mind, as well as the usual risk, cost, security, and scalability considerations.

Step 1—Determining Acceptable Performance Specifications

In the section on data storage, we categorized data into immediately available, at hand, and in archives, arriving at three rough access speed ranges (nanoseconds, milliseconds, and longer). Just because RAM can be accessed in nanoseconds doesn't mean any data kept in RAM will automatically be processed at that speed, however. A large database with thousands or millions of records takes seconds and even minutes to process, depending on the number of records, the type of query used, and the type of calculations (if any).

Modern PC, server, and workstation processors (Intel Pentium, PowerPC, and Alpha RISC designs) are capable of extremely fast processing for most standalone applications, and multiple processor, parallel processor, and clustered architectures offer even more speed in the same hardware range. For specialized applications that are calculation intensive, involve many variables, or must produce realtime output in high volume (such as animated simulations), high-performance or supercomputer hardware may be required.

One measure of processing speed is millions of instructions per second. But sheer processing speed doesn't give a true picture of a processor's power to perform operations specific to the application program you have in mind. Benchmarking software was created to provide comparison between CPUs and their associated hardware for similar types of work.

For example, the Standard Performance Evaluation Corporation (SPEC) builds source code benchmark suites. They test the CPU, cache, RAM (memory), and compiler. For this type of benchmark, the impact of I/O, graphics, operating system, and network is insignificant.

The same company (and others) also builds tools for various specific situations. These tools provide comparison points for combinations of CPUs and associated hardware performing known workload amounts using known applications.

Step 2—Evaluating Total Workload Under All Conditions

If you've ever displayed CPU usage in Windows NT you know that most of the time the processor isn't doing too much. But lock up your system and you might notice CPU usage hit and stay at 100 percent. It's not doing anything productive for you, but it's doing lots of it.

Networked systems have the same characteristics. They may have little activity for long periods of time, interspersed with heavy demand for short periods of time. Your users only care about total workload when it affects their own ability to use the functions they need.

Capacity planning is the term for evaluating expected workload in computer systems, both for the individual processors and the networks connecting them. Theoretical, peak, sustained, and average loads can be estimated, and with these estimates you may determine your present and forecasted hardware needs.

Step 3—Determining Appropriate Hardware Architectures

For systems expected to receive a high number of concurrent requests for data, a powerful I/O subsystem is required, as well as a CPU with multitask capability. For example, if you intend to host high-volume Web sites on a server, you'll need to ensure that the server (or servers) can process many "hits" per day. And if you're connecting a database, doing ecommerce (meaning secure transactions), or serving up large files, you'll need an extremely fast system (CPU, graphics, I/O, and so on) to cope with the processing required.

Using performance measurements related to the workload you intend to process, determine the CPU and system architecture suitable for your applications. For instance, Visualysis intends to create complex 3D animations on individual workstations, then render them in a "render farm" of connected machines dedicated solely to rendering. Because creating complex 3D applications is very RAM- and calculation-intensive, Visualysis has purchased workstations running Windows NT with 128MB of RAM; plenty of cache; large (9 GB), fast (7 ms) hard disk drives; high-performance graphics subsystems with 32MB of RAM; and dual Pentium 400 MHz processors. For the render farm, the company will utilize a high-bandwidth network connecting several specialized graphics workstations optimized for rendering.

Whatever type of workload you process, indicators of processing requirements are usually always apparent, whether it's polygon count, record size or number, floating-point operations, and so on. For each critical application, find the indicator that gives the most reliable measure of processing time and use it to gauge required hardware. By the way, I like to save money as much as the next guy, but when I buy computers, I always buy one level below the cutting edge. It's not the cheapest stuff, but it has the advantage of being proven, stable, and a lot less expensive.

Chapter 3
Data Organization

In Depth

This chapter examines real-world data gathering techniques, data modeling, and classification of data for database applications. Believe it or not, much of the work we do in this area is based on common sense, although you might feel that it's common sense taken to the extreme.

Effective data collection is the foundation for all processes upon which we rely to get things done. The most well-designed system is useless without it. Even a "perfect" system (designed exactly to spec) won't work with bad data—the familiar "garbage-in, garbage-out" syndrome. Unfortunately for you if you're a designer, users won't blame themselves for improperly entering data (or not entering it at all), they'll just say "It doesn't work," and you'll be blamed. Who said life was fair, anyway?

Data modeling is the technique used to make sense of the relationships between things we want to collect data about. Every organization employs business rules, policies, and so on to guide daily operations, and data modeling uses these business rules like two-by-fours in the construction of database structures.

Drowning In Data

Data is all around us. It's ours for the taking if only we'll sample it. In fact, the problem isn't finding enough data, it's sampling the right data using the right methods. Our first question should be "What's the minimum data I need to satisfy the requirements of the process to be supported?"

And when we're talking about the right data, we mean the correct data in many senses of the word. The data must be:

• Sampled into an acceptable format using the correct data type.

• Accurate to an acceptable level.

• Timely (available when and where we need it).

• Up to date to an acceptable level.

Collecting the right data starts with using the right methods. These methods are called data gathering techniques.

Data Gathering Techniques

Generally, we can categorize data gathering techniques into two types: manual and automated. Each has costs, risks, and benefits associated with it, and each is appropriate under different circumstances.

Manual Data Gathering Techniques

The data gathering technique we're probably all most familiar with is the form. Someone hands you a form; you fill it out and return it. Someone else then enters the data into a system, or perhaps the data just sits there in hard copy until it's needed again or eventually goes into a landfill. This is a manual data gathering method. It seems simple enough, but let's examine it in detail:

1. Assuming the fields listed on the form have been identified according to the requirements outlined by the systems analyst, the form design must be created.

2. After the design is approved, the form must be printed and distributed.

3. When a transaction is required, the person requesting the data must retrieve the proper form and provide it to the person filling it out.

4. The person filling it out must do so legibly, accurately, and with the right data in each field.

5. Assuming the form is filled out correctly, the person requesting the data must retrieve the form and forward it to the person entering the data or file it in the correct place.

6. If it's stored in hard copy format, someone must review and compile the data manually whenever summary data is required.

Manually collected data is expensive to obtain, expensive to store, and prone to errors of many kinds throughout the process. Unless the cost of automation is prohibitive for your circumstances or the data requirement is so inconsequential and short term that it really doesn't matter, avoid manual methods.

There's a security consideration, though. Manually collected data can be more difficult to steal for the same reasons it's difficult to obtain, store, and summarize. An employee bent on stealing data can't just download a file to disk and walk out or hack into your system from a remote location (perhaps without you being aware of the theft). Although this is a very crude form of security, more than a few organizations still depend upon it.

Automated Data Gathering Techniques

One of the most familiar automated data gathering methods is the bar code reader at the grocery store. Collecting the data is just a matter of placing the item you want to purchase in front of the reader for less than a second. The data then automatically travels in electronic form to everywhere it's required: the sales to-taling function in the system, your receipt, and the data repository. With the "club" cards in common use today, the stores also extract personal information with every purchase, and coupon redemption has been automated with the addition of imprinted bar code symbols.

The automated versus manual trade-off, in most cases, is a higher initial cost to implement but lower costs for gathering (and possibly using) the data. However, automating the process also means a lot more data will usually be collected, used, and stored, so there may not be a direct savings to your bottom line. Automation may simply make you a more effective marketer, improve your customer service, provide better strategic analysis, and so on. If your competitors are also automat-ing, the entire benefit to your organization may simply be that you've "kept up with the Joneses," without monetary benefit or improvement in market share.

Automated data collection can take many forms:

• Security cameras collect data.

• Chemical sensors collect data.

• Answering machines collect data.

The point is, you probably have a vast data collection network in place already, with some parts manual and some parts automated but ineffectively utilized. As you proceed with your systems analysis, note every instance of data collection currently in use, and evaluate each for integration opportunities.

Automated data collection can be outlined as follows:

1. Assuming the data has been identified according to the requirements outlined by the systems analysis, design the collection format.

2. Once the format is approved, create and deploy it.

3. When a transaction (collection event) is required, all elements of the transaction must be present and working properly. For instance, when buying something at the store, the required elements are you, the item being purchased, the bar code reader, the clerk, and the system supporting the process.

4. Each element of the collection process must perform its function properly, collecting the right data accurately. In the case of the store purchase, this implies that someone at a previous time has correctly entered the price matching the code of the item you're purchasing.

5. The system must properly retrieve, forward, process, and store the data.

6. When the data is required for summarization, the system must retrieve, forward, process, and store the new data properly as well.

Data Collection Integration

So how can existing and proposed data collection methods be integrated into an effective data collection foundation? First, sort collection methods into manual and automated collection methods; second, sort them into analog and digital methods; and third, rank them according to their accessibility and security.

For instance, suppose you run a research lab testing chemicals for antibacterial properties on a variety of surfaces. You find that your researchers happen to use several methods to collect data:

- Paper forms to record the initial conditions and make comments

- Video cameras to monitor test areas and ensure test conditions are not violated

- Photography with 35mm cameras to record progress and changes in the samples at set intervals

- Data acquisition sensors to record environmental conditions such as temperature and humidity

- Bar code readers and electronic forms to quickly collect and enter results at each interval and at the end of the experiment

Manual

The paper form is obviously a manual data collection method, but so is the use of a 35mm camera to record progress. Both methods are considered manual because the data is recorded by a person and it's analog data stored in a nonelectronic format.

Automated

The use of video cameras, data acquisition sensors, bar code readers, and electronic forms are automated methods, even though it may seem that some of them have a manual component. Strictly speaking, typing data into an electronic form on a laptop is a manual process, but we term it automated because the data is collected in electronic format.

Analog

All manual methods are by definition analog. The use of an automated method, such as video cameras, is analog as well. The importance of this distinction is that it means a further transformation will have to take place before automated processing and storage can occur.

Digital

Automated methods that record data in digital format are obviously digital, but the formats aren't necessarily useful or compatible as collected. This is a key consideration that leads us to our next criterion—accessibility.

Accessibility

Accessibility refers to the ability of the data collection elements to produce data that can be processed, stored, and distributed effectively and efficiently. For example, suppose the video camera in our scenario can utilize a video capture device to produce digitized data. This capability doesn't guarantee that:

- Enough data can be included to support the process in question (human intervention may still be required to interpret the images and enter the interpretation in a database).

- The data can be transmitted effectively over our network or the Internet (it may need compression).

- Other applications will be able to use it (it may need conversion).

- It can be stored effectively (it may need summarization and further compression).

Of course, making data accessible does not mean you can afford to compromise security. Every effort must be made to ensure the data goes only to the right people at the right time.

Security

Collecting data and making it accessible isn't the end of the job. The data must be accessible at the right points in the process and only to those people or other processes that are required and authorized to use it. Although we discuss security in depth in later chapters, it's important to note that security can be breached in many ways, and data collection methods are the first place to begin closing the holes.

The Integration Process

Now that you have an inventory of existing data collection methods and assuming that you also have generated the requirements of the proposed system, you can lay an effective foundation. Start by examining the minimum data required to support the new process without regard for any other data collection considerations. Each data element should be listed in the systems analysis, as well as its attributes (such as timeliness, accuracy, and so on).

Next, evaluate each collection methodology first for performance then for cost. This may seem counterintuitive; after all, why consider a system that you can't afford? But there are valid reasons for doing just that:

- Technology is rapidly dropping in price.

- Your competitors are adopting automation (and new rivals are constantly popping up with completely new systems).

3. Data Organization

- You may be unaware of strategic advantages the ideal data collection system can confer.

Even if you can't afford them, you can't afford not to fully review what the best systems have to offer.

If, after designing your ultimate system, it greatly exceeds your budget, gradually eliminate those items that contribute the least to performance while contributing the most to costs. Keep in mind that performance means security and ease of use as well as speed. Ideally, the method that immediately (and easily) converts all the required data into a preprocessed digital format ready to be distributed and stored securely, at the lowest overall cost, is the one to choose.

But don't forget to plan for the future. Differentiate between areas of high and low data-collection requirements growth. For example, your Web server may need to stay very secure while scaling up rapidly as more customers order over the Internet (and wouldn't you love to have that problem). On the other hand, if you're running a "virtual" company with few permanent employees, the process of collecting new employee data might be well served by a fairly static little database application running on your desktop collecting the data via electronic forms.

In the final analysis, data collection methods are similar to the water pipes in your home. They should be unobtrusive, deliver what's expected when and where it's required, and be affordable and leakproof. And manual data collection methods, the systems equivalent of carrying buckets of water from the creek into your house, are rapidly fading into history. We're obviously in favor of automated data collection methods (wherever appropriate), so perhaps you're interested in how to build them into the overall system. That's where schemas and data models come into play.

Schemas And Data Models

If you're a user, you might have suspected that the IT folks were scheming to make your life miserable, so the word *schema* might seem appropriate. However, every field has its jargon, and the IT world is no different. The definition of *schema* for IT purposes is a description of the structural rules of a database.

A schema is distinct from a data dictionary in that the data dictionary is used during systems analysis to record information collected about every aspect of the system being analyzed (data elements, users, hardware and software, files and forms, databases and schemas currently being used, and so on). The schema is the structure of a database that will eventually support the process (or processes) developed from the improvement effort of which the systems analysis is a part.

To put it a little more plainly, you construct the data dictionary to record your findings during the analysis, but you design the schema to support the approved solution. And as we mentioned in Chapter 1, this data dictionary should not be confused with the data dictionary we'll develop specifically for use with the database application itself.

Driven By Data Model

Like a child's plastic model of a fighter aircraft, a data model should certainly be realistic, but it would not be mistaken for the real thing. Data models and schemas are very close to the same thing, but the term *data model* refers to the concepts by which the structure of a database is organized while the schema refers to the way the elements of the structure are organized within that conceptual framework.

In addition, the database is said to occupy various states (or instances) during its lifetime that include the following:

- *Empty*—When the schema has been defined but the database contains no data.

- *Initial*—When the database has been loaded with data but no changes have been made.

- *Updated*—When changes have been made during usage (this portion is the bulk of a database's lifetime, ordinarily).

- *Valid or invalid*—After changes have been made, the condition of the database is said to be either valid or invalid, depending upon whether or not the DBMS is able to maintain the rules by which the database schema is defined.

Together, the data model and the schema serve as the structure of our database behind the scenes, and various data models serve various purposes within that structure, as we'll see next.

Types Of Data Models

Data models are used to describe concepts for the physical storage and retrieval of data (low-level models), the internal representation of data (intermediate-level models), and real-world views of data (high-level models). These levels roughly correspond to the internal schema (low-level or physical data model), the conceptual schema (intermediate-level data model), and the user-view schema (high-level data model).

ITs select and use various data models to support schemas at these levels to provide insulation between the way data is organized on the hardware, within the application, and by users. Users (or other processes) should see only the data they need to see, the way they need to see it. They shouldn't have to know in exactly what file or on what server a particular piece of information is stored before they can formulate a query to retrieve it. Users should be able to just point and click, like magic!

3. Data Organization

This three-level architecture enables applications to achieve separation of the user from the physical file structures, and thus makes all the complex operations in the background transparent to the user. The intermediate level mediates requests by users for data stored in the low-level system and also maintains the cohesiveness of the application as a whole.

This architecture keeps physical and logical data independent. Changes in the structure of each level leave the other levels unaffected. Microsoft's Access 2000 supports data independence quite well. For instance, you can change the structure of a table without redefining the structure of associated reports. Your only requirement is to modify the data source in a report when you change the name of its underlying table or add new fields (if desired) if you've added new fields to the table.

The Entity-Relationship (ER) Data Model

Traditionally, the design of a database application begins with requirements collection and analysis (the process and systems analysis) and the selection of a proposed solution. The proposed solution will include a conceptual design of the database system intended to support the solution, and the conceptual design will be modeled using some data model. In this section, we'll discuss the ER data model and how it defines real-world things and actions in constructing a database.

Entities

The ER model is popular, and the major database packages are designed to support the ER interpretation of the world. The ER model describes things as *entities*; for instance, a person would ordinarily be considered an entity. The general rule is any unique thing you're concerned with is an entity.

Attributes

Entities can have *attributes*. For instance, a person has a gender, and Gender can be considered an attribute of the entity Person. Interestingly, even if a person dies, the entity representing him or her can live on forever (kind of like Elvis). The attribute indicating a person's status (dead or alive) would simply contain the entry "dead", or perhaps a date of death.

Entities may have many attributes, and attributes come in many flavors. Some attributes only take on a single value, such as a birth date. Others may have several values, such as Performance Awards.

Attributes can be *composite* or *simple*. For instance, the composite attribute of a phone number includes a three-digit area code. Simple attributes can't be broken down into simpler data components.

Attributes can be *stored* or *derived*. For example, a person's age can be stored directly as data, or it can be derived from his or her birth date (by calculating the number of years between birth date and the system date). Obviously, in most cases it would be best to derive this attribute to avoid constant manual record updates.

Attributes can take on a special value called the *null* value. Null is different from zero or a blank space. Zero is a value, as is a blank space. The null value means either *not applicable* or *unknown*. For example, the country code for phone numbers isn't applicable for U.S. residents, while social security numbers (SSNs) may simply be unknown. Unknown (as a null value) can be further categorized as either *missing* or *not known*. For example, it's a fair bet that a U.S. resident has an SSN, so if it's unknown, it's probably missing, while "not known" means we don't even know if it exists (a fax number, for instance).

Relationships

In the real world, entities often have *relationships* with other entities. For instance, a person may work for a company, and, if so, it can also be said that the company employs that person. The person and the company are both entities, while *works for* is the relationship of the person to the company and *employs* is the relationship of the company to the person.

Although it appears that we're discussing two relationships, there's only one. The one relationship just means different things depending upon the *role* of the entity. In fact, in some relationships the same entity can play several roles. For example, a person working on a project as part of a team can both provide information to and ask information of the team, all while working on the project. Relationships such as these are called *recursive* relationships.

There are several kinds of relationships, including *one-to-one*, *one-to-many*, and *many-to-many*. Suppose, for instance, you work in a company that has a strict business rule of one (and only one) desktop computer assigned to each person. As an entity, you'll have a one-to-one relationship with the desktop computer assigned to you.

Assuming you'll work on many projects during your time with the company, you'll have a one-to-many relationship to your projects (each project is only worked on by one person). But if we assume others also work on the same projects, the relationship between projects and those who work on them will be many-to-many (many people work on each project, and each person works on many projects).

Finally, more than two entities can exist for each relationship (although two is most common). For example, suppose you work on projects. The *works on* relationship is created by the two entities involved. Now suppose a progress review team periodically reviews all projects. The relationship works on now encompasses three entities: you, the projects, and the review committee. The number of entities involved in a relationship is termed the *degree* of the relationship. Relationships involving two entities are called *binary* relationships; those including three entities are called *ternary* relationships.

Classification Of Data Within The Schema

At this stage in the database design game, we're concerned with building a schema to logically depict the things (and the relationships between these things) that we'd like to keep track of and make decisions about. But before we begin building our schema, we need to understand some jargon.

Entities And Data Types

The ER data model identifies an entity as a physical thing with attributes. This is equivalent to a *record* in a database or the data for each individual person or thing. An *entity type* is the set of fields (attributes) that make up the record, for all records in the table. An *entity type name* is the name given to the table holding the records. An *entity set* is the set of records currently in the table. The entity type can be called the *intension* for a set of entities, and the entity set itself can be called the *extension* of the entity type.

Keys

Within an entity type, some attributes contain values that, by definition, must always be unique. Unique (key) values allow each entity (or record) in the table to be distinguished from every other entity. This property is useful for linking one entity type to another, such as people to projects or companies to products. Also, it's common for an entity type to have several, unique key attributes. When this occurs, the database designer chooses one from among the several keys to be the *primary key*.

You may have noticed key values occurring in everyday life. Each transaction on your credit card has a key value, and the vehicle identification number on your car should also be unique. *Composite keys* are made from several attributes and may only take on a unique value when connected.

For example, the transaction numbers on your credit card may be the combination of your account number, the date and time, and the store where you made the purchase. Individually, each of these values may be repeated many times within the attributes of the entity type—Transactions—in your credit card company's database, but together they uniquely identify that one particular transaction you made in that store, on that day, at that time.

Weak Entity Types

If an entity has no key attributes of its own, it's termed a *weak entity type*. Entities such as this always owe their existence to another entity type called the *owner* entity. If your company maintains buildings on the company campus and if each building has perhaps one or two conference rooms with a variety of attributes (phone lines, overhead projector, Internet access, and so on), conference rooms may be a weak entity type always owned by the facility that contains it.

In the relational database model (discussed in Chapters 4 and 5), weak entity types are related to their owners using a *foreign key*, the primary key value of the owner entity. If the entity being related to happens to have a key value of its own for some reason, the existence dependence relationship still holds, but the entity isn't a weak entity type.

Value Ranges

Value ranges (also called *value sets* or *domains*) apply to attributes and govern the values they may assume. Attributes frequently can only exist in a limited range of values. For example, if we assume that all employees live in the U.S., then the value of their zip codes must be taken from the set of valid zip codes in the U.S. No other value can be allowed, and if one is present, we immediately know it's an error.

Password is an example of an attribute whose value range is nearly unlimited (at least for good passwords) because it's chosen at random and may assume almost any value. Gender obviously only requires two values, M or F (but with advances in genetic engineering, who knows how long this will hold true).

If there can be only one value for an attribute, then it can be assumed and need not be entered unless it's needed for some other purpose. For instance, if you construct a table containing everyone born in the year 1975, it's unnecessary to include a field for the year of birth, unless you must perform some calculation requiring the year of birth. The easiest way to enter this kind of data is with a default value, and we'll discuss default values in greater depth later in this book.

Be careful when leaving out assumed data. The Y2K (Year 2000) problem was born this way, when programmers coded year dates with only the last two characters, on the assumption that the other two characters would never be needed during the life of the programs.

Data Types

Knowing the value range of an attribute allows you to figure out what data type to use. As we discussed in Chapter 2, the kind of data an attribute (or field) will hold determines the data type to use, and data type is directly related to storage requirements.

Relationships

In the real world, relationships between entities can take almost any form and come in almost any quantity. The sun has a relationship to you, namely *shines on,* while your relationship to the sun could be labeled *tanned by.* This is a *direct* relationship in that there are no intermediary relationships. If you put sunblock on, you could say that your relationship with the sun is mediated by the sunblock, and the relationship would become *indirect.*

Relationships often occur between groups of things. Many projects may be worked on by one person or by many people. A strict one-to-one, one-to-many, or many-to-many relationship among things is noted by the relationship's *cardinality ratio.*

Some relationships are merely *statistical.* For instance, when a medicine is tested upon thousands of folks without negative side effects for 99 percent of the population, we can say that the statistical relationship it has with people is *beneficial to* people, while the relationship people have to it is *benefit from.*

The *participation constraint* reflects the level of participation between entities in a relationship. When there's *total* participation, an entity may not exist if it doesn't also participate in a particular relationship. This is sometimes called *existence dependency.* A good example of this is the relationship of Orders to Customers. You probably don't want orders created without being connected to a customer, so you would specify total participation between Orders and Customers. Note that you could still have Customers without Orders. The participation constraint in that direction is *partial*, meaning that some Customers will have Orders but not all.

Relationships can be thought of as attributes in that we could define each instance of a relationship between a Customer and an Order as an attribute of either the Customer or the Order. This way of looking at relationships will become important to us in later chapters when we examine relational database application development.

It's important to make these distinctions because when we build a data model we're modeling the real world within the data model, essentially creating a *miniworld.* Within the miniworld, relationships we build represent the business rules by which the miniworld operates, and they are a fundamental structural component. Changing them at a later time can dramatically change the way the database operates, so we need to get them right the first time.

Structural Constraints

By setting value ranges, cardinality ratios, participation constraints, relationship and entity types, and so on, we're building logical operational rules into our schema.

These rules will translate into database operations when we perform the actual construction. Sometimes we need the freedom to break these rules when exceptions occur, and that's why database design is an art rather than a science. Intuition and professional judgment play a big role in designing a practical database, rather than a perfect one.

If you've ever kept records, you know that there are always exceptions to the rules. Sometimes you need the ability to add a record that falls outside the business rules—a special case. If the database has been designed to allow for this, perhaps with a flag to highlight special status, it may be easier to use and maintain than one that has every business rule hard-coded into the structure. Knowing when to apply this approach is part of the art of database design.

We've covered lots of ground, mostly about esoteric jargon used in the professional database design world. At this point, you may feel like falling asleep, but believe me there are practical advantages to formally following through with this part of the database design process. By taking the time to understand these terms, you'll see that they relate fairly well to process engineering terms covered in Chapter 1. And the process engineering terms relate fairly well to your daily work. For instance, each resource used in the construction of a product can be considered an entity with attributes, and the relationships between entities often bear a similarity to the relationships between the products and resources.

Knowing the language (and perspectives) of systems analysts and process engineers is the first step toward harnessing the power of these disciplines to achieve real-world benefits.

3. Data Organization

Immediate Solutions

This section provides a step-by-step guide to data collection and the overall design of a database structure, construction of a schema diagram and data model mapping, along with detailed instructions for identifying entities, attributes, and relationships. We also illustrate schema and data model symbols and cover typical database requirements.

Inventorying And Integrating Data Collection Methods

Data collection methods are the eyes, ears, nose, and skin of our automated information production system. Ideally, data should be automatically absorbed from the surrounding environment, processed, and made available with little or no effort by us. Three major steps are required for building an effective and efficient data collection system:

- Inventorying current data collection capabilities.

- Developing proposed capabilities.

- Integrating data collection capabilities into one system that will support the proposed process.

Step 1—Inventorying Data Collection Methods

For the current process, whatever that might be, examine every data element and its origin. Don't assume anything, or you might miss critical data sources. For instance, suppose a report contains an employee's ID number. Does the employee supply this data during the data collection process, or does the system supply it by referencing the employee database? Every time the system supplies data, the system is making assumptions about where to get the data and about the accuracy of the data it's supplying. Moreover, system-supplied data is usually invisible to users.

It's better to list each data element with its associated source and any other parameters (methodology, timeliness, quality, and so on). Your list should follow the sequence of any work-flow diagrams you've created during the systems analysis and process engineering portions of your process redesign effort. Categorize data collection methods as manual or automated. If the process for collecting data seems to be partially manual and partially automated, you need to define the data supplied by each portion of the process as separate data elements.

Note the costs associated with data collection at each sampling point. For instance, if a worker must stop what he's doing to record the hours he's worked on a particular process, the five minutes spent doing that should be charged to the collection of that data at the employee's hourly rate. The same goes for automated data collection methods. If recurring costs are $1,000 per day for an automated data collection system, and one million samples are taken per day, the cost of each sample is one tenth of a cent.

The end result should be a list of all current data elements and their associated data collection methods, along with the parameters of the data being collected. It should be straightforward to follow the list as data is collected throughout the current process using work-flow diagrams.

Step 2—Developing Proposed Data Collection Methods

Examine the difference between the current and proposed processes. Are new data elements required to support the new process? Can old data elements be thrown out? Are there any elements the system could supply? Think about all the data elements you'd like to have without considering cost or demands on the system. Generate a nice, long list, including the same information as the list of current data elements, and make sure it follows your proposed work-flow diagram.

Evaluate the methodologies you could use to collect each proposed data element. Try to push automated methods as close to the point of origination as possible. For instance, where paper forms are used to collect data from customers, could an electronic stylus work? If it makes you feel more comfortable, list several methods for each, and note the trade-offs (electronic collection may be faster or require less conversion but cost more up front, for instance). Later, with all the facts in place, you can decide which method to use.

Keep in mind multiple use of data collection mechanisms. A motion-detection system that turns on the lights when a person enters a room can also collect data about the amount of usage a particular room gets and perhaps also feed the security system if a person is in the room after hours. But watch out for the pitfalls of making too many assumptions about data supplied by a system. The fact that a person is in a room after hours does not necessarily mean the alarm should sound or that an intrusion has occurred. Careful evaluation of the meaning of data in relation to how it was collected is critical to a well-designed system.

Step 3—Integrating Current And Proposed Data Collection Methods

Merge the two lists of data elements and collection methodologies into one. Throw out any data elements that aren't required, then examine the remaining list. Your goal should be to build a system that supplies the data necessary to support the proposed process at the least cost, with adequate quality and with the least change possible.

Although it would be nice to have a completely automated data collection system, this isn't always practical. Consider the possibility that the power might fail, that data may be misinterpreted, or that the costs of a completely automated system are simply too high for the application at hand. If you find you must maintain a manual backup for an automated system, perhaps you should forego the automated system and just use the manual method at all times. It might cost more to operate than the automated system but less than both the automated system and the manual backup.

In the end, your list should include the following:

- All data elements required for the new process.
- The required quality of each data element (accuracy, timeliness, and so on).
- Assumptions when data is collected or supplied indirectly.
- All techniques employed to gather the data.
- Costs associated with these techniques.
- Contingency data collection techniques and their costs.

In addition, it should be easy to follow the data elements throughout the sequence of a work-flow diagram.

Data Modeling And The Database Design Process

The fundamental structure of a database is modeled as a diagram consisting of entities, attributes, and relationships. We'll assume you've already performed the necessary data and requirements gathering and are ready to begin modeling the structure of the database using the ER data model.

Step 1—Assembling Requirements

The data you've gathered during systems analysis and process engineering includes requirements of many types: business rules, things which must be tracked, data elements required during work flow, decision points, and so on. Begin applying your data model by organizing all requirements by type. Careful analysis of the collected requirements will help categorize them properly.

Keep in mind that functional requirements are separate from database requirements. Functional requirements specify the data processing that must occur;

database requirements refer to data elements that must be present at each stage of the process.

For example, suppose a medical office accepts patients with private insurance, MediCare, or no insurance plan at all. The office would want to track payment plans and options for each customer, for each visit, and for all services rendered. The data elements relating to the customer (name, address, phone number, insurance plan, and so on) are considered database requirements. The production of a current account status report would be a functional requirement (it would assist in customer service at the point in the process when the customer calls to complain about a bill).

Step 2—Building The Conceptual Schema

Once the various database and functional requirements have been assembled and analyzed, it's time to begin building the high-level conceptual schema and data flow diagrams that contain them and dictate the relationships between them. The conceptual schema is usually a diagram that shows each entity and its attributes, with lines depicting relationships. Data flow diagrams are developed from analysis of the functional requirements and resemble work-flow or process diagrams. The decision points (or transactions) specified by data-flow diagrams are termed the *High-Level Transaction Specification*.

A conceptual schema diagram's purpose is to make it easy to share your vision of the things to be tracked or accounted for (the entities) and how they're related (the relationships) with other interested parties. The elements of your schema diagram should correspond to elements in the data-flow diagrams, which should, in turn, be easy to match up to process diagrams. Both kinds of diagrams should be easy for users to understand and should contain no missing data or conflicts with other processes/systems.

At this point, it's very important to bring the users in again for a review and perhaps even a sign-off on the diagrams. Although you don't discuss performance specifications or technical issues, users must validate that the information produced at each stage is complete and will support their processes. Now is the time to find problems, holes, or inconsistencies because it's much cheaper to rearrange a diagram than to reprogram a database.

Step 3—Data Model Mapping

The high-level conceptual schema must next be transformed into the *Logical Database Design*, using the structures available in whatever DBMS package you're using (in our case, Access 2000). This means mapping data elements into data types, attributes into fields, entities into tables, and relationships into joins. From there, it's easy to proceed to the design of the overall DBMS application program.

Defining Entity Types

Entities, the fundamental things we want to track with our eventual database application, are the first things we'll define when beginning to design our schema. You can think of entities as nouns, while the relationships between them are like verbs. For instance, Customers and their Orders are things (or nouns), while the relationship, Purchased By, between Customers and Orders sounds like an action (or verb).

Step 1—Defining Things To Track

Even if you've got a clear idea of what you want to produce or what process you must support, there's no guarantee that this will immediately translate into all the items you must track to produce the required data. Therefore, the best way to begin is simply to jot down everything you can think of that could possibly be an entity.

Don't exclude anything. People are an obvious entity, for instance, but others may not be so obvious. Entities can easily masquerade as attributes of other entities. For instance, it may seem like items ordered are an attribute of Orders, but in most cases, they're entities in their own right.

Remember also that entities can be conceptual things, such as dreams, grade point averages, or time periods. There may be no physical thing to point to, but an idea can be an entity type all the same.

Step 2—Grouping Entity Types Into Logical Categories

Employees, customers, patients, supervisors, scientists, and so on all share one common trait: they're people. People live, die, breathe, eat, get sick, get paid (hopefully), and so on. Buildings, open areas, conference rooms, offices, homes, and so on also share a common trait: they have spatial dimensions. The point here is to group entity types by common traits that we're likely to care about for the same reason. A building, a sick patient, and pond scum may all share a common color (sickly green), but we're unlikely to care about this for the same reason.

Grouping entity types by shared traits makes it easier to define attributes and relationships later on in the process because the parameters of unusual entity types can more easily be recognized by the traits they share with more common entity types.

Step 3—Dividing Entity Type Categories Into Active And Passive

People can initiate actions. Your typical parking lot can't initiate an action. Although both are entity types, one is active and the other is passive. Active entity types may have actions initiated upon them (a manager may award a bonus to an employee), but passive entity types never initiate actions (a parking lot doesn't file a request to be repainted).

After grouping your entity types into categories, it's usually easy to then group the categories into active and passive super-groups. There are two reasons to do this. If you notice that an entity type no longer fits into its group properly (a building may have an alarm system that initiates an alarm sequence when the building is entered after hours), perhaps you should regroup the alarm system entity type into another category, say automated sensing devices.

Another reason to break categories into active and passive groups is that it will help to define the roles these entity types play when you're defining relationships later on. Active entity types are much more likely than passive entity types to have multiple one-to-many relationships with other entity types.

Step 4—Determining Which Entities Require Keys

Some entities need to remain unique within their entity type. Employees will remain unique, in most cases, so we don't accidentally award a bonus to the same person twice.

Other entities (weak entities) that may not require a key are usually on the many end of a relationship, and they may contain a *partial key*. Award Preference (for companies that allow employees to choose what they'd like as an award, in lieu of cash) is a good example of this. The entity type, Award Preference, may contain only one attribute: Preference. Entities recorded within this entity type would have multiple records with the same Preference. The partial key (Preference) relates particular entities within this entity type to entities within the Employee entity type via what is called an *identifying relationship*. The entity type to which Award Preference is related (Employees) is called the *identifying owner*.

Weak entities, such as our example above, are by definition related to another entity type and can't exist without that relationship. The reverse is not always true, however. Some entity types have a total participation constraint (existence dependency) with another entity type and, yet, still have keys of their own.

Defining Attributes

Attributes take on many forms, and their definition in the schema determines, to a great extent, practical data processing capabilities. Poorly defined attributes may make it difficult or impossible for those programming the database application to meet specifications. In addition, the workarounds used to cope with bad attribute design may be complex and difficult to maintain. Use the following guidelines for defining attributes that make the most sense in light of the requirements.

Step 1—Identifying Composite Attributes

People are usually identified by their names, so we know we'll want to list Name as an attribute. But wait! If you recall, Name is actually a composite attribute because it includes first, middle, and last names (and maybe several others). How do we determine whether to leave it composite or break it down into separate attributes?

The answer to this question can be found in our requirements. Although we could conceivably search for a person by last name even if the entire name made up one attribute, it's immensely easier to separate an individual's name then search only on the one name. So should we split up the names into their own attributes? The answer is very likely yes because at some point in the process someone will probably want to search for an individual by last name.

By the same token, an address is a common composite attribute within many databases. Should we split out the street number from the street name or the suite or apartment number from the rest of the address? Here again, the answer is probably in our requirements. For this case, the answer is probably no because it's unlikely that anyone would want to search for all the employees using hazardous materials who happen to live on a particular street. If a search such as this were required to support the process, you can bet it would be clearly spelled out (assuming the requirements were adequately specified).

In general, the determination as to whether to split composite attributes into their atomic data elements depends upon the searches (and other data processing) you expect to do using that data. If you're in doubt, lean toward using atomic data. Well-defined atomic data can always be concatenated back together, but composite data is difficult to split apart after data entry. In addition, when data is entered as a long string, it's difficult to ensure that extra spaces haven't been entered, that certain parts are correctly capitalized, and so on.

Step 2—Defining Attribute Values

Attributes can take on a single value or multiple values or even be derived from stored attributes. In our conceptual schema, we'll identify the type of attribute using various symbols for each of these traits, so we want to list the attribute type before constructing the diagram.

Single- and Multivalued Attributes

Take the attribute Address, for example. If we assume there's only one address per person, then we conclude that this attribute is single-valued. But suppose the person maintains a home address and a business address and our requirements tell us we'll have to know both to communicate effectively with him or her. Does this mean the attribute should become multivalued? Probably not.

Note that multivalued attributes are not the same as composite attributes. Composite attributes contain several pieces of data, each of which is a part of the same thing (an address, for instance). Multivalued attributes may contain atomic or composite values, but a single attribute may contain several values, each of which represents the same thing (college degrees, addresses, and so on). As an example of a multivalued attribute, you might have a person who plays soccer, football, and tennis. If one of the attributes in your database is Sports Played, then that attribute might have several values, and therefore be a multivalued attribute.

So how do we decide what to do? In the case of Address, we probably want to know what address to mail things to. Perhaps it would be best to label this attribute Mailing Address, and store any other addresses in a memo field (particularly if there's little reason to suspect the other address might ever be used for mailing purposes). In fact, unless we know there'll be some cases where it's essential to record secondary addresses (if they exist), such as during an emergency, it's probably best to leave that data out of the database altogether.

In the case of college degrees, it might be useful to know the educational level of our employees for human resources statistical purposes or perhaps when bidding on a contract. If so, rather than make the attribute multivalued, perhaps we should add attributes for each common level of educational achievement: High School, Trade School, Bachelor's Degree, Master's Degree, Doctorate, and so on. We could then easily compile records based on these criteria. Our requirements should tell us whether we're likely to do this with the database we're creating.

So when is it acceptable to use a multivalued attribute? The answer is when there's little processing that must be performed on that value. For instance, if you stock lockable briefcases in your store and some have only one locking mechanism while others have two, go ahead and store both values in the same attribute. Chances are you'll never sort briefcases by type of locking mechanism. If a customer asks for this data when inquiring about a particular briefcase, it'll appear onscreen when you call up the record.

One final note about multivalued attributes. When you have a question about them, consider making a special entity type just for that attribute. In our briefcase example, perhaps the entity type could be called Special Features, and it could list all the special features a briefcase might have. That way, you can associate the briefcase with as many features as you like without expanding the entity type of all items you stock to encompass every special feature possible for every item.

Step 3—Defining Stored Vs. Derived Attributes

Some required attributes won't be listed in the attributes list or shown on the conceptual schema diagram, but they're there nonetheless. Age is a very common example. Age can be derived using the difference between the Birth Date attribute and the current value of the system clock.

Determining the need for an Age attribute is part of generating requirements. It's likely to be part of the functional requirements (derived using data processing techniques) and will probably begin flowing through the process whenever the first decision or transaction requiring an Age value occurs.

For this reason, it's important to check the functional requirements while building your list of required data elements. Although it's easy to see when, where, and why Birth Date is essential for the derivation of Age, the need for other data elements may not be nearly so obvious.

Step 4—Defining Key Attributes

Key attributes set a particular entity apart from all other entities by accepting only unique values. Their purpose is to ensure that no two entities (records) have the same value in at least one field, thereby ensuring that each entity represents a different thing (person, building, department, and so on).

ID Attributes

In modern database design, it's common to include one attribute for this purpose, typically called Employee ID, Customer ID, Department ID, and so on. Why not use Home Phone Number as the key attribute for your employees? After all, no two employees should have the same phone number, right? Obviously, considering the possibility that a husband and wife, roommates, or some other combination of people might live at the same address and use the same phone, this isn't a good idea. In fact, for just about any piece of data there's always the possibility that a valid (or at least temporarily valid) exception will occur.

Using a specially created ID attribute has other advantages as well. DBMSs often incorporate a data type that automatically increments the key value by one each time a new entity is recorded. This data type can be compact, automatically unique, and serve as an indicator of the sequence in which records were added. And because it's built in, it runs quickly.

Composite Keys

Sometimes there's a need for composite keys. These are keys made of two or more existing attributes. The existing attributes may be unique by themselves (some entities have more than one unique attribute), or they may individually be nonunique. Nonunique attribute values, when combined, must form a unique, nonrepeating value to make a composite key.

Use composite keys when you need to build an entity that's based on other entities. For instance, suppose an employee requests that a certain hazardous material be issued for a particular process on a unique item being manufactured. You'd want to keep a record of the employee, the material, the process, and the item being manufactured, as well as the date and time of issue and the amount issued.

For this entity type (let's call it HazMat Issues) the person, material, process, or item might not be unique because it may all apply to other entities (records) within this entity type. However, if we assume that each process is performed only once to each item being manufactured, then the four attributes, taken together, form a unique value that should never be repeated. Using these four attributes actually helps enforce the business rules holding the database together because if someone tries to perform the same process with the same material another time (in violation of the rules) the database will not accept the entry.

Defining Relationships

Relationships are the glue that hold entities together. Note that for a given entity type (the set of attributes making up the entities in the type) there may be many entities (records). Note also that each entity may play several roles in relation to other entities. In fact, entities may play roles among themselves (as in the example of the employee who manages some employees while being managed, in turn, by others).

Step 1—Listing Relationships Between Entities

Make a list of all relationships between entities, without considering the role each entity plays in the relationship. For instance, if you have entities called Customers and Orders, you could list the relationship as Purchase.

Step 2—Identifying The Roles Played

Name the roles played by each entity type in the relationship. In the relationship noted in Step 1, the roles played are Makes Purchase (the role played by the Customer) and Purchased By (the role played by the Order).

Next, note whether a particular role is recursive, as in the case of the entity type Employees, where some employees are also managers. In this case, if you've defined an entity type called Managers and another called Employees, you would eliminate the entity type Managers and list it as a relationship instead, a recursive relationship among employees with each other. Eventually, all our relationships will be defined as entity types, but not until we begin the process of mapping the entities and relationships in our schema into a particular DBMS application.

Step 3—Defining The Cardinality Ratio

For each relationship, determine how the entities will be affected by each other as data is entered. How many Orders might a Customer have? Zero? One? Many? The answer in this case is most likely all three possibilities, so the cardinality ratio is one-to-many, going from Customers to Orders.

Step 4—Defining The Participation Constraint

Ask yourself: Can a Customer exist without an Order? The answer is probably yes, so there's no requirement for total participation of Customers in a Purchase relationship with Orders. But can (or should) an Order exist without a Customer? The answer is probably no, so there's a requirement for total participation of Orders in a Purchase relationship with Customers. At this stage, the role of each entity comes into play.

Step 5—Defining Attributes Of Relationships

Remember we talked about viewing relationships as entity types? Even though we're not defining relationships as entity types yet, we're going to assign them attributes of their own during schema construction. Consider the relationship between Manager and Branch. If we term the relationship Manage, we can then assign an attribute Start Date to the relationship itself.

Although Start Date is an attribute of the relationship Manage (between the Manager and the Branch), it could also be considered an attribute of either entity type. Because there's a one-to-one relationship between Manager and Branch (for any given time period, only one manager manages a branch and only one branch is managed by a manager) the Start Date could be part of the Manager entity type or the Branch entity type.

If there's a one-to-many relationship between entity types, an attribute of this kind can only be assigned to the entity type on the many side of the relationship. Suppose for example that there are many Employees working for a Branch. Each employee will begin participating in the Works For relationship on a particular Start Date. In our schema, this attribute will be part of the relationship itself, but we could make it an attribute of the Employees entity type. It would not work as an attribute of the Branch entity type, however, because there would be a different value for each employee.

If a many-to-many relationship exists between entity types, the attribute must be defined as an attribute of the relationship, not of either of the entities. For instance, Employees may work for many Customers, and Customers may utilize the services of many Employees. By definition, the number of hours spent in each case is a product of the combination of Employee-Customer and cannot be tracked as part of either individual entity type.

Constructing A Schema Diagram

The first step (following requirements collection) in constructing a database is to build a schema diagram. The schema diagram shows all the entities, their attributes, and their relationships. Before you start drawing, there are a few things to do.

Step 1—Listing All Entity Types

Make a list of all entity types required. Entity types are things like people, buildings, experiments, departments, medications, orders, and so on. Assign a short, descriptive name for each entity type, such as Employees, or Buildings. Don't skimp on your list; we'll whittle it down later.

For example, suppose you're charged with creating an application that will track hazardous materials used in a manufacturing facility. You might need to keep track of:

- People using hazardous materials—Employees.
- The materials themselves—Hazardous Materials.
- The areas in which they're used—Buildings.
- The processes during which they're used—Processes.
- The waste streams resulting from their use—Waste Streams.
- Each usage—HazMat Usage.
- The list of materials issued—HazMat Issue.
- The responsible authority (supervisor) in the area—Supervisor.
- Storage containers—HazMat Locker.
- Safety gear (respirators, protective clothing, and so on)—Personal Protective Gear.
- Supplementary materials (paint brushes, paper cups, and so on)—HazMat Usage Materials.
- Measuring equipment (scales, flow meters, and so on)—HazMat Issue Gear.

Each of these things may be depicted as an entity in its own right. Entity types are depicted in the schema diagram using a rectangular box, and weak entity types (those without key attributes) are depicted using a box within a box (see Figure 3.1).

Step 2—Categorizing Entities By Trait, Then As Active Or Passive

After listing entity types, categorize them according to similar traits. Employees and Supervisors are both people, and this tells us instantly that they are both probably members of the same group with a special, recursive relationship to themselves. We can now eliminate Supervisor as an entity type of its own, and later on we'll add a relationship to our list to account for this.

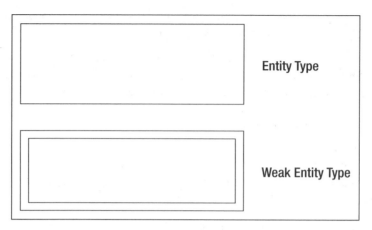

Figure 3.1   Entity type symbols.

The only entity types in our list that might initiate actions are Employees, Supervisors, Processes, and HazMat Issue Gear. We've already eliminated Supervisors as an entity type of its own, so we're left with just the three. If there's a part of the entity types Process or HazMat Issue Gear (automated warning systems, for instance) that should be defined as an entity type itself, now is the time to do so.

Let's assume Processes may initiate an action (such as an automatic shutdown sequence) but that HazMat Issue Gear contains no automated functions. To account for this, you'd define an entity type named Automated Emergency Actions and review the systems analysis to determine whether there are any other entity types that should be part of the same category. By definition, Automated Emergency Actions are active but have no smaller portions that are active within them, so we can now proceed to the next step.

Step 3—Identifying All The Attributes Of Listed Entities

When you have a comprehensive, categorized list of all the entities that might end up in the database, begin listing the attributes of each entity. Using the hazardous waste example, we can start by listing each attribute for our first entity, people who use hazardous materials. The attributes you could list include:

- *Employee ID*—The key attribute of Employee.
- *Name*—A composite attribute consisting of first and last name and middle initial.
- *Grade*—The rank of the employee for pay purposes.
- *Shop*—The subsection of the branch in which the employee works.
- *Process Certifications*—The processes that the employee is certified to perform.

- *Safety Training Date (for hazardous materials)*—The most recent safety training attended by the employee.

- *Weeks Since Last Safety Training*—The number of weeks since the last time the employee received safety training.

- *Current Phone Number*—The phone number where the employee can be reached in the plant.

- *Location*—The building where the employee works.

Interestingly, at this point you may find you have the capability to make a connection between the database you're designing and existing databases. Most likely, someone in your organization has already created a central database storing employee data. If so, and if you can tap into it, you can avoid building a duplicate employee entity in miniature. In fact, if you can verify that the existing database will adequately support the process you're working on (the data is high quality and updated in a timely fashion), you *should* connect the two to eliminate confusion, to reduce labor spent updating and maintaining records, and to increase data consistency. Chances are, even if it is technically complex to integrate the two, the value of having one correct data source more than outweighs the cost of doing so.

Let's assume that there's an Employee database maintained by your company (pretty likely, wouldn't you say?) and that it contains the employee's name, address, home phone number, ID number, and so on. That would mean we could eliminate the Name and Grade attributes from our list of attributes for employees. Why? Because we can establish a one-to-one relationship between our database and the company Employees database using the key attribute, Employee ID. But wait. Would it be convenient to have Employee Name data reside in our application as well as the company Employee database? Probably, so we might want to keep the Name attribute as part of our schema. It's a judgment call, and we'll examine this issue in more detail in later chapters.

The rest of the attributes are all clearly single-valued ones directly related to the Employee and within the context of Hazardous Materials Usage, except for Process Certifications. Unless an Employee performs only one process (unlikely in most situations), he or she will probably maintain certifications for several processes at a given time. This means the attribute is multivalued. Process Certifications is actually a relationship between Process and Employees because Employees can be Certified For a particular Process, and Processes can be Certified On by Employees.

The only derived attribute is Weeks Since Last Safety Training. That attribute is derived from the difference between Last Safety Training Date and the current date, whatever that might happen to be.

Single-valued attributes are depicted in the schema diagram as a circular or oval shape with the name of the attribute inside, while multivalued attributes use an oval within an oval. Key attributes are shown by an underline beneath the name of the attribute. Composite attributes, such as Name, are depicted with an oval for the primary attribute and additional ovals for each atomic attribute of the composite. Derived attributes are depicted by an oval composed of dashed (rather than solid) lines. Figure 3.2 shows the symbols used for each type of attribute.

Step 4—Identifying Relationships Between Listed Entity Types

The identification and diagramming of relationships between entities is a subject for careful consideration because this is one of the essential steps in building business rules into your database. Your first step in identifying relationships between entity types is to list all the relationships you can think of between the entities you've categorized then draw relationship symbols around them. Relationships are depicted with diamond shaped boxes holding the name of the relationship inside, and identifying relationships (those establishing a relationship from an identifying owner entity type and a weak entity type) are depicted with a diamond within a diamond. Both symbols are shown in Figure 3.3.

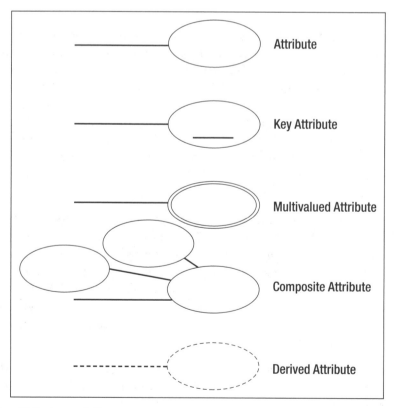

Figure 3.2   Attribute symbols.

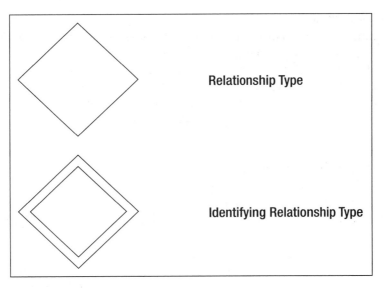

Figure 3.3   Relationship symbols.

Various aspects of relationships can be defined by:

- Cardinality ratio
- Participation constraints

Cardinality Ratio

Relationships fall into three basic categories: one-to-one, one-to-many, and many-to-many. Although the roles played by actual entities may describe hundreds of different scenarios and business rules, DBMSs commonly allow only a few. In our example, the relationship between Employees and Shop can be termed Work For. Because an Employee can work for only one Shop at a time while a Shop employs many Employees, the cardinality ratio between Employee and Shop (within relationship Works For) is many-to-one.

The cardinality ratio between HazMat Locker and Hazardous Materials is many-to-many because many materials can be stored in many lockers. The cardinality ratio between Process and Hazardous Materials would be many-to-many because a process could use many materials and a material could be used during many processes.

As you can see, the best way to identify the cardinality ratio is simply to verbalize a simple statement defining the relationship between entity types. From there, the cardinality ratio should be easy to identify.

Cardinality ratio is depicted in our schema diagram with the number 1 on the one side of a relationship and a capital M on the many side of the relationship (Access uses the infinity symbol instead of M). Figure 3.4 shows these symbols in common use.

Participation Constraint

In a similar fashion, a simple statement of business rules can help define participation constraints. For instance, suppose all hazardous material must be listed in the specifications of a Process before being procured, stocked, or used. This rule means that Hazardous Materials have total participation in the entity type Process. In fact, it means that, unless there's a Process calling for a particular Hazardous Material, that particular Hazardous Material can't exist within the entity type, Hazardous Materials.

By the same token, a Process can exist without any Hazardous Material associated with it. In this example, we'd define this as partial participation by Process in Hazardous Materials. Participation constraints are shown using single lines for partial participation and double lines for total participation (see Figure 3.5).

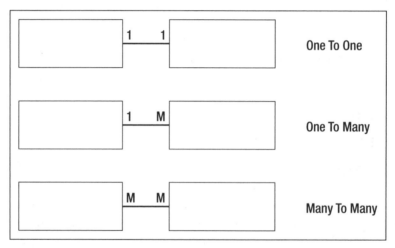

Figure 3.4   Depicting cardinality ratio.

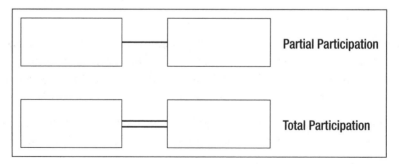

Figure 3.5   Depicting participation constraints.

Part II

Database Fundamentals

Chapter 4

Relational Databases

In Depth

This chapter extends entity relationship (ER) concepts to the parent-child relationship (PCR), a hierarchical schema that closely resembles the structures found in many modern database programming applications. We also begin a discussion of functional dependencies and the normal forms, mathematical constructs useful in database development, structured query language (SQL), and considerations for the general process of transforming a database into an application program.

At this point, we start building structures that can be translated into objects within Access 2000 and modifying these structures to optimize our eventual database application. Although we won't refer directly to Access 2000 very frequently yet, if you've used the program or its predecessors, you'll note the similarities to concepts discussed in this chapter.

Our use of hierarchical (or PCR) structure allows us to incorporate structures that, by their nature, optimize searches and other database functions. Normalization and the use of relational mathematics further optimizes our application and helps eliminate errors. Finally, a short discussion of SQL and how an application grows from a database provides a bridge from the theory to the realities of database design.

The objective of this chapter is to offer designers, users, and managers some insight into the terminology used and the reasons for applying ER, PCR, and normalization techniques. Access 2000 contains a number of wizards that will perform these routines and suggest better database designs; knowing how and why simply leads to better database design from the start and helps when compromises must be made.

Designing A "Good" Database

Like any other complex product, a database serving a particular purpose must sometimes trade off performance or functionality in one area for better performance in other areas. A trade-off that results in lowered speed is one thing, but a trade-off that results in the production of "bad" (erroneous) data is quite another thing.

Specific rules can be followed to create "good" data. Other rules keep storage size lean and others speed up searches. Performance starts with the schema. "Good" database design thus attempts to produce only accurate data while optimizing performance, with the realization that performance may mean different things to different designers or users.

Fundamentally, a good database design produces semantically correct results. For instance, we can simply state "No order can exist without there first being a customer to which the order is attached." In database terms, we can relate all orders to customers, and specify that a customer must exist before an order can be generated. The DBMS will ensure the rules are followed and disallow the creation of orders not attached to a customer. Essentially, what we would logically state, the DBMS enforces programmatically. The relational model offers techniques with which to build these logical structures.

The Relational Model Of Data

Introduced by Dr. Edgar F. Codd (1970), the relational data model is based on the *relation*, what we might think of as a table of values. Each row within the table contains fields, and the values in each field are related to each other. In fact, the entity recorded in that row is *described* by the values in the fields of that row.

In Chapter 3, we described the entity-relationship model in detail, and you'll find it resembles the relational model in many respects. The relational model simply extends the ER model and formalizes it into structures that can be manipulated more easily with standard database operations. Although some very simple databases may not require extension to the relational model, in practice the majority of databases do. Before we jump into how the relational model works, let's go over a few terms specific to the model.

Relational Terms

Now, just when we're approaching what look like familiar terms (*field*, *record*, *table*, and so on) we jump into a whole new set of names for these items. In relational terminology, a row is called a *tuple*, the name of a field (or column header) is called an *attribute* (as mentioned in Chapter 3), and a table is referred to as a *relation*. The data type describing the types and ranges of values that are allowed in each field is called a *domain*. A more detailed explanation of each follows.

Domains

It's interesting to note that domains define ranges of values as well as data types in the strict sense of the word. As we covered in Chapter 2, the term *data type* in common DBMSs refers to the storage size of the value and the operations that may be performed upon it. Domains also reference all the permissible values, which may be less than the values of the data type itself.

For instance, the Integer data type is stored as 16-bit (2-byte) numbers ranging in value from -32,768 to 32,767. A field for employee age may use the Integer data type (perhaps you want to be able to average employee ages for statistical purposes), but you might limit the values possible in this field to between 18 and 70. Therefore, the domain for this field would be all integers between 18 and 70. In addition, you'd specify that the unit of measure for this domain is Years. Even though the number of years may consist of more than one digit, it is logically an atomic value.

Formally, domains are supposed to consist of atomic values, values that can't be subdivided further, rather than composite values, as we discussed in Chapter 3. But how do we tell the difference? If a phone number consists of the area code and local number, should we define the entire number as a domain of all valid phone numbers in the U.S.? Or should we define the first three characters as a field of their own (area code) and the next seven numbers as also a field (local numbers)? We can choose to define the fields and domains either way, depending upon whether we expect to perform any functions on a particular segment of data. If we're going to manipulate records by area code, then it's best to define area code as its own field. If not, keep the entire number in one field. Once the domains have been defined, we can assemble them into the constituents of a table, or relation.

Relations

In the relational model, tables are called relations, implying that the values in each field are related to their row, and the rows are related to each other because the domains of their fields are the same. This makes intuitive sense, because both your name and your social security number are related to you, as well as your address, phone number, and age (although there could be someone else who has the same name, age, and other identifying characteristics as you). In a listing of people in your state, the individual records would be related because they all take their field values from the same groups (domains). For example, the phone number value in one of the records can be taken from the same group of valid phone numbers for your state as any other phone number value in the entire table.

The definition of a given domain and the interpretation we make about the values in a field from that domain may change over time, and these changes can affect our database design. It's possible that fields in a row could share a domain. For instance, valid phone numbers within a state include both home phone numbers and fax numbers. Although the phone numbers for both fields come from the same domain, the way we interpret the data (based on the field name) may influence our use of it. In this case, we wouldn't bother to call the fax number because there's little likelihood a person would answer. In any case, the set of values related to each other are called tuples.

Tuples

Tuples are records, and a relation (table) can hold many of them. The order of the tuples doesn't matter logically, even though physically there's always an order applied (first record, second record, last record, and so on). The order of attribute (field) values within a tuple doesn't logically matter either, although a consistent order is always applied physically for storage purposes. Only certain types of attribute values are allowed, as we discuss next.

Attributes

Composite or multivalued attributes aren't allowed in the relational model; composite attributes must be broken down into their atomic components, and multivalued attributes must be represented by separate relations. If the value of an attribute is unknown, it takes on a special value called *null*, meaning the value is unknown, not applicable, or nonexistent. Attributes and the values they can assume can be manipulated to apply some business rules to the database design, using constraints.

Constraints On The Relational Model

During the systems analysis phase of our database design exercise, we conducted interviews to gather business rules. Business rules can be applied to the database we design by incorporating them into the constraints on our relational model. Constraints (domain, key, and so on) can usually be interpreted directly from statements made by current process users, if the analyst is listening carefully.

Domain Constraints

Suppose we're formulating a system for calculating GPA at a school. We can constrain the values of the domain, LetterGrade, to a subset of all possible values for its data type (text, A through Z plus numbers and special characters), as we've discussed. Better yet, we could make a list of the only values capable of being applied correctly (the list of all possible letter grade values = A, B, C, D, and F, for example). Domain constraints limit the values a particular attribute can assume, while key constraints limit the duplication of values.

Key Constraints

Here's a thought. Can you think of any circumstance in which it would be desirable to have two records in the same table with identical values in each field? If all the values of two or more records were identical, then there'd be no characteristics to distinguish one from another. After the first identical record, all the others would be duplicates, adding no additional data.

But wait! What if we defined a table that contained only two fields: a foreign key (the same value as a key field in another table) and one other entry that's the same in each record. Wouldn't many of the records in this table have identical entries? The answer is yes, and you could use a structure such as this to record the number of items an entity is associated with. For instance, you could record the number of cans of tomato sauce a person bought, but your database design would be incorrect.

A valid relation (table) would use a numeric field to count the number of cans, not a separate relation. If each can had some distinct identity (such as time of purchase, type of sauce, and so on), then a separate relation could be used, but that relation would then conform to good database design because all its records would be unique.

The point we're making here is that a properly designed table can contain only unique records, although for some attribute values the records may be identical. The smallest combination of attributes that still uniquely identifies a record is called a *key*; any combination larger than that is called a *superkey*. A relation might have more than one key (each called *candidate keys*), but the rule of thumb is to choose the one that has the fewest attributes. The chosen one is called the *primary key*. Primary keys are an essential ingredient in building integrity constraints.

Integrity Constraints

The definition of a table and its fields is called a *relation schema*, whereas the definition of the relationships between relations is called a *relational database schema*. To properly define relationships between relations, we need to set integrity constraints.

Entity integrity declares that no primary key value can be null. This simply means that there must always be a value in that field for each record created. This only makes sense because the primary key value uniquely identifies the record.

Referential integrity specifies that if a record in one table refers to a record in another table, the other table must actually contain the record to which it refers. We've already alluded to this several times in previous chapters, using the Customers and Orders example.

A *foreign key* is used to make the connection between relations in which referential integrity is established. The foreign key is a field (attribute) in one table that holds the value of the primary key from another table to which the record refers. With the constraints we've discussed in place, the DBMS will prevent any insert, delete, and edit operations from taking place if the constraints are violated.

Insert, Delete, And Edit Operations

The attribute (field) values of inserted or edited records must conform to domain, key, entity, and referential integrity. Delete operations will fail if referential integrity is violated. These operations are only a few of all the operations available to us for the production of information. Relational algebra is another set of operations that generates information from the data in our database.

Relational Algebra

The design of relations is heavily influenced by the processes these relations must support. Effective support of processes means accurate and timely information production. Using relations to produce information requires queries, the database tools used to select and retrieve useful data from relations. Relational algebra and other relational operations are the construction materials used to build queries.

Relational algebra is so called because it's concerned with mathematical operations that can be used to manipulate tables (relations). These operations form the basis upon which relational calculus rests, as well as many common query operations we take for granted in modern database applications. Although it's not necessary to write out and perform these operations each time you create a query in Access 2000, understanding the fundamentals can help you eliminate errors in query design.

Relational algebra operations include:

- Union
- Intersection
- Difference
- Cartesian product

Relation operations include:

- Select
- Project
- Joins
- Aggregate functions

Relation operations are at the heart of SQL and common functions every relational database performs, as we discuss next.

Relation Operations

The select and project operations were specifically designed for use with relational databases. Applying them to relations results in new relations that we can name. We can make the result a part of the database, or we can simply use it to proceed to another step. The select operation is frequently the first operation performed in a query.

Select

As its name implies, the select operation retrieves a set of tuples (a subset of the original relation) that conform to a *selection condition*. For instance, if you want to generate a list of all customers located in Kansas, you would apply the selection condition State = Kansas against the relation Customers (assuming the relation Customers has an attribute called State). The result would be a new relation containing all the same attributes as the Customers relation but with tuples (records) only where the selection condition was met (only records where the value of State is equal to Kansas).

TIP: *Most likely, you'd have set the attribute (field) as a two-character field using the two-character designation for states to reduce the likelihood of errors occurring because of variations in the way state names were entered. In fact, a good design would have created a separate relation solely for the purpose of maintaining the list of all possible two-character state values for lookup purposes.*

Selection conditions use *Boolean expressions* to make up *selection clauses*. Boolean expressions include comparison operators such as equals, less than, less than or equal to, greater than, greater than or equal to, and not equal to. Notice that ordered values such as numbers, dates, or alphabetical characters can be operated upon with all the comparison operators, while unordered values such as color or state can only be operated upon by equals or not equal to.

The Boolean operators AND, OR, and NOT can be used to specify multiple conditions against an attribute or several attributes. For instance, suppose you want to retrieve all customers located in Kansas or Texas. Using the example above, you'd apply the selection condition State = Kansas OR State = Texas to the Customers relation. The result would be all tuples where state equals either Kansas or Texas.

Notice that by applying the selection condition State = Kansas AND State = Texas the query would fail because there should be no cases where State equals both Kansas and Texas for the same tuple. The AND operator might be used to retrieve customers where you're concerned with the values in two attributes though. For instance, if you want to retrieve customers located in Kansas who have more than $1,000,000 in annual sales, you'd apply the selection condition State = Kansas AND Annual Sales > 1,000,000 to the Customers relation. The project operation differs from select in that the result of a project operation is a relation that contains certain attributes from a relation but not from others.

Project

The project operation allows you to retrieve all tuples from the original relation but specify only some of the attributes. For instance, if you want to retrieve only customer names and titles from the relation Customers, you'd apply the project operation name and title to Customers.

But what if two different customers had the same name? To produce a valid relation, all tuples must be distinct or unique. The project operation automatically discards any tuples that are duplicates across all existing attributes. In this case, it would be advisable to include the key of the original relation (perhaps Customer Number) to ensure that no customers were missed.

Relational Algebra Expressions

An accepted shorthand exists for writing relational algebraic expressions; it's the equivalent of writing a formula rather than using English to describe mathematical expressions. However, our purpose here is to clearly explain the basics to designers, users, and managers. Therefore, we refrain from using this technique and concentrate on prose and examples that will do the job acceptably. For excellent resources about these subjects, including the shorthand used to write these expressions, please see the bibliography.

Relational algebra expressions can be combined or applied one by one with temporary results at each stage. Intermediate relations created in each step can be named, as we mentioned, and subsequent operations applied to them. Some operations can be applied in any order; others must be applied in a given sequence for correct results. Also, attributes can be renamed during this process.

Logically, this makes sense. A select operation would work regardless of the order in which it was applied because each additional condition would be applied to the remaining tuples. Project operations must be applied in a given order, though, because discarding some attributes and/or tuples means they aren't available later. Both select and project operations are logical operations, as opposed to mathematical set operations.

Set Operations

Set operations include union, intersection, difference, and join. They derive from mathematical set theory and are useful because relations are defined as sets of tuples. Set operations work with several relations (unlike relation operations that are applicable only to a single relation at a time), and their result is a new relation, again, one that we can name.

Before a set operation can be processed on two relations, the relations must be *union compatible*. They must have the same number of attributes, and these attributes must have the same domain (their values must be from the same pool of values; that is, home phone numbers and fax numbers all come from the same pool of all valid phone numbers). A description of each set operation follows.

Union

When a union is applied to two relations, the result consists of all the tuples in *either* relation, with duplicate values (across all attributes) eliminated. Suppose we apply a union to the relation Customers of Northwest Region and another relation, Customers of Southwest Region, in which both relations contain Customer Number and Customer Name. This creates a relation containing the name and number of all customers from both regions, minus any duplicates (a single customer with locations in both regions, for example).

Intersection

Applying an intersection to two relations generates a listing of all the tuples in *both* relations. Tuples not found in both relations are discarded, as are multiple instances of the same tuple. Using the example above, the result of an intersection would be only those customers who have locations in both regions, most likely a much smaller list. Like the AND operator, values retrieved must be present in the first relation and in the second relation.

Difference

Applying a difference operation to two relations lists all the tuples in one relation that aren't found in the other. Tuples in the first relation that are also in the second relation are discarded. Using our Customers example, the result would be only customers in the first region who aren't also located in the second region.

Notice that you could apply a union or an intersection in either direction, but the difference holds only for one direction. This means that the results wouldn't match were you to apply a difference from the Northwest Region to the Southwest Region and vice versa.

Other Operations

Unsurprisingly, we can perform other operations as well. Some of these are actually built from operations we've already discussed, but it's more convenient to use them directly than to use several simpler operations in sequence.

Cartesian Product

The Cartesian product operation is actually an intermediate operation that's usually used in combination with a select operation to produce a join (we'll discuss that next). A Cartesian product operation applied to two relations generates a new relation with all the attributes of both original relations and a tuple equaling the product of one relation times the other relation.

This operation isn't very useful by itself precisely because it's the product of both original relations. Most of the tuples it contains have no valid information. For instance, suppose we take the Cartesian product of the relations Customers and Orders. The result will be a relation containing all attributes of Customers (Customer Number, name, address, phone number, and so on) plus all the attributes of Orders (Order Number, Customer Number, date, amount, shipping costs, and so on). If there are 10 Customers and 50 Orders the result will contain 500 tuples, as though each customer made every order (and, of course, we know this to be untrue).

However, applying a select operation (in which tuples are selected when the attribute Customer Number from the Customers relation equals Customer Number from the Orders relation) results in a relation containing only those tuples that represent unique orders for each Customer.

Join Operations

The join operation combines the Cartesian product and select operations into one efficient operation that produces a new relation from the original relations. This new relation contains all the attributes of both relations as well as tuples in which the join condition is met. This means join conditions include the *equijoin*, in which an attribute from one relation contains a value equal to the value of an attribute from the other relation. The two attributes are called *join attributes*.

The join attributes must be from the same domain (for instance, you could use Department Number in the Departments relation and Department Number in the Employees relation to apply a join returning all the employees in each department). Tuples without a Department Number (a null value in Department Number) won't be included in the result. A *natural join* is an equijoin with the excess join attribute removed. There's no need to show Department Number twice in the final result, so the natural join removes it.

Join operations can use comparison operators such as greater than, less than, and so on, rather than just equals. The number of tuples in the final result may range from zero to the product of the number of tuples in each relation. For example, if we have a list of 10 Orders and a list of 50 Items, the result of a join operation could be zero tuples if none of Items were part of any Order, to 500 tuples if every Item were on every Order. The ratio of tuples in the result to possible tuples is called *join selectivity*.

Outer Join And Outer Union Operations

Sometimes it's desirable to generate a result that contains more tuples than a standard or natural join does. Using the *left outer join*, for instance, generates all the tuples of a natural join plus tuples from the left relation (the first one) in which the join condition isn't met. A *right outer join* includes just the opposite, and a *full outer join* includes tuples in which the join condition is met as well as tuples from each relation in which the condition isn't met. Note that the full outer join is unlike the Cartesian product, in which every tuple in both relations is matched with every tuple in the other relation. With no matching tuple in one or the other relation, the result is automatically filled in with a null value.

The *outer union*, on the other hand, produces a new relation by combining the original relations regardless of whether they're union compatible. For instance, if we applied an outer union to the relations Hazardous Materials and Waste Materials we would end up with a relation listing all materials that are waste products of our factory, but only some of the tuples would have values for the Hazardous Properties attribute. Waste materials that aren't classified as Hazardous would have null values for this attribute.

Aggregate Functions

Aggregate functions lump together (or aggregate) groups of values and include sum, average, standard deviation, maximum, minimum, count, and so on. They can be applied across an entire relation (count the number of projects in the relation Projects), or they can be applied separately to each group within a relation (count the number of projects assigned to each Department Number in the relation Projects). Any attribute in the relation Projects could potentially be used to divide projects into groups, but of course some will make much more sense than others.

Note that the final result will contain one additional attribute to hold the value generated by the aggregate function. For instance, if we're calculating the average volume of items on orders, the final relation will have both the volume of each item and another attribute showing the average volume within that order. If we leave out the item volume attribute (using the Project operation), the result will show only orders and the average volume. And if we leave out everything but the average volume attribute, the result will be a single tuple containing the average volume across all orders in the original relation. Another method of achieving the same results is to use relational calculus.

Relational Calculus And Query By Example

Relational calculus is similar to relational algebra in that any retrieval operation (or sequence of operations) that can be specified in relational algebra can also be specified in relational calculus. The primary differences are that only one expression is required in relational calculus and relational calculus is *nonprocedural*; that is, there's no description of the sequence of operations required to produce the correct result. Relational calculus operates on the values contained in tuples or the domains of those values.

Relational Calculus

Relational calculus falls basically into two categories: *tuple relational calculus* and *domain relational calculus*. Essentially, tuple relational calculus first specifies the attributes of a tuple to be retrieved, then the conditions that must be met (including conditions involving other relations). Domain relational calculus operates in a similar way except that it uses the domain of individual attributes, rather than tuples, in defining retrievals. Expressing queries using relational calculus is simplified by Query By Example (QBE).

Query By Example (QBE)

Perhaps you've been wondering when we'd get to something that looks familiar, like something you see in Microsoft Access. QBE is it. Officially, QBE is a relational query language that's articulated by filling in examples of the relations to be queried. Many modern DBMSs use QBE as the foundation for queries (the original was developed by IBM Research).

Any query that can be expressed using relational algebra or relational calculus can be expressed using QBE. QBE's big advantage is that using it is intuitive because the examples are functional representations of the relations to be queried. The example screen usually has a place where relations can be inserted, as well as another area resembling a little spreadsheet, with the attribute names across the top heading up columns that can be filled in. The user may fill in specific values to be retrieved for some attributes, while other attributes might get wild-card characters. In traditional QBE, the symbol P. (a capital P followed by a period) denotes a column to retrieve. If the user places a comparison operator, such as a less-than symbol (<) in a column, QBE knows the value of that attribute must meet the condition specified to be retrieved. Any values on the same row are assumed to be connected by the logical AND; values on separate rows are connected by the logical OR.

QBE can specify join operations by placing a wild-card character in the join attributes from the original relations in the QBE statement. This generates a query that retrieves only those tuples in which the join attributes contain matching values. Microsoft Access makes it even easier by allowing you to visually specify joins between relations and to edit the nature of those joins (making them left, right, or full outer joins by right clicking the join lines in the query screen). QBE is much different than SQL, but both query methods have their proponents.

SQL

SQL stands for structured query language. It's pronounced sequel and, as a matter of fact, was initially called SEQUEL (for structured English query language). Several versions are currently supported, and new versions are constantly in the works.

The American National Standards Institute (ANSI) and the International Organization for Standardization (ISO) have been instrumental in creating standard versions of SQL, but, as usual, vendors frequently implement their own versions to support features that differentiate their products from their competitor's. Our usage of SQL commands in this chapter is for example purposes only and should not be taken as representative of Microsoft Access SQL, which will be properly defined and discussed in later chapters.

SQL Commands

In SQL terms, table is equivalent to relation, row is equivalent to tuple, and column is equivalent to attribute (thank goodness!). SQL's many capabilities can be used to define entire databases, including schemas, tables, fields (columns), data types, queries, views, and so on. Each function in SQL is written in regular English with a fairly straightforward syntax, as we see in the next section.

Creating Tables

For instance, the SQL command **CREATE TABLE Customers** will create a table named Customers within a database. Of course, you must specify the database (schema) within which to create the table, and you'll typically want to create fields and their data types to go with it. In addition, you can set up primary and foreign keys, the tables they reference, and referential integrity. A fully formed table declared using SQL might look like this:

```
CREATE TABLE COMPANY.CUSTOMERS
     (      NAME          VARCHAR(20)    NOT NULL,
            ADDRESS       VARCHAR(40),
            CNUMBER       CHAR(6)        NOT NULL,
     PRIMARY KEY(CNUMBER));
```

Using SQL syntax, a table named Customers would be created in the database named Company. It would have three fields: Name, Address, and CNumber (Customer Number). CNumber would be the primary key, and neither CNumber or Name could have null values.

Schemas and tables can be deleted using the **DROP SCHEMA** and **DROP TABLE** commands, and the **DROP** commands can be modified by the **RESTRICT** and **CASCADE** options. When used for deleting schemas, the **RESTRICT** option works only if the schema has no elements in it; using the **CASCADE** option drops all tables, domains, and other elements. When used for deleting tables, the **RESTRICT** option prevents table deletion if there are constraints dependent upon the table (such as with referential integrity), whereas **CASCADE** deletes all constraints along with the table.

Finally, tables can be modified in SQL using the **ALTER TABLE** command. Columns can be added or deleted, the data type and other parts of a column definition can be changed, and table constraints can be added or deleted. The **RESTRICT** and **CASCADE** options are frequently used to satisfy the remaining constraints on the table.

Creating Queries

Queries are created in SQL using the **SELECT** command, not to be confused with the select operation in relational algebra. Although there are similarities in some areas, the SQL **SELECT** command has many abilities not inherent in the select operation, as we shall see.

A simple select query might use three commands: **SELECT**, **FROM**, and **WHERE**. If we want to retrieve all customers in the Northwest region it might look like this:

```
SELECT      CNUMBER, NAME, REGION
FROM        CUSTOMERS
WHERE       REGION="Northwest"
```

The **SELECT** command tells the DBMS what fields to return values for, in this case Customer Number, Name, and Region. The **FROM** command specifies the table to get the values from, and the **WHERE** clause is a conditional expression specifying the retrieval of records only in which certain values are found. The result of this query would be a table containing three fields consisting only of records in which Region equals Northwest.

Join conditions can be specified using the **FROM** command, and the command can include several table names, provided fields with the same name in different tables are prefixed with the name of the table they come from (like CUSTOMER.NAME and SUPPLIER.NAME). To make the join, SQL allows use of the logical AND condition in the **WHERE** clause so you can set the primary key of one table equivalent to the foreign key of another table. A SQL query such as this might look like the following:

```
SELECT      CNUMBER, SNUMBER, CUSTOMER.NAME, SUPPLIER.NAME
FROM        CUSTOMERS, SUPPLIERS
WHERE       CUSTOMER.NAME=SUPPLIER.NAME
```

This SQL query would return a table with records only of customers and suppliers where the name is the same, and it would also contain only four fields: Customer Number, Supplier Number, Customer Name, and Supplier Name. Effectively, this is the same as the select, project, and join operations we discussed in relational algebra.

If the **WHERE** clause isn't included in our SELECT query, SQL assumes all records meet our criteria (or lack of it) and includes all records in the result. If we've specified several tables in the **FROM** command, SQL creates a Cartesian product (cross product) of all records. As you can imagine, an error of this type could produce extremely large results, so it pays to be very careful with **WHERE** commands. Finally, we can specify all fields by using an asterisk (*) after the **SELECT** command, rather than having to include the name of every field.

SELECT queries produce duplicate tuples, rather than eliminating them like relational operations. If duplicate records are undesired, they can be eliminated using the **DISTINCT** option in the **SELECT** command. SQL also uses the relational algebra operations **UNION**, **EXCEPT** (difference), and **INTERSECT**, and in these cases, duplicate records are eliminated.

SQL queries can be nested, one inside the other, to produce results in which values must be compared with values based on a query. The nested query is called the *inner query*, so, of course, the query in which it's nested is called the *outer query*. Each record retrieved by the outer query is first evaluated against the results of the inner query to see if the **WHERE** clause is true. If so, it's included in the result.

Finally, SQL queries are capable of the following common query actions:

- *Using explicit values or null*—SQL queries can be written to evaluate against a set of explicit values or the null value rather than values found in a table.

- *Renaming fields*—Fields can be renamed in SQL statements then referred to in the same statement. This is accomplished using the **AS** command.

- *Using aggregate functions*—SQL queries can make use of aggregate functions via **SUM**, **MIN**, **MAX**, and other aggregate commands. These functions can be applied to groups when **GROUP BY** is inserted.

- *Using arithmetic operators*—Plus, minus, multiplied by, and divided by can be used on numeric values in a query. The result is a table with an additional field containing the new value, plus any other fields specified.

- *Using string operators*—The **LIKE** operator matches strings (or substrings) if they contain the same values, and wild-card characters can be substituted for single or groups of characters if desired. The concatenate operator (pipes, or ||) appends one string to another.

- *Sorting values*—SQL queries can sort (order) values in ascending or descending order using the **ASC** and **DESC** commands in the **ORDER BY** clause. The default sort order if **ORDER BY** is used is ascending.

SQL also contains facilities for inserting new records, deleting records, editing records, generating views (temporary or virtual tables), creating indexes, and many other normal database functions. These functions can be embedded within other programming languages as well.

However, Microsoft Access contains a very intuitive graphical user interface (GUI) for accomplishing most of these functions, so the primary concern here should be to understand enough about SQL to use it most effectively in those situations where it's called for. Writing Visual Basic for Applications (VBA) is a prime example. In practice, it's sometimes easiest to use the GUI to create a query, then invoke the Microsoft SQL View to incorporate the SQL into your code. But we need to review a few more aspects of data modeling first, such as the Parent-Child Relationship (PCR).

The Parent-Child Relationship (PCR)

One way of stating a common semantic rule in databases is to use the PCR in a *hierarchical schema*. Despite its new-age, politically correct connotations, the PCR in this context actually has a scientific meaning. Specifically, it refers to a one-to-many relationship between entity types, now called *record types*. Record types are a collection of data items or fields. Together, these two data structuring concepts compose the hierarchical data model.

The *parent record type* is, of course, the record type on the *one* side of the relationship, and the *child record type* is the record type on the *many* side. Each instance of a PCR type consists of one record of the parent record type and zero or more records of the child record type. Sounds logical enough, right?

Many hierarchies composed of many record and PCR types may exist within a hierarchical database schema, and each record type may contain many fields (or data items), each with its own data type. Although the schemas, PCRs, record types, and data items can become somewhat confusing, clarity can be discovered again by thinking of them as simply the data types, fields, tables, relationships between tables, and hierarchies that can so easily be built directly in Access 2000 or any other modern DBMS.

Defining A Hierarchical Schema

Hierarchical schemas are defined by the following set of characteristics:

- The granddaddy of all record types, called the root of the schema, is not a child record type of any other record type.

- Every other record type may be a parent record type but is also a child record type in one parent record type.

- A parent record type can have zero or more child record types. If it has more than one child, the child types are ordered from left to right in the hierarchical diagram.

- A record type with no children is called a leaf.

In our "Immediate Solutions" section we'll define parent child relationships on an example database to show how it's done. For now, we'll press on to the refinement of your database design with normalization and functional dependencies.

Functional Dependencies, Normalization

We've discussed many ways relational databases can be constructed and the languages, notations, and schemas used to do so. The concepts of functional dependency and normalization provide tools we can use to evaluate the effectiveness and efficiency of one approach compared to another. These concepts apply both to base tables physically stored in the system somewhere and to virtual tables (views) that are generated and regenerated on the fly. Remember, your goal is an effective database design, not necessarily a perfect one.

Database Design Goals

Generally, the goals of database design are to:

- Produce an easily understandable structure.
- Use as little storage space and provide as much speed as possible (efficient).
- Create an effective database.

Sometimes an effective design makes compromises between speed, storage space, and clarity to achieve a workable balance. After all, what good is a fast, small database that no one understands?

Semantic Clarity

A design that's easy to understand is desirable for practical reasons; namely, if it's easy to explain, it will be easy to ensure that it meets users' needs. (You were planning on talking it over with the users, right?) Making each table refer to only one entity is a good rule of thumb. Basically, this means only one field will refer to each related entity within a table.

For example, if you make a table for customers, omit fields about the region where the customer is located; instead, create a separate table called Regions for that information and connect it using a Region Number field in the Customers table. It's easier to explain, and it uses less storage space because the data doesn't have to be repeated for each new customer in the same region. Of course, your design may still produce errors (anomalies).

Anomalies

Poor design can also lead to errors or *anomalies*. These can be categorized as:

- Insertion anomalies
- Deletion anomalies
- Modification anomalies

Mixing entity types can cause insertion anomalies because we have to know the correct values for both (or many) entities before we can insert a new entity record. For instance, by mixing customers and regions, we would need to know all the correct values for a region before we could create a new customer record. In practice, this would probably be quite difficult or expensive to accomplish because the person inserting a new customer is unlikely to have that information at hand, and should they, it's unlikely that the data would be identical to previously entered data.

Of course, you could build in a function to retrieve the data for them from other records, but which one would you use if there were differences? The easiest, simplest approach is to use the Region Number field we discussed earlier. That would automatically point to the correct record in the Region table, and should the data need updating, one update would automatically serve as an update for all pointers to it, no matter where they reside. This resolves the modification anomaly as well.

The deletion anomaly occurs when we delete records with mixed entities. If our company is going through a transition period and we delete all customer records from our database, we also delete all references to regions, even though that may not be desirable as part of the current housecleaning effort. Storing region data in a separate table eliminates this anomaly.

One thing to keep in mind is that occasionally situations call for mixed entities in one table, perhaps for performance reasons (faster queries, for example). Make sure to prominently note such occurrences so that any anomalies created can be dealt with programmatically. And be aware that you may be opening the door to more null values and invalid records.

Null Values And Invalid Records

Suppose we build a Customers table. It would seem obvious that we should include company name, address, phone number, point of contact, and so on. But should we include annual sales? Suppose we'd like to enter it, if known, but it's unknown or not applicable in many cases? Leaving this field in the Customers table means there will be many null values, wasting space and making aggregate functions more difficult to process. The better approach is to put infrequently known values in a table of their own (referenced by the Customer Number in this case).

Invalid records can be created if your design calls for joins that don't use primary or foreign keys. For instance, suppose you joined customers to regions by state rather than by region number. Should parts of a state be in two or three regions (hey, it could happen), you'd end up with two or three customer records when only one is appropriate. Careful evaluation of potential results can alert you to the possibility of invalid records appearing after joins (sometimes even using primary or foreign keys is not enough to prevent them), and, of course, they must be eliminated. After eliminating null values and invalid records as much as possible, we turn our attention to functional dependencies.

Functional Dependency

A functional dependency (FD) between fields in a table means that the data found in one or more fields is dependent upon the data found in the other field(s). The atomic weight of an element is functionally dependent upon the isotope of an element because, if we know the isotope, we also know there is only one possible value for the atomic weight. However, if multiple values are present, this means no functional dependency exists, as in the case of atomic weight and element name. One element name can have several atomic weights associated with it because there are many elements with more than one isotope.

Essentially, a functional dependency defines a constraint on the schema of a relation that must remain intact for all values entered. It's defined when the schema is constructed, not from values entered later, and becomes part of the business rules enforced by the DBMS. Elaborate notational systems and inference rules are used to describe functional dependencies, but they're beyond the scope of this book. Please refer to the bibliography and the appendix of additional resources for excellent sources of further reading on the subject. Understanding and recognizing functional dependencies is a key part of the normalization process.

Normalization

Functional dependencies assist our understanding of normalization. Normalization is a formal set of tests to determine the suitability of a particular database design. Applying the tests to a design tells us the *normal form* to which a design conforms, and thereby helps us locate design errors and improvement candidates. Typically, poor designs can be improved by breaking fields out of larger tables into their own, separate (smaller) tables. A description of normal forms follows.

First Normal Form (1NF)

A relation (table) conforms to first normal form if it has no attributes (fields) that are composite or multivalued. No fields should exist where it's permissible to enter several values, and no values made up of smaller, discrete (single) values should exist. Thus, 1NF prevents us from building relations inside relations (tables) or tuples (records).

Relations not in 1NF are improved by either creating additional fields (for composite attributes) or by creating additional relations (for multivalued attributes).

Second Normal Form (2NF)

The next step in good database design is to evaluate relations from the standpoint of 2NF. The second normal form calls for full functional dependency, meaning that every attribute in the table is fully dependent upon the primary key attribute. The primary key may be composed of one or of several attributes, but other attributes in the table must depend upon both of them for a full functional dependency to exist.

Consider our example of atomic weights, isotopes, and element names. Notice that many other attributes may be included in the relation (boiling point, density, and so on), but we're interested only in the three mentioned. Were we to use atomic weight as the primary key (because atomic weight is one of the unique values associated with an element/isotope), a functional dependency would exist because both the element name and isotope can take on only one value for a given atomic weight. But in using an element name as the primary key (because no two element names would be identical), no functional dependency would exist between element name and isotope or atomic weight.

Bringing the latter case to 2NF would require that we make an additional relation using either atomic weight or isotope number as the primary key, with element name as the foreign key. In this relation, each unique record could have only one value for element name and, thus, would be in 2NF. It doesn't matter that two records could have the same value for element name because uniqueness is determined by isotope or atomic weight, not element name. In practice, though, the easier improvement is to pick a primary key that satisfies 2NF rather than build additional tables, as the former case suggests.

Third Normal Form (3NF)

The third normal form is achieved when a relation is in 2NF and there are no *transitive dependencies*. Transitive dependencies are present if one or more fields is functionally dependent upon another field that's not a primary key (or part of it) but is itself functionally dependent upon the primary key. Essentially, we're trying to eliminate dependencies of dependencies.

Using our periodic table example again, we could say that atomic weight is the primary key, the element name is functionally dependent upon atomic weight, and the location of the element within the periodic table is functionally dependent upon the element name. Because element name isn't a key for this relation, keeping all these fields in the same relation is poor design. A better design would create another relation keyed by Element Name, with Table Location as an attribute (along with any other properties that are specific to the element itself rather than the atomic weight or isotope).

Other Normal Forms

Database researchers have developed other normal forms (Boyce-Codd Normal Form, named in part for Edgar F. Codd, the person who first proposed the normalization process, and several higher-level normal forms). These forms can be applied to reveal violations of constraints that may produce problems when the database is finally in use, but these constraints are generally difficult to identify, so higher-level normal forms aren't ordinarily employed. Normalizing to 3NF is usually enough to begin the process of building the actual database.

Data Processing Considerations

When you've completed the database design process, you should have a set of diagrams that clearly illustrate all the entities and their relationships in your solution. Your next step as a designer is to ensure that users understand and agree upon the elements of the design. Once users have agreed that the schemas diagrammed capture the essence of the entities they wish to track, as well as information they'd like to generate from those entities, it's time to build the physical database, beginning with the system catalog.

The System Catalog

The *system catalog* is a relational database within the DBMS that's used to store information about the structure of any databases created within the DBMS. This data is called *metadata*, meaning it's information about information. Because the system catalog is a database itself, it can be accessed using the query, update, and maintenance methods available with the DBMS to those who have permission.

A system catalog holds all information about any database created within the DBMS, including schemas, data types, fields, tables, keys, and any other constructs within a given database or databases. User and group security information are also contained in the system catalog.

Some of the data in the system catalog is defined during the construction process; other data changes are defined as the database is used. If a change is made to the definition of a table (by adding a new field, for instance), that change is recorded in the system catalog. Should a user be added or deleted, that change is recorded in the system catalog. The current state of the system catalog can be displayed or printed by the database administrator (DBA) as needed to assist in the maintenance process, and the system catalog can also be used to assist in query optimization and other important data processing considerations.

Query Processing And Optimization

Queries are the primary means by which data in a database is manipulated. Queries can be performed infrequently or many times a second and can affect millions of records or just one. Queries can retrieve data from a single physical table or across multiple tables and queries. Because queries are such a fundamental part of the support a database provides to a process and because they can vary so widely in the amount of storage and processing resources they require, queries in a well-designed database are usually optimized. Before optimization, however, the query must be converted from its initial entry form to something the DBMS can handle. This is called query processing.

Query Processing

Before a query—whether expressed in a high-level query language, such as SQL, or taken from a GUI—can be executed, it must be processed. Processing involves scanning to identify the language components of the query, parsing to check the syntax, and validating to ensure that field and table names are valid. The next step is the creation of an internal representation of the query, called a *query tree* or *query graph*. Now the query is ready for execution, and optimization can take place.

Query Optimization

Because a typical query can be executed correctly in many ways, the DBMS has to formulate an *execution strategy*. This involves the generation of one or more workable strategies followed by evaluation against an internal set of rules to reveal the best strategy (although, in practice, it may not be the ultimate best but, rather, the best of those generated). This evaluation process is known as *query optimization*.

Optimization decisions are made by the built-in query optimizer module. They're based on algorithms that help order relational operations efficiently (heuristic rules) and that estimate the resources consumed with each strategy. It's important to note that a fundamental understanding of the ways data is stored and the ways relational operations are processed can guide the database designer toward higher-performance designs.

For example, consider a very simple query that selects every employee record in which the first name equals John. Even though First Name is not the primary key (Employee Number is the primary key) we can set an *index* on First Name to speed up queries such as this. The index should always retain pointers to first names in alphabetical order, even though many records are added with no apparent order in the First Name field. Therefore, when the query is performed, it'll reference the index rather than the records directly and will easily be able to find all the records in which first name equals John. Without the index, every record in the table would have to be searched (the *brute force* approach) taking a lot more resources (including time). And as we'll see in the next section, there are quite a few things (transactions) happening in a multiuser database, so we need to conserve power and storage space wherever possible.

Transaction Processing

Manipulating the data in a database frequently involves changing the data permanently. In this context, permanently means that the change is physically written wherever the data is stored (perhaps on a hard disk drive somewhere). Of course the data could be changed again a second later by the same user (or another user somewhere else), but this is different from retrieving data and making changes that are not *committed* to physical storage.

Changes of this type are called *transactions* that are composed of operations. A read operation in a transaction occurs when data is retrieved from a database and copied to a variable (perhaps it's displayed in an Access form you've designed). A write operation in a transaction occurs when data is copied from the variable back into the database. Because a transaction isn't complete until both operations are performed, you can see how errors could creep in if the transaction fails along the way.

Suppose your data entry clerk pulls up a customer record and enters a new order. Should power to the computer die between the time the record is retrieved and the record is later saved, the new order won't show up. Moreover, if the change to the orders table is completed and the change to the items ordered table isn't, the customer record may indicate an order without any items ordered. It's easy to see that transactions must be completely performed in the proper sequence, or problems will result.

Concurrency Control

These problems are compounded when multiple users are working with the same database at the same time. If a data entry clerk retrieves a record to edit it and someone else does the same record before the first updates are committed, the value of the first transaction may be lost.

Microsoft Access provides concurrency control in the form of locking mechanisms that prevent multiple users from using the same data at the same time. The price of accuracy is lower performance, depending upon the locking level chosen. Of course, if there's little chance that users will access the same data simultaneously, then the most optimistic locking (the least restrictive locking method) can be used, with better results. The possibility of many users trying to use the same fields, records, or tables dictates a highly restrictive locking method, with a commensurate fall-off in performance. Regardless of the form of concurrency control, a recovery method must be available in case of disaster.

4. Relational Databases

Recovery And The System Log

A variety of situations can cause transactions to fail during execution, such as system crashes, processing errors, hard disk failures, or even full-scale disasters such as floods. But by carefully preparing for the most common disasters, you'll have enough data to recover backed up on a tape or erasable CD-ROM somewhere. Recovery data is stored in the system log.

Transactions, by their nature, have a beginning, an ending, and an after ending, either an abort or commit. As the transaction proceeds, it becomes active, partially committed, either failed or fully committed, and terminated. These are defined as *transaction states*, and their progress is recorded in the system log while data is recorded in the database. If a disaster strikes, the initial state of the database can be recovered from the system log, and the database can be reconstructed up to the last committed transaction before the disaster. But not all disasters are hardware glitches; some are caused by poor security.

Security

You're probably aware that whenever you use a "club card" at the grocery store, your purchases are matched to the personal information you provided when you filled out the application. It's the price you pay for the discounts you receive. The store is, in effect, paying you to tell them what products and brands you use. But suppose the information were to fall into the wrong hands. It's possible that someone could generate a profile of the type of person you are (smoker, drinker, spendthrift, and so on) as well as composing a partial "audit trail" of your life (where you were at what time of day, did you have cash for the purchase, and so on).

Naturally, grocery stores want to preserve the perception that they'll be the only users of the data and that the data will only be used for legitimate purposes. (You did read the fine print in the terms of the agreement, didn't you?) So they have an interest in ensuring the security of the data. And they're not the only ones. These days, most everyone recognizes the need to keep data and databases safe and secure.

Like most decisions, determining how much security you need depends on the costs, benefits, and risks/threats involved. Evaluating the best approach means considering scenarios in which security could be breached and the consequences of that breach. It's not always strictly quantifiable, though. Quantifying the costs, benefits, and risks/threats is a great starting point, but in the end, the amount of security you establish depends on your comfort level (or your paranoia level, whichever is more meaningful to you).

Security is a double-edged sword. Too much can be unnecessarily expensive, reduce performance, and negatively impact the processes supported by the database. Too little can put you at risk on several fronts (not all of which are immediately obvious). The problem is that security issues cover a much broader spectrum than just keeping data away from the wrong people. Although we can't cover each topic in great detail, we can help designers, users, and managers understand the basics and how to arrive at the optimum security strategy for a given situation. Evaluating the items in the following listing is a good place to start:

- Physical security
- Communications security
- Structure and access security

Physical Security

Physical security means making sure only authorized people can actually get to the machines containing the data and making sure the data is safe in case disaster strikes. Just about any computer is going to be physically located in a lockable room, unless the machine is portable. The room could be made quite secure with special locks and monitoring equipment, as well as being hardened against disaster (underground, fireproof, and so on). Other enhancements, such as temperature and humidity control, power conditioning, alarm systems, and particulate removal systems, help to ensure reliable operation of critical hardware.

Communications Security

Physically securing the hardware and keeping it safe and running reliably is just the first step. Most database systems will be used in a networked environment or will run on computers connected to a network or the Internet. Deferring for a moment other security considerations, encryption may provide the level of communications security needed to give you peace of mind.

Structure And Access Security

If we assume that your computers are physically secure and that your communications are secure, your next step is to evaluate access to the database and the data within it. During the design process, relatively little security may be in place because the design is most likely a collaborative effort, with designers, users, and managers all contributing. Security increases (meaning access to the working model is restricted) as the design approaches the required functionality; more labor is invested in it, and it begins to take on the characteristics of the finished product.

Eventually, a production version is placed in service and security must be fully enforced so only the DBA can modify the objects in it. The structure can no longer be added to, deleted from, or changed by any member of the design team (unless they're working for the DBA), and the files may be converted to a distributable run-time version that can't be modified with the original design tools.

4. Relational Databases

In addition, the DBA may open user accounts, create groups, and set permissions on database objects for groups. The DBA, of course, has complete control over the database, but users may have access only to selected objects, then only at the level set for the group they participate in and only for the actions allowed by the applied permissions. Some security schemes implement multilevel security by associating classification levels with objects and users/groups. In any case, security considerations must be accounted for during the entire life cycle of the database and can affect the database design structure. To get a real feel for how to implement what we've discussed, let's put some of what we've learned into practice.

Immediate Solutions

In this section, we're going to illustrate the concepts developed in the "In Depth" section, so we'll use, as an example, the construction of an educational database containing the periodic table and data about its known constituents. We'll assume the groundwork has been laid and the ER model has already been constructed.

The entities, relationships, and attributes defined so far can be seen in Table 4.1.

Figure 4.1 shows the ER diagram of the entities, relationships, and attributes we've created based on what we know about elements (presumably we learned this from users during interviews).

As we discussed in Chapter 3, entities are depicted using rectangular boxes, relationships are shown in diamond shapes, and attributes are shown in ovals. The cardinality ratio is noted with the number 1 or the letter M near the relationship between entities, and single or double lines represent the level of participation by entities in a relationship. Notice the derived attribute (Number of Isotopes) attached to the Isotopes entity, the fact that Properties and Products are weak

Table 4.1   ER model components for the periodic table database.

Entities And Relationships	Attributes
Elements	Name, Symbol, Number, Atomic Weight, Stable, Year Isolated, Natural, Periodic Table Position
Isotopes	Atomic Mass, Number Of Isotopes
Products	Name
Locations	Country
Properties	Boiling Point, Melting Point, Density, State, Color
Family	Name, Family Type
Found In	Natural Substance
Used In	Quantity Per Use
Member Of	
Properties Of	
Isotope Of	

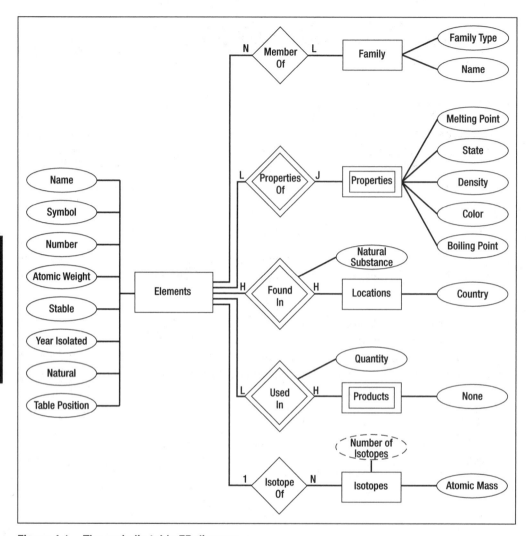

Figure 4.1   The periodic table ER diagram.

entities (depicted as boxes within a box), and the identifying relationships (de-picted as diamonds within diamonds).

The data type of each attribute and its valid domain is listed in Table 4.2. Some of the attribute names include the name of the entity they belong to for the sake of clarity. Notice the domains are essentially constraints on the values that can be assigned to the attributes they're associated with. Following ER to relational mapping, there'll be several additional attributes (foreign keys), but their data type and domain will be identical to the primary keys from which they're derived (although their names might be different, again, for clarity).

Table 4.2   Attribute data types and domains.

Attribute	Data Type	Domain
Element Name	Text	The names of the elements (or number if unnamed)
Symbol	Text	The symbols of the elements
Number	Text	The atomic numbers of the elements
Atomic Weight	Numeric	The range of numbers corresponding to atomic weights
Stable	Boolean	Yes/No
Year Isolated	Date	Four-character years
Natural	Boolean	Yes/No
Table Position	Text	Numbers < 1,000
Family Name	Text	Family names of elements
Family Type	Text	Description of family type
Boiling Point	Numeric	Temperature values < 1,000,000 K
Melting Point	Numeric	Temperature values <1,000,000 K
State	Text	Solid, liquid, or gas
Density	Numeric	Values <1,000 g/ml
Color	Text	Colors
Natural Substance	Text	Naturally occurring substances
Country	Text	Names of countries
Product Name	Text	Names of products
Quantity	Numeric	Values as a percent
Atomic Mass	Numeric	Values < 1,000
Number of Isotopes	Numeric	Derived as values < 1,000

From the information given, we can build a relational data model and go on to set up our database.

Extending The ER Model To The Relational Data Model

It's a short leap from the ER model to the relational model, primarily building relations (tables) from entities, creating new relations from relationships, and building the attributes that link them. When complete, a listing of relations and their attributes comes in handy, especially if you choose to construct your database purely with SQL.

Step 1—Creating Relations From Entities

Convert entities to relations. For instance, Elements, Family, Properties, Locations, Products, and Isotopes all become relations. Choose one key from among the candidate keys to be the primary key. Our choice for the primary key of the relation Elements will be Atomic Number. Primary keys for Family and Isotopes are Family Name and Atomic Mass. Properties and Products are weak entity types and have no primary keys. If the ER diagram includes composite attributes, include their components as simple attributes in the relation.

Step 2—Creating Foreign Keys (Referential Integrity Constraints)

Create foreign keys for Elements, Properties, Products, and Isotopes. The foreign keys will be attributes with the same domain as the primary keys of the entities to which they are related. For Elements, we include the primary key of Family (Family Name) as a foreign key. For Properties, Products, and Isotopes, we include the primary key of Elements (Atomic Number).

Include the attribute, Quantity, from the relationship, Used In, as an attribute of the new relation, Products, because Products is on the many side of the relationship with Elements. The relationships, Member Of, Properties Of, Used In, and Isotope Of, have cardinality ratios less than many-to-many and can be discarded because foreign keys represent them.

Step 3—Creating Relationship Relations

For relationships with a many-to-many cardinality ratio, create a relation that includes the primary key from both entities the relationship is related to. In our case, we make a relation called Found In that includes the primary keys of Elements and Locations (Atomic Number and Country). Natural Substance remains an attribute of Found In.

Step 4—Listing Relations And Attributes

At this point, it's useful to list the newly created relations and their attributes, as shown in Table 4.3. Note that the combination of Atomic Number and Country in Found In results in a composite primary key for this relation.

Table 4.3   List of periodic table relations and attributes.

Relations	Attributes
Elements	Name, Symbol, Number (Primary Key), Atomic Weight, Stable, Year Isolated, Natural, Table Position, Family Name (Foreign Key)
Family	Family Name (Primary Key), Family Type
Properties	Atomic Number (Foreign Key), Boiling Point, Melting Point, State, Density, Color

(continued)

Table 4.3   List of periodic table relations and attributes (continued).

Relations	Attributes
Found In	Atomic Number (Foreign Key), Country (Foreign Key), Natural Substance
Locations	Country (Primary Key)
Products	Name, Atomic Number (Foreign Key), Quantity
Isotopes	Atomic Mass (Primary Key), Atomic Number (Foreign Key)

Now that we have a clear idea what elements we're working with, we can begin to build queries to get useful data from the database.

Constructing Queries With Relational Operations

In this section, we give examples of each type of query and show step-by-step how to put it into terms that make sense using relational algebra or relational calculus. The queries will start with a question, Q, and conclude with the answer, A.

Select Query 1

Q: Retrieve the records of all elements that are unstable.

A: Perform the following steps:

• Select, where Stable = No, records from Elements.

• Name the new relation Unstable Elements.

The query above retrieves all records from the relation, Elements, where the value of Stable is No, then creates a new relation with these records called Unstable Elements.

Select Query 2

Q: Retrieve the records of all elements that are both unstable and natural.

A: Perform the following steps:

• Select, where Stable = No AND Natural = Yes, records from Elements.

• Name the new relation Natural Unstable Elements.

The query above retrieves all records from the relation, Elements, where the value of Stable is No and (using the Boolean operator AND) the value of Natural is Yes, then creates a new relation with these records called Natural Unstable Elements.

Project Query 1

Q: Retrieve the number, symbol, and name of all elements.

A: Perform the following steps:

- Project, from Elements, the attributes Number, Symbol, and Name.

- Name the new relation Element Specifics.

The query above retrieves all the records from the relation, Elements, but only the attributes Number, Symbol, and Name, then creates a new relation with these records called Element Specifics.

Select And Project Query 1

Q: Retrieve the number, symbol, and name of all unstable elements.

A: Perform the following steps:

- Select, where Stable = No, records from Elements.

- Name the new relation Unstable Elements.

- Project, from Unstable Elements, Number, Symbol, and Name.

- Name the new relation Unstable Element Specifics.

The query above retrieves all the records from the relation, Elements, in which the value of Stable is No. Next, it creates a new relation called Unstable Elements, retrieves all the records from Unstable Elements but only the attributes, Number, Symbol, and Name, then creates a new relation with these records called Unstable Element Specifics.

Union Query 1

Q: Produce a list containing all elements that are unstable, are used in medicines, or both.

A: Perform the following steps:

- Select, where Stable = No, records from Elements.

- Name the new relation Unstable Elements.

- Project, from Unstable Elements, the attribute, Atomic Number.

- Name the new relation Unstable Elements N.

- Select, where Product Name = Medicine, records from Products.

- Name the new relation Elements Used In Medicine.

- Project, from Elements Used In Medicine, the attribute, Atomic Number.

- Name the new relation Elements Used In Medicine N.

- Merge the single-attribute relations with the Union operation.

- Name the new relation Elements Unstable, Used In Medicine, Or Both.

The query above retrieves all the records from the relation, Elements, in which the value of Stable is No and creates a new relation called Unstable Elements. It then trims the attribute list to Atomic Number only and names the new relation Unstable Elements N. Next, it retrieves all the records from the relation, Products, in which the value of Product Name is Medicine and creates a new relation called Elements Used In Medicine. It then trims the attribute list to Atomic Number only and names the new relation Elements Used In Medicine N. Finally, to process the Union operation it adds the records in the first relation to the records in the second relation, eliminates duplicate records, and names the final relation Elements Unstable, Used In Medicine, Or Both.

Intersection Query 1

Q: Produce a list containing all elements that are unstable and are used in medicines.

A: Perform the following steps:

- Select, where Stable = No, records from Elements.

- Name the new relation Unstable Elements.

- Project, from Unstable Elements, the attribute, Atomic Number.

- Name the new relation Unstable Elements N.

- Select, where Product Name = Medicine, records from Products.

- Name the new relation Elements Used In Medicine.

- Project, from Elements Used In Medicine, the attribute, Atomic Number.

- Name the new relation Elements Used In Medicine N.

- Merge the single-attribute relations with the Intersection operation.

- Name the new relation Elements Unstable And Used In Medicine.

The query above retrieves all the records from the relation, Elements, in which the value of Stable is No and creates a new relation called Unstable Elements. It then trims the attribute list to Atomic Number only and names the new relation Unstable Elements N. Next, it retrieves all the records from the relation, Products, in which the value of Product Name is Medicine and creates a new relation called Elements Used In Medicine.

It then trims the attribute list to Atomic Number only and names the new relation Elements Used In Medicine N. To process the Intersection operation it compares the records in the first relation to the records in the second relation, keeps those that match, eliminates duplicate records, and names the final relation Elements Unstable And Used In Medicine.

Difference Query 1

Q: Produce a list containing all elements that are unstable and are not used in medicines.

A: Perform the following steps:

- Select, where Stable = No, records from Elements.
- Name the new relation Unstable Elements.
- Project, from Unstable Elements, the attribute, Atomic Number.
- Name the new relation Unstable Elements N.
- Select, where Product Name = Medicine, records from Products.
- Name the new relation Elements Used In Medicine.
- Project, from Elements Used In Medicine, the attribute, Atomic Number.
- Name the new relation Elements Used In Medicine N.
- Reduce the single-attribute relations with the Difference operation.
- Name the new relation Elements Unstable And Not Used In Medicine.

The query above retrieves all the records from the relation, Elements, in which the value of Stable is No and creates a new relation called Unstable Elements. It then trims the attribute list to Atomic Number only and names the new relation Unstable Elements N. Next, it retrieves all the records from the relation, Products, in which the value of Product Name is Medicine and creates a new relation called Elements Used In Medicine.

It then trims the attribute list to Atomic Number only and names the new relation Elements Used In Medicine N. To process the Difference operation, it discards any records in the first single-attribute relation that match those in the second relation (as well as those in the second relation after comparison) and names the final relation Elements Unstable And Not Used In Medicine.

Aggregate Function Query 1

Q: Produce a list, including Name, Number, Symbol, and Stable, showing the number of elements that are stable, the number of elements that are unstable, and the average atomic weight of each group.

A: Perform the following steps:

- Group, by the attribute, Stable, records from Elements.
- Count the records in each group.

- Assign that value to its group in a new attribute called Count Of.
- Average the Atomic Weight values for each group.
- Assign that value to its group in a new attribute called Avg. Weight.
- Project the attributes Stable, Count Of, and Avg. Weight.
- Name the new relation Count-Avg. Atomic Weight Stable-Unstable Elements.

The query above groups all the records in Elements by the attribute, Stable, then counts the number of records and puts that value in a new attribute called Count Of. It then averages all the values for Atomic Weight in each group and puts that value in a new attribute called Avg. Weight. Next, it projects the attributes, Stable, Count Of, and Avg. Weight, eliminates duplicates, and produces a new relation named Count-Avg. Atomic Weight Stable-Unstable Elements.

Query By Example 1

Q: Retrieve the name, symbol, atomic number, and atomic weight of all stable, natural elements isolated before 1900.

A: Use the following QBE selection grid:

Name	Symbol	Number	Atomic Weight	Stable	Year Isolated	Natural
P.	P.	P.	P.	Yes	<1900	Yes

The query above lists the values for name, symbol, atomic number, and atomic weight for each record in which the value of the attribute, Stable, is Yes, the value of the attribute, Year Isolated, is less than 1900, and the value of the attribute, Natural, is Yes.

Having shown how queries flow using relation operators, let's now move on to using SQL. You'll find SQL very similar to relation operators in flavor, and SQL is a boon to those who appreciate an English-like shorthand.

Using SQL

In this section, we'll use SQL to build our periodic table database. The steps taken mimic (in simplified form) similar measures you'd take to create a database using SQL in the real world.

Step 1—Creating The Database And Tables

Use the Create Schema and Create Table statements to create a schema and tables for the periodic table database.

```
CREATE SCHEMA PERIODIC TABLE
CREATE TABLE ELEMENTS
        ( NAME                  VARCHAR(30)         NOT NULL,
          SYMBOL                VARCHAR(3)          NOT NULL,
          NUMBER                VARCHAR(3)          NOT NULL,
          ATOMIC WEIGHT         DECIMAL(3,6)        NOT NULL,
          STABLE                BIT                 NOT NULL,
          YEAR ISOLATED         DATE,
          NATURAL               BIT,
          TABLE POSITION        VARCHAR(3)          NOT NULL,

        PRIMARY KEY (NUMBER),
        FOREIGN KEY (FAMILY NAME) REFERENCES FAMILY(NAME));

CREATE TABLE FAMILY
        ( NAME                  VARCHAR(30)         NOT NULL,
          TYPE                  VARCHAR(50),

        PRIMARY KEY (NAME));

CREATE TABLE PROPERTIES
        ( ATOMIC NUMBER         VARCHAR(3)          NOT NULL,
          BOILING POINT         DECIMAL(10,2),
          MELTING POINT         DECIMAL(10,2),
          DENSITY               DECIMAL(10,2),
          STATE                 VARCHAR(10),
          COLOR                 VARCHAR(20),

        FOREIGN KEY (ATOMIC NUMBER) REFERENCES ELEMENTS(NUMBER));

CREATE TABLE FOUND IN
        ( ATOMIC NUMBER         VARCHAR(3)          NOT NULL,
          COUNTRY               VARCHAR(40)         NOT NULL,
          NATURAL SUBSTANCE     VARCHAR(50),

        FOREIGN KEY (ATOMIC NUMBER) REFERENCES ELEMENTS(NUMBER),
        FOREIGN KEY (COUNTRY) REFERENCES ELEMENTS(NUMBER);

CREATE TABLE LOCATIONS
        ( COUNTRY               VARCHAR(40)         NOT NULL,

         PRIMARY KEY (COUNTRY));

CREATE TABLE PRODUCTS
        ( NAME                  VARCHAR(50)
```

```
        QUANTITY                DECIMAL(10,2)
        ATOMIC NUMBER           VARCHAR(3)              NOT NULL,

        FOREIGN KEY (ATOMIC NUMBER) REFERENCES ELEMENTS(NUMBER));

CREATE TABLE ISOTOPES
      ( ATOMIC MASS             DECIMAL(10,2)           NOT NULL,
        ATOMIC NUMBER           VARCHAR(3)              NOT NULL,

        PRIMARY KEY (ATOMIC MASS),
        FOREIGN KEY (ATOMIC NUMBER) REFERENCES ELEMENTS(NUMBER));
```

Step 2—Populating The Database

Use the Insert Into statement to add values to records/fields in the order in which the fields appear in each record.

```
INSERT INTO ELEMENTS
VALUES ( 'HYDROGEN','H','1','1.0079','Y','1776','1','1'),
       ( 'HELIUM','He','2','4.00260','Y','1895','1','2')
```

Values can be added to additional records/fields as long as each row is separated by a comma.

Step 3—Creating Queries

Now you're ready to create queries on your SQL database, like the following example that's similar to Select Query 2, retrieving the name, symbol, and number of all the stable, natural elements.

```
SELECT      NAME, SYMBOL, NUMBER
FROM        ELEMENTS
WHERE       STABLE=NO AND NATURAL=YES
ORDER BY    NUMBER
```

Although we've already constructed a simple database and queries with SQL, there are other steps that should be explicitly performed whenever a database is constructed. They're easy to overlook or minimize, so let's walk through them here.

Applying Parent-Child Relationships

When dealing with entities that appear to contain lots of one-to-many relationships, it is frequently appropriate to employ the PCR data model (while a discussion of the PCR data model is appropriate to enhance our understanding of data models in general, bear in mind that it is only a bridging concept to get us to the relational data model, used by most modern DBMS programs). Parent-child relationships can be applied in the following manner:

Step 1—Determining The Root Record Type

For our periodic table database, Family is the root record type because it does not participate as a child record in any PCR type.

Step 2—Determining The Parent Record Types

Family, Elements, and Locations are Parent record types. Elements is also a Child record type because it participates in the PCR type (Family, Elements). Locations is also a Child record type because it participates in the PCR type (Elements, Locations).

Step 3—Determining The Child Record Types

Properties, Products, and Isotopes are Child record types, and we can also apply the term *leaf* because they're not parent record types in any other PCR type.

Determining Functional Dependencies And Normalizing

Normalization is the process of simplifying, reducing excess data, reducing null values, and eliminating the occurrence of erroneous records in a database design. The following steps take you through the process for our periodic table database.

Step 1—Clarifying The Purpose Of The Database In Plain English

Write out a statement that explains the implied rules of the database using the simplest possible terms. For instance: "The purpose of this database is to store data regarding the known elements, such as name, symbol, atomic number, atomic weight, stability, year isolated, natural or man-made, and table position. Each record in the Elements table represents one element. It's related to its properties by the primary key of each element (its number), to its family (if any) by family name, to locations where it's found by the table Found In, to products it's used in and its isotopes by its number."

Step 2—Reducing Excess Data

If we started with a large, flat-file periodic table database, many records would contain duplicate values. For instance, suppose we included all the data for each element in every record for the Isotopes table. The result would be many duplicate values, plus the possibility of errors creeping into our data upon updates.

Therefore, your job, at this step, is to break your database into smaller tables that don't have the possibility of update anomalies or excess data. Do this by examining your data model diagram and separating the attributes into smaller tables until no anomalies exist.

Step 3—Reducing Null Values

Null values tend to occur wherever fields exist that frequently don't have a value. Perhaps the value is unknown, or perhaps it's simply not applicable in all (or most) cases. Whatever the reason, good designs will take these fields and make a separate table out of them that's linked to the primary table with a foreign key. Again, this can be done by analyzing the fields in use and separating potential null fields.

Notice that for the periodic table example, much of the separation of fields into smaller, logical tables has already occurred during the design process, as well as the establishment of primary and foreign keys.

Implementing Concurrency Control And Recovery

Maintaining concurrency means making sure all transactions processed against the database are performed sequentially, no matter how they're stored and processed (meaning even batch transactions get done one after the other in the correct order). Locking is the primary technique used to exercise control over concurrency. Timestamp ordering is another popular method.

It makes sense to assume that if one person is using a particular data item, record, or query, no one else should use that same chunk of information until the first user is done with it. However, this can lead to problems. Your solution depends upon the kind of usage you expect your database to get.

Step 1—Determining Usage Requirements

Should many users be likely to use the same records frequently, the probability of interference between their transactions increases. In cases such as this, tighter locking must occur. If the probability of conflicting transactions is small, looser locking is appropriate.

Step 2—Selecting A Locking Strategy

Locking strategies include the following categories:

- Binary locks
- Shared and exclusive locks
- Two-phase locking

4. Relational Databases

Binary Locks

Binary locks are either locked or unlocked. If locked, no other user can access that object until the lock is unlocked. If another operation depends upon that object, that operation must wait until the lock is released. Thus, multiple transactions depending upon that object must form a queue. This type of locking is very restrictive.

Shared And Exclusive Locks

Shared and exclusive locks (also called multiple-mode locks) can be share-locked, exclusive-locked, or unlocked. The advantage of this locking scheme is that many transactions can read share-locked items, while exclusive-locked items are restricted to a single transaction. This is less restrictive, but there's another piece to the puzzle.

Using our periodic table database as an example, a job well done will draw many users, but they'll all have read-only access, so a shared-locking protocol is appropriate.

Two-Phase Locking

A locking protocol, called two-phase locking, has been developed to guarantee that the transactions are performed in the correct order (serializability). Two-phase locking ensures that transactions take place in the proper order by forcing all locking operations to occur before any unlock operations within a given transaction.

Typically, conservative two-phase locking (locking all items before the transaction begins execution) and strict two-phase locking (preventing release of locks until commit or abort) are combined to ensure concurrency without creating deadlocks.

Step 3—Implementing Deadlock Prevention

Deadlocks occur when two transactions are each waiting for an object the other one has already locked. Using strict and conservative two-phase locking will solve the deadlock problem but can limit use of the system concurrently too much. Other schemes apply priority systems to transactions so older transactions can be processed first.

The resolution of your locking strategy should then be followed by the implementation of a security strategy. Generally speaking, the implementation of a security strategy follows a logical series of steps, as shown in our next section.

Implementing Security

Use the following checklist as you proceed through the design cycle to help you decide what security measures to use and how extensive they must be.

Step 1—Evaluating Security Requirements

Any process using information will accumulate data, process it into information, and most likely make it available again at some later point. At each stage, the costs of collecting and processing it, as well as its intrinsic value, grow. It's tempting to archive it all under lock and key, so to speak, but, in fact, two of the most important considerations are determining what information can be discarded safely and determining when it can be tossed.

Just as information must be made available during the process, security must be maintained. The level of security maintained must reflect the risks of loss, theft, tampering, and other damage, as well as statutory and customer service requirements. Essentially, if it cost you a bundle to gather and process the information or if you stand to lose a bundle if it's lost or stolen, better take appropriate security measures. And when you destroy the information, better make sure it's really gone.

Turning again to our periodic table database example, we want everyone in the world to have access because it's going to be an educational database. We want to maintain control of the design, but there's no risk involved with losing the data.

Step 2—Evaluating Security Alternatives

Even the most bulletproof computer room is still subject to unexpected events: power outages, human error, earthquakes, and so on. Although it's important to ensure the physical security of your systems, communications security and access security are just as important, if not more so. After all, stealing a car is easy if you happen to have the keys, right?

Weight your requirements more towards communications and access security, and be willing to spend more money there. A well-designed backup system will protect your data when the building burns down, but once it escapes into the hands of an unscrupulous character, you can't get it back.

Step 3—Selecting A System Security Strategy

Your system security strategy should encompass communications security, access security, and structural security. Consider the following for communications security:

• Will the database be on a network, available to multiple users?

- Will those users include external users?

- Will those users be using the Internet, dialing in via modem, or using some other telecommunications technology?

- Will they have the capability to conduct their business in a secure way, including the initial login?

Your network administrator should be handling most of these issues, but some considerations specific to databases must have answers. We'll cover the specifics as they relate to Access in later chapters, but be aware that a secure network does not necessarily mean a secure database.

Setting access security (*discretionary access control*) means your DBA builds user and group accounts to manage access. The DBA has complete access to all functionality (although specific areas may be deliberately shielded, the DBA can still compromise security in other ways). Assuming you've been prudent in your choice of DBA, this person shouldn't be a security risk. How the DBA manages access presents risks, though.

Typically, the DBA will create users and groups, grant groups privileges to tables, forms, queries, reports, and other objects in a particular database, then assign users to groups. The purpose of the groups is to allow the granting of privileges once, rather than setting and revoking multiple privileges over and over each time a person comes on board, gets a new job, or leaves the company. Common security holes occur when people having the wrong privileges are assigned to the wrong group or misuse their privileges. Two fundamental prerequisites for a secure system should be applied:

- Properly budgeting the time it takes to manage user and group accounts.

- Having a well-designed process in place so the right people are notified when people change jobs or responsibilities.

Structural security (*mandatory access control*) concerns building levels of security into your database at the object level. It's combined with access security to give an extra measure of protection for highly sensitive material. For instance, suppose documents exist within a group that only some of the users should have the ability to review. The capability to mark those documents as highly secure (top secret, secret, confidential, and so on) means that even if 20 users are assigned to a group, only those who possess the right security clearance can view the document. As you can imagine, this added level of security can be costly to implement and maintain, but its use has been justified in many organizations. It's like a group of specialists working on a top secret project. Just because they work in the same office and generally have privileges to the same information doesn't mean everyone should be allowed access to all the information stored there.

It may seem that the material we've just covered is somewhat dense and technical, but it's just an overview that lays the foundation for the exciting (but challenging) topics we discuss in Chapters 6 and 7, including decision logic and decision support systems, distributed databases and client-server architecture, deductive and active databases, and neural networks. But first, Chapter 5 reviews and relates Chapters 1 through 4 to Microsoft Access 2000.

Chapter 5

Database Structures

In Depth

This chapter reviews many of the concepts discussed in the first four chapters, with an eye toward integrating them with modern methods of database design. We now begin to focus on Microsoft Access specifically and pull together previous discussions as they relate directly to Access.

Data Management Concepts

A database management system, or DBMS, is considered a basic component of data processing and is a collection of programs that are constantly running processes. They're used to control the activities required to store, retrieve, and manage data in one or more databases. Most DBMSs available today, such as Microsoft Access, can manage not only multiple data columns, rows, and tables within a database but multiple databases as well.

The DBMS software product first came about in the early 1960s when software-developing scientists realized that every time they built an application they duplicated code to handle the data functions of store, retrieve, and maintain. Over time, the programs that perform these same functions became a separate, generic system. This new separate, generic data management system could be used for multiple applications. Moreover, these different applications needed only to contain calls to access the data management system to perform specific data operations.

This data management system evolved into the DBMSs of today. Besides reducing the need for duplicating code, DBMSs provide many other benefits, including:

- Scalability
- Better developer productivity
- Shared data
- Security
- Data integrity management, redundancy, and consistency
- Data independence

The first benefit of a DBMS, such as Microsoft Access, is that it is scalable. In other words, the DBMS is able to grow and expand so that it can run across many machines or stay on a single machine. A DBMS is a single software system that runs many individual processes, like an operating system. The DBMS can share a machine's resources, such as CPUs and disks, or it can use them all itself. Because the DBMS can run in many different configurations, it's considered scalable. Most DBMSs start on a single machine, sharing that machine's resources with other applications and processes. As the DBMS increases in the amount of data it stores and the number of applications it services, it needs more resources. The database administrator, or DBA, then starts to scale the DBMS to a different configuration that satisfies users' growing processing needs. In general, as you begin to scale your Access applications to larger user bases, you'll likely also consider moving up to an even more scalable database, such as Oracle or Microsoft's SQL Server. Using Access 2000, you can very easily build front ends for SQL Server that will build on your existing investment in Access.

Because the DBMS is a standalone software system that can grow to meet users' application and data storage needs, the developers building the applications can spend more time concentrating on their applications. Developing time and costs are lower because the DBMS already has the data processing functions built in. In addition, the developer doesn't have to rebuild these functions into the application software. Whenever developers need their application to interact with the database, a call to the DBMS is placed within the application code that tells that DBMS which data to find and what to do with it.

The DBMS also allows for data sharing because the DBMS is a single, scalable system that's easy to access by one application or multiple, different applications. Most modern-day DBMS systems (including Microsoft Access) allow many users, using either the same application or multiple applications, to access the data stored within a single database.

The next benefit of a DBMS is security because it can be programmed to allow or restrict any user's access to specific data columns, rows, tables, or databases. Within Access, you'll generally implement security with a series of passwords providing different levels of access to the database.

However, the DBMS is capable of enforcing rules beyond security issues. Data integrity, consistency, and redundancy rules can also be enforced. For example, a DBMS can be given the responsibility of ensuring that data types are correct, that multiple data items aren't stored, and that the data meets a specific criteria, such as true or false or a specific state such as Nevada, Arizona, or California.

The final benefit of a DBMS is that it maintains different views of the data and the databases it manages. These DBMS-provided views, usually referred to as *schemas*, are broken down into three different types: physical (or internal), conceptual, and user (or external). The physical schema is the actual layout of the data and databases in their physical locations on the disk or tape. The conceptual view is how the data and the databases look in column, row, and table layout. The user view is also in column, row, and table layout or in a user-readable form layout, but it's tailored to each user's security access levels. With these views, the DBMS provides *data independence*. Data independence means the applications and users are separate and have no impact on the representations of the actual data they use. For example, if a physical location is changed for an entire database within the DBMS, the conceptual and user views don't change, which means that you don't need to change or recompile the applications that use the data (providing the applications are capable of looking for the data). For example, if an application changes a field's name from *Soc_Sec_Number* to *SSN*, the conceptual and physical views don't have to change. Data independence saves a lot of time and effort for both the application developers and the DBAs charged with maintaining the database.

Although most DBMSs provide, to a lesser or greater extent, all of the benefits this section details, some will provide better or more complete implementations of the benefits. Most DBMS types also provide certain type-specific benefits that will often play a role in your decision of what database type to use.

Understanding The History Of Database Types

The first type of DBMS to receive standard use throughout the data processing community in the 1960s was file processing. The actual data was kept within *flat files*, which are simple text-based files. As these files became larger, the speed and efficiency of data access degraded. By the early 1970s, file processing was replaced by the hierarchy and network-style DBMSs. The *hierarchy DBMS* used structured trees to store data. On the other hand, the *network DBMS* used records to store each data entity. Both of these DBMSs allowed for larger, more robust databases with faster and more efficient access. However, because they didn't provide the best data independence, they were replaced by the current type of DBMS—relational.

TIP: *Although most databases that businesses use today and all databases that you design with Microsoft Access are relational, the hierarchical database is making something of a comeback in the database industry. The sheer volume of data that many companies maintain, combined with the fact that relational databases aren't always the best way to manage certain types and systems of data, has resulted in database developers and industry professionals creating a new type of hybrid database that combines elements of both relational databases and hierarchical databases.*

Relational databases are the result of Dr. E. F. Codd's frustrations with the standard database management systems available at the time. A researcher at IBM in 1969, Dr. Codd discovered that algebraic concepts can be applied to the database world in which data can be organized into tables containing columns and rows. Each column, row, and table must adhere to specific relationships.

Relational database management systems, or RDBMSs, gained popularity in the late 1970s and became the standard by the mid-1980s. While there are many reasons for the popularity of RDBMS systems, arguably the most important are their ease of design and administration when compared with hierarchical databases.

There are four major types of RDBMS product users. These users include the DBA, the system administrator or SA, the application developer, and the application user. The DBA is the person generally responsible for keeping the RDBMS running. The SA is responsible for the operating system and the machine on which the RDBMS is running. An application developer builds the applications that access the RDBMS. Finally, the application user is the person who runs the application to access the data in the RDBMS and performs specific tasks on that data.

All user applications that access the RDBMS are considered clients, and the actual RDBMS (that is, the data itself) is considered the server. The client-server process is natural in the RDBMS world because the RDBMS is its own software process, running throughout the day and waiting for tasks to perform. These tasks are specified by the accessing client applications, which run for the duration of the task. There are many types of clients. Some are provided by Microsoft or other third-party vendors to perform tasks such as database backups and system checks. Other clients are user-built applications that perform tasks such as collecting data to store or creating and printing reports on the information stored in the database.

TIP: *When you work with Access databases, whether the database and the application that accesses it are on the same machine or on different machines, the database (and the Microsoft Jet engine, which implements the RDBMS) is always the server, and the application (whether designed within the Access environment or in some other development tool, such as Microsoft Visual Basic) is always the client.*

A client can have the RDBMS server perform one of four basic tasks. These tasks are select, insert, update, or delete. A select task is also known as a *query* because it looks at a specific set of data and returns that data to the client. An insert task actually adds new information, usually an entire row, into the database. An update task changes existing data. A delete task actually removes an entire row of data from the database.

The two different types of clients that perform these tasks are batch and online. A batch client performs many tasks for a long period of time, usually without involving a user. For example, a batch process can read thousands of addresses from a file and store them or insert them into the database. Each set of tasks performed by the batch client is considered a transaction. A single transaction can contain many long tasks or a few short ones.

An online client is an example of a process that uses transactions containing a few short, quick, single-minded tasks. In contrast to a batch client, which runs a single transaction containing hundreds of tasks that might run for minutes or hours until completed, an online transaction contains a few tasks and should complete within seconds. Known as OLTP, or online transaction processing, this client is usually run by a user sitting at a keyboard performing his or her own tasks. When that user needs to retrieve or store data, the application makes a quick access to the DBMS.

The databases used by these clients are sometimes considered the most important part of day-to-day business. A database is usually set up to represent a specific view of a company's business world. For example, a company that sells auto parts could have three major areas of its business world represented in databases: parts inventory, customers, and orders. All a company needs to know about its day-to-day activities resides in the company's databases, and the applications it builds are the way to access that data.

Most databases are under a gigabyte in size, but some can grow to be quite large. They utilize the most popular application client—OLTP. Batch processing was very popular in the 1970s and 1980s, but with the decrease in desktop equipment prices, companies can afford to have more online users. Most of this book is dedicated to building these business-world databases in Microsoft Access, tuning these databases for efficient access, and building application clients to access these databases.

TIP: *Microsoft Access has an effective size limitation of 1 gigabyte. If you try to build Access databases larger than 1 gigabyte, the Jet engine's responses to actions against the database are unpredictable and may include loss of data, corruption of existing data, and faulty responses to queries. Generally, if your databases will be larger than several hundred thousand records, you should consider using another, more scalable development platform (such as Oracle or SQL Server) for your database implementation.*

Sometimes companies build extremely large databases called *data warehouses*. Although most databases contain a company's world of information, a data warehouse contains the universe of an entire corporation. Data warehouses aren't generally used to perform daily OLTP activities. A data warehouse is used to perform intense data analysis, called *data mining*. These databases can be expected to grow into a terabyte or larger in size. Note that data warehouses generally consist of multiple copies of other databases.

A database consists of one or more tables; if more than one table is included in a database, the entities described in the tables must be related by at least one attribute class (field) that's common to two of the tables. The formal statistical name for a database is *heterogeneous universe*—a recently coined alternative term is *universe of discourse*. This book adheres to the term *database*. Object-oriented databases (OODBs) don't conform strictly to the atomicity rules for attributes. Similarly, the OLE Object field data type of Jet databases isn't atomic because the data in the fields of the OLE Object field data type contains both the object's data (or only the presentation for a linked object) and a reference to the application that created the object. The object type of the content of Jet OLE Object fields may vary from record to record.

A *query* is a method by which you obtain access to a subset of records from one or more tables that have attribute values satisfying some criteria. There are a variety of ways to process queries against databases. You'll learn how to process queries against databases with the Jet database engine in later chapters. You also can use queries to modify the data in tables, known as cross-tab and action queries, which you'll also learn more about later in this book.

Understanding the benefits and limitations of RDBMS systems (and, for that matter, hierarchical database systems) is easier to do when you consider the different kinds of database systems that you may encounter. Whether it is an old Rolodex card system or a modern day client-server system distributed around the world, any system that maintains information in the manner described previously can be considered a database system.

Classifying Database Systems

The history of digital computers is inexorably tied to the concurrent development of database methodology. It's probably a safe estimate that at least 80 percent of worldwide computer resources and programming activities are devoted to database applications.

The first military and commercial applications for tabulating machines and digital computers were devoted to retrieving, calculating, and reporting on data stored in the form of punched cards. For example, a deck of cards containing the names and addresses of customers constituted a database table. Another deck of punched cards containing information on the invoices issued to customers for a given period represented another table. Using a collating device, you could shuffle the two decks so that a new deck was created wherein each customer card was followed by the cards detailing the orders for that customer. You could then use the cards to print a report in which the customer's card provided a report subheading and all of the orders for the customer were printed under the subheading. Cards from other decks could be collated into the two-level deck to create more detailed reports. Early tabulating machines included the capability to create customer subtotals and order grand totals. Figure 5.1 shows the effect of collating two decks of cards to print a report of invoices.

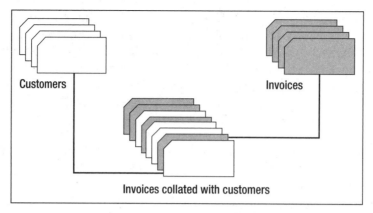

Figure 5.1   Collating two decks of punched cards to create a report of invoices.

The obvious problem with the punched-card collation technique was that every time you wanted a different report, you had to separate (decollate) the cards back into their original decks and then manually run a different set of collation processes. Replacing tabulating machines with computers equipped with nine-track magnetic tape drives solved many of the problems associated with moving decks of cards back and forth between collators. You transferred the data from a sorted deck of cards to a magnetic tape, then mounted the tapes you needed on tape drives and let the computer combine (merge) the data on the "table" tapes onto a new tape whose data was identical to that of a collated deck of punched cards. Then you could print a report from the data on the newly recorded tape.

Punched-card decks and magnetic tapes are sequential devices. Finding a particular record requires that you search from the first card of the deck or first record of a tape and read each card or record until you find a match (or determine that no matching record exists). When high-capacity, random access data storage devices (such as disk drives) became available, searching for a particular record became much faster, even if you had to read each record in the table. To speed the process, sorting and indexing methods were developed to minimize the number of records the computer had to read until matching data was found. Probably the most important work in this field was volume 3 of Stanford University professor Donald E. Knuth's *Art of Computer Programming* series, *Sorting and Searching*, published by Addison-Wesley in 1973, which remains in print today (ISBN 0-201-03803-X).

Advances in computer technology that directly followed the creation and widespread use of the random access disk drive have occurred primarily in the form of architectural, rather than conceptual, changes to both hardware and software. The pace of improvement in the operating speed and the rate of cost reduction of computer hardware has far outdistanced the rate of progress in software engineering, especially in database design and programming methodology. You can substantially improve the performance of an ill-conceived and poorly implemented database design simply by acquiring a faster computer. The price of a new computer is usually much less than the cost of reengineering an organization's legacy database structure. Ultimately, however, poor database designs and implementations result in a severe case of organizational inefficiency. One of the purposes of this chapter is to provide a sufficient background in database design to make sure that the database structures you create don't fall into this category. The simplest type of database is the flat-file database, which you will learn more about in the next section.

Flat-File Databases

The simplest database form consists of one table with records having enough columns to contain all of the data you need to describe the entity class. The term *flat-file* is derived from the fact that the database itself is two-dimensional—the number of table fields determine the database's width, and the quantity of table records specify its height. There are no related tables in the database, so the concept of data depth, the third dimension, doesn't apply. Any database that contains only one table is, by definition, a flat-file database if the database requires that the tables be flat. (Most true relational databases require flat tables; however, the power of relations is in the establishment of the connections between the tables.)

Flat-file databases are suitable for simple telephone and mailing lists. Ranges of cells, which are designated as "databases" by spreadsheet applications, also are flat-files. A mailing-list database, as an example, has designated fields for names, addresses, and telephone numbers. Data files used in Microsoft Word's print merge operations, for example, constitute flat-file databases.

You run into problems with flat-file databases when you attempt to expand the use of a mailing-list database to include sales contacts, for example. If you develop more than one sales contact at a firm, there are only two ways to add the data for the new contact if you're using a flat-file database:

- Add a new record with duplicate data in all fields except the Contact and, perhaps, the Telephone Number field.

- Add new fields so you can have more than one Contact Name and Telephone Number field per record. In this case, you must add enough Contact field pairs to accommodate the maximum number of contacts you expect to add for a single firm. The added fields are called *repeating groups*.

Neither of these choices is generally attractive because both choices are extremely inefficient—particularly when you're dealing with a database of contacts hundreds of contacts in size. Both methods can waste a considerable amount of disk space, depending on the database file structure you use. Adding extra records duplicates data, and adding new fields results in many records that have no values (nulls) for Multiple Contact and Telephone Number fields. Adding new fields causes trouble when you want to print reports. It's especially difficult to format printed reports that have repeating groups.

Regardless of the deficiencies of flat-file databases, many of the early mainframe computers only offered flat-file database structures. All spreadsheet applications offer "database" cell ranges that you can sort by a variety of methods. Although spreadsheet "databases" appear to be flat, this is seldom truly the case. Figure 5.2 may help you visualize the spreadsheet model.

One of the particular problems with spreadsheet databases is that the spreadsheet data model naturally leads to inconsistencies in attribute values and repeating groups. Time-series data contained in worksheets is a classic example of a repeating group. The section "Organizing Entity Classes" (which appears later in this chapter) shows you how to deal with inconsistent entity classes that occur in worksheet "databases," and the "Normalizing Table Data" section describes how to eliminate repeating groups.

Clearly, flat-file databases are not necessarily the most efficient means to deal with complex data structures. Because flat-file databases are so limited in scope and capability, database developers must take advantage of other database models to efficiently manage data. Two of those models are the network and hierarchical models, as the next section details.

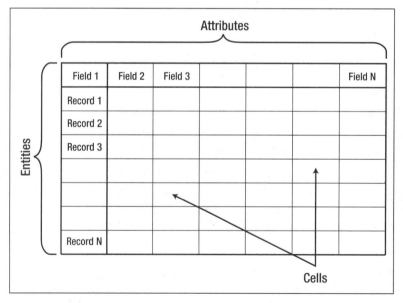

Figure 5.2   A simple database laid out in a spreadsheet format.

The Network And Hierarchical Database Models

The inability of flat-file databases to efficiently deal with data that involved repeating groups of data led to the development of a variety of different database structures (called *models*) for mainframe computers. The first standardized and widely accepted model for mainframe databases was the *network model* developed by the Conference on Data System Languages (CODASYL), which also developed Common Business-Oriented Language (COBOL) to write applications that manipulate the data in CODASYL network databases. Although the CODASYL database model has its drawbacks, an extraordinary number of mainframe CODASYL databases remain in use today. Billions of lines of COBOL code are in use every day in North America to manage these databases.

CODASYL databases substitute the term *record type* for table, but the characteristics of a CODASYL record type are fundamentally no different from the properties of a table. CODASYL record types contain *pointers* to records of other record types. A pointer is a value that specifies the location of a record in a file or in memory. For example, a customer record contains a pointer to an invoice for the customer, which, in turn, contains a pointer to another invoice record for the customer, and so on. The general term used to describe pointer-based record types is *linked list*; the pointers link the records into an organized structure called a *network*. Network databases offer excellent performance when you're seeking a set of records that pertain to a specific object because the relations between records (pointers) are a permanent part of the database. However, the speed of network databases degrades when you want to browse the database for records that match specific criteria, such as all customers in California who purchased more than $5,000 worth of product A in August 1998.

TIP: *The problem with CODASYL databases is that database applications (primarily COBOL programs) need to update the data values and the pointers of records that have been added, deleted, or edited. The need to sequentially update both data and pointers adds a great deal of complexity to transaction-processing applications for CODASYL databases.*

IBM developed the *hierarchical model* for its IMS mainframe database product line, which uses the DL/1 language. The hierarchical model deals with repeating groups by using a data structure that resembles an upside-down tree: Data in primary records constitutes the branches and data in repeating groups are the leaves. The advantage of the hierarchical model is that the methods required to find related records are simpler than the techniques needed by the network model. As with the CODASYL model, a large number of hierarchical databases are running on mainframe computers today.

Despite their common existence in the mainframe world, hierarchical databases did not translate well to the PC-based client-server model. Instead, relational databases are the most common database structure in the PC-based client-server model.

The Relational Database Model

As you've learned, the *relational database model* revolutionized the database world and enabled PCs to replace expensive minicomputers and mainframes for many database applications. The relational database model was developed in 1970 by Dr. E. F. Codd of IBM's San Jose Research Laboratories. The primary advantage of the relational model is that there's no need to mix pointers and data in tables. Instead, records are linked by *relations* between attribute values. A *relation* consists of a linkage between records in two tables that have identical attribute values. Figure 5.3 illustrates relations between attribute values of relational tables that constitute part of a sales database.

Because relational tables don't contain pointers, the data in relational tables is independent of the methods used by the database management system to manipulate the records. A relational database management system is an executable application that can store data in and retrieve data from sets of related tables in a database. The RDBMS creates transitory *virtual pointers* to records of relational tables in memory. Virtual pointers appear as they're needed to relate (*join*) tables and are disposed of when the relation is no longer required by a database application. The "joins" between tables are shown as lines in Figure 5.3. Joins are created between primary key fields and foreign key fields of relational tables. The primary and foreign key fields of the tables of Figure 5.3 are listed in Table 5.1.

Table 5.1   The primary and foreign keys of the tables depicted in Figure 5.3.

Table	Primary Key	Foreign Key
Customers	Customer Num	None
Invoices	Invoice	Customer Num
Invoice Items	Invoice and Product	Invoice

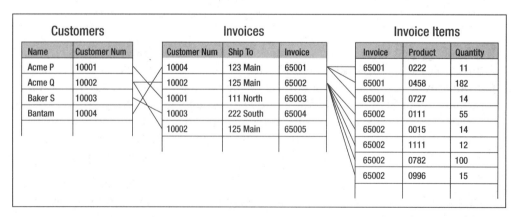

Figure 5.3   Each table within the database has relationships with other tables in the database.

Relational databases require duplicate data among tables but don't permit duplication of data within tables. You must duplicate the values of the primary key of one table as the foreign key of dependent tables. A *dependent table* is a table that requires a relationship with another table to identify its entities fully. Dependent tables often are called *secondary* or *related tables*. Thus, the Invoices table is dependent on the Customers table to supply the real-world name and address of the customer represented by values in the Customer Num field. Similarly, the Invoice Items table is dependent on the Invoices table to identify the real-world object (in this case an invoice) to which records are related.

Three types of relations are defined by the relational database models, each of which is described in the following list:

- *One-to-one* relations require that one and only one record in a dependent table can relate to a record in a primary table. One-to-one relations are relatively uncommon in relational databases.

- *One-to-many* relations enable more than one dependent table to relate to a record in a primary table. The term *many-to-one* is also used to describe one-to-many relations. One-to-many relations constitute the relational database model's answer to the repeating-groups' problem. Repeating groups are converted to individual records in the table on the "many" side of the relation. One-to-many relations are the most commonly found relations.

- *Many-to-many* relations aren't true relations because many-to-many relations between two tables require an intervening table, called a *relation* table, to hold the values of the foreign keys. (Relational-database theory only defines relations between two tables.) If Figure 5.3 had included a Products table to describe the products represented by the Product field of the Invoice Items table, then the Invoice Items table would serve as a relation table between the Invoices and Products tables. Some relation tables only include foreign key fields.

TIP: *One situation for which a one-to-one relationship is useful is in an employees table in which the employees' names, addresses, and telephone numbers need to be available to many database users; however, information about salaries, benefits, and other personal information should be restricted to a need-to-know basis. Databases, such as Jet, don't provide column-level permissions, so you create a one-to-one relationship between the table that contains the nonconfidential data and the one that contains confidential information. Then you grant read-only permission to everyone (the Users group) for the nonconfidential table and grant permission only to a limited number of users for the confidential table.*

The proper definition of the relations between entity classes and the correct designation of primary and foreign keys constitute the foundation of effective relational database design methods. The relational database model is built on formal mathematical concepts embedded in relational algebra. Fortunately, you don't need to be a mathematician to design a relational database structure. A set of five rules, discussed in a forthcoming section of this chapter, define the process of creating tables that conform to the relational model.

Designing a relational database structure, however, does require a database management tool. Most relational databases use a tool called a *manager*, which the next section explains in detail.

Types Of Relational Database Managers

The preceding description of the relational database model made the important point that the properties of a relational table object (such as the data in the object) are independent of the methods used to manipulate the data. This means you can use any relational database management application to process the data contained in a set of relational tables. For example, you can export the data in the tables of an IBM DB2 mainframe database as a set of text files that preserve the tables' structure. You can then import the text files into tables created by another database management system. Alternatively, you can use Jet, an ODBC driver for DB2, and a network gateway to the DB2 database to access the data directly. The independence of data and implementation in relational databases also enables you to attach tables from one database type to another. You can join the attached tables to the native tables in your Jet database without going through the export-import exercise. Thus, you can design a relational database that can be implemented with any relational database manager.

TIP: *Relational database managers differ in the types of data you can store in tables and in how you name the fields of tables. Many RDBMSs, such as SQL Server, include the **long varbinary** field data type, which you can use to store image data in tables. However, other RDBMS products, including the most commonly used versions of IBM's DB2, don't support **long varbinary** fields or their equivalent. Similarly, you can embed spaces and other punctuation symbols in Jet tables and field names, but you can't in most other RDBMS tables. If you're designing a database that the user may eventually port from the original RDMBS to another relational database implementation, make sure you use only the fundamental field data types and conform to the table- and field-naming conventions of the least versatile of the RDBMS products.*

There are, to be sure, substantial differences in how relational database systems are implemented. These differences are often overlooked by persons new to database management or persons converting from a mainframe database system to a desktop database manager. The following sections discuss how mainframe, minicomputer, and client-server databases differ from traditional desktop database managers.

Relational SQL Database Management Systems

Full-featured client-server relational database management systems separate the database management application (server or *back end*) from the individual (client) applications that display, print, and update the information in the database.

Client-server RDBMSs, such as Microsoft SQL Server, run as a process on the server computer. Most client-server systems in use today run under either the Unix operating system or the Windows NT operating system. The client-server RDBMS is responsible for the following activities:

- Creating new databases and one or more files to contain the databases. (Several databases may reside in a single fixed disk file.)

- Implementing database security to prevent unauthorized persons from gaining access to the database and the information it contains.

- Maintaining a catalog of the objects in the database, including information on the owner (creator) of the database and the tables it contains.

- Generating a log of all modifications made to the database so the database can be reconstructed from a prior backup copy combined with the information contained in the log (in the event of a hardware failure).

- Preserving referential integrity, maintaining consistency, and enforcing domain integrity rules to prevent corruption of the data contained in the tables. Most client-server RDBMSs use preprogrammed triggers that create an error when an application attempts to execute a query (whether a selection query or an action query) that violates the rules.

- Managing concurrency issues so multiple users can access the data without encountering significant delays in displaying or updating data.

- Interpreting queries transmitted to the database by user applications and returning or updating records that correspond to the criteria embedded in the query statement. Virtually all client-server RDBMSs use statements written in structured query language (SQL) to process queries—thus the generic name, SQL RDBMS.

- Executing *stored procedures*, which are precompiled queries you execute by name in an SQL statement. Stored procedures speed the execution of commonly used queries by eliminating the necessity for the server to optimize and compile the query. The ActiveX Data Objects (ADO) included with Visual Basic 6.0 and Access 2000 are designed expressly for executing server-stored procedures.

Separate database applications (front ends) are responsible for creating the query statements sent to the database management system and for processing the rows of data returned by the query. Front ends handle all of the data formatting, display, and report-printing chores. One of the primary advantages of using a SQL RDBMS is that the features in the preceding list, such as security and integrity, are implemented by the RDBMS itself. Therefore, the code to implement these features doesn't need be added to each different front end application. In general, the front-end and back-end (two-tier database model) have been further clarified

5. Database Structures

and better implemented in the three-tier client-server architecture. The next section details the three-tier client-server architecture.

Three-Tier Client-Server Architecture And LOBjects

The stored procedures of client-server databases used to execute predefined queries and maintain database integrity use SQL plus proprietary SQL language extensions such as Transact-SQL, used by Microsoft and Sybase SQL Server products, and Sybase SQL Anywhere, used only by Sybase SQL Server. SQL is a set-oriented, not a procedural, programming language. Therefore, dialects of SQL aren't well suited to writing programs for validating data in accordance with complex business rules. What follows is an example of a complex business rule:

> The current credit limit of a customer is equal to the customer's maximum credit limit, less uncontested open invoices and orders in process, unless the customer has outstanding, uncontested invoices beyond terms plus 10 days, or if the total amount of contested invoices exceeds 50 percent of the total amount of open invoices. Should a pending order exceed the customer's calculated credit limit, or any customer payment is behind terms plus 10 days, approval must be obtained from the credit manager prior to accepting the order.

Such a business rule is impossible to program as a conventional, linear SQL stored procedure because the last condition requires the credit manager to intervene in the process.

Three-tier client-server architecture adds a processing layer between the front-end client and the back-end server. The processing layer, often called a *Line-Of-Business object* (LOBject), processes requests from client applications, tests the requests for conformance with programmed business rules, and sends conforming requests to the back-end RDBMS, which updates the affected tables. Visual Basic (and other Windows-based program languages, including Visual Basic for Applications, which Access 2000 includes) lets you create OLE *Remote Automation Objects* (RAOs) that reside on an application server, which need not be the server that runs the RDBMS. Each client application using the LOBject creates its own instance of the RAO. Figure 5.4 illustrates the architecture of a three-tier client-server application that uses Microsoft Mail or Microsoft Exchange to process credit approvals (or rejections) for the scenario described in the preceding paragraph.

Just as there are different types of relational databases, so too are there different types of relational database managers. Most managers fall into the traditional style, which the next section details.

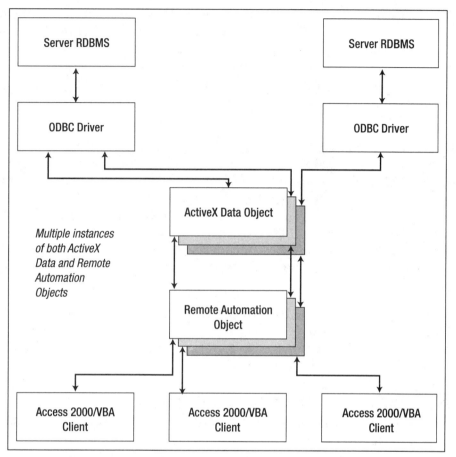

Figure 5.4   Using a three-tier client-server application to process complex business rules.

Traditional Desktop Relational Database Managers

Traditional desktop database managers, such as dBASE and Paradox, combine their database management features with the interpreter or compiler that executes the application's source code. The early versions of these products enabled you to create quite sophisticated database applications that would run on PCs with only 256K of RAM. The constraints of available RAM in the early days of the PC required that the database management portion of the desktop DBM's code include only those features that were absolutely necessary to make the product operable. Therefore, products of this type, which also include early versions of FoxPro and Clipper for DOS, don't truly qualify as full-fledged relational database management systems and are more properly termed *database file managers*. You implement the "relational" and the "management" features through the application source code you write.

The components of the dBASE and Paradox DBMs that manipulate the data contained in individual tables don't provide all of the built-in features of true relational database management systems listed in the preceding section. (The exception is the desktop products' capability to create a file that contains one table.) You need to write application code to enforce referential and domain integrity, and a one-DOS-file-per-table system doesn't lend itself to the easy establishment of secure databases.

The commercial success of dBASE (especially dBASE III and IV) and Paradox for DOS created a user base of perhaps six million. (Borland claims there are four million dBASE users worldwide. By comparison, Microsoft claims that there are over twenty million Access and Jet engine users worldwide.) Therefore, dBASE and Paradox product upgrades need to be backward compatible with tens of millions of dBASE (.DBF and .DB) files and billions of lines of dBASE and PAL code. New features, such as file and record locking for multiuser applications and the capability to use SQL to create queries, are add-ins (or tack-ons) to the original DBMS.

Microsoft Access goes one step further than the traditional manager. Access, both the manager and the RDBMS itself, are hybrid versions, providing the user with powerful ways to make the RDBMS perform at advanced levels, without requiring additional add-ins or "helper" products.

Microsoft Access: A Hybrid RDBMS

Microsoft Access is a cross between a conventional desktop DBMS and a complete, full-featured RDBMS. Access uses a single database file that includes all of the tables native to the database. Access's Jet database engine enforces referential integrity for native tables at the database level, so you don't need to write Visual Basic for Applications (VBA) program code to enforce the integrity of your data. Jet enforces domain integrity at the field and table levels when you alter the value of a constrained field. Jet databases include system tables that catalog the objects in the database, and concurrency issues are handled by the database drivers.

Access lets you break the back-end/front-end barrier that separates RDBMSs from desktop DBMSs. Application code and objects, such as forms and reports, can be included in the same database file as the tables. Microsoft used Access's capability to include both front-end and back-end components in a single .MDB file as a strong selling point. It soon became apparent to Access developers that separating application and database objects into individual .MDB files was a better design. You create a Jet database that contains only tables and attach these tables to an Access .MDB file that provides the front-end functionality. User names and passwords are stored in a separate .MDW workgroup (formerly .MDA) library file; this is necessary because a Jet .MDB file contains only one database. Here again, you can put sets of unrelated tables in a single .MDB file. Jet's proprietary flavor of SQL is the native method of manipulating data in tables; it's not an afterthought. The Jet DLLs that implement the database functionality are independent from the msaccess.exe file that includes the code you use to create forms and reports. Jet databases are about as close as you're likely to get to a RDBMS in a low-cost, mass-distributed software product.

Using Jet .MDB database files with Visual Basic (and VBA) front ends approximates the capabilities and performance of client-server RDBMSs at a substantially lower cost for both hardware and software. If you're currently using one-file-per-table legacy DBMSs, consider attaching the tables to a Jet database during the transition stage while your new 32-bit Windows front ends and your existing applications need to simultaneously access the tables. Once the transition to Visual Basic front ends is completed, you can import the data to a Jet database and take full advantage of the additional features .MDB files offer. If you outgrow the Jet database structure, it's a quick and easy port to SQL Server 6.5 (and an even easier port to 7) and the Microsoft SQL Server ODBC or OLE DB driver.

TIP: *You no longer need a copy of Microsoft Access to take advantage of Access's built-in enforcement of referential integrity and the security features of Jet databases. Visual Basic 5 and 6 and the Jet 3.5, 3.51, and 4.01 Data Access Objects provide programmatic implementation of referential integrity and security. The Jet database engine and the 32-bit Jet ODBC driver also support the SQL **FOREIGN KEY** and **REFERENCES** reserved words to define relationships during table creation. However, don't implement the SQL-92 **CHECK** reserved word, which enables you to enforce domain integrity with ranges or lists of values that constrain attribute values. Microsoft Access 2000 will help you to quickly recoup your investment in database design because Access lets you establish relationships in a graphic Relationships window, supplies a simple method for adding field-level and table-level constraints, provides a graphic Query-by-Design window, and generates Jet SQL statements for you, among other powerful design features.*

Designing a database in Microsoft Access is simple—you can use the tools that the IDE provides you to quickly implement almost any relational database structure. However, it is important to determine what the database's structure will be before you even start to create the actual database implementation. In general, you will use a technique known as data modeling to help you determine what the database structure should be.

Modeling Data

The first step in designing a relational (or any other) database is to determine what objects need to be represented by database entities and what properties of each of these objects require inclusion as attribute classes. The process of identifying the tables required in the database and the fields that each table needs is called *data modeling*. You can take two approaches during the process of data modeling:

- *Application-oriented* design techniques start with a description of the type of application(s) required by the potential users of the database. From the description of the application, you design a database that provides the necessary data. This is called the *bottom-up* approach, because applications are ordinarily at the bottom of the database hierarchy.

- *Subject-oriented* design methodology begins by defining the objects that relate to the subject matter of the database as a whole. This approach is called *top-down* database design. The content of the database determines what information front-end applications can present to the user.

Although application-oriented design can enable you to quickly create an *ad hoc* database structure and the applications to accomplish a specific goal, bottom-up design is seldom a satisfactory long-term solution to an organization's information needs. It's common to find several application-oriented databases within an organization that have duplicate data, such as independent customer lists. When the firm acquires a new customer, each of the customer tables needs to be updated. This is an inefficient and error-prone process.

Subject-oriented database design is a far more satisfactory method. You might want to divide the design process into department-level or workgroup-related databases, such as those in the following list:

- A *sales* database that has tables based on customer, order and line item, invoice and line item, and product entity classes.

- A *production* database with tables for parts, suppliers, bills of material, and cost accounting information. The product and invoice tables of the sales department's database would be attached to the production database.

- A *personnel* database with tables for employees, payroll data, benefits, training, and other subjects relating to human resources management. The production and sales databases would attach to the employees table—production for the purposes of cost accounting purposes and sales for commissions.

- An *accounting* database, with tables comprising the general ledger and subsidiary ledgers, would attach to the majority of the tables in the other databases to obtain access to current finance-related information. Accounting databases often are broken down into individual orders, accounts receivable, accounts payable, and general ledger databases.

No fixed set of rules determines which shared tables should be located in what database. These decisions are often arbitrary or are based on political, rather than logical, reasoning. Department-level databases are especially suited for multiuser Jet databases running on peer-to-peer networks with 30 or fewer users.

Each department can have its own part-time database administrator who handles backing up the database, granting and revoking the rights of users to share individual tables in the database, and periodically compacting the database to regain the space occupied by deleted records.

The first step in the actual modeling of data (after you determine which type of design you intend to use) is to diagram the databases that you will use to store the data. The next section explains database diagramming in detail.

Database Diagrams

Diagramming relations between tables can aid in visualizing database design. *Entity-relationship* (ER) diagrams, also called *entity-attribute-relation* (EAR) diagrams, are one of the most widely used methods of depicting the relations between database tables. Peter Chen first introduced the ER diagramming method in 1976. An ER diagram consists of rectangles that represent the entity classes (tables). Ellipses above the table rectangles show the attribute class (field) involved in the relation. Pairs of table rectangles and field ellipses are connected by parallelograms to represent the relation between the fields. Figure 5.5 illustrates an ER diagram for the Customers and Invoices tables of the database described in Figure 5.3 and Table 5.1.

The *1* and ∞ adjacent to the table rectangles indicate a one-to-many relationship between the two tables. In the original ER diagram type, Chen uses m to represent many. However, because the Access 2000 relationships dialog box uses the infinity symbol to represent the *many* side of a one-to-many relationship, it's consistent to do so here.

ER diagrams describe relations by predicates. One of the definitions of *predicate* is "a term designating a property or relation." If you remember diagramming sentences in grammar school English classes and relate that knowledge to the diagram in Figure 5.5, you'll observe that "Customers" is the subject, "are sent" is the

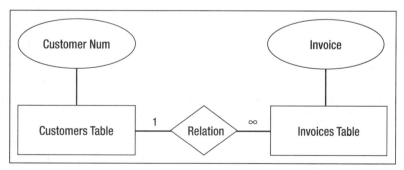

Figure 5.5   A simple ER diagram that shows the relationship of the Customers and Invoices tables.

predicate, and "invoices" is the predicate object of a complete sentence. ER diagrams are capable of describing virtually any type of allowable relation between two tables by adding additional symbols to the basic diagram shown in Figure 5.5. A very large number of ER diagrams are required to define relationships between the numerous entities in enterprise-wide databases. Because of the complexity of such ER diagrams, you will generally use a modeling tool to assist you in database design.

Using Modeling Tools For Database Design

Designing databases to accommodate the information requirements of an entire firm is a major undertaking. Therefore, computer-aided software engineering (CASE) tools often are used for the design of complex database systems. CASE tools for database design usually include the following capabilities:

- *Business model generation*—The first step in the use of a high-end CASE tool is to create an operational model of an enterprise, which consists of defining virtually every activity involved in operating the organization. Accurately modeling the operations of a large firm as it relates to information requirements is an extraordinarily difficult and time-consuming process.

- *Schema development*—A database *schema* is a diagram that describes the entire information system pictorially, usually with less detail than that offered by ER diagrams. The schema for a large information system with a multiplicity of databases can cover an entire wall of a large office or conference room.

- *Relation diagramming*—Some CASE tools support several methods of diagramming relations between tables. Most, but not all, CASE tools support ER diagrams, as well as other pictorial methods, such as Bachman diagrams.

- *Data dictionary development*—A *data dictionary* is a full description of each table in the database and each field of every table. Other properties of tables and fields, such as primary keys, foreign keys, indexes, field data types, and constraints on field values, are included.

- *Repository creation*—A *repository* is a database that's part of the CASE tool. The repository contains all the details of the structure and composition of the database. Data in the repository is used to create schema, relation diagrams, and data dictionaries. The repository is also responsible for maintaining version control when you change the database's design. Microsoft and Texas Instruments have joined forces to develop an object-oriented repository for 32-bit Windows database development (the Microsoft Repository, which you'll learn more about later in this book).

- *Database generation*—After you've designed the database, the CASE tool creates the SQL Data Definition Language (DDL) statements necessary to create the database and its tables. You then send the statements to the RDBMS, which builds the database for you.

- *Data flow diagramming*—Some database CASE tools include the capability to create data flow diagrams that describe how data is added to tables and how tables are updated. Data flow diagrams, however, are application related, not database-design related. Therefore, data flow diagramming capability is not a prerequisite for qualification as a CASE database tool.

Mainframe database developers have a variety of CASE tools from which to choose, and there are several CASE tools that serve the client-server market, such as Popkin Software's Data Architect. Developers using desktop DBMSs haven't been so fortunate. No commercial CASE tools with the basic features in the preceding list are currently available for Xbase and Paradox developers.

Database modeling tools are a simplified version of CASE tools for information system development. Modeling tools omit the business modeling aspects of CASE tools but implement at least the majority of the features described in the preceding list. An example of a database modeling tool designed specifically for Jet databases is Visio Corporation's Visio Professional. Visio Professional is a full-fledged database design system that you can use to create Jet databases from structured English statements that define entity and attribute classes. Visio Professional employs a unique database-diagramming method, called Object-Role Modeling (ORM), derived from the Natural Language Information Analysis Method (NIAM) and Binary Relationship Modeling (BRM) database design methodologies. A Formal ORM (FORM) diagram for the classic instructor-course-room database model, included as a tutorial example with Visio Professional, appears in Figure 5.6. Terry Halpin of the University of Queensland, who devised ORM, has written a 500-page, college-level textbook, *Conceptual Schema & Relational Database Design*, 2d ed (Prentice Hall Australia, 1995, ISBN 0-13-355702-2) that explains ORM in detail.

Visio Professional uses a language called Formal Object Role Modeling Language (FORML) to describe entity classes, attribute classes, and relations between entities. The semantics of FORML are similar to the subject/predicate statements of ER diagrams. In ER diagramming, you draw the pictorial elements then add the callouts that describe the elements. Using FORML, you start with a structured English sentence that states a fact about an object.

After you've entered as many facts as you can collect about each object that's to be represented in your database, you run Visio Professional's fact compiler to create the database design. The fact compiler adds table and field definitions to the repository database then builds the FORM diagram. FORM diagrams are more compact than ER diagrams, so it's practical to fully depict all fields of tables and relations between tables in the database schema. An even more compact schema is provided by Visio Professional's Table Browser window as shown in Figure 5.7.

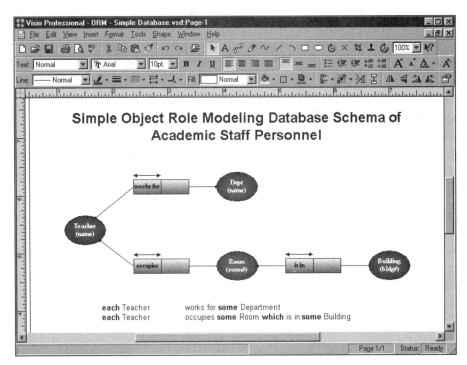

Figure 5.6   A simple FORM model for the relationship between teachers, departments, and classrooms and buildings.

The Table Browser window shown in Figure 5.7 displays eight of the 12 tables that constitute Visio Professional's tutorial database. You can hide or minimize the individual windows that display the details of a table to reduce display clutter. Relations between table fields are depicted by lines that terminate in "+" symbols, which represent the "one" side, and " >" symbols, which represent the "many" side of a one-to-many relation.

Experienced database designers might conclude that a database modeling tool such as Visio Professional is "overkill" for relatively simple database design projects. If you've designed a number of complex databases, you can probably create a relational table structure by rote. Although entering FORML sentences to describe entity and attribute classes might seem tedious, the benefits of FORM far outweigh the cost of the time needed to write object descriptions. You get an object repository, schema, table diagram, FORM diagram, and data dictionary, plus Visio Professional creates the Jet database tables for you. An additional benefit is that FORM diagrams are comprehensible to clients who aren't database experts. Therefore, your client can validate a database design before you commit to creating your database applications. This avoids the sinking feeling that pervades database developers when they hear their clients utter those dreaded words,

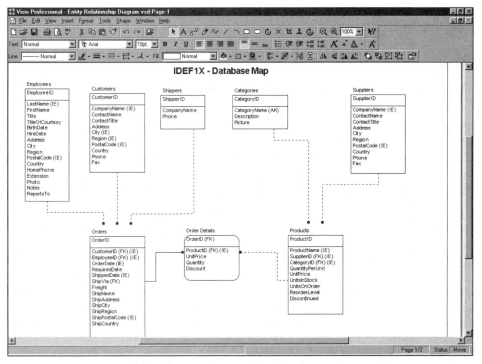

Figure 5.7 The Table Browser window within Visio Professional displays table information and relationships.

"Uh, we forgot to tell you about. . ." Visio Professional also includes a reverse-engineering feature that lets you "reverse engineer" your Jet databases to create a FORM diagram stored in Visio Professional's repository. One of the major benefits of using Visio Professional is your ability to track changes to database schema in a manner similar to that of Microsoft Visual SourceSafe.

Rules For Relational Database Design

If you use a modeling tool to create your database structure, the modeling tool automatically creates tables that comply with the basic rules of relational database design. Database developers, however, often are faced with the task of importing or using existing data that isn't in a suitable format for a relational database. It's quite common for database developers to be presented with the task of transforming data contained in spreadsheet "databases" into tables of a relational database. Another scenario is the conversion of a poorly designed, dysfunctional database or a CODASYL network database that contains repeating groups into a proper relational structure. (COBOL permits the use of the *GroupName* OCCURS *Several* TIMES statement to create repeating groups in network databases.)

The sections that follow describe the methods you use to transform nonrelational data to fully relational form.

Organizing Entity Classes

In the "Flat-File Databases" section of this chapter, you learned that the worksheet data model often contains inconsistent entities in rows. The stock prices example, shown in Figure 5.8, is a sample Excel worksheet whose structure violates every rule applicable to relational database tables except attribute atomicity. STOCKS is a worksheet that lists the New York Stock Exchange's (NYSE) closing, high, and low prices for shares and the sales volume of 25 stocks for a five-day period. Rows contain different entities and columns B through F are repeating groups. The Stocks5.xls workbook in Excel 2000 format, which is included on the accompanying CD-ROM, is used in the examples that follow. You'll find Stocks5.xls in the \Chap05 folder.

You need to separate the entity classes according to the object each entity class represents. The four entity classes of the STOCKS worksheet of the Stocks5.xls workbook are the closing price, the highest transaction price, the lowest transaction price, and the trading volume of a particular stock on a given day. To separate the entity classes, you need to add a column so that the stock is identified by its abbreviation in each row. You can identify the data entities by their classes—Close, High, Low, and Volume—plus the abbreviation for the stock, which is added to the new column with a simple recorded Excel VBA macro. You then sort the data with the Entity and Key columns. The result of this process appears, as shown for the Stocks1 worksheet, in Figure 5.9.

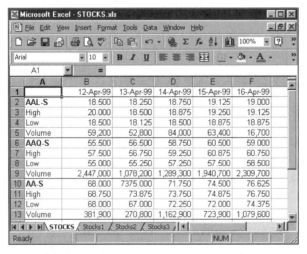

Figure 5.8   The Stocks5.xls database within Microsoft Excel—a good example of poor database design.

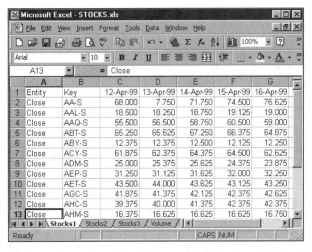

Figure 5.9   The Stocks1 worksheet with entities sorted by entity class.

TIP: *The Dates column represents a mixed entity type (three prices in dollars and the volume in shares), but each entity is now identified by its type. Therefore, you can divide the entities into separate tables at any point in the transformation process.*

Now you have a table that contains entities with consistent attribute values because you moved the inconsistent stock name abbreviation to its own attribute class, Key, and replaced the stock abbreviation in the Entity column A to a value consistent with the Entity attribute class, Close. However, the repeating-groups problem remains.

TIP: *Manual worksheet methods of manipulating tabular data are used in this chapter because worksheet techniques, such as selecting, cutting, and pasting groups of cells, represent the easiest and fastest way to change the structure of tabular data. If you need to transform a large amount of worksheet data into relational tables, you should use VBA OLE Automation methods or create general-purpose VBA macros in the worksheet application to automate the transformation process.*

Normalizing Table Data

The process of transforming existing data into relational form is called *normalization*. Normalization of data is based on the assumption that you've organized your data into a tabular structure wherein the tables contain only a single entity class. Here are the objectives of data normalization:

• To eliminate duplicated information contained in tables

• To accommodate future changes to the structure of tables

• To minimize the impact of changes to database structure on the front-end applications that process the data

The sections that follow describe the five steps that constitute full normalization of relational tables. In most cases, you can halt the normalization process at the third normal form. Many developers bypass the fourth and fifth normal forms because these normalization rules appear arcane and inapplicable to everyday database design.

The First Normal Form

The first normal form requires that tables be flat and contain no repeating groups. A data cell of a flat table may contain only one atomic (indivisible) data value. If your imported data contains multiple data items in a single field, you need to add one or more new fields to contain each data item before moving the multiple data items into the new field.

The Northwind.mdb sample database with Access 2000 includes a table, **Customers**, whose **Address** field contains data that violates the first normal form because some cells contain a two-line address. Figure 5.10 shows the **Customers** table of Northwind.mdb in form view.

The multiline address for Consolidated Holdings violates the atomicity rule. Therefore, you need another field, such as **Location**, to contain the second line of two-line entries in the **Address** field. For parcel delivery services, such as Federal Express, you need the physical address in the **Location** field for firms that use postal boxes to receive their mail.

TIP: If you're an XBase or Paradox developer, you might think that adding a field to contain the physical location portion of the address causes unwarranted expansion of the size of the **Customers** table. This isn't the case with Jet tables because Jet databases use variable-length fields for the **Text** field data type. If an entry is missing in the location field for a customer, the field contains only the **Null** value in databases that support **Null** values. The size is an issue applicable to fixed-width xBase and Paradox table fields, because you must provide enough width to accommodate both lines of the address, whether one or two fields are used to contain the address data. Jet tables use variable-length fields for **Text** entries. An alternative to adding a **Location** field is to create a separate table for location data that has an optional one-to-one relation with the **Customers** table. This is a less efficient process than accepting **Null** or blank values in records that don't have **Location** values.

Eliminating repeating groups is often a tougher process when you're transforming worksheet data. Four of the five columns of stock price data shown in the preceding Figure 5.9 are repeating groups. The "quick and dirty" method of eliminating repeating groups is a series of copy, cut, paste and fill operations. You add another column to specify the date for each entry. You then cut and paste the cells for the four repeating groups into the column renamed from the beginning date of the series to PriceVolume. The final step is to sort the data on the Entity, Key, and Date fields. A portion of the resulting worksheet (Stocks2)

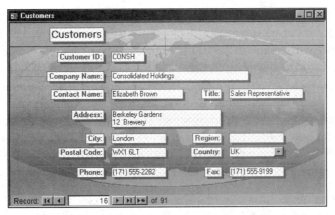

Figure 5.10 The Customers table of Northwind.mdb violates the first normal form.

appears in Figure 5.11. Instead of 101 rows for the 25 stocks, you now have 501 rows and what appears to be a large amount of duplicated data. However, your data is now in first normal form.

The Second Normal Form

The second normal form requires that all data in nonkey fields of a table be fully dependent on the primary key and on each element (field) of the primary key when the primary key is a composite primary key. "Fully dependent on" is a synonym for "uniquely identified by." It's clear from examining the data shown in Figure 5.11 that the only nonkey column of Stocks2 is PriceVolume. The Entity, Key, and Date fields are members of the composite primary key. The sorting process used in the preceding section proves this point.

	A	B	C	D
1	Entity	Key	Date	PriceVolume
2	Close	AA-S	12-Apr-99	68.000
3	Close	AA-S	13-Apr-99	7.750
4	Close	AA-S	14-Apr-99	71.750
5	Close	AA-S	15-Apr-99	74.500
6	Close	AA-S	16-Apr-99	76.625
7	Close	AAL-S	12-Apr-99	18.500
8	Close	AAL-S	13-Apr-99	18.250
9	Close	AAL-S	14-Apr-99	18.750
10	Close	AAL-S	15-Apr-99	19.125
11	Close	AAL-S	16-Apr-99	19.000
12	Close	AAQ-S	12-Apr-99	55.500
13	Close	AAQ-S	13-Apr-99	56.500

Figure 5.11 The STOCKS worksheet transferred to the first normal form within the Stocks2 worksheet.

A controversy has developed among database designers as to whether or not objects that have a common attribute class, such as price, should be combined into a single table with an identifier to indicate the type of price, such as List, Distributor, or OEM for products or, in this case, Close, High, and Low transaction price for the day. This process is called *subclassing* an entity. There's no argument, however, that the volume data deserves its own worksheet, at least for now, so you cut the volume data from Stocks2 and paste it to a new worksheet called Volume. You can delete the Entity column from the Volume sheet because the name of the sheet now specifies the entity class. The data in the Volume sheet, with field names added, is shown in Figure 5.12.

Each entity now is uniquely identified by the two-part composite primary key comprising the Key and Date fields. You can import the data from the Volume sheet into a table from any application that supports importing Excel 2000 tables contained in a workbook—Access 2000, for example. Both the Stocks2 and Volume worksheets contain data in second normal form.

The Third Normal Form

The third normal form requires that all nonkey fields of a table be dependent on the table's primary key and independent of one another. Thus, the data in a table must be normalized to second normal form to ensure dependency on the primary key. The issue here is the dependencies of nonkey fields. A field is dependent on another field if a change in the value of one nonkey field forces a change in the value of another nonkey field.

At this point in the normalization process, you have the following three choices in how to design the table(s) to hold the stock price data:

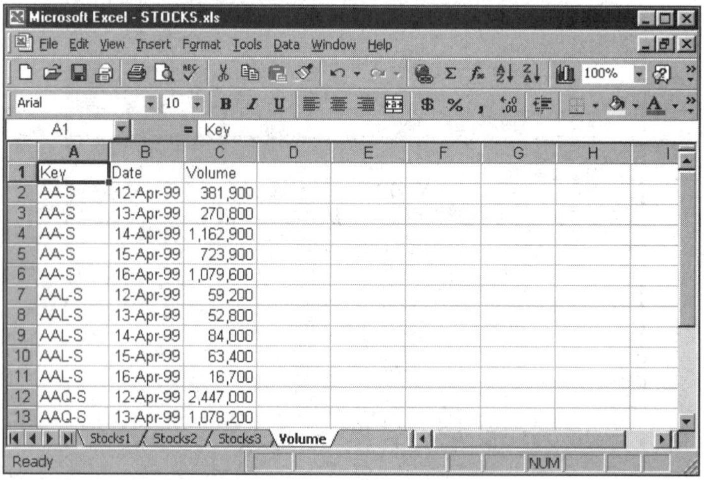

Key	Date	Volume
AA-S	12-Apr-99	381,900
AA-S	13-Apr-99	270,800
AA-S	14-Apr-99	1,162,900
AA-S	15-Apr-99	723,900
AA-S	16-Apr-99	1,079,600
AAL-S	12-Apr-99	59,200
AAL-S	13-Apr-99	52,800
AAL-S	14-Apr-99	84,000
AAL-S	15-Apr-99	63,400
AAL-S	16-Apr-99	16,700
AAQ-S	12-Apr-99	2,447,000
AAQ-S	13-Apr-99	1,078,200

Figure 5.12 The Volume worksheet in second normal form.

- Leave the data remaining in the Stocks2 worksheet as is and create one Prices table, using the Entity column to subclass the price entity. This method requires a three-field composite key.

- Create a Prices table with three columns—High, Low, and Close—using Key and Date as the composite primary key. You could even add the volume data to the Volume field and have only one record per stock-day.

- Create three separate prices tables—High, Low, and Close—and use Key and Date as the composite primary key. In this case, you don't subclass the entities.

The decision on your available choices for a table structure that meets the third normal form is a judgment call based on the meaning of the term *independent*. For example, you must determine whether stock prices and trading volumes are truly independent of one another. You must also determine whether the opening, high, and low prices are dependent upon the vagaries of the stock market and the whims of traders and are, thus, independent of one another. These concerns mix the concepts of dependence and causality. Although it's likely that a higher opening price will result in a higher closing price, the causality is exogenous to the data itself. *Exogenous data* is data that's determined by factors beyond the control of any of the users of the database. The values of the data in the table are determined by data published by the NYSE after the exchange closes for the day. Therefore, the values of each of the attribute classes are independent of one another, and you can choose any of the three methods to structure your stock prices table(s).

Over-Normalizing Data And Performance Considerations

After you've determined that your data structure meets the third normal form, the most important consideration is to avoid over-normalization of your data. *Over-normalization* is the result of applying too strict an interpretation of dependency at the third normal stage. Creating separate tables for High, Low, and Close prices, as well as share-trading Volume, is overkill. You need to join three tables in a one-to-one relationship to display the four data values for a stock. This will be a very slow process unless you create indexes on the primary key of each table. You have four tables, so you need four indexes, and even after indexing, the performance of your stock prices database won't be as fast as a table that contains all of the values. Plus, the four indexes will be larger than a single index on a table that contains fields for all four attributes.

The rule for third normal form should have two corollary rules:

- Combine all entities of an object class that can be uniquely identified by the primary (composite) key and whose nonkey values either are independent of one another or are exogenous to the database and all related databases into a single table, unless the combination violates the fourth normal form. Combining entities into a single table is called *integrating data.*

- Decompose data into tables that require one-to-one relationships only when the relationship is optional or when you need to apply security measures to nonkey values and only when your RDBMS does support column-level permissions. *Decomposing data* means breaking a table into two or more tables without destroying the meaningfulness of the data.

Therefore, the answer to the question of which structure is the best (which was posed in the preceding section) is answered by the suggested corollary rules for the third normal form. Create a new Stocks3 worksheet with fields for the High, Low, and Close prices, as well as for the trading Volume. Then paste the appropriate cells to Stocks3 and add field names. Figure 5.13 shows the result of this process.

TIP: *A more elegant method of transforming worksheet data with repeating data groups to third normal form is to use Excel's Pivot feature to perform some of the transformation operations for you. (The Pivot feature is related to the* ***TRANSFORM*** *and* ***PIVOT*** *statements of Jet SQL.)*

The Fourth Normal Form

The fourth normal form requires that independent data entities not be stored in the same table when many-to-many relations exist between these entities. If many-to-many relations exist between data entities, the entities aren't truly independent; therefore, such tables usually fail the third normal form test. The fourth

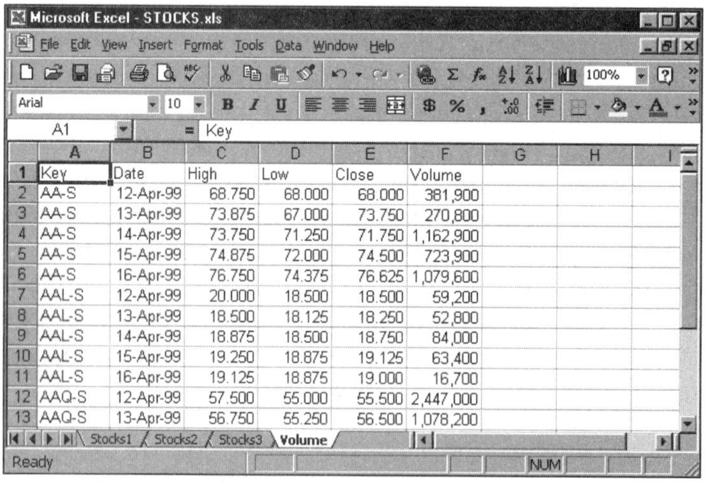

Key	Date	High	Low	Close	Volume
AA-S	12-Apr-99	68.750	68.000	68.000	381,900
AA-S	13-Apr-99	73.875	67.000	73.750	270,800
AA-S	14-Apr-99	73.750	71.250	71.750	1,162,900
AA-S	15-Apr-99	74.875	72.000	74.500	723,900
AA-S	16-Apr-99	76.750	74.375	76.625	1,079,600
AAL-S	12-Apr-99	20.000	18.500	18.500	59,200
AAL-S	13-Apr-99	18.500	18.125	18.250	52,800
AAL-S	14-Apr-99	18.875	18.500	18.750	84,000
AAL-S	15-Apr-99	19.250	18.875	19.125	63,400
AAL-S	16-Apr-99	19.125	18.875	19.000	16,700
AAQ-S	12-Apr-99	57.500	55.000	55.500	2,447,000
AAQ-S	13-Apr-99	56.750	55.250	56.500	1,078,200

Figure 5.13 The result of transforming the data into the third normal form.

normal form requires that you create a relation table that contains any data entities that have many-to-many relations with other tables. The stock prices data doesn't contain data in a many-to-many relation, so this data can't be used to demonstrate decomposition of tables to the fourth normal form.

The Fifth Normal Form

The fifth normal form requires that you be able to exactly reconstruct the original table from the new table(s) into which the original table was decomposed or transformed. Applying the fifth normal form to your resulting table is a good test to make sure you didn't lose data in the process of decomposition or transformation. The Stocks3 worksheet contains every piece of data contained in the original STOCKS worksheet; therefore, with enough cutting, pasting, and sorting, you could restore it. It's often a tedious process to prove compliance with the fifth normal form. Fortunately, compliance with the fifth normal form rule doesn't require that you be able to use ANSI SQL statements to reconstruct the original table.

Once you create a normalized database, you will generally achieve quick, responsive performance when accessing the data within the database—at least until the database contains significant amounts of data. However, it is likely that your database performance will start to worsen as your tables get larger. One of the most important techniques you can use to improve performance is indexing, as the next section details.

Indexing Tables For Performance And Domain Integrity

The primary purpose of adding indexes to tables is to increase the speed of searches for specific data values. If you want to display all persons named Smith in the LastName field of a table, creating an index on the LastName field results in a substantial improvement in the search performance. Without an index, the database manager must start at the beginning of the table and test every record for the occurrence of "Smith" in the LastName field. If you create an index on the LastName field of the table, the searching operation uses the index, not the table itself, to find the first record in which LastName = 'Smith'.

Joining two tables by the primary key field(s) of one table and the foreign key field(s) of another table is a special case of searching for records. When you join two tables, the search criterion becomes **Table2.ForeignKey = Table1.PrimaryKey**. The index must match every foreign key value with a primary key value. Without an index on both the primary key field(s) and the foreign key field(s), joining large tables can take a very long time.

The sections that follow describe the indexing methods in common use with today's desktop DBMSs and client-server RDBMSs, the structure of database tables and indexes, and how to choose the fields of tables to index so that you achieve optimum application performance.

Table Indexing Methods

An index, in simplified terms, consists of a table of pointers to records or groups of records. The records that contain pointer values, usually with an unsigned long integer data type, are organized in a binary hierarchy to reduce the number of tests required to find a record that matches the search criteria. Indexes traditionally refer to the three levels of the hierarchy as the root, branch, and leaf level. (Here again, the analogy to an inverted tree is used.) However, the number of levels in the branch hierarchy actually depends on the number of records in the indexed table. The root leads to one of two branches, and each branch leads to another branch until you reach the leaf level, which is indivisible. The leaf level of the index contains the pointers to the individual records or, in the case of Jet and most client-server databases, the pages that contain the records. The branches contain pointers to other branches in the index or to the leaves.

The exact method of indexing field values varies with the database manager you use; dBASE (NDX and MDX files), FoxPro (IDX and CDX), Clipper and CA-Clipper (NTX), Paradox (PX), Btrieve, and Jet indexes vary in structure. (Btrieve and Jet don't store indexes in separate files, so no file classifications are given for these two databases.) Regardless of the indexing method, indexing techniques reduce the number of records that must be searched to find the first record matching the search criteria. The most efficient indexes are those that find the first matching record with the fewest number of tests (passes) of the value of the indexed field.

Records And Data Pages

Traditional desktop DBMs store fixed-width records in individual files and store indexes on the fields of the file in one or more index files. FoxPro 2 and dBASE IV (as well as more recent versions of both products) enable you to store multiple indexes for a single table in a single CDX and MDX file, respectively. The table files used by these database managers have fixed-length records, so you can identify a record by its offset (its distance, in bytes) from the beginning of the data in the file, immediately after the header portion of the file. Therefore, pointers to records in these files consist of offset values.

Jet and the majority of client-server databases store indexes as special structures (not tables) within the database file. These database types support variable-length fields for Text (the **varchar** type), Memo (the **long varchar** type), and OLE Object and Binary field data types (the **varbinary** and **long varbinary** types). To prevent the tables from becoming full of holes when you delete records or extend the length of a variable-length field, Jet and SQL Server databases use pages to store data, rather than records. Jet and SQL Server pages are 2K in length, corresponding to the standard size of a cluster on a fixed disk of moderate size formatted by Windows 95 or DOS. (As the size of fixed disk partitions grow, so does the size of the clusters. As an example, the cluster size of a 1 gigabyte file using DOS's and Windows 95's FAT16 file system is 32K.) Therefore, if you increase the number of characters in a text field, the worst-case condition is that the RDBMS must move 2K of data to make room for the data. Without enough empty space (called *slack*) in the page to hold the lengthened data, the RDBMS creates a new page and moves the data in the record to the new page. Figure 5.14 illustrates the structure of the 2K data pages employed by Jet and SQL Server databases with about 1.7K of variable-length records and roughly 350 bytes of slack.

WARNING! *The only drawback to the page-locking methodology is that you lock an entire page when updating a record in the page. If the record you're updating is very small, the lock can affect a number of records that you aren't editing. If you use the optimistic locking technique offered by Jet and SQL Server, the lock is likely to be transparent to other database users, especially if your front-end application is very fast. Tables in dBASE and Paradox use record locking, which affects only the single record being edited.*

Btrieve table files include data pages and index pages. Data pages consist of separate fixed-length and variable-length pages. The size of all pages within a Btrieve file must be equal. You can specify the size of the pages in the range of from 512 to 4,096 bytes when you create the table. Choosing the correct page size for the type of data and the average length of records in the table can have a profound effect on the performance of Btrieve databases.

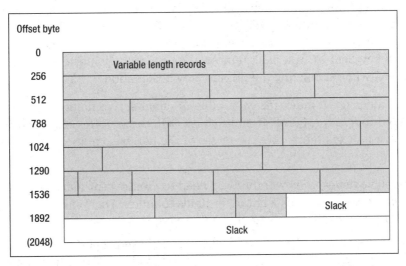

Figure 5.14   The structure of the 2K data pages Jet and SQL Server used for storage.

Balanced B-Tree Indexes

The most common method of indexing tables is the balanced binary tree (B-tree) method originally proposed by Russian mathematicians G. M. Adleson-Velski and E. M. Landis in 1963. Before the B-tree method, editing, inserting, and deleting indexed fields of records caused the index trees to become lopsided, increasing the number of passes required to find the record or page with a matching value. The balanced B-tree method reorganizes the tree to ensure that each branch connects either to two other branches or to a leaf. Therefore, the B-tree index needs to be reorganized each time you add or delete a record. B-tree indexes speed decision-support queries at the expense of transaction-processing performance. In a B-tree index structure, the length of a search path to a leaf is never more than 145 percent of the optimum path.

Choosing Fields To Index

A truism in the database industry regarding the indexing of the fields of tables states: Index only the fields you need to index to enhance the performance of your database front ends, and don't index any other fields. The more indexes you add to a table, the longer it takes to update entries that affect the value(s) of indexed field(s) and to add a new record, which requires updating all indexes. The problem here is knowing which fields improve application performance. The first step is to determine what your options are. The following list discusses how the database types, supported by the Jet database engine, handle the indexing of primary key fields.

Jet tables, for which you specify primary key field(s) in a **TableDef** object, have no-duplicates indexes that are automatically created by the Jet database engine on these field(s). Most client-server databases that you connect to with the ODBC application programming interface (API) also have no-duplicates indexes on primary key field(s), although the indexes usually aren't created automatically. A no-duplicates index prevents the addition of a record with duplicate values in the primary key field(s). You can't remove the primary key index or specify "duplicates OK" without deleting the primary key designation.

Specify a clustered index for each table of client-server databases that support clustered indexes. (Microsoft and Sybase SQL Server offer clustered indexes.) Clustered indexes reorganize the pages of the database in the order of the clustered index.

After you've determined whether you need to create a (primary) key field(s) index, you need to consider what other fields to index. The following list provides some suggestions that apply to all database types:

- Use short codes to identify entities that don't have properties designed to identify the entity, such as part numbers for products. Creating indexes on long text fields, such as product names, unnecessarily increases the size of the index table, slows performance, and wastes disk space.

- Indexes based on numeric values usually have better performance than indexes based on character fields. Using auto-incrementing fields—Access's **AutoNumber** (formerly Counter) field data type, for example—as a primary key field sometimes is feasible when you import existing data.

- Index the foreign key field(s) that participate in joins with other tables.

- Index the foreign key fields that your client will search most often.

- Don't create a separate index for the indexed fields of the composite primary key. Almost all database management systems enable searches on partial key matches, so such an index would duplicate the existing primary key index.

Avoid using the **Like "*Criteria"** statements in Jet SQL and **LIKE '%Criteria'** statements in ANSI SQL. Queries that contain these statements can't use indexes.

Don't try to create indexes on fields of the long data types—**long varchar** (Jet Memo fields) or **long varbinary** (Jet OLE Object fields). Neither the Jet database engine nor the client-server RDBMSs are capable of creating indexes on these field data types.

TIP: *The Jet database engine uses query optimization techniques to choose which indexes to use when your application processes a SQL query.*

If you follow the rules in the preceding list, you aren't likely to go too far wrong in choosing the fields of your tables to index. If you're using Jet tables and have a copy of Microsoft Access, comparing the performance of queries with and without foreign key indexes is a simple process. Jet indexes, as a whole, are much smaller than dBASE and FoxPro indexes. Therefore, you can relegate disk space issues to a lower priority when determining how many indexes to add to a Jet table.

TIP: *You need at least several hundred records to test the effect of indexing foreign key fields on your application's performance. The more records, the better the test. If you or your client observe that the performance of your Visual Basic front end deteriorates as the number of records in the database increases, you may have failed to add an index to an important foreign key. You won't need to change your application's code to utilize the new indexes, except where you use **Seek** operations on **Recordset** objects of the Table type, which you can now safely replace with **Find**. . . methods on **Recordset** objects of the Dynaset and Snapshot types. The Jet database engine's query optimizer automatically uses the new index when the new index aids a query's performance.*

---

5. Database Structures

Immediate Solutions

This section provides a step-by-step guide to identifying data types and systems within your organization, as well as evaluating the costs of maintaining and using certain of these data types. You'll also learn the basics of creating new data-storage systems for your organization.

Identifying Legacy Data

Data collection methods are the eyes, ears, nose, and skin of our automated information production system. Ideally, data should be automatically absorbed from the surrounding environment, processed, and made available with little or no effort by us. Follow two major steps for building an effective and efficient data collection system: inventorying current data collection capabilities, developing proposed capabilities, and integrating them into one system that will support the proposed process.

Step 1—Determining Current Data Storage Locations

Before you can identify legacy data within your organization, you must first determine where data is currently stored. Identifying these storage locations is a crucial first step in identifying legacy data that you may want your new information systems to access or reference. Common locations for legacy data include:

- Filing cabinets
- Mainframe computers
- Older, PC-based data storage systems
- Card-based computer systems
- Tape or other sequential storage media systems
- Rolodexes or other card files

Identifying all the locations in which you may have legacy data stored is a time-consuming process. You should generally involve each department in your organization in the identification process, as departments will typically know what data they maintain better than you will.

Step 2—Identifying Usefulness Of Legacy Data

Determining the current locations of your legacy data is only the first step. You'll often find that much legacy data is either no longer used or isn't cost-efficient to convert to a newer database system. You must carefully analyze the costs associated with converting legacy data into a newer database before you begin. Considerations to keep in mind include the following:

- Usefulness of the data

- Necessity for regular access to the data

- Structure of the data (hierarchical, relational, or free-form)

- Time to design applications to manage the data

For instance, if a particular secretary in the executive section of your organization maintains a Rolodex-style card file of contacts for that executive, and no one else in the organization accesses that data, it may not be worthwhile to convert the existing data to the database; simply enter new contacts in a database. However, if all the secretaries maintain separate contact lists, it may be worthwhile to implement a database that all the secretaries share that has all their contact lists, sorted and filtered by the name of the person the contact is for.

Data Quality

After you determine what data is extant within your organization and begin to consider how useful and necessary that data is, you must also consider the issue of *data quality*. Data quality refers to the accuracy, currentness, usefulness, and other features of the data you're considering converting. Determining the quality of the data is a crucial step before you actually begin to convert or update the data.

Step 1—Identifying Data Consistency

Often, with legacy data, you'll find that, though you have large amounts of data, the data itself may not be consistent. For example, the secretary's Rolodex cards may contain only phone numbers for some contacts, while containing fax numbers, pager numbers, mobile numbers, and even email addresses for others. Although this particular example may be trivial (you're only talking about five additional fields to resolve it), you can imagine the difficulty of converting data if, for example, your company uses a five-digit invoice field that has rolled over in the last several years. Such a rollover would make tracking the invoices on the invoice number field impossible because of duplication.

Moreover, determining whether the data is in consistent formats is also important. For example, if two secretaries already use programs to manage card files, and one program has the street number and address in separate fields, while the other has the street number and address in the same fields, converting these databases to a new database will require extra processing.

Identifying data consistency requires a more "hands-on" approach to the data than identifying legacy data types does. You must have access to the data and the opportunity to check a sufficient sample of the data to determine its consistency.

Step 2—Identifying Data Accuracy

In addition to identifying the consistency of the data, you must also verify the accuracy of the data. For example, if over half of the people in the executive's card file are no longer at the numbers that the secretary has on file, converting these records is a waste of time and energy.

More importantly, consider a situation in which your legacy data reaches back five years or more. It's more than likely that prices, inventory counts, storage locations, and possibly even the products that your company sells will have changed in that time. In such situations, identifying not only that the data is present but that what it reflects is accurate for the time is crucial, particularly if you're in a business that sells physical production. Ensuring that prices are accurate reflections of historical data without corrupting your current-day data is very important.

Typically, you'll need to use outside or corroborating data sources to verify the accuracy of the data you're considering converting. You must also be careful to ensure that these other sources of data are accurate to protect yourself against verifying data against a bad sample.

Data Usability

After you've verified the quality of your legacy data, you must next verify that data's usability. In other words, it isn't enough to verify that the data is quality data, you must next determine if the data is useful. You saw some of this in the previous section when we discussed concerns such as the validity of phone numbers. However, even if a phone number is valid, it isn't particularly usable if the information relates to a supplier your company no longer does business with.

More importantly, if the data is in a form that isn't easily convertible to a database (for example, if your business is a law firm, and all your individual court files are in folders), the data's usability is at question. In the law firm example, you'd probably want to index all the hard copies, scan them to enable free-text searches, and so on. If your law firm has 1,000 clients, and each client has an average of 100 pages per file (which is minimal—many law firm files run to thousands of pages or more), that's 100,000 individual pages to scan in, index, and cross-reference.

Of these 100,000 pages, perhaps only 15,000 are really critical. However, you can't simply discard the other 85,000 pages of the files (both because it's illegal and because you might need them some time). In this case, the data isn't particularly usable without specific software and hardware implementations that help you get the data into the database.

Evaluating Costs

Throughout the previous sections, a common theme has been concern with return on investment (ROI) from the conversion of legacy data to newer data stores. Evaluating all the previous concerns (about usability, accuracy, and so on) are simply ways of determining the cost of converting your legacy data into a newer database.

Determining costs of a conversion is very important in business today, whether you're an independent contractor or a management information system (MIS) manager for the company who's responsible for data conversion. Determining costs of conversion can generally be done in three steps, as detailed here.

Step 1—Determining The Cost Of New Database Development

When evaluating the cost of converting legacy data, the first concern is the cost of developing the new database. To determine the cost of developing the new database, you must take into account the database program cost itself, the cost of a programmer to design the database, and the cost of a database administrator to maintain the new database. It's common for database design costs to run into the thousands of dollars. For example, if you pay a developer $25 an hour, and it takes that developer a month to design and implement your custom database, the cost of that developer alone is $4,000 for the month.

Step 2—Determining The Cost Of Converting Legacy Data

After you determine the cost of creating the new database, you must next determine the cost of converting the legacy data for the database. This cost may include programming costs for a programmer to design a program to automatically convert the database information into the new tables. However, it will almost always include data entry costs (either to enter all the data or to handle cases in which the data doesn't convert correctly) and will generally also include the cost of verifying that the data has converted correctly. Typically, most companies will use spot-checking to determine whether the data has converted correctly throughout a database. After you convert the data, your next step is one of the most difficult (and generally most expensive)—teaching users to use the new system.

Step 3—Determining The Cost Of Training Users To Use The New System

Whenever you implement new software within your organization, you'll find that training costs are associated with that implementation. At a bare minimum, you'll have the cost of providing actual training to your users (which may vary from one hour to one day, depending on your program's complexity). Additionally, you'll have the ongoing productivity cost associated with teaching them to use a new program. Finally, you'll likely have increased costs within your support department from supporting and providing assistance on the new program.

All these costs alone may not be over-burdensome, but when you add them up (particularly if you're rolling out a large database to a significant number of users), you can potentially incur greater costs from rolling out the database than you did from the development of the database and the roll out of the database front end.

Creating New Data

Your final alternative, which is generally not acceptable to most businesses, is to create new data, rather than transforming or importing your company's legacy data. Generally, this is only a solution in situations where one or more of the following cases is true:

- The amount of data to convert is so minimal that the benefit of conversion over re-creation is nonexistent.

- The structure of the data is such that it can't efficiently be converted to the new database—for example, if the data is hierarchical in structure and the new database is relational.

- The cost of converting the data is prohibitive when compared to the ROI for doing so, and starting from scratch has a lower cost and the same or better ROI.

- The data in the legacy storage is either unusable, inaccessible, or in some other form that prevents you from effectively using the data within the new database.

- You determine that the legacy data isn't crucial within your organization and decide to simply maintain the data indefinitely in the older database system (or filing cabinet, or so forth) and use a "day-forward" construction in which the data in the database begins at some set point in time and continues forward from that date.

Chapter 6

Advanced Database Systems

In Depth

This chapter explores advanced database architectures and the networks required to support them. Simple concepts related to storage and processing of data in standard database formats provide the foundation for building complex and powerful applications that can energize any organization. Computer scientists and researchers around the world examine the relationship between data, algorithms, and hardware looking for ways to reduce storage requirements and improve processing speed. We outline current efforts across the board, and illustrate the connection between specific "hot topics" in the industry and real-world problems they solve. In Chapter 7, ideas elucidated in this and previous chapters are brought together as we construct a data warehouse.

One of the common themes throughout the history of humankind's attempts to build computing machines is the desire to create a machine that can "think." That is, a machine that could examine the same set of facts as a human being, apply logic and experience, and make a decision or come up with an answer that we (as humans) would perceive as correct.

When a human being is faced with a simple question—such as What is the sum of two numbers?—the answer is straightforward and can be derived using a simple algorithm. Because of the nature of the problem and the ease with which it can be translated into logic and instructions for a machine, people have found it relatively easy to build machines that can solve these problems and get a "correct" answer.

On the other hand, when facing a complex problem or one that isn't easily translated into logical terms, such as image recognition, we find it much more difficult to make machines that find the "correct" answer. Interestingly, humans can easily recognize images accurately, demonstrating the tremendous difference between the way humans and modern computers process data.

Under the general heading of artificial intelligence (AI), new technologies that mimic aspects of human reasoning are in development, and some of these technologies have proven themselves in the commercial marketplace. Expert systems, fuzzy logic, neural networks, vision systems, voice recognition, and so forth are examples. Although the names and processing structures are all different, these technologies share some characteristics.

For instance, both the human brain and the CPU are composed of large numbers of individual processing units (neurons and transistors). By itself, a single processing unit is capable of only a simple and decidedly unexciting calculation, yes or no, on or off, fire or don't fire. Adding a very straightforward processing path can make a set of processing units capable of calculating sums, for example. Compared to neurons computer hardware is many times faster, essentially perfect (except for programming errors or hardware failure), and untiring, so computers excel at simple calculations such as this.

When more complex tasks are preformed, another factor comes into play: the optimization of processing structures. For example, when light falls on your retina or on a charge-coupled device (CCD), signals are generated that travel to either your brain or a processing unit. Your brain has a multitude of highly specialized structures specifically designed to process the incoming signals (using many neurons in parallel) into comprehensible images. The computer has only very limited and crude routines (comparatively) to conduct the same kinds of processing and, for the most part, performs the processing sequentially. Even with vastly superior speed at the individual processing unit level, computer hardware and software fall far short of the ability of the human brain (but this is changing).

Technologies aimed at reproducing or mimicking the brain's abilities generally rely on the ingenuity of programmers to simulate processing (call it post-processing, to borrow from the image acquisition lexicon) taking place in the brain. Because computer hardware is so much faster than neurons, programmers can sometimes use brute-force methods, but they usually try to build algorithms matching those found in the brain.

Database technology plays a central role in advanced processing systems because it provides a convenient and fairly well-understood format for storing and retrieving data. With the advent of databases that can store (or reference) any kind of data, as well as storage and retrieval systems that are constantly being improved and refined, distributed databases form the basis for many "smart" systems. The networks that connect distributed databases and the resources they carry are the subject of this chapter.

Networking And Database Architectures

Naturally, choosing a database architecture is driven, at least in part, by the requirements of the processes to be supported. Deriving the best architecture from this somewhat simplistic statement is quite an exercise in most cases, however. Let's start by continuing our examination (started in Chapter 5) of the evolution of client-server architectures and their current uses, then we'll make the connection to advanced systems and the architectures most suited to supporting them.

Client-Server Architectures

Much of computing history revolves around single computers and single computer programs, and in fact, most science fiction assumed computers would eventually become massively powerful but remain individual systems. The primary drawback to single-system architectures, of course, is that performance doesn't usually scale well no matter how much more powerful the processor becomes.

Host-Based Processing

Masquerading as a distributed system, host-based application processing consists of a single-system (perhaps an IBM or possibly a PC more recently) with terminals attached. The terminals are called "dumb" because they serve only to display output and accept input. No processing is performed on the terminals.

Master-Slave Processing

In master-slave processing, much the same scenario exists as in host-based processing, except that the terminals are capable of very limited processing, such as field validation and text editing. An IBM 3090 with cluster controllers and intelligent terminals is an example.

Client-Server Processing

Client-server architectures distribute resources, application programs, and services and use load balancing to achieve better performance with current hardware and software. Like the old saying: If one is good, two must be better (although there are many caveats to this). For a database server (see Figure 6.1), a client database application running on a PC would send a request to read data from the

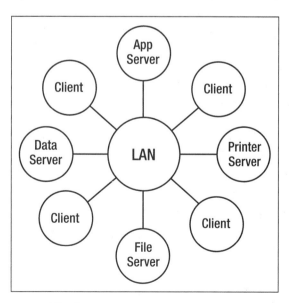

Figure 6.1   Client-server architecture.

server database application. The server processes the request locally, then sends only the records requested to the client. Effective client-server applications require fast and reliable communications links, cooperation between clients and server, application division among clients and server, and server control over resources and requests.

Each node on the local area network (LAN), whether it's a computer, printer, server, or other resource, can access the other nodes and use the services they provide. In fact, the distinction between clients and servers is fading somewhat as more and more servers act as clients, and clients act as servers. Many more types of servers are now available: application, transaction, systems management, data, and so on. Synchronizing operations across several network protocols, operating systems, and physically disparate locations is the challenge faced when developing a distributed database application.

Next Generation Networks And Computing Architectures

The attributes of a successful architecture include support for multiple users, scalability, high performance and throughput, adequate and easy to increase storage and processing, minimal downtime, and support for many types of data (text, audio, video, 3D, and so on). Large-scale concurrent use of resources is the hallmark of modern database applications, regardless of what the designer's original intentions were. Because usage typically increases over the life of an application, processing, networking, and storage hardware should be easy to scale up, while remaining available around the clock.

Each piece of hardware and software resident on a network has a set of capabilities and performance specifications available for processing its own and other requirements. As we've discussed previously, many CPU cycles are wasted on individual PCs while the human being operating it decides what to do next; and the days of buying a separate printer for each person in the office are long gone. Whenever these capabilities can be shared, consolidated, run in parallel, or otherwise put to the performance of a common task, the result is increased performance at a lower cost and with higher speed (unless the overhead communication and interconnection costs outweigh the advantage). With networking and processing architectures continuing to improve, integration of computing resources will naturally follow. As the old adage says, "The network *is* the computer."

Networks And Databases

Your choice of networking hardware, software, and topology (assuming you've a choice) may have a significant impact on your network's ability to support the database solution you design. We'll review networking basics in this chapter to establish the connection between hardware and software and to familiarize managers and users with the terminology used and advantages and drawbacks of each network type. For more information on the subject, you can find a good primer in Appendix B of Karanjit S. Siyan's *Windows NT Server 4, Professional Reference,* published by New Riders in 1996 (ISBN 1562058053).

In Chapter 2, we discussed the open systems interconnection (OSI) model and basic network topologies, and we'll resume our discussion with a more in-depth look at topologies, media, networking standards, and bandwidth.

For a short discussion, it helps to think of networks as groups of stations (computers, printers, and so on) connected by communications links (wiring, fiber optics, wireless and infrared signals, and so on) using a variety of communications protocols to accomplish their central mission, the sharing of resources (files, applications, storage space, processing power, and so on). A limited number of stations can be linked at different distances depending upon the wiring media and network type, and larger networks can be built using internetworking connection devices.

Networking Standards

The Institute of Electrical and Electronic Engineers (IEEE) publishes standards that define how networks should operate. One important standard is IEEE 802.3, that defines the standard for Ethernet networks (although differences between the actual spec and Ethernet do exist), and another is IEEE 802.5, that defines the standard for Token Ring networks. These standards primarily specify hardware (such as network interface cards and wiring media) and how networks communicate at the lowest levels.

The first two layers of the OSI model (physical and data link) are directly related to the scope of the IEEE 802 standards (see Figure 6.2). IEEE 802 divides the OSI data link layer into two distinct parts: the media access control (MAC) and the logical link control (LLC). The physical layers of the OSI model and IEEE 802 specifications correspond.

The MAC portion of the data link layer supports media access to a shared physical medium, and various network types use their own MAC techniques. The LLC portion of the data link layer is the same for IEEE 802 networks, meaning layers farther up the OSI model can use the same communication mechanisms no matter what hardware is used. Communication between the upper layers and the LLC is effected by means of Link Service Access Points (LSAPs). The LLC provides three types of service for the upper layers:

- *Unacknowledged datagram*—Provides no feedback about order or delivery of packets

- *Virtual-circuit*—Makes a connection to ensure packets arrive without errors and in the correct order

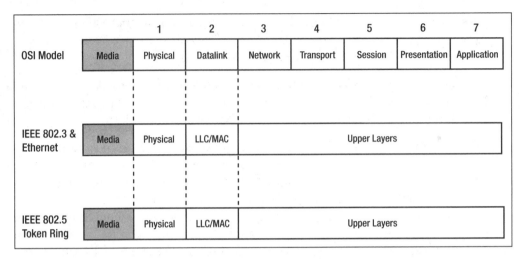

Figure 6.2   The relation between the OSI model and the IEEE 802 standard.

- *Acknowledged datagram*—Provides feedback and corrects packets if necessary

Regardless of the wiring media used (the physical layer), the network can be set up according to IEEE 802 standards. Wiring comes in several flavors, each with its own characteristics.

Physical Wiring Media

Computers can be connected to each other using physical wiring, wireless (radio) devices, and infrared devices. In fact, any method of transmitting signals between computers can be used; the constraints that lead to using the most popular choices are cost, bandwidth, and reliability (a string between two cans just isn't practical).

Because the bulk of networks use physical wiring to connect computers, we'll focus on various types of wire and fiber optic cable in this section. For instance, common wiring choices include:

- *Coaxial cable*—Coaxial cable is like the cable TV wiring in your home. It has a wire inside that sends the signal, and the shielding around the inner wire transmits the return signal.

- *Twisted-pair*—Twisted pair (TP) wiring contains two wires wrapped around each other (a lot like telephone wire), and comes in shielded twisted pair (STP) and unshielded twisted pair (UTP) varieties. One wire sends and one wire returns signals.

- *Shielded cables*—Shielded cable contains wires inside a braided-wire jacket. The jacket shields the wires from electrical interference.

- *Fiber-optic cable*—Fiber-optic cable transmits signal as pulses of light, through a medium made of glass or plastic. Because the signals are light they aren't subject to electrical interference, but because the "wires" are made of glass it's more difficult and more expensive to install.

The physical wiring between computers is just part of the story. The question of how network nodes can be made to communicate data efficiently, given the constraints on passing signals across wires, has led to the development of several popular communications methods.

Ethernet

Many LANs use Ethernet standards for network communications. Ethernet was developed by Dr. Robert M. Metcalfe, David Boggs, and others for Xerox, and it was published as a standard by Xerox, Digital Equipment Corporation, and Intel in 1981.

When a station on an Ethernet LAN is active, it "listens" for transmissions before sending. Transmissions (termed carrier) cause the station to avoid transmitting its own carrier until the channel is free (following a wait of 9.6 microseconds). Still, transmissions sometimes interfere (these are called collisions). Stations detect and repair collisions as they occur. The name for this scheme is Carrier Sense Multiple Access with Collision Detection (CSMA/CD).

Ethernet LANs are made up of segments constructed of wiring (such as UTP or coaxial cable) to which each node is connected, with terminators at both ends. You can put as many as 1,024 stations on a single segment, and segments made of coaxial cable can be 500 meters long; by joining segments you can reach a maximum length of 2,500 meters (although this can be stretched a little). Segments wired with UTP must be smaller because of noise and loss of signal. Ethernet networks can run at 100Mbps, but many are still operating at 10Mbps. Ethernet is similar (but not identical) to IEEE 802.3.

Token Ring

Token Ring refers to another popular method for building a LAN. Stations on the network are connected point-to-point in ring fashion (although, physically, the network wiring resembles a star because the links flow to and from a central hub). Token Ring networks can be wired using ordinary media such as coaxial cable, twisted-pair, and fiber-optic cable. Data is communicated via tokens passed from station to station, where only the station possessing the token may transmit.

IEEE 802.5 sets the data rate for Token Ring LANs at 1, 4, and 16Mbps. The maximum number of stations is 260 (using STP cables), but it's advisable to keep the number of stations on any given ring relatively small (under 100) for troubleshooting purposes. Token Ring networks are often constructed as multiple rings combined into one using Multistation Access Units (MAU). Although you can connect stations to a single MAU from as far as 100 to 300 meters (depending upon the type of cabling used), it's better to use the lower limits of 100 to 45 meters because you don't want to have to rewire all stations when it's time to build a multiple MAU network. Of course, you could always use a nonstandard technology such as ARCnet or LocalTalk.

ARCNet And LocalTalk

Attached resource computer network (ARCNet) was developed in the '70s by Datapoint Corporation, but it has limited usage among LANs in general partly because of its low data rate (2.5Mbps) and partly because it remained essentially a proprietary system long after Ethernet had broad acceptance in the marketplace. Up to 255 stations can be attached to an ARCNet LAN with a token passing method to communicate between stations. The maximum distance (according to the SPEC) between a station and hub is 2,000 feet, and ARCNet LANs can be expanded to miles in size.

LocalTalk is a proprietary (Apple Computer) method of connecting Macintosh computers to a LAN. The data rate of LocalTalk networks is slow (230Kbps) and the network can be a maximum of 300 meters in size, with 32 devices present on each segment. Rather than detecting collisions between packets (as Ethernet does) LocalTalk uses Carrier Sense Multiple Access with Collision Avoidance (CSMA/CA) to attempt to avoid collisions between packets.

Naturally, all network communications methods we've discussed allow for expansion. And such expansion of a network increases available resources and allows communications between even more widely separated stations.

Expanding Your Network

Ideally, we'd like to be able to increase network bandwidth, add stations, and locate stations anywhere without limitations. However, limits exist in the real world, but, fortunately, workarounds are also available, each with its own costs, tradeoffs, and benefits. If (or perhaps I should say when) you realize a need to expand your network, connect networks of different types, increase bandwidth, or simply add stations to an existing network, you'll probably use repeaters, bridges, and routers.

Repeaters

Repeaters are like amplifiers. They simply repeat signals from one LAN segment to another. Before repeating the signal, they usually recondition the signal by increasing the power level (amplification), retime it, and forward it to all ports except the one from which the signal came. Repeaters are quite mechanical and use only the physical layer of the OSI model, meaning they've no logic running to process information about the packets they receive and can't access addressing data. Therefore, all signals are repeated, even packet collisions and other garbage. Stations on a Token Ring LAN individually perform repeater functions, so repeaters aren't usually used. When connecting different types of networks, though, a bridge must be used.

Bridges

Bridges are smarter than repeaters and can connect different types of networks together (Ethernet and Token Ring, as shown in Figure 6.3 for example). In this instance, a bridge will have network cards of both kinds to which each network is connected (Ethernet to Ethernet and Token Ring to Token Ring). The bridge serves as translator between the two network types.

Because bridges need to translate packets between various network types, they need processing power onboard; and because they must process some packets before forwarding, they're built with onboard storage. In addition, bridges can only accomplish their functions with access to the data link layer of the OSI model.

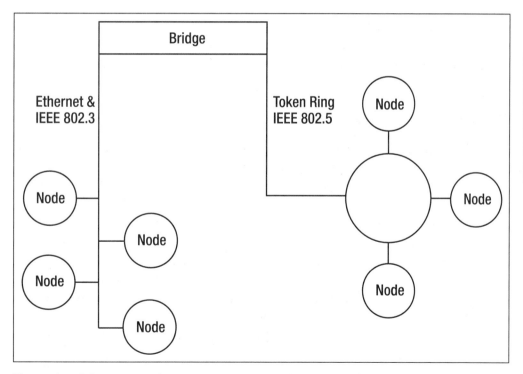

Figure 6.3   Bridge connecting Ethernet and Token Ring networks.

By virtue of their processing power, translation ability, and access to the data link layer, bridges isolate networks, resolve some traffic bottlenecks, and ensure that collisions and tokens don't cross from one network to the next. However, bridges make no decisions about the status of the network as a whole. That's called routing, and routers are the devices used.

Routers

Routers are a lot smarter than bridges or repeaters; they actually read the address of each packet. They compute the best path for a packet to reach its destination by evaluating parameters such as number of hops, time delay, bandwidth, and link status along the path. Routers are more complex, expensive, and difficult to install and to maintain, but they're indispensable for interconnecting large LANs.

As we discussed in Chapter 2, routers must "speak" many protocols to connect LANs of different types. Routers read source and destination addresses of packets (on the network layer) to forward packets properly and, therefore, must maintain an internal database called a routing table that contains information about either every node on the network or just local nodes. The maintenance of routing tables is a significant part of router operations.

Determining the best hardware and network architecture for a database application is just the beginning. Once your application is distributed and ready to run, you'll want to automate as much of the data capture process as possible. We've discussed data types and data acquisition; now we'll examine automating these functions.

Automated Data Import Systems

In Chapters 2 and 3, we discussed the presence of data all around us and made mention of the fact that there is plenty of data already in electronic form residing in legacy systems. Binary data is also constantly being generated under different operating systems and in various file formats on user's individual machines, on customer and supplier machines, and by other organizations that provide data to us.

Much of the data that's available may come to our system in a format other than what we'd prefer, and we may have little or no control over the format of this data. A constant need exists to import data into a format that's native to the operating system and applications we're running.

Ideally, we can automate the acquisition and conversion of incoming data (and outgoing data as well, for that matter). Microsoft Access and Microsoft programs in general (as well as Microsoft's competitors, of course) have efforts underway to alleviate much of this data format incompatibility, but until everyone is speaking the same language (data-wise) we'll still have to develop import and export systems.

The Life Of Data

Data is captured, transmitted, converted, stored, and deleted over its lifetime, and it takes on many forms while undergoing these manipulations. We can think of these functions as being distributed across three general phases: capture, usage, and long-term storage. To efficiently make data available across the organization over its life, we need to ensure its purity and translate it into a common format (or formats).

As we discussed in Chapter 2, for data to be meaningful, it must contain not only values but also some indication of the units and dimension being measured. One dimension not always tracked but normally implied is time. As human beings, in the absence of other context, we normally assume an undated data value refers to the present (current, existing) situation or state of things.

One metaphor for data capture is the "snapshot." It means the data captured represents the state of things at the time it was captured. In truth, however, all data is suspect because errors can occur in the capture process that invalidate the data. You can catch or compensate for some human or machine, but some errors masquerade as valid data and can permeate the system as a whole, especially when subsequent processes rely on it with little human intervention. Data validation mechanisms incorporated into data entry points are the first line of defense against invalid data.

The first thing to do is "clean up" or sanitize data after it's been captured. Missing, inconsistent, or out-of-tolerance data can be identified fairly easily, but without reference to the original source, we can't be 100 percent sure changes are accurate. For instance, if three entries read "Mr. J. Smith" at a given address and one entry reads "Mr. H. Smith", can we assume that the "H" is incorrect, or might it be that another Mr. Smith lives at the same address? And at what point in the process does cleanup take place? In practice, we're always cleaning up data, but it's best to establish cleanup points as soon in the process as possible to reduce the amount of erroneous data flowing through the system.

After the initial capture and cleanup, data is frequently transmitted to another location (although, looking at all the sources of data available to a typical organization, large amounts of data are local-use only, as it should be). Before transmission, a compression and sometimes an encryption process is often employed. And much of the data at this stage isn't transmitted to a central repository but to intermediate locations for operational usage. Chances are, the data will now be summarized, in many cases, before being put to work to satisfy day-to-day operating requirements. Its format won't be standardized, and some information may be lost because of roll up.

An automated data importation system must, at least, pull data from these intermediate locations, convert it to common formats, and make it available to users across the network. If critical data is being lost along the way because of roll up, the automated system must extend further along the chain, close to the data capture point. The difference between the two is frequently an order of magnitude in cost, time, training, and everything else that goes into building a new process and solution.

Conversion Utilities

Digital data is the common thread that relates data from birth to death, and today's most disparate capture points typically can convert that data into formats that, although they may not be common, can at least be translated into common formats. Your job is to decide which formats are most common and to encourage people at the intermediate usage points to use these formats. You must then build or install conversion utilities (either off the shelf or custom) that translate these intermediate formats into the common formats you need.

Deciding which formats to use may be a matter of mapping the formats used throughout the organization by operating system, application, and process supported (see Figure 6.4). Critical processes, wide usage, and future growth of artificial or market-driven standards should guide your decision making. Of course, there's nothing that says you can't change currently used formats, but it may not be practical, depending upon the scale and reach of your project. Although most formats relate to the application program that can read them, encryption is a special type of format that deserves extra attention.

Encryption Utilities

From birth to death, sensitive data must be secured to protect the interests of the organization. Trade secrets, strategies, negotiations, and the like can damage an organization if they fall into the wrong hands, and it's common knowledge that corporate espionage is on the rise.

Encryption utilities frequently use algorithms based on the difficulty of factoring prime numbers to encode data so only the authorized receiver can decode it. In fact, some of the algorithms are so powerful that the U.S. government prohibits export of software containing them.

Encryption utilities protect data but at the price of adding to processing overhead (for rapidly encoding and decoding transmissions) and network overhead

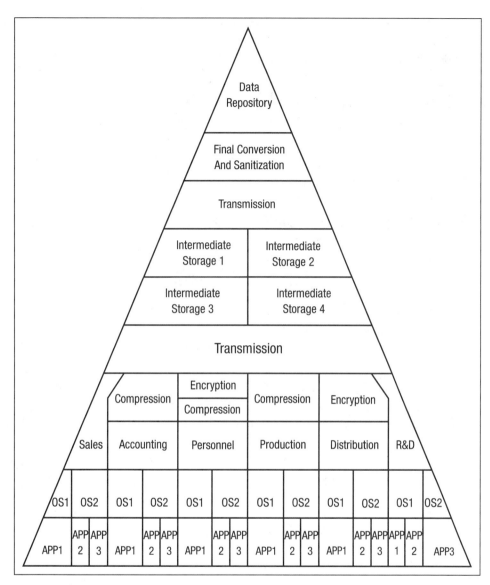

Figure 6.4   Map of common formats.

(additional data is required for each byte sent). Even so, encryption makes sense under many circumstances, and provisions should be made to convert encrypted data from its initial format to a common format even if it's still kept encrypted. In fact, when data is accumulated and made available in a common format, there may even be a need to impose a higher level of encryption because so much data is available in one place.

Naturally, when data has been captured and converted to a common format, you'll need somewhere to store it, both daily backups and long-term archives. Getting the data into the storage system is the subject of the next section.

Archive And Backup Systems

One of the major steps in creating a data warehouse (covered in depth in Chapter 7) is building mechanisms into transaction processing systems to store or accumulate transaction data. Typically, legacy systems initially store this data as records in operational tables, but as the amount of data grows, blocks of records are moved out of these tables and into archive storage.

Archive storage systems automate the process of marking records for archiving, removing old records from current operational tables, and safely storing the records somewhere else, oftentimes on a different media altogether (such as optical disks). Archive systems are sometimes confused with backup systems, but important distinctions exist between the two. Backup systems back up current data for restoration in case of accident, while archive systems store only selected portions of current data (specific time periods such as quarterly data, for example). Note that backup systems can be included as part of an overall archiving system.

Automatic archiving systems are closely linked with data marts and data warehouses (discussed in Chapter 7) and should directly support their functions. They form a bridge between the requirements of the operational data systems and the informational data systems. Operational systems need to be purged of old records frequently to stay uncluttered and fast, and your data repositories can be constructed to archive old records efficiently while performing their other functions.

Backup Systems

You've probably educated everyone in your organization about the need to frequently back up important data, but even the best of us still forget once in awhile. You probably also have critical data under a backup regimen that's adequate. Your challenge, now that data is so distributed and critical data can reside just about anywhere, is to find a way to create a backup system and policy that supports processes across the organization, whether the data is on a PC or a mainframe or anywhere in between.

Ideally, every computer in your organization would always be completely backed up, in realtime, so any accident would simply mean a downtime equaling the time it takes to issue a new system and copy the image to the new hard disk drive. In practice, this isn't practical for distributed computers, such as PCs (as opposed to fixed systems such as mainframes, minis, and so on), in terms of required storage, connectivity, bandwidth, cost, and other considerations.

You can approach this, however, by automating the backup system as much as possible. Human beings are notorious for forgetting to back up files, so buy or construct a utility that makes it easy for them to set backup directories and time backups for whenever they're connected to the network. Allow them to temporarily suspend backups if they're connecting remotely and can't afford the time or cost of running a full backup the moment they connect.

Backup Hardware

Back up distributed computers to hard disk drive systems rather than tapes and other linear, slower media. The point of a backup is to get the person up and running as quickly as possible in case of an accident. Trying to find the right tape, running the restore routine, and getting the data back to its original condition is time consuming and difficult compared to the much easier (and faster) process of recovering data from a networked drive, and the cost of hard disk storage has dropped dramatically. Using a redundant array of inexpensive disks (RAID), also known as redundant array of independent drives, in which multiple inexpensive hard disk drives are connected together and can be swapped out without bringing the system down or losing data is a common approach.

Successful backup systems should be unobtrusive, easy to use, reliable, easy to restore from, and inexpensive. Archiving systems should possess similar traits, but also contribute some unique functions that lend them to use with data warehousing.

Archiving Systems

Archiving systems differ from backup systems in several ways. They're geared towards removing selected records from current operational systems, and they're frequently used for data mining and other informational, strategic purposes (rather than just storehouses of static data). You can thus separate archiving systems into two main categories:

- *Informational*—Informational archiving systems remain accessible for day-to-day usage as well as for data mining and strategic planning. Sales transactions are a good example. A salesperson may need to access the sales history of a client to determine whether a discount is warranted based on prior purchases. By the same token, a marketing person may need to summarize sales by region over the last few years to determine if changes to marketing strategy are called for. Informational data, though it may officially be in the archives, should remain online and accessible to support these functions.

- *Long-term storage*—Storage data is infrequently accessed (usually only in special cases) and is often data (such as images of documents) that may not be summarized. Cancelled checks are an example. Each check may be scanned front and back and the resulting image stored digitally or on microfilm. It's stored offline, but may be recalled and copied if the need arises.

For informational data in archive systems, it's very common to build archiving routines into the database solution. It's important to examine the systems analysis and process engineering documents carefully to make intelligent decisions as to the frequency and type of archiving that should occur for any given data. If the database resides at various points on the local area network/wide area network (LAN/WAN), the archiving system must be able to locate and identify all data to be archived. The next section illustrates such distributed database requirements.

Databases On A LAN/WAN And The Web

Placing a database on a LAN/WAN is a common method of ensuring that all internal users of the database have access (assuming they have access to the LAN/WAN). Microsoft Access offers several ways to accomplish this task, such as splitting the database into two parts: the data (tables) and the data manipulation functions (forms, reports, queries, and so on).

These days, LANs and WANs are frequently organized as intranets, local implementations of Transmission Control Protocol/Internet Protocol (TCP/IP) taking advantage of the easy and ubiquitous Web-based paradigm of information delivery. In addition, many people already have Internet access at work and at home and are familiar enough with Web sites and email that additional training isn't required when the company decides to provide more information resources across the company Intranet.

Another advantage of using Internet standards such as TCP/IP, Hypertext Markup Language (HTML), and Simple Mail Transfer Protocol (SMTP) is the company owns whatever it develops and uses, rather than paying large development and usage fees for proprietary solutions. For example, the development of Web pages is open to anyone who understands HTML, just as anyone who speaks English can freely speak to anyone who understands English. In the following discussion we'll talk in terms of the Web whenever we're referring to intranets, extranets, or the Internet.

Browsers, The Web, And Databases

The major players on the browser scene, Microsoft and Netscape, are battling for market share by adding new features at a very rapid pace, and sometimes the features they add make their browsers incompatible with each other. For the most part, however, Web pages are equally at home on either browser and also have the advantage of being platform independent. One development effort, if carefully designed to avoid browser incompatibilities, can support multiple platforms, browsers, and users.

Connecting a database to a Web site is now such a common task that the only requirements are the Web page, the database, and a few simple tools (such as

Active Server Pages, an open database connectivity [ODBC] driver, and a text editor). But, of course, there's much more to it than simply making the connection. The database application must be designed with the Web in mind, meaning periodic data exports in Web format to keep the Web site up-to-date, as well as additional security, storage, and archiving concerns. The company Webmaster is going to be responsible for coordinating these activities, and must understand the internal network, the Web, databases, and the Internet in general.

Data Delivery

Although internal networks deliver data at up to 100Mbps, there'll be many occasions when users are limited to much slower speeds. Some database applications will be available only to internal users and can, therefore, offer resources that just wouldn't be practical over the Internet in general. Fortunately, many applications require only the delivery of text (email) or text-based records. The limitations of data delivery over the Internet, in general, are based on the hierarchy of analog modems, Integrated Services Digital Network (ISDN), and cable modems, although some customers or users may have T1 or faster communications links.

Plain Old Telephone Service (POTS) to home or office is analog, but the majority of the infrastructure consists of digital communications links and switching devices. Dedicated point-to-point links can be established and discarded at will, over the entire world. New technologies are competing, but telephone service is the means by which most of the world does (and will continue to for some time) make the connection to the Internet. Data rates throughout the world probably average no more than 14.4Kbps, but a significant portion of the U.S. population now runs 28.8, 33.6, and 56Kbps modems. Because ISDN and cable modems have been slow to deploy for most of the population, a growing number of dual modem lines are in use, with data rates approaching 100Kbps.

ISDN was one of the first digital-data-over-the-phone-lines technologies to be deployed, and it's being deployed quite rapidly at present Other technologies, such as cable networks and digital subscriber lines (DSL), are superior and cost much less, but they're unavailable to the majority of potential users.

ISDN can transfer data at a variety of rates, but the basic rate most of us are familiar with is 64Kbps. ISDN transmits and switches data using two transfer modes (methods):

- *Circuit switching*—Circuit switching establishes dedicated connections that remain constant while in use. Network resources are dedicated to the users for the life of the connection. This is somewhat inefficient, however, because many transmissions tend to be less than continuous. Speech itself is full (on the order of 50 percent) of large and small silences, but circuit switching remains predominant because quality reconstruction of speech is sensitive to lag. If you've ever used Internet telephone service over ISDN (or especially over an analog modem) you know what we mean.

- *Packet switching*—Packet switching, touched on in Chapter 2 and this chapter, breaks data up into packets copied across the network. Processing overhead and the natural lags inherent in the Internet reduce the applicability of this technique to voice delivery, but increased efficiency in the use of network resources and the increased capability that comes from digitized communications offers advantages for other types of communications.

ISDN channels can be combined to provide a higher data rate of 128Kbps (minus overhead), but cable modems provide the fastest data rates at the lowest price— from 1 to 10Mbps. Although cable modems are inexpensive to install and operate, they've been deployed only in limited areas of the U.S. and share resources with other users on the segment. Heavy simultaneous use can consume available band-width, consequently reducing the average data rate per user, and users can "peep" into other users transmissions with the right software.

Phone companies are fighting back against the deployment of cable modems with DSL technologies that offer comparable data rates, but the prices are generally higher and deployment is quite limited so far. In any case, users requiring high bandwidth may not be able to afford it (or it may not be available in their area), so the data rate required to support your application should be carefully compared to users' capabilities in terms of the natural information rate.

Natural Information Rate

Network applications have a natural information rate that isn't necessarily de-pendent upon the actual bit rate. For instance, if you're sampling audio using hardware and software that generate 64Kbps (the sampling rate per second times the number of bits per sample) then that's the bit rate you'll be transmitting at. During periods of silence, no information will be transmitted; however, the si-lence will be reconstructed on the other end via the 64Kbps data stream. The natural information rate is the data rate after compression equivalent to the rate needed to transmit only the information that changes. It's directly associated with the actual amount of information that needs to be transferred to reconstruct the original data stream (more about this in the next section).

The most important characteristics of the natural information rate are the peak value, the average value, and the variability (or burstiness) of the source (see Figure 6.5). If the natural information rate exceeds the transfer rate, quality will suffer; under the opposite conditions, inefficient use of network resources is the result. This has led to many variations of streaming audio (and video) that trans-mit packets stored in a buffer until enough is accumulated to compensate for the

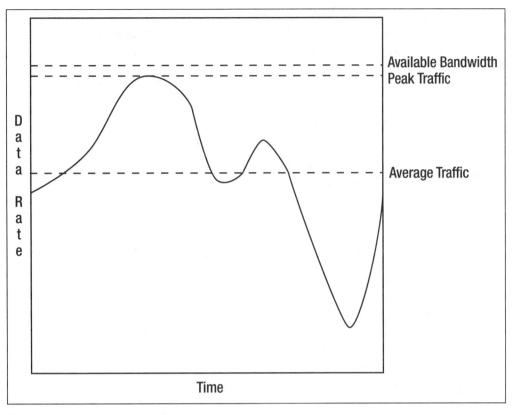

Figure 6.5   Data rates over time.

natural lags of the Internet. Buffering of delivered data sources is just one of many techniques used to deliver large amounts of continuous, multimedia data, such as video and audio.

Multimedia Delivery Systems

Your local cable-TV company runs a multimedia delivery system. For the most part, it's a broadcast, realtime, noninteractive system, but it still qualifies as a multimedia delivery system. However, most organizations today would like a multimedia delivery system that's two-way, interactive, and on-demand (rather than just realtime). Fortunately, today's networks are capable of this feat, though they must utilize extensive compression to achieve it.

High-volume binary storage devices, high-bandwidth delivery mechanisms, and powerful routing devices are at the core of modern multimedia delivery. As you may have noticed, audio and video on the Internet are still not close to what your local cable company delivers to your TV set, so our discussion will be based on what an organization can do on an Ethernet LAN.

Video is analog electrical signals that can be transmitted or stored, then played back at 30 frames per second (fps). If a video signal is digitized, each frame of digital data must contain enough information to fill a computer screen. The data required to fill the screen each second is equal to the total pixels (resolution) times the number of bits (generally 24 bits per pixel for full color) times the number of frames per second. Pure, uncompressed, digitized video consumes tens of megabytes per second, and can rapidly overload storage and transmission devices.

Compression

Depending upon the measurement, units, and dimensions represented by data, different compression schemes may be required. Compression is the process of representing the information contained in data with fewer bits. For instance, a line can be represented as a series of black pixels across the screen using bits of data for the color value and location of each pixel. It can also be represented as starting and ending coordinates for black pixels and a formula calculating the location of each pixel in between. Clearly, for many lengths of line the formula and coordinates could be represented with fewer bits. The result would be the same information output with less bits input. In this example, there's no loss of data, but some compression methods produce adequate results even with some data loss.

Video and audio are good candidates for compression because for many points in a typical video or audio file no change occurs, or the results of change can be deduced. Losses are common to achieve the high compression rates necessary for storage and transmission, but results can often be good enough to serve the purpose at hand. Other types of data, such as text, numbers, and executable files, must never lose data during the compression process but can still be compressed to varying degrees.

The words compression and decompression are combined into the term *codec* to refer to the algorithms used to compress video and audio for storage and delivery, then play it back. Video playback software includes Apple's QuickTime for the Mac and Windows, Microsoft's Video for Windows and ActiveMovie, while the codecs used are MPEG-1 and MPEG-2 (MPEG stands for Moving Pictures Experts Group), Motion JPEG (JPEG means Joint Photographic Experts Group), Indeo (Intel video), and Cinepak (developed by Apple and SuperMac).

Another standard is on the horizon as well—MPEG-4. Due to be finalized (at least version 1) in November 1998, it allows for separate coding of video "objects," meaning individual objects (video, 3D, audio, and so on) can be "layered" onto any given scene. It allows for much greater control over the composition of displayed scenes and better coding efficiency.

Because these codecs lose data, each is optimized to suit different platforms. For more recent (and more powerful) systems, MPEG-2 is the codec of choice and with hardware acceleration can play back high-resolution (704×480) video at 30 fps. The quality and content of the original recording, along with the quality of the encoding system and encoding techniques used, have a significant impact on the final output produced.

Delivery

In the world of television, we're used to realtime, analog broadcasts. Simple information about the scheduling of TV shows is a billion-dollar industry in the country, and most of us dutifully "tune in" at the appropriate times. Videocassette recorders (VCRs) changed our habits somewhat, so now we can record favorite shows and rent movies. But we'd all like to have several things in a video delivery system, whether at home or at work:

- *On-demand access (video on demand)*—Selecting and playing back the footage we want, whether a finished production or raw clips, releases us from the time constraints traditional video imposes.

- *Interactivity (shopping, searching, and so on)*—Two-way communication enriches the medium many times over. One possibility, for instance, is the selection of varying paths through the information presented.

- *Editing capability (video capture, nonlinear editing, and so forth)*— Digitized video is similar to other data in that it can be edited, although the tools and talent required aren't trivial.

To deliver these capabilities, video must not only be captured and digitized, but additional information must be stored with each separate show or clip to construct a searchable database. The greater the amount of additional data stored, the more cost is involved (for identifying, entering, storing, and retrieving data), but much greater capabilities are created.

One promising packet-switching technique is Asynchronous Transfer Mode (ATM). Developed in the early '80s, it utilizes fast packet switching, an offshoot of conventional packet switching. ATM packets are small (53 bytes), fixed in size, and demonstrate a low overall delay, making them more suitable to delivery of video. ATM uses error correction only at either end of the transmission, and unlike other packet switching techniques, ATM is connection oriented, so flow control and error correction don't place as heavy a burden on transmission rates.

MPEG frames can be mapped to ATM frames efficiently, meaning ATM is a good mode for the transmission of MPEG packets. As these standards grow and improve, expect to see video and multimedia delivery mature and converge with ordinary analog broadcasting techniques.

6. Advanced Database Systems

Immediate Solutions

This section details criteria for selecting database architecture, building a network to support a database solution, and automating data importation. We provide examples of simple networks, intranets and extranets, and run through the most significant parts of any decision-making process involving the delivery of knowledge to the desktop, regardless of what architecture or hardware you select.

Optimizing Solutions For A Network Architecture And Type

Client-server architectures are the most practical and serviceable choice for most database applications, but you may be restricted to using existing network and database architectures depending upon the breadth of your solution, available funds, and the availability of legacy networks. What you need and what you want may be two different things, but at a minimum you'll have to determine how to make your solution accessible everywhere it's required to support a process, given whatever limitations exist. Whether you must use existing resources or you're lucky enough to be able to build a new network from scratch, upgrade the network to a higher data rate, or expand the network to accommodate more users, the following steps will prove useful in optimizing your solution to fit.

Step 1—Examine Process Support Requirements

Systems analysis and process engineering documents should tell you:

- How many processes or tasks are supported by the application. If just one process or task is supported, can it be consolidated into a function performed on just one station? If multiple processes are supported, does one station perform the bulk of them, or are they distributed across the network?

- How frequently they interact with the application. Constant updates and retrievals will impact existing traffic much more than occasional communications.

- Where on the network they're located. Lots of traffic across a large network is more costly than the same traffic traveling across one network segment.

Step 2—Evaluate Processes And Tasks As Proposed

Even though you may have a fairly firm idea of how you want work and data to flow throughout your organization, you can use a concept called *abstraction* to consolidate and align processes and tasks into more manageable inputs and outputs across the network. For instance, suppose you have dozens of users entering data over the course of a week, but the data is used to generate reports only at the end of the week. Rather than create dozens of individual connections to the central server, you can use one of the entry machines to collect and consolidate inputs and send them in batches when network activity is low each evening.

Step 3—Update The Solution

At this point, it's worth the extra effort to build new versions of processes and tasks into the original solution and examine their effect on all parameters of the solution. Are there going to be any additional delays in providing data to related processes? Is the quality of the information going to suffer? Compromises are okay, as long as you understand what they entail.

Step 4—Apprise Customers-Users Of Any Changes

Take the time to meet again with customers/users to make sure they understand how changes might affect their working situation. Remember, the solution is theirs (if you've done your homework), and they need to understand how these changes will affect them and why they're necessary. They might also become your allies in gaining additional funding if the changes you need to make don't integrate well with their idea of how processes and tasks should be accomplished. Get them on your side!

Even though you may have optimized workflow to the greatest extent possible, there'll still be many times when the network must be upgraded to accommodate new traffic. The size, data rate, carrying and switching capacity, and other fixed parameters of your network can be estimated in comparison with the requirements of your solution and existing traffic, leading you to an idea of what's needed to enable adequate performance under load.

Sizing A Network For A Database

Before adding a large-scale database to the other applications on your network, you'll want to estimate the impact it may have on network traffic. Depending upon your projections, you may want to add components and/or bandwidth to ensure excellent access. You may also decide to modify your database deployment strategy to reduce network traffic, particularly from segment to segment (discussed in several later sections).

Estimating Network Traffic

The traffic generated by usage of a particular application depends on a few basic variables: users, frequency of access, result sets, and network overhead. The amount and variability of traffic levels as well as the way traffic is distributed across the network play important roles in network expansion and database deployment decisions.

Step 1—Determine The Number And Location Of Users

Using Step 1 of the previous section as a guide, estimate the number and location of users both existing and projected. Depending upon the database application and the processes it's intended to support, you may have only one user or dozens (and perhaps the entire organization). Looking forward, a successful application tends to draw additional users to it, especially if it's easy to use and contains good data. Plan for growth in the number of users and the frequency with which they use the application.

To get an idea of the distribution of users across the network, make a chart (see Figure 6.6) showing the physical network segments and the components on each, including the wiring, bridges, hubs, routers, switches, communications links, and nodes (computers, printers, and so on). Note user functions at each node, and relate user functions to processes in your systems analysis. This map will be out of date whenever major functions change location but can serve as an adequate guide for a time.

Step 2—Determine Required Access Bandwidth Over Time

During the systems analysis phase, you should've generated a list or diagram of processes required to support the mission of the company, as well as an estimate of the number of times these processes occur. For instance, completing the weekly status report may require 20 separate queries of the proposed application. Each query represents data traveling across the network. Because each query may occur at a different time of day and will probably mandate varying amounts of data, it's important not only to estimate the average traffic but also to estimate peak and sustained amounts throughout the day, week, month, and so on.

Estimate the level of traffic across the segments of the network and create probable traffic level charts (at the natural information rate) for the new application. Keep in mind that good network engineering practice (like any other engineering) is to estimate high (conservatively), meaning you should build in a fairly large margin for error, growth, and unusual occurrences. Users have the funny habit of suddenly deciding to all use the same application at the same time.

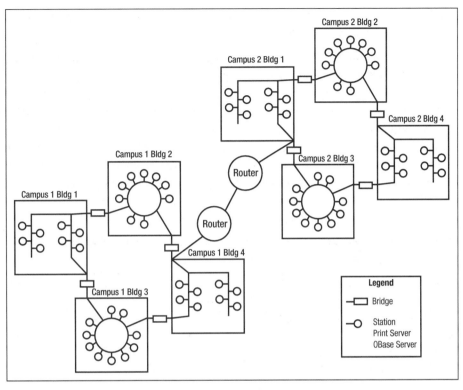

Figure 6.6   An example of a network, its users, and its processes.

Step 3—Evaluate The Potential For Network Disruption

Unless you're building a brand-new network, any application you create will be added to the application mix already present on the network. You can use existing log records and usage charts to build a usage profile for current network traffic plus proposed network traffic.

Step 4—Compare Network Costs Vs. Network Capabilities

Assuming you determine there's a need to expand the capabilities of your network, you'll want to evaluate the additional capabilities new network components offer versus the capabilities they provide. Using the network chart you developed in Step 1, examine the potential for network bottlenecks. It does no good to upgrade from 10BaseT to 100BaseT if some other components of your network don't have the capability to support the increased bandwidth.

Step 5—Simulate Network Traffic Levels

Static comparisons of estimated traffic levels are a good tool, but dynamic simulations of network traffic with existing and proposed applications running under real-world conditions provide the best picture of what you can expect when you actually deploy the new application.

Average traffic levels are really no guide at all for sizing a network because communications links and switches must be capable of handing peak and sustained traffic loads. A good rule of thumb is to build a network that can handle twice the peak traffic loads (Figure 6.5 shows a network in need of upgrade). This will provide an acceptable margin for growth, as well as an indicator of approaching network saturation as growth occurs and will greatly reduce the possibility of network outages. Remember, people expect the network to remain available at all times. Just because it's unreasonable doesn't mean people don't assume it's so.

Automating Data Import Systems

Automation is desirable because it reduces error, increases speed, and relieves tedium, but it costs. Building an automated system means engineering out variability as much as possible, so there's less chance the automated system will encounter an unrecognized situation. Errors made by automated systems propagate much more quickly than errors made by people precisely because they're automated and, therefore, faster.

Engineering out variability implies a clear understanding of inputs to the system, provisions for unusual or out-of-tolerance (error) conditions, and straightforward rules for producing adequate outputs with correct inputs. One of the normal benefits of automating data import systems is standardization of data and format of outputs (we'll discuss this in more depth in Chapter 7).

To begin the process of automating data import systems, we must identify sources of data and the formats they operate in. From there, we proceed to determine how we want the inputs translated and how outputs will be made available to users.

Step 1—Identify All Current And Expected Data Formats

Data can arrive at our system from just about anywhere, in just about any format, periodically or continuously, by Web, internal network, floppy disk, data entry, and on and on. For data supporting crucial processes, not only should we take steps to ensure that production doesn't fail, we should try to make this data conform to our processing and storage systems as early in the capture phase as possible (in general).

Other considerations need to be taken into account, however. The point at which data is converted to one (or several) output formats may be affected by transmission requirements, the capabilities of the capture device, security, and the requirements of the process it supports. For example, should image data be compressed before transmitting it to a central storage unit? Is it feasible to compress it within the capture device, or is a separate system required? Would the data be more difficult to intercept and use in its raw format? Answering these questions helps clarify where and when to convert data and also gives you an idea of how much conversion may be necessary.

But regardless of our efforts to capture data in formats we can use directly, for the foreseeable future there'll always be significant amounts of data that must be translated, sanitized, and otherwise converted before we can use it. To build a picture of what we're dealing with, create a chart showing the types and amounts of data in each format, the means by which it's captured and transmitted, and how it connects to the processes it supports.

Step 2—Identify The Output Format For Each Input Data Stream

Although it would be pleasant and elegant to convert all data to the same format for later use, this isn't yet practical. Many types of data don't lend themselves to manipulation in standard formats, so we'll end up with several formats. The end format for each input data stream must be identified to gauge conversion requirements and the load that'll be placed on hardware and software under operating conditions.

Step 3—Evaluate Commercial-Off-The-Shelf (COTS) Software For Data Conversion

Hundreds of packages on the market convert data to standard formats, and many of these also assist in sanitizing data. Making the choice may be simple in some cases, but the sheer number of packages, options, and combinations of capabilities can often be overwhelming. Although, from one standpoint, the choice of package (or custom development) is a business decision (what will it cost versus the capabilities it offers?), many other factors also need to be considered, such as:

- Ease of installation, setup, and use
- Interoperability and programmability
- Range of formats converted and range of output formats

Sometimes you'll find that the IT staff has expertise using a particular package, and that (plus the fact that the package is already a sunk cost) can be the deciding factor. And don't forget that many desktop applications can be easily configured to automatically convert data into a number of output formats, reducing the load on bulk conversion routines later in the processing cycle.

6. Advanced Database Systems

Step 4—Program Any Remaining Conversion Utilities Required

Chances are good that, even after installing a COTS package to perform most of the sanitization and translation, your IT folks will still have to program a few routines and utilities to integrate importation processes with the rest of your network and applications. Even though it can be an expensive proposition, mitigate the expense by making sure any conversion routines are written with a standard interface and can be reused later for similar data formats and conversion requirements.

Step 5—Conduct Testing To Ensure Data Is Properly Converted

As with any production system, pretesting and small-scale production testing is warranted. Simulate deployment on a nonproduction system. Deploy the system on a limited basis and evaluate its performance. The results of these tests can make final production release much less frightening.

Creating Archive And Backup Systems

Your system administrator already has critical data on mainframes and minis backed up and archived automatically. Your job as solution developer is to provide the administrator with enough data about your proposed solution, so he can estimate any additional resources required to accommodate the new data streams. Your other (and more difficult) job is to ensure that critical data residing on PCs under the control of users is kept safe. This is no easy task.

Very likely, some people in your organization back up all critical data on a daily basis or even as soon as they produce it. These folks are also just as likely to use floppy disks for backup. They're conscientious, and they don't trust some unknown or unseen backup methods with their data. They tend to think of the data as theirs, rather than as company property. At the other end of the spectrum are folks who assume that if the data was that important the company would automatically back it all up, so they don't even need to worry about it. And a few of your folks will actually use the most effective methods of backing up their data according to a realistic assessment of the value of the data and the time involved in backing it up.

So you can assume that you've a range of backup behaviors established within your organization. Like any behaviors, they can be changed with education, but all the ordinary caveats about change apply. The easiest thing to do is build automation into the application, so backups and archiving will take place transparently.

Step 1—Differentiate Between Backup And Archive

As usual, the systems analysis and process engineering diagrams and documents should provide clues about which data must be backed up and which should be archived (and sometimes both). Identify every expected piece of data falling into either category.

Step 2—Develop A Backup Plan

Part of educating users about backups is getting them to save all working data into their own working and archive folders. Finished products go into their archive folder, while projects they're still working on go into their working folder. They can then subdivide the working folders into subfolders based on how they like to work. If users want to separate files by application type or if they like to keep all files for a given project in the same folder, it doesn't make a big difference.

Step 3—Develop An Archiving Strategy

Archiving data may occur infrequently, or it may happen as soon as new records or files are created, depending upon the needs of other processes. Because archived data should probably be drawn from central sources (rather than users' computers) after it has been converted and sanitized, it's easier to develop an archiving strategy than a backup strategy. Identify the records or folders that must be forwarded to the archives, the frequency with which they must be forwarded, and any additional processing that must take place to store the data in the archives. Make the entire process automatic, and don't forget to include indicators to the system administrator when the archives are getting full or otherwise need attention.

Step 4—Estimate Backup And Archive System Requirements

Being familiar with the processes, tasks, and backup-archive requirements, you're in a position to estimate total storage requirements and types. Provide your system administrator with an estimate of total requirements (and include network traffic as well) over the life of the solution. Project usage growth and potential scalability, so the system administrator can estimate the impact to the system as a whole.

Step 5—Simulate Normal Usage And Test Data Restoration

Before deploying backup and archiving systems, deploy and debug them to make sure the right data is going to the right places at the right times. It's especially critical to test data restoration from backup systems because many older backup technologies aren't very user-friendly in this regard.

Implementing Databases On A LAN/WAN

Sharing data and information over a LAN or WAN is an effective way to increase productivity. Users are aware of this but tend to take it for granted because they've always shared information, just not via the network. Before there were networks, people exchanged files using "sneakernet" and floppy disks. Before computers, people exchanged data with memos and reports. To users, the only thing new is the speed and their ability to complain that "the network was down" when they miss a deadline.

Consequently, as soon as a user develops a database that someone else needs access to, the user attempts to share the database across the network. Users will place the database in a shared directory and make it accessible over the network, or they'll make copies and email them to other users. Pretty soon several copies of the database are floating around, none of which are synchronized or being used for the same purpose. Data becomes outdated, new objects are created willy-nilly, and before long users are blaming the IT staff (who else?).

IT staffers need to ensure that everyone in the organization uses proper database development and distribution techniques. These techniques are outlined in the following steps:

Step 1—Review The Structure Of The Database

Larger databases commonly consist of an application front end (using Access, for instance) and a robust back end (such as Microsoft's SQL server). Smaller database solutions may use only Access, especially stand-alone applications. Chapter 5 covers restrictions on size and concurrent users for Access-only databases.

Step 2—Optimize The Database

Most databases contain optimization tools that'll make suggestions for changing the structure of an application to improve query speed, such as creating indexes, breaking larger tables into several smaller ones, normalizing data, and so forth. Most of the suggestions should be followed, unless you know there's a good reason to choose a particular structure.

In addition, you may need to separate the database into data tables to be stored on a server (or servers) and application objects such as queries, forms, and reports. Application objects can be copied and distributed to multiple users while data remains limited to a central server, and if several servers are required, replication and synchronization can be used to maintain data consistency.

Step 3—Separate The Database Into Production And Staging Versions

Two copies of the database will likely be required, one for use in production and one for further development and maintenance (staging). The production version will probably have a limited but well-tested set of data tables and application objects, as well as fully assigned users, groups, and permissions. The staging version will contain sample data representative of production data and will be accessible only to developers.

Most maintenance tasks will first be performed on the staging version, tested, and released only when warranted sound. Significant maintenance changes should always be incorporated into systems analysis and process engineering documents and reviewed by users. A schedule for routine maintenance is helpful, especially if it means taking the production version down for any length of time.

Step 4—Optimize The Production Version

The production version should be reoptimized before release followed by fully printed documentation corresponding to the current version number. This is especially important with smaller databases serving only a few people. The data in these smaller applications can end up being critical to the organization for unforeseen reasons, and if no documentation is available, it can be very difficult to decipher the true meaning of the application's contents.

Step 5—Assign Permissions To Application Objects And Data

Production applications, as we alluded to earlier, should have users, groups, and permissions assigned to their objects to ensure access is only allowed where appropriate. Although routine administration of the application may rest with another party after your development effort is complete, you need to build an initial set of users, groups, and permissions to get the ball rolling. By the way, also print this list for subsequent administrators and make it part of the documentation package.

Step 6—Distribute And Maintain The Production Version

Your last task is to distribute the data tables and application objects to currently defined users, notify them that the functions are available, and establish a feedback mechanism so errors, deficiencies, and suggestions for improvement can be collected. In later chapters we'll discuss how to set up training programs so people will actually use the applications as intended.

Publishing Databases On The Intranet/Extranet/Internet

Everyone wants to be a Webmaster, right? Actually, it's often a no-win situation because the Webmaster has final responsibility for everyone's content but has little control over what tools people use, the level of sensitivity of the information, or capabilities built into the Web server.

Connecting a database to a Web site is a common request because people get tired of updating static content rather quickly. They soon come to realize that building and maintaining a database and offering limited access to it is a much easier way of distributing the right information to the right people with a minimum of hassle. And they'll look to the Webmaster to provide the expertise not only in designing and maintaining the Web site but in creating the connection to the database. A clear understanding of database publishing on the Web is, of course, a prerequisite.

Step 1—Ensure The Database Meets Company Standards

Before starting the process of connecting a database to the Web, examine the database design and ensure the portions to be connected to the Web are the minimum required to provide the functionality needed. Make sure no critical or sensitive information is contained within the database unless it must be, and keep the tables as small as possible. Employ an archiving system to remove input data from the database on a regular basis, the more frequently the better. Optimize the database for data delivery across the internal or external networks.

Step 2—Classify The Data In The Database

Some of the data will probably be sensitive to a degree, and certainly there should be restrictions placed on users, maybe to several levels. Classify the data according to sensitivity and usage requirements, and create a system of users and groups to control access to each area or type of information in the database. Make sure the data proposed for posting or access follows company guidelines.

Step 3—Document Responsibility For Database Maintenance

Typical Web-based databases contain content provided by both the Webmaster and individual departments across the company. Usually the Webmaster has a standard template for company content, especially content provided to customers and other outsiders. This content may include company logos, menus, and navigation graphics, as well as layout and color schemes. Individual departments must conform to the standard template, even within the confines of result sets produced by the database. The Webmaster may be called upon to modify output pages of the database to remain compliant with company templates.

Individual departments within the company will frequently update the database from their own workstations, but the first person to be called when inaccurate data is displayed is the Webmaster, so it's crucial to document who is responsible for content in each individual area within the organization. Each department should assign a person (and probably an alternate) to manage the content it's responsible for. This person should be familiar with all aspects of the department's content, including how it's created, managed, posted, and removed, and this person should understand the workings of the Web, the database application, and the connections between the two.

Step 4—Arrange For Web Space, Security, And Web Server Maintenance

The system administrator for the network will likely have control of storage space, servers, and communications links inside and outside the company, as well as deployed operating systems and network security. The Webmaster must make arrangements with the system administrator for Webspace supported by adequate servers and communications links to provide access as desired by internal and external customers.

The Webmaster should also develop a structure and usage parameters for the proposed content, including directories, content types, restricted access areas, sensitivity rating, and expected traffic. Delivered to the system administrator, these specifications provide the information necessary to properly set up and maintain the space. For a database-connected application, database drivers, scripts, users, groups, and other constructs will have to be created by the system administrator's staff.

Step 5—Create The Web Interface

Once the Web site content and the database have been created, an interface between the two must be built. Depending upon the process supported, various capabilities must be incorporated into the interface, usually as HTML query forms and HTML-related template output files. The original systems analysis and process engineering should serve as a guide to the kinds of access required.

Step 6—Install And Test The Database, Then Deploy

After building all the components, install them on the Web server in an unused directory and test the interface and database live on a small scale. Ask users to try to find what they're looking for, and debug the application as problems, errors, and deficiencies crop up. Make sure to ask users who are totally unfamiliar with the database and Web site (but not necessarily the content or purpose for providing it) to see if they can find their way around and accomplish the tasks supported by the application. After initial testing and debugging reveals and

6. Advanced Database Systems

removes the obvious difficulties, deploy the Web site content and database as planned.

Step 7—Monitor Usage Of The Web Site

Every time someone accesses a particular page on your Web site your system can record that access. If you use cookies (short strings of data deposited on users' computers to track them as they access your site) you can build user profiles that tell you plenty about what they like or dislike about your site. The system administrator should have all the necessary tools available for monitoring accesses to the Web site. These tools can tell you much about accesses, for instance:

• Who is accessing the site and what pages they're accessing

• When they're accessing the site and what links they're clicking on

• How long they stay with a particular page

• What information they've requested

• What amounts of bandwidth are being used

Monitoring usage of the Web site goes hand-in-hand with modifying the Web site to make it more user-friendly, more accessible, and easier to navigate, as well as providing insight into whether the Web site is accomplishing its objectives.

Creating A High-Volume, Multimedia Delivery System

Video and related multimedia files, ranging from home delivery of movies to delivery of training materials inside a corporation, can be delivered through many different applications. In this section we'll explore the development of a video-on-demand system that supplies full-length motion pictures to consumers with a small delay. Generally speaking, network architecture, storage systems, video database, and delivery techniques all play a part in the development of any video or multimedia delivery system.

Step 1—Determine The Characteristics Of The Delivered Material

In this case, the primary material to be delivered is compressed video, but certainly other data will be traversing the network in support of delivery. Customer information, requests, and shopping data may all be transmitted, as well as realtime commands from game players (for interactive movies).

Regarding the compressed video, before encoding video studios, evaluate video sources to determine quality levels. VHS tapes are at the low end of the spectrum and probably won't satisfy their customers' requirements, while digital videotape formats may serve quite well. Content also makes a difference. Because video compression is sensitive to high-motion content, action sequences benefit from the use of better codecs. Therefore, full-length movies will tend to use more recent codecs such as MPEG-2 and the soon-to-be-released MPEG-4. The transport stream defined for MPEG-2 specifies fixed length packets of 188 bytes for transmission on digital networks.

Step 2—Evaluate The Characteristics Of The Delivery Network

Assuming delivery is to be via the Internet, you can rest assured that the majority of potential customers won't have the bandwidth required to create video of acceptable quality for at least a few more years. However, as the number of users with cable modem or DSL access increases, selected applications may be viable in selected niche markets. Categorize your potential user base by type of access and compare their demographics with the movies you intend to offer. You should be able to arrive at some conclusion about which movies to offer based on the markets that can receive them.

Step 3—Adapt Delivered Video Formats To The Delivery Network

Another method for increasing the availability of your product to the general public is to modify the source data to fit other formats. For instance, you can further compress MPEG data to stream through lower bandwidth access devices using proprietary compression techniques and tools. The caveat here is that quality is reduced accordingly, and customers may not be willing to pay much for a product of lower quality.

Step 4—Test, Debug, And Improve All Aspects Of Delivery

Your video database is the primary tool you'll use for storing and managing the content you deliver. To use a video rental store metaphor, it'll be your store—clerks, search mechanism, and sales functions all rolled into one. You might even use it to decide on the fly which compression and delivery technique to use. Before deploying it, test it extensively to make sure it performs flawlessly.

6. Advanced Database Systems

Part III

Modern Database Implementation

Chapter 7

Data Warehousing

In Depth

This chapter covers the construction of data warehouses, the term used for the organization, processing, and distribution of data from operational sources. As we discussed in previous chapters, data is all around us and much of the data we collect may be useful for other than the immediate requirements of the processes it supports. Getting some use out of the massive volumes of data available is quite a feat, however, because unique problems are involved. Storage and distribution technologies, as well as database architecture, processing, and summarization issues are all significant factors in data warehouse design.

The term warehouse evokes images of large buildings designed to hold vast quantities of goods in storage. Materials stored in warehouses are brought in, stored, and moved out. The bulk of the work involved in processing materials through a warehouse mainly concerns movement and tracking, not adding value (in fact, warehouses add cost to products or to materials).

Data warehouses are much different and might best be described by the term *data repository*. Data accumulates in the data warehouse and is gradually processed into cleaner, clearer, more summarized versions (adding value along the way). The data warehouse is meant to support primarily strategic requirements rather than the day-to-day operational needs of an organization.

One of the best reasons to build a data warehouse is to keep data consistent across the organization. For example, today's sales figures for a retail organization can be defined in many ways, depending on who is accumulating the numbers and what is being considered. The sales clerk in the store might offer one figure, but an accountant might give an entirely different number based on corrections, returns, discounts, and other adjustments. Because so many parts of an organization tend to accumulate and use data for their own reasons, the value of having a central source that imports, transforms, cleans, consolidates, and integrates operational data into a consistent, rationally-organized repository available across the organization is immediately evident.

Another benefit of using a data-warehouse approach is establishing a universal interface for retrieving and processing data. As many companies and organizations adopt Web-based interfaces and systems for the distribution of data, the ease with which key people can use (or post their own) data climbs, and learning curves fall. Although Microsoft Access is not the database tool to use for the back

7. Data Warehousing

end of a data warehouse, its simple yet powerful interface, Web-integration features, and ubiquity on the desktop make it the ideal candidate for use on the front end.

Creating an effective data warehouse means building an environment that's consistent, easy to use, and formidable. The elements of an effective environment are described in this chapter, and we provide a foundation for their application in our examples.

Building A Data Warehouse (Macro Level)

Data warehouses are currently a hot topic in database circles because they're conceptually pure and elegant. They call for the creation of a centralized, integrated, sanitized source of data that's easy to understand and easy to navigate. Unfortunately, hiding all the complexity behind such a magical interface is a monstrous task, and many complete books have been written covering just this one subject. We won't be able to cover every detailed aspect of such an important topic, but we'll give you enough information in this chapter and in the next to make informed decisions when dealing with vendors or the management of your organization.

In previous chapters, we discussed data and data gathering, explaining that data is gathered by organizations in many ways, for many reasons, not all of which are connected, understood, or supportive of the organization's core processes. A thorough systems analysis should have built a complete picture of all existing data, and the proposal process should have generated a list of all data elements required to support proposed processes. Therefore, you should be in a position to define how data will flow into your data warehouse environment (assuming that you intend to create and use one).

Should you build a data warehouse? Without addressing the cost or technologies you might use (which are dependent upon the risks and potential return on investment, as always) the answer is an unqualified yes. Even for very insignificant information production systems, using data warehouse concepts makes sense.

Remember, a data warehouse is not a specific piece of software or hardware; it's actually a way of organizing data for a particular use. As we mentioned in earlier chapters, change is constant, and organizations that can make strategic use of data to gain a competitive advantage have a better chance of surviving than those that don't. A data warehouse makes it possible to capture and analyze data from disparate sources, revealing trends that otherwise would have been lost in the cacophony of information that floods our senses every day.

And keep in mind that data accumulated in a data warehouse is informational data, not operational data. The distinction here is that a given item of data (perhaps a record of the pay received by an employee on a certain payday) may be useful operationally but not for planning purposes. For instance, the employee may complain that her paycheck was shorted, and reviewing the individual record can (or should) verify the amount paid. But to plan the budget for payroll next quarter, it might be more helpful to query the accumulated records in the data warehouse to find out the percentage by which payroll deviated from the yearly average last year (assuming conditions are similar this year).

The Data Warehouse Paradigm

As Alex Berson and Stephen J. Smith note in *Data Warehousing, Data Mining, and OLAP*, published by McGraw-Hill in 1997 (ISBN 0-07-006272-2), a paradigm shift is underway in the computing and information systems world. Rather than relying on a single computer, master-slave or host-based system, or an ordinary relational database, users today know that data may reside in many locations and must be accessible as transparently as possible.

This paradigm shift is evidenced by the emergence of object request brokers (ORB), middleware, manipulation of more complex data types, and the installation of highly parallel computing systems for processing very large databases (VLDB). Object request brokers are an evolutionary development arising from the general shift towards reusable, object-oriented program designs. Middleware refers to software that mediates requests from a variety of clients to a variety of servers. Highly parallel computing systems were discussed in Chapter 2, and obviously are often required when processing exceptionally large databases.

The creation of a data warehouse hinges upon your ability to convert operational data stores, wherever and whatever they might be, into informational data. The differences between the two can be summarized as shown in Table 7.1.

As you can imagine, large organizations today (and any organization dealing with data from many sources) find their data in many formats, in many places, sometimes pristine and sometimes full of errors and inconsistencies. Operational data is replaced with new data every time a transaction is performed, and transactions

7. Data Warehousing

Table 7.1   Operational and informational data differences.

Operational Data	Informational Data
Sourced from data entry	Sourced from operational data stores
Organized by application	Organized by subject
Constantly updated	Updated less frequently
Constantly accessed	Access varies
Usage is predictable	Usage varies

commonly occur throughout the day. Depending on the age and size of the organization a lot of data sources and archives could exist, each with its own (sometimes proprietary) format and structure. And because much of the data is entered manually, its validity is suspect.

These problems will only get worse. Companies are now accumulating, storing, and selling information in massive quantities. Organizations that once faced the prospect of integrating their own internal data sources must now contend with integrating data from across the Web, from customers and suppliers, and from government agencies.

These are the primary goals served by creation of a data warehouse:

- Pull data together from disparate sources.
- Translate it into compatible formats.
- Weed out duplicate or erroneous data.
- Summarize and consolidate data.
- Make data available in a structure that serves the analytical needs of management (informational data).

Characteristics Of A Data Warehouse

Data warehouse technology can be purchased from many vendors, and each vendor has its own idea of the necessary attributes of a data warehouse. Some common themes run throughout, however. Typically, data warehouses contain the following:

- A relational database management system (RDBMS) optimized for analysis by a few users, rather than rapid updates by many users, capable of containing very large amounts of data.
- One or a few large tables that are updated periodically (once per day) rather than frequently each day.
- Tools to extract and clean up data from virtually any kind of format.
- A metadata catalog to make navigation of the data easy.

The RDBMS

The RDBMS is often specially designed to take advantage of parallel computing architectures such as symmetric multiprocessors (SMP), massively parallel processors (MPP), and clustered processors. In addition, it may support special indexing structures and multidimensional databases.

Data Transformation

Operational data from many sources feeds the very large tables in a data warehouse, and this data is reformatted, sanitized, filtered, and summarized into one or several common formats. Names and relationships of data are standardized, excess data is removed, summaries or derived values are calculated, and missing data is supplied automatically when possible. Any inconsistencies (such as different units of measure or different methods for representing the same facts) are ironed out.

Metadata

Metadata is like a book's table of contents. It's not the information itself, but it tells you about the information and guides you to it effectively. Metadata in a data warehouse is also like the page containing copyright information. It gives you technical information about the information in the book.

Data warehouses contain a metadata catalog that describes where the data comes from and how it's transformed, what it means, its history, and other items useful to the warehouse designers. It also contains navigation, format, and validity information for users. The metadata catalog, as the primary means by which users interact with the overall warehouse, should support easy manual and programmed access to the data.

Building And Using A Data Warehouse

Assembling the components of a data warehouse is as much a matter of identifying existing (legacy) systems, tools, and data as it is buying new hardware or software. Usually legacy systems support a fairly well-defined set of processes, and the processes your solution supports should be clearly noted by now. Comparing legacy systems and data to the requirements of proposed solutions should provide clues about additional hardware and software needed. However, keep in mind that the growth of a data warehouse is quite complex and calls for the implementation of a data warehousing strategy, not just a "buy it and install it" mentality.

One way data warehouses can evolve is from *data marts*, which are like little data warehouses designed to support the needs of only one department or division (usually supporting one core process). Although everyone would ideally use the same data warehouse throughout the organization because many organizations already have what amount to data marts in place, often a more viable strategy is to merge these individual marts together over a period of time. It's harder but usually works better than throwing everything out and starting from scratch.

Data Marts

The data mart concept, as we've alluded to, is a mini data warehouse environment employed by a single user. Of course, we're not referring to just one person but, instead, to one or more people using a particular set (or sets) of data for one subject area. Data marts are sometimes precursors of data warehouses, and integrating them into a data warehouse environment after they've been incorporated into the workings of the organization can be quite challenging.

Data marts follow the same construction processes as data warehouses: data acquisition, transmission, reformatting, storage, and reporting. By their nature they fall into two categories—dependent and independent. Independent data marts stand alone; dependent data marts depend on the data warehouse to process and segregate data for them. Independent data marts are useful in and of themselves but fail to take advantage of the key benefit of data warehouses, namely the consistency of data created by data integration within the data warehouse. Basically, if you already have data marts, you should most likely integrate them with your data warehousing strategy. When you've no data marts, build the data warehouse first, then build dependent data marts from the warehouse.

How do you know when you need to develop data marts? A good starting point for a data warehousing strategy is to determine the most urgent data requirements across your entire organization, then choose a data warehousing architecture, and build your first data mart using that architecture. Make sure the architecture is scalable, so you can add additional marts later within the framework of the warehouse. You can achieve results more quickly this way, on a smaller budget, with the support of only the department that urgently needs the mart, and the project will be easier to understand and complete because it's somewhat smaller and less all-encompassing. However, you'll still have the foundation laid for a full-blown data warehouse as you proceed, an important part of which is the data acquisition storehouse.

Data Acquisition Storehouses

Data acquisition is different from most other types of data collection. Consider a situation in which a research group is conducting experiments to collect data. In this case, the experiments focus on changes in airflow and performance characteristics relative to changes in the design of an airfoil. The research group might design a scale model, mount it inside a wind tunnel, and attach sensors that detect drag and other variables while the wind tunnel is in operation.

Data acquisition hardware will capture analog signals emanating from sensors on the model and in the mounting hardware, convert the analog signals to digital data, and transmit the data to a specially designed PC for storage. Part of the data stored (time and date) will be generated by the PC.

This type of data usually amounts to raw, numerical values that only have meaning in the context of the program that interprets them, and the amount of data can be massive. Building a storehouse to accumulate this type of data is fundamentally different from the requirements of archives for text data (such as employee payroll records and sales data). In fact, any type of data that doesn't fall into the category of American Standard Code for Information Interchange (ASCII) characters can present difficulties for storage and retrieval systems.

Because so much data comes from so many unusual sources today (audio, video, raw numerical data, formatted file types, spatial data, and so on) vendors are building special tools to manipulate this type of data (frequently called Binary Large OBjects, or BLOBs). The best of these tools has the ability to define metadata about these objects in standard terms, so key aspects of these objects are easily searchable. The new tools also have the capability to search and manipulate the raw data within these objects as is. In essence, these tools understand the data inside a BLOB as though they were native acquisition or manipulation programs. Storing and accessing all data types so they can be easily be retrieved makes the job of generating information from these data sources simpler for today's information generation tools.

Information Generation Tools

Getting data out of a data warehouse involves the IT department, managers, and users. The IT department will need to develop complex queries and reports because no one else has the required expertise, and they'll also be called upon to advise and educate users and managers about the capabilities of the warehouse architecture and the context (meaning) of the data inside. Managers will need to understand the data, how to extrapolate from its operational sources, and how it's used for planning and strategic purposes. Users will need to understand how the data supports their processes and conscientiously incorporate usage of it into their routine decision making. Both managers and users will need to learn enough about the warehouse and the tools it offers to program many of their own query and reporting mechanisms because IT can't be expected to (nor should it) program every ad hoc query that pops up.

Naturally, developers have created many tools to assist in the process of finding, retrieving, processing, and reporting data residing in the warehouse. Some of these tools are dedicated applications, while others are completely programmable tools, and still others fall somewhere in between. The benefit of using a program such as Microsoft Access is that most people are already somewhat familiar with it (and the interface of Windows-based programs in general).

Even so, Access also has many powerful capabilities for advanced users, including complete programmability and easy integration with other applications. One big advantage is that most knowledge workers can (and should) be trained to build their own applications, thereby leveraging the IT staff, lessening the cost of development, and further educating the knowledge worker base. Of course, you might argue that it doesn't make sense to have an expensive executive developing her own solutions, but this argument simply doesn't hold water anymore. It's like arguing that a theoretical scientist shouldn't perform mathematical calculations when a grad student could do them for much less money. Understanding the data, where it comes from, how it's derived, what it means, and how to operate the tools that produce it is such an integral part of the job that no executive can afford to "delegate" that part to a subordinate.

When the standard set of query and reporting tools in an application such as Access is insufficient (because of the complexity of the queries or special programming required), custom programs can be written to gather and format particular sets of data. This is more costly and usually falls on the relatively limited resources of the IT department. It's costly in another way as well, in that custom-programmed applications may have a very limited life, don't translate easily for other uses, require collaboration between the user and the IT staff member(s), and may take longer to build than the specific requirement for data lasts. Nevertheless, application programming tools (such as Visual Basic) are frequently very useful and will remain a part of the arsenal of tools available for digging data out of the warehouse.

Finding Valuable Information

Operational data has intrinsic value. The amount a customer paid during the last billing cycle is intrinsically valuable because it answers an immediate, specific, and unidimensional question. Informational data, on the other hand, is valuable because it establishes relations between data values. The individual values themselves have no intrinsic informational value, but together they can answer some very interesting questions, such as what percentage of customers are overdue this month versus the percentage overdue last month. Even more exciting, it can sometimes indicate to us what percentage might be overdue next month.

To relate data values to one another, statistical algorithms examine data sets and attempt to find correlations between two or more sets of values. Basically, the algorithms are looking for patterns. Although this can be done by people (and often is), human beings find it boring to sift through mounds of values, and they frequently make mistakes. People are notorious for arriving at inaccurate conclusions from a given set of data, and humans also aren't very good at examining data with a large number of related dimensions.

Patterns are regularities in data, nothing more. Random data is devoid of patterns (although they can occur by chance in random data), but patterns reoccur on a regular basis. Patterns form the basis for models because when data is missing the pattern can be used to fill in, whether the missing data occurs in sequences that have already occurred or in sequences that will occur in the future.

Models based on patterns sometimes lead to the development of laws, rules of thumb, and so forth. For instance, scientists noting the change in pressure and temperature in a sealed vessel in relation to changes in volume would first record the changes as data, then attempt to determine the correlation between the two. Upon clear evidence that the value of pressure is inversely proportional to the value of volume, they might conclude that a physical law is at work. The data might not show an exact correlation, but because it's likely measurement errors and not fundamental properties of the universe, their theory would probably assume exact values for an imaginary "perfect" case. And when a marketing manager notes that "for every 1,000 direct mail pieces we send out we get a 2 percent response rate," again the data might not show this exactly, but it makes a very good rule of thumb.

Machines don't do all pattern detection, however. To make patterns easier for people to detect, we commonly express data visually as charts, graphs, pictures, and so forth. Depending upon the type of data we're searching, we can also use our other senses by turning data into sound, vibrations, and other sensory input. Because our brains are hard-wired for pattern detection across many of our senses, taking advantage of all our senses is smart and efficient.

Finding valuable data is, therefore, a matter of finding patterns in the data and constructing a logical predictive model from the patterns. Then, as new data pours in, it can be examined with an eye toward producing a strategy based upon the model. Of course, we'd like to make our models much more sophisticated than our direct mail example above, so we employ computers and complex algorithms to find patterns and construct models from the billions of records and data values in our warehouse. Constructing models from patterns can be done using expert systems, although, in general, expert systems are built by human beings, based on their years of experience, rather than patterns ferreted out of data via pattern-detection algorithms.

Expert Systems

There was a time when I was an aircraft mechanic (a jet-engine mechanic to be precise). Part of my duties included troubleshooting engine problems, and I followed a precise set of guidelines that, step by step, eliminated potential causes of the problem until only one was left, which usually turned out to be the culprit. Occasionally, I used my experience to tell me when to deviate from prescribed procedures.

If I were programming an expert system, I would formulate these rules into decision points managed by an *inference engine*, the logical heart of an expert system. At each step in a process, users can feed in inputs that the inference engine evaluates to derive the next step. Step by step a path is followed that, when the

7. Data Warehousing

inputs are valid and the expert logic is sound, will result in the correct solution of a problem. Rules in an expert system are similar to programming constructs, creating an if/then loop. The inputs are called *antecedents,* and the results are called *consequents.* Expert systems can proceed forward from problem to solution, or they can proceed backward from hypothesis (scenario) to required starting conditions.

Although expert systems were hailed as a way to capture and formalize the vast amounts of knowledge that exist only in the minds of experts, drawbacks apply. For one, they take a major effort to program, and shouldn't be considered a trivial undertaking. Also, even the experts frequently don't understand why things work the way they do, they just know how. Not knowing why means any fundamental change (whether detectable or not) may alter and render the system invalid. Finally, expert systems tend to make decisions in an "all-or-nothing" style. When a part is bad intermittently, or its output is low but still within limits, the expert system may not take this into account. Fuzzy logic was developed to account for just these kinds of situations.

Fuzzy Logic

Fuzzy logic is one of the terms that entered the common vocabulary with a meaning different than what was intended. People often use it to refer to thinking that's not quite straight, but, in fact, it's an attempt to provide computers with the ability to approximate in a somewhat human fashion.

People frequently think in terms of degree. For instance, the weather is cold or hot (or really cold and burning hot), clothes are clean or dirty (or perhaps filthy dirty), salaries are high or low (or perhaps extremely high), and so on. Rather than fixed values, we're usually thinking in ranges, and these ranges are often compared to other ranges (see Figure 7.1). For instance, we might think a ball player's salary is extremely high when we make minimum wage, but we might think it's reasonable when we make millions per year ourselves.

Computers can simulate this kind of thinking with fuzzy logic because, instead of using hard and fast values to make decisions, a computer programmed to use fuzzy logic uses a range of values from 0.0 to 1.0. Values towards the center of a range tend to be closer to 1.0 for that range, and values at the extremes of a range tend to be closer to 0.5 for that range and 0.5 for the range they're close to becoming a part of. For instance, when we make minimum wage and we're using that range to determine the appropriateness of someone else's salary, we might feel that salaries within 500 percent of our own are reasonable, salaries between 500 percent and 5000 percent higher are high, and salaries above 5000 percent higher are extremely high. A lawyer's salary of 4900 percent higher than our own would have a value of approximately 0.55 for the high range and approximately 0.45 for the extremely high range, meaning it's "pretty darn high."

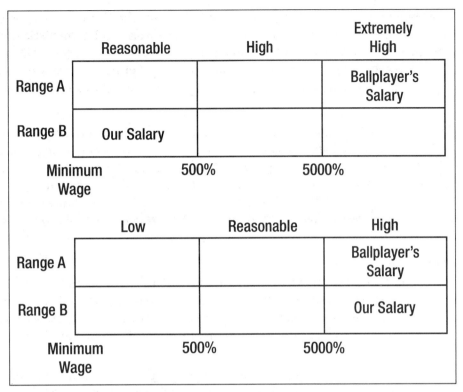

Figure 7.1   Fuzzy logic value ranges.

Now, what can be done knowing that a value is "pretty darn high"? In practice fuzzy logic systems resemble expert systems, because they both use rules and an inference engine to process inputs and arrive at conclusions. The difference is fuzzy logic systems are better at coping with imprecise data and can provide answers that are easier for humans to understand. Fuzzy logic systems are also easier to build because they can use imprecise terms or general ranges rather than exact yes/no values. In any case, pattern matching, model making, expert systems, and fuzzy logic are all techniques useful in the quest to mine data from the data warehouse.

Data Mining

Like so many terms in the IT world, data mining is overused and overhyped, so much so that it's easy to forget the real significance of the concept. What we're really talking about is getting the most out of the trillions of bits of data that flow into organizations every day. The data tells us a great deal about the actual state of the world today, almost as if on a small scale we could imitate God and actually know what is happening everywhere, all the time. The patterns within it give us valuable clues to what is going to happen next when our models are clever enough. Of course, there's a great debate over whether the world is deterministic or not (and, therefore, whether we could model the future even with perfect data), but these philosophical questions are the subject of another book. Here, we're concerned with mining valuable data (see Figure 7.2) and using that data to predict the future.

The essence of data mining, as opposed to other esoteric technologies for deducing knowledge from data introduced over the years, is that data mining is meant to be done by the user or manager, not statisticians, programmers, or analytical geniuses. Users should be able to browse data easily and visually in many ways, finding unusual relationships, comparing facts along common dimensions, and conveying their results quickly to other users. One very useful tool is online analytical processing.

OLAP

The popular term for knowledge generation via data warehouses is online analytical processing (OLAP), which refers to one of the tools used to perform data mining (as well as more common types of data retrieval and reporting). OLAP tools utilize a multidimensional data model following 12 guidelines formulated by Dr. Edgar F. Codd:

1. Multidimensional conceptual view. The data is portrayed in an inherently multidimensional way so users can easily navigate the various dimensions and hierarchies present in the data.

2. Transparency. The tool presents the user with a consistent and similarly formatted view of data no matter what its original format or source.

3. Accessibility. The tool retrieves only the data required for the current analysis, but can retrieve data from any and all available sources.

4. Consistent reporting performance. All queries and reports are retrieved in essentially at the same time, as far as the user is concerned (this one is very tough).

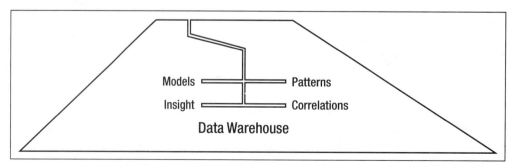

Figure 7.2   Mining data.

5. Client-server architecture. The system utilizes the standard client-server architecture, making it possible to integrate within standard networks and database solution architectures.

6. Generic dimensionality. The dimensions used share the same structure and capabilities.

7. Dynamic sparse matrix handling. Because some data matrices contain low levels of data (compared to null values) the system must actively modify its physical storage models for optimum retrieval times.

8. Multiuser support. The system must support multiple, concurrent users.

9. Unrestricted cross-dimensional operations. The system must be able to roll up or summarize data across any dimensions present.

10. Intuitive data manipulation. All data manipulations should be possible via the graphic user interface (GUI), rather than requiring the user to enter structured query language (SQL).

11. Flexible reporting. The system must allow the user to arrange data (cells, columns, rows, and so on) via the GUI.

12. Unlimited dimensions/aggregation levels. The system must not be restricted in the number of dimensions or aggregation levels (up to resources available in the hardware).

Dr. Codd's guidelines were later expanded to 18, and he received criticism because these rules seemed to favor the products of the vendor that sponsored his work in this area. Other vendors subsequently proposed their own sets of rules, each focusing on aspects of their own products. Another definition that has proved useful and seems to be independent of the vendor is fast analysis of shared multidimensional information (FASMI). It's more concise but generic and delivers the basic ideas quite well:

- The system should be fast, providing responses in one to five seconds. This implies very fast, probably parallel, processors, as well as speedy storage and transmission hardware.

- The system should support all data analysis and modeling methods and do so in an intuitive and user-friendly way.

- The system should support data sharing for multiple users, performing multiple functions with all the permissions, locking, and security features necessary to conduct business or communicate data.

- The system should offer a multidimensional data structure, showing all the ways data can be related.

- The system should provide enough data, from wherever it's located, to support the production of information (and, thereby, knowledge). In particular,

7. Data Warehousing

the system should be capable of retrieving very large amounts of data and processing it automatically when necessary.

In any case, many tools on the market can help you get massive amounts of data into users' hands and help them manipulate it efficiently. One formal way users can put data to work supporting processes is called the decision support system.

Decision Support Systems

One technology at the heart of Knowledge Design (KD) is the decision support system (DSS). As its name implies, a decision support system attempts to provide the data required to support decisions. As such, it must supply not only data about current or historical events, but also data about the context in which a decision must be made in the present. This implies that enough information is available to make a decision (or that the decision must be made now, regardless of the amount of data available), and also that it's reasonable to conclude that the decision indicated will accomplish the desired goal.

Over the years, businesses and other organizations have automated process after process. They started with the processes that lent themselves most easily to automation, such as payroll processing. Payroll processing follows a fairly well-defined set of rules, and the output is printed checks (or direct deposits more recently). One result of the automation of payroll processing is the accumulation of data (about pay amounts, personnel paid, and pay days) in flat-file or relational databases. Unfortunately, the data models and schemas used to process payroll (and other online transaction processing [OLTP] requirements) aren't necessarily handy for analysis in support of business decisions.

Decision Support (Star) Schemas

In contrast to simple, relational database schemas connecting relatively small tables via primary keys, decision support schemas often connect one or a few very large tables to many much smaller tables. Each of the smaller tables contains what are called dimensions, hence the name *multidimensional data model*. As we discussed in Chapter 2, for data values to have meaning, the units and dimensions of the data must be identified. In the case of decision support schemas, special types of relational database schemas called *star* and *snowflake* are used (see Figure 7.3).

In a star schema, data is broken into two categories: facts and dimensions. These are similar to entities and attributes. For example, the Northwest Sales Office may be one of the entities tracked in your operational information system. The dollar value of sales for Product A in Quarter 2 is a fact, and the Northwest Sales Office is a dimension of this fact (as are Product A and Quarter 2).

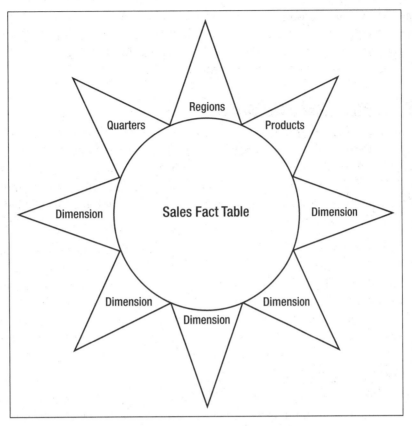

Figure 7.3   The star schema.

The name star schema comes from the arrangement of many dimension tables around the very large fact table. The snowflake schema is an extension of the star schema. Not only do fact tables contain raw, numerical data values, they also contain presummarized data for each dimension to alleviate the need to summarize massive amounts of data each time a new query is initiated. There is, however, a point at which presummarization causes storage and retrieval problems, because of the nature of the calculations.

Consider a large fact table and several dimension tables. When each fact in the fact table is to be cross-referenced with each dimension in the dimension tables, the result set grows exponentially with each new dimension added. Also, because there may be no data in many of the result set fields, the result set tends to be full of empty data values. Application vendors design innovative indexing and join strategies to alleviate performance problems related to retrieving data. When, however, you're dealing with only a subset of all facts and dimensions available (rather than everything possible), you can reduce the size of presummarized data sets and, thereby, minimize retrieval times. This minimization of data sources is central to the development of intelligent databases because intelligent actions (by your solution) depend on the creation of knowledge, which in turn frequently depends on easily assimilable data sources.

Intelligent Databases

Going one step further than decision support systems, intelligent databases combine the attributes of a successful process into a completely automated system that actually thinks in place of people (albeit in a rather crude and limited way). As we've discussed previously, it takes data to build information, and it takes information to provide knowledge. Intelligence lies in mixing knowledge with the power to effect actions.

For example, data is collected via bar code readers in a supermarket. That data is processed into information about the amount of goods in stock on the shelves for each location. When this information is combined with previously accumulated information about sales rates for a given time of year, the knowledge that some items will (most likely) soon be out of stock can be generated. When that knowledge is combined with information about restocking delivery times and the capability to generate a restocking purchase order automatically, you have what can be termed an intelligent database.

Unlike expert systems that generate answers to specific questions under controlled conditions, intelligent databases can do more than make deductions, they can initiate actions. Computer controlled trading is another example of intelligent databases in action. Combining information about a holder's current portfolio, market conditions, and previous results allows the database application to "know" when to buy or sell (and which stocks, as well).

Intelligence comes from adding two things to a database: the capability to analyze data on the fly to detect unique conditions, and the capability to make a decision and accomplish an action based on that decision. Although adding intelligence can make for a very powerful system, the risks increase every time a new action capability is added.

The risks stem from the fact that computers take actions based on a limited set of facts not tempered by experience, common sense, or judgment. Computers and database systems have no innate ability to respond to unforeseen conditions with creative solutions and may not even recognize a new situation when it presents itself. For example, suppose you've programmed your database to buy more of a given product when stock levels fall below a certain level. You certainly don't want this to occur when the product is in the midst of a recall, yet there may be no easy way of building knowledge of that possibility into the program. In fact, recognizing any of hundreds of other possibilities that we take for granted as human beings is the forte of artificial intelligence, a collection of techniques useful for refining knowledge from the vast mounds of data accumulating on our data warehouses.

Artificial Intelligence

Because we're human, we tend to think in concepts via structures that are familiar to us. For example, when we want to communicate our ideas about a situation to someone else, we might draw a picture. When we use a computer, we're more comfortable with a computer that can draw us a picture as well (which is how we've ended up with the GUI). If computers were truly intelligent, we often muse, they would speak to us, draw for us, feel as we feel, and it would make communication between human and machine ever so much easier. Of course, we're conveniently forgetting how often it's difficult to communicate effectively with other people, precisely because they're human.

Nevertheless, one of the most important roles of artificial intelligence (AI) is to allow computers to understand our problems in human terms and to convey their understanding in ways we can easily relate to. Data visualization is the formal term for effective communication of data, information, or knowledge, and until speech recognition becomes commonplace, it's going to be the best we can do.

One of the data miner's most popular tools is the 3D immersive data browser. Actually, you can use Virtual Reality Modeling Language (VRML) and a Web interface to accomplish this kind of interactive data browsing environment. Using metaphors and icons for data, segments, trends, alerts, series, and so on, the 3D data surfer can quickly see trouble spots, opportunities, and anomalies. Combined with artificial intelligence techniques, data visualization represents a powerful tool for bringing relevant data quickly to the users who need it most while making sure they understand what has been provided and why they need it right now. These techniques are at the core of KD, but applying them requires more background on the nature of artificial intelligence.

The Nature Of Artificial Intelligence

In Chapter 6, we began a discussion of AI and neural networks, focusing on the way humans interpret meaning and arrive at conclusions in the real world, versus the way computers are constructed to calculate. Depending upon the applications you have in mind and the processes your solution must support, you may find it advantageous to include artificial intelligence via a neural network or some other mechanism.

Thinking Computers

Although research into the development of AI began as far back as the 1950s, and early successes with checkers and chess playing machines made its development seem straightforward, further developments came at a much higher price. Current research makes it clear that although building computing systems that excel at a particular function (even those that seem to be clearly the province of humans) is possible, building computer systems with a range of capabilities comparable to the average person (including basic common sense and creativity) isn't.

The difficulty lies in the fact that there are two requirements for common sense and creativity. One is the ability to discern the universe on human terms, and the other is a reason to care. Human beings are born with the ability (or acquire it rather quickly) to gather data and format it into useful constructs: memories, people, places, things, and so forth. Common sense is born of the millions of experiences and memories we accumulate, many of which we never consciously recall. Computers, on the other hand, must be constructed (in hardware and software) to perform a crude imitation of these functions, and building fuzzy logic routines to evaluate data in a "human" fashion is still a very young art.

In addition, humans feel pleasure and pain and come to understand at a very early age that actions often have unpredictable consequences. Knowing we can be hurt, or die, or bring pleasure to ourselves and others gives us a reason to care, to learn, and to develop creative solutions. Just having a body with immediate access to the functions it gives to us is an incredible driver toward "human" behavior. Computers, though, almost never achieve even the most rudimentary sense of the universe or their own place in it. Having no knowledge of their own mortality, no feeling of pain or pleasure, they have no incentive to formulate actions that accomplish goals. Essentially, they have no goals, they just operate as long as the power is on and a program is running.

The solution to developing computers that can think like humans is to play at being God. Build a 3D environment with artificial (or real) people in it, and build little software babies with all the most essential attributes of real people to populate it. Raise them as though they were human, and they'll gradually take on human characteristics. Eventually, the software "person" will mature (as you've programmed it to) and should be capable of making decisions with just as much creativity and common sense as any ordinary human being. The downside, of course, is precisely the same thing. People are often irrational, emotional, and illogical, and your "thinking" computer will have all the same flaws.

So the question of whether to include "thinking" systems in your own solution basically revolves around the effects you're trying to achieve. For now, when you want human thought, it's easier and more practical to use real people (that's what your staff is for). When you want to automate certain aspects of work that can be defined pretty tightly, there are many systems available that can work inside these parameters, even though they may not be very creative or demonstrate much common sense (decision trees and neural networks, for example). Decision trees (see Figure 7.4) follow a decision-making pattern much like humans use.

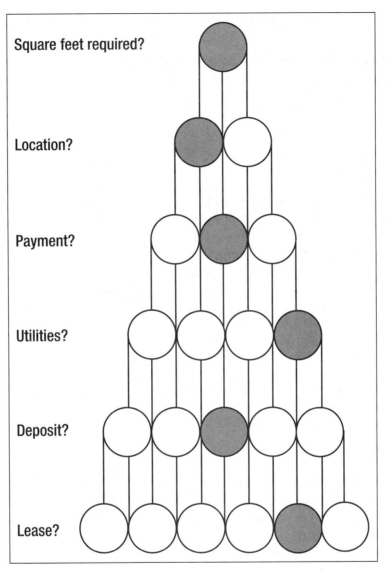

Figure 7.4   A decision tree.

Decision Trees

A decision tree is a straightforward method of building a predictive model based on logical premises about a business problem. It's valuable precisely because it's straightforward (unlike neural networks, which build their models automatically but in a complex and hard-to-understand way), and therefore inspires confidence. It's a lot like the process you go through when making a standard business decision, only the rules are formulated into a model that you can understand explicitly even though you use it as a programmed application. For example, you might think through the following scenario when deciding what office space to move into:

- How many square feet of space are required?
- What's the location?
- How much is the monthly payment?
- Will the owner pay utilities?
- How much is the deposit?
- How long is the lease?

Notice that some of the questions have yes or no answers, and others have several answers. As you ask each question, you refine and reduce the set of potential locations until you're left with only the locations that meet your needs. When a question has multiple answers (in this case, for instance, there might be several ranges of affordable leases, depending upon whether utilities are paid and so forth). It works the same way in a database. Perhaps you have several thousand employees in your organization, and they're paid increases based on performance as measured by 10 rating factors. You can use a decision tree to determine the amount of increase each employee deserves by sifting their performance ratings through a series of questions related to the ratings they received for each factor. You'll find that decision trees are very similar to neural networks but are much easier to explain to your users. That in itself is a significant point in favor of them.

Neural Networks

Neural networks are an increasingly popular technology employed to discern patterns from vast quantities of detail data. Although they run on everything from ordinary PCs to supercomputers, the structures they use to process information are modeled after the brain. Like ordinary modeling techniques, neural networks are used in situations where the requirement is to predict future results, rather than merely to uncover facts about the past. However, they're designed to build predictive models automatically, but the models aren't evident to the user, nor are they directly programmable by the user.

Neural networks are often run on single processor systems, but they're composed of many *linked nodes* that cooperatively solve problems and identify patterns in data. The nodes are comparable to the neurons in your brain, and the weight each applies to a particular set of data is dependent upon the rules the network has incorporated as its operational strategy. Neural networks learn by doing, meaning each time they perform a process, they can use feedback about their success or failure to modify the weights on each node (hopefully to increase the probability of success next time).

Data mining is an especially important application for neural networks because they can be "trained" to identify patterns in vast amounts of data that a human being would probably never see. Moreover, they can be set to examine quantities of data according to a schedule and can be made intelligent enough to alert managers and users whenever an interesting or alarming trend is developing. And best of all, they don't need to be explicitly programmed with every rule.

How Neural Networks Work

There is a significant amount of work involved in building neural networks, even though they often are prestructured for particular business problems. For example, you can buy neural networks formulated for grading insurance risks, credit, and so forth. Whether you buy one prestructured or you train it yourself, it will have the following components:

- A user interface and, perhaps, a programming language. You'll install it on your system, train it by exposing it to data, and perhaps set it to automatically interact with other programs on your system with the scripting language.

- Input nodes that are data entry areas for making predictions where the outcome isn't known.

- Output nodes that reflect the answer or prediction given a set of values at the input nodes.

- Hidden nodes that operate in a kind of "black box" way, affecting the outcomes but unseen by the user.

Before you can enter data into the input nodes, you must arrange the data into some kind of relative sequence: bad to good, high to low, and so forth. The data must be assigned a numerical value because the network makes calculations upon it with other numerical values. This means you'll have to find some way to take nonnumerical data and convert it to numbers of a specific kind (usually 0.0 to 1.0).

Your answers will arrive at the output nodes in numerical form, so to get the actual answer, you'll have to convert the answers from numbers to something understandable. For instance, when yes is equal to 1.0, an answer of .97 would indicate a yes answer, and you can set your application to produce that answer whenever the numerical value is above 0.50. You can even set it to produce a range of answers (such as "not only no, but hell no", "not likely", "probably", "very likely", and "yes indeedy").

To train your neural network yourself can be quite a tedious job. As you feed each training record in, the network will "make a guess" at the correct answer and you'll let it know when it's right or wrong, and by how much. The degree of error the network finds between its guess and the right answer directly affects the degree by which the network changes its model. Each time it receives another training record, it adjusts its model more and more closely to reality, thereby increasing the probability of successful predictions. Even though it automatically builds its own model internally, you still have to train it one record at a time.

Like any model, however, neural networks are only as good as the models inside them, and when some fundamental factor changes, they may make terrible predictions. For this reason, it's important to periodically feed in more real data, in effect retraining them.

Immediate Solutions

This section gives an example of the decision-making process as it occurs during the design of a data warehouse at the macro level and demonstrates the relationship of decision support systems to data warehouses. We build a data acquisition storehouse and a data mart, connect them together to form the basis for a data warehouse, and go on to describe the building of an intelligent database and deploying a neural network.

Building A Data Warehouse (Macro Level)

The first question to answer, if you're considering building a data warehouse, is whether or not to build one. Will the benefits outweigh the costs? What are the risks involved? How long will it take, and are there other areas where the company would benefit more from the expenditure of precious resources? These are business questions that can partially be answered by simply evaluating the costs, benefits, and risks, but determining whether or not to build a data warehouse has more fundamental implications.

The future of the entire organization is at stake. For years, businesses have stumbled along, automating parts of processes here and there, putting networks in place and connecting computers, and hoping to eventually get a bottom-line return for all their efforts. Yet analysts are still finding few hard productivity gains across industries, as a whole. At the same time, try to find anyone familiar with computers who would willingly go back to using manual methods. There must be something going on.

Essentially, building a data warehouse is about changing the culture of our organizations at their most basic levels. Instead of people collecting, transforming, manipulating, and reporting data independently, they learn to use sophisticated tools to pull it from a very clean, well-documented, and consistent source. Like iron ore that's mined, smelted, and processed into high-quality, high-strength steel, data becomes a very strong and pure raw material for the construction of high-quality decisions across the organization. The benefits are hard to measure, but they're there nonetheless, and they're very real. You simply won't want to go back.

Step 1—Establish Your Stategy

During systems analysis and process engineering, all available data was documented. You should also have mapped data collection, formats, and transmission methods, as well as any compression and encryption, when you automated the importation of data as discussed in Chapter 6. Now your job is to evaluate all sources of data heading toward the repository and to decide whether you can populate the repository directly from this data or whether you need to build another system from the top down. The key question is, are existing data flows fairly compatible or mostly incompatible?

When data marts have already been developed, the data reaching the intermediate stages may be formatted for wholly different uses in totally incompatible formats and structures. Sometimes these are proprietary and simply don't lend themselves to integration. In addition, there may be vested interests that fight to keep data in formats they're used to. More than just a business decision, how to develop your warehouse (and the formats to use) can easily become a political decision. But whatever you do, however you approach it, you must always focus on the fact that the final format and structure of the data warehouse has two opposing goals: It must collect all data into consistent and equivalent units and dimensions, and it must serve the complete requirements of everyone (now and in the future) who needs to use it.

Step 2—Select The Design

Rather than a finished product, a data warehouse is the epitome of constant improvement. The design of a data warehouse should reflect a continuous dialog between IT, managers, and users about what drives the business, what processes the organization values and strives to achieve, and what the organization's customers want. The data warehouse needs to accommodate massive quantities of data from many sources (some of which aren't even used yet). It needs to be easy to understand and easy to navigate, yet contain the most powerful and sophisticated tools for retrieving and processing data that's available. It should be easily scalable, able to take advantage of the best processing technologies, yet cost-effective and transparent to users. Although the components that go into your data warehouse may be complicated, custom-designed, and expensive, one salient point is clear today: Use a Web interface.

Using a Web interface is a no-brainer. Across the country, across the world, on the evening news, and in your local library, everyone is already being trained and getting used to the Web interface. From the CEO to the whiz kids coming out of high school to the new customer (Aunt Mary down on the farm), everyone understands how to point and click and fill in forms with a Web interface. There's really no data that can't be conveyed and displayed with a well-designed Web page, no matter how complex, interconnected, and customized the database applications are behind it.

So here again, you have two requirements at opposite ends of the spectrum. First, you have to select the most powerful tools to get the job done (and you have to foresee the future of these tools and formats while you're at it), and at the same time, you have to find and become great at using the most standard of interfaces, the Web.

Step 3—Determine Data Warehouse Contents

The contents of your data warehouse will be data that's consistent but not necessarily less detailed than the data sources it comes from. The data model (or models) you use will affect users' abilities to quickly retrieve and process the data they need, so you must carefully weigh indexing and modeling systems for performance. Vendors often use performance indicators that reflect the strengths of their own products (see Chapter 8 for a detailed discussion of popular products and performance). The best tactic is to ask vendors to suggest modeling and performance enhancement techniques using some of your own data, but this can be an expensive proposition depending upon how realistic you want the simulation to be. After all, your data won't remain static and neither will its formats as your organization improves over the years.

In addition, your data warehouse will contain a healthy dose of metadata. The construction tools you use should make it easy to generate metadata with as little effort as possible, and the data generated should be easy for everyone to understand without taking up an excessive amount of room or becoming hard to navigate.

Step 4—Conceive The Structure Of The Warehouse

Because many organizations already have some form of data mart (or marts) in place, your initial job may be to take one of them and rebuild it into the foundation for the rest of the data warehouse. You can start by using a nine-step process devised by Ralph Kimball. In 1996, Ralph Kimball authored a well-regarded work, *The Data Warehouse Toolkit: Practical Techniques for Building Dimensional Data Warehouses*, published by John Wiley & Sons (ISBN 0471153370). In it he described the following steps to structuring a data warehouse:

Choose The Subject Matter

Because your ultimate objective is to support processes across the organization, and because organizations tend to be divided up by the core processes they perform (such as marketing, production, distribution, IT, and so on), it makes sense to choose subject matter by core process. Choose the subject matter for each area within the data warehouse you're transforming.

Decide What The Fact Table Represents

It's likely that the core processes you're transforming existing data marts to support require only a few fact tables and some of the dimensions available to do the job. Selecting the tables and dimensions depends upon the supported processes and their requirements.

Identify And Calibrate The Dimensions

The dimensions to be used must be singled out and made consistent across all sources. We use the word *calibrate* rather than the word *conform* because the objective here is to make sure all dimensions relate facts using the same scales, regardless of whether they refer to the same general dimension (time, for instance, can be measured on the scale of seconds, hours, days, weeks, and so on).

Choose The Fact Sets

This is primarily a matter of deciding what values among the universe of facts available will be used: how far back in time, from what regions, from what organizations, for what customers, and so on. Although you might ordinarily use only facts already being gathered, a good systems analysis will point out additional facts that may need to be gathered.

Store Precalculations In The Fact Table

To speed retrieval, it's often necessary to precalculate many values in advance, one of the reasons data warehouses can grow so large. To keep your warehouse manageable, you must precalculate only the values that are most likely to be used frequently.

Round Out The Dimension Tables

Most dimension tables will contain gaps, incorrect or missing values, that must either be entered, corrected, or filled with placeholder values.

Choose The Duration/Scope Of The Database

Similar to choosing fact sets, choosing the duration/scope of the database is done by limiting the scope of data sources: a particular time frame (window), several locations, a certain organization, and so on.

Track Slowly Changing Dimensions

The data warehouse needs to be recalibrated from time to time to cope with the slow change of some dimensions, and this is accomplished by tracking changes to dimensions.

Select Query Priorities And Query Strategies

Begin your data warehouse with a set of priorities and strategies for performing queries that reflect anticipated data requests, but manage these priorities and strategies actively to find the optimum for any given situation. Often, what you start out with won't be optimum, no matter how well you analyze the situation and requirements to begin with.

Step 5—Extract, Convert, And Sanitize Data

After the structure of the data warehouse is finished you still need to begin the process of populating the warehouse by extracting records from available sources and converting and sanitizing them. You'll most likely need several extraction and conversion tools, especially as more and more data sources are stored in the warehouse. Extraction, conversion, and sanitization are ongoing tasks, so you should make provisions to automate them as much as possible as well.

Step 6—Create A Metadata Catalog

One of the most important steps in creating your data warehouse is the assembly of metadata. After all, metadata is the only guidepost users have to find the data they're looking for. Metadata should be in terms they understand. When you use jargon, use jargon they understand, not computer terms or the formal, official names for things. When the organization says "capacity" when it means "throughput," use "capacity" for that fact.

Step 7—Train Managers And Users

Even the best, most well-designed data warehouse, metadata, and navigation system will still be difficult for users to comprehend and use effectively. Good old Lotus 1-2-3 was a marvel in its time, and it saved billions of labor hours (and tedious labor hours they were, too). But think about how long it took you to learn to use it, even though it had a GUI before Microsoft did. Whatever tool you choose, your users will need to use it for quite some time before they're proficient simply because it's so powerful. As a matter of fact, the power of an application can be related in almost direct proportion to the learning curve required.

Users typically learn best when they have a reason to learn, so part of your strategy might be to deploy tools (and the training that goes with them) incrementally when conditions occur that make using the tools profitable. For instance, when production managers must perform an annual analysis of machinery utilization within their respective areas, train them to use data from the warehouse via a data browser. Showing them specifically how it can help them accomplish their annual analysis can lead to rapid adoption, with the side benefit that they'll understand how to use the tool the next time they have a similar report due.

Following these steps is valuable when converting legacy systems into a data mart, but what about building a data mart from scratch? Much the same process is followed, but there are significant differences discussed in our next section.

7. Data Warehousing

Implementing A Data Mart

Building a data mart is, in essence, the same as building a mini data warehouse. Data sources, legacy systems, and analytical tools that must be integrated into the mart will already be in use. The primary difference, especially when building a standalone system, is that the data mart supports the purpose of only one department or core process group.

Step 1—Identify Core Processes

Refer to the systems analysis and process engineering documents to determine the core processes supported within the area of interest. All data inputs and required outputs should be listed.

Step 2—Determine Opportunities For Informational Data Support

The purpose of a data warehouse or data mart is to provide analytical data for strategic and planning purposes, not day-to-day operations. For instance, when a salesperson needs a price check, the operational system provides it. When a salesperson needs to estimate an appropriate discount on a large ticket item by comparing unit costs with discounts given recently to other customers with similar sales volumes, the data mart should provide that information.

Step 3—Select Tools

When you're building a standalone data mart from scratch, you can review the formats of existing data sources and analytical tools and try to use something similar (or at least familiar) for building and using the data mart. When you're transforming an existing, proprietary data mart to a standard data mart (to serve as the foundation for an eventual data warehouse), you may have to throw out legacy tools and start over. Make sure users know why you're doing this, how the change will affect them, and offer plenty of training to get them back up to speed. In addition, this would be a good time to collaborate with users again because their input is much more valuable than your insight when it comes to the work they're trying to do.

Step 4—Evaluate Data Mart Impact

Additional resources will undoubtedly be required to support a new application or environment, unless you're lucky enough to be throwing away a huge legacy system while you're at it. New data sources, data conversion, networking, data storage, processing, and other resources must be factored into the equation to provide the kind of service users demand. All the usual business decisions must be made using total costs, benefits, and risks as guidelines.

Building A Data Acquisition Storehouse

Storing raw data for analysis later can be accomplished with a data acquisition storehouse. This storehouse is one of the intermediate areas where data flows to after it's captured, and it's somewhat unlikely that this data will ever be placed directly into a data warehouse (although this is beginning to change as data warehouses gain BLOB handling tools). You must make provisions for a multitude of data types, a relational database tool to manage the acquired data effectively, and high-speed connections for storing and accessing data effectively.

Step 1—Define Data Types

Each type of data you might store in a data acquisition storehouse has its own special requirements for efficient storage. Some types can easily be compressed, though others don't lend themselves to compression (or at least not much). Data type and retrieval requirements indicate the type of storage medium required and the data model for storage.

Step 2—Outline The Storage Process

Like harvested produce, acquired data is gathered, preprocessed, delivered, postprocessed, and stored for its shelf life, after which it's often transferred to archival storage or deleted. The entire storage process should be well defined, with checkpoints, alerts, and end points noted. You don't want to keep any data that's "gone bad," likewise you don't want to throw away data that's still valuable. A clear outline of the sources and uses for data in the storehouse can make programming much easier.

Step 3—Appoint User Representatives And Build Metadata

Each user group can be segmented according to the products it produces, and this tells you a little about the types of data they acquire and store. These representatives can also tell you a great deal about the metadata required for the job. For instance, when you store engineering drawings for a group, you want to make it easy for them to find particular drawings without necessarily having to open the CAD application and review the contents of each drawing. This implies that someone from the group has identified the most important elements in each drawing and entered them into the relational database.

Step 4—Configure Relational Database Interface

Users are going to want an interface that's easy to use for finding their drawings, and they don't want to have to formulate queries each time they need to find a particular project or set of projects. But rather than assign someone from IT to perform this task, it's an ideal opportunity to train your representative to do the relatively simple GUI interface programming using a tool like Microsoft Access. This person can enter data for each project, store projects within the storehouse, manage the files, maintain the database, build simple canned queries and reports, and modify the database as user requirements change. Only when the representative needs consulting services should IT get involved.

Step 5—Train Users

Users tend to have their own way of doing things, and because acquired data is often associated with projects or production (rather than being used to run the business itself), users can be very picky about using the storehouse. As a matter of fact, users will fight you tooth and nail to keep their old ways of storing data, unless they have the benefit of training to convince them otherwise. Not only should you train them, you should make it clear why the new method is going to make their jobs easier, make them more productive, make their data safer, and so on. Most of all, you should give them clear and convincing reasons to trust you with their data. After all, which of their customers is going to buy the tired old excuse "IT lost my data"?

Building A Decision Support System

Decision support systems don't just provide information, they specifically provide enough of the right types of information to allow the user to make valid decisions. They actually produce knowledge of a situation, including the call to action (like a well-made commercial).

When you've created a data mart or data warehouse, you're already halfway there. All the data you need for your decision support system should be gathered, stored, sanitized, and consolidated for rapid retrieval. The only thing you have left to do is automate its appearance across your organization.

Step 1—Identify Supported Decisions

Referring once again to the systems analysis and process engineering documents, identify the processes that need automated support. Unlike general data mart supported processes, these processes are, more likely, going to offer opportunities for automation. For instance, if you're an operator working in a nuclear power plant, you might be working in a large control room full of gauges, dials, and switches. When a meltdown is imminent, do you want to be informed of this fact by a slightly higher reading on a temperature gauge in the corner? A better method of conveying knowledge in this situation would be to have some kind of mild but attention-getting alarm sound, followed by a readout on the main screen informing you of the nature of the problem as well as what corrective action to take, and how long you have in which to take action. Also helpful would be other counteractions to take when the primary fix doesn't work.

Step 2—Determine Automation Requirements

Does the your decision support system require an expert system? Fuzzy logic? Intelligence? A neural network? The kind of software application used depends upon the requirements of the decisions to be made, and each has its own special costs and strengths.

Step 3—Simulate Real-World Conditions

The last thing you want to do is deploy your system in the real world without testing it properly. Collision avoidance alarm systems in air traffic control towers make a good example. Diverting aircraft from collision courses is an admirable goal for an alarm system, and detecting, calculating the potential for, and averting possible collisions is well within the capabilities of modern hardware and software. But common sense tells us that avoiding a collision with another aircraft is great unless we're diverted straight into another aircraft, a building, or the ground. It's important to test decision support systems not just for the alternatives they choose but for the alternatives they dismiss.

Step 4—Monitor, Maintain, And Improve

The world changes constantly, but, basically, software and computer systems don't. Sometimes we can program them to change in response to certain conditions, but mostly we don't try to do this because it's difficult to tell what changes will be relevant. We must monitor the real world for significant change, and when it occurs, modify (or maintain) our decision support system. When the opportunity arises for significant improvement, it can be incorporated in the next maintenance cycle.

7. Data Warehousing

Employing Artificial Intelligence With Data Visualization

Artificial intelligence is as yet amorphously defined and means many things to many people. Perhaps it's best to think of AI as a collection of techniques you can use to make a solution do your thinking for you. Although it isn't a panacea, there are some situations in which it comes in very handy. For example, when you're building an automatic phone answering system you might want to consider using artificial intelligence systems to actively manage your lines, the messages played back, and service centers used. To allow a very small staff to manage such a call center, you'd want to have the system handle as many of the calls as possible automatically. But when a situation occurs beyond the scope of the system, you'd want it to transparently hand the call over to a human operator.

Step 1—Set System Rules

Outline all the choices, rules, decisions, and so forth that you want the system to use. When necessary, refer to the sections on setting up a decision tree or a neural network to decide just how you want to handle incoming calls. Keep in mind that, for many organizations, how a customer is treated by their automatic phone system is a good part of the customer service interaction as well as the customer's perception of the company.

Step 2—Set Values For Alerts

The point at which the system decides to hand the call of to a human operator could be dependent upon how well customers like the treatment they're receiving from the machine. For instance, when people can't get the answer they're looking for after about three levels of choices, it might be best to let them speak to a company representative. But when data shows that for the particular set of menu choices your company offers, customers are willing to wade through five levels, the system should let them continue until they've hit the fifth level.

Step 3—Decide Alert Methods

When lines are overloaded and waiting times are increasing, do you let the system decide to start transferring calls to another call center, or do you have a person intervene and make the decision? If you decide to bring a person into the picture, how are you going to make them aware of the situation and what corrective actions would likely be helpful? These are the decisions you need to make before hand.

I tend to favor the dashboard approach, with gauges and dials displaying an analog representation of the values in question. When threshold values are exceeded, displayed values change color (red, perhaps) or begin to blink. One way or another, they need to call attention to themselves and should also indicate how far out-of-tolerance the situation has become. Of course, you can use many analogies, so it's up to your imagination as to how to portray data in a way the user will effectively understand.

Step 4—Inform The User Of Alternatives

Informing the user which corrective actions will probably lead to success is more difficult. Depending upon the situation, the "commonsense" approach may make things worse. Artificial intelligence really helps under these circumstances because computers can rapidly evaluate a multitude of variables and suggest actions, whereas, a human might take too long or make errors.

Installing An Expert System

Whenever you have a group of people doing a routine (but possibly complex) job, it's a natural candidate for an expert system. The fact that it's routine implies that there are well-established rules, and because it's currently being done successfully, the knowledge is resident in your employees to do it. Your job is to extract that knowledge and put it to work.

Step 1—Gather Recorded Information

Often, much of the data you need to build an expert system is already in instructions, training manuals, and reference texts in the work area. Ask users for a list of everything they use to perform their functions, and collect it.

Step 2—Interview Subject Matter Experts

Before you can build the rules the expert system will follow, you need to find out what the rules are, and the way to do that is to interview Subject Matter Experts (SMEs). SMEs know every aspect of their job, what works and what doesn't, and, sometimes, even why.

Interview them as politely as possible, and consider appointing a member of their group to perform the interviews. You might have to provide some training to this person, but chances are the SMEs will be more straightforward with a person who has a similar background, and they'll all be speaking the same jargon, so they'll understand each other. Have your representative record everything that's said without attempting to categorize the facts or relationships yet.

Step 3—Formulate Rules

Away from the SMEs, meet with your representative and categorize all facts, relationships, procedures, decision sets, courses of action, and so forth into a series of logical rules. Use your rep as a sounding board to determine how to prioritize, weight, and sequence various steps, as well as the conditions under which each course of action is appropriate.

State rules in if-then terms. For instance, if A=6 and B=9, perform step 1. Much like writing the logic for a simple computer program, building rules for an expert system can be done with a flow chart (as shown in Figure 7.5).

Step 4—Program The Inference Engine

The expert system package you obtain will have an interface and perhaps a script-like programming language that lets you enter the rules, specifications, and values you've derived into the inference engine. Make sure you carefully document your entries as you make them, so others can follow your steps and maintain the system.

7. Data Warehousing

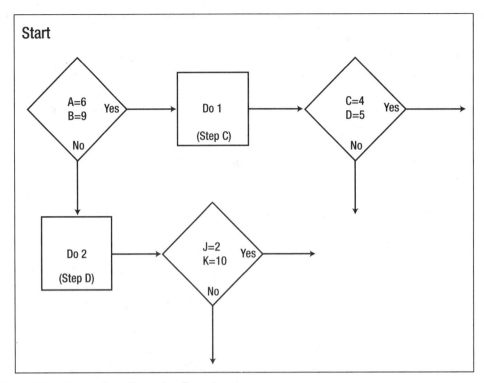

Figure 7.5 An expert system rules flow chart.

Mining Data Using A Decision Tree

Creating a decision tree is appropriate when you have lots of data to mine but have fairly straightforward rules to work with. If you can formulate the rules into a series of yes-no questions, you have a good candidate for analysis and prediction with a decision tree. The following steps illustrate how decision tress are built in practice, using a simplified manual example. Automated tools that are available can perform much of the labor involved.

Step 1—Find Predictive Data

To begin building your decision tree, you need to have data available that shows actual outcomes based on historical records. For example, if you have records of 20 factors related to leased office space over the past five years and sales results for the offices leased, you have enough information to train the decision tree.

Step 2—Decide What Questions To Ask

As you build the tree, you need to supply questions by which it will process data. Some questions (predictors) may have little correlation to the answer you're seeking though others may be very significant. For instance, when you want to know what locations will be good for business, the numerical portion of the street address probably has little or nothing to do with it (although in some areas a very low street address implies prestige). The best questions segment the data in a way that's relevant to the answer of interest.

Step 3—Check Remaining Data

After asking a question and segmenting the data, review data in each segment to see whether you've gotten the refinement you're looking for. For example, if you ask what ZIP code the location is in, you might find that some locations have higher sales than others. This will be evident in the remaining data.

Step 4—Continue Building And Refining

Ask each question in sequence and refine the tree after each question by checking the remaining data. When you're finished asking all the questions, you can double-check the tree against a new set of data, and if you're not satisfied with its predictive power, you can rerun the questions using a different sequence, different questions, or different values for questions.

Deploying A Neural Network

Although vendors imply that neural networks are easy to set up and maintain, significant work may be required to get your data into the proper format for processing and to state the business problem of interest and valid answers in a way the network can deal with. Therefore, deploying a neural network is serious and should be carefully evaluated before implementation.

Some vendors include consulting services with their neural network products, giving implementation a higher probability of success. This is a common practice throughout the high-end business tools world, but prices are several orders of magnitude higher as well, making for a much different business decision than buying a copy of Access.

To deploy a neural network (using Figure 7.6 as an example), you would follow these general steps:

Step 1—Define The Business Problem

Suppose you want to estimate attrition rates for several categories of employees next year. Formally stated, you want to know the number of employees in these categories who will likely leave the company for FY99. The factors affecting a decision to leave the company are age, type of work, and income. These factors

7. Data Warehousing

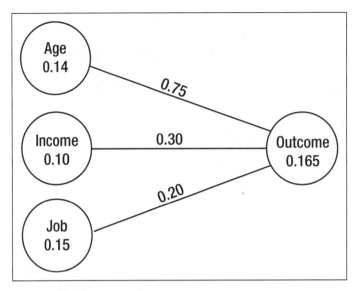

Figure 7.6   A neural network.

must be represented as numerical values between 0.0 and 1.0, so all the values in the domain are equivalently defined. For instance, when the actual values represent an age range of 21 to 41, age 31 would equal 0.50.

Step 2—Define The Answer

The answer is found by evaluating each employee according to the factors mentioned in Step 1. The answer is defined as a numerical value between 0.0 and 1.0, with proximity to 0.0 indicating a high propensity for leaving the company and proximity to 1.0 indicating a low propensity.

Step 3—Define The Weights

Nodes are connected by links, and links are assigned weights that modify the values assigned to each node to arrive at an answer. Links take on their weights by repeatedly being exposed to data indicating the value of factors and actual outcomes. For example, when age demonstrates a very small correlation with attrition in predicting whether a person will leave the company, its weight will be reduced accordingly.

Step 4—Make Predictions

Once you've trained the network with enough data, you can use it to make a decision in a real case where the outcome is unknown. For instance, suppose you have your neural network set up and trained using hundreds of real case records. Now, suppose you feed it (enter into its input nodes) a real record, and let's say the record is for a plumber, age 25, making $24,000 per year working in the plant maintenance department. In addition, suppose the range of ages employed at the plant is from age 18 to age 68, the range of salaries is from $12,000 to $132,000, and plumbing has historically been highest in attrition.

Calculate their age value (68 − 18 = 50, 25 − 18 = 7, and 7 ÷ 50 = 0.14). Next, calculate their salary value (132,000 − 12,000 = 120,000, 24,000 − 12,000 = 12,000, and 12,000 ÷ 120,000 = 0.10). Finally, calculate their occupation value (on a scale of 0.0 to 1.0 let's assume plumbing rates 0.15 among all the occupations in the company).

If age is the most significant predictor of attrition potential, the link between age and outcome would have the highest weight. For instance, when most records show a strong correlation between age and attrition, the link between age and outcome might be 0.75, while the link for occupation might be 0.30 and the link for income might be 0.20. The outcome in this case would be 0.165. However, suppose age has an inverse relationship to outcome, meaning that the older a person gets the more likely he is to leave the company. The weight might show a negative value, pushing the outcome closer to 0.0 as age rises, rather than the opposite.

This is a very simplified version of a neural network, shown only to illustrate, in general terms, how they operate. Links can be very complex formulas that take on a variety of interesting weights as node values change. The more closely link weights correlate to observed outcomes given real values, the better the model performs in predicting actual outcomes.

7. Data Warehousing

Chapter 8

Applications And Operating Systems

In Depth

This chapter addresses practical applications and operating systems (apps and OSs) issues, namely how to decide whether to buy or make apps and OSs, and how to find and use them if you do decide to buy. Although some apps and OSs cost very little or nothing, depending upon the licensing terms, costs for ownership and maintenance must still be evaluated.

That we need apps and OSs to build solutions almost goes without saying, but bringing it up allows us to examine fundamental decisions from a fresh perspective. With so many buzz words, so much hype, and so many complementary, similar, opposing, and just plain strange definitions and categories of software, even recognizing requirements is difficult. Like a jigsaw puzzle in which the pieces constantly change size, shape, and color, the software market often defies understanding. New software species are born, acquire names, become standardized, and wink out of existence like high school clothing fashions. Acronym builders and naming committees are working overtime to come up with the next cool-sounding appellation for the latest trend, fad, standard, app, OS, program, and the hardware required to run it.

Competition drives the software market, regardless of what people think about Microsoft or other proprietary software makers. Anyone with an education, a computer, and existing software packages can build an OS or an application. Granted, you'll have huge hurdles to leap over going from homespun apps to high market-share winners, but in fact mind share is what makes the difference. Consumers (users) care about only three things: How much does it cost? Does it work? and How fast is it? Of course, within the context of "Does it work?" lurk all sorts of smaller concerns: How much space does it take up? How compatible is it? How secure is it? Will the company that makes it be there tomorrow? and so forth. These smaller concerns separate the garage startups from the "real" companies, but there's still plenty of room for new players even so. All in all, if you give users software that has a significant new capability, is substantially cheaper, faster, more secure, or more compatible, they won't care who made it, they'll use it.

In the X86 PC world, one major and a few minor OSs are available to choose from, as well as many thousands of software programs and applications and a tremendous amount of hardware combinations. The Macintosh PC world is ruled by Apple Corporation, and although there were clones for a time, Apple has now

8. Applications And Operating Systems

closed that door and is again the only company producing Macintoshes. A small but devoted band of Commodore/Amiga PC users continue to hang on, as well as other PC hobbyist-type groups working with lesser-known but still fascinating software and operating systems.

The legacy mainframe and minicomputer world is dominated by proprietary operating systems and applications often built by the hardware manufacturers themselves. Software in this category is usually very expensive (in relative terms) but very robust, highly secure, and well tuned to the hardware it resides within. In addition, third-party applications or add-on makers are rare (because of the proprietary nature of the parent OS and apps), and specialized technical support, consulting, and warranties are frequently offered.

Still, you'll find many alternatives to commercial off-the-shelf (COTS) packages. Especially in the PC world, shareware and freeware are very common. Shareware is usually a demo or lighter version of a production package, while freeware is frequently fully-featured versions of high-performance software without technical support. All in all, so many rapidly changing options make determining the need for a particular piece of software and deciding how to obtain and use it partly a matter of luck and perseverance, rather than great analytical skill. This chapter is devoted to providing the background necessary to make the most of what skills you have; hopefully, luck will follow.

Applications And OSs

Software can be divided into operating systems that make hardware perform and applications that do the work. From arcane assembly routines embedded into read-only memory (ROM) to basic input/output systems (BIOSs) in complementary metal-oxide semiconductors (CMOS) to random access memory (RAM) chips, to full-fledged graphical user interface (GUI) operating systems and network operating systems that do everything but clean your screen, operating systems and their little brothers serve to provide a platform upon which work can get done.

BIOSs

The BIOS is the first piece of software a computer encounters when power is applied (see Figure 8.1). It's embedded in CMOS chips but can be upgraded if necessary. On PCs, a battery holds BIOS settings when power is off, allowing the current time and date, as well as other crucial data, to persist. On startup, the BIOS performs the power-on self test (POST) and boots the computer from the floppy or hard disk drive.

The BIOS also controls things such as the setting of the computer's internal clock, bus speed, hardware interrupts, and so forth. As computer hardware has grown

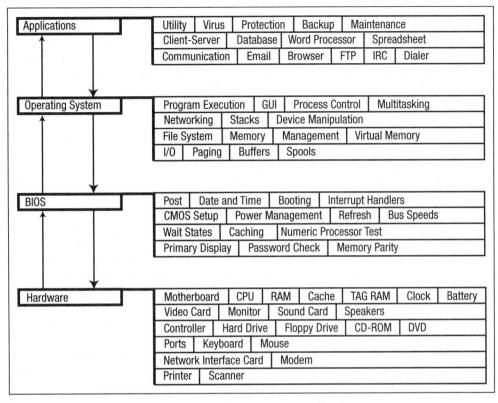

Figure 8.1 The role of the BIOS, operating system, and applications.

more complex, the settings used to control it have grown more numerous and complex as well. Different settings can affect performance, so understanding the settings of your particular model and its associated peripherals is crucial to getting the most from your overall solution.

The BIOS provides hardware interrupts to maintain an interface between various hardware components (the keyboard and CPU, for instance). When a key is pressed, it generates an electrical signal that travels to the CPU. The signal, known as an interrupt, notifies the CPU to stop (interrupt) what it's doing and respond to the keystroke. You'll find numerous interrupts for the many devices operating within an ordinary computer.

In one form or another, all computers have BIOSs, whether they're mainframes, minis, workstations, PCs, handhelds, or simply embedded CPUs. Modern operating systems are a step above the BIOS and have much more elaborate (and hotly debated) functions.

8. Applications And Operating Systems

OSs

Operating systems mediate communications between application programs and the BIOS, and, thereby, the hardware itself. The OS typically provides a file system and support for the CPU running it. Application programs utilize the operating system to accomplish their functions, although exactly which functions are rightfully part of the operating system and which belong to applications is a matter of intense debate. Some operating systems are actually embedded within components (the realtime operating system), while others load each time from storage (like the operating system in your desktop or laptop).

OS Characteristics

Although Microsoft's Windows versions, variations of Unix, and the Macintosh operating system constitute the majority of operating systems available, many research projects are pointing the way to the future. One characteristic of operating systems in general is the number of bits processed, as in 8-, 16-, 32-, and 64-bit operating systems. More bits processed per cycle indicates faster performance, but there are exceptions to that general rule.

Another common characteristic is multithreaded, multitasking capability, meaning the OS can perform multiple tasks simultaneously. Some OSs are truly multitasking, while others simply divide their time into small time slices, performing only one task at a time but switching so often it seems they're working on multiple processes at the same time.

Other operating systems can operate in parallel across networks; object-oriented OSs deal with everything as a hierarchy of objects; and some OSs even allow various components of themselves to be replaced during operation.

Network Operating Systems

Network operating systems (NOSs) typically run on a network server and function to connect individual computers together. Although some NOSs are designed to run "above" other operating systems, most are really just extensions of standard operating systems. Windows NT is an example of an operating system that can function as a network operating system, and Unix clones are also in this category. Operating systems, of course, support other programs, such as applications and utilities.

Applications And Utilities

Application programs, including utilities, do everything else, although the line between application programs and operating systems is the site of a ferocious battle because of the perception that operating system market share provides a natural monopoly. The government may end up deciding what components belong inside the operating system and what are independent applications and utilities.

Application programs can be as simple as the clock, calculator, and text editor that come with Windows or as complex as a program development environment. Utility programs also range from the simple to the complex but are generally defined as programs that perform functions related to keeping your computer running efficiently, rather than performing functions related directly to some task you wish to accomplish. Microsoft Access 2000 is an example of an application program, and it's a dual-use program in that it can be used directly to accomplish database functions but can also be used to build database applications that run independently of it. Older versions of Access can be considered legacy software, although the term generally refers to older, mainframe-type applications.

Legacy Software

The term for all your existing software, including operating systems, applications, utilities, and so on is legacy software. As you conduct your internal survey to determine what you currently have available, keep in mind that the software itself is only part of the equation. Training, technical support, special licensing and contractual conditions, and especially personal biases all come into play. Even something as simple as changing email programs can lead to disruption, lowered morale, and frequent complaints.

The general rule is never change basic systems unless it's unquestionably necessary. Adding a new solution or system on top of legacy systems is difficult enough. Still, quite a few good reasons do exist to change underlying applications and operating systems, not all of which can be defined in strictly quantifiable, bottom-line terms.

For instance, the Year 2000 (Y2K) problem is raising, in many organizations, the question of whether to embark on a wholesale upgrade of all legacy systems or to implement a piecemeal fix, system by system. The costs are enormous either way, but frequently there are substantial benefits in overhauling the entire system. After all, putting an entirely new system in place might reduce maintenance costs, increase efficiency, and enable you to build better documentation. Middleware is one of the types of software being considered, although it is a class of software and not a particular application type.

Middleware

Modern networks are composed of many different types of operating systems, database applications, hardware configurations, and so forth. These different "species" of systems need to be accessible to each other, not just at the communications (lower network layers) level but at the applications level as well. Specialized programs that connect and translate between many back-end and front-end applications transparently comprise middleware. Middleware is just about as much buzzword as actual software category, but it helps to focus your attention on the need for software that provides a bridging mechanism (or gateway) for communications between legacy mainframe data repositories and front-end applications.

An Application/OS Survey

In Chapter 2, we did a quick survey on the Internet and found tens of operating systems available, some free, some commercial, some outdated, and some standard. Conducting a survey of what's out there before you make a decision is always warranted, if only to remind you of why you chose the OS or application you did. And who knows, maybe something worthwhile will come along. Things are changing rapidly and show no signs of slowing down. There are several viable survey methods you can use.

Survey Methods

You can use many available methods for gathering data about existing or in-development software projects, and they all have varying degrees of effort and efficacy. The software industry is known for hype, misdirection, and spin, and all too often, promised products or features never materialize. Part of this is because of the fast-changing and highly competitive arena in which software manufacturers operate, but there's also a healthy dose of good, old-fashioned marketing and business strategy at work. Unfortunately, the consumer is left to sort out facts from claims, performance from sham, software from "vaporware." Just knowing the right questions to ask is hard, but there are ways to protect yourself. And protect yourself you must, especially on the Web.

The World Wide Web (WWW) And The Internet

Using the Web, of course, is absolutely the fastest, most convenient way to obtain information about most subjects, especially about computers. But the very things that make it fast, convenient, and comprehensive also make it suspect. Anyone can post information and make it appear authoritative and, with the right tools, can seriously undermine the credibility of even the most respected sources.

Newsgroups are also helpful, but take care not to assume every claim represents an unbiased opinion (in fact, newsgroup postings are notable for their bias, but at least you can usually see both sides of the story).

Print Media

Print magazines, newsletters, and even junk mail are also good sources of software reviews. Magazines, in particular, have the advantage of employing laboratories devoted to nothing but testing software under various conditions. Because they make their money advertising for the software industry, they have their own biases but should be able to at least give you an in-depth picture of newly developed or released applications. And when you subscribe to a maga-zine, you'll instantly be enrolled for one of the best ways to collect printed in-formation about software, junk mail. I know it's a pain, but if you throw it all in a pile, it'll be there when you need leads. Junk mail sometimes even contains specs, so it's not all trash.

Specifications

When you buy a circuit board, you can usually get fairly comprehensive technical specifications with it. You can determine the materials making up the board and its components, the physical and electrical properties, the form factor, and so forth. Unlike hardware specifications, software is specified mostly in intangibles (things that must be measured indirectly). Software specifications include such things as the amount of hard disk drive space required for a standard installation, RAM consumed during normal operations, how quickly certain functions will be performed on a particular piece of hardware, algorithms, data structures, com-patibility lists, and so on.

Basic application parameters are normally pretty easy to measure (the amount of hard disk space required, for instance) while performance specifications can vary tremendously depending upon the installation platform, hardware configuration, other applications installed, and so forth. In addition, performance specs vary dynamically in relation to changes in other running applications. Therefore, it's important to uncover both static and dynamic performance specifications.

Some performance standards are available (we touched on these in Chapter 2), but they can easily be misused, so it's a good idea to run your own tests if you've the means and the time. Performance testing packages and associated documen-tation can be somewhat expensive, not just to run but to set up, yet the informa-tion you gain from using them might make or break your project. Of course, performance standards are only reliable when testing is done on the right con-figuration, as noted in the installation requirements.

Installation Requirements

Every application or OS should provide documentation concerning the hardware it runs on and the minimum recommended configurations. Included in the instal-lation requirements are CPU type, RAM requirements, and any peripheral devices required. Ignore the minimum requirements except as guidelines about the type of systems on which the software can run. Even recommended hardware may not be suitable for your particular solution. And don't forget, you can always make whatever software you need if you don't find anything suitable on the market. The question is, should you?

The Make-Or-Buy Decision

Like most anything else, your company can choose to make its own software rather than buy it. Whether or not this will be practical (less costly in terms of time or money) is a wholly different question. Time and money aren't the only factors to consider; resources available and ultimate use of the software must also be taken into account. Some companies have found themselves entering new businesses and markets once they complete development of a particularly useful application.

Building Your Own Applications

Building applications can be accomplished on many levels. For instance, if a user builds a database application, technically that's homegrown software. At the same time, if someone in your company builds a customized driver in assembly language, that's also homegrown software. The difference is in the amount of specialized technical knowledge required, the tools used, the time it takes, and the uses to which the end product can be put. Database applications are constructed on software that's designed to be very easy for end users to learn and create with, while drivers written in assembly require special tools and special training and are usually built only by programmers on the IT staff. A database application may end up being used in some form or another by the entire company, while a driver may be used on just one or on a few machines on the network.

At this point, you should have a reasonably clear idea of what software components are necessary to complete your solution, and you should be ready to begin hunting for them. Assuming that for certain components you don't find anything suitable during your trip through cyberspace, you may need to build them yourself (or contract the work out). In addition, you may find certain applications that your existing staff has the skill to build more cost-effectively than a straight purchase from a vendor. Auditing the capabilities of your existing IT staff is the prerequisite for making this determination.

Conducting a comprehensive audit is most likely a part of the duties of IT managers already (if not, it should be), considering how crucial IT skills are to any organization today, and how hard it is to get well-qualified IT personnel. Your audit should note the following:

- All current employees, contractors, and available talent.

- Specialized skills, knowledge, and abilities.

- Labor costs of each.

- Current projects, priorities, and time frames.

It's very important to estimate the amount of time qualified employees or contractors have available to spend on new projects, as well as the priority of other projects that might slip. And don't forget users. Involve them in construction of front ends and interfaces if practical. Face-to-face conversations with user and IT managers are crucial to gaining the support and commitment you'll need for successful application development. While you're at it, you can get some feedback about other products and companies in or on the periphery of the market.

Business Directions

The market for products you may build is important because the overall business direction of your company should be considered when you're deciding whether to build or to buy. If you're currently building specialized software that's useful within your business domain, chances are that others will find it useful as well. If it's not such a competitive weapon that you must keep it secret, it might be profitable to sell to other companies. A surprising number of success stories float around about companies having done this, starting from a position totally outside software development. But, as with any decision of this kind, you must carefully evaluate the costs, risks, and potential benefits of such a move, including the possibility that companies whose sole business is software production might come to view you as a competitor.

Any serious attempt to penetrate a market or build a new niche in an existing market must be accompanied by careful evaluation of the players and products in or around that market. For example, if you embark on the development of a data conversion utility that would have value across the entire industry you're in, you may very well end up with a marketable and profitable product. However, if you make the investment to build the utility then make the investment to turn it into a marketable product, existing players may decide to counter with products or marketing strategies of their own, quickly wiping out your marketing investment (and its associated benefits). Chapter 9 contains a more detailed discussion of the internal and external marketing factors that come into play in the development of any solution or solution component. The following section presents some of the factors that make for competitive applications.

Application/OS Evaluation

Applications and OSs come in a bewildering number of versions, optimized for various platforms, cultures, hardware configurations, and compatibility with other software. Evaluating a particular package, plug-in, or utility (beyond cost) comes down to determining how it stacks up against the competition and whether or not it'll work with your legacy systems and existing organization within the bounds of the solution you're proposing.

Key Attributes

These are key attributes of well-built software:

- An easy-to-use interface
- Small size
- High quality
- Fast and efficient performance
- Standardization
- Compatibility
- Networkability
- Security

Each of these attributes is important, but they don't necessarily apply to all software packages. Some applications have no human interface whatsoever, for example.

Interface

Interfaces are evolving toward speech, but not every application needs a good interface or speech to perform well. Some applications will never interact with people or only interact rarely with systems administrators. The command-line interface can be a very quick and effective means for administering an application, with the added benefit that it makes it more difficult for an inexperienced user to accidentally make unwanted changes.

Size

The cost of software size is relative to storage size, retrieval speeds, and storage costs, but smaller applications tend to be more tightly written and contain only essential features. We prefer smaller applications that perform the functions they were designed for to larger applications that contain a feature for every suggestion that was ever made during the Beta period. Storage requirements also vary according to the type of installation chosen, meaning that you may be able to exercise a certain amount of control over the amount of storage space your users need by specifying a customized installation for all users.

Quality

Regarding quality, much has been written about the total lack of quality control in the software industry. Everyone knows software always has bugs, and consumers usually find most of them (but hopefully during the Beta period). Even hardware has bugs. Some bugs are deadly, some serious, and some merely annoying. The nature of bugs makes them difficult to measure because if you could measure them up front, you could fix them.

Even so, a manufacturer's track record can give you an indication of future performance on the bug front, and watching how they handle bugs such as Y2K can give you an indication of how you'll be treated. An up-front approach, with plenty of notice given, responsibility taken, and patches developed and delivered regularly means you stand a better chance of getting the basic support you deserve.

Before roundly criticizing the software industry for producing defective products, remember that most products have defects of some type or another. Medicine is often sold for years before horrible side effects are discovered, and automobiles are subject to regular recalls. Complex products provide valuable, unusual, and hard-to-duplicate services and features for our modern life, and bugs are the price we pay. Deserving of criticism, however, are attempts to avoid responsibility for the consequences of known bugs or a lack of forthright action to notify the public and fix the offending code.

Performance

Programs accomplish a particular task in many ways, but the most efficient programs accomplish them with elegant algorithms that are small, run fast, and don't use up an excessive amount of processing or memory resources. Gauging the performance of a particular application is more than just measuring how fast it runs; performance is also measured by how well it performs each function. For instance, one algorithm for cleaning up images may perform very quickly but produce lower-quality results than a slower algorithm. And determining performance of various algorithms is most likely going to mean an indirect evaluation anyway because manufacturers don't warm to the idea of releasing details of the inner workings of their applications or how they write their source code.

To judge the performance of a particular package, you need to decide what performance means to you. If your solution needs the best possible processing speed, best retrieval times, finest quality for a given function, strongest security, and so forth, you need to decide what trade-offs you're willing to make.

Standardization

Standards can be set by cooperative committees or associations, and they can also evolve based upon market share (the de facto standard). Like it or not, applications tend to work better when running with related applications from the same manufacturer. And manufacturers tend to have little regard for how well a competitor's products work with their own, except when the competitor's product is the standard.

As a buyer, you may have little realistic choice for operating systems or applications given the set of legacy applications you're faced with. But you can be creative, and in the long term, it's in your own best interests to support several alternative approaches. For example, Windows NT is gaining ground as an operating system for the server market, but quite a few companies are considering experimenting with Linux as an alternative. Linux is more difficult to install and run, but it's very robust, has a significant user base, and can be had for free (although many people use the commercial Red Hat version for which technical support is provided for a nominal fee).

In terms of communications protocols, Internet Protocol (IP) is the standard on the Internet, so you know you're going to use it (or a version of it). Here's a case in which the standard is obviously beneficial and is open as well, meaning it is developed and published for the benefit of all users and manufacturers by an independent body?

Compatibility

Like standardization, compatibility is about how easily a program can be used with others, although it refers more to file formats than operating systems or communications protocols. An application can do everything it does in a non-standard (but hopefully more efficient) way, but if it can convert to a standard or intermediate file format, it can still be an extremely good alternative.

Another aspect of compatibility, though, resides in the user interface. If an application or operating system is available in a wide variety of languages, characters, input and output methods, and so forth, it's very compatible and makes a better choice.

Networkability

If an application comes with utilities that allow it to be easily distributed across a network, communicate with itself or other applications across a network, and share processing, memory, and storage resources across a network, it has good networkability. Some applications, by their nature, don't work well across a network though, so it's important to understand the nature of the application as well as the capabilities of your legacy network.

Security

Operating systems play a greater role in security than applications, in general, simply because they tend to be more responsible for enforcing security. Microsoft Access 2000 does provide more functionality than ordinary application programs in that it uses a rather unusual model for making applications secure.

Security features include the ability to set up users and groups, object permissions, and encrypt/decrypt data. Security usually involves various levels of password protection, authorization, authentication, and encryption strength. Some applications are completely unsecure, while others conform to security standards set by the federal government and other standards-making organizations.

Typical Application/OS Licensing

Buying software is unlike buying most other products. Because software is intellectual property in a form that's easily duplicated (in fact, duplication is usually essential for installation), software companies have a well-founded fear of pirating—illegal duplication of their goods. Even elaborate copy protection schemes are unable to prevent pirating and customers dislike them intensely because they make legitimate use of the software cumbersome.

Software manufacturers, therefore, construct complex and multifaceted licensing agreements that take effect as soon as the shrink-wrapped carton is opened or the software is installed. These agreements limit the number of computers the software can be installed on, your rights to use or sell the product you've purchased, even your ability to examine the code. At the same time, these agreements attempt to limit your recourse if anything happens, although they usually include a statement notifying you that you may have additional rights or some sections may not be applicable, depending upon your state of residence at the time of purchase.

Common Licensing Terms

Fortunately, software manufacturers often put some common terms in their licensing agreements, so the job of deciphering what applies and how to comply with it is made somewhat simpler. Common terms also make it easier to compare one package to another, but don't expect everything to be straightforward. Complex packages frequently have complex terms, and it can be difficult to extract enough data to compare apples to apples.

Users And Seats

Manufacturers commonly negotiate one of several types of licensing arrangements for networked software: per seat, per concurrent use, total users, unlimited users, and so on. A clause requiring the buyer to maintain logs and records of usage is sometimes included in the terms of the license, meaning extra effort will be required on your part to enforce these provisions. You can minimize the labor involved in managing usage by installing automated license monitoring software.

Making Copies

You're ordinarily allowed to install commercial software on only one computer, but sometimes you can also install the software on a portable computer, the idea being that you would use either one or the other but not both simultaneously. Some manufacturers also allow you to install and/or run the application from a network computer (across an internal network), and most allow for additional backup copies to be made as well. Overall, the idea is to allow a single user to use the software at a given time, without too much concern for where it's installed, as long as there's not much chance someone else will be able to use it concurrently.

Resale

Typical licensing terms restrict your ability to resell, lease, rent, or otherwise re-capture value from your investment. The term *license* itself implies that, rather than buying the product, you're buying only a limited use of the product, and that right to use can be revoked. One notable exception to this exclusion allows you to sell your right to use the software if you transfer all copies and materials, including upgrades, and uninstall (erase) the software from your computer.

Modification, Decompiling, And Reverse Engineering

By the same token, you're restricted from taking the software apart, decompiling it, or modifying it. You must use it as it is, and you can't use just the parts that you like, except as provided for by the manufacturer.

Runtime Licenses

Microsoft Access 2000 comes in a development version that offers a *runtime* license. A runtime license allows you to distribute an executable version of the program with applications you create, although the runtime version only runs your application and won't let users do any development of their own. This is a convenient way to produce finished applications you can sell and is very inexpensive, considering that other database application development manufacturers sometimes charge significant royalties for each application you sell.

The Purchasing Process

Making a decision to obtain a particular application or OS is the beginning of a purchasing process that can either be rewarding and effective or frustrating, expensive, and time-consuming. Exercising control over who you deal with, what information is exchanged, and the terms of the deal gives you a better chance of producing a positive outcome, but, of course, there's no guaranteed method for success.

You should know all of the important parameters, such as the particular product, version, street prices, extras, volume discounts, purchase volumes expected, and so on. You should also know the range of prices your company has authorized you to pay. Armed with this information, you can then find an appropriate contact within the manufacturing company or vendor to deal with. If possible, deal directly with the manufacturer. Sometimes this is just not done, and sometimes there's important value added by vendors. In fact, some solutions come as a package deal, relieving you of the burden of dealing with several manufacturers. Like buying a light fixture, you would buy the complete "solution" from a hardware store, not the individual pieces from several lighting materials manufacturers.

Negotiation

From a negotiation standpoint, it's best to deal through one person rather than a sales team. Too often, sales teams can muddy the waters and provide the vendor with opportunities to dilute the focus of a customer's purchasing efforts. Even if a sales team is assembled and offered as a "resource" to you, make sure only one person speaks for the group and has the authority to make decisions. It's easier to pursue a purchasing strategy when dealing with an individual.

Purchasing strategies

The size of your order today, and its potential for the future, indicates your status to vendors. Other factors also come into play, such as how large and well known your company is. Day-to-day purchases of applications and OSs in small quantities may not seem important (and may, in fact, not be), but added together, they can make a significant difference to the vendor's bottom line, and so they can provide you with a bargaining chip. If your company is a major and respected player in your industry, the prestige conferred upon manufacturers and vendors you do business with can also make a difference. In fact, you may even get products at cost or free, just so your suppliers can get bragging rights.

Projecting an aura of strength boosts your position, and the key is relative knowledge. The best bargainers can guess your actual position by asking a few questions and watching your face, so mentally prepare yourself by gathering as much information as you can beforehand. Know what the limits are (prices and delivery schedules/terms you can accept), then start low and squeeze whenever possible.

Marketing Strategies

Companies market their wares using a variety of methods and channels, including straight retail purchase, lease, volume discounts, package deals (bundling), resale, partnership programs, and even multilevel marketing. Other than straight purchases, these programs are usually designed to offer you incentives to buy and use their products that don't exist in an ordinary business relationship. For instance, if you're selling or pushing their products toward your clients you're less likely to use their competitor's products. Therefore, it's best to avoid these deals unless you intend to also be a reseller with one supplier.

Acquisition

When was the last time you saw a missing material report on your email system? Things do get lost, misrouted, stolen, or simply not delivered sometimes. Although you undoubtedly have a superbly effective shipping and receiving process in place, events beyond your control can ruin your carefully laid installation plans. Moreover, software delivery may be partly or wholly via the Internet, complicating verification that the required materials were delivered on time, intact, and undamaged. Notifying the shipping and receiving department of impending shipments and creating clear documentation for distribution will uncomplicate your life and assist users later on when upgrades arrive.

Storage

For software that comes with manuals, disks, containers, and especially physical copy protection devices, secure storage is important. You may want to remove registration documents, printed licenses, authentication, special offers, reference manuals, master disks, and so forth for separate storage from user manuals or user disk copies. Making users responsible for storing materials associated with desktop applications may seem like a good idea, but it's really more trouble than it's worth. When they lose the manuals, or the disks, they'll just call you anyway, so it's best to retain control over these materials.

Total Cost Of Ownership

Purchase price is straightforward and should be relatively easy to determine and evaluate, so we'll spend our efforts discussing other costs that aren't so well defined. Unsurprisingly, purchase price isn't the only cost involved in buying a new OS or application. Just the cost of finding and evaluating appropriate packages can be substantial if tallied up. Looking at the purchase of new applications from a life-cycle perspective will make you appreciate all associated costs.

A comprehensive assessment of costs is fundamental to any evaluation of competing applications and OSs and serves as an outline for budgeting and task scheduling. For example, training costs may be a significant component of overall costs of introducing a new OS, irrespective of your estimates of training expenditures for the database solution as a whole. Costs incurred during each phase of ownership should be estimated, and the process usually provides a few unexpected surprises if only because of the rapid pace of change in the marketplace. Sometimes a new and seemingly very inexpensive product is actually the result of a well-executed strategy to shift costs from a highly visible part of your purchase to a hidden part of your purchase, as with companies that reduce costs by scrimping on technical support.

Training And Installation Costs

Users, managers, and the IT staff are all easy-to-recognize training targets when new software is planned for purchase. However, you should also consider people external to the organization, such as customers, suppliers, governmental agency regulators, examiners, inspectors, and anyone else needing to access your services. As we've said, using a Web interface for external access requirements makes sense in most situations. Even so, you'll need to spend some effort notifying people of your new service, as well as training them to use it properly. You might put this effort into making the interface self-explanatory or into specific customer training after you implement the new service, but either way it'll cost you.

For insiders, different levels and types of training may be called for (see Chapter 13 for an in-depth discussion of typical training requirements and methodologies), such as classes, training presentations and training manuals, computer-based training, instructional videos or animations, and possibly high-level presentations for upper managers or executives.

Maintenance Costs

Maintenance can be divided into two categories: preventive and unscheduled. Unscheduled maintenance must be performed when some unknown defect appears, but we all know that software is never entirely free of bugs. Just because some maintenance requirements are unknown doesn't mean they should be unplanned. You can and should incorporate provisions for unscheduled resources into your maintenance plans, and you should be proactive in both categories.

Keeping up with known bugs and security holes, patches, service releases, and upgrades is simply part of IT's job. Estimating costs for doing so is just a matter of doing business, but don't be surprised if managers assume you'll just fold these costs into whatever your current responsibilities are. After all, if you're constantly improving your own processes, your costs should be diminishing, so your people can handle a new work load without a budget increase, right? Proving that this assumption is incorrect for a particular case is the IT manager's job.

Y2K And Other Beasts

The whole controversy about who is responsible for fixing Y2K problems is bringing more visibility to software warranties in general. Some companies are offering to fix Y2K bugs in their software (that were created knowingly by their programmers, albeit with good intentions) for a fee. Software buyers, of course, might assume that software manufacturers would stand behind their work and take offense to the idea of paying twice for essentially the same software. It seems the definition of a finished product and the conditions under which it'll work as expected is still a gray area, for the most part, although we expect things will be more well defined after the millenium.

Numerous other Y2K-like issues are coming to the surface these days because of Y2K, and chances are it'll be good for the software consumer as well as future programmers. For one thing, I doubt that anyone will assume that the software he writes today will have disappeared in another 20 years.

Immediate Solutions

This section shows how to formulate requirements for applications and OSs given the mix of components currently deployed, and how to objectively review products on the market by examining technical specifications and evaluating available products. We look at bargaining tactics and negotiating strategies, total cost of ownership, and maintenance and upgrading issues. The goal of this section is to provide you with the tools necessary to decide whether to buy or make apps and OSs and to develop a smooth, uncomplicated, and efficient process for performing purchasing, installation, and maintenance functions.

Identifying Application And OS Requirements

Your existing (legacy) hardware and software systems form a structure upon which your solution will be overlaid. The only exception to this is when you build an entirely new process from scratch, and even then, you must still deal with the legacy in people's minds, namely the OSs and applications they're already familiar with. Think of your proposed solution as a sculpture carved, not in three spatial dimensions, but in the dimensions of software attributes, such as space required, cost, performance, and so forth. Your job is to identify "holes," deficiencies in legacy systems, that must be filled by new software to round out the dimensions of the finished, sculptured solution.

Step 1—Review Systems Analysis Documents

Again, the systems analysis and process engineering documents should provide lists of existing software systems and processes supported. These lists should note not just the types, names, or versions of current software but operational parameters (technical specifications) as well, such as performance, space required, security, transmission speed, and so on.

Step 2—Compare Legacy Capabilities To Proposal Requirements

On the opposite end, proposal documents should provide a similar list of requirements (and possibly some potential candidates) to fulfill the proposal. Simply matching existing capabilities to proposed requirements can sometimes do the job, but there may be times when there's no direct correlation. In these cases you need to either fill in the blanks, or label the mismatch a deficiency.

Step 3—Map Deficiencies

Once you've identified all deficiencies, you can begin the process of characterizing them according to common traits, using your knowledge of software capabilities as a guide. For instance, a deficiency in the area of security might be fulfilled by a specialized security utility or by a change of operating system. The appropriate "shape" of the component that must fill this role is up to you to decide, but the scope of your solution offers clues. A small project affecting only one department probably shouldn't drive a company-wide operating system change, but a larger project might warrant such a change.

Step 4—Define Applications/OSs Fulfilling Mapped Deficiencies

Once the rough outline or "shape" of applications or OSs required to fill deficiencies is complete, it's time to match it with software that's on the market. You'll find that this is when you need to be at your most creative because some deficiencies simply have no good match on the market. If no good matches are found, you might be forced to develop an application yourself or change your proposed solution substantially.

Step 5—Estimate Costs, Benefits, Risks Of Alternatives

Each variation of your chosen solution needs to be evaluated fully for its impact on the overall process flow in your organization, using the systems analysis and process engineering documents as a guide. This process doesn't have to be long or extensive (if it grows very large, you'll know it's time to go back to the drawing board and start over), but it should be comprehensive and involve users. The last thing you want to do is surprise users with a totally different component or interface.

Conducting An Application And OS Survey

That the Internet contains a wealth of information about computers and software is an understatement, and most of your programmers are very well aware of resources for finding, evaluating, maintaining, and updating software, as well as building their own or modifying open source code. At the point when you want to research specific programs, applications, or OSs, especially if you want to assemble a comprehensive picture of what's available, it's just a matter of focusing the knowledge and efforts of these people toward the software you have in mind. If you're going to do most or part of the research yourself, take some time to interview programmers and others in your organization or in special interest groups in your area (or on the Internet) for insight about available software or research projects that might produce something of interest.

Step 1—State Your Goals And Objectives

Clearly articulate the software requirements you need to fill and your time frame. Request backup documentation for claims about specific application characteristics and also sources of information. Provide an electronic document to fill out because you're more likely to get all the information you need that way. It's also a good idea to note on the document that the information provided is confidential. Avoid leaking the information from people in your company directly to potential suppliers. Remember to include a deadline in your request, and sell them on the idea by telling them how the new solution will benefit them directly.

Step 2—List Important Characteristics

Make a place on your request for every characteristic that's critical to the application, such as size, memory requirements, features, compatibility, and so forth. List all aspects of the characteristic. For instance, if you're looking for an application that can provide virus protection, make sure to request information on the types of viruses that it can protect against (macro viruses, boot sector viruses, and so on). List characteristics in order of importance, but categorize them logically so your researchers can easily find them and associate similar characteristics.

Step 3—Gather Potential Candidates

Compare potential candidates using a matrix of features, costs, benefits, and risks. Estimate the risks yourself or have someone whose judgment you trust do it (manufacturers are unlikely to provide an accurate or unbiased assessment of the risks of using their products).

Print and online computer magazines devote themselves to reviewing and evaluating commercial software extensively and often post recent reviews online, complete with feature/performance matrices scored using their own laboratories, loading utilities, and hardware/software/network configurations. The Usenet is another valuable source of information, with hundreds of groups devoted to every imaginable OS and application.

Step 4—Perform A Cursory Check Of Suitability

If possible, download a demo or Beta version of the product and install and test it yourself. Using the product yourself (or having an IT person do so) is a very different experience than simply reading documentation and reviews. Beta products, of course, can be expected to fail in earlier versions, but demo software should work as advertised. Significant problems with either are a warning flag.

Reviewing Technical Specifications

Each potential candidate has its own set of pros and cons, and some of them can be found in the technical specifications—the fine print of software. Specific information about platforms and hardware requirements is in the technical specs, as well as what features are included, what file formats are used, what optimizations are available, and so on. Before you start, you should know exactly what specs are most important for your solution.

Step 1—Define Desired Specifications

You should be able to glean the exact technical specifications required from the list of important characteristics you made during your survey of the marketplace. You'll need to clean up the specs and put them in the same terms, of course, but the process shouldn't be that difficult. For desktop commercial applications, it's very common to find minimum and recommended specifications, and we suggest using at least the recommended hardware or above. After all, just because an application or OS will run, doesn't mean it'll run *well*.

Step 2—Review Documentation

Most manufacturers will provide some type of documentation, but how it's provided and what it covers varies tremendously. Try reading life insurance policies to compare coverage and costs and you'll get the idea. That leaves you, the unfortunate consumer, with the task of sorting out the various claims, specs, features, requirements, and so forth. Even getting the documentation from the Internet can be difficult and time-consuming. In fact, one measure of a good company is how easy to read and comprehensive their documentation is. In any case, try to list all the specifications of each application in common terms, to make later comparison easier.

Step 3—Compare Required Vs. Claimed Specifications

Having done your homework and clearly laid out all your requirements, you'll now be surprised to learn that you didn't consider some things. Manufacturers with a customer orientation always try to anticipate their customer's needs, and if they do it well enough, they'll build in features you didn't even know you wanted until you found them.

Matching your requirements to those found in a particular product sounds straightforward enough, but often, it means translating their terms, converting their units of measurement, and even defining a logical interpretation of the abilities and limits of the package in question. Just remember to compare apples to apples, as the old saying goes.

Step 4—Verify Claimed Specifications

In the endless game of software development, makers try to one-up each other by announcing planned features that encourage you to wait until their product is released before you buy. All too often these features are "vaporware," never to be seen again. Even if the maker fully intends to include them, the production programming team may be unable to deliver on time. Before you accept written specifications, attempt to verify their existence (and that they actually work) independently.

Deciding Whether To Buy Or Make Software

An objective analysis of the pros and cons regarding buying or making software may not be all there is to the decision, but it's clearly the best first step. If the analysis shows strong disadvantages against making your own, any decision to proceed toward internal construction should be viewed with suspicion. However, if strong disincentives don't exist but the advantages are only marginal, there may be good (but intangible) reasons for pursuing development in-house. For projects requiring programming talent, there may be an opportunity for your IT staff to stretch their legs and expand their capabilities. For projects requiring less extensive programming (Access front ends are a prime candidate), getting users involved in construction can have the important benefit of creating more user buy-in and ownership. In either case, the first step is to evaluate all existing resources.

Step 1—Evaluate Existing Resources

Depending upon what type of software you're considering developing, you may have too many, too little, or inappropriate resources. In each case, your knowledge and utilization of existing resources is the key to effective in-house software development. Take stock of everyone and everything available, including workstations, network facilities, software development resources, and so on.

Step 2—Estimate Development Costs

Cost estimating is simply a matter of totaling all resource costs per unit. The trick is to allow for inevitable delays, overruns, unexpected difficulties, and new requirements. Even a small, well-planned development effort will run into unforeseen problems, and they'll cost you both time and money.

Break out your estimate into categories, using your project management task details as a guide:

• Scope, specifications

- Modules, user interface, integration, testing, debugging, final acceptance
- Documentation, training materials
- Distribution, installation

Assign each category costs according to the resources it consumes. For example, development of the user interface may require 120 hours of programming labor, using the same amount of time on a programming workstation loaded with the appropriate tools. And don't forget, it may also require another 20 hours of graphic design for the icons, logos, and other artwork to make it truly easy to navigate and to understand.

Step 3—Estimate Total Ownership Costs

Total ownership costs (TOC) reflect life cycle costs for the acquisition, deployment, maintenance, and disposal of an application or operating system. To gain an appreciation of these costs, you can consult the documentation provided by the manufacturer, but for larger applications, it may be best to perform your own studies (and you'll need to do so if you want to compare the costs of building your own). Figure 8.2 shows how the life of an application can be depicted over time.

Divide the life cycle of software into phases. Each phase carries its own unique activities, localized to one person or group or distributed across the organization. Estimate the costs in each category in a manner similar to estimating costs for development of the application alone, with costs assigned per resource utilized per unit. If an application requires the use of specialized hardware, be sure to include the additional costs in your estimates.

For example, if you expect the application will require two hours of maintenance for updates each fiscal year, to each station, then you'd multiply labor hours times stations to get the figure per year, then multiply that by the expected life (in years) of the application.

Step 4—Estimate Risks And Benefits

Some companies develop lots of their own utilities and applications, even though they're not software development companies per se, because of the nature of their work. Game developers tend to build lots of their own tools, for instance. If you develop applications within your company, there'll be times when it appears that marketing your in-house applications to other companies is a good way to develop additional sources of revenue.

Risks abound, however, and not just that you might be selling valuable tools to your competitors. Entering a new business or a new market niche may entail developing entirely new processes within your business—new sales and distribution channels—and put new loads on existing resources. Carefully weigh the risks

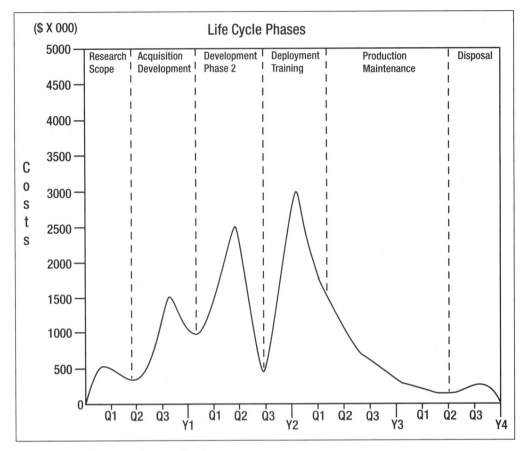

Figure 8.2   Life cycle of an application.

and benefits of selling in-house applications, and treat it as you would any other new venture.

For example, suppose you develop the world's greatest file format converter for 3D animation files, and you get lots of use out of it. Your development costs total $1 million in programmers time and other costs, and you'd like to recoup some of that by selling a few packages to other companies with similar needs.

Do your marketing homework first, and find out what other products are on the market, what their capabilities are, and how they're priced. You can use information you'll collect in the next step to determine what's out there. Then prepare a break-even analysis to estimate how many units you'd have to sell and at what price to achieve the kind of return you want. Make sure to conservatively estimate (meaning estimate on the high side) the costs you'll incur to enter and successfully penetrate the market, just as you would with any other product you're planning to introduce.

If you find that you've few competitors and you can price the finished package at $10,000 each and your marketing and sales expenses would total $100,000, then you can recoup all your development and sales costs selling only 110 copies. If the market will only bear sales of 50 copies, you'll at least make your marketing and sales expenses back plus a portion of your development costs. But real risks exist, such as the possibility that a competitor might introduce a product just like yours at half the price and steal most of the market or that nobody is as interested in the product as you had hoped. You've got to factor in the possibility that you could lose the entire $100,000 marketing and sales investment.

Step 5—Develop Risk Mitigation Strategies

On the other hand, developing an application in-house could be the perfect strategy for several reasons. In the same way that automobile manufacturers subsidize internal finance companies to make it easier to buy their cars, companies that have a frequent need for specialized software often subsidize development houses so they can spread the associated costs and risks. You might not always make your money back, but if you needed the software anyway and can share it without damaging yourself competitively, then by all means do so.

Evaluating Candidate Applications And OSs

Now that you've reduced the size of your list of potential candidates to only those that show a good match with your solution requirements, it's time to compare each candidate against the others to reach your final choice. The basic product you're buying (or developing) is software, and its usefulness depends on the attributes mentioned previously: interface, size, quality, performance, standardization, networkability, compatibility, and security.

Software, though, is only part of the equation. Documentation, training, widespread use, technical support, consulting, licensing terms, delivery format and method, and how well the application fits into your legacy systems are also pertinent. Weighing these factors objectively should be your first step, but don't forget to use your subjective judgement as well. A matrix showing the ranking of each alternative attribute by attribute is helpful, but in the end, the final decision should be made with your personal judgment of the value of each package and the company behind it as well.

Step 1—Rank Features/Limitations In A Matrix

Combine previously built matrices into a larger matrix that contains the important characteristics of all candidates, with the most important characteristics at the top. Some characteristics won't be easy to compare, such as features one application has that another doesn't or differences in licensing terms. These features should be evaluated in the context of your legacy systems and the specific solution you're developing.

Step 2—Calibrate And Score Characteristics

Convert units of measure to common terms and assign a score to each factor based on the range of the factor. For instance, various candidate applications require different amounts of hard disk drive space, and let's suppose the amount of space varies from 21MB to 36MB for a typical installation. The range is therefore 15MB. If we assume a cost of $0.50 per megabyte for storage over the life of the application, then the cost per unit installed ranges from $10.50 to $18.00, a range of $7.50. Depending upon the number of units installed, storage costs could almost double. This sounds like a large increase (almost 100 percent), but if only a few units are installed, the incremental cost is negligible.

Step 3—Use Your Judgment

Some factors are difficult to weight by any totally objective system. The particular likes and dislikes of your users, learning curves, manufacturer's reputation, and so forth can all have a significant impact on the success of your project but don't lend themselves to evaluation by scoring. Ultimately, you'll have to use your judgment, but don't hesitate to ask the experts. You and your staff may be called upon to support the new software, but users will work with it every day, and satisfying their perceived needs is at least as important as satisfying their actual needs.

Negotiating Terms

Buying a single software package off the shelf of your local office warehouse might not seem like an opportunity to negotiate a deal, but it's a deal just as much as buying thousands of copies from a manufacturer over a period of years. No matter what the size of the deal, you can always negotiate for a better price or terms/conditions. The question is: How much can you get for the time and effort you spend? Like most other business decisions, you should consider the cost/benefit/risk trade-offs.

Bargaining is best done from a position of strength, and your strength lies in superior information, both about yourself and those you're buying from. You're strongest when you've no pressing need to purchase, when many alternatives are available, and when the size of your order will make a significant impact on the seller's bottom line. Even if none of these factors are in your favor, keeping that information from the seller and building the appearance of a position of strength may be enough to get you a better deal. So start by determining the parameters of your position.

Step 1—Identify Parameters

How much flexibility is there in your installation schedule? If the entire project is at risk of slippage or failure because of delays in procurement, you've little bargaining room and your position degrades as the installment date approaches.

How many sellers or manufacturers are there? Can you build it yourself, realistically? Can you cobble it together from several packages? Can you change your strategy entirely to eliminate the need without killing the entire project? Even if there's no viable alternative, knowing your position and asking yourself these questions can help you give the impression later of having alternatives.

What price can your company afford? What terms? When does it have to be delivered, and how much support are you going to need for consulting and training? Again, knowing your own position and any alternatives you have is the first step toward eliminating or minimizing detriments and maximizing your bargaining strengths.

Step 2—Collect Intelligence

How many sellers or manufacturers are there? How big are they? How are their sales? Are they startup companies, are they building toward an IPO, are they weakened by competition? What is their position in the market, and how badly do they need to make this sale? Even small sales are negotiable, and even pressing an individual salesperson can get you a discount on a small purchase, if they're looking to make a quota.

Companies will sometimes give you software outright simply to have a prestigious customer to point to when making other deals in the future, so if you're dealing with a startup, you can often get extremely good deals from them. Of course, you're taking a chance because they probably can't offer the same levels of service or stability as a large, more well-known company.

Step 3—Solicit Bids Or Proposals

If possible, advertise to solicit bids. Accepting offers puts you in a very nice position because it lets you set all the terms, collect intelligence, and review at your leisure, knowing bidders are already interested enough to submit a bid. Be careful to ask the right questions, though, or you may end up with a low bid that delivers an inferior product (or is unable to deliver at all). Ask for guarantees, warranties, and performance bonds if necessary.

For smaller purchases, you'll probably have more choices available, so let suppliers or their reps know you're shopping around. They'll be eager to beat their competitors and may make the first move in offering special incentives.

Step 4—Select Potential Suppliers And Bargain

List all potential suppliers and their attributes. Draft a strategy for dealing with each one, and if possible, get them bargaining against one another. For larger deals, it may be worthwhile to put a spin on your company's public image to give the appearance of a position of strength. For instance, a press release noting the strengths of your in-house programming staff indicates the ability to create necessary apps independently, even if there's no way your own staff will have the time to do so (but the seller won't know that).

Keep potential suppliers interested, but as soon as you've definitively selected against a supplier let them know. Depending upon the type and size of order you're planning on making, suppliers may spend an enormous amount of effort preparing elaborate bids and proposals, and you want to do them the courtesy of letting them know how much you appreciate their efforts by treating them fairly.

Step 5—Close The Deal

Even small deals can be viewed as larger deals if you lump multiple small purchases together. Even though there are advantages to getting yourself the best possible deal each time, building a long-term relationship with a supplier has its own benefits as well. Your supplier may become more stable and should certainly learn to anticipate your needs. In addition, your own staff will learn to work with that supplier. The thing to watch out for is becoming complacent or dependent upon one or a small number of suppliers.

The deal should clearly spell out all terms over the life cycle of the application, including any volume discounts (discount amounts and qualification requirements), technical support, and disposal requirements, as we discuss next.

Acquisition, Registration, And Storage

Acquisition can be a one-time event for a given solution, or it can spread over years as an application is procured, used productively, and becomes obsolete. Setting up a workable plan for acquiring, registering, and storing software and its physical components is just a formal way of communicating with people you may never see in person (because of physical or temporal separation). For example, the fellow manning the receiving station might need special instructions about how to handle your shipment of software, and the person receiving patches or periodic technical support releases could use a reference if they're hired long after you've moved on. A simple but clear document outlining requirements for each purchase and shipment is the means to convey this information.

Step 1—Set Acquisition Policy

Regardless of where or by what means the software is delivered, you want to make sure delivery information is transmitted to a central location. That way you can easily verify whether the manufacturer is living up to the terms of the agreement you just made. Lay out delivery terms, delivery method, and delivery locations with the manufacturer in your purchase documentation. Keep in mind that any of these terms might change, either on the manufacturer's end or your own, and the new terms might very well be beneficial to both parties. Ensure that there's some kind of notification process when terms change so your employees will be cognizant of any changes.

You can deliver software and updates in many viable ways because the product is primarily information. It can come as a shrink-wrapped package, with manuals, disks, and packaging, or as a data stream over the Internet. It might be delivered as one package to one location or many data streams to thousands of locations. Of course, verifying that you've received everything you paid for, on schedule, is a bit more difficult in the latter case.

Step 2—Notify Shipping And Receiving

Laying out the terms of the deal in the documentation makes the job of shipping and receiving personnel less stressful because they don't have to find the purchasing person to understand what should be happening. As a matter of fact, posting the documentation to your intranet for their perusal is a good idea (but then, most internal communications benefit from the intranet).

Another helpful idea is laying out a delivery schedule. Because you are, in effect, signing the shipping and receiving folks up to perform certain actions on certain days, providing them with a schedule is a polite way of helping them plan their work. And if you plan to allow users to receive software or updates at their stations, you need to find a way to verify receipt automatically. Don't leave it up to the users because they have their own jobs to do.

Step 3—Receive Deliveries

Your shipping and receiving process should mandate documentation of receipt of software, whether it's done by the shipping and receiving department or individually by users scattered across the organization. Make documenting receipt as easy as possible (automatic if possible). If deliveries don't occur or aren't documented, personally follow up to verify what happened. If you wait too long to notify the manufacturer that you didn't get everything you were promised, it may be much more difficult to track the shipment or reorder.

8. Applications And Operating Systems

Step 4—Unpack, Review Contents, And Store

If your purchase is delivered as just a data stream across the Internet, verify beforehand what files the data stream consists of, what compression method (if any) will be used, the exact size of the file, and any encryption protocols, keys, or certificates are required on your end. See if you can arrange for delivery of an individual file set, for testing purposes, before allowing distribution of the files throughout your company. Before unpacking the files, place them on a machine not connected to your intranet but configured in a similar manner to other machines that'll be running the application. Unpack the files, install them, and test the application with antivirus software and under loads similar to what it'll encounter during production use.

If your purchase is delivered as physical packages with manuals, disks, certificates, and so forth, have it delivered to a central location (or locations), unpacked, verified, and stored safely. As you go about installing it on various machines, create documentation for each machine the application is installed to, then store the documentation with the disks and manuals.

Step 5—Register Applications

You should be able to register the purchase in a batch of registrations, but for some purchases, you'll have to register them individually. Set a registration policy (registration name, organization, and so on) then follow up to ensure that your registration records match that of the manufacturer, so you can get the technical support you deserve later on. If freebies or special deals are offered with the purchase, decide in advance how you want to handle them. By rights, any special offers are the property of the company (like frequent-flyer miles received for company-paid travel), and allowing some people to use them but not others may create friction in the company.

If there's a special licensing mechanism that must be utilized to verify the number of legitimate users, make sure it's properly installed and enforced. Make sure users are aware of it (and the penalties for violating it), so they'll be more likely to abide by it.

Step 6—Dispose Of Applications

Like most other products, software has a life cycle, usually ending with deletion and disposal. There may be terms in your purchase agreement calling for specific steps to be taken when you remove and dispose of your purchase. If not, having a sensible disposal policy is preferable to simply throwing out the old manuals and deleting the applications. For example, if you have older software (disks, manuals, and so on) you can sometimes donate it to schools, churches, or nonprofit organizations for a tax credit. And sometimes the manufacturer will specify a particular method of destruction calling for magnetically erasing data from disks and destroying documentation and certificates, not just dumping them in a landfill. Either way, set out policy in advance when you make the purchase. Doing so will allow you to estimate costs more closely and help out those who need to carry out disposal a few years down the road.

Installation And Maintenance

To use a cliché, installation and maintenance are where "the rubber meets the road." Installation strategies can be as simple as initiating a batch copying process to every machine on a network or as cumbersome and tedious as sending a technician to each machine in the plant for individualized manual installation. Even installing a single application on a single machine can be perilous if that machine somehow supports a critical process. The alternatives available to you dictate which strategies you can use and, thereby, the effectiveness of your installation and maintenance plans and policies. Developing appropriate plans is the first step toward success in each area.

Step 1—Develop An Installation Plan

Development of an appropriate installation plan is dependent upon the machines on which new software will be installed, currently installed software, the processes currently being supported by them, any requirements to run the two concurrently, available training resources, and the installation method you choose. For example, if you install manually, you'll need to schedule technicians during the appropriate time frames and provide them with the materials and tools they need. Building a plan around working hours for a given department is helpful, as is making sure the technicians are able to answer questions about how users can expect the new software to react to their existing applications.

Step 2—Implement Installation

As a general rule, installers should back up existing data before installing new software. They should also check for the appropriate hard disk space and make sure the machine undergoing installation actually has the configuration they expect. Notify users beforehand, so they can help with the backup and so alleviate their fears. These are the machines on which they earn their livelihood, so they have a right to be concerned.

Step 3—Set Maintenance Policy

To keep things running smoothly, machines must receive regular maintenance, and software is no exception. Unfortunately, quite a bit of the maintenance software requires falls into the unscheduled category, so building an efficient maintenance policy can be difficult.

The first thing to do is quantify and categorize all known or suspected maintenance requirements. For example, security holes are likely to be exposed in most networked or client-server applications and most OSs. A portion of the maintenance budget should be set aside for closing security holes, for labor to research, obtain, and install patches, and for notifying users if necessary. The money to set aside can be estimated according to the number of labor hours required, which should be scheduled by technician type as part of the overall plan.

Step 4—Schedule Maintenance

Critical systems may run at all times of the day, while desktop systems usually run only during working hours. A good chunk of maintenance will end up being scheduled at night, and you'll probably pay a nighttime differential premium to your technical staff. Even so, some systems must be maintained according to their own schedule, and disruptions can't be avoided.

Schedule maintenance for the least possible disruption while at the same time minimizing maintenance labor costs by doing work at the most convenient hours as much as possible. For applications that must be up all the time, this can be difficult, and you may have to set aside extra machines to run in parallel while maintenance is taking place. Desktop users can sometimes use their laptops for a few hours rather than shutting down completely.

Step 5—Set Upgrade Policy

Upgrades almost always sound good, but we've found that it's often better to avoid upgrades for 90 to 180 days, especially comprehensive upgrades of basic systems such as OSs and major applications. Unlike patches and service releases, upgrades intentionally introduce new features that come with their own set of bugs, capabilities, and compatibility problems. Waiting until the inevitable new bugs are discovered and ironed out is the prudent course of action, with a side benefit that an understanding of how to efficiently use the upgrade (present in the user community and available technical support knowledge bases) also improves.

Step 6—Schedule Upgrades

Upgrades can be effectively accomplished during routine maintenance actions, so they should be scheduled together, but be careful not to try to do too much all at one time. Troubleshooting problems with an upgrade is made more difficult when you're not exactly sure what caused the problem, the upgrade or the maintenance. Either way, expect an increased volume of trouble calls in the days following an upgrade because users will undoubtedly be getting adjusted to the new software and may not notice problems with drivers, other applications, or common utilities for a few days (until they use them again).

Chapter 9

Marketing

In Depth

This chapter is for application and solution developers who are building databases for use both inside and outside of their organizations. One of the most difficult hurdles developers face is how to market their applications properly; all too often, we deliver solutions in search of a problem, or we ignore customers' own perceptions of their needs and instead concentrate on our view of their problems. Lacking buy-in, the result is a solution that "doesn't work," when we know in fact that it does work and if they would only open their eyes, learn the program, and use it as intended, it would work very well indeed.

The sad fact is, as an industry and as individuals, we often market solutions poorly. In doing so, we do a disservice not only to ourselves, but to the programmers, designers, computer scientists, systems engineers, and everyone else who sweats blood to produce elegantly effective software, as well as the customers who dearly need the features and performance it provides. And yet there are people who seem to sail right through the rough waters of pleasing the customer, miraculously able to take even the tiniest improvement and make it seem like the best thing since sliced bread. It all boils down to perception.

Perception is a strange concept because it cannot be analyzed directly, it constantly changes (in fact, thinking about it can change it), and everybody's perceptions are uniquely their own. Many studies have been done to quantify perception and how various things affect it, but most have met with only moderate success. Still, the human mind seems to go out of its way to avoid predictable behavior, and we all sometimes have difficulty predicting our next move.

Inside our heads are many bits and pieces of personalities, likes and dislikes, considerations, biases, facts, fantasies, fears, and memories of just about everything we've ever encountered, all floating around at various levels of our consciousness. Sometimes they bob to the surface, sometimes they hide submerged, waiting for just the right moment to appear (wanted or unwanted). The "rational mind" is anything but, and marketers know how to influence all of us (at least some of the time).

But there's more to marketing than just persuasion. Depending upon the nature of the product and to whom your marketing efforts are directed, you may need to educate your audience as well as play to their biases. Everyone's heard the old expression "You can lead a horse to water, but you can't make him drink." In this context, it means that you can give a person the facts, but you can't make him understand them. So sometimes marketing means giving the horse an incentive to drink (or a disincentive not to).

So why do we feel that marketing is important enough to include a chapter about it in this book? Assuming you've done a great job of meeting the needs of your customers and users, in the end, how well your solution is marketed and how many people adopt it is the only measure of your success. In marketing terms, the *product, price, place,* and *promotion* must be carefully selected for the consumers we have in mind, our *target market*.

But how do we find out what makes our users tick? And who are they, anyway? How do we reach them and convince them to adopt our solution or buy our product? Those are marketing questions, and in this chapter, you'll learn how to identify the characteristics and motivations of your target market to help sell your solution successfully.

Your Target Market

Whether you're making a small database for yourself, a larger system for your company, an end product to sell to a client, or a standalone product for consumers, you need to appeal to a particular market, or perhaps several markets. The amount of effort you spend on marketing should be commensurate with the difficulty you expect to face selling it to that market. If you're selling it to yourself and a few colleagues, it may not take much to convince this small group to use it, but if you're selling it on the open market, it's a much different story.

No product appeals to all consumers universally, so building an effective marketing strategy starts with identifying differences between the populations that make up your markets. The term "target market" implies that you're aiming your promotional strategy toward specific groups, which are based on characteristics that make them unique. And by the way, it never hurts to make people feel unique.

Stakeholders

Identifying your target market can be a bit of a wild goose chase. For example, babies are not the target market for diapers; their parents are. Babies are the "end users" perhaps, but their parents must be convinced that your brand is the one to buy. By the same token, a senior manager may be the official decision maker when it comes to using a database you create, but the office assistant may be the actual user and make the actual decision. The point is, there may be several stakeholders with input on the decision, some of whom are not easily recognizable. Within an organization, your systems analysis should give you some clues, but outside your organization, you may have to do some detective work to find out who makes purchase or usage decisions (we'll examine how these decisions are made in "Marketing Models" later in this chapter).

Internal Markets

Determining who the stakeholders are is a matter of understanding what each party or group gets out of the product. For example, some folks may enter data into your proposed application, while others may analyze the data for decision-making purposes. Suppose your team has found a way to vastly improve decision making with only a modest increase in data entry. If it's not cost effective to automate the increased data entry, then someone will have to do it manually. This could have a negative impact on data entry clerks, sales clerks, office assistants, or other primary users. Not surprisingly, they may be unhappy about this because very few people find data entry anything other than a tedious, annoying chore. On the other hand, analysts may find that the increased data lets them make much better decisions, which would have a positive impact on them.

Moreover, employee compensation plans may reward the analysts for better performance while penalizing the data entry clerks, who will probably make a few more mistakes. This is a classic example of how company policy can sabotage the best efforts of the IT department and another reason for encouraging change from the bottom up. If those who might feel a negative impact can be encouraged to participate and obstacles to their participation can be removed, your "product introduction" should be well received. External markets tend to be affected by the same kinds of factors.

External Markets

As a database designer, you might be called upon to connect your internal database to the company Web site so outside suppliers or customers can automate their interactions with you. For some developers (or some applications), external markets are consumers for standalone programs. In either case, making external markets aware of the applications, teaching them to use the applications properly, and achieving "buy-in" or anticipated sales volume all rest on identifying positive and negative impacts to stakeholders/customers.

Today's customers appreciate (and expect) a few very common database tools connected to Web sites, for example, or an automated call-management system such as order-tracking queries. Customers benefit because they can determine the status of their orders quickly, often without human intervention. The organization benefits because overhead is lower and customer service is improved. If a bar-coding system that makes data entry easier is installed, even the order-processing employees may perceive beneficial effects, resulting in increased morale. As stakeholders, all these groups should be more satisfied, happier, and more inclined to enthusiastically accept the changes you're proposing. And having identified the stakeholders, you can then proceed to use marketing research to find out what makes them tick.

9. Marketing

Marketing Research

Marketing plays a prominent role in our society, and we tend to think of it as advertising. However, the true goal of marketing is to deduce and then meet the needs of consumers. The most effective marketing reaches all the way back to product design, affecting the characteristics of the product or service, what features are included or discarded, and how it is presented to the consumer. Marketing research, therefore, is an attempt to determine exactly what consumers want (and they often aren't even sure themselves) and how they want it.

Marketing research is inexact, but it can be useful statistically. For instance, if you determine that the average age of employees in your company is 40+, that fact could have a bearing on how you introduce new applications. Younger employees are likely to be comfortable with automated applications, while older folks will tell you about how they used to use slide rules (it wasn't all that long ago!).

Sources Of Marketing Research Data

Typically, marketing research is divided into two categories: primary sources and secondary sources. Primary sources, counterintuitively, are your second step. Secondary sources refer to published studies that may be relevant to your needs, whereas primary sources are studies you undertake when secondary sources don't provide sufficient data. Secondary sources are plentiful at your local business college and, therefore, really just take up your time (or the time of that new assistant just out of business school). Primary sources are much more expensive because they must be designed and performed properly to yield useful information. Unless you have a capable marketing department with the time to devote to a study for your proposed application, you'll probably have to hire a consulting company to perform the study.

Secondary Sources

If you've taken Economics 101, you know that capitalist economies employ market forces to moderate supply and demand, but communist economies attempt to use central planning to predict supply and demand. Because of the chaotic, unpredictable nature of the multitude and manifold buying and selling decisions that make up any economy, communism fails to work efficiently for any length of time, whereas capitalism, with its decentralized decision making, tends to be self-regulating. Of course, neither system is perfect, and keeping a capitalist economy humming but still reasonably fair to all parties involved takes some intervention and regulation as well.

One result of the need for some government intervention in an economy is the production of prodigious amounts of government-sponsored studies concerning input and output across the economy as a whole. There are thousands upon thousands of official government reports produced annually for the economies of the world, reports that track production and consumption of literally everything we make and every service we provide. Not only is raw data produced, but there are summaries at every level as well. You can find this information at civic libraries, at universities, and sometimes on the Web. If you want your data in electronic form, online and updated recently, you may have to pay a fee.

The drawback of precollected, canned reports is that they may not address the specific question you have in mind. Sometimes you can use available data to extrapolate or estimate the specific numbers you need. If not, you must consider performing primary research.

Primary Research

When you endeavor to produce new data from scratch, you are conducting primary research (and there is more discussion about this in the next section). It may be a marketing survey, test marketing, focus groups, and even Beta testing. In fact, Beta testing is an example of how marketing reaches all the way back to the very design of the product in an attempt to create a satisfying one. No primary research should be conducted without carefully considering the company's objectives, however. A poorly designed study may yield great quantities of very expensive data that still cannot be used to draw useful conclusions, and in the worst case, you could actually cause a predisposition against your product even before the final design is set.

The problem is that the act of conducting marketing research—whether it's a survey, Beta-testing program, focus group, or whatever—affects the participants' perceptions. Perhaps you know a developer who, with the best of intent, presented an immature "rough draft" of his solution to a potential user, only to find the project cancelled because the early feedback was so overwhelmingly negative. The best course is to carefully design the research program so statistically accurate answers are produced and to account for the effect surveys and market-testing programs can have on consumers and users. View your primary research efforts as another component of your marketing campaign in general, related to market measurement as you track the progress of your campaign.

Market Measurement

All markets have a size that can be measured in market share, sales volume, units sold, perceptions changed, and so forth. As with most business problems, measuring the size of a market allows us to establish a benchmark for subsequent measurement of the success of our strategy and provides clues for improvement. Knowing how to conduct marketing research prepares us to measure markets accurately, or at least accurately enough to make informed decisions.

Please note that we're discussing both ordinary product sales (such as the sale of a standalone application to the general public) and the level of buy-in created (as in the number of users who adopt your solution). Clearly, although you may not generate dollar figures when you're giving away software, creating a Web-connected application, or providing a solution inside your own company, it's important to be able to measure the number of people who are persuaded to adopt your application. Both types of "sales" can be measured, and there are several commonly used terms that describe market size in regard to market measurement (they each provide a different perspective about the size or composition of a market):

- *Market potential*—If you (and everyone else who is selling) could sell all the products or change all the perceptions that are possible, you would have fulfilled the market potential. In economic terms, you would have reached everyone who was willing and able to buy.

- *Market forecast*—Your market forecast is the amount of units you expect to sell or the number of opinions you expect to change. It includes everyone in the market on the selling side. It will always be lower than the market potential because no one can expect to sell to everyone in the market or to convince 100 percent of the target market to change their minds.

- *Sales potential*—Sales potential is a measure of what you or your company can potentially sell in a given time period. You can measure it as dollar sales or as units sold, and you can substitute the number of users for units sold when you are marketing to users who are not necessarily buyers. As with market potential, it measures the sales potential for the entire market, not just what you realistically expect to sell.

- *Sales forecast*—Your sales forecast is the amount—in dollars, units sold, or adopting users—that you (or your company) expect to sell in a given time frame using a particular marketing plan. If you plan to use two entirely different marketing plans across several national regions, for instance, you will develop two sales forecasts so the success of each marketing plan can be measured and compared.

- *Market share*—Market share is the ratio of company sales to industry sales. For example, if you sell 1M worth of your solution to the market and your competitors sell 9M, your market share is 10 percent (1M + 9M = 10M, 10M ÷ 1M = 10%). If you're selling a solution within your company, you can use legacy solutions or competing methods as a comparison. For example, if 10 users adopt your solution and 90 users continue to use legacy solutions or alternative methods, your internal market share is 10 percent, using the same method of calculation.

- *Sales penetration*—Sales penetration is the ratio of your total sales to your sales potential figure. For example, if sales potential is estimated at 100 units sold in the first quarter and you've sold 10 units, your sales penetration is 10 percent. By the way, if your sales forecast for the first quarter is 10 units, then you've achieved exactly what you predicted.

Market measurement does not have to stop here. You can continue to develop measures (yardsticks) for any aspect of marketing you desire, depending upon those features of the market that are important to your marketing campaign. For instance, you might want to build measures of how consumers (and the market they represent) change over time or how competitors react to your marketing efforts. If you create incentives for purchase or adoption, competitors may counter with even better offers. Gauging changes in consumer desires and competitive response (and planning for them) can help you avoid costly strategies that may not produce results. Several approaches are useful for accurate market measurement.

Measurement Approaches

Measuring markets or sales can yield fairly precise results for times past ("Hindsight is 20/20," as the saying goes), but foretelling the future is guesswork. However, there are methods that can be used to refine guesses about the future to make them more accurate. Rather than pure speculation, you can predict with some confidence the size of markets and the level of sales you can expect. Of course, your predictions will be based on estimates that assume market conditions will remain stable or change in predictable ways. A downturn in the economy, the introduction of a new product by a competitor, changes in the number, size, or marketing strategy of competitors, and so on may have unforeseen impacts. Even something as simple as news reports can spur on or dry up sales of a given product. These forces are at work inside companies as well, so they can affect adoption of new solutions by your target users.

Estimates of market variables are imperfect (hence the term "estimate"), but some are based on less subjective data. Measurement methods using *time series* analysis, *input-output* analysis, and *correlation and regression* analysis are considered objective, while consensus, experience, opinion, and educated speculation are considered subjective. Even so, subjective methods are valuable and may be quite accurate if properly obtained.

Subjective Methods

Subjective methods of market measurement use a modeling approach for calculating size, either adding from the bottom up or subtracting from the top down. For example, if you add up (or take a sample and extrapolate) all projections from customers of their own expected purchases, you can accumulate an estimate of market potential. By the same token, if you start with the size of the world economy and subtract all other industries and markets, you should be left with an estimate of market potential. Whether you're using subjective or objective methods, approaching the problem from the bottom up or the top down is useful, and you can choose your approach on the basis of personal preference or the information available (retrieved during the course of marketing research).

Included within the subjective classification are polling company managers, interviewing sales reps, and surveying distributors or customers. Company managers and sales reps may be inclined toward optimism (or pessimism, depending upon their stake in the matter), but distributors and customers should be fairly unbiased, although it may be difficult to get them to spend the time to make an accurate estimate of their own intentions.

You can sometimes increase overall estimate accuracy by balancing one set of estimates against another. This is where your judgment and experience are crucial. Comparing subjective results to objective results is also helpful for building a realistic picture of the market. Hopefully, any glaring errors will surface in the comparison.

Objective Methods

With objective methods, estimates are based on hard figures, known quantities that are then subject to extrapolation. The time series analysis is based on known sales volume, units, or users extrapolated into the future (the *trend line*). For example, if sales of accounting applications have risen 5 percent each year for the past 10 years, we can assume that sales of such software will rise again 5 percent next year, as illustrated in Figure 9.1.

The danger, of course, is that what we're really dealing with is a very simple model of sales based on one set of figures. There's no guarantee that next year's sales will follow the same pattern. The underlying variables supporting this model

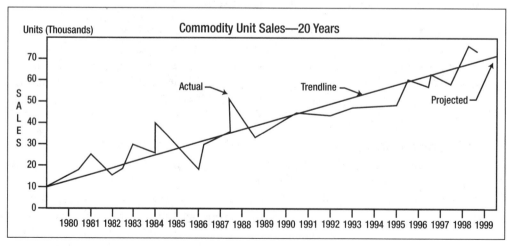

Figure 9.1   Time series analysis graph.

could easily change, and in the end, you're relying on your judgment and experience about the market. In any case, most models will not be nearly so simple or predictable.

Another useful modeling technique is the input-output analysis. Here, we're basing our estimates on the relationship between our product and another product, one for which we may have better estimates of future demand. For example, suppose we have a firm projection that 2M copies of Microsoft Office 2000 will be shipped in the next year, and we know that 8 percent of Office upgrade users will buy a particular application from us (based on previous sales to Office upgrade users). We can then generate a sales forecast of 160,000 units in 1999. The accuracy of our model depends on the stability of the relationship between both products and the accuracy of the primary product's sales projections.

More complex (and presumably more accurate) models can be developed using correlation and regression analysis (shown in Figure 9.2). This type of analysis starts by identifying independent variables affecting the behavior of a dependent variable—in our case, unit sales or user adoption of a database application. The behavior of the dependent variable is correlated with known or projected values (sometimes estimated as a high or low range of values), and regression methods are applied to produce an equation that predicts future values of the dependent variable. The model is thus supported by a mix of variables that, for a time, may be quite representative of the significant factors governing the actual situation and, therefore, may be a good predictor of future events.

Surveys And Test Marketing
Surveys and test marketing fall into a gray area between subjective and objective methods. Surveys are essentially opinion polls that are developed and conducted

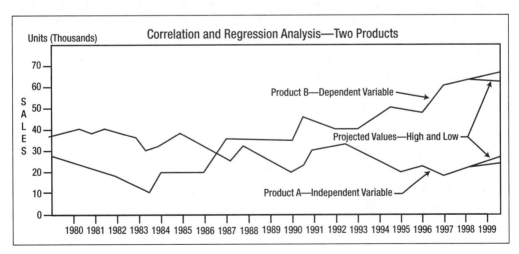

Figure 9.2   Correlation and regression analysis graph.

as accurately as possible. However, because they are the aggregation of opinion, they can be influenced by the biases of pollsters and often are. In fact, in our attention-driven economy, more and more people are refusing to even take polls. This raises the question of how representative the remaining population is. After all, they apparently have nothing better to do.

Test marketing has a similar failing; what people say or do as a test market group may be very different than what ordinary consumers do in the store. You have probably observed the same effect within your own organization when introducing a new application. Bringing people in for training makes them feel special, and so perhaps they try to please you or make you feel good about your efforts. Later on, they may privately discuss their feelings about the pros and cons of the application. Beta testing can have a similar effect.

Beta-Testing Programs

The software industry has been roundly criticized for its inability to consistently (if ever) produce and release bug-free products that work as advertised. And yet, software companies are some of the most successful at involving customers in the earliest product design stages and finding out (although not necessarily delivering) what customers really want. The fact is, software can have any features you care to design in, but that same unlimited flexibility makes it extremely difficult to build in or predict perfect reliability. The very nature of the product forces developers to work closely with clients and consumers when designing and testing software, and any Beta-testing program must be viewed as an element of your overall marketing strategy.

There are several pitfalls to avoid, however. Never introduce a Beta that doesn't at least install and run or one that crashes incessantly for no apparent reason. Don't label it a Beta candidate until you can at least identify the parameters within which its basic functions will work. Provide incentives to Beta testers, not just philosophical reasons for spending the time and effort to help you make the next killer app. And make sure you get feedback that identifies target market characteristics as well as potentially valuable marketing information, not just bug reports. You want to know how people *feel* about your product under development, not just what's technically wrong with it.

Well-designed surveys, test marketing efforts, and Beta-testing programs conducted under unbiased conditions can be revealing. Just making the effort can sometimes prepare a positive environment in which to implement your final version or promote the release candidate. Plus, the wealth of data you gather will lay the groundwork for your next phase, segmenting your target market.

Market Segmentation

Markets are made up of people, and people have thousands of characteristics that make them individuals. Various groups sometimes share similar characteristics (in fact, being part of a particular group can be a characteristic itself). Sometimes, you can find a correlation between the characteristics shared by members of group and their behavior. You may not be able to predict what a single person will do in response to your marketing efforts, but you might be able to predict statistically what the group will do.

Buying behaviors are called *transaction variables*, and they are used to divide a market into similar segments according to how its members respond to buying opportunities. Transaction variables that are useful in segmenting a market include total purchase amounts; frequency of purchases; model, brand, or type purchased; whether buyers are early adopters or in the late majority; and so on. Segmenting a market involves correlating transaction variables with buyer variables, which produces knowledge about what appeals might encourage a person known to possess certain characteristics to engage in buying behavior that is common to his market segment. The characteristics that buyers share within a particular segment are called *buyer variables*.

Buyer Variables

Buyer variables include geographic region, demographics, social class, and so on. The influence and effect of each variables is as much dependent upon the times we live in as the physical realities we face. Figure 9.3 shows typical buyer variables and transaction variables. For example, many American people today prefer to see themselves as living in a classless society and may not respond well to messages appealing to various class levels. Years ago, appeals to class distinctions were much more effective and were not regarded as almost unethical. Geographic variables, on the other hand, persist, and appeals to differences based on geographic location are often plainly made. Interestingly, they are not necessarily unappealing to members from outside the geographic area. (When was the last time you took offense to a truck commercial featuring cowboys?)

Geographic Regions

The size and proximity of geographic areas is the first level of classification by location. Obviously, population groups in other countries share common differences, but population groups in regions, provinces, states, cities, and even towns are often distinct as well. Within these areas, population groups can be further divided by the concentration of people, meaning urban (high concentrations), suburban (intermediate concentrations), and rural (low concentrations). Geographic distinctions sometimes mark groups speaking a particular language (or language type), maintaining a certain culture or religion, and having other more subtle characteristics.

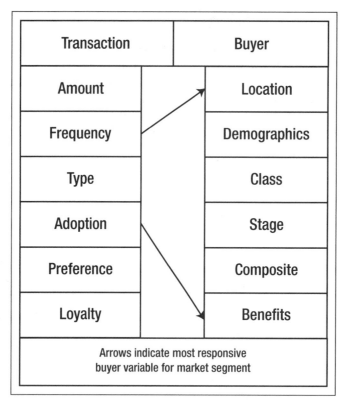

Figure 9.3   Typical buyer and transaction variables

Location and other underlying characteristics affect buying behavior or adoption within organizations much as they affect the general public. Although companies attempt to build a cohesive "corporate culture," geographic dispersion is conducive to the development of "islands of individuality" within an organization, each with its own notions of appropriate acceptance of new applications or business processes.

In both cases, modern communications technology tends to make people feel that they are all part of a common group. At the same time, modern transportation technology reduces geographic separation (at least in terms of the time it takes to overcome distance). We'll probably never be one homogenous group across the planet, but the World Wide Web is making us ever more so. Still, there are other differences that will always define unique groups, called demographics.

Demographics

Our target market is composed of individuals who make buying decisions, and defining them opens the way to analyzing the characteristics they share. Once you've discovered who the decision makers are and have a rough idea of how decisions are made, you can focus on the things that make them unique, including their demographics. Demographics are measurable characteristics that groups of people share (although sometimes you can have a group of only one), such as age, education, gender, marital status, household size, occupation, and so forth. These characteristics can be associated with a propensity to believe certain things, to buy certain things, to act in certain ways. Appealing to the things that make a group of people unique is a well-known and effective tactic for generating interest and influencing buying (or buy-in) decisions. If sales are your objective, then knowing what characteristics members of your audience share is a good place to start devising a strategy.

Although some demographic traits are less helpful than others in predicting buying behavior, a significant advantage of standard demographics is the relative ease with which they can be obtained. Going back to our example in earlier chapters of the grocery store club cards, think of the data that was requested on the form you filled out. Imagine that data being correlated with everything else a good sleuth can find on the Internet and then being further correlated with all the purchases you make. The stores at which you shop may end up with a better idea of what you'll purchase next than *you* have.

Composite Variables

Social class is an example of a set of buyer variables that are grouped together to make one, a composite buyer variable. It consists of education, occupation, and sometimes income, residence location, and other factors (depending on whose interpretation is used). Family life cycle is another composite variable, assembled from age, marital status, children, and so on. For obvious reasons, families at various stages tend to purchase more of some items and less of others. For example, families with newborns or very young children tend to buy diapers, toys, baby food, and TVs. Games and educational software would probably fit into this category (although Grandma and Grandpa might also tend to purchase the same items as gifts for the grandkids).

Subjective Buyer Variables

Buyer variables that are useful in market segmentation are sometimes arrived at via surveys and tests, thus making them more subjective than those based on hard facts. Nevertheless, a strong correlation can be found in them, and it's worth noting that even variables based on objective numbers don't necessarily relate to buying behaviors more closely than those based on subjective variables. *Personality* is one such variable, and there are a multitude of personality tests that can be used to indicate significant personality traits. *Self-image* and *lifestyle* are also subjective variables, and surveys can provide statistically comparable data about them. Even though they are subjective measures, if the surveys and tests are conducted properly, the answers can be accumulated statistically and can indicate group behavior, if not individual behavior.

9. Marketing

Personality, self-image, and lifestyle may not necessarily be as important in the final buying decision as they are in your marketing strategy for assisting your target market in reaching that decision. Knowing the attitudes individuals harbor can make it much easier to persuade them that the application you're developing will be of benefit to them. All of these factors are important when you decide what marketing model (decision-making model) to follow as you build your marketing strategy and plans.

Marketing Models

Understanding the characteristics that define your target market and how they are related to buying behaviors is just the first element of a successful marketing strategy. People often make decisions in mysterious ways, but marketing research indicates the presence of conscious and subconscious stepping-stones along the way to the final decision. They can be modeled in a fashion similar to decision-tree models (as depicted in Figure 9.4) used in decision support systems, but there is disagreement about how valid the models are. Nevertheless, modeling how your users might make a decision to accept or reject the solution you build for them can provide important clues about what marketing strategy might have the most positive influence.

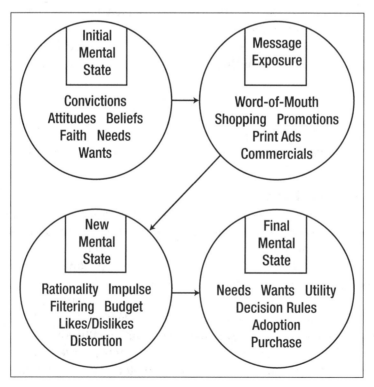

Figure 9.4   Online service adoption decision-making model.

Every group is composed of people who, for one reason or another, tend to reach similar decisions after a time. That is part of what makes them a group. How they arrive at those attitudes is the subject of much debate (group dynamics), but some factors tend to be applicable to all groups. For example, most groups can be divided into leaders and followers, or more generally, into a pecking order. There is also an element of authority in most organizations; a team, section, or branch usually has someone with appointed authority. Some leaders lead by doing, others lead opinions (the opinion leader), and the majority of folks in the group follow their lead. In most groups, there are a few dissenters, but unless they become leaders, their influence remains negligible.

Individuals and groups both have decision-making dynamics that can be modeled, although experts disagree on what model is most accurate for any given circumstance. Marketing models tend to follow similar paths (like decision trees), but they often aim at subconscious biases and fears to work their magic. Finding and perhaps modifying the right marketing model tells you what path you need to follow with your marketing strategy.

Marketing Strategy Development

The development of any strategy (marketing or otherwise) requires an understanding of and a commitment to the goals and objectives of the organization, an assessment of the organization's strengths, weaknesses, and available resources, and the experience to discriminate between actions having low and high probabilities of producing the desired outcome. The first step in developing a marketing campaign is establishing a marketing strategy, and the actual plan of action (or plan of attack, whichever you prefer) should be born as a consequence of strategic decisions.

There are two primary parts for successful marketing campaigns, but both are not required for every implementation. The first is education, which includes (hopefully) facts and persuasion. The second is a call to action, meaning there is something specific you want the person or group to do or not do. Sometimes both are mixed together in marketing communications, and sometimes they are deliberately segregated by media or separated in time. Your objective is to educate the audience by giving them the facts they need in a way they can understand and to persuade them to perceive things in a way that is favorable to you. If they already understand the situation and perceive it in the preferred way, then all you should have to do is ask them to take action. Action can be both positive and negative, as in asking someone to try your product (positive) or asking someone to avoid other products (negative).

The marketing model you've chosen should give you an indication of the media to use and how to shape the messages you deliver so your audience will be receptive.

9. Marketing

Especially if you need to educate your audience before they reach the frame of mind in which a purchase or adoption decision can be made, you need them to be in a receptive and enthusiastic state.

Consumer (User) Education

There's a reason why "timing is everything" for inventions and new products. No matter how great the benefits or how dazzling the new technology, if people aren't ready for it, they won't accept it, like it, buy it, or use it. Most humans naturally fear the unknown, the different, and even change itself. When you have the world's greatest mousetrap but the world isn't ready for it, education can sometimes bridge the gap. The trick is to figure out what people really need to know in order to understand why they need your mousetrap, how it's better than all the others, and how to use it properly once they have it.

Relatively few people need to know how to eat an apple, or why, but that doesn't stop produce companies from running ads or sponsoring studies about the nutritional benefits of eating apples or how delicious they taste. Of course, some of this advertising is just an excuse to remind us that apples are there, but some of it is truly educational. And it never hurts to spend a little effort to educate those whose cultural background does not include the habit of eating apples (or baking apple pies). Educational efforts should focus specifically on the attributes that make the product worthy of attention, why those attributes constitute improvements over other products, how they're related to benefits delivered, and how consumers or users can tap those benefits for themselves.

Users also require education, not just about how to use a new application, but why it is best for themselves and the company. Especially where there is little direct benefit to the individual, it's worthwhile to spend some effort convincing users that adoption of the application will at least bring them indirect benefits. Users may also need to be educated about the scope of their jobs and the extent of their jobs' data-driven requirements. It's not uncommon to find knowledge workers using only experience to perform their jobs, flying by the seat of their pants, as it were. They may be totally unaware that there is data available to assist them as they manage their responsibilities, that they are mandated to process it before arriving at certain decisions, or that there are tools available to help them process the data, much less a new and improved tool. Calling such people to action is futile unless they understand their position.

The Call To Action

After delivering educational and persuasive messages, it's time to ask people to behave as you would like them to, but not necessarily in obvious terms. Rather than a direct appeal, perhaps you can pick a related behavior they feel comfortable with and associate it with the action you intend for them to carry out. You've laid the groundwork in their minds, but to get them to act, you need to "ask for the sale" one way or another.

If users or consumers fear something about the new application or service, it may be appropriate to use incentives or disincentives to precipitate action. Even in the most authoritarian organizations, simply ordering people to use a new product or service will usually have little effect, but the proper education, call to action, and incentives can be excellent motivators. For example, suppose you are encouraging the production department to use a new reporting tool to update, track, and adjust production costs and output on a daily basis. Managers are on board because they'll be able maintain much better control over production and solve problems before they get out of hand, but foremen and workers don't pay much attention because it's an added burden, and unfamiliar as well. Rather than beating frontline employees to death about using the system, a better approach would be to appeal to their pride by establishing a cost/schedule limit of some kind (most any deadline, crisis, event, or milestone will serve, and you can make one up if you have to).

Make sure they are of aware of and understand the new reporting tool (education), articulate the reasons they must meet the deadline in terms that appeal to their sense of pride and professionalism ("One for the Gipper," that sort of thing), and make the deadline tight enough that failure is probable without use of the tool (incentive/disincentive). The leaders among the group will quickly decide that adopting the tool is the best course of action; otherwise, followers in the group may have the opportunity to displace them as leaders, and they wouldn't want that. Next thing you know, your frontliners will be using the tool as if they had been using it all their lives and claiming that they actually conceived of it and pushed you into building it for them. Then it's time for you to take a little bow, but make sure they receive most of the credit. After all, their "ownership" is what made it work.

The scenario just outlined is an example of how you can use the power of education, persuasion, and incentives to accomplish your marketing objectives, but there is a great deal more to it than that. Formal marketing plans are the basis of well-designed marketing campaigns, and implementation is no different than any other business activity. It must be planned, executed, measured, and modified during execution like most other programs or projects.

Marketing Planning And Implementation

Careful planning can make the difference between an effective campaign and one that actually backfires. People hate to be patronized, but they love to be stroked. People hate to be lied to, but they love a little exaggeration. Who offers the message (and how) is at least as important as the message itself (remember "The medium is the message"?). The medium, the time of day, the semantic content of the words, the imagery in the pictures—any impact on the senses at all affects how the message is perceived.

Delivering The Message

There are many means available to deliver your message (or messages). Television, radio, print (newspapers, magazines, books), billboards and signs, personal communication, the Web, matchbook covers, the side of a blimp—you name it, someone will try it. You need to consider the following key factors:

- *The nature of the message*—Is the message positive or negative? Is it educational or a call to action, or is its purpose to establish an ambiance or frame of mind?

- *Common perceptions about the medium*—Is the medium perceived as honest, straightforward, unbiased? Is the medium live, recorded, historical? From where does your target market usually get messages of this type?

- *Common perceptions about the deliverer*—Does the message come from someone you can trust? Do you trust the Pillsbury Doughboy? Do you trust your senator? Do you trust managers or users, and do they trust the IT department?

- *Situational factors about the message*—What time of day (or time of year) will the message be delivered? With what images does the delivery associate the message? What sounds? How long is the message, and how many times will it be repeated? What other messages are delivered in conjunction with your message (what program is on during its delivery, or what magazine articles are nearby)?

Your plan should include a time line of actions (commercial advertisements, conventions, training sessions, Beta-testing programs, and so on). It should also make clear what numbers you expect to see at each phase and some method for relating those numbers back to the actions you took. For example, if you expect your print ads to influence 20 percent of a given target market, you should be able to survey a sample of those folks and find out the rate at which print ads influenced them.

After contracting for the resources required to produce and deliver your messages and initiating your campaign, you need to follow up with further measurement to correct your course as you go. Competitors respond, consumers change their minds, and no implementation is perfect. If you take measurements frequently and take corrective action where needed, you'll conduct a successful campaign.

Immediate Solutions

This section illustrates the steps to take to build a solid marketing strategy, whether you're "selling" your solution to an in-house group or on the commercial market. Although it may not be necessary to conduct a full-blown marketing survey for small, internal applications that don't get wide usage, understanding the steps involved and giving them their due increases the probability that your solution will be successful.

We're concerning ourselves with two primary situations here: developing an application for use by company employees or the public without a monetary transaction and selling complete, standalone applications to the general public. If you happen to be developing solutions for other companies as a consultant, you can apply the nonmonetary transaction case to yourself because your sales job to the company itself has already been done and you need to market your solution to the users within the other company.

The development of a sound plan of action involves the usual steps of defining the parameters within which you're operating, setting goals and objectives, arriving at a strategy for accomplishing them, measuring the results, and taking corrective action. There are some interesting and unique-to-marketing things to consider along the way, and the following steps will help to clarify the dos and don'ts.

As an example marketing campaign for this chapter, we'll use a customer service application developed for a fictitious company called Parts Plus. Parts Plus sells replacement parts for industrial and consumer items across several industries: home appliances, sporting goods, electronics, computers, office equipment, manufacturing and scientific gear, and so forth. With so many unique items for sale covering such a wide cross section of equipment types, Parts Plus has a major problem coping with consumer (both individual and corporate) requests for information concerning proper usage, care, servicing, and warranties for its products.

The Parts Plus IT staff has been developing a database application connected to its Web site as a front-end application to serve its customers automatically, 24-7. The staff is now working with the marketing department to create and conduct an effective marketing campaign with the following objectives:

- To find out who might use the service and how much their use of the service would save the company now and in the future.

- To determine what potential users want in such a service and to modify the design of the service to accommodate those wants.

- To segment the market according to usage patterns and to understand the characteristics shared within user populations so an effective marketing strategy and plan can be formulated.

- To make potential users aware of the service, educate them about what benefits it confers, and show them how to use it effectively.

- To track implementation progress, competitors' responses, and degree of marketing success and then revise the plan as necessary to maintain progress toward stated marketing goals.

The IT and marketing managers at Parts Plus enjoy an especially productive working relationship, and they have collaborated on projects several times in the past with positive results. They start by brainstorming about the target market.

Identifying Your Target Market

Your target market is made up of people who, for some reason or another, stand to be affected by the solution you're developing. They have a stake in the outcome and are therefore called stakeholders. Easiest to identify are the primary users; assuming you've done your job well, proper use of the application should result in benefits to the users. Remember, though, that sometimes the beneficiaries are not the users themselves. Data-entry clerks are users, too, even though they may never analyze the data they've entered. For them, the new solution may merely add to their data-entry burden. It's important to identify all stakeholders, even those for whom the impacts are negative rather than positive.

The target market for Parts Plus can be found by using a process of elimination. Out of all the people on the planet, which ones are willing and able to use the proposed customer service system and also have the need to do so? How do they decide that it is a better alternative for fulfilling their customer service needs than visiting the store or calling in? Before you begin market measurement and marketing model development in earnest, you need to understand how your target market thinks on a macro level. You can start by simply making a list of potential users.

Listing Potential Users

Categorize all potential users according to whether they enter, analyze, maintain, update, delete, or otherwise interact with data in the system and whether they do so as primary users (users actually at the workstation), secondary users (users reviewing summaries or reports), or tertiary users (users who may not interact with the data or abstracts from it but feel a positive or negative impact nevertheless). List everyone you can think of, including their place within the systems analysis or their position outside the company.

For Parts Plus, the list is made up of everyone inside the company who maintains the system or is affected by the results of customer usage, as well as the customers themselves. Make sure to include as much data about users and those affected by usage as you can: organizational position, demographics, what relationship they have with the application, and so forth.

Checking Systems Analysis And Processing Engineering Documents

Review systems analysis and process engineering documents (both existing and proposed) to understand how users and customers perceive the solution and the data it provides compared to how they perceive legacy systems. Consider the impact new applications may have on their role. For Parts Plus, customers are already fed up with the legacy method of providing customer service and are ready for something new, but they are suspicious of claims about improved customer service from a company that doesn't perform well at present.

Defining Usage Circumstances

Note the timing, frequency, method, and expected results when the application communicates with them and vice versa. Summarize and analyze call-in records to find out who calls in, when, for how long, and what problems they're calling about. Correlate this data with any demographics data you've been able to accumulate. You can use this data later when you begin to segment the market by transaction variables. The calling records for Parts Plus indicate that the majority of calls share the following commonalities:

- 70 percent of calls occur within two days of initial purchase regardless of the item purchased.

- Calls are usually received in the afternoon and evening, but there are a significant number of calls after 11:00 P.M. but before 3:00 A.M..

- Callers stay on the line for 15 to 18 minutes after the call is answered by a technician.

- Most callers ask for directions about how to use the product properly, and less than 10 percent call to report a defect or problem.

Based on this information, a number of things can be said about how people reach a decision to use the customer service call-in system. Most consumers put Parts Plus products to work right away, and that's when they need help the most. They work typical schedules, but some work after hours into the night, and they need a source of information that can be accessed anytime. Their questions are not routine, so they stay on the line a significant amount of time before getting the answers they need. The products are fairly well manufactured but accompanying manuals or training materials are not doing a good enough job of educating consumers (either that or the nature of the products is too complex for people to feel comfortable without some hand-holding).

Listing User Characteristics

Users tend to share certain characteristics when they share stakes in a solution. Unlike demographics, which may vary among a group of users, characteristics such as occupation, job responsibilities, processes supported, usage requirements, and so on are common across the user group. These characteristics nevertheless must be accounted for in the marketing plan, and appealing to them can increase your odds of successful introduction of an application. Parts Plus customers fall into the ordinary segments, but the internal employees affected by the customer service system are mainly composed of existing customer service representatives who earn relatively low wages, are typically younger, and are typically fairly new to the company.

Verifying The Usage Model

It's easy to make assumptions about how data should be used, and it often seems obvious that a particular user or customer needs a given piece of data to make a decision or accomplish a selected task. Users are fickle and quite finicky, and each person may have a different approach to his or her job or to the task of getting something new to work properly. What seems important to you might not be important to the user/consumer at all. Targeted Parts Plus users are customer service representatives who will be maintaining the new system while keeping the old call-in system going in parallel. They'll have to be proficient at entering data into the new system while taking calls from the old system, and they will probably see some of their friends transferred to other departments as the work load diminishes. As you can see, how they use the new system and their role as members of the target market may be more complex than you originally anticipated.

Customers may also have a complex role to play within the target market. For example, they may decide that some of their questions are better answered by a live person rather than a computerized system. Taking the time to interview users and customers to determine exactly how they individually fulfill the requirements of their job or their needs often allows you to make small but significant changes in the final product rather than building a "one-size-fits-all" solution.

Conducting Marketing Research

Most universities have business departments, and there is a large volume of existing marketing research that you can tap into at small expense. Performing valid marketing research studies is costly, complex, and difficult to do quickly. Parts Plus has plenty of previous marketing studies that show who its typical customers are (including demographics and other characteristics), but a Beta-testing effort is in order to refine the service so it will be easy to navigate.

Depending upon your needs and the scope of your project, you may be able to get by with a modest research effort, or you might need to allocate significant dollars and time. If you can estimate costs and benefits of formal marketing studies (primary research) with reasonable precision, you can use that information to help decide whether to pursue them or not. But before you get started, put together a marketing research plan.

Planning Marketing Research

Marketing research is sometimes as easy and straightforward as counting units sold and to whom, or it can be as difficult and imprecise as looking into a crystal ball. You'll need to do a little reverse engineering, starting with the numbers you know you need and working your way backward to determine intermediate numbers at each stage, as well as where the holes are. Your marketing research plan should articulate why each number or set of numbers is required, determine how accurate the numbers must be, and offer an indication of what source might be used to obtain them.

The marketing manager for Parts Plus has resurrected past marketing studies that detail what factors are common to Parts Plus customers, including what they buy and when, what traits they share, and how many times they come back for more of the same or similar products. He realizes that what he doesn't know is how many of them have the means to access an online service effectively, how computer literate they are, or the impact a customer's poor navigation skills might have on internal customer service reps.

Checking Secondary Sources

The cheapest and easiest way to get the data you need is to consult all secondary sources: your local business school library, the Internet, previous marketing studies you've performed, and so forth. The drawback is that these sources often contain reams of data that may not be quite what you're looking for, and it takes time to peruse them to find out whether they can be used. Our Parts Plus marketing manager already has some of the data he needs from previous studies, so he goes online to find out what else is available. He finds that there are good numbers

9. Marketing

(available for free) regarding the number of households that possess computers and have Internet access, but there is no direct data on how many additional calls might be generated on the legacy call-in customer service system because of customer inability to use the automated system.

Developing Survey Tools

Our marketing manager realizes he should develop some kind of estimate about the impact computer literacy will have on the effectiveness of the proposed customer service system. He asks the IT manager to work with him to build a test of the system overflow into the Beta-testing program, specifically to answer that question. Both managers decide that each call-in customer will be asked if they found what they need on the online system for a period of days during the Beta test. If the call-in customer doesn't know about the Beta test, she will be offered an incentive to try it. The customer service representative will then direct her to the Web site but ask her to please call back if she can't find her answer. In the course of the subsequent problem-solving session with the rep, all those who call back will be asked politely what the difficulty was. A survey conducted in this manner makes customers feel as if they're being offered more options rather than fewer, and it also gathers data about which customers can use an online system as well as what problems they had using it. Finally, it allows managers to gauge how many folks will call back after trying it.

Evaluating Results

Results should be summarized in a formal report, even when the data is brief, the results seem obvious, and indications are plain. For instance, the marketing and IT managers for Parts Plus prepare a report pulling together all data they've accumulated about customers, customer service reps, and customer service requests. Based on the data, they realize that they must put more effort into making the Web site easy to navigate, making customers aware of its existence, and putting lots of "how-to" information on it. Emphasizing these areas will facilitate reductions in usage of the old call-in system as well as relieve stress on customer service reps, which will help achieve the overall goals of the customer service system.

Measuring The Potential Market

Gauging the size of a market is important to you as an IT manager or software marketing manager, and it is important to your company as well. Parts Plus has an idea of who its target market is, but it needs to formally estimate the size and growth of its target market over the next several years. Many of the marketing and production decisions you make will be based on the size of the market, and many of the decisions others in your company make will be based on the same data. Although it is more an art than a science, there are steps you can follow to at least do it consistently, and you'll learn quite a bit more about it as you go. The first step is to figure out what it is you want to measure and how accurately.

Determining Measurement Goals

Parts Plus is designing a Web-based database (an automated customer service application) for use by its customers. The obvious assumption is that everyone in the world should use it, but the actual market will most certainly be restricted to those who can and will. Not everybody can access the Web, and of those who can, not everyone will use the automated customer service application. In addition to the measurements already made, you would want to measure how many potential customers there are, how many will have access to the Web, and how many might prefer to use an automated response system in the years to come. Parts Plus expects its customer service application to last at least three years in its present form, and they would like to see 70 percent to 90 percent of customer service requests fulfilled by it across that time frame.

Choosing A Measurement Approach

The type of measurement you're interested in making is expressed in units called customers. You must determine the time frame to measure, how frequently customers will use the service, and how accurate your numbers must be. The Parts Plus marketing department already has good counts of existing customers as well as good projections of potential customers (and sales forecasts, too). That should satisfy the first measure and correlate to the time frames it has chosen to work with.

The life cycle of your application should drive the time frames you use, especially if there are still decisions to be made concerning cost/benefits of deploying the application. For an application such as this, it's more important (and more difficult) to be accurate on the high end rather than the low end because, on the Web, your maximum expected usage drives your total expenditures for hardware, software, and bandwidth.

Analyzing Market Variables

Imagine waves of new customers buying your company's products, and suppose the products are desirable but happen to have a rather large learning curve (have you bought a flatbed scanner recently?). This is the situation in which Parts Plus finds itself. Some of the same variables that produce excellent sales results could also generate lots of users for their customer service application. If sales are high and the learning curve is high but usage figures are extremely low, that's an indication that there are other variables at work.

Choosing which customer service avenue to utilize is a funny decision. For routine matters, a Web site is preferable (for someone with easy Internet access) to an 800 number; 800 numbers employ verbal menu choices that may take a long time to traverse, and even the best call centers get overloaded from time to time. On the other hand, customers may believe that talking directly to a person is the only way to solve what they perceive as a unique problem, and therefore, they may ignore the Web site (even if the information they want is easily available).

Estimating Current Market Size

Estimating market potential and sales potential (the size of the entire market and the amount of sales a given company can expect) may not seem to be necessary in our current case (a customer service application on the Web). But suppose the majority of sales occur through distributors and all service is supplied by the manufacturer. You may only be able to estimate how many people will come to the Web site by looking at total market sales and then correlating percentage of sales to your products. This is a common situation, and it means that you may need to estimate both market potential and sales potential to get a clear picture of potential adoption and usage for your customer service application. Parts Plus retails directly to consumers, so it has a clear picture of how many customers it has and who they are.

Projecting Future Market Size

You can facilitate the projection of the size of future markets with research. Secondary sources, model development, and test marketing methods are traditionally used, and the method selected is determined by the costs involved and the accuracy required. Costs and accuracy relate to the risks involved; if you're risking lots of money or resources (or even the image of your company), it makes sense to invest more in research.

Because even the best models and data are fairly mechanical representations of a fluid reality, and because software markets, technology, and perceptions are changing so rapidly, you'll also need to exercise your judgment when predicting market size. In some cases, you may even need to influence the direction of the market (as you've undoubtedly seen larger companies attempt). Distasteful as they may seem (especially when done by others), hype and vaporware can serve a company well and should not be taken lightly. At the very least, you must be able to recognize them and account for them in your own estimates.

Parts Plus bases its estimates of the future market for its automated customer service application on estimates of sales for its products over the next three years, converted from dollar figures to units sold. Each item sold represents a certain number of customer service requests in the first two weeks, corresponding to the number of hits the Web site can expect. The marketing manager further categorizes products sold by the number of service calls taken in the past (for each category) and extrapolates from there to determine how much information to place in the system for each product category.

Segmenting Your Market

Once you've measured the market, you can begin breaking it down into segments that share identifiable transaction variables, and then you can analyze the populations of those segments for shared traits (buyer variables). Disregarding for a moment the connection between shared traits and likely response to your marketing efforts, this step is an exercise in understanding the components of your market.

Not only should you begin to get a statistical feel for your customers or users, you should also develop a sense of what makes them tick. If you're lucky enough to have market segments that share characteristics with yourself or people you know well, disassociate yourself from your work for a moment and think about how you or your friends would react to the introduction of a new application or automated service. Would you use it, or would you ignore or reject it? What have you done in the past? Hasn't there been at least one occasion where you rejected a new application because you didn't understand it, because it was implemented on the wrong platform (in your eyes), or because you didn't like the people proposing it? Put yourself in the shoes of your prospective customers, see things through their eyes, forget about optimism and your desire for a successful application, and you'll gain a whole new perspective. The ability to do this objectively is a talent that will help you avoid costly mistakes and will spur your creative juices when a difficult sales job is called for.

Identifying Transaction Variables

Transaction variables are behaviors you can expect members of a particular segment to perform when given the opportunity. Most markets contain a mix of transaction variables, meaning some groups will not buy, some will buy occasionally, some will buy in large or small quantities, some will buy immediately and some will take their time, and so on.

In the case of a Web-based customer service system, there will be people who will, for example, use or not use, use frequently or occasionally, or use in response to a particular problem. You can estimate usage patterns from existing customer service records for your call center or from other automated customer service systems for which research data is available in secondary sources.

As an example, let's say Parts Plus estimates that 20 percent of its customers will never use a Web-based customer service system, 10 percent will use it frequently for every minor or imagined problem they encounter, 30 percent will use it frequently in the first 45 days after purchase of the company's product, and 40 percent will use it occasionally (and randomly) over the life of the product. The marketing manager does a preliminary segmentation of the markets by these four transaction variables and then begins the process of attributing buyer variables to each portion of the market.

Identifying Buyer Variables

Within each preliminary segment, there may be several population groups sharing traits that might make them susceptible to various marketing appeals. For example, perhaps the 20 percent who never use the service are composed of young professionals who already understand the product well and older folks who don't have (or want) access to the Web. Maybe the 10 percent who use it frequently are located in rural areas too far from a store to stop by for customer service and also happen to have lower education levels and therefore need more hand-holding.

Essentially, your job is to carefully examine the people falling into each category and discern what traits they share. Information about their traits should be available from your target market research and can be exposed by running their data through a cross-tab application. Along one dimension runs the segment they belong to, and along the other dimension runs the traits they share, as shown in Figure 9.5.

Transaction \ Buyer	Location	Demographics	Class	Stage	Composite	Benefits
Amount	0	20	0	0	80	0
Frequency	20	40	0	10	0	30
Type	0	30	0	40	20	10
Adoption	40	20	0	10	0	30
Preference	0	10	50	20	10	10
Loyalty	40	10	40	10	0	0

Buyer variable percentage across segments—segmented by transaction variable

Figure 9.5   Cross-tab graph of market segments and traits.

Determining Connections Between Variables

In the preceding step, you assembled all the buyer variables that seem to be present in each preliminary market segment. In this step, your goal is to make a careful analysis of those variables to determine the nature of the connection between buyer and transaction variables. Do the 40 percent who only access the service occasionally do so because they're well educated, because they have a higher income and a better understanding of the product, or because they have less time to spend? The answers may not be obvious, and extra study may be warranted.

Examining Preliminary Variables For Subtle Differences

Depending on the groupings you find in each segment, it may be necessary to further subdivide segments and the population groups within them. In our Parts Plus example, if everyone in the market has a high income, the marketing manager may have to differentiate between them on the basis of where that income comes from. Is it earned, inherited, or from investments? Are there more subtle differences in buying behaviors based on smaller gradations of income within their income group? Do they tend to spend more or less of the income they receive? Especially where there appears to be no significant difference between groups that would connect them to a particular transaction variable (you find similar groups in all segments), you need to refine your data until significant variables appear.

Mapping Segments To Significant Variables

There may be several significant variables for each group after the preceding step is completed, but to develop an effective marketing strategy, you must determine the most significant variables and rank them in order. For example, you might find that, within the 30 percent who access the system heavily in the first 45 days after purchase, 90 percent have no more than a high school education and 70 percent consider themselves aggressive and bright. They access the system heavily because they are determined to understand the product. Education and self-image appear to be the significant traits in this case, in that order.

Selecting Segments To Serve

If 10 percent of your target market is going to access the service excessively, do you need to make an appeal to them to use the service? Maybe not. Will a negative appeal or more education encourage them to use the system more wisely or effectively? Probably not. Is there any point in aiming your marketing efforts at them, and if you did, would it result in better ratings for customer satisfaction? Again, the answer is likely to be no (or negligible). On the other hand, catering to the 30 percent who are heavy users or the 40 percent who use the system occasionally should bring positive results. The point is, marketing efforts will be wasted or counterproductive with some groups, so you need to begin making some decisions about which segments you want to serve. You can do this by deciding whether marketing efforts can affect the group in question and whether the potential benefits are worth the effort.

Choosing/Developing Marketing Models

The marketing model you choose depends on several factors: whether you're interested in persuading individuals or groups, the traits shared by populations of each market segment, and how closely models match the characteristics of those populations. Sometimes it's necessary to modify existing models so they conform to your requirements. This is another area where your experience and professional judgment are required, and the job is not an easy one because the variables supporting each model don't always affect the outcome in a linear fashion.

Evaluating Existing Models

Start by gathering the most recent research on models of consumer buying behavior or adoption patterns. There are always a few models being developed, modified, refined, or discarded—some new, some fashionable, some out-of-favor. Look for a model that addresses products in your industry, populations in your selected market segments, and traits that your populations share. Examine the decision path of each model, especially where you already have an idea of the message you want to communicate. The marketing manager at Parts Plus has found a model that seems to work for well-educated, high-income folks and shows a fairly straightforward decision path influenced by print ads and word of mouth. It is considered a strong candidate for driving the Parts Plus marketing strategy.

Applying Models

Having selected a model or a small set of models to work with, your next step is to apply them to the factors you're working with. Each model represents a series of decision points people must pass through, and the interaction of message delivery/reception and the inner workings of the model determine its impact on the targeted population. At each stage, the model should predict how many people, given optimum exposure to the message, incorporate the desired perception into their thought processes. To determine an overall estimate (or range of estimates) for success of the campaign, you must input estimates of positive influence for each targeted population at each stage of the model. Application of the model to the target markets for Parts Plus reveals that as many as 70 percent of potential users can be brought to the conclusion that using the automated customer service system can effectively serve their needs.

Modifying Models

Because models are based on attributes of statistically average populations and variations in perceptive functions, you can modify them to assume characteristics more like your actual populations in order to estimate the probability of a significant difference in their response rates. It might be worthwhile to do this with several alternative models to find the best possible model to use.

Choosing The Best Fit

In the end, the model you choose to use is just a tool to help you do your job and avoid obvious mistakes. No model is perfect, and conditions change rapidly. The real benefit is that you have done your homework and are basing your decisions on more than just your experience and professional judgment. Even the best model could indicate a poor or counterproductive strategy, though, so be prepared to alter your plans if reality indicates that the model has gone sour.

Developing Your Marketing Strategy

Building your marketing strategy means taking into account everything you know about your target market and selected segments, deciding what appeal has the best chance of helping you accomplish your objectives, and figuring out the best way to implement your strategy. Influencing people or groups is an art, not a science, and creativity counts. It's a fact that, in today's economy, there are so many messages being communicated that getting someone's full, undivided attention is problematic at best. Your strategy should include components designed to address the decision-making process at every step of the way, and they should do so in a way that leaves consumers with the right impression.

Building Initial Strategy

Your strategy should be based on the marketing model you plan to follow, and you should consider the existing perceptions of consumers and what decisions they need to make to lead them to the behavior you desire. Parts Plus, for example, knows it needs to make sure potential users are aware of how easy it is to use automated customer service systems. The marketing manager also asks the following questions:

- Do customers and internal users view these systems favorably, or do they see them as complicated, hard to navigate, and unhelpful?

- What is the primary means by which they can be educated about customer service systems, and which delivery method is most likely to have the desired result?

- Are there opinion leaders who, if convinced, will convince others to follow?

Answering questions such as these helps decide how to approach message delivery for each decision point and usually leads to several strategy alternatives. To verify the usefulness of alternatives, you should use test marketing or Beta testing.

Conducting Test Marketing/Beta Testing

During your marketing research phase, you may have conducted some test marketing to help determine how consumers respond to new products or services, but another round of test marketing (or Beta testing) may be in order to determine how consumers respond to marketing efforts you intend to carry out. If necessary, plan a small-scale marketing effort to test the accuracy of the model you're following for each of the alternative strategies you've developed.

Modifying Strategy

The strategy you ultimately choose will be the one that appears to have the best chance of helping you to accomplish your goals within your cost parameters. Of course, if there appear to be no viable alternatives, perhaps it's time to go back to the drawing board and rethink the product you're planning to introduce. It doesn't necessarily mean the product is not good; perhaps it's just not cost effective to try to sell it to the market you would like to serve.

On the other hand, if there are modifications you can make to the strategy that result in significant gains, perhaps you're better off making those changes. Just be sure to retest and revise as necessary. In our Parts Plus example, the marketing manager has concluded that the best way to make customers aware of the automated system is to plant Web sites related to each major product group on the Internet, using domain names and Meta tags that increase the probability of high rankings in frequently used search engines. Because the population of users likely to utilize the service is familiar and comfortable with search engines, they should be receptive to finding information about customer service options there.

Developing A Marketing Plan

The development of your marketing plan includes formulation of the budget, listing of all required resources, estimates of their impact at each stage (from the marketing model application), how each step is related to the next, and what steps are dependent upon preceding steps for success. In fact, the marketing manager for Parts Plus has put all phases and milestones of the marketing plan into a project-management tool for easy assignment of resources and task interconnection.

Implementing Your Marketing Plan

Putting a marketing plan in action means spending resources according to a time line. Essentially, that means making contact with people—if not personally, then remotely. All of your messages should be crafted beforehand, but some will be custom-made and personally delivered (although perhaps by a professional speaker, trainer, or marketing representative) on the spot while others will be stored and delivered automatically.

For messages delivered in person, you'll be setting up meetings, offering training sessions, or participating in trade shows and conventions. For building consumer awareness and encouraging user adoption in the mass media, you'll be contracting with advertising firms, creating commercials and ads, scheduling time on radio or TV, and buying space in publications. You may also employ many other common advertising vehicles, such as slogans, URLs, and email addresses on business cards, letterhead, brochures, and promotional items. And don't forget to make it easy for potential customers and users to provide feedback via email, newsgroups, chat rooms, bulletin boards, Web-based response forms, regular mail, and perhaps an 800 number. Feedback becomes very important later on when you're trying to find out if your plan is working as intended.

Establishing A Time Line

The marketing model you choose and the strategy you've developed should tell you what time line you need to follow to properly deliver your message. You'll be constrained somewhat by delivery options in the open marketplace, and there will be limitations on delivery options even for a small, in-house training and deployment effort. Depending upon the nature of your objective, you might need to be especially sensitive to your targeted population's need to assimilate and digest your messages. For example, it may take two or three repetitions of your message to bring the majority of a selected population to the next step along the decision-making path, and going to the step after that prematurely could make your whole plan backfire. In fact, you'll be doing at least some follow-up surveying, test marketing, or Beta testing while you implement, and depending upon how formal this feedback collection process is, you may need to allow significant delays at each step to effectively accomplish your objective.

Acquiring Resources

The media you choose for message delivery depends on cost, availability, and your marketing strategy. Check the costs (not just for using the media but for advertising agency commissions and commercial development), and then check for availability corresponding to the time line you've chosen. Media companies are very good about providing statistical analyses regarding viewership, reader-ship, or whatever measure is used to gauge effectiveness, but you may want to check independent sources to verify what you'll be getting.

Implementing Your Plan

Implementation is the process of getting the ball rolling, and it deserves its own step because it's not like flipping a switch. It's more like tipping the first domino in a long string of dominoes. You've got to make sure they're properly set up in the first place, and you've got to chase after them to make sure they keep falling in sequence.

The marketing manager for Parts Plus makes a deal with the IT manager about registering domain names, building Web sites, and registering links and descrip-tions with all the popular search engines. Additionally, agreements are made to put URLs in company literature, especially anything having to do with customer service, and to run a few ads in trade publications for each of the product lines.

Verifying Implementation

How do you make sure your ads are running in every place you've contracted and at the right times, in the right frequencies, with the right information? That is, are you getting the exposure you paid for? You could watch every TV program, read every magazine, go to every trade show, and so on, but that may not be practical. If you are running a substantial commercial operation, chances are good that you'll have to designate a representative to follow up on each specific media or event. If you have an advertising agency, they may perform this function, but it can be costly and there's nothing like seeing it yourself to inspire confidence. The media companies themselves are sometimes mandated to provide proof that they've run your ads according to their contracts (the FCC makes radio stations keep detailed records and recordings of commercials they've aired, for instance), so that might help. In some cases, you'll have to wait for ratings numbers to be published to find out what kind of exposure you received.

Taking Corrective Actions

Media companies sometimes make mistakes, domain names are sometimes al-ready taken, and there are no guarantees that a search engine will allow a particu-lar URL to be registered or that the desired ranking can be achieved. However, you can get at least some assurances that mitigating actions will be taken to alle-viate the negative effects of errors or omissions, and you'll need to follow up to make sure remedies are applied as soon as possible to ensure as little disruption to your marketing plans as possible.

The IT manager for Parts Plus knows that search engine rankings are an impor-tant factor in the overall marketing campaign and directs the IT staff to continue modifying Web-site content until a top-20 ranking is achieved for at least 3 key-words on each product line's Web site. Thereafter, the IT staff is directed to re-visit the search engines once per quarter to maintain ranking levels.

Measuring And Adjusting Your Marketing Strategy

Naturally, as you implement your marketing plans, conditions will change, some-times in direct response to what you're doing. Competitors take notice and re-spond, consumers react, users begin to adopt. Now you're in the game, you've set a course toward your objectives, and you'll need to gauge progress and make course corrections as you travel. Unfortunately, it takes time to get a reading on the effectiveness of your campaign, analyze the results, and conclude the best way to get back on track. Like a large ship under full steam, changing course takes time as well. Prudent managers are ready to measure progress as effec-tively as possible from the outset and have several planned alternatives at hand, ready for immediate use.

Measuring Results

You can use the same formal measurement tools (surveys, test marketing, and so forth) you used to conduct your initial marketing research, but they often take too long to implement. Your best bet is to gather and analyze customer responses, complaints, or just plain gossip winding its way along the grapevine. Frank dis-cussions with people you trust among user groups or in consumer populations should alert you directly to any major problems, and you should be able to quickly identify not just the nature of the problem but how the targeted group is reacting to it. For example, if you've been reading negative comments on the bulletin board you set up about navigating your customer service system, invite people who've made the comments to call in and talk about it. Get enough personal information to find out what population they belong to for your analysis later.

Analyzing Results

Although you can make some decisions based on gut feeling (and as a manager, that's your job sometimes), it's best to analyze results formally when you can get enough data and there's time. Assemble all feedback data you've received on a regular basis and characterize it as well as you can. Data from well-documented formal sources is easy enough to collect and use, but don't ignore bits and pieces of data just because they're harder to identify. For instance, suppose you've got-ten incomplete, offhand reports from various sources about problems, negative reactions, confusion about your message, or perhaps simply a lack of communi-cation (the message is not getting through). To effectively use partial data, do

9. Marketing

your best to guess at the population providing the report, the message delivery method, and the decision point (of the marketing model) at which the difficulty appears. Then you can begin to modify your marketing strategy to accommodate this feedback

Revisiting Strategy Development, Revising, And Reimplementing

With new data in hand, you can go back to your original strategy development and rebuild your models. Following the same process you used to conceive your first strategy and plan, decide where you would make changes or choose different alternatives. If another viable strategy doesn't present itself fairly clearly, it may be that you need to choose another model entirely or even rethink the underlying product or service. When you have a new strategy, develop it into a new plan and reimplement; then repeat as necessary.

Part IV

Microsoft Access 2000 Overview

Chapter 10

Access 2000 Technologies

In Depth

This is a short chapter, the purpose of which is to give you a taste of what the new version of Access, Access 2000, is all about. This chapter offers a quick overview of Access 2000 (in-depth analyses of Access 2000 features can be found starting in Chapter 14), a look at Access's new features, and a review of the new technologies found in Access. There are many new ways to gather, process, report, visualize, and communicate data, and understanding your current and future choices is essential to your competitive edge. Any good database program should allow you to store and retrieve your data, but doing so easily and effectively is not as simple as it sounds. The amount of data addressed, the speed of retrieval, the ability to communicate and share data with others, as well as security, transaction capability, and user friendliness, all play important roles in deciding what package to use. Microsoft Access 2000 is well known as a leader in desktop database software, and each of these areas is consistently improved every time a new version is released.

In the preceding chapters, we've discussed databases in general: how they're designed and built, how they integrate with other software and hardware, their impact on an organization's processes, and how to involve users so application development is successful. In this chapter, we begin a discussion of the specifics of Microsoft's Access 2000, a highly integrated component of Office 2000. Access 2000 provides several very important features that make it easy to bring users in to our development efforts.

Compatibility is always an issue, and Access 2000 is likely to be on most users' desktops. It's inexpensive, widely used, and fairly easy for the average user to learn. Simple applications can be made in just minutes (or less using the built-in wizards), but Access is programmable, secure, and a multiuser program as well. Users feel comfortable with it (at least more comfortable than with pure SQL or high-powered database solutions), so they begin to develop on their own. Then it's just another step to absorbing user-developed functionality into SQL Server and spreading it across the organization as a full-featured solution.

Before we venture into the most powerful features of Access and the complex aspects of programming solutions with it, let's quickly review the basics here. We won't touch on everything, but we will relate some of the newest features and how they add to what you already know about Access in its previous incarnations.

Access 2000

Microsoft's Access 2000 is the latest version of the Access desktop database series. The design goals include simplicity, ease of use, and powerful features; conflicting objectives to say the least. New Web compatibility, new data analysis tools, and a choice of database engines make Access bigger and more powerful than ever, and the interface does a credible job of simplifying things. Still, there's a lot going on. One of the most important new features is the ability to create Data Access Pages, and you'll find pages a new basic object type in your Access Database window.

Data Access Pages

As a front end, Access can connect to data anywhere in the organization, given the proper access. Because it is simple enough for typical users (with a little training), your IT staff can effectively serve as consultants, rather than programmers, for the most part. And with Data Access Pages (DAPs), users can share information over an intranet or the Web rather than only with those who also have Access.

Data Access Pages are essentially redesigned forms and reports made of HTML that access data from the Web. You build them in a special DAP designer in Access (see Figure 10.1). Once you've built your DAPs, they can then be edited later and remain bound to the data source you originally specified. DAP pages are stored as separate HTML files outside the traditional Access database file (MDB), so they can be shared easily.

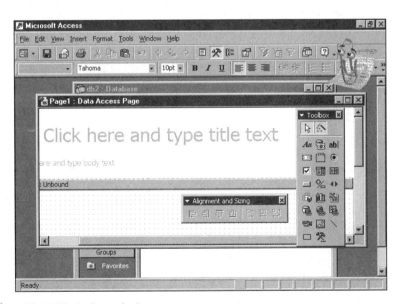

Figure 10.1 The DAP designer in Access.

Database Engines

Microsoft employs separate database engines to power Access 2000 and other Office products. In Access 2000, you have a choice of two engines: an improved Jet and the new Microsoft Database Engine (MSDE). Jet is more compatible with Access 97 and previous databases, whereas MSDE offers better scalability than SQL Server 7. Jet installs by default, but you can choose to use MSDE. MSDE is Microsoft's stated strategic direction, something to keep in mind when choosing your engine.

By the way, Microsoft also includes what it calls an "upsizing wizard," which can migrate Access databases to SQL Server fairly painlessly. Existing Jet databases are converted to SQL Server databases, including table structure, data, indexes, validation rules, defaults, autonumbers, and relationships. No changes are made to reports, queries, macros, or security.

Other New Features

Access 2000 contains many new features that make it easier to use with other Office applications, as well as making it easier to learn. Here's a quick overview:

- *Backward compatibility*—You can save databases to previous versions so it's easier to share them with people who haven't upgraded yet. Note the downward conversion dialog box in Figure 10.2.

- *Name Autocorrect*—No more having to dig through an entire application when you change a field name in a table. Older versions require changing field names in every object referencing the field, but now Access will automatically change the names of fields (and other objects) in all related applications. This is a

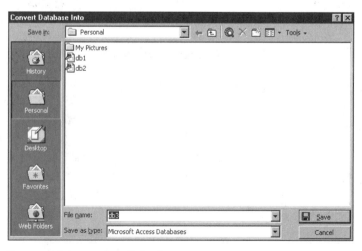

Figure 10.2   Downward conversion dialog box.

major time-saver. Of course, you can always turn off this feature if you don't need it for some reason.

- *Conditional formatting*—A real reporting boon, conditional formatting allows you to set conditions (which change the look of the report depending on the values encountered) on report fields. One value triggers one look while the next triggers another. Now your reports are truly customized.

- *Subdatasheets*—Opening a table in Datasheet view allows you to see any linked subtables, meaning it's much easier to browse data in Access.

- *Properties changes*—You can now change properties in forms without going into Design view, a big plus when tweaking forms for that perfect final look.

- *Relationships window printing*—A simple idea, but one that has been lacking in previous versions; namely, the ability to print a hard copy of the Relationships window.

- *Control grouping*—Grouping makes life easier wherever it applies, and now it applies to controls. You can add controls to a group and change their properties together rather than individually, as you needed to before.

- *Report snapshots*—Another simple but previously unavailable (until Access 97, SR-1) capability allows you to save a snapshot of a report for later printing or distribution.

- *Automatic compaction*—Access can automatically compact databases upon closing if the file size is quite large (you can specify size in percentage terms). This relieves the user of having to check and compact manually.

All in all, Access 2000 offers quite a few reasons to upgrade. And if you're considering more powerful databases to handle more users, you can still use Access 2000 as a front end without trouble. Microsoft has included a special file format that connects your Access 2000 databases directly to SQL Server for incredible scalability.

Scalability

As data grows more and more plentiful, and competition sharpens, more sophisticated analysis of existing data in larger and larger quantities becomes ever more important. Naturally, Microsoft incorporated new data-analysis tools into Access 2000 to respond to this need. In addition to new Web-based data-analysis tools, there are tools that merge the desktop database functionality of Access 2000 with the back-end data store capabilities of SQL Server. The connecting technology is called Microsoft Access Projects (or Microsoft Access Data Projects, with the suffix .ADP).

When you build an Access database, the default choice is to use the Jet engine for storing your data. Now you have a choice of several other engines as well, including SQL Server 6.5 and SQL Server 7. Microsoft Access Project provides the link. And because SQL Server is client-server based, Access 2000's wizard functionality has been extended to provide support within the client-server arena. Typical users will find the power and scalability refreshing, and Access's ease of use (and familiar interface) leverages their existing skills.

Access 2000 Interface

The basic interface Access uses remains similar but not unchanged. As you can see in Figure 10.3, the object choices and manipulation buttons (Open, Design, New) are present, but also visible are the first choices for whatever object you've selected (in this case, table creation modes).

As you scan the Database window, notice the new Pages object in the list on the left-hand side. If you click on it, you'll see that you can create Data Access Pages in much the same way as you create ordinary objects in Access, in Design mode and by using wizards. And if you've installed the rest of the Office suite, you'll notice that many components of the interface are similar across all the applications.

Objects, Wizards, And VBA

Microsoft products all include wizards, which essentially are small applications that lead the user by hand through a series of dialog boxes to accomplish relatively complex tasks in short order. Even the most unfamiliar user can ordinarily accomplish quite sophisticated actions with a wizard, and oftentimes the results are so well done that advanced users use them as a shortcut. That said, getting the most out of wizards is really a combination of knowing what they do and knowing how to do it for yourself. Then you can understand the sometimes unclear directions on each screen and the outcomes they'll produce.

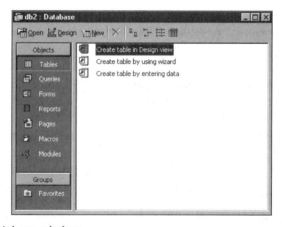

Figure 10.3   The Database window.

Each object in Access can be created by using wizards, and the level of detail is extensive. For example, combo box controls on forms have their own wizard. In fact, there is a button on the toolbox that specifically turns wizards on and off for control creation.

Visual Basic for Applications (VBA) design gets a new look as well (see Figure 10.4, an example from the Northwind database sample included with Access 2000). A Project window, Startup window, and Code window are all present by default, and you can set options for other windows.

Security And Sharing

Security in Access 2000 works much like it did in earlier versions, with a few new features. The User-level Security Wizard is easier to use, and modules behind forms and reports are now protected by a VBA password. You can still set a database password or change the Workgroup ID and create users and groups with permissions for each individual object. One major area of concern is how to protect your database when you use DAP technology.

Data access pages combine an HTML file (stored on your system in another location) and a shortcut (stored in your Access database file). To prevent changes to

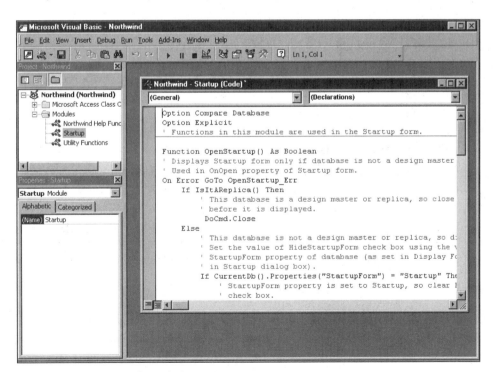

Figure 10.4   The VBA design window.

the shortcut or its HTML file, you must use the file system (NTFS in Windows NT, for instance) to set security.

To implement user-level security, you must make sure the connection information for the DAP contains the location of the correct Workgroup ID file and that there are no passwords set for the database as a whole. Also, make sure you don't save the username and password with the page, or any user can access the database with it. Finally, DAPs use the Microsoft Office Data Source Control (MSODSC) to connect to a data source. There is the possibility that someone could try to access the database illegally with a Visual Basic script, but you can prevent this by properly setting the data access mode.

The Web And The Internet

Access 2000 has plenty of features designed to make it easy to publish and share data, such as DAPs. Within Access, there is a new object type called Pages. It refers to Data Access Pages, and in Design view, it consists of a designer that lets you visually create DAPs. You can edit the contents of the page on screen and drag and drop objects into it. Editing changes can be made to the page by any application that supports the Microsoft Component Object Model (COM), such as Word and FrontPage. Once you've designed a page, you can then connect (or bind) it to the appropriate data source.

When you build a page without a database open, the program will ask you for connection information. You can either enter this data when you create the page or enter it later, and if you change the location of the database to which it's bound, you'll have to modify the connection information. Any pages you create within an open database are automatically connected to it.

HTML Round-Tripping

Office applications, including Access, all add special formatting to documents to make them work with their respective application programs. HTML documents, by their nature, abhor special formatting. Access allows the creation and editing of HTML documents with special formatting, which means extra data must be connected to an HTML file to make it work with Office applications as well as the Web. Microsoft calls the process of adding extra data *round-tripping* and calls HTML files "a full-fidelity companion file format" to the Office binary file format.

Access DAPS use HTML, Cascading Style Sheets, and Extensible Markup Language (XML) to build, format, and preserve HTML and special formatting details. XML is heavily used to provide a means of translating nonvisual document properties into an HTML-compatible format without breaking the user's browser.

Sharing Information Across The Web

Ordinarily, when you create a database, you think in terms of entering, retrieving, and outputting data for a specific reason, perhaps for a datacall, a canned report, or your colleagues' needs. Because we're all rapidly being connected via the Web and intranets, and because business processes are changing so quickly, the need to easily share information is critical. Proprietary solutions just don't fit anymore, just as proprietary phone systems don't work. For the Web and an intranet, using common standards is the obvious choice. But connecting data from a database to a Web page has historically meant convoluted and complex programming—a problem solved to a large extent with the arrival of data access pages. Now it's just another step in the design and construction process.

In Access 2000, you can create new Web pages or open any existing Web page in the page designer. You can add controls and data-bound fields, and you can do just about any other Access-style editing you would usually do. DAP supports VBScript and JavaScript, and you can also include Office 2000 Web Components (Spreadsheet, Chart, and Pivot Table).

Access Web Tools

Access provides tools specifically for working with DAPs and new functionality as well. You can group DAP pages or dynamically link them, meaning users can delve into data behind summary data (unlike traditional, static HTML pages). The DAP toolbox allows you to easily add Web controls when designing your DAP forms and reports, and the Field List lets you pop data-bound fields directly into your DAP page via a live link to the underlying database. And hyperlink handling is much improved. Now you can link from object to object without VBA code.

Immediate Solutions

This section takes you through the steps required to preview Access 2000, understand the new technologies in Access 2000, and use common Access capabilities.
If you are a first-time user, you'll find the steps here illustrate basic usage of Access 2000 (and are similar to those used in previous versions). If you are an advanced user, you may want to skip forward a few chapters, unless you would like
a review of the basics and highlights of new Access technologies.

Touring Access 2000

Access 2000 installs about as easily as any other desktop database product on the
market, and running it from the Start button produces the main screen in a few
seconds. First you'll be invited to open any existing databases or create a new
one, and then you'll see the familiar Database window.

Launching Access 2000

Click on Start, choose Programs, then Microsoft Access from the menu to launch
Access. The screen shown in Figure 10.5 will be displayed. There is not much
new here, except for the reference to DAPs as database objects.

Creating A Blank Database

You can create a blank database when Access is first opened or later using the
File|New command. The name for a blank database (chosen by Access) is db2.
After Access creates your blank database, you'll see the initial Database window
and have the opportunity to create any Access objects you desire within the database: tables, forms, queries, reports, pages, macros, and modules.

Examining/Setting Options

Clicking on Tools|Options gets you to the Options dialog box, where you can set
the basic options for Access usage (see Figure 10.6).

In the Options dialog, you'll see various tabs:

- *View*—For specifying objects to show, the columns to show in a macro
  window, and click options for the Database window

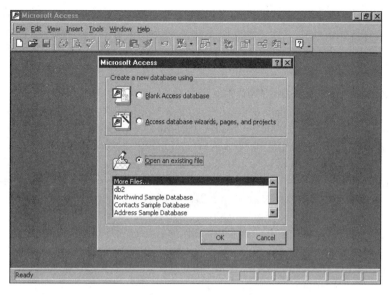

Figure 10.5   The main screen of Access 2000.

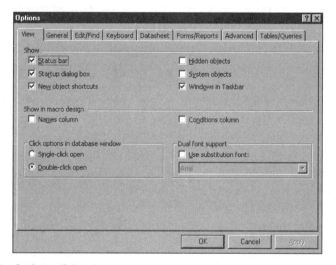

Figure 10.6   The Options dialog box.

- *General*—For setting margins, a few Web options, Name Autocorrect, and database sort order

- *Edit/Find*—For manipulating editing, finding, and filtering

- *Keyboard*—For changing keyboard behavior

- *Datasheet*—For setting default datasheet options

- *Forms/Reports*—For setting the default Form or Report template

- *Advanced*—For changing Dynamic Data Exchange (DDE), Object Linking and Embedding (OLE), and open database connectivity (ODBC) defaults

- *Tables/Queries*—For setting field types and sizes

Creating A Basic Table And Form

Access offers you two choices for creating any object: You can use Design mode or you can use a wizard. Create a basic table by clicking on the Table object choice and then clicking on the New button on the Database window (if you double-click on the Table object choice, you'll go straight to the Design window). Next, you'll have the option to choose again from five choices: Datasheet View, Design View, Table Wizard, Import Table, and Link Table. Choose Design View and you'll be presented with the Table Design window. Just enter field names, specify data types and sizes, and you're off. If you follow the same procedure to make a form, you'll find there are seven choices: Design View, Form Wizard, AutoForm: Columnar, AutoForm: Tabular, AutoForm: Datasheet, Chart Wizard, and PivotTable Wizard.

Using Microsoft Access Wizards

Rather than use Design view to create objects from scratch, it's often easier to use wizards to create the initial design and then modify it. Clicking through a series of dialog boxes may not be very satisfying, but it gets a lot of the routine work done. You can select tables for forms, queries, pages, and reports, and you can select styles. Each wizard typically gives you the option of immediately opening the resulting object in Design view for further work.

Using The Table Wizard

The Table Wizard can be started by double-clicking on the Table Wizard option for the Table object. It's a series of screens (beginning with the one shown in Figure 10.7) that use prebuilt template tables as the foundation for the table you're creating.

Notice the many template tables offered. You can choose Business or Personal tables, and you can select whatever fields you like or add new ones. On subsequent screens, you can create a primary key and name the table, and thankfully, Microsoft has reduced the number of screens you must traverse to finish your table.

Using The Form Wizard

The Form Wizard reduces the process of building forms to a few simple steps. Just specify the table to bind to and the style and name of the form, and presto! Figure 10.8 shows the results of clicking through the screens using most of the defaults. As you can see, a little more work is required to clean up the form, so you'll probably want to edit your forms immediately after opening them.

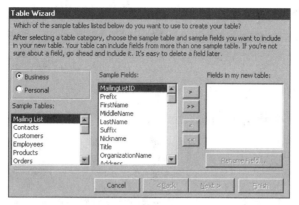

Figure 10.7   The first screen of the Table Wizard.

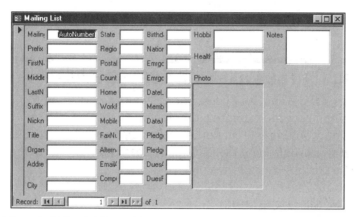

Figure 10.8   A form built by the Form Wizard.

Using The Query Wizard

The Query Wizard is one of the simplest to use; just double-click to start it from the Database window and pop through a few screens (Figure 10.9 shows the first screen), and your query appears. It's a typical query-by-example (QBE) query, and you can easily modify and customize it once you've created it. The easiest way is to work backward, adding all the fields first and then reducing the number as you tweak it.

Using The Report Wizard

If you have no printer installed, the Report Wizard won't complete its task. Other than that, it operates in much the same manner as the Form and Query Wizards operate, although you have the option of setting sorting and grouping options as you follow the screens through the wizard.

10. Access 2000
Technologies

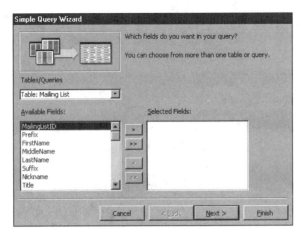

Figure 10.9   The first screen of the Query Wizard.

Publishing On The Web With Access 2000

Publishing on the Web with Access is finally just about as simple as creating normal forms and reports in Access, thanks to Data Access Pages. You can create
pages as you would create any other object in Access. There is a new DAP designer that works quite a bit like a visual HTML editor except that it allows you to
add familiar Access controls as you go.

Building HTML Documents

If you have existing HTML documents, you can edit them to include DAP controls, or you can start from scratch or use the DAP Wizard. The DAP Wizard operates in the same fashion as the Report Wizard. After it creates a page, the DAP
Wizard will open it so you can make further changes. Our example is shown in
Figure 10.10.

Editing HTML Documents

You can edit DAP documents pretty much the same way you would in any visual
HTML editor. You can add and edit text, change fonts and styles, add hyperlinks
and pictures, even insert movies and shapes. Turn the toolbox on (choose
View|Toolbox) and special Web-based tools will appear. You can also turn on the
Web toolbar so you can browse while you build (choose View|Toolbars|Web). The
following new tools are available in the toolbox:

- *Bound HTML*—Creates an HTML object for entering HTML or scripts that
  can't be created by using other controls. To examine the tags or script

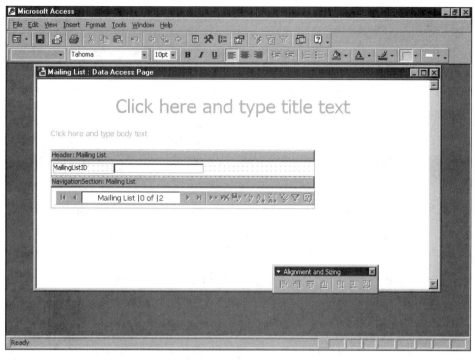

Figure 10.10   A DAP created by the DAP Wizard.

behind these controls, choose View|HTMLSource and the window shown in
Figure 10.11 will open.

- *Expand*—Creates Expand and Contract buttons for users to open and close
  page sections.

- *Record Navigation*—Creates a record navigation button.

- *Office Pivot Table, Chart, and Spreadsheet*—Inserts data-analysis tools.

- *Bound Hyperlink and Hyperlink*—Creates hyperlinks to other documents or
  pages. The Hyperlink button opens the Insert Hyperlink dialog box shown in
  Figure 10.12.

- *Hotspot Image*—Creates an ordinary image map from an image file.

- *Movie*—Creates a video object linked to a file.

Previewing HTML Documents

Choose File|Preview to start Internet Explorer 5 and display your DAP inside it. If
you haven't saved your page, you'll be prompted to do so before Internet Explorer starts. Once inside Internet Explorer, you'll have the same view any other
user has. Just remember that there are lots of Netscape users out there, and you're
not going to get the same functionality (although the basic HTML will work fine).

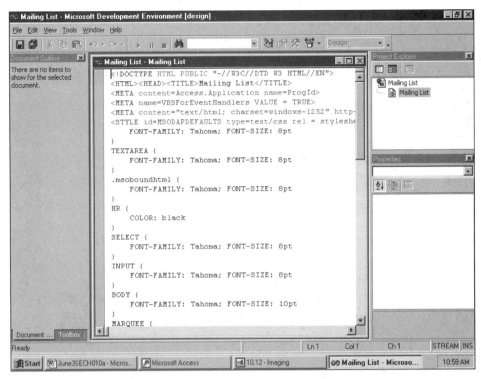

Figure 10.11   The Microsoft Development Environment with HTML source.

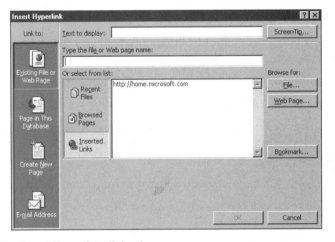

Figure 10.12   The Insert Hyperlink dialog box.

Incorporating Advanced Technologies

With so many new technologies to consider, it can be difficult to decide just what to use, and where. There are trade-offs with all of them, and sometimes simpler is better, or just as useful. Many text-based applications are still functioning fine and don't need replacing, but they warrant a closer look if you're designing a new system. A good rule of thumb is to evaluate the complexity of the application. For example, a cashier application for a fast-food restaurant may need to record 35 food or beverage items, each with a fixed price and set tax rates, using cash only (no credit card purchases). On the other hand, an application that researches and records sales and purchase data for a car dealer might require a complex, graphical user interface (GUI) connected to the manufacturer's Web site as well as the finance company's database.

Reviewing The Solution Interface

If you look once more at your systems-analysis and process-engineering documents, you should get a clear indication of the points at which people must interact with data, as well as the nature of the interaction. Ask yourself how much data they need, in what format it would work best, and whether or not the underlying data and application can support new technologies efficiently. For example, if you know you're going to be satisfying the requirements of a growing number of users, perhaps using MSDE would be a better choice than using Jet. On the other hand, if you're sticking with lots of prebuilt Access databases constructed in earlier versions, maybe the best choice is Jet after all.

Comparing Technology Features And Benefits

For each interaction point, list the features that may be beneficial and then evaluate the trade-offs between features and benefits. For instance, perhaps it would be useful to have a voice alert a cashier accepting a $50 bill to deposit the bill in the drop box rather than the cash register. However, to incorporate this feature, you may require processing greater than the terminal can support, which means you'll need to upgrade the terminals. If it is not already planned, upgrading terminals is a costly way to achieve the capability necessary to support this feature, and therefore, it may not be a worthwhile feature to include. By the same token, upgrading to SQL Server has significant costs, including increased administrative and maintenance costs as well as purchase price.

Evaluating And Selecting Features For Incorporation

As each feature is evaluated for costs and benefits, those with the benefits necessary to support inclusion should be selected and built into the system. Before making a decision on any one feature, outline the costs, benefits, and requirements of all the features you would like to have and examine whether it would be appropriate to include quite a few of them as a whole. Sometimes one or a few features require upgraded hardware or software that can drive the entire solution to new levels of capability and performance, so there's no point in evaluating each feature piecemeal when it's time to select which ones you'll include.

Chapter 11

New Features And Trends In Access 2000

In Depth

In the preceding chapter, we looked at target markets for Access. In the next chapter, we'll look more closely at some of the specific considerations for purchasing and installing Access 2000 in your enterprise. In this chapter, we'll look at some of the new features of Office 2000 and, more specifically, Access 2000. We'll also consider some of the trends—such as the move toward Web-based computing—that the designers at Microsoft took into account during the creation of the newest version of Office.

Specifically, we'll look at some of the ways in which the Office 2000 platform, through its Component Object Model (COM) foundation and its close integration with other products—particularly products from Microsoft—provides a much improved enterprise solution over Office 97. We'll also consider the improvements to the new Jet 4 engine. We'll close with a brief discussion of the benefits of using BackOffice as an integrated server platform and the integration of Office with those back-end products.

The Office 2000 Services Platform

The architectural flexibility of Office is made possible by its support of a consistent object model throughout the suite, including a rich set of interfaces and events based on the industry-standard COM specification. This object model, and the interfaces and events it supports, helps enterprises and developers reuse and build upon Office services. The Office 2000 Services Platform identifies the key desktop client applications that Office 2000 provides.

Here are a few examples of the services Office 2000 can provide:

- *Web publishing*—Office 2000 now allows publishing and storing of binary or HTML documents on a Web server. It also permits control over various replication and offline scenarios for users accessing and updating files.

- *Data access and reporting*—Office 2000 offers new support for accessing OLE DB and ActiveX Data Objects (ADO) recordsets within Excel, in addition to creating multidimensional reports from SQL Server online analytical processing (OLAP) services.

- *Business intelligence*—Word, Excel, Access, and other Office 2000 applications provide wizards and standard templates for common business-analysis functions.

- *Collaboration*—This service allows all Office documents and any HTML files to be shared and changed. Trigger events can prompt users when files are updated.

- *Data analysis and tracking*—This service provides a new lightweight set of Office ActiveX controls that can be used for creating Web-based data tracking and reporting solutions; there is also support for server-side scripting. These controls include the **PivotTable** control, which provides a thin-client method that users can take advantage of to manipulate data on a remote server in a wide variety of methods.

Reduced Cost Of Ownership

One of the most commonly discussed information technology topics today is the total cost of ownership of personal computing and how to reduce it. Reducing the cost of owning Office is one of Microsoft's top priorities for Office 2000, which is reflected in new administrative capabilities as well as in the continued quest for making personal computing as easy as possible.

Most important for large organizations is the fact that most file formats between Office 2000 and Office 97 are compatible. This means that Office 97 and Office 2000 users can exchange most documents natively. Office 97 will be able to open any Office 2000 file without a converter. However, certain formatting options available in Office 2000 will not round-trip—that is, convert to Office 97 and back—because Office 97 does not recognize them. The only exception to the full round-tripping support is Access—because of new support for Unicode within the product (Access did not previously support this file format). Access 2000 is, however, able to down-rev save—that is, convert the 2000-compatible binary to a 97-compatible binary—to Access 97.

In addition, Office 2000 includes such new features as the option of one world-wide executable. This executable can be installed on almost any language version of the Windows operating system. Similarly, Office 2000 includes self-repairing applications that automatically detect and fix errors to files or Registry settings that are needed to launch successfully. The Office Custom Installation Wizard and the Office Profile Wizard make it simple and efficient to customize how Office 2000 installs in your organization. Better support for roaming profiles makes it possible for Office 2000 users to work using their own preferences and settings regardless of what computer they are working on as long as it uses the same operating system.

Additional Office 2000 features can help reduce the cost of supporting these applications (for example, support for the security features in the operating system, customizable Help, and other usability improvements). All of these features are available to all users regardless of the other products in use.

Some capabilities, however, are better implemented at the desktop or at the server operating system level. If typical system administration problems are fixed at the operating system level, the administrator will, in the end, have an entire desktop that is easier to administer—rather than just four or five applications that are easier to administer. The following sections describe features that further reduce the cost of ownership when Office 2000 is combined with other software.

Operating System Shell Update

Windows 2000 Workstation, Windows 98, and Internet Explorer 4.01 all include an updated shell that supports additional functionality in Office 2000. A service pack will be available for updating the shell in Windows 95 and Windows NT Workstation 4.

Install On Demand

Install on Demand is a feature that will automatically install an Office 2000 feature or application if necessary. So, for example, if a user has installed some—but not all—Office components, the missing components will be installed when the user first tries to access them. You will learn more about the Install on Demand feature in later chapters, particularly Chapter 13.

Web Folders

Web folders make it possible to view Web servers from Windows Explorer just as you would view network servers or local hard drives. Office 2000 supports the ability to cut, copy, and paste (or drag and drop) documents from a Web server to a network server or local hard drive or from a local hard drive or network server to a Web server. This makes it easier to use content found on the Internet or an intranet or to have average users post content to an intranet site or intranet staging server.

Windows 2000 Extends Office 2000

Windows 2000 Workstation promises to significantly extend the reliability, security, networking, and performance advantages of Windows NT 4. Most importantly, when combined with Windows 2000 Server, Windows 2000 Workstation is the only desktop operating system to support all of the manageability capabilities built into Office 2000. These capabilities should help businesses reduce their Total Cost of Ownership (TCO) for the Office 2000 product by up to one-half when compared with other Windows environments.

The Windows 2000 Workstation operating system will include new technologies (such as IntelliMirror) that combine the power and flexibility of distributed computing with a tightly managed environment. IntelliMirror management technologies work by "intelligently mirroring" a user's data, applications, system files, and administrative settings on Windows 2000-based servers.

By supporting features that are enabled by Windows 2000, Office goes further in reducing the cost of ownership than it could on its own. To learn more about improvements in Windows 2000 that Office takes advantage of, see the Microsoft Windows 2000 preview site on the Microsoft Web site.

Increased Integration With The Web

Office 2000 increases integration with the Web by providing tools for easy creation of Web content, easy publication to the Web, and simplified retrieval of Web content. Many of these features are enabled entirely by Office and are independent of the browser or server software your organization is using. The following new features are among the most notable:

- *HTML file format*—Saving files to HTML format is as easy as saving to the native application file format and has greatly improved accuracy in the conversion, as well. In addition, information is stored in the file to improve using it again in the original application. So, for example, if the user creates a spreadsheet and saves it to HTML, all of the elements will look right in a browser. And if the user opens that file again in Excel 2000, formulas will recalculate, PivotTable dynamic views will pivot, and other features will work as if the file had remained in Excel format. In other words, the Excel spreadsheet will round-trip from its binary format (*.XLS), to HTML, and back to its binary format without significant data loss.

- *Enhanced application features*—Some applications have added features to support commonly used HTML formats. For example, Word has added support for using frames to create a table of contents, with a linking TOC in the left-hand frame rather than embedded within a document as is appropriate for a printed document.

- *Save to the Web*—Not only is it easier to save to the HTML format, it is also easier to save a document as a Web page on a Web server. Simply navigate a Web server as you would a network server and save a file there. Plus, this means that Office 2000 users can more easily share documents with people using FrontPage 2000 to create Web sites. For example, you can save a Word document as HTML right into a FrontPage-based Internet or intranet site.

Some of the new functionality in Office 2000 is actually enabled by combining Office with either a specific level of browser functionality, Web server functionality, or both.

Improved Integration With And Support For The Enterprise

Over the years, Office has consistently taken advantage of new standards, helping it to be both a client in the enterprise and a personal productivity tool. Every iteration of Office shipped in the past five years has supported Object Linking and Embedding (OLE) as well as its descendent, ActiveX, so you can use other applications to program Office. Previous versions of Office also supported other enterprise standards, such as Open Database Connectivity (ODBC), Microsoft Mail, and Lotus Notes. Office 2000 adds improved data access, enhanced corporate reporting tools, and improved ability to create custom solutions to the broad features of earlier versions.

Data Access

Office supports all of the previous technologies supported by earlier Office versions, but improvements such as improved text importing tools in Excel have been added for all customers. Office has also improved its integration and support for SQL Server, including improved performance and new capabilities in SQL Server 7.

OLE DB

Access 2000 supports OLE DB, a recently introduced standard for data access. With OLE DB, Access 2000 databases can connect directly to SQL Server instead of going through the Jet engine, the traditional default database engine in Access. Power users and developers can now create solutions that combine the ease of use and speedy development of the Access interface (client) with the scalability, performance, and reliability of SQL Server versions 6.5 and higher. Processing occurs in SQL Server for a true client-server solution. Power users and developers can develop SQL Server databases using the Access interface, and end users will find that performing data entry with SQL Server back ends and Access front ends is as easy to do as it is with any other Office applications.

Access 2000 Client-Server Tools

Because earlier versions of Access have been known for their easy-to-use wizards, Microsoft has extended this functionality into the client-server development tools. A variety of wizards make it easier for Access developers to create a client-server database. Most developers will appreciate the ability to use popular Access wizards—such as the Report Wizard, Form Wizard, Control Wizard, and Button Wizard—against a SQL Server back end. These wizards have been updated to support the new client-server architecture.

Client-Server Design Tools

With an Access Data Project, new design tools allow users to create and manage SQL Server objects—including tables, views, stored procedures, and database diagrams—from the Design view. This makes it easier for current Access users and developers to extend their database knowledge to the client-server environment. You will learn more about Access Data Project design in Chapters 15 and 33.

SQL Server-Based Administration Tools

Access 2000 allows users to perform and manage common administration tasks in SQL Server, including tasks such as replication, backup and restore, and security. This means that users can use Access 2000 on the client to perform SQL administrative tasks.

Enhanced Web Queries

For those organizations with connectivity to the Web or an intranet, Office 2000 includes enhanced support for the Excel Web Queries feature. The new Web Query Wizard makes it much easier to import data from the Web into Excel. This wizard walks users through the process of bringing data from a Web page into Excel 2000 and helps create the query file as they choose the Web page, the desired content for importing, and the type of formatting. Web query pages can be refreshed automatically on a scheduled basis.

Office Web Components

Office 2000 includes three new Office Web components—a Spreadsheet component, a Chart component, and a PivotTable component—that make corporate data available through any browser. The Spreadsheet component provides basic spreadsheet functionality in the browser, allowing users to enter text and numbers; create formulas; recalculate, sort, and filter data; and perform basic formatting. It supports frozen panes for keeping header rows and columns visible while scrolling through data, as well as in-cell editing and resizable rows and columns. The Chart component provides interactivity and automatic updates as the underlying data changes.

The PivotTable component is similar to PivotTable views in Excel 2000 and provides a dynamic way to view and analyze database information in the browser. The PivotTable component is created in either Access or Excel and resides on a Data Access Page (DAP). This component lets users browse data, dynamically sort and filter it, group it by rows or columns, create totals, and focus on the details behind the totals. It helps users work efficiently with large or small amounts of data. Although the author of the Data Access Page determines the initial view, the user can access the Field List Chooser to drag and drop the dynamically linked fields directly onto the page.

New Features In Jet 4

As a developer, you'll see that many of the most important improvements to the Office 2000 suite (and Access in particular) can be found in the changes and improvements to the Jet engine, which underlies Access development. For Access 2000, Microsoft has released the newest upgrade to the engine, Jet 4. The following sections detail some of the most significant improvements to the engine and the way it manages data.

Unicode Support

All character data—that is, data stored in columns defined as the Access data types **Text** and **Memo** or data that is equivalent to the Jet SQL data types **CHAR**, **VARCHAR**, and so on—is stored in the Unicode two-byte character representation format. It replaces the Multi-byte Character Set (MBCS) format used in previous versions of the Jet database engine for storing character data for certain languages. For example, both Japanese and Chinese can only be stored in a Unicode format. When Jet 3.x or earlier databases are converted to 4.0 format, data in **Text** and **Memo** columns will be converted from MBCS to Unicode based on the locale information or sort order of the Jet 3.x databases. It is not based on the current locale of the operating system on which the conversion is done.

To accommodate the change to Unicode data and enable all existing data to be successfully converted, Microsoft increased the internal unit of storage, the *page size*, from 2K (2,048 bytes) to 4K (4,096 bytes). This, in turn, doubled the maximum database size for Jet databases, allowing them to go from a maximum size of 1.07GB to 2.14GB.

Although the Unicode representation of character data requires more space to store each character (two bytes instead of just one byte), columns with string data types can be defined to automatically compress the data, if possible. So, for most character sets, character data can be stored in a compressed format, so the use of the Unicode representation, ironically, actually improves your ability to reduce the database size. There is some impact, however, based on whether character data is stored in columns defined as Access **Text** or Access **Memo**. Access **Memo** columns have a limitation with respect to compression. How to enable Unicode compression, when it is enabled by default, and where it applies is described later on in this chapter.

Note that noncharacter data types, such as **Integer**, **Currency**, **Date/Time**, and so on, are unaffected by the adoption of Unicode.

NT-Compatible Sorting

Implementing the Unicode representation for the storage of character data enabled the Jet database engine to develop and use a sorting mechanism that is based on the native Windows NT sorting functionality. This sorting mechanism uses NT Locale IDs (LCIDs) and it supports all sort orders also supported by Windows NT.

The sorting mechanism is used by Jet when it is running on Windows NT so that all the newer sorts are supported regardless of which version of Windows NT is being used. The sorting mechanism is also used by Jet when it is running on Windows 9x, so it's possible to properly sort on Windows 9x all of the languages available on Windows NT instead of just the system default language that Windows 9x supports in its ANSI sorting. The sorting mechanism ensures consistency in sorting across operating systems.

Overview Of Data Type Changes In Jet 4

To make it easier to upsize Jet databases to SQL Server databases, for better compatibility between Jet and SQL Server, and for the sake of replication, Jet data types have been aligned with those of SQL Server to a greater degree. In some instances, this has also provided for greater compatibility with ODBC data sources that can be accessed through the Jet engine.

> **WARNING!** As with much of the ANSI SQL 92 enhancements to Access, many of the changes in data types are only available from ADO and the Jet OLE DB Provider.

Changes To The Character Type

Better known as the **Text** type, the **Character** type has the most changes in the newest version of the engine. Maximum length for a field remains at 255 characters; however, Unicode support now makes this maximum length viable for all languages by storing data in 510 bytes.

Changes To The Memo Type

Also known as the **Long Text** type, the **Memo** type now supports a maximum length (in bytes) of approximately 2.14GB. This would be about 1.07GB characters—because each character requires two bytes for its Unicode representation. However, this limit is not particularly real because the maximum size of a Jet database is also 2.14GB.

Changes To The Currency Type

Remote data that is typed as **SQL_DECIMAL** or **SQL_NUMERIC** (for example, SQL Server **Decimal** or **Numeric**) and accessed with ODBC by the Jet engine is no longer automatically mapped to the Jet **Currency** type. If the precision and scale of the linked column exactly matches the precision and scale of SQL Server **Money** (19,4) or **Smallmoney** (10,4), Jet will continue to map it to **Currency**. If the precision is less than or equal to the maximum Jet **Decimal** precision (28), Jet will map it to **Decimal**. All other cases will map to **Double**.

Note that, depending on the mapping, Access will no longer automatically add a currency symbol to its display of numbers. This means that, if you have an Access application in which you want currency symbols to be displayed, you must alter the precision and scale of the column types in SQL Server to match those of the built-in SQL Server **Money** or **Smallmoney** types. To prevent currency symbols from being displayed, it is possible now to alter the precision and/or scale to avoid those values when defining **SQL_DECIMAL** or **SQL_NUMERIC** columns.

The New Decimal Data Type

The **Decimal** data type is new in Jet 4. It is an exact numeric data type that holds values from (1028)-1 through -(1028)+1. You can define both precision and scale, (1,0) up to (28,28). The default precision and scale is (18,0).

Remote data that is typed as **SQL_DECIMAL** or **SQL_NUMERIC** and accessed with ODBC by the Jet engine will be mapped to **Decimal** if the following two cases are true:

- Precision and scale of the linked column does *not* exactly match the precision and scale of **Money** (19,4) or **Smallmoney** (10,4).

- The precision is less than or equal to the maximum Jet **Decimal** precision (28).

Note that this data type is not supported in either the Data Access Object (DAO) model or from SQL data definition language (DDL) in DAO. It is supported only in ADO and the Access User Interface. Decimal columns will appear in the Access Table designer as **Number**, with a field size of **Decimal**. Note that **Number** remains a SQL synonym for **Double**, however.

Auto-Increment Columns And The IDENTITY Keyword

With prior releases, auto-increment columns were only available through the use of the **Counter** and **AutoIncrement** keywords in SQL DDL. With Jet 4, the use of the new **IDENTITY** keyword is also supported.

TIP: *Through ADO and the Jet OLE DB provider, Jet 4 allows you to specify that the auto-increment column be based on any supported numeric data type (with the default remaining **Long**) when the **IDENTITY** keyword is used. However, if you specify a data type that does not map to a Jet **Long** (types other than **Long**, **Int**, **Integer**, or **Integer4**), Jet 4 will drop the auto-increment attribute for the column and simply make it the data type specified.*

Compressed String Data Types

Most string data type columns that are less than 4K in size in Jet 4 can now be stored in a compressed format. If this feature is enabled when the data is created, data will be compressed as it is stored and uncompressed when it is retrieved from the column.

This attribute was added for string data types because of the change to the Unicode character representation format. Unicode characters uniformly require two bytes for each character. For existing Jet databases that contain predominantly character data, this could mean increased database size when they are converted to Jet 4. Yet the Unicode representation of many character sets—those formerly denoted as Single-Byte Character Sets (SBCSs)—can easily be compressed to a single byte.

Memo columns/fields can also be defined to store data in a compressed format, although the compressed data must fit within 4,096 bytes or less. This means that, within a given table, for a given **Memo** field, some of the data may be compressed and some may not.

New SQL Extensions

Many enhancements were added to the Jet 4 SQL implementation to support new functionality and to make it conform more closely to the ANSI SQL 92 specification. Many of these enhancements also make it easier to write SQL statements that will interoperate between Jet and SQL Server.

The Jet 4 database engine supports two forms of SQL syntax: one mode that supports the same Jet SQL commands used in previous versions of Access and another new mode that supports new Jet SQL commands and syntax and is more compliant with the ANSI SQL 92 standard. Through the Access 2000 user interface, a user can only use the SQL syntax that was used in the previous version of Access. The newer SQL syntax is only available when used inside modules that use ADO and the Jet OLE DB provider. When using the Jet OLE DB provider through ADO, users will be able to execute the newer SQL syntax using temporary queries (that is, queries that are not stored and are used as part of a recordset's source) and through stored queries (by using the new **Create View** and **Create Procedure** statements). Although all stored queries created through the Jet OLE DB provider will be accessible through ADO and the Jet OLE DB provider, they will not be visible to users through the Access User Interface.

It is possible to create and modify a stored query in an Access database by using the ADO Extensions 2.1 for both DDL and the Security object library (ADOX). However, if you do so, your query won't be visible in the Access Database window or any other part of the Access user interface. If you do know the name of the query, however, you can reference it in Access objects that allow you to physically type in the name of the query. You can still run stored queries created by using ADOX from ADO code.

Database Security Support

Support for using SQL statements to define database security constraints has been added to the Jet engine. Instead of using either DAO or ADO for things such as adding users and groups, setting and unsetting privileges on database objects, administering passwords, and so on, you can use the following SQL syntax:

```
CREATE/ADD/ALTER/DROP USER/GROUP
```

Later chapters will discuss database security in greater detail. For now, simply know that you have significantly more control over how you implement your security in Access 2000 than you did in earlier versions of Access.

Views

Support for the definition of views has been added to Jet. This capability is built on top of Jet's stored query functionality and offers almost exactly the same capability. The view syntax, however, permits you to make this functionality portable to other SQL databases when it is written within the limitations of ANSI view semantics. Views are discussed in greater detail in Chapter 15.

Stored Procedures

Support for the definition of stored procedures has been added to Jet. This capability is built on top of Jet's stored query functionality for action queries (queries based on update, delete, select into, and drop statements) and **SELECT** queries that contain parameters. Stored procedures are discussed in greater detail in Chapter 15.

Transactions

Jet SQL now includes extended support for the invocation and termination (committing or rolling back) of transactions. Although ANSI SQL specifies that a new transaction is started automatically following a **Commit** or **Rollback**, Jet does not follow this model. Thus, an additional transaction verb is defined to explicitly start transactions. Note that Jet does not automatically start transactions. Transactions are covered in detail in later chapters.

Connection Control

The connection control (also known as passive shutdown) feature prevents users from connecting to a database. This capability is useful for a database administrator who needs to acquire exclusive access to a database to perform maintenance (e.g., compacting the database) or make updates to the database schema or applications.

When connection control is invoked, users currently connected to a database will remain unaffected until they disconnect. At that point, they would simply be unable to reconnect until connection control was revoked.

Bidirectional Replication With SQL Server

With previous versions of Jet, SQL Server data could be replicated to a Jet database, but changes made in the Jet database could not be used to update the SQL Server database. Replication was unidirectional, from a SQL Server publisher to a Jet subscriber.

With version 4 of the Jet database engine and version 7 of SQL Server, support for bidirectional replication between Jet and SQL Server has been added. Not only can changes made to data in a SQL Server database be replicated to a Jet database, but changes made to that data in Jet can be synchronized to and reconciled with the SQL Server database.

There are some limitations, as detailed in the following list:

- Only data may be replicated between Jet and SQL Server. Access application objects (e.g., forms, reports, macros, and modules) cannot be replicated to SQL Server and will continue to reside only in a Jet database.

- The only topology supported in the Jet/SQL Server replication structure is *hub and spoke*. In such an environment, the SQL Server is always the hub. The Jet replicas at the spokes cannot synchronize with other Jet replicas; they can synchronize only with the SQL Server hub.

Resolving Replication Conflicts

In previous versions, Jet replication differentiated between synchronization conflicts and synchronization errors. Synchronization conflicts occurred when two users updated the same record in two different databases in a replica set. Synchronization of the two databases would take place, but only one of the two sets of changes would be applied to both databases. Thus, one user would always lose data in the synchronization. Synchronization errors occurred when a change to data in one database in a replica set could not be applied to another database in the replica set because it would violate a constraint such as referential integrity or uniqueness.

With Jet 4 replication, the events that cause synchronization conflicts and synchronization errors are both viewed simply as synchronization conflicts, and a single mechanism is used to record and resolve them, which makes resolution of such problems easier. When a conflict occurs, a "winning" change will be selected and applied, and the "losing" change will be recorded as a conflict at all replicas. The new Conflict Resolution Wizard can then be used to reconcile and resolve synchronization conflicts. Note that the same Conflict Resolution Wizard can be used with either SQL Server 7 or Jet 4 replicable databases.

Column-Level Conflict Resolution

In Jet 3.5, conflicts were determined at the row level. In other words, if two users in two different replicas changed the customer record for the same customer but each changed a different field in the record, the two records would conflict when the replicas were synchronized. Suppose one changed the ZIP code and the other changed the phone number. Note that, although the changes themselves do not conflict, because they are two separate fields, a synchronization conflict would still occur as conflicts were determined at a record level.

Jet 4 implements column-level (field-level) conflict resolution, meaning changes to the same record in two different replicas will cause a synchronization conflict only if the same column or field is changed. Thus, in the preceding scenario, there would no longer be a synchronization conflict because the two users changed the values of different columns. Column-level tracking of changes and conflict resolution will significantly reduce the potential for conflicts and simplify the maintenance of replicated databases.

Jet column-level change tracking and conflict resolution will work in conjunction with the corresponding SQL Server 7 capability when Jet/SQL Server replication is used.

Column-level conflict resolution is the default when a database is made replicable. To specify row-level conflict resolution for a table, it must be set prior to making the table replicable.

New Access Project Storage Format

In Jet 3.5 Replication, individual Access objects (forms, reports, modules, and so on) could be identified and tracked, allowing changes to individual objects to be synchronized. In other words, if an Access form changed in the design master replica and no other objects changed, only the changes to the form were replicated when the replica set was synchronized.

However, in Access 2000, all Access objects are stored in a single Binary Large Object (BLOB) within the database file or in a separate Access Data Project file (referred to as an ADP file). In this format, the individual objects can't be identified or tracked by Jet replication. What this means is that, if the Access project in the design master is made replicable, any single object is modified and then the entire project is replicated when a replica set is synchronized. However, you can choose to not make the Access project replicable when you create the design master. In this case, the Access project in each of the replicas is not replicable and all objects created in a replica are local.

Replica Visibility

Jet 4 replication defines three degrees of visibility for replicas. A replica's visibility can be defined as *global, local,* or *anonymous.*

Local and anonymous replicas provide a way of controlling topology. Anonymous replicas are important for Internet-based replication where you don't want to keep track of the number of times the database is downloaded over the Web. The following list provides more detailed information about each degree of replica visibility:

- *Global replica*—A replica that can synchronize with all other global replicas in a replica set. A global replica can also synchronize with any replica it created, with some exceptions. (The descriptions of local and anonymous replicas that follow will enumerate the exceptions.) When a Jet database is made replicable, its visibility is set to global. If you developed with Jet 3.5 replication, you will be familiar with the characteristics of global replicas because all replicas created with Jet 3.5 are global replicas.

- *Local replica*—A replica that can synchronize only with its parent replica, which is a global replica. A local replica can't synchronize with other replicas in the replica set. Local replicas permit finer control of the topology of a replica set. For example, they can be used to enforce a star topology at individual sites where you want to ensure that synchronization between the sites goes through a global hub at each site.

- *Anonymous replica*—Like a local replica, an anonymous replica is one that can synchronize only with its parent, a global replica. The purpose of having anonymous replicas is to permit large numbers of replicas that participate in a replica set, to reduce the amount of information stored about a replica set, and to reduce processing overhead. This is consistent with supporting replica sets whose subscribers are distributed across the Internet. Unlike a local replica, a global replica cannot schedule synchronization with an anonymous replica. An anonymous replica initiates synchronization with its parent.

Other limitations of replicas include the following—important considerations to keep in mind when developing a replica topology in your organization:

- Local and anonymous replicas can only synchronize with the parent replica that created them. If the parent replica is moved, it will receive a new ReplicaID and will no longer be visible to its local or anonymous replicas.

- Local and anonymous replicas will not be supported for Briefcase replication.

- Local and anonymous replicas cannot be converted into a design master.

- You can create replicas from a local or an anonymous replica. The new replica will inherit the same properties as the original replica, except for the ReplicaID. So from a local replica, you can only create a local replica, and from an anonymous replica, you can only create an anonymous replica.

- A SQL Server 7 global (publishing) replica will be able to create a Jet replica with any of the three degrees of visibility. However, a SQL Server 7 local or anonymous replica cannot create Jet replicas.

Benefits Of Increased Web Support Within Office

Current trends in business and computing are driving business people in ever larger numbers to use intranets and the Internet to share information with one another and with customers. In the early days of the Internet, only Web developers understood how to create and publish Web pages. Other users were limited to reading what these developers published. This has changing vastly in the last few years as a wide variety of Web-development tools have become available to users.

In Office 2000, the trend toward easier Web-page design and implementation is another step forward. Because Word, Excel, Access, and PowerPoint all support HTML as a native file format, all Office 2000 documents are Web-ready by default. And because Web-server support is integrated into the Office 2000 File Save and File Open dialog boxes, publishing an Office 2000 document to a Web server is as easy as saving a file on your own computer's hard disk.

But publishing a spreadsheet or database document to the Web is only half the story. The other half is enabling other people to interact with the published document and gain information specific to their interests—not just the publisher's. For example, if you create a spreadsheet to analyze a product's profitability given various input costs, a user's ability to enter new values and recalculate the results is a key factor in the document's value. Likewise, if you create Excel PivotTable dynamic views or Access forms, reports, or queries, other users must be able to sort, filter, pivot, or enter new values themselves.

The problem, of course, is in determining how this interaction translates to the Web. Web browsers can't sort, filter, or recalculate totals on Web pages. Office 2000 includes Office Web Components to let Access and Excel users share their documents on the corporate intranet and still preserve the interactivity that adds so much value to the information.

The Office Web Components

The Office Web Components are a collection of COM-based ActiveX controls for publishing spreadsheets, charts, and databases to the Web. They take full advantage of the interactivity provided by Internet Explorer. When you use Internet Explorer to browse a Web page that contains an Office Web Component, you interact with the page right in your browser—you can sort, filter, enter values for formula calculations, expand and collapse details, pivot data, and so on. The ActiveX controls provide the interactivity. Moreover, the Web Components are fully programmable, enabling easy development of custom pages to fit your specific needs. The Office Web Components include a spreadsheet, a PivotTable dynamic view, a data source, and a chart.

Spreadsheet Component

The spreadsheet component provides a recalculation engine, a full-function library, and a simple spreadsheet user interface in Web pages. Calculations can refer to spreadsheet cells or to any control on the page or URL that uses the Internet Explorer document object model. Office 2000 users can create Web pages with spreadsheet components by saving Excel workbooks as Web pages and by selecting the option to publish the page interactively.

PivotTable Component

The PivotTable dynamic views component enables users to analyze information by sorting, grouping, filtering, outlining, and pivoting. The data can come from a spreadsheet range, from a relational database (such as an Access or SQL Server database), or from any data source that supports multidimensional OLE DB. When an Excel user saves a PivotTable or QueryTable dynamic view as an interactive Web page, the page contains a PivotTable component. Web pages with PivotTable components can also be designed directly in the Access DAP designer. You will learn more about the PivotTable components and their use within Data Access Pages in later chapters.

Data Source Component

The data source component is the reporting engine behind Data Access Pages and the PivotTable component. It manages communication with back-end database servers and determines which database records can be displayed on the page. For example, if a Data Access Page displays customers and orders, the data source component retrieves the order records for the customer being displayed and manages the sorting, filtering, and updating of those records in response to user actions. It relies on ActiveX Data Objects for plumbing and is fully programmable and customizable.

Chart Component

The chart component graphically displays information from the spreadsheet, from the PivotTable dynamic views, or from the data source component. Because it is bound directly to other controls on the page, it updates instantly in response to user interactions with the other components. For example, you can chart a PivotTable view that displays sales by region. Then, in the browser, you can pivot to display sales by product, and the chart will update automatically without round-tripping to the Web server. When an Excel user saves a workbook containing a chart as an interactive Web page, the page contains a chart component. Office Web Component charts can also be created and edited directly in the Access Data Access Pages designer.

Building Solutions Based On Office Web Components

All Office Web Components are fully programmable with ActiveX automation. Any container that supports COM can reference the type library of the components; just set a reference from your VBA, Visual Basic, or other programming project to the Office Web Components. The object models for the Office Web Components are fully documented in Office 2000 Help and are available in any object browser that supports COM-type library inspection, such as the Visual Basic object browser.

TIP: *If you have trouble locating information on the object model, the object model Help file is contained within msowcvba.chm, which Office installs within the Office\1033 subdirectory of your Office 2000 installation directory.*

Server-Side Solutions With Office Web Components

Office Web Components can be used in server-side Active Server Page (ASP) solutions with Internet Information Services, allowing developers to hide the formulas on which their calculations were based or to build a solution that runs on any browser. In server-based solutions (because the controls are not active at the client), the user interface that the controls provide can't collect input from the user: The command bars, field lists, and input grids are not present. It is the developer's responsibility to collect input from the user with standard HTML input controls and to then—using this input as parameters—use their object models to manipulate the components on the server and return results to the user.

All Web Components support server-side result sets. The spreadsheet will typically be used to perform a calculation, storing the result in a range. The value of that range is then shipped down to the client as HTML text. Both the chart and the PivotTable components support an Export Picture method. In server-side solutions, developers can manipulate their object models based on user input—

perhaps using an input box to select a value on which to filter results, for example—and then send results down to the client browser as a GIF. Even though the components do not need to be installed on the client in this scenario, an Office 2000 license is still required at the client to view pages that are generated by using the Web Components on the server. However, this model will let your users use Navigator or some other browser to access the pages you generate.

Benefits Of An Integrated Server Platform

Throughout this chapter, and in other chapters in this book, you have seen how integration with other products, both inside the Microsoft family and out, was a core design consideration for Office 2000 products. Despite their (natural) desire to have you use only Microsoft products, their development teams have recognized that you may use different sets of Microsoft products or even a wide array of non-Microsoft products. Integration also lies at the core of Microsoft's design philosophy for the BackOffice family of applications and BackOffice Server. Server products in the family are fully integrated with Windows NT Server and with each other. In addition, solution developers benefit from an integrated application-development framework, allowing them to focus on delivering business solutions instead of designing an application infrastructure.

This integration also enables other key benefits when it is combined with Microsoft products on the network's front end, including reduced cost of PC ownership, enhanced interoperability in the enterprise, and simplified management. The following sections briefly discuss some of these benefits.

Reducing Cost Of Ownership

Reducing the cost of ownership of a solution is on the tip of almost every IT manager's tongue today. BackOffice, when combined with Office 2000, can help make reduction in TCO more accessible by delivering a unified applications and services platform that is easier to learn and use and easier to deploy and manage.

Unified Environment

To deliver effective business solutions, many enterprises feel that the greatest benefits are achieved with a unified platform with a single security model, single network infrastructure, single data-access model, and single application-development framework. The end result is platform on which it easier to develop applications and is easier to use and manage—which of course has a positive impact on cost of ownership.

The single security model that all applications and services leverage provides users with a common entry point (a single logon) for all network access. This way, desktop users don't have to maintain multiple accounts, passwords, and profiles for different enterprise systems or applications. In addition, Web security and integrity can be maintained by enforcing permissions for files and directories on the workgroup or enterprise Web server(s). This also makes it easier for administrators to perform many of their crucial tasks. The integration of Office 2000 with the Windows NT (and Windows 2000) security model also expedites the sharing of information among Office 2000 users.

This all happens in a comprehensive and consistent manner across server, host, and desktop environments. In addition, BackOffice provides Office desktops with services for X.509 certificates for secure communications and encryption across the Internet.

The single data-access model also helps reduce cost of ownership by providing universal data access across the enterprise, whether that data resides in flat-file databases on the desktop, relational databases on a Windows NT Server, or legacy databases on a mainframe. This is accomplished through ActiveX Data Objects. As you have seen (and as you will learn in more detail in later chapters), ADO is a set of high-level application programming interfaces (APIs) that enables component-based applications to query different data stores with a consistent set of interfaces. It provides connectivity to any ODBC-compliant database or any OLE DB data source.

ADO components can be driven with any ActiveX scripting language (such as JScript or VBScript) from an ASP within a Web-based application or directly within a 32-bit Windows-based application. These components can also be managed with Microsoft Transaction Server (MTS) to build highly reliable and scalable applications. ADO provides a technology framework in which you can integrate all of your corporate data into component applications. It also gives you an easy way to build applications that can access different data stores.

Office and BackOffice together deliver a unified network infrastructure, with common directory services, numerous communications options, and intranet and Internet services. Office uses these technologies to provide users with universal data access on the local area network (LAN) or wide area network (WAN), across the Internet, and over a dial-up line. In addition, broad support for networking standards and protocols allows administrators to integrate Office and BackOffice applications into their existing network architecture, reducing deployment costs and protecting their current IT investments.

Easy To Learn And Use

As a developer, you are probably well aware that users are always more comfortable with what they know. The immediate benefit of a solution built from the Office and BackOffice platform is that users are presented with an interface that they use every day rather than a whole new set of proprietary tools. For example, financial analysts can use Excel to build reports from historical sales data stored on a mainframe without having to go through the aggravation of exporting that mainframe data to some other local file structure.

Administrators of Office-based and Web-based applications benefit in the same way because the tools used to manage applications and services are consistent across the platform, letting IT personnel learn new technologies quickly. It is also easier for end users to learn new Web-based business applications that use the Office Web Components because the same features and functionality they are used to in Office can be made part of the new interface.

Manageable learning curves and easy-to-use tools contribute to lowering cost of ownership and increasing user productivity, with fewer Help desk and support calls.

Enterprise Interoperability

One of the most important features that BackOffice provides Office desktop users is access to data, applications, and services residing on heterogeneous legacy systems in the enterprise, such as AS/400s, MVS mainframes, Unix hosts, and NetWare servers. Some of the most important interoperability features are discussed here:

- *Directory integration*—In Windows 2000, the Active Directory Services Interface (ADSI) provides integration with Novell Directory Services (NDS), Lightweight Directory Access Protocol (LDAP)-based realms, and Kerberos realms, presenting a unified name space to administrators in a heterogeneous environment.

- *Macintosh integration*—Services for the Macintosh allow Windows NT Server to provide an integrating platform for mixed PC and Macintosh networks.

- *Email integration*—Through messaging standards support and tools for interoperability and coexistence, Office 2000 users can connect to, use, or migrate from existing enterprise messaging platforms. X.500 support, X.400 support, Internet Mail (SMTP/MIME), Notes Mail, and industry-standard protocol connectors enable you to communicate with Internet, X.400-based, SMTP-based, and other email environments.

- *Database integration*—Office 2000 users can access a wide range of existing data sources using tools such as replication, direct connectivity, and application services, tying desktop users into the enterprise data environment.

Enterprise Manageability

Both Office 2000 and BackOffice fit into a comprehensive management framework for the enterprise, whether you want to use tools to manage other environments or manage servers and desktops from a larger network-management system.

Each member of the BackOffice family of applications has support for Simple Network Management Protocol (SNMP) alerts and traps, providing interoperability with SNMP-based management tools and network-management applications. Further, Systems Management Server (SMS) can forward SNMP traps as well as receive traps from other SMS stations or network-management solutions.

All BackOffice applications share consistent Windows-based administration techniques and use the Windows NT Server/Windows 2000 Server administration tools. This lets you use the administration tools you know today. Every BackOffice component can be administered from a single seat: over the LAN, over the Internet, and from a remote dial-in. In addition, this management model enables Web-based administration.

Systems Management Server enables you to manage clients in a heterogeneous working environment over popular LAN and WAN protocols. It can manage clients running most modern-day operating systems.

Office and BackOffice also integrate into the Zero Administration for Windows initiative, which provides greater control and manageability of desktops in Windows-based environments. This includes support for Web-Based Enterprise Management (WBEM) in desktop and server applications, support for emerging standards for the Common Information Model (CIM), and integrated support for Windows Management Instrumentation (WMI) and the Distributed Management Interface (DMI) in the operating system.

Both Office and BackOffice provide snap-ins for the Microsoft Management Console (MMC), an extensible display framework for hosting management applications. From the snap-ins, administrators can create tools that are customized for specific tasks or management functions and distribute them to other administrators. For example, a Web administrator could have a custom taskpad for managing document libraries, Web sites, and Office Web Server Extensions.

Using Office 2000 With BackOffice

There are many new features that are "switched on" when Office 2000 is used with BackOffice and that also enable you to build a broad range of applications. Using the new Office Web Components, Office Web Server Extensions, and integrated features of the BackOffice platform, developers, administrators, and users are exposed to a whole new way of interacting with information. For more information on such features, refer to the Help file that comes with Office 2000 as well as Microsoft white papers on BackOffice integration with Office (available from the Microsoft Web site).

Immediate Solutions

Finding Support Resources For Office 2000 And BackOffice

In addition to this book and other resources available in your local bookstore, a good place to look for help with support problems is Microsoft. Office 2000's online Help files are extensive—whether or not you use the assistant—and much of what you need to know can be discovered right from your computer. However, should you need further assistance, there are several excellent online resources at the Microsoft Web site that can help you solve difficult problems with your Access implementations:

- The Microsoft Knowledge Base addresses Office 2000 questions and issues. You can reach the knowledge base at **support.microsoft.com**.

- The Microsoft Technet site is a source of in-depth technical information and resources for deploying and supporting Office 2000. You can reach Technet at **www.microsoft.com/technet**.

- If your organization does not have its own Microsoft Certified Solutions Developers (MCSDs), Microsoft will refer you to a Microsoft Certified IT professional in your area who can help you evaluate the capabilities of Office 2000 or troubleshoot a problem you encounter. For more information, see the Microsoft Web site.

- The Microsoft Office Enterprise Center has a great deal of information related to Office 2000, most of which focuses on managing your organization's computing resources. You can visit the Enterprise Center at **www.microsoft.com/office/enterprise**.

- For extensive information on the BackOffice family of products, you can visit Microsoft's BackOffice Web site at **backoffice.microsoft.com**.

Chapter 12

Access Purchasing
And Installation

In Depth

In previous chapters in this section of the book, we've gone from a general analysis of Relational Database Management Systems to a more in-depth analysis of Access 2000 and what it offers you in your enterprise. In this chapter, we'll assume that you have decided to deploy Access in your organization (and most likely Office 2000 right along with it) and move on to a closer analysis of some of the issues surrounding the purchase and installation of the Access 2000 product.

In Chapter 13, we'll consider some of the issues that surround training your users on Access 2000 and the distribution options for Access throughout your enterprise. We'll also revisit some of the different Office packages and consider some of the alternatives you have for installing different versions of the Office 2000 suite in different locations within your organization.

Determining Who Needs Access And How To Obtain It

The first question for most IT departments considering an Access 2000 deployment will be "How many copies do we need?" The second question, which ties closely with the first, will likely be "How much is it going to cost?" Careful evaluation of what computers in your organization require the Access product and what computers can simply receive distributables is at the core of these questions.

As you'll learn in greater detail in later chapters, you don't actually need to purchase the Access development environment to distribute Access applications throughout your organization. In fact, the only people who truly need the Access Interactive Development Environment (IDE) are your developers. Everyone else in your organization really only needs the Access distributable files. As you'll see later on, deploying the Access IDE throughout your organization will create security and maintenance issues for your Access applications that you are better off avoiding.

That said, it's important to recognize that Microsoft offers several different versions of the Office suite, some that include Access and others that do not. The following section explores the different versions of the Office suite in detail.

Understanding The Different Suite Configurations Microsoft Offers

As you have learned, Microsoft offers several different suite configurations for Office 2000 from which you can choose when you're making your purchasing decisions. Office 97 included four different suites—Standard, Small Business, Professional, and Developer. Office 2000 adds a new suite type, Premium.

Microsoft designed the Premium suite to meet the needs of three basic groups: software enthusiasts, users in large organizations, and IT professionals who not only want to create content for the Web, but also want to create and manage the Web sites that house that content. In addition to the new Premium edition, Microsoft has restructured the other suites to ensure that you can trade up to Professional or Premium suites without losing any of the tools available in the Standard and Small Business versions.

With Office 97, for example, a user who upgraded from the Small Business edition to the Professional edition was forced to give up Small Business Tools and Publisher. But with Office 2000, users making this upgrade will receive both of these applications in Professional.

The following list describes Microsoft's intended audience for each Office suite, as well as the applications each suite contains:

- *Small Business*—Office 2000 Small Business provides small businesses with a core set of tools to help them manage their businesses more effectively. This suite includes the new 2000 versions of Word, Excel, Outlook, Publisher, and Microsoft Small Business Tools.

- *Standard*—Office 2000 Standard is designed for customers with basic computing needs. It provides customers with the newest versions of the core set of Office applications. The four applications packaged with the Standard edition are Word, Excel, PowerPoint, and Outlook.

- *Professional*—Office 2000 Professional expands on the tools contained within the Standard edition and is designed for organizations that need a wide range of productivity tools for publishing and sharing documents on the Web. This suite features Word, Excel, Outlook, PowerPoint, Access, Publisher, and Microsoft Small Business Tools. This is likely the package that you will install on most workstations within your organization.

- *Premium*—Office 2000 Premium takes the Office Professional package and expands it even further, providing a comprehensive set of tools to create and manage Web sites. It also provides additional tools to help enhance Web sites and printed documents with attractive, custom graphics. The Premium edition includes the FrontPage Web-site creation and management tool and

PhotoDraw, a new business graphics software package, as well as Word, Excel, Outlook, PowerPoint, Access, Publisher, and Microsoft Small Business Tools.

- *Developer*—Office 2000 Developer is targeted at the developer who is building solutions with Office and Office components. It includes all the applications contained in Office 2000 Premium; Visual Basic 6; tools and documentation for building, managing, and deploying solutions with Microsoft Office; and an unlimited runtime license for runtime applications designed with Access (which is important for effective purchasing and installation).

Clearly, Microsoft has provided some valuable alternatives. One of the most important things to keep in mind, however, is that, as long as you have at least one registered copy of Office Developer (or Visual Basic 6, for that matter), you can redistribute as many copies as you need of all the applications that use the Access database engine. The crucial consideration in this case, and do not lose sight of this, is that you can *only* distribute runtime engines with the license Microsoft grants to you. If you try to distribute unlicensed copies of the Access development environment, you will be in violation of copyright law.

New Features In Access 2000

One of the most important considerations that you will have to take into account when you're considering how you'll install Access 2000 in your organization is what new features the product offers over your existing database product (which may or may not be an earlier version of Access). Evaluating those features is also an important step in determining how many copies to purchase. In addition to the traditional range of development tools that Access 2000 offers (that is, features that were also found in earlier versions), Access also adds more productivity features, improved database Web document creation, increased integration with SQL Server, and a tight office programmability model. The following sections detail most of the new features and some of the benefits they offer you.

Access Database Window

When you first run the Access IDE, the first thing you'll notice is the new database window. Microsoft changed the database window to accommodate the new objects exposed in Access 2000, to make the use of the window a little more intuitive, and to make the program's interface consistent with the new user interface metaphor used throughout Office 2000. Figure 12.1 shows the new database window in Access 2000.

The window is radically different from the database window in earlier versions of Access, such as Access 97, whose database window is shown in Figure 12.2.

As you can see, there is a lot more "going on" in the database window for Access 2000. Some of the most important changes to the window include the following:

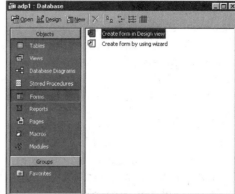

Figure 12.1   The new database window in Access 2000. The left window is for the standard MDB file, and the right window is for the new Access Data Project.

Figure 12.2   The Access 97 database window.

- A Pages tab for Data Access Pages.

- New tabs for views, stored procedures, and database diagrams when Access Data Projects are used (a new way from your Access programs to access SQL Server back ends through a thin-client front end).

- A user interface that is consistent with the model displayed in the Outlook bar—specifically, new toolbar styles and menu variations.

- A Listview control for listing objects within the window; in fact, the window's views can be changed to control how you view the icons for objects (which is similar to how you can change the window's views in Windows Explorer).

- New **<object>** items in the list of objects for easy access to wizards and designers.

- The ability to create defined groups that contain any type of Access object.

In addition to the changes to the database window, Access also changes the way you will view other objects within their own specific windows.

Subdatasheets

Access 2000 lets the user browse hierarchical data in Datasheet view. The user can view subdatasheets inline with table, query, form, and subform datasheets. The subdatasheet can be bound to a table, query, or form. In Access 2000, instead of seeing a single table or record source in the datasheet, the user can insert subdatasheets to view related data.

For example, suppose a user is viewing the **Wine List** table in a Wine Collection database. The **Wine List** table has a one-to-many relationship with the **Wine Purchases** table. Instead of being able to see only the data in the **Wine List** table, the user can see the list of purchases for a bottle of wine in a subdatasheet under each category row. The user is now able to drill down whenever relationships between tables exist. Figure 12.3 shows this use of subdatasheets in action.

Name AutoCorrect

Access 2000 automatically fixes common side effects that occur when a user or developer makes name changes to Access objects from the Access user interface. To accomplish this, Access stores both a unique identifier with each object that is created and name mapping information that allows Access to correct binding errors when they occur. When Access detects that an object has been changed since the last Name AutoCorrect, it will perform a complete name fix-up on all items for that object when the first binding error occurs.

A typical example of this is when a user changes the name of a field in a table and that field is also being used in queries, forms, and reports. In previous versions of Access, the queries, forms, and reports would be broken—that is, they wouldn't recognize the new field name—when a field name was changed. In Access 2000, the field name is automatically updated throughout Access objects and the user is not required to do any work to keep using the application.

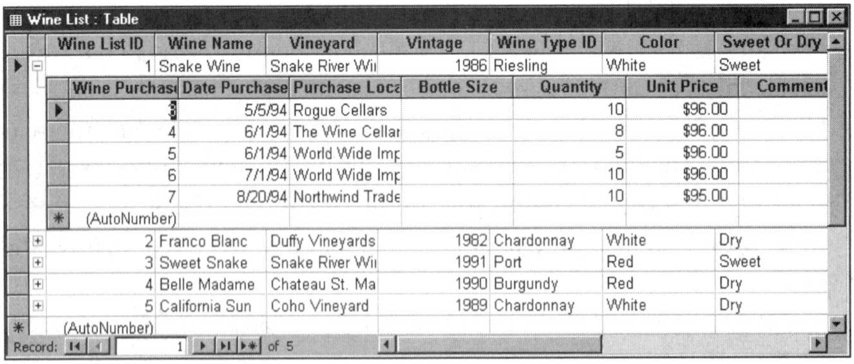

Wine List ID	Wine Name	Vineyard	Vintage	Wine Type ID	Color	Sweet Or Dry
1	Snake Wine	Snake River Wil	1986	Riesling	White	Sweet

	Wine Purchas	Date Purchase	Purchase Loca	Bottle Size	Quantity	Unit Price	Comment
	3	5/5/94	Rogue Cellars		10	$96.00	
	4	6/1/94	The Wine Cellar		8	$96.00	
	5	6/1/94	World Wide Imp		5	$96.00	
	6	7/1/94	World Wide Imp		10	$96.00	
	7	8/20/94	Northwind Trade		10	$95.00	
*	(AutoNumber)						

Wine List ID	Wine Name	Vineyard	Vintage	Wine Type ID	Color	Sweet Or Dry
2	Franco Blanc	Duffy Vineyards	1982	Chardonnay	White	Dry
3	Sweet Snake	Snake River Wil	1991	Port	Red	Sweet
4	Belle Madame	Chateau St. Ma	1990	Burgundy	Red	Dry
5	California Sun	Coho Vineyard	1989	Chardonnay	White	Dry
(AutoNumber)						

Record: 1 of 5

Figure 12.3   The use of subdatasheets lets the user easily drill down along relationships.

WARNING! *Although this feature is useful and helps protect against silly mistakes, you should not count on it to solve problems with name changes. You should always make sure you take the time to check all references to a changed object, especially before you deploy an application.*

Conditional Formatting

One of the most frustrating limitations with previous versions of Access was the inability of the interface to assist in quickly and easily formatting fields based on the value of data. To address this problem, Access 2000 introduces conditional formatting. Choose the Format menu Conditional Formatting option and Access will display the Conditional Formatting dialog box, which is shown in Figure 12.4.

When the developer first opens the Conditional Formatting dialog box, Access populates it with the default formatting information—which shows the current format for the field. This default behavior helps to bridge the formats applied elsewhere (through the property sheet and other dialogs) and this dialog, where the formatting is all brought together. The developer will be able to control the format of fields on both forms and reports based on the values of the fields or on user-defined functions. Developers will thus be able to specify multiple conditions for each field.

Convert Database To Prior Access Version

For the first time, Access users can now down-save a database into a previous version of Access, making it easier to share database files with users of different versions. Access will save the database as an Access 95 database so it is available to users of Access 95, Access 97, and Access 2000.

Note that saving a database in a previous version's binary format may cause unexpected problems. For example, all Data Access Pages will be lost from the database. Additionally, programming features specific to the newest version of Access (such as management of seed values for **Autonumber** fields) will not execute correctly in earlier versions of Access.

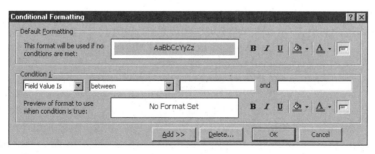

Figure 12.4   The Conditional Formatting dialog box.

Data Access Pages

In addition to changes in the development environment, Access 2000 adds an exciting and powerful new object to its offerings. The new Data Access Pages (DAPs) let you effectively design forms and reports for direct deployment to the Web or a corporate intranet. DAPs are a major improvement over Access 97's ability to publish your Access objects by converting them to Web formats. The major limitation of publishing was that the conversion often fell short and users sometimes didn't get what they were hoping for.

Data Access Pages help solve this problem because they are targeted for the browser. There's no conversion process involved in the publishing of DAPs; they are HTML files that you design in Access and run in the browser. Data Access Pages bring the ease of use of Access forms and reports to data-bound HTML files.

Data Access Pages are essentially HTML pages with data-binding capabilities. The pages can be run within the Access shell or in the Microsoft Internet Explorer 5 browser software. Unlike forms and reports, Data Access Pages are stored outside the Access database file (MDB) as an HTML file. Users can also email Data Access Pages to each other, allowing other users to view data-bound Data Access Pages in Outlook.

> **WARNING!**   Data Access Pages will only work with Internet Explorer 5. If you are publishing to a mixed environment, you will most likely still want to find other ways to Web-publish your data.

Access can open any existing HTML file in the data access page designer. Once a page is opened in Access, you can add data-bound fields to it. To build a Data Access Page, you can simply work with the new data access page designer. It uses Internet Explorer for its design surface and has familiar tools such as a property sheet, a field list, a toolbox, and wizards. The controls that you place on Data Access Pages are HTML intrinsic and ActiveX controls and are similar to the controls that are used for building forms. Data Access Pages also have an object model comparable to an Access form, and they support writing script in VBScript or JScript. The benefit is powerful, useful HTML pages developed in an environment that is closely integrated with Access.

Data Access Pages are more than a simple forms package for the Internet. Grouped Data Access Pages provide users with a totally new way to interact with data, giving them the opportunity to drill in and work with hierarchical data in an interactive manner, which has not been possible before. Bringing the richness of hierarchical data to HTML pages is one of the key benefits of Data Access Pages. The Office 2000 Web Components (including a Spreadsheet Component, the PivotTable Component, and the PivotChart Component) let you easily build interactivity and high-powered data analysis and reporting into your DAPs.

Connectivity To Enterprise Data

Access 2000 lets you connect to SQL Server directly by using OLE DB instead of going through the Jet database engine (through linked tables). When a user chooses this approach, Access will create an Access project (an Access Data Page [ADP] file instead of an MDB file) which will store forms, reports, macros, and modules. The data-related objects (tables, views, relationships, and stored procedures) are all stored on the SQL server. This new, thin-client structure allows power users and developers to build Access 2000 applications that work directly against a SQL Server-based back end. To provide Access users with the tools they need to develop databases easily, Access 2000 integrates the DaVinci visual database design tools.

SQL Server Integration

The SQL Server integration features that have been built into Access 2000 (Microsoft Access projects, DaVinci integration, etc.) are targeted toward the high-end Access user or developer who is knowledgeable about SQL Server and generic client-server issues and techniques. The user interface changes are therefore tailored to this user, a fact that is evident because they are not particularly easy to use. However, they are very clean and functional.

You will learn more about client-server design and its benefits in later chapters. For now, you should understand that the newest version of Access simultaneously simplifies the development of client-server applications and empowers the Access developer to make better client-server applications.

When using an Access project file, the user can connect directly to either SQL Server 6.5 (with Service Pack 3), SQL Server 7, or the Microsoft Data Engine (MSDE). In all configurations, Access supports the creation and manipulation of SQL objects, including tables, views, stored procedures, triggers, and database diagrams. Database diagrams represent a functional superset of the Access Relationships window—that is, they let you create relationships, in addition to performing other tasks. These objects—tables, views, stored procedures (with support for parameters), and SQL strings—are all valid data sources for Access forms and reports and Data Access Pages.

Client-Server Design

There are four key items users need to consider when deciding whether they will use Jet or SQL Server for their database engine. The determination you make for these items will control how you implement your database designs. The four considerations are as follows:

- *Simplicity*—Jet is far easier to use and administer than SQL Server. This makes Jet a good starting place for relatively simple database applications. Users should only move to SQL Server when they need the advantages it offers, such as scalability and true client-server support.

- *Data integrity*—SQL Server is a client-server database. Jet is a file-server database. The big advantage of SQL Server is its ability to run queries and log transactions. If anything goes wrong during a write to the database (disk error, network failure, power failure, etc.), SQL Server can recover because it logs the transactions. When the system comes back up, SQL Server will revert back to the last consistent state. Because Jet cannot log transactions, the database may be corrupted if anything goes wrong. You would need to revert to your last backup copy.

- *Number of simultaneous users (performance)*—SQL Server can handle more simultaneous users than Jet. Jet's limit depends on what the users are doing. Reading data is a relatively low-impact task and Jet can handle up to 255 simultaneous users. The practical limit is between 50 and 250 users, depending on what your application is designed to do. SQL Server can scale to a much higher number of users.

- *Amount of data*—Jet can handle up to 1GB of data per MDB file in Access 97 and up to 2GB of data in Access 2000. You can create larger databases by using tables that are linked to several different MDB files. SQL Server has a much higher limit, effectively running to the terabytes. SQL Server also has a performance advantage over Jet for large sets of data and many simultaneous users. Because Jet is a file-server system, the query processing must happen on the client. This involves moving a lot of data over the network for large databases. SQL Server runs the query on the server. This loads the server more than Jet, but it can reduce the network traffic substantially (especially if the users are selecting a small subset of the data).

In short, SQL Server is the right choice for systems that involve important trans-actions (e.g., financial transactions) or store mission-critical data (24 hour/day, 7 day/week systems). When deciding between Jet and SQL Server, developers should ask themselves, "If this database goes down for a couple of hours, will it be ac-ceptable or a huge problem?" The more important the database is, the more SQL Server should be the database of choice.

Programmability

Access 2000 lets you use the Microsoft Scripting Environment (MSE), a new shared scripting IDE, to develop scripts for Data Access Pages. MSE lets you work with HTML events and Object events and properties within your Data Access Pages to create an event-based model comparable to working with Access forms. You will learn more about the MSE in Chapter 35.

Worldwide Support

In Access 2000, Microsoft has added Unicode support, which will let you and your users store and display text in many languages. For example, if you created an application that contained address information for international clients, you would be able to see a Japanese name next to a Russian name in your table. This will give international users much greater flexibility when they are creating databases. This feature also allows for multiple-language support in forms and reports.

With the addition of Unicode support to Access 2000, users will have the ability to store all character sets within one database. Some characters require more storage space than others. For example, a database containing Chinese characters will be larger in size than a database containing only alphanumeric characters. Access will automatically compress data contained in fields to minimize the size of the database.

Access 2000, along with all other Office applications, supports the Global Interface feature. With the Microsoft Office 2000 Language Pack, users will be able to select the language to be used in the Access user interface.

New Jet Features

As you know, the Jet engine is the underlying technology that drives Access databases. In the Access 97 release, the Jet engine was version 3.5. Access 2000 contains several major improvements to the Jet database engine, for which Microsoft has now changed the version number to Jet 4. New Jet 4 features include the following:

- Full Unicode support, as described previously.
- Row-level locking.
- An enhanced conflict/error model.
- Enhanced counters. Jet **Autonumber** fields now support seed and increment settings (from Data Access Object [DAO] code only).
- A native OLE DB provider that provides a native interface directly to Jet.
- New SQL syntax (optional ANSI-compliant SQL queries).

System Requirements

In general, Access 2000 will run on any computer that supports Windows 98 or NT 4. However, you are generally best served if you ensure that any computer running Access 2000 has at least 32MB of memory and several hundred megabytes of free disk space (for the swap file).

Additionally, taking full advantage of the features of Access 2000—particularly Data Access Pages—requires that you install Microsoft's Internet Explorer 5 on your system. Although Access (and Office) will work correctly with earlier versions of Internet Explorer, you'll get the most out of the features in Access 2000 only if IE5 is installed.

> **WARNING!   Help and certain other features of Office will not work at all if you do not at least have IE4 installed. In general, and particularly if your users will be doing any work with the help files or with the Web, you should go ahead and install IE5 onto computers on which you install Office.**

Installing Access 2000 On A Single Computer

Although the specifics of the Access installation are covered in Chapter 22, it is worthwhile to note several key points here about the Access and Office installation. One of the most important points is that the new Office installation updates the Windows Installer, which keeps a close eye on your applications and responds whenever you request a feature that you did not originally install. Be warned, however, that from time to time, when a user selects a feature that may not have been installed initially, Access (or any other Office application) will request the Office CD-ROM to install support. You should closely evaluate the level of support you intend to provide to your users for the use of such features because the configuration of individual Office suites on computers throughout your organization may vary widely.

Additionally, if the user does not have IE5 installed on his computer, the Access installer will prompt the user to install IE5. Generally, you should keep a close eye on the features users install from IE5. For example, if you are using Outlook as your messaging solution, you probably won't want users to have access to Outlook Express, which could result in significant confusion on their part when they try to find their email.

Finally, and this corresponds to the first point regarding the Windows Installer, the Office installation *by default* does not install many features of the product. Instead, the installation marks the features as Load On 1st Use and then installs them from the CD-ROMs when the user tries to access the features. This would not necessarily be a major problem, except the Premium Edition of the Microsoft Office suite includes six CD-ROMs, which can become a significant administration issue when multiplied by hundreds of users.

In Chapter 13, we'll consider some of the possible deployment strategies in more detail, with a specific focus on how to reduce the total cost of ownership (TCO) for the Office 2000 products.

Registration Wizard

The installer finishes its installation with a new Registration wizard, which requires that you register the product. This is a change from earlier versions of Office—in fact, if you do not register the product, it will eventually stop working (after 50 executions). The nice thing about the new Registration wizard is that it is based entirely on email and performs most of its processing with the click of a button. If your computer is on a LAN connected to the Internet, the Registration wizard will often finish its processing within about 10 seconds.

In the next chapter, we'll explore some of the training issues and deployment strategies surrounding a successful deployment of the Access 2000 product. However, the key to a successful deployment is early determination of what versions of the Office product you'll use within your organization and how you'll deploy Access throughout the organization. Before you continue with the next chapter, you should closely evaluate the considerations laid out in this chapter and ensure that you can effectively make the proper decision about what Office 2000 products you'll need, how many you'll need, and when to buy them.

Immediate Solutions

Finding Support Resources For Access 2000

In addition to this book and other resources available in your local bookstore, the best place to look for help with support problems is to Microsoft. Access 2000's online help files are extensive—whether or not you use the assistant—and much of what you need to know can be discovered right from your computer. However, should you need further assistance, there are several excellent online resources at the Microsoft Web site that can help you solve difficult problems with your Access implementations:

- The Microsoft Knowledge Base addresses Office 2000 questions and issues. You can reach the Knowledge Base at **http://support.microsoft.com**.

- The Microsoft Technet site is a source of in-depth technical information and resources for deploying and supporting Office 2000. You can reach Technet at **http://www.microsoft.com/technet**.

- If your organization does not have its own Microsoft Certified Solutions Developers (MCSDs), Microsoft will refer you to a Microsoft Certified IT professional in your area who can help you evaluate the capabilities of Office 2000 or troubleshoot a problem you encounter. For more information, see the Microsoft Web site.

- The Microsoft Office Enterprise Center has a great deal of information related to Office 2000, most of which focuses on managing your organization's computing resources. You can visit the Enterprise Center at **http://www.microsoft. com/office/enterprise**.

Chapter 13

Access 2000 Distribution And Training

In Depth

After determining how many copies of Access to purchase for your organization and considering how you'll ultimately deploy Access in your organization, you must consider specific details of how you'll implement the deployment. Additionally, you should craft a plan for how you will train users in the new product once it is deployed.

In this chapter, we'll consider strategies and techniques for the deployment of Access in your organization. The deployment techniques we'll discuss range from a machine-by-machine deployment to the use of other products, such as Systems Management Server (SMS), to control the deployment of your application. We'll also discuss some of the common training techniques and how you can apply them to your distribution.

When you are considering deployment techniques, the primary focus is always on Total Cost of Ownership (TCO), a dollars-and-cents method of analyzing the cost to install and maintain a product. In fact, one of Microsoft's primary concerns in the development of the new Office 2000 suite was the improvement of the product's deployment capabilities and the reduction of the suite's TCO.

In the following sections, we'll consider some of the new support built into the Office 2000 suite. Afterward, we'll discuss some of the other options you have for effective deployment of the product.

Deployment Considerations

Deploying Access and the rest of the Office suite is intimately connected with the type of environment to which you want to deploy and the method you will use in the deployment. For the purpose of this discussion, we'll consider three general categories of deployment:

• Local machine deployment, where you install Access and Office onto a single machine that may be connected to the Internet but is not connected to a network.

• Local area network deployment, where you install Access and Office onto client machines in a local area network (LAN), preferably from a single, central management point.

- Wide area network deployment, where you install Access and Office onto client machines in a wide area network (WAN). You may use a single, central management point at the center of the network or you may use a distributed set of management points spread out over the WAN.

Understanding the implications of these different distribution methodologies requires first that you understand some of the improvements made to the Office product itself. The biggest improvement comes in the suite's installation code. Developers at Microsoft have created an entirely new architecture for the installation, and Microsoft feels that the new architecture is so superior that it has actually made the installation program (called the Windows Installer) part of the operating system for future releases. The Installer will run as a service; moreover, Microsoft has indicated that using the Installer (rather than custom installation code) will likely be part of the new Windows 2000 operating system's logo recommendations.

New Windows Installer Technology

At the root of most of the new features in Microsoft Office 2000 that reduce TCO is the new installation program, the Windows Installer service. The Windows Installer service differs from earlier installation programs in many ways. However, it specifically will help you address the following deployment concerns:

- Managing shared resources
- Helping to consistently enforce the same set of installation rules on client computers
- Providing for easy customization of the installation process
- Helping users install only the components they need, while also helping them easily install additional components at a later time (depending on how you have customized the installation, this feature may not be available)
- Diagnosing and repairing configuration problems at application runtime—a process that you can see clearly if you leave earlier versions of Office running on the same system

Because addressing issues of this nature is a concern for the installation of all desktop software, the Office 2000 installation actually adds the Windows Installer to the operating system as a service. Moreover, the folks at Microsoft have indicated that the new Windows Installer will ship with Windows 2000 Workstation. They have also indicated that they will provide a service pack for Windows 9x and Windows NT 4 that includes the new service.

WARNING!   Unfortunately, the Package and Deployment Wizard that comes with Office 2000 Developer Edition does not take full advantage of the new Windows Installer service. Do not expect that it will do so. If logo requirements are a concern for your development process, you should not use the Package and Deployment Wizard.

Understanding Differences In The New Service

Most existing installation programs use procedural scripts to copy files, add Registry keys, and create shortcuts. The developer creates those scripts and specifies important issues about them—such as when to copy over existing system files and controls, for example. In this environment, if the user chooses the Typical installation option, the installation program runs through a script (from beginning to end) that determines which files to copy and where, adds Registry keys, and creates application shortcuts. When the script is done, setup is finished and the installation program has no further interaction with the application.

If a user needs an additional component later, she needs to know how to start the setup program again, how to add or remove components, and exactly which component she needs. This problem is even more significant when you consider that many modern-day installation packages or programs use some type of compressed storage, such as a cabinet (CAB) file. The user must then know not only what files she needs but also what cabinet file contains the files she needs, or the setup program must run again and provide additional options to the user. Needless to say, adding a single additional feature to a program or installation can result in significant wasted time while the user tries to put together the necessary steps.

The Windows Installer service, on the other hand, views all applications as comprising three logical building blocks: components, features, and products. A *component* is a collection of files, Registry keys, and other resources that are all installed as a unit. Although components are not exposed to the user, having discrete units that go together provides increased flexibility and management to both the developer and the administrator. Because multiple files, Registry keys, or shortcuts can exist together in one component, developers can ensure that mutually dependent files are installed or uninstalled together. In addition, one part of a component provides a resource that tracks the component to enable the Windows Installer to verify whether it exists and is properly installed.

Because resources are managed on the component level rather than on a file level, the Windows Installer is better able to accurately track the files, Registry keys, or shortcuts that are shared by more than one application. If an application that uses a shared component is removed, that shared component will not be removed unless no other applications on the system are using it. This solves two common desktop-maintenance problems: removing resources that are still needed and leaving resources behind that are not needed. Furthermore, because the Windows Installer runs as a service, it is able to constantly evaluate components and ensure that they are installed correctly.

Features are the pieces of an application that a user can choose to install. Features are nothing more than components that are grouped together and can be installed in a variety of ways. (Features—and installing them—are covered later in this chapter.) For now, consider the model shown in Figure 13.1, which depicts how a fictional feature might be composed of multiple components.

Products are single products such as Office 2000 or Microsoft Word. Products comprise one or more features. Each product is described to the Windows Installer with a package file. This package file is a database that is optimized for installation performance, and it describes the relationships between features and components for a given product. At installation, the Windows Installer service opens the package file and uses the information to determine the installation operations that must be performed for that product. Figure 13.2 shows a model of how a product contains features, which in turn contain components.

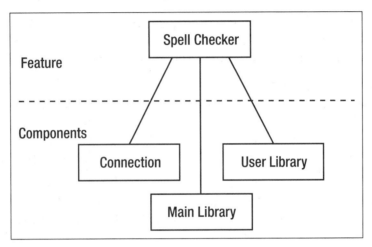

Figure 13.1   A feature is composed of components.

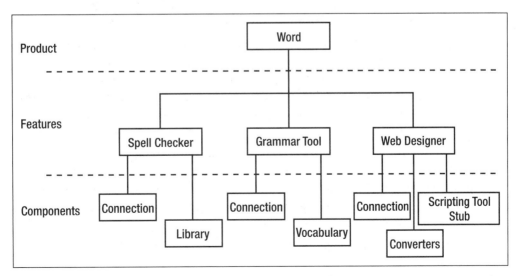

Figure 13.2   A product contains features and their components.

The Windows Installer also provides a management application programming interface (API). Through this API, the Windows Installer can manage all file paths for an application to better accommodate features such as roaming user support, Install on Demand, and runtime resiliency. Later sections in this chapter explain these features in more detail.

Greater Support For Customization

For many administrators, one of the biggest issues in previous versions of Office was the difficulty they encountered in customizing the installations to meet their specific enterprise needs. Although Microsoft made the installations customizable, all the control that an administrator might want never seemed to be exposed.

Because the new Windows Installer model exposes installation flexibility to the feature level (each feature, remember, consists of a group of components), the administrator has more control than before in how the installation proceeds.

Flexible Execution Methods

In the past, administrators had to decide whether to install applications on the local machine or to run them from a server; there was little flexibility for a mixed decision. In addition, to maintain control and shield the user from the installation process, an administrator had to simultaneously install every application that a user might need.

With Office 2000, administrators have several choices about where the software runs, with feature-by-feature flexibility (meaning that some features can be set to run from certain locations while others can be set to run from other locations):

- *Run from Local Machine*—With this method, the software is installed on the local computer, providing the best performance and the fewest networking issues, such as bandwidth drain or downtime.

- *Run from Source*—With this method, the software runs from the source— which can be a CD-ROM, a server, or even a terminal server—reducing the hard-drive requirements at the local computer and the work involved in the central administration of updates. This method uses more network resources, including server space and bandwidth, and depends on the network being accessible at all times.

- *Install on Demand*—With this method, a feature or component is not installed until the user tries to use it for the first time, at which time the Windows Installer will handle the installation. This method, although useful, may also create issues, particularly if the initial installation was handled from a CD-ROM rather than a server or other central source.

- *Don't Install*—With this method, the feature or component is not available to the user at all.

Needless to say, these options expose a great deal of flexibility to the administrator, letting you choose the most appropriate means to handle *each feature* of the product within your organization. These options serve many purposes, but some common examples include the following:

- Users of laptops with sufficient hard-drive space will be best served with all software installed and running from the local machine. Performance is improved, and all features are available regardless of their connectivity status.

- Users with older computers and little hard-drive space might want to either run the least-used features or applications from the source or run all of the software from the source. The computer's performance might suffer, but a hardware upgrade can be avoided or postponed.

- A large organization that has both central IS and business unit IS teams might choose to install typical installation features to the local machine and make other features available on demand. This reduces the necessary amount of preplanning and the number of different configurations while making all features available to the user. In addition, the business unit IS team can customize the choices for its use.

With early versions of Office, an administrator who wanted to customize the way Office was installed for a large group of users had to open and hand-edit a large ASCII text file known as an *STF file*. This file was not easy to understand, but it was, unfortunately, very easy to corrupt. It was difficult for even the most knowledgeable administrators to customize, and it was not supported by product support services.

For both Office 95 and Office 97, Microsoft provided the Network Installation Wizard, which made it easier to customize the Office installation, but the choices were somewhat limited. In many cases, administrators still found themselves hand-editing the STF file.

With Office 2000, the Windows Installer service provides so much flexibility that it is possible to give the administrator virtually unlimited choices for customization. There are several tools packaged with Office 2000 to simplify such customization. The following sections provide a brief overview of the tools and their use.

Office Custom Installation Wizard

The Custom Installation Wizard uses the traditional wizard interface to take the administrator step-by-step through virtually any customization, such as individual application options. The administrator chooses which features to install, where to install them, and how the installation should run. Upon completion, the Custom Installation Wizard produces a customized file called the *transform file* (to which it appends the .mst suffix), which works with the Windows Installer to implement the administrator's installation options and provides the command line for running Office the way the administrator prefers. The Custom Installation Wizard allows the administrator to more easily configure and deploy Office in a way that meets the needs of the environment.

Moreover, if the company chooses the Office Premium edition, FrontPage is part of the integrated setup. FrontPage will then work with all the tools described in the next two sections to help with deployment and maintenance. In fact, these tools even work if the company has to deploy FrontPage first to groups of people—rather than forcing you to install the tools prior to the FrontPage installation.

Office Profile Wizard

The Office Profile Wizard makes it possible for the administrator to adjust any of the more than 1,500 user-customizable settings in Office 2000—from the color of the background in Word to the default file formats to use in each application, the administrator has complete control. The administrator simply installs Office 2000 to a computer and uses the applications to change the desired settings. When the administrator then runs the Office Profile Wizard, the Wizard takes a snapshot file (indicated by the .OPS suffix) of those changes from the default settings. The OPS file is then built into the MST file produced by the Custom Installation Wizard to implement all the administrator's changes upon installation on other computers.

Office Removal Wizard

The Office Removal Wizard is an improved version of the Office Cleanup Wizard that was introduced in Office 97. Because of the new features provided to the operating system and applications by the new Windows Installer service, it is possible to remove previous installations of Microsoft Office more completely and accurately. This wizard provides the administrator with a wide variety of options to assist in the removal of Office versions 4.x through 2000.

Automatic Recovery Support

The Windows Installer tracks every action it undertakes in installing Office 2000, including any elements from a previous version that are removed. If setup does not complete successfully, the installer automatically recovers (or rolls back) all changes, restoring the desktop to its previous working condition. Users do not experience downtime or the frustration of not knowing how to restore their desktops to a working condition. Once setup installs successfully, this information is discarded.

TIP: *You will notice that much of what the new Windows Installer does is concerned with what is known as atomicity. The new service tries to ensure that every action it performs that relates to a specific goal occurs; if the actions don't occur, they are not made permanent. For example, if your Windows Registry is full and the Installer is unable to write all the necessary Registry information for the Office Suite, the Installer (depending on your actions) may roll back all or part of the installation because that component (containing the Registry entries) was not completed successfully.*

As a direct result of the distributed computing model, this atomic model is becoming more and more common in all applications that you see today. The new Installer service is an excellent example of what can be accomplished in any type of object-oriented programming when the developers apply a strong eye to detail and specifics.

Support For Scalability

In today's offices and enterprises, there is, more than ever, a wide disparity in the types of machines the network and the administrator must support. Although the PC desktop is still the dominant computer system in the enterprise, the growth in the number of other, terminal-style systems within a common enterprise environment has not been ignored by the developers at Microsoft. In fact, the new Office 2000 suites support installation on three general types of computer systems:

- *Traditional Windows-based PC*—Whether on a desktop or a laptop computer, Microsoft Office 2000 continues to exploit the power of the Windows operating system and PC technology to the fullest.

- *Microsoft Windows NT 4, Terminal Server Edition*—Terminal server is a super-thin client that runs 32-bit applications from a Windows NT server on older, less powerful computers (such as 286s and 386s). Office 2000 has been developed to support this configuration (be forewarned, though—it will almost certainly be significantly slower than a full PC installation because of bandwidth and processing constraints).

- *Net PC*—The Net PC is a new type of simple, easy to manage Windows-based PC for the corporate environment. Net PCs are ideal for task-oriented users who need the local processing, local storage, and familiar user environment and administrators who need full control to centrally manage the Net PC users' environment. Office 2000 also supports the Net PC environment (again, however, you may be concerned with speed because of bandwidth and processing constraints).

Ongoing Maintenance And Support

In the past, after the Microsoft Office product was installed, the setup program finished and few features contributed to the ongoing maintenance and support of the product. With Office 2000, Microsoft has added several specially designed features to make it easier to migrate to Office 2000 and maintain the product after migration. Understanding these new features and taking advantage of them will help to make your deployment run more smoothly.

A few common issues made it difficult to upgrade to a newer version of desktop applications software. Arguably, the most important was that no simple way existed to restore the desktop (and the underlying operating system) to its previous state if the application's setup did not complete successfully. Common problems included the following:

- A lack of ability to migrate custom user settings

- Differences in file formats that made it difficult to share documents with other users who did not have "the latest and greatest" version of the application

- Interoperation issues that made it difficult or impossible to use different versions of the same software on the same computer

The following sections detail some of the improvements Office 2000 includes to help solve some of these issues.

Automatic User Settings Migration

While upgrading a user from a previous version of Office, the setup program can compare the user's current settings to the original defaults and therefore understand which customizations the user made in the previous version. The Windows Installer then automatically migrates the user's changes in the previous version to Office 2000. Any settings that were not customized are replaced with the new defaults for Microsoft Office 2000.

This new, automated migration feature is critical for reducing TCO because it helps makes the user's transition to the new product more painless. Bringing over custom settings (such as the default location for documents in Word) saves the user significant amounts of customization time during the migration.

Binary File Format

Office 2000 and Office 97 file formats are compatible (unlike Office 95 and Office 97 formats). Office 97 will be able to open any Office 2000 file without a converter. However, certain formatting options available in Office 2000 will not transfer over to Office 97 because Office 97 does not recognize these features.

> **WARNING!** *The major exception to this rule is Access 2000, because of new support for Unicode field types. Access 2000 can save a database as an Access 97 database but will truncate all fields with Unicode support. Carefully evaluate the construction of your Access 2000 databases before downward-revising them.*

For organizations migrating from versions of Office prior to Office 97, file formats will be different in Office 2000. The administrator has several options for making it easier for users to share files—from deploying converter packs to setting the default file format in Office 2000 applications to their earlier formats, such as Word for Windows 6 or Microsoft Excel 5.

Support For Multiple Concurrent Versions

When an organization is migrating to the latest version of Microsoft Office, it is sometimes necessary for some users to have more than one version of an application running simultaneously on the same computer. This includes help-desk personnel and administrators, as well as users who might use custom solutions that have not yet been migrated. Office 2000 can run on a computer in tandem with an earlier version of Office (or any of its individual applications) without causing conflict problems.

TIP: *If your users use earlier versions of Office, each time they run an Office 2000 application, they will see a dialog box from the Windows Installer indicating that it is cleaning up information. This dialog box is simply making sure that everything is correct with the Office 2000 application—it does not indicate a problem with either pre-existing or the Office 2000 installations.*

Maintenance Issues

One of the biggest issues with system maintenance has always been DLL conflicts and other issues surrounding the components that make up modern-day software programs. Office 2000 includes significant improvements in avoiding DLL conflicts, the easy removal or addition of components as needed, and support for roaming users and system policies. Some of the most important features of the suite are detailed in the following sections.

Install On Demand

Install on Demand (or install on first use) is a blanket term that actually covers two different scenarios. Its goal is to make it simpler to get the right features to the right user at the right time.

Many administrators want to have some way to make an application available to a user without having to actually install the application. For example, a department might have a window of 30 days in which to upgrade to the next version of Office. Some users might have custom solutions that need testing and might want to upgrade closer to the end of that window, while others would prefer to upgrade immediately. Alternatively, suppose only a few people in a department use a particular application. Rather than installing the application on all desktops, the administrator would simply make it easily available to those users who want it.

The Windows Installer makes it possible to *advertise* an application without actually installing it. A shortcut is placed on the Windows taskbar so the user can see the application, but the application is not actually installed until the user chooses to use it (hence the notion of install on first use). The benefit in this case is that users don't need to be trained, nor do they need to call the help desk to add an application; yet they can still access an application's additional functionality as their needs change. This feature works for any 32-bit version of Windows that includes the Installer service, including Windows 98 and any 32-bit version of Windows with Microsoft Internet Explorer 4.01 Service Pack 1 and the shell update (Windows 95 or Windows NT 4).

In a large organization, it is extremely difficult and time consuming for an administrator to try to track each feature that any given user might need at any given time. Furthermore, users' needs will often change—and not only when they change jobs or departments. With Office 2000, the administrator can choose to deploy the Typical installation option and choose Install on Demand as the installation state for all other features. These features are then made available to the user via the user interface (menus, toolbars, and dialog boxes) and are installed without user intervention (outside of a yes/no prompt) the first time the user accesses them. With Install on Demand, the Office 2000 standard installation that an organization creates can be more efficient without inconveniencing individual users who need additional features.

Improved Support For Roaming Users And System Policies

Office has supported system policies and roaming users since the release of Office 97—but a bit incompletely. With Microsoft Office 2000, all user-customizable options are stored in the **HKEY_CURRENT_USER** hive rather than in the **HKEY_CURRENT_MACHINE** hive of the Windows Registry. Because any of these settings can be changed for each individual user in Office 2000, the support for system policies and roaming users is now much more complete. Administrators can control the desktop better, and users can have the correct access to their settings and software regardless of what computer they are using, as long as it is running the same operating system as the computer containing their preset preferences.

Built-In, Ongoing Application Support

Most of the features mentioned in the previous sections reduce the cost of supporting users with Office 2000. Office 2000 goes further, however, in targeting issues that directly affect the cost of supporting Office throughout the life of a version. The new suite includes several improvements—both conceptual and accessible—that will help you support Office throughout the enterprise more efficiently.

Application Resiliency

Microsoft defines "resiliency" as an application's capability to keep running regardless of what the user or another application installation does to the existing installation. In other words, an application should be able to continue to operate correctly regardless (for all intents and purposes) of changes the user may make to other applications or to the operating system. Two specific features of Office

2000 provide resiliency, which Microsoft refers to as *self-repairing applications* and the *Detect and Repair* feature.

- *Self-Repairing Applications*—Each time an Office 2000 application is started, the application (using the Windows Installer) does a quick check of the files that are critical for its use. If any of those files are damaged or missing, the application will send a request to the Windows Installer to fix the problem file or files by copying new files from the source, changing a Registry reference, or using whatever other technique the installer deems appropriate. This check is so quick that, in general (unless there is a problem), the user won't notice the time it takes to complete it.

- *Detect and Repair*—Because of the speed with which it performs its processing, the Office 2000 self-check is not completely comprehensive—in fact, it only focuses on the application's critical files. Therefore, it is possible (or even likely) that, from time to time, a file or setting that is deemed less critical could be damaged and prevent the Office application from operating properly. The Detect and Repair feature, which the user can launch from the Help menu, checks the entire application and makes the necessary repairs.

What all this means for you, the administrator, is that, if a user accidentally deletes a critical DLL while trying to free up hard-disk space, the Office 2000 application will repair itself automatically. If the DLL is not critical, the user can repair the application by using the Detect and Repair feature from the Help menu. Calls to your organization's help desk are thus reduced; moreover, the need to have an analyst physically access the problem computer is much less likely, allowing for significantly more efficient management of the systems throughout your enterprise.

Interactive Help And Customizable Alerts

Interactive Help and Customizable Alerts are powerful features that can help you integrate Office 2000 into your unique environment. Interactive Help (implemented through the Office Assistant) allows the Help dialog to complete the suggested task automatically. Users don't need to step through the solution; the Assistant does it for them. Customizable Alerts allow administrators to add a link in an error message to tell users where to go for additional resources and help.

For example, suppose users try to print a document from Word and it fails because the server that supports the users' printer is down. Without a Customized Alert, users get a fairly generic error message. With a Customized Alert, users might click on a hyperlink that takes them to a support desk Web page; the page shows which servers and/or printers are down and suggests other printers to use instead, with complete instructions or automation for doing so.

Systems Management Server Overview

In addition to the features that are built in to Office 2000 to assist in the deployment of Office across an enterprise, there are several methods you can use in your environment. Arguably, the most common would be Microsoft's Systems Management Server (SMS) or a similar product. Although the following sections will detail SMS, similar principles would apply to any other network management product of this type.

SMS is an extremely powerful product to help network administrators control an organization's entire network. SMS is designed to help administer large enterprise-wide networks, but is flexible enough to maintain even small networks. It is extremely versatile and able to handle networks with a wide variety of configurations.

However, with this power, using SMS requires careful planning and an understanding of the network's configuration to be the most effective. Planning how your SMS sites are arranged helps to implement an effective SMS strategy. SMS takes advantage of features found in Windows NT and uses another BackOffice product, SQL Server, for its record keeping. SMS can be used on a single server in an organization, or SMS tasks can be divided between different servers.

SMS Features

SMS provides a large array of features to help the network administrator control the network. SMS is also quite versatile in its configuration to better serve the needs of different network designs. It takes advantage of Windows NT and BackOffice features, such as using SQL Server as its information store. SMS tasks can also be distributed on other servers in the network to reduce the load on one server. Conversely, SMS can run on a single server for smaller network environments.

SMS provides some of the following features to help network administrators control the network:

- Hardware inventory
- Software inventory
- Software distribution
- Network application management
- Network performance analysis
- Network configuration information
- Remote client troubleshooting and support

The primary program the administrator will use with SMS is the SMS Administrator program, which provides the user interface between the administrator and the SMS services.

Although all SMS's features are important, in this chapter, we will concern ourselves only with software distribution and remote client troubleshooting and support because they are the only topics that directly relate to deployment issues.

Software Distribution

When you are considering deployment options for your Office software, the most important feature of Systems Management Server is its capability to distribute software across the network. SMS's software-distribution feature is very versatile, allowing automated setup options and both mandatory and expiring distributions. Previously, most administrators had two options for installing software on networked computers: Take the application's disks or CD-ROM to each individual machine and run the setup program, or create a network share and instruct the user to install the program off the share. The first method was time consuming, and the second relied on the expertise of the user to configure the software correctly.

SMS's capability to deliver software across the network and allow automated setups helps the software-distribution process become more efficient. As with SMS's other features, larger organizations or organizations with remote computers may find this capability more useful. SMS can be used to distribute both optional and mandatory software packages. Mandatory packages are useful when a network administrator wants all the network users to install a software program. SMS also can set expiration dates for software distributed over the network. This means that, if the software distributed by SMS is not installed by a certain date, the software is no longer available for installation.

SMS makes software distribution very convenient, but when you use SMS, always be sure to distribute software that you understand and comply with the license agreement of the software. Many companies, including Microsoft, are very specific about licensing agreements and will enforce them.

TIP: When you work with SMS, be aware that, unless you are using the Windows 2000 version of SMS, SMS may cause problems with the Windows Installer.

Remote Help Features

As discussed earlier in this chapter, with any type of machine, problems do occur. Most users on the network don't know much about the internal workings of computer hardware and software and require assistance to fix problems. The situa-

13. Access 2000 Distribution And Training

tion is sometimes further complicated by the user not knowing how to effectively describe the problem to the administrator. The Office 2000 automated components will most likely provide significant assistance in managing such issues, but it is also likely that the user will nevertheless, sooner or later, call the help desk or administrator.

Systems Management Server provides the administrator with utilities designed to help a user via remote administration of a network computer. The administrator can see exactly what is occurring on the screen of a user's computer and perform all of the on-screen tasks as if he or she were actually sitting at that computer. Although this feature may not be as useful for a network contained in a single building, it is useful for administrators who have to handle network users on the opposite end of the country or even across town.

SMS's Remote Control feature is a powerful tool for providing support to network users. Especially in geographically dispersed network configurations, the Remote Control feature saves time and trouble for an administrator who would otherwise have to be physically at the problem workstation.

However, on-screen viewing of a network computer isn't the only remote help feature found in SMS. An administrator can also do a remote reboot or execute a program on the remote machine. An SMS administrator can also view dynamic configuration and memory information that isn't stored in the SMS database of a remote computer. All of these remote functions enable the SMS administrator to provide better support to remote network users.

Training Considerations

Training users on how to use their Office installation is arguably one of the largest expenses for most enterprises. If you are a developer or administrator, however, the job is not typically yours to address—the human resources department or the training division will generally be responsible for ensuring that users are trained correctly.

When evaluating and planning the move to Office 2000, you should nevertheless be aware of some of the training considerations and how to best address them in internal discussions regarding the training of users.

Office 2000 Training Assistance

Unlike earlier versions of software, even earlier versions of Office software, Office 2000 provides extensive built-in support to help the user learn how to perform new activities and use the software.

The core of the Office 2000 training and assistance program can be found in the *Office Assistants*. Office Assistants were first introduced with Office 97, and their role has been expanded and clarified in Office 2000. The Office Assistants are capable of responding to plain-text queries more efficiently than they were in the earlier version, and Microsoft has also expanded the contents of the underlying help file to provide more information and more useful responses to users.

The Assistants generally "hang-out" on screen (they are movable, so the user can move them if they get in the way). When users runs into trouble, they can simply double-click on the Assistant to open a window that includes suggestions on what help topics the user might need to access, as well as a plain-text search area in which the user can enter questions. Figure 13.3 shows the Links Assistant within Access after double-clicking.

Once the user opens the Help file, they can go to one of several summary pages that detail how to perform tasks; for example, a user can seek help on how to "expand or collapse a subdatasheet" by expanding the view within the help file tree. Rather than searching for "data," "datasheet," "subdatasheet," or "expand," the user can easily view options in a hierarchical manner. Figure 13.4 shows the help window after expanding the view and selecting the help query.

Outside Training

For most organizations, migrating users to an entirely new platform (for example, from the WordPerfect Office suite to the Microsoft Office suite or from Macintosh to Windows 98) generally requires more extensive training. Depending on the size of your organization, your training department might be able to handle the load.

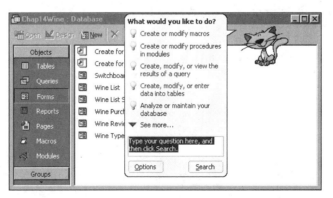

Figure 13.3   The Links Assistant displays a help window.

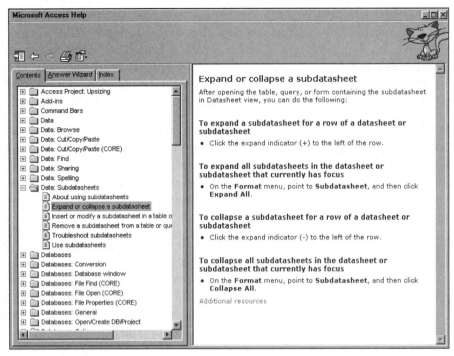

Figure 13.4   Navigating help is more intuitive than it used to be.

Alternatively, and more commonly, you can seek out an organization that is certified by Microsoft to perform training on the Office 2000 suite. Such an organization will provide both high-level and low-level training on the product and will generally train your users faster and better than you, as an administrator or developer, could. For more information on outside training organizations, consult your local yellow pages or search on the Internet.

Immediate Solutions

Finding Additional Microsoft Deployment Support

Arguably, the most important deployment support information can be found within the Office 2000 Resource Kit, the administrators' and support professionals' guide to Office. Additionally, Microsoft has published a large number of white papers about deployment on the Microsoft Web site at **www.microsoft.com/office/ enterprise**. The following list includes some of the deployment-related white papers:

- *Deployment Framework*—This document provides a framework for planning a deployment and making deployment decisions.

- *Deployment Guides and Roadmaps*—These guides and road maps provide a specific road map and recommendations for deploying Office 2000 within a given environment.

- *Actual RDP Deployment Case Studies*—These are technical case studies that detail how specific organizations deployed Office 2000 in their environments and what they learned. Organizations studied include Microsoft Information Technologies Group (ITG) as well as participants in the Rapid Deployment Program (RDP).

Taking The Microsoft Certified Office Administration Course

As with many of its important products, Microsoft offers a complete, hands-on Microsoft Certified Technical Education Center (CTEC) Office administration course. Topics in this course include installing Office, using Web-based capabilities, supporting collaboration, supporting coexistence and migration, extending and customizing help, planning a deployment, and maintaining and troubleshooting Office 2000. For more information on this course and other courses related to the deployment and maintenance of Office, including certification as an Office Professional, see the Microsoft Training and Certification Web site at **www.microsoft.com/train_cert**.

Part V

Microsoft Access 2000 Usage

Chapter 14

Access For Personal And Small Office/Home Office Use

In Depth

Access 2000 is a powerful database product. Access has come a long way since its early days as a simple add-on to the Office package. Although you'll find many uses for Access databases, one area in which Access shines is in personal and small office/home office (SOHO) use. In this chapter, we'll briefly explore some of the considerations for designing databases for these two environments. We'll then spend most of the chapter considering three of the wizards provided with Access and how you can use them to create and customize simple databases.

Using Simple Databases

Database creation with Access is designed to be as painless as possible—particularly the creation of simple databases to meet common needs. Unlike larger database products (such as Oracle or SQL Server), getting started with Access is easy—you can build your first databases in just minutes, whether you are using the wizards or designing the databases directly.

Database Creation Options

As with most products in the Office family, Access provides you with a set of predefined templates that you can use to create many common types of databases. However, Access also lets you create tables for your database directly. It also lets you import databases from other locations—for example, from Excel spreadsheets.

Because spreadsheets are, for many people, easy to use, many home and small business users may already have large numbers of spreadsheets in which they store important information. Importing those spreadsheets into Access is a snap; Access will help you through the entire import process, providing you with prompts and information along the way.

You can also import data from many other locations, including Lotus 1-2-3 spreadsheets, dBase databases, and even simple text files or Web documents.

Common Uses For Simple Databases

That said, however, you might be asking yourself, "Why would I need to use a database in my home or small business? What benefits does it bring to the table? Do I really maintain enough data to make using a database worthwhile?"

The answers to these questions will, of course, depend on your computing environment and what type of information you need to maintain. However, most of us maintain a much larger amount of information than we expect—information that will often be useful to analyze or that we might subsequently provide to others for their use.

Personal Uses

For most people, it's difficult to make a strong argument for using databases to maintain personal information. For example, many people use Quicken or Microsoft Money to maintain their personal checkbooks, bills, and other information. Those programs both use databases, and because you are using a program that someone else has invested all the time and effort into specializing to fit your needs, why would you design something similar yourself? The answer is, you probably wouldn't. However, there are volumes of other information that many of us need to (or at least should) keep track of to protect our interests and assets.

One of the best examples of this type of solution is a home inventory database. As you may or may not know, most insurance companies will only reimburse you fully in the event of a loss (such as a fire) if you can provide a full and complete accounting of your possessions. The best way to do that is to maintain a home inventory in an off-site location, such as a safety deposit box. Maintaining home inventory information is a perfect fit for a database.

However, home inventories are very generalized—there may be other, more specific information you want to maintain about your possessions that might be helpful for other reasons. For example, if you are a wine collector, you might want to keep information about every bottle of wine you own: where you bought it, what winery it is from, and so on. Additionally, you'll most likely want to retain information about how much you liked the wine, whether or not it is something to reorder, and so on.

Although it may or may not have any residual value, another fun application of databases many people choose to take advantage of is tracking CD collections, book collections, recipes, and so on.

SOHO Uses

Making the argument for SOHO uses is much simpler. The easiest example, of course, is maintaining an inventory of products—the ability to track products, generate invoices, and so on is a useful one to have. Additionally, contacts are the core of any small business—maintaining them in an accessible and useful manner is important. Although many companies still use Rolodexes, it is a simple matter to design a database that maintains all your contact information. With the proliferation of small scanners and Access's storage capabilities, creating a database that also includes a scan of a business card (and will even dial the telephone number of the contact for you) is a similarly straightforward matter.

Additional databases, for billing, writing checks, and maintaining other important information, are also useful to the small office. Access's power lets you then combine those databases and the information they contain to simplify all types of management activities.

The complete integration of Office makes it simple for you to integrate information such as presentations, appointments, even links to the files that comprise your presentations, all within the same database.

Finally, the new Web-publishing features of Access make it possible for you to take your simple corporate database—for example, your inventory and order-taking system—and publish a front end to the Web. Such publishing gives you an international presence, letting you take orders from someone in Frankfurt as easily as you take orders from someone around the corner.

Mail Merges

Probably the most common use for databases in smaller companies, however, is creating mail merges. A *mail merge* lets you create a form letter, define the labels for the envelopes, and then merge those items with data from your database. Mail merges let you generate hundreds or even thousands of letters simply, with a few keystrokes. Even better, by using mail merges efficiently, you can perform many automation tasks, including the following:

- Automatically sort by ZIP code and region, simplifying the process of receiving bulk mailing rates from the post office.

- Generate target mailings based on past account actions—for example, if you are having a toner sale, you can make sure that only those clients who typically order more than three toners at a time receive the mailing.

- Include client-specific information in your letters. For example, if you are having a toner sale, you might open the letter by writing, "Dear Jane, We noticed that you haven't ordered any toner since August 8, 1998. If you are running low, now is the time to order...."

It is a stunningly simple process to perform a mail merge with an Access database from within Microsoft Word. You'll see a brief example of how to do a mail merge in the Immediate Solutions section of this chapter.

Making The Determination To Use A Database

Deciding *where* within your business to use a database is often as important as deciding to use one. Despite the benefit of databases for even the smallest company, you must often make a cost-versus-benefits evaluation for each possible database application to ensure that using a database is the appropriate solution in that environment.

It's important to consider the following points when you are deciding whether or not a database is an appropriate solution:

- *Data reuse*—If you'll be reusing the data in ways that you had perhaps not originally intended, a database is generally a good solution. For example, if you are getting married, you might want to place the names of all your invited guests into a database, simplifying the process of sending thank-you cards. You can then reuse the database later to, for example, generate your annual holiday card list.

- *Accessibility*—If you plan to access the data regularly—for example, for sales contacts—using a database is generally appropriate.

- *Variation*—If your data is likely to change frequently, or if you will make regular additions and deletions to it, a database may be an efficient solution. For example, if you acquire art often, it makes sense to store information about your art in a database so you can easily update your records without having to redo your entire list of art.

- *Volume*—If you expect that the amount of similar data that you will have to store might grow rapidly, using a database can greatly simplify your life. For example, if you have a small business that sells crafts, you might start off using paper invoices and tracking your inventory in a spreadsheet. However, if your business starts to grow rapidly, a database may help you manage such information more efficiently.

As a rule, a database will help you in most situations where information is involved. But be careful—don't just use a database for the sake of using one. If you buy a lot of videos, for example, you might be tempted to keep a record of them in a database. But if you never use the database for any purpose other than to just put that video information into it, it is probably a waste of time. The real power of databases comes with the using the information they maintain, not simply storing the information itself.

14. Access For Personal And Small Office/ Home Office Use

Immediate Solutions

As you have learned, Access 2000 provides several database templates to help you get started with database design. In the following sections, we'll explore some of the templates that Access provides that are appropriate for personal use and for small office or home office use.

Creating An Address Book Database

Some of the database templates provided with Access 2000 are useful for creating a database that tracks names and addresses for you. There are two templates that are appropriate for creating such databases—the Address Book template and the Contact Management template. The Contact Management template is more complex. The Address Book template creates a simple, one-table database and is a worthwhile place to begin working with databases.

The database specified by the template is useful for tracking names and addresses on a more personal level; it includes information such as name, spouse name, children's names, birthdays, and so on. To create the database, perform the following steps:

1. In the New Database dialog box, double-click on the Address Book icon. Access will display the Save As dialog box.

2. Assign the database a name appropriate to your environment (for example, My Addresses, Kids Addresses, etc.). Click on Create to save the new database. Access will open the Database Wizard and display information about the template.

3. In the first screen of the Database Wizard, click on Next to move to the field selection dialog box.

4. Within the field selection dialog box, Access will display the possible fields that you can use with the database (as specified by the template). In addition to the fields you would expect, Access also lets you select optional fields—such as a **Children Names** field, a **Nickname** field, and a **Hobbies** field (the optional fields are shown in italics within the dialog box). Figure 14.1 shows the Database Wizard with the **Address Information**

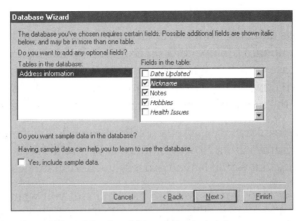

Figure 14.1 The Database Wizard for the Address Book database.

table currently selected and optional **Hobbies** and **Nickname** fields added to the table.

5. As you will see with most of the database templates, Access (through the Database Wizard) will place sample data within the table to help you design and use it, if you request the data. If you have not worked with a particular template before, it is generally a good idea to select the Yes, Include Sample Data check box. Click on Next to continue.

6. In the next window of the Database Wizard, select a background for the program to use with all the forms for the database. The Chap14Addr.mdb database, a sample address book database contained on this book's companion CD-ROM, uses the Clouds background style. After you select a background style, click on Next to move to the next dialog box in the wizard.

7. Select an output type for your reports. Because the Address Book database is for personal use in this case, you might want to select the Soft Gray style. After you select the output type, click Next to move to the last dialog box.

8. In the last dialog box, choose a title for the database (which will appear on the switchboard). You can also opt to include a picture on every report for the database. This picture might be a scanned-in image of you or some other personal notation for the people in your address book. After you name the database (and add the picture if you choose to do so), click on Finish to create it. Access will display a series of dialog boxes and progress bars while it is creating the database.

When Access finishes designing the database, it will display a switchboard that lets you add information about addresses into the database. It also lets you generate reports on the names contained within the database.

Should you wish to modify the database design, doing so is relatively easy. To open the Access database window, click on the Close box in the upper-right corner of the switchboard (do not click on Exit This Database; if you do, Access will close the database entirely). When you click on the Close box, Access will display the database window, minimized in the lower-left corner of the Access client area. If you click on the minimized window, Access will display the database window.

The Address Book database is pretty straightforward; you would most often use it for personal information. However, there are certain things that you can do to add functionality that would let you process the information is more useful ways.

For example, suppose you're going to England and you want to view everyone you might be able to visit while you're there. Then, suppose you want to send them a letter to tell them you are coming and would like to see them. Doing so within Access (especially if you use Word as well) is an easy process. To achieve these goals, you need to do the following with the database:

1. Create a new query that returns information only about people in the U.K.

2. Make a copy of the current Addresses form and associate it with the new query.

3. Write the letter in Word using the mail merge function and generate your form letters.

The following sections detail how to perform each of these steps.

Creating A New Query With U.K. Information

The easiest way to get U.K.-specific information is to create a simple query that only returns records with the **Country** field equal to "UK". In real life, you might want to create a *parameterized query*, which would let you specify different countries for different situations. However, for simplicity, we'll only consider the one specific case here. To create the new query, perform the following steps:

1. Within the Database window, make sure the Queries object is selected. Next, click on the Create Query in Design View option. Access will open the query designer and place the Show Table dialog box in front of it.

2. Within the Show Table dialog box, double-click on the **Addresses** table entry. Access will add the table to the top of the query designer. Next, click on Close to close the Show Table dialog box.

3. At the top of the query designer, select all the fields (except *) and drag and drop them into the field selectors at the bottom of the designer.

4. Within the **Country** field (you may have to scroll over to see it), enter the criteria **Like 'UK'** in the **Criteria** field. You may also want to add sorting to the **LastName** and **FirstName** fields. If you do, however, make sure the

LastName field is to the left of the **FirstName** field—otherwise, your query will be sorted by the **FirstName** of the addressees.

5. Click on the Close button to close the designer. Access will prompt you to save the new query, which you should do as **qryUKAddresses**.

Viewing The U.K. Entries From A Form

Now that you have designed a query, you may want to review your query's results. You can do so either from a report or from a form that only reviews U.K. records. If you add a form that only reviews U.K. records, you can interact with the query. To create a form that works with the new **qryUKAddresses** query, perform the following steps:

1. Within the Database window, make sure that you are viewing the Forms objects.

2. Right-click on the Addresses form and select Copy from the pop-up menu. Next, right-click anywhere in the Forms area of the database window and choose Paste from the pop-up menu. Access will prompt you to assign a new name to the form. Save the form as **frmUKAddresses**. Access will add the new **frmUKAddresses** form to the set of form objects.

3. Next, select the new form and click on the Design icon on the toolbar. Access will open the form in Design view.

4. If the Properties window is not currently displayed, click on the Properties button on the toolbar to display it. Within the Properties window, make sure it is referencing the Form object and click on the Data tab.

5. Using the drop-down combo box, change the value of the Record Source property to point to the **qryUKAddresses** query.

6. Click on the Form View icon on the toolbar to view the form's data. If you used the sample data for the database, you will see a single entry in the form—just as you would have expected. Close the form—Access will prompt you to save the changes to its design.

Now that the form is in place, you should make it accessible from the program's switchboard. That is the task we will tackle in the next section.

Adding The New Form To The Switchboard

Now that the form and query are created, you should add the form to the switchboard for the program. Because the switchboard lets the user navigate through all the other objects in the database, it should let them view the results from the new query as well. To modify the switchboard, perform the following steps:

1. Within the Database Window, select Database Utilities from the Tools menu. Select the Switchboard Manager option from the Database Utilities submenu. Access will display the Switchboard Manager dialog box.

2. In the Switchboard Manager dialog box, double-click on the Main Switchboard (default) option. Access will open the Edit Switchboard Page dialog box.

3. Click on the New button. Access will open the Edit Switchboard Item dialog box. Within the dialog box, enter the text as "UK Addresses", the command as "Open Form in Edit Mode", and the form as "frmUKAddresses". Click on OK. Access will return to the Edit Switchboard Page dialog box.

4. As you can see, the manager added the new command to the bottom of the switchboard—not the best place for it. You can use the Move Up button to move the item up in the list. Click on the button three times to move the item to below the Enter/View Addresses entry.

5. Click on Close to close the dialog box. Access will return you to the Switchboard Manager dialog box. Click on Close to close the Switchboard Manager.

To check your new entry, double-click on the **Switchboard** item in the Forms objects section. Access will open your new switchboard, as shown in Figure 14.2.

Creating A Mail Merge From The New Query

As discussed earlier in this chapter, one of the most common uses for databases in the personal and small business environments is for a mail merge. In this case, you're going to send a letter out to all of your U.K. contacts to let them know that you are coming over next month and that you hope to see them. For this example, you can load the Chap14Addr.doc file from the companion CD-ROM and then perform the following steps to make a mail merge from the document:

1. Within Word, select Mail Merge from the Tools menu. Word will open the Mail Merge Helper, as shown in Figure 14.3.

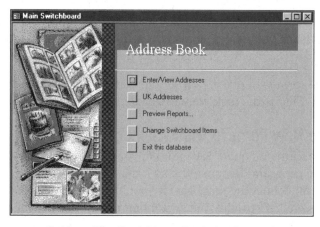

Figure 14.2   The new switchboard for the Address Book database after the additions.

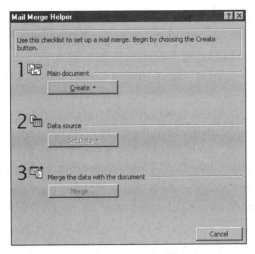

Figure 14.3   The Mail Merge Helper dialog box within Microsoft Word.

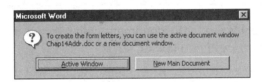

Figure 14.4   The form letter source dialog box.

2. Click on the Create button and select Form Letters from the resulting drop-down list. Word will display the dialog box shown in Figure 14.4, which lets you select either the current window or a new window as the source for the form letter. You have already loaded the letter you'll use, so click on the Active Window button.

3. When you return to the Mail Merge Helper dialog box, click on the Get Data button, which lets you select a data source for the merge data. Select Open Data Source from the drop-down menu.

4. Within the Open Data Source dialog box, change the selection in the Files Of Type drop-down list to MS Access databases and select the Chap14Addr database. Windows will process for a few minutes, and then Word will display the Microsoft Access dialog box in front of the Mail Merge Helper. Select the Queries tab and double-click on the **qryUKAddresses** option in the list.

5. Word will display a dialog box with a warning that there are no merge fields within the document and prompt you to edit the document. Click where indicated to edit the document.

6. In the document, go to the space between the data field and the greeting. Next, click on the Insert Merge Field drop-down list and select the

FirstName field. Word will display the field name within << and >>. Type a space after the >> and insert the **LastName** field. Press Enter to move to the next line.

7. On the next line, insert the **Address** field. Press Enter to move to the next line.

8. On the next line, insert the **City** field followed by a comma and a space. Then insert the **StateOrProvince** field followed by a space. Next, insert the **Country** field, also followed by a space. The last field to insert on this line is the **PostalCode** field. Press Enter to move to the next line.

9. Use the arrow keys to move down to the line that begins with "Hello" and insert the **FirstName** field again after the word "Hello" and before the comma.

TIP: *The companion CD-ROM includes the Chap14AddrWFIELDS document, which shows what the letter should look like after you finish inserting the merge fields.*

Now that all the fields are in the document, you're ready to merge with the database. To do so, perform the following steps:

1. Select Mail Merge from the Tools menu. Access will display the Mail Merge Helper dialog box.

2. Within the Mail Merge Helper dialog box, click on the Merge button. Word will display the Merge dialog box, which lets you control certain features of the merge. For this example, simply click on the Merge button to begin the merge.

3. Word will merge the data in the Access database with the merge document, yielding a new document that contains the form letters in sequence, sorted by last and first name.

Creating A Book Collection Database

One of the database templates provided with Access 2000 is useful for creating a database that tracks your book collection. The template, which is called Book Collection.mdz, can be run from the New dialog box.

The database specified by the template is useful for tracking book, author, and quotation information. To create the database, perform the following steps:

1. From within the New Database dialog box, double-click on the Book Collection icon. Access will display the Save As dialog box.

2. Assign the database a name that is appropriate to your environment (for example, Personal Collection, Business Collection, Textbooks, etc.). Click on Create to save the new database. Access will open the Database Wizard and display information about the template.

3. In the first screen of the Database Wizard, click on Next to move to the field selection dialog box.

4. Within the field selection dialog box, Access will display the possible fields that you can use with the database (as specified by the template). In addition to the fields you would expect, Access also lets you select optional fields—such as an ISBN field (which would contain the book's unique reference number), an OLE data field to hold a photograph of the author, and so on. Figure 14.5 shows the Database Wizard with the **Book Information** table currently selected.

5. As you will see every time you work with the database wizards, Access will place sample data within the table to assist you in its use and design, if you so request. If you have not worked with a particular template before, it is generally a good idea to select the Yes, Include Sample Data check box.

6. In the next window of the Database Wizard, select a background for the program to use with all the forms for the database. The Chap14Book.mdb database, a sample book database included on the companion CD-ROM, uses the International background style. Select a background style and click on Next to move to the next dialog box in the wizard.

7. Select an output type for your reports. Because the Book Collection database is for personal use in this case, you might want to select the Casual style. If you intend to use the output from the database for insurance purposes or for some other professional reason, you can use a different style. The Chap14Book.mdb database uses the Casual style.

14. Access For Personal And Small Office/ Home Office Use

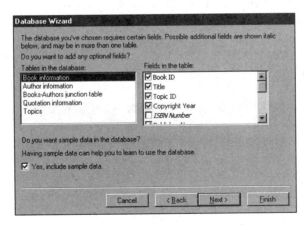

Figure 14.5   The Database Wizard for the Book Collection database.

8. In the last dialog box, choose a title for the database (which will appear on the switchboard). You can opt to include a picture on every report for the database. This picture might be a scanned-in image of you or some other personal notation for the books in your collection. After you name the database (and add the picture if you choose to do so), click on Finish to create the database. While it is creating the database, Access will display a series of dialog boxes and progress bars, as shown in Figure 14.6, to alert you to its progress.

When Access finishes designing the database, it will display a switchboard that lets you add information about books, quotations, authors, and topics into the database. It also lets you generate reports on the books contained within the database.

Should you wish to modify the database design, doing so is relatively easy. To open the Access database window, click on the Close box in the upper-right corner of the switchboard (do not click on Exit This Database; if you do, Access will close the database entirely). Access will display the database window, minimized in the lower-left corner of the Access client area. If you click on the minimized window, Access will display the database window.

If you want to create, for example, a new type of report, perhaps one by genre, you'll need to perform three steps:

1. Add a **Genre** table to the database (to keep with normalization rules).
2. Add genre information to the **Books** table.
3. Create a new report that groups data by genre.

The following sections detail how to perform each of these steps.

Adding A **Genre** Table To The Database

Because you will probably want to make looking up data for the genre as easy as possible, you should place genre information within its own table. Adding a new table to the database to store genre information is a simple process. To do so, perform the following steps:

Figure 14.6   The Database Wizard progress dialog box.

1. Within the Database window, make sure the Tables object is selected. Next, click on New. Access will open the New Table dialog box.

2. Within the New Table dialog box, select the Design View option and click on OK. Access will display the Table1:Table dialog box.

3. In the first row, enter "GenreID" as the field name and "Autonumber" as the type. You may also want to enter a comment, such as "Primary key for the Genre table".

4. In the next row, enter "Genre" as the field name and "Text" as the type. You may also want to enter a comment, such as "Genre name; no more than 50 characters".

5. Next, click on the row selector for the first row. Access will highlight the entire row. Click on the Primary Key button on the toolbar to make the first row the primary key for the database.

6. Click on the Close button in the upper-right corner of the designer to close it. Access will prompt you for a name to use with the table. Name the table Genre.

After you finish the table's design, you should add some genres to the table. For example, the Chap14Book.mdb database has four genres: nonfiction, drama, science fiction, and educational. Entering genres before you link the table to the other tables makes it easier to visualize the changes in the other tables. In the next section, you'll explore how to add the genre information to the **Books** table.

Adding The Genre Information To The **Books** Table

Adding the Genre information to the **Books** table is actually a two-step process. In this process (which you'll generally follow whenever you add a new, related table to a database), you'll first add a foreign key referencing the table to the **Books** table. Then, you'll use the Lookup Wizard to specify where the foreign key should get its value. When you're finished, the field will display a combo box that users can use to select the genre by name.

To add a foreign key to the **Books** table, perform the following steps:

1. Within the Database window, open the **Books** table in Design view.

2. Use the mouse or the Tab key to move to the last row in the designer. Enter "GenreID" as the field name and "Number" as the data type. Make sure the Field Size property is set to Long Integer for the field. You may also want to enter a description, such as "Foreign key to the Genre table".

3. Next, select the Lookup tab for the field. Within the Display Control property, use the drop-down list to select Combo Box as the control type.

4. Click on the expression builder for the Row Source field to build the query of the values to obtain. Access will display the Query Builder window with the Show Table dialog box in front.

5. Double-click on the **Genre** table entry within the Show Table dialog box. Access will add the **Genre** table to the top of the query designer. Close the Show Table dialog box.

6. Within the top portion of the query designer, double-click on the * field (which will add all fields to the query). Alternatively, if you want to sort the genres alphabetically, you can add each field manually and then apply the sort. When you finish, click on the Close button to close the query designer. Access will return you to the Books:Table designer.

7. Set the Bound Column property to 1 (the ID field for the **Genre** table). Next, set the Column Count property to 2. Finally, to ensure that the combo box doesn't display both the key and the value, set the Column Widths property to 0";2".

8. Click on the Close button to close the designer. Access will prompt you to save your changes to the table's design.

If you now go into the table to edit its values, you can scroll to the right side of the table and enter new values for the **GenreID** field by using a drop-down combo box, as shown in Figure 14.7.

Normally, you would now have to change the design of the form for book entry to allow for a genre entry on a form. However, we'll leave that as an exercise for

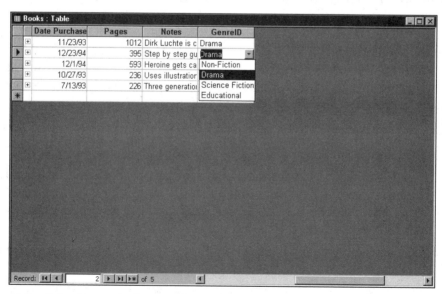

Figure 14.7   Using the combo box to add a genre to an entry.

later and move on to creating a new report that sorts output by genre. Then we'll briefly discuss how to add an entry for the new report to the switchboard.

Creating A New Report Grouped By Genre

The whole point of adding the new genre category was to let us print out our book list by book type. To that end, let's create a new report—one which is grouped first by genre, then by author, and finally sorted by book title. To do, we will perform two steps: First, we'll design a custom query to use as the foundation of the report, then use the Report Wizard to design the actual report itself. To create the query, perform the following steps:

1. Within the Database window, select the Queries object. Next, click on the Create Query in Design View option. Access will display the query designer with the Show Table box in front.

2. Within the Show Table box, double click on the **Authors**, **BooksAuthors**, **Books**, **Genre**, and **Topics** tables. Click on Close to create the Show Table dialog box.

3. Next, select the fields and tables that you want in the query. The query in the Chap14Book.mdb database contains the **Title**, **DatePurchased**, and **Pages** fields from the **Books** table. It also contains the **Genre** field from the **Genre** table, the **Topic** field from the **Topics** table, and the **FirstName** and **LastName** fields from the **Authors** table. When you finish making your selections, click on the Close button to close the designer. Access will prompt you to save the query. The Chap14Book.mdb database's query is named **qryBooksByGenre**, but you can name yours as you wish.

Now that the query is ready, its time to create the report. To create the report, perform the following steps:

1. Within the Database Window, select the Reports object. Next, click on the Create Report By Using Wizard option. Access will display the Report Wizard.

2. From the Tables/Queries drop-down list, select the Query: qryBooksByGenre (or whatever you named your query) option. Then click on the >> button to select all fields. Click on Next to move to the next dialog box in the wizard.

3. Within the grouping levels dialog box, click first on the **Genre** field. Next, click on the **LastName** field. When you finish, you will have two grouping levels within your report. Click on Next to move to the sorting options dialog box.

4. Within the sorting options dialog box, select the **Title** field as the first field by which to sort. Click on Next to move to the next dialog box.

5. The next two dialog boxes let you select some formatting options. For each, select the form layout that meets your needs and click on Next.

6. In the last dialog box, name the report **Books By Genre**. Click on Finish to close the wizard. Figure 14.8 shows the newly created report.

You could customize these steps further; for example, it would be nice to have the query combine the **LastName** and **FirstName** fields into an **AuthorName** field for grouping.

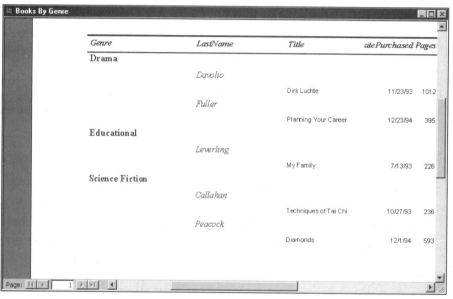

Figure 14.8   The **Books By Genre** report in Print Preview.

Creating A Wine Collection Database

The last database template we'll discuss in this chapter is provided with Access 2000 and is useful for tracking a wine collection. It will maintain information about bottles of wine, their vineyards, where they were purchased, and so on. The template, named Wine List, can be run from the New dialog box. To create the database, perform the following steps:

1. From within the New Database dialog box, double-click on the Wine List icon. Access will display the Save As dialog box.

2. Assign the database a name that is appropriate to your environment (for example, Home Collection, Restaurant Collection, etc.). Click on Create to

save the new database. Access will open the Database Wizard and display information about the template.

3. From the first screen of the Database Wizard, click on Next to move to the field selection dialog box.

4. Within the field selection dialog box, Access will display the possible fields that you can use with the database (as specified by the template). In addition to the fields you would expect, Access also lets you select optional fields—including the percentage of alcohol in the bottle and where you purchased the bottle.

5. In the next window of the Database Wizard, select a background for the program to use with all the forms for the database. The Chap14Wine.mdb database, a sample Wine Collection database included on the companion CD-ROM, uses the Stone background style. After you select a background style, click on Next to move to the next dialog box in the wizard.

6. Select an output type for your reports. Because the Wine Collection database will probably generate reports that you send to your insurance agent, attorney, or some other professional, you probably want to select the Corporate style. The Chap14Wine.mdb database uses the Corporate style.

7. In the last dialog box, choose a title for the database (which will appear on the switchboard); you can also opt to include a picture on every report for the database. This picture might be a scanned-in image of you or some other personal notation for the wine in your collection. After you name the database (and add the picture if you choose to do so), click on Finish to create the database. While it is creating the database, Access will display a series of dialog boxes and progress bars to alert you to its progress.

When Access finishes designing the database, it will display a switchboard that lets you add information about wines in your collection—including when and where you purchased each bottle—as well as information about different wine types into the database. It also lets you generate reports on the wines within your collection—by Type, by Vintage (year), and by Vintner.

Should you wish to modify the database design, doing so is relatively easy. To open the Access database window, click on the Close box in the upper-right corner of the switchboard (do not click on Exit This Database; if you do, Access will close the database entirely). Access will display the database window, minimized in the lower-left corner of the Access client area. If you click on the minimized window, Access will display the database window.

If, for example, you also wanted to track information about reviews for each bottle of wine within the database, you would need to perform four steps to do so:

1. Add a **Reviews** table to the database (to keep with normalization rules).

2. Establish a relationship with the **Wine List** table to affiliate each review with a bottle of wine.

3. Add a command button to display and add reviews.

4. Create a new report that displays the reviews for each wine.

The following sections detail how to perform each of these steps.

Adding A **Reviews** Table To The Database

Because you will probably want to make looking up data for the reviews as easy as possible, you should place review information within its own table. Adding a new table to the database to store review information is a simple process. To do so, perform the following steps:

1. Within the Database window, make sure the Tables object is selected. Next, click on New. Access will open the New Table dialog box.

2. Within the New Table dialog box, select the Design View option and click on OK. Access will display the Table1:Table dialog box.

3. In the first row, enter "ReviewID" as the field name and "Autonumber" as the type. You may also want to enter a comment, such as "Primary key for the review table".

4. In the next row, enter the foreign key to the **Wine List** table, naming it **WineListID** and setting its type as Number.

5. In the next row, enter "Reviewer" as the field name and "Text" as the type.

6. In the next row, enter "Review" as the field name and "Text" as the type. Make the field size 255 to leave some room for review information.

7. In the next row, enter "NotableQuote" as the field name and "Text" as the type.

8. Click on the Close button at the upper-right corner of the designer to close it. Access will prompt you for a name to use with the table. Name the table **Reviews**.

After you finish the table's design, you should add some reviews to the table. For example, the Chap14Wine.mdb database has four reviews for different bottles of wine specified in the collection. In the next section, you'll explore how to add the relationship information for the reviews to the relationships definitions for the database.

Adding The Relationship Information To The Database

To effectively use the new **Reviews** table, you must relate it to the **Wine List** table on the Foreign Key that you added to the table. You will do this from the

Relationships window in the Access Interactive Development Environment (IDE). To set up the necessary relationship, perform the following steps:

1. Within the Database window, select Relationships from the Tools menu. Access will display the Relationships window.

2. Click on the Show Table icon on the toolbar to display the Show Table dialog box. Within the Show Table dialog box, double-click on the **Reviews** entry to add the table to the Relationship window. Next, click on Close to close the Show Table dialog box.

3. Click on the **WineListID** field in the Wine List window and drag it over to the **WineListID** field in the Reviews window. Access will display the Edit Relationships dialog box.

4. Within the Edit Relationships dialog box, click on Create to create the one-to-many relationship between the fields. You may also want to enforce referential integrity across the relationship; it is a good idea in this situation. When you finish, the Relationships window will look like Figure 14.9.

Now that you have created the relationship between the tables, it is time to create the new form to enter the review information. You will do so in the next section.

Adding A New Form To Display Review Information

Although you can create the new form for reviews from scratch, it is easier to copy and then modify the **Wine Purchases** form. To create the new **Wine Reviews** form, perform the following steps:

1. Within the Database Window, select the Forms object. Next, right-click on the **Wine Purchases** form icon. Select Copy from the pop-up menu that Access displays.

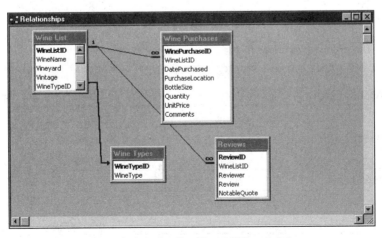

Figure 14.9   The Relationships window for the Chap14Wine database.

2. Within the Database Window, right-click anywhere and select Paste from the pop-up menu. Access will ask you to name the new form. Name the new form Wine Reviews and click on Save.

3. Now that the form is created, you need to change the information it displays to coincide with the **Reviews** table. To begin, click on the new **Wine Reviews** form object and then click on the Design button on the toolbar. Access will open the form in Design view.

4. Make sure the Properties window is displayed and then edit the **Record Source** field for the form to the following SQL query value:

```
SELECT DISTINCTROW [Reviews].*
FROM [Reviews]
WHERE (([Reviews].[WineListID]=[forms]![Wine List]![WineListID]));
```

5. The query will change the data source for the form, but you still need to change the values within the fields and labels to correspond to the new table. Table 14.1 shows the control name, the property name, and the new value to set it to for the controls on the form.

6. The last step to prepare the form is to edit the code within the form's **On Open** event and delete the code within the form's **On Activate** event. Specifically, change the code within the event to read as follows:

```
Private Sub Form_Open(Cancel As Integer)
  If Not IsLoaded("Wine List") Then
    MsgBox "Open the Review form using the Review button " & _
        Chr(10) & Chr(13) & "on the Wine List form."
  Cancel = True
  End If
End Sub
```

Table 14.1   The changes to make to the Wine Reviews form.

Control	Property	New Value
WinePurchaseID Label	Caption	ReviewID
	Name	ReviewID Label
WinePurchaseID	Control Source	ReviewID
	Name	ReviewID
DatePurchased Label	Caption	Reviewer
	Name	Reviewer Label
DatePurchased	Control Source	Reviewer
	Format	[none]

(continued)

Table 14.1   The changes to make to the Wine Reviews form (continued).

Control	Property	New Value
	Input Mask	[none]
	Width	2.0"
	Name	Reviewer
PurchaseLocation Label	Caption	NotableQuote
	Name	NotableQuote Label
PurchaseLocation	Control Source	NotableQuote
	Width	2.0"
	Height	0.375"
	Name	NotableQuote
Quantity, Quantity Label		[deleted]
UnitPrice, UnitPrice Label		[deleted]
Comments Label	Caption	Review
	Name	Review Label
Comments	Control Source	Review
	Top	1.4583"
	Height	0.9375"
	Name	Review

Now that you have the new form all fixed up, the next step is to add the command button to the **Wine List** form. To do so, perform the following steps:

1. Within the Database Window, select the Forms object. Next, click on the **Wine List** form and click on Design. Access will display the form in Design view.

2. Within the Toolbox, click on the Command Button icon. Make sure the Wizard button at the toolbox's top is also enabled. At the bottom of the form (in the footer section), next to the **Wine Purchases** button, add a new button with the same dimensions. Access will display the Command Button wizard.

3. Within the Command Button wizard, select Form Operations from the Categories list and Open Form from the Actions list, as shown in Figure 14.10. Click on Next.

4. Within the next dialog box, select **Wine Reviews** as the form to open. Click on Next to move to the next dialog box.

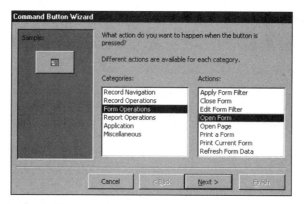

Figure 14.10   The Command Button wizard, set to open a form.

5. Access will ask whether it should open all the records for the form. Because you have constrained the records by the query on which the form is keyed, you'll display all the records. Click on Next.

6. In the next dialog box, enter "Wine & Reviews" as the caption for the button. Click on Next to move to the last dialog in the wizard.

7. Name the button **cmdWineReviews** and click on Finish to exit the wizard.

You can now bring up reviews on wines in your collection, as shown in Figure 14.11.

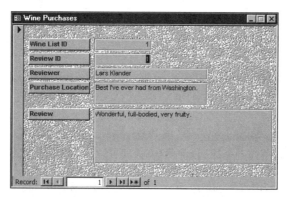

Figure 14.11   The new Reviews dialog box.

Chapter 15

Using Access In A
Corporate Environment

In Depth

As you have seen, Access is a useful tool for designing simple and complex databases for use in the home or small office. However, the real power of Access 2000 is unleashed when you use it to create corporate databases. In fact, with its new features, Access 2000 is an excellent tool for both standalone database development and full client-server development with the Microsoft SQL Server 7.0 back end. In this chapter, we'll briefly explore some of the things you should consider when you're designing databases for the corporate environment, and then spend most of the chapter considering some database design issues for companies. We'll show you how you can create and customize a simple database using one of the wizards provided with Access. We'll also consider upsizing a database to SQL Server, and finally, we'll show you how you can use the Microsoft Data Engine, a standalone version of SQL Server, to design SQL Server databases natively from Access.

Using Simple Databases

Database creation with Access is designed to be as painless as possible—particularly when you're creating simple databases to meet common needs. Unlike with larger database products (such as Oracle or SQL Server), getting started with Access is easy—you can build your first databases in just minutes, whether you're using the wizards or designing the databases directly.

Moreover, with the new client-server designer, you can also design SQL Server databases from within Access in just minutes. You'll see the simplicity of this process in the Immediate Solutions section of this chapter.

Common Uses For Simple Corporate Databases

With all the buzz in the computer industry about client-server databases, online transaction processing, and other moves toward distributed processing environments—and with the amount of data that an organization might feasibly have—it is often difficult to interpret the possible benefits of databases within your organization. Moreover, it is often extremely difficult to determine whether an application should be designed for a standalone, workgroup, or client-server configuration. The following sections outline for you some important points to keep in mind about database design for the corporate environment.

Uses For Standalone Database

The simplest type of database is, as you might intuitively expect, a standalone database. In this context, a standalone database is one that stores all of its data on a single computer; the front end runs on the same computer, and the database is not accessible from other computers on the network.

One of the nice features of Access—particularly Access 2000—is its ability to easily scale up to broader usage if you should determine you need it. Historically, converting from a local access implementation to a client-server solution was difficult at best (and sometimes almost impossible) unless you created an application to manually export the data to the new database. With Access 2000, such considerations are not quite so important—you can use the Upsizing Wizard included with Access to scale the database up to SQL Server.

In any event, standalone databases should meet the following requirements, most of which focus on who will use the database:

- The database should maintain information that will likely only be important to a single user, such as an index of documents on the local computer.

- The database should maintain information that is not duplicated in any other database in the organization, and it should bear no relationship to data in any other database in the organization.

- No other user should ever need to access the data in the database.

- There should be no benefit in trying to combine the data with other data in other databases in the organization.

As you can see, the constraints on standalone development are pretty stiff; in fact, most standalone databases violate one or more of these rules. For example, to simplify making phone calls and performing mail merges, a secretary might maintain a list of people that his or her boss calls on a regular basis. In most cases, it is likely that much of the data not only exists somewhere else, it's probably in some other form—for example, if the people are vendors or customers, they are probably in the company's ordering and purchasing database system.

The implications of this problem don't really become clear until you multiply that single secretary by the 50 other secretaries in the office. Suddenly, you have 50 databases, all of which duplicate certain centrally stored information, and all of which probably duplicate information stored within other, counterpart databases. Clearly, a better solution is to provide all of the secretaries with limited access to the ordering and purchasing database. You could then link the local application to additional tables where the users can input other contacts (that is, contacts not existing elsewhere already) and specific information about those contacts. With a complete security model and efficient design, all the secretaries could use the same database without exposing confidential information to other secretaries.

However, the design issues for such an application are significantly greater than those for creating a simple, standalone contact manager (Access even provides a wizard for creating such a database). In such a case, many IS professionals would opt to create the local databases rather than solve all the problems contained in the creation and maintenance of a central database. Needless to say, such decisions in your organization may or may not have a long-term impact on productivity, and there may be other considerations (such as the manager's preference) that come into play in creating a solution.

Uses For Workgroup Installation

Making the argument for database uses in workgroup environments is much simpler. In many organizations, certain types of information (such as sales contacts and subcontractors used only by a specific department) may have meaning only in certain workgroups in the organization. In such cases, workgroup installations will often be appropriate.

You can think of a workgroup installation as one in which a database is shared among a limited number of users (usually no more than 10). Additional constraints on workgroup installations include the following:

- Security should be a minor issue because many workgroup installations will not have the capability to support a stringent security model as a true client-server environment would.

- Ongoing data entry should be minimal—protecting against locking errors and similar problems.

- The amount of data should be reasonable; any database exceeding several thousand records is likely a good candidate for client-server.

- The database should have meaning only within the workgroup—the data should not be duplicated elsewhere or related to other data elsewhere in the organizaton.

- Users outside the workgroup should have no need for access to the data.

Although the constraints on workgroup implementations are looser than the constraints on standalone development, there are still many good reasons you should *not* develop workgroup implementations of your databases. The primary determination, again, rests on considering the return on investment you'll get by creating multiple databases that duplicate each other rather than ensuring that your enterprise does not duplicate data in any of its applications.

This goal is respectable, but it is generally not realistic—there will almost always be data duplicated in some locations within an organization. However, it often comes down to *how much* data will be duplicated. Duplicating a few or even a few hundred records may not be a major consideration (depending on the size of your organization). But duplicating thousands of records probably justifies assigning a database or application designer to ensure that the duplications are minimized or eliminated.

As with standalone databases, there are likely to be specific considerations—generally personnel rather than technical considerations—that will drive the creation of workgroup databases in your organization. Although your overall goal may be to move to client-server databases for all data, you will most likely find limitations on that goal in many environments.

Uses For Databases In Client-Server Environments

The most common use for databases in the corporate environment, and without question the most appropriate design for databases in the corporate environment, is the client-server model. In this model, all the data is maintained in a single central location or a series of central locations. Individual users access the data by using applications specifically designed to reach it. Security is greatly improved, and client-server databases can handle many more transactions (and can handle them more efficiently) than either of the other two models. In general, a client-server implementation will use SQL Server, Oracle, or some other highly scalable database product as its back end and some type of application as its front end. In this book, we will consider Access front ends to client-server back ends. Client-server constructions should meet the following requirements:

- Data should be shared throughout the organization.
- There should be significant benefits to combining disparate pieces of data from different segments of the organization.
- The quantities of data should be sufficient that scalability is an issue.
- The number of users should be sufficient that scalability is an issue.
- Security should be a concern.
- The network backbone should be capable of handling the data passed back and forth to the server.
- The database should become large enough that different storage models are important.
- The database might accept large quantities of transactions that will succeed or fail as whole transactions.
- The database should be accessed by a highly distributed client base—perhaps even from the Internet.

In general, the majority of organizations will find that their mission-critical data—whatever it may be—is best serviced in the client-server environment. Such databases are stable, particularly if the server platform they are on is also stable. In the vast majority of cases, client-server databases may need to handle thousands, even millions of transactions without a hiccup—a feat that most Access databases are simply not capable of performing.

Client-Server Design Issues

So, if Access isn't really capable of true client-server design, why discuss it in a book dedicated to Access programming? With the addition of new Access Data Projects (ADPs), the new Access 2000 supports client-server design at a level never before possible in Access. Access projects let you actually design client-server databases directly against an SQL Server back end and maintain them from within Access. Moreover, the project is essentially a very thin client against the back end database.

The support within Access for new Data Access Pages (DAPs) makes designing Web pages that work against an SQL Server database easier than ever before. The Access Database window even supports new objects to help you work with SQL Server databases when you create an ADP, as shown in Figure 15.1.

As you can see, when you are working with an ADP, the Database window adds support for Views, Database Diagrams, and Stored Procedures and removes queries from the accessible objects. The following sections briefly discuss these new objects, and we'll also look briefly at database diagrams.

Views allow you to specify exactly how a user will see data. They can be thought of as stored queries. Stored procedures are precompiled SQL statements. Because

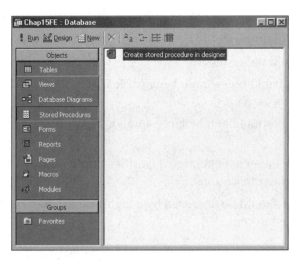

Figure 15.1   Working with an ADP within the Database window.

stored procedures are precompiled, they run much more quickly than straight SQL queries do—they are, functionally, equivalent to Jet query objects created in Access. Triggers can be very complex, and several rules govern how and when they should be created. Triggers allow you to ensure data integrity, domain integrity, and referential integrity within your database.

Creating And Manipulating Views

Views allow you to horizontally and vertically partition information from one or more tables in the database. In other words, with a view, you can allow the user to see only selected fields and selected rows. Views can also be created to show derived information. In addition, views have the following advantages:

- You have more control over what the user can see. This is useful for both security and ease of use. Users don't have to look at "extra" information that they don't require.

- You can simplify the user interface by creating views of often-used queries. This will allow a user to run a view with a simple statement rather than supplying parameters every time the query is run.

- You can heighten security. Users can only affect what you let them see. This may be a subset of rows or columns, statistical information, or a subset of information from another view.

- You can use the BCP utility to export data from a view.

There are rules and restrictions you should be aware of when you are creating views:

- When you are creating a view, any database objects that are referenced by the view are verified.

- When you are running a view, you must have SQL Server's **SELECT** permission on the objects referenced in the view definition. This means that you could potentially create a view that you can't run. Permissions on views are checked each time that view is run, not when it is created.

- You can't alter a view once it has been created. To modify a view, you must drop the view and then re-create it.

- If you drop objects referenced within a view, the view still remains. You will receive an error message the next time you attempt to run that view.

- Temporary tables can't be referenced in a view. This also means that you cannot use a **SELECT INTO** clause in a view.

- If you create a child view based on a parent view, you should be aware of what the parent view is doing. You could run into problems if the parent view is large and complex.

- Data in a view is not stored separately. This means that if you modify data in a view, you are modifying the data in the base tables.

- Triggers and indexes can't be created on a view.

You will learn more about views in later chapters.

Stored Procedures

Stored procedures are precompiled SQL statements that are stored at the SQL Server (on the server machine). Because stored procedures are precompiled, they provide the best performance of any type of query. There are many system-stored procedures defined with an **sp_** prefix that gather information from system tables and are especially useful for administration. You can create your own user-defined stored procedures as well.

Understanding The Benefit Of Stored Procedures

Stored procedures are extremely fast database objects that are stored on the SQL Server itself. When you run a stored procedure for the first time, it is run in the following manner:

1. The procedure is parsed into its component pieces.

2. The components that reference other objects in the database (tables, views, and so on) are checked for their existence. This is also known as *resolving*.

3. Once resolving is complete, the name of the procedure will be stored in the **sysobjects** table and the code to create the stored procedure will be saved in **syscomments**.

4. Compilation continues and, during compilation, a blueprint that defines how to run the query is created. This blueprint is often called a normalized plan or a query tree. The query tree is saved in the **sysprocedures** table.

5. When the stored procedure is first executed, the query plan is read and fully compiled into a procedure plan and then run. This saves you the time of reparsing, resolving, and compiling a query tree every time you run the stored procedure.

Another added benefit of using a stored procedure is that, once the stored procedure is executed, the procedure plan will be stored in the procedure cache. This means that, the next time you use that stored procedure, it will be read directly from the cache and run. This gives you a huge performance boost over running a standard SQL query again and again.

You can use stored procedures to encapsulate business rules. Once encapsulated, these rules can be used by multiple applications, thus giving you a consistent data interface. This is also advantageous in that, if functionality needs to change, you only need to change it in one place rather than once for each application. All in all, stored procedures can be summarized as offering the following benefits:

- Performance is boosted for all stored procedures, but even more so for stored procedures that are run more than once because the query plan is saved in the procedure cache.

- With stored procedures, you can pass in arguments and get data returned too.

- Stored procedures can be set up to run automatically when SQL Server starts up.

- Stored procedures can be used to extract data or modify data (not at the same time).

- Stored procedures are explicitly invoked. Unlike triggers, stored procedures must be called by your application, script, batch, or task.

Working With Triggers

In this section, you'll learn about a special type of stored procedure called a *trigger*. Triggers are automatically invoked when you try to modify data that a trigger is designed to protect. Triggers help secure the integrity of your data by preventing unauthorized or inconsistent changes from being made. For example, suppose you have a customers table and an orders table. You can create a trigger that will ensure that, when you create a new order, it will have a valid customer ID to which it can attach. Likewise, you could create the trigger so that, if you tried to delete a customer from the customers table, the trigger would check to see if there were any orders still attached to that customer and, if so, halt the delete process.

Triggers don't have parameters and can't be explicitly invoked. This means that you must attempt a data modification to fire off a trigger. Triggers can also be nested up to 16 levels. Nested triggers work like this: A trigger on your orders table might add an entry to your accounts receivable table that would, in turn, fire a trigger that checks to see if the customer has any overdue accounts receivable and notifies you if he or she does.

Performance-wise, triggers have a relatively low amount of overhead. Most of the time involved in running a trigger is used up by referencing other tables. The referencing can be fast if the other tables are in memory or a bit slower if they need to be read from disk.

Triggers are always considered a part of the transaction. If the trigger or any other part of the transaction fails, it is rolled back.

In the past (before SQL Server 6.5), triggers were the only means of enforcing referential integrity. However, you now have the ability to use Declarative Referential Integrity (DRI), which makes most triggers unnecessary. You can create triggers directly from the Access Interactive Development Environment (IDE) without using any of the SQL Server management tools.

Essentially, you'll use triggers (rather than the Relationships window that you use with Access-created databases) to enforce referential integrity.

Using Database Diagrams To Create Databases

You can use database diagrams to create, edit, or delete database objects for SQL Server or Microsoft Database Engine (MSDE) databases while you're directly connected to the database in which those objects are stored. Database diagrams graphically represent tables, the columns they contain, and the relationships between them. You can use database diagrams to do the following:

- Simply view the tables in your database and their relationships.

- Perform complex operations to alter the physical structure of your database.

When you modify a database object through a database diagram, the modifications you make are not saved in the database until you save the table or the database diagram. Thus, you can experiment with "what if" scenarios on a database's design without permanently affecting its existing design or data.

In any event, when you finish working with a database diagram, you can make the following choices:

- Discard your changes.

- Save the changes to selected tables in the diagram or the entire database diagram and have the changes modify the server database.

- Save the Transact-SQL code that your changes to the diagram would invoke against the database in a change script. If you save a change script instead of saving your changes to the database, you then have more options as to its application. You can either apply the change script to the database at another time using a tool such as Microsoft SQL Server's iSQL command-line utility, or further edit the change script in a text editor and then apply the modified script to the database.

You control the timing, type, and extent of the changes to your database by choosing how changes to the database diagram affect the server database.

Creating And Modifying Database Objects

As noted previously, you can use a database diagram to create and modify database objects, including the following objects:

- Tables

- Table columns and their properties

- Indexes

- Constraints

- Table relationships

You can modify tables and their columns directly in a database diagram. You modify indexes, constraints, and relationships through the Properties window for a table in your diagram.

Creating And Managing Database Diagrams

Needless to say, database diagrams duplicate functionality available to you else-where from the Access Database window. However, database diagrams simplify your interaction with the SQL Server by letting you view both abstract and de-tailed information simultaneously in a somewhat more intuitive interface. In gen-eral, you can use database diagrams to:

- Manipulate database objects without having to write Transact-SQL code.

- Visualize the structure of your database tables and their relationships.

- Provide different views of complex databases.

- Experiment with database changes without modifying the underlying database.

- Create new objects and relationships.

- Alter the structure of your database.

Using Database Diagrams To Perform Database Operations

You can create database diagrams of varying complexity, from diagrams that con-tain just one table to diagrams that contain hundreds of tables. When you first create a diagram, you are presented with a blank diagram surface to which you can add tables. In the diagram, you can:

- Add tables by dragging them from the Show Table window, other open diagrams, or the view designer.

- Create new tables that have not yet been defined in the database.

- Edit the tables and their properties you have added to or created within the diagram.

- Edit the database objects, such as constraints and indexes, that are attached to the tables in the diagram.

- Create relationships between tables.

- Delete tables or relationships from the diagram.

- As mentioned previously, save a SQL change script, which places the Transact-SQL code for your changes in a file so that you can later apply them to the database or perform further editing upon them.

- Save your diagram to update the database with your changes.

It is important to note that changes that you make outside of the database diagram will pass through to the diagram. For example, if you add a table to the diagram, then proceed to add additional fields (columns) to the table from the Table designer, when you return to the diagram, that table will indicate your new fields (columns) within the designer.

Using Database Diagrams To Graphically Lay Out Your Tables

You can perform a variety of diagramming operations in a database diagram without affecting the object definitions in your database. You can customize the appearance of your diagram to meet your development needs in the following ways:

- Use the keyboard or mouse to move around in a diagram.
- Select and move tables and relationship lines.
- Change the size and shape of tables.
- Remove tables from the diagram without deleting them from the database.
- Change the magnification of a diagram.
- Open the Properties window to view properties for the objects in your diagram.

These operations affect the appearance of your diagram, but they do not affect the structure of your database. We will further explore database diagrams, and other advanced features of working with SQL Server and the MSDE, in Chapter 33.

Immediate Solutions

As you have learned, Access 2000 provides several database templates to help you get started with database design. In the following sections, we'll explore one of the many database templates Access provides that is appropriate for corporate use. We will also explore the creation and use of an Access Data Project with the MSDE engine.

Creating A Time And Billing Database

One of the database templates provided with Access 2000 is useful for creating a database that tracks your time and billing information. The template, named Time and Billing.mdz, can be run from the New dialog box.

The database specified by the template is useful for tracking time and billing information, including client information, project information, time card information, and more. To create the database, perform the following steps:

1. From within the New Database dialog box, double-click on the Time and Billing icon. Access will display the Save As dialog box.

2. Assign the database a name appropriate to your environment (for example, Partners, Associates, Project Billings, etc.). For this example, we'll name the database Chap15TB.mdb. Click on Create to save the new database. Access will open the Database Wizard and display information about the template.

3. From the first screen of the Database Wizard, click on Next to move the field selection dialog box.

4. Within the field selection dialog box, Access will display the possible fields that you can use with the database, as specified by the template. In addition to the fields you would expect, Access also lets you select optional fields—such as a **Referred By** field (which would contain additional information about who referred the client), an **Employee Number** field (which contains additional information about your employees), and so on. Figure 15.2 shows the Database Wizard with the **Information About Employees** table currently selected.

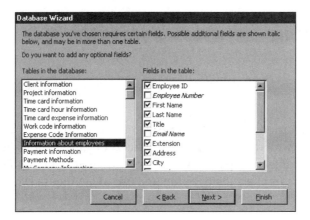

Figure 15.2   The Database Wizard for the Time and Billing database.

5. As you will see with all the database wizards, Access will place sample data within the table to assist you in its use and design. If you have not worked with a particular template before, it is generally a good idea to select the field indicating the wizard should place data within the database. In any event, click on Next to move to the next dialog box in the wizard.

6. In the next window of the Database Wizard, select a background for the program to use with all the forms for the database. The Chap15TB.mdb database, a sample database packed on the companion CD-ROM, uses the Sumi Painting background style. Click on Next to move to the next dialog box in the wizard.

7. In the next dialog box, select an output type for your reports. Because the Time and Billing database is for corporate use in this case, you might want to select the Corporate style. The Chap15TB.mdb database uses the Corporate style. After selecting an output type for your reports, click on Next to move to the last dialog box in the wizard.

8. In the last dialog box, choose a title for the database (which will appear on the switchboard). You can opt to include a picture on every report for the database. This picture might be a scanned-in image of your corporate logo or some other notation for the forms. After you name the database (and add the picture if you choose to do so), click on Finish to create the database. Access will display a series of dialog boxes and progress bars while it is creating the database.

When Access finishes designing the database, it will display a prompt for you to enter information that the database will use about your company. The application will display the dialog box for you to make your entry, as shown in Figure 15.3.

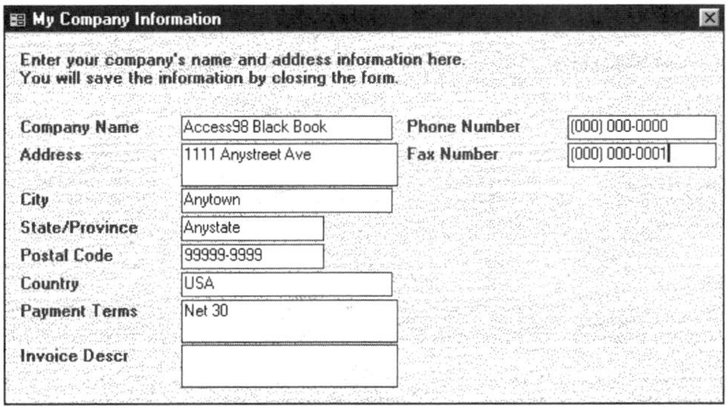

Figure 15.3   The dialog box within which you should enter company information for the database.

After you enter the information and close the form, Access will display the switchboard for the database. This switchboard lets you add information about clients, time cards, employees, and so on into the database. It also lets you generate reports about clients, billings, and more.

Should you wish to modify the database design, doing so is relatively easy. To open the Access database window, click on the Close box in the upper-right corner of the switchboard (do not click on Exit This Database; if you do, Access will close the database entirely). When you click on the Close box, Access will display the database window, minimized in the lower-left corner of the Access client area. If you click on the minimized window, Access will display the database window.

If, for example, you want to create a new type of report, perhaps one that simply outputs the work codes and their descriptions in the database, you can do so by performing the following two steps:

1. Add a **Description** field to the **Work Codes** table.

2. Create a new report that outputs work codes and descriptions.

The following sections detail how to perform these steps.

Adding a **Description** Field To The **Work Codes** Table

As pure representations, work codes are useful for displaying time card information, but there may be times when you want to associate and display a description with each work code—for example, for accounting audits or other regular internal reviews. To add a **Description** field to the **Work Codes** table, perform the following steps:

1. Within the Database window, make sure the Tables object is selected. Click on the Work Codes icon and then click on the Design icon in the toolbar. Access will display the **Work Codes** table in Design view.

2. Within the table designer, tab to the third row. Enter "Description" as the field name and "Text" as the type. You may also want to enter a comment, such as "Textual explanation of work code".

3. Click on the Close button in the upper-right corner of the designer to close it. Access will prompt you to save the table.

After you finish the table's design, you should add some work codes to the table. For example, the Chap15TB database has five work codes: 300, 301, 302, 400, and 401. Each work code also has a brief description entered. Note that the even hundred-numbered work codes describe what type of client the other work codes are—for example, 300 corresponds to "Banking Clients" and 301 corresponds to "Bob's National Bank." In the next section, you'll add a label and text box to the form to correspond to the description of the work code in the table.

Changing The Appearance Of The **Work Codes** Form

After you add the new field to the table, you should then add a corresponding data-bound field to the form that lets the user easily add the additional information into the table. To add the new field to the form, perform the following steps:

1. Within the Database window, make sure the Forms object is selected. Next, open the **Work Codes** form in Design view.

2. After Access displays the form designer, click on the Field List icon on the toolbar to display a list of fields available for that form. Within the Field List dialog box, click on the **Description** field and drag it onto the form below the Work Code field and text box.

3. Using the Form design tools, align the new bound text box and its supporting label. When you finish aligning the new controls, your form should look similar to the one in Figure 15.4. After you finish designing the form, close the designer. Access will prompt you to save the new form; do so, saving it as the **Work Codes** form.

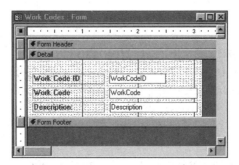

Figure 15.4   The form designer after you have added the new field to the form.

Creating A New Report Of Work Codes

The whole point of adding the new **Description** field was to make it possible to print out work codes in a report that contains meaningful explanations of the codes themselves. To that end, let's create a new report—one that is grouped by code and then description. To do so, we'll use the Report Wizard to design the report. To create the report, perform the following steps:

1. Within the Database Window, select the Reports object. Next, click on the Create Report By Using Wizard option. Access will display the Report Wizard.

2. From the Tables/Queries drop-down list, select the Table:Work Codes entry. Then click on the > button to select the **WorkCode** and **Description** fields. Click on Next to move to the next dialog box in the wizard.

3. Within the Grouping Levels dialog box, click on the **WorkCode** field. Next, click on the Grouping Options button. Within the resulting dialog box, select the Grouping Interval as **1st Letter**. If this field were numeric, we might have it change by hundreds; if the field used leading zeros, we might have it change by the first three letters, and so on. Click OK to close the Grouping Interval dialog box, then click on Next to move to the sorting options dialog box.

4. Within the Sorting Options dialog box, select the **WorkCode** field as the field to sort by. Click on Next to move to the next dialog box.

5. The next two dialog boxes lets you select some formatting options. In each dialog box, select the form layout that meets your needs and click on Next.

6. In the last dialog box, name the report Work Codes. Click on Finish to close the wizard. Figure 15.5 shows the newly created report.

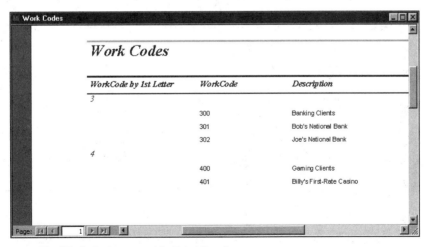

Figure 15.5   The Work Codes report in Print Preview.

You'll notice in the figure that the wizard automatically truncates the field to show only its first letter—which will likely be confusing for the user. Instead, we want to display the entire field in the grouping level. The next section explains how to make the necessary design change.

Changing The Report's Appearance

As you saw in the preceding section, the wizard can be helpful for quickly and easily creating reports, but customizing the report to appear the way you want it to will still generally require action on your part. The **Work Codes** report isn't displayed exactly as we want it to be. To change the display, we simply need to go into the Design view for the report. To make the change, perform the following steps:

1. If the preview window is still open, click on the Design View icon in the upper-left corner of the screen. Otherwise, within the Reports object of the Database window, click on the report and then click on Design. Access will display the report in Design view.

2. Within the designer, under the WorkCode Header section of the report, you'll see a label that contains the expression **=Left$([WorkCode], 1)**. To clean up the report, we simply need to change the specification for this field. Click on the field and press Alt+Enter to open the Properties window.

3. Within the Properties window, change to the Data tab. Within the Control Source property, you'll see the expression that is displayed in the label. If you click on the drop-down list to the right of the property, Access will display a list of available fields. Select the **WorkCode** field.

4. Click on the Preview icon to see the changed report. It should look like Figure 15.6, which solves the problem with the truncated work codes.

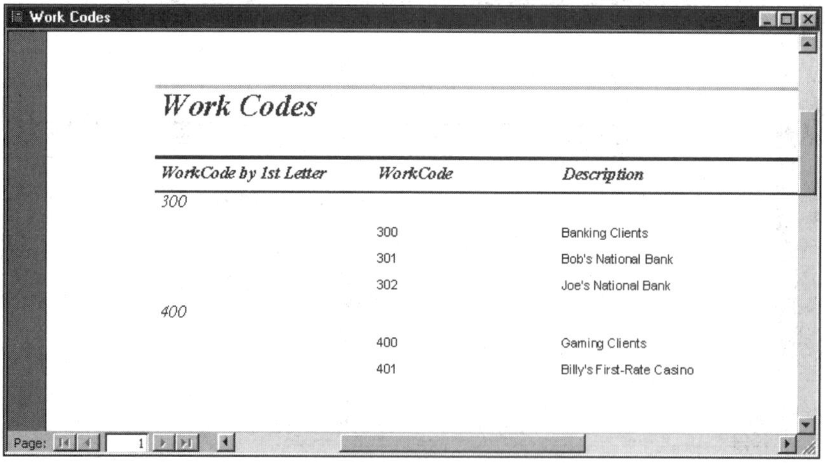

Figure 15.6   The changed report displays an entire work code.

You should also probably change the header for the first column and perhaps add additional information (such as the description) to the top of each grouping level as well. These steps are, however, left as exercises for you. Finally, you should add the new report to the switchboard.

Installing The MSDE

If your network already uses SQL Server 7, you can create ADPs directly against the SQL Server across the network. Alternatively, you can use the MSDE, installed locally, to create the connections and the SQL Server database. For simplicity's sake, in this chapter we'll create a database with the MSDE. You must first install the MSDE onto your local, development machine (Access will not do it automatically). To install the engine, perform the following steps:

1. Insert the Office 2000 CD-ROM 1 into the CD-ROM drive. Using Windows Explorer, navigate to the \SQL\X86\Setup directory.

2. Within the directory, double-click on the file named SetupSQL.exe. Windows will start to run the MSDE installation program.

WARNING! *If you have installed one of the SQL Server 7 Betas onto your development machine, and the build is earlier than Build 516, the MSDE will not install. In some cases, removing the SQL Server Beta from the machine may not be enough; you may actually need to install either a later Beta of SQL Server or the release version so that the MSDE will recognize the program code and helper DLLs that it needs.*

After executing the file, follow the prompts to install MSDE onto your computer. When you finish the installation, the installer will prompt you to reboot your machine. You must do so before you can use the MSDE for project design.

Starting The SQL Server Service

After you install the MSDE engine and reboot the system, your computer will come back up with the SQL Server service icon in the system tray. However, you will notice that the icon has a red circle over it, which indicates that the service is not currently running. To start the service (a necessary step to use the MSDE), perform the following steps:

1. Double-click on the SQL Server service icon in the system tray. Windows will display the SQL Server Service Manager.

2. The Server combo box should contain the name of the computer on which the service is running, and the dialog box should indicate that the service is stopped. Click on the Start/Continue button to start the service. Additionally, if you plan to use the MSDE regularly during development, you may want to instruct the service to start automatically when the operating system boots. If so, click on the check box to instruct the service manager. When you finish, the dialog box should look similar to the one in Figure 15.7.

In addition, the icon in the system tray should change to a green arrow pointing right. You can either close the Service Manager dialog box entirely or minimize it, depending on whether or not you plan to be using the Service Manager regularly.

Figure 15.7   The SQL Server Service Manager after you start the service.

Upsizing An Existing Database To SQL Server

One of the new features of Access 2000 is its provision for easy upsizing of your databases to SQL Server 7. The easiest way to perform an upgrade of this type from within the Access IDE is through the Database Upsizing Wizard. To use the Upsizing Wizard on the Chap15TB database, perform the following steps:

1. Choose Open from the File menu and open the Chap15TB.mdb database.

2. Choose Database Utilities from the Tools menu. Within the submenu, select the Upsizing Wizard option. Access will display the dialog box shown in Figure 15.8.

3. For this exercise, use the Create New Database option—although you can upsize into an existing database if you so choose. Click on Next to move to the next dialog box.

4. You will be prompted to select a SQL Server to use for the database, as well as a login ID and password for a user who has create rights on the database. Finally, it prompts you to name the new SQL Server database. After you perform these actions, click on Next to move to the next dialog box.

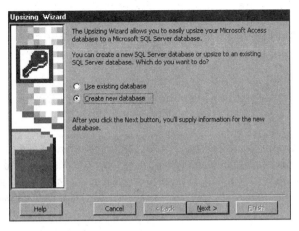

Figure 15.8 The opening dialog box of the Upsizing Wizard.

5. You will be prompted to select which tables to export to the SQL Server. Click on the >> button to export all the tables. Click on Next to move to the next dialog box.

6. The next dialog box lets you export table attributes in addition to data (see Figure 15.9). From within the dialog box, accept the defaults and click on Next to move to the next dialog box.

7. In the next dialog box, you can opt to keep your existing application as is, change the application to support links to the SQL Server tables, or create an ADP to connect to the table. Select the Create A New Access Client/ Server Application option and accept the default name. Click on Next to move to the next dialog box.

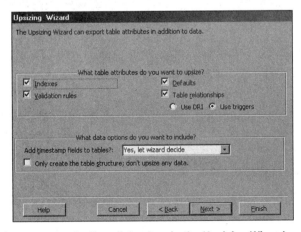

Figure 15.9 The data export selection dialog box in the Upsizing Wizard.

8. After you click on Finish in the last dialog box, the Upsizing Wizard will use the information that you have entered to create the new SQL Server database and the ADP to access the database.

The new ADP will maintain all of your current forms and reports, but it will not maintain any data locally—instead, all data will be maintained in the new SQL Server.

WARNING!   Before you upsize a database to SQL Server, make sure all of the table names correspond to SQL Server naming rules. Specifically, in the Chap15TB.mdb database, make sure there are no spaces in any of the table names. Because of new features in Access 2000, you can rename the tables without having to rebuild all the queries and other objects in the database.

Working With The Access Data Project

As with standard Access databases, you must first create the data project before you can begin to work with it. To create an ADP, perform the following steps:

1. Choose New from the File menu. Access will display the New dialog box.

2. Within the General tab of the dialog box, double-click on the Project (New Database) icon. If you are designing a project to work with an existing SQL Server 7 back end, you can choose the Project (Existing Database) icon. We'll be creating a new database as we create the project.

3. After you double-click on the Project (New Database) icon, Access will display the File New Database dialog box. Click on Create to save the new project as Chap15FE.adp. Access will display the Microsoft SQL Server Database Wizard.

4. Within the first combo box, enter the name of the server for the SQL Server database (which you can obtain from the SQL Server Service Manager or from your network administrator).

5. Enter a login ID and password of an account with Create Database privileges on the server. Finally, enter "Chap15BESQL" as the name of the new database. Click on Next to move to the last dialog box in the wizard.

6. Click on Finish. The MSDE engine will create the SQL Server database and return you to the Database window.

As you saw earlier in this chapter, the Database window has some additional objects that a normal MDB window doesn't have—Views, Database Diagrams, and Stored Procedures. You'll learn more about the objects in later chapters.

Creating The Tables

As you saw earlier, the first step to creating the database is to create the tables that will reside in the database. When you do this through an ADP, the tables are automatically created on the SQL Server, and the links to the Server data are automatically created in the project. We'll use a database example similar to others that you have seen, a simple order entry database. The following sections detail how to create the tables in the database.

Creating The **BillTo** Table

The first table to create is the **BillTo** table. This table will maintain address information about the customer, which the program will (ultimately) use to maintain billing information for each customer. The design of the table is pretty straightforward—as will be the design of the most of the tables. To design the table, perform the following steps:

1. Double-click on the Create Table In Design View option within the Database window. When you do so, Access may display the prompt shown in Figure 15.10. If so, go ahead and install the Client Server Visual Design Tools. You will need to insert the Office 2000 CD-ROM 1 into the drive to do so.

2. After installing the Design Tools, Access will display the Table 1:Table Design view window. It will also prompt you to enter a name for the table. Enter the name as **BillTo** and click on OK.

3. As you can see, the Design window is somewhat different than the Access table Design window. However, most of what you know will translate; we'll explore specifics of the SQL Server design tools in Chapter 33. Within the window, specify the fields within the table as shown in Table 15.1.

4. Scroll to the right and click in the **IsRowGuid** check box for the **Customer Num** field. The designer will place a checkmark in the box and set the default value for the field to **(newid())**.

5. Click in the **AllowNulls** check box for the **CustomerNum** field. The designer will remove the checkmark from the box.

6. Click on the gray selector box to the left of the **CustomerNum** field. Access will highlight the entire field.

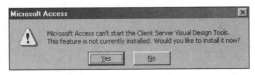

Figure 15.10 The Client Server Visual Design Tools installation prompt.

Table 15.1   The fields in the *BillTo* table.

Field Name	Data Type	Length
CustomerNum	uniqueidentifier	16
CustomerFirst	char	25
CustomerLast	char	25
Address1	char	25
Address2	char	25
City	char	25
State	char	2
Zip	char	10
Phone	char	14
Fax	char	14

7. Click on the primary key button on the toolbar. Access will display a primary key symbol in the selector. When you finish the steps, the designer will look similar to Figure 15.11.

8. Click on the Close button on the window to close the designer. Access will prompt you to save the design changes.

TIP: *Depending on how many records will actually be in the table, using the **uniqueidentifier** field for your primary key is probably overkill—it is, after all, a 16-byte number, which means that it will generate more IDs than there are computers on the Internet before it repeats. In general, you could probably get by with a **long integer** as the key value. We're simply using it here to show you its availability.*

Creating The **ShipTo** Table

The second table to create is the **ShipTo** table. This table will maintain shipping address information about the customer, which the program will (ultimately) use

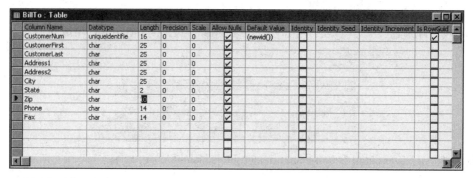

Figure 15.11   The designer after you create the **BillTo** table.

to keep records about where orders were shipped. As with the **BillTo** table, the design of the table is pretty straightforward. To design the table, perform the following steps:

1. Double-click on the Create Table In Design View option within the Database window. Access will display the Table 1:Table Design view window. It will also prompt you to enter a name for the table. Enter the name as **ShipTo** and click on OK.

2. Within the window, specify the fields within the table as shown in Table 15.2.

3. Scroll to the right and click in the **IsRowGuid** check box for the **ShipToNum** field. The designer will place a checkmark in the box and set the default value for the field to **(newid())**.

4. Click in the **AllowNulls** check box for the **ShipToNum** field. The designer will remove the checkmark from the box.

5. Click on the gray selector box to the left of the **ShipToNum** field. Access will highlight the entire field.

6. Click on the primary key button on the toolbar. Access will display a primary key symbol in the selector.

7. Click on the Close button on the window to close the designer. Access will prompt you to save the design changes.

Creating The **OrderLookup** Table

The next table to create is the **OrderLookup** table. This table will maintain shipping address information about the customer, which the program will use to link

Table 15.2   The fields in the *ShipTo* table.

Field Name	Data Type	Length
ShipToNum	uniqueidentifier	16
CustomerNum	uniqueidentifier	16
CustomerFirst	char	25
CustomerLast	char	25
Address1	char	25
Address2	char	25
City	char	25
State	char	2
Zip	char	10
Phone	char	14
Fax	char	14

15. Using Access In A Corporate Environment

the customer information to the order information. To design the table, perform the following steps:

1. Double-click on the Create Table In Design View option within the Database window. Access will display the Table 1:Table Design view window. It will also prompt you to enter a name for the table. Enter the name as **OrderLookup** and click OK.

2. Within the window, specify the fields within the table as shown in Table 15.3.

3. Click on the gray selector box to the left of the **CustomerNum** field. Hold the Shift key down and click the mouse on the gray selector box to the left of the **OrderNum** field. The designer will highlight all three fields.

4. Click on the primary key button on the toolbar. Access will display a primary key symbol in the selector next to the three fields indicating that the primary key will be derived from their combined values.

5. Click on the Close button on the window to close the designer. Access will prompt you to save the design changes.

Creating The **Orders** Table

Next, we'll create the **Orders** table. This table will maintain order information and combine the line items from the **OrderDetail** table with the date and total information it contains when it displays the invoice. To design the table, perform the following steps:

1. Double-click on the Create Table In Design View option within the Database window. Access will display the Table 1:Table Design view window. It will also prompt you to enter a name for the table. Enter the name as **Orders** and click on OK.

2. Within the window, specify the fields within the table as shown in Table 15.4.

3. Scroll to the right and click in the **IsRowGuid** check box for the **OrderNum** field. The designer will place a checkmark in the box and set the default value for the field to **(newid())**.

4. Click in the **AllowNulls** check box for the **OrderNum** field. The designer will remove the checkmark from the box.

Table 15.3   The fields in the OrderLookup table.

Field Name	Data Type	Length	AllowNulls
CustomerNum	**uniqueidentifier**	16	False (unchecked)
ShipToNum	**uniqueidentifier**	16	False (unchecked)
OrderNum	**uniqueidentifier**	16	False (unchecked)

*Table 15.4   The fields in the **Orders** table.*

Field Name	Data Type	Length
OrderNum	uniqueidentifier	16
OrderDate	datetime	8
DeliveryDate	datetime	8
Total	money	8

5. Click on the gray selector box to the left of the **OrderNum** field. Access will highlight the entire field.

6. Click on the primary key button on the toolbar. Access will display a primary key symbol in the selector.

7. Click on the Close button on the window to close the designer. Access will prompt you to save the design changes.

Creating The **ItemInformation** Table

The next table to create is the **ItemInformation** table. This table will maintain specific information about items. You should create this table before the **OrderDetail** table so that you can simply use a lookup between the tables to fill in the **ItemNumber** field in the **OrderDetail** table. To design the **ItemInformation** table, perform the following steps:

1. Double-click on the Create Table In Design View option within the Database window. Access will display the Table 1:Table Design view window. It will also prompt you to enter a name for the table. Enter the name as **ItemInformation** and click OK.

2. Within the window, specify the fields within the table as shown in Table 15.5.

3. Scroll to the right and click in the **IsRowGuid** check box for the **ItemNum** field. The designer will place a checkmark in the box and set the default value for the field to **(newid( ))**.

4. Click in the **AllowNulls** check box for the **ItemNum** field. The designer will remove the checkmark from the box.

5. Click on the gray selector box to the left of the **ItemNum** field. Access will highlight the entire field.

*Table 15.5   The fields in the **ItemInformation** table.*

Field Name	Data Type	Length
ItemNum	uniqueidentifier	16
Description	varchar	50
Price	money	8

6. Click on the primary key button on the toolbar. Access will display a primary key symbol in the selector.

7. Click on the Close button on the window to close the designer. Access will prompt you to save the design changes.

Creating The **Discount** Table

Next, we'll create the **Discount** table (which is the next-to-last table in the database). This table will maintain specific information about discounts. You should create this table before the **OrderDetail** table so you can simply use a lookup between the tables to fill in the **DiscountNum** field in the **OrderDetail** table. To design the **Discount** table, perform the following steps:

1. Double-click on the Create Table In Design View option within the Database window. Access will display the Table 1:Table Design view window. It will also prompt you to enter a name for the table. Enter the table's name as **Discount** and click on OK.

2. Within the window, specify the fields within the table as shown in Table 15.6.

3. Scroll to the right and click in the **IsRowGuid** check box for the **DiscountNum** field. The designer will place a checkmark in the box and set the default value for the field to **(newid( ))**.

4. Click in the **AllowNulls** check box for the **DiscountNum** field. The designer will remove the checkmark from the box.

5. Click on the gray selector box to the left of the **DiscountNum** field. Access will highlight the entire field.

6. Click on the primary key button on the toolbar. Access will display a primary key symbol in the selector.

7. Click on the Close button on the window to close the designer. Access will prompt you to save the design changes.

Creating The **OrderDetail** Table

The last table to create is the **OrderDetail** table. This table will maintain specific information about discounts. To design the **OrderDetail** table, perform the following steps:

Table 15.6   The fields in the Discount table.

Field Name	Data Type	Length
DiscountNum	uniqueidentifier	16
DiscountValue	decimal	9
DiscountDescription	varchar	50

1. Double-click on the Create Table In Design View option within the Database window. Access will display the Table 1:Table Design view window. It will also prompt you to enter a name for the table. Enter the table's name as **OrderDetail** and click OK.

2. Within the window, specify the fields within the table as shown in Table 15.7.

3. Scroll to the right and click in the **IsRowGuid** check box for the **OrderItemID** field. The designer will place a checkmark in the box and set the default value for the field to **(newid( ))**.

4. Click in the **AllowNulls** check box for the **OrderItemID** field. The designer will remove the checkmark from the box.

5. Click on the gray selector box to the left of the **OrderItemID** field. Access will highlight the entire field.

6. Click on the primary key button on the toolbar. Access will display a primary key symbol in the selector.

7. Click on the Close button on the window to close the designer. Access will prompt you to save the design changes.

Table 15.7   The fields in the *OrderDetail* table.

Field Name	Data Type	Length
OrderItemID	uniqueidentifier	16
OrderNum	uniqueidentifier	16
ItemNum	uniqueidentifier	16
DiscountNum	uniqueidentifier	16

15. Using Access In A Corporate Environment

Chapter 16

Using Access For Scientific And Medical Purposes

In Depth

In previous chapters, you've seen some of the many applications of Microsoft Access. You've considered applications both in the small office/home office (SOHO) environment and in the larger, more corporate environment. You've also considered the implications for client-server development with Access and how you can easily scale Access applications up to SQL Server applications using the tools Microsoft provides.

Although the applications for Access are probably too numerous to count, in this chapter we would like to consider a third major cross-section of business for which Access can be used. Specific issues unique to both the science and engineering fields and the medical field make Access a good match for many applications in both. In this chapter, we'll briefly explore some of the considerations when designing databases for these two environments, and we'll then spend the rest of the chapter considering the design of a simple database application to track, report, and graph data from a series of samples. We will begin with the discussion of database uses.

Using Databases

Although most of us may not consider it often, the science and engineering fields, as well as the medical field, lend themselves well to the maintenance of large amounts of data in a location that allows for easy recall. Aside from databases that track conceptual information—such as engineering diagrams or synthetic molecules—databases are exceptionally useful for tracking information from testing of concepts.

Consider for a moment a chemist in a small laboratory who is testing the effectiveness of a new solvent at eliminating a specific waste product. That chemist may perform hundreds of tests with that solvent, with all outside factors being identical, simply to determine the solvent's real efficiency. In such a testing environment, the chemist must be able to keep records of every single test, including the amount of solvent used, the effectiveness, the time it took for the solvent to work, and so on.

In the subsequent sections, we'll evaluate some of the common uses for databases in these environments, both from a management perspective and from a usefulness perspective. We'll first consider the benefits of using databases to manage other documents and similar pieces of information within your organization.

Using Databases To Manage Other Documents

One of the best uses for Access in an engineering environment is as a means of tracking the company's archive of diagrams, schematics, blueprints, and so on. Many of the most common computer-based tools for generating such documents—such as AutoCad—support the Visual Basic for Applications (VBA) object model.

Support for VBA means that you can easily link such applications to an Access database—in fact, you can create hooks within the AutoCad application. Such hooks, for example, might force the user to enter information about the document into the database that maintains the archive information before the user can write the file to the hard drive.

Such hooks and interoperability are all a function of ActiveX Automation (formerly called OLE Automation, or object linking and embedding). Later sections in this chapter explain ActiveX Automation (also known simply as Automation) in detail.

This type of construction is also useful in the medical environment—particularly if the user is able to scan hard-copy medical records for a patient into the computer, then link to them from the database. Such hard-copy records management is one of the fastest growing areas of information services in the medical industry. Although Access may not be the best solution in larger medical offices—because of the size limitations on databases—it will often be an excellent solution for smaller offices.

However, despite the usefulness of databases in tracking information about other information—for example, documents—you will nevertheless most often use databases to track database-specific information. The following section discusses some of the uses for such databases within medical and scientific organizations.

Using Databases To Track Ongoing Information

The other common use for databases in these fields is tracking large volumes of information of a consistent type. For example, the situation detailed earlier in this chapter, in which the chemist is performing a large number of repetitive tests of a single product, is an excellent use for a database in tracking scientific information.

In the medical field, the uses for databases are even more pronounced. Arguably the most important of these uses would be in the tracking of patient information, not just appointments and billing information but ongoing specifics about the patient, such as his or her vital signs. Lab results and other information the doctor might acquire about the patient are also very useful.

How is this data more useful than that tracked for each patient on his or her chart, though? Primarily in predictive medicine—that is, using the data within the database to gather long-term information about the patient in a single area, providing the doctor with necessary information to make a prediction about either the patient's illness or to analyze the success of a particular set of treatments.

In fact, databases in the medical profession could, in the long term, provide for great improvements in patient care, letting doctors spend more time with the patient and less time analyzing long streams of data. As we've seen with the other most common applications of database, the benefit of the database is found in the gathering of information into a single, useful source. The human factor can then interpret the data to provide a more accurate diagnosis. In addition, advances in computing technology will help the physician avoid other problems—such as prescription conflicts, and so on.

Understanding the usefulness of tracking other types of information in a database—such as references to scanned documents—requires that you have at least a basic understanding of ActiveX Automation. The following sections briefly explain how Automation works and its usefulness to the developer.

ActiveX Automation Explained

Windows users have come to expect seamless integration between products. They aren't concerned with what product you use to develop their application; they just want to accomplish their tasks. Often Word, Excel, AutoCad, or some other product is best suited for a particular task that your application must complete. It's your responsibility to pick the best tool for the job. This means you must know how to communicate from your application directly to that tool.

All of this means that you can no longer learn only about the product and language that you select as your development tool. Instead, you must learn about the other applications available to your end users. Furthermore, you must learn how to communicate with these applications.

OLE Automation is the capability of one application to control another application's objects. This means that your Access application can launch Excel, create or modify a spreadsheet, and print it, all without the user having to directly interact with the Excel application. Many people confuse ActiveX Automation with the process of linking and embedding. OLE 1.0 provided you with the ability to create compound documents, meaning that you could embed an Excel spreadsheet in a Word document or link to the Excel spreadsheet from within a Word document. This capability was exciting at the time and is still quite useful in many situations, but ActiveX (in addition to everything that OLE 1.0 provides) introduces the capability for one application to actually control another application's objects. This is what ActiveX Automation is all about.

TIP: *Developers often refer to ActiveX Automation as OLE Automation because ActiveX is a descendent of OLE, and object linking and embedding, as a phrase, defines more completely how your application uses Automation objects.*

Just as you can control other applications using Automation, your Access application can be controlled by other applications such as Excel or a VBA application. This means that you can take advantage of Access's marvelous report writer from your Visual Basic application. In fact, you can list all the Access reports, allow your user to select one, then run the report, all from within a Visual Basic form.

Needless to say, Automation is a powerful and important tool—a crucial one, in fact, in expanding the usefulness of applications within an office. While understand the low-level hows and whys of Automation is beyond the scope of this chapter (and, to a large extent, this book), it is worthwhile to understand some of the terminology, and how it is applies to your development process.

Automation Terms

Before you learn how ActiveX Automation works, you need to understand a few OLE terms. ActiveX Automation requires an Automation client and an Automation server. The Automation client application is the one that's doing the talking. It's the application that's controlling the server application. Because this book is about Access, the examples in this chapter show Access as an Automation client, meaning that the Access application is controlling the other application (Excel, Word, and so on). The Automation server application is the application being controlled. It contains the objects that are being manipulated. Excel is acting as an Automation server when Access launches Excel, makes it visible, creates a new worksheet, sends the results of a query to the worksheet, and graphs the spreadsheet data. It's Excel's objects that are being controlled, Excel's properties that are being changed, and Excel's methods that are being executed.

Another important component of ActiveX Automation is a Type Library. A Type Library is a database that lists the objects, properties, methods, and events exposed by an Automation server application. Type Libraries allow the server application's objects, properties, and methods to be syntax-checked by the Access compiler. Furthermore, in using a Type Library, you can get help on another application's objects, properties, and methods from within Access.

The Object Model of an Automation server application contains the set of objects that are exposed to OLE client applications. The objects within the Object Model are called object types. When you write ActiveX Automation code, you create and manipulate instances of an object type. These instances are called *objects*.

Most modern-day applications will let you control them through the user of Automation. Access is no exception; in fact, Access has a very high level of Automation support. The following section discusses how you can control Access from other applications in greater detail.

Controlling Access From Other Applications

Many times, you'll want to control Access from another application. For example, you might want to run an Access report from a Visual Basic or Excel application. Just as you can tap into many of the rich features of other products such as Excel from within Access, you can utilize some of Access's features from within another program. Fortunately, it's extremely easy to control Access from within other applications.

An overview of the Access object model can be found in Access Help. Unless you're very familiar with the Access object model, you should look at this graphical representation of Access's object model before you attempt to use ActiveX Automation to control Access. Access launches with its **Visible** property set to False. You can change the **Visible** property of the application object to True to make Access visible. If the instance of the object was created using ActiveX Automation, it terminates when its object variable is destroyed.

Immediate Solutions

As you've learned in previous chapters, Access 2000 provides a useful means for creating databases for many different situations. In this chapter we focused on potential technical and medical applications of the database software. In the following section, we'll consider the development of a simple database to track sample data, displaying it both within reports and in a chart.

Creating The Test Data Database

As you've seen, databases have valuable applications when working within testing environments and maintaining data from such tests. The simple database that you'll design in the following sections will maintain information about effectiveness as a percentage and will maintain information by date, time, and test name. To begin the design, you must first create a blank database. To do so, perform the following steps:

1. Select File|New or click on the New icon on the toolbar. Access will display the New Database dialog box.

2. Select the General tab within the New Database dialog box and double-click on the Database icon. Access will display the Save As dialog box.

3. Name the database as Chap16Samps.mdb. Click Create to save the new database. Access will open the Database window.

Creating The **TestNames** Table

The first table to create is the **TestNames** table. This table will maintain the information about IDs and naming for tests. It's essentially a lookup table for the **TestInfo** table's **TestID** field. The design of the table is very straightforward—it contains only two fields. To design the table, perform the following steps:

1. Double-click on the Create Table In Design View option within the Database window. Access will display the Table 1:Table Design view window.

2. Within the window, specify the fields within the table as shown in Table 16.1.

3. Click the mouse on the gray selector box to the left of the **TestID** field. Access will highlight the entire field.

Table 16.1   The fields in the *TestNames* table.

Field Name	Data Type	Description
TestID	**AutoNumber**	Primary key for the **TestNames** table
TestName	**Text**	Plain text name for the test

4. Click on the primary key button on the toolbar. Access will display a primary key symbol in the selector.

5. Click on the Save button on the toolbar to save the table. Name the table as **TestNames**.

6. When you finish, click on the Close box for the Design view of the table to close the table designer. Access may prompt you to save the changes to the table's design.

Creating The **TestInfo** Table

The second table in the database is the **TestInfo** table. This table will maintain all the remaining testing information, including the date and time of the test and the effectiveness of the test. To design the table, perform the following steps:

1. Double-click on the Create Table In Design View option within the Database window. Access will display the Table 1:Table Design view window.

2. Within the window, specify the fields within the table as shown in Table 16.2.

3. Click the mouse on the gray selector box to the left of the **SampleID** field. Access will highlight the entire field.

4. Click on the primary key button on the toolbar. Access will display a primary key symbol in the selector.

5. Click on the Save button on the toolbar to save the table. Name the table as **TestInfo**.

6. Click in the Data Type box for the **TestID** field. On the Properties page at the bottom of the dialog box, click on the Lookup tab.

Table 16.2   The fields in the *TestInfo* table.

Field Name	Data Type	Description
SampleID	AutoNumber	Primary key for the **TestInfo** table
SampleDate	Date/Time	Date for the sample
SampleTime	Date/Time	Time for the sample
TestID	Number (Long Integer)	Foreign key to the **TestNames** table
Effectiveness	Number (Single)	Effectiveness of the particular test

7. Change the Display Control to a Combo Box. Access will display additional properties in the tab. In the Row Source property, either use the Query Builder (click on the ellipsis) or enter the Row Source property as follows:

```
SELECT TestNames.TestID, TestNames.TestName
FROM TestNames;
```

8. Set the Bound column property to 1, and the Column Count property to 2. Within the Column Widths property, set the values to be 0";2".

9. Click in the Data Type box for the **SampleDate** field. On the Properties page at the bottom of the dialog box, click on the General tab.

10. Within the **Format** property for the field, set the format for the field to Medium Date.

11. Click in the Data Type box for the **SampleTime** field. On the Properties page at the bottom of the dialog box, click on the General tab.

12. Within the **Format** property for the field, set the format for the field to Medium Time.

13. When you finish, click on the Close box for the Design view of the table to close the table designer. Access will prompt you to save the changes to the table's design.

Adding The Relationship Information To The Database

To effectively use the new tables, you must relate them to each other. You'll do this from the Relationships window in the Access Interactive Development Environment (IDE). To set up the necessary relationship, perform the following steps:

1. Within the Database window, select Tools|Relationships. Access will display the Relationships window.

2. Click on the Show Table icon on the toolbar to display the Show Table dialog box (Access may display the dialog box automatically). Within the Show Table dialog box, double-click on both the tables to add them to the Relationship window. Next, click on Close to close the Show Table dialog box.

3. Within the **TestNames** table's window, click on the **TestID** field and drag it over to the **TestID** field in the **TestInfo** table's window. Access will display the Edit Relationships dialog box.

4. Within the Edit Relationships dialog box, click on the Enforce Referential Integrity checkbox. Access will display two additional options; click on both the Cascade Update Related Fields check box and the Cascade Delete Related Fields check box. Click on Create to create the relationship.

16. Using Access For Scientific And Medical Purposes

When you finish specifying the relationships, the Relationships window will look similar to Figure 16.1.

When you close the Relationships window, Access 2000 will prompt you to save your changes. Make sure you do so, or none of your newly-defined relationships will be saved to the database.

Creating The Forms For The Database

After you create the basic tables, you should then create input forms for the database. Because the database is so simple, we can simply use the wizards to create the necessary forms. To create the form for the entry of test names, perform the following steps:

1. Within the Database window, change to the Forms tab. Next, open the wizard, either by double-clicking on the Create Form By Using Wizard shortcut or by using the New dialog box.

2. Within the first dialog box of the wizard, select the table source as **TestNames**. Next, click on the >> button to place both fields onto the form. Click the Next button to move to the next dialog box in the wizard.

3. On the next dialog box, choose a columnar layout for the form. Click Next when you finish.

4. Choose any background you like for the form; the Chap16Samps.mdb database on the companion CD-ROM uses the Blends background. Click Next after you make your selection.

5. In the last dialog box of the wizard, change the default name of the form to **frmTestNames**. Click Finish to close the wizard. Access will display the form. Close the form.

To create the second form, perform the following steps:

1. Within the Database window, make sure the Forms tab is still selected. Next, open the wizard, either by double-clicking on the Create Form By Using Wizard shortcut or by using the New dialog box.

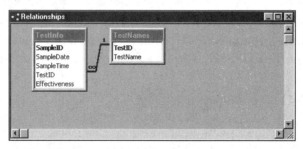

Figure 16.1   The Relationships window for the Chap16Samps database.

2. Within the first dialog box of the wizard, select the table source as **TestInfo**. Next, click on the >> button to place all five fields onto the form. Click the Next button to move to the next dialog box in the wizard.

3. On the next dialog box, choose a columnar layout for the form. Click Next when you finish.

4. Choose any background you like for the form; the Chap16Samps.mdb database on the companion CD-ROM uses the Blends background. Click Next after you make your selection.

5. In the last dialog box of the wizard, change the default name of the form to **frmTestInfo**. Click within the option box so you can work with the design of the form. Click Finish to close the wizard. Access will display the form in design view.

6. You'll notice in the design view that the **TestID** field uses a text box, rather than a combo box, as we set it to in the table design. To make this correct, we simply need to transform the field, as detailed in the following section.

Transforming The **TestID** Text Box

As the last section explained, we need to transform the text box for the **TestID** field to a combo box to keep it consistent with the lookup method that we've set for it previously. To transform the text box, perform the following steps:

1. Within Design view, right-click on the **TestID** data-bound text box. Access will display a pop-up menu.

2. Within the pop-up menu, select the Change To option and select the Combo Box option from the resulting submenu. Access will change the control to a combo box.

3. If the Properties window isn't displayed, press Alt+Enter to display the window. Within the window, change to the Data tab. In the Row Source property, either use the Query Builder (click on the ellipsis) or enter the Row Source property as follows:

```
SELECT TestNames.TestID, TestNames.TestName
FROM TestNames;
```

4. Set the Bound column property to 1. Next, change to the Format tab of the Properties window.

5. Within the Properties window, change the Column Count property to 2. Within the Column Widths property, set the values to be 0";2".

6. Next, click on the **TestID** label and change the **Caption** property to read "Test Name:". After you finish, close the Properties window.

The only other change you need to make is to enable the user to add additional test names by spawning the form for the **TestNames** table. To do so, perform the following steps:

1. If the Toolbox isn't currently displayed, click on the Toolbox icon on the toolbar. Access will display the Toolbox.

2. Within the Toolbox, make sure the Wizards button is depressed, then select the Command Button icon.

3. Create a small command button next to the combo box. Access will display the Command Button Wizard.

4. Within the Command Button Wizard, select the Form Operations option in the left list box and the Open Form option in the right list box. When you finish, click on Next to move to the next dialog box in the wizard.

5. The next dialog box lets you select what form to open. Select the **frmTestNames** form and click on the Next button.

6. In the next dialog box, instruct Access to open the form and show all records. Click Next to move to the next dialog box.

7. In the next dialog box, instruct Access to display text on the command button and input the text as "…". Click Next to move to the last dialog box in the wizard.

8. Assign the name to the command button as **cmdShowTestNames**. Click Finish to close the wizard.

Access may make the command button too large; if so, you can use the Sizing controls to size the button correctly. When you finish, the form should look similar to Figure 16.2 when in Form view.

After you finish the form's design, you should close the form and save the changes. Then, you should enter some sample data into the tables. The Chap16Samps.mdb database already includes sample data. After you enter sample data, the next step is to create a report that displays the data. However, before you create the report,

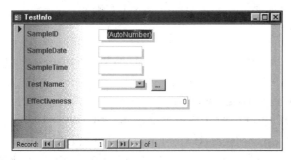

Figure 16.2   The **TestInfo** form in Form view.

the best way to get the underlying data for the report is to use a query that combines the two tables. You'll create the query in the next section.

Creating A New Query For The Report To Use

The easiest way to get the information for the report is to create a simple query that combines the records from the two tables. In real life, you might want to create a *parameterized query*, which would let you specify different tests so a given report would only return test information about a single test. However, for simplicity, we'll only consider a query to return all the information here. To create the new query, perform the following steps:

1. Within the Database window, make sure the Queries object is selected. Next, click on the Create Query In Design View option. Access will open the query designer and place the Show Table dialog box in front of it.

2. Within the Show Table dialog box, double-click the **TestInfo** table entry and the **TestNames** table entry. Access will add the tables to the top of the query designer. Next, click Close to close the Show Table dialog box.

3. At the top of the query designer, select the **SampleDate, SampleTime,** and **Effectiveness** fields from the **TestInfo** table. Also, select the **TestName** field from the **TestNames** table.

4. Click on the Close button to close the designer. Access will prompt you to save the new query, which you should do as **qryTestSamples**.

Creating A New Report

Now that the query is ready, it's time to create the report. To create the report, perform the following steps:

1. Within the Database Window, select the Reports object. Next, click on the Create Report By Using Wizard option. Access will display the Report Wizard.

2. From the Tables/Queries drop-down, select the Query:qryTestSamples option. Then click on the >> button to select all fields. When you finish, click on Next to move to the next dialog box in the Wizard.

3. Within the Grouping Levels dialog box, double-click on the **TestName** field. When you finish, you'll have a single grouping level within your report. Click Next to move to the Sorting Options dialog box.

4. Within the Sorting Options dialog box, select the **SampleDate** field as the first field to sort by. Next, select the **SampleTime** field as the second field to sort by.

5. Next, click on the Summary Options command button. Access will display the Summary Options dialog box. Within the dialog box, select the Avg check box. Click on OK to return to the Report Wizard. Next, click on the Next button to move to the next dialog box.

6. The next two dialog boxes let you select some formatting options. For each, select the form layout that meets your needs, and click on Next.

7. In the last dialog box, name the report as Samples By Test Name. Click Finish to close the Wizard. Figure 16.3 shows the newly created report.

Now that you have the report you wanted, you have only two more steps to perform to finish the design of the database—the creation of the chart form and the design of the switchboard to help the user navigate the database application.

Creating The Chart Form

Our overall goal in the project's design was to create a project that would let us perform two basic tasks: chart data over time and display testing results in a report. Although a vast number of ways are available in which to create chart support within an Access form, the easiest way by far is to use the Chart Wizard. For simplicity's sake, we'll use the Chart Wizard to design the charting form in this database. To create the charting form, perform the following steps:

1. Within the Database window, change to the Forms tab. Next, click on the New button on the toolbar. Access will display the New dialog box.

2. Within the New dialog box, select the Chart Wizard as the method to use, and choose the **qryTestSamples** query as the source for the chart. Click on OK to start the wizard.

3. The next dialog box instructs you to select the fields it should use to design the chart. Select all the fields except the **SampleTime** field. Click Next to move to the next dialog box.

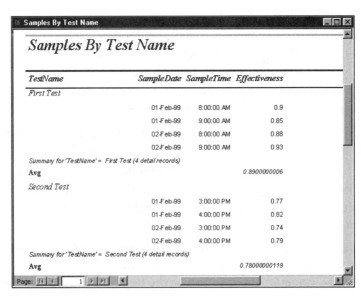

Figure 16.3   The Samples By Test Name report in Print Preview.

4. From the list of available charts, select the Line chart. Click Next to move to the next dialog box.

5. Access will display the dialog box shown in Figure 16.4, within which you can customize the layout of the chart. Several things need to be customized here: First, double-click on the SumOfEffectiveness icon. Access will display the Summarize box. Within the dialog box, select Average. Access will summarize the displayed information by average value. Click OK to close the Summarize dialog box.

WARNING! If you specify data for both the Axis and the Series on a chart, you must summarize the information in some way. The Chart Wizard won't (and actually can't) create the chart if you don't.

6. Next, double-click on the SampleTimeByMonth icon. Access will display the Group dialog box. The default is Month; change the default to reflect your data entries. For the Chap16Samps database, the setting is Day. After you make the changes, click OK to close the Group dialog box and Next to move to the last dialog box in the Wizard.

7. The last dialog box lets you specify a name for your chart—in this case, name it **frmSampleResults**. Click Finish to close the Wizard.

When you finish, the chart should look similar to Figure 16.5.

When you close the form, Access will prompt you to save its design. Save the form as **SampleResults**.

Creating The Switchboard For The Project

The only significant step left to take is to create a switchboard to let the user more easily navigate the project. To create the switchboard, perform the following steps:

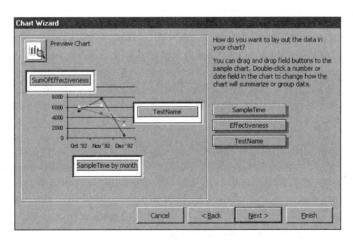

Figure 16.4   The Wizard dialog box which lets you control how data in the chart is displayed.

16. Using Access For Scientific And Medical Purposes

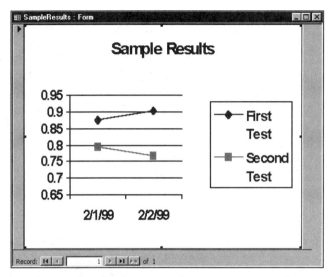

Figure 16.5   The **frmSampleResults** form contains a chart.

1. Select Tools|Database Utilities. Within the submenu, select the Switchboard Manager option. Access will display a dialog box informing you that no switchboard exists and prompting you to decide whether it should create one. Select Yes. Access will display the Switchboard Manager.

2. Within the Switchboard Manager, click on the Edit button. Access will display the Edit Switchboard Page dialog box.

3. Within the Edit Switchboard Page dialog box, click on the New button. Access will display the Edit Switchboard Item dialog box. Within the dialog box, enter the item text as "Enter/View Sample Data". Enter the command as "Open Form in Edit Mode" and select **frmTestInfo** from the list of forms. Click OK to close the dialog box and return to the Edit Switchboard Page dialog box.

4. Within the Edit Switchboard Page dialog box, click on the New button. Access will display the Edit Switchboard Item dialog box. Within the dialog box, enter the item text as "Enter/View Test Names". Enter the command as "Open Form in Edit Mode" and select **frmTestNames** from the list of forms. Click OK to close the dialog box and return to the Edit Switchboard Page dialog box.

5. Within the Edit Switchboard Page dialog box, click on the New button. Access will display the Edit Switchboard Item dialog box. Within the dialog box, enter the item text as "Display Chart of Sample Data". Enter the command as "Open Form in Edit Mode" and select **frmSampleResults** from the list of forms. Click OK to close the dialog box and return to the Edit Switchboard Page dialog box.

6. Within the Edit Switchboard Page dialog box, click on the New button. Access will display the Edit Switchboard Item dialog box. Within the dialog box, enter the item text as "Display Report of Sample Data". Enter the command as "Open Report" and select the **Samples By Test Name** report. Click OK to close the dialog box and return to the Edit Switchboard Page dialog box.

7. Within the Edit Switchboard Page dialog box, click on the New button. Access will display the Edit Switchboard Item dialog box. Within the dialog box, enter the item text as "Close Application". Enter the command as "Exit Application". Click OK to close the dialog box and return to the Edit Switchboard Page dialog box.

8. Click Close to close the Edit Switchboard dialog box. Click Close again to exit the Switchboard Manager.

Launching The Switchboard Automatically

You'll probably want the switchboard to launch automatically when you start the database. To do so, perform the following steps:

1. From the Database window, select Tools|Startup. Access will display the Startup dialog box.

2. In the Display Form/Page combo box, select Switchboard. You may also want to disable the Database window; if so, remove the check mark from the Display Database Window option. When you finish, the dialog box will look similar to Figure 16.6.

3. Click OK to close the Startup dialog box and return to the Database window.

The next time you open the database, Access will automatically display the switchboard.

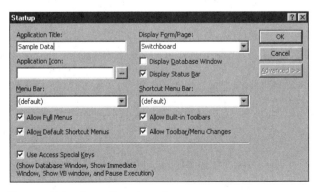

Figure 16.6   The Startup dialog box after your changes.

Part VI

Database Application Design Reference

Chapter 17

Problem Definition And Design Planning

In Depth

Several steps are involved in developing an effective database design. As with all types of applications, the process begins with a *requirements analysis*. In terms of relational database design, this phase answers questions regarding what data elements must be stored, who will access them, and how they'll be accessed.

The second step is to define the logical database. This phase isn't concerned with how the data will be stored physically but with how information is grouped logically. The requirements are translated into a model that provides a level of abstraction from the physical database, representing data in terms of business entities and relationships, rather than in terms of tables and fields. This logical database design is often depicted in an *information diagram*, discussed further in later chapters.

Physical design is the final phase in which individual data elements are given attributes and defined as fields in tables. This phase also deals with performance considerations relating to the creation of indexes, database design issues (such as Table database and Application database splits), query design, and the physical layout and location of the data files on the disk. The Access Interactive Development Environment (IDE) is used or Data Definition Language (DDL) SQL statements are written to create database objects.

A simple contact manager will be used as a sample application throughout this chapter, illustrating the concepts and techniques presented for each phase of the design process. Let's begin, then, by considering the first step in the design-planning phase, as discussed in the following section.

Requirements Definition

System requirements are typically gathered through a series of interviews with the end users. This is an iterative process in which systems designers provide structure to the ongoing dialogue, document findings, and solicit feedback from the users. Although requirements definition isn't normally considered part of the design process (but rather part of the planning process), the design is driven by the requirements, and the two processes often overlap. For example, the logical model may bring out new requirements that weren't recognized in the earlier phases of analysis. It's important, however, to identify all requirements before developing a physical design, because design decisions and hardware purchasing decisions are ineffective without a full understanding of system requirements.

A common technique used to define and document database requirements is to develop a data dictionary. As the name implies, a data dictionary simply lists and defines the individual data elements that must be stored. An initial draft of the data dictionary for a simple contact manager might look like Table 17.1.

Although this is a good way to start defining database requirements, obvious shortcomings should stand out to you. The data dictionary doesn't describe how these individual items are related. It also lacks information regarding how the data is created, updated, and retrieved, among other things.

Table 17.1   Data dictionary for the contact manager sample application.

Item	Description
Last name	The individual contact's last name
First name	The individual's first name
Middle initial	The individual's middle initial
Contact type	Standardized description indicating whether this individual represents a client, a prospect, a vendor, or some other type of contact
Individual notes	Additional information related to the individual
Company	The name of the company the individual represents
Company notes	Additional information about the individual's company
Address line 1	Line 1 of the individual's street address
Address line 2	Line 2 of the individual's street address
Address line 3	Line 3 of the individual's street address
City	City name for the individual's mailing address
State	State name for the individual's mailing address
Zip code	ZIP code for the individual's mailing address
Address type	Standardized description indicating whether this is a work, home, or some other type of address
Phone number	The individual's area code and phone number
Phone type	Standardized description indicating whether this is a home, office, or other type of phone number
Date contacted	The date this individual was contacted
Contacted by	The name of the salesperson or employee who contacted this individual
Contact method	Standardized description indicating whether the individual was contacted by phone, mail, fax, or some other method
Contact reason	Standardized description of the reason that the individual was contacted
Contact notes	Additional information related to this specific contact

17. Problem Definition And Design Planning

A functional specification documents the system requirements in plain English and should fill in details concerning who'll be using the system, when, and how. Information concerning the number of concurrent users accessing the system, how frequently records are inserted and updated, and how information will be retrieved are particularly important topics to be covered in the functional specification. These factors will help determine hardware and software licensing requirements and have a significant impact on issues relating to performance, security, and database integrity.

The functional description for the sample contact manager might include a summary similar to the text that follows:

> The system will be available to 40 sales representatives, 5 sales managers, 26 sales assistants, 6 purchasing agents, 1 purchasing department manager, and 2 purchasing assistants, for a total of 80 users. Of these 80 possible users, it is expected that a maximum of 20 would be actively using the system at any given time. Purchasing department personnel should have access only to purchasing department contacts, and sales department personnel should have access only to sales contacts.

> All users may add information regarding a specific contact at any time, but while sales representatives and purchasing agents can add new prospects, only assistants can add new vendors and clients (after obtaining proper approval from a manager). Sales representatives and purchasing agents should have access only to their accounts and prospects, but managers should have full access to the entire database for their specific departments.

> One assistant from each department will be designated as a system administrator. Only the system administrators will be able to add and modify address, phone, contact types, contact methods, and contact reasons. With the approval of a manager, a system administrator will be able to reassign a vendor or client to a new purchasing agent or sales representative.

> For audit purposes, every time information is added or modified, the individual who made the modification, and the date and time that the information was modified, should be recorded.

In this case, the functional specification adds several new data elements to the requirements, in addition to pertinent information regarding access and security. The functional specification and data dictionary are often developed simultaneously because one document may provide relevant information that should be reflected in the other.

TIP: *You'll often combine the information in the functional specification and the data dictionary into a graphical representation of the database's contents. Chapters 5 and 19 discuss the appearance of the graphical representation in more detail.*

An important part of requirements analysis is to anticipate the needs of the users because they won't always be able to fully explain the system requirements on their own. Based on information we already know about the contact management application, you (or the other system designers) may have the following follow-up questions, among others:

- Will a contact have only one address and phone number? One company? One type?

- How does a prospect become a client or vendor?

- How are client and vendor accounts assigned to sales representatives and purchasing agents initially?

- How are client and vendor account numbers assigned?

- Can contact and audit information be archived? If so, after how many months?

Obviously, these are just a few of the questions that come to mind. In practice, the functional description should describe the system to the fullest extent and detail possible. The importance of thorough requirements analysis and documentation is often underestimated. Put simply, poor requirements definition will most likely result in poor or inadequate design because these requirements provide the foundation for the later phases of design, including the logical and physical data models. However, presuming you have effectively designed and stated your requirements, you will then move on to the design of the logical model. The following section describes the logical model in detail.

The Logical Model

A common way to represent the logical model is through an entity relationship (ER) diagram, which you learned about briefly in Chapter 5. For the purposes of this type of model, an *entity* is defined as a discrete object for which items of data are being stored, and a relationship refers to an association between two entities.

In the contact manager example, there are five main entities for which data is being stored:

- Individuals (with whom contacts are made)

- Addresses

- Phone numbers

- Contacts (communications with individuals)

- Employees

The relationships between these entities can be summarized in plain terms:

- Employees have access to zero, one, or many Individuals.
- Individuals have one or many Addresses.
- Individuals have one or many Phone Numbers.
- Employees make zero, one, or many Contacts.
- Individuals have zero, one, or many Contacts.

These entities and their relationships can be represented graphically by an ER Diagram, as shown in Figure 17.1.

In the figure, observe how the one-to-one or many and one-to-zero, one, or many relationships are represented. One-to-one and one-to-zero or one relationships can be represented using similar notation. This may seem to be a simplistic approach to modeling the application's data, but it's often a good first step. In larger applications with hundreds of entities, these models can become extremely complex.

This model can be taken a step further by defining attributes for each entity. An entity's attributes are the individual items of data to be stored that relate specifically to the object. The attributes for each entity in the contact manager application are listed in Table 17.2.

Note that several items of information are missing. The audit information mentioned in the functional specification is omitted. This can be handled by adding a

17. Problem Definition And Design Planning

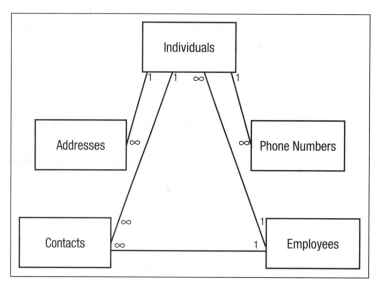

Figure 17.1   An ER Diagram for the contact manager sample application.

Table 17.2 *Simple entity and attribute definitions.*

Entity	Attribute
Employees	Employee number
Employees	User ID
Individuals	Last name
Individuals	First name
Individuals	Middle initial
Individuals	Company
Individuals	Individual notes
Individuals	Company notes
Contacts	Contact date
Contacts	Contacted by
Contacts	Contact reason
Contacts	Contact method
Contacts	Contact type
Contacts	Contact notes
Addresses	Address line 1
Addresses	Address line 2
Addresses	Address line 3
Addresses	City
Addresses	State
Addresses	ZIP code
Addresses	Address type
Phone numbers	Phone number
Phone numbers	Phone type

LastUpdateUserID and **LastUpdateTimeStamp** attribute to each entity. More important, there are attributes missing that are required to relate entities to each other. These data items must be handled somewhat differently because they aren't "natural" attributes belonging to a specific entity.

This is a highly abstract view of the data concerned only with broad categories of data (entities) and the logical relationships between them. The ER model, although good at representing basic data concepts, isn't of much use when it comes to physical implementation. The relational model helps bridge this gap.

The relational model is characterized by its use of keys and relations, among other things. The term *relation* in the context of relational database theory shouldn't be confused with a relationship. A relation can be viewed as an unordered, two-dimensional table, in which each row is distinct. Relationships are built between relations (tables) through common attributes. These common attributes are called *keys*.

There are several types of keys, and they sometimes differ only in terms of their relationships to other attributes and relations. A primary key uniquely identifies a row in a relation, and each relation can have only one primary key, even if more than one attribute is unique. In some cases, it takes more than one attribute to uniquely identify each row in a relation. The aggregate of these attributes is called a concatenated key or a composite key. In other cases, a primary key must be generated. The entity Individuals in the preceding example illustrates this point. Although it may be likely, there's no guarantee that the combination of the entity's attributes will be unique. A new attribute should be created based on generated values to make Individuals a relation (in general, in Access 2000, you accomplish this through the use of an **Autonumber** field, which uniquely identifies each record in the table).

Another type of key, called a *foreign key*, exists only in terms of the relationship between two relations. A foreign key in a relation is a nonkey attribute that's a primary key (or part of the primary key) in another relation. This is the shared attribute that forms a relationship between two relations (tables). Primary and foreign key relationships are illustrated in Table 17.3.

In the table, the note (**PK**) indicates that the attribute is the primary key of the relation, while the note (**FK**) indicates that the attribute is a foreign key.

Referring back to the example, the entities' attributes can be extended to fulfill the audit requirements and make the model relational. Note that the ID attribute

Table 17.3.   Entity attributes (relational model).

Entity	Field Description
Employees	Employee number (**PK**)
Employees	User ID
Employees	Last update user ID
Employees	Last update date/time
Individuals	ID (**PK**)
Individuals	Last name
Individuals	First name

(continued)

Table 17.3. *Entity attributes (relational model) (continued).*

Entity	Field Description
Individuals	Middle initial company contact type
Individuals	Assigned employee (**FK**)
Individuals	Individual notes
Individuals	Company notes
Individuals	Last update user ID
Individuals	Last update date/time
Contacts	Contacts ID (**PK**)
Contacts	Individual ID (**FK**)
Contacts	Contacted by (**FK**)
Contacts	Contact date
Contacts	Contact reason
Contacts	Contact method
Contacts	Contact notes
Contacts	Last update user ID
Contacts	Last update date/time
Addresses	ID (**PK**)
Addresses	Individual ID (**FK**)
Addresses	Address line 1
Addresses	Address line 2
Addresses	Address line 3
Addresses	City
Addresses	State
Addresses	ZIP code
Addresses	Address type
Addresses	Last update user ID
Addresses	Last update date/time
Phone numbers	ID (**PK**)
Phone numbers	Individual ID (**FK**)
Phone numbers	Phone number
Phone numbers	Phone type
Phone numbers	Last update user ID
Phone numbers	Last update date/time

is a generated primary key in each relation in which it appears. The reasons for this will be explained in further detail in the following section on performance considerations.

Numerous limitations and redundancies are in this model. For example, if one individual works for more than one company, he or she must be stored as two separate individuals to be associated with both companies. Redundancies are also introduced when multiple contacts share the same address and phone number.

To solve such problems, you must normalize the data. You've learned the basics of normalization in previous chapters, and will discuss them again in later chapters. Normalization is one of the most important concepts for you to understand and apply effectively in relational database design.

The Normalization Process

The process known as normalization is a technique used to group attributes in ways that eliminate these types of problems. More specifically, the goals of normalization are to minimize redundancy and functional dependency. Functional dependencies occur when the value of one attribute can be determined from the value of another attribute. The attribute that can be determined is said to be functionally dependent on the attribute that's the determinant. By definition, then, all nonkey attributes will be functionally dependent on the primary key in every relation (because the primary key uniquely defines each row). When one attribute of a relation doesn't uniquely define another attribute, but limits it to a set of predefined values, it's called a *multivalued dependency*. A *partial dependency* exists when an attribute of a relation is functionally dependent on only one attribute of a concatenated key. *Transitive dependencies* occur when a nonkey attribute is functionally dependent on one or more other nonkey attributes in the relation.

Normalization is measured in terms of normal forms, and the process of normalization consists of taking appropriate steps to reach the next normal form. The normal forms are described in detail in Chapters 5 and 19, so we won't review them further here. The design of the Chap17.mdb database, however, complies with normalization rules through the fourth normal form.

The Physical Model

The physical database consists of tables, forms, queries, reports, indexes, and other database management items. Dependencies exist between these elements that impose an order on the design process. The process often starts with designing the smallest units of physical storage and proceeds, in order, to each successively larger unit of storage. Overall capacity and performance considerations provide constraints to the design and should be considered at every step. As with logical modeling, developing a physical design can be a somewhat iterative process.

TIP: *Although Access really starts at the table level for design issues, as you develop more advanced client-server applications, you'll likely move to SQL Server, Oracle, or some other product at the back end. In such cases, you'll be able to control the design of your tables with an increased level of granularity—that is, you will have more control over the level of atomicity of components of the database.*

Assigning Field Names And Data Types

Designing the physical database begins with assigning field names and data types. The attributes of a field determine how it will be physically stored in the database by defining its data type and maximum length. The data type and length of a field should be carefully chosen at design time because it's sometimes difficult to change these attributes after data has been loaded.

TIP: *Chapter 23 discusses the creation of tables in detail and includes a table which describes each of the data types in Access and their uses. For more information on Access data types, refer to Chapter 23.*

You should consider additional factors besides the nature of the data and its length when selecting a data type for a field. For example, with the **Number** data type, the declared precision and scale greatly affect how the data is stored. If not fully understood, these values may not behave as intended. For example, assume that a field has been declared as **Number** with the subtype **Long Integer**. If you then try to store a fractional value into that field, Access will do one of two things (depending on how the assignment is attempted):

- Generate an error indicating that the value is invalid.
- Truncate the value and store it as a **Long Integer**, rather than as a real number.

Moreover, these considerations are important if you intend to use the data in computations—multiplying a **Long Integer** by a **Single** will generally result in a loss of precision, making the results inaccurate.

Using the contact manager application example, the field types for the **Addresses** table might be defined as shown in Table 17.4.

Defining the field's attributes is also an important step in capacity planning. From this information, the maximum record size for each table can be determined. This combined with an estimate of the total number of rows helps determine the amount of storage required to house the data.

Table 17.4   Definition of the field names and data types of the Addresses table in the contact manager sample application.

Field Name	Data Types
ID	AutoNumber
EntityType	Number (Long Integer)
Entity ID	Number (Long Integer)
Address Line 1	Text
Address Line 2	Text
Address Line 3	Text
City	Text
State	Text
Zip Code	Text
Address Type	Number Long Integer
Last Update User ID	Text
Last Update Date/Time	Date/Time (Medium Date)

The next step is to begin creating DLL scripts that will be used to create the tables. This may seem like a step toward implementation, but DDL can be used as a tool for capacity planning and the design of tablespaces and data file layout.

*TIP: In Access, you won't use DDL as much as you might in other designers. However, you're likely to use DDL from Visual Basic for Applications (VBA), particularly for tasks such as creating simple, temporary tables. If the application works against a Data Access Objects (DAO) database, you can also use **TableDef**, **Field**, and other related objects in the DAO model to specify the database's construction. See Chapter 28 for more information on DAOs.*

The DDL for creating tables consists of defining field names and attributes, primary keys and indexes, and other specifics of table design.

Performance Considerations

When designing the physical database, performance is an important consideration. There are numerous factors related to the design that will affect the overall performance of the database. These factors include the data model itself, indexing, the location of the data on the network, the physical location of the data on the disks, and size and number of relations on a table.

A factor that can heavily impact overall performance stems from the logical model. The degree of normalization in the model often comes down to a trade-off between flexibility and performance. In the example of normalization presented in the section on the logical model, several relations were created that improved the flexibility of the model, as shown in Table 17.5.

Separating company information from the **Individuals** table added a considerable amount of flexibility. This allowed individuals to be related to more than one company, and it allowed addresses and phones to be related to either an individual or to a company. Another nice feature of the normalized model is that it allows any number of phones and addresses to be related to an individual or to a company.

The end result of all this is a very flexible (but possibly overly complex) data model. Assume, for example, that one of the primary uses of the database is to generate a listing of the names of contacts and their companies, addresses, and phone numbers. This is a fairly complex query and illustrates a potential flaw in the model: Although addresses and phones can be related to either companies or individuals, there is nothing in the model that allows phones and addresses to be related to an individual at a company.

Assume, then, that you create, as a workaround, a third entity type for an individual at a company, then you impose a rule that the **IndividualID** is used for that entity in which an entity's ID is required as a foreign key. The phone list can be generated under this scenario, but it requires joining nine tables. **Individuals** must be joined to **Addresses**, **PhoneNumbers**, and **Individual-Company Relation**, which must be joined to **Companies** to get the company name, and **Addresses** must be joined to **Cities** and **States**. In addition, **PhoneNumbers** and **Addresses** must be joined to **Phone Types** and **Address Types** to get their respective, standardized type descriptions. Although joining nine tables isn't a particularly difficult task, if the database contains millions of individuals, the number of joins can have a very significant impact on performance. If this report is generated up-to-the-minute online and the database has a high volume of transactions, the impact is further magnified.

Denormalization, the opposite of normalization, can be used to improve performance under these circumstances. By combining some of the relations, the number of joins can be reduced without sacrificing flexibility.

Table 17.5   *Junction table used to relate Individuals to Companies.*

Individual-Company Relation	Companies	Individuals
Individual ID (**FK**)	ID(**PK**)	ID(**PK**)
Company ID (**FK**)	Company	Type
	Company notes	

With a slightly denormalized model, only seven tables must be joined to generate the list, and no flexibility is lost. Note that the foreign key constraints must be removed from **IndividualID** and **CompanyID** on the **Addresses** and **Phone Numbers** tables because one or the other might be **NULL**. The following code shows a SQL statement that you might use to create a report after this denormalization:

```
SELECT First_Name, Middle_Init, Last_Name, Company_Name,
    Address_Types.Type, Address_Line1, Address_Line2,
    Address_Line3, City, State, Zip, Phone_Types.Type,
    Phone_Number
FROM Individuals, Individual_Company_Relation,
    Companies, Addresses, Phone_Numbers,
    Address_Types, Phone_Types
WHERE Individuals.ID = Individual_Company_Relation.Individual_ID
    AND Individual_Company_Relation.Company_ID = Companies.ID
    AND Individual_Company_Relation.Individual_ID =
        Addresses.Individual_ID
    AND Individual_Company_Relation.Company_ID = Addresses.Company_ID
    AND Individual_Company_Relation.Individual_ID =
        Phone_Numbers.Individual_ID
    AND Individual_Company_Relation.Company_ID =
        Phone_Numbers.Company_ID
    AND Addresses.Address_Type = Address_Types.ID
    AND Phone_Numbers.Phone_Type = Phone_Types.ID
```

Additional denormalization could improve performance further but probably at the cost of flexibility.

The previous example can also be used to illustrate the importance of indexes. Indexes can be created on single or multiple fields and may or may not be unique. When creating an index on multiple fields, the order in which the fields are declared is particularly important because most modern database engines treat the value of such an index as an aggregate. The field that will be used the most should be declared first in a multifield index. In the previous example, the **Individual_Company_Relation** table is a prime candidate for an index. If both fields are indexed in aggregate, the table itself should never be read. **Individual_ID** should be declared as the first field in the index because it's used for one more join.

The creation of indexes should be planned very carefully because improper use of indexes can have a damaging effect on performance. Even where indexes improve the performance of **SELECT** statements, they have a negative impact on **INSERT**s and **UPDATE**s, because the indexes must be modified in addition to the tables.

The fields and their attributes themselves play a role in performance as well. Wherever possible, integers should be used as keys because they can be compared faster than any other data type. Field and table constraints should be avoided because they must be checked whenever a value is inserted or updated. Although these constraints are often necessary, integrity should be enforced by other means when it's possible to do so safely.

Immediate Solutions

Defining A Problem And Planning A Design

As you have learned in this chapter, three general steps are required for effective database design. Performing these steps each time you design a database will help you ensure that all your databases are designed to be as effective and efficient as possible.

Step 1—Performing A Requirements Analysis

In the requirements analysis phase of development, you should determine what data elements must be stored, who will access them, and how they will be accessed and stored. Three steps are part of this process:

1. Interview users in the target deployment environment for the database. If you're an application developer, these users will be within the department where you intend to deploy the database. If you're developing for retail release, these users will be people within your target market. Make sure you interview a cross-section of your target market; for the internal department, make sure you interview not only the department managers but also all the different types of employees who will be using the database.

2. Based on the feedback from your interviews, define a *data dictionary*, which specifies and details all of the different data items you'll be storing within the database. This comprehensive list should include not only field names but also descriptions of each item. Although it's impossible to normalize your data at this point, begin looking for relationships between different data objects. Finally, note in the data dictionary any data which the application will be retrieving from external sources.

3. Again, based on the feedback from your interviews, define a *functional description*, which specifies and details the ways in which you'll store data in the database, how users can retrieve the data, and what form the retrieval will take. For example, if users want to be able to dial the telephone directly from a record, and you've agreed to provide them with such functionality, it should be described within the functional description. You should focus as well on describing reports, forms, queries, and other specific database objects in detail within the functional description, though you don't need to describe them in such terms.

After developing the data dictionary and functional description, review them with a small sampling of your interviewing group. This is necessary to make sure you haven't missed any important data storage or application design issues. While reviewing your design with the end users at every phase in the application design process is important, resolving all possible issues before you begin the logical design of the application will greatly simplify your long-term development process.

After you've reviewed your data dictionary and functional description with the users, you can begin the design of the logical database, as described in the next section.

Step 2—Defining The Logical Database

The second step in any good design sequence is to define the logical database. During this phase of development, you won't deal with how the data will be stored physically—that is, its actual structure on the disk drive—but instead with how information is grouped logically within the database. Depending on the complexity of your application (and your corporate standards), this step may take the form of a series of sketches or may take the form of a more complete *information diagram*.

For the information diagram design, you'll translate the requirements established in Step 1—including both the data dictionary and the functional description. You must then translate these requirements into a model that provides a level of abstraction from the physical database. This model should represent data in terms of business entities and relationships, rather than in terms of tables and fields.

In other words, even if you're developing an application for a single department, that department may contain three business entities. You can visualize these entities as follows:

* Engineers who need specifics about projects

* Field managers who only need to know their contacts at the project subcontractors

* In-office managers who need to know rollup data about budgets and costs

Your information diagram, then, should represent these three entities. Although all three may access the same data, or subsets or supersets of that data, they all need the data in different forms. Your information diagram should show how the data and functionality within the application will be used to provide them with the data they need in the form they need it.

For example, a single data dictionary containing subcontractor information may describe both general and specific information about the subcontractor. The field manager may only need to know contact information about the subcontractor—

a few fields, available immediately. Engineers may need to know more about the subcontractor—what other projects it's worked on, what its safety rating has been, and so on. Such requirements may justify reports or a series of forms allowing them to drill down into information that may be problematic. In-office managers need to review rollup data about budgets and costs and may be the only ones with access to any of that information in a combined form. However, they should also be able to drill down into data to determine what other data the viewed data derives from; and they'll likely need both forms (for working with the data) and reports (for delivering the data in meetings).

As you can see, logical design tries to model the data in a way consistent with the end user's business model and needs. Your focus in this phase of development, again, is on making sure that you're effectively responding to the user's needs—and business-entity-based design will help you to do that more effectively.

As with the data dictionary and functional description, after developing the logical design, review it with a small sampling of your interviewing group—in this case, one individual from each of the groups you've established. Reviewing how well you meet the goals with the people they're applicable for is important—because although a manager may have a good idea what the engineers need, he or she will never have as good of an idea as the engineers themselves.

After you've reviewed your logical design with the users and obtained their agreement that your design meets their needs, you can begin the physical design of the database, as described in the next section.

Step 3—Defining The Physical Database

Physical design is the final phase in the design of an application. In this phase of design, individual data elements are given attributes and defined as fields in tables. Once you've performed this initial part of the design—making sure all the data within your dictionary is included, including references to any external data—you can begin to design the parts of the database that will bring it into accordance with your functional description and logical design.

During the design phase, you'll also deal with performance considerations, such as the use and creation of indexes, as well as the specifics of the database's design. For example, a common issue you must address is whether the database containing the data itself and the database containing the user interface are saved as the same file or separate files. Furthermore, you'll design the queries that make up the database, set the physical layout and location of the data files on the disk, and create all necessary supporting objects for the user interface (UI).

When creating items in the UI, queries, and other parts of the application that allow the user to manipulate the underlying information in ways consistent with the functional description and the logical design, you should make sure to closely consult the logical design. Consulting the logical design while you're developing the database will help to ensure your application's physical design remains consistent with its logical design.

The physical design of the application is, without question, the most time-consuming part of application or database creation. In the next chapter, we'll consider more of the specifics surrounding physical application design, particularly the application's user interface.

Chapter 18

Planning And Design

In Depth

It's likely that your first production-database application designed with Access 2000 will be used for decision-support purposes. Industry sources estimate that decision-support applications constitute 75 percent or more of all of the database applications in operation today. When you create a decision-support application for utilization with an existing relational database, you don't need to be concerned with database design, maintaining referential and domain integrity, or concurrency problems. (You do, however, need to take consistency issues into account if you're summarizing data.)

The purpose of a decision-support application is to transform raw data into useful information. Your primary task is to provide the users of your application with a simple, straightforward method of obtaining the data they need. This chapter begins by discussing how to organize the data you're converting into useful information with decision-support applications. The chapter also discusses designing the user interface to make your application easy to understand. Finally, the chapter reviews examples of the Access 2000 code needed to create the graph, chart, and grid objects that display the selected information to the user.

Organizing The Data Behind A Decision-Support Front End

The objective of most of today's decision-support applications is to replace printed reports with on-screen presentations of information. A successful decision-support application supplies information at your fingertips—both within the Access environment and, optimally, throughout your organization. For midlevel managers and below, the display of information on a PC—either a single, shared PC for a presentation or individual PCs in their offices—is the most common presentation platform. At the upper echelon of the corporate ladder, the information is often displayed on large-screen or projection video systems using one PC in a conference setting.

While organizing the data behind the front end is a complex, multistep process, specifying the sources of the data the front end will use is the first and defining step. The following section discusses data sources in detail.

Specifying The Data Sources

The usual relationships of data sources and information systems for a typical manufacturing company appear in the hierarchical structure shown in Figure 18.1. Data-entry and transaction-processing activities are primarily confined to the lowest level of the hierarchy: operational databases. (The operational database level of the hierarchy is often called the "trench" or the "data trench.") The levels above the operational databases involve little or no data entry; these upper levels in the hierarchy are referred to as information systems (IS) or management information systems (MIS). The diagram in Figure 18.1 divides the information-systems category into functional information systems at the directorate and vice president's level and planning and forecasting information systems used by top management and corporate staff.

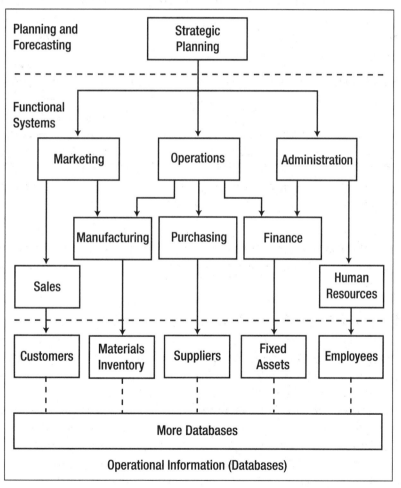

Figure 18.1   The hierarchy of information systems and databases for a manufacturing firm.

Depending on the size of the company and the type of computer hardware the firm uses, the operational databases may be located in a centralized mainframe system or distributed across several database servers in a client-server relational database management systems (RDBMS) environment. Combinations of mainframe and client-server environments are common for firms in the process of downsizing and distributing their operational databases. A small manufacturing firm might have all its operational databases in the form of multiple standalone database files that reside on a single file server.

If you're developing database applications for a firm with $10 million or more in annual sales, be prepared to deal with the connectivity issues raised by a wide variety of network operating systems and database management systems. These issues may include legacy data, legacy networks, and legacy network and hierarchical database management systems (DBMSs). It's common for developers of database front ends to spend more time solving connectivity problems, both DBMS- and network-related, than they spend designing, coding, and testing the entire front-end application.

You also may need to integrate data from online data sources into your database front-end application. Credit information from Dun and Bradstreet and TRW, stock prices from the Dow Jones News Service, and real estate transaction data are just a few of the uses for the data communication features of Access 2000. Another data source you may need to incorporate in your applications is the CD-ROM. Virtually all the 1990 census data is now available from the U.S. Bureau of the Census in exportable database format on CD-ROMs, and many companies publish phone, business, and other directories on CD-ROMs.

Once you have identified where your data is coming from, you can then start to consider the characteristics of the data you will be using. The first step is determining how much detail you want to display in your front end, as discussed in the next section.

Determining The Level Of Detail Required

Before the advent of the RDBMS and client-server computing technology, the principal source of functional information, as well as planning and forecasting information, was a multitude of printed reports. Each report was the product of a batch operation that required a program, usually written in COBOL, to execute the embedded SQL or other instructions that create a formatted report. In many cases, reports were created with more than the optimal level of detail because of a lack of programming resources to write, test, and deploy production programs to summarize the data. The capability for users of client applications to create their own ad hoc queries with whatever degree of detail they desire is the driving force behind the front-end application generator market.

Unless you're dealing with data that has been rolled up (the subject of the next section), your decision-support, front-end application accesses tables in operational databases. The level of detail you provide in a decision-support application usually varies inversely with the position of the users in the organizational hierarchy. As you progress upward in the corporate organizational chart, tabular data gives way to graphs and charts for trend analysis, and the frequency of reporting slows from daily to monthly. The list that follows describes the three basic categories of decision-support applications:

- *Executive summaries and planning information*—These consist of graphs and charts that depict financial performance versus internal projections and prior fiscal periods often against the results reported by competitors. This category of report is most likely to require integration of data from online sources operated by data utilities or from firms that specialize in providing online econometric data.

- *Functional summaries*—Reports of orders for the director of sales or daily cash-flow reports from the director of finance, for example, are most often run weekly. At the directorate level, tabular data is the rule. The data from the directors' reports usually is consolidated into monthly reports issued at the vice pres-ident's level. Graphs compare current operating results with recent historical data, usually for a one-year period or less.

- *Operational data summaries*—These are required by supervisory personnel to evaluate day-to-day performance at the departmental or regional level. Credit managers, for example, need realtime access to the payment histories of customers placing new orders. Exception-reporting applications, which are used on the shop floor (for example, applications that identify parts shortages or quality-control problems), may need to run on an hourly or shift basis. Tabular formats, rather than graphic presentations, are most common at the operational level.

Figure 18.2 is a diagram showing the layers of information that constitute typical marketing-decision support applications corresponding to the three categories in the preceding list.

The executive summary for the marketing VP consolidates sales of all products in all regions. The functional summary for the director of sales includes sales of a particular product line in all regions. The operational data viewed by the regional sales manager reports sales in one region for all products.

One of the principal objections of management personnel to MIS reports, whether displayed online or in the form of computer printouts, is excessive detail. If you use a 9-point MS Sans Serif font with a tightly spaced grid in your Access reports, you can display several times as much data on a single line of a single report as is

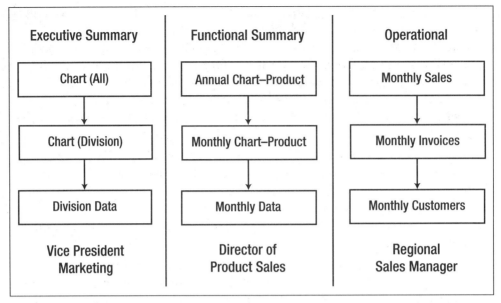

Executive Summary	Functional Summary	Operational
Chart (All)	Annual Chart–Product	Monthly Sales
Chart (Division)	Monthly Chart–Product	Monthly Invoices
Division Data	Monthly Data	Monthly Customers
Vice President Marketing	Director of Product Sales	Regional Sales Manager

Figure 18.2   Levels of information detail in summary and operational decision-support applications.

possible with a straight, 40-character width fixed output device. For management, it's the aggregated data that's important, together with exception highlighting. If you need to provide one or two levels of detail behind the summary data, first offer the detail behind the exceptions, then make additional detail information an option.

When you decide to show less data in your reports, depending on how you determine what data you will show, you may be performing a *rollup*—combining actual data to generate output data. One of the most important considerations in creating rollups is data consistency; another is application performance. The following section discusses both considerations in detail.

Maintaining Performance And Data Consistency With Rollups

Impatience is another personal trait that tends to increase with the level of authority and responsibility in an organization. Operatives in "the trenches" may be satisfied with an application that takes a minute or more to present a screen of data—an Access application running as a front end against a SQL Server back end can easily take 60 seconds to update, depending on the server's location and the size of the operative query. If your summary queries (especially cross-tab queries) need to traverse tens of thousands of records containing line items for a year's collection of invoices, you're certain to face an unsatisfied client when you deliver your production front end.

The traditional (and still the best) approach to maintaining adequate performance for time-series, decision-support applications is to consolidate time-based detail data into new tables. This process is called *rolling up data*. Consolidating data, other than creating monthly and yearly rollups for accounting purposes, has been relatively uncommon in PC-based database applications. Intel Pentium PCs running at clock speeds of 450MHz or greater have now become the most popular CPUs for database servers, and the cost of fixed disk storage is now as low as $25 per gigabyte. Therefore, the economic disincentive of replicating data is minimal.

Although rolling up data violates the no-duplicated-data rule for relational databases (because rolled up data is derived from existing tables), you'll probably want to aggregate data when your summary queries need to process more than a few thousand records. The following list details some of the most important guidelines for how and when to roll up data:

- Avoid cascading rollups when possible. A *cascading rollup* is a rollup operation that summarizes data that's been rolled up at a greater detail level. If a retroactive change to the underlying detail occurs, you need to reaggregate each level in the process.

- Roll up data at intervals likely to be the least subject to retroactive changes. An example is three-month rollups for corporations whose quarterly financial reports are subject to independent audit. Monthly rollups may be necessary to achieve acceptable application performance, but monthly rollups shouldn't be cascaded into quarterly aggregations because retroactive changes may be made in the underlying operational databases. Quarterly rollups are based on records in the operational databases.

- Never roll up data at the operational-database record level. An example of rolling up data at the operational level is the **Order Amount** field of the **Orders** table of the Northwind Traders database that was provided with Microsoft Access 2.0. This design abnormality was corrected in all newer versions of the sample database, including the one that ships with Access 2000. However, in Access 2, the value in the **Order Amount** field was the sum of the product of the **Order Quantity** and **Unit Price** fields of the line item records in the **Order Details** table for a single order. In such an environment, changes that occurred in the **Order Details** table, including partial shipments, had to be immediately rolled into records in the **Orders** table to maintain data consistency. Rollups should never have to be executed on a realtime basis.

- Roll up data during periods of transaction-processing inactivity, such as nights or weekends. One of the advantages of rolling up data is the elimination of consistency errors that can occur when you aggregate detail information being updated simultaneously. You can write a stored procedure that runs unattended on the server to roll up data at predetermined intervals if your application uses SQL Server or another client-server RDBMS that supports stored procedures.

In the typical information-system hierarchy illustrated in preceding Figure 18.1, rollups of sales, manufacturing, purchasing, finance, and human resources operational databases occur at the director level. Another rollup further consolidates data for the vice presidents of marketing, operations, and administration.

The performance improvement you can achieve by rolling up data enables you to design Access 2000 decision-support applications that replace slide shows created with PowerPoint or similar Windows-presentation applications. Using a presentation application to export and re-create graphs and tables in the form of slides is an inefficient, time-consuming process. Many firms now prepare monthly or weekly presentations by transferring summary data to presentation slides. A well-designed Access 2000 decision-support application can return its development cost many times by eliminating the data import and conversion steps. Your Access 2000 presentation application needs to be totally bulletproof, and you'll probably want to store the rolled up data on a local fixed disk to avoid the embarrassment that attends the appearance of blank screens or messages that read "Unable to connect to server" during the presentation.

TIP: *This type of presentation support is best implemented in Access 2000 through the use of Data Access Pages (DAPs) and some of the controls that come with Access, such as the PivotTable list control. You'll learn more about how to use design techniques to improve presentation of data in later chapters.*

Once you have your data sources identified, you need to implement a query strategy. The following sections discuss query strategies in detail.

Query Strategies

The sections that follow discuss some of the issues you need to resolve before you commit to a particular strategy to obtain the **Recordset** objects on which to base your decision-support applications.

Persistent Vs. Impersistent Queries

Decision-support applications that consist of a fixed feature set are likely candidates for the use of persistent **QueryDef** objects. You can only store **QueryDef** objects in Jet databases, so if you're planning to roll up data from client-server or mainframe databases, a Jet database is the most appropriate database type to store the rolled up data.

You can pretest your SQL statements by using Access 2000's query designer application to create and store **QueryDef** objects for rollup or direct queries. Access's query designer gives you a chance to preview the result of your query and to fine-tune the SQL statement that creates the **QueryDef**. Once you have the SQL statement optimized, you can substitute parameters for the independent variables you set to return records for specific regions, products, or time spans.

Alternatively, you can write the Jet SQL statement for a query, then pass the value of the SQL statement as a **String** variable to the **strSource** argument of an **OpenRecordset** statement in module code (or a **Connection** object, if you're using Active Data Objects [ADO]). The SQL statements of persistent **QueryDef** objects are stored, after parsing and optimizing, by the Jet database engine. The SQL statements you pass to the **OpenRecordset** method need to be parsed and optimized before being executed. In most cases, using a parameterized **QueryDef** object for rollups is faster than the **OpenRecordset** method with a SQL statement.

To optimize performance of your application, you need to test both persistent and impersistent versions of your queries. Access's Performance Analyzer is useful for comparing the performance of a **QueryDef** object versus executing a SQL statement dynamically.

Using Parameterized QueryDef Objects

If you're only changing one or two elements of a query, such as record-selection criteria in a **WHERE** clause, consider using a parameterized **QueryDef** object. Using a parameterized **QueryDef** object in an Access database is similar to passing arguments to stored procedures in SQL Server databases. The Jet SQL syntax required for you to specify that you intend to pass one or more parameters to the SQL statement of a QueryDef object is as follows:

```
PARAMETERS ParamName1 DataType1[, ParamName2 DataType2 [, ...]];
```

Parameters (**ParamName#**) and their corresponding SQL data types (**DataType#**) are passed in comma-separated pairs to a named parameter placeholder in the SQL statement, as shown here:

```
PARAMETERS State Text, DateStart DateTime, DateEnd DateTime;
SELECT * FROM Orders
WHERE [ShipRegion] = State
  AND [OrderDate] BETWEEN DateStart AND DateEnd;
```

The comma that separates the pair of parameter names and the SQL parameter data type is required. The semicolon (;) that terminates the list of parameters is also necessary. The values of the parameter names you pass can't match field names contained in any of the tables that participate in the query. If you insist on using illegal punctuation in your parameter name value (such as spaces or hyphens), enclose the parameter names within square brackets.

The permissible values for the **SQLType#** parameter component are listed in the SQL Parameter Type column of Table 18.1. Table 18.1 lists the conventional field data type name, the SQL parameter data type, the **Variant** data subtype, and the corresponding Visual Basic for Applications (VBA) fundamental data types for each of the SQL parameter data type identifiers corresponding to Microsoft open database connectivity (ODBC) SQL data types, not the American National Standard Institute's (ANSI) SQL data types.

The **Binary** and **Value** data types aren't supported by Access 2000 or Jet 4. You can't create a field of the Jet **Binary** or **Value** field data type; however, Microsoft Access offers **Binary** and **Value** options in the **Data Type** combo box of the Query Parameters dialog. As mentioned elsewhere in this book, Microsoft uses the **Binary** field data type for the System ID (SID) value of the **MSysAccounts** table of System.mdw. If you really want to use the **Binary** data type, you can make a copy of the System.mdw table with another name, import the table into an Access database, then alter the design of the table as desired.

You pass the value of the parameter—but not the SQL parameter data type—to the **QueryDef** object in the second to the last of the following generic statements:

```
Dim dbName As Database
Dim qdfQueryDef As QueryDef
Dim rstResult As Recordset
```

Table 18.1   Correspondence of Jet database field, Jet SQL parameter type, and Access 2000 data types.

Field Data Type	SQL Parameter Type	Variant Data Subtype	VBA Data Type
Yes/No	Bit	2	**Integer**
Byte	Byte	2	**Byte**
Number (Integer)	Integer	2	**Integer**
Number (Long Integer)	Long	3	**Long**
Number (Single)	IEEESingle	4	**Single**
Number (Double)	IEEEDouble	5	**Double**
Currency	Currency	6	**Currency**
Date/Time	DateTime	7	**Variant**
Text	Text	8	**String**
OLEObject	LongBinary	8	**String**
Memo	LongText	8	**String**
Binary	Binary	8	Not supported
Value	Value	N/A	Not supported

```
Set dbName = OpenDatabase("DatabaseName")
Set qdfQueryDef = dbName.QueryDefs("QueryName")
qdfQueryDef!ParamName = typDesiredValue
Set rstResult = qdfQueryDef.OpenRecordset([intOptions])
' Use Recordset
```

You must use the bang symbol (!) as the separator between **qdfQueryDef** and **ParamName**; using a period (.) separator generates a "Property not found" error message. You can also use the **Parameters** collection.

The object identifier for the **OpenRecordset** method is the **QueryDef** object, not the **Database** object. When you specify a **QueryDef** object as the object identifier for the **OpenRecordset** method, you don't supply a **strSource** or **objSource** argument. If you supply either of these arguments, you receive an "Invalid argument" error message.

An example of the use of a parameterized **QueryDef** object is given in the section titled, "Displaying Detail Data With The **MSFlexGrid** Control," that follows later in this chapter. You'll learn more about the code in this section in Chapter 28.

Designing Rollup Queries

Rollup queries are make-table queries you execute from within an Access 2000 application. Rollup queries use the SQL aggregate **SUM** function to total numeric values contained in tables of operational databases. Typically, a rollup query creates a new table with the following fields:

- *Period*—One or more fields that identify the range of dates for which the operational data is summed. You can use separate fields for the year and subperiod (quarter, month, or week). You also can combine these two fields with a coding system, such as 1999Q4 (fourth quarter of 1999), 199912 (December 1999), or 1999W52 (last week of 1999). As a rule, you'll find that using separate fields for the year and subperiod makes subsequent record selection simpler.

- *Attribute*—One or more optional fields that describe an object class or object. Attributes include categories of products, individual products, geographic regions, or persons (individual salespeople, for instance).

- *Value*—One or more numeric fields that contain the result of the summation of the values of operational database records for the period. If you use more than one value field in the rollup table, the operational database table must contain each of the fields. For example, you can sum both the **Quantity** and **[Unit Price]*Quantity** values of a table containing invoice line items to obtain total units sold and total sales, then divide total sales by total units sold to obtain average unit price.

The easiest method of developing rollup queries is to create a group of summary make-table query objects in Access. You then write a simple Access 2000 application to execute the query objects you created (you could even key the invocation of the make-table queries to something as simple as a command button).

The Chap18Dec.mdb sample database, which is included on the accompanying CD-ROM, contains several make-table query objects. (It also provides the rolled up data required by the sample decision-support forms in the sections later in this chapter.) The Jet SQL statement of the **qryMonthlySalesRollup QueryDef** object that creates the data for a graph might look similar to the following (and does, in the sample database):

```
SELECT Format(Orders.[ShippedDate],"yyyy") AS Year,
    Format(Orders.[ShippedDate],"mm") AS Month,
SUM([Order Details].[UnitPrice]*[Order Details].Quantity*
    (1-[Order Details].Discount)) AS Sales
INTO tblSalesRollupMonth
FROM Orders, [Order Details]
WHERE Orders.[OrderID]=[Order Details].[OrderID]
GROUP BY Format(Orders.[ShippedDate],"yyyy"),
    Format(Orders.[ShippedDate],"mm")
HAVING Format([Orders].[ShippedDate],"yyyy") = "1998";
```

The SQL statement differs from ANSI SQL syntax in the use of the VBA **Format**() function to return parts of dates (in the **Year** and **Month** fields) and in the **GROUP BY** and **HAVING** clauses. If this query was executed with the SQL pass-through option (that is, if it was running against a SQL Server or other back end), you'd replace the **Format** function with the appropriate ANSI SQL scalar function, **YEAR** or **MONTH**. The **GROUP BY** aggregations you use must correspond exactly to the corresponding **SELECT** descriptors in your SQL statement.

The **SUM( )** SQL aggregate function totals the net sale amount, taking into account the discount, if any, offered to the customer on a particular product. The **INTO** statement identifies the name of the table that's created by the query. The initial **GROUP BY** criterion that groups orders by the year in which the order was shipped is included in the **GROUP BY** clause because you might want to specify more than one year in the **HAVING** clause with an **AND** operator.

If the **tblSalesRollupMonth** table doesn't exist, the query creates the table. If the **tblSalesRollupMonth** table exists, the existing table is deleted before the new table is created.

Most of the other make-table **QueryDef** objects in Chap18Dec.mdb are more complex than the **qryMonthlySalesRollup** query. You can examine the syntax of each **QueryDef** object by opening the **QueryDef** object in the Access Interactive Development Environment's (IDE's) SQL view.

TIP: *You may encounter a special problem with some rollup queries in Jet databases that use **AutoNumber** or **Counter** field types. The Jet database engine doesn't permit you to create tables that have more than one **AutoNumber** field. If your rollup queries try to combine data from two or more tables and if you include more than one **AutoNumber** field in the rollup table, the query will fail. For example, if you try to use a rollup query like **qryMonthlySalesRollup** (included in the Chap18Dec.mdb sample database for this chapter) directly on the **Categories** and **Products** tables in the Northwind.mdb sample database supplied with Access, it won't work. The error occurs because the query attempts to create a new table containing the **ProductID** (from the **Products** table) and the **CategoryID** (from the **Categories** table) fields. Unfortunately, both of these fields are **AutoNumber** fields. The **qryMonthlySalesRollup** query works in the Chap18Dec.mdb sample database because the **Categories** and **Products** tables have had all their **AutoNumber** fields converted to **Number** fields with a **Long Integer** format.*

*When creating your own rollup tables, you may first need to isolate the data you want in an intermediary table, then change the **AutoNumber** field data types to **Number** fields with **Long Integer** format to create the rollup tables you desire.*

To execute make-table queries with VBA code, you apply the **Execute** method to the **QueryDef** object. The **Execute** method is applicable only to action queries; you receive an error message if you attempt to apply the **Execute** method to a **SELECT** or **TRANSFORM** (crosstab) query that returns rows. As an example, the following code executes each of the six make-table **QueryDef** objects in Chap18Dec.mdb:

```
Dim dbDecSupport As Database
Set dbDecSupport = CurrentDb()
dbDecSupport.Execute "qryMonthlySalesRollup", dbFailOnError
dbDecSupport.Execute "qryMonthlySalesRollupCategory", dbFailOnError
dbDecSupport.Execute "qryMonthlySalesRollupProduct", dbFailOnError
dbDecSupport.Execute "qryQuarterlySalesRollup", dbFailOnError
dbDecSupport.Execute "qryQuarterlySalesRollupCategory", dbFailOnError
dbDecSupport.Execute "qryQuarterlySalesRollupProduct", dbFailOnError
```

Alternatively, you can substitute a make-table query statement for the name of a **QueryDef** object. In some previous versions of Access, the **ExecuteSQL** method was used for SQL pass-through queries to create tables from a client-server database connected by the ODBC API. The **ExecuteSQL** method is obsolete; you now use the **Execute** method with the **dbSQLPassThrough** option flag for client-server queries.

While creating predefined queries is an important part of database design, you will find that no developer can predict all the possible combinations of queries. Users may want data in different formats than what you have provided, may want to combine data in different ways, and so on. Building in support for user queries that users can create on the fly is the discussion in the next section.

18. Planning And Design

Implementing Ad Hoc Queries

One of the incentives for purchasing database front-end application generators is their users can generate their own ad hoc queries against large databases. The intensity of the desire to create ad hoc queries usually is inversely proportional to the individual's position in the corporate hierarchy. In the upper corporate echelons, executives want the click of a single button to deliver the summary information they need. At the operational level, managers and supervisors want the opportunity to choose from a multiplicity of record-selection options.

When an unhindered user executes a **SELECT** * query against large mainframe or client-server databases, it can bring even the highest performance RDBMS to its knees. Accidentally or intentionally returning all of the records in a monster table can cause severe network congestion, at least until the user's RAM and disk swap file space is exhausted. The worst-case scenario is the accidental creation of a Cartesian product by the omission of a join condition when more than one table is involved in a query. Some RDBMSs detect this condition and refuse to execute the query. Others, such as applications that use the Jet database engine, attempt to return every combination of records in the tables.

Don't create decision-support applications that enable users to enter their own **SELECT** statements against production databases. Use combo boxes or list boxes to restrict the fields to be displayed and to add required **WHERE** clause record-selection criteria.

Now that you have considered many of the issues related to the actual data that you will display within your front end, you can begin to design the front end itself. The following sections discuss the creation of the user interface.

Designing The User Interface

Windows achieved its commercial success because Windows 3.x had a graphic interface that most users preferred to the DOS command-line prompt. Windows 9x took that early interface to the next level, making it easier to use and more intuitive. Windows applications now dominate the PC software market because they use design elements which, at least in most cases, conform to the Common User Access (CUA) architecture developed by IBM in the 1980s. The CUA specification describes the design and operation of menus and other common control objects, such as checkboxes, radio (now option) buttons, and message boxes.

The primary objective of the CUA specification is to create uniformity in the overall appearance and basic operational characteristics of computer applications. CUA principles apply to character-based DOS applications executed on PCs and to mainframe sessions running on 3270 terminals. The user interface of Microsoft Windows 3.x, Windows 9x, Windows NT, and IBM OS/2 for PCs, XWindows and

Motif for Unix systems, and MacOS all conform in most respects to IBM's basic CUA specification. Therefore, if you're accustomed to Word for the Macintosh, you can quickly adapt to using Word for the PC.

The sections that follow describe some of the basic requirements of the user interface for database decision-support applications designed for use at the upper-management level. Subsequent chapters in this book provide similar guidance for more flexible decision-support applications and data-entry (online transaction-processing) applications.

Optimizing Application Usability

The usability of mainstream Windows applications ultimately determines the products' success in the software market. Feature-list comparisons in product advertising and magazine reviews may influence the purchasing decisions of individual users, but the primary purchasers of Windows applications are large corporations. The objective of these corporate purchasers is to minimize the time and training expenses required for their personnel to learn and to use the applications effectively. Thus, applications are rated by their usability, a wholly subjective attribute. An application that one user finds intuitive and easy to use may be totally incomprehensible to another user.

Testing applications for usability is an art, not a science, and it's a primitive art at best. Commercial firms that conduct usability tests on major software products can charge $250,000 or more for testing relatively simple Windows applications. Microsoft (needless to say) has invested tens of millions of dollars in usability testing of their operating system and applications products. It's quite unlikely that the applications you create will undergo commercial usability tests. Instead, your client may simply inform you that he or she doesn't understand how to use your application without reading the manual. When that happens, your application has just failed the ultimate usability test.

The following sections describe characteristics of applications that achieve high usability ratings and show you how to implement these characteristics in the forms that constitute a simple executive-level, decision-support application.

Striving For Simplicity

When you design decision-support applications, your watchword is *simplicity*. Application simplicity is achieved by applying the following rules to your application design:

Don't add features to an application that aren't needed to accomplish the client's fundamental objective. When in doubt, don't implement a feature that isn't in the minimum capabilities list. Wait for the client to request additional features. If you need special features to test the application, hide these features from other users.

18. Planning And Design

Don't attempt to display more than one type of information on a single form. For example, don't combine graphs and tabular information on the same form. Instead, hide the graph window and show the window with the tabular data.

The preceding two rules are especially important for executive-summary, decision-support applications, because top executives are unlikely to be PC power users. A simple, intuitive user interface and a limited feature list are the two primary characteristics of professional-quality, executive-summary applications.

Figure 18.3 illustrates the first form of a hypothetical executive-summary, decision-support application that displays sales information for a one-year period. A button bar is the primary navigation device for the application, enabling the user to make the following choices:

- Display total corporate sales by month, using a line graph that also includes lines representing the statistical arithmetic mean and the best-fit slope for the period.

- Display monthly sales by division, with a stacked vertical bar chart or an area chart.

- Display sales by product for the year to date or for a particular quarter or month, in pie chart format.

- Attach the current object or parts of the object displayed by the form to an email message that requests additional data about a particular element of an object. The graph, chart, or selected cells of a grid control in the window is copied to the clipboard, then pasted into an email message.

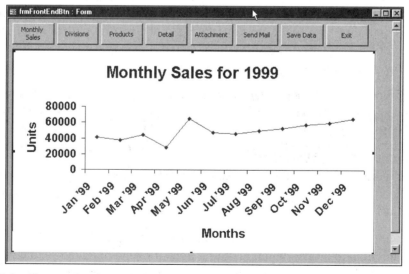

Figure 18.3   The opening form of an executive-summary, decision-support application.

- Create an email message that requests information about, or that makes comments on, the object pasted into the message.

- Save the current data, messages, and annotations in a file for future reference.

- Exit the application when finished with the review of the current data.

The data source for the forms for Figures 18.3 through 18.6 is Chap18Dec.mdb, which is contained on the accompanying CD-ROM. Chap18Dec.mdb uses tables attached from Crosstab.mdb and expects to find Crosstab.mdb in the same directory as the file. Data for the year 1998 is shown in these examples because 1998 is the latest year for which 12 months of data is available in Northwind.mdb, on which Crosstab.mdb is based. If you installed either Crosstab.mdb or Chap18Dec.mdb in a location other than their default directory, you need to change the values in the code that point to the default directory, and you need to reattach the Crosstab.mdb tables to Chap18Dec.mdb.

The following list describes the design principles embodied in the decision-support form shown in Figure 18.3:

- The form uses Windows 95's standard neutral gray background to present a conservative appearance and to avoid strong contrast with colored objects. Large areas of white or vivid colors are distracting to the user of an application.

- There's no opening form or splash screen. A splash screen is a form or design element that identifies the application. (An example of a splash screen is the copyright message that appears when you first launch Word, Excel, or other mainstream Windows applications.) You may need an initial login window to obtain the password required to start the application and to log the user into a secure database.

- The button bar presents large targets for the mouse. Each tab has a caption to explain the purpose of the button. Button bars and toolbars that substitute for common menu choices are common in today's Windows applications. Alternatively, you can use Access 2000's 32-bit Toolbar control to provide a toolbar that matches those of other 32-bit Windows applications.

- A menu is provided to enable the user to make choices that aren't implemented by tabs. In production applications, a menu choice duplicates the action of each tab or button on a toolbar.

- The form is designed to occupy almost all of the display area in normal mode. The form doesn't have sizable borders (**BorderStyle = 1, Fixed Single**), and no maximize button is provided (**MaxButton = False**), so the width of the form is forced to correspond to the total width of the tab set. When you're designing the application for presentation, set the size of the form to the entire display area—but make sure that your application is smart enough to analyze the display area and to analyze the terminal on which the application is running, and respond appropriately.

The preferred user interface for decision-support applications is the multiple-document interface (MDI) child forms that display documents (graphs, charts, and tables) with common menus and button bars.

The form shown in Figure 18.3 (and the forms of Figures 18.4 and 18.5, which follow) can serve as the foundation of the form designs for the majority of decision-support applications you might need to design.

The VBA code that supplies the values on which the graphs shown in this chapter are based is described in the section, "Creating Graphs From Rolled-Up Data," later in this chapter.

Maintaining Consistency

Both external and internal consistency of the user interface is a principal requirement of a properly designed Windows application. The following list describes these two types of consistency:

- External (exogenous) consistency means that the appearance and behavior of your application is similar to other mainstream Windows applications. When, for example, your client primarily uses Office applications, the appearance and operational characteristics of your application should be modeled on Excel, Outlook, or some other application.

- Internal (endogenous) consistency implies that the appearance of all of the forms and the behavior of all of the controls on the forms that constitute your application is similar. If the behavior of a button or menu choice needs to differ under certain conditions, change the appearance of the icon (change a color, for example) or alter the **Caption** property value for the menu choice.

Here are the rules for maintaining external application consistency:

- Choose a mainstream Windows application as the model for your application's button bar or toolbar. Microsoft Exchange is a good choice as a model for button bar forms, and Excel's standard toolbar represents a good starting point for forms needing more than eight buttons.

- Buttons with icons identical to or similar to icons found in other mainstream applications should perform the same or similar functions in your application.

- Use a consistent font for button captions. Microsoft uses the 8.25-point MS Sans Serif Roman font for most button captions and as the default typeface for numeric values; your application should follow suit. Roman is the term for a font with no attributes—for example, no bolding, italics, or underlining.

- Use a common menu and button bar on an MDI parent form and employ MDI child forms or subforms or some other sequencing technology to present graphs, charts, and grid controls based on your application's queries.

- Windows 9x common dialogs (used for opening and saving files, as well as for other common operations) and message boxes usually have a sculpted appearance and a light gray background.

You need to meet the following criteria to maintain internal consistency:

- All the forms that constitute the application should have a similar appearance. Background colors, typeface families, and the size of display elements should remain constant throughout the application. It's easier to read sans serif fonts, such as Arial and MS Sans Serif, than fonts with serifs, such as Times New Roman or MS Serif. Use the bold attribute for label captions, graph and chart labels and legends, and numerical values in grid controls. Use standard bitmapped and TrueType fonts that are supplied with Windows 9x; let users change the fonts to their own favorites but only if absolutely necessary.

- The location and sequence of navigation devices should remain constant for all forms. Buttons and menu choices that appear on more than one form always appear in the same sequence and in the same position (where feasible).

- Icons used to identify objects or operations should have the same appearance in all forms. If the images you use for the icons adequately represent and distinguish the objects or operations, you can eliminate captions in second-level forms in which you need more buttons than will fit in a single row if the buttons have captions.

Figure 18.4 is an example of a form that uses a toolbar-style row of buttons, rather than a button bar. The toolbar form is internally consistent with the button bar form shown in Figure 18.3. The difference between a toolbar and a button bar is that the buttons of a toolbar are placed within a designated area of the form (usually at the top). A background margin surrounds individual buttons or groups of buttons in toolbars. Using smaller buttons without captions often is necessary when you have more buttons on forms than can be accommodated by the width of the display.

Identifying Toolbar Button Functions

It's difficult to create a collection of small icons (about 24×24 pixels) that unambiguously represents a variety of operations. Figure 18.5 illustrates the use of a Toolbar control with tooltips (pop-up labels built into the toolbar button object) that appear when the mouse pointer is positioned on the surface of the button. The Toolbar control was introduced in Visual Basic 4 and made its way over to

18. Planning And Design

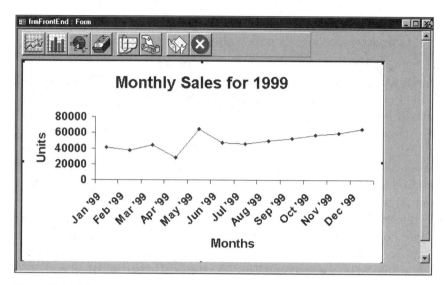

Figure 18.4   Using toolbar-style buttons instead of a button bar.

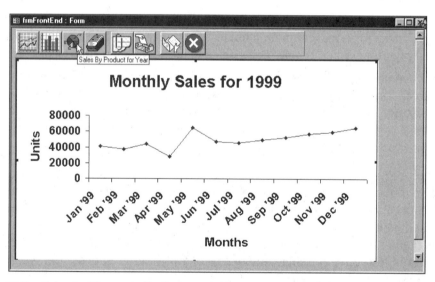

Figure 18.5   Using tooltips and a Toolbar control for buttons on a form.

Access with Access 97. The toolbar in Figure 18.5 is a single object containing a collection of button objects. The tooltips that appear are a property of the button. To make these tooltip labels appear, you simply set the **ToolTipText** property of the particular button. All of the code needed to display and hide the tooltips is intrinsic to the Toolbar control.

By using the Toolbar control, you can easily create a "look and feel" for your applications similar to that found in Office 2000. By changing the **Visible** property of a

Toolbar control, you can provide your application with multiple toolbars; the Toolbar control even has an **AllowCustomize** property which, if **True**, permits your application's user to customize the toolbars in your application.

Using tooltips for the buttons in a Toolbar control is a better method of identifying the purpose of a button than displaying the same information in a status bar at the bottom of a form. No eye movement is necessary to read the adjacent label caption, whereas a substantial eye movement is required to traverse the display from the top toolbar to the bottom status bar. Minimizing the eye movement required to accomplish each of the application's tasks is one of the principles of good user interface design.

Once you have determined the navigational items that you will use within your application's interface, you can design those items. The following section discusses the creation of graphics for use with your application's navigation.

Creating And Using Graphical Command Buttons And Toolbars

The documentation that accompanies Access 2000 describes how to use the graphics capabilities of Access 2000 but provides little or no practical advice for adding images to command buttons and other controls. The "Immediate Solutions" section describes how to obtain the bitmapped images you need for your toolbar buttons and how to create Windows bitmap (BMP) files with Windows Paint. This section also details how to add the image contained in a BMP file to the **Picture** property of a command button.

In additional to navigational graphics, your applications should generally also support the display of summary information in graphical form. In general, such information will display best with a chart or a graph, as discussed in the next section.

Creating Graphs From Rolled-Up Data

The Microsoft Chart ActiveX control (version 6) that's included with Access 2000 enables you to create a variety of graphs and charts from data supplied by your application's queries. This chapter distinguishes between the terms *graph* and *chart*. A graph consists of data points, usually connected by lines. A chart uses two-dimensional objects, such as bars or other filled-screen areas, to represent the data. Graphs and charts usually employ display colors or print patterns to distinguish sets of data. All the graphs and charts in the sample forms discussed in this chapter use rolled-up data created by the set of make-table queries discussed in the preceding section of this chapter.

18. Planning And Design

Just as you will often display rolled-up data in a chart form, your applications will often want to display detail data in a grid- or spreadsheet-style display. You have several options of how to do this, including sub-datasheets and controls. The following section discusses one of the controls you can use, the Microsoft FlexGrid control.

Displaying Detail Data With The MSFlexGrid Control

The FlexGrid control is Access 2000's primary method of displaying the tabular detail behind a graphical presentation (without using the Spreadsheet control or a subform). Unlike subforms, the FlexGrid control can't be linked to a **Recordset** object directly. For the FlexGrid control, however, you can write a simple VBA routine to display data created by the **qryMonthlyProductSalesParam** query from the **Products** table and the **qryMonthlyProductSalesCrosstab** query of Chap18Dec.mdb. The SQL statements used to create the two **QueryDef** objects that you use to generate a Snapshot-type **Recordset** object (which you manipulate to supply data to the grid) are as follows:

```
TRANSFORM Sum(tblProductRollupMonth.Sales) AS SumOfSales
SELECT tblProductRollupMonth.[ProductID]
FROM tblProductRollupMonth
GROUP BY tblProductRollupMonth.[ProductID]
PIVOT tblProductRollupMonth.Month
    IN ("01","02","03","04","05","06","07","08","09","10","11","12");
PARAMETERS CategID Text;
SELECT Products.[ProductID], Products.[ProductName],
    [01], [02], [03], [04], [05], [06], [07], [08], [09],
    [10], [11], [12]
FROM qryMonthlyProductSalesCrosstab, Products,
    qryMonthlyProductSalesCrosstab RIGHT JOIN Products
    ON qryMonthlyProductSalesCrosstab.[ProductID] =
    Products.[ProductID]
WHERE Products.[CategoryID]=CategID;
```

The SQL **TRANSFORM** statement creates a crosstab query that it returns as a Snapshot-type **Recordset** object that consists of the **ProductID** field's column and 12 monthly columns labeled 01 through 12. One row is created for each product. The **IN** predicate is added to ensure that the query returns 12 columns, even if no data is available for all of the months of the year. The **SELECT** statement uses the **Recordset** object created by the **TRANSFORM** statement as if the **Recordset** were a persistent table.

TIP: *Using a Snapshot-type rather than a Dynaset-type **Recordset** object usually is faster when your query result set contains less than about 100 rows. (Summary decision-support forms should never contain large numbers of rows.) Decision-support applications don't modify data, so there's generally no reason to specify a Dynaset-type **Recordset** for most summary queries.*

The purpose of the parameterized **SELECT** query is to ensure that all rows for products within a category designated by the **CategID** parameter appear in the resulting **Recordset**, regardless of whether sales of the product occurred during the year, and to supply a column containing the name of the product. An SQL **RIGHT JOIN** clause is needed to make all of the products in the category appear. You need to use Jet SQL for the **JOIN** statement because the Jet database engine doesn't recognize the ANSI SQL =* operator that designates a right join.

The code with the data from the parameterized **qryMonthlyProductSalesParam** query doesn't vary greatly from the code used to create graphs with multiple data sets. You can see the operative code within the mdlGrid.bas VBA code file.

If your queries return relatively few (less than 100) rows to a FlexGrid control, the performance of your Access 2000 application is likely to be much better than an identical VB application created with a DBGrid control bound to a Dynaset-type **Recordset** of a Data control. As the number of rows increases, the DBGrid control gains the advantage because Jet only returns 100 or so records to **Recordset** objects of the Dynaset type before painting the subform. If you fill the FlexGrid control in the **Form_Load** event handler with the data from a few hundred or more rows, your form takes substantially longer to open.

18. Planning And Design

Immediate Solutions

Obtaining And Modifying Button Bitmaps

Access 2000 includes a plethora of icons and bitmaps you can use to decorate conventional, 3D command and group pushbuttons or as the button faces for toolbar buttons. All of the buttons used in the button bar and toolbar forms in Figures 18.3 through 18.5 are based on icons Access 2000 installs in your Clip Art folders (if you instruct it to do so). Figure 18.6 displays a list view of the icons provided in the Icons\Arrows folder, which you can also use within your applications. (Because these are ICO files, Windows 9x is able to display the actual icon image in the directory listing; you'll need to use the QuickView option from the Explorer pop-up menu or the Paint program to view the appearance of the sample bitmaps supplied with Access 2000.)

You may use either ICO or BMP files to provide the **Picture** properties of buttons.

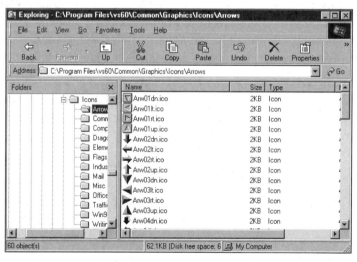

Figure 18.6   Some of the icons provided within the Icons\Arrows folder.

Generating Bitmaps With Desktop Publishing Packages

Many full-featured, vector-based drawing packages are available on the market today. Most include a variety of clip art images you can use (or adapt for use) as button faces in your applications. Some desktop publishing applications come with several thousand clip art images on the CD-ROM. In addition, you can purchase CD-ROM disks packed with nothing but various clip art images.

When you open the icons or clip art images in commercial publishing packages, the image is typically much larger than you need or want for a button bitmap. Generally, you must reduce the image to create a bitmap that's approximately 0.25 inch high. Add a light gray background color to the image so the background matches the default background color of Access 2000 buttons. You'll probably have to export the image from its original clip art format, which is usually some type of vector drawing format, rather than a bitmap. When you export the clip art image, export it to a 16-color Windows bitmap (BMP) format file.

Adding Code To Show And Hide Forms

The event handler for the event that responds when the user clicks on a button in the button bar or toolbar (except the button that represents the currently se-lected form) should use the **Show** method to open the new form. It should then use the **Hide** method to make the current form temporarily disappear. If the form you select hasn't been opened, the **Show** method automatically executes the **Load** method. (Using the **Load** method by itself doesn't create an instance of a form's window.) You can force a form's **Load** method to execute every time by using the VBA **Unload** statement instead of the **Hide** method.

The generalized code structure for showing and hiding forms is this:

```
Sub btnButtonName_Click
  frmNewFormName.Show
  [DoEvents]
  frmCurrentFormName.Hide
End Sub
```

To prevent your application from disappearing from the display, apply the **Show** method to the new form before you **Hide** the currently open form. The optional **DoEvents** statement enables Windows to process the messages necessary to dis-play the **frmNewFormName** form before hiding the window that displays the current form. **DoEvents** is necessary only when you load a form that has a sub-stantial amount of code that needs to be executed when the **Form_Load** event of the new form is triggered.

18. Planning And Design

Generating Line Graphs

The graph showing monthly sales for 1999, as shown in Figure 18.3 earlier in this chapter, uses Chap18Dec.mdb's **tblSalesRollupMonth** table created by the **qryMonthlySalesRollup** make-table query from data contained in Crosstab.mdb. Most of the properties of the graph are set in design mode. When you view the Monthly Sales for 1999 graph in design mode, the data points that create the sales line are created by a random number generator. In run mode, dynamic properties and the values of each data point are supplied by your code.

Unless you want to create an animated graph, in which displaying the individual data points is delayed by a timer control, you send the data to the Chart custom control in the **Form_Load** event. The companion CD-ROM includes the necessary code for the drawing of the chart within the **Form_Load** event of the **frmChartDisplay** form.

Chapter 19

Database Construction

In Depth

After you complete the analysis of what you want or need to maintain within your databases and after you've sketched out a model for what your database will contain—including the business rules, information rules, and other crucial parts of the database model—you can create the database. Converting conceptual and real-world rules to database design specifics is arguably one of the most difficult tasks the database developer faces.

In this chapter, we'll consider some of the specific steps you must follow to convert your design to an implementation. We'll look briefly at some overriding concepts of table design, return once again to normalization rules, and also consider some of the issues surrounding relationships and queries as they relate to design specifics. In the "Immediate Solutions" section of this chapter, we'll consider some of the important documentation steps you should take when creating the database from the design. We'll also discuss some of the important integration issues you must consider (and how the integration process might work) when designing an application that will be expected to work with other applications in your organization.

Converting The Design To Implementation

This chapter presumes that you've completed an information design diagram that you'll then use to create the database. The information design diagram should, at a minimum, include generalized layouts of all the information the database will maintain and important relationships between the data in the database. Optimally, the information design diagram will include all of the following:

- A listing of all atomic data you'll maintain—for example, a customer's phone number, extension, and receptionist's name.

- A diagram of the relationships between the data in specific locations and the data in other locations—for example, a customer number may have relationships to an invoice table, which, in turn, would have a relationship to an accounts receivable query, and so on.

- A list of queries that will combine information from multiple tables and information describing what the queries will maintain.

- A list of all reports the application will generate, including the underlying tables or queries that return the data the reports use.

Figure 19.1 shows an example of an information diagram and the information that the diagram must maintain. We'll use the information diagram in Figure 19.1 as the model for our database design throughout the rest of this chapter.

As you should be able to tell from the diagram, the figure describes a simple point-of-sale system. The goal is to track customers and orders, as well as sales. The system makes certain presumptions about the nature of the sales the company performs, which should be obvious from the simplicity of the diagram. Some of the most important assumptions include the following:

- Customers pay for orders as soon as they're placed, and all orders are paid for the same way (cash).

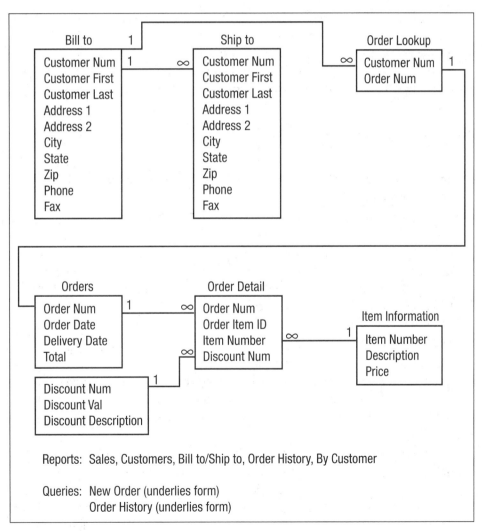

Figure 19.1   The information diagram for the Chap19.mdb database.

- Customers may have multiple Ship To addresses, which may or may not be the same as the Bill To address, but in no case should a customer have more than one Bill To address.

- Customers are purchasing only items—not services, per se. In the event customers were purchasing services (such as landscaping services in addition to plants), you would have to create more relationships to allow for the differences in billing services rather than products.

- Order information isn't changed materially after the order is entered initially—if it were, the **Total** field in the **Orders** table would belong instead in one of the queries, and would likely be generated on the fly, rather than being a static value.

- Whatever discounts the company offers are always within certain predefined criteria, and are also not set on the fly—for example, a 10 percent discount is always for a specific purpose. Moreover, customers don't have discount levels associated with them individually, indicating that the only time the company offers discounts is during a sale or other similar companywide discount offering.

- The reports will generate simple summary information. The four specified reports will indicate total sales by date, a full customer list, a list of customers having both Bill To and Ship To addresses that contains both addresses, and an order history by customer. The last report lets you track what products a customer has ordered in the past, how often, and so on.

- The queries the database will support will likely be the underlying information sources for both the reports and the forms, as any type of useful information you might want to retrieve from the database will require the combination of information from one or more tables. Although the outline only describes queries for the forms, the designer is likely to find during implementation that he also uses queries for the reports. In fact, over the course of the chapter, you'll see how using a query will help you build the reports.

- The information diagram also details the relationships the table will support. Clearly, the designer knows a little about database design, even going so far as to use indicators describing the nature of the relationship between tables— one-to-one, one-to-many, and so on. However, even if these weren't in the diagram, deducing what the relationships would be is a relatively straightforward process.

- In certain cases, you'll probably want to use a lookup to return certain information; for example, you'll want the **Description** field from the **ItemInformation** table to be accessed from a lookup in the **Order** form. However, you'll also want to maintain further information about the lookup's nature—because you'll want to use the **ItemNumber** field to determine the **Price** to display within the order form.

Although there's much more information to be gleaned from this simple sketch, these bullet points should give you a pretty good idea of the type of information you can, and should, be able to draw out pretty easily from a good information diagram. You should also be able to see potential holes in the diagram before you begin your design—for example, the question raised previously as to whether or not the discount information should be associated with customers.

TIP: *A good information diagram can be the difference between a relatively smooth database design and a process that takes longer than it should, requires additional input from the users, and generally just drags on indefinitely. You should always make sure your information diagrams—particularly before you begin the design of an application that you intend to deploy throughout your organization—contain an accurate and complete depiction of the information you'll need to maintain within the database.*

Furthermore, good information diagrams will save users time, forcing them to think through design issues with you well in advance of the application's deployment, saving them frustration as well. In short, good design means good implementation, and the more involved the end users and the others who'll actually access the information are, the sooner in the process, the better your final application will be when you deploy it.

Once you're comfortable that your design is accurate and complete, you can begin to convert the design to a database implementation. You will learn how to do so in the next section.

Creating The Tables The Information Diagram Specifies

The first step in creating the tables is to make sure that all of the information in the original diagram is normalized. Remember, as you've seen in multiple, previous chapters, five levels of normalization are specified in the principles of database design:

- *First normal form*—The first normal form requires that tables be flat and contain no repeating groups. A data cell of a flat table may contain only one atomic (indivisible) data value. If your imported data contains multiple data items in a single field, you need to add one or more new fields to contain each data item before moving the multiple data items into the new field.

- *Second normal form*—The second normal form requires that all data in nonkey fields of a table be fully dependent on the primary key and on each element (field) of the primary key when the primary key is a composite primary key. "Fully dependent on" is a synonym for "uniquely identified by."

- *Third normal form*—The third normal form requires that all nonkey fields of a table be dependent on the table's primary key and be independent of one another. Thus, the data in a table must be normalized to second normal form to ensure dependency on the primary key. The issue here is the dependencies of nonkey fields. A field is dependent on another field if a change in the value of one nonkey field forces a change in the value of another nonkey field.

- *Fourth normal form*—The fourth normal form requires that independent data entities not be stored in the same table when many-to-many relations exist between these entities. If many-to-many relations exist between data entities, the entities aren't truly independent; therefore, such tables usually fail the third normal form test. The fourth normal form requires you to create a relation table containing any data entities that have many-to-many relations with other tables.

- *Fifth normal form*—The fifth normal form requires that you be able to exactly reconstruct the original table from the new table(s) into which the original table was decomposed or transformed. Applying the fifth normal form to your resulting table is a good test to make sure you didn't lose data in the process of decomposition or transformation.

Ensuring that your design meets these criteria before you start the implementation will save you much time later. In the design that we've seen for this chapter, the diagram meets (in general), all of the forms, with certain allowances for the limitations of Access. However, you should also consider the use of keys within your implementation, as discussed in the next section.

Considering Primary And Foreign Keys In The Implementation

In addition to ensuring that your table design meets the specifics of the information detailed within the diagram, you should also consider the creation and maintenance of a primary key for each table within the database. In the information diagram in Figure 19.1, the diagram itself indicates both the primary and foreign keys for all the tables that make up the database. As you learned in earlier chapters, a *primary key* is a unique value that references every single record in the table. In general, a primary key will be an autosequencing number, which Access will automatically increment for you each time the user enters a new record. However, there may also be times when you'll use other field types for a primary key, or, as seen in the **OrderLookup** table, you'll use a combination of fields to indicate the primary key. In the **OrderLookup** table, neither the **CustomerNum** foreign key nor the **OrderNum** foreign key will ever be unique—at least not with any level of confidence.

However, because both keys are unique within their own tables, the combination of the two fields should be unique within the **OrderLookup** table. Therefore, when you design the table, you should specify that the combination of the two fields will be the primary key for the table. Alternately, you could add a third field to the table which contained an **Autonumber** field and specify that field as the primary key, but doing so lends no benefit to the database's design, and in actuality will result in the waste of space within the database. Moreover, adding a third field to the cross-referencing table creates an unnecessary level of complexity within the table as to the table's purpose that may confuse or even mislead another developer working with the table at a later date.

Creating The Application Database And The Table Database

As you've learned in previous chapters, it's always beneficial to design your tables as two different sets of tables—one that actually maintains the data within the database (the Table database) and one that maintains only links to the data but also contains all of the front-end information (the Application database). In Access 2000, this consideration is even more important because of the relative simplicity of migration to a client-server platform. The Application database can then be converted to an Access Data Project (ADP), while the Table database can be easily migrated to SQL Server 7 with the Upsizing Wizard.

In the "Immediate Solutions" section of this chapter, after you create the Table database, you'll then create the Application database, within which you'll place the queries, forms, and reports that access the data within the database. Once you have created the table objects within the database, you should go ahead and define the relationships between those objects, as discussed in the next section.

Specifying The Database Relationships

After you design the tables that will comprise the database, you must then specify the relationships between the tables. Again, the information diagram in Figure 19.1 provides a more-than-adequate guide to the creation of relationships between the tables. Moreover, the diagram also specifies the direction of the relationships and their definitions. In most cases, however, your initial diagram of the database's construction won't include the relationship information that you'll eventually use in the design of the database. You should, instead, be ready to add that information to the diagram as you go along.

Although the Database Documenter tool (which you'll learn more about in later chapters) can help you keep a close track on the design of your database, you're often better served to maintain a sketch of the database. Such a sketch helps (or, better yet, a model created in a program such as Visio, as described in Chapter 5); you can instantly reference and review database information in a more visual or graphic manner. Furthermore, the diagram can help you more easily understand the design of your database and the goals you're trying to achieve. Although the documenter will provide you with much valuable information about specifics of the database's design, it's not quite as helpful in providing easily-reviewable summary information that access in seconds.

TIP: *When specifying relationships between tables in the database, keep a close eye on how you design the tables because they can help you to more easily determine these relationships and can even automate some parts of their creation. For example, if you specify the **ItemNumber** field in the **OrderDetail** table as being a lookup on the **ItemNumber** field in the **ItemInformation** table, Access will specify that underlying relationship between the primary and foreign keys in the two tables for you, saving you extra work.*

When you design relationships, you will do so within the Table database. The Application database will then be able to take advantage of those relationships for its design. The tables in the Application database will be tables linked to the Table database (which contains the actual data), as discussed in the following section.

Creating The Linked Tables

After you create the tables that will reside in the Table database, you must then begin the creation of the Application database. If you'll be using Access 2000 for both the front end and the back end (as is the case with this particular application), you should simply create a new Access database and link the tables in the front end to the tables in the back end.

If you'll be using Oracle or another third-party product for the server database, you'll use a similar process, making sure that your front end is set up to do SQL pass-through queries to the back end. This technique is described in greater detail in later chapters.

If you're using SQL Server for the back end on the server, you may want to consider using an ADP for the Application database. The ADP structure creates a very thin front end that maintains no data locally on the client machine and further uses triggers and other techniques specific to the SQL Server back end.

In any event, you will want to design queries (or stored procedures) that will access the data in the table database. The following section discusses query design issues.

Designing The Database's Queries

After you create the tables and specify the relationships between them, the next step in the database's design is the creation of the queries the database will use to display information in forms and reports. Using the split-table model that we've discussed previously, the queries will be the first object you create after you create the linked tables in the Application database. The queries should reference values in the linked tables (which will then, of course, pull the information from the actual tables containing data in the Table database).

As you can see from Figure 19.1, the information diagram should provide, at a bare minimum, guidance as to what fields and tables will be joined. Optimally, the diagram should provide appropriate information about what fields to join on, the nature of the joins themselves, and any other specific and appropriate information the query's design.

Your queries should solve most of the issues involved in combining the tables in preparation for the creation of the forms and reports that will comprise the front end for the database. When you finish designing the queries, you should then have an intuitive guide to the design of the forms and reports that the front end will use.

Additionally, you may want to create cross-tab queries that you'll use solely with your reports—for example, to create an Orders-by-Month report. Such cross-tab queries, when created and stored locally, will speed the performance of your reports.

Finally, you should evaluate during the design process what queries will remain static—that is, won't require input from the user—and what queries may change each time they're invoked. For example, a cross-tab query may automatically return the last 12 months' information, or you might want to parameterize the query so the user can control how much historical data the query returns.

After you create the tables and the queries—conceptually, after you create the tools to store and return data—you'll need to create the user interface, to accept from and display the data to the user. The first part of the user interface's design is in the creation of forms, which is discussed in the next section.

Designing The Application Database's Forms

As you saw in the previous section, once you create the queries that will return the vast majority of the information for the application, you can go ahead and create the forms that your Application database will use. If you've designed the queries correctly, you should be able to simply use the Form Wizard to create most of your forms—at least their basic appearance.

After using the Form Wizard to create the templates for your forms, you can use the Design view to add additional controls to the forms—navigation controls, controls that invoke subforms or execute Visual Basic for Applications (VBA) code, and so on.

Additionally, you'll probably want to design some sort of switchboard to help navigate through the project. Depending on how you implement your reports, you may be able to create the switchboard after you finish designing the forms. Alternately, you may need to wait until after you've created all the reports before you design the switchboard, so you can simply invoke the reports directly from the switchboard. Design of the application database's reports is discussed in the next section.

Designing The Application Database's Reports

The last step in creating the front end—with the notable exception of program code that you need to add to the application—is the creation of the reports that you'll provide the user. Like form generation, you should be able to create the majority of your reports directly from the queries you've already created for the project.

The Report Wizard will help you create the outlines for your reports—outlines that you can then customize in the Design view, just as you did the form design. In general, however, the majority of the customization you'll do with the reports will be cosmetic—making sure fields are wide enough, making sure that the layout of the report when printed is visually appealing and consistent with current reporting methods, and so on.

After you create all the reports, depending on whether any of the reports use parameterized queries or not, you can add the reports (or the forms that call them) to the switchboard for the project. Once the creation of the reports is completed, the lion's share of the implementation of your design is complete.

After you finish the design, you should check the design with data, perform entry steps, try to make the program not work, and so on. This early testing of your application—particularly if you're careful to try to screw up every feature—will not only make you look better in your organization but will also make the Alpha and Beta testing of your application more efficient and useful.

Beta testing steps, methods, and considerations, as well as some final design considerations, are considered in Chapter 20. However, once you complete each of the general steps laid out in this chapter, your application will be "ready to go."

Closing On Implementation From Design

Obviously, the steps laid out in this chapter form a general model you should apply each time you create a database application from a model. Just as obviously, the steps laid out in this chapter don't allow for or address all of the possible considerations you'll likely have when designing "real-world" implementations. Additional considerations that you should evaluate during the application design process include the following:

- Macros and/or VBA code to automate your application

- VBA code to make your application more responsive to user input

- Field-level validations or, in the case of ADPs and databases that use pass-through queries, error handling and triggers to process field-level validations at the server

- Replication and backup issues, support for which should be built into all your applications

- Error handling to process any unknown occurrence gracefully, letting your application recover from bad input or other unexpected user actions

- A Help file to provide the user with context-sensitive assistance in the use of the database and the fields and controls on forms in the database

Each of these topics is discussed in greater detail in later chapters; for now, simply understand that they exist and that you must address them. In fact, addressing these particular problems with each database you design will make the difference between a product that "works" on the sufferance of its users, and a product that users like and will use as an important business tool in their day-to-day operations.

Immediate Solutions

As you saw in the "In Depth" section of this chapter, taking a database design and implementing it is simply an issue of performing the correct steps in the correct sequence. In the following sections in this chapter, we'll discuss each of these steps in sequence. When you finish this section, you'll have a database modeled directly on the diagram contained in Figure 19.1.

Creating The Tables

As you saw earlier, the first step in creating the database is to create the tables that will reside in the Table database (we'll create the table links within the Application database later in this chapter). To create the first new database, perform the following steps:

1. From within Access 2000, select the File menu New option. Access will display the New dialog box, as shown in Figure 19.2.

2. Within the New dialog box, double-click on the Database icon. Access will close the New dialog box and display the File New Database dialog box, which lets you name and save the new database. Name the new database as Chap19BE.mdb (for back end), and click on Create.

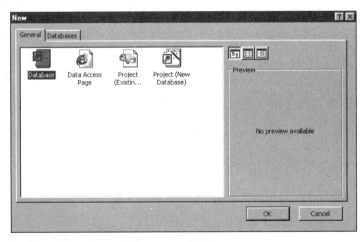

Figure 19.2   The New dialog box within Access 2000.

Access will create the database and display the Database window, with the Tables object selected. From here you'll create the tables, one at a time, as detailed in the following sections.

Creating The **BillTo** Table

The first table to create is the **BillTo** table. This table will maintain address information about the customer, which the program will (ultimately) use to maintain billing information for each customer. The design of the table is pretty straightforward—as will be the design of most of the tables. To design the table, perform the following steps:

1. Double-click on the Create Table In Design View option within the Database window. Access will display the Table 1:Table Design View window.

2. Within the window, specify the fields within the table as shown in Table 19.1.

3. Click the mouse on the gray selector box to the left of the **CustomerNum** field. Access will highlight the entire field.

4. Click on the primary key button on the toolbar. Access will display a primary key symbol in the selector.

5. Click on the Save button on the toolbar to save the table. Name the table as **BillTo**.

6. Click in the Data Type box for the **Phone** field. On the properties page at the bottom of the dialog box, click in the Input Mask property field to enter an input mask. Click on the ellipsis to run the Input Mask Wizard (Access may prompt you to save the table).

Table 19.1   The fields in the BillTo table.

Field Name	Data Type	Description
CustomerNum	AutoNumber	Primary key for the **BillTo** table
CustomerFirst	Text	Customer's first name
CustomerLast	Text	Customer's last name
Address1	Text	First line of customer address
Address2	Text	Second line of customer address
City	Text	Customer city
State	Text	Customer state
Zip	Text	Customer ZIP
Phone	Text	Customer phone
Fax	Text	Customer fax

7. Within the Input Mask Wizard, select the Phone Number mask and click Next. Access will display the next dialog box, which lets you modify the input mask. Accept the default, and move to the next dialog box by clicking Next.

8. Within the next dialog box, select the option to store the data with the symbols in the mask, as shown in Figure 19.3.

9. Click Finish to close the Wizard. Access will apply the input mask to the **Phone** field.

10. Repeat Steps 6 through 9 to apply an input mask to the **Fax** field. When you finish, click on the Close box for the Design view of the table to close the table designer. Access will prompt you to save the changes to the table's design.

Creating The **ShipTo** Table

The second table to create is the **ShipTo** table. This table will maintain shipping address information about the customer, which the program will (ultimately) use to keep records about where orders were shipped. As with the **BillTo** table, the design of the table is pretty straightforward. To design the table, perform the following steps:

1. Double-click on the Create Table In Design View option within the Database window. Access will display the Table 1:Table Design View window.

2. Within the window, specify the fields within the table as shown in Table 19.2.

3. Click the mouse on the gray selector box to the left of the **ShipToNum** field. Access will highlight the entire field.

4. Click on the primary key button on the toolbar. Access will display a primary key symbol in the selector.

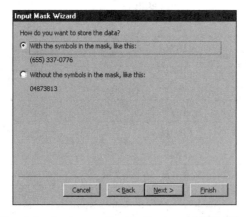

Figure 19.3   Choosing the data storage method in the Input Mask Wizard.

Table 19.2   The fields in the *ShipTo* table.

Field Name	Data Type	Description
ShipToNum	AutoNumber	Primary key for the **ShipTo** table
CustomerNum	**Number** (long integer)	Foreign key to the **BillTo** table
CustomerFirst	Text	Ship to customer's first name
CustomerLast	Text	Ship to customer's last name
Address1	Text	First line of ship to customer address
Address2	Text	Second line of ship to customer address
City	Text	Ship to customer's city
State	Text	Ship to customer's state
Zip	Text	Ship to customer's ZIP
Phone	Text	Ship to customer's phone
Fax	Text	Ship to customer's fax

5. Click on the Save button on the toolbar to save the table. Name the table as **ShipTo**.

6. Click in the Data Type box for the **Phone** field. On the properties page at the bottom of the dialog box, click in the Input Mask property field to enter an input mask. Click on the ellipsis to run the Input Mask Wizard (Access may prompt you to save the table).

7. Within the Input Mask Wizard, select the Phone Number mask and click Next. Access will display the next dialog box, which lets you modify the input mask. Accept the default, and move to the next dialog box by clicking Next.

8. Within the next dialog box, select the option to store the data with the symbols in the mask.

9. Click Finish to close the Wizard. Access will apply the input mask to the **Phone** field.

10. Repeat Steps 6 through 9 to apply an input mask to the **Fax** field. When you finish, click on the Close box for the Design view of the table to close the table designer. Access will prompt you to save the changes to the table's design.

Creating The **OrderLookup** Table

The next table to create is the **OrderLookup** table. This table will maintain shipping address information about the customer, which the program will use to link the customer information to the order information. To design the table, perform the following steps:

1. Double-click on the Create Table In Design View option within the Database window. Access will display the Table 1:Table design view window.

2. Within the window, specify the fields within the table as shown in Table 19.3.

3. Click the mouse on the gray selector box to the left of the **CustomerNum** field and drag the mouse down until all three fields are highlighted.

4. Click on the primary key button on the toolbar. Access will display a primary key symbol in the selector next to the three fields—indicating that the primary key will be derived from their combined values.

5. Click on the Save button on the toolbar to save the table. Name the table as **OrderLookup**.

Creating The **Orders** Table

The next table to create is the **Orders** table. This table will maintain order information, combining the line items from the **OrderDetail** table with the date and total information it contains when displaying the invoice. To design the table, perform the following steps:

1. Double-click on the Create Table In Design View option within the Database window. Access will display the Table 1:Table design view window.

2. Within the window, specify the fields within the table as shown in Table 19.4.

3. Click the mouse on the gray selector box to the left of the **OrderNum** field. Access will highlight the entire field.

4. Click on the primary key button on the toolbar. Access will display a primary key symbol in the selector.

*Table 19.3   The fields in the **OrderLookup** table.*

Field Name	Data Type	Description
CustomerNum	**Number** (long integer)	Foreign key to the **BillTo** table
ShipToNum	**Number** (long integer)	Foreign Key for the **ShipTo** table
OrderNum	**Number** (long integer)	Foreign key to the **Orders** table

*Table 19.4   The fields in the **Orders** table.*

Field Name	Data Type	Description
OrderNum	**AutoNumber**	Primary key for the **Orders** table
OrderDate	**Date**	Date of the order
DeliveryDate	**Date**	Date the order was delivered
Total	**Currency**	Total for the order

5. Click in the Data Type box for the **OrderDate** field. On the properties page at the bottom of the dialog box, click in the Format property field and set the format as Medium Date.

6. Click in the Data Type box for the **DeliveryDate** field. On the properties page at the bottom of the dialog box, click in the Format property field and set the format as Medium Date.

7. Click on the Save button on the toolbar to save the table. Name the table as **Orders**.

Creating The **ItemInformation** Table

The next table to create is the **ItemInformation** table. This table will maintain specific information about items. You should create this table before the **OrderDetail** table so you can simply use a lookup between the tables to fill in the **ItemNumber** field in the **OrderDetail** table. To design the **ItemInformation** table, perform the following steps:

1. Double-click on the Create Table In Design View option within the Database window. Access will display the Table 1:Table design view window.

2. Within the window, specify the fields within the table as shown in Table 19.5.

3. Click the mouse on the gray selector box to the left of the **ItemNumber** field. Access will highlight the entire field.

4. Click on the primary key button on the toolbar. Access will display a primary key symbol in the selector.

5. Click on the Save button on the toolbar to save the table. Name the table as **ItemInformation**.

Creating The **Discount** Table

The next table to create (and the next-to-last table in the database) is the **Discount** table. This table will maintain specific information about discounts. You should create this table before the **OrderDetail** table so you can simply use a lookup between the tables to fill in the **DiscountNum** field in the **OrderDetail** table. To design the **Discount** table, perform the following steps:

1. Double-click on the Create Table In Design View option within the Database window. Access will display the Table 1:Table design view window.

Table 19.5   The fields in the *ItemInformation* table.

Field Name	Data Type	Description
ItemNumber	AutoNumber	Primary key for the **ItemInformation** table
Description	Text	Description of the item
Price	Currency	Price of the item

2. Within the window, specify the fields within the table as shown in Table 19.6.

3. Click the mouse on the gray selector box to the left of the **DiscountNum** field. Access will highlight the entire field.

4. Click on the primary key button on the toolbar. Access will display a primary key symbol in the selector.

5. Click on the Save button on the toolbar to save the table. Name the table as **Discount**.

Creating The **OrderDetail** Table

The last table to create is the **OrderDetail** table. This table will maintain specific information about discounts. To design the **OrderDetail** table, perform the following steps:

1. Double-click on the Create Table In Design View option within the Database window. Access will display the Table 1:Table design view window.

2. Within the window, specify the fields within the table as shown in Table 19.7.

3. Click the mouse on the gray selector box to the left of the **OrderItemID** field. Access will highlight the entire field.

4. Click on the primary key button on the toolbar. Access will display a primary key symbol in the selector.

5. Click in the Data Type box for the **ItemNumber** field. On the properties page at the bottom of the dialog box, click on the Lookup tab.

6. Change the Display Control to a Combo Box. Access will display additional properties in the tab. In the Row Source property, either use the Query Builder (click on the ellipsis) or enter the Row Source property as follows:

Table 19.6   The fields in the *Discount* table.

Field Name	Data Type	Description
DiscountNum	AutoNumber	Primary key for the **Discount** table
DiscountVal	**Number** (single)	Discount in percentages (.20 =-20%)
DiscountDescription	Text	Description of the discount

Table 19.7   The fields in the *OrderDetail* table.

Field Name	Data Type	Description
OrderItemID	AutoNumber	Primary key for the **OrderDetail** table
OrderNum	**Number** (long integer)	Foreign key to the **Orders** table
ItemNumber	**Number** (long integer)	Foreign key to the **ItemInformation** table
DiscountNum	**Number** (long integer)	Foreign key to the **ItemInformation** table

```
SELECT ItemInformation.ItemNumber, ItemInformation.Description
FROM ItemInformation;
```

7. Set the Bound column property to 1, and the Column Count property to 2. Within the Column Widths property, set the values to be 0";2".

8. Repeat Steps 5 through 7 for the **DiscountNum**, except set the Row Source property as follows (either manually or using the Query Builder):

```
SELECT Discount.DiscountNum, Discount.DiscountDescription
FROM Discount;
```

9. When you finish, save the table as **OrderDetails**.

TIP: *Depending on how you do the design of the **OrderDetails** table, Access may let you do the setup detailed in Steps 5 through 8 using the Lookup Wizard. In such a case, simply ensure that the Query Builder returns the primary key and the description field from each of the lookup tables, and that the first column is hidden in the combo box.*

Adding The Relationship Information To The Database

To effectively use the new tables, you must relate them to the other tables in the database using the guidelines established in the information diagram. You'll do this from the Relationships window in the Access Interactive Development Environment (IDE). To set up the necessary relationships, perform the following steps:

1. Within the Database window, select the Tools menu Relationships option. Access will display the Relationships window.

2. Click on the Show Table icon on the toolbar to display the Show Table dialog box (Access may display the dialog box automatically). Within the Show Table dialog box, double-click on all the tables to add them to the Relationship window. Next, click on Close to close the Show Table dialog box.

3. Within the **BillTo** table's window, click on the **CustomerNum** field and drag it over to the **CustomerNum** field in the **OrderLookup** table's window. Access will display the Edit Relationships dialog box.

4. Within the Edit Relationships dialog box, click on the Enforce Referential Integrity checkbox. Access will display two additional options; click on the Cascade Update Related Fields check box. Click on Create to create the relationship.

5. Within the **BillTo** table's window, click on the **CustomerNum** field and drag it over to the **CustomerNum** field in the **ShipTo** table's window. Access will display the Edit Relationships dialog box.

6. Within the Edit Relationships dialog box, click on the Enforce Referential Integrity checkbox. Access will display two additional options; click on the Cascade Update Related Fields check box. Click on Create to create the relationship.

7. Within the **ShipTo** table's window, click on the **ShipToNum** field and drag it over to the **ShipToNum** field in the **OrderLookup** table's window. Access will display the Edit Relationships dialog box.

8. Within the Edit Relationships dialog box, click on the Enforce Referential Integrity checkbox. Access will display two additional options; click on the Cascade Update Related Fields check box. Click on Create to create the relationship.

9. Within the **Orders** table's window, click on the **OrderNum** field and drag it over to the **OrderNum** field in the **OrderLookup** table's window. Access will display the Edit Relationships dialog box.

10. Within the Edit Relationships dialog box, click on the Enforce Referential Integrity checkbox. Access will display two additional options; click on the Cascade Update Related Fields check box. Click on Create to create the relationship.

11. Within the **ItemInformation** table's window, click on the **ItemNumber** field and drag it over to the **ItemNumber** field in the **OrderDetails** table's window. Access will display the Edit Relationships dialog box.

12. Within the Edit Relationships dialog box, click on the Enforce Referential Integrity checkbox. Access will display two additional options; click on the Cascade Update Related Fields check box. Click on Create to create the relationship.

13. Within the **Discount** table's window, click on the **DiscountNum** field and drag it over to the **DiscountNum** field in the **OrderDetails** table's window. Access will display the Edit Relationships dialog box.

14. Within the **Orders** table's window, click on the **OrderNum** field and drag it over to the **OrderNum** field in the **OrderDetails** table's window. Access will display the Edit Relationships dialog box.

15. Within the Edit Relationships dialog box, click on the Enforce Referential Integrity checkbox. Access will display two additional options; click on the Cascade Update Related Fields check box. Click on Create to create the relationship.

When you finish specifying the relationships, the Relationships window will look similar to Figure 19.4.

Close and save the Relationships window and the relationships it defines. Now that you've created the relationship between the tables, it's time to create the Application database for the application. You'll do so in the next section.

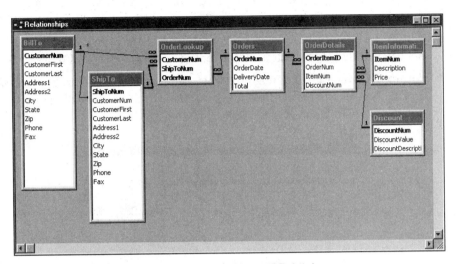

Figure 19.4   The Relationships window for the Chap19BE database.

Creating The Application Database

To create the Application database, perform the following steps:

1. From within Access 2000, select the File menu New option. Access will display the New dialog box.

2. Within the New dialog box, double-click on the Database icon. Access will close the New dialog box and display the File New Database dialog box, which lets you name and save the new database. Name the new database as Chap19FE.mdb (for front end), and click on Create.

Access will create the database and display the Database window, with the Tables object selected. From here you'll create the links to the tables, one at a time, as detailed in the following section.

Linking To The Tables In The Back End

To set up the Application database to access the tables in the Table database, you simply need to create linked tables to the database. To do so, perform the following steps:

1. Select the File menu Get External Data option. Within the submenu, select the Link Tables option. Access will display the Link dialog box.

2. Within the Link dialog box, double-click on the Chap19BE.mdb listing. Access will display the Link Tables dialog box, as shown in Figure 19.5.

3. Within the Link Tables dialog box, click on the Select All option. Next, click on OK. Access will create links to the tables within your Application database, as shown in Figure 19.6.

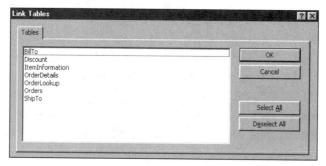

Figure 19.5   The Link Tables dialog box, for connecting to the back-end database.

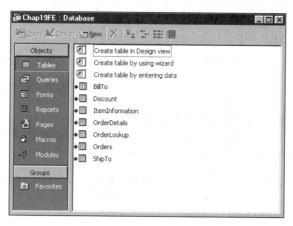

Figure 19.6   The Database window after the addition of the linked tables.

Creating Queries In The Front End

Creating queries in the front end is a relatively simple process, creating the queries against the linked tables. To create the query that displays all the detail information for an order in the front end using the wizard, perform the following steps:

1. Within the Database window, click on the Queries object. Next, double-click on the Create Query By Using Wizard option. Access will display the Simple Query Wizard.

2. Within the Tables/Queries combo box, select the **Table:Orders** table. Move all four fields to the Selected Fields combo box.

3. Within the Tables/Queries combo box, select the **Table:OrderDetails** table. Move the **OrderItemID**, **ItemNumber**, and **DiscountNum** fields to the Selected Fields combo box.

4. Within the Tables/Queries combo box, select the **Table:ItemInformation** table. Move the **Price** field and the **Description** field to the Selected Fields combo box.

5. Within the Tables/Queries combo box, select the **Table:Discount** table. Move the **DiscountValue** field and the **DiscountDescription** field to the Selected Fields combo box.

6. Click on the Next button to move to the next dialog box in the wizard. Choose a Detail query and click Next to move to the next dialog box.

7. Name the query as **qryOrders** and click Finish to save the query.

The other queries that the database uses are all designed and included within the Chap19FE.mdb database for you.

Chapter 20

Implementation—Beta Testing And Bug Checking

In Depth

Once you've constructed an application, it's very important to test the application and ensure that it works correctly before deploying the application into its final location. Effective testing and error checking can make the difference (particularly for in-house applications) between an application that's widely accepted and used within your organization and an application that people use but don't like, or even worse, that people don't use at all.

In general, your delivery process should consist of three major benchmarks. At each step along the way, you should be sure to perform bug checking and debugging of your implementation. Specifics of your bug checking, debugging, and error-handling procedures will vary, depending on the hardware and corporate environment you're deploying to, your corporate or departmental standards, and more.

Over the remainder of this chapter, we'll explore the basic model of implementation delivery that you should build your application around. We'll then evaluate some of the powerful debugging techniques that Access 2000 supports and wrap up the chapter by discussing some of the error-handling techniques that every application should use. We will also evaluate the creation of error logs and error forms, an often underused but crucial piece of the evaluation and testing process. The first consideration is in deploying the application, which is discussed in the following sections.

Deploying The Application

After all the planning, design, and programming, you might think that you're ready for your ultimate goal—deploying the application. In fact, for many programmers new to Access, the ability to develop the application rapidly—in a matter of weeks or even days—will result in the almost irresistible temptation to immediately deploy the new application. You can then eliminate the application from your list of things to do—a list of things that, if your information systems (IS) department is like most, is probably longer than you'll ever finish.

However, deploying an application before its time is generally a bad decision. The amount of time that you'll spend servicing and patching the application, combined with the level of frustration that most of your users will reach as the result of an application that doesn't work correctly, will more than offset any benefit you achieve by deploying the application quickly.

So, determining how to deploy your application is a crucial process. Depending on the scope of your application, and what environment you'll deploy it to, your application may require some or all of the steps detailed in the following sections. You'll have to make that determination on a case-by-case basis. Note, however, that everything that follows presumes that you've performed the processes defined in Chapters 17, 18, and 19—planning the application out with the end user, prototyping, and so on. By the time you reach the Alpha testing phase of your application's design, you and your users (or the user representative) should have been working closely together for some time to optimize the design of your application. The best place to start when considering a deployment is with the design of the process you will use in the deployment, which the next section discusses.

Describing The Overall Process

Although probably as many different deployment schedules and programs exist as there are developers, in general, most developers deploy applications along a schedule or program consistent with that shown in Figure 20.1.

Note from the figure how important user feedback is at every stage of the application's development. Note also that the vast majority of the user feedback—particularly feedback about functionality—should occur during the Alpha testing period of the process. By the time you release the first Beta of your application,

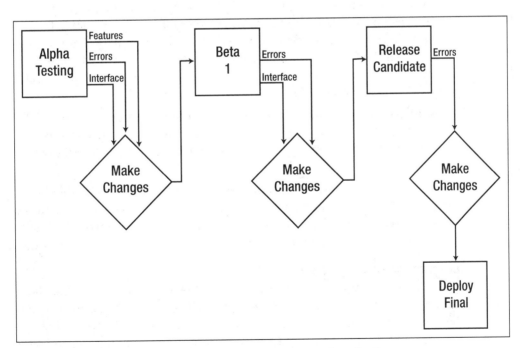

Figure 20.1   The generalized program for the deployment of applications.

your code should be "locked down"—the only changes you make should be either cosmetic (to the application's appearance) or to fix bugs and errors in the application's logic or implementation. The first part of the deployment, then, is the Alpha testing phase, which the next section describes.

Understanding The Alpha Testing Portion Of The Procedure

The Alpha testing portion of the procedure is arguably the most critical time in application development. Because all changes to the application's functionality should occur as a response to the Alpha testing process, ensuring that you have a complete Alpha test is very important to effective deployment. Functionality changes after Alpha testing may include creation of additional functionality, removal of certain features, or changes to the way the application handles certain parts of its processing.

When Alpha testing, be sure to keep the following considerations in mind:

- Involve users from each group that will use the application in the Alpha testing process. If you're developing for in-house deployment, one user from every level in the department where the application will be deployed should use the application. For example, a human resources application might be Alpha-tested by 10 people, including secretaries, HR managers, and the directory of the division.

- Force users to evaluate the program completely. When you simply deploy the Alpha then ask users what they think, you'll generally *not* get valuable feedback. Provide your Alpha testers with a definitive questionnaire that forces them to use all the features the application supports. Provide them with additional writing space that's easy to access, so they can make notes about problems they encounter or features they think are missing.

- Give users definitive timelines for completion of the Alpha evaluation. You'll generally find that you get more complete, useful information from users when you force them to complete their evaluation within a predetermined amount of time.

- Let users know that you won't accept their evaluations if you think they're incomplete. Make sure that management is ready to work with you to enforce this policy—particularly upper-level management because the worst offenders are, typically, department or division managers.

Understanding Beta Testing Phase 1

After you deploy the Alpha test and receive your feedback from the users, allot a specific amount of time to implement the appropriate changes. Be careful to evaluate the user's comments—some suggestions that come out of Alpha testing may be inconsistent with what you and the users have previously agreed on as the specifics of the application. You'll often find that users want additional features added to the application at the Alpha stage—once they figure out just what you can do for them in their application.

Depending on the environment in your office, you may be able to push out your Beta testing dates to add new features for such users. However, in most situations, you must be ready to tell users they'll need to wait for the next release of the program to reach that functionality. In such cases, you can use the specification forms that you designed and used in Chapters 17 and 18 to let users know that the application is complete based on the specifications agreed to and signed by yourself and the users.

In any event, after you make all the necessary application changes that grow out of the Alpha testing step, you're ready to deploy the first Beta test of the application. At this phase in the development cycle, users should understand that all changes that occur after the Beta test are in response to application errors or are cosmetic changes to the interface. Betas, then, should be "feature-complete."

You can think of the steps in the testing process as being akin to the application of various levels of sandpaper to wood. Before you ever release the Alpha test, your wood should be shaped and shaved and honed to a reasonably close approximation of its final design. Your work that results from the Alpha test should be like using a coarse-grained sandpaper on the wood. By the time you get to the Beta test, the wood should be pretty much ready to go—all that you'll be doing is applying the fine-grained sandpaper to the wood. Changes you make after the Beta test simply ensure that any remaining rough edges are gone before you apply the varnish and fix the wood into its permanent state.

When Beta testing, be sure to keep the following considerations in mind:

- Involve users from each group that will use the application in the Beta testing process. If possible, try to ensure that everyone who provided Alpha-testing services also provides Beta-testing services. Additionally, try to get some users who weren't involved in the Alpha test involved in the Beta test. Finally, ensure that the users who will be using the application the most are heavily involved in the Beta test.

- Force users to evaluate the interface for the program completely and make sure that they don't encounter errors at any point. When they do encounter errors, force them to log the errors. Again, provide your Beta testers with a definitive questionnaire that forces them to use all the features the application supports. Provide them with easily accessible additional writing space to make notes about problems they encounter. Though the Beta questionnaire will be similar to the Alpha questionnaire, there should be significant differences—particularly, the Beta questionnaire shouldn't discuss features at all.

- Give users definitive timelines for completion of the Beta evaluation. As with the Alpha evaluation, you'll generally find that you get more complete, useful information from users when you force them to complete their evaluation within a predetermined amount of time.

- Again, let users know that you won't accept their evaluations if you think they're incomplete.

Understanding Beta Testing Phase 2—The Release Candidate

After you complete the first Beta test and make any changes that result, you'll generally deploy the so-called Release Candidate of your application. This delivery should be, for all intents and purposes, the proposed final version of your application. The reason for the deployment of this version as a Beta is to let people check it for errors resulting from your responses to the earlier parts of the Beta testing process. Inadvertent though it is, programmers often discover they've introduced new errors into the applications during the process of repairing other errors. Deploying the Release Candidate gives you one more chance to ensure that your application is bug-free.

When Release Candidate testing, be sure to keep the following considerations in mind:

- Everyone involved in the Beta testing should test the Release Candidate. If possible, try to ensure that everyone in the department or company receiving the application gets to perform some testing on the Release Candidate.

- Force users to evaluate the application only for errors. When they do encounter errors, force them to log the errors. Again, provide your Release Candidate testers with a definitive questionnaire that forces them to use all the features that the application supports. Let users know, before they begin the test, that the only useful feedback at this point in the evaluation is feedback on application errors—feature-based feedback will be responded to in the next release of the application.

- Give users definitive timelines for completion of the Release Candidate evaluation.

- Again, let users know that you won't accept their evaluations if you don't think they're complete.

TIP: *You may find that your application development cycle goes through more than a single Beta release. In any event, no matter how many Betas you release, it's generally a good idea to have a Release Candidate version deployed before you finalize the application. Such a release gives you a last chance to fix any errors that may have been introduced late in the process or that you failed to fix after any of the earlier steps in the Beta process.*

Time For Testing Phases

A final consideration for your testing process is the amount of time you should allocate for each phase in the process. Determining how much time to allow yourself—both for the tests themselves and for you to perform the changes the tests result in—will vary depending on the application's complexity.

A good rule of thumb is that the testing and deployment process, in total, should add up to about one-third of the entire development time for the application, although it may be more in certain situations. In other words, if it took you two months to develop the application initially, you should allot another month for the testing and deployment process.

Again, as with most development guidelines, you'll find that your own specifications will vary, depending on your environment and the application that you're developing.

In any event and as should be painfully obvious to you by this point, the one thing that you must accept is that no application is ever perfect—especially not on the first draft. In fact, for most applications, no matter how many drafts you go through, the application still won't be perfect. Using error trapping within your applications is crucial to creating "bulletproof" deployments. However, learning effective debugging techniques will go a long way toward eliminating errors. In the next sections, we discuss some of these techniques and their importance.

Understanding Why Debugging Is Important

A good programmer isn't necessarily one who can get things right the first time. To be fully effective as a Visual Basic for Applications (VBA) programmer, you need to master the art of debugging—the process of troubleshooting your application. Debugging involves locating and identifying problem areas within your code and is a mandatory step in the application-development process. Fortunately, the Access 2000 environment provides excellent tools to help you with the debugging process. By using these debugging tools, you can step through your code, setting watchpoints and breakpoints as needed.

Utilizing the VBA debugging tools is significantly more efficient than taking random stabs at fixes to your application. A strong command of the Access 2000 debugging tools can save you hours of trial and error. In fact, it can make the difference between a successfully completed application-development process and one that continues indefinitely with problems left unsolved. There are many considerations in addressing bugs within your program code; obviously, the best way to address bugs is to avoid ever creating them. The following sections describe some of the techniques you can use to avoid the creation of bugs.

Avoiding Bugs In The First Place

The best way to deal with bugs is to avoid them. Proper coding techniques can really help you in this process. The use of **Option Explicit**, strong typing, naming standards, and tight scoping can help you to eliminate bugs in your code. The following sections discuss each of these techniques in detail.

Using Option Explicit

Option Explicit requires that all your variables be declared before they're used. Including **Option Explicit** in each Form, Code, and Report module helps the VBA compiler to find typos in the names of variables.

As discussed in detail in Chapter 27, the **Option Explicit** statement is a command that you can place in the General Declarations section of any Code, Form, or Report module. The **Option Explicit** command can be manually inserted into each program, or you can instruct the VBA Interactive Development Environment (IDE) to insert it automatically by selecting Require Variable Declaration from the Modules tab within the Options dialog box.

Using Strong Typing

Strong typing your variables is also discussed in Chapter 27. To strong type a variable means to indicate what type of data is stored in a variable at the time that it's declared. For example, **Dim intCounter As Integer** initializes a variable that contains integers. If elsewhere in your code you assign a character string to **intCounter**, the compiler will catch the error.

Using Naming Standards

Naming standards can also go a long way toward helping you to eliminate errors. The careful naming of variables makes your code easier to read and makes the intended use of the variable more obvious. Problem code tends to stand out when naming conventions have been judiciously followed. Naming standards are covered in later chapters and are outlined in detail in the appendices.

Using Variable Scoping

Finally, giving your variables the narrowest scope possible reduces the chances of one piece of code accidentally overwriting a variable within another piece of code. You should use **Local** variables whenever possible. Use **Module-Level** and **Global** variables only when it's necessary to see the value of a variable from multiple subroutines or multiple modules. For more information about the issues surrounding variable scoping, consult Chapter 27.

Clearly, there are many things you can do during your development phase to minimize the number of bugs in your application. That being said, it is impossible to create a program that works seamlessly without broad testing of the application—there are simply too many variables in the Windows environment. Knowing that you can't completely prevent bugs, the next step is to try to minimize them by effective testing on your part. The following sections discuss some of the additional tools at your disposal for eliminating bugs.

Nothing Can Kill All The Bugs

Unfortunately, no matter what you do to prevent problems and errors, they still creep into your code. Probably the most insidious type of error is a logic error. A logic error is sneaky because it escapes the compiler. A logic error means that your code compiles but simply doesn't execute as planned. This type of error might become apparent when you receive a runtime error or when you don't get the results you expected. This is where the debugger comes to the rescue. One of the most important features of the debugger is the Immediate window, discussed in the next section.

Harnessing The Power Of The Immediate Window

The Immediate window serves several purposes. It provides you with a great way to test VBA and user-defined functions, it enables you to both inquire about and change the value of variables while your code is running, and it allows you to view the results of **Debug.Print** statements. To open the Immediate window while in a Code, Form, or Report module, do one of two things:

1. Press Ctrl+G on the keyboard.

2. Select the View menu Immediate window option. The Immediate window is pictured in Figure 20.2.

The Immediate Solutions section of this chapter discusses some of the uses of the Immediate window in more detail. However, you can only use the Immediate window from within the debugger—which, of course, implies that you must run the debugger. The following section describes ways in which you can start the Access debugger.

Invoking The Debugger

You can invoke the Access debugger in several ways:

- Place a breakpoint in your code.
- Place a watchpoint in your code.

```
Immediate
We Are Now In Function1()
 10
We Are Now In Func2()
Lars Klander
```

Figure 20.2   The Immediate window lets you test functions, and manage and change the value of variables.

- Press Ctrl+Break while the code is running.

- Insert a **Stop** statement in your code.

A breakpoint is an unconditional point at which you want to suspend code execution. It's temporary in that it's in effect only while the database is open. In other words, breakpoints are not saved with the database.

A watchpoint is a condition under which you want to suspend code execution. For example, you might want to suspend code execution when a **Counter** variable reaches a specific value. A watchpoint is also temporary; it's removed once you close the database.

A **Stop** statement is permanent. In fact, if you forget to remove **Stop** statements from your code, your application will stop execution while the user is running it. The most common method to invoke the debugger, then, is to use breakpoints. Managing breakpoints is a key skill for any effective programmer. The following section details some of the ways in which you can use breakpoints to help troubleshoot problems in your program code.

Using Breakpoints To Help You Troubleshoot

As mentioned, a breakpoint is a point at which execution of code will be unconditionally halted. Multiple breakpoints can be set in your code, and you can add and remove breakpoints as your code is executing.

A breakpoint allows you to halt your code execution at a suspicious area of code. This enables you to examine everything that's going on at that point in your code execution. By strategically placing breakpoints in your code, you can quickly execute sections of code that are already debugged, stopping only at problem areas.

Three steps are involved in setting a breakpoint:

1. Place your cursor on the line of code where you want to invoke the debugger.

2. Insert a breakpoint in one of three ways: Press your F9 function key, click the gray Breakpoint bar in the Code window, or select the Debug menu Toggle Breakpoint option.

3. Run the form, report, or module containing the breakpoint. VBA suspends execution just before executing the line of code where you placed the breakpoint. It displays a rectangular outline around the statement that's about to execute.

Now that your code is suspended, you can step through it one line at a time, change the value of variables, and view your call stack, among other things.

Keep in mind that a breakpoint is actually a toggle. When you want to remove a breakpoint, press F9 or click on the red dot that indicates the breakpoint. Breakpoints will be removed when the database is closed, when another database is opened, or when you exit Access.

After you hit a breakpoint, you will commonly want to continue processing from the breakpoint, allowing you to closely monitor what the application is doing. This process is known as *stepping through code*, and the following sections describe your options for stepping through code in detail.

Stepping Through Code

Access 2000 gives you two main options for stepping through your code. Each one is slightly different. The Step Into option allows you to step through each line of code within a subroutine or function, whereas the Step Over option executes a procedure without stepping though each line of code within it. Knowing the right option to use to solve a particular problem is an acquired skill of experienced developers. However, the basics of using the different methods are discussed in the following sections.

Step Into

When you've reached a breakpoint, you can continue executing your code one line at a time or continue execution until another breakpoint is reached. To step through your code one line at a time, select Step Into from the Debug toolbar, press F8, or select the Debug menu Step Into option.

The Debug statements are about to print to the Immediate window. Let's take a look. Open the Immediate window. None of your code has printed anything to the Immediate window yet. Press F8 (step) three more times until you've executed the line **Debug.Print iTemp**. Notice the results of the **Debug.Print** statements.

Now that you've seen how you can display things to the Immediate window, let's take a look at how you can use the Immediate window to modify values of variables and controls. Start by changing the value of **iTemp**. Click in the Immediate window and type **iTemp = 50**. When you press Enter, you actually modify the value of **iTemp**. Type **?iTemp** and you'll see that Access echoes back the value of 50.

Executing Until The Next Breakpoint Is Reached

Assume that you've reached a breakpoint but you realize that your problem is further down in the code execution. In fact, the problem is actually in a different function. You might not want to continue to move a step at a time down to the offending function. Use the Procedure drop-down menu to locate the questionable function, then set a breakpoint on the line where you want to continue stepping. You're now ready to continue code execution until Access reaches this line.

To do this, click Continue on the toolbar, press F5, or select the Run menu Continue option. Your code continues to execute, stopping at the next breakpoint.

Using Step Over

Sometimes you already have a subroutine fully tested and debugged. In such cases, you may want to continue stepping through the routine that you're in, but you don't want to watch the execution of subroutines. In this case, you use Step Over. To step over a subroutine or function, click Step Over on the toolbar, press Shift+F8, or select the Debug menu Step Over option. The code within the subroutine or function that you're stepping over will execute, but you won't step through it.

No matter how you step through or over the code in your application, you are likely to eventually need to step to a specific statement. Such a process is called *setting* the statement, and the next section describes the technique in detail.

Setting The Next Statement To Execute

After you've stepped through your code, watched the logical flow, and modified some variables, you might want to reexecute the code beginning at a prior statement. To do this, click anywhere in the line of code where you want to commence execution. Next, select the Debug menu's Set Next Statement option or press Ctrl+F9. Notice that the rectangle indicating the next line of code to be executed is now over that statement. You can then step through the code using F8, or you can continue normal code execution using F5. Access allows you to set the next line to be executed within a procedure only. This feature can be used to reexecute lines of code or to skip over a problem line of code.

You've learned how to set breakpoints, step through and over code, use the Immediate window, set the next line to be executed, and continue to run until the next breakpoint is reached. Once you've reached a breakpoint, it's often important to see which functions were called to bring you to this point. This is where the Calls feature can help. Information about Calls is displayed within the Calls window, discussed in the following section.

The Calls Window

To bring up the Calls window, select the Calls button from the toolbar or select the View menu Call Stack option. The window shown in Figure 20.3 appears.

When you want to see the line of code that called a particular function or subroutine, double-click that particular function or click the function, then click Show. Although your execution point isn't moved to the calling function or subroutine, you're able to view the code within the procedure. If you want to continue your

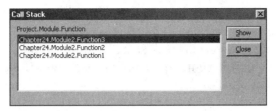

Figure 20.3　The Call Stack window traces function calls.

code execution, press F8. You'll be moved back to the procedure through which you were stepping, and the next line of code will execute. When you press F5, your code executes until another breakpoint or watchpoint is reached. When you want to return to where you were without executing additional lines of code, select the Debug menu's Show Next Statement option.

One of the most important considerations when stepping through code is tracking the ongoing value of a variable or expression. Displaying ongoing information about a variable or expression's value while debugging is known as *setting a watch*, a technique which the next section describes.

Working With Watch Expressions

Sometimes it's not enough to use the Immediate window to test the value of an expression or variable. You might want to keep a constant eye on the expression's value. An important feature in Access 2000 is the ability to set watchpoints. You can set a watchpoint before running a procedure or while code execution is suspended. After a Watch expression is added, it appears in the Immediate window. As you'll see, you can create several types of watchpoints.

Instant Watch

An Instant Watch is the most basic type of watchpoint. To add an Instant Watch, highlight the name of the variable or expression you want to watch and click the Instant Watch button on the Debug toolbar, select the Debug menu Quick Watch option, or press Shift+F9. The Quick Watch dialog box, shown in Figure 20.4, appears.

Figure 20.4　The Quick Watch dialog box lets you quickly view the value of a variable or add an expression as a permanent watchpoint.

You can click Add to add the expression as a permanent watch or select Cancel to view the current value without adding it as a watchpoint. While watchpoints are valuable for trying to determine the cause of an error, they will not help you resume execution after the runtime error. For that, you will need to work directly with the debugger. The following sections describe techniques you can use to resume execution within your application after a runtime error.

Continuing Execution After A Runtime Error

As you're testing, you often discover runtime errors that are quite easy to fix. When a runtime error occurs, a dialog box will appear to alert you to the error. If you select Debug, you'll be placed in the Code window, on the line that generated the error. After rectifying the problem, you can simply click the Continue button on the toolbar or select the Run menu Continue option to continue the application's processing after the error.

Resetting Code

After an error has occurred, VBA often displays a message giving you the option of resetting your code. If you opt to reset your code, all variables (including Publics and Statics) lose their values. You can also select Reset from the toolbar. You must decide whether it's better to proceed with your variables already set or to reset the variables, then proceed.

Needless to say, the debugger is an excellent tool for bug-proofing your applications. When used together with the information that its various component windows provide to you, the debugger can help you respond to almost any coding problem. However, like most program components, it does have its limitations. The following section discusses some of the issues to be aware of when working with the debugger.

Things To Watch With Debugging

Although the Access debugger is excellent, the debugging process itself is wrought with an array of potential problems:

- The debugging process can interrupt code execution, especially when forms are involved. When this occurs, the best bet is to place **Debug.Print** statements in your code and examine what happened after code execution is complete.

- Along the lines of the previous problem, it's difficult to debug code where **GotFocus** and **LostFocus** events are coded. Moving to the Immediate window causes the **LostFocus** event to be triggered. Returning to the form causes the **GotFocus** event to be triggered. Once again, a great solution is **Debug.Print**. You might also consider writing information to an error log for your review after code execution has completed.

- Code that uses **Screen.ActiveForm** and **Screen.ActiveControl** or other **Screen.Active** constructions will cause serious problems with the debugging process. When the Immediate window is active, there's no active form and no active control. Avoiding these lines in your code wherever possible will alleviate this problem.

- Finally, be aware that resetting code can cause problems. If you're modifying environmental settings, you're left with whatever environmental settings your application code changed. If you continue execution after the error without resetting, all sorts of other problems could occur. It's a good idea to code a special utility routine that resets your environment.

Understanding all of these considerations is important. Why it's important is simple—no matter how good a programmer you are, your programs will still have errors. Recognizing that, and taking steps to alleviate the problem, is the discussion of the next section.

Handling Runtime Errors

Errors happen, even in the absence of programmer error. It's necessary to protect your programs and your data from the adverse effects of errors. You accomplish this through the process of error handling.

Error handling is also known as error trapping. Error handling is the process of intercepting Jet or VBA's response to an error. It enables the developer to determine the severity of an error and to take the appropriate action in response to the error.

Without error handling, the user of your application is forced to abruptly exit from your application code. Consider the following example:

```
Private Sub cmdCallError_Click()
  Call TestError(txtValue1, txtValue2)
End Sub


Sub TestError(Numerator As Integer, Denominator As Integer)
  Debug.Print Numerator / Denominator
  MsgBox "I am in Test Error"
End Sub
```

The click event behind the command button calls the routine **TestError**, passing it the values from two text boxes. **TestError** accepts these parameters and attempts to divide the first parameter by the second parameter. When the second parameter is equal to zero, a runtime error occurs. Because there is no error handling in effect, the program terminates.

The error message the user receives provides four choices—Debug, Continue, End, and Help. If users choose Debug, the module window appears, and they're placed in Debug mode on the line of code causing the error. When users select Continue (this isn't always available), Access ignores the error and continues with the execution of the program. If users choose End, the execution of the programming code terminates. When the application is running with the runtime version of Access, the application shuts down and users are returned to Windows. With error handling in effect, you can attempt to handle the error in a more appropriate way whenever possible.

Error-handling code can be added to the error event procedure of a form or report. It can also be added to any VBA subroutine, function, or event routine. The previous code can easily be modified to handle the error gracefully. The code that follows gives an example of a simple error-handling routine:

```
Sub TestError(Numerator As Integer, Denominator As Integer)
  On Error GoTo TestError_Err
  Debug.Print Numerator / Denominator
  MsgBox "I am in Test Error"
  Exit Sub

TestError_Err:
  If Err = 11 Then
    MsgBox "Variable 2 Cannot Be a Zero", , "Custom Error Handler"
  End If
  Exit Sub
End Sub
```

This code is found in a module called **basError** contained in the database named Chap20.mdb.

The routine now invokes error handling. If a divide-by-zero error occurs, a message box displays, alerting the user to the problem. Upon the occurrence of an error, the screen appears as in Figure 20.5.

Working With Error Events

Every form and report contains an error event procedure. This event is triggered by any interface or Jet database engine error. It's not triggered by a programming error that the Access developer has made.

Figure 20.5   The simple Custom Error Handler implemented by the code.

Errors often occur in the interface of a form or report, as well as in the Jet database engine. For example, a user might try to enter an order for a customer who doesn't exist. Rather than displaying Access's default error message, you might want to intercept and handle the error in a particular way.

After an error occurs within a form, its error event is triggered. In the following code, you can see **Sub Form_Error**. It contains two parameters. The first parameter is the number of the error; the second parameter is the way you want to respond to the error. The error number is an Access-generated number.

This code, found within the Chap20.mdb database, tests to see whether a referential integrity error has occurred. When it has, a message box is displayed asking whether the user wants to add the customer. If the user answers yes, the customer form is displayed:

```
Private Sub Form_Error(DataErr As Integer, Response As Integer)
  Dim intAnswer As Integer

  If DataErr = 3201 Then  'Referential Integrity Error
    intAnswer = MsgBox("Customer Does Not Exist... _
        Would You Like to Add Them Now", vbYesNo)
    If intAnswer = vbYes Then
      DoCmd.OpenForm "frmCustomer", , , , acAdd, acDialog
    End If
  End If
  Response = acDataErrContinue
End Sub
```

> **WARNING!**   *Be aware that this sample only traps referential integrity errors. It doesn't handle any other error.*

The **Response = acDataErrContinue** line is very important. It instructs Access to continue the code execution without displaying the standard error message. The other option for **Response** is **AcDataErrDisplay**. It instructs Access to display the default error message.

TIP: *When you want to get a list of all the errors that can occur in Access, as well as a description of what each error number means, search for Error Codes in the help index. A list appears, containing each error number and a description of the error. You can click on an error description to get a more detailed explanation of the error.*

Using On Error Statements

An **On Error** statement activates error handling. Each routine must contain its own **On Error** statement when you want that routine to do its own error handling.

Otherwise, error handling is cascaded up the call stack. If no **On Error** statements are found in the call stack, VBA's own error handling is invoked.

By using an **On Error** statement, you can cause the application to branch to error-handling code, resume on the line immediately following the error, or attempt to reexecute the problem line of code.

You must decide the most appropriate response to a particular error. Sometimes it's most appropriate for your application to halt in response to an error. At other times, it's best to have the routine skip the offending line entirely. By combining the use of **On Error Goto**, **On Error Resume Next**, and **On Error Resume**, you can handle each error appropriately.

On Error Goto

The statement **On Error Goto <label>** tells VBA that from this point forward, if an error occurs, it should jump to the label specified within the statement. This is the most common form of error handling.

The label specified in the **On Error** statement must be within the current procedure, and it must be unique within a module. The following code illustrates a simple example of error handling:

```
Sub SimpleErrorHandler(iVar1 As Integer, iVar2 As Integer)
  On Error GoTo SimpleErrorHandler_Err
  Dim sngResult As String

  sngResult = iVar1 / iVar2
  Exit Sub

SimpleErrorHandler_Err:
  MsgBox "Warning! Error!"
  Exit Sub
End Sub
```

Some important things can be learned from this simple routine. The routine receives two integer values. It then invokes the error handler. When an error occurs, execution continues at the label. Notice that this routine contains two **Exit Sub** statements. When you remove the first **Exit Sub** statement, the code falls through to the label regardless of whether an error occurred. The **Exit Sub** statement at the bottom gracefully exits the procedure, setting the error code back to zero.

Including The Error Number And Description In The Error Handler

The previous error-handling code didn't provide a very descriptive message to the user. The **Description** and **Number** properties of the **Err** object assist in providing the user with more meaningful error messages. The **Err** object is covered in detail later in this chapter in the section "The Err Object." For now, let's look at the **Description** and **Number** properties to see how they can enhance an error-handling routine. To display the error number and description, you must modify the error-handling code to look like this:

```
SimpleErrorHandler_Err:
  MsgBox "Error #" & Err.Number & ": " & Err.Description
  Exit Sub
```

This time, instead of hard coding the error message, you display the error number and VBA's internal error string. The resulting error message looks like Figure 20.6. The **SimpleErrorHandler** routine, as well as all the examples that follow, can be found in the **basError** module of the Chap20.mdb database.

Using On Error Resume Next

On Error Resume Next continues program execution on the line immediately following the error. This construct is generally used when it's acceptable to ignore an error and continue code execution. The following is an example of such a situation:

```
Sub ResumeNext()
  On Error Resume Next
  Kill "AnyFile"
  MsgBox "The App Didn't Die, But the Error Was: " & Err.Description
End Sub
```

The **Kill** statement is used to delete a file from disk. If the specified file isn't found, an error results. You only delete the file if it exists, so you're not concerned about an error. **On Error Resume Next** is very appropriate in this situation because there's no harm done by resuming execution after the offending line of code.

Using On Error Goto 0

On Error Goto 0 is used for two purposes:

- When you want Access to return to its default error handler

- To have Access return to the error handler of a routine above the current routine

Figure 20.6   An error message with an error number and error string.

Generally, you don't want Access to return to its default error handler. You might do this only if you were, for some reason, unable to handle the error, or if you were in the testing phase and not yet ready to implement your own error handler.

The reason that you want Access to return the error to a higher level routine is much more clear. You do this when you want to "centralize" the error handling, meaning that one routine might call several others. Rather than placing error-handling code in each routine that's called, you can place the error handling in the calling routine.

Using Resume, Resume Next, And Resume <LineLabel> Statements

When you're in your error-handling code, you can use the **Resume**, **Resume Next**, and **Resume <LineLabel>** statements to specify how you want VBA to respond to the error. **Resume** attempts to reexecute the offending line of code, **Resume Next** resumes execution after the offending line of code, and **Resume <LineLabel>** continues execution at a specified Line Label. The following sections cover these statements in detail.

The Resume Statement

As mentioned previously, the **Resume** statement resumes code execution on the line of code that caused the error. This statement must be used with extreme care because it can throw the code into an unrecoverable endless loop. Here is an example of an inappropriate use of the **Resume** statement:

```
Function BadResume(sFileName As String)
  On Error GoTo BadResume_Err
  Dim strFile As String

  strFile = Dir(sFileName)
  If strFile = "" Then
    BadResume = False
  Else
    BadResume = True
  End If
  Exit Function

BadResume_Err:
  MsgBox "Error"
  Resume
End Function
```

This function is passed a file name. The **Dir** function searches for the file name and returns **True** or **False** depending on whether the specified file name is found.

The problem occurs when the drive requested isn't available or doesn't exist. This code throws the computer into an endless loop. To remedy the problem, your code should be modified to look like this:

```
Function GoodResume(sFileName As String)
  On Error GoTo GoodResume_Err
  Dim strFile As String

  strFile = Dir(sFileName)
  If strFile = "" Then
    GoodResume = False
  Else
    GoodResume = True
  End If
  Exit Function

GoodResume_Err:
  Dim intAnswer As Integer

  intAnswer = MsgBox(Error & ", Would You Like to Try Again?", vbYesNo)
  If intAnswer = vbYes Then
    Resume
  Else
    Exit Function
  End If
End Function
```

In this example, the error handler enables the user to decide whether to try again. Only when the user's response is affirmative does the **Resume** occur.

The Resume Next Statement

Just as you can invoke error handling using an **On Error Resume Next**, you can place a **Resume Next** statement in your error handler:

```
Sub ResumeNextInError()
  On Error GoTo ResumeNextInError_Err
  Kill "AnyFile"
  MsgBox "We Didn't Die!"
  Exit Sub

ResumeNextInError_Err:
  Resume Next
End Sub
```

In this example, the code is instructed to go to the label called **ResumeNextInError_Err** when an error occurs. The **ResumeNextInError_Err** label issues a **Resume Next**. This clears the error and causes execution to continue on the line after the line in which the error occurred.

The Resume <LineLabel> Statement

The **Resume <LineLabel>** command enables you to specify a line of code where you would like code execution to continue after an error occurs. This is a great way to eliminate the two **Exit Sub** or **Exit Function** statements required by the error-handling routines that you've looked at so far. Here's an example:

```
Sub ResumeLineLabel(iVar1 As Integer, iVar2 As Integer)
  On Error GoTo SimpleErrorHandler_Err
  Dim sngResult As String

  sngResult = iVar1 / iVar2
SimpleErrorHandler_Exit:
  Exit Sub

SimpleErrorHandler_Err:
  MsgBox "Error #" & Err.Number & ": " & Err.Description
  Resume SimpleErrorHandler_Exit
End Sub
```

Notice that this routine contains only one **Exit Sub**. If no error occurs, Access drops through the **SimpleErrorHandler_Exit** label to the **Exit Sub**. If an error *does* occur, the code within the **SimpleErrorHandler_Err** label executes. Notice that the last line of the label resumes execution at the **SimpleErrorHandler_Exit** label.

This method of resolving an error is useful because any code required to execute as the routine is exited can be written in one place. For example, object variables might need to be set equal to **Nothing** as the routine is exited. These lines of code can be placed in the exit routine.

The error-handling that we have examined so far has been relatively straightforward—the processing should be somewhat intuitive. However, error-handling is not always so clear. One of the biggest problems encountered by developers new to Access is the way Access will pass errors up from a routine to its calling routine. The following section discusses this method, known as *cascading errors*.

Understanding The Cascading Error Effect

If Access finds no error handling in a particular subroutine or function, it looks up the call stack for a previous error handler. This is illustrated with the following code:

```
Sub Function1()
  On Error GoTo Function1_Err
  Debug.Print "I am in Function1"
  Call Function2
  Debug.Print "I am back in Function1"
  Exit Sub

Function1_Err:
  MsgBox "Error in Function1"
  Resume Next
End Sub

Sub Function2()
  Debug.Print "I am in Function2"
  Call Function3
  Debug.Print "I am still in Function2"
End Sub

Sub Function3()
  Dim sngAnswer As Single

  Debug.Print "I am in Function3"
  sngAnswer = 5 / 0
  Debug.Print "I am still in Function3"
End Sub
```

In this situation, the error occurs in **Function3**. Because **Function3** doesn't have its own error handling, VBA refers the error back to **Function2**. **Function2** also doesn't have any error handling. **Function2** relinquishes control to **Function1**. VBA executes the error code in **Function1**. The real problem occurs because of the **Resume Next**. The application continues executing within **Function1** on the statement that reads **Debug.Print "I am back in Function 1"**. This type of error handling is dangerous and confusing. It's therefore best to develop a generic error-handling routine that's accessed throughout your application. Any functional error-handling routine that provides useful feedback to the user will need to use the **Err** object, discussed in the next section.

The Err Object

The **Err** object contains information about the most recent error that occurred. As with all Access objects, it has its own built-in properties and methods. The properties of the **Err** object are listed in Table 20.1.

The **Err** object has only two methods: **Clear** and **Raise**. The **Clear** method enables you to clear an error condition explicitly. The **Clear** method is used primarily when you write code that uses the **On Error Resume Next** statement. The

Table 20.1   Properties of the Err object.

Property	Description
Number	The number of the error that has been set
Description	The description of the error that has occurred
HelpContext	The Context ID for the help file
HelpFile	The path and file name of the help file
LastDLLError	The last error that occurred in a 32-bit DLL
Source	The system in which the error occurred (which is extremely useful when you're using object linking and embedding [OLE] automation to control another application, such as Excel)

On Error Resume Next statement doesn't clear the error condition. Remember, there's no reason to issue the **Clear** method explicitly with any type of **Resume**, **Exit Sub**, **Exit Function**, **Exit Property**, or **On Error Goto**. The **Clear** method is implicitly issued when these constructs are used. The **Raise** method of the **Err** object is covered in the next section.

Raising An Error

The **Raise** method of the error object is used in the following situations:

- When you want to generate an error on purpose (for example, in testing)

- When you want to generate a user-defined error

- When no code in the error routine handles the current error and you want to allow other parts of the call stack to attempt to handle the error

- When you want to nest an error handler

Using the **Raise** method to generate an error on purpose and create a user-defined error is covered in the following sections.

Generating An Error On Purpose

Many times, you want to generate an error when testing, so you can test out your own error handling. Rather than figuring out how to "cause" the error condition, you can use the **Raise** method of the **Err** object to accomplish this task. Here's an example:

```
Sub RaiseError()
  On Error GoTo RaiseError_Err
  Dim sngResult As String

  Err.Raise 11
  Exit Sub
```

```
RaiseError_Err:
  MsgBox "Error #" & Err.Number & ": " & Err.Description
  Exit Sub
End Sub
```

This code invokes an error 11 (divide by zero). By generating the error, you can test the effectiveness of your error-handling routine.

Creating User-Defined Errors

Another important use of the **Raise** method of the **Err** object is the generation of a custom error condition. Use this when you want to have something that doesn't generate an Access error but does generate a user-defined error you can send through the normal error-handling process. Because the **Raise** method enables you to set *all* the properties of the **Err** object, you can create a user-defined error complete with a number, description, source, and so forth. Here's an example:

```
Sub CustomError()
  On Error GoTo CustomError_Err
  Dim strName As String

  strName = InputBox("Please Enter Your Name")
  If Len(strName) < 5 Then
    Err.Raise Number:=99999, _
        Description:="Length of Name is Too Short"
  Else
    MsgBox "You Entered " & strName
  End If
  Exit Sub

CustomError_Err:
  MsgBox "Error # " & Err.Number & " - " & Err.Description
  Exit Sub
End Sub
```

Although it's very simple, this example illustrates an important use of generating user-defined errors. The code tests to see whether the value entered has less than five characters. If it does, a user-defined error (number 99999) is generated. The routine drops into the normal error-handling routine. Later in the chapter, you'll explore how to create a generic error handler. By passing user-defined errors through your generic error handler, all errors—user-defined or not—are handled in the same way. For now, however, let's move on to a consideration of the **ErrorsCollection** collection, which differs somewhat from the VBA **Err** object.

The ErrorsCollection

The **ErrorsCollection** is part of Access's Jet engine. It stores the most recent *set* of errors that have occurred. This is important when dealing with Data Access Objects (DAO) and open database connectivity (ODBC). With either DAO or ODBC, one operation can result in multiple errors. When you're concerned with each error generated by the one operation, you need to look at the **ErrorsCollection**. It has the same properties as the **Err** object. If you want to view the errors stored within the **ErrorsCollection**, you must loop through it, viewing the properties of each **Err** object. The code to do so looks like this:

```
Sub ErrorsCollection()
  On Error GoTo ErrorsCollection_Err
  Dim db As Database

  Set db = CurrentDb
  db.Execute ("qryNonExistent")
  Exit Sub

ErrorsCollection_Err:
  Dim ErrorDescrip As Error
  For Each ErrorDescrip In Errors
    Debug.Print ErrorDescrip.Description
  Next ErrorDescrip
  Exit Sub
End Sub
```

The routine loops through each **Err** object in the **ErrorsCollection**, printing the description of each error contained within the collection. Note how the application uses the **For Each** construct to loop through all the current errors in the collection—a more powerful technique than simply displaying the most recent error contained within the **Err** object.

Immediate Solutions

Working With The Immediate Window

The best way to get familiar with the Immediate window is to use it to perform specific debugging tasks. The following sections detail some of the ways that you can use the Immediate window when debugging your code.

Testing Values Of Variables And Properties

The Immediate window allows you to test the values of variables and properties as your code is executing. This can be quite helpful when you're trying to determine what is actually happening within your code.

To practice with the Immediate window, you don't even need to be executing code. While in Design view of a form, report, or module, all you need to do is place yourself in the Code window. If the Immediate window isn't visible, select the Immediate Window option from the View menu. Follow these seven steps to see how this works:

1. Open any module.

2. Press Ctrl+G on the keyboard.

3. Run the **frmTest** form found in the Chap20.mdb database on your CD-ROM.

4. Click anywhere on the Immediate window to activate it.

5. Type **?Forms!frmTest!ClientID.Value**. The **ClientID** of the current client will appear on the next line.

6. Type **?Forms!frmTest!CompanyName.Visible**. A **True** or a **-1** will appear on the next line, indicating that the control is visible.

7. Type **?Forms!frmTest!Address.BackColor**. The number **-2147483643** will appear on the next line, specifying the background color of the address control.

Setting Values Of Variables And Properties

You can invoke the Immediate window in two ways. You can press Ctrl+G or select the View menu Immediate Window option. An advantage of Ctrl+G is that, whereas the View menu Immediate Window menu item is available only within a Module window, Ctrl+G invokes the Immediate window without the Code window being active.

Not only can you display things to the Immediate window, you can use the Immediate window to modify the values of variables and controls as your code is executing. This feature becomes even more valuable when you realize you can reexecute code within a procedure after changing the value of a variable. Here's how this process works:

1. Invoke the Immediate window if necessary. Remember, this can be accomplished from any Form, Report, or Code module or by pressing Ctrl+G.

2. Type **Forms!frmTest!ContactTitle.Value = "Hello"**. The contact title of the current record should change to "Hello".

3. Type **Forms!frmTest!CompanyName.Visible = False**. The **CompanyName** control on the **frmTest** form should become hidden.

4. Type **Forms!frmTest!Address.BackColor = 123456**. The background color of the **Address** control on the **frmTest** form should turn green.

The Immediate window is an extremely valuable testing and debugging tool. The previous examples barely begin to illustrate its power and flexibility.

Changes you make to data while working in the Immediate window are permanent. On the other hand, changes you make to the properties of controls or the values of variables aren't saved with the form or report.

Clearing The Immediate Window

The Immediate window displays the last 200 lines of output. As additional lines of code are added to the Immediate window, older lines disappear. When you exit completely from Access and return to the Immediate window, it will be cleared. When you want to clear the Immediate window at any other time, follow three steps:

1. Use Ctrl+Home to go to the top of the Immediate window.

2. Hold down your Shift key and press Ctrl+End to go to the last statement in the Immediate window.

3. Press the Del key.

Practicing With The Built-In Functions

In addition to being able to test and set the values of properties and variables using the Immediate window, you can test any VBA function. To do this, type the function and its arguments in the Immediate window, preceded by a question mark. Here are some examples:

```
?datepart("m",date)
```

This example returns the month of the current date.

```
?dateadd("m",1,date)
```

This example tells you the date one month after today's date.

```
?datediff("d",date(),#12/31/00#)
```

This example tells you how many days exist between the current date and the end of the millennium (contrary to popular belief, the new millenium starts on January 1, 2001).

Executing Subroutines, Functions, And Methods

In addition to allowing you to test any VBA function, the Immediate window allows you to test any user-defined subroutine, function, or method. This is a great way to debug your user-defined procedures. To see how this works, take the following steps:

1. Open the **basExamples** module found in the Chap20.mdb database on your sample code CD.

2. Invoke the Immediate window if it isn't already visible.

3. Type **?ReturnInitsFunc("Lars", "Klander")**. This calls the user-defined function **ReturnInitsFunc**, sending "Lars" as the first parameter and "Klander" as the second parameter. The value L.K. should appear in the Immediate window. This is the return value from the function.

4. Type **Call ReturnInitsSub("Dave", "Mercer")**. This calls the user-defined subroutine **ReturnInitsSub**, sending "Dave" as the first parameter and "Mercer" as the second parameter. The value D.M. should appear in a message box.

5. Notice the difference between how you call a function and how you call a subroutine. Because the function returns a value, you must call it using a question mark. On the other hand, when calling a subroutine, you use the **Call** keyword.

You can also call a subroutine from the Immediate window using the following syntax:

```
RoutineName Parameter1, Parameter2, ....
```

Notice that when you omit the **Call** keyword, the parameters must *not* be enclosed in parentheses.

Printing To The Immediate Window At Runtime

The ability to print to the Immediate window is useful because you can test what is happening as your code is executing, without having to suspend code execution.

It's also valuable to be able to print something to a window when you're testing, without interfering with the user-interface aspect of your code. You can test a form without being interrupted then go back and view the values of variables and so on. Here's how the process works:

1. Type **Call LoopThroughCollection**. This calls the user-defined subroutine **LoopThroughCollection**. The values Dogs, Cats, Horses, and Goldfish should appear. These values were printed to the Immediate window by the routine.

2. Open the form **frmDebugPrint** in Form view.

3. Tab from the First Name to the Last Name.

4. Tab back to the First Name.

5. Type your First Name.

6. Change to Design view of the form.

7. Go to a Code window.

8. Open the Immediate window. Notice all the statements that were printed to the Immediate window. These **Debug.Print** statements were coded in all the appropriate Form and Control events.

Using The Debugger

The best way to get familiar with the debugger is to get hands-on experience setting and stopping code execution at a breakpoint.

Start by creating a form called **frmDebugForm** that contains a command button called **cmdDebug**. Give the button the caption "Test Code". Place the following code in the **Click** event of the command button:

```
Sub cmdDebug_Click ()
  Call Function1
End Sub
```

Create a module called **basFuncExamples**. Enter three functions into the module:

```
Sub Function1 ()
  Dim iTemp As Integer

  iTemp = 10
  Debug.Print "We Are Now In Function1()"
```

```
      Debug.Print iTemp
      Call Function2
   End Sub

   Sub Function2 ()
      Dim sName As String

      sName = "Lars Klander"
      Debug.Print "We Are Now In Func2()"
      Debug.Print sName
      Call Function3
   End Sub

   Sub Function3 ()
      Debug.Print "We Are Now In Function3()"
      MsgBox "Hi There From The Function3() Procedure"
   End Sub
```

Now you should debug. Start by placing a breakpoint within the **Click** event of **cmdDebug** on the line that reads **Call Function1**. Here are the steps to follow to do so:

1. Click anywhere on the line of code that says **Call Function1**.

2. Press your F9 function key, click in the gray bar to the left of the line to break on, or select the Debug menu's Toggle Breakpoint option. However you set the breakpoint, the VBA editor will place a dark red circle to the left of the line and highlight the line in the same color.

3. Go into Form view and click the Test Code button. Access suspends execution just before executing the line where you placed the breakpoint. VBA displays a rectangular yellow outline around the line and highlights the same line, indicating that it's about to execute that line, as shown in Figure 20.7.

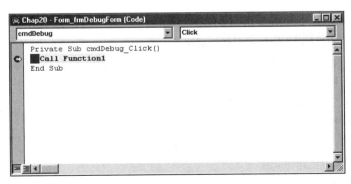

Figure 20.7   Code execution halted at a breakpoint.

Adding A Watch Expression

As you saw earlier in this chapter, you can add a Watch expression using the Quick Watch. Adding a watchpoint this way doesn't give you full control over the nature of the watch, however. When you need more control over the watch, select the Debug menu Add Watch option. The Add Watch dialog box is shown in Figure 20.8.

TIP: *If you add an Instant Watch, or you add a watch using the Debug menu Add Watch option, you can easily customize the specifics of the Watch by double-clicking the Watch in the Watch window.*

The Expression text box is used to enter a variable, property, function call, or any other valid expression. It's important to select the procedure and module in which you want the expression to be watched. Next, indicate whether you want to simply watch the value of the expression in the Immediate window, break when the expression becomes True, or break whenever the value of the expression changes. The two latter options are covered in detail in the sections that follow.

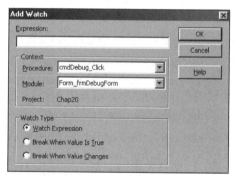

Figure 20.8   The Add Watch dialog box.

Editing A Watch Expression

After you've added a watch, you might want to edit the nature of the watch or re-move it entirely. The Edit Watch dialog is used to edit or delete a Watch expression:

1. Activate the Immediate window.

2. Select the expression you want to edit.

3. Select the Debug menu Edit Watch option. The dialog box pictured in Figure 20.9 appears.

4. Make changes to the watch, or click Delete to remove it.

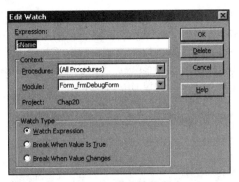

Figure 20.9   The Edit Watch dialog box lets you modify the specifics of a watch expression once you've added it.

Breaking When An Expression Is True

A powerful aspect of a Watch expression is that you can break whenever an expression becomes **True**. For example, you can break whenever a **Public** variable reaches a specific value. You might want to do this when a **Public** or **Private** variable is somehow being changed and you want to find out where. Consider the following code, found in the **basFuncExamples** module stored on the companion CD-ROM in Chapter 20's directory:

```
Sub ChangeGlobal1()
  gintCounter = 50
  Call ChangeGlobal2
End Sub

Sub ChangeGlobal2()
  gintCounter = gintCounter + 10
  Call ChangeGlobal3
End Sub

Sub ChangeGlobal3()
  Dim intCounter As Integer

  For intCounter = 1 To 10
    gintCounter = gintCounter + intCounter
  Next intCounter
End Sub
```

You might find that **gintCounter** is somehow reaching a number greater than 100 and you aren't sure how. To solve the problem, add the watchpoint pictured

in Figure 20.10. Notice that the expression you're testing for is **gintCounter >
100**. Figure 20.10 shows the breakpoint as set to break the code whenever the
expression becomes **True**. To test the code, type **ChangeGlobal1** in the Immediate window. The code should break in the **ChangeGlobal3** routine, indicating
that this routine is the one causing the problems.

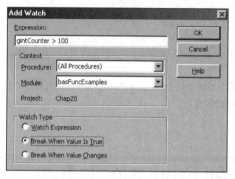

Figure 20.10   Defining a watch that makes the execution break whenever the specified
expression evaluates as True.

Breaking When An Expression Has Changed

Instead of breaking when an expression becomes **True**, you might want to break
whenever the value of the expression changes. This is a great way to identify the
place where the value of a variable is mysteriously altered. Like Break When Expression Is True, this option is great for tracking down problems with **Public** and
Private variables. Notice the watchpoint being set in Figure 20.11.

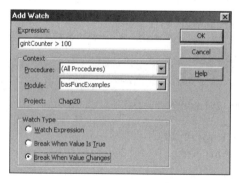

Figure 20.11   Creating a watch that will cause code execution to break whenever the value of
the expression has changed.

It's in the context of all procedures within all modules. It's set to break whenever the value of **gintCounter** is changed. When you execute the **ChangeGlobal1** routine, you'll find that the code halts execution within **ChangeGlobal1** immediately after the value of **gintCounter** is set to 50. If you press F5 to continue execution, the code halts within **ChangeGlobal2** immediately after **gintCounter** is incremented by 10. In other words, every time the value of **gintCounter** is modified, the code execution breaks.

Such a watch is useful when you find that you're returning unexpected values from a variable. In general, you'll find in such situations that you're inadvertently incrementing the value within a loop of some type.

Clearing An Error

When an error occurs, the **Err** object remains set with the error information until one of the following clears the error:

- **Resume**, **Resume Next**, or **Resume <LineLabel>**
- **Exit Sub**, **Exit Function**, or **Exit Property**
- Any **Goto** statement
- Explicitly using the **Clear** method on the **Err** object

Until the error is somehow cleared, all the information remains set within the **Err** object. After the error is cleared, no information is found within the **Err** object.

Creating A Generic Error Handler

A generic error handler is an error handler that can be called from anywhere within your application. It's capable of responding to any type of error.

A generic error handler keeps you from having to write specific error handling into each of your subroutines and functions. This enables you to invoke error handling throughout your application in the most efficient manner possible.

You can take many approaches in creating a generic error handler. A generic error handler should provide the user with information about the error, enable the user to print out this information, and log the information to a file. A generic error handler should be able to be called from every procedure within your application.

The **On Error** routine (in this case, the label **CodeSampleSub_Err**) of every procedure that does error handling should look like the error-handling routine contained within the following subroutine:

```
Sub CodeSampleSub()
  Dim strSubName As String

  strSubName = "CodeSampleSub"
  On Error GoTo CodeSampleSub_Err
  MsgBox "This is the rest of your code...."
  Err.Raise 11
  MsgBox "Past the Error!!"
  Exit Sub

CodeSampleSub_Err:
  Dim intAction As Integer

  intAction = ErrorHandler(intErrorNum:=Err.Number, _
      strErrorDescription:=Err.Description, _
      strModuleName:=mstrModuleName, _
      strRoutineName:=strSubName)
  Select Case intAction
    Case ERR_CONTINUE
      Resume Next
    Case ERR_RETRY
      Resume
    Case ERR_EXIT
      Exit Sub
    Case ERR_QUIT
      End
  End Select
End Sub
```

This error-handling routine within **CodeSampleSub** creates an **Integer** variable that holds the return value from the error system. The **intAction** variable is used to hold an appropriate response to the error that has occurred. The error routine calls the generic error-handling function named **ErrorHandler**, passing it the error number (**Err.Number**), a description of the error (**Err.Description**), the name of the module containing the error, and the name of the subroutine or function containing the error. The name of the module is stored in a Private constant named **mstrModuleName**. The Private constant is declared in the General section of the module and needs to be created for every module that you make. The name of the subroutine or function is stored in a local variable called **strSubName**. With this approach, you create a local string and assign it the name of the sub at the beginning of each procedure. This requires upkeep because procedure names can change, and you need to remember to change your string. When the code returns from the **ErrorHandler** function, a return value is placed in the **intAction** variable. This return value is used to determine the fate of the routine.

Now that you've seen how to implement error handling in your procedures, it's time to take a look at the function that's called when an error occurs. First, however, you need to see the constants and user-defined type that the error-handling function will use to perform its processing before you analyze the function itself. The declarations are shown here:

```
Public Const ERR_CONTINUE = 0  'Resume Next
Public Const ERR_RETRY = 1 'Resume
Public Const ERR_QUIT = 2  'End
Public Const ERR_EXIT = 3  'Exit Sub or Func


Type typErrors
   intErrorNum As Integer
   strMessage As String
   strModule As String
   strRoutine As String
   strUserName As String
   datDateTime As Date
End Type


Public pError As typErrors
```

The preceding code is placed in the general section of **basHandleErrors**, found on the companion CD-ROM in Chapter 20's subdirectory. The type structure (**typErrors**) that's declared holds all the pertinent information about the error. The public variable **pError** holds all the information from the type structure. The constants are used to help determine the fate of the application after an error has occurred. Here is the **ErrorHandler** function (also within the **basHandleErrors** module):

```
Function ErrorHandler(intErrorNum As Integer, _
    strErrorDescription As String, _
    strModuleName As String, _
    strRoutineName As String) As Integer
  With pError
    .intErrorNum = intErrorNum
    .strMessage = strErrorDescription
    .strModule = strModuleName
    .strRoutine = strRoutineName
    .strUserName = CurrentUser()
    .datDateTime = Now
```

```
            End With
            Call LogError
            Dim db As Database
            Dim snpRS As Recordset

            Set db = CurrentDb()
            Set snpRS = _
                db.OpenRecordset("Select Response from tblErrors Where " & _
                "ErrorNum = " & intErrorNum, dbOpenSnapshot)
            If snpRS.EOF Then
              DoCmd.OpenForm "frmAppErrors", WindowMode:=acDialog, _
                  OpenArgs:=ErrorHandler
              ErrorHandler = ERR_QUIT
            Else
              Select Case snp.Response
                Case ERR_QUIT
                  DoCmd.OpenForm "frmAppErrors", WindowMode:=acDialog, _
                      OpenArgs:="Critical Error:  Application will Terminate"
                  ErrorHandler = ERR_QUIT
                Case ERR_RETRY
                  ErrorHandler = ERR_RETRY
                Case ERR_EXIT
                  DoCmd.OpenForm "frmAppErrors", WindowMode:=acDialog, _
                      OpenArgs:="Severe Error:  Processing Did Not Complete"
                  ErrorHandler = ERR_EXIT
                Case ERR_CONTINUE
                  ErrorHandler = ERR_CONTINUE
              End Select
            End If
          End Function
```

The **ErrorHandler** function receives the error number, error description, module name, and subroutine or function name as parameters. It then fills in the **pError** type structure with the information that it was passed, as well as the current user and date. Next, it calls a routine that logs the error into an Access table. The routine looks up the severity of the error code in an Access table called **tblErrors** to decide the most appropriate way to handle the error. If the error code isn't found in the error table, an error form is displayed and a return value is sent to the calling function, indicating that application execution is to be terminated. If the error code is found in the **tblErrors** table and determined to be critical or severe, an error form displays before control is returned to the calling routine. In any case, a severity code for the error is returned to the calling function. The details involved in each step of the process are discussed in the following section.

Logging The Error

The **SQLLogError** routine is responsible for logging all the error information into an Access table. Because users often decide not to print out the error form or provide you with inaccurate information about what was happening when the error occurred, it's important that you log each error so that you can review the error log at any time. Moreover, users—even beta testers—will often neglect to tell you about the error. Keeping a close log of errors is a crucial part of beta testing your application. Errors can be logged to either a text file or a data table. This section shows you both methods of logging your error. Start with logging your errors to a table. The **SQLLogError** routine looks like this:

```
Sub SQLLogError()
  Dim sSQL As String

  DoCmd.SetWarnings False
  sSQL = "INSERT INTO tblErrorLog (ErrorDate, ErrorTime, UserName, " & _
      "ErrorNum, ErrorString, Module, Routine) "
  With pError
    sSQL = sSQL & "VALUES ( #" & .datDate & "#, #" & _
        .datTime & "#, '" & .strUserName & "', " & _
        .intErrorNum & ", '" & .strMessage & "', '" & _
        pError.strModule & "', '" & pError.strRoutine & "')"
  End With
  DoCmd.RunSQL sSQL
  DoCmd.SetWarnings True
End Sub
```

This routine uses a SQL statement to add a record to your error table. The record contains all the information from the structure called **pError**. The information is logged to a table called **tblErrorLog**. The structure of this table appears in Figure 20.12.

The alternative is to write the information to a textual error log file:

```
Sub TextLogError()
  Dim intFile As Integer

  intFile = FreeFile
  Open CurDir & "\ErrLog.Asc" For Append Shared As intFile
  Write #intFile, "A2000BBLogError", Now, Err, Error, CurrentUser()
  Close intFile
End Sub
```

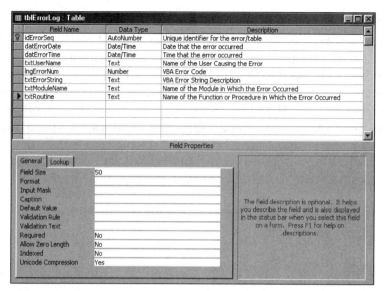

Figure 20.12   The structure of the tblErrorLog table.

This code uses the low-level file functions **Open** and **Write** to open and write to an ASCII text file. All the pertinent information about the error is written to this text file. The routine then uses the **Close** command to close the text file. The potential advantage of this routine is that if the problem is with the database (for example the network is down), the error logging process still succeeds.

Determining The Appropriate Response To An Error

After the error has been logged, you're ready to determine the best way to respond to the error. By making your error system data driven, you can handle each error a little differently. The structure of the **tblErrors** table appears in Figure 20.13.

This table should contain a list of all the error numbers for which you want to trap. It should also contain two fields—**ErrorNum** and **Response**. When an error occurs, the **ErrorHandler** function searches for a record with a value in the **ErrorNum** field that matches the number of the error that occurred. The **ErrorHandler** function uses the following code to locate the error code within the **tblErrors** table:

```
Dim db As Database
Dim snpRS As Recordset

Set db = CurrentDb()
Set snp = db.OpenRecordset("Select Response from tblErrors Where " & _
```

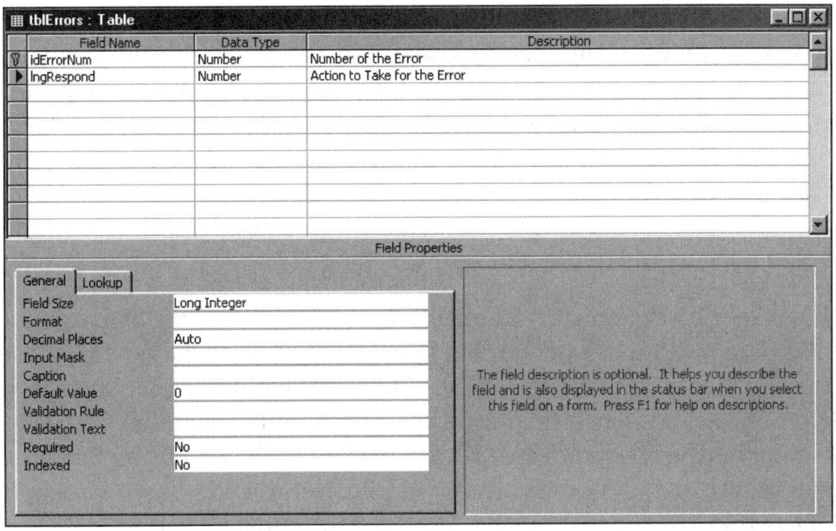

Figure 20.13   The structure of tblErrors.

```
      "ErrorNum = " & intErrorNum, dbOpenSnapshot)
If snpRS.EOF Then
  DoCmd.OpenForm "frmAppErrors", WindowMode:=acDialog, _
      OpenArgs:="ErrorHandler"
  ErrorHandler = ERR_QUIT
Else
  Select Case snpRs!Response
    Case ERR_QUIT
      DoCmd.OpenForm "frmAppErrors", WindowMode:=acDialog, _
          OpenArgs:="Critical Error:  Application will Terminate"
      ErrorHandler = ERR_QUIT
    Case ERR_RETRY
      ErrorHandler = ERR_RETRY
    Case ERR_EXIT
      DoCmd.OpenForm "frmAppErrors", WindowMode:=acDialog, _
          OpenArgs:="Severe Error:  Processing Did Not Complete"
      ErrorHandler = ERR_EXIT
    Case ERR_CONTINUE
      ErrorHandler = ERR_CONTINUE
    End Select
End If
```

This part of the **ErrorHandler** function creates both a **Database** and a **Recordset** object variable. It opens a Snapshot type of **Recordset** using a **Select** statement. The **Select** statement searches a table called **tblErrors**. When a match is found, the **Response** field is used to determine the response to the error. Notice in the code that if the error number isn't found in **tblErrors**, default error handling occurs, which means that the code handles all other errors as a group. (Note: This is the application's default error handling, not Access's.) If the error number is found, the **Response** field is evaluated and the appropriate action is taken (via the case statement). If it isn't found, the **frmAppErrors** form is opened and the **ERR_QUIT** constant value is returned from the **ErrorHandler** function. In this way, you need to add to the table only specific errors you want to trap for.

When no records are found within **tblErrors** that match the SQL statement, the **frmAppErrors** form is opened, and the return value for the function is set equal to the constant value **ERR_QUIT**. When the error number is found within **tblErrors**, the Response field from the Snapshot is evaluated. If the Response field contains the constant value **ERR_QUIT** or **ERR_EXIT**, the **frmAppErrors** form is displayed before the constant value is returned to the offending function or subroutine. If the Response field contains the constant value for **ERR_RETRY** or **ERR_CONTINUE**, the constant value is returned without displaying the **frmAppErrors** form.

The return value from the **ErrorHandler** function is used as follows:

```
Sub SampleCrashSub()
  Dim strSubName As String

  strSubName = "SampleCrashSub"
  On Error GoTo SampleCrashSub_Err
  MsgBox "This is the rest of your code...."
  Err.Raise 11
  MsgBox "Made it Past the Error!!"
  Exit Sub

SampleCrashSub_Err:
  Dim intAction As Integer

  intAction = ErrorHandler(intErrorNum:=Err.Number, _
     strErrorDescription:=Err.Description, _
     strModuleName:=mstrModuleName, _
     strRoutineName:=strSubName)
  Select Case intAction
    Case ERR_CONTINUE
      Resume Next
    Case ERR_RETRY
      Resume
    Case ERR_EXIT
      Exit Sub
```

```
      Case ERR_QUIT
          End
   End Select
End Sub
```

In this example, the **SampleCrashSub** procedure generates an error 11 (divide by zero). Because **tblErrors** contains the number zero in the **Response** column, and the **ERR_CONTINUE** constant is equal to three, the error form is displayed and the **SampleCrashSub** procedure is exited with an **Exit Sub**.

Creating An Error Form

Creating an error form—a form whose sole purpose is to display error information within your application—is an important part of both the bug-testing process and the normal distribution of an application. The code in the error form's load event calls two subroutines, as you can see in the following reprint of the **Form_Load** event's code:

```
Private Sub Form_Load()
  Call GetSystemInfo(Me)
  Call GetErrorInfo(Me)
  Me!lblAction.Caption = Me.OpenArgs
End Sub
```

The first subroutine is called **GetSystemInfo**. It performs several Windows application programming interface (API) calls to fill in the system information on your form. Using API calls is necessary because, although the VBA programming model that Access 2000 provides you with has significant access to a powerful and useful model, VBA is unable to perform or is inefficient at performing certain tasks. In such cases, declaring an external Windows API call is often the best (or only) alternative. In the case of the error form, reading memory information and obtaining other operating system information of the type the form displays is generally best accomplished using the API. The code for the **GetSystemInfo** function, which performs all the API function calls, is as shown here:

```
Sub GetSystemInfo (frmAny As Form)
  'Get Free Memory
  Dim MS As MEMORYSTATUS

  MS.dwLength = Len(MS)
  GlobalMemoryStatus MS
```

```
With frmAny
  .lblMemoryTotal.Caption = Format(MS.dwTotalPhys, "Standard")
  .lblMemoryAvail.Caption = Format(MS.dwAvailPhys, "Standard")

  'Get Version Information
  Dim OSInfo As OSVERSIONINFO

  OSInfo.dwOSVersionInfoSize = Len(OSInfo)
  If GetVersionEx(OSInfo) Then
    .lblOSVersion.Caption = OSInfo.dwMajorVersion & "." _
        & OSInfo.dwMinorVersion
    .lblBuild.Caption = OSInfo.dwBuildNumber And &HFFFF&
    If OSInfo.dwPlatformId = 0 Then
      .lblPlatform.Caption = "Windows 95"
    Else
      .lblPlatform.Caption = "Windows NT"
    End If
  End If

  'Get System Information
  Dim SI As SYSTEM_INFO

  GetSystemInfo SI
  .lblProcessor.Caption = SI.dwProcessorType
End With
End Sub
```

These API calls require the following **Declare** statements and application-defined types. The functions and types are both defined by the Win32 API. You can find these declarations in a module on the CD-ROM under Chapter 20's directory called **basErrAPI**:

```
Option Compare Database
Option Explicit

Private Type MEMORYSTATUS
  dwLength As Long
  dwMemoryLoad As Long
  dwTotalPhys As Long
  dwAvailPhys As Long
  dwTotalPageFile As Long
  dwAvailPageFile As Long
  dwTotalVirtual As Long
  dwAvailVirtual As Long
End Type
```

```
Type OSVERSIONINFO
  dwOSVersionInfoSize As Long
  dwMajorVersion As Long
  dwMinorVersion As Long
  dwBuildNumber As Long
  dwPlatformId As Long
  strReserved As String * 128
End Type


Private Type SYSTEM_INFO
  dwOemID As Long
  dwPageSize As Long
  lpMinimumApplicationAddress As Long
  lpMaximumApplicationAddress As Long
  dwActiveProcessorMask As Long
  dwNumberOfProcessors As Long
  dwProcessorType As Long
  dwAllocationGranularity As Long
  dwReserved As Long
End Type


Public Declare Sub GlobalMemoryStatus Lib "kernel32" _
    Alias "GlobalMemoryStatus" (lpBuffer As MEMORYSTATUS)
Private Declare Function GetVersionEx Lib "Kernel32" _
    Alias "GetVersionExA" (lpOSInfo As OSVERSIONINFO) As Boolean
Public Declare Sub GetSystemInfo Lib "kernel32" _
    Alias "GetSystemInfo" (lpSystemInfo As SYSTEM_INFO)
```

TIP: *You can also use the API Text Viewer, which ships with all versions of Visual Basic and which can also be found on the Office 2000 Resource Disk, to locate and copy these functions and other API functions into your programs.*

The second subroutine, called **GetErrorInfo**, fills in the labels on the error form with all the information from your structure:

```
Sub GetErrorInfo(frmAny As Form)
With frmAny
  .lblErrorNumber.Caption = pError.intErrorNum
  .lblErrorString.Caption = pError.strMessage
  .lblUserName.Caption = pError.strUserName
  .lblDateTime.Caption = Format(pError.datDateTime, "c")
  .lblModuleName.Caption = pError.strModule
  .lblRoutineName.Caption = pError.strRoutine
End Sub
```

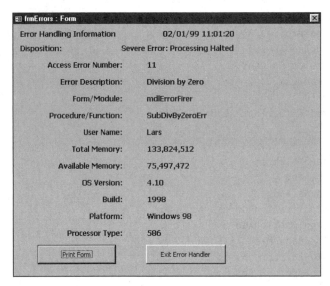

Figure 20.14   The frmAppErrors form created by the form's Load event.

Finally, the disposition of the error, sent as an **OpenArg** from the **ErrorHandler** function, is displayed in a label on the form. The error form appears in Figure 20.14.

Printing The Error Form

Users are often not very accurate in describing an error and the corresponding error message. It's therefore important to give them the ability to print out their error message—preferably in some standard output that they can then fax to you. The following code will print your error form:

```
Sub cmdPrintErr_Click()
  On Error GoTo Err_cmdPrintErr_Click
  DoCmd.PrintOut

Exit_cmdPrintErr_Click:
  Exit Sub

Err_cmdPrintErr_Click:
  MsgBox Err.Description
  Resume Exit_cmdPrintErr_Click
End Sub
```

Preventing Your Own Error Handling From Being Invoked

When you're testing your application, you don't want your own error handling to be triggered. Instead, you want VBA's error handling to be activated. The trick is in the Options dialog. Select the Tools menu Options option. Within the Options dialog box, click on the Modules tab. Check the option Break on All Errors. As long as this option is set, your error handling is ignored and Access's default error handling is invoked. Using this setting, you can turn error handling on and off from one central location.

Chapter 21

Completing The Implementation

In Depth

In Chapter 20, we focused on some of the specific design issues associated with release of a database implementation. Beta testing, user feedback, and interface analysis are all crucial steps in the process of releasing a product.

However, once you release the product, you'll very rarely end up not improving it. In fact, in most environments, there'll be problems that, no matter how hard you work on during the Beta testing, won't be known until the application is fully deployed. Many can be solved using methods similar to those discussed in Chapter 20—particularly if your implementation is for a local network or entirely internal to your company, in which patch deployment is likely to be standard practice.

Even after you iron out all of the bugs in your programs, though, other issues need to be considered once the application is deployed. In this chapter, we'll consider some of these. Specifically, we'll consider application optimization, application documenting, and maintenance techniques. You won't necessarily use all these techniques for every application—but they're definitely important for you to know, so you can effectively resolve problems when they do arise.

Optimizing Your Application

In a world where hardware never seems to keep up with software, it's important to do everything you can to improve the performance of your application. The next several sections in this chapter will help you to optimize your applications for speed and reduce the memory and hard disk space required by them.

Optimization is the process of reviewing your operating environment, VBA code, application objects, and data structures to ensure they're providing for optimum performance. In a nutshell, optimization is the process of making your application leaner and meaner.

Users become frustrated when an application runs slowly. In fact, if users aren't warned about a slow process, they often reboot or shut down the power on the machine *while* a process is running. Needless to say, such an action can have significant results on the integrity of the data in the application.

To help reduce the chance of a user rebooting the computer during a lengthy process, it's generally a good idea to provide the user with some sort of indication that a process will take awhile. This can be accomplished using a message box that appears before processing begins or by providing a status bar that shows the progress of the task being completed.

Many things can be done to optimize an application's performance—ranging from using a front-end tool such as the Performance Analyzer, to fastidiously adhering to certain coding techniques. The following sections highlight all (or at least the vast majority) of the major things that you can do to optimize the performance of your applications.

Improving Application Performance By Modifying Hardware And Software Configurations

The *Access environment* refers to the combination of hardware and software configurations under which Microsoft Access is running. These environmental settings can greatly affect the performance of an Access application.

The easiest way to improve the performance of an Access application is to upgrade the hardware and software configuration it's running on. This form of optimization requires no direct intervention from the developer. A side benefit of most of the environmental changes you can make is that any improvements made to the environment will be beneficial to users in all of their Windows applications.

Improving the environment involves more than just adding some RAM. It can also mean optimally configuring the operating system and the Access application.

The Need For More Hardware

The bottom line is that Windows and Access 2000 both crave hardware—the more, the better. The faster your users' machines, and the more memory the machines have, the better. Additional hardware might not be the least expensive solution, but it certainly is the quickest and easiest thing you can do to improve the performance of your application.

RAM Is The Critical Factor

Memory is what Access craves most, whether you're running under the full version of Microsoft Access or using the runtime version of the product. Microsoft Access requires 12MB of RAM just to run under Windows 9x, its standard operating environment. Although 12MB of RAM is required, 16MB of RAM is recommended by Microsoft. Under Windows NT, Access requires a minimum of 16MB of RAM. Both requirements can climb dramatically if your user is running other applications or if your application utilizes object linking and embedding (OLE) automation to communicate with other applications. Put in a very straightforward way, the more RAM you and the users of your application have, the better. Having 32MB of RAM creates a great environment for Access 9x. In fact, when every one of your users has at least 32MB of RAM, you can stop reading this chapter because everything else covered here is going to provide you with only minor benefits compared to adding more RAM. If you're like most of us, and not every one of your users has a Pentium 120 with 32MB of RAM, read on.

WARNING!   Developers should have a bare minimum of 32MB of RAM installed on their machines. Most developers agree 64MB of RAM is required if you intend to do any serious development work.

Defragment Your User's Hard Disk

As your computer writes information to disk, it attempts to find contiguous space on disk within which to place data files. As the hard disk fills up, files are placed in fragmented pieces on the hard disk. Each time your application attempts to read data and programs, it must locate the information scattered over the disk. This is a very time-consuming process. Therefore, it's helpful to defragment the hard disk on which the application and data tables are stored, using a utility such as the Disk Defragmenter that ships with Windows 9x.

The process of defragmenting a hard disk can easily be automated using the System Agent included as part of the Microsoft Plus! pack. The Microsoft Plus! package is sold as an add-on to Windows 95, but most of its products are included with Windows 98. The System Agent, one of the many components included with the Microsoft Plus! package, is a useful tool that enables you to schedule when and how often the defragmentation process occurs.

TIP: *The System Agent is included with Windows 98.*

Compact Your Database

Just as the operating system fragments your files over time, Access itself introduces its own form of fragmentation. Each time you add and modify data, your database grows. The problem is when you delete data or objects within your database, your database doesn't shrink. Instead, Access leaves empty pages available in which new data will be placed. But these empty pages aren't necessarily filled with data. The empty space can be freed using the Compact utility, which is part of the Microsoft Access software. The Compact utility frees excess space and attempts to make all data pages contiguous. Compact your database frequently, especially if records or database objects (for example, forms and reports) are regularly added and deleted. The Compact utility can be accessed only when no database is open. To open it, select the Tools menu Database Utilities option. You can find the Compact Database option from this menu.

Don't Use Compressed Drives

Regardless of the compression utility you're using, disk compression significantly degrades performance with Access 2000. This is documented in the README file.

Tune Virtual Memory: Tweak The Swap File

Although Windows 9x attempts to manage virtual memory on its own, you might find it useful to provide Windows 9x with some additional advice. To modify the size of the swap file, right-click on My Computer. Select Properties, then select the Performance tab. Click the Virtual Memory button. It might be useful to change the size of the swap file or move it to a faster disk drive or a drive that's connected to a separate controller card. However, any changes you make might adversely affect performance. It's important that you evaluate whether any changes you make will help the situation—or, perhaps, make things worse.

TIP: *If Access 2000 or Windows is running on a compressed drive, you can improve performance by moving the swap file to an uncompressed drive. If possible, the swap file should be located on a drive or partition solely dedicated to the swap file or a drive or partition that's rarely accessed by other applications. This helps to ensure the swap file remains in a contiguous location on disk.*

Run Access And Your Application Locally

In general, it's best to install both the Access software and your application objects on each user's local machine. Only the data tables should be stored on a network file server. Otherwise, you'll be sending DLLs, OLE Objects, help files, type libraries, executables, *and* database objects all over the network cable.

Do Everything You Can To Speed Up Windows

In many companies, you'll often find the users with the slowest machines and the least memory have the most accessories running. These accessories include multimedia, fancy wallpaper, and other common utilities. When performance is a problem, you might try experimenting to see whether eliminating some of the minor applications improves the performance of your application. If it does, encourage the user to eliminate the frills, get more memory, or accept your application's performance.

Another tip to make Windows 9x run faster is to shut down and restart on a regular basis. Memory tends to become fragmented and applications run more slowly. Although you can often go weeks or months in Windows NT without rebooting, most developers find it beneficial to reboot their Windows 9x machine at least once a day.

Change Access's Software Settings

In addition to the more obvious measures just outlined, some minor software tweaking can go a long way toward improving performance. Adjusting several settings in the Windows registry can dramatically improve performance. These changes all involve the registry's indexed sequential access method (ISAM) section. The properties you might want to change include **MaxBufferSize** and **ReadAheadPages**. Both of these settings determine how the Jet engine utilizes memory.

MaxBufferSize controls the maximum size of the Jet engine's internal cache. By default, it's set to optimize performance on most machines. It does this by reading data in 4K pages and placing the data in a memory cache. The data in the cache is readily available to forms, reports, tables, and queries. Lowering the value for **MaxBufferSize** frees memory for other tasks. This might be helpful on a machine with a minimal memory configuration.

ReadAheadPages controls the number of 4K data pages the Jet database engine reads ahead when performing sequential page reads. This number can range from 0 to 31, with the default at 16. The higher the number, the more efficient Access is at reading ahead so data is available when you need it. The lower this number, the more memory is freed up for other tasks.

As you configure any of these settings, remember: What is good for one machine isn't necessarily good for the next. The settings for each machine need to be optimized with its unique hardware configuration in mind. However, in the vast majority of situations, you will not have access to all the hardware. To minimize performance problems, you should make sure your application is optimized. The Performance Analyzer can help you to optimize your application's performance.

Letting The Performance Analyzer Determine Problem Areas

You can do many things to improve the performance of an application. Most of them require significant attention and expertise on your part. The Performance Analyzer is a tool that does some of the work for you. It's a tool that analyzes the design of an Access application and suggests techniques that can be used to improve the application's performance. Many of the techniques the Performance Analyzer suggests can be implemented automatically.

To use the Performance Analyzer, select the Tools menu Analyze submenu Performance option. The dialog shown in Figure 21.1 appears.

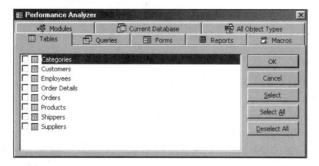

Figure 21.1   The Performance Analyzer dialog box.

Select the individual tables, queries, forms, reports, macros, modules, and relationships you want the Performance Analyzer to examine. After you click OK, the Performance Analyzer analyzes the selected objects. While it's analyzing, it will display a dialog box alerting you to the status of the analyzer. When it has completed the analysis process, the Performance Analyzer will display one of two dialog boxes. The first, which you'll almost never receive on the first pass, tells you the analyzer has no suggestions. The second, more common, dialog box provides you with a list of suggested improvements to the selected objects. Figure 21.2 shows the Performance Analyzer dialog box containing suggested improvements.

The suggested improvements are broken down into recommendations, suggestions, ideas, and items that were automatically fixed. Suggested improvements include things such as the addition of an index or conversion of an OLE object. For example, after analyzing the database shown in Figure 21.2, the performance analyzer suggested the creation of some additional relationships. It also suggested the creation of several indexes on different tables comprising the database.

When you then click on a suggestion and click Optimize, Access will automatically perform the optimization for you on your behalf—provided the optimization isn't too complex for Access.

Designing Tables To Optimize Performance

Now that you've seen the changes you can make to your environment to improve performance, let's talk about the changes you can make to your data structures to optimize performance. Such changes include eliminating redundant data, utilizing indexes, selecting appropriate field data types, and various query techniques.

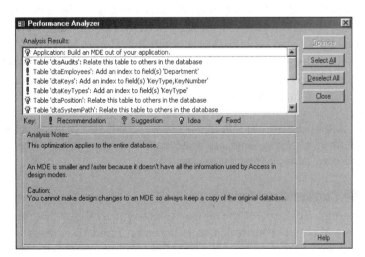

Figure 21.2   The Performance Analyzer dialog box containing suggested improvements.

Optimizing The Data Structure

Optimizing performance by tweaking the data structure is imperative for good performance. No matter what else you do to improve performance, poor data design can dramatically degrade the performance of your application. All other optimization attempts are futile without proper attention to this area.

You can spend days and days optimizing your data. These changes must be well thought out and carefully analyzed. They're often made over time as problems are identified. Such changes can include those discussed in the following sections.

Normalization, Again

As you've been told many times before, normalize your data. Normalizing data is the number one improver of performance in most cases. Data that appears in multiple places can significantly slow down your application. An example of that would be a company address appearing in both the **Customer** table and the **Orders** table. This information should be included only in the **Customer** table. Queries should be used to combine the address and order data when needed.

On The Other Hand, Maybe Not

When it comes to performance, unfortunately, no hard and fast rules apply. Although most of the time you gain performance by normalizing your data structure, at other times denormalizing the data structure can help. This is generally the case in which you forever find yourself creating a particular join over and over again. You can try denormalizing the data to see whether dramatic performance improvements result. Remember, denormalization has definite downsides regarding data integrity and maintenance.

Use Indexes Liberally

It's amazing how far an index can go in improving performance. Fields on both sides of a join should be indexed, and any fields or combination of fields on which you search should also be included in an index. Create indexes for all columns used in query joins, searches, and sorts, and create primary key indexes rather than unique indexes and unique indexes rather than nonunique indexes. The performance improvements rendered by indexes are profound.

> **WARNING!**   *Although indexes can dramatically improve performance, you shouldn't create an index for every field in a table. Indexes have their downside. Besides taking up disk space, they also slow down the process of adding, editing, and deleting data.*

Select The Correct Data Type

When defining a field, select the shortest data type available for storing the data. For example, if you'll be storing a code between 1 and 10 within the field, there's no reason to select **Double** for a numeric field. Using the wrong data type not only slows performance, it can also cause your application to rapidly swell in size.

Similarly, execution of long, non-compiled SQL queries can also slow the performance of your application. Instead, you should design and save your queries before execution—compiled queries run much more quickly.

Designing Queries To Optimize Performance

Optimizing your queries requires lots of practice and experimentation. For example, some queries involving a one-to-many relationship run more efficiently when the criteria is placed on the "one" side of the relationship. Others run more efficiently when the criteria is placed on the "many" side. Let's start with some basics that can go a long way toward improving the performance of your queries and your application as a whole (you'll learn more about working with queries in Chapter 24):

- Include as few columns in the result set as possible.

- Try to reduce the number of complex expressions contained in the query. Although including a complex expression in a query eliminates the need to build the expression into each form and report, the performance benefits gained are sometimes worth the trouble.

- Use the **Between** operator rather than greater than (>) and less than (<).

- Use the SQL **Count(*)** statement rather than the **Count([column])** statement.

- Group Totals queries by the field that's in the same table you're totaling. In other words, if you're totaling cost multiplied by price for each order in the **Order Detail** table, group by the **OrderID** within the **Order Detail** table, not the **OrderID** within the **Orders** table.

Now that you've seen what you can do with the design of your queries to improve performance, its worthwhile to consider a couple of simple techniques you can employ to improve the performance of your queries.

A simple but often neglected method of optimizing queries is to deliver your queries compiled. A query compiles when you open it in Datasheet view then simply close it. When you modify a query, then save it, it isn't compiled until the query runs. Delivering precompiled queries ensures they run as quickly as possible.

Finally, it's important that you compile your queries using the same amount of data your application will contain because Jet's query optimizer optimizes the query differently, depending upon the amount of data it finds. If you build a query using 100 records that will run on a live table containing 100,000 records, the query won't be properly optimized. You must rerun and resave your query using the correct quantity of data if you want the query to be properly optimized.

Just as pre-creating your queries will optimize their performance, changes to your code will often improve performance. The next section discusses some of the changes that can result in a significant improvement.

Making Coding Changes To Improve Performance

No matter what you do to optimize the operating-system environment and improve your data design, poor code can continue to bog you down. A properly optimized application is optimized in terms of the environment, data design, and code. Just as poor table design can degrade performance, poor coding techniques can also have a dramatic negative effect on performance. Changes to your code include the elimination of variants and dead code, the utilization of built-in collections, and the use of specific object types. An important code-related optimization is to deliver your modules precompiled.

The following changes and techniques can all aid in the improvement of performance. It's important to recognize that any one change won't make much of a difference. However, an accumulation of all of the changes, especially where code is being reexecuted in a loop, can make a significant impact on the performance of your application.

Use The Smallest Data Type Possible

Variant variables are the slowest. They carry a lot of overhead because they're resolved at runtime. Remember, the following statement declares a variant type of variable:

```
Dim intCounter
```

To strong type this variable as an integer, for example, your code must be modified to look like this:

```
Dim intCounter As Integer
```

Not only should you strong type your variables, but you should also use the smallest data type possible. Remember data types such as **Boolean**, **Byte**, **Integer**, and **Long** are the smallest and, therefore, the fastest. These are followed by **Single**, **Double**, **Currency**, and (finally) **Variant**. Of course, if you must store very large numbers with decimal points into a variable, you can't pick **Single**. Just keep in mind that it's wise to select the smallest data type appropriate for the use of the variable.

Use Specific Object Types

Just as the general variant data type is inefficient, generic object variables are also inefficient. The **MakeItBold** subroutine uses a generic object variable:

```
Private Sub cmdMakeBold_Click()
  Call MakeItBold(Screen.PreviousControl)
End Sub

Sub MakeItBold(ctlAny As Control)
  ctlAny.FontBold = True
End Sub
```

On the other hand, the **SpecificBold** subroutine uses a specific object variable:

```
Private Sub cmdSpecificBold_Click()
  Call SpecificBold(Screen.PreviousControl)
End Sub

Sub SpecificBold(txtAny As TextBox)
  txtAny.FontBold = True
End Sub
```

The difference is the **SpecificBold** subroutine expects to receive only text boxes. It doesn't need to resolve the type of object it receives and is, therefore, more efficient.

Use Inline Code

Some people have a tendency to call out to procedures for everything. This is good from a maintenance standpoint but not from an efficiency standpoint. Each time Visual Basic for Applications (VBA) calls out to a procedure, additional time is taken to locate and execute the procedure. This is particularly evident when the procedure is called numerous times. You need to decide how important maintainability is compared to speed.

Toggle Booleans Using Not

One of the most common errors made by new programmers is to assign values to variables using more complex and slower means then necessary. One of the best examples of this can be found when working with **Boolean** variables. The following code is very inefficient:

```
If bFlag = True Then
  bFlag = False
Else
    bFlag = True
End If
```

It should instead be modified to look like this:

```
bFlag = Not bFlag
```

Besides requiring fewer lines of code, this expression evaluates much more quickly at runtime.

Use The Built-In Collections

The built-in collections are there whether you use them or not. By using the **For Each...Next** construct and a collection of objects (which you'll learn more about in Chapter 27), you can write very efficient code. Consider the following example:

```
Sub FormCaption()
  Dim frm As Form

  For Each frm In Forms
    frm.Caption = frm.Caption & " - " & CurrentUser()
  Next
End Sub
```

Here, you're using the **Forms** collection to quickly and efficiently loop through each form, changing the caption on its title bar.

Use Transactions—But Only If It Helps

In versions of Access earlier than Access 95, transactions dramatically improved performance. Using explicit transactions, the data is written to disk only once, upon the call to **CommitTrans**. All changes between a **BeginTrans** and a **CommitTrans** are buffered in memory. Because disk access is the slowest thing on a computer, this technique offered you major performance benefits in versions of Access prior to Access 95.

The difference with Access 95 and later versions is that the Jet 3.x/4.x engine implicitly buffers transactions. Most of the time Jet's own transaction handling offers better performance than your own. At other times, you can improve on what Jet does on its own. The only way to know for sure is to do your own benchmarking. Each situation will be different.

Eliminate Unused Dim And Declare Statements

As you modify your subroutines and functions, you often declare a variable, then never use it. Each **Dim** statement takes up memory whether you use the variable or not. Furthermore, **Declare** statements, which are used to call external library functions, also take up memory and resources. They should be removed if the library functions aren't being used.

Eliminate Unused Code

Most programmers experiment with various alternatives for accomplishing a task. This often involves creating numerous test subroutines and functions. The problem is most people don't remove this code when they're done with it. This "dead code" is loaded with your application and, therefore, takes up memory and resources. Several third-party tools are available that can help you to find both dead code and variable declarations. The Performance Analyzer can also assist you with the process of eliminating dead code and variables.

Use The Me Keyword

Sometimes, you might use a code invocation, such as **Forms!frmHello!txtHello,** to refer to a control on the current form. It's more efficient to refer to the control as **Me!txtHello** because VBA searches only in the local name space. Although this makes your code more efficient, the downside is the **Me** keyword only works within form modules. It doesn't work within code modules. This means you can't include the **Me** keyword in generic functions that are accessed by all of your forms.

Use String Functions When Possible

Many of the string processing functions come in two forms—one with a dollar sign (**$**) and one without. A common example is **Left(sName)** versus **Left$(sName).** It's more efficient to use the version with the dollar sign whenever possible. The functions with the dollar sign return strings rather than variants. When a string variable is returned, VBA doesn't need to perform type conversions. Note that you should only use this **$** version if **sName** is a **String** variable—not a **Variant**.

Use Dynamic Arrays

Array elements take up memory regardless of whether they're being used. Therefore, it's sometimes preferable to use dynamic arrays. The size of a dynamic array can be increased as needed. If you want to reclaim the space used by all of the elements of the array, you can use the **Erase** keyword as follows:

```
Erase aNames
```

If you want to reclaim some of the space being used by the array without destroying data in the elements you want to retain, use **Redim Preserve**.

```
Redim Preserve aNames(5)
```

This statement sizes the array to six elements. (It's zero-based.) Data within these six elements is retained.

> **WARNING!** *You need to be careful when using dynamic arrays with **Redim Preserve**. When you resize an array using **Redim Preserve**, the entire array is copied in memory. If you're running in a low-memory environment, this can mean virtual disk space will be used, slowing performance—or worse than that, the application can fail if both physical and virtual memory are exhausted.*

Use Constants Whenever Possible

Constants improve both readability and performance. A constant's value is re-solved upon compilation. The value the constant represents is written to code. A normal variable has to be resolved as the code is running, because VBA needs to obtain the current value of the variable.

Use Bookmarks

A bookmark provides you with the most rapid access to a record. If you're plan-ning to return to a record, set a variable equal to that record's bookmark. It's very easy to return to that record at any time. Here's an example:

```
Sub BookMarkIt()
  Dim db As Database
  Dim rst As Recordset
  Dim varBM As Variant

  Set db = CurrentDb()
  Set rst = db.OpenRecordset("tblSample", dbOpenSnapshot)
  varBM = rst.Bookmark
  Do Until rst.EOF
    Debug.Print rst!RecordID
    rst.MoveNext
  Loop
  rst.Bookmark = varBM
  Debug.Print rst!RecordID
End Sub
```

The bookmark is stored in a variable before the **Do Until** loop is executed. After the **Do Until** loop executes, the **Recordset**'s bookmark is set equal to the value contained within the string variable.

Set Object Variables Equal To Nothing

Object variables take up memory and associated resources. Their value should be set equal to **Nothing** when you're done using them. This conserves memory and resources. To do so is a simple matter, as shown in the following code:

```
Set oObj = Nothing
```

Deliver Your Application With The Modules Compiled

Applications run more slowly when they aren't compiled. Forms and reports load more slowly, and the application requires more memory. If you deliver your appli-cation with all of the modules compiled, they don't need to be compiled on the user's machine before they're run.

To easily recompile all modules, select the Run menu Compile All Modules option with the Module window active. This command opens and compiles all code in the application, including the code behind forms and reports. You must follow the Run menu Compile All Modules command with the File menu Save All Modules command. Doing so preserves the compiled state of the application. If you compile all modules and don't save the compiled state, you might as well not have compiled in the first place.

TIP: *Don't bother selecting the Run menu Compile All Modules command if you plan to make additional changes to the application. An application becomes decompiled whenever the application's controls, forms, reports, or modules are modified. Even something as simple as adding a single control to a form will cause the application to lose its compiled state. Therefore, it's important to perform the Run menu Compile All Modules command and the File menu Save All Modules command immediately before you distribute the application.*

Organize Your Modules Well

VBA code can theoretically be placed in any module within your application. The problem is a module isn't loaded until a function within it is called. After a single procedure in a module is called, the entire module is loaded into memory. Furthermore, if a single variable within a module is used, the entire module is loaded into memory. As you might imagine, if you design your application without much thought, every module in your application will be loaded.

If you place similar routines all in one module, that module is loaded and others aren't loaded. This means if users are using only part of the functionality of your application, they'll never be loading other code modules. This conserves memory and, therefore, helps to optimize your application's performance.

Designing Forms And Reports To Improve Performance

Several things can be done to forms and reports to improve your application's performance. These include techniques to quickly load the forms and reports, tips and tricks regarding OLE objects, and special coding techniques that apply only to forms and reports.

Designing Forms To Improve Performance

Because forms are your main interface to your user, making them as efficient as possible can go a long way toward improving the user's perception of performance within your application. Additionally, many of the form optimization techniques are extremely easy to implement.

Form-optimization techniques can be categorized in two ways: those that make the forms load more quickly, and those that enable you to more efficiently manipulate objects within the form.

The larger a form is and the more controls and objects you've placed on it, the less efficient that form will be. Make sure controls on the form don't overlap. It's also extremely beneficial to group form data onto logical pages. This is especially important if your users have insufficient video RAM. Objects on subsequent pages shouldn't be populated until the user moves to that page.

Forms and their controls should be based upon saved queries. Include only fields required by the form in the form's underlying query. Avoid using **Select *** queries. Because Access is so efficient at internally optimizing the manipulation of query results, this improves the performance of your forms. To take further advantage of the power of queries, reduce the number of records the query returns, loading only the records you need at a particular time.

OLE objects take far more resources than do images. If an OLE bitmapped object doesn't need to be changed, convert it to an image. To accomplish this, click on the object and select the Format menu Change To option.

Avoid the use of subforms whenever possible. Access treats a subform as a separate form, so it takes up significant memory.

Make sure the **RowSource** for a combo box includes only the columns needed for the combo box. Index on the first field that appears in the combo box. This has a dramatic effect on the speed at which a user can move to an element of the combo box. Also, whenever possible, make the first visible field of a combo box a text field. Access converts numeric fields to text as it searches through the combo box to find a matching value.

A general rule regarding the performance of forms is to place all database objects, except data, on each user's machine. This eliminates the need for Access to constantly pull object definitions over the network.

Another tip that can help you to dramatically improve the performance of your forms is to use the default formatting and properties for as many controls as possible. This acts to significantly improve performance because only the form and control properties that differ from the default properties are saved with the form.

TIP: *If the majority of controls have a set of properties that are different from the default control for the form, you should change the default control for the form, then add controls based on the default. Access thus saves only the properties of the default control and doesn't need to store the properties for each control placed on the form. This can result in dramatic performance improvements.*

Designing Reports To Improve Performance

Many of the report-optimization techniques are the same as the form-optimization techniques. Reducing the number of controls, avoiding overlapping controls, basing reports on queries, and avoiding OLE objects are all techniques that improve the performance of reports as well as forms.

A special technique that can be used to improve the performance of reports involves the **NoData** event. This event is fired when a report is opened and no data is returned by the record source of the report.

While improving performance at runtime is a goal of every developer, most developers avoid addressing another important issue: documentation. Documenting your system will help you to modify and improve it later, and will also help to protect your company's interests and investment in the application. The following sections discuss documenting in detail.

Documenting Your System

Back in the days of mainframes and very formal centralized Management Information System (MIS) departments, documentation was a mandatory requirement for the completion of an application. Today, it seems as if all types of people are developing applications: administrative assistants, CEOs, sales managers, MIS professionals, and so on. To make matters worse, many of us who consider ourselves MIS professionals never received any formal systems training. Finally, the demand to get an application up and running, and then move on to the next application is more prevalent than ever. As a result of all of these factors, it seems documentation has gone by the wayside.

Despite all of the reasons why documentation doesn't seem to happen, it's as important to properly document your application today as it was in the mainframe days. Documentation provides you and your users with the following benefits:

- It makes the system easy for you and others to maintain.

- It helps to state the purpose and function of each object within the application.

Preparing Your Application To Be Self-Documenting

Fortunately, Access ships with an excellent tool to assist you with the process of documenting your database. This tool is called the Database Documenter. Although this tool can be used without any special preparation on your part, a little bit of work as you build the components of your application can go a long way toward enhancing the value of the output supplied by the Database Documenter.

Documenting Your Tables

The Database Documenter prints all field and table descriptions entered in the design of a table. Figure 21.3 shows a table in Design view. Notice the descriptions for each of the fields. These descriptions provide additional information

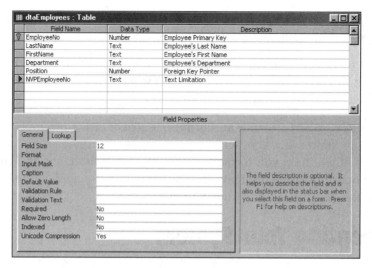

Figure 21.3   Descriptions for some of the fields in the table.

that isn't readily obvious by looking at the field names. The Table Properties window also contains a Description property. This property will be included in the documentation for the table when it's printed in the Database Documenter.

In addition to enhancing the output from the Database Documenter, entering a table description also assists you and the users of your database when working with the tables in the database. Figure 21.4 shows the Database window after descriptions have been entered for the tables in the database. Notice that the description of each table appears in the Database window.

TIP: *You must have the View Details option set in order to view descriptions.*

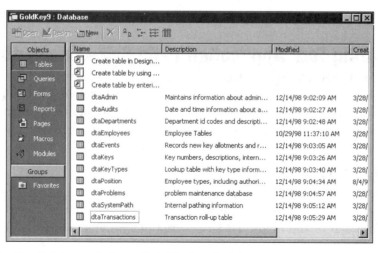

Figure 21.4   The Database window with table descriptions.

Documenting Your Queries

Just as you can enhance the output the Database Documenter provides for tables, you can also enhance the output the Database Documenter provides for queries. Figure 21.5 illustrates the Query Properties window.

As you can see, the **Description** property has been filled in with a detailed description of the purpose of the query. Figure 21.6 shows the description of an individual column within a query. Both the query and field descriptions are included in the output provided by the Database Documenter.

Documenting Your Forms

Documentation isn't limited to table and query objects. A form has a **Description** property. It can't be accessed from the Design view of the form. To view or modify the **Description** property of a form, follow these steps:

1. Make the Database window the active window.

2. Click with the right mouse button on the form for which you want to add a description.

3. Select Properties. The Object Properties dialog appears.

4. Enter a description in the Description text box.

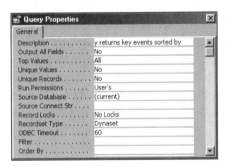

Figure 21.5   The Query Properties window with a description of the query's purpose.

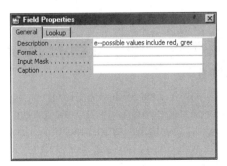

Figure 21.6   The description of an individual column within a query.

5. Click OK. The description you entered appears in the Database window, and it also appears in the output from the Database Documenter.

Documenting Your Reports

Reports are documented in exactly the same manner as forms are documented. Reports have a **Description** property that must be entered from the Object Properties dialog. Remember, to access this dialog, you right-click on the object within the Database window, then select properties.

Documenting Your Macros

Macros can be documented in significantly more detail than forms and reports. Each individual line of the macro can be documented. Not only does this provide documentation within the Database Documenter, macro comments become code comments when you convert a macro to a Visual Basic module. In addition to documenting each line of a macro, you can also add a description to the macro. As with forms and reports, to accomplish this, right-click on the macro from the Database window and select properties.

Documenting Your Modules

The importance of documenting your modules can't be emphasized enough. This is accomplished using comments. Of course, not every line of code needs to be documented. You should document all areas of your code you think aren't self-explanatory. Comments will assist you when you revisit the code to make modifications and enhancements. They also assist anyone who'll ever be responsible for maintaining your code. Finally, they provide the user with documentation about what your application is doing. Comments print with your code modules, as illustrated later in this chapter, in the section "The Database Documenter." As with the other objects, you can right-click on a module to assign a description to the module.

While the majority of the documentation for your application should occur within the components of the database, you may also want to add documentary information to the database as a whole. The following section discusses database documentation.

Using Database Properties To Document The Overall Database

In addition to enabling you to assign descriptions to the objects within the database, Microsoft Access enables you to document the database as a whole. This is accomplished by filling in the information included in the Database Properties window. To access a database's properties, select the File menu Database Properties option or right-click on the title bar of the Database window and select Database Properties. The Database Properties dialog is a tabbed dialog. The tabs include

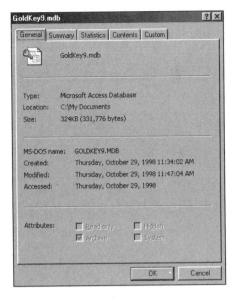

Figure 21.7   The Database Properties dialog box.

General, Summary, Statistics, Contents, and Custom. Figure 21.7 shows the Database Properties dialog box.

The following is a list of the tabs of the Database Properties dialog and a description of what they contain:

- *General tab*—The General tab displays general information about your database. Included on the General tab are the date the database was created, its size, its MS-DOS name, and its file attributes.

- *Summary tab*—The Summary tab, shown in Figure 21.8, contains modifiable information that describes the database and what it does. This tab includes the database title, its subject, and comments about the database.

- *Statistics tab*—The Statistics tab contains statistics about the database, such as when it was created, last modified, and last accessed.

- *Contents tab*—The Contents tab, shown in Figure 21.9, includes a list of all of the objects contained within the database.

- *Custom tab*—The Custom tab enables you to define custom properties associated with the database. This is useful in a large organization with numerous databases where you want to be able to search for all of the databases containing certain properties.

Documenting database properties and the properties of objects within the database is clearly important. However, taking that documentation and putting it into a useful form can often be something of a challenge. To assist in the process, Access 2000 includes the Database Documenter, explained in the next section.

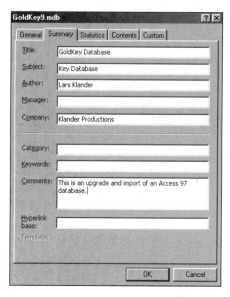

Figure 21.8   The Summary tab of the Database Properties dialog box.

Figure 21.9   The Contents tab of the Database Properties dialog box.

The Database Documenter

The Database Documenter is an elegant tool that's part of the Access application.
It enables you to selectively produce varying levels of documentation for each of
the objects within your database. Here's how it works:

1. Make sure the Database window is the active window.

2. Select the Tools menu Analyze submenu Documenter option. The Database Documenter dialog box appears, as shown in Figure 21.10 (you'll notice it looks similar to the Performance Analyzer).

3. Use the tabbed dialogs to select the type of object you want to document.

4. Click the check box to the left of each object you want to document. You can use the Select All command button to select all objects of the selected type.

5. Click the Options button to refine the level of detail that's provided for each object. Depending on which object type was selected, different options are displayed. Database Documenter options are covered later in this chapter, in the "Documenter Options" section.

6. Repeat Steps 3 through 5 to select all database objects you want to document.

7. Click OK when you're ready to produce the documentation.

After you've selected all of the desired objects and options and have clicked Okay, the Object Definition window appears. This Print Preview window allows you to view the documentation output for the objects you selected, as shown in Figure 21.11.

The Object Definition Print Preview window is just like any other Print Preview window. You can view each page of the documentation and can send the documentation to the printer. Just as with most tools at your disposal in Access, you can set certain options in the Documenter to help make it most closely fit your needs. The following section details some of those options.

Documenter Options

By default, the Database Documenter outputs a huge volume of information for each object that's selected. For example, each control on a form is documented,

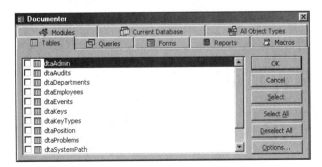

Figure 21.10   The Database Documenter dialog box.

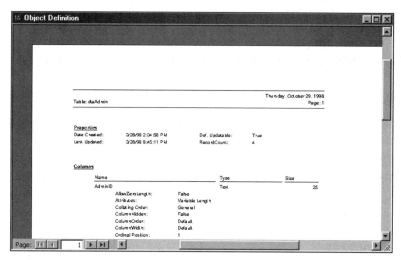

Figure 21.11   The Object Definition Print Preview window after documenting.

including every property of the control. It's easy to produce 50 pages of documentation for a couple of database objects. Besides being a tremendous waste of paper, this volume of information is overwhelming to look at. Fortunately, you can refine the level of detail that's provided by the Documenter for each category of object you're documenting. This is accomplished using the Options button of the Database Documenter dialog. The Table Definition options are pictured in Figure 21.12.

Notice you can specify whether you want to print table Properties, Relationships, and Permissions By User And Group. You can also indicate the level of detail you want to display for each field: Nothing; Names, Data Types, And Sizes; or Names, Data Types, Sizes, And Properties. For table indexes, you can opt to include Nothing; Names And Fields; or Names, Fields, And Properties.

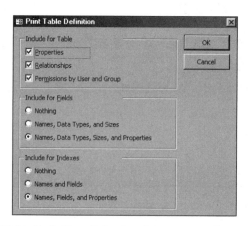

Figure 21.12   The Print Table Definition dialog box lets you specify output options.

If you select Queries from the Object Type drop-down, then click Options, the Print Query Definition dialog box will appear. The Print Query Definition dialog enables you to select the level of detail to be output for the selected queries. You can opt whether or not to include Properties, SQL, Parameters, Relationships, and Permissions By User And Group for the Query. You can also select the level of detail you'll include for each column of the query and for the indexes involved in the query.

The Forms and Reports options are similar to one another. The Print Form Definition dialog box lets you specify whether you want to print Properties, Code, and Permissions By User And Group for the form. For each control on the form, you can opt to print nothing, the names of the controls, or the names of the controls and their properties. The Print Report Definition dialog offers the same options.

For macros, you can select whether you want to view macro Properties, Actions And Arguments, and Permissions By User And Group. For modules, you can opt to view Properties, Code, and Permissions By User And Group.

As you can see, the Database Documenter offers you much flexibility in the level of detail it provides. Of course, if you haven't filled in the properties of an object (for example, the **Description**), it does you no good to display the properties. However, whatever level of detail you choose, the Documenter will always generate a report. That report is useful for hard-copy output, but is not particularly useful for online management. The following section details some of the options you have when working with the report.

Producing Documentation In Other Formats

After you've produced the documentation and it appears in the Object Definition Print Preview window, you can output it to other formats. To do this, select the File menu Output To option from the Print Preview window. The Output To dialog box appears. You can output the documentation to Microsoft Excel, to a Rich Text Format file, to HTML, or to an MS-DOS text file. After selecting the desired format, click OK. Access prompts you for a name for the new file. It then proceeds to create the file and even launches you into the appropriate application, based on the file format you select—Excel if you select Excel, Word if you select Rich Text Format, your default browser if you select HTML, and Notepad if you select MS-DOS Text.

Writing Code To Create Your Own Documentation

Most of the time, what information is provided by the Database Documenter is sufficient. At times, you won't like the format the Database Documenter selects— or more importantly, you might want to document properties of the database objects not available through the user interface. It's in these situations that you can opt to enumerate the database objects using code and output them to a custom report format. The "Immediate Solutions" section of this chapter contains an example of how to enumerate the objects in a database.

In addition to documentation tasks and the performance issues we have discussed previously, there are certain other maintenance tasks that you should perform regularly. The following sections discuss some of those techniques.

Database Maintenance Techniques

Although there isn't too much you need to do to maintain an Access database, you must know a couple of important techniques to ensure your databases are maintained as effectively as possible. The two techniques you must be familiar with are *compacting* and *repairing*. In short, compacting a database means removing unused space, and repairing a database involves repairing a damaged database (MDB file). Both of these processes and the various ways you can accomplish them are covered in this chapter.

Compacting Your Database

As you and the users of your application work with a database, the database grows in size. To maintain a high state of performance, Access defers the removal of discarded pages from the database until you explicitly compact the database file. This means as you add data and other objects to the database and remove data and objects from the database, the disk space that was occupied by the deleted objects isn't reclaimed. This results not only in a very large database (MDB) file, but also in a degradation in performance as the physical file becomes fragmented on disk. Compacting a database accomplishes the following tasks:

- Reclaims all space occupied by deleted data and database objects.

- Reorganizes the database file so the pages of each table within the database are contiguous. This serves to improve performance because as the user works with the table, the data within the table is located contiguously on the disk.

- Resets Counter fields so the next value will be one more than the last *undeleted* counter value. For example, if in testing you've added many records that you delete just before placing the application in production, compacting the database resets all of the counter values back to one.

- Re-creates the table statistics used by the Jet engine when queries are executed and marks all queries to be recompiled the next time they're run. These are two very important related benefits of the compacting process. If indexes have been added to a table or the volume of data in the table has been dramatically changed, the query won't execute efficiently. This is because the stored query plan that Jet uses to execute the query is based on inaccurate information. When the database is compacted, all table statistics and the query plan for each query are updated to reflect the current state of the tables within the database.

TIP: *It's a good idea to defragment the hard disk where the database is stored before performing the compact process. This ensures that as much contiguous disk space as possible is available for the compacted database.*

How To Compact A Database

The following three methods exist for compacting a database:

- Use commands provided within the user interface.

- Click on an icon you set up for the user.

- Use the **CompactDatabase** method from code.

Regardless of the method you select for the compact procedure, the following conditions must be true:

- The user performing the compact procedure must have the rights to open the database exclusively.

- The user performing the compact procedure must have Modify Design or Administer permission for all tables in the database.

- The database must be available to be opened for exclusive use. This means no other users can be using the database.

- There must be enough disk space available for both the original database and the compacted version of the database. This is true even if the database is compacted to a database by the same name.

The "Immediate Solutions" section details the steps to perform to compact a database. It is important to note that compacting a database will not fix a database which may have been damaged, unless you use the Compact And Repair option from the Interactive Development Environment (IDE). However, in general, to fix a database, you must use the repair process, detailed in the following section.

Repairing A Database

The repair process is used when a database has been damaged. Damage can occur to a database when the power is interrupted while the database is open or for several other reasons. Regardless of the cause, a damaged database can often be salvaged using the repair utility. As with the compact process, the repair process can be executed from within the Access interface using a desktop shortcut or using Data Access Objects (DAO) code. To perform the repair process, the follow conditions must be met:

- The user performing the repair process must have the rights to open the database exclusively.

- The database must be available to be opened for exclusive use. This means no other users can be using the database.

It's a good idea to back up the database before attempting to repair it because it's possible for the repair process to do further damage to the database. Also, don't use the repair process as a substitute for carefully following backup procedures. The repair process isn't always successful. Nothing is as foolproof as a regularly executed backup process.

TIP: When a database is repaired, it might increase in size. This is because the repair process actually creates a series of temporary indexes to assist with the repairs. It's therefore a good idea to compact a database after you repair it. This can be accomplished using the combination of the **/Repair** and **/Compact** switches. When you specify both command-line switches, Access always repairs the database first, before compacting it.

Immediate Solutions

Optimizing String Comparisons With The **Len** Function

Using the **Len** function is more efficient than testing for a zero-length string. Here's what the code for both tests looks like:

```
Sub SayNameZero(strName As String)
  If strName <> "" Then
    MsgBox strName
  End If
End Sub

Sub SayNameLen(strName As String)
  If Len(strName) Then
    MsgBox strName
  End If
End Sub
```

The **SayNameLen** function is easier for VBA to evaluate and, therefore, runs more quickly and efficiently. Additionally, string operations by the nature are slow; try and use numeric operations whenever you can to speed processing.

Optimizing Comparisons With **True** And **False**

This example is very similar to the previous one. It's better to evaluate for **True** and **False** instead of zero. Here's an example:

```
Sub SayEarningsZero(lngEarnings As Long)
  If lngEarnings <> 0 Then
    MsgBox "Salary is " & lngEarnings
  End If
End Sub
```

The following code would run more efficiently:

```
Sub SayEarningsTrue(lngEarnings As Long)
  If lngEarnings Then
```

```
      MsgBox "Salary is " & lngEarnings
    End If
End Sub
```

Using Variables To Optimize Object References

If you're going to repeatedly refer to an object, you should declare an object variable and refer to the variable rather than the actual control. Here's an example:

```
Forms!frmAny!txtHello.FontBold = True
Forms!frmAny!txtHello.Enabled = True
Forms!frmAny!txtHello.Left = 1
Forms!frmAny!txtHello.Top = 1
```

This is a very scaled-down example, but if numerous properties are being changed or if this code is being called recursively, an object variable can be used to make the code more efficient.

```
Private Sub cmdChangeObject_Click()
  Dim txt As TextBox

  Set txt = Forms!frmHello!txtHello
  txt.FontBold = True
  txt.Enabled = True
  txt.Left = 100
  txt.Top = 100
End Sub
```

Using **With...End With** To Optimize Object Operations

Another way to optimize the code in the previous example is to use a **With...End With** construct. The code would look like this:

```
Private Sub cmdChangeObjectWith_Click()
  With Forms!frmHello!txtHello2
    .FontBold = True
    .Enabled = True
    .Left = 100
    .Top = 100
  End With
End Sub
```

Optimizing Using Action Queries

Besides being easier to code, it's much more efficient to execute a stored query than to loop through a recordset, performing some action on each record. Consider the following example:

```
Sub LoopThrough()
  Dim db As Database
  Dim rst As Recordset

  Set db = CurrentDb()
  Set rst = db.OpenRecordset("tblSample", dbOpenDynaset)
  Do Until rst.EOF
    rst.Edit
      rst!IncreaseField = rst!IncreaseField + 1
    rst.Update
    rst.MoveNext
  Loop
End Sub
```

The preceding code loops through a recordset, adding one to each project total estimate. Contrast this to the following code:

```
Sub ExecuteQuery()
  Dim db As Database

  Set db = CurrentDb
  db.Execute "qryIncreaseField"
End Sub
```

This code executes a stored query called **qryIncreaseField** (which should contain an **Update** query). The query runs much more efficiently than the **Do Until** loop.

Using Code To Enumerate Objects In The Database

By using DAO-based code, you can enumerate any of the objects within your database. The following is an example:

```
Sub EnumerateTables()
  Dim db As Database
  Dim tdf As TableDef
  Dim fld As Field
```

```
      Dim fSystem As Boolean
      Dim fAttached As Boolean

      Set db = CurrentDb
      DoCmd.SetWarnings False
      For Each tdf In db.TableDefs
        fSystem = tdf.Attributes And dbSystemObject
        fAttached = tdf.Attributes And dbAttachedTable
        DoCmd.RunSQL "INSERT INTO tblTableDoc" _
            & "(TableName, DateCreated, LastModified, " _
            & "SystemObj, AttachedTable ) " _
            & "Values (""" & tdf.Name & """, #" _
            & tdf.DateCreated & "#, #" _
            & tdf.LastUpdated & "#, " _
            & fSystem & ", " & fAttached & ")"
      Next tdf
      DoCmd.SetWarnings True
  End Sub
```

The **EnumerateTables** routine documents various information about the tables in the database. It uses a **For...Each** loop to loop through all of the table definitions in the database. For each table in the **TableDefs** collection, it determines whether the table is a system table or a linked table. It then executes a SQL statement, inserting all of the requested information about the table definition into a table called **tblTableDoc**. This table could then be used as the foundation for a report. Of course, when you use appropriate **For...Each** loops and properties, *any* information about *any* of the objects in the database can be obtained using the same technique.

Compacting And Repairing Using The User Interface

The Access user interface provides the user with a fairly straightforward interface to the compact and repair operations. To compact and repair a database using the user interface, perform the following steps:

1. Close all open databases.

2. Select the Tools menu Database Utilities submenu Compact and Repair Database option. The Database to Compact From dialog box will appear.

3. Select the database you want to compact and click Compact. The Compact Database Into dialog box will appear.

4. Select the name for the compacted database. This can be the same name as the original database name or it can be a new name. Click Save. Access will compact and repair the database.

Providing A Shortcut To The Compact Process

A very simple way to provide the user a means by which to compact a database is to create an icon that performs the compact process. This is accomplished using the **/Compact** command-line option. The **/Compact** command-line option compacts the database without ever opening it. The shortcut looks like this:

```
c:\MSOffice\Access\Msaccess.exe c:\Databases\Chap21.MDB /Compact
```

To create a shortcut, follow these steps:

1. Open the folder where your application is installed.
2. Click with the right mouse button on the application (MDB) icon for your database.
3. Select Create Shortcut. Windows 9x will create the shortcut.
4. Next, click with the right mouse button on the shortcut you just created.
5. Select the Properties option from the menu.
6. Click the Shortcut tab.
7. In the Target box, click to the right of the command line and add the **/Compact** option.

Compacting Using Code

Using the **CompactDatabase** method, you can compact a database using code. The **CompactDatabase** method is performed on the **DBEngine** object. It receives the old database and new database as parameters. In addition, it receives the following optional parameters:

- *Locale*—An optional string determining the collating order in which the data in the compacted database will be sorted. This option is used when you're working with a database in which the data is stored in another language and you want the data collated in a particular language.

- *Options*—Used to specify whether you want the compacted database to be encrypted as well as what version you want the database to be compacted into. The two constants that can be used for encryption are **dbEncrypt** and **dbDecrypt**. If you don't specify either of these constants, the compacted database will have the same encryption status as the original source database. An additional constant can be specified within the **Options** argument. This constant determines the version of the data within the compacted database. The **CompactDatabase** method converts only data, not the objects within the database.

• **Password**—Enables you to supply the password for a database that's password protected.

The following code compacts and encrypts a database called Chap21.mdb. It uses the **dbLangGeneral** locale, which is appropriate for English, German, French, Portuguese, Italian, and Modern Spanish. The compacted database will be called Chap21S.mdb.

```
Sub CompactDB()
  DBEngine.CompactDatabase "c:\databases\Chap21.mdb", _
      "c:\databases\Chap21S.mdb", _
      dbLangGeneral, dbEncrypt
End Sub
```

For this code to execute successfully, remember that the Chap21 database must be closed and the user running the code must have the right to open the database exclusively. Furthermore, the user must have Modify Design or Administer permissions for all tables within the database.

Providing A Shortcut To The Repair Process

Just as the **/Compact** command-line switch can be used to compact a database, the **/Repair** command-line switch can be used to repair a database. The format is as follows:

```
c:\MSOffice\Access\Msaccess.exe c:\Databases\Chap21.mdb /Repair
```

To create a shortcut, follow these steps:

1. Open the folder in which your application is installed.

2. Click with the right mouse button on the application (MDB) icon for your database.

3. Select Create Shortcut. Windows 9x will create the shortcut.

4. Next, click with the right mouse button on the shortcut you just created.

5. Select the Properties option from the menu.

6. Click the Shortcut tab.

7. In the Target box, click to the right of the command line and add the **/Repair** option.

Repairing The Database Using Code

Just as you can compact a database using code, you can also repair it using code. The following subroutine illustrates this process:

```
Sub RepairDB()
  Dim db As Database
  On Error Resume Next

  Set db = OpenDatabase("c:\databases\Chap21.MDB")
  If DBEngine.Errors.Count > 0 Then
    If Err = 1000 Then 'Database Corrupt
      MsgBox "Database is Corrupt..Attempting to Repair"
      DBEngine.RepairDatabase "c:\databases\Chap21.MDB"
    End If
  End If
End Sub
```

The **RepairDB** subroutine attempts to open the Chap21 database. If an error occurs on the **OpenDatabase** method, the **On Error Resume Next** statement causes the next line of code to execute. The next line of code evaluates whether the error was number 1000, indicating the database is corrupt. If so, the **RepairDatabase** method is performed on the **DBEngine** object using the name of the damaged database as an argument.

Part VII

Microsoft Access 2000 GUI And VBA Programming Reference

Chapter 22

Installation, Setup, And Configuration

In Depth

In this chapter, we'll consider some basic principles of application design, as well as lay out the strategies you'll probably use when creating applications with Access 2000. After the high-level perspective on design considerations, you'll work your way briefly through the installation of Access on your local computer. After installation, you'll be introduced to the Access 2000 interface. Finally, we'll consider issues relating to the creation of basic databases using the Access 2000–provided wizards.

You should know about several tricks of the trade that can save you a lot of time in the development process and help to ensure that your applications are as optimized as possible for performance. This chapter addresses these strategies and also explains several commonly misunderstood aspects of the Jet engine, the Access Runtime engine, and security.

Splitting Tables And Other Objects

In a multiuser environment, it's almost imperative that the tables that make up your system be placed in one database and the rest of the system objects be placed in another database. For simplicity, this book refers to the database containing the tables as the Table database and the database containing the other objects as the Application database. The two databases are connected by linking from the Application database to the Table database. This strategy offers the following advantages:

• Maintainability

• Performance

• Scalability

Assume for a moment that you distribute your application as one Access database—stored within a single MDB file. Your users work with your application for a week or two, writing down all problems and changes. It's time for you to make modifications to your application. Meanwhile, live data has been entered into the application for two weeks. You make a copy of the database (which includes the live data) and make all the fixes and changes. This process takes a week. After you finish your work on the database, you're ready to install your copy of the database back to the network.

Unfortunately, the users of the application have been adding, editing, and deleting records all week. Copying your file back now will eliminate all their changes—not the best option, obviously. Data replication can help you with this problem. The simplest solution is to split the database objects so the tables (your data) are in one MDB file, and the rest of your database objects (your application) are in a second MDB file. When you're ready to install the changes, all you need to do is to copy the Application database to the file server. The new Application database can then be installed on each client machine from the file server. In this way, users can run the new copy of the application from their machines. The database containing your data tables remains intact and is unaffected by the process.

The second benefit of splitting the database objects concerns performance. Your Table database obviously needs to reside on the network file server so the data can be shared among the users of the system. There is no good reason why the other components of the database need to be shared. Access provides optimal performance when the Application database is stored on each local machine. This method not only dramatically improves performance, but it also greatly reduces network traffic. When the Application database is stored on the file server, the application objects and code need to be sent over the network each time an object in the database is opened. If the Application database is stored on each local machine, only the data needs to be sent over the network. The only complication of this scenario is that each time the Application is updated, it needs to be redistributed to the users—a small inconvenience relative to the performance benefits that are gained through this structural split.

The third benefit of splitting tables from the other database objects relates to scalability. Because the tables are already linked, it's easy to change from a link to a table stored in Access's own proprietary format to any open database connectivity (ODBC) database, such as Microsoft SQL Server. This capability gives you quick and dirty access to client-server databases. If you've already thought through the design of your system with linked tables in mind, the transition is that much easier. Don't be fooled, though, by how easy this sounds. Many issues are associated with using Access as a front end to client-server data that go far beyond a matter of simply linking to the external tables. Some of these issues are covered in this chapter, and many others are covered in Chapter 31.

A few special types of tables should be stored in the Application database rather than in the Table database. Tables that rarely change should be stored in the Application database on each user's local machine. An example would be a State table. In most situations, this table rarely, if ever, changes. On the other hand, it's continually accessed to populate combo boxes, participate in queries, and so on. By placing the State table on each local machine, you improve performance and reduce network traffic. Temporary tables should also be placed on each local machine. This is more a necessity than an option. When two users are running the same process at the same time and that process utilizes temporary tables, a conflict occurs as one user overwrites the other's temporary tables. Placing temporary tables on each local machine improves performance and eliminates the chance of potentially disastrous conflicts.

If you've already designed your application and have included all the tables in the same database as the rest of your database objects, don't despair. You can use the Database Splitter Wizard to divide up your database. The Database Splitter Wizard, linked tables, and many other issues relating to effective use of Access in a multiuser environment are covered in Chapter 31.

Using Access As A Front End

If you're planning to use Access as a front end to other databases, you need to consider a few issues. In fact, the whole design methodology of your system will differ depending on whether you plan to store your data in an Access database or on a back-end database server.

In a system where your data is stored solely in Access tables, the Jet engine part of Access provides all data retrieval and management functions. All security, data validation, and the enforcement of referential integrity are handled by the Jet engine.

In a system where Access acts as a front end to client-server data, the server provides the data management functions. The server is responsible for retrieving, protecting, and updating data on the back-end database server. In a situation wherein Access mimics a front end, the local copy of Access is responsible only for sending requests and getting either data or pointers to data back from the database server. When you're creating an application in which Access behaves as a front end, capitalize on Access's strengths as well as on the server's strengths, which can be a very challenging endeavor.

Things You Need To Worry About In Converting To Client-Server

The transition to client-server isn't always a smooth one. You need to consider several things when you're developing a client-server application or planning to eventually move your application from an Access database to a back-end database:

- Not all field types supported in Access are supported in every back-end database.

- Any security that you implement in Access isn't converted to your back-end database.

- Validation rules that you set up in Access need to be reestablished on the back end.

22. Installation, Setup, And Configuration

- Referential integrity isn't supported on all back ends. If it's supported on your back end, it's not automatically carried over from Access.
- Queries involving joins that were updatable within Access aren't updatable on the back-end server.

This list is just an overview of what you need to think about when you're moving an application from an Access database with attached tables to a back end or when you're developing specifically for a back end. Many of these issues have far-reaching implications.

For example, when you set up validation rules and validation text within your application, the rules need to be rewritten as triggers on the back end. This isn't your only problem. If a validation rule is violated on the back end, you'll get a returnable error code. You have to handle this returnable error code using error handling within your application, displaying the appropriate message to your user. The **Validation Text** property can't be used.

Benefits And Costs Of Client-Server Technology

With all the issues discussed in the previous section, you might ask why you should bother with client-server technology. It does provide significant benefits but involves large costs in time and money to implement properly. In each case, you need to evaluate whether the benefits of client-server technology outweigh the costs. The major benefits of client-server technology include the following:

- Greater control over data integrity
- Increased control over data security
- Increased fault tolerance
- Reduced network traffic
- Improved performance
- Centralized control and management of data

The major costs of client-server technology include the following:

- Increased development costs
- Hardware costs for the server machine
- Setup costs for the server database

These lists summarize the major costs and benefits of client-server technology; they're meant only to alert you to what you need to think about when evaluating the movement of your data to a back-end database server. These and other issues are covered in more detail in Chapter 31. It is important to note, however, that these costs are relatively minor when compared with the cost of mainframe or other more traditional, large-scale implementations.

22. Installation, Setup, And Configuration

Your Options When Using Access As A Front End

Client-server technology isn't an all-or-none proposition, nor is there only one way to implement it using Access as a front end. One option is to use Access as a true front end. This means that all data is stored on the server, and all queries are processed on the server. This approach is implemented using Pass-through queries rather than stored Access queries. With Pass-through queries (covered in Chapter 31), a back-end–specific SQL statement is passed to the back end rather than being processed by Access.

To make Access a true front end, you must also disable its natural ability to bind data to forms and reports. After you've done all this you've eliminated all the features that make Access a strong product in the first place. Unfortunately, you haven't eliminated all the overhead associated with the functionality that you removed. When you want to use this approach, you're better off developing the entire application in a lower-overhead environment such as Visual Basic (or by using Access Projects).

Another approach is a hybrid method in which you use a combination of attached tables, SQL Pass-through queries, and local Access tables. The idea is that you take advantage of Access's functionality and strong points wherever possible. Pass-through queries are used to perform functions that can be performed more efficiently by communicating directly to the back end or that aren't available at all using Access SQL. To further improve performance, many tasks can be performed locally and communicated to the server as one transaction after any initial validation has been done. Data can also be downloaded to Access in bulk so additional processing is done locally. Many possibilities exist, and each is appropriate in different situations. It takes experience and experimentation to determine the combination of methods that optimize performance in a given situation.

What This All Means To You Right Now

This section has provided an overview of the issues you need to consider when you're building an application for client-server deployment or with the idea that it might be moved to a client-server environment in the future. More detailed information is given in Chapter 31. The issues behind developing client-server applications were highlighted here to reduce the chances of unexpected grief in the future. When you read through the book with these issues in mind, you'll be a much happier developer. If you're using Access as a front end, make sure that you take special note of any warnings regarding the development of client-server applications as you read this book, particularly in the more advanced chapters.

Basing Forms And Reports On Queries

The record source for a form or report can be based on a table object, a query object, or a SQL statement. By basing forms and reports on stored queries, you can dramatically improve the performance and flexibility of your applications. In most cases, you don't need to display all fields and all records on a form or report. By basing a form or report on a query, you can better limit the data that's transferred over the network. These benefits are most pronounced in a client-server environment. When you base a form or report on a table object, Access sends a SQL statement that retrieves all fields and all records from the database server. On the other hand, when the record source for the form or report is a query, just the fields and records specified within the query are returned to the workstation.

Many developers don't realize that basing a form or report on a stored query is more efficient than basing the same form or report on a SQL statement. When you save a query, the Access database Jet engine creates a *Query Plan*. This plan contains information regarding the most efficient method of executing the query. When the query is saved, the Jet engine looks at the volume of data as well as available indexes. It determines the optimal method of executing the query and stores the method as the Query Plan. This plan is used whenever a form or report based on that query is executed. When a form or report is based on a SQL statement, the optimization process occurs when the form or report is opened and the Query Plan is executed on the fly.

When basing a form on table data, you can't control the order of the records in the form, nor can you base the form on more than one table. You can't limit the records displayed on the form until after the form is opened. By basing a form on a query, you can control the criteria for the form, as well as the default order in which the records are displayed. Everything just mentioned applies to reports as well, except the order of the records. The order of the records included on a report is determined by the sorting and grouping of the report itself.

Many other techniques are available to you when displaying a form based on a large recordset. Form techniques are covered in detail in later chapters.

Understanding The Access Runtime Engine

Many developers misunderstand what Access has to offer out of the box. New developers often think they can't develop applications in Access because their company refuses to buy each user a copy of Access, or that they need to buy some other tool (such as Visual Basic) so that they can "compile" their applications. These are just two of the many misconceptions that exist regarding exactly what Access does and doesn't have to offer.

Features Of The Access Product

As you know, Access 2000 comes with the Microsoft Office 2000 Professional and Premium editions. Most features of Access 2000 are included in the Professional edition; some interactive functionality with Web design is disabled unless you install the Premium edition. The most basic but important feature of the full, interactive development environment for the Access product is a royalty-free distribution license that allows you to distribute unlimited copies of your application without your users having to own copies of Access. Instead, you build applications from Access and then create distribution versions which you send to users. The installations of the distribution versions include the necessary helper files (such as dynamic-linked libraries), so that users can run the application without installing the Access product. These helper files, when considered as a single entity, comprise the *Access Runtime Engine*. Users can run the application with the runtime engine you distribute to them. Office 2000 also includes the Microsoft Office Developer (MOD) CD-ROM (which ships with the Premium version of Office and includes the runtime engine). The MOD also provides several additional development tools:

- The Microsoft Access Language Reference and Microsoft Office 2000 Data Access Reference.

- A Package and Deploy Wizard that helps you to create disks containing compressed files with everything necessary to install and run your application.

- A host of additional object linking and embedding (OLE) custom controls. These controls can be used to significantly enhance the functionality of your application and can be distributed to your users as part of your MOD license. Although most OLE custom controls come with Access 2000, the MOD does provide others not included with the basic package.

- The Microsoft Replication Manager. This tool assists you with the replication process by allowing you to schedule updates between replicas, determine which objects in the database are replicated, visually display all the replicas in a replica set, and manage multiple replica sets. Note that this Replication Manager is more extensive than simple briefcase-based replication, which the Access 2000 product supports automatically (Tools menu, Replication option).

- The Windows 9x Help Compiler and accompanying documentation. The Windows 9x Help Compiler is covered in later chapters.

- The Windows Application Programming Interface (API) Viewer. This tool contains all the Declares, Constants, and Type Structures used with the 32-bit Windows API. It allows you to easily copy the function, constant, and type declarations into your code modules.

TIP: *If you have Visual Studio or Visual Basic Professional or Enterprise Edition installed on your computer, you'll find that many of these tools are included with both of these products. You may want to evaluate what is currently installed on your system before purchasing the MOD.*

Differences Between The Standard And Runtime Versions Of Access

It's important that you understand the differences between the standard and runtime versions of Access. The following differences have definite implications in the way you develop any applications that you expect to run from the runtime version:

- The Database, Macro, and Module windows aren't available in the runtime environment.

- No Design views are available in the runtime environment.

- Filter windows aren't available in the runtime version, including Filter-by-Form.

- No built-in toolbars are available in the runtime environment.

- Many windows, menus, and commands are invisible in the runtime environment. For example, the Window menu Hide option and Window menu Unhide option commands are invisible. Although these and other commands aren't visible, their functionality is generally accessible using code.

- You must build error handling into your runtime applications. When you don't, the application displays a generic message and exits to the desktop when an error occurs.

- You must build your own custom help files for each runtime application.

- Various keystrokes aren't available in your application.

Some of the disabled features protect your applications. For example, the absence of the Database and Design windows means that your users can't modify your application while running it under the runtime version of Access. Other disabled features translate into additional coding for you. One example is the absence of the Query-by-Form feature. This feature, available in the full version of Access, allows your users to easily filter form information. The absence of this feature can mean extra work for you.

Preparing An Application For Distribution

With all the features absent from the runtime version of Access, it's not surprising that you must take some special steps to prepare your application for distribution. Some of the steps are specific to running from the runtime version, but most are steps that you should take so your application appears professional to the user. Six steps are involved in preparing your application for distribution with the runtime version of Access:

- Basing your application around forms

- Adding startup options to your database

- Securing the objects within your application
- Building error handling into your application
- Adding a help file to your application
- Building custom menus and toolbars to be associated with forms and reports within your application

Your application should be based around and controlled via forms. It should generally begin with a main switchboard that allows the user to access the other components of your application. The main switchboard can bring the user to additional switchboards, such as a data entry switchboard, a report switchboard, or a maintenance switchboard. Switchboards can be built using an add-in called the Switchboard Manager, or they can be designed as custom dialogs. Building a switchboard as a custom dialog is covered in later chapters, as is using the Switchboard Manager to create switchboards. The main advantage of using the Switchboard Manager is that it allows you to quickly and easily create a polished application interface. The primary advantage of custom switchboards is the flexibility and freedom that they provide.

You set a form as the starting point for your application by modifying the startup options for your database. Set these options by selecting the Tools menu Startup option. The Startup dialog box will appear, as shown in Figure 22.1.

Using this dialog, you can set startup options for your application, including a startup form, an application title, and an icon that appears when your application is minimized.

As you'll learn in the next section, a database isn't secure just because you're running it from a runtime version of Access. Without security, your application can be modified by anyone with a full copy of Access. Securing your database objects is, therefore, an important step in preparing your application for distribution. Security is covered in detail in later chapters.

When error handling isn't built into your application and an error occurs while your user is running your application from the runtime version of Access, the

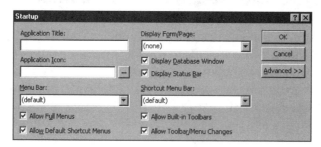

Figure 22.1   The Startup dialog box.

user is rudely exited out of the program. The user doesn't receive an appropriate error message and is left to wonder what happened. It is, therefore, vital that you add error handling to the procedures within your application.

In most cases, you want your users to be provided with custom help specific to your application. To add custom help to your application, you must build a help file and attach parts of the help file to forms and controls within your application.

Finally, because built-in toolbars aren't available in the runtime version and most of the features on the standard built-in menus are disabled, you should build your own toolbars and menus that are associated with specific forms and reports. This touch adds both polish and functionality to your application.

After you complete these steps, you're ready to take some final steps to ready your application for distribution:

- Test your application using the **/Runtime** switch.
- Create setup disks or perform a network install using the Package and Deploy Wizard.
- Install your application on a machine that has never run a copy of either the standard or runtime version of Access.
- Test your application on the machine; make sure it runs as expected.

Before you bother running the Package and Deploy Wizard (a somewhat lengthy process), it's best that you run your application using the **/Runtime** switch. This switch simulates the runtime environment, allowing you to simulate user actions under the runtime version of Access. Taking this step will generally save you a lot of time and energy. It finds most, if not all, of the problems associated with running under the runtime version.

After you test your application using the **/Runtime** switch, you're ready to run the Package and Deploy Wizard. The Package and Deploy Wizard allows you to create setup disks or perform a network install. When your users are ready to install your application, they run the installation program using **A:\Setup** (or the appropriate network drive and path). They're presented with a professional-looking, familiar setup program similar to that included with most Microsoft products.

After you run the Package and Deploy Wizard, it's important that you test your application by running the install on a machine that has never contained a copy of either the standard or runtime version of Access. Install and fully test your application. Make sure that you experiment with every feature. When you're done testing, delete everything but the zip file and unzip the zip file into the Windows System directory (so that it contains all the files that it contained before the installation of your program). The whole idea is to test your application on a machine containing no Access-related files. This ensures that all required files are included on your setup disks. After you test your application, restore the machine to its original state so you can use the machine to test your next installation.

TIP: *You should use a utility such as PKZIP, WinZip, or some other archiving tool to compress all the files in the test machine's Windows System directory or back up the entire Windows directory to another directory before the installation.*

Although this process cleans up much of what was changed as a result of installing the application, it doesn't fully restore the machine to its original state because the registry is modified during the install process. If you want to fully restore the machine to its original state, you must back up the registry before the install and restore the registry after you're done testing the application.

> **WARNING!**   *PKZIP is a shareware utility. It can be obtained from PKware, Inc. It's important to properly register the utility when you begin to use it. This involves sending the appropriate fee to PKware, Inc., in Brown Deer, Wisconsin. The fee and full address can be obtained by typing "PKZIP/?" or visiting the PKware Web site at http://www.pkware.com. Other utilities are similar.*

The Access Runtime Engine: Summing It Up

You've just read an overview of the differences between the full and runtime versions of Access. If you plan to distribute an application with the runtime version of Access, remember which features are available to your users; otherwise, you'll be in for some big surprises.

Executable File Vs. Access Database: What It Means To You

Many developers mistakenly think that distributing an application with the runtime version of Access is equivalent to distributing an executable file. A database that's distributed with the runtime version of Access can be modified just like any other database.

A user can run your application using the runtime version of Access. All the rules of running an application within the runtime version apply. This means that while running under the runtime version of Access, the user can't go into Design view, can't create his or her own objects, doesn't have access to the built-in toolbars, and so on.

This same user can install his or her own copy of the standard Access product. Using the standard version of Access, the user can open the same database. If the objects within the database haven't been secured, the user can modify the application at will.

In short, a database prepared with the Package and Deploy Wizard is no different than any other database. The Package and Deploy Wizard doesn't modify an MDB file in any way. It simply compresses all the files necessary to run your application, including the database and runtime engine, and creates a network install or distribution disks containing the compressed files. Therefore, unlike an environment where an EXE prohibits users from viewing or modifying your code, only the implementation of security protects the design of your application.

The Importance Of Securing Your Database

By now, you should understand the importance of securing your application. Setting up security is a fairly complex but extremely worthwhile process. Security can be set up at either a group or a user level. You can assign rights to objects, and these rights can be assigned to either individual users or a group of users. Figure 22.2 shows the User and Group Permissions dialog box (which you can access from the Tools menu Security submenu User and Group Permissions option).

As you can see, rights can be assigned for each object. In the case of a table, the user or group can be assigned rights to read, insert, update, and delete data as well as read, modify, or administer the design of the table. Different groups or users can be assigned different rights to an object. For example, one group can be assigned rights to add, edit, and delete data. Another group can be assigned rights to edit only, and another group to view only. An additional group can be denied the right to even view the data.

Available rights differ for tables, queries, forms, reports, macros, and modules. The types of rights that can be assigned are appropriate to each particular type of

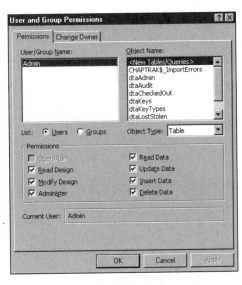

Figure 22.2   The User and Group Permissions dialog box.

object. When security has been properly invoked, it can't be violated, no matter how someone tries to access the database objects (including using the runtime version of Access, a standard copy of Access, programming code, or even a Visual Basic application). When properly secured, the database is as difficult to illegally access as an executable file.

Installing Access 2000

Now that you've spent some time focusing in on the strategies that you'll likely use when developing databases, you must install the Access 2000 product before you can actually begin to design any databases.

Installing the Access 2000 product is a pretty straightforward process—the setup program looks similar to the setup program for every other Microsoft product, with some improvements to the process that will be explained later in this section. Figure 22.3 shows the Office 2000 setup program's startup screen.

After you enter the data the page requests, click on Next. The setup program will display the End User License Agreement. Read the agreement closely, and agree to the terms if you accept them.

WARNING!   *Access won't install if you don't accept the license agreement.*

The next screen lets you select where to install Office. One of the nice improvements to the setup program is that it displays information for you about the drives available and lets you know whether the installation will work. Figure 22.4 shows the Install Location dialog box.

Figure 22.3   The startup screen for the setup program.

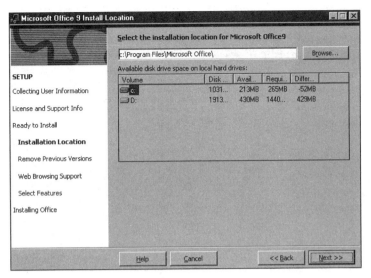

Figure 22.4   The Install Location dialog box.

Note within the dialog box how the image indicates that there isn't enough space on this computer's C: drive to install the suite. If you try to continue from this point, the program will return an error because of the lack of available disk space. Instead, you must first change the installation directory to another drive.

After selecting the target installation directory, click Next. Office 2000 will search your system's Registry to determine whether any previous installations of Office are present. When there are, the wizard will display an informational dialog box alerting you to the presence of the previous installations of Office. You can't remove these versions from within the installation wizard; however, you don't need to remove them for Office 2000 to run correctly. In fact, you can run both Access 97 and Access 2000 simultaneously on the same computer without problems. Click Next to move to the next dialog box.

Microsoft Office 2000 is optimized to run best with Internet Explorer (IE) 5. The next dialog box in the wizard prompts you to select a version of IE for your installation. You can upgrade your system to IE5, or you can simply maintain the current version of IE installed on your system, provided that version is at least IE4.01. Office 2000 is optimized for IE5, and if you don't have a compelling reason for keeping an earlier browser, you should install IE5 on your computer. After making your decision regarding Internet Explorer installation, click Next. The Installation Wizard will display the Select Features dialog box.

This dialog box looks considerably different from most previous installation programs from Microsoft. They've abandoned the old check box for a treeview-based model, as you can see in Figure 22.5.

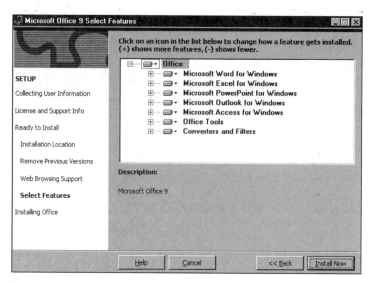

Figure 22.5   The initial display of the Select Features dialog box.

Each portion of the installation has its own "branch." Because we're most concerned with Access installation, we'll look only at the Access branch in this dialog box. To look at the Access branch, click on the "+" sign next to the Microsoft Access for Windows item. The dialog box will expand, providing a list of optional installation features for Access. Note that some of these features have a small, yellow "1" on their icon, as shown in Figure 22.6.

This icon means that the program will load this feature from the CD-ROM the first time you try to use it. This is a very powerful new feature of the installer, minimizing the amount of time necessary to get up and running and minimizing the footprint of the program. In the case of the Additional Wizards, for example, the user must select an icon that represents one of these wizards—at which point, Access will automatically prompt the user to place the CD-ROM in the drive so Access can install the wizard fully on the computer.

In fact, the new installer provides four settings for each installation option—run from the computer, run from the CD-ROM, install on first use, and Not Available. Figure 22.7 shows the settings drop-down menu for the Sample Databases icon in the Select Features dialog box.

In general, because you'll be developing applications with this installation, you should install everything in the Access branch unless your disk space is at a premium. After you finish making your selections (both in the Access branch and the other branches of the dialog box), click Install Now to install the application(s).

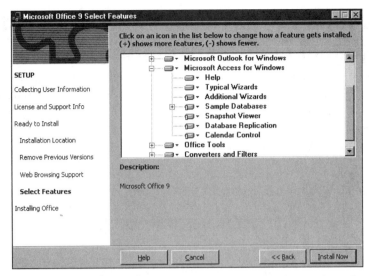

Figure 22.6   The Select Features dialog box after expanding the Access branch.

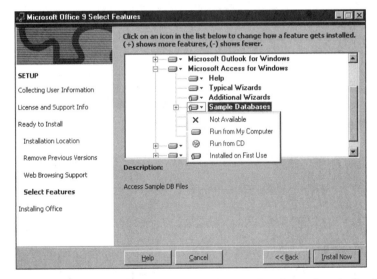

Figure 22.7   The settings drop-down menu for the Sample Databases icon in the Select
Features dialog box.

The Office 2000 setup will commence, copying files to your hard drive until the
installation is complete, at which point it will prompt you to register the software
(which you should do) and reboot the computer. Reboot the computer to complete the installation, and run Access 2000 from the Start menu before beginning
the next section.

Introduction To The Access 2000 Interactive Development Environment (IDE)

Every time you open Access 2000, the program will display the opening dialog box, which lets you either create a new database or open existing databases. Because you haven't created any databases, you should choose to create a new database at this point. Figure 22.8 shows the dialog box after you have chosen to create a new database using a wizard.

After you select the Access Wizards option and click okay, Access will display the New dialog box, shown in Figure 22.9.

Figure 22.8   The opening dialog box of the Access 2000 IDE.

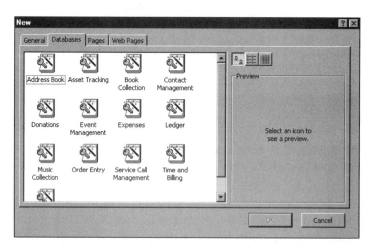

Figure 22.9   The New dialog box shows wizards that you can use to create databases.

As you can see, Access provides you with the means to create a variety of databases using only a wizard. The "Immediate Solutions" section of this chapter details how to use the database wizard to create a simple Asset Tracking database.

After you create the new database using the Wizard, Access will let you open it automatically in the IDE. The remaining sections in this chapter, which detail information about the IDE, will presume that you've created the Asset Tracking database and have it open in the IDE.

Understanding The Windows In The Access Interface

The Database window is the center from which you'll do much of your work with Access databases. As you can see, the window has a series of icons representing various Access objects down its left-hand side and corresponding entries for the objects on the right-hand side. For example, when you click on the Reports object, Access will display the list of reports for the **AstTrk1** database, as shown in Figure 22.10.

From each of the windows, you can add new tables, queries, forms, reports, pages, macros, and modules to the database. You can also edit and modify existing objects of each type. You'll learn more about each of these processes in the following chapters.

Every other window that you'll need to work with your databases will also appear within the Access IDE, with one notable exception—the Visual Basic editor window. When you edit a module, Access will spawn the Visual Basic for Applications (VBA) editor, as shown in Figure 22.11.

You'll learn more about the VBA editor in later chapters.

22. Installation, Setup, And Configuration

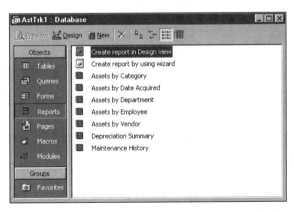

Figure 22.10   The Database window displaying information about the Reports attached to the database.

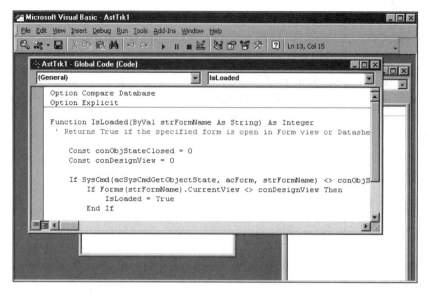

Figure 22.11   The Visual Basic for Applications editor.

Expanding Menus

One of the most interesting and useful new features of the new Access 2000 IDE is the expandable menus. These menus will automatically expose additional choices when the user pauses with the mouse over a specific menu for a given period of time. To understand this better, consider Figure 22.12.

As you can see in the figure, the menu initially displays nine options and an expansion arrow at the menu's bottom. However, when you pause over the menu or click on the expansion arrow, the menu will grow to fifteen options, as shown in Figure 22.13.

Figure 22.12   The Tools menu before expansion.

Figure 22.13   The Tools menu after expansion.

This new feature is part of Microsoft's ongoing efforts to maximize accessibility within applications. The original nine options are the most commonly used options, and the additional six represent other choices you may need to make, but won't use quite as frequently.

Every menu in the new IDE, with the exception of the File menu, provides this expansion option. Moreover, some submenus also provide this option to give the user more choices.

Using Help From The IDE

For the new developer and for the developer interested in finding out more about new features of Access 2000, online help is an invaluable resource. You can access online help by pressing F1, clicking on the Help button on the toolbar, or selecting one of the options from the Help menu.

Help for Access 2000 comes in two primary forms. The first form, which you'll likely use most often, is a sorted set of searchable documents that lets you find out information about a specific object, command, or task. Alternately, you can use the Office 2000 assistant (Rocky the dog, by default), who lets you ask plain-text questions in the manner of the Windows 9x Answer Wizard.

Immediate Solutions

Creating A Database With The Asset Tracking Wizard

To create a new database with the Asset Tracking wizard, perform the following steps:

1. From the New dialog box, select the Databases tab. Within the Databases tab, double-click on the Asset Tracking icon. Access will display the File New Database dialog box.

2. Within the File New Database dialog box, enter the name of the database within the file name field. Name the database as **AstTrk1**. Click the Create button to create the database. When you click the Create button, Access will open the Database Wizard dialog box.

3. The first dialog in the Database Wizard explains what the database will store. It's purely informational. Click Next to move to the next dialog box.

4. The next dialog box lets you add optional fields to the tables that will comprise the database. For example, in Figure 22.14 the **DepartmentID** and **VendorID** fields have been added to the **Asset Information** table.

   For the sample database in this chapter, add the **DepartmentID** and **VendorID** fields as optional fields to the **Asset Information** table. After you add the optional fields, click Next to move to the next dialog box in the Database Wizard.

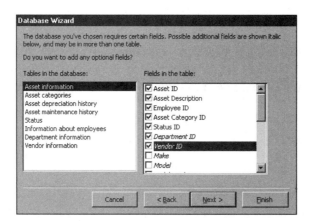

Figure 22.14   The dialog box that lets you add additional fields to the table definitions.

5. The next dialog box lets you select a background for the forms in the database. The default is **Blends**, and that's what you'll use for this database. You can preview the other styles by clicking on each one. When you finish, click Next to move to the next dialog box.

6. The proceeding dialog box lets you select a style for your printed reports from the database. Because this is likely a corporate database, you can select the **Corporate** style. You can preview the other styles by clicking on each one. When you finish, click Next to move to the next dialog box.

7. The dialog box that follows lets you name the database for internal purposes, and place a picture on all reports from the database if you so choose. When you do opt to display a picture, use the Picture... button to select the picture file for the image. Click Next when you finish to move to the next dialog box.

8. The last dialog box in the Database Wizard lets you select whether to open the database after the wizard creates it. It also lets you view help on using a database. When you click Finish in this dialog box, the wizard will construct the database.

When the wizard finishes constructing the database, it'll open the Database window, as shown in Figure 22.15.

Figure 22.15   The Database window for the **AstTrk1** database.

22. Installation, Setup, And Configuration

Viewing Database Properties

You can view general information about a database in one of two ways. You can select the File menu Database Properties option, or you can right-click at the top of the database window and select the Database Properties option from the pop-up menu. Figure 22.16 shows the Database Properties dialog box.

Figure 22.16   The Database Properties dialog box displays general information about the database.

22. Installation, Setup, And Configuration

Chapter 23

Developing Tables And Relationships

In Depth

Throughout the remaining chapters in this book, you'll focus on specific implementation issues and techniques for Microsoft Access 2000. These chapters will take you from table design and implementation through implementing Web front ends for Access. Throughout, you'll focus on the development of Access applications, maintaining a consistent eye toward the development philosophies and issues detailed in Chapter 22 and earlier chapters.

In this chapter, you'll focus specifically on the development of Access tables and the design of relationships between these tables. Effective table design and, to a lesser extent, relationship specification will make or break your applications. Everything else you do in Access (or any other database product, for that matter) is dependent on the basic design of the tables making up the database. This chapter's goal is to provide you with solid groundwork in the creation of Access 2000 tables, using the database design theory previous chapters have laid out— from normalization to specifics of the Access 2000 implementation.

Building A New Table

You can add a new table to an Access 2000 database in several ways. These include using a wizard to assist you with the design process, designing the table from scratch, building the table from a spreadsheet-like format, importing the table from another source, and attaching to an external table. The first three methods are discussed here. The other two, importing and attaching, are explained in later chapters in this book.

Regardless of which method you choose, you'll have two means of creating the new database. Within the database window, you can click on one of the Access 2000 provided shortcuts for table creation, as shown in Figure 23.1.

As you can see, the database window will let you create tables from design view, from the wizard, or by entering data into a spreadsheet-like format. Alternately (or when you plan to import or attach), you can start by selecting the Table tab of the database window and clicking on the New button. Access will display the New Table dialog box. This dialog box lets you select the method you want to use to build your table.

Figure 23.1 The Database window provides shortcuts for table creation.

Building A Table Using A Wizard

When you select Table Wizard from the New Table dialog (or when you use the Wizard shortcut), Access will display the Table Wizard dialog box. The first step in the Table Wizard dialog box lets you select specific fields from one of many predefined tables. The tables are categorized as either Business or Personal. If you select Business, a set of business-related tables appears, such as mailing lists, customers, and employees. When you select Personal, you see a set of tables relating to Personal topics, such as addresses, household inventory, and recipes. Select one or more of these tables as the basis for your database.

After you've selected a predefined table, you can specify which fields from that table you want to include in your custom table. Do so by double-clicking on the desired field, or click on the > button. Figure 23.2 shows the Table Wizard after selecting the **EmployeeID**, **FirstName**, **LastName**, **Title**, **Extension**, **DateHired**, and **Salary** fields from the table template called **Employees**.

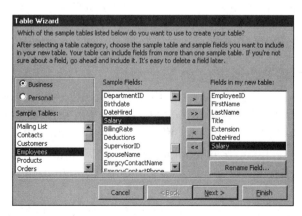

Figure 23.2 The Table Wizard lets you create custom tables from predefined formats.

TIP: *The Table Wizard lets you rename fields within your custom table. To do so, click the Rename Field button in the Wizard.*

After you've selected the desired table and fields, click Next. Access will display a dialog box requesting a name for the table. This Table Wizard step allows you to name your table and indicate whether you want Access to set the primary key for you. Primary keys are covered in more detail later in this chapter. It's always a good idea for every table to contain a primary key because it's used to uniquely identify each record. When you don't tell Access to set a primary key, you're given the opportunity to designate your unique field as the primary key at a later time. If you haven't entered a unique identifier (some field that uniquely differentiates each record from the next) for the table, select Yes. Access adds an **AutoNumber**-type field to your table and designates it as the primary key. It's a good idea to let Access set the primary key, but if you don't, the primary key or any other attributes of the table can be modified at any time. The naming conventions for table names are similar to those for field names, except the standard for table names is that they begin with the tag **tbl**.

In the third step (the fourth step when you choose to specify your own primary key) of the Table Wizard, Access attempts to identify any relationships between the new table and any existing tables. The process of establishing relationships is an important part of Access development. Relationships enable you to normalize your database and to once again *flatten out* the data structure at runtime. They also help you to ensure the integrity of data within your application. For example, you can define a relationship so orders can't be entered for customers who don't exist. Although Access automatically identifies relationships if it can, you can modify or add relationships by clicking on the Relationships button. When you're satisfied with the relationships, click Next.

The final dialog box lets you indicate whether you want to view the design of the table, enter data into the table, or let Access automatically build both the table and a data-entry form for you.

Designing A Table From Scratch

Designing tables from scratch is a method of creating a table that offers flexibility and encourages good design principles. When you create tables from scratch, keep in mind some important considerations about fields and field names:

- Field names can be up to 64 characters long. For practical reasons, try to limit them to between 10 and 15 characters—enough to describe the field without making the name difficult to type.

- Field names can include any combination of letters, numbers, spaces, and other characters, excluding periods, exclamation points, accents, and brackets.

We recommend that you stick to letters. Spaces in field names cause inconvenience when you're building queries, modules, and other database objects.

- Field names can't begin with leading spaces. In fact, as mentioned previously, field names shouldn't contain any spaces at all.

- Try not to duplicate property names or the names of other Access objects when naming your fields. Although your code might work in some circumstances, you might get unpredictable results in others.

So that a potential movement to client-server is as painless as possible, be aware that not all field types are supported by every back-end database. Furthermore, most back-end databases impose stricter limits than Access does on the length of field names and the characters that are valid within field names. To reduce the number of problems you encounter when you migrate your tables to a back-end database server, take into consideration these issues when you're naming the fields in your Access tables.

Building A Table From A Datasheet

Building a table from a datasheet might seem easy, but it's not a very good way to build a table. This method of table design makes it easy to introduce severe design flaws into the table. Although this method was added as an "enhancement" to Access 95, and has been a part of all the subsequent iterations of Access, it was added primarily for spreadsheet users getting adjusted to the database world. In general, you shouldn't use the datasheet method to design your tables because it's both inefficient and error prone.

Selecting The Appropriate Field Type For Your Data

The data type you select for each field in your table can greatly affect the performance and functionality of your application. Several factors should influence your choice of data type for each field in your table:

- The type of data that's stored in the field

- Whether the contents of the field need to be included in calculations

- Whether you need to sort the data within the field

- The way you want to sort the data within the field

- How important storage space is to you

The type of data you need to store in a field has the biggest influence on the data type you select. For example, if you need to store numbers that begin with leading zeros, you can't select a **Number** field because leading zeros entered into a

Number field are ignored. This factor is a consideration for data such as ZIP codes (some begin with leading zeros) and department or billing codes.

If the contents of a field need to be included in calculations, you must select either the **Number** or **Currency** data type. You can't perform calculations on the contents of fields defined with the other data types. The only exception to this rule are **Date/Time** fields, which can be included in date/time calculations.

It's important to consider whether you need to sort or index the data within a field. **Memo** and **OLE** fields can't be sorted; therefore, you shouldn't select these field types if the data within the field must be sorted or indexed. Furthermore, you must consider the *way* you want the data to be sorted. For example, within a **Text** field a set of numbers would be sorted in the order in which they appear (that is, 1, 10, 100, 2, 20, 200) because the data within the **Text** field is sorted in a standard ASCII sequence. On the other hand, within a **Number** or **Currency** field the numbers would be sorted as expected (that is, 1, 2, 10, 20, 100, 200). You might think you would never want the data sorted in a standard ASCII sequence, but it might make sense to sort certain data, such as department codes, in this fashion.

Finally, consider how important disk space is to you. Each field type takes up a different amount of storage space on your hard disk, which might be a factor when you're selecting a data type for a field.

Nine field types are available in Access: **AutoNumber**, **Currency**, **Date/Time**, **Hyperlink**, **Memo**, **Number**, **OLE Object**, **Text**, and **Yes/No**. Information on the proper uses for each field type and the amount of storage space occupied by each type is summarized in Table 23.1.

The most difficult part of selecting a field type is knowing which type is best in each situation. The following detailed descriptions of each field type and when each is used should help you with this process.

Understanding AutoNumber Fields

AutoNumber field values are automatically generated when a record is added; in Access 2000 **AutoNumber** fields can be either sequential or random. The random assignment is excellent when multiple users are adding records offline because it's unlikely that Access will assign the same random value to two records. A special type of **AutoNumber** field is a **Replication ID**. This randomly produced unique number helps with the replication process by generating unique identifiers used in the process of synchronizing database replicas.

You should note a few important things about sequential **AutoNumber** fields. When a user deletes a record from a table, its unique number is lost forever. Likewise, when a user is in the process of adding a record but cancels, the unique

Table 23.1   Appropriate uses and storage space for Access field types.

Field Type	Appropriate Uses	Storage Space
AutoNumber	Unique sequential or random numbers; examples include invoice numbers and project numbers	4 bytes (16 bytes for replication ID)
Currency	Currency values; examples include amount due and price	8 bytes
Date/Time	Dates and times; examples include date ordered and birth date	8 bytes
Hyperlink	Text or combinations of text and numbers stored as text and used as a hyperlink address; an example is **http://www.coriolis.com**	Each part of the three parts of a **Hyperlink** data type can contain up to 2048 characters.
Memo	Long text and numeric strings; examples include notes and descriptions	Ranges from 0 to 64,000 bytes
Number	Data that will be included in calculations (excluding money); examples include ages and codes such as employee ID or payment method	1, 2, 4, or 8 bytes, depending on the field size selected
OLE Object	Objects such as Word documents or Excel spreadsheets; examples include business plans, graphical presentations, employee reviews, and budgets	0 bytes to 1 gigabyte depending on what is stored within the field
Text	Data containing text, a combination of text and numbers, or numbers that don't need to be included in calculations; examples include names, addresses, department codes, and phone numbers	Based on what is actually stored in the field; ranges from 0 to 255 bytes
Yes/No	Fields that will contain one of two values (yes/no, true/false); examples include paid and tenured	1 bit

counter value for that record is forever lost. If this behavior is unacceptable, you can generate your own counter values.

Understanding Currency Fields

The **Currency** field type is a special type of number field appropriate when currency values are being stored in a table. **Currency** fields prevent the rounding off of data during calculations. They hold 15 digits of whole dollars plus accuracy to the hundredths of a cent. Although extremely accurate, this type of field is very slow.

Any changes to the **Currency** format made in the Windows Control Panel are reflected in your data. Access doesn't automatically perform actual conversion of currency amounts—it simply displays them as your settings specify.

Understanding Date/Time Fields

The **Date/Time** field type is used to store valid dates and times, allowing you to perform date calculations and ensure that dates and times are always sorted properly. Access actually stores the date or time internally as an 8-byte floating point number. **Time** is represented as a fraction of a day. Any date and time settings that you establish in the Windows Control Panel are reflected in your data.

Understanding Hyperlink Fields

Hyperlink fields are used to store Uniform Resource Locator (URL) addresses. A hyperlink address can have up to three parts: *displaytext*—the text that appears in a field ; *control address*—the path to a file (Uniform Naming Convention [UNC] path) or page (URL); or *subaddress*—a location within the file or page. The easiest way to insert a hyperlink address in a field or control is to click **Hyperlink** on the Insert menu.

Understanding Memo Fields

Memo fields can hold up to 64K of text. This amount of storage can hold up to 16 pages of text for each record. **Memo** fields are excellent for any types of notes you want to store with table data. Remember that you can't sort by a **Memo** field.

Understanding Number Fields

Number fields are used to store data that must be included in calculations. When currency amounts are included in calculations or the calculations require the highest degree of accuracy, use a **Currency** field rather than a **Number** field. The **Number** field is actually several types of fields in one because Access 2000 offers six sizes of numeric fields. **Byte** can store integers from 1 to 255, and **Integer** can hold whole numbers from -32,768 to 32,767. **Long Integer** can hold whole numbers ranging from less than -2 billion to more than 2 billion. Although all three of these sizes offer excellent performance, each type requires an increasingly larger amount of storage space. Two of the other numeric field sizes, **Single** and **Double**, offer floating decimal points and, therefore, much slower performance. **Single** can hold fractional numbers to seven significant digits; **Double** extends the precision to 14 significant digits. The final size, **Replication ID**, is available only in Access 2000. It provides a unique identifier required by the data synchronization process.

Understanding OLE Object Fields

OLE Object fields are designed to hold data from any OLE server application registered in Windows, including spreadsheets, word-processing documents, sound, and video. Many business uses exist for OLE fields, such as storage of resumes, employee reviews, budgets, or videos.

Understanding Text Fields

Most of your fields will be **Text** fields. Many developers don't realize that it's best to use **Text** fields for any numbers not used in calculations. Examples are phone numbers, part numbers, and ZIP codes. Although the default size for a **Text** field is 50 characters, up to 255 characters can be stored in a **Text** field. Because Access allocates disk space dynamically, a large field size doesn't use hard disk space, but you can improve performance when you allocate the smallest field size possible. The maximum number of characters allowed in a **Text** field can be controlled by the **FieldSize** property.

Understanding Yes/No Fields

Use **Yes/No** fields to store a logical true or false. What's actually stored in the field is **-1** for **Yes** and **0** for **No**. The display format for the field determines what the user actually sees (Yes/No, True/False, On/Off). **Yes/No** fields work efficiently for any data that can have only a true or false value. Not only do they limit the user to valid choices, they take up only 1 bit of storage space.

Now that you understand the types of fields that you can use when you design tables, it is important to understand what you can accomplish by manipulating certain properties of those fields. The next sections discuss the various field properties and their use.

Working With Field Properties

After you've added fields to your table, you need to customize their properties, and field properties allow you control how data is stored as well as what data can be entered into the field. The properties available differ depending on which field type is selected. You can find the most comprehensive list of properties under the **Text** field type, as shown in Figure 23.3. The following section describes each field property.

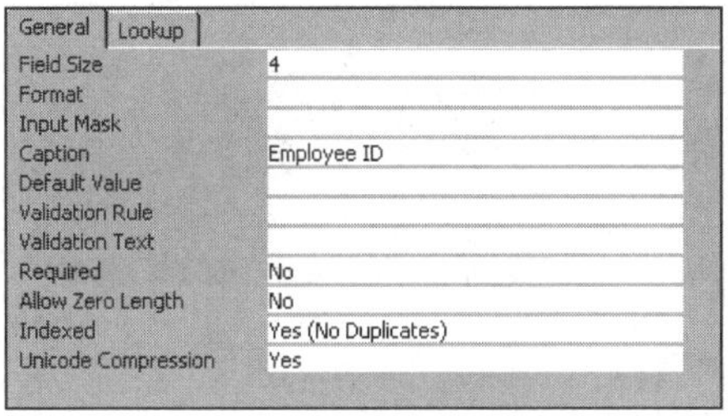

Figure 23.3   The field properties available for a **Text** field.

Limiting What's Entered Into A Field

The first property is **Size**. It's available for **Text** and **Number** fields only. As previously mentioned, it's best to set the field size to the smallest type or value possible. A small size improves performance for **Text** fields, and a small size means lower storage requirements and faster performance for **Number** fields.

Determining How Data Is Displayed

The second property is **Format**. This property is available for all but **OLE Object** fields. It allows you to specify how Access displays your data. Access allows you to select from predefined formats or to create your own custom formats. The formats available differ depending on the data type of the field. For example, Access allows you to select from a variety of **Date/Time** formats, including Short Date (7/7/96), Long Date (Sunday, July 7, 1996), Short Time (7:17), and Long Time (7:17:11AM). The formats for a **Currency** field include Currency ($1,767.25), Fixed (1767.25), and Standard (1,767.25).

Determining What Data Goes Into A Field

Another important property is Input Mask. It's available for **Text**, **Number**, **Date/Time**, and **Currency** fields. Whereas the **Format** property affects the display of data, the Input Mask property controls what data is stored in a field. You can use the Input Mask property to control, on a character by character basis, what type of character (numeric, alphanumeric, and so on) can be stored as well as whether a particular character is required. The Input Mask Wizard, shown in Figure 23.4, helps you create commonly used input masks. Here's an example of a resulting mask:

```
000-00-0000;;_
```

This input mask forces the entry of a valid social security number. Everything that precedes the first semicolon designates the actual mask. The character

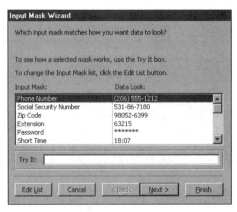

Figure 23.4   The Input Mask Wizard assists with the process of entering an input mask.

between the first and second semicolon determines whether literal characters (the dashes, in this case) are stored in the field. The zeros force the entry of the digits 0 through 9. The dashes are literals that appear within the control as the user enters data. When you enter a 0 in this position, literal characters are stored in the field, and when you enter a 1 or leave this position blank, the literal character isn't stored. The final position (after the second semicolon) indicates what character is displayed to show the space where the user types the next character (in this case the underscore).

Here is a more detailed example. In the mask \(**999**") "**000\-0000;;**_ the first backslash causes the character that follows it (the parenthesis) to be displayed as a literal. The three nines allow for optional numbers or spaces to be entered. The parenthesis and space within the quotation marks are displayed as literals. The first three zeros require values *0* through *9*. The dash following the next backslash is displayed as a literal. Four additional numbers are then required. The two semicolons have nothing in between them, so the literal characters aren't stored in the field. The second semicolon is followed by an underscore, so an underscore is displayed to indicate the space where the user types the next character.

Using The Caption Property

The next property available is the **Caption** property. The text placed in this property becomes the caption for fields in Data Sheet view. It's also used as the caption for the attached label added to data-bound controls when you add them to forms and reports. The **Caption** property becomes important whenever you name your fields without spaces. Whatever is in the **Caption** property overrides the field name for use in Datasheet view, on forms and on reports.

It's important to set the **Caption** property for fields *before* you build any forms or reports that use the fields. When a form or report is produced, Access looks at the current caption. If the caption is added or modified at a later time, captions for that field on existing forms and reports aren't modified.

Using The Default Value Property

Another important property is the Default Value property. You use this property to specify the default value that Access places in the field when the user adds new records to the table. Default values, which can be either text or expressions, can save the data-entry person a lot of time. They don't in any way validate what is entered into a field.

Default values are automatically carried into any queries and forms containing the field. Unlike with the **Caption** property, this occurs whether the default value was created before or after the query or form was created.

Using The Validation Rule Property

Whereas the Default Value property suggests a value to the user, the Validation Rule property limits what the user can place in the field. The validation rule can't be violated; the database engine strictly enforces validation rules. As with the Default Value property, this property can contain either text or a valid Access expression. User-defined functions can't be included in the Validation Rule property. References to forms, queries, or tables can't be included in the Validation Rule property.

When you set the Validation Rule property but not the Validation Text property, Access automatically displays a standard error message whenever the validation rule is violated. To display a custom message, you must enter something in the Validation Text property.

Using The Validation Text Property

Use the Validation Text property to specify the error message that users see when they violate the validation rule. The Validation Text property must contain text; expressions aren't valid in this property.

Using The Required Property

The **Required** property is very important because it determines whether you require that a value be entered into the field. This property is useful for foreign key fields, where you want to ensure that data is entered into the field. It's also useful for any field that contains information that's required for business reasons (company name, for instance).

Using The Allow Zero Length Property

The Allow Zero Length property is similar to the **Required** property. Use it to determine whether you'll allow the user to enter a zero-length string (""). A zero-length string isn't the same as a null (absence of an entry). A zero-length string indicates that the data doesn't exist for that particular field. For example, a foreign employee might not have a social security number. By entering a zero-length string, the data-entry person can indicate that the social security number doesn't exist.

The **Required** and Allow Zero Length properties interact with each other. If the **Required** property is set to Yes and the Allow Zero Length property is set to No, you're being very strict with your users. Not only must they enter a value, that value can't be a zero-length string. Suppose the **Required** property is set to Yes and the Allow Zero Length property is also set to Yes. In such a case, you're requiring users to enter a value, but that value can be a zero-length string. If the **Required** property is set to No and the Allow Zero Length property is also set to No, you're allowing users to leave the field null (blank) but not allowing them to enter a zero-length string. Finally, setting the **Required** property to No and the Allow Zero Length property to Yes means you're being the most forgiving to your users. In this case, they can leave the field null or enter a zero-length string.

Using The Indexed Property to Speed Up Searches

The final property is the **Indexed** property. Indexes are used to dramatically improve performance when the user searches a field. It's generally best to err in the direction of including too many indexes rather than too few.

TIP: *To create multifield indexes, use the Indexes window. To create a multifield index, create an index with one name and with more than one field.*

Indexes speed up the searching, sorting, and grouping of data. The downside is they take up hard disk space and slow down the process of editing, adding, and deleting data. Although the benefits of indexing outweigh the downsides in most cases, you shouldn't index every field in each table. Create indexes only for fields, or combinations of fields, for which the user searches or sorts. Finally, never index **Yes/No** fields. They're only 1 bit and can only take on one of two values. For these reasons, indexes offer no benefits with **Yes/No** fields.

Using Unicode Compression

As you may or may not be aware, Windows provides support for language independence through the use of the Unicode standard. The Unicode standard allows for support of many different character types (such as Kanji, the Japanese character set) through the use of double-byte representation of letters in the alphabet. (A greatly simplified definition, but sufficient for the discussion here.)

The new Unicode Compression property lets you instruct Access to automatically handle compression of strings entered into a field using Unicode—letting Access optimize the amount of storage space necessary for the string. Use of this field will be particularly important to you if your database is destined for international distribution; otherwise, unless you are in a country (such as Japan) that requires Unicode support for all its applications, you probably won't find yourself using this field often.

As you have seen, properties help you control the actions of fields within your tables. You have also seen how properties let you control the interaction of your users with the tables themselves and control the format in which the users must enter data. In the following sections, you will learn more about other specific features of table design and how their effective use can help you make your tables more efficient and improve performance.

Understanding The Importance Of The Primary Key

The most important index in a table is called the Primary Key index. This index ensures the uniqueness of the fields that make up the index and also provides a default order for the table. It's mandatory that you set a primary key for the fields that participate on the one side of a one-to-many relationship. To create a Primary Key index, select the fields that you want to establish as the primary key and click on the Primary Key button on the toolbar.

Working With The Lookup Feature

By using the Lookup Wizard, you can instruct a field to look up its values in another table or query or from a fixed list of values. You can display the list of valid values in a combo or list box. A lookup is generally created from the foreign key (many side) to the primary key (one side) of a one-to-many relationship.

The Lookup Wizard can be invoked by selecting Lookup Wizard from the list of data types for the field. The first dialog of the wizard asks whether you want to look up the values in a table or query or whether you want to input the values. In general, you should always look up the values in a table or query. This makes your application extremely easy to maintain. The second dialog of the wizard asks you to indicate the table or query that will be used to look up the values. Select a table or query and click Next. The third dialog appears. This step of the Lookup Wizard asks you which field in the table or query will be used for the lookup. The fourth step of the Lookup Wizard gives you the opportunity to control the width of the columns in your combo or list box.

Finally, the wizard allows you to specify a title for your combo box. When you click Finish, all the appropriate properties are filled in by the wizard (Access will also ask you to save the table). These properties appear on the Lookup tab of the field, as shown in Figure 23.5.

The Display Control property is set to Combo Box, indicating that a combo box will be used to display the valid values. This occurs whether the user is in Data Sheet view or within a form. The Row Source Type indicates that the source for the combo box is a table or query. The Row Source property shows the actual structured query language (SQL) **SELECT** statement used to populate the combo

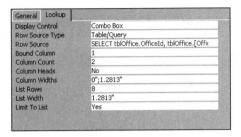

Figure 23.5 The field properties set by the Lookup Wizard.

box. Other properties show which column in the combo box is bound to what data, how many columns are in the combo box, the width of the combo box, and the width of each column in the combo box. These properties are covered in more detail in later chapters.

In addition to field properties, Access provides you with control over the properties of entire tables. Some of these properties are extremely important for table design, as you will see in the following section.

Working With Table Properties

Table properties allow you to specify properties that apply to the table as a whole. To access them, click on the Properties button on the toolbar in the Design view of a table. The **Description** property is used mainly for documentation purposes. The Validation Rule property is used to specify validations that must occur at a record level rather than at a field level. For example, a different credit limit might exist depending on the state that a customer is in. In that case, what is entered in one field is dependent on another field. The validation rule might look something like this:

```
[State] In ("CA","NY") And [CreditLimit]<=2500 Or _
    [State] In ("MA","AZ") And [CreditLimit]<=3500
```

This validation rule requires a credit limit of $2,500 or less for California and New York and a limit of $3,500 or less for Massachusetts and Arizona. It doesn't specify a credit limit for any other states. Table-level validation rules can't be in conflict with field-level validation rules.

The Validation Text property determines the message that appears when the user violates the validation rule. When it's left blank, a default message appears.

The **Filter** property is used to indicate a subset of records that appears in a datasheet, form, or query. The Order By property is used to specify a default order for the records. The **Filter** and Order By properties aren't generally applied as properties of a table.

TIP: *Adding descriptions to your tables, queries, forms, reports, macros, and modules goes a long way toward making your application self-documenting. This helps you, or anyone who modifies your application, to perform any required maintenance on the application's objects.*

While table properties are important for the effective management of tables and can provide great assistance when performing tasks such as documentation, they are typically very mutable. For example, an Order By value might reflect one order at a given point and a completely different order at another point during execution. However, certain definitions about the table are critical for runtime processing—the most important of which, indexing, is explained in the next section.

Using Indexes To Improve Performance

As mentioned in the section on the Indexed property, indexes can help you to dramatically improve the performance of your application. Create indexes for any fields you sort, group, join, or set criteria for. Queries can greatly benefit from indexes, especially when created for fields included in your criteria, fields used to order the query, and fields used to join two tables included in the query.

In fact, you should always create indexes for fields on both sides of a join. If your users will be using the Find dialog, indexes can help to dramatically reduce the search time. Remember, the only downsides to indexes are the disk space they require and the small amount of time it takes to update them when adding, deleting, and updating records. You should always perform benchmarks with your own application, but you'll probably find indexes helpful in almost every situation.

As you will learn in greater detail later, relationship definitions can make or break application performance—even more so than indexes. The following sections discuss relationships and their importance to Access development.

Introduction To Relationships

A relationship exists between two tables when a key field from one table is matched to a key field in another table. The fields in both tables usually have the same name, data type, and size. Relationships are a necessary by-product of the data normalization process covered in detail in Chapter 5 and referenced constantly elsewhere throughout this book. It's the process of eliminating duplicate information from your system by splitting information into several tables, each containing a unique value. Although data normalization brings many benefits, you need to relate the tables in your system so your users can view the data in the system as a single entity. After you've defined relationships between tables, you can build queries, forms, and reports that combine information from multiple tables. In this way, you can reap all the benefits of data normalization and ensure that your system provides users with all the information they need.

Types Of Relationships

Three types of relationships can exist between tables in a database: one-to-many, one-to-one, and many-to-many. Setting up the proper type of relationship between two tables in your database is imperative. The right type of relationship between two tables ensures the following:

- Data integrity
- Optimal performance
- Ease of use in designing system objects

The reasons behind these benefits are covered throughout this chapter. However, before you can understand the benefits of relationships, you must understand the types of relationships available.

One-To-Many Relationships

A one-to-many relationship is by far the most common. In a one-to-many relationship, a record in one table can have many related records in another table. A basic example is a relationship set up between a **Customers** table and an **Orders** table. For each customer in the **Customers** table, you want more than one order in the **Orders** table. On the other hand, each order in the **Orders** table can belong to only one customer. The **Customers** table is on the one side of the relationship, and the **Orders** table is on the many side. To implement this relationship, the field joining the two tables on the one side of the relationship must be unique. In the example of customers and orders, the **CustomerID** field that joins the two tables must be unique within the **Customers** table. When more than one customer in the **Customers** table has the same **CustomerID**, it's not clear which customer belongs to an order in the **Orders** table. For this reason, the field that joins the two tables on the one side of the one-to-many relationship must either be a primary key or have a unique index. In almost all cases, the field relating the two tables is the primary key of the table on the one side of the relationship. The field relating the two tables on the many side of the relationship is called a foreign key.

One-To-One Relationships

In a one-to-one relationship, each record in the table on the one side of the relationship can have only one matching record in the table on the many side of the relationship. This relationship isn't common and is used only in special circumstances. Usually, when you've set up a one-to-one relationship, you should have instead combined the fields in both tables into one table, rather than using a relationship between two tables. You should create a one-to-one relationship only for one of the following reasons:

- The number of fields required for a table exceeds the number of fields allowed in an Access table.

- Certain fields included in a table need to be much more secure than other fields included in the same table.

- Several fields in a table are required for only a subset of records in the table.

The maximum number of fields allowed in an Access table is 255. There is rarely a compelling reason why a table should ever have more than 255 fields. In fact, before you even get close to 255 fields, take a close look at the design of your system. On the extremely rare occasion that having more than 255 fields is appropriate, you can simulate a single table by moving some of the fields to a second table and creating a one-to-one relationship between the two. As you design more and more databases, however, you will likely find that in even the most complex systems, you rarely have a table with more than 25 fields.

The security issue is another reason to separate into two tables data that logically would belong in the same table. An example would be a table containing employee information. Certain information, such as employee name, address, city, state, ZIP code, home phone, and office extension, might need to be accessible by many users of the system. Other fields, including the hire date, salary, birth date, and salary grade, might be highly confidential. Field-level security isn't available in Access. You can simulate field-level security using a special attribute of queries called Run with Owners Permissions. The alternative to this method is to place all the fields that can be accessed by all users in one table and the highly confidential fields in another. Only certain users are given access to the table containing the confidential fields.

The last reason to define one-to-one relationships is when certain fields in a table will be utilized for only a relatively small subset of records. Take for example an **Employee** table and a **Vesting** table. Certain fields would be required only for employees who are vested, and only a small percentage of the company's employees might be vested. It wouldn't be efficient in terms of performance or disk space to place all the fields containing information about vesting in the **Employee** table. This would be especially true if the vesting information required a large volume of fields. By breaking the information into two tables and creating a one-to-one relationship between them, you can reduce disk-space requirements and improve performance. This improvement is particularly pronounced when the **Employee** table happens to be large.

Many-To-Many Relationships

In a many-to-many relationship, records in both tables have matching records in the other table. A many-to-many relationship can't be defined in Access. Instead, you must develop this type of relationship by adding a table called a Junction table. The Junction table is related to each of the two tables as one-to-many relationships. An example is an **Orders** table and a **Products** table. Each order probably contains multiple products, and each product is found on many different orders. The solution is to create a third table called **Order Details**. The **Order Details** table is related to the **Orders** table in a one-to-many relationship based on the **OrderID** field. It's then related to the **Products** table in a one-to-many relationship based on the **ProductID** field.

Establishing Relationships

Relationships between Access tables are established in the Relationships window. While you can establish relationships using code (which is explained in later chapters), you will generally find that the graphical model provided by the Relationships window is easiest to work with.

To open the Relationships window, click Relationships on the toolbar with the Database window active. Looking at the Relationships window, you can see the type of relationship that exists for each table. All the one-to-many relationships defined in a database are represented with a join line. When referential integrity has been enforced between the tables involved in a one-to-many relationship, the join line between the tables appears with the number 1 (one) on the one side of the relationship and an infinity symbol on the many side of the relationship.

Important Notes About Establishing Relationships

You need to remember a few important things when establishing relationships. If you're unaware of these important issues, you could find yourself in some difficult situations with your relationships.

It's important to understand the correlation between the Relationships window and the actual relationships that you have established within the database. The Relationships window lets you view and modify the existing relationships. When you establish relationships, the actual relationship is created the moment you click Create. You can delete the tables from the Relationships window (by selecting them and using your Delete key), but the relationships still exist. The Relationships window provides a visual blueprint of the relationships that have been established. When you modify the layout of the window by moving tables around, adding tables to the window, or when removing tables from the window, you're prompted to save the layout when you close the Relationships window. Access isn't asking whether you want to save the relationships you have established; it's simply asking whether you want to save the visual layout of the window.

When adding tables to the Relationships window using the Show Tables dialog, it's easy to accidentally add the same table to the window multiple times. The relationships window can either hide tables behind the Show Tables dialog or display the tables below the portion of the Relationships window you're viewing. When this occurs, you'll see multiple occurrences of the same table when you close the Show Tables dialog. Each occurrence of the table is given a different alias. You must remove the extra occurrences.

Using the Show Tables dialog, you can also add queries to the Relationships window. Although it's rarely used, this is useful when you regularly include the same queries within some other query and want to permanently establish a relationship between them.

When you remove tables from the Relationships window (which doesn't delete the relationships) and you want to once again show all relationships that exist in the database, click Show All Relationships on the toolbar. This button shows all existing relationships.

Referential Integrity

Establishing a relationship is quite easy. Establishing the right kind of relationship is a little more difficult. When you attempt to establish a relationship between two tables, Access makes some decisions based on a few predefined factors:

- A one-to-many relationship is established when one of the related fields is a primary key or has a unique index.

- A one-to-one relationship is established when both of the related fields are primary keys or have unique indexes.

- An indeterminate relationship is created when neither of the related fields is a primary key or has a unique index. Referential integrity can't be established in this case.

Referential integrity is a series of rules that are applied by the Access Jet database engine to ensure that the relationships between tables are properly maintained. At its most basic level, referential integrity rules prevent the creation of orphan records in the table on the many side of the one-to-many relationship. For example, after establishing a relationship between a **Customers** table and an **Orders** table, all orders in the **Orders** table must be related to a particular customer in the **Customers** table. Before you can establish referential integrity between two tables, the following conditions must be met:

- The matching field on the one side of the relationship must be a **Primary Key** field or must have a unique index.

- The matching fields must have the same data types. With the exception of **Text** fields, they must also have the same size. For example, **Number** fields on both sides of the relationship must have the same size (for example, **Long Integer**).

- Both tables must be part of the same Access database.

- Both tables must be stored in the proprietary Access file (MDB) format (in other words, they can't be external tables from other sources).

- The database containing the two tables must be open.

- Existing data within the two tables can't violate any referential integrity rules. For example, all orders in the **Orders** table must relate to existing customers in the **Customers** table.

- Although **Text** fields involved in a relationship don't have to be the same size, it's prudent to make them the same size. Otherwise, you degrade performance as well as risk the chance of unpredictable results when creating queries based on the two tables.

After referential integrity has been established between two tables, the following rules are applied:

- You can't enter a value in the foreign key of the related table that doesn't exist in the primary key of the primary table. For instance, you can't enter a value in the **CustomerID** field of the **Orders** table that doesn't exist in the **CustomerID** field of the **Customers** table.

- You can't delete a record from the primary table when corresponding records exist in the related table. As an illustration, you can't delete a customer from the **Customers** table when related records exist in the **Orders** table (records with the same value in the **CustomerID** field).

- You can't change the value of a primary key on the one side of a relationship when corresponding records exist in the related table. For example, you can't change the value in the **CustomerID** field of the **Customers** table when corresponding orders exist in the **Orders** table.

When any of the preceding three rules are violated and referential integrity is being enforced between the tables, Access 2000 will display an error message informing you of the reference violation.

Access's default behavior is to prohibit the deletion of parent records that have associated child records and to prohibit the change of a primary key value of a parent record when that parent has associated child records. You can override these restrictions by using the Referential Integrity options that are available in the Relationships dialog when you establish or modify a relationship.

Using The Cascade Update Related Fields Option

The Cascade Update Related Fields option is available only when referential integrity has been established between the tables. With this option selected, the user isn't prohibited from changing the primary key value of the record on the one side of the relationship. Instead, when an attempt is made to modify the field joining the two tables on the one side of the relationship, the change is cascaded down to the **Foreign Key** field on the many side of the relationship.

There's no need to select the Cascade Update Related Fields option when the related field on the one side of the relationship is an **AutoNumber** field. An **AutoNumber** field can never be modified. The Cascade Update Related Fields option has no effect on **AutoNumber** fields.

It's very easy to accidentally introduce a loophole into your system. When you create a one-to-many relationship between two tables but forget to set the **Required** property of the **Foreign Key** field to Yes, you allow the addition of orphan records.

Using The Cascade Delete Related Records Option

The Cascade Delete Related Records option is available only when referential integrity has been established between the tables. With this option selected, the user can delete a record on the one side of a one-to-many relationship, even when related records exist in the table on the many side of the relationship. For instance, a customer can be deleted even when the customer has existing orders. Referential integrity is maintained between the tables because Access automatically deletes all related records in the child table.

When you attempt to delete a record from the table on the one side of a one-to-many relationship, you'll get the usual warning message. On the other hand, when you try to delete a record from the table on the one side of a one-to-many relationship and related records exist in the child table, Access will display a different warning telling you that you're about to delete the record from the parent table and any related records in the child table.

The Cascade Delete Related Records option isn't always appropriate. It's an excellent feature, but use it prudently. Although it's usually appropriate to cascade delete from an **Orders** table to an **Order Details** table for instance, it's generally not appropriate to cascade delete from a **Customers** table to an **Orders** table. This is because you generally don't want all your order history deleted from the **Orders** table if, for some reason, you want to delete a customer. Deleting the order history causes important information, such as your profit and loss history, to change. Therefore, it's appropriate to prohibit this type of deletion and handle the customer in some other way, such as marking the customer as inactive. On the other hand, when you delete an order (because it was canceled, for example), you probably want the corresponding order detail information to be removed as well. In this case, the Cascade Delete Related Records option is appropriate. You need to make the appropriate decision in each situation, based on business needs.

The important thing is to carefully consider the implications of each option before making your decision.

Understanding The Benefits Of Relationships

The primary benefit of relationships is the data integrity that they provide. Without the establishment of relationships, users are free to add records to child tables without regard to entering required parent information. After referential integrity is established, you can select Cascade Update Related Fields or Cascade Delete Related Records, as appropriate, which saves you a lot of code in maintaining the integrity of the data in your system. Most relational database management systems require that you write the code to delete related records when a parent record is deleted or to update the foreign key in related records when the primary key of the parent is modified. By selecting the Cascade Update and Cascade Delete options, you're sheltered from having to write a single line of code to accomplish these common tasks.

Relationships are automatically carried into your queries. This means that each time you build a new query, the relationships between the tables within it are automatically established based on the relationships that you have set up in the Relationships window. Furthermore, each time you build a form or report, relationships between the tables included on the form or report are used to assist with the design process. Whether you delete or update data using a datasheet or a form, all referential integrity rules automatically apply, even when the relationship is established after the form is built.

Using Indexes With Relationships

The field that joins two tables on the one side of a one-to-many relationship must be a **Primary Key** field or must have a unique index so referential integrity can be maintained. If the index on the one side of the relationship isn't unique, there's no way to determine to which parent a child record belongs.

An index on the field on the many side of the one-to-many relationship is optional. It serves to improve the performance of any processing involving the relationship. Make sure that you set the index to Yes (Duplicates OK); otherwise, you've created a one-to-one rather than a one-to-many relationship.

Immediate Solutions

Designing Tables In Design View

To design a table in Design view, perform the following steps:

1. From the Database window, use either the Create table in design view shortcut or the New button on the toolbar to open the Table Design View window.

2. Define each field in the table by typing the name of the field in the Field Name column. If you prefer, you can click on the Build button on the toolbar. Access will display the Field Builder dialog box shown in Figure 23.6. This builder allows you to select from predefined fields with predefined properties. Of course, the properties can be modified at any time.

3. Within the Design View window, tab to the Data Type column. Select the default field type or text or use the drop-down combo box to select another field type.

4. Tab to the Description column. What you type in this column appears on the status bar when the user is entering data into the field. This column is also great for documenting what data is actually stored in the field.

5. Continue entering fields as desired. When you need to insert a field between two existing fields, click on the Insert Rows button on the toolbar. The new field is inserted above the field that you were on. To delete a field, click on the Delete Rows button on the toolbar.

6. When you finish entering field names, click the Save button on the toolbar, or select the File menu Save option. Access will prompt you to save the new table; Access will also prompt you to specify a primary key for the table.

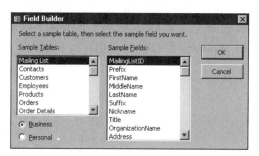

Figure 23.6   The Field Builder dialog box enables you to select from predefined fields with predefined properties.

Creating Tables From Datasheet Mode

When you decide to use the Datasheet method to create tables, perform the following steps:

1. Select Datasheet view from the New Table dialog or select the Create New Table By Entering Data shoutcut from the database window. The Datasheet window, which you can use to build tables, will appear.

2. Rename each column by double-clicking on the column heading (for example, **Field1**) that you want to change. Type the name for your field, then press Enter.

3. Enter data into the datasheet. Be sure to enter the data in a consistent format. For example, when your table includes a column for hire date, make sure that all entries in that column are valid dates and that all dates are entered in the same format. Access uses the contents of each column to determine the data type for each field. Inconsistent data entry confuses Access and causes unpredictable results.

4. After you have added all the columns and data that you want, click on the Save button on the toolbar. Access will prompt you to enter a table name.

5. Access will then ask whether you want to add a primary key.

6. Access assigns data types to each field based on the data you've entered. To look at the design of the resulting table when Access is done, click on the Design View button on the toolbar.

7. Add a description to each field. This helps to make your table self-documenting.

8. If you forget a field and need to insert it later, click with the right mouse button on the column heading of the column to the right of where you want to insert the new column. A context-sensitive menu appears. Select Insert Column. A column is inserted. It can be renamed by double-clicking on the column heading.

Working With Fields

For the following examples, build a table with the fields and types listed in Table 23.2. After you define the table, save it as **tblCustomers**.

Setting Field Sizes

Setting field sizes (as well as most other field properties) is relatively straightforward. To set the **Size** property of the **State** field to two characters, click anywhere within the field and type "2" in the **Size** property at the bottom of the

Table 23.2   The field definitions of the table to use for the examples.

Field	Type
CompanyID	AutoNumber (this is also the Primary Key)
CompanyName	Text
State	Text
PhoneNumber	Text
ContactDate	Date/Time
CreditLimit	Currency

Design View window. Switch to Datasheet view and name the table **tblCustomers**. Try to enter data into the **State** field. Notice that only two characters can be entered.

Setting The Format Property

Set the Format property of the **ContactDate** field to **Medium Date**. Switch to Datasheet view and enter some dates in the format mm/dd/yy. Notice that they appear in the format 12-Jan-99.

Using The Input Mask Wizard

Use the Input Mask Wizard to add a mask for the **PhoneNumber** field. To do this, perform the following steps:

1. Click anywhere in the **PhoneNumber** field, then click in the Input Mask property. Click on the ellipse to the right of the Input Mask property. Access will display the Input Mask Wizard.

2. Select Phone Number from the list of available masks. Click Next to move to the next dialog box in the Wizard.

3. Access will prompt you to specify whether or not you want to use the default input mask. Click Next to move to the next dialog.

4. Within the next dialog box, select the option of not storing the literal characters within the field. Click Finish to exit the Wizard.

Switch to Data Sheet view and enter a phone number. Notice how your cursor skips over the literal characters. Try leaving the area code blank. Access should allow you to do this. Now try to enter a letter in any position. Access should prohibit you from doing this. Attempt to leave any character from the seven-digit phone number blank. Access should prohibit you from doing this.

> **WARNING!**   When you employ an input mask, the user is always in overtype mode. This behavior is a feature of the product and can't be altered.

Setting The Default Value Property

Enter the default values specified in Table 23.3 for the **State**, **ContactDate**, and **CreditLimit** fields.

Switch to Data Sheet view and add a new record. Notice that default values appear for the **State**, **ContactDate**, and **CreditLimit** fields. You can override these defaults if you wish.

Setting The Validation Rule Property

Add the validation rules specified in Table 23.4 to the fields within your table.

Switch to Data Sheet view. After you save the table, the message shown in Figure 23.7 appears.

When you select Yes, Access attempts to validate all existing data using the new rules. When any errors are found, you're notified that errors occurred, but you aren't informed of the offending records, as shown in Figure 23.8.

You need to build a query to locate all records violating the new rules. If you select No, Access doesn't attempt to validate your existing data. You aren't warned of any problems.

Table 23.3   The default values for several fields in the tblCustomers table.

Field	Default Value
State	CA
ContactDate	=Date()
CreditLimit	1000

Table 23.4   Validation rules to add to several fields in the tblCustomers table.

Field	Validation Rule
State	In (CA, AZ, NY, MA, UT)
ContactDate	<= Date()
CreditLimit	Between 0 And 5000

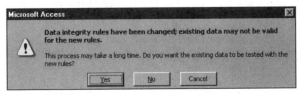

Figure 23.7   The validation prompt for the new rules.

Figure 23.8   The validation error message you receive when all data doesn't fit the new rules.

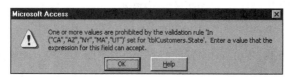

Figure 23.9   The default validation error message.

After you've entered Data Sheet view, try to enter an invalid state into the **State** field. Access will display the message shown in Figure 23.9.

As you can see, this isn't the friendliest message, which is why you should create a custom message using the Validation Text property.

Validation rules entered at a table level are automatically applied to forms and queries built from the table. This occurs whether the rule was entered before or after the query or form was built. When you create a validation rule for a field, Access doesn't allow **Null** values to be entered in the field. This means that the field can't be left blank. When you want to allow the field to be left **Null**, you must add the **Null** to the validation expression: **In (CA, AZ, NY, MA, UT) or Is Null**.

Setting The Validation Text Property

Add the information detailed in Table 23.5 to the Validation Text properties of the **State**, **ContactDate**, and **CreditLimit** fields.

Try entering invalid values for each of the three fields. Observe the error messages.

Setting The Required Property

Within the Table Design view, set the Required property of the **CompanyName** and **PhoneNumber** fields to Yes. Switch to Data Sheet view and attempt to add a

Table 23.5   Validation text for the validated fields.

Field	Validation Text
State	The State Must Be CA, AZ, NY, MA, or UT
ContactDate	The Contact Date Must Be On or Before Today
CreditLimit	The Credit Limit Must Be Between 0 and 5000

new record, leaving the **CompanyName** and **PhoneNumber** fields blank. Make sure you enter a value for at least one of the other fields in the record. When you try to move off the record, Access will display an error message and force you to either edit or discard the record.

Setting The Allow Zero Length Property

Within the Design View window, add a new **Text** field to the **tblCustomers** table called **ContactName**. Set the **Required** property for the field to Yes. Attempt to add a new record and enter two quotes ("") into the **ContactName** field. Access will display an error message indicating that you must enter a valid value for the field. Return to the design of the table. Change the Allow Zero Length property to Yes. Go to Data Sheet view and try to enter two quotes into the **ContactName** field. This time you should be successful.

Setting The Indexed Property

Within the Table Design View window, set the Indexed property of the **CompanyName**, **ContactName**, and **State** fields to Yes (Duplicates OK). Click on the Indexes button on the toolbar. Access will display the Indexes window, with entries corresponding to those shown in Figure 23.10.

Notice the Index Name of **PrimaryKey**. This is the name for the Primary Key index. Note that the Primary and Unique properties for this index are both set to Yes.

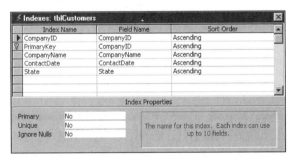

Figure 23.10 The Indexes window after you add some indexes to the table.

Establishing A Relationship Between Two Tables

To establish a relationship between two tables, perform the following steps:

1. Open the Relationships window.

2. If you've never opened the Relationships window of a particular database, the Show Table dialog appears. Select each table you want to relate, and click Add.

23. Developing Tables And Relationships

3. Once you've established relationships in the current database, the Relationships window appears.

4. If the tables you want to include in the relationship don't appear, click on the Show Table button on the toolbar. To add the desired tables to the Relationships window, click to select a table, and click Add.

5. Repeat Step 4 for each table you want to add. To select multiple tables at once, use Shift to select contiguous tables or Ctrl to select noncontiguous tables, and click Add. Click Close when you're done.

6. Click and drag the field from the table on the one side of the relationship to the matching field in the table on the many side of the relationship. The Edit Relationships dialog box will appear, as shown in Figure 23.11.

7. Determine whether you want to establish referential integrity (covered in the next section) and whether you want to cascade update related fields or cascade delete related records (covered in the next section).

8. Click Create. Access will create the relationship.

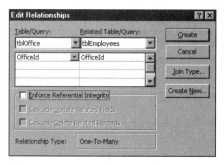

Figure 23.11   The Edit Relationships dialog box.

Working With The Relationships Window

To work with the Relationships window, create a new database and add tables called **tblCustomers**, **tblOrders**, and **tblOrderDetails**. Each table should have the following fields:

- **tblCustomers**: **CustomerID**, **CompanyName**, **Address**, **City**, **State**, **ZipCode**

- **tblOrders**: **OrderID**, **CustomerID**, **OrderDate**, **ShipVIA**

- **tblOrderDetails**: **OrderID**, **LineNumber**, **ItemID**, **Quantity**, **Price**

In the **tblCustomers** table, set the **CustomerID** field as the primary key. Set the size of the field to 5. All other fields can be left with their default properties.

In the **tblOrders** table, set **OrderID** to the **AutoNumber** field type. Make the **OrderID** the **Primary Key** field. Set the length of the **CustomerID** field to 5. Add an index to this field. Set the field type of the **OrderDate** field to **Date**.

In the **tblOrderDetails** table, set the field type of the **OrderID** field to **Number**, and make sure that the size is **Long Integer**. Add an index to this field. Set the type of the **LineNumber** field to **Number** with a size of **Long Integer**. The primary key of the table should be based on the combination of the **OrderID** and **LineNumber** fields. The **ItemID** and **Quantity** fields should be **Number** type with a size of **Long Integer**. The **Price** field should be **Currency** type.

To build the relationships, perform the following steps:

1. To open the Relationships window, click Relationships on the toolbar with the Database window active (or select the Tools menu Relationships option).

2. With the **tblCustomers** table in the Show Table dialog box selected, hold down your Shift key and click to select the **tblOrderDetails** table.

3. Click Add to add all three tables to the Relationships window.

4. Click Close to close the Show Table dialog box.

5. Click and drag from the **CustomerID** field in the **tblCustomers** table to the **CustomerID** field in the **tblOrders** table.

6. When Access displays the Relationships dialog box, click the Create button within the dialog box.

7. Repeat the process, clicking and dragging the **OrderID** field from the **tblOrders** table to the **OrderID** field in the **tblOrderDetails** table.

Modifying An Existing Relationship

Modifying an existing relationship is easy. Access gives you the ability to delete an existing relationship or to simply modify the nature of the relationship. To permanently remove a relationship between two tables, follow these steps:

1. With the Database window active, click Relationships on the toolbar.

2. Single-click on the line joining the two tables whose relationship you want to delete.

3. Press the Delete key. Access will ask you to verify your actions. Click Yes.

You'll often want to modify the nature of a relationship rather than remove it. To modify a relationship, follow these steps:

1. With the Database window active, click Relationships on the toolbar.

2. Double-click on the line joining the two tables whose relationship you want to modify.

3. Make the required changes.

4. Click OK. All the ordinary rules regarding the establishment of relationships apply.

Testing Referential Integrity

To test for referential integrity, work within the Relationships window.

1. To open the Relationships window, select the Database window and click Relationships on the toolbar.

2. Within the Relationships window, double-click on the join line between **tblCustomers** and **tblOrders**. Access will display the Edit Relationships dialog box.

3. Within the Edit Relationships dialog box, click on the Enforce Referential Integrity check box.

4. Click OK to exit the Edit Relationships dialog box.

5. Repeat Steps 2 through 4 for the relationship between **tblOrders** and **tblOrderDetails**.

Go into **tblCustomer** and add a couple of records. Take note of the **CustomerIDs**. Go into **tblOrders**. Add a couple of records, taking care to assign **CustomerIDs** of customers that exist in the **tblCustomers** table. Now try to add an order for a customer whose **CustomerID** doesn't exist in **tblCustomers**. When you've set up the relationships correctly, Access will display an error message.

As another test, try to delete from **tblCustomers** a customer who has no orders. You should get a warning message, but you should be allowed to complete the process. Now try to delete a customer who has orders. You should be prohibited from deleting the customer. Attempt to change the **CustomerID** of a customer who has orders. You shouldn't be able to do this, either.

Implementing The Cascade Delete Related Records Option

To implement and test the Cascade Update Related Fields option, perform the following steps:

1. Modify the relationship between **tblCustomers** and **tblOrders**.

2. Within the Edit Relationships dialog box, click on the Cascade Update Related Fields check box.

3. Modify the relationship between **tblOrders** and **tblOrderDetails**.

4. Within the Edit Relationships dialog box, click on the Cascade Delete Related Records check box. There's no need to Cascade Update Related Fields because the **OrderID** field in **tblOrders** is an **AutoNumber** field.

Attempt to delete a customer who has orders. You should still be prohibited from doing this because you didn't select Cascade Delete Related Records. Change the Customer ID of a customer in **tblCustomers** who has orders. This change should be allowed. Take a look at the **tblOrders** table. The **CustomerID** of all corresponding records in the table should now be updated to reflect the change in the parent record.

Another test you can perform is to add some order details to the **tblOrderDetails** table. Try to delete any order that has detail within the **tblOrderDetails** table. You should receive a warning, but you should be allowed to complete the process.

23. Developing Tables And Relationships

Chapter 24

Creating Queries

In Depth

Understanding Queries And When You Should Use Them

A Select query is a stored question about the data stored within the tables of your database. Select queries are the foundation of much of what you do within Access. They underlie most of your forms and reports, allowing you to view the data you want, when you want. You use a simple Select query to define the tables and fields whose data you want to view and also to specify the criteria to limit the data that the query's output displays. A Select query is simply a query of a table or tables that displays data only. It doesn't modify data in any way. More advanced Select queries are used to summarize data, provide the results of calculations, or cross-tabulate your data. You can use Action queries to add, edit, or delete data from your tables, based on selected criteria.

Select queries are relatively straightforward—they select data from one or more tables and return that data within the context of a single result. You'll learn specifics of Select query implementations in the "Immediate Solutions" section of this chapter. However, Access also supports another type of query, an *Action query*, which you can use to perform actions *on* a database, rather than simply returning data *from* a database.

Understanding Access SQL

As you have learned in previous chapters, Access Structured Query Language (SQL) is the language that underlies Access queries, so you need to understand a little bit about Access SQL, where it came from, and how it works. Access SQL allows you to construct queries without using the Access Query By Example (QBE) grid. One instance when you'll need to do this is when you must build a SQL statement on the fly in response to user interaction with your application. Furthermore, certain operations supported by Access SQL aren't supported by the graphical QBE grid. You must build these SQL statements in SQL view of the Query Builder.

Understanding SQL And Its Origins

SQL is a standard from which many varying dialects have emerged. It was invented at an IBM research laboratory in the early 1970s and first formally described in a research paper released in 1974 at an Association for Computing Machinery meeting. Access SQL is a dialect of SQL. It's a hybrid of the SQL-86 and SQL-92 standards.

At the very least, you need to understand the basic constructs of SQL. These constructs allow you to select, update, delete, and append data using SQL commands and syntax. SQL is actually made up of very few verbs. The most commonly used verbs are discussed in the next section.

Understanding SQL Syntax

SQL is easy to learn. When retrieving data, you simply build a **SELECT** statement. **SELECT** statements comprise various clauses that determine the specifics of how the data is selected. Once executed, **SELECT** statements select rows of data and return them as a recordset.

The SELECT Clause

The **SELECT** clause is used to specify what columns you want to retrieve from the table(s) whose data is being returned to the recordset. The simplest **SELECT** clause looks like this:

```
SELECT *
```

This **SELECT** clause retrieves all columns from a table. However, if you wanted to retrieve only certain columns from a table, you might construct the **SELECT** clause as shown here:

```
SELECT LocationID, ManagerName
```

This **SELECT** clause retrieves only the LocationID and ManagerName columns from a table. Not only can you include columns that exist in your table, you can include expressions in a **SELECT** clause. For example, you might create the following query:

```
SELECT LocationID, [City] & ", " & [State] & "   " &
    [ZipCode] AS Address
```

This **SELECT** clause retrieves the LocationID column as well as a pseudocolumn called Address that includes an expression that concatenates the City, State, and ZipCode columns.

The FROM Clause

The **FROM** clause is used to specify the table(s) or query(ies) from which the records should be selected. It can include an alias that you'll use to refer to the table. The **FROM** clause looks like this:

```
FROM tblLocations AS Locations
```

In this case, the name of the table is **tblLocations**. The alias is Locations. If you combine the **SELECT** clause with the **FROM** clause, the SQL statement looks like this:

```
SELECT LocationID, ManagerName FROM tblLocations
```

This **SELECT** statement retrieves the LocationID and ManagerName columns from the **tblLocations** table.

The WHERE Clause

The **WHERE** clause is used to limit the records that are retrieved by the **SE-LECT** statement. A **WHERE** clause can include up to 40 columns combined by the keywords **AND** and **OR**. A simple **WHERE** clause looks like this:

```
WHERE State = "NV"
```

Using an **AND** to further limit the criteria, the **WHERE** clause looks like this:

```
WHERE State = "NV" AND ContactTitle Like "Store Man*"
```

This **WHERE** clause limits the records returned to those in which the state is equal to "NV" and the ContactTitle begins with "Store Man." Using an **OR**, the **SELECT** statement looks like the following:

```
WHERE State = "NV" OR State = "CA"
```

This **WHERE** clause returns all records in which the state is equal to either "NV" or "CA." Compare this with the following example:

```
WHERE State = "NV" OR ContactTitle Like "Store Man*"
```

This **WHERE** clause returns all records in which the state is equal to "NV" or the ContactTitle begins with "Store Man." For example, the store managers in California will be returned from this **WHERE** clause. The **WHERE** clause combined with the **SELECT** and **FROM** clauses looks like this:

```
SELECT LocationID, ManagerName FROM tblLocations
    WHERE State = "NV" OR State = "CA";
```

The ORDER BY Clause

The **ORDER BY** clause determines the order in which the returned rows will be sorted. It's an optional clause and looks like this:

```
ORDER BY ClientID
```

The **ORDER BY** clause can include more than one field:

```
ORDER BY State, LocationID
```

When more than one field is specified, the left-most field is used as the primary level of sort. Any additional fields are the lower sort levels. Combined with the rest of the **SELECT** statement, the **ORDER BY** clause looks like this:

```
SELECT LocationID, ManagerName FROM tblLocations
    WHERE State = "NV" OR State = "CA"
    ORDER BY LocationID;
```

The JOIN Clause

Often you'll need to build **SELECT** statements that retrieve data from more than one table. When building a **SELECT** statement based on more than one table, you must join the tables with a **JOIN** clause. The **JOIN** clause differs depending on whether you join the tables with an **INNER JOIN**, a **LEFT OUTER JOIN**, or a **RIGHT OUTER JOIN**. Here's an example of an **INNER JOIN**:

```
SELECT DISTINCTROW tblLocations.LocationID,
    tblLocations.StoreName, tblProjects.ProjectName,
    tblProjects.ProjectDescription
    FROM tblLocations
    INNER JOIN tblProjects
    ON tblLocations.LocationID = tblProjects.LocationID;
```

Notice that four columns are returned in the query result. Two columns are from **tblLocations** and two are from **tblProjects**. The **SELECT** statement uses an **INNER JOIN** from **tblLocations** to **tblProjects** based on the **LocationID** field. This means that only clients that have projects are displayed in the query result. Compare this with the following **SELECT** statement:

```
SELECT DISTINCTROW tblLocations.LocationID,
    tblLocations.StoreName, tblProjects.ProjectName,
    tblProjects.ProjectDescription
    FROM tblLocations
    LEFT JOIN tblProjects
    ON tblLocations.LocationID = tblProjects.LocationID;
```

This **SELECT** statement joins the two tables using a **LEFT JOIN** from **tblLocations** to **tblProjects** based on the **LocationID** field. All clients are included in the resulting records whether or not they have projects.

The word **OUTER** is assumed in the **LEFT JOIN** clause, which is used when building a Left Outer Join.

Using The ALL, DISTINCTROW, And DISTINCT Clauses

The **ALL** clause of a **SELECT** statement means that all rows meeting the **WHERE** clause are included in the query result. When the **DISTINCT** keyword is used, Access eliminates duplicate rows, based on the fields that are included in the query result. This is the same as setting the Unique Values property to Yes in the graphical QBE grid. When the **DISTINCTROW** keyword is used, Access eliminates any duplicate rows based on all columns of all tables included in the query (whether or not they appear in the query result). This is the same as setting the Unique Records property to Yes in the graphical QBE grid.

The GROUP BY Clause

The **GROUP BY** clause is used to calculate summary statistics. A **GROUP BY** clause is created when you build a Totals query using the graphical QBE grid. Consider the following example:

```
SELECT DISTINCTROW tblLocations.State, tblCustomers.City,
    Sum(tblOrders.Retail) AS SumOfRetail
    FROM tblCustomers
    INNER JOIN tblOrders
    ON tblCustomers.CustomerID = tblOrders.CustomerID
    GROUP BY tblLocations.State, tblCustomers.City;
```

This **SELECT** statement returns the state, city, and total freight for each state/city combination. The **GROUP BY** clause indicates that detail for the selected records isn't displayed. Instead, the fields indicated in the **GROUP BY** clause are displayed uniquely. One of the fields in the **SELECT** statement must include an aggregate function. This result of the aggregate function is displayed, along with the fields specified in the **GROUP BY** clause.

Using The HAVING Clause

A **HAVING** clause is similar to a **WHERE** clause but differs in one major respect: It's applied after the data is summarized rather than before. Consider the following example:

```
SELECT DISTINCTROW tblCustomers.State, tblCustomers.City,
    Sum(tblOrders.Retail) AS SumOfRetail
    FROM tblCustomers
    INNER JOIN tblOrders
    ON tblCustomers.CustomerID = tblOrders.CustomerID
    GROUP BY tblCustomers.State, tblCustomers.City
    HAVING (((Sum(tblOrders.Retail))>100));
```

In the example, the criterion **> 100** will be applied after the aggregate function **Sum** is applied to the grouping.

Applying What You've Learned

You can practice entering and working with SQL statements in two places:

- The SQL View window of a query
- Visual Basic for Applications (VBA) code

You'll take a look at both of these techniques in the "Immediate Solutions" section.

Action Queries

Access Action queries let you easily modify data without writing any code. In most cases, Action queries are actually more efficient than accomplishing the same task using code. Four types of Action queries are available: Update, Delete, Append, and Make Table. Update queries let you modify data within a table. You'll use Delete queries to remove records from a table. Append queries let you add records to an existing table, while Make Table queries create an entirely new table.

Update Queries

Update queries are used to modify all records or records meeting specific criteria. They can be used to modify the data within one field or several fields (or even tables) at one time. An example would be a query that increases the salary of everyone within a given organization in Nevada by 10 percent. As mentioned, using Update queries is usually more efficient than accomplishing the same task using VBA code. They are, therefore, the most common means that developers use to modify table data. The "Immediate Solutions" section of this chapter details how to create an Update query.

In general, the common naming convention specifies that you should name Access Update queries with the prefix, "qupd". Each type of Action query should be given a prefix indicating what type of query it is. Table 24.1 specifies all the proper prefixes for Action queries.

Table 24.1   Naming prefixes for Action queries.

Type of Query	Prefix	Example
Update	qupd	qupdChangeTaxes
Delete	qdel	qdelRetiredEmployees
Append	qapp	qappRemoteLocationData
Make Table	qmak	qmakTemporaryClientData

All Access queries are stored as SQL statements. The SQL behind an Access Update query looks similar to the following:

```
UPDATE DISTINCTROW tblVendors SET tblVendors.DefaultDueDate = 30
    WHERE (((tblVendors.Group)="B"));
```

The actions taken by an Update query, as well as by all Action queries, can't be reversed. You must exercise extreme caution when running any Action query.

It's important that you recognize that if the Cascade Update Related Fields Referential Integrity setting is turned on and the Update query attempts to modify a primary key field, the foreign key of all corresponding records in related tables will be updated. If the Cascade Update Related Fields option isn't turned on and referential integrity is being enforced, the Update query won't let the query modify the offending records.

Delete Queries

Rather than simply modifying table data, Delete queries are used to permanently remove records from a table whether they're old records from a table or all orders that occurred in a previous year. Delete queries permanently remove all records meeting the specified criteria. The "Immediate Solutions" section of this chapter details how to create a Delete query.

The SQL behind a Delete query looks similar to the following:

```
DELETE DISTINCTROW tblRetiredEmployees.DateRetired
    FROM tblRetiredEmployees
    WHERE (((tblRetiredEmployees.DateRetired)<Date()-730));
```

It's often useful to view the results of an Action query before you actually affect the records included in the criteria. To view the records that will be affected by the Action query, click the Query DataSheet View button on the toolbar before you select Run. All records that will be affected by the Action query appear in Datasheet view. If necessary, you can temporarily add key fields to the query to get additional information about the records that are about to be affected.

It's important to remember that if the Cascade Delete Related Records Referential Integrity setting is turned on, all corresponding records in related tables will be deleted. If the Cascade Delete Related Records option isn't turned on and referential integrity is being enforced, the Delete query won't allow the offending records to be deleted. If you want to delete the record(s) on the one side of the relationship, you'll first need to delete all the related records on the many side of the relationship.

Append Queries

Append queries let you add records to an existing table. This is often done during an archive process. The records that are to be archived are first appended to the history table using an Append query. They're then removed from the master table using a Delete query. The "Immediate Solutions" section of this chapter details how to create an Append query.

The SQL behind an Append query looks similar to the following:

```
INSERT INTO tblRemoteLocations (LocationID, EmployeeID, DateEntered)
    SELECT DISTINCTROW tblRemoteLocations.LocationID,
    tblRemoteLocations.EmployeeID,
    tblRemoteLocations.DateEntered
    FROM tblRemoteLocations
    WHERE (((tblRemoteLocations.DateEntered)
    Between #1/1/98# And #12/31/98#));
```

Append queries don't allow you to introduce any primary key violations. If you're appending any records that duplicate a primary key value, Access will alert you to the error with a message box. If you proceed with the append process, only those records without primary key violations will be appended to the destination table.

Make Table Queries

Whereas an Append query adds records to an existing table, a Make Table query is used to create a new table. The new table is often a temporary table used for intermediary processing. Such a temporary table is often created to freeze data for the period of time that a report is being run. By building temporary tables and running the report from these tables, you ensure that users can't modify the data underlying the report during the reporting process. Another common use of a Make Table query is to provide a subset of fields or records to another user. The "Immediate Solutions" section of this chapter details how to create a Make Table query.

The SQL for a Make Table query looks like the following:

```
SELECT DISTINCTROW tblRemoteLocations.LocationID,
    tblRemoteLocations.EmployeeID,
    tblRemoteLocations.DateEntered, [DateEntered]+365 AS ArchiveDate
    INTO tblTemporaryData
    FROM tblRemoteLocations
    WHERE (((tblRemoteLocations.LocationID) Between 1 And 10));
```

Special Notes About Action Queries

Additional warning messages appear when running Action queries from the Database window or when using code. You can suppress this message, and all other query messages, from within your program code using the **SetWarnings** method of the **DoCmd** object. The code looks like this:

```
DoCmd.SetWarnings False
```

To suppress warnings by modifying the Access environment, select Options from the Tools menu. Within the Options dialog box, click the Edit/Find tab. Remove the check mark from the Action Queries check box.

There's a major difference between suppressing warnings using the **DoCmd** object and suppressing warnings through the Tools menu Options option. Setting warnings using the **DoCmd** object centralizes control within the application. On the other hand, using the Tools menu Options option to suppress warnings affects all applications run by a particular user.

Action Queries Vs. Processing Records Using Code

As mentioned earlier in this chapter, Action queries can generally be significantly more efficient than VBA code. Consider the following example:

```
Sub ModifyPrice()
  Dim db As DATABASE
  Dim rs As Recordset
  Set db = CurrentDb()
  Set rs = db.OpenRecordset("tblOrderDetails")
  Do Until rs.EOF
    If rs!UnitPrice > 1 Then
      rs.Edit
      rs!UnitPrice = rs!UnitPrice - 1
      rs.UPDATE
    End If
    rs.MoveNext
  Loop
End Sub
```

This subroutine loops through **tblOrderDetails**. If the **UnitPrice** of a record is greater than 1, the price is reduced by 1. Compare the **ModifyPrice** subroutine to the following code:

```
Sub RunActionQuery()
   DoCmd.OpenQuery "qupdUnitPrice"
End Sub
```

As you can see, the **RunActionQuery** subroutine is significantly easier to code. Conceptually, the **qupdUnitPrice** query should accomplish the same tasks as the **ModifyPrice** subroutine. In most cases, the Action query runs more efficiently.

Special Query Properties

Access 2000 queries have several properties that can dramatically alter their behavior. To access a query's properties, click with your right mouse button on a blank area in the top half of the Query window and select Properties. The Properties window appears, as shown in Figure 24.1. The three properties important to the discussion of Query behavior and, therefore, discussed in the following sections are Unique Values, Unique Records, and Top Values.

Unique Values

The Unique Values property, when set to Yes, causes the query output to contain no duplicates for the combination of fields included in the query output. For example, a query might return customer information sorted by City and State. Normally, because the Unique Values property defaults to No, you would likely see many duplications of the city and state within the list of customers. However, if you set the Unique Values property to Yes, each combination of city and state will appear only once (and only the first customer record for that city and state combination will be displayed by the query).

Unique Records

The default value for the Unique Records property is No—a significant change from previous versions of Access, where the default value was Yes. If the value of the Unique Records property is Yes, it will cause the **DISTINCTROW** statement to be included in the SQL statement underlying the query. The Unique Records property applies only to multitable queries. It's ignored for queries including only one table. The **DISTINCTROW** statement allows the results of a multitable query to be updatable by ensuring that each record included in the query output is unique.

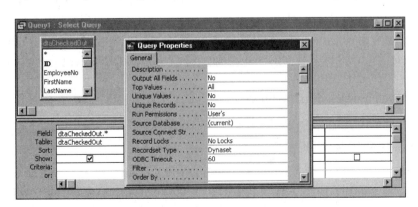

Figure 24.1   The Properties window showing Query information.

Top Values

The Top Values property allows you to specify a certain percentage or a specific number of records that the user wants to view in the query result. For example, you can build a query that outputs the country/city combinations that have the top 10 sales amounts. You can also build a query that shows the country/city combinations in which sales ranked in the top 50 percent. You can specify the Top Values property in different ways; the "Immediate Solutions" section of this chapter details several ways that you can specify them.

You might be surprised to discover that the Top Values property doesn't always seem to accurately display the correct number of records in the query result. This is because all records with values that match the value in the last record are returned as part of the query result. Consider a table with 100 records. The query asks for the top 10 values. Twelve records will appear in the query result if the 10th, 11th, and 12th records all contain the same value within the field being used to determine the top value.

Optimizing Queries

The Microsoft Jet database engine includes an Optimizer. This Optimizer looks at how long it takes to accomplish each task involved in the process of producing the required query results. It then produces a plan for the shortest path to accomplishing the desired results. This plan is based on several statistics:

- The amount of data in each table included in the query
- How many data pages are in each table
- The location of each table included in the query
- What indexes are available in each table
- Which indexes are unique
- Other statistics

The Query Compilation Process

These statistics are updated whenever the query is compiled. For a query to be compiled, it must be flagged as needing to be compiled; this happens when any of the following occurs:

- Changes are saved to the query
- Changes are saved to any tables underlying a query
- The database is compacted

Once a query has been flagged as needing to be compiled, it won't be compiled until the next time the query is run. The compiling process generally takes one to four seconds, and during this time, the updating of all statistics occurs, and a new optimization or Query Plan is produced.

Because a Query Plan is based on the number of records in each table included in the query, you should open and save your queries each time the volume of data contained within a table changes significantly. This is especially true when you're moving your query from a test environment to a production environment. If you test your application with a few records in each table and the production data contained within the table soon grows to thousands of records, your query will be optimized for only a few records and won't run efficiently.

Analyzing A Query's Performance

When analyzing the time it takes for a particular query to run, it's important to time two tasks:

- How long it takes for the first screen of data to display

- How long it takes to obtain the last record in the query result

The first measurement is fairly obvious; it measures the amount of time it takes from the moment the Run button is selected on the toolbar until the first screen of data is displayed. The second measurement is a little less obvious; it involves waiting until the "N" value in "Record 1 of N" at the bottom of the query result displays. The two measurements might be the same if the query returns only a small number of records. This is because the Jet engine decides whether it's more efficient to run the query then display the query results or to display partial query results then continue running the query in the background.

The Performance Analyzer can be used to analyze your queries to determine whether additional indexes will improve query performance. It's important to run the Performance Analyzer with the volume of data that will be present in the production version of your tables.

Things You Can Do To Improve A Query's Performance

You can do many things to improve a query's performance. These include, but aren't limited to, the following techniques:

- Index fields on both sides of a join.

- Add only the fields that you actually need in the query results to the query grid. If a field is required for criteria but doesn't need to appear in the query result, clear the Show checkbox on the query grid.

- Add as many indexes as possible. This slows down the process of inserting, updating, and deleting records, but the trade-off is usually well worth it.

- Always index on fields used in the criteria of the query.

- Compact the database often. During the compacting process, Access attempts to reorganize a table's records so that they reside in adjacent database pages, ordered by the table's primary key. This improves performance when the table is being scanned during the query process.

- When running a multitable query, test to see whether the query runs faster with the criteria placed on the one side or the many side of the join.

- Avoid adding criteria to calculated or nonindexed fields.

- Select the smallest field types possible for each field. For example, create a **Long Integer CustID** field rather than specifying the **CompanyName** field as the primary key for the table.

- Avoid calculated fields in nested queries. It's always preferable to add calculations to the higher-level queries.

- Rather than including all expressions in the query, include some expressions on form and report controls. The downside to this is that the expression will need to be repeated and maintained on each form and report.

- Use Make Table queries to build tables out of query results that are based on tables that rarely change. An example is a State table. Rather than displaying a unique list of states on all the states currently included in the Customer table, build a separate State table and use that in your queries.

- When using **Like** in the query criteria, try to place the asterisk at the end of the character string rather than at the beginning. When the asterisk is placed at the end of a string, as in **Like Th***, an index can be used to improve query performance. If the asterisk is placed at the beginning of a string, as in **Like *Sr**, no index can be used.

- Use **Count(*)** rather than **Count([fieldname])** when counting how many records meet a particular set of criteria.

- Use **Group By** as little as possible. When possible, use **First** instead. For example, if you're totaling sales information by order date and order number, you can use **First** for the order date and group by order number. This is because all records for a given order number automatically occur on the same order date.

- Use "Rushmore" technology to speed query performance wherever possible. Rushmore technology improves the performance of certain queries. Rushmore technology is discussed in the following section.

Probably one of the most important things to learn from the tips listed here is that you shouldn't follow them blindly. Like form design, most developers agree that query optimization is an art rather than a science. What helps in some situations might actually do harm in others. It's important to do benchmarks with your actual system and data.

Rushmore Technology

As mentioned in the previous section, Rushmore is a data-access technology that can be used to help improve the processing of queries. This technology can be utilized only when certain types of expressions are included in the query criteria, but it won't automatically speed up all your queries. A query must be constructed in a certain way for it to benefit from Rushmore.

A query containing an expression and comparison operator as the criteria for an Indexed field can be optimized by Rushmore. The comparison operator must be <, >, =, <=, >=, <>, **Between**, **Like**, or **In**. The expression can be any valid expression, including constants, functions, and fields from other tables. Examples of optimizable expressions include the following:

```
[Age] > 50
[OrderDate] Between #1/1/96# And #12/31/96#
[State] = "CA"
```

Rushmore can also be used to optimize queries, including complex expressions, that combine the SQL **AND** and **OR** operators. If both expressions are fully optimizable, the query will be fully optimized. If only one expression is fully optimizable and the expressions are combined with an **AND**, the query will be partially optimized. If only one expression is fully optimizable and the expressions are combined with an **OR**, the query won't be optimized.

Keep in mind a few important considerations about Rushmore:

- Queries containing the **NOT** operator can't be optimized.
- The **COUNT(*)** function is highly optimized by Rushmore.
- Descending indexes can't be utilized by Rushmore unless the expression is =.
- Queries on open database connectivity (ODBC) data sources can't utilize Rushmore.
- Multifield indexes can be utilized by Rushmore only when the criteria is in the order of the index. For example, if an index exists for the **LastName** field in combination with the **FirstName** field, it can be used to search on **LastName** or on a combination of **LastName** and **FirstName**, but it can't be used in an expression based solely on the **FirstName** field.

The Jet engine will automatically invoke the Rushmore technology when it can to optimize queries that meet the Rushmore restrictions. Unfortunately, other than closely following the rules detailed in this section, there is no way to be certain whether or not your query is Rushmore-optimizable.

Crosstab Queries

A Crosstab query is one that summarizes query results by displaying one field in a table down the left side of the datasheet view and additional facts across the top of the datasheet. For example, a Crosstab query can summarize the number of orders placed each month by a salesperson. The name of each salesperson can be placed within the left-most column of the query output. Each month can be displayed across the top of the query output. The number of orders placed would appear in the appropriate cell of the query output, as shown in Figure 24.2.

Crosstab queries are probably one of the most complex and difficult queries to create. For this reason, Microsoft has provided a Crosstab Query Wizard. The methods for creating a Crosstab query with and without the Crosstab Query Wizard are explained in the "Immediate Solutions" section.

Important Notes About Crosstab Queries

Regardless of how a Crosstab query is created, you should be aware of some special caveats when working with Crosstab queries:

- You can select only one value and one column heading for a Crosstab query. Multiple row headings can be selected.

- The results of a Crosstab query are never updatable.

- You can't define criteria on the Value field. If you do, you receive the error message "You can't specify criteria on the same field for which you enter Value in the Crosstab row." If you must specify criteria for the Value, you must build a Crosstab query that's based on a Totals query. The criteria must be placed in the Totals query on which the Crosstab query is based.

- All parameters used in a Crosstab query must be explicitly declared in the Query Parameters dialog.

Understanding Outer Join Queries

Outer Joins are used when you want the records on the one side of a one-to-many relationship to be included in the query result regardless of whether matching records exist in the table on the many side of the relationship. Consider a Customers table and an Orders table. In many situations, the user will want to include only customers with orders in the query output. An Inner Join (the default Join type) accomplishes this task. In other situations, the user will want all customers to be included in the query result whether they have orders or not. This is when an Outer Join is necessary.

SalepersonName	Total Of Value	Aug 98	Jul 98	Jun 98
Dave	$2,000.00	$3,000.00	$2,000.00	$1,000.00
Lars	$2,000.00	$3,000.00	$2,000.00	$1,000.00

Figure 24.2   An example of a Crosstab query showing the number of orders placed by each employee by month.

There are two types of Outer Joins, *Left Outer Joins* and *Right Outer Joins*. A Left Outer Join occurs when all records on the one side of a one-to-many relationship are included in the query result regardless of whether any records exist on the many side of the relationship. A Right Outer Join exists when all records on the many side of a one-to-many relationship are included in the query result regardless of whether any records exist on the one side of the relationship. A Right Outer Join should never occur, unless referential integrity isn't being enforced. The "Immediate Solutions" section of this chapter details how to establish an Outer Join.

Understanding Self-Join Queries

A Self-Join allows you to join a table to itself. This is often done so information in a single table can appear to exist in two separate tables. The classic example is with employees and supervisors. Two fields are included in the employees table. One field includes the **EmployeeID** of the employee being described in the record. The other field specifies the **EmployeeID** of the employee's supervisor. If you want to see a list of employees and their supervisors, you'll need to use a Self-Join. You will learn more about how to build a Self-Join query later in this chapter.

Self-Relationships can be permanently defined in the Relationships window. You'll often do this so referential integrity can be established between two fields within the same table. In the example of employees and supervisors, a permanent relationship with referential integrity can be established to ensure that supervisor ID numbers aren't entered with employee ID numbers that don't exist.

Building Union Queries

A Union query allows you to combine data from two tables with similar structures. Data from each table is included in the output. For example, say you have a **tblCustomer** table and a **tblCustomerArchive** table. The **tblCustomer** table contains active customers, and the **tblCustomerArchive** table contains archived customers. The problem occurs when you want to build a report that combines data from both tables. A Union query lets you resolve these problems, as you will see later in this chapter.

Pass-Through Queries

Pass-Through queries allow you to send uninterpreted SQL statements to your back-end database when you're using something other than Jet. These uninterpreted statements are in the SQL specific to your particular backend. Although the Jet database engine sees these SQL statements, it makes no attempt to parse or modify them. Pass-Through queries are used in several situations:

- The action you want to take is supported by your back-end database server but not by Access SQL or ODBC SQL.

- Access or the ODBC driver is doing a poor job parsing the SQL statement and sending it in an optimized form to the back-end database.

- You want to execute a stored procedure on the back-end database server.

- You want to ensure that the SQL statement is executed on the server.

- You want to join data from more than one table residing on the database server. If you execute the join without a Pass-Through query, the join is accomplished in the memory of the user's PC after all the required data has been sent over the network.

Although Pass-Through queries provide many advantages, they aren't a panacea. Pass-Through queries have a few disadvantages:

- When you send SQL statements specific to your particular database server, you need to rewrite all the SQL statements if you switch to another back-end.

- The results returned from a Pass-Through query aren't updatable.

- Jet does no syntax checking of the query before passing it on to the back-end.

The "Immediate Solutions" section details how to build a Pass-Through query.

The Propagation Of Nulls And Query Results

Null values can wreak havoc with your query results because **Null** values propagate. To resolve this issue, you'll probably use an expression to add the two values that look similar to the following:

```
TotalPrice:IIF(IsNull([Field1]),0,[Field1] +
    IIF(IsNull([Field2]),0,[Field2]))
```

This expression uses the **IIF** function to convert the **Null** values to zero before the two field values are added together.

Building Subqueries

Subqueries allow you to embed one **SELECT** statement within another. By placing a subquery in the criteria of a query, you can base one query on the result of another. You might, for example, want to create a query that finds all the customers without orders. The SQL statement would look like the following:

```
SELECT DISTINCTROW tblCustomers.CustomerID,
    tblCustomers.CompanyName, tblCustomers.ContactName
    FROM tblCustomers
    WHERE (((tblCustomers.CustomerID) Not In
    (Select CustomerID from tblOrders )))
```

This query first runs the **SELECT** statement, **SELECT CustomerID From tblOrders**. It uses the result as criteria to the first query.

Immediate Solutions

This section provides a step-by-step guide to building queries. Although the sub-sections are generally in the order that you'll likely perform the tasks, you should refer to the jump table at the beginning of this chapter to identify the sections that will help you solve specific problems.

Creating A Basic Query

Creating a basic query is easy because Microsoft has provided you with an intuitive drag-and-drop interface. There are two ways to start a new query in Access 2000. The first way involves selecting the Query tab from the database window and then clicking New. The New Query dialog box will appear, as shown in Figure 24.3.

This dialog box enables you to select whether you want to build the query from scratch or use one of the wizards to assist you. The Simple Query Wizard walks you through the steps involved in creating a basic query. The other wizards help you create three specific types of queries: Crosstab, Find Duplicates, or Find Unmatched. If you select Design view rather than one of the wizards, the Show Table dialog box will appear, as shown in Figure 24.4.

The Show Table dialog box enables you to select the tables or queries that supply data to your query. Access doesn't care whether you select tables or queries as the foundation for your queries. You can select tables or queries by double-clicking on the name of the table or query you want to add, or by clicking on the table,

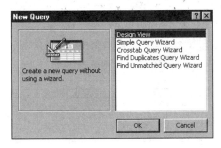

Figure 24.3   The New Query dialog box.

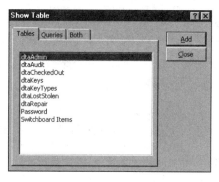

Figure 24.4   The Show Table dialog box.

then clicking Add. You can select multiple tables or queries by using the Shift key to select a contiguous range of tables or the Ctrl key to select noncontiguous tables. After you've selected the desired tables or queries, click Add, then click Close. Doing so will bring you to the Query Design window, as shown in Figure 24.5.

An alternative to the method just described is to select a table from the Tables tab and select New Query from the New Object tool drop-down on the toolbar. This is a very efficient method of starting a new query based on only one table because the Show Table dialog never appears.

You're now ready to select the fields you want to include in the query. Notice that the Query Design window is divided into two sections. The top half of the window shows the tables or queries that underlie the query you're designing. The bottom half of the window shows any fields that will be included in the query output. A field can be added to the Query Design grid on the bottom half of the Query Design window in the following ways:

- Double-click on the name of the field that you want to add.

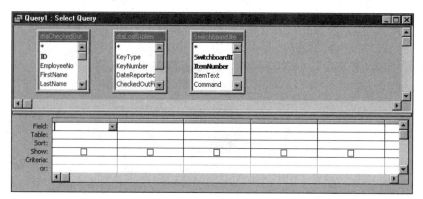

Figure 24.5   The Query Design window.

- Click-and-drag a single field from the table on the top half of the Query window to the Query Design grid in the bottom half of the window.

Select multiple fields at the same time using your Shift key to select a contiguous range of fields or your Ctrl key to select a noncontiguous range of fields. You can double-click the title bar of the field list to select all fields. Then click-and-drag any one of the selected fields to the Query Design grid in the bottom half of the window.

Running A Query

The easiest way to run a query is to select the Run button from the toolbar (which looks like an exclamation point). You can click on the View button on the toolbar to run a query, but this method works only for Select queries, not for Action queries. The Query View button has a special meaning for Action queries. Clicking Run is preferable because you don't have to worry about what type of query you're running. After running a Select query, you should see what looks like a data sheet, with only the fields that you selected. To return to the design of the query, click on the View button.

Removing A Field From The Query Design Grid

To remove a field from the Query Design grid, follow these steps:

1. Locate the field that you want to remove.
2. Click on the small gray button (column selector) immediately above the name of the field. The entire column of the Query Design grid will become black.
3. Press the Delete key or select Delete from the Edit menu.

Inserting A Field After The Query Is Built

The process for inserting a field after a query is built differs, depending on where you want the new field to be inserted. If you want it to be inserted after the existing fields, it's easiest to double-click on the name of the field you want to add. If you prefer to insert the new field between two existing fields, it's best to click-and-drag the field you want to add, dropping it on the column that you want to appear to the right of the inserted column.

Moving A Field To A Different Location On The Query Design Grid

Although you can move a column while in the Datasheet view of a query, you may want to permanently alter the position of a field in the query output. This can be done for the convenience of the user or, more importantly, because you'll use the query as a foundation for forms and reports. The order of the fields in the query becomes the default order of the fields on any forms and reports you build using any of the wizards. You can save yourself a lot of time by setting up your queries effectively.

Follow these steps to move a single column:

1. Select a column while in Design view of the query by clicking on its column selector (the small, gray button immediately above the field name).

2. Click the selected column a second time, and drag it to a new location on the Query Design grid.

Follow these steps to move more than one column at a time:

1. Drag across the column selectors of the columns you want to move.

2. Click any of the selected columns a second time, and drag them to a new location on the Query Design grid.

Moving a column in the Datasheet view doesn't modify the underlying design of the query. If you move a column in Datasheet view, subsequent reordering in the Design view is not reflected in the Datasheet view. In other words, Design view and Datasheet view are no longer synchronized, and you must reorder both manually.

Saving Your Query

To save your query at any time, click on the Save button on the toolbar. You're prompted to name your query. Query names should begin with the tag "qry" so you can easily recognize and identify them as queries. It's important to understand that when you save a query, you're saving only the definition of the query and not the actual query result.

Ordering Your Query Result

When you run a new query, you will notice that the query output appears in no particular order (unless you added an **Order By** clause). However, you'll generally want to order the query output. This can be accomplished by using the Sort row of the query grid. To order your query result, follow these steps:

1. Click within the Query Design grid in the Sort cell of the column that you want to sort.

2. Use the drop-down combo box to select an ascending or descending sort.

Sorting By More Than One Field

Often, you'll want to sort your query output by more than one field. To accomplish this, the columns you want to sort must be placed in order from left to right on the Query Design grid, with the column you want to act as the primary sort on the far left and the secondary, tertiary, and any additional sorts following to the right. If you want the columns to appear in a different order in the query output, they must be moved manually after the query has been run.

Refining Your Query With Criteria

So far, you've learned how to select the fields you want and how to indicate the sort order for your query output. One of the important features of queries is the ability to limit your output by selection criteria. Access allows you to combine criteria using any of several operators to limit the criteria for one or more fields. The operators and their meanings are covered in Table 24.2.

Table 24.2 Access operators and their meanings.

Operator	Meaning	Example	Result
=	Equal to	="Sales"	Finds only those records with "Sales" as the field value.
<	Less than	<100	Finds all records with values less than 100 in that field.
<=	Less than or equal to	<=100	Finds all records with values less than or equal to 100 in that field.

(continued)

Table 24.2   Access operators and their meanings (continued).

Operator	Meaning	Example	Result
>	Greater than	>100	Finds all records with values greater than 100 in that field.
>=	Greater than or equal to	>=100	Finds all records with values greater than or equal to 100 in that field.
<>	Not equal	<>"Sales"	Finds all records with values other than "Sales" in the field.
And	Both conditions must be true	Created by adding criteria on the same line of the query grid to more than one field	Finds all records where the conditions in both fields are true.
Or	Either condition can be true	"CA" or "NY" or "UT"	Finds all records with the value of "CA", "NY", or "UT" in the field.
Like	Compares a string expression to a pattern	Like "Sales*"	Finds all records with the value of "Sales" at the beginning of the field.
Between	Finds all records with the range of values	Between 5 and 10	Finds all values of 5 through 10 (inclusive) in the field.
In	Same as Or	In("CA", "NY","UT")	Finds all records with the value of "CA", "NY", or "UT" in the field.
Not	Same as not equal	Not "Sales"	Finds all records with values other than "Sales" in the field.
Is Null	Finds nulls	Is Null	Finds all records where no data has been entered in the field.
Is Not Null	Finds all records not null	Is Not Null	Finds all records where data has been entered in the field.

Criteria entered for two fields on a single line of the Query Design grid is considered an **AND**, which means that both conditions need to be true for the record to appear in the query output. Entries made on separate lines of the Query Design grid are considered an **OR**, which means that either condition needs to be true for the record to appear in the query output.

Working With Dates In Criteria

Access provides you with significant power in adding date functions and expressions to your query criteria. Using these criteria, you can find all records within a certain month, on a specific weekday, or between two dates. Table 24.3 provides several examples.

The **Weekday(date, [FirstDayOfWeek])** function is built to work based upon your locale and how your system defines the first day of the week. **Weekday( )** used without the optional **FirstDayOfWeek** argument defaults to **vbSunday** as the first day. A value of zero defaults the **FirstDayOfWeek** to the system definition. Other values can also be set. (See the online help for **WeekDay( )** for more information.)

Table 24.3   Sample date criteria.

Expression	Meaning	Example	Result
Date()	Current date	Date()	Records with the current date within a f field.
Day(Date)	The day of a date	Day ([OrderDate])=1	Records with the order date on the first day of the month.
Month(Date)	The month of a date	Month ([OrderDate])=1	Records with the order date in January.
Year(Date)	The year of a date	Year ([OrderDate]) =1991	Records with the order date in 1991.
Weekday(Date)	The weekday of a date	Weekday ([OrderDate])=2	Records with the order date on a Monday.
Between Date And Date	A range of dates	Between #1/1/98# and #12/31/98#	All records in 1998.
DatePart(Interval, Date)	A specific part of a date	DatePart("q", [OrderDate])=2	All records in the second quarter.

Creating Calculated Fields

One of the rules of data normalization is that the results of calculations shouldn't be included in your database. You can output the results of calculations by building these calculations into your queries. You can display the results of the calculations on forms and reports by making the query the foundation for a form or report. You can also add controls to your forms and reports containing the desired calculations. In certain cases, this can serve to improve performance.

The columns of your query result can contain the result of any valid expression, including the result of a user-defined function. This makes your queries extremely powerful. For example, the following expression could be entered:

```
Left([FirstName],1) & "." & Left([LastName],1) & "."
```

This expression will give you the first character of the first name followed by a period, the first character of the last name, and another period. An even simpler expression would be:

```
[UnitPrice]*[Quantity]
```

This calculation will simply take the UnitPrice field and multiply it by the Quantity field. In both cases, the resulting expression will be named automatically by Access. To give the expression a name such as **Initials**, you must enter the expression as follows:

```
Initials:Left([FirstName],1) & "." & Left([LastName],1) & "."
```

The text preceding the colon is the name of the expression—in this case, **Initials**.

You can enter any valid expression in the Field row of your query grid. Notice that field names included in an expression are automatically surrounded by square brackets unless your field name contains spaces. If a field name includes any spaces, you must enclose the field name in brackets. Otherwise, your query won't run properly, which is just one of the many reasons why field and table names shouldn't contain spaces.

Creating Update Queries

As you learned earlier in this chapter, you'll use Update queries to modify all records or records meeting specific criteria. To build an Update query, follow eight steps:

1. Click the Queries tab of the Database window and click New.

2. Select Design View and click OK.

3. The Show Table dialog appears. Select the table(s) or query(ies) that will participate in the Update query and click Add. Click Close when you're ready to continue.

4. To indicate to Access that you're building an Update query, open the Query Type drop-down on the toolbar and select Update Query. You can also use the Query menu Update Query option.

5. Add fields to the query that will either be used for criteria or will be updated as a result of the query.

6. Add any desired criteria.

7. Add the appropriate Update expression.

8. Click Run on the toolbar. The message box pictured in Figure 24.6 appears. This message can be suppressed programmatically, if desired. Click Yes to continue. All records meeting the selected criteria are updated.

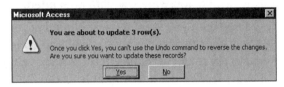

Figure 24.6   The Confirmation dialog box for the Update query.

Building A Delete Query

Follow four steps to build a Delete query:

1. While in Design view of a query, use the Query Type drop-down to select Delete Query. You can also use the Query menu Delete Query option.

2. Add desired criteria to the Query Design grid.

3. Click Run on the toolbar. The message box pictured in Figure 24.7 appears. This message can be suppressed programmatically, if desired.

4. Click Yes to permanently remove the records from the table.

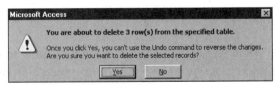

Figure 24.7   The Confirmation dialog box for the Delete query.

Building An Append Query

To build an Append query, follow five steps:

1. While in Design view of a query, use the Query Type drop-down to select Append Query. You can also use the Query menu Append Query option. The dialog box pictured in Figure 24.8 appears.

Figure 24.8   The Append Query dialog box.

2. Select the table to which you want the data appended.

3. Drag all fields whose data you want to be included in the second table to the Query Design grid. If the field names in the two tables match, Access automatically matches the field names in the source table to the corresponding field names in the destination table. If the field names in the two tables don't match, you need to explicitly designate which fields in the source table match which fields in the destination table.

4. Enter any criteria in the Query Design grid.

5. To run the query, click Run on the toolbar. A message box will appear to confirm the append action. This message can be suppressed programmatically, if desired. Click Yes to complete the process.

Creating A Make Table Query

Six steps are required to create a Make Table query:

1. While in Design view of a query, use the Query Type drop-down to select Make Table. You can also use the Query menu Make Table option. The dialog box pictured in Figure 24.9 appears.

2. Provide Access with the name of the new table. Click OK.

3. Move all the fields you want included in the new table to the Query Design grid. It's common to include the result of an expression in the new table.

4. Add any desired criteria to the Query Design grid.

Figure 24.9   The Make Table dialog box.

5. Click Run on the toolbar to run the query. A message box will appear to confirm the Make Table action. This message can be suppressed programmatically, if desired.

6. Click Yes to complete the process.

If you attempt to run the same Make Table query more than one time, the table with the same name as the table you're creating is permanently deleted. Access will display a message box confirming that you wish to delete the original table.

Creating A Crosstab Query Using The Crosstab Query Wizard

Eight steps are required to design a Crosstab query using the Crosstab Query Wizard:

1. Select the Queries tab from the Database window, and click New.

2. Select Crosstab Query Wizard, and click OK.

3. Select the table or query that will act as a foundation for the query. If you want to include fields from more than one table in the query, you'll need to base the Crosstab query on another query containing the desired tables and fields. Click Next.

4. Select the field(s) whose values you want to use as the row headings for the query output. Click Next.

5. Select the field whose values you want to use as the column headings for the query output. Click Next.

6. If the field you selected for a heading is a Date field, the Crosstab Query Wizard requests that you specify the interval you want to group by. Select the desired date interval, and click Next.

7. The next step of the Crosstab Query Wizard asks you to specify what number you want calculated for each column and row intersection. Click Next.

8. The final step of the wizard allows you to specify a name for your query. When you're done, click Finish.

Figure 24.10 shows a completed Crosstab query in Design view. Several attributes of the completed query are important. Notice the Crosstab row of the Query Design grid. The **SalespersonName** is specified as a row heading. The **SalespersonName** field is used as a Group By for the query. The following expression is included as a Column Heading:

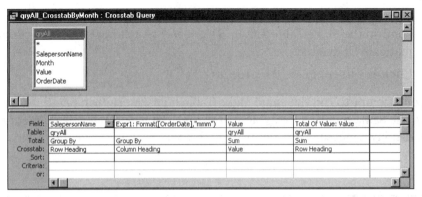

Figure 24.10   A completed Crosstab query.

```
Format([OrderDate],"mmm")
```

This expression returns the order date formatted to display only the month. This expression is also used as a Group By for the query. The **OrderID** is specified as a value. The Total cell for the column indicates that this field will be counted (as opposed to being summed, averaged, and so on).

Notice the column labeled "Total of OrderID." This column displays the total of all the columns within the query. It's identical to the column containing the value except for the alias in the field name and that the Crosstab cell is set to Row Heading rather than Value.

Creating A Crosstab Query Without Using The Crosstab Query Wizard

Although you can create many of your Crosstab queries using the Crosstab Query Wizard, you should know how to build a Crosstab query without the wizard. This gives you the ability to modify existing Crosstab queries and to gain the ultimate control over the creation of new queries. To build a Crosstab query without the use of the Crosstab Query Wizard, follow 12 steps:

1. Click the Queries tab of the Database window, and click New.

2. Select Design View, and click OK.

3. Select the table or query that will be included in the query grid. Click Add to add the table or query, then click Close.

4. Use the Query Type drop-down to select Crosstab (or use the Query menu Crosstab option).

5. Add the fields you want to include in the query output to the Query Design grid.

6. Click the Crosstab row of each field you want to include as a row heading. Select Row Heading from the drop-down.

7. Click the Crosstab row of the field you want to include as a column heading. Select Column Heading from the drop-down.

8. Click the Crosstab row of the field whose values you want to cross-tabulate. Select Value from the Crosstab drop-down, and select the appropriate aggregate function from the Total drop-down.

9. Add any desired date intervals or other expressions.

10. Specify any criteria for the query.

11. Change the sort order of any of the columns as desired.

12. Run the query when you're ready.

Using Fixed Column Headings

If you don't use fixed column headings, all the columns are included in the query output in alphabetical order. For example, if you include month names in the query result, they appear as Apr, Aug, Dec, Feb, and so on. By using fixed column headings, you tell Access the order in which each column appears in the query result. Column headings can be specified by setting the Column Headings property of the query.

All fixed column headings must match the underlying data exactly; otherwise, information will be omitted inadvertently from the query result. For example, if the column heading for the month of June was accidentally entered as "June", and the data output by the format statement included data for the month of "Jun", all June data will be omitted from the query output.

Establishing An Outer Join

To establish an Outer Join, you must modify the join between the tables included in the query:

1. Double-click the line joining the tables within the Query Design grid.

2. The Join Properties window appears. To create a Left Outer Join between the tables, select Option 2 (select Option 3 if you want to create a Right Outer Join).

3. Click OK to accept the join. An Outer Join should be established between the tables.

Figure 24.11 shows the Join Properties window.

The SQL statement produced when a Left Outer Join is established looks similar to the following:

```
SELECT DISTINCTROW tblCustomers.CustomerID, tblCustomers.CompanyName
FROM tblCustomers
LEFT JOIN tblOrders
ON tblCustomers.CustomerID = tblOrders.CustomerID;
```

A Left Outer Join can also be used to identify all the records on the one side of a join that don't have any corresponding records on the many side of the join. To do this, simply enter "Is Null" as the criteria for any field on the many side of the join.

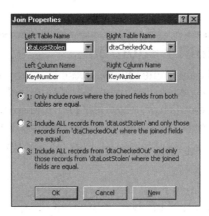

Figure 24.11   The Join Properties window.

Building A Self-Join Query

As you learned earlier in this chapter, there may be times when you need to build a Self-Join query. To build a Self-Join query, perform the following steps:

1. Click the Queries tab of the Database window, and click New.

2. Select Design View, and click OK.

3. From the Show Tables dialog, add the table to be used in the Self-Join to the query grid two times. Click Close. Notice that the second instance of the table appears with an underscore and the number 1.

4. To change the alias of the second table, click with the right mouse button on top of the table in the Query Design grid, and select Properties. Change the Alias property as desired.

5. To establish a join between the table and its alias, click-and-drag from the field in one table that corresponds to the field in the aliased table.

6. Drag the appropriate fields to the Query Design grid.

7. Click on the View button on the toolbar to display the query in Datasheet view.

Building A Union Query

To build a Union query, perform the following steps:

1. Click the Queries tab of the Database window, and click New.

2. Select Design View, and click OK.

3. Click Close from the Show Tables dialog without selecting a table.

4. Select the Query menu SQL Specific submenu Union option. A SQL window appears.

5. Type in the SQL **UNION** clause. Notice that you can't switch back to the Design view of the query. A common SQL **UNION** clause might look similar to the following, which merges the **tblNewAccounts** table with all records in the **tblCustomers** table with **OrderAmounts** larger than 1,000.

```
TABLE [tblNewAccounts] UNION ALL
SELECT *
FROM tblCustomers
WHERE OrderAmount > 1000;
```

6. Click on the Run button on the toolbar to execute the query.

Creating Pass-Through Queries

Building a Pass-Through query is pretty straightforward. To build a Pass-Through query, perform the following steps:

1. Click the Queries tab of the Database window, and click New.

2. Select Design View, and click OK.

3. Click Close from the Show Tables dialog, without selecting a table.

4. Select the Query menu SQL Specific submenu Pass-Through option. The SQL Design Window appears.

5. Type in the SQL statement in the dialect of your back-end database server.

6. View the Query Properties window and enter an ODBC connect string.

7. Click the Run button on the toolbar to run the query.

Passing Parameter Query Values From A Form

The biggest frustration with Parameter queries occurs when multiple parameters are required to run the query. The user is confronted with multiple dialogs, one for each parameter included in the query. The following steps explain how to build a Parameter query that receives its parameter values from a form:

1. Create a new Unbound form (that is, create the form in Design View, but do not attach a data source to the form).

2. Add text boxes or other controls to accept the criteria for each parameter that will be added to your query.

3. Name each control in a way that lets you readily identify the data that it contains.

4. Add a command button to the form. Instruct the command button to call the Parameter query (with a **DoCmd** statement or similar construction).

5. Save the form.

6. Add the parameters to the query. Each parameter should refer to a control on the form. In other words, the Criteria book should have contents similar to the following:

```
Like frmUnbound.txtTextBox1.Text
```

7. Right-click the top half of the Query Design grid, and select Parameters. Define a data type for each parameter in the Parameters dialog. To continue with the sample in Step 6, you might define the Parameter type as Text (the default).

8. Save and close the query.

9. Fill in the values on the criteria form, and click the command button to execute the query. It should execute successfully.

Chapter 25

Creating Forms And Reports

In Depth

Considering Forms

As you saw in Chapter 23, creating the database design is only the first step in the development of an Access 2000 solution. Although many supporting components are available that you'll generally want to implement together with your Access databases, the three most commonly used components are forms, queries, and reports. In the last chapter, you examined queries more closely. In this chapter, you'll consider the uses and purposes of forms and reports.

Developers often think that forms exist solely for the purpose of data entry. On the contrary, forms serve many different purposes in Access. Some of the most common uses are as shown in the following list:

- Displaying and editing data for data entry
- Navigating through the application
- Providing messages to the user, either in the form of custom dialog boxes or through the use of ActiveX controls
- Printing hard copies of data-entry information

Probably the most common use of an Access form is as a vehicle for displaying and editing existing data or adding new data. Fortunately, Access provides numerous features that enable you to build forms that greatly ease the data-entry process for your users. Access also makes it easy for you to design forms that allow your users to view data but not modify it, view and modify data, or add new records only.

Although not everyone immediately thinks of an Access form as a means of navigation through an application, forms are quite strong in this area. Figure 25.1, for example, shows a form created with the Switchboard Manager in Access 2000.

Although the Switchboard Manager makes the process of designing a switchboard form extremely easy, you'll find any type of switchboard easy to develop. You can be creative with switchboard forms by designing forms that are both utilitarian and exciting.

You can also use Access to create custom dialog boxes. These dialog boxes can be used to display or retrieve information from your users. For example, you might use a dialog box to retrieve a set of parameters for a query or report.

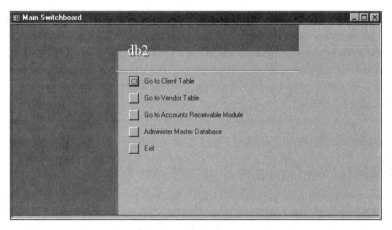

Figure 25.1   A simple switchboard form created within the Switchboard Manager.

Another strength of Access is its ability to produce professional-looking printed forms. In many other products, it's difficult to print a data-entry form. Sometimes the entire form needs to be re-created as a report. In Access, printing a form is simply a matter of clicking a button. Additionally, you have the option of creating a report that displays the information that your user is entering, the results of a query, and so on. You'll learn more about reports later in this chapter.

Access provides many styles of forms. The data in a form can be displayed one record at a time, or you can allow the user to view several records at once. Forms can be displayed modally, meaning that the user must respond and close the form before continuing, or displayed so that the user can move through the open forms at will. The important thing to remember is that many uses and styles of forms are available. You'll learn about them throughout this chapter and throughout the book. As you read this chapter, remember that your form's designs are, in general, limited only by your imagination.

Describing The Form's Components

Access forms contain three sections, each of which has its own function and behavior:

• Header

• Detail

• Footer

The Detail section of a form is the main section. It's the section that's used to display the data of the table or query underlying the form. As you'll see, the Detail section can take on many different looks; it's very flexible and robust.

The Header and Footer sections of the form are used to display information that doesn't change from record to record. Command buttons that control the form are often placed in the header or footer of the form. An example would be a command button that allows the user to view all the projects associated with a particular client. Controls can also be used to help the user navigate around the records associated with the form. An example appears in Figure 25.2. The user can select from the valid list of employees. After the user selects an employee from the combo box, the user is moved to the appropriate record.

Selecting The Correct Control For The Job

Windows programming in general, and Access programming in particular, isn't limited to just writing code. Your ability to design a user-friendly interface will often determine the success of your application. Access and the Windows programming environment offer a variety of controls; each is appropriate in different situations. The next sections discuss each control, outlining when and how you should use each one.

Labels

Labels are used to display information to your users. Attached labels are automatically added to your form as you add other controls such as text boxes, combo boxes, and so on. They can be deleted or modified as necessary. Their default captions are based on the Caption property of the field that underlies the control to which they are attached. If nothing has been entered into the Caption property of the field, the field name is used for the caption of the label.

The Label tool, found in the toolbox, can be used to add any text to the form. Click the Label tool, and click and drag the label to place it on the form. Labels

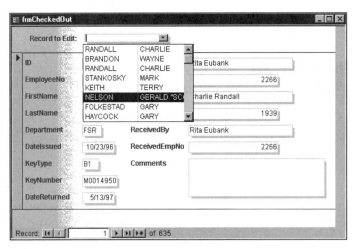

Figure 25.2   Adding a combo box to a form to speed record selection.

are often used to provide a description of the form or to supply instructions to users. Labels can be customized by modifying their font, size, color, and so on. They can't be modified by the user at run time, but they can be modified at run time using Visual Basic for Applications (VBA) code.

Text Boxes

Text boxes are used to obtain information from the user. Bound text boxes display and retrieve field information, whereas unbound text boxes gather information from the user that's not related to a specific field in a specific record. For example, a text box can be used to gather information from a user regarding report criteria.

Text boxes are automatically added to a form when you click and drag a field from the field list to the form and the Display Control property for the field is set to Text Box. Another way to add a text box to a form is to select the Text Box tool from the toolbox. Click to select the Text Box tool and then click and drag to place the text box on the form. This process adds an unbound text box to the form. If you want to bind the text box to data, you must set its Control Source property.

Combo Boxes

Access offers several easy ways to add a combo box to a form. If the Display Control property of a field has been set to Combo Box, a combo box is automatically added to a form when the field is added to the form. The combo box automatically knows the source of its data as well as all its other important properties.

If the Display Control property of a field has not been set to Combo Box, the easiest way to add a combo box to a form is to use the Control Wizard. The Control Wizard, when selected, helps you to add combo boxes, list boxes, option groups, and subforms to your forms. Although all the properties set by the Combo Box Wizard can be set manually, using the wizard saves both time and energy. If you want the Combo Box Wizard to be launched when you add a combo box to the form, make sure the Control Wizard tool in the toolbox has been pressed (switched on) before you add the combo box. You'll learn more about adding combo boxes to your forms in the "Immediate Solutions" section of this chapter.

Combo boxes are extremely powerful controls. Though covering them in much detail is beyond the scope of this book, you'll use and analyze them in several different implementation environments over the course of the examples and solutions.

List Boxes

List boxes are very similar to combo boxes but differ from them in three major ways:

- They consume more screen space.

- They let the user select only from the list that's displayed. This means that you can't type new values into a list box (as you can with a combo box).

- They can be configured to allow the user to select multiple items.

As with a combo box, the Display Control property of a field can be set to List Box. If the Display Control property has been set to List Box, a list box is added to the form when the field is clicked and dragged from the field list to the form.

The List Box Wizard is almost identical to the Combo Box Wizard. (You'll learn about both Wizards in the "Immediate Solutions" section of this chapter.) After running the List Box Wizard, the List Box properties affected by the wizard are the same as the Combo Box properties.

Check Boxes

Check boxes are used when you want to limit your user to entering one of two values. The values entered can be limited to Yes/No, True/False, or On/Off. You can add a check box to a form in several ways:

- Set the Display Control property of the underlying field to Check Box, then click and drag the field from the field list to the form.

- Click the Check Box tool in the toolbox, then click and drag a field from the field list to the form. This method adds a check box to the form even if the Display Control property of the underlying field isn't a check box.

- Click the Check Box tool in the toolbox, then click and drag to add a check box to the form. The check box you've added is unbound. To bind the check box to data, you must set the Control Source property of the control.

Option Buttons

You can use option buttons alone or as part of an option group. An option button alone can be used to display a True/False value, but this isn't a standard use of an option button (check boxes are standard for this purpose). As part of an option group, option buttons force the user to select from a mutually exclusive set of options. An example is payment type—credit card, cash, check, and so on.

Toggle Buttons

Like option buttons, toggle buttons can be used alone or as part of an option group. A toggle button by itself can display a True/False value, but this isn't a standard use of a toggle button. Toggle buttons are more commonly used as part of an option group, as discussed in the next section.

Option Groups

Option groups allow the user to select from a mutually exclusive set of options. They can comprise check boxes, toggle buttons, or option buttons. The most common implementation of an option group is option buttons.

The easiest way to add an option group to a form is to use the Option Group Wizard. To ensure that the Option Group Wizard will run, make sure the Control Wizards button in the toolbox is selected. Click Option Group in the toolbox, then click and drag to add the option group to the form. The Option Group Wizard is launched. You'll learn about the Option Group Wizard later in the "Immediate Solutions" section.

Morphing A Control From One Format To Another

When you first build a form, you might not always make the best choice for the type of control to display each field on the form. Alternately, you might make what you think is the best choice for the control only to find out later that it wasn't exactly what your user had in mind. However, in Access 2000, it's easy to *morph*, or convert, the type of control. For example, you can morph a list box into a combo box by changing only a few properties.

Text Box To Combo Box

One of the most common types of conversions is from a text box to a combo box. To morph a text box to a combo box, click with your right mouse button on the text box. Select Change To, then select the type of control you want to morph the text box to. The types of controls available depend on the type of control you're morphing. For example, a text box can be converted to a label, list box, or combo box, as shown in Figure 25.3.

After morphing a text box to a combo box, you'll need to modify the appropriate Control properties to make the combo box perform correctly. The Row Source, Bound Column, Column Count, and Column Widths properties need to be filled in. Select the appropriate table or query for the row source. If you select a table,

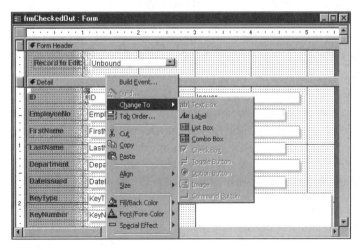

Figure 25.3 The possible targets when you morph a text box.

then click on the ellipsis, you're prompted to create a query based on the table. After selecting Yes, you can build a query containing only the fields that you want to include in the combo box. You're then ready to select the bound column. The bound column is used to store data into the underlying table. For example, the user might select the name of a project that a payment is being applied to, but the **ProjectID** will be stored in the Payments table. You need to set the column count to the number of columns selected in the underlying query. The column widths can be set so that Access hides the key column.

Combo Box To List Box

Converting a combo box to a list box is a much simpler process than converting a text box to a combo box or list box because combo boxes and list boxes share so many properties. To morph a combo box to a list box, simply click with the right mouse button on the combo box and select the Change To submenu List Box option.

Understanding And Using Form Properties

Forms have many properties that can be used to affect the look and behavior of the form. The properties are broken down into four categories—Format, Data, Event, and Other. To view a form's properties, you must select the form in one of two ways:

- Click the Form Selector (the small gray button at the intersection of the horizontal and vertical rulers).

- Select the Edit menu Select Form option.

After you select the form, you should choose the View menu Properties option to display the form's properties. Alternately, you can right-click on the form and select the Properties option from the pop-up menu.

Working With The Properties Window

After a form has been selected for design work, setting form properties (and the properties of any form components) is a simple task. Determining what form properties to set isn't quite so simple; many people have suggested that form design is more of an art than a science, requiring nothing so much as experience to develop quality interfaces. To view the properties for a form, click the Properties button on the toolbar to view its properties. Access will display the Properties window. The Properties window is shown in Figure 25.4.

Notice that the Properties window consists of five tabs: Format, Data, Event, Other, and All. Many developers prefer to view all the form's properties at once (in which case you can select the All tab), but a form has a total of over 75 properties. Rather than viewing all 75 properties at once, try viewing the properties by

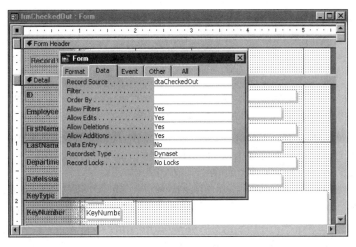

Figure 25.4   The Properties window when working with the form in design mode.

category. The Format category includes all the physical attributes of the form. These attributes affect the form's appearance. An example is the form's background color. The Data category includes all the properties that relate to the data to which the form is bound. An example is the form's underlying record source. The Event category contains all the Windows events to which a form can respond. For instance, you can write code that executes in response to the form being loaded, becoming active, displaying a different record, and so on. The Other category contains a small number of properties that don't fit into any of the other three categories.

Working With The Important Form Properties

As mentioned, forms have 75 properties. Thirty-one of these properties are Event properties, which you'll learn more about in Chapter 26. This section covers Format, Data, and Other properties of forms.

Format Properties Of A Form

The Format properties of a form affect its physical appearance. Forms have 24 Format properties, as detailed in the following list:

- *Caption*—The Caption property sets the text that appears on the title bar of the form. This property can be customized at run time. An illustration would be to include the name of the current user or specify the name of the client for whom an invoice is being generated.

- *Default View*—The Default View property allows you to select three options; whichever option you select will become the default view for the form.

- *Single Form*—Only one record can be viewed at a time.

- *Continuous Form*—As many records as will fit within the form window are displayed at one time, each displayed as the detail section of a single form.

- *Datasheet*—Displays the records in a spreadsheet-like format, with the rows representing records and the columns representing fields.

- *Views Allowed*—The Views Allowed property determines whether the user is allowed to switch from Form view to Data Sheet view or vice versa. The Default View property determines the default display mode for the form, and Views Allowed determines whether the user is permitted to switch out of the default view.

- *Scroll Bars*—The Scroll Bars property determines whether scroll bars appear if the controls on the form don't fit within the form's display area. You can select from vertical and horizontal, neither vertical nor horizontal, just vertical, or just horizontal.

- *Record Selectors*—A record selector is the gray bar that appears to the left of a record when the user is in Form view or the gray box that appears to the left of each record when the user is in Data Sheet view. A record selector allows the user to select a record to be copied or deleted. The Record Selectors property determines whether the record selectors appear. If you provide the user with a custom menu, you can choose to remove the record selector to ensure that the user copies or deletes records using only functionality specifically built into your application.

- *Navigation Buttons*—Navigation buttons are the controls that appear at the bottom of a form, allowing the user to move from record to record within the form. The Navigation Buttons property determines whether the navigation buttons are visible. Set the Navigation Buttons property to No for any dialog forms. You might want to set the Navigation Buttons property to No for data-entry forms and add your own toolbar or command buttons that enhance or limit the functionality of the standard buttons. For instance, in a client/server environment, you might not want to give users the ability to move to the first or last record. This type of record movement can be very inefficient in a client/server architecture.

- *Dividing Lines*—The Dividing Lines property is used to indicate whether you want a line to appear between each record when the default view of the form is set to Continuous Forms.

- *Auto Resize*—The Auto Resize property determines whether the form is automatically sized to display a complete record.

- *Auto Center*—The Auto Center property is used to specify whether you want the form to be automatically centered within the Application window whenever it's opened.

- *Border Style*—The Border Style property is far more powerful than its name implies. The options for the Border Style property are None, Thin, Sizable, and Dialog. The border style is often set to None for splash screens, which means that the form has no border. A Thin border isn't resizable; the Size command isn't available within the Control menu. This setting is a good choice for pop-up forms, which remain on top even when other forms are given the focus. A Sizable border is standard for most forms. It includes all the standard options within the Control menu. A Dialog border is thick. A form with a border style of Dialog can't be maximized, minimized, or resized. When the border style of a form is set to Dialog, the Maximize, Minimize, and Resize options aren't available within the Control menu of the form. The Dialog border is often used along with the Pop-Up and Modal properties to create custom dialog boxes.

- *Control Box*—The Control Box property is used to determine whether a form has a Control menu. Use this option sparingly. One of your responsibilities as an Access programmer is to make your applications comply with Windows standards. If you look at the Windows programs you use, you find very few forms without Control Menu boxes. This should tell you something about how you should design your own applications.

- *Min Max Buttons*—The Min Max Buttons property is used to indicate whether the form has minimize and maximize buttons. The available options are None, Min Enabled, Max Enabled, and Both Enabled. If you remove one or both buttons, the appropriate options also become unavailable in the Control menu. The Min Max Buttons property is ignored for forms with a border style of None or Dialog. As with the Control Box property, most programmers will rarely use this property.

- *Close Button*—The Close Button property determines whether the user is able to close the form using the Control menu or by double-clicking on the Control icon. In setting the value of this property to No, you must provide your user with another way to close the form; otherwise, the user might have to reboot his or her computer to close your application.

- *Whats This Button*—The Whats This Button property is used to specify whether you want the Whats This button added to the form's title bar. This feature works only when the form's Min Max Buttons property is set to No. When set to Yes, the user can click on the Whats This button, then click on an object on the form. Help for the selected object is displayed. If the selected object has no help associated with it, help for the form is displayed. For a form that has no help associated with it, Microsoft Access Help is displayed.

- *Width*—The Width property is used to specify the width of the form. This option is most often set graphically by clicking and dragging to select an appropriate size for the form. You might want to set this property manually when you want more than one form to be exactly the same size.

- *Picture, Picture Type, Picture Size Mode, Picture Alignment, and Picture Tiling*—The Picture properties allow you to select and customize the attributes of a bitmap to be used as the background for a form.

- *Grid X, Grid Y*—The Grid X and Grid Y properties can be used to modify the spacing of the horizontal and vertical lines that appear in the form when in Design view. By setting these properties, you can affect the precision of the placement of objects on the form when the Snap to Grid option is active.

- *Layout for Print*—The Layout for Print property is used to specify whether screen or printer fonts are used on the form. To optimize the form for printing rather than display, set this property to Yes.

- *Palette Source*—The Palette Source property is used to determine the source for the selectable colors for a form.

Data Properties Of A Form

You'll use the Data properties of a form to control the source for the form's data, to specify what actions the user can take on the data within the form, and to determine how the data within the form is locked in a multiuser environment. A form contains 10 Data properties, detailed within the following list:

- *Record Source*—The Record Source property is used to indicate the Table, Stored Query, or SQL statement on which the form's records are based. After you've selected a record source for a form, the controls on the form can be bound to the fields within the record source. The Field List window is unavailable until the record source of the form has been set. The record source of a form can be changed at runtime. This aspect of the Record Source property allows you to create generic, reusable forms that can be used in many situations.

- *Filter*—The Filter property is used to automatically load a stored filter along with the form. Many developers prefer to base a form on a query that limits the data displayed on the form. The query can be passed parameters at runtime to customize exactly what data is displayed.

- *Order By*—The Order By property is used to specify in what order the records on a form appear. This property can be modified at runtime to change the order in which the records appear.

- *Allow Filters*—The Allow Filters property lets you control whether records can be filtered at runtime. When this option is set to No, all filtering options become disabled to the user.

- *Allow Edits, Allow Deletions, Allow Additions*—These properties let you specify whether the user can edit data, delete records, or add records from within the form. These options can't override any permissions that have been set for the form's underlying table or queries.

- *Data Entry*—The Data Entry property is used to determine whether your users can only add records within a form. Set this property to Yes if you don't want your users to be able to view or modify existing records but you do want them to be able to add new records.

- *Recordset Type*—The Recordset Type property gives you three options: Dynaset, Dynaset (Inconsistent Updates), and Snapshot. Each of these options offers different performance and updatability. The Dynaset option creates a fully updatable recordset. The only exceptions to this rule involve records or fields that aren't updatable for some other reason. An example is a form based on a query involving a one-to-many relationship. The join field on the one side of the relationship is updatable only if the Cascade Update Related Records feature has been enabled. The Dynaset option allows all tables and bound data to be edited. The Snapshot option allows no updatability.

- *Record Locks*—The Record Locks property is used to specify the locking mechanism that will be used for the data underlying the form's recordset. Three options are available. The No Locks option provides optimistic locking. Access doesn't attempt to lock the record until the user moves off the record. This option can lead to potential conflicts when two users simultaneously make changes to the same record. No Locks is the least restrictive locking mechanism. The All Records option is used to lock all records underlying the form for the entire time the form is open. This is the most restrictive option and should be used only when it's necessary for the user of the form to ensure that other users can view, but not modify, the form's underlying recordset. The Edited Record option locks a 2K page of records as soon as a user starts editing the data within the form. This option provides pessimistic locking. Although it averts conflicts by prohibiting two users from modifying a record at the same time, this option can lead to potential locking conflicts.

Other Properties Of A Form

In addition to the form properties detailed in the previous sections, some form properties appear only under the Other tab (and under the All tab). These properties control a variety of different features, as shown in the following list:

- *Pop-Up*—The Pop-Up property is used to indicate whether the form always remains on the top of other windows. This property is often set to Yes, in conjunction with the Modal property, for custom dialog boxes.

- *Modal*—The Modal property is used to indicate whether focus can be removed from a form while it's open. When the Modal property is set to Yes, the form must be closed before the user can continue working with the application. As mentioned, this property is used in conjunction with the Pop-Up property to create custom dialog boxes.

- *Cycle*—The Cycle property is used to control the behavior of the Tab key within the form. The options for the Cycle property are All Records, Current Record, and Current Page. When the Cycle property is set to All Records, users are placed on the next record when they press Tab from the last control on the form. When the Cycle property is set to Current Record, users are moved from the last control on a form to the first control on the same record. The Current Page option refers only to multipage forms. With a multipage form, when the Cycle property is set to Current Page, users tab from the last control on the page to the first control on the same page. All three options are affected by the tab order of the objects on the form.

- *Menu Bar*—The Menu Bar property is used to specify a menu bar associated with the form. The menu bar is created using the Menu Builder.

- *Shortcut Menu, Shortcut Menu Bar*—The Shortcut Menu property is used to indicate whether a Shortcut menu is displayed when the user clicks with the right mouse button over an object on the form. The Shortcut Menu Bar property allows you to associate a custom menu with a control on the form or with the form itself.

- *Fast Laser Printing*—The Fast Laser Printing property is used to determine whether lines and rectangles print along with the form. Setting this property to Yes dramatically improves the performance when printing the form to a laser printer.

- *Help File, Help Context ID*—The Help File and Help Context ID properties are used to associate a specific help file and topic with a form.

- *Tag*—The Tag property is an extra property that can be used to store miscellaneous information about the form. This property is often set and monitored at run time to store necessary information about the form.

- *Toolbar*—You can use the Toolbar property to specify the toolbar to use for a form or report. You create these toolbars by using the Customize subcommand of the Toolbars option on the View menu or by using the ActiveX Toolbar control.

- *HasModule*—You can use the HasModule property to specify or determine whether a form or report has a class module. Setting this property to No can improve the performance and decrease the size of your database.

- *Allow Design Changes*—You can use the Allow Design Changes property to specify whether changes can be made to the appearance of a form from within any view, or if they can be made only from within the Design View window.

Considering The Available Control Properties

Although many different properties are available for forms, these properties will be consistent from form to form. Control properties, on the other hand, will vary significantly, depending on the type of control that you're working with. The more common properties are covered in this section. More individualized properties are covered throughout the book as they apply to a specific topic, and you can find more about any property from within the Access online help file.

Format Properties Of A Control

Though control properties differ, Access will group them into the same four categories that it groups form properties into: Format, Data, Event, and Other. The first of the other property sets is the Format category. The Format category's values will vary; however, some of the most common properties are shown in the following list:

- *Format*—The Format property of a control is used to determine the way the data within the control is displayed. The format for a control is automatically inherited from its underlying data source. This property is used in only two situations:

  - When you want to override the Format setting set for the field

  - When you want to apply a format to an unbound control

  You can select from a multitude of predefined values for the format of a control, or you can create a custom format. Many developers often modify this property at runtime to vary the format of a control, depending on a certain condition. For example, the format for a social security number is different from the format for a corporate federal tax identification number.

- *Visible*—The Visible property is used to indicate whether a control is visible. This property can be toggled at runtime, depending on specific circumstances. An example is a question on the form that applies only to records where the gender is set to Female. If the user sets the gender to Male, the question shouldn't be visible.

- *Display When*—Use the Display When property when you want certain controls on the form to be sent only to the screen or only to the printer. The three options are Always, Print Only, or Screen Only. An example of the use of the Display When property is a label containing instructions. You might want the instructions to appear on the screen but not on the printout.

- *Scroll Bars*—The Scroll Bars property is used to determine whether scroll bars appear when the data within the control doesn't fit within the size of the control. The options are None and Vertical. Many developers will often set the Scroll Bars property to Vertical when the control is used to display data from a Memo field. The scroll bar makes it easier for the user to work with a potentially large volume of data contained within the Memo field.

- *Can Grow, Can Shrink*—The Can Grow and Can Shrink properties apply only to the printed version of the form. The Can Grow property, when set to Yes, expands the control when printing so all the data within the control fits on the printout. The Can Shrink property applies when no data has been entered into the control. When this property is set to Yes, the control shrinks when no data has been entered so blank lines won't be printed.

- *Left, Top, Width, Height*—These properties are used to set the position and size of the control.

- *Back Style, Back Color*—The Back Style property can be set to Normal or Transparent. When set to Transparent, the background color of the form shows through the control. This is often the preferred setting for an option group. The Back Color property of the control is used to specify the background color (as opposed to text color) for the control. If the back style of a control is set to Transparent, the back color of the control is ignored.

- *Special Effect*—The Special Effect property is used to add 3D effects to a control. The options for this property are Flat, Raised, Sunken, Etched, Shadowed, and Chiseled. Each of these effects provides a different look and feel for the control.

- *Border Style, Border Color, Border Width*—These properties affect the look, color, and thickness of the border of a control. The Border Style options are Transparent, Solid, Dashes, Short Dashes, Dots, Sparse Dots, Dash Dot, and Dash Dot Dot. The Border Color property is used to specify the color of the border. You can select from a variety of colors. The Border Width property can be set to one of several point sizes. If the Border Style of a control is set to Transparent, the Border Color and Border Width of the control are ignored.

- *Fore Color, Font Name, Font Size, Font Weight, Font Italic, Font Underline*—These properties control the appearance of the text within a control. As their names imply, they allow you to select a color, font, size, and thickness for the text, as well as to determine whether the text is italicized or underlined. These properties can be modified in response to an event that occurs at runtime. An illustration would be to modify the text color of a control if the value within that control exceeds a certain amount.

- *Text Align*—The Text Align property is often confused with the ability to align controls. The Text Align property affects how the data is aligned *within* a control.

- *Decimal Places*—The Decimal Places property is used to specify how many decimal places you want to appear within the control. This property is used in conjunction with the Format property to determine the appearance of the control.

Data Properties Of A Control

Just as you'll typically affiliate a form with a data source—in the form of a table or query—you'll typically affiliate the controls on your form with specific items within that data source. Generally, each field in the data source will correspond to one control in the form's detail area. The following list describes the common control data properties to help you format the control's output correctly:

- *Control Source*—The Control Source property is used to specify the field from the record source that's associated with that particular control. A control source can also be any valid Access expression.

- *Input Mask*—The Format and Decimal Places properties affect the appearance of the control, but the Input Mask property affects what data can be entered into the control. The Input Mask of the field underlying the control is automatically inherited into the control. If no Input Mask is entered as a field property, the Input Mask can be entered directly in the form. If a Format property and an Input Mask property of a control are different, the Format property affects the display of the data within the control until the control receives focus. When the control receives focus, the Input Mask property prevails.

- *Default Value*—The Default Value property of a control determines the value that's assigned to new records entered within the form. This property can be set within the field properties. A default value set at the field level is automatically inherited into the form. The default value set for the control overrides the default value set at the field level.

- *Validation Rule, Validation Text*—The validation rule and validation text of a control perform the same function as the validation rule and validation text for a field. Because the validation rule is enforced at the database engine level, the validation rule set for a control can't be in conflict with the validation rule set for the field to which the control is bound. If the two rules conflict, the user is unable to enter data into the control.

- *Enabled*—The Enabled property determines whether you allow a control to receive focus. When set to No, the control appears dimmed.

- *Locked*—The Locked property determines whether the data within the control can be modified. When the Locked property is set to Yes, the control can receive focus but can't be edited. The Enabled and Locked properties of a control interact with one another. Table 25.1 summarizes their interactions.

Table 25.1   How Enabled and Locked properties interact.

Enabled	Locked	Effect
Yes	Yes	The control can receive focus. Its data can be copied but not modified.
Yes	No	The control can receive focus. Its data can be edited.
No	Yes	The control can't receive focus.
No	No	The control can't receive focus. Its data appears dimmed.

Other Properties Of A Control

Just as with forms, in addition to the Format and Data properties, most controls will have some other, miscellaneous properties, which Access groups together under the Other tab in the Properties window. The following list describes some of the most commonly listed properties:

- *Name*—Employ the Name property to name the control. This name is used when you refer to the control in code. It's also displayed in various drop-downs that show all the controls on a form. It's very important to name your controls because Named controls improve the readability of your code and facilitate the process of working with Access forms and other objects (and naming doesn't mean Text1, Text2; it means meaningful names for Access objects).

- *Status Bar Text*—The Status Bar Text property is used to specify the text that appears in the status bar when the control receives focus. This property setting overrides the Description property that can be set in the design of a table.

- *Enter Key Behavior*—The Enter Key Behavior property determines whether the Enter key causes the cursor to move to the next control or add a new line within the current control. This setting is often changed for text boxes used to display the contents of Memo fields.

- *Allow AutoCorrect*—The Allow AutoCorrect property is used to specify whether the AutoCorrect feature is available within the control. The AutoCorrect feature automatically corrects common spelling errors and typos.

- *Auto Tab*—The Auto Tab property, when set to Yes, automatically advances the cursor to the next control when the last character of an input mask has been entered. Some users like this option and others find it annoying, especially if they must tab out of some fields but not others.

- *Tab Stop*—The Tab Stop property is used to determine whether the Tab key can be used to enter a control. It's appropriate to set this property to No for controls whose values rarely get modified. The user can always opt to click in the control when necessary.

- *Tab Index*—The Tab Index property is used to set the tab order for the control. Most developers generally set the Tab Index property using the View menu Tab Order property, rather than by setting the value directly within the Tab Index property of the control.

- *Shortcut Menu Bar*—The Shortcut Menu Bar attaches a specific menu to a control. The menu bar appears when the user clicks with the right mouse button on the control.

- *ControlTip Text*—The ControlTip Text property is used to specify the tooltip associated with a control. The tooltip automatically appears when the user places the mouse pointer over the control and leaves it there for a moment.

- *Help Context ID*—The Help Context ID property is used to designate the Help topic that's associated with a particular control.

- *Tag*— The Tag property is an extra property that you can use to store information about a control. Your imagination determines how you use this property. The Tag property can be read and modified at runtime.

Bound, Unbound, And Calculated Controls

Important differences exist between bound and unbound controls. Unbound controls are used to display information to the user or gather information from the user that isn't going to be stored within your database. Examples of unbound controls include the following:

- A label providing instructions to the user

- A logo placed on a form

- A combo or text box placed on a form so that the user can enter report criteria

- A rectangle placed on the form to logically group several controls

Bound controls are used to display and modify information stored in a database table. A bound control automatically appears in the form specified in its Display Control property. The control automatically inherits many of the attributes that were assigned to the field to which the control is bound.

A Calculated control is a special type of control that displays the results of an expression. The data within a Calculated control can't be modified by the user. The control's value automatically changes as the values within its expression are changed. For instance, the Sales Total within an invoice form would change as the Price or Quantity of different objects is changed.

Understanding The Importance Of Reports In Access

As you've learned, the Forms that you can use within Access will let you format the data in your database in many different fashions that make accessing the data much easier for your users. However, there are many cases when you'll want to generate output (either hard-copy reports or on-screen reports) that can't be easily reflected in a form. In such cases, you'll probably want to generate a report to display the information.

Types Of Reports Available

The reporting engine of Microsoft Access is very powerful, with a wealth of features. Many types of reports are available in Access 2000, several of which are detailed in the following list:

- Detail reports
- Summary reports
- Cross-tabulation reports
- Reports containing graphics and charts
- Reports containing forms
- Reports containing labels
- Reports including any combination of the above

Detail Reports

A Detail report provides an entry for each record included in the report. You can then group the detail within the report. You can also provide subtotals, grand totals, and summaries within detail reports.

Summary Reports

A Summary report provides summary data for all the records included in the report. For example, you might print a report that displays only total sales by quarter and by year. The underlying detail records that compose the summary data aren't displayed within the report. A summary report itself contains no controls in its Detail Section. All controls are placed in report Group Headers and Footers that are grouped on the quarter and year of the ship date. Because no controls are found in the Detail Section of the report, Access prints summary information only.

Cross-Tabulation Reports

Cross-tabulation reports display summarized data grouped by one set of information on the left side of the report and by another set across the top of the report. For example, you might create a report that displays total sales by product name and employee. Cross-tabulation reports are always based on a Crosstab query and generally require a fair amount of VBA code because each time the report is run, a different number of employees might need to be displayed in the columns of the report. In other words, the number of columns needed might be different each time the report is run.

Reports Containing Graphics And Charts

Research proves that people more successfully retain data displayed as pictures rather than numbers. Fortunately, Access makes the process of including graphics and charts in your reports quite easy. You can effortlessly design reports that include a combination of both numbers and charts. You'll add a chart to a report in the "Immediate Solutions" section of this chapter.

Reports Containing Forms

A report that emulates a printed form is a common need. The Access Report Builder, with its many graphical tools, enables you to quickly produce reports that emulate the most elegant of data-entry forms. The use of graphics, color, fonts, shading, and other special effects give the form a professional look and feel. Creating a report that looks similar to a form is a simple process, which you'll learn more about in the "Immediate Solutions" section of this chapter.

Reports Containing Labels

Creating mailing labels in Access 2000 is easy. They're simply a special type of report with a page setup indicating the number of labels across the page and the size of each label.

Understanding The Sections Of A Report

Reports can contain many parts, referred to as sections of the report. A new report is automatically made up of three sections:

- Page header
- Detail section
- Page footer

The Detail Section of a report is the main section used to display the detailed data of the table or query underlying the report. Certain ones, such as Summary reports, contain nothing in the Detail Section, but contain data in Group Headers and Footers.

The Page Header of a report is the portion that automatically prints at the top of every page. It often includes information such as the title of the report. The Page Footer automatically prints at the bottom of every page, and it often contains information such as the page number and date. Each report can contain only one Page Header and one Page Footer.

In addition to the three sections that are automatically added to every report, a report can contain the following sections:

- Report header
- Report footer
- Group headers
- Group footers

In a given report, you can add one, some, or all of the additional sections. Figure 25.5 shows a report in design mode with each of the sections displayed.

A Report Header prints once, at the beginning of the report, while the Report Footer prints once, at the end of the report. Each Access report can contain only one Report Header and one Report Footer. The Report Header is often used to create a cover sheet for the report. It can contain graphics or other fancy effects, adding a professional look to a report containing important information. The most common use of the Report Footer is for grand totals. It can also include any other summary information for the report.

In addition to Report and Page Headers and Footers, an Access report can contain up to 10 Group Headers and Footers. Report groupings separate data logically and physically. A Group Header prints before the detail for the group, and the Group Footer prints after the detail for the group. For example, you can group customer sales by country and city, printing the name of the country each time the country changes and the name of the city each time the city changes. You can total the sales for each country and city. The country and city names

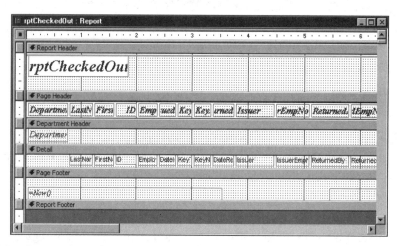

Figure 25.5   A report in design mode, showing the three sections of the report.

are placed in the country and city Group Headers. The totals are placed in the country and city Group Footers.

Reports are a complex topic that you've only scratched the surface of here. However, it's worthwhile to recognize that reports are, generally, very easy to create either with the Report Wizard or in Report Design View. You'll create several reports in the "Immediate Solutions" section.

Immediate Solutions

This section provides a step-by-step guide to building forms and reports. Although the subsections are generally in the order that you'll likely perform tasks, you should refer to the jump table at the beginning of this chapter to identify sections that help you solve specific problems.

Creating A New Form

You can create a new form in several ways. The most common is to select the Forms tab of the database window and click New. The New Form dialog box will appear, as shown in Figure 25.6.

This dialog box lets you select from the multitude of options available for creating a new form. Forms can be created from scratch using Design view or with the help of six wizards. The wizards are covered briefly before you move on to the process of creating a form from scratch. Even the most experienced of developers employs the Form Wizard to complete certain tasks.

Creating A Form With The Form Wizard

To create a form using the Form Wizard, select Form Wizard from the New Form dialog and click OK. The Form Wizard is launched. The first step of the Form Wizard prompts you for the name of the table or query that you want to use as the

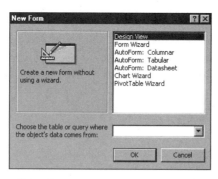

Figure 25.6   The New Form dialog box.

foundation for the form. Whether you're creating a form using a Form Wizard or from Design view, it's always better to base a form on a query. Using a query as the foundation for a form provides better performance, allows for more flexibility, and enables you to create a form based on data from multiple tables. Figure 25.7 shows the Tables/Queries drop-down combo box.

You can see within the figure that all the tables are listed, followed by all the queries. After you select a particular table or query, click the OK button to move the next dialog box in the wizard. As you can see in Figure 25.8, the fields included in the query or table are displayed in the list box on the left of the new dialog box.

To select the fields that you want to include on the form, double-click on the name of the field or click on the field, then click on the > button.

After you've selected the desired fields, click Next. The third step of the Form Wizard lets you specify the layout for the form you're designing. You can select from Columnar, Tabular, or Datasheet; the most common choice is Columnar. Click Next after selecting a form layout. The third step of the Form Wizard allows you to select a style for your form. You can select from several predefined styles, as shown in Figure 25.9.

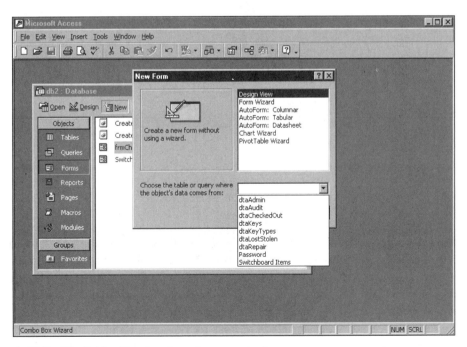

Figure 25.7   The Tables/Queries drop-down combo box.

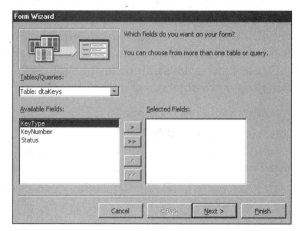

Figure 25.8   The second dialog in the Wizard displays the fields of the selected Table or Query.

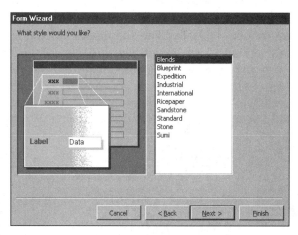

Figure 25.9   The predefined form styles.

Don't be concerned about changing your mind at a later time; all the properties set by the wizard can be easily modified in Design view after the form has been created. Click Next after selecting a style.

The final step of the Form Wizard allows you to provide a title for your form. Unfortunately, the title of the form becomes the name of the form as well. For this reason, type the text you want to use as the name of the form. You can worry about changing the title in Design view of the form. This step of the Form Wizard also lets you specify whether you want to view the results of your work or open the form in Design view. It's usually best to view the results, then modify the form's design after you've taken a peek at what the Form Wizard has done. To complete the Wizard, click Finish.

Another way to start the Form Wizard is to click on the Tables or Queries tab, then click on the table or query on which you want the form to be based. Use the New Object drop-down on the toolbar to select Form. The New Form dialog appears. Select Form Wizard. You don't need to use the Tables/Queries drop-down to select a table or query. The table or query that you selected before invoking the wizard is automatically selected for you.

TIP: *If you want Access 2000 to create a default form for you on the table without a Wizard, select the Autoform option from the New Object drop-down on the toolbar.*

Creating A Form From Design View

Although the Form Wizards are extremely powerful and useful, in many cases it's better to build a form from scratch, especially if you're building a form that's not bound to data. To create a form without the use of a wizard, click the Forms tab, then click New. The New Form dialog appears. Select Design view (the default choice). If your form will be bound to data, use the drop-down included in the New Form dialog to select the table or query that will serve as the foundation for the form. Click OK. The Form Design window will appear as shown in Figure 25.10.

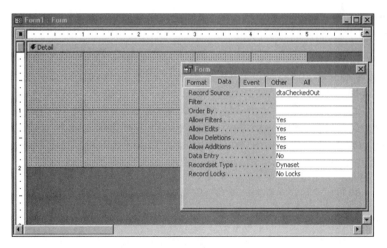

Figure 25.10   The Form Design window.

Adding Fields To The Form

Fields can be easily added to a form using the Field List window because the Field List window contains all the fields that are part of the record source for the form. For example, in Figure 25.10 the record source of the form is

dtaCheckedOut. The fields listed in the Field List window are the fields that are part of the query. The record source for the form is the table or query that underlies the form. To add fields to a form, follow these steps:

1. Make sure the Field List window is visible. If it's not, click on the Field List button on the toolbar.

2. Locate the field you want to add to the form. Click and drag the field from the field list to the location on the form where you want the field to appear. The location you select becomes the upper-left corner of the text box. The attached label appears to the left of where you dropped the control.

To add multiple fields to a form at the same time, select several fields from the field list. Use the Ctrl key to select multiple noncontiguous fields or the Shift key to select multiple contiguous fields. For example, hold down your Ctrl key and click on three noncontiguous fields. Each field is selected. Next, click a field, hold down your Shift key, and click another field. All fields between the two fields are selected. Click and drag any of the selected fields to the form. All selected fields are added to the form at once.

Selecting Form Objects

The easiest way to select a single object on a form is to click on it. When the object is selected, you can move it, size it, or change any of its properties. Selecting multiple objects is a bit trickier and can be done in several ways. Different methods are more efficient in different situations. To select multiple objects, you can hold down the Shift key and click on each object that you want to select. Each selected object is surrounded by selection handles, indicating that it's selected. Figure 25.11 shows a form with four selected objects.

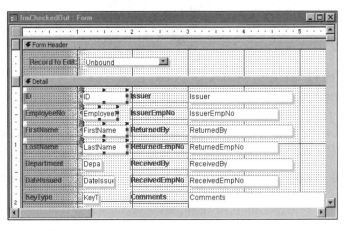

Figure 25.11   A form with four selected objects.

You can also select objects by lassoing them. To lasso objects, the objects must be located close to one another on the form. Place your mouse pointer on a blank area of the form (not over any objects), then click and drag. You'll see that a thin line appears around the objects that your mouse pointer is encircling. When you let go, any objects that were anywhere within the lasso, including those that were only partially surrounded, are selected. If you want to deselect any of the selected objects to exclude them from the selection, hold down your Shift key and click on the object you want to deselect.

One of the other useful ways to select multiple objects is to use the horizontal and vertical rulers that appear at the edges of the Form Design window. Click and drag within the ruler. Notice that as you click and drag on the vertical ruler, two horizontal lines appear, indicating which objects will be selected. As you click and drag across the horizontal ruler, two vertical lines appear, indicating the selection area. When you let go of your mouse, any objects that are anywhere within the lines are selected. As with the process of lassoing, to remove any objects from the selection, hold down your Shift key and click on the object you want to deselect.

Moving Things Around On The Form

To move a control along with its attached label, you don't need to select it first. Place your mouse over the object and click and drag. An outline appears, indicating the new location of the object. When the object reaches the desired position, release the mouse. An attached label automatically moves with its corresponding control.

To move more than one object at a time, you must first select the objects that you want to move. Select the objects using any of the methods outlined in the previous section. Place your mouse over any of the selected objects and click and drag. An outline appears, indicating the proposed new position for the objects. Release the mouse when you've reached the desired position.

Sometimes, you want to move a control independent of its attached label, which requires a special technique. If you click on a control, such as a text box, you see that as you move your mouse over the border of the control, a hand appears with five fingers pointing upward. If you click and drag, both the control and the attached label move as a unit. The relationship between them is maintained. Placing your mouse pointer over the larger handle in the upper-left corner of the object makes the mouse pointer appear as a hand with only the index finger pointing upward. If you click and drag here, the control moves independently of its attached label. The relationship between the objects changes.

Aligning Objects To One Another

Access makes it easy to align objects. Figure 25.12 shows two objects that aren't aligned.

Notice that the attached labels of both the objects are selected. To left-align any objects (even objects of different types), select the objects that you want to align, then select the Format menu Align submenu Left option. The selected objects will become left-aligned, as shown in Figure 25.13.

You can align the left, right, top, or bottom edges of any objects on a form. You can also align the center of each object.

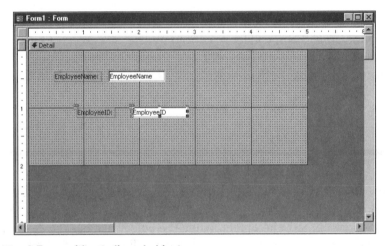

Figure 25.12   A Form without aligned objects.

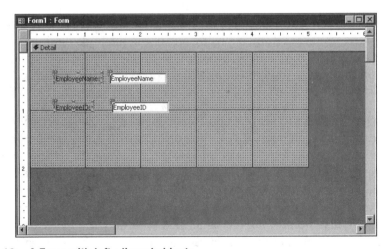

Figure 25.13   A Form with left-aligned objects.

Don't confuse the Format menu Align feature with the Align tools on the Formatting toolbar. The Format menu Align feature aligns objects one to the other, whereas the Align tools on the Formatting toolbar align the text of an object within its borders.

Using The Snap To Grid Feature

The Snap to Grid feature determines whether the objects snap to the gridlines on the form as you move and size them. This feature is found under the Format menu. If you turn this feature off (it's a toggle), objects can be moved and sized without regard for the gridlines.

Most developers leave the Snap to Grid feature on all the time. However, you can use a special trick to temporarily deactivate the feature when needed. To do this, hold down your Ctrl key as you click and drag to move objects. The Snap to Grid setting is ignored.

Power Sizing Techniques At Your Disposal

Just as there are several ways to move objects, there are several ways to size objects. When an object is selected, each handle (except for the handle in the upper-left corner of the object) can be used to size the object. The handles at the top and bottom of the object allow you to change the height of the object. Those at the left and right of the object allow you to change the width of the object. The handles in the upper-right, lower-right, and lower-left corners of the object allow you to change the width and height of the object simultaneously. To size an object, place your mouse pointer over a sizing handle and click and drag. You can select multiple objects and size them at the same time. Each of the selected objects increases or decreases in size by the same amount. The relative sizes of the objects remain intact.

Access provides several powerful methods of sizing multiple objects, found under the Format menu Size submenu:

- *To Fit*—Sizes the selected objects to fit the text within them.

- *To Grid*—Sizes the selected objects to the nearest gridlines.

- *To Tallest*—Sizes the selected objects to the height of the tallest object within the selection.

- *To Shortest*—Sizes the selected objects to the height of the shortest object within the selection.

25. Creating Forms And Reports

- *To Widest*—Sizes the selected objects to the width of the widest object within the selection.

- *To Narrowest*—Sizes the selected objects to the width of the narrowest object within the selection.

Probably the most confusing of the options is the Format menu Size submenu To Fit option. It's somewhat deceiving because it doesn't perfectly size text boxes to the text within them. Because of the varying nature proportional fonts, it isn't possible to perfectly size a text box to the largest possible entry that it contains. You can generally visually size text boxes to a sensible height and width. Use the Size property of the field to limit what's typed in the text box. If the entry is too large to fit in the allocated space, the user can scroll to view the additional text.

Controlling Object Spacing

Access provides excellent tools to help you space the objects on your form an equal distance from one another. To make the vertical distance between selected objects equal, select the Format menu Vertical Spacing submenu Make Equal option.

You can make the horizontal distance between objects equal using the Format menu Horizontal Spacing submenu Make Equal option. Other useful related commands are the Format menu Vertical Spacing submenu Increase (or Decrease) option and the Format menu Horizontal Spacing submenu Increase (or Decrease) option. These commands maintain the relationship between objects while proportionally increasing or decreasing the distance between them.

Modifying Object Tab Order

The tab order for the objects on a form is determined by the order in which you add the objects to the form. This order isn't necessarily appropriate for the user. It might become necessary to modify the tab order of the objects on the form. To do so, select the View menu's Tab Order option. The Tab Order dialog box appears, as shown in Figure 25.14.

This dialog box offers two options. Use the Auto Order command button to tell Access to set the tab order based on the location of each object in a section on the form. If you want to customize the order of the objects, click and drag the gray buttons to the left of the object names listed under the Custom Order heading to specify the tab order of the objects.

Figure 25.14   The Tab Order dialog box.

You must set the tab order for the objects in each section of the form separately. To do this, select the appropriate section from the tab order dialog, then set the order of the objects in the section. In Figure 25.14, the Form Header and Form Footer are unavailable because the selected form doesn't have a header or footer.

Adding A Combo Box To A Form

To add a combo box to a form, select the Combo Box tool in the toolbox. Click and drag to place the combo box on the form. The Combo Box Wizard is launched. The first step of the Combo Box Wizard appears in Figure 25.15.

You're asked whether you want the combo box to look up the values in a table or query, whether you prefer to type the values yourself, or whether the combo box will be used to search for a particular record. The first option should be used if your combo box is going to be used to select the data that's stored in a field. An

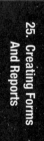

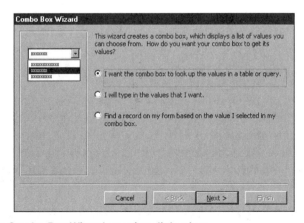

Figure 25.15   The Combo Box Wizard opening dialog box.

example would be the state associated with a particular client. Most developers rarely, if ever, use the second option, which requires that you type the values for the combo box. Populating a combo box this way makes it difficult to maintain. Every time you want to add an entry to the combo box, your application must be modified. The third and final option is appropriate when you want the combo box to be used as a tool to locate a specific record. An example is a combo box, placed in the header of a form, that displays a list of valid customers. After selecting a customer, the user is moved to the appropriate record. This option is available only when the form is bound to a record source.

The second step of the Combo Box Wizard lets you to select a table or query to populate the combo box. For optimal performance, you should select a query. The third step of the Combo Box Wizard allows you to select the fields that appear in your combo box.

The fourth step of the Combo Box Wizard lets you specify the width of each field in the combo box. Access will recommend that the key column for the table or query be hidden. The idea is that the user will see the meaningful English description while Access worries about storing the appropriate key value into the record.

The fifth step of the Combo Box Wizard lets you specify whether you want Access to simply remember the selected value or to store it in a particular field in a table.

The sixth and final step of the Combo Box Wizard prompts for the text that becomes the attached label for the combo box. The Finish button completes the process, building the combo box and filling in all its properties with the appropriate values.

Adding An Option Group To A Form

The first step of the Option Group Wizard, shown in Figure 25.16, lets you type the text that will be associated with each item in the option group.

The second step of the Option Group Wizard gives you the option of selecting a default choice for the option group. This choice comes into effect when a new record is added to the table underlying the form. The third step of the wizard allows you to select values associated with each option button. The text displayed with the option button isn't stored in the record. Instead, the underlying numeric value is stored in the record.

The fourth step of the Option Group Wizard asks whether you want to remember the option group value for later use or whether you want to store the value in a

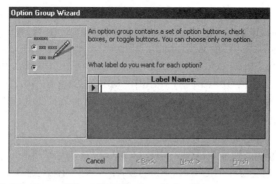

Figure 25.16   The Option Group Wizard's opening dialog box.

field. The fifth step of the Option Group Wizard allows you to select from a variety of styles for the option group buttons. You can select among option buttons, check boxes, and toggle buttons. You can also select from etched, flat, raised, shadowed, or sunken effects for your buttons. The wizard lets you preview each option. The sixth and final step of the wizard lets you to add an appropriate caption to the option group.

It's important to understand that the Option Group Wizard sets properties of the frame, the option buttons within the frame, and the labels attached to the option buttons. The control source of the frame and default value of the option group are set by the Option Group Wizard. Each individual option button is assigned a value, and the caption of the attached labels associated with each button is set.

Creating A New Report

You can create a new report in several ways. The most common is to select the Reports tab of the Database window and click New. The New Report dialog box will appear, as shown in Figure 25.17.

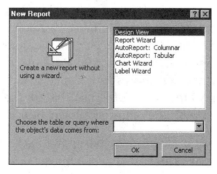

Figure 25.17   The New Report dialog box.

This dialog box allows you to select from the many options available for creating reports. They can be created from scratch using Design view, but they can also be created with the help of five wizards. Three of the wizards help you build standard reports, one helps you build reports containing charts, and the last wizard automates the process of creating mailing labels. The Report Wizards are so powerful that most developers use one of them to build the initial foundation for almost every report they create.

Creating A Report With The Report Wizard

To create a report using the Report Wizard, select Report Wizard from the New Report dialog and click OK. The Report Wizard is launched. The first step of the Report Wizard prompts you for the table or query that will supply data to the report. It's best to base your reports on queries. This improves performance and enhances your ability to produce reports based on varying criteria.

After you've selected a table or query, you can select the fields that you want to include on the report. The fields included in the selected table or query are listed in the list box on the left. To add fields to the report, double-click on the name of the field you want to add or click on the field name and click >.

After you've selected a table or query and the fields you want to include on the report, click Next. You're prompted to add group levels to the report. Group levels add report groupings to the report. Add them if you need to visually separate groups of data or include summary calculations (subtotals). Report groupings are covered later in this chapter. If your report doesn't require groupings, click Next.

The third step of the Report Wizard prompts you for sorting levels for your report. Because the order of a query underlying a report is completely ignored by the report builder when the report is run, it's necessary that you designate a sort order. You can add up to four sorting levels using the wizard. After you select the fields you want to sort on, click Next.

The fourth step of the Report Wizard prompts you for the layout and orientation of the report. The layout can be Vertical or Tabular. Tabular reports are the most common, displaying report data in columns going across the report. Vertical reports display one record at a time, with each of the fields displayed one beneath the other down the report. The orientation can be Portrait or Landscape. This step of the Report Wizard also allows you to specify whether you want Access to attempt to adjust the width of each field so that all the fields fit on each page. After supplying Access with the required information, click Next.

The fifth step of the Report Wizard enables you to select a style for your report. The available choices are Bold, Casual, Compact, Corporate, Formal, and Soft

Gray. Access allows you to preview each look before you make a decision. Any of the style attributes applied by the Report Wizard, as well as any other attributes of the report defined by the wizard, can be modified in Report Design view at any time after the wizard has produced the report. After you've selected a style, click Next.

The final step of the Report Wizard prompts you for a title for the report. This title will be used as the name and the caption title for the report. Most developers provide a standard Access report name and modify the caption after the Report Wizard has completed its process. You're given the opportunity to preview the report or modify the report's design. If you opt to modify the report's design, you're placed in Design view. The report can then be previewed at any time. Figure 25.18 shows the preview of a completed report.

Another way to start the Report Wizard is to click on the Tables or Queries tab, then click on the table or query on which you want the report to be based. Use the New Object drop-down on the toolbar to select Report. The New Report dialog box will appear. Within the New Report dialog box, select Report Wizard. You don't need to use the Tables/Queries drop-down to select a table or query. The table or query you selected before invoking the wizard is automatically selected for you.

Creating A Report From Design View
Although you'll usually get started with most of your reports using a Report Wizard, you should understand how to create a new report from Design view. To create a report without the use of a wizard, click the Reports tab, then click New.

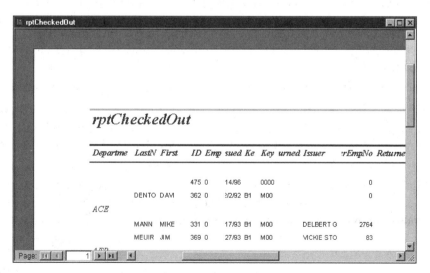

Figure 25.18   The preview of a completed report—note the truncated titles and fields generated by the wizard.

The New Report dialog appears. Click Design View, then use the drop-down to select the table or query on which the report will be based. Click OK. The Report Design window appears.

Adding Fields To The Report

Fields can most easily be added to a report using the Field List window. With it open, click and drag a field from the field list onto the appropriate section of the report. Just as with forms, multiple fields can be added at one time. Use the Ctrl key to select noncontiguous fields or the Shift key to select contiguous fields, then click and drag the fields to the report as a unit.

One problem with adding fields to a report is that both the fields and the attached labels are placed in the same section of the report. This means that if you click and drag fields from the Field List window to the Detail Section of the report, both the fields and the attached labels will appear in the report. If you're creating a tabular report, this isn't acceptable. You need to cut the attached labels and paste them within the Page Header section of the report.

Selecting Report Objects

To select a single report object, click on the object you want to select. Selection handles appear around the selected object. When the object is selected, you can modify any of its attributes (properties), or you can size, move, or align the object.

To select multiple objects so that you can manipulate them as a unit, use one of the following techniques:

- Hold down the Shift key as you click on multiple objects. Each object you click on is added to the selection.

- Place your mouse pointer in a blank area of the report. Click and drag to lasso the objects you want to select. When you let go of the mouse, any object that's even partially within the lasso is selected.

- Click and drag within the horizontal or vertical ruler. As you click and drag, lines appear indicating the potential selection area. When you release the mouse, all objects within the lines are selected.

Moving Objects Around In The Report

If you want to move a single control along with its attached label, click on the object and drag it to a new location. The object and the attached label move as a unit. To move multiple objects, use one of the methods covered in the previous section to select the objects you want to move. After the objects are selected, click and drag any of them. The selected objects and their attached labels move as a unit.

Moving an object without its attached label is a trickier process. When placed over the center or border of a selected object (not on a sizing handle), the mouse pointer appears as a hand with all five fingers pointing upward. When the mouse pointer appears as a hand, the selected object and its attached label move as a unit, maintaining their relationship to one another. When you place your mouse pointer directly over the selection handle that appears in the upper-left corner of the object, the mouse pointer appears as a hand with the index finger pointing upward. If you click and drag with the mouse pointer in this format, the object and the attached label move independently of one another, so you can alter the distance between them.

Aligning Objects To One Another On The Report

To align objects to one another, select the objects you want to align. Select the Format menu Align option, then select Left, Right, Top, Bottom, or To Grid. The selected objects align with each other.

You must be aware of a few special criteria when aligning report objects. If you select several text boxes and their attached labels and attempt to align them, Access attempts to align the left sides of the text boxes with the left sides of the labels. To avoid this problem, you need to align the text boxes separately from their attached labels.

During the alignment process, Access never overlaps objects. For this reason, if the objects you're aligning don't fit, Access is unable to align them. For example, if you attempt to align the bottom of several objects horizontally and they don't fit across the report, Access aligns only the objects that fit on the line. You can also use tools such as Snap to Grid, just as you did with forms, when you design your reports.

Chapter 26

Creating Macros And Modules

In Depth

Although macros shouldn't be used to develop the routines that control your applications—a task better left to modules, which you'll learn about briefly later in this chapter and in depth in Chapter 27—a few specific application-development tasks can be accomplished only by using macros. Therefore, it's important to understand at least the basics of how macros work. Furthermore, using Access 2000 macros can often help you to get started with the application-development process, because Access 2000 macros can be converted to Visual Basic for Applications (VBA) code. This means that you can develop part of your application using macros, convert the macros to VBA code, and proceed with the development process. Although it's not recommended that you use this approach if you're a serious developer, it does provide a great jump-start for those new to Access or Windows development in general.

Understanding Macros

Most serious developers, do the vast majority of automation and specialized design with VBA. A macro is a set of one or more actions that each perform a particular operation, such as opening a form or printing a report. Macros can help you to automate common tasks. For example, you can run a macro that prints a report when a user clicks a command button.

A macro can be one macro composed of a sequence of actions, or it can be a macro group. You can also use a conditional expression to determine whether in some cases an action will be carried out when a macro runs.

If you have numerous macros, grouping related macros in macro groups can help you to manage your database more easily. To display the names of macros for a macro group, click Macro Names on the View menu in the Macro window.

Understanding Modules

While a macro is a specific task set that performs a sequence of actions, a module contains a collection of VBA declarations and procedures that are stored together as a unit. Two types of modules are available—modules associated with a specific form or report, and modules that stand alone, known as *class modules*.

Modules differ from macros primarily in two ways. First, macros perform a pre-specified series of steps, or actions, that take advantage of built-in Microsoft

Access features. Second, macros provide only a limited set of actions for you to take advantage of and do not directly allow for the creation of your own functions, unlike VBA. Macros are useful for performing certain specific tasks, but are limited in scope. Modules, on the other hand, expose the entire VBA model, providing you with a broad set of functions, including calls to the Windows application programming interface (API), to truly make your applications highly functional.

Considering Macros Vs. Modules

Clearly, in certain cases using macros makes sense and in other cases, using modules makes more sense. Some general rules govern when you should use each. Typically, choose macros if your design requirements meet most or all of the following:

- If you need to prototype your application quickly. Macros make it simple to open, close, and manipulate forms and reports, which makes it easier for you to rapidly mock up the application's flow.

- If you're really not concerned about bulletproofing your application. Because macros can't trap for errors, Access will handle any runtime errors that occur while your application is running. If you're providing an application for your own purposes or for in-house use, it may not be worth your while to trap for errors.

- If you need to trap keystrokes or provide a macro that runs automatically without any command-line interference. Each of these actions requires a macro (although you can trap keystrokes from VBA, it's a little more difficult).

On the other hand, you should use VBA for most of the other tasks you want to perform. It should be your programming model of choice for larger applications, because you can easily document, comment, and control VBA code. Additionally, you must use VBA code if you need to perform any of the following tasks:

- Call functions in dynamic-link libraries (DLL), including any and all Windows API functions.

- Control transaction processing—specifically, rollbacks and commitments of partially completed sets of actions.

- Use scoped variables (a scoped variable is a variable that's visible to program code only in certain parts of your application).

- Provide commented printouts of your application. (In fact, you can print out macros—but it's much more difficult to document them in-depth than it is to document VBA code.)

26. Creating Macros And Modules

TIP: *In the Access 2000 VBA implementation, you can create menus and toolbars directly from code, using the* **CommandBars** *collection and the* **CommandBar** *object. You can also use the* **KeyDown** *and* **KeyPress** *events from within form modules to capture keystrokes, though you're still better served to use macros for global keystroke interception.*

Using Macros Within Your Access Applications

In general, as detailed previously, there are three specific situations where you'll use macros within your applications: trapping keystrokes globally, providing user-defined menus, and executing a macro from the command line or automatically at startup.

Using The AutoKeys Macro

By default, Access looks for a macro named **AutoKeys** to control the global key mappings for an application. When you specify a value within the macro, you'll assign it to a specific key set. The syntax for the macro names that you can use is shown within Table 26.1.

Just as with any other macro that you create, the Action column of the macro can contain any of the standard macro actions and can use the **RunCode** action to invoke VBA code from the given keystroke.

Table 26.1   The macro syntax for the AutoKeys macro group.

Syntax	Key Combinations
^A or ^2	Ctrl + any letter or number
{Fn}	Any function key, 1 through 12
^{Fn}	Ctrl + any function key, 1 through 12
+{Fn}	Shift + any function key, 1 through 12
^+{Fn}	Ctrl + Shift + any function key, 1 through 12
{Insert}	Insert key
^{Insert}	Ctrl + Insert key
+{Insert}	Shift + Insert key
^+{Insert}	Ctrl + Shift + Insert key
{Delete}	Delete key
^{Delete}	Ctrl + Delete key
+{Delete}	Shift + Delete key
^+{Delete}	Ctrl + Shift + Delete key

To separate the key mapping, simply place a new macro name (actually, the keystroke set to map) on a new row. Access will stop playing back each macro when it runs across a new name in the macro group. You can also separate each macro from the next with a blank line and perhaps, some comments.

Figure 26.1 shows the macro editor after adding a pair of macros to the file. In this case, if the user presses the Ctrl+F1 key combination, the application will display a simple message box and beep at the user. If the user presses the Ctrl+P key combination, the application will print the currently open object.

Limitations Of The AutoKeys Macro

As you can see in Table 26.1, a lot of key combinations are noticeably absent from the keys you can map within the **AutoKeys** macro. Specifically, you can't trap the following key combinations from within the **AutoKeys** macro:

• Alt + function keys

• Alt + Insert key

• Alt + Delete key

• The Esc key

• Cursor movement keys (alone or in combination with Ctrl, Shift, or Alt)

• Alt + A through Alt + Z (which Access reserves for hot-key use)

As you'll learn later, you can trap these keys—but only from within your VBA code for the application.

Figure 26.1   The macro editor after creating a pair of keystroke combinations.

Restricting Key Playback To Specific Situations

Although keys that you assign to the **AutoKeys** macro will normally take effect anyplace in the Access environment, you can limit the situations where the macro will take effect. If you set a *condition* in the macro sheet's Condition column, the macro attached to the particular keystroke will be invoked only if the condition is met. For example, in Figure 26.2, the Ctrl+F1 macro that you saw previously has been modified to limit its execution to occur only if the user is viewing a form when the user invokes the macro.

You can also use the **RunCode** action and invoke VBA code that determines whether or not to perform the action. For example, you can use a **RunCode DoMsgBox** invocation within the macro and include the following code within a module:

```
Function DoMsgBox()
   If Application.CurrentObjectType = A_FORM Then
     MsgBox "Invoke the VBA Code", vbOKOnly, "Test Box"
     Beep
   End If
End Function
```

Running A Macro Automatically

For many applications, you'll want Access to take a specific action or series of actions automatically every time the user loads the application. Although Access will let you use the Tools menu Startup option to load forms at startup, you need

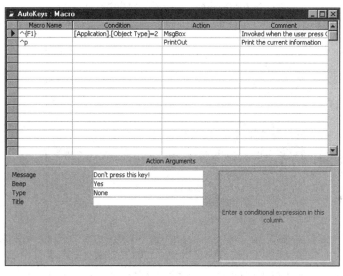

Figure 26.2   The Macro window after adding a condition to the Ctrl+F1 macro.

to use a macro to perform more complex processing. The macro that you'll use must be named **AutoExec**, and after you create it, Access will automatically execute the macro each time the database loads.

Loading Other Macros At Startup

In addition to specifying the **AutoExec** macro, you can also manually instruct an application to load and execute a specific macro at startup by including the macro's name in the command-line invocation of the application, as shown here:

```
MSACCESS AppName.mdb /xMacroName
```

Access will run the macro name that follows the **/x** switch as soon as it loads the application. You might, for example, create a series of shortcuts on the desktop that load different parts of an application as the startup screen, and use a custom macro to open that portion of the application.

TIP: *If your application uses an **AutoExec** macro and you also specify a macro to execute at startup, Access will first run the **AutoExec** macro and then run the specified macro.*

Bypassing The AutoExec Macro

If you create a macro that runs automatically every time you load an application, it's almost inevitable that a time will come when you'll want to run the application without running the macro. To bypass the **AutoExec** macro, simply press and hold the Shift key while the application loads. Access will load the application, but will bypass the macro.

If your application is running in the Access runtime environment (rather than the development environment), the runtime engine will ignore the Shift key and will execute the **AutoExec** macro normally. In other words, there's no way for users not using the development environment to bypass the macro.

Using The DoCmd Object

Most macro commands can be performed in VBA code using the **DoCmd** object. The macro action becomes a method of the **DoCmd** object. The arguments associated with each macro action become the arguments of the method. For example, the following method of the **DoCmd** object is used to open a form:

```
DoCmd.OpenForm "frmCheckedOut", acNormal, "", _
    "[tblCheckedOut]![OutDate]>Date() -30", _
    acEdit, acNormal
```

The **OpenForm** method of the **DoCmd** object opens that form that appears as the first argument to the method. The second argument indicates the view in which the form will be opened. The third and fourth arguments are used to specify a Filter and Where Condition, respectively. The fifth argument of the **OpenForm** method is used to specify the Data Mode for the form (Add, Edit, or Read Only). The sixth argument is used to indicate the Window Mode (Normal, Hidden, Minimized, or Dialog).

Finally, VBA makes available an additional seventh argument that you can use within your program, the optional **openargs** argument. You can use this string expression to set the form's **OpenArgs** property. This setting can then be used by code in a form module, such as the **Open** event procedure. You can also refer to the **OpenArgs** property in macros and expressions.

For example, suppose that the form you open is a continuous-form list of clients. If you want the focus to move to a specific client record when the form opens, you can specify the client name with the **openargs** argument, and then use the **FindRecord** method to move the focus to the record for the client with the specified name.

TIP: *This argument is available only in VBA; you cannot use it if you create the macro solely from the macro window.*

Notice the intrinsic constants that are used for the **OpenForm** arguments; these greatly aid in the readability of the code. You can find the arguments in the Access online Help for each **DoCmd** method.

Understanding The Methods Of The DoCmd Object

In short, almost every action that you can perform from within a macro—from applying a filter to transferring text—can be done using the **DoCmd** object. Most of the methods you'll use will have a list of parameters that correspond exactly with the action arguments for the method's action-equivalent.

However, there are some actions that don't have an equivalent **DoCmd** method, as shown in the following list:

- **AddMenu**—You should use the VBA methods of adding menus to your applications.

- **MsgBox**—Use the VBA **MsgBox** function instead.

- **RunApp**—Use the VBA **Shell** function instead to run another application.

- **RunCode**—Run the target function directly in VBA instead.

- **SendKeys**—Use the VBA **SendKeys** statement instead.

- **SetValue**—Set the value directly in VBA instead.

- **StopAllMacros**—There's no VBA equivalent to this action.

- **StopMacro**—There's no VBA equivalent to this action.

Immediate Solutions

Creating And Running A Macro

To create a macro, click the Macros tab, and click New. The Macro Design window will appear. This window allows you to build a "program" by adding macro actions, arguments, names, and conditions to the macro.

Macro actions are like programming commands or functions. They instruct Access to take a specific action—for example, to open a form. Macro arguments are like parameters to a command or function. They provide Access with specifics regarding the selected action. For example, if the macro action instructs Access to open a form, the arguments for that action tell Access which form is to be opened and how it's to be opened (Form, Design, or Datasheet view or Print Preview). Macro names are like subroutines. Multiple subroutines can be included within one Access macro. Each of these routines is identified by its macro name. Macro conditions allow you to determine when a specific macro action will execute. For example, you might want one form to open in one situation and a second form to open in another situation.

Adding Macro Actions

As mentioned, macro actions instruct Access to perform a task. You can add a macro action to the Macro Design window in several ways. One method is to click a cell within the Macro Action column, and click to open the drop-down menu, as shown in Figure 26.3.

A list of all the macro actions appears. Select the desired action from the list, and it's added instantly to the macro. Use this method of selecting a macro action if you aren't sure of the name of the macro action and want to browse the available list.

After you've been working with macros for a while, you'll know which actions you want to select. Rather than opening the drop-down and scrolling through the entire list of actions, you can click a cell within the Action column and begin to type the name of the macro action you want to add. Access locates the first macro action beginning with the character(s) you type.

The **OpenTable**, **OpenQuery**, **OpenForm**, **OpenReport**, and **OpenModule** actions are used to open a table, query, form, report, or module, respectively. These

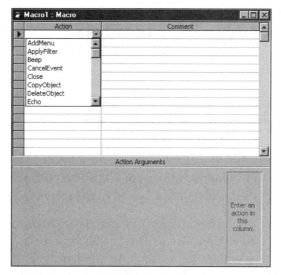

Figure 26.3   The macro editor's Action drop-down menu.

actions and associated arguments can all be filled in quite easily using a drag-and-drop technique, as detailed in the following list:

1. Use the Window menu Tile option to tile the Database window and the Macro Design window on the desktop.

2. Select the appropriate tab from the Database window. For example, if you want to open a form, select the Forms tab.

3. Click-and-drag the object you want to open to the Macro Design window. The appropriate action and arguments are automatically filled in by Access. Figure 26.4 shows an example where the **frmCheckedOut** form was dragged and dropped onto the Macro Design window.

The process of dragging and dropping a table, query, form, report, or module onto the Macro Design window saves you some time, because all the macro action arguments are automatically filled in for you. Notice in Figure 26.4 that six action arguments are associated with the **OpenForm** action: Form Name, View, Filter Name, Where Condition, Data Mode, and Window Mode. The process of dragging and dropping the **frmCheckedOut** form to the Macro Design window filled in three of the arguments for the **OpenForm** action. The name of the form (**frmCheckedOut**), the view (Form), and the window mode (Normal) were all automatically filled in. Macro action arguments are covered more thoroughly in the next section.

Figure 26.4   The macro editor after dragging and dropping a form into the macro action.

Setting Action Arguments

A macro action argument is like a parameter to a command or function. The macro action arguments that are available differ depending on what macro action has been selected. The macro action arguments give Access specific instructions on how to execute the selected macro action. Some macro action arguments force you to select from a drop-down containing appropriate choices; others allow you to enter a valid Access expression. Macro action arguments are automatically filled in when you click-and-drag a Table, Query, Form, Report, or Module object to the Macro Design window. In all other situations, you must supply Access with the arguments required to properly execute a macro action. To specify a macro action argument, perform the following five steps:

1. Select a macro action.

2. Press the F6 function key on the keyboard to jump down to the first macro action argument for the selected macro action.

3. If the macro action argument requires that you select from a list of valid choices, click to open the drop-down for the first macro action argument associated with the selected macro action. All the available choices will appear.

4. If the macro action argument requires that you enter a valid expression, you can type the argument into the appropriate text box, or you can solicit assistance from the Expression Builder. An example is the Where Condition argument of the OpenForm action. After you click the Where Condition text box, an ellipsis appears. If you click on the ellipsis, the Expression Builder dialog is invoked.

5. To build an appropriate expression, select a database object from the list box on the left, then select a specific element from the center and right-hand list boxes. Click Paste to paste the element into the text box. Click OK to close the Expression Builder dialog.

It's important to remember that each macro action has different macro action arguments. Some of the macro action arguments associated with a particular macro action are required, whereas others are optional. If you need help on a particular macro action argument, click the specific argument. Access provides you with a short description of the selected argument. If you need additional assistance, press the F1 key. Access will display Help for the macro action and all its arguments.

Specifying Macro Names

Macro names are like subroutines. They allow you to place more than one routine within a macro. This means that you can create many macro routines without having to create a large volume of separate macros. It's appropriate to include macros that perform related functions within one particular macro. For example, you might build a macro that contains all the routines required for form handling and another that contains all the routines required for report handling. Only two steps are needed to add macro names to a macro:

1. Click the Macro Names button on the Macro Design toolbar. The Macro Names column will appear.

2. Add macro names to each macro subroutine.

The Macro Names column of the macro is a toggle. You can hide it and show it at will, without losing the information within the column.

Specifying Macro Conditions

At times, you'll want a macro action to execute only when a certain condition is True. Fortunately, Access allows you to specify the conditions under which a macro action executes. To do so, perform the following steps:

1. Click the Conditions button on the Macro Design toolbar. The Macro Conditions column appears.

2. Add conditions to each macro action as desired. To add conditions with the Expression Builder, click the right mouse button on the Conditions column and select the Build option.

Running An Access Macro

The process of executing a macro varies depending on what you're attempting to accomplish. A macro can be run from the Macro Design window, from the Macros tab, by being triggered from a Form or Report event, or by selecting a Menu or Toolbar option. The first three cases are discussed here, while the last two will be discussed in Chapter 27.

Running A Macro From The Macro Design Window

A macro can be executed easily from the Macro Design window and can be run without subroutines. Click Run on the Macro Design toolbar. Each line of the macro is executed unless conditions have been placed on specific macro actions.

From Macro Design view, you can run only the first subroutine within a macro. To run a macro containing subroutines, click Run on the Macro Design toolbar. The first subroutine within the macro will execute. As soon as the second macro name is encountered, the macro execution will terminate.

Running A Macro From The Macros Tab

To run a macro from the Macros tab of the Database window, follow these two steps:

1. Click the Macros tab of the Database window.

2. Double-click the name of the macro you want to execute, or click the name of the macro and click Run.

If the macro you execute contains macro names, only the macro actions within the first subroutine will be executed.

Triggering A Macro From A Form Or Report Event

Four steps are needed to associate a macro with a Form or Report event:

1. Select the object you want to associate the event with.

2. Open the Properties window, and click to select the Event properties.

3. Click the event that you want the macro to execute in response to.

4. Use the drop-down to select the name of the macro you want to execute. If the macro contains macro names, make sure you select the correct macro name subroutine.

26. Creating Macros And Modules

Modifying An Existing Macro

You've learned a lot about macros. You've learned how to create a macro, add macro actions and their associated arguments, create macro subroutines by adding macro names, and conditionally execute the actions within the macro by adding macro conditions. Once a macro has been created, you can modify it. Enter Design view for the macro by performing the following steps:

1. Click the Macros tab of the Database window.

2. Select the macro you want to modify.

3. Click Design.

The design of the macro will appear. You can now insert new lines, delete existing lines, move the macro actions around, or copy macro actions to the macro you're modifying or to another macro.

Inserting New Macro Actions

To insert a macro action in an existing macro, perform the following steps from the macro editor:

1. Click the line above which you want the macro action to be inserted.

2. Press the Insert key, click the Insert Rows button on the toolbar, or select the Insert menu Rows option. Access will insert a new line in the macro at the cursor.

To insert multiple macro actions, you must perform a slightly different series of steps from the macro editor as follows:

1. Place your cursor on the line above the line where you want the new macro action lines to be inserted. Click the Macro Action Selector. Macro Action Selectors are the gray boxes that appear to the left of the Macro Action column.

2. Click-and-drag to select the same number of Macro Action Selectors as the number of macro actions you want to insert.

3. Press the Insert key, click the Insert Rows button on the toolbar, or select the Insert menu Rows option. Access will insert all the new macro lines above the macro actions that you selected.

Deleting Macro Actions

To delete a single macro action, perform the following steps:

1. Click the Macro Action Selector of the macro action you want to delete. Macro Action Selectors are the gray boxes that appear to the left of the Macro Action column.

2. Press the Delete key, click the Delete Rows button on the toolbar, or select the Edit menu Delete Rows option.

To delete multiple macro actions, perform the following steps:

1. Click-and-drag to select the Macro Action Selectors of all the macro actions you want to delete. All the macro actions should become black.

2. Press the Delete key, click the Delete Rows button on the toolbar, or select the Edit menu Delete Rows option.

Moving Macro Actions

You can move macro actions in a few ways, including dragging and dropping and cutting and pasting. To move macro actions by dragging and dropping, perform the following steps:

1. Click-and-drag to select the macro action(s) you want to move.

2. Release the mouse button.

3. Place your mouse cursor over the Macro Action Selector of any of the selected macro actions.

4. Click-and-drag. A black line appears, indicating where the selected macro actions will be moved.

5. Release the mouse button when the black line is in the appropriate location.

TIP: *If you accidentally drag-and-drop the selected macro actions to an incorrect place, use the Undo button on the Macro Design toolbar to reverse your action.*

To move macro actions by cutting and pasting, perform the following steps:

1. Click-and-drag to select the Macro Action Selectors of the macro actions you want to move.

2. Click Cut on the Macro Design toolbar (or use Ctrl+X or the Edit menu Cut option).

3. Click within the line above which you want the cut macro actions to be inserted. Don't click the Macro Action Selector.

4. Click Paste (or use one of the alternate Paste options). The macro actions are inserted at the cursor.

WARNING! *Don't click the Macro Action Selector of the row where you want to insert the cut macro actions unless you want to overwrite the macro action you have selected. If you don't click to select the Macro Action Selectors, the cut lines are inserted into the macro without overwriting any other macro actions. If you click to select Macro Action Selectors, Access will overwrite existing macro actions.*

Copying Macro Actions

Macro actions can be copied within a macro or to another macro. To copy macro actions within a macro:

1. Click-and-drag to select the Macro Action Selectors of the macro actions you want to copy.

2. Click Copy on the Macro Design toolbar (or use Ctrl+C or the Edit menu Copy option).

3. Click within the line above which you want the copied macro actions to be inserted. Don't click any Macro Action Selectors unless you want to over-write existing macro actions (see Warning in previous section).

4. Click Paste (or use one of the alternate Paste options). Access will insert the macro actions at the cursor.

To copy macro actions to another macro:

1. Click-and-drag to select the Macro Action Selectors of the macro actions you want to copy.

2. Click Copy on the Macro Design toolbar (or use Ctrl+C or the Edit menu Copy option).

3. Open the macro that will include the copied actions.

4. Click within the line above which you want the copied macro actions to be inserted.

5. Click Paste (or use one of the alternate Paste options). Access will insert the macro actions at the cursor.

Adding Comments To Your Macros

Just as it's useful to document any program, it's useful to document what you're trying to accomplish within your macro. These comments can be used when you or others are attempting to modify your macro at a later time. They can also be used as documentation, because they print when you print the macro.

To add a comment to a macro, click the Comment column of the macro and begin to type. In general, your comments for macros are limited to one line (256 characters). As detailed earlier in this chapter and explained in depth in Chapter 27, macros don't provide the depth of commenting support that VBA does, which is one of the many reasons why VBA is, in general, a better choice for programming Access databases.

Testing A Macro

Access doesn't provide very sophisticated tools for testing and debugging your macros. However, it does provide a method by which you can step through each line of a macro. To do so, perform the following steps:

1. Open the macro in Design view.

2. Click Single Step on the toolbar.

3. To execute the macro click Run (the exclamation point) on the toolbar. Access will execute the first line of the macro. The Macro Single Step dialog box will then appear, as shown in Figure 26.5.

   This dialog shows you the Macro Name, Condition, Action Name, and Arguments. In the figure, the Macro Name is **mcrTest1**, the Condition evaluates to True, and the Action Name is **OpenForm**. The **OpenForm** arguments are **frmCheckedOut**, Form, and Normal.

4. To continue stepping through the macro, click Step. If you want to halt execution of the macro without proceeding, click Halt. To continue normal execution of the macro without stepping, click Continue.

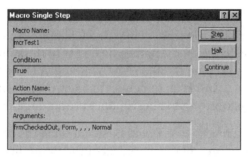

Figure 26.5   The Macro Single Step dialog box.

Converting A Macro To VBA Code

Now that you've discovered all the limitations of macros, you might be thinking about all the macros you've already written that you wish you'd developed using VBA code. Or, after seeing how easy it is to accomplish certain tasks using macros, you might be disappointed to learn how limited macros are. Fortunately, Access 2000 comes to the rescue—it's easy to convert an Access macro to VBA code. Once the macro has been converted to VBA code, the code can be modified just like any VBA module. The process of converting an Access macro to VBA code consists of six steps:

1. Open the macro you wish to convert in Design view.

2. Select the File menu Save As option. Access 2000 will display the Save As dialog box.

3. Within the As drop-down, change the selection from "Macro" to "Module".

4. Change the name of the macro—at the very least, be sure to precede the macro name with "mdl" rather than "mcr." After you change the selection and the module name, the Save As dialog box will look similar to Figure 26.6.

5. Click the OK button. The Convert Macro dialog box will appear. Within the dialog box, you can indicate whether you want to add error handling to the generated code and whether the code should include your original macro comments. After making your choices, click on the Convert button.

6. If the conversion is successful, you'll receive an indication from Access that the conversion completed. Click the OK button.

The converted macro appears under the list of modules with "Converted Macro-" followed by the name of the macro. Click Design to view the results of the conversion process. Figure 26.7 shows the results of a sample conversion process.

The macro is converted into distinct subroutines, one for each macro name. Note that VBA doesn't assign the same name to each subroutine but, rather, leaves a placeholder for you to assign the name you desire to the subroutine. The macro is complete with logic, comments, and error handling. All macro conditions are converted into **If...Else...End If** statements. All macro comments are converted into VBA comments. Basic error-handling routines are automatically added to the code.

When you convert a macro to a Visual Basic module, the original macro remains untouched. Furthermore, all of the objects in your application will still call the macro. It's important that you realize that to effectively utilize the macro conversion options, you must find all places where the macro was called and replace the macro references with calls to the VBA function.

Figure 26.6   The Save As dialog box from the macro editor.

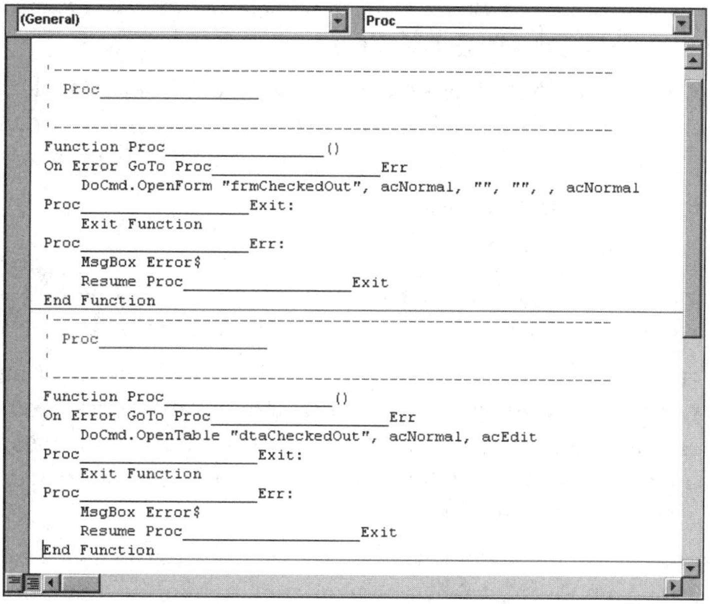

```
(General)                        ▼   Proc_____              ▼
 '----------------------------------------------------------------
 ' Proc_____
 '
 '----------------------------------------------------------------
 Function Proc_____()
 On Error GoTo Proc_____Err
     DoCmd.OpenForm "frmCheckedOut", acNormal, "", "", , acNormal
 Proc_____Exit:
     Exit Function
 Proc_____Err:
     MsgBox Error$
     Resume Proc_____Exit
 End Function
 '----------------------------------------------------------------
 ' Proc_____
 '
 '----------------------------------------------------------------
 Function Proc_____()
 On Error GoTo Proc_____Err
     DoCmd.OpenTable "dtaCheckedOut", acNormal, acEdit
 Proc_____Exit:
     Exit Function
 Proc_____Err:
     MsgBox Error$
     Resume Proc_____Exit
 End Function
```

Figure 26.7   The converted macro within the VBA editor.

Creating An **AutoExec** Macro

As you've learned, you can use either an **AutoExec** macro or Startup options to determine what occurs when a database is opened—although the Startup options tend to be more limited than the **AutoExec** macro is.

Many developers, because they prefer to include as few macros in their applications as possible, tend to designate a startup form for their application. The startup form calls a custom "AutoExec"-style routine when it's opened. You'll learn more about this method in Chapter 27.

The process of creating an **AutoExec** macro is quite simple. It's just a normal macro saved with the name **AutoExec**. An **AutoExec** macro usually performs tasks such as hiding or minimizing the Database window and opening a Startup form or switchboard—or directly invoking VBA code to perform complex processing.

When you're opening your own database to make changes or additions to the application, you'll probably not want the **AutoExec** macro to execute. Remember, you can prevent the **AutoExec** macro from executing by holding down your Shift key as you open the database.

Creating An **AutoKeys** Macro

As you've learned, an **AutoKeys** macro lets you redefine keystrokes within your database. You can map selected keystrokes to a single command or to a series of commands. Follow the following steps to build an **AutoKeys** macro:

1. Open a new macro in Design view.

2. Make sure the Macro Name column is visible.

3. Enter a Key Name in the Macro Name column. Allowable Key Names are defined in Table 26.1 and can also be found within the Access Help file.

4. Select the macro action you want to associate with the Key Name. You can apply conditions and arguments just as in a normal macro. You can have Access execute multiple commands in one of three ways: Associate multiple macro actions with a Key Name, perform a **RunCode** action, or perform a **RunMacro** action.

5. Continue adding Key Names and macro actions to the macro as desired. Separate each Key Name by one blank line to improve readability.

6. Save the macro as **AutoKeys**. The moment you save the macro, the Key Names are in effect, and the keystrokes are remapped. The **AutoKeys** macro comes into effect automatically each time you open the database.

It's generally not a good idea to remap common Windows or Access keystrokes. Your users become accustomed to certain keystrokes having certain meanings in all Windows applications. If you attempt to alter the definition of these common keystrokes, your users will become confused and frustrated. Therefore, it's important to use keystroke combinations that are rarely, if ever, used within Windows.

Chapter 27

Using Modules And Visual Basic For Applications

In Depth

Introduction To Visual Basic For Applications (VBA)

Visual Basic for Applications (VBA) is the development language for Microsoft Access 2000. It provides a consistent language for application development within the Microsoft Office suite. The core language, its constructs, and the environment are the same within Microsoft Access 2000, Microsoft Visual Basic, Microsoft Excel, Microsoft Word, and Microsoft Project. The differences between these environments are the built-in objects specific to each application. For example, Access has a **Recordset** object, and Excel has a **Workbook** object. Each application's objects have appropriate properties (attributes) and methods (actions) associated with them. This chapter provides an overview of the VBA language and its constructs.

Simple Access applications can be written using macros, as you learned in Chapter 26. However, although macros are great for quick prototyping and the most basic of application development, most serious Access development is done using the VBA language. Unlike macros, VBA provides the ability to perform all the following programming actions:

- Work with complex logic structures, such as case statements and loops

- Utilize constants and variables

- Take advantage of functions and actions not available in macros

- Loop through and perform actions on recordsets

- Perform transaction processing

- Create and work with database objects from within program code

- Implement error handling

- Create libraries of user-defined functions

- Call Windows application programming interface (API) functions

- Perform complex Dynamic Data Exchange (DDE) and object linking and embedding (OLE) automation commands

The VBA language allows you to use complex logic structures. Whereas macros allow you to perform only simple **If...Then...Else** logic, the VBA language provides a wealth of logic and looping constructs. These constructs are covered later in this chapter. The VBA language also enables you to declare and work with variables and constants. These variables can be *scoped*–that is, assigned meaning only within certain portions of your application—and passed as parameters to subroutines and functions. As you'll see later, variables and constants are an integral part of any Access application. These features aren't available within macros.

Many important features of the VBA language aren't available through macro actions. In trying to develop an application using only macros, you won't be able to take advantage of many of the rich features available in the VBA language. In addition, many of the actions that are available in both macros and modules can be performed much more efficiently using VBA code.

Complex Access applications often require that your program be able to loop through a recordset, performing some action on each member of the set. There's no way to accomplish this task using Access macros. In using VBA language, the process of looping through recordsets isn't only possible, it's very flexible. Using Data Access Objects (DAO) and ActiveX Data Objects (ADO), you can add, delete, update, and manipulate data. You'll learn about DAO and ADO in Chapter 28.

When manipulating sets of records, you usually want to ensure that all processing completes successfully before your data is permanently updated. Macros don't allow you to protect your data with transaction processing. Using the DAO **BeginTrans**, **CommitTrans**, and **Rollback** methods, you can ensure that your data is updated only if all parts of a transaction complete successfully. Transaction processing, if implemented properly, can dramatically improve the performance of your application, because no data is written to disk until the process completes. Chapter 28 explains transaction processing in detail.

Access macros won't let you create or modify database objects at runtime. Often, your more complex applications will require that you do so, which you can, easily, from the VBA language. Using VBA, you can create databases, tables, queries, and other database objects. You can also modify existing objects. The practical applications of VBA's power are many—virtually unlimited. An example is when users are allowed to build queries on the fly. You might want to give them the ability to design a query using a front end that you provide and store the query so they can run it again at a later time. You can use either DAO or ADO to provide such capability.

Access macros don't let you implement error handling. If an error occurs while an Access macro is executing in the runtime version of Access, the user is exited out of the application (and, therefore, the Access runtime). Using error-handling techniques, you can determine exactly what'll happen when an error occurs during the execution of your application.

VBA also makes it easier for the developer to write code libraries of reusable functions and to design and to debug complex processes. If you're developing even moderately complex applications, you can create generic function libraries that can subsequently be used with all of your Access applications. It's extremely difficult, if not impossible, to accomplish this using macros.

Many powerful functions not available with the VBA language are available as part of Windows itself. The Windows API refers to over 1,000 Windows functions that Microsoft exposes to developers. You can't take advantage of these functions from an Access macro. On the other hand, by using VBA code, you can declare and call upon these functions, improving both the performance and functionality of your applications.

DDE and OLE Automation enable you to communicate between your Access applications and other applications. Although DDE is an older technology than OLE Automation, it's still used to communicate with many applications that don't support OLE Automation. OLE Automation is used to control OLE server applications, and good examples of these server applications are Microsoft Excel and Microsoft Project. Using OLE Automation, you can control these applications' objects. You'll learn more about the OLE model later in this chapter.

In summary, although macros can provide a quick fix to a simple problem, their limitations mean you'll need to use VBA language for the development of complex solutions. To make the transition from macros to modules easier, Microsoft has provided a feature that allows you to convert any macro to VBA code, which you learned about in Chapter 26.

Understanding Access Code Modules, Form Modules, And Report Modules

VBA code is written in units called subroutines and functions. These subroutines and functions are stored in modules. Modules can be global, or they can be specific to a particular form or report. Global modules are often referred to as Access modules. They're created using the Modules tab of your Database window.

Modules specific to a form or report are generally referred to as Form and Report modules. Their code is often referred to as *Code Behind Forms* (CBF). You'll create and store the code written behind a form or report within that form or report. That code, in turn, will be triggered during execution by events occurring within the form or report.

A subroutine (also known as a procedure) is a procedure that responds to an event or performs some action. An Event subroutine is a special type of subroutine that automatically executes in response to an event, such as a mouse click on a command button or the loading of a form. A function is a special type of subroutine that can return a value, and therefore, can appear with equations or on the right side of an assignment. A subroutine, on the other hand, can't return a value.

Understanding The Module's Components

Whether you're dealing with an Access Module, Report Module, or Form Module, you'll see a General Declarations section at the top of the module. As the name implies, this is where you can declare variables and constants that you want to be visible to all the functions and subroutines within the module. These variables are referred to as module-level or **Private** variables. You can also declare **Public** variables within the General Declarations section of a module. You can see and modify **Public** variables using any function or procedure in any module within the database.

Public variables in Access 2000 replace Access 2's **Global** variables (although Access 2000 still supports the **Global** keyword). However, subtle differences exist between **Public** and **Global** variables. These differences are discussed later in this chapter.

A module is also made up of user-defined subroutines and functions. For example, Figure 27.1 shows a subroutine called **SendMessage**. Notice that the Object drop-down shown in the figure says General. This is because the subroutine called **SendMessage** isn't associated with a particular object.

Access 2000 has an environment option called Full Module View. This option, when checked, enables you to see multiple subroutines and functions within a

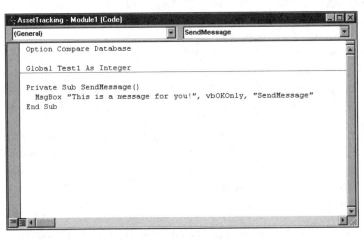

Figure 27.1 The **SendMessage** subroutine within a VBA editing window.

module at one time. In Figure 27.1, the editor is set to Full Module View. If you disable the Full Module View setting, you'll see only the code for the current subroutine or function within the module's editing window.

Understanding The Option Explicit Statement And Its Use

Option Explicit is a VBA statement that can be included in the General Declarations section of a module, form, or report. When you place **Option Explicit** in a General Declarations section, your program code must declare all variables within that module, form, or report before the program tries to use the variables.

Understanding Other Procedures That Modules May Contain

In addition to a General Declarations section and user-defined procedures, forms and reports contain event procedures. These procedures are associated with a particular object on a form. Notice in Figure 27.2 that the Object drop-down says **cmdTest1**. This is the name of the object whose event procedures you're viewing. The drop-down on the right shows all the events that can be coded for a command button. Each of these events creates a separate event procedure.

Event Procedures Made Easy

Event procedures are automatically created when you write event code for a control. For example, the procedure **Private Sub cmdHello_Click( )** is created when you place code in the **Click** event of the command button named **cmdHello**.

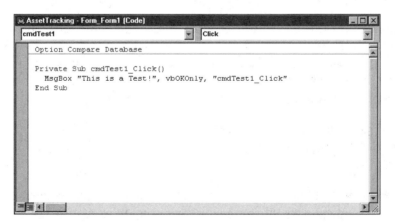

Figure 27.2   The **Click** event procedure for the **cmdTest1** command button.

Calling Event And User-Defined Procedures

Event procedures are automatically called when an event occurs for an object. When a user clicks on a command button, for example, the **Click** event code for that command button executes.

The standard method for calling user-defined procedures is to use the **Call** keyword—for example, **Call HelloSub**. You can also call the same procedure without using the **Call** keyword by simply invoking the procedure directly, with a call to **HelloSub**.

This violates standards, however, because the **Call** keyword indicates that you're calling a user-defined procedure or event procedure. The **Call** keyword makes the statement self-documenting and easier to read. A user-defined procedure can be called from an event procedure or from another user-defined procedure or function.

Scope And Lifetime Of Procedures

Procedures can be **Public**, **Private**, or **Static**. Whether you declare a procedure as **Public**, **Private**, or **Static** determines its *scope* (where it can be called from) and its *lifetime* (how long it'll reside in memory). The placement of a procedure can dramatically affect the functionality and performance of your application.

Understanding Public Procedures

A **Public** procedure can be called from anywhere in the application. Procedures declared in an Access module are automatically **Public**. This means that, unless you specify otherwise, procedures you place in a Code module can be called from anywhere within your application.

You might think that two **Public** procedures can't have the same name. Although this was true in earlier versions of Access, it's not true in Access 2000. When two **Public** procedures share a name, the procedure that calls them must explicitly state which of the two routines it's calling. This is illustrated by the following code snippet, contained within a form:

```
Private Sub cmdGoodBye_Click()
  Call basUtility.GoodByeMsg
End Sub
```

The **GoodByeMsg** procedure is found in two Access code modules. The prefix **basUtility** indicates that the procedure you want to execute is contained within the Access code module called **basUtility**.

Procedures declared in a Form or Report module are automatically **Private** to the form or report in which they're declared. This means they can be called only from another procedure within that form or report. Procedures in Form and Report modules can be explicitly declared as **Public** using the **Public** keyword. This means they can be called from anywhere within the application.

As an illustration, assume you have a procedure called **IAmPublic** within the form called **frmTest1**. Although the procedure is found within the form, it can be called from anywhere within the application. The only consideration you need to keep in mind is that the form containing the procedure must be open. The **IAmPublic** procedure, therefore, can be called from anywhere within the application using the following syntax:

```
Sub PublicFormProc()
  Call Forms.frmTest1.IAmPublic
End Sub
```

Understanding Private Procedures

Procedures declared in a Form or Report module are automatically **Private**. This means they can be called only from within the form or report where they're declared. If you want a procedure that's declared in an Access module to have the scope of that module, meaning that it can be called only from another procedure within the module, you must explicitly declare it as **Private**.

Understanding Scope Precedence

Private procedures always take precedence over **Public** procedures. When a **Private** procedure has the same name as a **Public** procedure, the code of the **Private** procedure is executed if it's called by any procedure within the module where it was declared. Naming conflicts don't occur between **Public** and **Private** procedures.

Static Procedures

Whenever a procedure is declared as **Static**, all the variables declared within the procedure maintain their values between calls to the procedure. This is an alternative to explicitly declaring each variable within the procedure as **Static**. Here's an example of a **Static** procedure:

```
Static Sub IncrementVars()
  Dim intCtr1 As Integer
  Dim intCtr2 As Integer
  Dim intCtr3 As Integer
  intCtr1 = intCtr1 + 1
  intCtr2 = intCtr2 + 1
  intCtr3 = intCtr3 + 1
```

```
    MsgBox "Variable values: " & intCtr1 & _
        " - " & intCtr2 & " - " & intCtr3
End Sub
```

Ordinarily, each variable in this procedure is reinitialized every time the procedure is run. This means that all 1s appear in the message box each time the procedure is run. Because the procedure is declared as **Static**, the variables within it retain their values from call to call. Each time the procedure is run, the values within the message box increase. This factor will become much clearer after the discussion of variables later in this chapter.

Naming Conventions For Procedures

The Leszynski Naming Conventions (LNC) suggest that all form and report procedure names be prefixed with the tag **cbf**. LNC standards add an optional scoping tag of *s* for **Static** procedures, *m* for **Private** procedures, and *p* for **Public** procedures. LNC standards suggest that you use the scoping tag only if you're creating software that will be widely distributed or released as public domain.

Considering Where To Place Your Code

Developers often wonder where to place code: in forms and reports or in Access modules. Each method has its pros and cons. Placing code in Access modules means that the code can be called easily from anywhere within your application, without loading a specific form or report. **Public** routines placed in Access Modules can also be called from other databases. For this reason, Access modules provide a great place to put generic routines you want readily available to you as part of a library.

All Access modules are automatically loaded when your database is opened, which is both good and bad. They're taking up memory whether their code is executed or not. On the other hand, Form and Report modules are loaded into memory only when the form or report is opened. This saves memory and resources, but a lot of code placed behind a form or report will take the form or report a long time to load. Users generally prefer a long application load time to slow execution while they're within the program, so place most of your code in Access modules. Another advantage of placing code behind forms and reports is that the form or report is very self-contained and, therefore, is portable. You can import the form or report into any other database and it will operate as expected. This object-oriented approach means the form requires nothing from the outside world.

As you can see, pros and cons exist for each methodology. As a general rule, when a procedure is specific to a particular form or report, place that procedure within the form or report. If it's widely used, place it in a module.

Working With Variables

You'll need to consider many issues when creating VBA variables. The way you declare a variable determines its scope, lifetime, and more. The following topics will help you to better understand the declaration of variables in VBA.

Declaration Of Variables

Of the several ways to declare variables in VBA, three are nonstandard and one is standard. In one instance, you can simply assign a value to a variable, declaring the variable at assignation—for example, **x = 10**. With this method of variable declaration, you really aren't declaring your variables at all; you're essentially declaring them as you use them. This method is quite dangerous as it lends itself to typos and other problems. Variables may have unknown values at given points, and because the variables are all **Variants** in such an environment, a program might be expecting a number and receive instead a text string.

The second nonstandard method you can use is to type **Dim intCounter**. The **Dim** statement declares the variable. The only problem with this method is you haven't declared the type of the variable to the compiler. It is, therefore, declared as being of type **Variant**.

Another common mistake is declaring multiple variables on the same line, as shown in the following code example:

```
Dim intCounter, intAge, intWeight As Integer
```

In this scenario, only the last variable is explicitly declared as an **Integer** variable. The other variables are implicitly declared as **Variants**.

The most efficient and bug-proof way to declare your variables is to strong type them to the compiler and declare only one variable per line of code, as shown in the following example:

```
Dim intCounter As Integer
Dim strName As String
```

As you can see, this type of declaration declares the name of the variable, as well as the type of data it can contain. This allows the compiler to catch careless errors, such as storing a string into an **Integer** variable. If implemented properly, by selecting the shortest practical data type for each variable, this method can also reduce the resources required to run your programs.

Considering Variants

Generally, try to eliminate the use of **Variants** whenever possible. Besides requiring a significant amount of storage space, **Variants** are also slow, because they must be resolved by the compiler—that is, the compiler must determine what the **Variant**'s effective type is at runtime. However, certain situations do warrant the use of a **Variant**. These situations include variables that need to contain different types of data at different times and instances where you must be able to differentiate between an empty variable (one that hasn't been initialized) and a variable containing a zero or a zero-length string. Moreover, **Variant** variables are the only types of variables that can contain the special value of **Null**. You'll learn more about **Empty** and **Null** values later in this chapter.

VBA Data Types

VBA offers several data types for variables. Table 27.1 shows a list of the available data types, the standard for naming them, the amount of storage space they require, the data they can store, and their default values.

Table 27.1   Data types and naming conventions.

Data Type	Naming Convention	Example	Storage of Data	Range	Default Value
Byte	byt	**bytValue**	1 byte	0 to 255	0
Boolean	bln	**blnAnswer**	2 bytes	True or False	False
Integer	int	**intCounter**	2 bytes	-32768 to 32767	0
Long (integer)	lng	**lngAmount**	4 bytes	-2147483648 to 2147483647	0
Single	sng	**sngAmount**	4 bytes	Very large	0
Double	dbl	**dblValue**	8 bytes	Extremely large	0
Currency	cur	**curSalary**	8 bytes	Very large	0
Date	dtm	**dtmStartDate**	8 bytes	1/1/100 to 12/31/9999	
Object Reference	obj	**objExcel**	4 bytes	Any object	
Fixed String	str	**strName**	10 bytes + String	0 to 2 billion	""
Var. String	str	**strName**	String	1 to 65,400	""
Variant /W Numbers	var	**varData**	16 bytes	Any numeric to double	Empty
Variant /W Characters	var	**varData**	22 bytes	Same as var. string	Empty
Type	typ	**typEmp**	Varies	Based on elements	

Considerations About Scope And Lifetime Of Variables

You've read about the different types of variables available in VBA. Variables can be declared as **Local**, **Private** (Module), or **Public** in scope. Always strive to include mostly **Local** variables in your code, because they're shielded from being accidentally modified by other routines. Let's take a closer look at how you can determine the scope and lifetime of variables.

Scope And Lifetime of Local Variables

Local variables are available only in the subroutine within which they were declared. Consider the following example:

```
Private Sub cmdOkay_Click
   Dim strAnimal As String
   strAnimal = "Chewie"
   Call ChangeAnimal
   Debug.Print strAnimal 'Still Chewie
End Sub
Private Sub ChangeAnimal
   strAnimal = "Kimba"
End Sub
```

This code behaves in one of two ways. If **Option Explicit** is in effect (meaning that all variables must be declared before they're used, as you learned earlier in this chapter), the code will yield a compiler error. If **Option Explicit** isn't in effect, **strAnimal** is changed to "Kimba" only within the context of the subroutine **ChangeAnimal**—and the value will still be "Chewie" within the **cmdOkay_Click** event procedure.

Understanding Static Variables

The following examples illustrate the difference between **Local** and **Static** variables. **Local** variables are reinitialized each time the code is called. Each time you run this procedure, the numeral 1 is printed in the Debug (Immediate) window:

```
Private Sub cmdLocal_Click()
   Dim intCtr As Integer
   intCtr = intCtr + 1
   Debug.Print intCtr
End Sub
```

Each time this code runs, the **Dim** statement at the procedure's beginning will reinitialize **intCtr**. This is quite different from the following code, which illustrates the use of a **Static** variable:

```
Private Sub cmdStatic_Click()
  Static sintCtr As Integer
  sintCtr = sintCtr + 1
  Debug.Print sintCtr
End Sub
```

Each time this code executes, the variable called **sintCtr** is incremented and retained. In other words, the first example will always output 1, while the second example will output 1, 2, 3, 4, and so on.

Considering Private Variables

So far, this discussion has been limited to variables that have scope within a particular procedure. Any procedure in the module within which they were de-clared can see Private (module-level) variables. These are declared by placing a **Private** statement, followed by the variable name (and the variable's type in most situations) within the General Declarations section of a Form, Report, or Access module:

```
[General Declarations]
Option Explicit
Private mintCounter As Integer
```

The value of a variable declared as **Private** can be changed by any subroutine or function within that module. For instance, the following subroutine changes the value of the **Private** variable **mintCounter** to 20. Notice the naming convention of using the letter *m* to prefix the name of the variable, which makes the variable stand out as **Private**. Use **Private** declarations only for variables that need to be seen by multiple routines but that all reside within the same code module. Strive to make most of your variables Local and to make your code modular and more bulletproof.

```
Private Sub cmdModule_Click()
  mintCounter = 20
  Debug.Print mintCounter
End Sub
```

Using Public Variables

Public variables can be accessed from anywhere within your application. They're usually limited to things such as login IDs, environment settings, and other vari-ables your entire application must see. Declarations of **Public** variables can be placed in the General Declarations section of an Access module or in a Form or Report module. The declaration of a **Public** variable will always appear similar to the following:

```
Option Explicit
Public gintCounter As Integer
```

Notice the prefix *g*, the naming convention prefix for a **Public** variable declared within an Access module. This standard is used because **Public** variables declared in an Access module are visible not only to the database within which they were declared but also to other databases. The prefix *p* should be used for **Public** variables declared in a Form or Report module. This prefix indicates that the variable is **Public** to the database but isn't visible to other databases. The following code, placed in the Click event of the **cmdPublic** command button, changes the value of the **Public** variable **pintCounter** to 50 (in this case, the variable should have been originally declared within a Form or Report module).

```
Private Sub cmdPublic_Click()
  pintCounter = 50
  Debug.Print pintCounter
End Sub
```

Adding Comments To Your Code

Comments are added to Access, Form, or Report modules using an apostrophe. The keyword **Rem** can also be used, but standards recommend using the apostrophe rather than **Rem**. The apostrophe can be placed at the beginning of the line of code or anywhere within the line of code. Anything following the apostrophe is considered a comment. Comments are color coded in Access 2000. Figure 27.3 shows code containing comments.

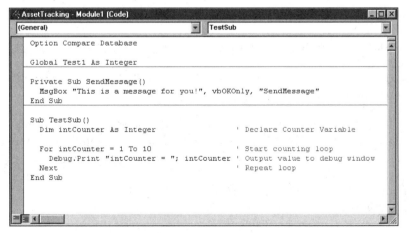

Figure 27.3   Code containing comments that clarify the code's purpose.

Understanding VBA Control Structures

VBA provides the developer with several different constructs for looping and decision processing. The following sections explain the most commonly used constructs.

Using The If...Then...Else Constructions

The **If...Then...Else** construct evaluates whether a condition is true or false. When the condition is true, VBA will perform the statement or statements that immediately follow the **Then** keyword. If the statement is false, VBA will perform the statement or statements that immediately follow the **Else** keyword, provided such statements exist. The **Else** is optional. You'll end the entire construct with the **End If** keyword, as shown in the following code:

```
Private Sub cmdIf_Click()
  If IsNull(Me!txtValue) Then
    MsgBox "You must Enter a Value"
  Else
    MsgBox "You entered " & Me!txtValue
  End If
End Sub
```

This code tests to see whether the text box called **txtValue** contains a **Null**. A different message is displayed depending on whether the text box value is **Null**.

One-line **If** statements are also permitted, although their usefulness is limited—they can only perform a single command after the **Then** keyword. A one-line **If** statement looks like this:

```
If IsNull(Me!txtvalue) Then MsgBox "You must Enter a Value"
```

This format for an **If** statement isn't recommended because it significantly reduces readability and usefulness.

Another valid keyword you can use with one or a series of **If** statements is the **ElseIf** keyword. An **ElseIf** enables you to evaluate an unlimited number of conditions within a single **If** statement. The following code is an example:

```
Sub MultipleIfs(intNumber As Integer)
  If intNumber = 1 Then
    MsgBox "You entered a One"
  ElseIf intNumber = 2 Then
    MsgBox "You entered a Two"
```

```
   ElseIf intNumber >= 3 And intNumber <= 10 Then
     MsgBox "You entered a Number Between 3 and 10"
   Else
     MsgBox "You Entered Some Other Number"
   End If
End Sub
```

The conditions within an **If** statement are evaluated in the order in which they appear. For this reason, it's best to place the most common conditions first within the **If** statement. When a condition is met, execution continues immediately after **End If**. If no conditions are met and there's no **Else** statement, execution also continues immediately after **End If**.

TIP: *If multiple conditions exist, it's almost always preferable to use a **Select Case** statement rather than an **If** statement. The exception to this rule is when you're using the **TypeOf** keyword to evaluate the type of an object.*

Using The Immediate If (IIf) Construct

An Immediate If (**IIf**) is a variation on an **If** statement. It's a function that returns one of two values depending on whether the condition being tested is true or false. The following code shows an example:

```
Function EvalSales(curSales As Currency) As String
  EvalSales = IIf(curSales >= 100000, "Great Job", "Sell More")
End Function
```

This function evaluates the parameter that's passed to see whether the parameter's value is greater than or equal to $100,000. If the value passed is greater than or equal to $100,000, the string "Great Job" is returned from the function; otherwise, the string "Sell More" is returned.

Both the true and false portions of the **IIf** are evaluated. This means that if a problem exists with either part of the expression (for example a divide by zero condition exists), an error occurs.

The **IIf** function is most often used in a calculated control on a form or report. Probably the most common example is an **IIf** expression that determines whether the value of a control is **Null**. If it is, you can have the expression return a zero or an empty string; otherwise, you can have the expression return the value contained within the control. The following is an illustration of an expression that evaluates the value of a control on a form:

```
=IIf(IsNull(Forms!frmOrders!Freight),0,Forms!frmOrders!Freight)
```

27. Using Modules And Visual Basic For Applications

This expression displays either a zero or the value for freight in the control called **Freight**. If the control is **Null** (that is, it contains no value), the code displays 0—otherwise, the code will display the value the control contains.

Using The Conditional If Statement (#If) For Conditional Compilation

Conditional compilation enables you to selectively execute blocks of code. This feature is useful in several situations:

- When you want certain blocks of code to execute in the demo version of your product and other blocks to execute in the retail version of your product

- When you are distributing your application in various countries and want certain blocks of code to apply to some countries but not to others

- When you want certain blocks of code to execute only during the testing of your application

Conditional compilation is accomplished by using the **#If...Then...#Else** directive, as shown in the following code:

```
Sub ConditionalIf()
  #If Language = "Spanish" Then
    MsgBox "Hola, Que Tal?"
  #Else
    MsgBox "Hello, How Are You?"
  #End If
End Sub
```

The compiler constant, in this case, **Language**, can be declared in one of two places. You can either declare it in the General Declarations section of a module or from within the Options dialog box (select the Tools menu Options option). A compiler constant declared in the General Declarations section of a module looks like the following:

```
#Const Language = "Spanish"
```

The disadvantage of this constant is that it can't be declared as **Public**. It's not possible to create **Public** compiler constants using the **#Const** directive. This means that any constants declared in the Declarations section of a module can only be used within that module. The major advantage of declaring this type of compiler constant is that it can contain a string. For example, the compiler constant **Language**, defined in the previous paragraph, is given the value Spanish.

Public compiler constants can be declared only from the Options dialog box (select the Tools menu Options option). Because they're **Public** in scope, compiler constants defined in the Options dialog box can be referenced from anywhere within your application. The major limitation on compiler directives set up in the Options dialog box is that they can contain only integers. For instance, you'd have to say Spanish = 1. You'll learn how to set up a compiler directive from the Options dialog box in the "Immediate Solutions" section of this chapter.

It's important to understand that using conditional constants isn't the same as using regular constants or variables along with the standard **If...Then...Else** construct. Regular constants or variables are evaluated at runtime, requiring processing time whenever the application is run. Conditional constants and conditional **If...Then...Else** statements control which sections of code are actually compiled. All resolution is completed at compile time. This eliminates the need for unnecessary processing at runtime.

Using The Select Case Statement

Rather than employing multiple **If...Then...Else** statements, it's often much clearer to use a **Select Case** statement. When VBA encounters a **Select Case** statement in your program, it evaluates the expression that follows the statement to produce a result. VBA then compares the result to each of the specified constant values that follow the **Case** keyword. If VBA finds a match, it will execute the statements immediately following the matching **Case** statement. To understand this better, consider the following:

```
Private Sub cmdCase_Click()
  Dim intResponse As Integer
  If IsNull(Me!txtValue) Then
    intResponse = 0
  Else
    intResponse = Val(Me!txtValue)
  End If
  Select Case intResponse
    Case 0
      MsgBox "You Must Enter a Number"
    Case 1 To 5
      MsgBox "You Entered a Value Between 1 and 5"
    Case 7, 11, 21
      MsgBox "You Entered 7, 11, or 21"
    Case Else
      MsgBox "You Entered an Invalid Number"
  End Select
End Sub
```

This subroutine first uses an **If** statement to evaluate whether the **txtValue** control contains a **Null**. If it does, the procedure stores a zero into the variable named

27. Using Modules
And Visual Basic For
Applications

intResponse. Otherwise, the value contained within **txtValue** is stored into **intResponse**. The **Case** statement evaluates **intResponse**. A 0 value displays a message box with the text "You Must Enter a Number". When the value is between 1 and 5 inclusive, the program displays a message box saying "You Entered a Value Between 1 and 5". Suppose the user enters 7, 11, or 21, the program displays an appropriate message. Finally, the **Case Else** statement captures all other cases and (in this particular example) displays a message indicating that the user entered an invalid number.

Using Looping Structures

Several looping structures are available in VBA. The two most commonly used are the **Do** loop and the **For** loop. In many cases, your programs must repeat one or more statements until the program meets a specific condition that doesn't necessarily involve a count. Consider a program that reads from one database and writes to another database; you may not know how many records you'll access until you reach the end-of-file (EOF) marker for the database. In such cases, you'll use a **Do** loop. When VBA encounters a **Do** statement in your program, VBA will test the condition specified. With a condition that's true, VBA performs the statements contained within the loop. A condition that's false means VBA will continue your program's execution at the first statement that follows the **Loop** keyword. You might implement a **Do** loop, then, as shown here:

```
Sub DoWhileLoop()
  Dim intCounter As Integer
  intCounter = 1
  Do While intCounter < 5
    MsgBox intCounter
    intCounter = intCounter + 1
  Loop
End Sub
```

This structure doesn't ensure that the code within the loop is executed at least once. When **intCounter** is greater than or equal to 5, the code within the loop is never executed. To get the code to execute unconditionally at least once, you need to use the following construct:

```
Sub DoLoopWhile()
  Dim iCounter As Integer
  iCounter = 5
  Do
    MsgBox iCounter
    iCounter = iCounter + 1
  Loop While iCounter < 5
End Sub
```

This code executes one time, even though **intCounter** is set to 5. The **Do While... Loop** evaluates before the code is executed and, therefore, doesn't ensure code execution. Because the **Do...Loop While** is evaluated at the end of the loop, it's guaranteed execution.

Alternatives to the **Do While...Loop** and the **Do...Loop While** are **Do Until...Loop** and **Do...Loop Until**. The **Do Until...Loop** construction works like this:

```
Sub DoUntilLoop()
  Dim intCounter As Integer
  intCounter = 1
  Do Until intCounter = 5
    MsgBox intCounter
    intCounter = intCounter + 1
  Loop
End Sub
```

This loop sets **intCounter** equal to 1. It continues to execute until **intCounter** becomes equal to 5. The **Do...Loop Until** construct is another variation:

```
Sub DoLoopUntil()
  Dim intCounter As Integer
  intCounter = 1
  Do
    MsgBox intCounter
    intCounter = intCounter + 1
  Loop Until intCounter = 5
End Sub
```

As with the **Do...Loop While** construct, the **Do...Loop Until** construct doesn't evaluate the condition until the end of the loop. The code within the loop is, therefore, guaranteed to execute at least once.

It's easy to unintentionally cause a loop to execute endlessly. The following code shows an example:

```
Sub EndlessLoop()
  Dim intCounter As Integer
  intCounter = 5
  Do
    Debug.Print intCounter
    intCounter = intCounter + 1
  Loop Until intCounter = 5
End Sub
```

27. Using Modules And Visual Basic For Applications

This code snippet sets **intCounter** equal to 5. The code within the loop increments **intCounter** then tests to see whether **intCounter** equals 5. If it doesn't, the code within the loop executes another time. Because **intCounter** never becomes equal to 5, the loop executes endlessly. Use Ctrl+Break to exit out of the loop. Ctrl+Break doesn't work in the runtime version of Access. *Note:* You can also use the **While...Wend** construction to perform looping actions. However, this construction is very limited in implementation and is generally not used in most modern-day programs.

Using The For...Next Loop

The **For...Next** loop construct is used when you have an exact number of iterations you want to perform. Unlike with the **Do** loop, you'll specify the number of times through the loop at the loop's beginning and definition. It looks similar to the following:

```
Sub ForNext()
  Dim intCounter As Integer
  For intCounter = 1 To 5
    MsgBox intCounter
  Next intCounter
End Sub
```

Note that **intCounter** is self-incrementing. The start and the stop values can both be variables. A **For...Next** construct can also be given a **Step** value. A **Step** value lets you increment the loop by any amount you desire. You'll use a **Step** value within a **For...Next** loop as shown in the following example:

```
Sub ForNextStep()
  Dim intCounter As Integer
  For intCounter = 1 To 5 Step 2
    MsgBox intCounter
  Next intCounter
End Sub
```

The loop repeats three times—once when **intCounter** equals 1, once when **intCounter** equals 3, and once when **intCounter** equals 5.

Using The With...End With Construction

The **With...End With** statement executes a series of statements on a single object. To limit the amount of typing and to increase the clarity of your code when applying a series of statements to a single object, VBA provides the **With...End With** construction. You'll use **With...End With** as shown in the following code:

```
Private Sub cmdWithEndWith_Click()
  With Me!cmdHello
    .BackColor = 16777088
    .ForeColor = 16711680
    .Value = "Access 2000 Black Book"
    .FontName = "Arial"
  End With
End Sub
```

This code performs four operations on the command button called **cmdHello**, found on the form on which it's run. The **BackColor**, **ForeColor**, **Value**, and **FontName** properties of the **cmdHello** text box are all modified by the code.

The **With...End With** statement provides two major benefits. The first is simply a matter of less typing: You don't need to repeat the object name for each action that you want to perform on the object. The second, more important benefit involves performance. Because the object is referenced once rather than multiple times, this code runs much more efficiently. The benefits are even more pronounced when the **With...End With** construct is found within a loop.

Using The For Each...Next Construction

The **For Each...Next** construction executes a group of statements on each member of an array or collection. The **For Each** construction works very similarly to the **For...Next** construction. The **For Each** construction iterates through the collection or array, moving through each object until it reaches the end of the collection. The following code snippit illustrates the use of this powerful construct:

```
Private Sub cmdForEachNext_Click()
  Dim ctl As Control
  For Each ctl In Controls
    ctl.ForeColor = 16711680
  Next ctl
End Sub
```

This code loops through each control on a form. The **ForeColor** property of each control on the form is modified. The **With...End With** construct is often used in conjunction with the **For Each...Next** construct. For instance, the following program code modifies three properties for each control in a collection:

```
Private Sub cmdForEachWith_Click()
  Dim ctl As Control
  For Each ctl In Controls
    With ctl
      .ForeColor = 16711680
```

```
        .FontName = "Arial"
        .FontSize = 12
      End With
    Next ctl
End Sub
```

This code loops through each control on the form. Three properties are changed for each control: **ForeColor**, **FontName**, and **FontSize**.

Before you put all this good information to use, remember that no error handling has yet been implemented within the code. If one of the controls on the form in the example doesn't have a **ForeColor**, **FontName**, or **FontSize** property, the code renders an error. Knowing the type of an object before you attempt to modify its properties can help you to prevent errors when dealing with the object.

Passing Parameters And Returning Values

Subroutines and functions can receive arguments (parameters), but only functions can return values. The following subroutine receives two parameters: **txtFirst** and **txtLast**. It then displays a message box with the first character of each of the parameters that was passed.

```
Private Sub cmdSendNames_Click()
  Call Initials(Me!txtFirstName, Me!txtLastName)
End Sub
Sub Initials(strFirst As String, strLast As String)
  MsgBox "Your Initials Are: " & Left$(strFirst, 1) _
      & Left$(strLast, 1)
End Sub
```

Notice that the text within the controls **txtFirstName** and **txtLastName** from the current form (**Me**) are passed to the subroutine called **Initials**. The parameters are received as **strFirst** and **strLast**. The first left character of each parameter is displayed in the message box.

The preceding code simply passes values then operates on these values. This next example uses a function to return a value:

```
Private Sub cmdNameFunc_Click()
  Dim strInitials As String
  strInitials = ReturnInit(Me!txtFirstName, _
      Me!txtLastName)
  MsgBox "Your initials are: " & strInitials
End Sub
Function ReturnInit(strFName As String, strLName As String) As String
```

```
    ReturnInit = Left$(strFName, 1) & Left(strLName, 1)
End Function
```

Notice that this sample calls a function **ReturnInit**, sending values contained within the two text boxes as parameters to the function. The function sets **ReturnInit** (the name of the function) equal to the first two characters of the strings. This returns the value back to the calling procedure (**cmdNameFunc_Click**) and sets **strInitials** equal to the return value.

Notice that the function **ReturnInit** is set to receive two string parameters. You know this because of the **As String** keywords that follow each parameter. The function is also set to return a string because the keyword **As String** follows the list of the parameters, outside of the parentheses. If you don't explicitly state that the function will return a particular type of data, it will return a variant.

Working With Built-In Functions

Visual Basic for Applications contains a rich and comprehensive function library. Some of the more commonly used functions and examples are listed in this chapter. You can use the online Help or the *Microsoft Access Language Reference* to become familiar with the rest. The "Immediate Solutions" section of this chapter provides examples of the common functions that you'll use.

Using The Object Browser To Simplify Function Access

The Object Browser enables you to easily browse Access's functions and add a function to your code. It even adds the function's parameters for you. Figure 27.4 shows the Object Browser.

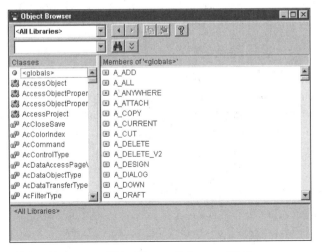

Figure 27.4   The Object Browser within Microsoft Access 2000.

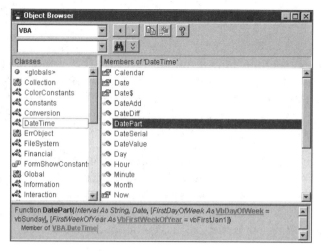

Figure 27.5   The Object Browser with the VBA Library referenced.

The example in Figure 27.4 shows the selection of a user-defined function selected from a module in a database. You can also select any built-in function. Figure 27.5 shows an example in which the **DatePart** function is selected from the VBA library. The Object Browser exposes all libraries referenced by the database.

Navigation Tips And Tricks

Effectively using the tips and tricks of the trade can save you hours of time. These tricks help you to navigate around the coding environment as well as to quickly and easily modify your code. They include the ability to easily zoom to a user-defined procedure, search and replace within modules, obtain help on VBA functions and commands, and split the Code window so two procedures can be viewed simultaneously.

Using The Zoom Feature

As you become more knowledgeable about VBA, you'll create libraries of VBA functions and subroutines. As you're viewing a call to a particular subroutine or function, you often want to view the code behind that function. Fortunately, VBA gives you a quick and easy way to navigate from procedure to procedure. Assume that the following code appears in your application:

```
Private Sub cmdOkay_Click()
    Dim iAgeInTen As Integer
    If IsNull(Me!txtName) Or IsNull(Me!txtAge) Then
        MsgBox "You must fill in name and age"
        Exit Sub
```

```
    Else
        MsgBox "Your Name Is: " & Me!txtName & _
            " and Your Age Is: " & Me!txtAge
        Call EvaluateAge(Val(Me!txtAge))
        iAgeInTen = AgePlus10(Fix(Val(Me!txtAge)))
        MsgBox "In 10 Years You Will Be " & iAgeInTen
    End If
End Sub
```

Let's say that you want to quickly jump to the procedure called **EvaluateAge** so you can take a better look at it. All you need to do is place your cursor anywhere within the call to **EvaluateAge** and press Shift+F2. You're immediately moved to the **EvaluateAge** procedure. Ctrl+Shift+F2 takes you back to the routine where you came from (in this case, **cmdOkay_Click**). This shortcut works for both functions and subroutines.

Using The VBA IDE Find And Replace Features

Often, you name a variable only to decide later that you want to change the name. VBA comes with an excellent find-and-replace feature to help you with this process. You can simply search for data, or you can search for a value and replace it with some other value.

The Find dialog allows you to search for text while the Replace dialog offers all the features of the Find dialog but also allows you to enter Replace With text. In addition, it lets you select Replace or Replace All. Replace asks for confirmation before each replacement, whereas Replace All replaces text without prompting for confirmation. In general, take the time to confirm each replacement. It's easy to miscalculate the pervasive effects of a global search and replace.

Using Context-Sensitive Help Within The IDE

A very useful but little-known feature of VBA is the capability to get context-sensitive help during coding. With your cursor placed anywhere within any VBA command or function, press the F1 key. You're given context-sensitive help on that command or function. Most of the help topics also give you the opportunity to view practical examples of the function or command within code. Figure 27.6 shows help on the **With...End With** construct.

Notice that the Help window includes the syntax for the command, a detailed description of each parameter included in the command, and remarks about using the command. At the top of the window you can see hypertext links to related topics ("See Also"), as well as a link to an example of the use of the **With...End With** construct. By clicking on Example, a specific example of the construct will appear. You can copy the example and place it into a module—a very useful way to learn about the various parts of the VBA language.

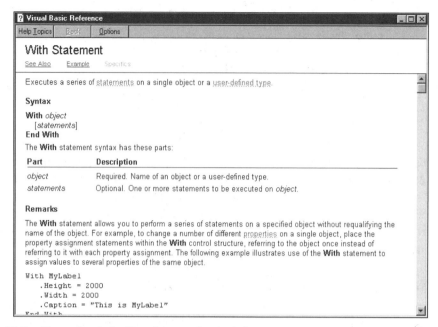

Figure 27.6   The online-help file reference for the **With...End With** construct.

Splitting The Code Window

The VBA Code window can be split so you can look at two routines within the same module at the same time. This option is useful if you're trying to solve a problem that involves two procedures or event routines in a large module. An illustration of a split Code window appears in Figure 27.7.

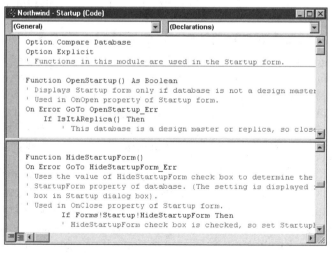

Figure 27.7   Splitting the Code window to view two routines.

Notice the splitter. By placing your mouse cursor on the gray splitter button just above the vertical scrollbar of the Code window and clicking-and-dragging, you can size each half of the window as desired. The window can be split only into two halves. After it has been split, you can use the Object and Procedure drop-downs to navigate to the procedure of your choice.

Only routines within the same module can be viewed in a particular Code window, but multiple Code windows can be open at the same time. Each time you open an Access, Form, or Report module, you're placed in a different window. Each module window can then be sized, moved, and split as desired.

Using The DoCmd Object To Perform Macro Actions

The Access environment is rich with objects containing built-in properties and methods. The properties can be modified and the methods can be executed using VBA code. One of the objects available in Access is the **DoCmd** object. This object enables you to execute macro actions in Visual Basic procedures. The macro actions are executed as methods of the **DoCmd** object. The syntax looks like this:

```
DoCmd.ActionName [arguments]
```

For instance, you can apply the prototype within a program as shown in the following example:

```
DoCmd.OpenReport strReportName, acPreview
```

The **OpenReport** method is a method of the **DoCmd** object that runs a report. The first two parameters that the **OpenReport** method receives are the name of the report you want to run and the view in which you want the report to appear (Preview, Normal, or Design). The name of the report and the view are both arguments of the **OpenReport** method.

Most macro actions have corresponding **DoCmd** methods that can be found within the online help file. Certain macro actions don't have corresponding **DoCmd** methods. They're **AddMenu**, **MsgBox**, **RunApp**, **RunCode**, **SendKeys**, **SetValue**, **StopAllMacros**, and **StopMacro**. **AddMenu** and **SendKeys** are the only two that have any significance to you as a VBA programmer. The remainder of the macro actions either have no application to VBA code or can be executed in better ways using VBA functions and commands. An example is the **MsgBox** action. The VBA language includes a **MsgBox** function that's far more robust than its macro action counterpart.

Many of the methods of the **DoCmd** object have optional parameters. If you don't supply an argument, its default value is assumed. You must use commas as place markers to designate the position of missing arguments. Here's an example:

```
DoCmd.OpenForm "frmOrders", , ,"[OrderAmount} > 1000"
```

The **OpenForm** method of the **DoCmd** object receives seven parameters. The last six parameters are optional. In the example, two parameters are explicitly specified. The first parameter is the name of the form, a required parameter. The second and third parameters have been omitted, meaning that you're accepting their default values. The commas, used as place markers for the second and third parameters, are necessary, because one of the parameters following them is explicitly designated. The fourth parameter is the **Where** condition for the form. This has been designated as the records where the **OrderAmount** is greater than 1,000. The remaining four parameters haven't been referenced, so default values for these parameters are used.

Understanding User-Defined Types And Their Usage

A user-defined type, known as a *structure* or *record*, allows you to create a variable that contains several pieces of information. User-defined types are often used to hold information from one or more records in memory. Because each element of a user-defined type can be instructed to hold a particular type of data, each element in the type can be defined to correspond to the type of data stored in a specific field of a table. A user-defined type might look like this:

```
Public Type TimeCardInfo
  TimeCardDetailID As Long
  TimeCardID As Long
  DateWorked As Date
  ProjectID As Long
  WorkDescription As String * 255
  BillableHours As Double
  BillingRate As Currency
  WorkCodeID As Long
End Type
```

Notice that the type of data stored in each element has been explicitly declared. The element containing the string **WorkDescription** has been declared with a length of 255. User-defined types make code cleaner by storing related data as a unit. A user-defined type exists only in memory and is, therefore, temporary. It's excellent for information that needs to be temporarily tracked at runtime. Because it's in memory, it can be quickly and efficiently read from and written to.

Working With Constants

A constant is a meaningful name given to a meaningless number or string. Constants can be used only for values that don't change at runtime. For instance, a tax rate or commission rate might be constant throughout your application. Three types of constants exist in Access:

- Symbolic
- Intrinsic
- System-defined

Symbolic constants are constants you create using the **Const** keyword. They're used to improve the readability of your code and make code maintenance easier. Rather than referring to the number .0875 every time you want to refer to the tax rate, you can refer to the constant **mccurTaxRate**. If the tax rate changes and you need to modify the value in your code, make the change only in one place. Furthermore, unlike the number .0875, the name **mccurTaxRate** is self-documenting.

Intrinsic constants are built into Microsoft Access—that is, they're part of the language itself. As an Access programmer, you can use constants provided by Microsoft Access, Visual Basic, DAO, ADO, and other libraries and controls that you include within your applications. You can also use constants provided by any object libraries you're using in your application.

System-defined constants are available to all applications on your computer. Only three system-defined constants exist: **True**, **False**, and **Null**.

Scoping Symbolic Constants

Just as regular variables have scope, user-defined constants have scope. For instance, you might create a **Private** constant, as shown here:

```
Private Const pccurTaxRate = 0.0875 As Currency
```

The following statement, when placed in the Declarations section of a module, creates a **Public** constant:

```
Public Const pccurTaxRate = 0.0875 As Currency
```

Because this constant is declared as **Public**, it can be accessed from any subroutine or function (including event routines) in your entire application. To truly understand the benefits of a **Public** constant, imagine a scenario in which numerous functions and subroutines are all referencing the constant named **pccurTaxRate**. Imagine what would happen if the tax rate were to change. Without the use of a constant, you'd need to search your entire application, replacing the old tax rate with the new tax rate. Because your **Public** constant is declared in one place, you can easily go in and modify the one line of code where this constant is declared.

By definition, the value of constants can't be modified at runtime. If you attempt to modify the value of a constant, you receive the VBA compiler error "Variable Required—can't assign to this expression."

Need to change the value at runtime? Consider storing the value in a table rather than declaring it as a constant. You can read the value into a variable when the application loads and modify the variable if required. If you choose, you can write the new value back to the table.

Working With Intrinsic Constants

Microsoft Access declares a number of intrinsic constants that can be used in Code, Form, and Report modules. They're reserved by Microsoft Access in that you can't modify their values or reuse their names, but they can be used at any time without being declared.

Use intrinsic constants whenever possible in your code. Besides making your code more readable, they make your code more portable to future releases of Microsoft Access. Microsoft might change the value associated with a constant, but it's not likely to change the name of a constant. All intrinsic constants appear in the Object Browser.

Working With Arrays

An array is a series of variables referred to by the same name. Each element of the array is differentiated by a unique index number. Arrays help to make coding efficient. It's easy to loop through each element of an array, performing some process on each element. Arrays have a lower and upper bound, and all array elements must be contiguous.

The scope of an array can be public, module, or local. As with other variables, this depends on where the array is declared and whether the **Public**, **Private**, or **Dim** keyword is used. The lower bound of an array is zero by default. All elements of an array must have the same data type.

Fixed arrays and dynamic arrays are two basic types of arrays. When declaring a fixed array, you give VBA the upper bound and the type of data it will contain. A fixed array means that you can't alter the array's size at runtime.

Often, however, you don't know how many elements your array needs to contain. In this case, consider declaring a dynamic array. Dynamic arrays can be resized at runtime. This can make your code more efficient, because VBA preallocates memory for all elements of a fixed array, regardless of whether data is stored in each of the elements. However, be careful if you aren't sure how many elements your array will contain because preallocating a huge amount of memory can be extremely inefficient.

Each type of array complements the other's drawbacks. As a VBA developer, you have the flexibility to choose the right type of array for each situation: Fixed arrays are the way to go when the number of elements doesn't vary widely. On the other hand, use dynamic arrays when the number of elements varies widely and you're sure you have enough memory to resize even the largest possible arrays.

Advanced Function Techniques

The advanced function techniques covered in this section allow you to get the most out of the procedures you build. The section begins by discussing the difference between passing your parameters by reference and passing them by value. Notice that the default method of passing parameters isn't necessarily the most prudent method, and optional parameters allow you to build flexibility into your functions. The second part of this section shows you how to work with optional and named parameters. Optional parameters allow you to omit parameters, but named parameters allow you to add readability to your code. Named parameters also shelter you from having to worry about the order in which the parameters must appear. After reading this section, you'll be able to build much more robust and easy-to-use functions.

Passing By Reference Vs. Passing By Value

By default, parameters in Access are passed by reference. This means that a memory reference to the variable being passed is received by the function. This process is best illustrated by an example:

```
Sub PassByRef()
    Dim strFirstName As String
    Dim strLastName As String
    strFirstName = "Lars"
    strLastName = "Klander"
    Call SubByRef(strFirstName, strLastName)
    Debug.Print strFirstName
    Debug.Print strLastName
End Sub

Sub SubByRef(strFirstParm As String, strSecondParm As String)
    strFirstParm = "Dave"
    strSecondParm = "Mercer"
End Sub
```

You might be surprised that the **Debug.Print** statements found in the subroutine **PassByRef** print "Dave" and "Mercer". This is because **strFirstParm** is actually a reference to the same location in memory as **strFirstName**, and **strSecondParm** is a reference to the same location in memory as **strLastName**. This violates the concepts of black box processing; a variable shouldn't be changeable by any routine other than the one within which it was declared. The following code eliminates this problem:

```
Sub PassByVal()
   Dim strFirstName As String
   Dim strLastName As String
   strFirstName = "Lars"
   strLastName = "Klander"
   Call SubByVal(strFirstName, strLastName)
   Debug.Print strFirstName
   Debug.Print strLastName
End Sub

Sub SubByVal(ByVal strFirstParm As String, _
    ByVal strSecondParm As String)
  strFirstParm = "Dave"
  strSecondParm = "Mercer"
End Sub
```

The **SubByVal** subroutine receives the parameters by value. This means only the values in **strFirstName** and **strLastName** are passed to the **SubByVal** routine. The **strFirstName** and **strLastName** variables, therefore, can't be modified by the **SubByVal** subroutine. The **Debug.Print** statements print "Lars" and "Klander".

In general, avoid passing parameters by reference. However, doing so makes good sense at certain times. Consider the following case:

```
Sub GoodPassByRef()
  Dim blnSuccess As Boolean
  Dim strName As String

  strName = "Coriolis"
  blnSuccess = GoodFunc(strName)
  Debug.Print blnSuccess
End Sub

Function GoodFunc(strName As String)
   If Len(strName) Then
       strName = UCase$(strName)
```

```
      GoodFunc = True
   Else
      GoodFunc = False
   End If
End Function
```

In essence, the **GoodFunc** function needs to return two values. Not only does the function need to return the uppercase version of the string that's passed to it, but it also needs to return a success code. Because a function can return only one value, you need to be able to modify the value of **strName** within the function. As long as you're aware of what you're doing and why you're doing it, there's no problem with passing a parameter by reference.

Some developers use a special technique to help readers of their code easily see whether the calling procedure is passing parameters by reference or by value. When they pass parameters by reference, they refer to the parameters using the same name in both the calling routine and the actual procedure they're calling. On the other hand, when they pass parameters by value, they refer to the parameters using different names in the calling routine and in the procedure they're calling.

TIP: *You can explicitly use **ByRef** and **ByVal** keywords to make it clear to readers whether a parameter is passed by reference or by value.*

Optional Parameters: Building Flexibility Into Functions

Access 2000 allows you to use optional parameters. In other words, it isn't necessary to know how many parameters will be passed. The function called **ReturnInit** in the following code receives the second and third parameters as optional. It then evaluates whether the parameters are missing and responds accordingly.

```
Function ReturnInit(ByVal strFName As String, _
     Optional ByVal strMI, Optional ByVal strLName)
  If IsMissing(strMI) Then _
     strMI = InputBox("Enter Middle Initial")
  If IsMissing(strLName) Then _
     strLName = InputBox("Enter Last Name")
  ReturnInit = strLName & "," & strFName & " " & strMI
End Function
```

This function could be called as follows:

```
strName = ReturnInit("Dave",,"Mercer")
```

As you can see, the second parameter is missing. The **IsMissing** function, which is built into Access, determines whether a parameter has been passed. After identifying missing parameters, you must decide how to handle the situation in code. In the sample, the function prompts for the missing information. Other possible choices include the following:

• Insert default values when parameters are missing

• Accommodate missing parameters in your code

The following example shows how you can use default values with optional parameters:

```
Function ReturnInit2(ByVal strFName As String, _
    Optional ByVal strMI, Optional ByVal strLName)
  If IsMissing(strMI) Then _
    strMI = "B"
  If IsMissing(strLName) Then _
    strLName = "Jones"
  ReturnInit2 = strLName & "," & strFName & " " & strMI
End Function
```

The example uses a default value of "B" for the middle initial and a default last name of "Jones". The following example, rather than automatically assigning default values that are likely meaningless, returns different values based on whether the optional parameters were included in the call or not, as shown here:

```
Function ReturnInit3(ByVal strFName As String, _
    Optional ByVal strMI, Optional ByVal strLName)
  Dim strResult As String

  If IsMissing(strMI) And IsMissing(strLName) Then
    ReturnInit3 = strFName
  ElseIf IsMissing(strMI) Then
    ReturnInit3 = strLName & ", " & strFName
  ElseIf IsMissing(strLName) Then
    ReturnInit3 = strFName & " " & strMI
  Else
    ReturnInit3 = strLName & ", " & strFName & " " & strMI
  End If
End Function
```

This example manipulates the return value, depending on which parameters it receives. When neither optional parameter is passed, just the first name displays. If the first name and middle initial are passed, the return value contains the first name followed by the middle initial. When the first name and last name are passed, the return value contains the last name, a comma, and the first name. Passing all three parameters means the function returns the last name, a comma, a space, the first name, a space, and the middle initial.

Using Named Parameters

In all the instances you've seen thus far, the parameters to a procedure have been supplied positionally. Named parameters enable you to supply parameters without regard for their position. This is particularly useful with procedures that receive optional parameters. Consider the following code:

```
strName = ReturnInit("Dave",,"Mercer")
```

Because the second parameter isn't supplied and because the parameters are passed positionally, a comma must be used as a place marker for the optional parameter. This requirement can become unwieldy when you're dealing with several optional parameters. The following example greatly simplifies the process of passing the parameters and also serves to better document what's happening:

```
strName = ReturnInit3(strFName:= "Dave",strLName:= "Mercer")
```

When parameters are passed by name, it doesn't matter in what order the parameters appear, as in the following code:

```
strName = ReturnInit3(strLName:= "Mercer",strFName:="Dave")
```

This call to the **ReturnInit3** function yields identical results in the last case as the call does in the first case, because passing by name eliminates the order concerns.

When using named parameters, each parameter name must be exactly the same as the name of the parameter in the function being called. Besides requiring intimate knowledge of the function being called, this method of specifying parameters brings one important disadvantage. If the author of the function modifies the name of a parameter, all routines that use the named parameter when calling the function will fail.

WARNING!   *In general, very few programmers use named parameters, and it is not a particularly useful or clear coding practice to adopt. Unless you have a specific reason to use named parameters, you should generally avoid them within your programs.*

Working With Custom Properties

Property procedures enable you to create custom runtime properties of user-defined objects. After you have defined custom properties, use **Property Let** and **Get** to assign values to and to retrieve values from custom properties. Custom properties provide you with flexibility in creating your applications. You can create reusable objects that expose properties to other objects by using custom properties.

Custom properties are **Public** by default and are placed in Form or Report modules, making them visible to other modules in the current database. They aren't visible to other databases.

Using The Property Let Keyword Combination

Property Let is used to define a property procedure that assigns a value to a property of a user-defined object. Using a **Property Let** is similar to assigning a value to a Public variable, but a Public variable can be written to from anywhere in the database with little or no control over what's written to it. You can control exactly what happens when a value is assigned to the property by using a **Property Let** routine. Here's an illustration:

```
Property Let TextEnabled(blnEnabled As Boolean)
  Dim ctl As Control

  For Each ctl In Controls
    If TypeOf ctl Is TextBox Then _
        ctl.Enabled = blnEnabled
  Next ctl
End Property
```

This routine receives a **Boolean** parameter. It loops through each control in the controls collection, setting the **Enabled** property of each text box to True or False, depending on the value of the **Boolean** variable that it was passed. You might be thinking that this code looks just like a subroutine. You're actually somewhat correct. It's a special type of subroutine that executes automatically in response to the change in the value of a custom property. The following line of code causes the code within the **Property Let** procedure to execute:

```
Me.TextEnabled = False
```

The value False is received as a parameter to the **Property Let** routine. All the text boxes become disabled. The **TextEnabled** property of the form can be called from any module in the database, causing the **Property Let** routine to execute.

Using The Property Get Keyword

Just as you can use **Property Let** to set the value of a custom property, you can use **Property Get** to define a property procedure that retrieves a value from a property of a user-defined object. The following code illustrates how you can use **Property Get** to retrieve a property value:

```
Property Get TextBoxValues()
  Dim ctl As Control

  For Each ctl In Controls
    If TypeOf ctl Is TextBox Then _
        TextBoxValues = TextBoxValues & ctl.Name & _
          " = " & ctl.Value & Chr(13)
  Next ctl
End Property
```

The **Property Get** routine loops through each control on the form. It retrieves the name and value of each text box, building a return value that's a concatenated string with the names and values of all the text boxes. The call to the **Property Get** routine looks like this:

```
Debug.Print Me.TextBoxValues
```

When the **Debug.Print** command executes, it retrieves the value of the **TextBoxValues** property of the form. The **Property Get** routine automatically executes whenever the code attempts to retrieve the value of the property. This routine can be executed by retrieving the property from anywhere within the database.

Working With Empty And Null

Empty and **Null** are values that can exist only for **Variant** variables. They're different from one another and different from zero or a zero-length string. At times, you need to know whether the value stored in a variable is zero, a zero-length string, **Empty**, or **Null**. It's possible to make this differentiation only with **Variant** variables.

Working With Empty

Variant variables are initialized to the value of **Empty**. It's often important to ascertain whether a value has been stored into a **Variant** variable. If a variant has never been assigned a value, its value is **Empty**, but as mentioned, the **Empty** value isn't the same as **Zero**, **Null**, or a zero-length string. It's important to be able to test for **Empty** in a runtime environment by using the **IsEmpty** function. The following code tests a **String** variable to see whether it's **Empty**:

```
Sub StringVar()
  Dim sName As String

  Debug.Print IsEmpty(sName)      ' Prints False
  Debug.Print sName = ""          ' Prints True
End Sub
```

The first **Debug.Print** statement prints **False** because the variable is equal to a zero-length string from its time of initialization as a **String** variable. VBA initializes all **String** variables to a zero-length string. The next sample tests a **Variant** variable to see whether it's **Empty**, as shown here.

```
Sub EmptyVar()
  Dim vntName As Variant

  Debug.Print IsEmpty(vntName)      ' Prints True
  vntName = ""
  Debug.Print IsEmpty(vntName)      ' Prints False
  vntName = Empty
  Debug.Print IsEmpty(vntName)      ' Prints True
End Sub
```

A **Variant** variable loses its **Empty** value when any value has been stored to it, including zero, **Null**, or a zero-length string. It can become **Empty** again only by storing the keyword **Empty** into the variable.

Working With Null

Null is a special value used to indicate unknown or missing data. It's important to recognize that **Null** *isn't* the same as **Empty**. Furthermore, one **Null** value isn't equal to another **Null** value. **Variant** variables can contain the special value called **Null**.

It's often important to ascertain whether specific fields or controls have ever been initialized. Uninitialized fields and controls have a default value of **Null**. By testing for **Null**, you can ensure that fields and controls contain values.

If you want to make sure that all fields and controls in your application contain data, you need to test for **Nulls**. Do this by using the **IsNull** function, as shown here:

```
Sub NullVar()
  Dim vntName As Variant
```

```
   Debug.Print IsEmpty(vntName)      ' Prints True
   Debug.Print IsNull(vntName)       ' Prints False
   vntName = Null
   Debug.Print IsNull(vntName)       ' Prints True
End Sub
```

Notice that **vntName** is equal to **Null** only after the value of **Null** is explicitly stored to it. It's important to know not only how variables and **Null** values interact, but how you can test for **Null** within a field in your database. A field contains a **Null** if data hasn't yet been entered into the field and the field contains no default value. In queries, you can test for the criteria "Is Null" to find all the records in which a particular field contains a **Null** value. When dealing with recordsets, you can also use the **IsNull( )** function to test for a **Null** value in a field. Here's some code that shows how to do so:

```
Sub LoopProjects()
  Dim db As DATABASE
  Dim rs As Recordset

  Set db = CurrentDb
  Set rs = db.OpenRecordset("tblProjects", dbOpenDynaset)
  Do While Not rs.EOF
    Debug.Print rs![ProjectID], rs![ProjectName]
    If IsNull(rs!ProjectBeginDate) Then _
        Debug.Print "Project Begin Date Contains No Value!!"
    rs.MoveNext
  Loop
End Sub
```

This example uses DAO objects, which you'll learn about in the next chapter. For now, you need to understand only that this code loops through each record in **tblProjects**. It uses the **IsNull( )** function to evaluate whether the **ProjectBeginDate** field contains a **Null** value. If the field does contain a **Null**, a warning message is printed to the Debug window.

```
Private Sub Form_Current()
  Dim ctl As Control

  For Each ctl In Controls
    If TypeOf ctl Is TextBox Then
      If IsNull(ctl.Value) Then
        ctl.BackColor = 16776960
      Else
        ctl.BackColor = 16777215
      End If
```

```
      End If
    Next ctl
End Sub
```

The code above loops through every control on the current form. If the control is a text box, the routine checks to see whether the value within the text box is **Null**. When the value is **Null**, the **BackColor** property of the text box is set to Aqua; otherwise, it's set to White.

You should know about some special characteristics of **Null**:

• Expressions involving **Null** always result in **Null**.

• A function that's passed a **Null** usually returns a **Null**.

• **Null** values propagate through built-in functions that return **Variants**.

The following code illustrates the propagation of **Nulls**:

```
Sub PropNulls()
  Dim db As DATABASE
  Dim rs As Recordset

  Set db - CurrentDb
  Set rs - db.OpenRecordset("tblProjects", dbOpenDynaset)
  Do While Not rs.EOF
    Debug.Print rs![ProjectID], rs![ProjectBeginDate] + 1
    rs.MoveNext
  Loop
End Sub
```

It's very common to create a generic routine that receives any value, tests to see whether it's **Null**, and returns a non-**Null** value. An example is the **ConvertNulls( )** function, as shown here:

```
Function CvNulls(vntVar1 As Variant, vntVar2 As Variant) As Variant
  ConvertNulls - IIf(IsNull(vntVar1), vntVar2, vntVar1)
End Function
```

This routine would be called as follows:

```
Sub TestForNull(vntSalary As Variant, vntCommission As Variant)
  Dim curTotal As Currency

  curTotal - ConvertNulls(vntSalary, 0) + _
      ConvertNulls(vntCommission, 0)
  MsgBox curTotal
End Sub
```

The **TestForNull( )** routine receives two parameters: salary and commission. It adds the two values together to determine the total of salaries plus commissions. Ordinarily, if the value of either parameter is **Null**, the expression results in **Null**. This problem is eliminated by the **ConvertNulls( )** function, which receives two parameters. The first parameter is the variable that's being tested for **Null**. The second is the value that you want the function to return if the first parameter is determined to be **Null**. The routine uses the combination of the **IIf** function and the **IsNull( )** function to evaluate the first parameter and return the appropriate value.

Taking Advantage Of Compilation Options

Microsoft Access provides you with a few alternatives for compilation. Understanding these alternatives can help you to decide whether compilation speed or the trapping of compilation errors is more important to you.

Compile On Demand

By default, VBA compiles your code only when the code in the module changes or when a procedure in one module is called by another module. Although this default setting can dramatically speed the compilation process, it can leave you wondering if you have a hidden error lurking somewhere within your application.

Here's a typical scenario. You open a form, make some simple changes, save the changes, and close the form. You repeat this process for a few additional forms. You also open a couple of modules to make some equally simple changes. During the testing process, you forget to test one or more of the forms and one or more of the modules. With the Compile On Demand option set to True (its default value), any errors won't be identified until the offending code is accessed.

Compile Loaded Modules

Whether the Compile On Demand feature is on or off, the Compile Loaded Modules tool, found on the Visual Basic toolbar, compiles only loaded modules. This means that all open Access, Form, and Report modules are compiled. The code within any closed modules, forms, and reports isn't compiled. If an error is found in any open module, the compilation process terminates, an error message is displayed, and your cursor is placed on the offending line of code.

Compile All Modules

The Compile All Modules feature is found under the Run menu. This menu item, when selected, compiles every module in the database, regardless of whether it's open. To save all code in the database in its fully compiled state, you must open the database exclusively, select the Compile All Modules feature, and select the

File menu Save All Modules option. This procedure not only ensures that the modules compile successfully, it ensures that they're saved in their compiled state so they don't need to be compiled again when the application is run.

Customizing The Interactive Development Environment

Before Access 95, Access programmers were given little opportunity to customize the look and feel of the interactive development environment (IDE). Fortunately, Access 95 provided major improvements in this area, which Access 2000 has perpetuated and expanded upon. To view the environment options, select the Tools menu Options option. Figure 27.8 shows the Editor tab of the Options dialog box. The various aspects of the dialog (which appear on both the Editor tab and the Editor Format tab) are discussed in detail in the remainder of this section.

Setting Coding Options

The coding options available to you include Auto Syntax Check, Require Variable Declaration, Auto List Members, Auto Quick Info, Auto Data Tips, and Auto Indent.

The Auto Syntax Check feature determines whether Access performs a syntax check each time you press Enter after typing a single line of code. Many developers find this option annoying. Many times you type a line of code and notice a typo in a previous line of code. You want to rectify the error before you forget. You move off the incomplete line of code that you're typing, only to receive an error message that your syntax is incorrect. If you turn off Auto Syntax Check,

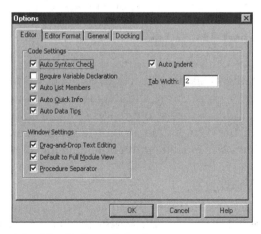

Figure 27.8   The Editor tab of the Options dialog box.

the editor will display the syntactically incorrect line in red, so you must simply watch your code closely.

The Require Variable Declaration option is a must. If this option is turned on, all variables must be declared before they're used. This important feature, when set, places the Option Explicit line in the Declarations section of every module. You're forced to declare all variables before they're used. Many innocent typos are identified by the compiler at compile time rather than by your users at runtime.

Finally, you can identify how many characters your text is indented each time the Tab key is pressed. Most programmers prefer a tab width of two over the default width of four. This slightly smaller tab width improves the readability of your code by consuming less screen real estate each time the Tab key is pressed.

Manipulating Code Color, Fonts, And Sizes

Access 2000 allows you to customize code colors, font, size, and tab width within the coding environment. It lets you specify the foreground and background colors for the Code window text, selection text, syntax error text, comment text, keyword text, and more. You can select from any of the Windows fonts and sizes for the text within the Code window.

All the customization options that have been discussed apply to the entire Access environment. This means that, when set, they affect all your databases.

Immediate Solutions

Changing The Editor's View Mode To Full Module View

To use the Full Module View environmental setting, perform the following steps:

1. From within VBA, select the Tools menu Options option. VBA will display the Options dialog box.

2. Within the Editor tab of the Options dialog box, click the Default to Full Module View option within the Window Settings frame. Click OK to exit the dialog box.

Setting The Editor To Automatically Require Explicit Declaration

In Access 2, it was necessary to manually enter the **Option Explicit** statement into each module, form, and report. You can globally instruct Access 2000 to insert the **Option Explicit** statement in all new modules, forms, and reports. To do so, perform the following steps:

1. From within VBA, select the Tools menu Options option. VBA will display the Options dialog box.

2. Within the Editor tab of the Options dialog box, click the Require Variable Declaration option. Click OK to exit the dialog box.

Accessing An Object's Event Code

As you've learned, you'll perform most responses to user actions from within event code for objects on your forms and reports. To access the event code of an object, perform the following steps:

1. Click on the object in Design view, and click on the Properties button on the toolbar, or right-click on the object and select Properties from the context-sensitive menu. Access 2000 will display the Properties dialog box.

2. Click on the Event properties tab.

3. Within the Event properties tab, select the property for which you want to write code (for example, the On Click event). Access 2000 will display a drop-down list.

4. Select Event Procedure from the drop-down list.

5. Click on the Ellipsis button. You're placed in the event code for that object.

Setting Up Compiler Directives

To set up a compiler directive, you can use either the Project Properties dialog box or code. To set up compiler directives from the Project Properties dialog box, perform the following steps:

1. If the VBA IDE isn't currently displaying the Project Explorer window, select the View menu Project Explorer option or press Ctrl+R. VBA will display the Project Explorer window.

2. Within the Project Explorer window, right-click the mouse on the Project name. VBA will display a pop-up menu.

3. Within the pop-up menu, select the Properties option. VBA will display the Project Properties dialog box, as shown in Figure 27.9.

4. Add the compiler directive to the Conditional Compilation Arguments text box. You can add more than one directive by separating each one with a colon. As mentioned, compiler directives entered in this way can contain only integers.

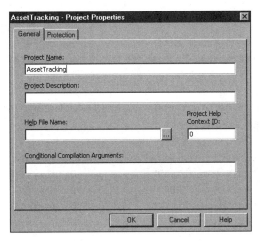

Figure 27.9   The Project Properties dialog box.

Alternately, you can set compiler directives within your program code. The code that you might create would look similar to the following:

```
Sub ConditionalIf()
  #If Language = 1 Then
    MsgBox "Hola, Que Tal?"
  #Else
    MsgBox "Hello, How Are You?"
  #End If
End Sub
```

Notice that **ConditionalIf** now evaluates the constant **Language** against the integer of 1.

VBA Commonly Used Functions

As you've learned, VBA includes complete support for most Visual Basic functions. Though the functions that VBA supports are far to numerous to detail here, the following sections explain some of the most commonly used functions.

Using The **Format** Function

The **Format** function formats expressions in the style you specify. The first parameter is the expression you want to format. The second parameter is the type of format you want to apply. The following procedure shows some examples of using the **Format** function with predefined values.

```
Sub FormatData()
  Debug.Print Format$(50, "Currency")      ' Prints $50.00
  Debug.Print Format$(Now, "Short Date")   ' Prints 2/4/96
End Sub
```

You can also create your own custom formats with the **Format** function, as shown in the following procedure:

```
Sub CustomFormatData()
  Debug.Print Format$(Now, "DDDD")    ' Displays the word for the day
  Debug.Print Format$(Now, "DDD")     ' Displays 3 - CHAR Day
  Debug.Print Format$(Now, "YYYY")    ' Displays 4 - digit Year
  Debug.Print Format$(Now, "WW")      ' Displays the Week Number
End Sub
```

Using The **Instr** Function

The **Instr** function returns the position in which one string resides within another. You'll often use the **Instr** function together with looping constructs to search strings for multiple occurrences of a matching string or to perform other advanced string operations. The following procedure shows how you might use the **Instr** function:

```
Sub InStrings()
  Debug.Print InStr("Lars Klander", "Klander") ' Returns 6
  Debug.Print InStr("Hello", "l")              ' Returns 3
End Sub
```

Note that **Instr** returns a 1-based value—meaning that the first character in the string is the 1 character, rather than the 0 character.

Using the **Left** Function

Your programs will often need to return certain portions of a string that you specify. You can use the **Left** (or **Left$**) function to return characters from the left-hand side of a string. **Left** returns the left-most number of characters that you specify from a string within a **Variant** (which VBA will automatically interpret as a **String**).

```
Sub LeftExample()
  Debug.Print Left("Hello World", 5)      ' Prints Hello
End Sub
```

If you know the value you're manipulating is a **String** (and not a **Variant**), you can use the **Left$** function (which is slightly faster than **Left**), as shown here:

```
Sub LeftExample()
  Dim HelloString As String

  HelloString = "Hello World"
  Debug.Print Left$(HelloString, 5)      ' Prints Hello
End Sub
```

Using The **Right** And **Right$** Functions

Just as you'll often need to return characters from the left side of a string, you'll also need to return characters from the right side of a string. The **Right** and **Right$** functions return the right-most number of characters in a string, as shown here:

```
Sub RightExample()
  Dim HelloVar
  Dim HelloString As String
```

```
        HelloVar = "Hello World"
        HelloString = "Hello World"
        Debug.Print Right(HelloVar, 5)        ' Prints World
        Debug.Print Right$(HelloString, 5)    ' Prints World
End Sub
```

Using The **Mid** And **Mid$** Functions

You'll often want to retrieve characters from some point in a string that's not the absolute left or absolute right side of the string. The **Mid** and **Mid$** functions return a substring of a specified number of characters in a string. This example starts at the fourth character and returns five characters:

```
Sub MidExample()
    Debug.Print Mid$("Hello World", 4, 5) 'Prints lo Wo
End Sub
```

Using The **UCase** Function

Sometimes, depending on your program's processing, you'll want to force all characters that appear within strings to be uppercase characters. In such situations, you can use the **UCase** function, which returns a string that's all uppercase, as shown here:

```
Sub UCaseExample()
    Debug.Print UCase$("Hello World")      ' Prints HELLO WORLD
End Sub
```

VBA also supports the **LCase** function that performs similar processing. However, **LCase** forces all characters in the string to be lowercase, rather than uppercase.

Using The **DatePart** Function

Historically, parsing dates and returning meaningful and accurate information has been a significant challenge for the programmer. However, VBA provides you with the **DatePart** function that you can use with variables of type **Date** or type **Variant** (providing the **Variant** contains a valid date value). The **DatePart** function returns the specified part of a date, as shown here:

```
Sub DatePartExample()
    Debug.Print DatePart("YYYY", Now)      ' Prints the Year
    Debug.Print DatePart("M", Now)         ' Prints the Month Number
    Debug.Print DatePart("Q", Now)         ' Prints the Quarter Number
    Debug.Print DatePart("Y", Now)         ' Prints the Day of the Year
    Debug.Print DatePart("WW", Now)        ' Prints the Week of the Year
End Sub
```

Using The **DateDiff** Function

Just as parsing dates used to be difficult for programmers, finding the difference—in days, minutes, hours, months, and so on—between two dates has always been challenging. Luckily, VBA provides the **DateDiff** function that helps you determine the interval of time between two dates. The **DateDiff** function is implemented as shown in the following example:

```
Sub DateDiffExample()
  Debug.Print DateDiff("d", Now, "12/31/99")      ' Days until 12/31/99
  Debug.Print DateDiff("m", Now, "12/31/99")      ' Months until 12/31/99
  Debug.Print DateDiff("yyyy", Now, "12/31/99")   ' Years until 12/31/99
  Debug.Print DateDiff("q", Now, "12/31/99")      ' Quarters until 12/31/99
End Sub
```

Using The **DateAdd** Function

Just as you'll often want to know the interval of time between two dates, you'll often want to add a fixed numbers of days or months or other time units to a date and yield the correct new date. VBA provides the **DateAdd** function that your programs can use to obtain the result of adding or subtracting a specified period of time to a date. The **DateAdd** function is implemented as shown here:

```
Sub DateAddExample()
  Debug.Print DateAdd("d", 3, Now)      ' Today plus 3 days
  Debug.Print DateAdd("m", 3, Now)      ' Today plus 3 months
  Debug.Print DateAdd("yyyy", 3, Now)   ' Today plus 3 years
  Debug.Print DateAdd("q", 3, Now)      ' Today plus 3 quarters
  Debug.Print DateAdd("ww", 3, Now)     ' Today plus 3 weeks
End Sub
```

Using The Object Browser

As you've learned, you can use the Object Browser to browse the functions available to your application. The following steps enable you to browse the available functions, select the function you want, and insert it into your code:

1. Select Object Browser from the toolbar or press F2. The Object Browser window appears.

2. Use the Libraries/Databases drop-down to select the library or database whose properties and methods you want to view.

3. The Object Browser window is divided into two parts. Select the module or class from the left list box.

27. Using Modules And Visual Basic For Applications

4. Select a property or method associated with that module or class from the right list box. Notice that the function and its parameters appear below the list boxes.

5. Click Paste Text to paste the function and its parameters into your code.

Opening The Find And Replace Dialog Box

You can simplify locating and changing values within your applications with the Find and Replace dialog box. To invoke the Find dialog box, select the Edit menu Find option or press Ctrl+F. The Find dialog appears in Figure 27.10.

Type the text you want to find in the Find What text box. Notice that you can search within the Current Procedure, Current Module, Current Database, or Selected Text. The Find Whole Word Only option tells the search engine not to find the text if it's part of another piece of text. For instance, if you select the Find Whole Word Only option and search for "Count", VBA doesn't find "Counter". Other options include toggles for case sensitivity and pattern matching.

To open the Replace dialog box, you can either click on the Replace button within the Find dialog box or press Ctrl+H.

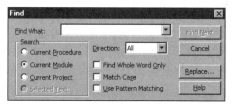

Figure 27.10   The Find dialog box within the VBA IDE.

Working With User-Defined Types

You'll often use user-defined types to clarify and simplify your program code. Within the next few sections, you'll learn how to create, declare, and effectively manipulate user-defined types.

Declaring A User-Defined Type

You declare a user-defined type using a **Type** statement. This statement must be placed in the Declarations Section of a module. The type can be declared as **Public** or **Private**. Types can't be placed in Form or Report modules. The **Type** statement will conform to the following prototype:

```
[Private | Public] Type VariableName
  ElementName1 [([subscripts])] As ElementType
  ElementName2 [([subscripts])] As ElementType
  [Further Element Names]
End Type
```

Creating A **Type** Variable

A **Type** variable is an instance of the type in memory. A **Type** variable must be declared before you can use the type by creating a Local, **Private**, Module-Level, or **Public** variable based on the type. Depending on where you place this declaration and how you declare it (**Dim**, **Private**, or **Public**), you'll determine its scope. All the same rules that apply to any other kind of variable apply to **Type** variables. For example, the following code creates a variable called **typChapter27** of user-defined type **ChapterStructures**.

```
Dim typChapter27 As ChapterStructures
```

If you place this **Dim** statement in the General Declarations section of a module, it's visible to all routines within that module. By placing it in a subroutine or function, it's local to that particular routine.

Storing Information From A Record Or Form Into A **Type**

After a **Type** variable has been declared, you can store data into each of its elements. The following code stores information from the form called **frmTimeCardHours** into a **Type** variable called **typTimeCardData**:

```
Private Sub cmdWriteToType_Click()
  Dim typTimeCardData As TimeCardInfo

  With typTimeCardData
    .TimeCardDetailID = Me!TimeCardDetailID
    .TimeCardID = Me!TimeCardID
    .DateWorked = Me!DateWorked
    .ProjectID = Me!ProjectID
    .WorkDescription = Me!WorkDescription
    .BillableHours = Me!BillableHours
    .BillingRate = Me!BillingRate
    .WorkCodeID = Me!WorkCodeID
  End With
End Sub
```

This code's advantage is that rather than creating eight variables to store these eight pieces of related information, it creates one variable with eight elements.

Retrieving Information From The Elements Of A **Type**

To retrieve information from your **Type** variable, simply refer to the name of the **Type** variable, followed by a period then the name of the element. The following code displays a message box containing all the time-card hour information:

```
Private Sub cmdDisplayFromType_Click()
  With typTimeCardData
    MsgBox "Timecard Detail ID Is" & .TimeCardDetailID & Chr(13) & _
        "Timecard ID Is " & .TimeCardID & Chr(13) & _
        "Date Worked Is " & .DateWorked & Chr(13) & _
        "Project ID Is " & .ProjectID & Chr(13) & _
        "Work Description Is " & Trim(.WorkDescription) & Chr(13) & _
        "Billable Hours Is " & .BillableHours & Chr(13) & _
        "Billing Rate Is " & .BillingRate & Chr(13) & _
        "Workcode ID Is " & .WorkCodeID
  End With
End Sub
```

Defining Your Own Constants

As mentioned previously in this chapter, a symbolic constant is declared using the **Const** keyword. A constant can be declared in a subroutine or function. It can also be declared in the General section of a Form or Report module. Constants can be strong-typed in Access 2000. The naming convention for constants consists of a suitable scoping prefix, the letter **c** to indicate that you're working with a constant rather than a variable, and the appropriate tag for the data type. The declaration and use of a **Private** constant would look like the following:

```
Private Const mccurTaxRate As Currency = .0875
```

This code, when placed in the Declarations section of a module, creates a **Private** constant called **mccurTaxRate** and sets it equal to .0875. An illustration of the constant used in code looks like this:

```
Function TotalAmount(curSaleAmount As Currency)
    TotalAmount = curSaleAmount + (curSaleAmount * mccurTaxRate)
End Function
```

This routine multiplies the **curSaleAmount**, received in as a parameter, by the constant **mccurTaxRate**. It returns the result of the calculation by setting the function name equal to the current sale amount plus the product of the two values. The advantage of the constant in this scenario is that the code is more readable than simply typing **TotalAmount = curSaleAmount + (curSaleAmount * .0875)**.

Viewing Intrinsic Constants

To view the constants that are part of the VBA language, select VBA from the Databases/Libraries drop-down of the Object Browser. Within the left-hand list box, select any of the available modules, classes, and enumerations. On the right-side, you'll see additional information. Constants are indicated by a gray box with an equal sign on the inside. For example, Figure 27.11 shows the Object Browser after selecting the **vbBlack** color constant.

Notice that all constant names begin with **vb**. All VBA constants are prefixed with **vb**, all Data Access Object constants are prefixed with **db**, and all constants that are part of the Access language are prefixed with **ac**. To view the Access language constants, select Access from the Databases/Libraries drop-down. To view the ActiveX Data Objects collection, select ADODB from the Databases/Libraries drop-down. To view the Data Access Object constants, add a reference to DAO to the project, then select DAO from the Databases/Libraries drop-down.

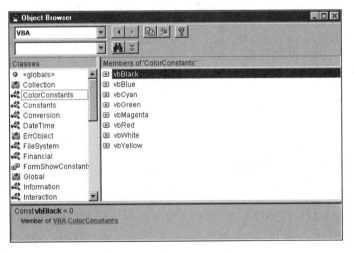

Figure 27.11   The **vbBlack** constant within the Object Browser.

Declaring And Working With Fixed Arrays

When declaring a fixed array, you give VBA the upper bound and the type of data that it will contain. The following code creates an array that holds six string variables:

```
Dim astrNames(5) As String
```

This array is fixed in that its size can't be altered at runtime. The following code gives an example of how you can loop through the array:

```
Sub FixedArray()
  Dim astrNames(5) As String
  Dim intCounter As Integer

  astrNames(0) = "Chewie"
  astrNames(1) = "Nana"
  astrNames(2) = "Kimba"
  astrNames(3) = "Savannah"
  For intCounter = 0 To UBound(astrNames)
    Debug.Print astrNames(intCounter)
  Next intCounter
End Sub
```

This code starts by storing values into the first four elements of a six-element array. It then loops through each element of the array, printing the contents. Notice that the **For...Next** loop starts at zero and goes until the upper bound of the array (5). Because the array is an array of strings, the last two elements of the array contain zero-length strings. If the array were an array of integers, the last two elements would contain zeros.

Another way to traverse the array is to use the **For Each...Next** construct. Your code would look like this:

```
Sub ArrayWith()
  Dim astrNames(5) As String
  Dim intCounter As Integer
  Dim vntAny As Variant

  astrNames(0) = "Chewie"
  astrNames(1) = "Nana"
  astrNames(2) = "Kimba"
  astrNames(3) = "Savannah"
  For Each vntAny In astrNames
```

```
    Debug.Print vntAny
  Next vntAny
End Sub
```

This code declares a **Variant** variable called **vntAny**. Instead of using a loop with **UBound** as the upper delimiter to traverse the array, the example uses the **For Each...Next** construct to traverse the array.

Declaring And Working With Dynamic Arrays

To create a dynamic array, you declare the array without assigning an upper bound. You do this by omitting the number between the parentheses when declaring the array. Here's an example:

```
Sub DynamicArray()
  Dim astrNames() As String
  Dim intCounter As Integer
  Dim vntAny As Variant

  ReDim astrNames(1)
  astrNames(0) = "Chewie"
  astrNames(1) = "Nana"
  For Each vntAny In astrNames
    Debug.Print vntAny
  Next vntAny
End Sub
```

A potential problem occurs when you try to resize the array:

```
Sub ResizeDynamic()
  Dim astrNames() As String
  Dim intCounter As Integer
  Dim vntAny As Variant

  ReDim astrNames(1)
  astrNames(0) = "Chewie"
  astrNames(1) = "Nana"
  ReDim astrNames(3)
  astrNames(2) = "Kimba"
  astrNames(3) = "Savannah"
  For Each vntAny In astrNames
    Debug.Print vntAny
  Next vntAny
End Sub
```

27. Using Modules And Visual Basic For Applications

You might expect that all four elements will contain data. Instead, the **ReDim** statement reinitializes all the elements, and only elements two and three will contain values. This problem can be avoided with the **Preserve** keyword. The following code behaves quite differently:

```
Sub ResizePreserve()
  Dim astrNames() As String
  Dim intCounter As Integer
  Dim vntAny As Variant

  ReDim astrNames(1)
  astrNames(0) = "Chewie"
  astrNames(1) = "Nana"

  ReDim Preserve astrNames(3)
  astrNames(2) = "Kimba"
  astrNames(3) = "Savannah"
  For Each vntAny In astrNames
    Debug.Print vntAny
  Next vntAny
End Sub
```

In this example, all values already stored in the array are preserved. The **Preserve** keyword brings its own difficulties, though. It can temporarily require huge volumes of memory, because during the **ReDim** process VBA creates a copy of the original array. All the values from the original array are copied to a new array. The original array is removed from memory when the process is complete. The **Preserve** keyword can present problems if you're dealing with very large arrays in a limited memory situation.

Disabling Compile On Demand

To disable the Compile On Demand feature, select the Tools menu Options option. Select the General tab and remove the check from Compile On Demand. You might notice a degradation in performance each time your code compiles, but this is time well spent.

Chapter 28

Working With DAO And ADO

In Depth

As you saw in Chapter 27, you can use the VBA programming language to perform advanced processing in your Access 2000 applications. When you perform such processing, you'll commonly find a need to manipulate database objects from code. Early versions of Microsoft Access, through Microsoft Access 97, supported the Data Access Objects (DAO), an object model that was directly tied to the Microsoft Jet engine, as the means of accessing Access databases. Understanding how to use DAO is crucial for working with Access databases developed in any of these earlier versions.

However, Microsoft introduced ActiveX Data Objects (ADO), a part of the object linking and embedding (OLE) DB object model, with Visual Studio 97 early in that year. Since that time, ADO has been extensively improved and expanded upon. Microsoft has indicated that there'll be no new versions of the DAO standard released, and that developers should use ADO for all new applications they design within Access 2000. In this chapter, you'll learn about DAO, how the model is formed, and how to use it. You'll also learn about ADO, the nature of the model, and how to use it. In the "Immediate Solutions" section of this chapter, you'll learn how to perform common tasks using DAO and ADO. The chapter will discuss DAO first because it's simpler, and you're more likely to be familiar with it.

Introduction To Data Access Objects

Data Access Objects are used to create, modify, and remove Jet engine objects through program code. They provide you with the flexibility of moving beyond the user interface to accomplish the manipulation of data and Jet engine objects. They can be used to perform the following tasks:

• Analyze the structure of an existing database

• Add or modify tables and queries

• Create new databases

• Change the underlying definitions for queries by modifying the Structured Query Language (SQL) on which the query is based

• Traverse through sets of records

• Modify table data

The Data Access Object Model

Figure 28.1 shows an overview of the Data Access Object Model for the Jet database engine—in Access 2000, the DAO 3.6 object library. At the top of the hierarchy is the Microsoft Jet database engine, referred to as the **DBEngine** object. The **DBEngine** object contains all the other objects that are part of the hierarchy. It's the only object that doesn't have an associated collection.

Each object within the Data Access Object Model is important to you because you'll manipulate the various objects at runtime using code so you can accomplish the tasks required by your application. The following is a description of each major object and how it affects you in your programming endeavors.

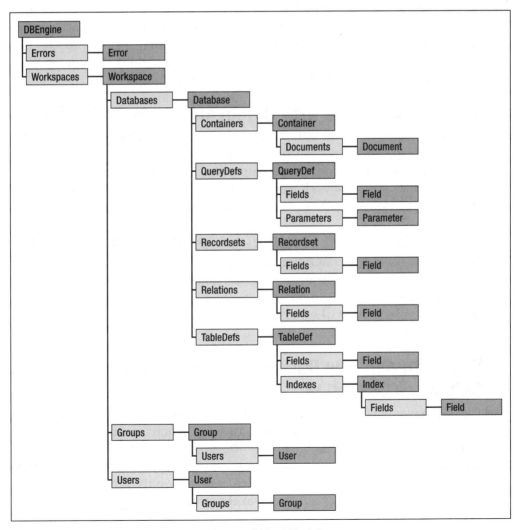

Figure 28.1   An overview of the Data Access Object Model.

WARNING!   *Because Microsoft is gradually phasing out DAO as a development platform, you'll find that you must add the DAO 3.6 Object Library to your projects from the Tools menu References option if you intend to use DAO within your projects. By default, Access 2000 will only load the ADO 2 library when you start a VBA project.*

Understanding The Workspace Object And Workspaces Collection

The **Workspaces** collection contains **Workspace** objects. Each **Workspace** object defines the area within which a particular user operates. All security and transaction processing for a given user takes place within a particular **Workspace**. You can create multiple **Workspaces** within your programs. This is of great value because, using this technique, you can log in as another user behind the scenes and accomplish tasks not allowed by the security level of the current user. For example, you can log in as a member of the Admins group, change the structure of a table that the current user doesn't have rights to, and log back out without the user of the system ever knowing that anything happened.

Understanding The User Object And Users Collection

The **Users** collection contains the **User** objects for a particular **Workspace**. Each **User** object represents a user account defined by a workgroup database. Because each user is a member of one or more groups, each **User** object contains a **Groups** collection that consists of each group that a particular user is a member of. **User** objects can be easily added and manipulated at runtime.

Understanding The Group Object And Groups Collection

The **Groups** collection contains all **Group** objects for a particular **Workspace**. Each **Group** object represents a group defined by a workgroup database. Because each group contains users, the **Group** object contains a **Users** collection that consists of each user who's a member of the group. Like **User** objects, **Group** objects can be added and manipulated at runtime.

Understanding The Database Object And Databases Collection

The **Databases** collection contains all the databases that are currently open within a particular **Workspace**. Multiple databases (and, therefore, multiple database objects) can be opened at the same time. These open databases can be either Jet databases or external databases. A **Database** object refers to a particular database within the **Databases** collection. It's easy to loop through the **Databases** collection, printing the name of each **Database** object contained within the collection. The code to do so might look similar to the following:

```
Sub EnumerateDBs()
  Dim wksLocal As Workspace
  Dim dbsLocal As Database
  Dim dbsLocal1 As Database
  Dim dbsLocal2 As Database

  Set wksLocal = DBEngine(0)
  Set dbsLocal1 = CurrentDb
  Set dbsLocal2 = ws.OpenDatabase("Northwind.MDB")
  For Each dbsLocal In wksLocal.Databases
    Debug.Print dbsLocal.Name
  Next dbsLocal
End Sub
```

This code loops through each open database within the current **Workspace** printing the name of each open database. It's also easy to perform all the other tasks required to build, modify, and manipulate database objects at runtime.

TIP: The **CurrentDb( )** function returns the currently-selected database, which in the case of VBA applications will be the database that the VBA program code is associated with. You'll learn more about the **CurrentDb( )** function later in this chapter.

Understanding The TableDef Object And TableDefs Collection

The **TableDefs** collection contains all the tables contained within a particular database. This includes all tables, whether they're open or not. The **TableDefs** collection also includes linked tables containing detailed information about each table. It's easy to loop through the **TableDefs** collection, printing various properties (for instance, the name) of each **TableDef** object contained within the collection. The code to do so might look similar to the following:

```
Sub EnumerateTables()
  Dim dbsLocal As Database
  Dim tblLocal As TableDef

  Set dbsLocal = CurrentDb
  For Each tblLocal In dbsLocal.TableDefs
    Debug.Print tblLocal.Name
  Next tblLocal
End Sub
```

This code loops through each **TableDef** in the current database, printing the name of each table in the database. It's easy to write code that adds, deletes, modifies, and otherwise manipulates tables at runtime.

TIP: *You'll find, as you work with **TableDefs**, that there are certain system-level tables in every Jet database that the database engine will create for you automatically. You'll be able to enumerate these tables and even print out their names within your programs, but you won't be able to directly modify these tables.*

Understanding The QueryDef Object And QueryDefs Collection

The **QueryDefs** collection contains all the queries contained within a particular database, as well as information about each query. It's easy to loop through the **QueryDefs** collection, printing various pieces of information about each query. The code for doing so would look like the following:

```
Sub EnumerateQueries()
  Dim dbsLocal As Database
  Dim qryLocal As QueryDef

  Set dbsLocal = CurrentDb
  For Each qryLocal In dbsLocal.QueryDefs
    Debug.Print qryLocal.Name
    Debug.Print qryLocal.SQL
  Next qryLocal
End Sub
```

This code loops through each **QueryDef** in the current database, and it prints the name and SQL statement associated with each **QueryDef**. It's easy to write code that adds, deletes, modifies, and otherwise manipulates queries at runtime.

Understanding The Field Object And Fields Collection

Fields collections are contained within the **TableDef**, **QueryDef**, **Index**, **Relation**, and **Recordset** objects. The **Fields** collection of an object is the collection of **Field** objects within the parent object. For example, a **TableDef** object contains **Field** objects that are contained within the specific table. Using the parent object, you can obtain information about its **Fields** collection. You might implement this technique as shown here:

```
Sub EnumFields()
  Dim dbsLocal As Database
  Dim tblLocal As TableDef
  Dim fldLocal As Field
  Set dbsLocal = CurrentDb
  For Each tblLocal In dbsLocal.TableDefs
    For Each fldLocal In tblLocal.Fields
      Debug.Print fldLocal.Name
```

```
        Debug.Print fldLocal.Type
      Next fldLocal
   Next tblLocal
End Sub
```

This code loops through each **TableDef** in the current database, printing the name and type of each field contained within the **Fields** collection of the **TableDef**. Code can also be used to add, delete, or change the attributes of fields at runtime.

Understanding The Parameter Object And Parameters Collection

As you know, Access queries can contain parameters created so the user can supply information required by the query at runtime. Each **QueryDef** object has a **Parameters** collection consisting of **Parameter** objects. You can write code to manipulate these parameters at runtime. The code looks similar to the following:

```
Sub EnumerateParameters()
   Dim dbsLocal As Database
   Dim qryLocal As QueryDef
   Dim prmLocal As Parameter

   Set dbsLocal = CurrentDb
   For Each qryLocal In dbsLocal.QueryDefs
     Debug.Print "*****" & qryLocal.Name & "*****"
     For Each prmLocal In qryLocal.Parameters
       Debug.Print prmLocal.Name
     Next prmLocal
   Next qryLocal
End Sub
```

This code loops through each **QueryDef** object within the current database. It prints the name of the **QueryDef** object then loops through its **Parameters** collection, printing the name of each parameter. **Parameter** objects can be added, deleted, and manipulated through code at runtime.

Understanding The Recordset Object And Recordsets Collection

Recordset objects exist only at runtime and are used to reference a set of records coming from one or more tables. The **Recordsets** collection contains all the **Recordset** objects currently open within the current **Database** object. **Recordset** objects are covered extensively later in this chapter.

Understanding The Relation Object And Relations Collection

The **Relations** collection contains all the **Relation** objects that describe the relationships established within a **Database** object. The following code loops through the current database, printing the **Table** and **ForeignTable** of each **Relation** object:

```
Sub EnumRelations()
  Dim dbsLocal As Database
  Dim relLocal As Relation

  Set dbsLocal = CurrentDb
  For Each relLocal In dbsLocal.Relations
    Debug.Print relLocal.Table & " Related To: " & relLocal.ForeignTable
  Next relLocal
End Sub
```

Relationships can be created, deleted, and modified at runtime using VBA code. However, you can only use DAO to do so.

Understanding The Container Object And Containers Collection

The **Containers** collection contains information about each saved **Database** object. Using the **Containers** collection, you can manipulate all the objects contained within the current database. Consider the following code, which does just that:

```
Sub EnumContainers()
  Dim dbsLocal As Database
  Dim cntLocal As Container

  Set dbsLocal = CurrentDb
  For Each cntLocal In dbsLocal.Containers
    Debug.Print cntLocal.Name
  Next cntLocal
End Sub
```

This code loops through the **Containers** collection, printing the name of each **Container** object. The results are Databases, Forms, Modules, Relationships, Reports, Scripts, Data Access Pages, SysRel, and Tables.

Understanding The Document Object And Documents Collection

A **Document** object represents a specific object in the **Documents** collection. You can loop through the **Documents** collection of a **Container** object. The code to do so might look similar to the following:

```
Sub EnumerateForms()
  Dim dbsLocal As Database
  Dim cntLocal As Container
  Dim docLocal As Document

  Set dbsLocal = CurrentDb
  Set cntLocal = dbsLocal.Containers!Forms
  For Each docLocal In cntLocal.Documents
    Debug.Print docLocal.Name
  Next docLocal
End Sub
```

This code sets a **Container** object to point to the forms within the current database. It then loops through each document in the **Container** object, printing the name of each **Document** object (in this case, the name of each form).

It's important to understand the difference between the **Forms** container and the **Forms** collection. The **Forms** container is part of the **Containers** collection, containing all the forms that are part of the database. The **Forms** collection contains all the forms open at runtime. The properties of each form in the **Forms** container differ from the properties of a form in the **Forms** collection.

Understanding The Property Object And The Properties Collection

Each Data Access Object has a **Properties** collection. The **Properties** collection of an object is a list of properties associated with that particular object. You can view or modify the properties of an object using its **Properties** collection. The code looks like this:

```
Sub EnumerateProperties()
  Dim dbsLocal As Database
  Dim cntLocal As Container
  Dim docLocal As Document
  Dim prpLocal As Property
  Set dbsLocal = CurrentDb
  Set cntLocal = dbsLocal.Containers!Forms
  For Each docLocal In cntLocal.Documents
    Debug.Print docLocal.Name
```

```
        For Each prpLocal In docLocal.Properties
           Debug.Print prpLocal.Name & " = " & prpLocal.Value
        Next prpLocal
     Next docLocal
  End Sub
```

This code loops through each form in the current database, printing all the properties of each **Form** object.

Understanding The Error Object And Errors Collection

The **Errors** collection consists of **Error** objects containing information about the most recent error that occurred. Each time an operation generates an error, the **Errors** collection is cleared of any previous errors. Sometimes a single operation can cause more than one error. For this reason, one or more **Error** objects might be added to the **Errors** collection when a single data access error occurs.

Understanding And Using The DBEngine Object

As mentioned, the **DBEngine** object refers to the Jet database engine, which is at the top of the Data Access Object hierarchy. The **DBEngine** object contains only two collections: **Workspaces** and **Errors**. When referring to the current database, you can use the **CurrentDB** function discussed in the next section, but when referring to any database other than the current database, you must refer to the **DBEngine** object, as in the following example:

```
Sub ReferToCurrentDB()
  Dim wksLocal As Workspace
  Dim dbsLocal As Database

  Set wksLocal = DBEngine(0)
  Set dbsLocal = wksLocal.OpenDatabase("Northwind.mdb")
  Debug.Print dbsLocal.Version
End Sub
```

This code creates a **Workspace** object variable that points at the current **Workspace**. The **OpenDatabase** method of the **Workspace** object is then used to open another database. The version of the database is printed by the routine.

Using The CurrentDB Function

Microsoft offers a shortcut you can use when creating an object variable that points to the current database. Using the **CurrentDB** function, you don't need to point at the **Workspace**, and you don't need to issue the **OpenDatabase** method.

Instead, set the **Database** object variable equal to the result from the **CurrentDB()** function. The code looks similar to the following (which you've seen a lot of throughout this chapter):

```
Sub UseCurrentDBFunc()
  Dim dbsLocal As Database
  Set dbsLocal = CurrentDb()
  Debug.Print dbsLocal.Version
End Sub
```

This code declares the **Database** object variable and then points it at the current database object. The **CurrentDB()** function can't be used to refer to objects that aren't part of the current database.

Understanding Recordset Types

A **Recordset** object is used to represent the records in a table or the records returned by a query. A **Recordset** object can be a direct link to the table, a dynamic set of records, or a snapshot of the data at a certain time. Recordset objects are used to directly manipulate data in a database. They let you add, edit, delete, and move through data as required by your application. Access 2000 supports three types of **Recordset** objects: Table, Dynaset, and Snapshot.

Using Dynaset-Type Recordsets

A **Recordset** object of the Dynaset type can be used to manipulate local or linked tables or the results of queries. A Dynaset is actually a set of references to table data that allows you to extract and update data from multiple tables, even tables from other databases. In fact, the tables in which data is included in a Dynaset can even come from databases that aren't of the same type (for example, Microsoft SQL Server, FoxPro, Paradox, and dBASE).

True to its name, a Dynaset is a dynamic set of records. This means that changes made to the Dynaset are reflected in the underlying tables, and changes made to the underlying tables by other users of the system are reflected in the Dynaset. Although a Dynaset isn't the fastest type of **Recordset** object, it's definitely the most flexible.

Using Snapshot-Type Recordsets

A **Recordset** object of the Snapshot type is similar to a Dynaset. The major difference is that the data included in the Snapshot is fixed at the time that it's created. The data within the Snapshot, therefore, can't be modified and isn't updated when other users make changes to the underlying tables. This trait can be an advantage or disadvantage. It's a disadvantage, of course, if it's necessary for the data in the recordset to be updatable. It's an advantage if you're running a report and want to ensure that the data doesn't change during the time in which the report is being run. You can, therefore, create a Snapshot and build the report from the Snapshot-type **Recordset** object.

Snapshots are more efficient with small result sets than Dynasets because, by nature, a Snapshot object creates less processing overhead. But regardless of their reduced overhead, Snapshots are actually less efficient than Dynasets when returning a result set with a large volume of data (generally over 500 records). This is because when you create a Snapshot object, all fields are returned to the user as each record is accessed. On the other hand, a Dynaset object contains a set of primary keys for the records in the result set. The other fields are returned to the user only when they're required for editing or display.

Using Table-Type Recordsets

A **Recordset** object of the Table type is often used to manipulate local or linked tables created using Microsoft Access or the Jet database engine. When you open a Table-type **Recordset** object, all operations are performed directly on the table.

Certain operations, such as a **Seek**, can be performed only on a Table type of recordset. You get the best performance for sorting and filtering records when using a Table type of recordset.

The downside of a Table type of recordset is that it can contain the data from only one table. It can't be opened using a Join or Union query. It also can't be used with tables created using engines other than Jet (for example, open database connectivity [ODBC] and other indexed sequential access method [ISAM] data sources).

Selecting Among The Types Of Recordset Objects Available

Deciding which type of recordset to use involves looking at the task to determine which type of recordset is most appropriate. When fast searching is most important and retrieving all the records isn't a problem, a Table is the best choice. If you must retrieve the results of a query and your result set needs to be editable, a Dynaset is the best choice. And when there's no need for the results to be updated but the results must consist of a relatively small subset of the data, a Snapshot is most appropriate.

Working With Recordset Properties And Methods

Like other objects, **Recordset** objects have properties and methods. The properties are the attributes of the **Recordset** objects, and the methods are the actions you can take on the **Recordset** objects. Some properties are read only at runtime; others can be read from and written to at runtime.

Creating A Recordset Variable

When working with a recordset, you must first create a **Recordset** variable. The **OpenRecordset( )** method is used to create a **Recordset** object variable. You must first declare a generic **Recordset** variable then point a specific recordset at the variable using a **Set** statement. The code to do so will generally look similar to the following:

```
Sub OpenTable()
  Dim dbsInfo As Database
  Dim rstClients As Recordset

  Set dbsInfo = CurrentDb()
  Set rstClients = dbsInfo.OpenRecordset("tblClients")
  Debug.Print rstClients.Updatable
End Sub
```

This code creates a **Database** object variable and a **Recordset** object variable. It then uses the **CurrentDB** function to point the **Database** object variable to the current database. Next, it uses the **OpenRecordset** method to assign the recordset based on **tblClients** to the object variable **rstClients**.

The type of recordset created is determined by the default type for the object or by a second parameter of the **OpenRecordset** method. If the **OpenRecordset** method is executed on a table and no second parameter is specified, the recordset is opened as the Table type. When the **OpenRecordset** method is performed on a query and no second parameter is specified, the recordset is opened as the Dynaset type. This default behavior can be overridden by passing a second parameter to the **OpenRecordset** method. The code to override the default behavior of **OpenRecordset** might look similar to the following:

```
Sub OpenDynaSet()
  Dim dbsInfo As Database
  Dim rstClients As Recordset
```

```
    Set dbsInfo = CurrentDb()
    Set rstClients = dbsInfo.OpenRecordset("tblClients", dbOpenDynaset)
    Debug.Print rstClients.Updatable
End Sub
```

This code opens the recordset as a Dynaset. The DAO library defines **dbOpenTable**, **dbOpenDynaset**, and **dbOpenSnapshot** as intrinsic constants you can use to open a **Recordset** object. A query can be opened only as a Dynaset or Snapshot **Recordset** object. The code to open a recordset based on a query (or a **QueryDef** object) appears as follows:

```
Sub OpenQuery()
  Dim dbsInfo As Database
  Dim rstClients As Recordset

  Set dbsInfo = CurrentDb()
  Set rstClients = dbsInfo.OpenRecordset("qryHoursByProject",
dbOpenSnapshot)
  Debug.Print rstClients.Updatable
End Sub
```

Finally, you can also open a **Recordset** object by passing in a SQL string. The **Recordset** object will return the results of the query as if you entered it within the SQL window of the Query designer. For example, you might use code similar to the following to create a recordset based on an incoming variable:

```
Sub OpenQuery(strQryParam as String)
  Dim dbsInfo As Database
  Dim rstEmployees As Recordset

  Set dbsInfo = CurrentDb()
  Set rstEmployees = _
      dbsInfo.OpenRecordset("Select * From tblStaff " & _
      "Where [Employee] Like '" & _
      strQueryParam & "'", _
      dbOpenSnapshot)
  Debug.Print rstEmployees.Updatable
End Sub
```

This code creates a **Database** object variable and a **Recordset** object variable. It then uses the **CurrentDB** function to point the **Database** object variable to the current database. Next, it uses the **OpenRecordset** method to assign the recordset based on the SQL statement and the incoming parameter to the object variable **rstEmployees**.

Understanding The Arguments That OpenRecordset Accepts

Microsoft provides several arguments that control the way in which a recordset is opened. The arguments and their uses are detailed in Table 28.1.

*Table 28.1   The constant arguments you can use with the **OpenRecordset** method.*

Constant	Usage
dbAppendOnly	When this option is used, records can be added to the recordset only. Existing data can't be displayed or modified. This option is useful when you want to ensure that existing data isn't affected by the processing. This option applies to Dynasets only.
dbSeeChanges	This option ensures that a user receives an error if the code issues an **Edit** method and another user modifies the data before an **Update** method is used. It is useful in a high-traffic environment when it's likely that two users will modify the same record at the same time. You can apply this option to Dynaset and Table recordsets only.
dbDenyWrite	When creating a Dynaset or Snapshot, this option prevents all other users from modifying the records contained with the recordset until the recordset is closed. Other users are still able to view the data contained within the recordset. When this option is applied to a Table type of recordset, other users are prevented from opening the underlying table.
dbDenyRead	Using this constant prevents other users from even reading the data contained within the recordset as long as the recordset remains open. This option can be used only on Table recordsets.
dbReadOnly	This option prevents your recordset from modifying data. If you don't want the data within the recordset to be updatable but you expect a large number of records to be returned and you want to take advantage of the record paging offered by Dynasets, you might want to open the recordset as a Dynaset.
dbForwardOnly	This argument creates a forward-scrolling Snapshot. This type of recordset is fast but limited in that you can use only the **Move** and **MoveNext** methods to move directly through the Snapshot.
dbSQLPassThrough	When the source of the recordset is a SQL statement, this argument passes the SQL statement to an ODBC database for processing. This option doesn't completely eliminate Jet; it simply prevents Jet from making any changes to the SQL statement before passing it on to the ODBC Drive Manager. The **dbSQLPassThrough** argument can be used only with Snapshots and read-only Dynasets.
dbConsistent	This argument applies to Dynasets. It allows consistent updates only. This is the default argument for Dynasets.
dbInconsistent	This argument allows for inconsistent updates, meaning that in a one-to-many join, you can update all columns in the recordset.

The arguments Table 28.1 describes can be used in combination to accomplish the desired objectives. The following example shows the use of an **OpenRecordset( )** argument:

```
Sub OpenRecordsetArgs()
  Dim dbsLocal As Database
  Dim rstLocal As Recordset

  Set dbsLocal = CurrentDb
  Set rstLocal = _
      dbsLocal.OpenRecordset("tblProjects", dbOpenDynaset, dbReadOnly)
  Debug.Print rstLocal.Updatable
End Sub
```

This code opens a Dynaset-type recordset as read only. It then prints the value of the **Updatable** property in the Immediate window.

Record Movement Methods

When you have a **Recordset** object variable set, you probably want to manipulate the data in the recordset. You can use several methods to traverse through the records in a recordset:

- **MoveFirst** moves to the first record in a recordset.
- **MoveLast** moves to the last record in a recordset.
- **MovePrevious** moves to the previous record in a recordset.
- **MoveNext** moves to the next record in a recordset.
- **Move[n]** moves forward or backward a specified number of records.

The following code shows some examples of how you can use the **Move** methods:

```
Sub RecordsetMovements()
  Dim dbsLocal As Database
  Dim rstLocal As Recordset

  Set dbsLocal = CurrentDb
  Set rstLocal = dbsLocal.OpenRecordset("tblProjects", dbOpenDynaset)

  Debug.Print rstLocal!ProjectID
  rstLocal.MoveNext

  Debug.Print rstLocal!ProjectID
  rstLocal.MoveLast
```

```
      Debug.Print rstLocal!ProjectID
      rstLocal.MovePrevious

      Debug.Print rstLocal!ProjectID
      rstLocal.MoveFirst

      Debug.Print rstLocal!ProjectID
      rstLocal.Close
   End Sub
```

This code opens a Dynaset. The record pointer is automatically placed on the first record of the Dynaset when the recordset is opened. The routine prints the contents of the **ProjectID** field then moves to the next record, printing its **ProjectID**. It then moves to the last record of the Dynaset, printing its **ProjectID**; moves to the previous record, printing its **ProjectID**; then moves to the first record, again printing its **ProjectID**. Finally, the **Close** method is applied to the **Recordset** object, properly closing the recordset and ensuring that all changes are written to disk.

Detecting The Limits Of A Recordset

Before you begin to traverse through recordsets, you need to understand two crucial **Recordset** properties, **BOF** and **EOF**. These properties are used to determine whether you've reached the limits of your recordset. The **BOF** property is True when the record pointer is before the first record, and the **EOF** property is True when the record pointer is after the last record. Here's a code sample that shows the use of the **EOF** property:

```
Sub FindRstLimits()
   Dim dbsLocal As Database
   Dim rstClients As Recordset

   Set dbsLocal = CurrentDb()
   Set rstClients = dbsLocal.OpenRecordset("tblClients", dbOpenSnapshot)
   Do While Not rstClients.EOF
      Debug.Print rstClients![ClientID]
      rstClients.MoveNext
   Loop
   rstClients.Close
End Sub
```

This code traverses through a Snapshot recordset, printing the value of the **ClientID** field for each record until it reaches the position after the last record in the recordset. It then exits the loop and closes the recordset.

You need to keep in mind some important characteristics of the **BOF** and **EOF** properties:

- If a recordset contains no records, both the **BOF** and **EOF** properties evaluate to True.

- The moment you open a recordset containing at least one record, the **BOF** and **EOF** properties are set to False.

- If the record pointer is on the first record in the recordset and the **MovePrevious** method is issued, the **BOF** property is set to True. When you attempt to use **MovePrevious** again, a trappable runtime error occurs.

- If the record pointer is on the last record in the recordset and the **MoveNext** method is issued, the **EOF** property is set to True. If you attempt to **MoveNext** again, a trappable runtime error occurs.

- When the **BOF** and **EOF** properties are set to True, they remain True until you move to a valid record.

- When the only record in a recordset is deleted, the **BOF** and **EOF** properties remain False until you attempt to move to another record—in which case they're set to True, and a trappable runtime error occurs.

Counting The Number Of Records In A Recordset

The **RecordCount** property of a recordset returns the number of records in a recordset that have been accessed. The problem with this is evident if you open a recordset and view the **RecordCount** property. You'll discover that the count is equal to 0 if there are no records in the recordset or equal to 1 if there are records in the recordset. The record count becomes accurate only if you visit all the records in the recordset. This can be done using the **MoveLast** method. In other words, if you want to gain an accurate count of all the records in a recordset, you should immediately move to the last record in the recordset and then back to the current position in the recordset, as shown here:

```
Sub CountRecords()
  Dim dbsLocal As Database
  Dim rstProjects As Recordset

  Set dbsLocal = CurrentDb()
  Set rstProjects = dbsLocal.OpenRecordset("tblProjects", dbOpenSnapshot)

  Debug.Print rstProjects.RecordCount        ' Prints 0 Or 1
  rstProjects.MoveLast
  Debug.Print rstProjects.RecordCount        ' Prints an accurate record Count
```

```
      rstProjects.Close
End Sub
```

The **MoveLast** method has its own problems, however. It's slow and inefficient, especially in a client/server environment. Furthermore, in a network environment, the **RecordCount** property becomes inaccurate as people add and remove records from the table. This means that if determining the record count isn't absolutely necessary, you should avoid it. The **RecordCount** property has one good use, though: It can be used to see whether there are any records in a recordset. When you're performing an operation that might return an empty recordset, you can easily use the **RecordCount** property to determine whether records were returned—if its value is 0, no records were returned; otherwise the recordset contains records.

Using The AbsolutePosition Property

The **AbsolutePosition** property returns the position of the current record. It's a zero-based value and can be used to specify where in a recordset a specific record was found. The following code shows how you might use the **AbsolutePosition** property:

```
Sub FindPosition(lngValue As Long)
   Dim dbsLocal As Database
   Dim rstProjects As Recordset
   Dim strSQL As String

   Set dbsLocal = CurrentDb()
   Set rstProjects = dbsLocal.OpenRecordset("tblProjects", dbOpenDynaset)
   strSQL = "[ProjectID] = " & lngValue
   rstProjects.FindFirst strSQL
   If rstProjects.NoMatch Then
      MsgBox lngValue & " Not Found"
   Else
      Debug.Print rstProjects.AbsolutePosition
   End If
End Sub
```

This code finds the first record with a **ProjectID** equal to the long integer received as a parameter. If the **ProjectID** is found, the value in the **AbsolutePosition** property of the record is printed.

> *WARNING! Don't rely on the presumption that the AbsolutePosition of a particular record will stay the same. The AbsolutePosition of a record changes as records are added or deleted or their order within the database is changed as the records are modified.*

Using The Bookmark Property

A **Bookmark** is a system-generated byte array that uniquely identifies each record in a recordset. The **Bookmark** property of a recordset changes as you move to each record in the recordset. It's often used when you need to store the current position in the recordset so you can perform some operation then return to the position after the operation is completed. Three steps are involved in this process:

1. Store the current **Bookmark** of the recordset to a **Variant** variable.

2. Perform the desired operation.

3. Set the **Bookmark** property of the recordset to the value contained within the **Variant** variable.

The operation looks similar to the following when you use it within your program code:

```
Sub UseBookMark()
   Dim dbsLocal As Database
   Dim rstProjects As Recordset
   Dim strSQL As String
   Dim vntPosition As Variant

   Set dbsLocal = CurrentDb()
   Set rstProjects = dbsLocal.OpenRecordset("tblProjects", dbOpenDynaset)
   vntPosition = rstProjects.Bookmark
   Do Until rstProjects.EOF
      Debug.Print rstProjects!ProjectID
      rstProjects.MoveNext
   Loop
   rstProjects.Bookmark = vntPosition
   Debug.Print rstProjects!ProjectID
End Sub
```

This code begins by opening a recordset and storing the **Bookmark** of the first record into a **Variant** variable. It then loops through each record in the recordset, printing the value within the **ProjectID**. After the loop is completed, the **Bookmark** property of the recordset is set equal to the **Variant** variable, setting the current position of the recordset back to where it was before the loop began processing.

Using The RecordsetClone Property

The **RecordsetClone** property of a form is used to refer to the recordset underlying the form. This property is often used when you want to perform an operation and then synchronize the form with its underlying recordset. The following code shows an example:

```
Private Sub cmdFindClient_Click()
  Me.RecordsetClone.FindFirst "ClientID = " & Me!txtClientID
  If Me.RecordsetClone.NoMatch Then
    MsgBox Me!txtClientID & " Not Found"
  Else
    Me.Bookmark = Me.RecordsetClone.Bookmark
  End If
End Sub
```

This routine performs the **FindFirst** method on the **RecordsetClone** of the current form. If the record is found, the **Bookmark** property of the form is set equal to the **Bookmark** of the recordset. This matches the form's position to the underlying recordset's position.

The Containers Collection

As you learned earlier in this chapter, a Container object maintains information about saved **Database** objects. The types of objects that are within the **Containers** collection are **Databases**, **Tables** (including **Queries**), **Relationships**, **SysRel**, **Forms**, **Reports**, **Scripts** (Macros), and **Modules**. The **Container** object is responsible for letting Jet know about the user interface objects. **Databases**, **Tables**, **Relationships**, and **SysRel** all have Jet as their parent object. **Forms**, **Reports**, **Scripts**, and **Modules** all have the Access application as their parent object.

Each **Container** object possesses a collection of **Document** objects. These are the actual forms, reports, and other objects that are part of your database. The **Document** objects contain only summary information about each object (date created, owner, and so on); they don't contain the actual data of the objects. To refer to a particular document within a container, you must use one of two techniques, as shown here:

```
Containers("Name")
Containers!Name
```

To list each **Container** object and its associated **Document** objects, you need to use code similar to the following:

```
Sub ListAllDBObjects()
  Dim dbsLocal As Database
  Dim conLocal As Container
  Dim docLocal As Document
```

```
    Set dbsLocal = CurrentDb
    For Each conLocal In dbsLocal.Containers
        Debug.Print "*** " & conLocal.Name & " ***"
        For Each docLocal In conLocal.Documents
            Debug.Print docLocal.Name
        Next docLocal
    Next conLocal
End Sub
```

This code loops through all the containers and within each container, all of the documents, listing each one.

Briefly Considering The Use Of DAO With ODBCDirect

The ODBCDirect **Workspace** provides an alternative when you only need to execute queries or stored procedures against a back-end server, such as Microsoft SQL Server, or when your client application needs the specific capabilities of ODBC, such as batch updates or asynchronous query execution. The DAO Object Model when working with ODBCDirect connections is slightly different than the DAO Object Model when working against Jet databases, as shown in Figure 28.2.

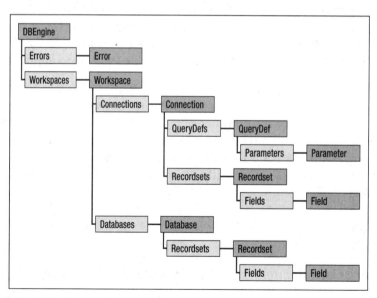

Figure 28.2   The ODBCDirect DAO Object Model.

Connecting To A Database Through ODBCDirect

A **Connection** object is similar to a **Database** object. In fact, a **Connection** object and a **Database** object represent different references to the same object. Properties on each of these two object types allow you to obtain a reference to the other corresponding object, which simplifies the task of converting ODBC client applications that use Microsoft Jet to use ODBCDirect instead. Use the **OpenConnection** method to connect to an ODBC data source. The resulting **Connection** object contains information about the connection, such as the server name, the data source name, and so on.

Using Queries With ODBCDirect

Although DAO doesn't support stored queries in an ODBCDirect workspace, a compiled query can be created as a **QueryDef** object and used to execute action queries and can also be used to execute stored procedures on the server. The **Prepare** property lets you decide whether to create a private, temporary stored procedure on the server from a **QueryDef** before actually executing the query.

Parameter queries can also be passed to the server, using **Parameter** objects on the **QueryDef**. The **Direction** property lets you specify a **Parameter** as input, output, or both or lets you accept a return value from a stored procedure.

Data Manipulation With ODBCDirect

Creating a **Recordset** object is a convenient way to query a database and manipulate the resulting set of records. The **OpenRecordset** method accepts a SQL string or a **QueryDef** object (stored query) as a data source argument. The resulting **Recordset** object features an extremely rich set of properties and methods with which to browse and modify data.

The **Recordset** object is available in four different types: Dynamic, Dynaset, Forward-Only, and Snapshot, which correspond to ODBC cursor types—Dynamic, Keyset, Forward-Only, and Static.

A batch update cursor library is available for client applications that need to work with a cursor without holding locks on the server or without issuing update requests one record at a time. Instead, the client stores update information on many records in a local buffer (or *batch*) and issues a batch update.

Asynchronous Method Execution

The **Execute**, **MoveLast**, **OpenConnection**, and **OpenRecordset** methods feature the **dbRunAsync** option. This allows your client application to do other tasks (such as loading forms, for example) while the method is executing. You can check the **StillExecuting** property to see whether the task is complete and terminate an asynchronous task with the **Cancel** method.

Introduction To ActiveX Data Objects

As you learned earlier in this chapter, DAO is the tried-and-true model for working with Jet databases. However, as Microsoft has continued to improve Access 2000 technology and as people have begun to use Access databases more and more as a desktop-based gateway to remote, client-server databases, developers have been requesting for some time that Microsoft make significant improvements to the DAO technology. Rather than investing significant time and energy in the improvement of DAO technology, Microsoft has, instead, rapidly improved the ActiveX Data Objects, making them a viable alternative to DAO. As you've seen, Microsoft intends to replace DAO entirely with ADO implementations in the next several years.

You, however, may be asking what the difference is between ADO and DAO—is there really a difference, and if so, what's the benefit to using ADO instead of DAO? To understand this issue, you must take a step back for a moment from ADO and consider the OLE DB, the underlying technology on which ADO is based.

When most developers and users thinks of data stores, they generally consider databases—both relational and hierarchical—as the most likely place to store data. If you think about it, however, volumes of data are stored on most computers that are nowhere near a database. For example, disk directories and email folders contain significant levels of important, useful information. In general, however, it has historically been very difficult, if not impossible, to take advantage of the data stored in such locations. Moreover, although you may need to access such data, your typical data source is likely to remain a relational database that supports the ODBC standard and is manipulated with commands written in SQL.

The general solution Microsoft offers to this problem is OLE DB, a set of Component Object Model (COM) interfaces that provide uniform access to data stored in diverse information sources. However, the OLE DB application programming interface is designed to provide optimal functionality in a wide variety of applications—meaning it isn't particularly simple. In fact, because OLE DB is COM based, it requires extensive manipulation of interfaces—making it somewhat more complex to work with than many other solutions.

To effectively use OLE DB from Access, you need an application programming interface (API) that's a bridge between your Access/VBA application and OLE DB. ADO is that bridge. ADO defines a programming model—the sequence of activities necessary to gain access to and update a data source. The programming model summarizes the entire functionality of ADO.

Understanding The ActiveX Data Objects Model

Figure 28.3 shows an overview of the ActiveX Data Objects Model. At the top of the hierarchy is the **Connection** object that contains all the other objects and collections that are part of the hierarchy. It's the only object that doesn't have an associated collection.

Each object within the ActiveX Data Objects Model is important to you because you'll manipulate the various objects at runtime using code, so you can accomplish the tasks required by your application. The following is a description of each major object and how you'll use it when programming with ActiveX Data Objects.

Understanding The Connection Object

A **Connection** object represents a unique session with a data source. It's akin to the DAO **Workspace** object, but doesn't have a parent engine object. Instead, the parent engine is specified within the connection string you use when initiating the **Connection** object. In the case of a client/server database system, the **Connection** will generally be equivalent to an actual network connection to the server. Depending on the functionality the database provider supports by the provider, some collections, methods, or properties of a **Connection** object may not be available. You can create **Connection** objects independently of any other previously defined object.

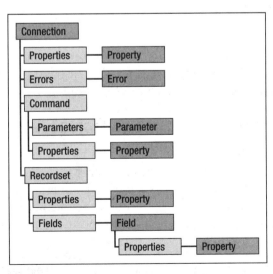

Figure 28.3   An overview of the ActiveX Data Objects model.

When using the collections, methods, and properties of a **Connection** object, you can do the following:

- Configure the connection before opening it with the **ConnectionString**, **ConnectionTimeout**, and **Mode** properties

- Set the **CursorLocation** property to invoke the Client Cursor Provider, which supports batch updates

- Set the default database for the connection with the **DefaultDatabase** property

- Set the level of isolation for the transactions opened on the connection with the **IsolationLevel** property

- Specify an OLE DB provider with the **Provider** property

- Establish, and later break, the physical connection to the data source with the **Open** and **Close** methods

- Execute a command on the connection with the **Execute** method and configure the execution with the **CommandTimeout** property

- Manage transactions on the open connection, including nested transactions if the provider supports them, with the **BeginTrans**, **CommitTrans**, and **RollbackTrans** methods and the **Attributes** property

- Examine errors returned from the data source with the **Errors** collection

- Obtain schema information about your database with the **OpenSchema** method

You can execute a query against a data source without using a **Command** object. Instead, you can pass a query string to the **Execute** method of a **Connection** object. However, a **Command** object is required when you want to persist the command text and reexecute it or use query parameters.

Understanding The Command Object And Commands Collection

When using ADO, you'll use a **Command** object to query a database and return records in a **Recordset** object, to execute a bulk operation, or to manipulate the structure of a database. Depending on the functionality the provider supports, some **Command** collections, methods, or properties may generate an error when referenced.

In general, the **Command** object replaces DAO **QueryDefs**, **TableDefs**, the **OpenRecordset** method, and more. With the collections, methods, and properties of a **Command** object, you can perform the following actions, among others:

- Define the executable text of the command—which will, in general, be a SQL statement—with the **CommandText** property.

- Define parameterized queries or stored-procedure arguments with **Parameter** objects and the **Parameters** collection (both of which are children of the **Command** object, as you can see in Figure 28.3).

- Execute a command and return a **Recordset** object if appropriate with the **Execute** method.

- Set the number of seconds a provider will wait for a command to execute with the **CommandTimeout** property—an especially useful technique when working with remote databases.

- Associate an open connection with a **Command** object by setting its **ActiveConnection** property. In other words, you can create a **Command** object, use it within one connection (that is, one database) and immediately thereafter associate it with another connection simply by changing this property.

- Pass a **Command** object to the **Source** property of a **Recordset** to obtain data.

To create a **Command** object independently of a previously defined **Connection** object, set the **Command** object's **ActiveConnection** property to a valid connection string. ADO still creates a **Connection** object, but it doesn't assign that object to an object variable. However, if you're associating multiple **Command** objects with the same connection, you should explicitly create and open a **Connection** object. If you don't set the **Command** object's **ActiveConnection** property to this object variable, ADO creates a new **Connection** object for each **Command** object, even if you use the same connection string, which can slow performance.

To execute a **Command**, simply call it by its **Name** property on the associated **Connection** object. The **Command** must have its **ActiveConnection** property set to the **Connection** object. If the **Command** has parameters, pass values for them as arguments to the method.

Understanding The Error Object And Errors Collection

The **Errors** collection contains all **Error** objects for a particular **Connection**. Any operation involving ADO objects can generate one or more provider errors. As each error occurs, the provider will place one or more **Error** objects into the **Errors** collection of the **Connection** object. When another ADO operation generates an error, ADO will clear the **Errors** collection, and the provider will then place the new set of **Error** objects into the **Errors** collection.

Each **Error** object represents a specific provider error, not an ADO error. ADO errors are exposed to the runtime exception-handling mechanism. In other words, the occurrence of an ADO-specific error will trigger an **On Error** event and appear in the **Err** object. However, because provider errors don't trigger the **On**

Error event, test the **Errors** collection to ensure proper performance after each task.

The set of **Error** objects in the **Errors** collection describes all errors that occurred in response to a single statement. Enumerating the specific errors in the **Errors** collection enables your error-handling routines to more precisely determine the cause and origin of an error and take appropriate steps to recover.

In addition to pure errors, some properties and methods will return warnings that appear as **Error** objects in the **Errors** collection but don't halt a program's execution. Such methods include the **Resync**, **UpdateBatch**, and **CancelBatch** methods for the **Recordset** object.

Understanding The ADO Recordset Object And Recordsets Collection

As you saw earlier in this chapter, the DAO **Recordset** object is one of the most important objects in data access management. If anything, the ADO **Recordset** object is even more important, as it fills more roles in the ADO structure.

A **Recordset** object represents the entire set of records from a base table or the results of an executed command. At any time, the **Recordset** object refers to only a single record within the set as the current record.

Just as with DAO, you'll use **Recordset** objects to manipulate data from a provider. When you use ADO, you manipulate data almost entirely using **Recordset** objects. All **Recordset** objects are constructed using records (rows) and fields (columns). Depending on the functionality supported by the provider, some **Recordset** methods or properties may not be available.

TIP: *ADOR.Recordset* and *ADODB.Recordset* are ProgIDs that you can use to create a *Recordset* object. The *Recordset* objects that result behave identically, regardless of the ProgID. The *ADOR.Recordset* is installed only with Microsoft Internet Explorer, while the *ADODB.Recordset* is installed with ADO. The behavior of a *Recordset* object is affected by its environment (that is, client, server, Internet Explorer, and so on). Recognizing that the object will perform differently in different situations is important because ADO supports Visual Basic, Scripting Edition (VBScript) and may, in fact, be invoked directly from a Web page.

As you learned earlier, four different cursor types are defined in ADO. A *cursor type* corresponds loosely to a recordset type as defined by DAO. The four ADO cursor types are as follows:

- *Dynamic cursor*—Allows you to view additions, changes, and deletions by other users, and allows all types of movement through the **Recordset** that don't rely on bookmarks. Furthermore, dynamic cursors allow bookmarks if the provider supports them. The Dynamic cursor is very similar to a Dynaset-type DAO **Recordset**.

- *Keyset cursor*—Behaves like a dynamic cursor, except it prevents you from seeing records that other users add and prevents access to records that other users delete. Data changes by other users will still be visible. It always supports bookmarks and, therefore, allows all types of movement through the ADO **Recordset**. As you can see, the Keyset cursor is also very similar to a Dynaset-type DAO **Recordset**.

- *Static cursor*— Provides a static copy of a set of records for you to use to find data or generate reports; it always allows bookmarks and, therefore, allows all types of movement through the **Recordset**. Additions, changes, or deletions by other users won't be visible. This is the only type of cursor allowed when you open a client-side (that is, from the Internet Explorer ADOR library) **Recordset** object. The Static cursor performs similarly to the DAO Snapshot-type **Recordset**.

- *Forward-Only cursor*— Behaves identically to a dynamic cursor except that it allows you to scroll only forward through records. This improves performance in situations where you need to make only a single pass through a **Recordset**. The Forward-Only cursor is consistent with the ODBCDirect DAO implementation of a Forward-Only **Recordset**.

Set the **CursorType** property before opening the **Recordset** to choose the cursor type, or pass a **CursorType** argument with the **Open** method. If you don't specify a cursor type, ADO will open a Forward-Only cursor by default.

Recordset objects can support two types of updating—immediate and batched. In immediate updating, all changes to data are written immediately to the underlying data source once you call the **Update** method. You can also pass arrays of values as parameters with the **AddNew** and **Update** methods and simultaneously update several fields in a record. If a provider supports batch updating, you can have the provider cache changes to more than one record then transmit them in a single call to the database with the **UpdateBatch** method. This applies to changes made with the **AddNew**, **Update**, and **Delete** methods. After you call the **UpdateBatch** method, you can use the **Status** property to check for any data conflicts to resolve them.

Understanding The Parameter Object And Parameters Collection

A **Parameters** collection contains all the **Parameter** objects of a **Command** object. As you learned earlier, a **Command** object has a **Parameters** collection made up of **Parameter** objects. Using the **Refresh** method on a **Command** object's **Parameters** collection retrieves provider parameter information for the stored procedure or parameterized query specified in the **Command** object. Some providers don't support stored procedure calls or parameterized queries; calling the

Refresh method on the **Parameters** collection when using such a provider will return an error.

You can minimize calls to the provider to improve performance if you know the properties of the parameters associated with the stored procedure or parameterized query you wish to call. Use the **CreateParameter** method to create **Parameter** objects with the appropriate property settings and use the **Append** method to add them to the **Parameters** collection. This lets you set and return parameter values without having to call the provider for the parameter information. If you're writing to a provider that doesn't supply parameter information, you must manually populate the **Parameters** collection using this method to be able to use parameters at all. Use the **Delete** method to remove **Parameter** objects from the **Parameters** collection if necessary.

ADO **Parameter** objects perform functions consistent with DAO Parameter objects. The primary difference is that, in ADO, you can only use **Parameter** objects with **Command** objects.

Understanding The Properties Collection

Each ActiveX Data Object has a **Properties** collection. The **Properties** collection of an object is a list of properties associated with that particular object. Some ADO objects have a **Properties** collection made up of **Property** objects. Each **Property** object corresponds to a characteristic of the ADO object specific to the provider. ADO objects have two types of properties: built-in and dynamic, as detailed here:

- *Built-in properties*—These properties are implemented in ADO and immediately available to any new object, using the **ADOObject.Property** syntax. They don't appear as **Property** objects in an object's **Properties** collection, so although you can change their values, you can't modify their characteristics.

- *Dynamic properties*—Defined by the underlying data provider, they appear in the **Properties** collection for the appropriate ADO object. For example, a property specific to the provider may indicate if a **Recordset** object supports transactions or updating. These additional properties will appear as **Property** objects in that **Recordset** object's **Properties** collection. Dynamic properties can be referenced only through the collection, using the **ADOObject.Properties(0)** or **ADOObject.Properties("Name")** syntax. In addition, a dynamic **Property** object has four built-in properties of its own, which you can use when enumerating through the **Properties** collection. The **Name** property is a string that identifies the property, while the **Type** property is an integer that specifies the property data type. The **Value** property is a variant that contains the property setting, and the **Attributes** property is a long value that indicates characteristics of the property specific to the provider.

You can't delete either kind of property. However, you can view or modify the properties of an object using its **Properties** collection, just as you could in DAO. The code to do so looks similar to the following:

```
Public Sub PropsAndAttribs
   Dim cnn1 As ADODB.Connection
   Dim rstEmployees As ADODB.Recordset
   Dim fldLoop As ADODB.Field
   Dim proLoop As ADODB.Property
   Dim strCnn As String

   ' Open connection and recordset.
   strCnn = "driver={SQL Server};" & _
      "server=HomeServ;uid=lmk;pwd=pwd;database=ServSamp"

   cnn1.Open strCnn
   Set rstEmployees = New ADODB.Recordset
   rstEmployees.Open "employee", cnn1, , , adCmdTable

   ' Display the attributes of the Employee table's properties.
   Debug.Print "Property attributes:"
   For Each proLoop In rstEmployees.Properties
      Debug.Print "   " & proLoop.Name & " = " & _
         proLoop.Attributes
   Next proLoop
   rstEmployees.Close
   cnn1.Close
End Sub
```

This code creates a connection to a SQL Server database, then opens a table called Employee on the database. Next, the program code loops through each **Property** object for the table, printing each object's name and attributes.

Working With ADO Recordset Properties And Methods

Like other objects, **Recordset** objects have properties and methods. The properties are the attributes of the **Recordset** objects, and the methods are the actions that you can take on the **Recordset** objects. Some properties are read only at runtime; others can be read from and written to at runtime.

Creating A Recordset Variable

When working with a recordset, you must first create a **Recordset** variable. The **Open** method is used to create a **Recordset** object variable. Begin by declaring a generic **Recordset** variable, then point a specific recordset at the variable using a **Set** statement. The code for this will generally look similar to the following:

```
Public Sub OpenRecordset()
  Dim cnn1 As Connection
  Dim rstEmployees As Recordset
  Dim strCnn As String

  ' Open connection.
  strCnn = "driver={SQL Server};" & _
      "server=HomeServ;uid=lmk;pwd=pwd;database=ServSamp"
  Set cnn1 = New Connection
  cnn1.Open strCnn

  ' Open employee table.
  Set rstEmployees = New Recordset
  rstEmployees.CursorType = adOpenKeyset
  rstEmployees.LockType = adLockOptimistic
  rstEmployees.Open "employee", cnn1, , , adCmdTable
End Sub
```

As you can see, the code creates a **Connection** object variable and a **Recordset** object variable. It then connects to a database on a SQL Server. Next, it assigns value to properties of the **Recordset** object, setting both the cursor type (to a Keyset cursor) and the locking to use on the recordset. Finally, it uses the **Open** method to assign the recordset based on the **employee stored procedure** to the object variable **rstEmployees**.

Understanding The Arguments The Open Method Accepts

You can see that the **Open** method accepts five parameters. Each of those parameters contains crucial information about the way ADO will open the recordset—parameters that ADO interprets in addition to the properties you set for the **Recordset** object. Much as it was worthwhile to examine the arguments to the **OpenRecordset** method, so too is it worthwhile to examine the parameters for the ADO **Open** method. However, all the parameters for the **Open** method are optional, provided you've set valid values in the **Recordset**'s properties. The prototype for the **Open** method is shown here:

```
recordset.Open Source, ActiveConnection, CursorType, LockType, Options
```

The **Source** parameter is a **Variant** that evaluates to a valid **Command** object variable name, a SQL statement, a table name, a stored procedure call, or the file name of a persisted **Recordset**. The **ActiveConnection** parameter is also either a **Variant** or a **String**. When a **Variant**, it must evaluate to a valid **Connection** object variable name; if a string, it must contain valid **ConnectionString** parameters.

The third parameter, **CursorType,** is a **CursorTypeEnum** value that determines the type of cursor that the provider should use when opening the **Recordset**. As you saw in the previous example, you can also set the cursor type in the **CursorType** property then ignore this parameter. Valid values for the **CursorType** property or parameter appear in Table 28.2.

The fourth parameter, **LockType,** is a **LockTypeEnum** value that determines what type of locking (concurrency) the provider should use when opening the **Recordset**. As you saw in the previous example, you can also set the lock type in the **LockType** property then ignore this parameter. Valid values for the **LockType** property or parameter appear in Table 28.3.

Table 28.2   Valid values for the *CursorType* property or parameter (as defined in the ADO object library).

Constant	Description
adOpenForwardOnly	(Default) Opens a Forward-Only–type cursor.
adOpenKeyset	Opens a Keyset-type cursor.
adOpenDynamic	Opens a Dynamic-type cursor.
adOpenStatic	Opens a Static-type cursor.

Table 28.3   Valid values for the *LockType* property or parameter (as defined in the ADO object library).

Constant	Description
adLockReadOnly	(Default) Read only; you can't alter the data.
adLockPessimistic	Pessimistic locking, record by record. The provider does what's necessary to ensure successful editing of the records, usually by locking records at the data source immediately upon editing.
adLockOptimistic	Optimistic locking, record by record. The provider uses optimistic locking, locking records only when you call the **Update** method.
adLockBatchOptimistic	Optimistic batch updates. Required for batch update mode as opposed to immediate update mode.

The fifth and final parameter is the **Options** parameter, a **Long** value that specifies how the provider should evaluate the **Source** argument if it represents something other than a **Command** object, or how the **Recordset** should be restored from a file where it was previously saved. Valid values for the **Options** parameter appear in Table 28.4 (note that the first five constants listed will also apply to the **CommandType** property).

Record Movement Methods With ADO

When you have a **Recordset** object variable set, you probably want to manipulate the data in the recordset. You can use several methods to traverse through the records in a recordset:

- **MoveFirst** moves to the first record in a recordset (you can't use this method with a Forward-Only cursor or with any **Recordset** object that doesn't support bookmarks).

- **MoveLast** moves to the last record in a recordset.

- **MovePrevious** moves to the previous record in a recordset (you can't use this method with a Forward-Only cursor or with any **Recordset** object that doesn't support bookmarks).

- **MoveNext** moves to the next record in a recordset.

- **Move[0]** moves forward or backward a specified number of records (you can't use this method to move backward with a Forward-Only cursor or with any **Recordset** object that doesn't support bookmarks).

*Table 28.4   Valid values for the **CommandType** property or parameter (as defined in the ADO object library).*

Constant	Description
adCmdText	Indicates that the provider should evaluate **Source** as a textual definition of a command.
adCmdTable	Indicates that ADO should generate a SQL query to return all rows from the table named in **Source**.
adCmdTableDirect	Indicates that the provider should return all rows from the table named in **Source**.
adCmdStoredProc	Indicates that the provider should evaluate **Source** as a stored procedure.
adCmdUnknown	Indicates that the type of command in the **Source** argument isn't known.
adCommandFile	Indicates that the persisted (saved) **Recordset** should be restored from the file named in **Source**.
adExecuteAsync	Indicates that the **Source** should be executed asynchronously.
adFetchAsync	Indicates that after the initial quantity specified in the **CacheSize** property is fetched, any remaining rows should be fetched asynchronously.

You'll invoke the ADO **Move** methods against a **Recordset** object just as you did in DAO programming, as shown here:

```
' rstLocal is an ADO DB Recordset
rstLocal.MoveNext
rstLocal.MoveLast
rstLocal.MovePrevious          ' Causes ADO error if bookmarks not supported
rstLocal.MoveFirst             ' Causes ADO error if bookmarks not supported
```

Detecting The Limits Of A Recordset

Just as with DAO **Recordsets**, ADO **Recordsets** contain the two crucial **Recordset** properties, **BOF** and **EOF**. These properties are used to determine whether you've reached the limits of your recordset. The **BOF** property is True when the record pointer is before the first record, and the **EOF** property is True when the record pointer is after the last record.

You need to keep in mind some important characteristics of the **BOF** and **EOF** properties as they apply to ADO **Recordsets**:

- If a recordset contains no records, both the **BOF** and **EOF** properties evaluate to True.

- The moment you open a recordset containing at least one record, the **BOF** and **EOF** properties are set to False.

- When the record pointer is on the first record in the recordset and the **MovePrevious** method is issued, the **BOF** property is set to True. Attempting to use **MovePrevious** again creates a trappable runtime error.

- If the record pointer is on the last record in the recordset and the **MoveNext** method is issued, the **EOF** property is set to True. Attempt to **MoveNext** again and a trappable runtime error will occur.

- When the **BOF** and **EOF** properties are set to True, they remain True until you move to a valid record.

- Deleting the only record in a recordset causes the **BOF** and **EOF** properties to remain False until you attempt to move to another record, in which case they're both set to True simultaneously, and a trappable runtime error occurs.

Counting The Number Of Records In A Recordset

The **RecordCount** property of a recordset returns the number of records in a recordset that have been accessed. If the **Recordset** object supports approximate positioning or bookmarks—that is, if invoking **Supports (adApproxPosition)** or **Supports (adBookmark)**, respectively, against the **Recordset** returns **True**—

this value will be the exact number of records in the **Recordset** regardless of whether it has been fully populated. If the **Recordset** object doesn't support approximate positioning, this property may be a significant drain on resources because all records will have to be retrieved and counted to return an accurate **RecordCount** value, just as they would with DAO objects.

Using The AbsolutePosition Property

The **AbsolutePosition** property returns the position of the current record. It's a one-based value in ADO—as opposed to a zero-based value in DAO. Use the property to specify where in a recordset a specific record was found. Additionally, the property might contain one of the following values:

- The **adPosUnknown** constant means that either the **Recordset** is empty, the current position is unknown, or the provider doesn't support the **AbsolutePosition** property.

- The **adPosBOF** value means that the current record pointer is at BOF (that is, the **BOF** property is **True**).

- The **adPosEOF** value means that the current record pointer is at EOF (that is, the **EOF** property is **True**).

Using The Bookmark Property

Just as with DAO, an ADO **Bookmark** is a system-generated byte array that uniquely identifies each record in a recordset. The **Bookmark** property of a recordset changes as you move to each record in the recordset. It's often used when you need to store the current position in the recordset so you can perform some operation and return to the position after the operation is completed. However, some ADO recordsets won't support bookmarks. Check the **Supports** (**adBookmark)** method before trying to use bookmarks on a database.

Using The Clone Property

The **Clone** method of a **Recordset** object lets you create multiple, duplicate **Recordset** objects, which you'll use particularly if you want to maintain more than one current record in a given set of records. Using the **Clone** method is more efficient than creating and opening a new **Recordset** object with the same definition as the original.

Note that changes you make to one **Recordset** object are visible in all of its clones, regardless of cursor type. However, once you execute the **Requery** method on the original **Recordset**, the clones will no longer be synchronized to the original. Furthermore, closing the original **Recordset** doesn't close any of its copies, and the reverse is also true; closing a copy doesn't close the original or any of the other copies.

WARNING!   In ADO, you can only clone a Recordset object that supports bookmarks. Bookmark values are interchangeable; that is, a bookmark reference from one Recordset object refers to the same record in any of its clones.

Considering The ADO Event Model And Asynchronous Operations

The ADO Event Model supports certain synchronous and asynchronous ADO operations that issue events before the operation starts or after it completes. An *event* is actually a call to an event handler routine.

Event handlers that are called *before* the operation starts allow you to examine or modify the operation parameters then either cancel the operation or allow it to complete. On the other hand, event handlers called *after* an operation completes are especially important because ADO 2 supports asynchronous operations. For instance, an application that starts an asynchronous **Recordset.Open** operation is notified by an **ExecutionComplete** event when the operation concludes. There are two families of events:

- **ConnectionEvents** are issued when a transaction on a connection begins, is committed, or is rolled back; when a **Command** executes; and when a **Connection** starts or ends. Table 28.5 lists the **ConnectionEvents**.

- **RecordsetEvents** are issued when you navigate through the rows of a **Recordset** object, change a field in a row of a **Recordset**, change a row in a **Recordset**, or make any change whatsoever in the **Recordset**. Table 28.6 lists the **RecordsetEvents**.

*Table 28.5   The **ConnectionEvents** that ADO supports.*

ConnectionEvent	Description
BeginTransComplete, CommitTransComplete, RollbackTransComplete	These transaction management events provide notification that the current transaction on the connection has started, committed, or rolled back.
WillConnect, ConnectComplete, Disconnect	These connection management events provide notification that the current connection will start, has started, or has ended.
WillExecute, ExecuteComplete	These command execution management events provide notification that the execution of the current command on the connection will start, or has ended.
InfoMessage	This informational event provides notification that there is additional information about the current operation (which you should then process within the event).

Table 28.6   The *RecordsetEvents* supported by ADO.

RecordsetEvent	Description
FetchProgress, FetchComplete	These retrieval status events provide notification of the progress of a data retrieval operation or notification that the retrieval operation has completed.
WillChangeField, FieldChangeComplete	These field change management events provide notification that the value of the current field will change or has changed.
WillMove, MoveComplete, EndOfRecordset	These navigation management events provide notification that the current row position in a **Recordset** will change, has changed, or has reached the end of the **Recordset**.
WillChangeRecord, RecordChangeComplete	These row change management events provide notification that something in the current row of the **Recordset** will change or has changed.
WillChangeRecordset, RecordsetChangeComplete	These recordset change management events provide notification that something in the current **Recordset** will change or has changed.

Understanding The Importance Of ADO's Events

Right about now you're probably asking yourself why you should care about ADO events. Most of the work you've been doing throughout this book has been with local databases—and DAO programming will halt the program's execution until, for example, the **Recordset** is filled, the update is complete, and so on. Although that *feature* makes writing programs easier—you always know that one thing is finished before you move on to the next—it isn't necessarily the most efficient way to access databases, *particularly* if the database is at a remote location.

Simply put, asynchronous processing (implemented through events in ADO) lets your program send a request to the data source (over a **Connection** object), *then go about its business until the data source responds.* In other words, you can write programs that let users perform other tasks while waiting for a **Recordset** to fill. With the **FetchProgress** event, you can even display a progress bar on screen that lets the user know how far along in the **Recordset** retrieval the database is. The possibilities for database programming are significant, and the level of functionality is far beyond what you could ever do in Access before.

TIP: *To use events (particularly for asynchronous processing) with ADO objects, you must first place the objects within a class module, and then expose the events from the class module. The ADO_Exam.mdb database contained on the companion CD-ROM and its program modules show how to use these events within your own programs.*

Immediate Solutions

Creating And Modifying Database Objects Using Code

In developing an Access application, it might be useful to add tables or queries, define or modify relationships, change security, or perform other data definition techniques at runtime. This can all be accomplished by manipulating the various Data Access Objects or ActiveX Data Objects. Each of the sections within the "Immediate Solutions" part of the chapter will detail how to perform specific actions, first using DAO, then using ADO.

To use the ADO code examples, you must install the Microsoft Access ODBC driver and create a Data Source Name (DSN) called Chap28 for the Access database file (Chap28.mdb) provided with the companion CD-ROM. To create a DSN, use the ODBC Data Source Administrator in Control Panel.

Adding A Table Using Code

Many properties and methods are available for adding and modifying Jet engine objects. The following code uses DAO to create a table, to add some fields, and to add a primary key index:

```
Sub CreateTable()                    'DAO Version
  Dim dbsLocal As Database
  Dim tdfLocal As TableDef
  Dim fldLocal As Field
  Dim idxLocal As Index

  Set dbsLocal = CurrentDb()                    ' Create new TableDef.
  ' Add field to Table Definition
  Set tdfLocal = dbsLocal.CreateTableDef("tblFoods")
  Set fldLocal = tdfLocal.CreateField("FoodID", DB_TEXT, 5)
  tdfLocal.Fields.Append fldLocal

  Set fldLocal = tdfLocal.CreateField("Description", DB_TEXT, 25)
  tdfLocal.Fields.Append fldLocal

  Set fldLocal = tdfLocal.CreateField("Calories", DB_INTEGER)
  tdfLocal.Fields.Append fldLocal
  dbsLocal.TableDefs.Append tdfLocal
```

```
    ' Designate the FoodID field as the Primary Key Index
    Set idxLocal = tdfLocal.CreateIndex("PrimaryKey")
    Set fldLocal = idxLocal.CreateField("FoodID")
    idxLocal.Primary = True
    idxLocal.Unique = True
    idxLocal.Fields.Append fldLocal

    ' Add the index to the Indexes collection
    tdfLocal.Indexes.Append idxLocal
End Sub
```

This code first creates a table definition called **tblFoods**. Before it can add the table definition to the **TableDefs** collection, it must add three fields to the table. Notice that the field name, type, and length are specified. After the table definition has been added to the database, indexes can be added to the table. The index added in the example is a primary key index.

Performing the same tasks is a bit different using ADO. In fact, because of ADO's design letting you access many different types of databases, you'll actually use SQL statements and the **Execute** method of the **Command** object to perform similar processing, as shown here:

```
Sub CreateTable()          ' ADO Version
  Dim cnnLocal As ADODB.Connection
  Dim cmdLocal As ADODB.Command

  ' Create Connection Object and open it on CHAP28.MDB
  Set cnnLocal = New ADODB.Connection
  cnnLocal.ConnectionString = "dsn=Chap28;UID=admin;PWD=;"
  cnnLocal.Open

  Set cmdLocal = New ADODB.Command
  Set cmdLocal.ActiveConnection = cnnLocal
  cmdLocal.CommandText = "CREATE TABLE tblFoods " _
      & "(FoodID TEXT (5), Description TEXT (25), Calories INTEGER);"
  cmdLocal.Execute

  cmdLocal.CommandText = "CREATE UNIQUE INDEX PrimaryKey " _
    & "ON tblFoods(FoodID) " _
    & "WITH PRIMARY DISALLOW NULL;"
  cmdLocal.Execute
End Sub
```

Removing A Table Using Code

Just as you can add a table using code, you can remove a table using code. The DAO code looks like this:

```
Sub DeleteTable()                    ' DAO Version
  Dim dbsLocal As Database

  Set dbsLocal = CurrentDb
  dbsLocal.TableDefs.Delete "tblFoods"
End Sub
```

The **Delete** method is issued on the **TableDefs** collection. The table you want to delete is passed to the **Delete** method as an argument.

Deleting tables with ADO will depend on the underlying database product that you use—some databases may not let you delete tables or indexes from SQL code and may require that you use a separate management product to perform such processing. However, for databases (such as Access 2000) that do support table deletions from SQL, you can use code similar to the following to delete a table with ADO:

```
Public Sub DeleteTable()             ' ADO Version
  Dim cnnLocal As ADODB.Connection
  Dim cmdLocal As ADODB.Command

  ' Create Connection Object and open it on CHAP28.MDB
  Set cnnLocal = New ADODB.Connection

  cnnLocal.ConnectionString = "dsn=Chap28;UID=admin;PWD=;"
  cnnLocal.Open

  Set cmdLocal = New ADODB.Command
  Set cmdLocal.ActiveConnection = cnnLocal
  cmdLocal.CommandText = "DROP TABLE tblFoods"
  cmdLocal.Execute
End Sub
```

Establishing Relationships Using Code

If you're creating tables using code, you'll want to establish relationships between these tables using code. Here's how:

```
Sub CreateRelation()
  Dim dbsLocal As Database
```

```
        Dim relLocal As Relation
        Dim fldLocal As Field

        Set dbsLocal = CurrentDb
        Set relLocal = dbsLocal.CreateRelation()
        With relLocal
          .Name = "PeopleFood"
          .TABLE = "tblFoods"
          .ForeignTable = "tblPeople"
          .Attributes = dbRelationDeleteCascade
        End With
        Set fldLocal = relLocal.CreateField("FoodID")
        fldLocal.ForeignName = "FoodID"
        relLocal.Fields.Append fldLocal
        dbsLocal.Relations.Append relLocal
    End Sub
```

This code begins by setting a **Relation** object to a new relationship. It then populates the **Name**, **Table**, **Foreign Table**, and **Attributes** properties of the relationship. After the properties of the relationship have been set, the field is added to the **Relation** object. Finally, the **Relationship** object is appended to the **Relations** collection.

TIP: *You can't create relationships with ADO; instead, use Joins to control the relationships of your data—or set the relationships from the Relationship window.*

Creating A Query Using Code

You might want to build your own query designer into your application and allow the users to save the queries they build. This requires that you build the queries yourself, using code, after the user has designed them. The code needed to build a query from DAO looks like this:

```
Sub CreateQuery()
  Dim dbsLocal As Database
  Dim qdfLocal As QueryDef
  Dim strSQL As String

  Set dbsLocal = CurrentDb
  Set qdfLocal = dbsLocal.CreateQueryDef("qryBigProjects")
  strSQL = "Select ProjectID, ProjectName, ProjectTotalEstimate " _
    & "From tblProjects " _
```

```
        & "Where ProjectTotalEstimate >= 30000"
    qdfLocal.SQL = strSQL
End Sub
```

This code uses the **CreateQueryDef** method of the **Database** object to create a new query definition. It then sets the SQL statement associated with the query definition. This serves to build and store the query.

It's important to understand that unlike the **CreateQueryDef** method of the database object, which immediately adds the query definition to the database, the **CreateTableDef** method doesn't immediately add the table definition to the database. The **Append** method of the **TableDefs** collection must be used to actually add the table definition to the database.

TIP: *You can create a temporary query definition by using a zero-length string for the name argument of the **CreateQueryDef** method.*

With ADO, you'll generally work with either stored procedures on the server, or you'll use the **Recordset** object's **Save** method to persist a recordset.

Modifying Table Data Using Code

So far, you've learned how to loop through and work with **Recordset** objects. Now you'll learn how to change the data contained in a recordset.

Changing Record Data One Record At A Time

You'll often want to loop through a recordset, modifying all the records that meet a specific set of criteria. The code required to accomplish this task looks like this:

```
Sub IncreaseEstimate()                    ' DAO Version
  Dim dbsLocal As Database
  Dim rstProjects As Recordset
  Dim strSQL As String
  Dim intUpdated As Integer

  Set dbsLocal = CurrentDb()
  Set rstProjects = dbsLocal.OpenRecordset("tblProjectsChange", _
    dbOpenDynaset)
  strSQL = "ProjectTotalEstimate < 30000"
  intUpdated = 0
  rstProjects.FindFirst strSQL
  Do While Not rstProjects.NoMatch
```

```
      intUpdated = intUpdated + 1
      rstProjects.Edit
        rstProjects.Fields("ProjectTotalEstimate") = _
            rstProjects.Fields("ProjectTotalEstimate") * 1.1
      rstProjects.Update
      rstProjects.FindNext strSQL
    Loop
    Debug.Print intUpdated & " Records Updated"
    rstProjects.Close
End Sub
```

This code finds the first record with a **ProjectTotalEstimate** less than 30,000. The code uses the **Edit** method to ready the current record in the Dynaset for editing and replaces the **ProjectTotalEstimate** with the **ProjectTotalEstimate** multiplied by 1.1. It then issues the **Update** method to write the changes to disk. Finally, the program uses the **FindNext** method to locate the next occurrence of the criteria.

Because most databases don't support the Jet engine **Find** methods, when working with ADO objects, you must create the recordset to update with a SQL **SELECT** statement, then move through the records in order, as shown here:

```
Sub IncreaseEstimate()                   ' ADO Version
  Dim cnnLocal As ADODB.Connection
  Dim cmdLocal As ADODB.Command
  Dim rstLocal As ADODB.Recordset
  Dim intUpdated As Integer

  ' Create Connection Object and open it on CHAP28.MDB
  Set cnnLocal = New ADODB.Connection

  cnnLocal.ConnectionString = "dsn=Chap28;UID=admin;PWD=;"
  cnnLocal.Open

  Set cmdLocal = New ADODB.Command
  Set cmdLocal.ActiveConnection = cnnLocal
  cmdLocal.CommandText = "SELECT * FROM tblProjectsChange " _
      & "WHERE ProjectTotalEstimate < 30000"
  rstLocal.CursorType = adOpenForwardOnly
  Set rstLocal = cmdLocal.Execute()

  intUpdated = 0
  Do While Not rstLocal.EOF
    intUpdated = intUpdated + 1
    rstLocal.Fields("ProjectTotalEstimate") = _
```

```
        rstLocal.Fields("ProjectTotalEstimate") * 1.1
    rstLocal.Update
    rstLocal.MoveNext
  Loop
  Debug.Print intUpdated & " Records Updated"
  rstLocal.Close
End Sub
```

Making Bulk Changes

Many of the tasks that you can perform by looping through a recordset can also be accomplished with an Update query. Executing an Update query is often more efficient than the process of looping through a recordset. If nothing else, it takes much less code. Therefore, it's important to understand how to execute an Update query through code.

Let's assume that you have a query called **qryChangeTotalEstimate** that increases the **ProjectTotalEstimate** for all projects in which the **ProjectTotalEstimate** is less than 30,000. The query is an Update query. The following code executes the stored query definition:

```
Sub RunUpdateQuery()                    ' DAO Version
  Dim dbsLocal As Database
  Dim qdfLocal As QueryDef
  Set dbsLocal = CurrentDb
  Set qdfLocal = dbsLocal.QueryDefs("qryIncreaseTotalEstimate")
  qdfLocal.Execute
End Sub
```

Notice that the **Execute** method operates on the query definition, executing the Action query.

Running Action queries from ADO is just as simple, as shown in the following code:

```
Sub RunUpdateQuery()                    ' ADO Version
  Dim cnnLocal As ADODB.Connection
  Dim cmdLocal As ADODB.Command

  ' Create Connection Object and open it on CHAP28.MDB
  Set cnnLocal = New ADODB.Connection
  cnnLocal.ConnectionString = "dsn=Chap28;UID=admin;PWD=;"
  cnnLocal.Open

  Set cmdLocal = New ADODB.Command
  Set cmdLocal.ActiveConnection = cnnLocal
```

```
    cmdLocal.CommandText = "UPDATE tblProjectsChange " _
      & "SET ProjectTotalEstimate = 30000 " _
      & "WHERE ProjectTotalEstimate < 30000;"
    cmdLocal.Execute
End Sub
```

As you can see, the program code simply assigns the Update query to the command object and executes the command.

Deleting An Existing Record

The **Delete** method enables you to programmatically delete records from a recordset. It works like this:

```
Sub DeleteCusts(lngProjEst As Long)
  Dim dbsLocal As Database
  Dim rstProjects As Recordset
  Dim intCounter As Integer

  Set dbsLocal = CurrentDb
  Set rstProjects = dbsLocal.OpenRecordset("tblProjectsChange",
dbOpenDynaset)
  intCounter = 0
  Do While Not rstProjects.EOF
    If rstProjects.Fields("ProjectTotalEstimate") < lngProjEst Then
      rstProjects.Delete
      intCounter = intCounter + 1
    End If
    rstProjects.MoveNext
  Loop
  Debug.Print intCounter & " Customer Records Deleted"
End Sub
```

This code loops through the **rstProjects** recordset. If the **ProjectTotalEstimate** amount is less than the value passed in as a parameter, the record is deleted. This task could also be accomplished with a **Delete** query.

The ADO **Delete** method works the same way—the only difference, of course, being that it uses ADO objects rather than DAO objects.

Adding A New Record

The **AddNew** method enables you to programmatically add records to a recordset. Here's an example:

```
Private Sub cmdAddRecord_Click()        ' DAO Recordset
  Dim dbsLocal As Database
  Dim rstProject As Recordset
```

```
    Set dbsLocal = CurrentDb()
    Set rstProject = dbsLocal.OpenRecordset("tblProjectsChange",
DB_OPEN_DYNASET)
    With rstProject
      .AddNew
        .Fields("ProjectName") = Me!txtProjectName
        .Fields("ProjectDescription") = Me!txtProjectDescription
        .Fields("ClientID") = Me!cboClientID
      .Update
    End With
    Me!txtProjectID = rstProject!ProjectID
End Sub
```

This code is used on an Unbound form called **frmUnbound**. The code issues an **AddNew** method, which creates a buffer ready to accept data. Each field in the recordset is then populated with the values from the controls on the form. The **Update** method writes the data to disk, and if you forget to include the **Update** method, the record is never written to disk. The last line of code is there to illustrate a problem: When an **AddNew** method is issued, the record pointer is never moved within the Dynaset. Even after the Update method is issued, the record pointer remains at the record it was on prior to the **AddNew**. You must explicitly move to the new record before populating the **txtProjectID** text box with the **ProjectID** from the recordset. This can easily be accomplished using the **LastModified** property, covered in the next section.

Again, you can use the ADO **Recordset** object's **AddNew** and **Update** methods to add records to a table or recordset. The code to perform the **AddNew** action would look similar to the following:

```
Private Sub cmdAddRecord_Click()            ' ADO Version
  Dim cnnLocal As ADODB.Connection
  Dim cmdLocal As ADODB.Command
  Dim rstLocal As ADODB.Recordset

  ' Create Connection Object and open it on CHAP28.MDB
  Set cnnLocal = New ADODB.Connection

  cnnLocal.ConnectionString = "dsn=Chap28;UID=admin;PWD=;"
  cnnLocal.Open

  Set cmdLocal = New ADODB.Command
  Set cmdLocal.ActiveConnection = cnnLocal
  cmdLocal.CommandText = "SELECT * FROM tblProjectsChange"
  rstLocal.CursorType = adOpenDynamic
  Set rstLocal = cmdLocal.Execute()
```

```
      With rstLocal
        .AddNew
          .Fields("ProjectName") = Me!txtProjectName
          .Fields("ProjectDescription") = Me!txtProjectDescription
          .Fields("ClientID") = Me!cboClientID
        .Update
      End With
      Me!txtProjectID = rstLocal.Fields("ProjectID")
    End Sub
```

Using The **LastModified** Property

The **LastModified** property contains a **Bookmark** of the most recently added or modified record. When you set the **Bookmark** of the recordset to the **LastModified** property, the record pointer is moved to the most recently added record. The code looks like this:

```
Private Sub cmdLastModified_Click()
  Dim dbsLocal As Database
  Dim rstProject As Recordset
  Set dbsLocal = CurrentDb()
  Set rstProject = dbsLocal.OpenRecordset("tblProjectsChange",
DB_OPEN_DYNASET)
  With rstProject
    .AddNew
      .Fields("ProjectName") = Me!txtProjectName
      .Fields("ProjectDescription") = Me!txtProjectDescription
      .Fields("ClientID") = Me!cboClientID
    .Update
    .Bookmark = rstProject.LastModified
  End With
  Me!txtProjectID = rstProject!ProjectID
End Sub
```

Notice that the **Bookmark** of the recordset is set to the **LastModified** property of the recordset.

> ***WARNING!*** *ADO doesn't support the LastModified property.*

Sorting, Filtering, And Finding Records

Sometimes you might need to sort or filter an existing recordset. You also might want to locate each record in the recordset that meets some specified criteria. The following techniques allow you to sort, filter, and find records within a **Recordset** object.

Sorting A Recordset

You can't actually change the sort order of an existing Dynaset or Snapshot. Instead, you create a second recordset based on the first recordset. The second recordset is sorted in the desired order. It works like this:

```
Sub SortRecordset()                         ' DAO Version
  Dim dbsLocal As Database
  Dim rstTimeCardHours As Recordset

  Set dbsLocal = CurrentDb
  Set rstTimeCardHours = _
     dbsLocal.OpenRecordset("tblTimeCardHours", dbOpenDynaset)
  Debug.Print "NOT Sorted!!!"
  Do While Not rstTimeCardHours.EOF
    Debug.Print rstTimeCardHours![DateWorked]
    rstTimeCardHours.MoveNext
  Loop
  Debug.Print "Now Sorted!!!"
  rstTimeCardHours.Sort = "[DateWorked]"
  Set rstTimeCardHours = rstTimeCardHours.OpenRecordset
    Do While Not rstTimeCardHours.EOF
    Debug.Print rstTimeCardHours.Fields("DateWorked")
    rstTimeCardHours.MoveNext
  Loop
End Sub
```

In this case, you're sorting a Dynaset that's based on the table **tblTimeCardHours**. The first time you loop through the recordset and print each date worked, the dates are in the default order (usually the primary key order). After using the **Sort** method to sort the recordset, the records appear in order by the date worked.

ADO doesn't support the **Sort** method; instead, you must sort the recordset before you assign it to the object. The following code shows how to do sorted and unsorted recordsets with ADO:

```
Sub SortRecordset()                         ' ADO Version
  Dim cnnLocal As ADODB.Connection
```

```
      Dim cmdLocal As ADODB.Command
      Dim rstLocal As ADODB.Recordset

      ' Create Connection Object and open it on CHAP28.MDB
      Set cnnLocal = New ADODB.Connection
      cnnLocal.ConnectionString = "dsn=Chap28;UID=admin;PWD=;"
      cnnLocal.Open

      Set cmdLocal = New ADODB.Command
      Set cmdLocal.ActiveConnection = cnnLocal

      cmdLocal.CommandText = "SELECT * FROM tblTimeCardHours"
      cmdLocal.Execute
      rstLocal.CursorType = adOpenForwardOnly
      Set rstLocal = cmdLocal.Execute()
      Debug.Print "NOT Sorted!!!"
      Do While Not rstLocal.EOF
        Debug.Print rstLocal.Fields("DateWorked")
        rstLocal.MoveNext
      Loop

      cmdLocal.CommandText = "SELECT * FROM tblTimeCardHours " & _
          "ORDER BY DateWorked"
      cmdLocal.Execute
      rstLocal.CursorType = adOpenForwardOnly
      Set rstLocal = cmdLocal.Execute()
      Debug.Print "Now Sorted!!!"
      Do While Not rstLocal.EOF
        Debug.Print rstLocal.Fields("DateWorked")
        rstLocal.MoveNext
      Loop
    End Sub
```

Filtering A Recordset

Filtering an existing recordset is similar to sorting one. The following example
is a variation of the previous one. Instead of sorting an existing recordset, it filters it.

```
Sub FilterRecordSet()
  Dim dbsLocal As Database
  Dim rstTimeCardHours As Recordset

  Set dbsLocal = CurrentDb
  Set rstTimeCardHours = _
      dbsLocal.OpenRecordset("tblTimeCardHours", dbOpenDynaset)
  Debug.Print "Without Filter"
```

```
   Do While Not rstTimeCardHours.EOF
     Debug.Print rstTimeCardHours![DateWorked]
     rstTimeCardHours.MoveNext
   Loop
   rstTimeCardHours.Filter = "[DateWorked] Between #1/1/95# and #1/5/95#"
   Debug.Print "With Filter"
   Set rstTimeCardHours = rstTimeCardHours.OpenRecordset
     Do While Not rstTimeCardHours.EOF
     Debug.Print rstTimeCardHours.Fields("DateWorked")
     rstTimeCardHours.MoveNext
   Loop
End Sub
```

The first time the code loops through the recordset, no filter is set. The program code then sets the filter, and the remaining code loops through the recordset again. The second time, only the records meeting the filter criteria are displayed.

Again, as with the **Sort** method, ADO doesn't support the **Filter** method.

Finding A Specific Record Within A Recordset

The **Seek** method enables you to find records in a **Table** recordset. It's usually the quickest method of locating data because it uses the current index to locate the requested data. It works like this:

```
Sub SeekProject(lngProjectID As Long)
  Dim dbsLocal As Database
  Dim rstProjects As Recordset

  Set dbsLocal = CurrentDb()
  Set rstProjects = dbsLocal.OpenRecordset("tblProjects", dbOpenTable)
  rstProjects.Index = "PrimaryKey"
  rstProjects.Seek "=", lngProjectID
  If rstProjects.NoMatch Then
    MsgBox lngProjectID & " Not Found"
  Else
    MsgBox lngProjectID & " Found"
  End If
End Sub
```

This code uses the primary key index to locate the first project with the project number that was passed to the function. It then displays a message box to indicate whether the value was found.

The **Seek** method can't be used to locate data in a Dynaset or Snapshot. Furthermore, it can't be used to search for records in an attached table, regardless of whether the attached table is an Access table or a client/server table. In this case, you must use the **FindFirst**, **FindLast**, **FindNext**, and **FindPrevious** methods. The **FindFirst** method finds the first occurrence of data that meets the criteria, and **FindLast** finds the last occurrence of such data. The **FindNext** and **FindPrevious** methods enable you to find additional occurrences of the data, as shown here:

```
Sub FindProject(lngValue As Long)
  Dim dbsLocal As Database
  Dim rstProjects As Recordset
  Dim strSQL As String

  Set dbsLocal = CurrentDb()
  Set rstProjects = dbsLocal.OpenRecordset("tblProjects", dbOpenDynaset)
  strSQL = "[ProjectID] = " & lngValue
  rstProjects.FindFirst strSQL
  If rstProjects.NoMatch Then
    MsgBox lngValue & " Not Found"
  Else
    MsgBox lngValue & " Found"
  End If
End Sub
```

This code uses the **FindFirst** method to find the first occurrence of the parameter that was passed in. Again, it displays an appropriate message box.

TIP: *You can use another trick to search a linked table. You can open the database that contains the linked table and seek directly on the table data.*

As you learned earlier, ADO doesn't support the **Find** methods. As you might expect, because ADO doesn't support Table-Only cursors, ADO doesn't support the **Seek** method either.

Running Parameter Queries

Access Parameter queries are very powerful. They enable the user to specify criteria at runtime. This ability is often helpful if your user wants to fill out a form at runtime and have the values on that form fed to the query. Consider the following code:

```
Sub RunParameterQuery(datStart As Date, datEnd As Date)   ' DAO Version
  Dim dbsLocal As Database
  Dim qdfLocal As QueryDef
  Dim rstLocal As Recordset
```

```
    Set dbsLocal = CurrentDb
    Set qdfLocal = dbsLocal.QueryDefs("qryBillAmountByClient")
    qdfLocal.Parameters("Please Enter Start Date") = datStart
    qdfLocal.Parameters("Please Enter End Date") = datEnd
    Set rstLocal = qdfLocal.OpenRecordset
    Do While Not rstLocal.EOF
      Debug.Print rstLocal.Fields("CompanyName"), _
          rstLocal.Fields("[BillAmount")
      rs.MoveNext
    Loop
End Sub
```

This subroutine receives two date variables as parameters, but it could just as easily receive form controls as parameters. It opens a query definition called **qryBillAmountByClient** and sets the values of the parameters called Please Enter Start Date and Please Enter End Date to the date variables passed into the subroutine as parameters. The query is then executed by issuing the **OpenRecordset** method on the **Recordset** object.

Using ADO to perform such processing is similar; you simply append the parameters to the command object before opening the recordset. The following code implements the process in ADO:

```
Sub RunParameterQuery(datStart As Date, datEnd As Date)
  Dim cnnLocal As ADODB.Connection
  Dim cmdLocal As ADODB.Command
  Dim rstLocal As ADODB.Recordset
  Dim prsLocal As ADODB.Parameters
  Dim prmLocal As ADODB.Parameter

  ' Create Connection Object and open it on CHAP28.MDB
  Set cnnLocal = New ADODB.Connection
  cnnLocal.ConnectionString = "dsn=Chap28;UID=admin;PWD=;"
  cnnLocal.Open

  Set cmdLocal = New ADODB.Command
  Set cmdLocal.ActiveConnection = cnnLocal

  cmdLocal.CommandText = "SELECT * FROM tblBillAmountByClient " & _
      "ORDER BY StartDate Where StartDate > ? And EndDate < ?"

  Set prmLocal = cmdLocal.CreateParameter("StartDate", adDate, adParamInput)
  prmLocal.Value = datStart
  cmdLocal.Parameters.Append prmLocal
  Set prmLocal = cmdLocal.CreateParameter("EndDate", adDate, adParamInput)
```

```
        prmLocal.Value = datEnd
        cmdLocal.Parameters.Append prmLocal
        Set prmLocal = Nothing

        rstLocal.CursorType = adOpenForwardOnly
        Set rstLocal = cmdLocal.Execute()
        Do While Not rstLocal.EOF
          Debug.Print rstLocal.Fields("CompanyName"),
    rstLocal.Fields("BillAmount")
          rstLocal.MoveNext
        Loop
    End Sub
```

Chapter 29

Using Class Modules With Access

In Depth

In previous chapters, you've learned about the different ways in which you can use Visual Basic for Applications (VBA) to add program code to your Access applications. As you've seen, you can use Form modules and Code modules to store and maintain program code. However, you'll often find you want to manipulate custom program code in a fashion that allows you to encapsulate programs within a single related area. This concept is known, generally, as *object-oriented programming*. In this chapter, we'll look at some of the issues surrounding the use of VBA class modules in your Access applications. You'll learn more about classes and objects and how to create your own classes and objects in VBA.

Understanding Objects

In the simplest sense, an object is a thing or a real-world entity. When programmers create programs, they write instructions that work with different objects (things), like variables or files. Different objects have different operations that your programs perform on them. For example, given a file object, your program might perform such operations as reading, writing, or printing the file. As you'll learn, VBA programs can define objects in terms of a class. An object's class defines the data the object will store and the functions that operate on the data. VBA programs often refer to the functions that manipulate the class data as methods. Some of your VBA programs, for example, might include the **Debug** and **RichTextBox** objects. In the case of these objects, methods such as **Debug.Print** and **RichTextBox.SelRTF**, are the operations on the objects. Within VBA, every form and control your program uses is an object. You'll more clearly understand much of what you'll learn in this section if you think about what you're learning in the context of forms and controls. All that being said, the purpose of visualizing each of these items as objects is to simplify programming with them—a process known (as mentioned above) as object-oriented programming, discussed in the next section.

Understanding Object-Oriented Programming

To programmers, an object is a collection of data and a set of operations, called *methods*, that manipulate data. Object-oriented programming is a way of looking at programs in terms of the objects (things) that make up a system. After you've identified the objects, you can determine the operations you or the user will usually perform on the object. If you have a document object, for example, common operations might include printing, spellchecking, faxing, or even discarding. Object-oriented programming doesn't require a special programming language.

You can write object-oriented programs in such languages as C++, Java, COBOL, and FORTRAN—though, in all fairness, it is much easier to do so in a language designed for such a purpose, like C++ or Java.

However, as you'll learn, languages described as object oriented usually provide class data structures that let your programs group the data and methods into one container that you can then reference from a single variable. As you'll also learn, object-oriented programming has many advantages. The two primary advantages of object-oriented programming are object reuse and ease of understanding. Fortunately, the objects that you write for one program you can often use in another. Rather than building a collection of function libraries, object-oriented programmers build *class libraries*. Likewise, by grouping an object's data and methods, object-oriented programs are often more readily understood than their non–object-based counterparts (at least after you learn the syntax of the programming language used). The best-known object-oriented languages are C++ and Java. In Office 95, Microsoft started migrating VBA toward an object-oriented language. Now, VBA is a very object-capable language.

Understanding Why VBA Isn't Truly Object Oriented

As you've learned, you can write object-oriented programs in almost any language, including VBA. However, you should recognize that VBA isn't considered a true object-oriented language. The two main reasons why programmers don't consider VBA an object-oriented language are its roots in BASIC and the number of predefined objects most programmers employ when they use VBA. As you probably know, the original BASIC language was a procedure-based language. In other words, every program started at some point A and finished at some point B, and the sequence of execution was in a relatively straight line. Later, BASIC gained the ability to call subroutines to perform branching activities. With the introduction of early versions of Visual Basic, and later VBA, BASIC became an event-driven language.

Nevertheless, even with all of the advances made in the BASIC language over the years, BASIC is still fundamentally a language that manages program flow with subroutines. Therefore, you can't refer to it solely as an object-oriented language. Additionally, as you'll learn in later sections, one of the primary benefits of classes in a true object-oriented language is the ability to inherit other classes' characteristics. Because you can't truly inherit characteristics from the controls the majority of VBA programmers use, these objects aren't sufficient to qualify VBA as an object-oriented language.

Despite the fact that VBA is lacking a few of the characteristics that generally are used to define object-oriented programming, it nevertheless provides you with several tools you can use to implement objects within your programs. The most common—and applicable—of these tools is the VBA class module. You will learn more about class modules in the following sections.

Understanding VBA Classes

As you write VBA programs, you'll often use structures (a program-defined type of value) to group related data. You can best view a VBA class as a responsive structure. A class stores data, manipulates data, and is capable of returning values to the invoking procedure. Consider, for example, the following structure definition:

```
Type Employee
  Name As String * 64
  Age As Integer
  SSN As String * 11                      ' Social security number
  Pay_Grade As Integer
  Salary As Single
  LastPayDay As Date
  Employee_Number As String * 11
End Type
```

If you use a class instead of a structure, you can actually process a **Last_Date_Paid** function within the class and automatically return the **LastPayDay** value whenever the user views an instance of the object. In fact, the **Last_Date_Paid** function will be a method of the class. A class, like a structure, describes a template for future variable declarations—it doesn't allocate memory for a variable. A class has a name (tag) and member fields. The following definition illustrates a simple class named **Employee**:

```
Private mvarEmpName As String              'local copy
Private mvarAge As Integer                 'local copy
Private mvarSSN As String                  'local copy
Private mvarPay_Grade As Integer           'local copy
Private mvarSalary As Single               'local copy
Private mvarEmployee_Number As String      'local copy

Public Function Last_Date_Paid(Name As String) As String
```

As you can see, the class definition is very similar to a structure. The only new items are the **Public** and **Private** labels. A later section in this chapter, "Understanding The **Public** Label," explains the **Public** label in detail.

Now that we have seen some of the basics of the implementation of classes in VBA, let's take a moment to step back and consider some of the underlying logic behind the creation of classes. In the following section, we will think about classes as they relate to some real-world objects—a technique that is often successful in making some sense out of the complexity of the object-oriented world.

Conceptualizing Classes

Classes and objects are some of the most difficult programming constructs for both beginning and advanced programmers to master. As you've learned, the best way to visualize classes and objects is by thinking about real-world objects. For example, my pet Kimba is a cat—a Persian cat, to be specific. In this case, the class would be either **Cats** or **Persians**, depending on how you construct your object model, and **Kimba** is the object. **Cats** share many characteristics—they have eyes, legs, a tail, a nose, and spots. However, each cat also has unique characteristics, such as name, sex, eye color, length of tail, and number of spots. The shared characteristics are items consistent throughout the class. In VBA, for example, one of these characteristics might be the **Click** event for any **Button** class. The unique characteristics, on the other hand, would be properties: the name of the object, the length of the object, and other properties that would make the object unique.

The goal of any object-oriented program is to make generalizations about every object you use within your program—whether it be a visual object, data object, or mathematical object, to name just a few—and to group these generalized objects together in their own classes. In true object-oriented languages, you'll actually derive many classes from other, more general classes. For example, you might derive the class **Persian** from **Cat**. Similarly, within Windows, you'll derive every visible object from the Windows-defined **CWin** class. In VBA, because it doesn't fully support inheritance, your classes probably won't separate as efficiently as you might prefer, but the classes you can create support much of the power of object-oriented programming.

> **TIP:** As you read other books and articles on object-oriented programming, you'll often encounter the term polymorphism. Polymorphism lets programs apply the same operation to objects of different types. Because polymorphism lets programmers apply the same operation to multiple types, polymorphism lets programmers use the same interface to access different objects. In C++, for example, virtual functions provide access to polymorphism. In the simplest sense, a virtual function is a pointer to a function the compiler resolves at runtime. Depending on the function to which a virtual function points, the operation the program performs will differ. As a result, a single interface (the virtual function) can provide access to different operations. Unfortunately, VBA doesn't support true polymorphism—you can simulate polymorphism with variant and optional parameters, but it's a cumbersome and often difficult process.

Hopefully, it is now much easier to see how classes can be useful and beneficial within your own programs. Now that you feel a little more comfortable with the theory behind classes, let's go ahead and design one, so that you get some experience with implementation.

Creating Classes

As you begin to create classes within VBA, you'll insert class modules into the VBA Interactive Development Environment (IDE). To better understand how classes work, we'll create a basic class in this section then discuss some of the issues about it in the rest of this chapter. To build your first class, perform the following steps:

1. From within the VBA IDE, select the Insert menu's Class Module option. VBA will add a new class module, **Class1**, to the project.

2. Within the Properties window, change the **Name** property for the class to **Employees**.

3. Although we'll expose information about each instance of the **Employees** class through properties, doing so is a two-step process. First, you must add local variable definitions to the General Declaration section of the project, as shown in the following code listing:

```
Private mvarEmpName As String              'local copy
Private mvarAge As Integer                 'local copy
Private mvarSSN As String                  'local copy
Private mvarPay_Grade As Integer           'local copy
Private mvarSalary As Single               'local copy
Private mvarEmployee_Number As String      'local copy
```

4. After you add the variable definitions to the class, you need to add two functions for each property to the class—one to return the property to the calling function, and one to set the property when called from the instancing location. The functions should look similar to the following—with, of course, variable name changes for each of the functions. This code, for example, sets and returns the **EmpName** property.

```
Public Property Let EmpName(ByVal vData As String)
   mvarEmpName = vData
End Property

Public Property Get EmpName() As String
   EmpName = mvarEmpName
End Property
```

You can see the entirety of the class file if you load it from the CD-ROM—it's in the Chap29 directory. The program code for the class is very similar to what you've already seen as to the programming of the class file.

Creating Classes Using The Class Builder Utility

If you have the Developer edition of Office 2000, Microsoft has provided the Class Builder utility, an add-in to the VBA IDE that you can use to create classes. To use the Class Builder utility to create another instance of the **Employees** class, perform the following steps:

1. Before you add a Class Module to the project, use the Add-Ins menu to add the Class Builder utility to the project, as shown in Figure 29.1.

2. Within the Add-In Manager, select the VB 6 Class Builder utility, then click on the Loaded/Unloaded checkbox and the Load On Startup checkbox. Click on OK to close the dialog box. The IDE will add the Class Builder utility to the Add-Ins menu.

3. From the Add-Ins menu, select the Class Builder utility. The VBA IDE will display the Class Builder dialog box.

4. Within the Class Builder dialog box, select File|New|Class. The VBA IDE will display the Class Module Builder dialog box.

5. Within the Class Module Builder dialog box, change the **Name** field to **Employees**. Click on the OK button. VBA will add the **Employees** class to the Class tree.

6. Select the Properties tab on the right side of the Class Builder window. Select File|New|Property. Visual Basic will display the Property Builder dialog box.

7. Within the Property Builder dialog box, enter **Age** into the **Name** field. Press the Tab key to move the **Data Type** field and select the Integer type. Click on the OK button. Visual Basic will add the **Age** property to the **Employees** class.

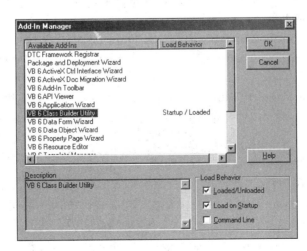

Figure 29.1   The Add-In Manager dialog box.

8. Select the Properties tab within the right side of the Class Builder window. Select File|New|Property. Visual Basic will display the Property Builder dialog box.

9. Within the Property Builder dialog box, enter **SSN** into the **Name** field. Press the Tab key to move the **Data Type** field and select the String type. Click your mouse on the OK button. Visual Basic will add the **SSN** property to the **Employees** class.

10. Select the Properties tab within the right side of the Class Builder window. Select File|New|Property. Visual Basic will display the Property Builder dialog box.

11. Within the Property Builder dialog box, enter **Pay_Grade** into the **Name** field. Press the Tab key to move the **Data Type** field and select the Integer type. Click on the OK button. Visual Basic will add the **Pay_Grade** property to the **Employees** class.

12. Select the Properties tab within the right side of the Class Builder window, then select File|New|Property. Visual Basic will display the Property Builder dialog box.

13. Within the Property Builder dialog box, enter **EmpName** into the **Name** field. Press the Tab key to move the **Data Type** field and select the String type. Click on the OK button. Visual Basic will add the **EmpName** property to the **Employees** class.

14. Select the Properties tab on the right side of the Class Builder window. Select File|New|Property. Visual Basic will display the Property Builder dialog box.

15. Within the Property Builder dialog box, enter **Salary** into the **Name** field. Press the Tab key to move the **Data Type** field and select the Single type. Click on the OK button. Visual Basic will add the **Salary** property to the **Employees** class.

16. Select the Properties tab within the right side of the Class Builder window. Select File|New|Property. Visual Basic will display the Property Builder dialog box.

17. Within the Property Builder dialog box, enter **Employee_Number** into the **Name** field. Press the Tab key to move the **Data Type** field and select the String type. Click on the OK button. Visual Basic will add the **Employee_Number** property to the **Employees** class. Figure 29.2 depicts the Class Builder window after you add properties to the **Employees** class.

18. Click on the Methods tab within the Class Builder window. Select File|New|Method. Visual Basic will display the Method Builder dialog box.

19. Within the **Name** field, enter **Last_Date_Paid**. Click on the + sign to the right of the **Arguments** field. Visual Basic will display the Add Argument dialog box.

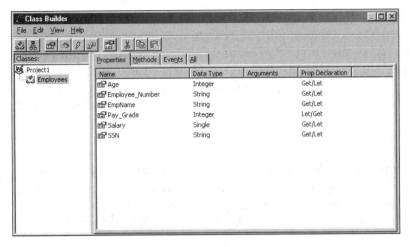

Figure 29.2   The **Employees** class and its properties.

20. Enter the name of the argument as Name. Select String from within the Data Type dialog box. Click on OK. Visual Basic will return to the Method Builder dialog box. Notice Visual Basic added the Name As String argument to the **Arguments** field.

21. Within the Return Type combo box, select String. Click on the OK button to exit the Method Builder dialog box. Visual Basic will add the **Last_Date_Paid** method to the list of methods the **Employees** class recognizes.

22. Select File|Update Project to add the new class descriptors to your project. Select File|Exit to exit the VB Class Builder utility. Note that Visual Basic has added the **Employees** class file to your project.

If you open the **Employees** class file, you'll notice the declarations within the listing that appeared earlier in this section. As you proceed through this book, you'll learn what the definitions mean and how you'll use them within your programs.

Understanding The Public Label

In the "Creating Classes Using The Class Builder Utility" section, you created a simple class, named **Employees**, that contained the **Public** label, as shown here:

```
Public Function Last_Date_Paid(Name As String) As String
```

Unlike a structure, with members that are all accessible to a program, a class can have members that the program can directly access using the **dot** operator, and other members (called private members) that the program can't access directly. The **Public** label identifies the class members the program can access using the **dot** operator. If you want the program to access a member directly, you must declare the member using the **Public** keyword.

Note that in this example, all the variables you declared in the previous section with the Class Builder utility appear to be private. Actually, the Class Builder utility has created property **Get** and **Let** functions to let your programs access the internal variables. In other words, if you have an object **DMercer**, which is an instance of the class **Employees**, and you want to assign the **Name** property, you'll assign the **Name** property using the **dot** operator, as shown here:

```
DMercer.Name = "David Mercer"
```

The concept of using interface functions to control properties is an important one, because of the control it provides in managing errant or inappropriate values. This concept is known, generally, as creating interfaces, or *information hiding*. There is more about information hiding in the next section.

Understanding Information Hiding

Information hiding is the process of hiding underlying implementation details of a function, program, or even a class. Information hiding lets programmers treat functions and classes as *black boxes*. In other words, if a programmer passes a value to a function, the programmer knows a specific result will occur. The programmer doesn't have to know how a function calculates a result but, instead, that the function works. For example, most programmers don't know the mathematics behind the **Atn** function, which returns an angle's arctangent. However, programmers know that if they pass a specific value to the function, a known result will occur. To use the function, the programmer must know only the input parameters and the values the **Atn** function returns.

In object-oriented programming, an object may have underlying implementation details. For example, a program may store a document's data in Word, Excel, or some other format. To use the document object, however, the program shouldn't have to know the format. Instead, the program should be able to perform read, write, print, and even fax operations without knowing the object details. To help programmers hide an object's underlying details, VBA lets you use the **Public** and **Private** keywords to divide class definitions. The program can directly access public data and methods, although it can't access the private data methods.

TIP: *As you read articles and books about object-oriented programming, you might encounter the term* encapsulation. *In the simplest sense, encapsulation is the combination of data and methods into a single data structure. Encapsulation groups together all the components of an object. In the "object-oriented" sense, encapsulation also defines how both the object itself and the rest of the program can reference an object's data. As you've learned, VBA classes let you divide your data into public and private sections. Programs can only access an object's private data using defined public methods. Grouping together an object's data and dividing your data into public and private sections protects the data from program misuses. In VBA, the class is the fundamental tool for encapsulation.*

Using The Private Keyword Within A Class

As you've learned, VBA lets you divide a class definition into public and private parts. The program can access directly the public data and methods with the **dot** operator. The program can't access the private data and methods. The following class definition shows the **Employees** class again, with private and public parts:

```
Private mvarEmpName As String             'local copy
Private mvarAge As Integer                'local copy
Private mvarSSN As String                 'local copy
Private mvarPay_Grade As Integer          'local copy
Private mvarSalary As Single              'local copy
Private mvarEmployee_Number As String     'local copy


Public Function Last_Date_Paid(Name As String) As String
```

The program can access directly the data and methods that reside in the public section with the **dot** operator. The only way the program can access the private data and methods, however, is through public methods. For example, the next section presents a program that manipulates both the public and private data.

Using Public And Private Data

As you've learned, VBA lets you divide a class definition into public and private data and methods. Programs can access the public data and methods using the **dot** operator. To access the private data and methods, however, the program must call the public methods. The program can't directly manipulate or invoke private data and methods. Before you create the program, however, you must add code to the **Last_Date_Paid** method. Double-click your mouse on the **Employees** class icon within the Project Explorer. VBA will open a Code window. Locate the **Last_Date_Paid** method and enter the following code:

```
Public Function Last_Date_Paid(Name As String) As String
  If UCase(Left(Name, 1)) < "L" Then
    Last_Date_Paid = ReturnDate(1)
  Else
    Last_Date_Paid = ReturnDate(2)
  End If
End Function
```

The **Last_Date_Paid** function (which the program code that invokes it will treat as a method) uses the function **ReturnDate**, which you haven't defined yet. To define the **ReturnDate** function, select Add-Ins|Class Builder. To add the **ReturnDate** function, perform the following steps:

1. Make sure that you've selected the **Employees** class within the Class Builder. If you haven't selected the **Employees** class, click on the Employees icon to select the **Employees** class.

2. Select File|New|Method. VBA will display the Method Builder dialog box.

3. Within the **Name** field, name the new method **ReturnDate**. Click on the + symbol to the right of the **Argument** field. VBA will display the Add Argument dialog box.

4. Within the **Name** field, type "WhichHalf". Select the DataType as Integer option. Click on OK. VBA will add the **WhichHalf As Integer** argument to the Method Builder dialog box.

5. Within the Method Builder dialog box, select the ReturnType as String. Click on the OK button. VBA will add the **ReturnDate** method to the **Employees** class.

6. Select File|Update Project. VBA will update the **Employees** class. Click on the *X* located in the top right-hand corner of the Class Builder window to exit the Class Builder.

7. If the **Employees** class Code window isn't open, open it by double-clicking on the Employees icon within the Project Explorer. VBA will display a Code window. Note that VBA has added the **ReturnDate** function just below the variable declarations. Click your mouse within the Code window and change the **Public** keyword preceding the ReturnDate header to **Private**. Add the following code to the **ReturnDate** function:

```
Private Function ReturnDate(WhichDate As Integer) As String
  Dim DateValue As Integer

  DateValue = CInt(Format(Date, "d"))
  Select Case WhichDate
    Case 1
      If DateValue < 15 Then
        ReturnDate = "First of the month"
      Else
        ReturnDate = "Fifteenth of the month."
      End If
    Case 2
      If DateValue > 7 And DateValue < 22 Then
        ReturnDate = "Seventh of the month."
      Else
        ReturnDate = "Twenty-second of the month."
      End If
  End Select
End Function
```

The **ReturnDate** function returns a string that indicates the last date paid to the calling function, **Last_Paid_Date**. However, because **ReturnDate** is a **Private** function, your programs can't access **ReturnDate** from anywhere outside of the class. To create a program to access the **Employees** class, perform the following steps:

1. Switch back to the Access window and add a new form to the project. Add a command button to the form.

2. Next, switch back to the VBA IDE and write the following code within the button's **Click** event:

```
Private Sub Command1_Click()
   Dim ThisEmployee As New Employees

   ThisEmployee.EmpName = "Dave Mercer"
   ThisEmployee.Age = "35"
   ThisEmployee.SSN = "999-99-9999"
   ThisEmployee.Pay_Grade = 100
   ThisEmployee.Salary = ThisEmployee.Pay_Grade * 100
   ThisEmployee.Employee_Number = "1"
   Debug.Print ThisEmployee.Last_Date_Paid(ThisEmployee.Name)
   Debug.Print ThisEmployee.ReturnDate
End Sub
```

When you've finished entering the code, save the project then try to execute the code by clicking on the command button. When you try to execute the program, VBA will display a "Method or data member not found" error message.

VBA won't execute the private method **ReturnDate** if you try to invoke it from within the program. Delete the offending line, and press F5 to continue execution. When you execute the program, VBA will display a message within the Immediate window, depending upon what day of the month it is when you execute the program. **Last_Date_Paid** can execute the **ReturnDate** method without difficulty because **ReturnDate** is only inaccessible from the main program.

One of the most difficult tasks programmers new to object-oriented programming face is determining what they should hide and what they should make public. As a general rule, the less the programmer knows about a class, the better. Therefore, you should try to use private data and methods as often as possible. In this way, programs have to use the object's public methods to access the object data. As you'll learn, if you force programs to manipulate object data with only public methods, you can decrease programming errors. In other words, you don't usually want a program to directly manipulate an object's data using only the **dot** operator. If you force users to use public methods to access private data, it will improve information hiding and make objects of your classes more stable.

TIP: *You've created a simple class that defines both public and private function members. As the number of methods provided with each class and the complexity of each method increases, so too will the number of functions you'll eventually define as public and private to handle the processing of the class. Remember that when you define methods (functions) within a class, you should only declare those methods that the class must expose (that is, make available to procedures outside the class) using the* **Public** *keyword. You should declare all other functions internal to the class using the* **Private** *keyword.*

Clearly, if what we have said so far is true, you should make the vast majority of your variables within the class **Private**, and provide the user with the means to access those variables. VBA, in fact, provides an easy set of tools for accessing private variables. In the next section, you will learn about these function types and how to use them.

Using The Property Let And Property Get Methods

As you've learned, you can use the VBA Class Builder to design a series of **Property Get** and **Property Let** functions within the **Employees** class module. You also learned that the **Property Get** and **Property Let** functions are interface functions, which you'll use to control the values the program tries to set for properties, among other things. You'll implement the **Property Get** and **Property Let** functions within your class modules, as shown here:

```
[Public | Private | Friend] [Static] Property Let name _
    ([arglist,] value)
  [statements]
  [Exit Property]
  [statements]
End Property

[Public | Private | Friend] [Static] Property Get name _
    [(arglist)] _
    [As type]
  [statements]
  [name = expression]
  [Exit Property]
  [statements]
  [name = expression]
End Property
```

The **Property Get** and **Property Let** functions have the components Table 29.1 describes.

Table 29.1   *The components of the* **Property Get** *and* **Property Let** *procedures.*

Component	Description
Public	An optional keyword that indicates the **Property Get** or **Property Let** procedure is accessible to all other procedures in all modules. If you don't use it in a module that contains an **Option Private** statement, the procedure isn't available outside the project.
Private	An optional keyword that indicates the **Property Get** or **Property Let** procedure is accessible only to other procedures in the class.
Friend	An optional keyword that indicates that the **Property Get** or **Property Let** procedure is visible throughout the project but not visible to a controller of an instance of an object.
Static	An optional keyword that indicates VBA preserves the **Property Get** or **Property Let** procedure's local variables between calls.
Name	The name of the **Property Get** or **Property Let** procedure. It follows standard variable naming conventions, except that the name can be the same as a corresponding **Property Get** or **Property Let** procedure in the same module.
Arglist	A required list of variables that represent arguments passed to the **Property Get** or **Property Let** procedure when the program calls it. The name and data type of each argument in a **Property Let** procedure must be the same as the corresponding argument in a **Property Get** procedure, and vice versa.
Value	A variable that contains the value the procedure is to assign to the property. When your program calls the procedure, the value argument must appear on the right side of the calling expression. The data type of value must be the same as the return type of the corresponding **Property Get** procedure. VBA requires the value argument for the **Property Let** procedure only. Attempts to set a value argument in a **Property Get** procedure will cause a runtime error.
Statements	Any group of statements for VBA to execute within the **Property Get** or **Property Let** procedure. The statements typically check the assigned value or the returned value for validity.
Type	An optional argument that determines the data type of the value the **Property Get** procedure returns. Type may be Byte, Boolean, Integer, Long, Currency, Single, Double, Date, String (except fixed length), Object, Variant, or user-defined type. The procedure can't return arrays of any type, but a Variant that contains an array can. The return type of a **Property Get** procedure must be the same data type as the last (or sometimes the only) argument in a corresponding **Property Let** procedure (if one exists) that defines the value assigned to the property on the right side of an expression.

TIP: *Every **Property Let** function must define at least one argument for the procedure it defines. That argument (or the last argument if there's more than one) contains the actual value for you to assign to the property when the program invokes the procedure the **Property Let** statement defines. Table 29.1 refers to that argument as value.*

If you don't explicitly specify the scope of a **Property** procedure using either the **Public**, **Private**, or **Friend** keyword, **Property** procedures are public. If you don't use the **Static** keyword, your program won't preserve the value of local variables between calls. You can use the **Friend** keyword only in class modules. However, procedures in any module of a project can access **Friend** procedures. A **Friend** procedure doesn't appear in the type library of its parent class.

Like a **Function** or **Property Get** procedure, a **Property Let** procedure is a separate procedure that takes arguments, performs a series of statements, and changes the value of its arguments. However, unlike a **Function** or **Property Get** procedure, both of which return a value, you can only use a **Property Let** procedure on the left side of a property assignment expression or **Let** statement. Conversely, you can only use a **Property Get** procedure on the right side of an expression in the same way you use a function or a property name when you want to return the value of a property.

As a general rule, you should design your class modules using **Property** procedures to ensure that bad input doesn't corrupt the data within the object. Once you have started working with class modules, it is only normal to be curious about the instancing of objects—that is, how the class module becomes an object. The next section discusses the process and provides some examples, too.

Understanding Object Instances

Many books and articles about object-oriented programming refer to *object instances*. In short, an object instance is an object variable. As you've learned, a class defines a template for future variable declarations. When you later declare an object, you create an object instance. In other words, when VBA allocates memory for a variable, it creates an object instance. All instances of the same class have the same characteristics. For the purposes of this book, an instance is a variable of a specific class.

Creating Object Instances

As you've learned, VBA doesn't allocate memory for classes until you create an instance of a class. You've also learned that VBA creates an instance, or object instance, when you create a variable of the Class type. Within VBA, you'll create variables having Class type using one of the following two methods:

```
Dim VariableName As New ClassName

Dim VariableName As Object
' Statements
Set VariableName = New ClassName
```

Either method is valid. However, just as when working with **Object** and **Control** variables, if you assign the **VariableName** to a specific type, it forces VBA to perform early binding. If instead you create an **Object** variable, and later assign the class type to that **Object** variable, VBA will perform late binding. In other words, if you use the **Dim** statement to create the variable of type Class, VBA will reserve that variable space at the beginning of the program (or whenever you declare **VariableName**). If you use the **Set** statement, VBA won't reserve the variable space for that class variable until the program reaches the assignment statement.

Understanding Inheritance

As you visualize how you might derive classes using inheritance, drawing pictures might help you to understand the relationships between classes. You'll find that one class you derive from one or more base classes might well become the base class for other classes. As you begin to define your classes, start with general characteristics and work toward specifics as you derive new classes.

For example, if you're deriving classes for types of automotive vehicles, your first base class might simply be **Autos**. **Autos** would contain characteristics common to all automotives, such as color, number of doors, tire size, engine size, number of passengers, and so on. Your next level might become more refined when you create the classes. The second level class types, **Cars** and **SUVs**, for example, would inherit the common characteristics that you defined in the **Autos** base class. As you further refine model types (for example, between a sedan and station wagon), however, you can use these second-level classes as base classes for other class definitions. Your base class levels will grow, conceptually similar to a family tree's growth, as shown in Figure 29.3.

Unfortunately, VBA doesn't support true inheritance. Although there are some methods you can use to avoid VBA's built-in constraints on inheritance, in general, you can't fully inherit classes, nor can you control how you inherit classes, as you can in C++. This book will design classes without inheritance.

Now that you have seen how you develop a class, and also how you instance that class into a single object, it is worthwhile to consider a little more closely the implications of how you define components of your class. Observe the suggestions carefully—they may save you a considerable amount of grief.

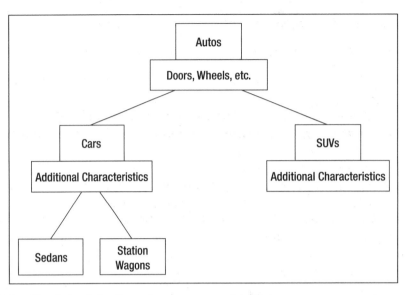

Figure 29.3   The Autos inheritance tree.

More On Private And Public Procedures And Functions

As you've learned, a private procedure or function is one that has limited scope. In other words, programs can only access a private procedure or function from within the area where the program defines the procedure or function. For example, only procedures within the same form can access a procedure within a form you declare as private. Similarly, procedures or functions that you declare as private within a module are visible or accessible only to other procedures or functions within the module. To let other programs (clients) access procedures or functions, you must make these procedures and functions public. Programmers refer to the process of letting other programs outside the class module access public functions within the class module as *exposing* these functions.

Private functions or procedures let you protect data from outside sources. The only way to retrieve and manipulate data in a private function or procedure is to call the routine from another public or private function or procedure within the same class module. Such indirect access to private functions or procedures lets the class (in this case, the ActiveX EXE) protect sensitive data. For example, imagine you have a private library of rare books in your house. A friend wants to read two of the books. However, you don't want anyone physically touching the books, because they're simply too valuable. If you let the friend physically touch the books, he may spill water on one, or worse, lose one. You must find a way to let your friend read the books without touching the books. So, you make a digital copy of each page and transfer the contents to a computer program. Now, your friend can read the books at his leisure without destroying anything. (Luckily, because the books are so old and rare, the copyright has expired, and you can make as many copies as you like.) In the same way, a private function would store the rare books. A public function would read the rare books on a computer screen without touching them.

New Objects In Access 2000

Access 2000 includes many new objects that improve the application's functionality. These objects also allow you, as a programmer, to strengthen your object-oriented programming skills. Many of these objects will be familiar to you, because they're actually extensions of existing Access and VB object types. The distinction between the old and new object types lies in the fact that the new object types generally reference a set of like objects to which a specific individual object belongs. This set of like objects is called a *collection* and forms the basis for understanding how data is organized and managed by Access 2000. Let's look at some of the new objects included with Access 2000, their collection designation, and how they're used.

AccessObject

AccessObject objects include information about a single object instance. They also describe forms, reports, macros, modules, data access pages, tables, queries, views, stored procedures, and database diagrams. Respectively, the aforementioned objects belong to the collections: **AllForms**, **AllReports**, **AllMacros**, **AllModules**, **AllDataAccessPages**, **AllTables**, **AllQueries**, **AllViews**, **AllStoredProcedures**, and **AllDatabaseDiagrams** collections. As a programmer, using **AccessObject** means that you'll have a common way to reference all objects of a given type. In other words, because an **AccessObject** object relates to an existing object, you don't create new **AccessObject** objects or delete existing ones. You typically reference an **AccessObject** object in a specific object collection by its **Name** property. For example, in the case of the Logon form you saw in Chapter 24, you might reference an instance of the form as an AccessObject using the syntax:

```
AllForms("Logon") AllForms![Logon]
```

You can see by this example that the **AccessObject Logon** is part of the **AllForms** collection.

AccessObjectProperty

AccessObjectProperty objects represent a built-in or user-defined characteristic of an **AccessObject** object. The **AccessObjectProperty** object is best understood by saying each **AccessObject** object contains an **AccessObjectProperties**

collection, and the objects comprising the **AccessObjectProperties** collection are, in fact, distinct **AccessObjectProperty** objects.

The objects themselves have two built-in properties: the **Name** property, which is a string uniquely identifying the property of the given object, and the **Value** property, which is a variant containing the property setting for the named object.

CodeData

As with the table and form objects you work with in Access 2000, the code that supports your programs is also stored in your Access 2000 database. When you refer to an **AccessObject** like a table or a form within your code, Access 2000 recognizes these references as **CodeData** objects. **CodeData** objects consist of the **AllTables**, **AllQueries**, **AllViews**, **AllStoredProcedures**, and **AllDatabase Diagrams** collections.

CurrentData

The **CurrentData** object refers to the objects stored in the current database by the source server application. As with the **CodeData** object, the **CurrentData** object is another way for Access 2000 to recognize references to stored data. However, in the case of the **CurrentData** object, the data being referenced isn't limited to data references embedded in your program code.

CurrentProject

In Access 2000, the set of all code modules in a database, including standard and class modules, is called a project. Projects typically have the same name as the database that they're associated with. The **CurrentProject** object refers to the Access 2000 entity by which the current Access 2000 project is referenced. You use the **CurrentProject** object just as you use the **Currentdb** object within the VBA models or components that make up your database. The difference is that **Currentdb** is a reference to the currently active database, and **CurrentProject** is a reference to the currently active Access 2000 project.

DataAccessPage

A **DataAccessPage** object refers to a particular Access 2000 data access page. You'll get better acquainted with data access pages in Chapter 35. For now, be aware that when you create a data access page, Access 2000 recognizes that page as a **DataAccessPage** object for reference purposes.

DefaultWebOptions

The **DefaultWebOptions** object contains a global set of properties used by Access when you save a data access page as a Web page or open a Web page. When you save a data access page, certain properties, like hyperlink color, hyperlink underlines, and settings for HTML encoding, are automatically set. The **DefaultWebOptions** object contains these properties that affect the characteristics of the overall document. These default properties may be set programmatically to affect all data access pages or specific data access pages.

FormatCondition

The **FormatCondition** object represents a conditional format of a combo box or text box control and is a member of the **FormatConditions** collection.

VBE

The **VBE** object is the root object that contains all other objects and collections represented in Visual Basic for Applications. Use the following collections to access the objects contained in the **VBE** object:

- **VBProjects** accesses the collection of projects.
- **Windows** accesses the collection of windows.
- **CodePanes** accesses the collection of code panes.
- **CommandBars** accesses the collection of command bars.

WebOptions

A **WebOptions** object refers to the specific Web option properties of an Access 2000 data access page. This object contains attributes used by Access 2000 when you save a data access page as a Web page or when you open a Web page. Using the **WebOptions** object, you can return or set attributes at either the application level or the data access page level.

TIP: *Be aware that attribute values differ from one data access page to another, depending on the value at the time the data access page was saved.*

Access 2000, in addition to incorporating new features, retains some important features—particularly as they concern objects—that you should be aware of. The following section discusses some of the objects found in earlier versions of the program that have been retained for this version.

Retained Objects In Access 2000

Although Access 2000 contains several new object types, it also maintains compatibility with previous versions of Access and their object types. The set of Access objects retained in Access 2000 that you're likely to use most often include these described in the following sections.

Application

The **Application** object still contains all Access objects and collections, including the **Forms**, **Reports**, **Modules**, and **References** collections, as well as the new **DataAccessPages** collection. The **Application** object also contains the **Screen**, **DoCmd**, **VBE**, **DefaultWebOptions**, **Assistant**, **CommandBars**, **DBEngine**, **FileSearch**, **ComAddIns**, **AnswerWizard**, and **LanguageSettings** objects. This object is typically used to apply methods or property settings to the entire Access 2000 application.

Control

The **Control** object represents a form, report, or section control that's within or attached to another control. All form or report controls belong to the **Controls** collection for the specific **Form** or **Report** object. Section controls belong to the **Controls** collection for the given section. Controls within a Tab control or Option Group control belong to the **Controls** collection for that control. Similarly, a Label control attached to another control belongs to the **Controls** collection for that control.

DoCmd

The **DoCmd** object has been retained, and its methods are used to run Access actions from Visual Basic. Actions perform tasks like closing windows, opening forms, and setting control values. Because the **DoCmd** object replaces the now-obsolete **DoCmd** statement, actions formerly used as arguments for the **DoCmd** statement are now methods of the **DoCmd** object.

Form

A **Form** object is a member of the **Forms** collection. The **Forms** collection is the set of all currently open forms. Reference to an individual **Form** object in the **Forms** collection is made by referring to the form by name or by referring to the form's index within the collection. (Individual forms are indexed beginning with zero.) Each **Form** object has a **Controls** collection, containing all controls used on a given form.

Module

Module objects refer either to a standard module or to a class module. The **Modules** collection contains all open **Module** objects, regardless of their type. **Module** objects in the **Modules** collection can be compiled or uncompiled.

Reference

The **Reference** object designates a reference to the type library of another application or project. When you create a **Reference** object, you set a reference dynamically from Visual Basic. The **Reference** object is a member of the **References** collection.

Report

A **Report** object references a specific Access report. These objects are members of the **Reports** collection, which consists of all currently open reports. Inside the **Reports** collection, individual reports are indexed beginning with zero. Consequently, you can refer to an individual **Report** object by referring to the report by name or by referring to its index within the **Reports** collection.

Screen

The **Screen** object is also retained in Access 2000. **Screen** objects reference specific forms, reports, or controls that currently have focus.

In general, an object alone may or may not be useful—or it may respond to a specific problem, whereas a complete solution requires managing groups of objects. To manage object groups, you use object collections, as discussed in the following section.

Access 2000 Object Collections

As you saw in previous chapters, Access 2000 supports Data Access Objects (DAOs) and their collections. These objects allow you to write programs to create and manipulate database components. Objects and collections contain properties that describe the nature of the components and methods used to manipulate them. Table 29.2 lists the current set of Access object collections by name, object type, and contents.

Table 29.2   Access object collections.

Name	Object Type	Description
AllDataAccessPages	AccessObject	Contains **AccessObject** for each data access page in the **CurrentProject** or **CodeProject** object.
AllDatabaseDiagrams	AccessObject	Contains **AccessObject** for each table database diagram in the **CurrentData** or **CodeData** object.
AllForms	AccessObject	Contains an **AccessObject** for each form in the **CurrentProject** or **CodeProject** object.

(continued)

Table 29.2   Access object collections (continued).

Name	Object Type	Description
AllReports	AccessObject	Contains **AccessObject** for each report in the **CurrentProject** or **CodeProject** object.
AllMacros	AccessObject	Contains **AccessObject** for each macro in the **CurrentProject** or **CodeProject** object.
AllModules	AccessObject	Contains **AccessObject** for each module in the **CurrentProject** or **CodeProject** object.
AllQueries	AccessObject	Contains **AccessObject** for each query in the **CurrentData** or **CodeData** object.
AllStoredProcedures	AccessObject	Contains **AccessObject** for each stored procedure in the **CurrentData** or **CodeData** object.
AllTables	AccessObject	Contains **AccessObject** for each table in the **CurrentData** or **CodeData** object.
AllViews	AccessObject	Contains **AccessObject** for each view in the **CurrentData** or **CodeData** object.
Connections	Connection	Provides data about a connection to an open database connectivity (ODBC) data source.
Containers	Container	Stores data about predefined object types.
Databases	Database	An open database.
DBEngine	DBEngine	The Microsoft Jet database engine.
Documents	Document	Contains data about saved, predefined objects.
Errors	Error	Contains data about any errors associated with this object.
Fields	Field	A column belonging to a table, query, index, relation, or recordset.
Groups	Group	A group of user accounts.
Indexes	Index	Predefined value ordering and uniqueness in a table.
Parameters	Parameter	A parameter for a parameter query.
Properties	Property	A built-in or user-defined property.
QueryDefs	QueryDef	A saved query definition.
Recordsets	Recordset	The records in a base table or query.
Relations	Relation	A relationship between fields in tables and queries.
TableDefs	TableDef	A saved table definition.
Users	User	A user account (Microsoft Jet workspaces only).
Workspaces	Workspace	A session of the Microsoft Jet database engine.

Immediate Solutions

Creating The Time-Based Class Module

The class modules described in the following sections will show you how to create a **DateStamp** class that contains a **DateStamp** property, a **TimeStamp** property, and a **DateTimeStamp** property. Begin to build the **DateStamp** class by performing the following steps:

1. Open the Chap29.mdb database.

2. Select Objects|Module button from the Access 2000 database window, then select Insert|Class Module from the Access 2000 menu bar. Access will open the Visual Basic Editor and create a new class module.

3. Select File|Save Chap29 from the Visual Basic Editor menu bar, then replace the name "Class1" with "DateStamp" in the Save As dialog box.

4. In the Declarations section of the class module window, create a private string variable with the name **mvarDateStamp**, as shown here:

```
Private mvarDateStamp As String
```

5. Select Class from the module window's Object drop-down menu, and enter the code for the **Class_Initialize( )** procedure:

```
Private Sub Class_Initialize()
  mvarDateStamp = Date
End Sub
```

6. Create a **Property Get** procedure by entering the following code into the code window:

```
Public Property Get DateStamp() As String
  DateStamp = mvarDateStamp
End Property
```

7. Select File|Save Chap29, then select File|Close And Return To Microsoft Access. Access will close the VBA IDE and return to the Database window. An icon will appear in the Access 2000 database window for the **DateStamp** class, as shown in Figure 29.4.

8. Select Objects|Module button from the Access 2000 database window, then select New from the window's toolbar to launch the VB Editor.

9. In the new module window, enter the following lines of code:

```
Sub ShowDateStamp()
  Dim Latest As New DateStamp

  MsgBox Latest.DateStamp
  Set Latest = Nothing
End Sub
```

10. Select File|Save Chap29, and save the new module with the name "ShowDateStamp".

11. Select Run|Run Sub/UserForm from the VBA Editor menu bar to run the **ShowDateStamp()** procedure. A successful run results in a message box.

Creating A **TimeStamp** Property

Now that you've grasped the mechanics of how to build and run a class module, let's add the **TimeStamp** property to the **DateStamp** class. To do so, perform the following steps:

1. From within the VBA IDE, open the **DateStamp** class module.

Figure 29.4 The new class module is represented by the DateStamp icon.

2. In the Declarations section of the class module window, create a private string variable with the name **mvarTimeStamp**, as shown here:

```
Private mvarTimeStamp As String
```

3. Select Class from the module window's Object drop-down menu, then change the code for the **Class_Initialize( )** procedure so it looks like the following:

```
Private Sub Class_Initialize()
  mvarDateStamp = Date
  mvarTimeStamp = Time
End Sub
```

4. Create a **Property Get** procedure for the new property by entering the following code into the code window:

```
Public Property Get TimeStamp() As String
  TimeStamp = mvarTimeStamp
End Property
```

To test your code, modify the **ShowDateStamp** procedure to display the value of the **TimeStamp** property—the reference will look like the following:

```
MsgBox Latest.TimeStamp
```

Creating A **DateTimeStamp** Property

To complete the design of the **DateStamp** class module, you should add the **DateTimeStamp** property to the module. To do so, perform the following steps:

1. From the VBA IDE, open the **DateStamp** class module.

2. In the Declarations section of the class module window, create a private string variable with the name **mvarDateTimeStamp**, as shown here:

```
Private mvarDateTimeStamp As String
```

3. Select Class from the module window's Object drop-down menu, then change the code for the **Class_Initialize( )** procedure so it looks like the following:

```
Private Sub Class_Initialize()
  mvarDateStamp = Date
  mvarTimeStamp = Time
  mvarDateTimeStamp = Now
End Sub
```

4. Create a **Property Get** procedure for the new property by entering the following code into the code window:

```
Public Property Get DateTimeStamp() As String
  DateTimeStamp = mvarDateTimeStamp
End Property
```

To test your code, modify the **ShowDateStamp** procedure to display the value of the **TimeStamp** property—the reference will look like the following:

```
MsgBox Latest.DateTimeStamp
```

Using **Property Let** With Class Modules

Now that you've seen how to create class modules that use programmatic functions and predefined defaults, let's look at how to customize an object property using the **Property Let** statement. In the case of this particular example, we're going to read some information from a text file. The code we'll write in the next two sections will let the user set a property corresponding to the file name, then we'll use the custom **ReadFile** method together with the property to read information into memory from a file. To do this, create a new class module in the project, called **FileClass**. Then, add the necessary code for the **FileName** property to the class, as shown here:

```
Private mvarFileName As String

Property Let FileName(NewName As String)
  mvarFileName = NewName
End Property

Property Get FileName() As String
  FileName = mvarFileName
End Property
```

Creating A Method

Now that you've seen how to create class modules that use programmatic functions and predefined defaults, let's look at how to set a method that can be invoked from outside the class module. To do so, you'll create a **Public** function inside the class module. The **ReadFile** method will open the file and read the text into a private variable of the class—and return a success value, as shown here:

```
Private mvarFileString As String

Public Function ReadFile() As Boolean
  Dim lstrLocal As String

  On Error Goto File_Error
  Open mvarFileName For Input As # 1
  Do While Not EOF(1)
    Line Input #1, lstrLocal
    MvarFileString = mvarFileString & lstrLocal
  Loop
  ReadFile = True
  Exit Function

File_Error:
  ' Didn't work
  ReadFile = False
End Function
```

Instantiating A Class Module

Module instantiation is a process of resource allocation and object re-creation. We'll examine this more closely in the next chapter. For now, let's instantiate a copy of **FileClass.** To do so, within the **ShowDateStamp** module, create a new procedure with the name **NewObject**, as shown here:

```
Sub NewObject()
  Dim FileObject As New FileClass

  FileObject.FileName = "sample.txt"
  If FileObject.ReadFile Then
    MsgBox "File Read Successfully!"
  Else
    MsgBox "File Not Read Succesfully!"
  End If
End Sub
```

The **Dim** statement functions in the same way as if you were declaring a variable. In other words, it allocates space to create the new object. **FileObject** identifies what the object will be called, and **As New FileClass** tells you that, when created, the new object will have the characteristics of the existing **FileClass** object. Notice, however, that the object itself hasn't been created. Actual object creation occurs when a property or method of the identified object is referenced in your procedure.

Chapter 30

Advanced Database Design Techniques

In Depth

In recent chapters, you've learned about both the fundamentals and advanced techniques of Access 2000 database design, as well as the issues surrounding manipulation of your Access 2000 databases—from Visual Basic for Applications (VBA) code, from macros, and from the different types of database objects that VBA provides you with. However, some important topics still remain to be considered in wrapping up the discussion of database design. In Chapter 31, we'll move on to development for the client-server database environment.

This chapter will discuss three important considerations to keep in mind when finishing your Access 2000 application—advanced form techniques, security techniques, and designing your own help files. The next section begins the discussion of advanced form techniques.

Using Advanced Form Management Techniques

You'll probably find that given Access's graphical environment, the majority of your development efforts will be centered around forms. It's imperative that you understand all the Form and Control events in addition to knowing which event you should code to accomplish what task. It's also important that you're aware of the types of forms that are available and how you can successfully achieve the look and feel you want for each form.

Many times you won't need to design your own form. Instead, you can take advantage of one of the built-in dialogs that are part of the VBA language or supplied as part of the Access development environment. Of course, you'll need to add menu bars and toolbars to your forms. Whatever types of forms you create, take advantage of all the tricks of the trade covered throughout this chapter.

Understanding The Form Events And Their Use

Microsoft Access traps for 30 Form events, each of which serves a distinct purpose. Events are also trapped for Form sections and controls. Although a brief explanation of each of the Form events is valuable, most of the events are relatively straightforward. Table 30.1 briefly explains the Form events.

Table 30.1   The Form events.

Event Name	Description
Activate	Occurs when the form receives focus and becomes the active window. It's triggered when the form is opened, when a user clicks on the form or one of its controls, and when the **SetFocus** method is applied using VBA code.
AfterDelConfirm	Occurs after the record is actually deleted, even if the deletion is canceled. If the **BeforeDelConfirm** event isn't canceled, the **AfterDelConfirm** event occurs after the confirmation dialog is displayed.
AfterInsert	Occurs after the record has actually been inserted. It can be used to requery a recordset when a new record is added.
AfterUpdate	Occurs after the changed data in a record is updated.
ApplyFilter	Occurs when the user selects the Apply Filter/Sort, Filter By Selection, or Remove Filter/Sort options. It also occurs when the user closes the Advanced Filter/Sort window or the Filter By Form window. You can use this event to make sure that the filter being applied is correct, to change the display of the form before the filter is applied, or to undo any changes you made when the **Filter** event occurred.
BeforeDelConfirm	Occurs after the **Delete** event but before the delete confirm dialog is displayed. If you cancel the **BeforeDelConfirm** event, the record being deleted is restored from the delete buffer, and the delete confirmation dialog box is never displayed.
BeforeInsert	Occurs when the first character is typed in a new record but before the new record is actually created. When the user is typing in a text or combo box, the **BeforeInsert** event occurs even before the **Change** event of the text or combo box.
BeforeUpdate	Fires before a record is updated. It occurs when the user tries to move to a different record or when the File menu Save Record option is executed. The **BeforeUpdate** event can be used to programmatically cancel the update process. It's used for this purpose when you want to perform complex validations. When a user adds a record, the **BeforeUpdate** event occurs after the **BeforeInsert** event.
Click	Occurs when the user clicks on a blank area of the form, on a disabled control on the form, or on the form's record selector.
Close	Occurs when a form is closed and removed from the screen, after the **Unload** event. It's important to understand that you can cancel the **Unload** event but not the **Close** event.
Current	Occurs each time focus moves from one record to another. The **Current** event is an appropriate place to put code that you want to execute whenever a record is displayed.
DblClick	Occurs when the user double-clicks on a blank area of the form, on a disabled control on the form, or on the form's record selector.

(continued)

Table 30.1   The Form events (continued).

Event Name	Description
Deactivate	Occurs when the form loses focus because a table, query, form, report, macro, module, stored procedure, view, Data Access Page, or the Database window becomes active. The Deactivate event isn't triggered when a dialog, a popup form, or another application becomes active.
Delete	Occurs when a user attempts to delete a record but before the record is actually removed from the table. This is the event in which to place code that allows the deletion of a record only under certain circumstances. If the **Delete** event is canceled, the **BeforeDelConfirm** and **AfterDelConfirm** events will never execute, and the record will never be deleted. When the user deletes multiple records, the **Delete** event occurs after each record is deleted. This enables you to evaluate a condition for each record and determine whether each record should be deleted.
Dirty	Occurs when the contents of a form change. When a **Dirty** event occurs, you can determine if the record can be changed. This allows you to perform generic checking any time a user tries to make an edit.
Error	Access fires this event whenever an error occurs while the user is in the form. Microsoft Jet database engine errors are trapped, but Visual Basic errors aren't. This event can be used to suppress the standard error messages that Jet would display. Visual Basic errors must be handled using standard **On Error** techniques.
Filter	Occurs whenever the user selects the Filter By Form or Advanced Filter/Sort options. You can use this event to remove the previous filter, enter default settings for the filter, invoke your own custom filter window, or prevent certain controls from being available in the Filter By Form window.
GotFocus	Occurs whenever a form receives the focus. The **GotFocus** event occurs for a form only if no visible, enabled controls are on the form.
KeyDown	Occurs if no controls are on the form or if the **KeyPreview** property of the form is set to Yes. When the **KeyPreview** property is set to Yes, all keyboard events are previewed by the form and occur for the control that has the focus. If the user presses and holds down a key, the **KeyDown** event occurs repeatedly until the key is released.
KeyPress	Occurs when the user presses and releases a key or key combination that corresponds to an ANSI code. It occurs if no controls are on the form or if the **KeyPreview** property of the form is set to Yes. The keystroke can be canceled by setting **KeyCode** to zero.
KeyUp	Occurs if no controls are on the form or if the **KeyPreview** property of the form is set to Yes. The **KeyUp** event occurs only once, regardless of how long the key is pressed. The keystroke can be canceled by setting the **KeyCode** parameter to zero.
Load	Occurs when a form is opened and the first record is displayed. It occurs after the **Open** event. The **Open** event of a form can cancel the opening of a form, but the **Load** event can't.

(continued)

Table 30.1   The Form events (continued).

Event Name	Description
LostFocus	Occurs whenever a form loses the focus. The **LostFocus** event occurs for a form only if no visible, enabled controls are on the form.
MouseDown	Occurs when the user clicks on a blank area of the form, on a disabled control on the form, or on the form's record selector. It occurs before the **Click** event fires. It can be used to determine which mouse button was pressed.
MouseMove	Occurs when the user moves the mouse over a blank area of the form, over a disabled control on the form, or over the form's record selector. It's generated continuously as the mouse pointer moves over the form. The **MouseMove** event occurs before the **Click** event fires.
MouseUp	Occurs when the user releases the mouse button. Like the **MouseDown** event, it occurs before the **Click** event fires and can be used to determine which mouse button was pressed.
Open	Occurs when a form is opened but before the first record is displayed. Using this event, you can determine exactly what happens when the form first opens.
Resize	Occurs when a form is opened and whenever the size of the form changes.
Timer	Occurs at regular intervals. It occurs only when the form's **TimerInterval** property is set. How often the **Timer** event fires depends on the value set within the **TimerInterval** property.
Unload	The **Unload** event occurs when a form is closed but before the form is actually removed from the screen. It's triggered when the user clicks Close on the File menu, quits the application by choosing End Task from the task list, quits Windows, or when your code closes the form. You can place code that ensures that it's okay to unload the form in the **Unload** event. You can also use the **Unload** event to execute any code that you want to have execute whenever the form is unloaded.

Understanding The Sequence Of Form Events

Effective programming and management of forms means that you must understand the order in which Form events occur. One of the best ways to learn about the order in which events occur is to place **Debug.Print** statements within the events that you want to learn about. Keep in mind that event order isn't an exact science—in fact, it's nearly impossible to guess the order in which events occur in all situations. It's helpful, though, to understand the basic order in which certain events do occur.

The Form-Opening Events

When the user opens a form, the following events occur, in the following sequence:

- **Open**
- **Load**

- **Resize**
- **Activate**
- **Current**

After these Form events occur, the **Enter** and **GotFocus** events of the first control fire next. Remember that the only place you can cancel the opening of the form is in the **Open** event.

Understanding The Form-Closing Events

When a user closes a form, the following events occur, in the following sequence:

- **Unload**
- **Deactivate**
- **Close**

Before these events occur, the **Exit** and **LostFocus** events of the active control are triggered.

Understanding The Form-Sizing Events

When a user resizes a form, what happens depends on whether the form is minimized, restored, or maximized. If the form is minimized, the following Form events occur, in the following sequence:

- **Resize**
- **Deactivate**

When the user restores a minimized form, the following events occur, in the following sequence:

- **Activate**
- **Resize**

When the user maximizes a form or restores a maximized form, only the **Resize** event occurs.

Understanding What Events Access Invokes In Other Common Situations

Three other common situations exist in which Access will invoke Form events: when the user moves from one form to another, when the user types a character, and when the user clicks the mouse button. When the user moves from one form to another, the **Deactivate** event occurs for the first form and the **Activate** event occurs for the second form. Remember that the **Deactivate** event doesn't happen if focus moves to a dialog, a popup form, or another application.

If the user types a character and the **KeyPreview** property of the form is set to True, the following Form events take place, in the following sequence:

- **KeyDown**
- **KeyPress**
- **Change**
- **KeyUp**

If you trap the **KeyDown** event and set the **KeyCode** to zero, the remaining events never occur. The **KeyPress** and **Change** events capture only ANSI keystrokes. These events are the easiest to deal with; however, you need to handle the **KeyDown** and **KeyUp** events when you need to trap for non-ANSI characters such as Shift, Alt, and Ctrl.

When the user clicks the mouse button, the following events occur, in the following sequence:

- **MouseDown**
- **MouseUp**
- **Click**

Understanding Section And Control Events

Sections have only five events: **Click**, **DblClick**, **MouseDown**, **MouseMove**, and **MouseUp**. These events rarely play a significant role in your application. However, each control type has its own set of events to which it responds. Many events are common to most controls. Other events are specific to certain controls. Furthermore, some controls respond to very few events. Table 30.2 details all the Control events.

Table 30.2   The Control events Access supports.

Event Name	Description
AfterUpdate	Applies to text boxes, option groups, combo boxes, list boxes, and bound object frames. It occurs after changed data in the control is updated.
BeforeUpdate	Applies to text boxes, option groups, combo boxes, list boxes, and bound object frames. It occurs before changed data in the control is updated.
Change	Applies to text and combo boxes. It occurs when data in the control changes. In the case of a text box, this event occurs when a character is typed. In the case of a combo box, it occurs when a value is selected from the list. Use this event when you want to trap for something happening on a character-by-character basis.

(continued)

Table 30.2   The Control events Access supports (continued).

Event Name	Description
Click	Applies to labels, text boxes, option groups, combo boxes, list boxes, command buttons, and object frames. It occurs when the user presses and releases a mouse button over a control. The **Click** event is triggered when the user clicks the mouse over an object, as well as in other situations. Access will also fire the **Click** event when the spacebar is pressed while a command button has the focus, when the Default property of a command button is set to Yes and the Enter key is pressed, and when the Cancel property of a Command button is set to Yes and the Escape key is pressed. Finally, Access will fire the **Click** event when an accelerator key for a command button is used.
DblClick	Applies to labels, text boxes, option groups, combo boxes, list boxes, command buttons, and object frames. It occurs when the user presses and releases the left mouse button twice over a control.
Enter	Applies to text boxes, option groups, combo boxes, list boxes, command buttons, object frames, and subforms. It occurs before a control actually receives the focus from another control on the same form. It occurs before the **GotFocus** event.
Exit	Applies to text boxes, option groups, combo boxes, list boxes, command buttons, object frames, and subforms. It occurs just before the **LostFocus** event.
GotFocus	Applies to text boxes, toggle buttons, option buttons, check boxes, combo boxes, list boxes, and command buttons. It occurs when focus moves to a control in response to a user action or when the **SetFocus**, **SelectObject**, **GoToRecord**, **GoToControl**, or **GoToPage** methods are issued in code. Controls can receive focus only if they're visible and enabled.
KeyDown	Applies to text boxes, toggle buttons, option buttons, check boxes, combo boxes, list boxes, and bound object frames. It occurs when the user presses a key while within a control and occurs repeatedly until the key is released. It can be canceled by setting the **KeyCode** parameter equal to zero.
KeyPress	Applies to text boxes, toggle buttons, option buttons, check boxes, combo boxes, list boxes, and bound object frames. It occurs when the user presses and releases an ANSI key while the control has the focus. It can be canceled by setting **KeyCode** equal to zero.
KeyUp	Applies to text boxes, toggle buttons, option buttons, check boxes, combo boxes, list boxes, and bound object frames. It occurs when a key is released within a control. It occurs only once, no matter how long a key is depressed.
LostFocus	Applies to text boxes, toggle buttons, option buttons, check boxes, combo boxes, list boxes, and command buttons. It occurs when focus moves away from a control in response to a user action or when the **SetFocus**, **SelectObject**, **GoToRecord**, **GoToControl**, or **GoToPage** methods are issued in code. The difference between the **GotFocus/LostFocus** and **Enter/Exit** events lies in when they occur. If focus is moved to another form or is returned to the current form, the **GotFocus** and **LostFocus** events of the control are triggered. The **Enter** and **Exit** events don't occur when the form loses or regains focus.

(continued)

Table 30.2   The Control events Access supports (continued).

Event Name	Description
MouseDown	Applies to labels, text boxes, option groups, combo boxes, list boxes, command buttons, and object frames. It occurs when the mouse button is pressed over a control and before the **Click** event fires.
MouseMove	Applies to labels, text boxes, option groups, combo boxes, list boxes, command buttons, and object frames. It occurs as the mouse is moved over a control.
MouseUp	Applies to labels, text boxes, option groups, combo boxes, list boxes, command buttons, and object frames. It occurs when the mouse is released over a control but before the **Click** event fires.
NotInList	Applies only to a combo box. It occurs when the user enters a value in the text box portion of the combo box that isn't in the combo box list. Using this event allows the user to add a new value to the combo box list. For this event to be triggered, the **LimitToList** property must be set to Yes.
Updated	Applies to a bound object frame only. It occurs when the object linking and embedding (OLE) object's data has been modified.

Understanding The Sequence Of Control Events

Just as Form events occur in a certain sequence when the form is opened, activated, and so on, control events occur in a specific sequence. When writing the event code for a control, it's important to understand the order in which events for the control occur.

The Events When Focus Moves From Or To A Control

When the focus is moved to a control, the following events occur, in the following sequence:

- **Enter**

- **GotFocus**

If focus is moving to a control as the form it's located on is opened, the Form and Control events occur in the following sequence:

- **Open** (form)
- **Activate** (form)
- **Current** (form)
- **Enter** (control)
- **GotFocus** (control)

When the focus leaves a control, the following events occur:

- **Exit**
- **LostFocus**

When the focus leaves the control because the form it's located on is closing, the following events occur:

- **Exit** (control)
- **LostFocus** (control)
- **Unload** (form)
- **Deactivate** (form)
- **Close** (form)

Events That Fire When The Data In A Control Is Updated

When you change data in a control and move the focus to another control, the following events occur:

- **BeforeUpdate**
- **AfterUpdate**
- **Exit**
- **LostFocus**

The following events occur after every character that's typed in a text or combo box, but before focus is moved to another control:

- **KeyDown**
- **KeyPress**
- **Change**
- **KeyUp**

In the case of a combo box, if the **NotInList** event is triggered, it occurs after the **KeyUp** event.

Referring To Me

The **Me** keyword is essentially an implicitly declared variable. It's available to every procedure within a Form or Report module. Using **Me** is a great way to write generic code within a form or report. You can change the name of the form or report, and the code will be unaffected. The following code is a good example:

```
Me.RecordSource = "qryProjects"
```

It's also useful to pass **Me** (the current form or report) to a generic procedure within a module. This is demonstrated in the following example:

```
Call ChangeCaption(Me)
```

The **ChangeCaption** procedure looks like this:

```
Sub ChangeCaption(frmAny As Form)
  If IsNull(frmAny.Caption) Then
    frmAny.Caption = "Form For - " & CurrentUser
  Else
    frmAny.Caption = frmAny.Caption & " - " & CurrentUser
  End If
End Sub
```

The **ChangeCaption** procedure, contained within a Code module, receives any form as a parameter. It evaluates the caption of the form it was passed. If the caption is **Null**, it sets the caption to **"Form for -"**, concatenated with the user's name. Otherwise, it takes that existing caption of the form it was passed and appends the user name. The **Me** keyword refers to any form in the project from within the form itself—no matter what type of form it is. You will find out more about the different form types in the next sections.

Understanding The Form Types

As you know, you can design a variety of forms using Microsoft Access. By working with the properties available within the Access form designer, you can create forms with many different looks and dramatically different types of functionality. This chapter covers all the major categories of forms, but remember you can build your own forms to meet your needs. However, don't lose track of maintaining consistency with the standards for Windows applications.

Use Single Forms To View One Record At A Time

One of the most common types of forms is a form that allows you to view one record at a time. A common example is a form that allows the user to view one customer record and move to other records as needed. Creating a Single form is easy and simply involves setting the Default View property of the form to Single Form.

Use Continuous Forms To View Multiple Records At A Time

Often, the user wants to be able to view multiple records at a time. This requires that you create a Continuous form that's built by setting the Default View property to Continuous Forms.

A common use of a Continuous form is a subform. You generally should show multiple records within a subform. The records that appear within the subform are all the records that relate to the record displayed in the main form.

Use Multipage Forms When Everything Doesn't Fit On One Screen

Scarcity of screen real estate is a never-ending problem. One of the solutions is a multipage form. To create a multipage form, view the form in Design view and place a Page Break control just before the start of the next page on the form. To insert a Page Break control, select it from the toolbox and click and drag to place it on the form.

When creating a multipage form, remember a few important steps:

- Set the Default View property of the form to Single Form.
- Set the Scroll Bars property of the form to Neither or Horizontal Only.
- Set the Auto Resize property of the form to No.
- Place the Page Break control exactly halfway down the detail area of the form if you want the form to contain two pages. When you want additional pages, divide the total height of the Detail section by the number of pages and place Page Break controls at the appropriate positions on the form.
- Size the Form window to fit exactly one page of the form.

Use Tabbed Forms To Conserve Screen Real Estate

An alternative to a multipage form is a Tabbed form. Access supports Tabbed forms with the Tab Control OCX (OCX stands for OLE custom control). Figure 30.1 shows how a multipage form can be designed to look like a Tabbed form.

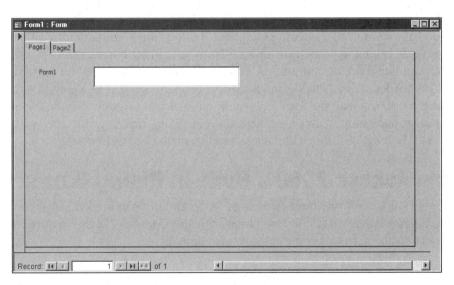

Figure 30.1   A multipage form designed as a Tabbed form.

Very little code is involved in making a Tabbed form work: In general, you can simply move between pages on the Tabbed form by clicking the tab for the form you want to move to.

Using Switchboard Forms To Control Your Application

A switchboard form is a great way to control your application. The Switchboard Manager is a tool designed to help you to easily create switchboards. The "Immediate Solutions" section of this chapter details how to create a switchboard form.

Splash Screen Forms: A Professional Opening To Your Application

Splash screens add professional polish to your applications and give your users something to look at while your programming code is setting up the application. It's easy to create a Splash Screen form. Consult the "Immediate Solutions" section of this chapter for further details on creating one.

You can also display a splash screen by including a bitmap file with the same name as your database (MDB) in the same directory as the database file. When the application is loaded, the splash screen—that is, the bitmap—displays for a couple of seconds. The only disadvantage to this method is that you have less control over when, and how long, the splash screen displays.

Use Dialog Forms To Gather Information

Dialog forms are generally used to gather information from the user. What makes them Dialog forms is that they're modal, meaning that the user can't proceed with the application until the form is handled. Dialog forms are generally used when you must obtain specific information from your user before the processing of your application can continue. A custom Dialog form is simply a regular form with a border style of Dialog and its Modal property set to Yes. Remember to give users a way to close the form. In addition to creating custom Dialog forms, you can also use many of Access 2000's built-in dialog boxes to interact with your users. The next sections will discuss built-in dialog boxes in detail.

Using Access 2000's Built-In Dialog Boxes

Access ships with two built-in dialogs: the standard Windows message box and the input box. Access 2000 also ships with the Common Dialog control, which gives you access to other commonly used dialogs.

Using The Message Box Dialog

A message box is a predefined dialog you can incorporate into your applications. Although it's predefined, it can be customized using parameters. The VBA language has a **MsgBox** statement and a **MsgBox** function. The **MsgBox** statement can only display a message, whereas the **MsgBox** function can display a message and return a value based on the user's response.

The message box contained within the VBA language is the same message box that's standard in most Windows applications, so it's already familiar to most Windows users. Rather than creating your own dialogs to obtain standard responses from your users, you should use the existing, standard interface.

Using The MsgBox Statement

The **MsgBox** statement receives five parameters: the message, the type of icon you want to appear, the title for the message box, and the help file and context ID that you want to be available if the user selects Help while the dialog is displayed. The statement looks like this:

```
MsgBox "This is a Message", vbInformation, "This is a Title"
```

This example displays the message "This is a Message". The information icon is displayed. The title for the message box is "This is a Title". The message box contains an OK button that's used to close the dialog.

Using The MsgBox Function

Whereas the **MsgBox** statement is normally used to display an OK button only, the **MsgBox** function enables you to select from various standard combinations of buttons to be included in the dialog. It returns a value indicating which button the user selected. The **MsgBox** function receives the same five parameters as the **MsgBox** statement. The first parameter is the message that you want to display. The second parameter is a numeric value indicating what buttons you want to display as well as the icon you want to display. Table 30.3 lists the values that can be numerically added to specify the buttons in the message box, which you pass as the second parameter.

TIP: *In general, try to use the intrinsic constants included in the table rather than numeric values. Doing so contributes to program clarity and helps you more easily modify the code.*

The values in Table 30.3 must be numerically added to one of the values in Table 30.4 if you want to include an icon other than the default icon in the dialog. Table 30.4 details the values you can use to indicate icons to display in the message box.

Table 30.3   Values indicating the buttons you want to display.

Buttons	Value	Intrinsic Constant
OK button only	0	**vbOKOnly**
OK and Cancel	1	**vbOKCancel**
Abort, Retry, and Ignore	2	**vbAbortRetryIgnore**
Yes, No, and Cancel	3	**vbYesNoCancel**
Yes and No	4	**vbYesNo**
Retry and Cancel	5	**vbRetryCancel**

Table 30.4   Values indicating the icons you want to display.

Icon	Value	Intrinsic Constant
Critical (Stop Sign)	16	**vbCritical**
Warning Query (Question)	32	**vbQuestion**
Warning Exclamation	48	**vbExclamation**
Information (I)	64	**vbInformation**

When using the **MsgBox** function, the dialog returns an integer value to the calling program. Table 30.5 lists the values returned from the message box function, depending on which button the user selected.

Using The InputBox Function

The **InputBox** function displays a dialog containing a simple text box. It returns the text the user typed in the text box and looks like this:

```
Sub InputBoxExample()
    Dim strName As String
    strName = InputBox("Please enter your name.", _
                    "Chapter 30", "Lars Klander")
    MsgBox "You Entered " & strName
End Sub
```

Notice that the first parameter is the message, the second is the title, and the third is the default value. The second and third parameters are optional. This subroutine displays the input box that appears in Figure 30.2.

Using The Windows Common Dialog Control

As mentioned, the Common Dialog control is an OCX that's included as part of Access 2000. It enables you to display Windows common dialogs, including File Save, File Open, File Print, File Print Setup, Fonts, and Colors.

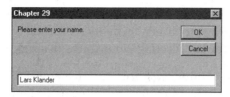

Figure 30.2   Using the **InputBox** function.

Table 30.5   Values that are returned from the message box function.

User Response	Value	Intrinsic Constant
OK	1	**vbOK**
Cancel	2	**vbCancel**
Abort	3	**vbAbort**
Retry	4	**vbRetry**
Ignore	5	**vbIgnore**
Yes	6	**vbYes**
No	7	**vbNo**

Often, you will want to control your program's interactions with the user not through the use of special dialog boxes, but rather through responsiveness on the part of your program's forms. One of the best way to make your form responsive is to use Access 2000's built-in form filtering support, as the next section details.

Taking Advantage Of Built-In Form-Filtering Features

Access has several form-filtering features that are part of the user interface. You can opt to include these features within your application, omit them from your application entirely, or control their behavior. For your application to control the behavior of the filter features, it needs to respond to the **Filter** event, which means that your application senses when a filter is placed on the data in the form. When it has sensed the filter, the code in the **Filter** event executes.

At times, you might want to alter the standard behavior of a filter command. For instance, you might want to display a special message to the user or take a specific action in your code. Another reason for responding to a **Filter** event could be that you want to alter the display of the form before the filter is applied. For example, if a certain filter is in place, you might want to hide or disable certain fields. When the filter is removed, you might want to return the appearance of the form to normal.

Fortunately, Access not only lets you know that the **Filter** event occurred, but it also lets you know how the filter was invoked. Armed with this information, you can intercept and alter the filtering behavior as desired.

When a user chooses Filter By Form or Advanced Filter/Sort, the **FilterType** parameter is filled with a value that indicates how the filter was invoked. If the user invokes the filter by selecting Filter By Form, the **FilterType** parameter equals the constant **acFilterByForm**. When the user invokes the filter by selecting Advanced Filter/Sort, the **FilterType** parameter equals the constant **acFilterAdvanced**. The following code demonstrates the use of these constants:

```
Private Sub Form_Filter(Cancel As Integer, FilterType As Integer)
  Select Case FilterType
    Case acFilterByForm
      MsgBox "You Just Selected Filter By Form!"
    Case acFilterAdvanced
      MsgBox "You Are Not Allowed to Select Advanced Filter/Sort!"
      Cancel = True
    End Select
End Sub
```

This code, placed in the **Filter** event for the form, evaluates the filter type. If Filter By Form was selected, a message box displays and the filtering proceeds as usual. When the user selects Advanced Filter/Sort, the user is told that he or she can't do this and the filter process is canceled.

Not only can you test for how the filter was invoked, you can intercept the process when the filter is applied. You accomplish this by placing code in the **ApplyFilter** event of the form, as shown in the following code:

```
Private Sub Form_ApplyFilter(Cancel As Integer, ApplyType As Integer)
  Dim intAnswer As Integer

  If ApplyType = acApplyFilter Then
    intAnswer = MsgBox("You just selected the criteria: " & _
        Chr(13) & Chr(10) & Me.Filter & _
        Chr(13) & Chr(10) & "Are You Sure You Wish to Proceed?", _
        vbYesNo + vbQuestion)
    If intAnswer = vbNo Then
      Cancel = True
    End If
  End If
End Sub
```

This code evaluates the value of the **ApplyType** parameter. If it's equal to the constant **acApplyFilter**, a message box is displayed verifying that the user wants to apply the filter. If the user responds Yes, the filter is applied; otherwise, the filter is canceled.

Often, especially in today's interconnected enterprise, your applications will need to provide response to users through other applications, or contain elements of those applications within themselves. The underlying Microsoft technology that supports such processing is known as OLE, and the next section provides a quick overview of both the technology and its common uses.

Including Objects From Other Applications: Linking Vs. Embedding

Microsoft Access is an OLE Client application, meaning it can contain objects from other applications. Access 2000 is also an OLE server application, which means Access has the capability to control other applications using program code. In this section, you learn how to link to and embed objects in your Access forms.

Using Bound OLE Objects

Bound OLE objects are tied to the data in an OLE field within a table in your database. An example is the **Photo** field that's part of the **Employees** table within the Northwind database. The field type of the **Employees** table supporting multimedia data is **OLE Object**. This means each record within the table can contain a unique OLE object. The **Employees** form contains a bound OLE control whose control source is the **Photo** field from the **Employees** table.

If you double-click on the photo of an employee, the OLE object can be edited *In-Place*, as shown in Figure 30.3.

The picture of the employee is actually embedded in the **Employees** table. This means the data associated with the OLE object is actually stored as part of the Access database (MDB) file, within the **Employees** table. Embedded objects, if they support the OLE 2.0 standard, can be modified In-Place. This is called *In-Place activation*.

Using Unbound OLE Objects

Unbound OLE objects aren't stored within your database. Instead, they're part of the form within which they were created. Like bound OLE objects, unbound OLE objects can be linked or embedded. You create an unbound OLE object on an Access form by adding an unbound object frame to the form.

You will often find that your applications need to perform preprocessing on your unbound forms to make them respond as you desire. While the **OpenArgs** property for forms has many uses—an almost infinite number, depending on how you

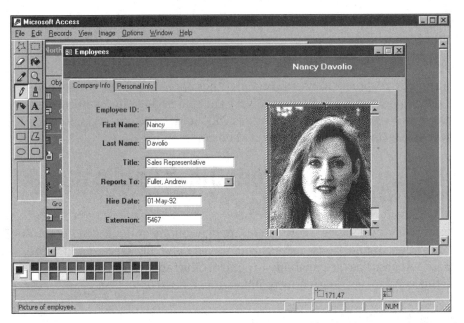

Figure 30.3   In-Place activation and editing of an OLE object in a record from the Microsoft
Northwind.mdb database.

process the arguments—you will always use **OpenArgs** to help your forms do
preprocessing if they need to. The following section explains the **OpenArgs** property in detail.

Using The OpenArgs Property

The **OpenArgs** property gives you a way to pass information to a form as it's
being opened. The **OpenArgs** argument of the **OpenForm** method is used to
populate the **OpenArgs** property of a form at runtime. It works as shown here:

```
DoCmd.OpenForm "frmPaymentMethods", , , , , acDialog, "GotoNew"
```

This code opens the **frmPaymentMethods** form when a new method of payment
is added to the **cboPaymentMethodID** combo box. It sends the
frmPaymentMethods form an **OpenArg** of "GotoNew". The **Load** event of the
frmPaymentMethods form should then look similar to the following:

```
Private Sub Form_Load()
  If Me.OpenArgs = "GotoNew" And Not IsNull(Me![PaymentMethodID]) Then _
     DoCmd.DoMenuItem acFormBar, 3, 0, , acMenuVer70
End Sub
```

This code evaluates the **OpenArgs** property of the form, moving to a new record if the **OpenArgs** property contains the text string "GoToNew" and the **PaymentMethodID** of the current record isn't **Null**. The **OpenArgs** property can be evaluated and used anywhere in the form. After the form is opened, your applications will often need to perform extended processing on the controls the form contains. While you learned a great deal about controls and their manipulations in Chapter 25, there are some advanced techniques that will often prove useful. The next section discusses some of these techniques as they relate to combo and list boxes.

Using Some Powerful Combo Box And List Box Techniques

Combo and list boxes are very powerful. Being able to properly respond to the **NotInList** event of a combo box, populate a combo box using code, and select multiple entries in a list box are essential skills of an experienced Access programmer. The following sections detail some of the power techniques you should know.

Handling The NotInList Event

As discussed earlier in this chapter, the **NotInList** event occurs when a user types a value in the text box portion of a combo box that isn't found in the combo box list. This event occurs only if the **LimitToList** property of the combo box is set to True. It's up to you whether you want to respond to this event.

At times, you might want to respond with something other than the default error message when the **LimitToList** property is set to True and the user attempts to add an entry. For example, if a user is entering an order and she enters the name of a new customer, you might want to react by displaying a message box asking whether she really wants to add the new customer. If the user responds affirmatively, you can display a customer form.

After you've set the **LimitToList** property to True, any code you place in the **NotInList** event is executed whenever the user attempts to type an entry that isn't found within the combo box. The following code shows an example:

```
Private Sub cboCompany_NotInList(NewData As String, Response As Integer)
  Dim intAnswer As Integer

  intAnswer = MsgBox("Company Does Not Exist.  Add (Yes/No)", _
      vbYesNo + vbQuestion)
End Sub
```

The problem with this code is that it warns the user of the problem but doesn't rectify the problem; thus, this code runs, and the default error handling kicks in. The **NotInList** event procedure accepts a response argument. This is where you can tell VBA what to do *after* your code executes. Any one of the three constants detailed in Table 30.6 can be placed in the response argument.

The following code, when placed in the **NotInList** event procedure of your combo box, displays a message asking the user whether she wants to add the customer. If the user responds No, she is returned to the form without the standard error message being displayed, but she still must enter a valid value in the combo box. If the user responds Yes, she is placed in the Customer form, ready to add the customer whose name she typed.

```
Private Sub cboCompany_NotInList(NewData As String, Response As Integer)
  Dim iAnswer As Integer

  iAnswer = MsgBox("Company Does Not Exist.  Add? (Yes/No)", _
      vbYesNo + vbQuestion)
  If iAnswer = vbYes Then
    DoCmd.OpenForm frmCustomer, acNormal, , , acAdd, acDialog
    Response = acDataErrAdded
  Else
    Response = acDataErrContinue
  End If
End Sub
```

Populating A Combo Or List Box With A Callback Function

As you know, it's easy to populate a combo or list box by setting properties of the control. This method is sufficient for many situations. In other situations, though, you might want to populate a combo or list box programmatically. One example is when you want to populate the combo or list box with values from an array. Another is when you want to populate the box with table or report names or some other database component.

Table 30.6   The available constants for the response argument.

Constant	Description
acDataErrAdded	This constant is used if your code adds the new value into the record source for the combo box. This code requeries the combo box, adding the new value to the list.
AcDataErrDisplay	This constant is used if you want VBA to display the default error message.
AcDataErrContinue	This constant is used if you want to suppress VBA's own error message, using your own instead. Access still requires that a valid entry be placed in the combo box.

To populate a combo or list box using code, create a Callback function. This function tells Access how many rows and columns will be in the combo or list box as well as what data will be used to fill the box. This function becomes the Row Source type for your combo or list box. Access calls the function and uses its information to populate the combo or list box. The "Immediate Solutions" section details how to create and implement a Callback function.

The function must contain five predetermined arguments. The first argument must be declared as a control, and the remaining arguments must be declared as variants. The function itself must return a variant. The parameters are listed in Table 30.7.

The List function is called several times. Each time it's called, Access automatically supplies a different value for the code, indicating the information that it's requesting. The code item can have the values shown in Table 30.8.

Table 30.7   The five predetermined arguments of a Callback function.

Argument	Description
fld	A control variable that refers to the combo or list box being filled.
id	A unique value that identifies the control being filled. It's useful when you're using the same function to populate more that one combo or list box.
row	The row being filled (zero-based).
col	The column being filled (zero-based).
code	A value specifying the information being requested.

Table 30.8   Possible code item values.

Code	Intrinsic Constant	Meaning	Returns
0	**acLBInitialize**	Initialize	Nonzero if the function can fill the list; False or Null if a problem occurs
1	**acLBOpen**	Open	Nonzero ID value if the function can fill the list; False or Null if a problem occurs
3	**acLBGetRowCount**	Number of rows	Number of rows in the list
4	**acLBGetColumnCount**	Number of columns	Number of columns in the list
5	**acLBGetColumnWidth**	Column width	Width of the column specified
6	**acLBGetValue**	List entry	List entry to be displayed in the column and row specified
7	**acLBGetFormat**	Format string	Format string used to format the list entry
8	**acLBClose**	Not used	
9	**acLBEnd**	End (last call)	Nothing

The function is automatically called once for codes 0, 1, 3, and 4. These calls initiate the process and determine the number of rows and columns that the combo or list box contains. The function is called twice for code 5, once to determine the total width of the box, and, again, to set the column width. The number of times that codes 6 and 7 are executed varies depending on the number of rows that are contained in the box (code 3). Code 9 is called when the form is closed or the combo or list box is queried.

Armed with this knowledge, you can take a good look at the **lstForms_Fill** function (contained in the Chap30.mdb file), the Callback function that's used to populate the list box. The purpose of this function is to populate the list box with a list of forms that was opened by the **CustomerPhoneList** form. The **CustomerPhoneList** form allows multiple instances of the Customers form to be opened and added to a collection. When the user closes the **CustomerPhoneList** form, the **CustomersDialog** form is opened, asking the user which instances of the Customers form he or she wants to leave open.

The Callback function begins by creating a form object variable based on the Customers form. Each element of the case structure seen in the routine is called as each code is sent by Access. Here's what happens:

- When Access sends the code of 0, the **colCustomerForms** variable is set equal to the **ReturnCollection** method of the **CustomerPhoneList** form. The **ReturnCollection** method of the **CustomerPhoneList** form contains a collection of open Customers forms. The function then returns a True.

- When Access sends the code of 1, the return value is a unique value equal to the return value of the **Timer** function.

- When Access sends the code of 3, the return value is set equal to the count of forms in the **colCustomerForms** collection.

- When Access sends the code of 4, the return value is set to 1 (one column).

- When Access sends the code of 5, the return value is set to -1, forcing a default width for the combo or list box.

Access then automatically calls code 6 by the number of times that was returned for the number of rows in the combo or list box. Each time code 6 is called, the form object variable is set equal to a different element of the form collection. The **CompanyName** from each form is returned from the function. The **CompanyName** return value is the value that's added to the list box.

All this work might seem difficult at first. After you've populated a couple of combo or list boxes, though, it's quite easy. In fact, all you need to do is copy the case structure that you see in the **lstForms_Fill** function and use it as a template for all your callback routines.

TIP: *Access 2000 also supports the **AddressOf** operator, which you can use to pass a function address to a Windows application programming interface (API) callback function. While callbacks in the Windows API are implemented somewhat differently than the example you saw in this section, the principle is the same. In general, callback functions enable your applications to receive series of information of indeterminate length from another location—in the case of the Windows API, from a system-level function.*

Handling Multiple Selections In A List Box

Access 2000 list boxes have a **Multiselect** property. When set to True, this property lets the user select multiple elements from the list box. Your code can then evaluate which elements are selected and perform some action based on the selected elements.

In addition to power control management techniques, there are important and useful techniques for managing subforms. The next section explains some of those tips and tricks in detail.

Power Subform Techniques

Many new Access developers don't know the ins and outs of creating and modifying a subform and referring to subform controls. Let's start with some important points you should know when working with them:

- The easiest way to add a subform to a main form is to open the main form and drag-and-drop the subform onto the main form.

- The easiest way to edit a subform after it's been added to the main form is to double-click on the subform control within the main form. If your double-click isn't successful, you need to click off of the subform object and double-click on it again.

The **LinkChildFields** and **LinkMasterFields** properties of the subform control determine which fields in the main form link to which fields in the subform. A single field name or a list of fields separated by semicolons can be entered into the **LinkChildFields** and **LinkMasterFields** properties. When they're properly set, these properties ensure that all records within the child form relate to the currently displayed record in the parent form.

Referring To Subform Controls

Many developers don't know how to properly refer to subform controls. You must refer to any objects on the subform through the subform control on the main form, as shown here:

```
Forms!frmCustomer!fsubOrders
```

This example refers to the **fsubOrders** control on the **frmCustomer** form. If you want to refer to a specific control on the **fsubOrders** subform, you must then point at its controls collection, as shown here:

```
Forms!frmCustomer!fsubOrders.Controls!txtOrderID
```

This code refers to the **txtOrderID** control on the form contained within the **fsubOrder** control on the **frmCustomer** form. To change a property of this control, you would extend the syntax to look like this:

```
Forms!frmCustomer!fsubOrders.Controls!txtOrderID.Enabled = False
```

This code sets the **Enabled** property of the **txtOrderID** control on the form contained within the **fsubOrders** control to False.

Now that you have seen some of the important design considerations to keep in mind when working with forms and controls—techniques, tips, and tricks that will make your applications that much better—there are several other considerations that you must address when finishing your applications. One of the most important issues for you to address, both from the perspective of securing your database's design from prying eyes and from the perspective of helping your clients ensure security throughout their databases, is the creation of security for your systems. The next sections discuss security considerations and implementations in detail.

Considering Database Security

After you design and develop a sophisticated application, you must ensure that the integrity of the application and the data that it maintains aren't violated. Microsoft Access gives you several options for securing your database. They range from a very simple method of applying a password to the entire database, to applying varying levels of security to each and every object in the database. The more intricate your security solution, the more difficult it is to implement. Fortunately, you can tailor the complexity of the security you implement to the level of security required by each particular application.

Establishing A Database Password

The simplest, least sophisticated, method of implementing security is to assign a password to the overall database. This means that every person wanting to gain access to the database must enter the same password. When access has been obtained to the database, all of the database's objects are available to the user. This type of security is referred to as share-level security.

Share-level security is the simplest and quickest security to set up. This method of security is adequate for a small business in which the users of the database want to ensure that no unauthorized people can obtain access to the data, but each person who *does* have access to the database has full access to all of its objects.

After you've assigned a password to a database, users are prompted for a password each time they open it. The Password Required dialog box appears each time the database is opened, as shown in Figure 30.4.

When the user has entered the valid password, he or she gains access to the database and all of its objects. In fact, the user can even remove the password by selecting the Tools menu Security submenu Unset Database Password option. The Unset Database Password dialog box only requires that you know the original password.

The preceding paragraphs outline all there is to know about setting a database password. Although it's extremely easy to understand and implement, it's also extremely unsophisticated. As you can see, a user either has or doesn't have access to the database, and it's very easy for any user who has access to the database to modify or unset its password.

> **WARNING!** *If you forget the password associated with a database, there's absolutely no way that you'll gain access to the database and its objects. It's therefore extremely important that you carefully maintain a list of the passwords associated with each database.*

To assign a password to a database, the user must be able to open the database exclusively. The right of a user to open a database exclusively can be granted or denied through the User and Group Permissions dialog. Assigning rights that permit or deny a user or a group exclusive open rights is explained later in this chapter.

Understanding Database Encryption

Before moving on to the more sophisticated methods of securing a database, it's important that you understand what *any* method of security does and doesn't provide for you. No matter how well you learn about and implement the techniques in this chapter, you won't be protected against someone attempting to read the data contained in your database. It's important that you're aware that even after you secure a database, someone with a disk editor can view the contents of the

Figure 30.4   The Password Required dialog box.

file. Although the data within the file won't appear in an easy-to-read format, the data is there and available for unauthorized individuals to see.

Fortunately, Access enables you to encrypt a database. The encryption process renders the data within the database indecipherable from word processors, disk utilities, and other products capable of reading text. When a database is encrypted, no one can decipher any of its data.

A database can be encrypted using the standard Access menus or by writing a VBA subroutine. In either case, the database that you're encrypting must not be open.

> **WARNING!** *It's always a good idea to back up the original database before you begin the encryption process. This ensures that if something goes wrong during the encryption process, you're still protected.*

When you encrypt a database, the entire database (not just the data) is encrypted. As you access the data and the objects within the database, Access needs to decrypt the objects so the user can use them and encrypt them again when the user is done accessing them. Regardless of the method of encryption you employ, the encrypted database degrades performance by about 15 percent. Furthermore, encrypted databases usually can't be compressed by most disk compression software utilities because compression software usually relies upon repeated patterns of data. The encryption process is so effective at removing any patterns that it renders most compression utilities ineffective. You need to make a decision as to whether this decrease in performance and the inability to compress the database file is worth the extra security that encryption provides.

Establishing User-Level Security

For most business environments, share-level security isn't sufficient. Therefore, it's necessary to take a more sophisticated approach toward securing the objects within your database. User-level security enables you to grant specific rights to users and groups within a workgroup. This means each user or group can have different permissions on the *same* object. With this method of security, each user begins by entering a user name and password. The Jet engine validates the user name and password and determines the permissions associated with the user. Each user maintains his or her own password, which is unrelated to the passwords of the other users.

With this method of security, users belong to groups. Rights can be assigned at the group level, the user level, or both. A user inherits the rights of his or her least restrictive group. This is highlighted by the fact that security is always on. By default, all users get rights to all objects because every user is a member of the group called Users. This group is, by default, given all rights to all objects. If you haven't implemented security, all users are logged on as the **Admin** user, who is a member of the Users group. The Jet engine determines that the **Admin** user has no password and therefore doesn't display an opening logon screen. Because members of the Users group by default get rights to all objects, it appears as if no security is in place.

With user-level security, you can easily customize and refine the rights to different objects. For example, one set of users might be able to view, modify, add, and remove employee records. Another set of users might be able to view only employee information. The last group of users might be allowed no access to the employee information, or they might be allowed access only to specific fields (such as name and address). The Access security model easily accommodates this type of scenario.

The major steps to implement user-level security include the following:

- Use the Workgroup Administrator to establish a new system database.
- Create a new user who'll be the administrator of the database.
- Make the user a member of the Admins group.
- Change the logon for the group by adding an administrator password for the workgroup.
- Remove the **Admin** user from the Admins group.
- Exit and restart Access, logging in as the new system administrator.
- Assign a password to the new system administrator.
- Open the database you want to secure.
- Run the Security Wizard, selecting the types of objects you want to be secured.
- Create Users and Groups who are members of the workgroup defined by the system database.
- Assign rights to Users and Groups for individual objects.

The first step to establishing user-level security involves setting up a workgroup. You then can define groups and users who belong to that workgroup and assign rights to these groups and users. Before you learn how to create groups and users, it's important for you to understand that groups and users are defined only in the context of a specific workgroup. Think of a workgroup as a group of users in a multiuser environment who share data and applications.

When you establish a new workgroup, Access creates a Workgroup Information File. The Workgroup Information File is where a unique identifier for the workgroup (called a WID), users, groups, and passwords are stored for a particular workgroup. All application databases can share the same workgroup file, or you can maintain separate workgroup files for different application databases.

Understanding The System.mdw File

As mentioned in the previous section, user and group security information is stored in a Workgroup Information File. The default name for this file is System.mdw. Each application database is associated with a specific Workgroup Information File. It's the combination of the information stored in the Workgroup Information File and the information stored in the database that grants or denies individual users access to the database or to the objects within it. Multiple databases can share the same Workgroup Information File, which contains the following:

- The name of each user and group

- The list of users that make up each group

- The encrypted logon password for each user that's defined as part of the workgroup

- Each user's and group's unique security identifiers (SIDs)

A SID is a machine-generated binary string that uniquely identifies each user or group. The system database contains the names and SIDs of the groups and users who are members of that particular workgroup and, therefore, share a system database.

Actually, you can create many Workgroup Information Files. The name of the Workgroup Information File currently being used is stored in the Windows registry. View it under the **HKEY_LOCAL_MACHINE** hive in a key called **\SOFTWARE\Microsoft\Office\9.0\Access\Jet\3.6\Engines\Jet**.

It's important that you record and store all workgroup information in a very safe place, so you can re-create it in case of an emergency. After entering the workgroup owner information, click OK. You're prompted for the name and location of the Workgroup Information File.

The Workgroup Information dialog enables you to enter the name and location of the workgroup file. After you type the name of a new workgroup file and click OK, you're asked to confirm the information. You're given one final opportunity to change any of the information. Click OK to confirm the information. Next, you're notified that the workgroup has been successfully created. You can then click Exit to close the workgroup administrator.

Joining A Different Workgroup

If different groups of users within your organization work with entirely different applications, you might find that it's appropriate to create multiple Workgroup Information Files. To access a database that's been properly secured with a specific Workgroup Information File, the database must be accessed while the user is a member of that workgroup. If the same user requires access to more than one database, each associated with a different Workgroup Information File, it might be necessary for the user to join a different workgroup. This can be accomplished using the Workgroup Administrator. To join a different workgroup, follow these steps:

1. Launch the Workgroup Administrator.

2. Select Join. The Workgroup Information File dialog appears.

3. Locate the name of the Workgroup File you want to join.

4. Click OK. You're notified that you successfully joined the workgroup.

Creating An Administrative User

When you've joined a workgroup, you're ready to create users and groups. You accomplish this from within Microsoft Access. Access comes with two predefined groups: the Admins group and the Users group. The Admins group is the system administrator's group account. This group automatically contains a member called Admin. Members of this group have the irrevocable power to modify user and group memberships and clear user passwords, so anyone who is a member of the Admins group is all-powerful within your system. The Admins group must contain at least one member at all times.

It's extremely important to create a unique workgroup identification (ID) from within the workgroup administrator. This is covered in the "Establishing A Workgroup" section later in this chapter. Otherwise, members of other workgroups can create their own workgroup file and grant themselves permissions to your database's objects. Furthermore, it's important to ensure that the **Admin** user doesn't own any objects and isn't given any explicit permissions. Because the **Admin** user is the same across all workgroups, all objects that Admin owns or has permissions to are available to anyone using another copy of Microsoft Access or Visual Basic.

The system also comes with a predefined Users group. This is the default group that's composed of all user accounts. All users are automatically added to the Users group and can't be removed from it. The Users group automatically gets all permissions to all objects. As with the **Admin** user, the Users group is the same across all workgroups. It's, therefore, extremely important that you take steps to remove all rights from the User's group, thereby ensuring that the objects in the database are properly secured.

The first step in this process is to create a new user who'll be the administrator for the database. To accomplish this, select the Tools menu Security submenu User and Group Accounts option. It doesn't matter which database you're in when you do this. It's only important that you're a member of the proper workgroup. Remember, you're defining Users and Groups for the workgroup, not for the database. The User And Group Accounts dialog box appears, as shown in Figure 30.5.

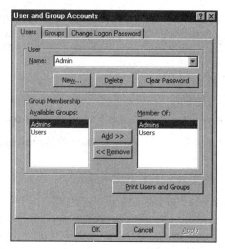

Figure 30.5   The User And Group Accounts dialog box.

The User and Group Accounts dialog enables you to create and delete users and assign their group memberships. It also enables you to create and delete groups and invoke a logon password for Microsoft Access. It's important to understand that even if you access this dialog from within a specific database, you're setting up users and groups for the *entire* workgroup. In other words, if you assign a password while you're a member of the standard System.mdw workgroup, and others on your network share the same System Workgroup File, everyone on your network will get prompted with a logon dialog when they attempt to launch Microsoft Access. If you don't want this to occur, you must create a new System Workgroup File before establishing security.

When you're sure that you're a member of the correct workgroup and are viewing the User and Group Accounts dialog, you're ready to create a new user who'll administrate your database. To establish a new administrative user, click New.

The New User/Group dialog box enables you to enter the user name and a unique Personal ID. This Personal ID isn't a password. The user name and Personal ID combine to become the encrypted SID that uniquely identifies the user to the system. Users create their own password when they log onto the system.

Making The Administrative User A Member Of The Admins Group

The next step is to make the new user a member of the Admins group. To do this, click Add with the new user selected from the User drop-down. The new user should appear as a member of the Admins group and of the Users group.

Changing The Password For The Admin User

After creating the new user and making him or her a member of the Admins group, you're ready to change the logon for the workgroup by adding a password for the **Admin** user. This is necessary so Access will prompt you with a Logon dialog when you launch the product. If Admin has no password, the Logon dialog never appears. Without a Logon dialog, you'll never be able to log on as the new user you just defined.

Before you exit and reload Access, remove Admin from the Admins group. Remember that the **Admin** user is the same in *every* workgroup. Because the Admins group has all rights to all objects in the database (including the right to assign and remove permissions to other users and objects), if you don't remove Admin from the Admins group, your database won't be secure.

You're now ready to close the User and Group Accounts dialog and exit Access. Click OK. Exit Access, and attempt to run it again. You'll be prompted with the Access Logon dialog box.

Log on as the new system administrator. You don't have a password at this point; only the **Admin** user has a password. At this point, it still doesn't matter which database is open.

After you've logged in as the new administrator, modify your password. To do this, select the Tools menu Security submenu User And Group Accounts option. Click the Change Logon Password tab. Remember that you can only assign a password for the user that you're logged on as.

Opening The Database You Want To Secure

After all of this work, you're finally ready to actually secure the database. Up to this point, it didn't matter which database you had open. Everything that you've done thus far has applied to the workgroup rather than to a particular database. Now, you must work with a specific database. Open the database that you want to secure. At the moment, the **Admin** user owns the database and members of the Users group have rights to all objects within the database.

Running The Security Wizard

The first thing you should do to secure the database is to use the Security Wizard. The Security Wizard revokes the rights from all users and groups except for the user that's currently logged on. It also creates a copy of the database; the ownership of the database and all of its objects are transferred to the user who is currently logged on.

To run the Security Wizard, select the Tools menu Security submenu User Level Security Wizard option. The Security Wizard dialog box will appear.

In the Security Wizard dialog box, select the objects that you want to secure. Notice you can secure all objects, or you can opt to secure just tables, queries, forms, reports, macros, or modules. After you click OK, you're prompted for the name of the secured database. The owner of a database can't be changed and *always* has rights to everything in the database. Because Admin is the owner of the database and Admin is the same in all workgroups, Access must copy all of the database objects to a new, secure database that's owned by the new user. Access in no way modifies the existing, unsecured database. Type a name for the new secure database, and then click Save. Access creates the new database, copies all of the objects to the new database, and removes all rights from all objects for the Users group in the new database. When the process is completed the dialog shown in Figure 30.6 will appear.

The Security Wizard dialog warns you that the new database has been secured and that the original database hasn't been modified in any way. The new database is owned by the new system administrator. All rights have been revoked from the Users group.

Creating Users And Groups

When you've established and joined a workgroup, you're ready to establish the users and groups who'll be members of the workgroup. Users represent individual people who'll access your database files, and they're members of groups. Groups are categories of users that share the same rights, which can be assigned at either the user level or the group level. It's easier administratively to assign all rights at the group level. This involves categorizing access rights into logical groups and assigning users to these groups.

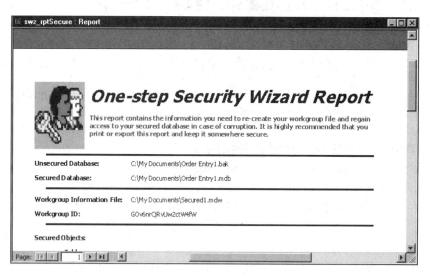

Figure 30.6   A successfully completed Security Wizard process.

If groups have been set up properly, the administration of the system is greatly facilitated. Should rights of a category of users need to be changed, they can be changed at a group level. When a user is promoted and needs additional rights, you can make that user a member of a new group. This is much easier than trying to maintain separate rights for each user. Users and groups can be added, modified, and removed using front-end interface tools, as well as through VBA code.

Regardless of how you choose to define groups and users, generally, create groups and assign users to the appropriate groups. It's important to think through the design of the organization as well as your application before you begin the mechanical process of adding the groups and users.

Types Of Permissions

To assign permissions appropriately, it's important that you understand the types of permissions available and what each type of permission allows the user to do. The types of permissions available are detailed in Table 30.9.

Some of the permissions listed in Table 30.9 implicitly include associated permissions. For example, a user can't update data in a table if he or she doesn't have the rights to read the data and the design of the table within which that data is located.

Table 30.9 The permissions you can set for users.

Permission	Description
Administer	Allows the user to set the database password, replicate the database, and change startup properties. A user with administer permission of a database object—such as a table, query, form, report, macro, or module—has full access to the object and its data. A user with administer permissions for an object can assign permissions for that object to other users.
Delete Data	Allows the user to delete records in a table or query.
Insert Data	Allows the user to add records to a table or query.
Modify Design	Allows the user to view and change the design of tables, queries, forms, reports, macros, and modules.
Open/Run	Allows the user to open a database, form, or report or run a macro.
Open Exclusive	Allows the user to open a database with exclusive access.
Read Data	Allows the user to view the data in a table or query.
Read Design	Allows the user to view tables, queries, forms, reports, macros, and modules in design view.
Update Data	Allows the user to view and modify table or query data, but it doesn't let the user insert and delete records.

Considering Some Other Important Security Issues

Although the discussion of security thus far has been quite thorough, a couple of issues surrounding the basics of security haven't yet been covered. They include additional issues with passwords, understanding how security works with linked tables, understanding and working with object ownership, and printing security information. These topics are covered in the sections that follow.

Passwords

When you create a user, no password is assigned to the user. Passwords can be assigned to a user only when that user has logged on to the system. The system administrator can't add or modify a user's password. It's important to encourage users to assign themselves a password the first time that they log on to the system. Using VBA code, the users can be forced to assign themselves a password.

Although you can't assign or modify a user's password, you can remove it. This becomes necessary when a user forgets his or her password.

Security And Linked Tables

When you've designed your application with two databases (one for tables and the other for the remainder of the application objects), it's necessary for you to secure both databases. Securing only the linked tables isn't sufficient!

A potential problem still exists. If a user has access to add, delete, and modify data from within your application, that user can open the database containing the data tables from outside your application and modify the data without going through the forms and reports you've designed. One solution to this problem is to revoke all rights from the tables. Base all forms and reports on queries that have the Run Permissions property set to Owner's. This provides users with the least opportunity to modify the data from outside of your system.

Ownership

Remember that the user who creates the database is the database's owner. This user retains irrevocable rights to the database. You can't change the owner of a database; you can only change the ownership of objects within the database. You can, in effect, change the owner of the database if you have rights to its objects, by creating a new database and importing all of the objects from the other database. This is automatically accomplished by the Security Wizard. By default, the creator of each object within the database is its owner.

Controlling Security With Program Code

You might not always be there to set up security for the users of your application. Of course, one alternative is to make sure they purchase their own copy of Access and instruct them on how to maintain security using the user interface. Access security is very complex, though, so this solution isn't very practical. In fact, if you're distributing your application to a large group of users, this option is an impossibility. Fortunately, you can build into your application code the capability to maintain all aspects of security directly. It's important that you provide your administrative users with the ability to establish and maintain security for their workgroups. This involves building a front-end interface to all of the security functionality provided by Access. Behind the scenes, you can use Data Access Object (DAO) code to implement the security functionality.

> **WARNING!**   Because ADO doesn't directly manage the Jet engine, you can't use ADO code to implement security functionality (although, once the security is in place, ADO can access the database very easily).

Maintaining Users And Groups Using Code

As you've already seen, it's important to create logical groups of users and assign rights to these groups. The user of your application might want to add or remove groups after you've distributed your application. You can use Group DAOs to create and manage group accounts at runtime.

Not only might you want to maintain groups using code, but you might also want to maintain users with code. You can employ User DAOs to create and manage user accounts at runtime. The "Immediate Solutions" section of this chapter details the code you can use for group and user management from your program code.

Working With Passwords

The administrative user often needs to add, remove, or modify users' passwords. By using the user interface, you can only modify the password of the user currently logged in, but by using code, you can modify any user's password, as long as you have administrative rights to do so.

Denying Users Or Groups The Ability To Create Objects

You might want to prevent the members of a workgroup from creating new databases or creating specific database objects. Preventing users from creating databases or other objects can only be accomplished using VBA code.

Denying Users Or Groups The Ability To Create Databases

Using DAOs, you can programmatically prohibit users from creating new databases. This is quite obviously a very powerful feature. The code looks like this:

```
Sub NoDBs(strGroupToProhibit)
    On Error GoTo NoDBs_Err
    Dim db As DATABASE
    Dim con As Container
    Dim strSystemDB As String

    'Obtain name of system file
    strSystemDB = SysCmd(acSysCmdGetWorkgroupFile)
    'Open the System Database
    Set db = DBEngine(0).OpenDatabase(strSystemDB)
    'Point to the Databases Collection
    Set con = db.Containers!Databases
    con.UserName = strGroupToProhibit
    con.Permissions = con.Permissions And Not dbSecDBCreate
NoDBs_Exit:
    Set db = Nothing
    Set con = Nothing
    Exit Sub
NoDBs_Err:
    MsgBox "Error # " & Err.Number & ": " & Err.Description
    Resume NoDBs_Exit
End Sub
```

The **NoDBs** routine receives the name of the user or group whom you'll prohibit from creating databases. It opens the system database and points to the containers collection. It then sets the permissions for the database to the existing permissions combined with **Not dbSecDBCreate**, thereby prohibiting the group or user from creating new databases.

Denying Users Or Groups The Ability To Create Other Objects

You might not want to prohibit users from creating new databases. Instead, you might want to prevent them from creating new tables, queries, or other objects within *your* application or data database file. The code is similar to that required to prohibit users from creating new databases, as shown here:

```
Sub NoTables(strGroupToProhibit)
    On Error GoTo NoTables_Err
    Dim db As DATABASE
```

```
   Dim con As Container
   Dim strSystemDB As String

   'Obtain name of system file
   strSystemDB = SysCmd(acSysCmdGetWorkgroupFile)
   'Point to the Current Database
   Set db = CurrentDb
   'Point to the Databases Collection
   Set con = db.Containers("Tables")
   con.UserName = strGroupToProhibit
   con.Permissions = con.Permissions And Not dbSecDBCreate
NoTables_Exit:
   Set db = Nothing
   Set con = Nothing
   Exit Sub
NoTables_Err:
   MsgBox "Error # " & Err.Number & ": " & Err.Description
   Resume NoTables_Exit
End Sub
```

The difference between this code and the code required to prohibit users from creating new databases is that this code points the database object variable at the current database rather than at the system database. It then points the **Container** object to the **Tables** collection. Other than these differences, the code is identical to the **NoDBs** routine.

Security And Client-Server Applications

It's important to understand that security for client-server applications must be applied on the back-end database server. You can request a logon ID and password from the user at runtime and pass them to the database server as part of the connection string, but Access security itself does nothing in terms of interacting with client-server data. Any errors that are returned from the back end must be handled by your application. You'll learn more about client-server applications in Chapter 31.

Developing A Help File

In a perfect world, you could create an application that wouldn't require any explanation. In this perfect world, your user could simply view any form in your application and *instantly* know how to use it. No assistance would be required. Unfortunately, the world isn't perfect. Even with the elegant graphical user interface that Windows provides, it's necessary that you provide users with guidance in using your application. This can be accomplished relatively easily by including Help files with it.

Considering Help From A User's Perspective

Before you venture into the process of creating a custom Help file, it's important that you become familiar with the basics of working with Windows 95/98 Help. This provides you with a context within which to develop your own Help files. These files should provide your users with the same look and feel as the Help files included with Access, Word, Excel, and the other standard products with which your users should already be familiar.

Planning The Help File

Before you worry about *how* to build a Help file, plan out what it will look like. What you provide in a Help file is determined by the type of users that will be working with your application. For instance, if your application will be distributed to a wide range of users, including those new to Windows, your Help file should include the most basic information. On the other hand, if your application is directed toward power users who are extremely adept at Windows and maybe even Access, your Help file should focus on assisting the user with the more complex aspects of your application. In general, it should contain the following:

- An introduction to your application.

- A description of each form and report that comprises your application.

- Instructions on how to use the various controls on your forms.

- A description of each toolbar and each tool contained on the toolbar.

- Instructions for carrying out tasks such as adding a client, deleting a client, or adding projects relating to a client.

Depending on the level of the users, you might want to provide additional detail, such as a description of terms, concepts, or Windows 95 or Access skills required for the use of your application.

Building The Help Components

When you've decided what to include in the Help file that will accompany your application, you're ready to begin the process of creating the actual file. The following is an overview of the tasks required to build a custom Help file:

- Build a Help Topic file (.RTF).

- Create a Map file (.MAP).

- Create a Contents file (.CNT).

- Create the Help Project file (.HPJ).

- Prepare the Help file to be compiled.

- Compile the Help Project file (.HLP).

- Add the Help file to your application.

Although creating a Help file is beyond the scope of this chapter, Microsoft has indicated that the Office 2000 Developer's Toolkit will include the Microsoft Help Workshop, an application you can use to design Help files.

Adding Custom Help To Your Applications

After you've created a compiled Help file, you need to let your application know that it's available. You must also associate different objects within your application with different help topics within the Help file. Each form and report has a Help File property and a Help Context ID property. The Help File property must be filled in with the name of a compiled Help file. The Help Context ID is the number you defined within the Map file. Each control on a form contains a Help Context ID property. If you fill in this property with a Context ID as specified in the Map file, the Help topic that has the Topic ID associated with the specified Context ID appears whenever that control has focus and the user presses F1.

Getting Help With Help: Authoring Tools

Many people feel that the process of creating the RTF Topic file in Microsoft Word (or using another word processor) is tedious and difficult. Fortunately, several third-party tools are on the market to assist you with this process.

RoboHELP is one of the more popular help-authoring tools. Available from Blue Sky Software, this excellent tool adds user-friendly toolbars, menu commands, and dialog boxes to Microsoft Word, significantly easing the process of creating the RTF file. Creating the footnotes and jumps as well as adding graphics to the RTF file becomes a matter of pointing and clicking. RoboHELP also facilitates the process of building help into your application by automatically creating and maintaining the Help Project and Map files for you.

Another popular help authoring tool is Doc-To-Help. This product, offered by WexTech Systems, enables you to create a printed manual and online help at the same time. Like RoboHELP, Doc-To-Help provides templates that add buttons and menu commands to Microsoft Word, making the process of developing the RTF file a matter of pointing and clicking.

TIP: *For more information or to purchase RoboHELP, contact Blue Sky Software at (619) 459-6365 or by fax at (619) 459-6366 or visit their Web site at **http://www.winhelp.com**. For more information or to order Doc-To-Help, contact WexTech Systems, Inc. at (212) 949-9595 or by fax at (212) 949-4007 or visit their Web site at **http://www.wextech.com**.*

30. Advanced Database Design Techniques

HTML-Based Help Files

With the release of Visual Studio 6 and Office 2000, Microsoft has moved their Help files away from the RTF-based help file and into a HTML-based Help file. Unfortunately, Microsoft hasn't made available tools (like the Help Workshop) to assist Help file developers. However, RoboHELP and Doc-To-Help, as well as most other third-party Help design software developers, provide support for creating HTML-based Help files.

Immediate Solutions

Using The **BeforeUpdate** Event

The **BeforeUpdate** event can be used to programmatically cancel the update process. It's used for this purpose when you want to perform complex validations. When a user adds a record, the **BeforeUpdate** event occurs after the **BeforeInsert** event. The Northwind database that ships with Access contains an excellent example of the use of a **BeforeUpdate** event, reprinted here:

```
Private Sub Form_BeforeUpdate(Cancel As Integer)
' Display a message box that says that product name is required.
   Dim strMsg As String, strTitle As String
   Dim intStyle As Integer

   If IsNull(Me![ProductName]) Then
     strMsg = "You must enter a product name before you leave the " & _
        "record."   ' Define message.
     intStyle = vbOKOnly + vbInformation ' Define buttons.
     strTitle = "Product Name Required"  ' Define title.
     MsgBox strMsg, intStyle, strTitle
     DoCmd.CancelEvent
   End If
End Sub
```

This code, found within the products form, determines whether the product name is **Null**. If it is, a message is displayed and the **CancelEvent** method is executed, canceling the update process.

Using The **Unload** Event

As you learned earlier in this chapter, the **Unload** event occurs when a form is closed but before the form is actually removed from the screen. It's triggered when the user clicks Close on the File menu, quits the application by choosing End Task from the task list, quits Windows, or when your code closes the form. You can place code that ensures that it's okay to unload the form in the **Unload** event. You can also use the **Unload** event to place any code that you want to have execute whenever the form is unloaded. Here's an example:

```
Private Sub Form_Unload(Cancel As Integer)
  '  If EnterOrEditProducts form is loaded,
  '  select it, requery CategoryID combo box,
  '  and set value of CategoryID combo box.
  Dim ctl As Control

  If IsLoaded("EnterOrEditProducts") Then
    Set ctl = Forms!EnterOrEditProducts!cboCategoryID
    DoCmd.SelectObject acForm, "EnterOrEditProducts"
    ctl.Requery
    ctl = Me!CategoryID
  End If
End Sub
```

This code checks to see whether the **EnterOrEditProducts** form is loaded. If it is, the **EnterOrEditProducts** form is selected, the **CategoryID** combo box is requeried, and the combo box's value is set equal to the **CategoryID** of the **AddCategory** form.

Creating A Switchboard Form

To create a Switchboard form using the Switchboard Manager, perform the following steps:

1. Select the Tools menu Database Utilities submenu Switchboard Manager option. Access will display the Switchboard Manager dialog box.

2. Within the Switchboard Manager dialog box, click the New button. Access will display Create New dialog box.

3. Within the Create New dialog box, enter the Switchboard form name, for example **frmMainSwitch**.

4. Press Enter or click on the OK button. Access will return to the Switchboard Manager dialog box.

5. Within the Switchboard Manager dialog box, click on the new switchboard. Next, click on the Edit button. Access will display the Edit Switchboard page dialog box.

6. Within the Edit Switchboard page dialog box, click on the New button. Access will display the Edit Switchboard Item dialog box.

7. Within the Edit Switchboard Item dialog box, enter values for the Text, Command, and Switchboard options. When finished, click OK.

8. Repeat Steps 6 and 7 until you have added all the switchboard options to the switchboard. When you finish, click Close to exit the Edit Switchboard page dialog box and click Close again to return to the database window.

Creating A Splash Screen Form

To create a Splash Screen form, perform the following steps:

1. Create a new form.

2. Set the Scroll Bars property to Neither, the Record Selectors property to No, the Navigation Buttons property to No, the Auto Resize property to Yes, the **AutoCenter** property to Yes, and the Border Style to None.

3. Make the form Popup and Modal.

4. Add a picture to the form. Set the properties of the picture.

5. Add any text you would like to put on the form.

6. Set the timer interval of the form to the amount of seconds that you want the splash screen to display.

7. Code the **Timer** event of the form as **DoCmd.Close**.

8. Code the **Unload** event of the form to open your main Switchboard form.

Because the **Timer** event of the Splash Screen form closes the form after the amount of time specified in the timer interval, the Splash Screen form unloads itself. While it's unloading, it loads the Switchboard form.

You can implement your Splash Screen form in many other ways. For example, you can call the Splash Screen form from a Startup form. The **Open** event of the Startup form simply needs to open the Splash Screen form. The problem with this method is that if your application loads and unloads the Switchboard while the application is running, the Splash Screen displays again.

Another popular method is to build a function that's called from an **AutoExec** macro. This startup function can display the splash screen, execute all the tasks required to set up your application, and unload the splash screen. The following code shows an example:

```
Function AutoExec()
   DoCmd.OpenForm "frmSplash"
   DoCmd.Hourglass True
   '***  Code to set up your application is placed here  ***
```

```
'*** End of Setup Code ***
DoCmd.OpenForm "frmSwitchboard"
DoCmd.Close acForm, "frmSplash"
DoCmd.Hourglass False
End Function
```

This code opens the **frmSplash** form. It then displays an hourglass and continues with any setup processing. When it's done with all the setup processing, it opens the **frmSwitchboard** form, closes the splash screen, and gets rid of the hourglass.

Using The **MsgBox** Function

As you've learned, you can use the **MsgBox** statement within your VBA code to display a message box providing information to a user. You can use the **MsgBox** function to display a message box requesting feedback from the user, as shown in the following code:

```
Sub MessageBoxFunction()
  Dim intResponse As Integer

  intResponse = MsgBox("Are You Sure?", vbYesNoCancel + vbQuestion, _
      "Confirmation Prompt")
End Sub
```

This message box displays Yes, No, and Cancel buttons. It also displays the Question icon. Figure 30.7 depicts the resulting message box.

The **MsgBox** function call returns a value that the program code then stores within the **Integer** variable **intResponse**. After you've placed the return value in a variable, you can easily introduce logic into your program to respond to the user's selection—generally using either an **If…Then** construct or a **Select Case** statement.

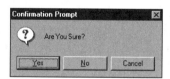

Figure 30.7   A message box requesting feedback from the user.

Inserting A New Object Into A Record

As you learned in this chapter, you can embed OLE objects within your Access databases. To insert a new object, perform the following steps:

1. Move to the record that will contain the OLE object.

2. Right-click on the OLE Object control and select Insert Object. The Insert Object dialog will appear, as shown in Figure 30.8.

3. Select an object type. Select Create New if you want to create an embedded object. Select Create from File if you want to link to or embed an existing file.

4. If you select Create from File, the Insert Object dialog changes to look like Figure 30.9.

5. Select Link if you want to link to the existing file. Don't click Link if you want to embed the existing file. If you link to the file, the Access table will contain a reference to the file as well as presentation data (a bitmap) for the object. If you embed the file, Access copies the original file, placing the copy within the Access table.

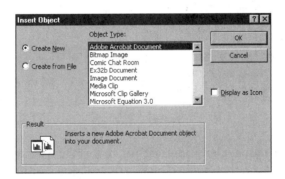

Figure 30.8   The Insert Object dialog box.

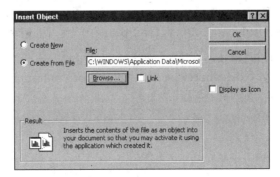

Figure 30.9   The Insert Object dialog box after you select Create from File.

6. Click Browse and select the file you want to link to or embed.

7. Click OK.

If you double-click on a linked object, you'll launch the source application for the object.

Building An **AutoExec** Routine To Launch The Application

You can create an **AutoExec** routine that launches your application automatically at startup. To do so, begin by modifying the **AutoExec** macro so it hides the Database window and calls an **AutoExec** function. The **AutoExec** function then might look similar to the following:

```
Function AutoExec()
  DoCmd.OpenForm "frmSplash"
  DoEvents
  DoCmd.Hourglass True
  ' *** OTHER PROCESSING HERE
  DoCmd.Hourglass False
  DoCmd.OpenForm "frmClients"
  If IsLoaded("frmSplash") Then
    DoCmd.Close acForm, "frmSplash"
  End If
End Function
```

The **AutoExec** routine opens the **frmSplash** form and issues a **DoEvents** command to give the form time to load before the routine continues processing (you could also use the windows **Sleep( )** API function). The program code then leaves a stub for you to perform additional processing while the program displays the hourglass mouse pointer. Finally, the program code turns off the hourglass, opens the **frmClients** form, and unloads **frmSplash** if it's still loaded.

The **AutoExec** routine is one way to launch an application. You can also use the **Startup** property to designate a starting point for your application.

Creating A Database Password

To assign a database password, perform the following steps:

1. Open the database to which you want to assign a password.

2. Select the Tools menu Security submenu Set Database Password option. The Set Database Password dialog box will appear.

3. Type and verify the password and click OK. The password is case sensitive.

Encrypting A Database From Access

To encrypt a database using Access's standard menus, perform the following steps:

1. Make sure no databases are open.

2. Select the Tools menu Security submenu Encrypt/Decrypt Database option.

3. Select the file you want to encrypt, and click OK.

You're prompted for the name of the encrypted database. If you select the same name as the existing file, Access deletes the original decrypted file when it determines that the encryption process is successful.

Establishing A Workgroup

To establish a new workgroup, you must use the Workgroup Administrator. It's a separate program you execute outside Microsoft Access. Under Windows NT, you can access the Workgroup Administrator by selecting the Microsoft Access Workgroup Administrator icon in the Microsoft Access program group. Under Windows 95, you must choose Run from the Start menu and browse to find the Wrkgadm.exe file. Of course, you can add a desktop shortcut to execute this file.

Upon entering the Workgroup Administrator, you're presented with the Workgroup Administrator dialog box. From the Workgroup Administrator dialog box, you can create a new workgroup, or you can join one of the existing workgroups. If you select Create, you're presented with the Workgroup Owner Information dialog box.

From the Workgroup Owner Information dialog box, you can enter a name, an organization, and a case-sensitive workgroup ID that will be used to uniquely identify the workgroup to the system. If you don't establish a unique workgroup ID, your database isn't secure. As you'll see, anyone can find out your name and organization. If you don't establish a workgroup ID, anyone can create a new system information file with your name and company, rendering any security that you implement totally futile.

Changing The Password For The **Admin** User

To change the password for the **Admin** user, click on the Change Logon Password tab of the User and Group Accounts dialog box (if it is not already open, you can do so from the Tools menu Security option). The User and Group Accounts dialog box will appear. Assign a new password and verify it. (There's no old password unless you think of the old password as blank.) Then click OK. This establishes a password for the **Admin** user. You can't establish a password for the new user you just defined until you log on as that user.

Removing The **Admin** User From The Admins Group

To remove the **Admin** user from the Admins group, perform the following steps:

1. Click to select the Users tab.

2. Select the **Admin** user from the Name drop-down.

3. Select Admins from the Member Of list box.

4. Click Remove.

Adding Groups From Access

To add a new group, perform the following steps:

1. Open the secured database and select the Tools menu Security submenu User and Group Accounts option.

2. Click the Groups tab of the User and Group Accounts dialog.

3. Click New. The New User/Group dialog box will appear.

4. Type the name of the group and enter a personal ID that uniquely identifies the group.

5. Click OK.

6. Repeat Steps 3 through 5 for each group you want to add.

Adding Users From Access

To add, delete, and modify users through the user interface, perform the following steps:

1. Select the Tools menu Security submenu User and Group Accounts option.

2. Click the Users tab if it isn't already selected.

3. Click New. The New User/Group dialog box will appear.

4. Enter the name of the user and the personal ID associated with the user. Remember that this isn't a password, but instead, it combines with the user name to create a unique identifier for the user.

5. Click OK.

6. Repeat Steps 3 through 5 for each user you want to define.

Assigning Each User To The Appropriate Group

Before you assign rights to users and groups, make each user a member of the appropriate group. A user can be a member of as many groups as you choose, but remember that each user gets the rights of his or her most forgiving group. In other words, if a user is a member of both the Admins group and a group with read-only access to objects, the rights of the Admins group will prevail. To assign each user to the appropriate groups, perform the following steps:

1. Select the Tools menu Security submenu User and Group Accounts option.

2. Click the Users tab if it isn't already selected.

3. Use the Name drop-down to select the user for whom you want to create group membership.

4. Click the name of the group to which you want to add the userand then click the Add button.

5. Repeat Steps 3 and 4 for each user to whom you want to assign group membership.

Remember that the users and groups you create are for the workgroup as a whole, not just for a specific database.

Assigning Rights To Users And Groups

When assigning rights, the key is to assign specific rights to each group, and ensure that all users are members of the appropriate groups. After that, you can assign each group specific permissions to the objects within your database. User and group information is maintained in the system database; permissions for objects are stored within system tables in the application database (MDB) file. After you've established a workgroup of users and groups, you must assign rights to specific objects in your database by following these steps:

1. Make sure that the database whose objects you want to secure is open.

2. Select the Tools menu Security submenu User and Group Permissions option. The User and Group Permissions dialog box will appear. Notice that as you click on each user in the User/Group Name list box, you will see that only the administrator has rights to any objects. If you click on the Groups radio button, you see that only the Admins group has any rights.

3. To assign rights to a Group, click the Groups option button. All of the available groups appear in the User/Group Name list box.

4. Use the Object Type drop-down to select the type of object you want to secure.

5. Use the Object Name list box to select the names of the objects to which you want to assign rights. Multiple objects can be selected using the Ctrl and Shift keys.

6. Mark the corresponding Permissions check boxes to select the appropriate permissions for the objects. The types of permissions available are discussed in the "Types Of Permissions" section earlier in this chapter.

7. Repeat Steps 4 through 6 for all objects to which you want to assign rights.

In general, assign groups the rights to objects, and simply make users members of the appropriate groups. Notice that you can use the Object Type drop-down to view the various types of objects that make up your database.

Clearing A User's Password

To clear a user's password, perform the following steps:

1. Select the Tools menu Security submenu User and Group Accounts option.

2. Use the Names drop-down to select the user whose password you want to clear.

3. Click Clear Password. The user's password is cleared.

Changing The Ownership Of A Database Object

To change the ownership of an object within the database, perform the following steps:

1. Select the Tools menu Security submenu User and Group Permissions option.

2. Within the User and Group Permissions dialog box, click the Change Owner tab.

3. Use the Object Type drop-down to select the type of object whose ownership you want to change.

4. Use the Object list box to select the objects whose ownership you want to change. You can use Ctrl and Shift to select multiple objects.

5. Select the Groups or Users option button.

6. Select the name of the group or user who'll become the new owner of the objects.

7. Click Change Owner.

8. Repeat Steps 3 through 7 for all objects for which you want to assign new ownership.

Printing Security Information

A list of each user and the groups that he or she is a member of can be printed quite easily. To do so, perform the following steps:

1. Select the Tools menu Security submenu User and Group Accounts option.

2. Click Print Users and Groups. The Print Security dialog box will appear.

3. Select whether you want to view Both Users and Groups, Only Users, or Only Groups.

4. Click OK.

TIP: *You can print the rights to different objects using the Database Documenter. See the Access 2000 online Help file for more information on this feature.*

Adding A Group From Code

You add a group from code by appending the **Group** object to the **Groups** collection. The code to do so will look similar to the following:

```
Function CreateGroups(GroupName As String, PID As String) As Boolean
   Dim wrk As Workspace
   Dim grp As GROUP

   On Error GoTo CreateGroups_Err
   CreateGroups = True
   Set wrk = DBEngine.Workspaces(0)
   Set grp = wrk.CreateGroup(GroupName, PID)
   wrk.Groups.Append grp
CreateGroups_Exit:
   Set wrk = Nothing
   Set grp = Nothing
   Exit Function
CreateGroups_Err:
   MsgBox "Error # " & Err.Number & ": " & Err.Description
   CreateGroups = False
   Resume CreateGroups_Exit
End Function
```

The function uses a **Workspace** variable and a **Group** variable. The **CreateGroup** method of the **Workspace** object receives two parameters: the name of the group and the personal ID (PID). The new group is referenced by the **Group** object variable, **grp**. The **Append** method, when applied to the **grp** object variable, adds a new group to the workspace. The function uses the value in **GroupName** as the name of the group to add and the value in **PID** as the PID for the group. After running this routine, you will see that a new group has been added to the workgroup (as can be viewed from the Tools menu Security submenu User and Group Accounts option).

Removing A Group

The code to remove a group is very similar to the code required to add a group. The following function, **RemoveGroups**, shows how you might use code to do this:

```
Function RemoveGroups(GroupName As String)
   Dim wrk As Workspace
```

```
     On Error GoTo RemoveGroups_Err
     RemoveGroups = True
     Set wrk = DBEngine.Workspaces(0)
     wrk.Groups.Delete GroupName
RemoveGroups_Exit:
   Set wrk = Nothing
   Exit Function
RemoveGroups_Err:
   If Err.Number = 3265 Then
     MsgBox "Group Not Found"
   Else
     MsgBox "Error # " & Err.Number & ": " & Err.Description
   End If
   RemoveGroups = False
   Resume RemoveGroups_Exit
End Function
```

The **RemoveGroups** function performs the **Delete** method on the groups collection of the workspace, using the value in **GroupName** as the name of the group to remove. If the group doesn't exist, an error number 3265 results. The program code will display an appropriate error message.

Adding A User From Code

You can add a user with code by appending a **User** object to the **Users** collection. The code to accomplish this looks similar to the following:

```
Function CreateUsers(UserName As String, PID As String) As Boolean
   Dim wrk As Workspace
   Dim usr As User

   On Error GoTo CreateUsers_Err
   CreateUsers = True
   Set wrk = DBEngine.Workspaces(0)
   Set usr = wrk.CreateUser(UserName, PID)
   wrk.Users.Append usr
CreateUsers_Exit:
   Set wrk = Nothing
   Set usr = Nothing
   Exit Function
```

```
CreateUsers_Err:
  MsgBox "Error # " & Err.Number & ": " & Err.Description
  CreateUsers = False
  Resume CreateUsers_Exit
End Function
```

This routine creates **Workspace** and **User** object variables. It associates the **Workspace** object variable with the current workspace and invokes the **CreateUser** method to add the user to the workspace. The values in the **UserName** and **PID** variables are passed to the **CreateUser** function as arguments. The **Append** method is then applied to the **Users** collection of the workspace to add the user to the collection of users within the workspace.

Assigning A User To A Group From Code

After you add the user, you must give the user group membership. Let's take a look at how you can add a user to an existing group; the following code adds a specified user to a specified group:

```
Function AssignToGroup(GroupName As String, UserName As String)
  Dim wrk As Workspace
  Dim grp As Group
  Dim usr As User

  On Error GoTo AssignToGroup_Err
  AssignToGroup = True
  Set wrk = DBEngine.Workspaces(0)
  Set grp = wrk.Groups(GroupName)
  Set usr = wrk.CreateUser(UserName)
  grp.Users.Append usr
AssignToGroup_Exit:
  Set wrk = Nothing
  Set grp = Nothing
  Set usr = Nothing
  Exit Function
AssignToGroup_Err:
  If Err.Number = 3265 Then
    MsgBox "Group Not Found"
  Else
    MsgBox "Error # " & Err.Number & ": " & Err.Description
  End If
  AssignToGroup = False
  Resume AssignToGroup_Exit
End Function
```

This code creates three object variables, **Workspace**, **Group**, and **User**. The **Workspace** variable is pointed at the current workspace. The **Group** variable is pointed toward the group specified in the **GroupName** parameter. The **CreateUser** method is used to point the **User** object variable to the user specified in the **UserName** parameter. You might wonder why you should use a **CreateUser** method even though the User Name must already exist for this code to run properly. This is because you must create another instance of the account before adding it to a group. Finally, the **Append** method is applied to the **Users** collection of the **Group** object to add the user to the group.

Removing A User From A Group From Code

Just as you'll want to add users to groups, you'll also want to remove them from groups. The following code implements the **RevokeFromGroup** function, which does the removing:

```
Function RevokeFromGroup(GroupName As String, UserName As String)
  Dim wrk As Workspace
  Dim grp As GROUP

  On Error GoTo RevokeFromGroup_Err
  RevokeFromGroup = True
  Set wrk = DBEngine.Workspaces(0)
  Set grp = wrk.Groups(GroupName)
  grp.Users.Delete UserName
RevokeFromGroup_Exit:
  Set wrk = Nothing
  Set grp = Nothing
  Exit Function
RevokeFromGroup_Err:
  If Err.Number = 3265 Then
    MsgBox "Group Not Found"
  Else
    MsgBox "Error # " & Err.Number & ": " & Err.Description
  End If
  RevokeFromGroup = False
  Resume RevokeFromGroup_Exit
End Function
```

This procedure establishes an object variable pointing to the group specified in the parameters. It then removes the specified user from the group by performing the **Delete** method on the **Users** collection of the group.

Removing A User From Code

Sometimes you want to remove a user entirely. The **RemoveUsers** function accepts a user name and will delete the user from the database, as shown here:

```
Function RemoveUsers(UserName As String) As Boolean
  Dim wrk As Workspace

  On Error GoTo RemoveUsers_Err
  RemoveUsers = True
  Set wrk = DBEngine.Workspaces(0)
  wrk.Users.Delete Me!txtUserName
RemoveUsers_Exit:
  Set wrk = Nothing
  Exit Function
RemoveUsers_Err:
  If Err.Number = 3265 Then
    MsgBox "User Not Found"
  Else
    MsgBox "Error # " & Err.Number & ": " & Err.Description
  End If
  RemoveUsers = False
  Resume RemoveUsers_Exit
End Function
```

The **RemoveUsers** function issues the **Delete** method on the **Users** collection of the workspace. This deletes the user entirely.

Assigning A Password To A User From Code

The administrative user can assign a password to any user. The code to do so looks similar to the following:

```
Function AssignPassword(UserName As String, Password As String)
  Dim wrk As Workspace
  Dim usr As User

  On Error GoTo AssignPassword_Err
  AssignPassword = True
  Set wrk = DBEngine.Workspaces(0)
  wrk.Users(UserName).NewPassword "", Nz(Password)
```

```
AssignPassword_Exit:
  Set wrk = Nothing
  Set usr = Nothing
  Exit Function
AssignPassword_Err:
  MsgBox "Error # " & Err.Number & ": " & Err.Description
  AssignPassword = False
  Resume AssignPassword_Exit
End Function
```

The **AssignPassword** function sets the **NewPassword** method of the **User** object specified in the **UserName** parameter. The first parameter, the old password, is intentionally left blank. Members of the Admins group can modify anyone's password but their own, without having to know the old password. The second parameter, the new password, is the value passed in the **Password** parameter. The **Nz** function sets the new password to a zero-length string if the administrative user didn't supply a new password.

Ensuring That A User Has A Password

You might want to ensure that users who log onto your application have a password. This can be accomplished with the following code:

```
Function AutoExec()
  Dim usr As User
  Dim strPassword As String

  Set usr = DBEngine(0).Users(CurrentUser)
  On Error Resume Next
  usr.NewPassword "", ""
  If Err.Number = 0 Then
    strPassword = InputBox("You Must Enter a Password Before Proceeding", _
        "Enter Password")
    If strPassword = "" Then
      DoCmd.Quit
    Else
      usr.NewPassword "", strPassword
    End If
  End If
End Function
```

The **AutoExec** function can be called from the startup form of your application. It points a **User** object variable to the **CurrentUser** and accomplishes this using the return value from the **CurrentUser** function as the user to look at within the **Users** collection. The **CurrentUser** function returns a string containing the name of the current user.

When an object variable is pointing at the correct user, the code attempts to set a new password for that person. When you modify the password of the current user, you must supply both the old password and the new password to the **NewPassword** method. If the old password is incorrect, an error occurs. In this case, if an error occurs, it means that the user has a password and nothing special needs to happen. In the absence of an error, you know that no password exists, so the user is prompted for a password. If the user doesn't supply one, the application quits. Otherwise, the new password is assigned to the user.

Assigning And Revoking Permissions To Objects Using Code

Often, you'll want to assign and revoke object permissions using code. Once again, this can be easily accomplished using DAO code. The following code assigns view rights for the table selected in a list of tables to the group selected from a list of groups in a combo box:

```
Private Sub cmdViewRights_Click()
  Dim db As DATABASE
  Dim doc As Document

  Set db = CurrentDb
  Set doc = db.Containers!Tables.Documents(lstTables.Value)
  doc.UserName = Me!cboGroupName.Value
  doc.Permissions = dbSecRetrieveData
End Sub
```

Notice that the code points a document variable to the table selected in the list box . The **UserName** property of the document is set equal to the group selected in the combo box. The Permissions property of the document is then set equal to **dbSecRetrieveData**. The **dbSecRetrieveData** constant indicates that the user has rights to read the definition and data within the table. A listing of the permission constants for queries and tables is listed in Table 30.10.

Notice that in the following example, the **dbSecRetrieveData** constant is combined with the **dbSecReplaceData** constant using a bit-wise **OR**. The **dbSecReplaceData** constant doesn't imply that the user can also read the table

Table 30.10 The permission constants for queries and tables.

Permission Constant	Permission Description
dbSecReadDef	Grants read permission to the definition of the table or query.
dbSecWriteDef	Grants permission to alter the definition of the table or query.
dbSecRetrieveData	Grants permission to read data stored within the table or query. Also, implicitly grants read permission to the definition of the table or query.
dbSecInsertData	Grants permission to insert new rows into the table or query.
dbSecDeleteData	Grants permission to delete rows from the table or query.
dbSecReplaceData	Grants permission to modify table or query data.

definition and data. As you might guess, it's difficult to edit data if you can't read it. It's therefore necessary that you combine the **dbSecRetrieveData** constant with the **dbSecReplaceData** constant to allow the user or group to read and modify table data.

```
Private Sub cmdModifyRights_Click()
  Dim db As DATABASE
  Dim doc As Document

  Set db = CurrentDb
  Set doc = db.Containers!Tables.Documents(lstTables.Value)
  doc.UserName = Me!cboGroupName.Value
  doc.Permissions = doc.Permissions Or _
      dbSecRetrieveData Or dbSecReplaceData
End Sub
```

Encrypting A Database Using Code

Earlier in this chapter, you learned how to encrypt a database using the user interface. If a database isn't encrypted, it isn't really secure because a savvy user can utilize a disk editor to view the data in the file. If you've distributed your application with the runtime version of Access and you want to provide your user with the ability to encrypt the database, you must write DAO code to accomplish the encryption process. The code looks like this:

```
Sub Encrypt(strDBNotEncrypted As String, strDBEncrypted As String)
    DBEngine.CompactDatabase strDBNotEncrypted, strDBEncrypted,_
        dbLangGeneral, dbEncrypt
End Sub
```

This subroutine receives two parameters. The first is the name of the database you want to encrypt. The second is the name you want to assign to the encrypted database. The **CompactDatabase** method is issued on the database engine. This method receives four parameters: the name of the database to encrypt, the name for the new encrypted database, the collating order, and other options. The other options parameter is where you use a constant to indicate that you want to encrypt the database.

Part VIII

Microsoft Access 2000 And Client-Server Development

Chapter 31

Client-Server Programming With Access 2000

In Depth

As you've probably seen quite clearly from the previous chapters in this book, programming for a multiuser environment—whether a pure client-server, distributed workgroup, or some other multiuser configuration—has issues of its very own. When you consider the fact that client-server today can also include Internet front ends, as well as connection to a wide variety of back ends, from SQL Server to Oracle, the innate complexity of client-server programming is only increased.

This chapter will work with you through the primary issues of client-server development, from configuring Access with the multiuser environment in mind to actually connecting Access to a back-end database. Later chapters in this section will focus on specific connectivity, as well as the use of new features, such as Access Data Pages (ADP) for the creation of more powerful and accessible front ends.

Designing Your Application With The Multiuser In Mind

When you develop applications that will be accessed over the network by multiple users, you must ensure that your applications effectively handle the sharing of data and other application objects. Many options are available for developers when they design multiuser applications. This chapter covers, among other things, the pros and cons of these options.

Multiuser issues are the issues surrounding the locking of data. These issues include deciding where to store database objects, when to lock data, and how much data to lock. In a multiuser environment, having several users simultaneously attempting to modify the same data can generate conflicts. As a developer, you need to handle these conflicts. Otherwise, your users will experience unexplainable errors or lost data.

Multiuser Design Strategies

Numerous methodologies exist for handling concurrent access to data and other application objects by multiple users. Each of these methodologies introduces solutions as well as problems. It's important to select the best solution for your particular environment.

Strategies For The Installation Of Access

You can choose two strategies for the installation of Access:

• Running Access from a file server.

• Running a separate copy of Access on each workstation.

Each of these strategies has associated pros and cons. The advantages of running Access from a file server are as follows:

• Allows for central administration of the Access software.

• Reduces hard disk requirements. The Access software takes up between 14 and 42 megabytes of hard disk space, depending on the type of installation. Although this can be reduced by using the Access runtime engine, local hard disk space can definitely be a problem. Installing Access on the file server at least partially eliminates this problem. It can totally eliminate the problem when dynamic link libraries are also installed on the file server.

• Access applications can be installed on diskless workstations.

Clearly, there are certain benefits to running Access from the file server. In some environments, such as those that use network computers or environments where you are running Windows NT Terminal Server (and therefore have computers that may have difficulties with or be entirely incapable of running Access locally), you may not have a choice as to your installation method. In other environments—such as those that use 100BaseT Ethernet, Gigabit Ethernet, or ATM—you may have more than sufficient bandwidth to support such an installation. However, although the advantages of installing Access on a file server might seem compelling, it has serious drawbacks, including the following:

• Every time the user launches an Access application, the Access EXE, DLLs, and any other files required to run Access are *all* sent over the network wire to the local machine. Obviously, this generates a significant volume of network traffic.

• Performance is generally degraded to unacceptable levels.

Because the disadvantages of running Access from a file server are so pronounced, it's generally more appropriate, in most networks, for you to install Access, or at least the Access runtime, on each user's machine.

Strategies For The Installation Of Your Application

Just as you can use different strategies for the installation of Access, you can also employ various strategies for the installation of your application, such as the following:

• Install both the application and data on a file server.

• Install the data on the file server and the application on each workstation.

In other words, after you've created an application, you can place the entire application on the network, which means that all of the tables, queries, forms, reports, macros, and modules that make up the system reside on the file server. Although this method of shared access keeps everything in the same place, you'll see many advantages to placing only the data tables in a database on the file server. The remainder of the objects are placed in a database on each user's machine. Each local application database is linked to the tables on the network. In this way, users share data but not the rest of the application objects.

The advantages of installing one database containing data tables on the file server and installing another database containing other application objects locally are as follows:

- Because each user has a copy of the local database objects (queries, forms, reports, macros, and modules), load time and network traffic are both reduced.

- It's very easy to back up data without having to back up the rest of the application objects.

- When redistributing new versions of the application, it's not necessary to be concerned with overwriting the application's data.

- Multiple applications can all be designed to use the same centrally located data.

- Users can add their own objects (such as their own queries) to their local copies of the database.

In addition to storing the queries, forms, reports, macros, and modules that make up the application in a local database, most developers also recommend that you store the following objects within each local database:

- Temporary tables
- Static tables
- Semistatic tables

Temporary tables should be stored in the database that's located on each workstation because when two users are performing operations that build the same temporary tables, you don't want one user's process to interfere with the other user's process. The potential conflict of one user's temporary tables overwriting the other's can be eliminated by storing all temporary tables in each user's local copy of the database.

You should also place static lookup tables, such as a state table, on each workstation. Because the data does not change, maintenance isn't an issue. The benefit is that Access doesn't need to pull that data over the network each time it's needed.

Semistatic tables can also be placed on the local machine. These tables are rarely updated. As with static tables, the major benefit of having these tables reside in a local database is that reduced network traffic means better performance, not only for the user requiring the data but also for anyone sharing the same network wire. Changes made to the semistatic tables can be transported to each workstation using replication. Replication is explained in detail later in this chapter.

The Basics Of Linking To External Data

Linking to external data, including data that isn't stored within another Access database, is covered extensively later in this chapter. However, at this point it's valuable to understand the three options available to you when linking to external data:

- Design the databases separately from the start.
- Include all objects in one database and split them manually when you're ready to distribute your application.
- Include all objects in one database and split them using the Database Splitter Wizard.

How to use all three of these options is detailed in the "Immediate Solutions" section of this chapter.

Be aware that when distributing an application using linked tables, it's necessary to write code to ensure that the data tables can be located from each application database on the network. When each user has the same path to the file server, this isn't a problem. If the path to the file server varies, you need to write a routine that ensures the tables can be located. If they can't be located, the routine should prompt the user for the location of the data. The "Immediate Solutions" section contains just such a routine.

Understanding Access's Locking Mechanisms

Although the preceding tips for designing network applications reduce network traffic, they in no way reduce locking conflicts, which, with the ever-increasing amounts of network bandwidth, may be a more significant consideration by far for your application. To protect shared data, Access locks a page (4K) of data as the user edits a record.

When a page of records is locked, multiple users can read the data, but only one user can make changes to the data. Data can be locked through a form and also through a recordset that isn't bound to a form. Three methods of locking for an Access application are listed here:

- Page locking
- Table and recordset locking
- Opening an entire database with Exclusive Access

With page locking, only the page containing the record that's being edited is locked. On the other hand, with table and recordset locking, the entire table or recordset containing the record that's being edited is locked. With database locking, the entire database is locked, unless the user opening the database has opened it for read-only access. When the user opens the database for read-only access, other users can also open the database for read-only access. The ability to obtain exclusive use of a database can be restricted through security.

It's important to note that the locking scheme to which you must adhere depends upon the source of the data that you're accessing. When you're accessing data on a database server using open database connectivity (ODBC), you'll inherit the locking scheme of the particular back end that you're using. When you're accessing indexed sequential access method (ISAM) data over a network, you'll get any record locking that the particular ISAM database supports. For example, if you're accessing FoxPro data, you have the capability to utilize record locking or any other locking scheme that FoxPro supports.

Locking And Refreshing Strategies

Access provides several tools for controlling locking methods in datasheets, forms, and reports. To configure the global multiuser settings, select the Tools menu Options option. Access will display the Options dialog box. Within the Options dialog box, click on the Advanced tab. The dialog box pictured in Figure 31.1 appears.

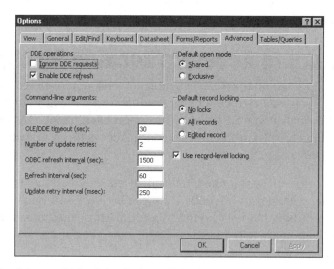

Figure 31.1   The Advanced tab of the Options dialog box.

The following multiuser settings can be configured from this dialog:

- Default Record Locking
- Default Open Mode
- Number of Update Retries
- ODBC Refresh Interval
- Refresh Interval
- Update Retry Interval

Default Record Locking

The Default Record Locking option enables you to specify the default record locking as No Locks (optimistic), All Records (locks entire table or dynaset), or Edited Record (pessimistic). This is where you can affect settings for all objects in your database. Modifying this option won't affect any existing queries, forms, and reports, but it'll affect any new queries, forms, and reports. These options are discussed later in this chapter as they apply to forms and recordsets.

Determining The Locking Mechanism For A Query

When you want to determine the locking method for a particular query, you can do this by modifying the Record Locks query property. Once again, the options are No Locks, All Records, and Edited Record. You can set this information within the Query Properties dialog box.

Determining The Locking Mechanism For A Form Or Report

Just as you can configure the locking mechanism for a query, you can also configure the locking mechanism for each form and report. Forms and reports have Record Locks properties, just as queries do. Changing these properties modifies the locking mechanism for that particular form or report.

TIP: *Reports don't provide the Edited Record choice for locking. The Edited Record option isn't necessary because report data can't be modified.*

Default Open Mode

The Default Open Mode of the Advanced Options dialog enables you to configure the default open mode for databases. By encouraging users to set this option within their own copies of Access, you prevent people from inadvertently opening up a database exclusively. Take a good look at the Access File Open dialog, as shown in Figure 31.2.

As you can see in the bottom-right corner of the File Open dialog box, you can choose the open mode. What the dialog box defaults to is determined by the Default Open Mode set in the Advanced Options dialog.

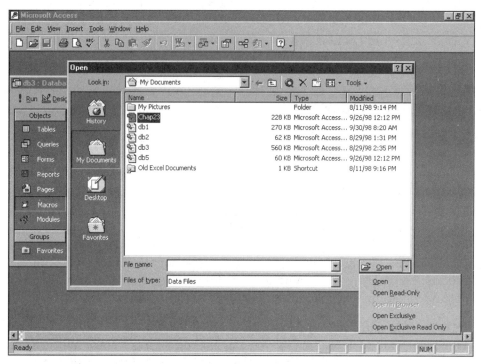

Figure 31.2   The File Open dialog box.

Number Of Update Retries

The number of update retries is used to specify how many times Access will reattempt to save data to a locked record. The higher this number is, the larger the chance that the update will succeed. The downside is that the user has to wait while Access continues attempting to update the data, even when there is no hope that the update will complete successfully. The default for this setting is 2. The value can range from 0 to 10.

ODBC Refresh Interval

The ODBC refresh interval determines how often your form or datasheet is updated with changes made to data stored in ODBC data sources. For example, assume that two users are viewing the same data stored in a back-end Microsoft SQL Server database. User 1 makes a change to the data. The ODBC refresh interval determines how long it'll be before User 2 sees the change. The higher this number is, the less likely it is that User 2 will see the current data. The lower this number is, the more network traffic will be generated. The default for this setting is 1,500 seconds (25 minutes). The value can range from 1 to 3,600 seconds.

Refresh Interval

The Refresh Interval is used to specify how long it takes for a form or datasheet to be updated with changed data from an Access database. This is very similar to the ODBC Refresh Interval, but the ODBC Refresh Interval applies only to ODBC data sources, and the Refresh Interval applies only to Access data sources. As with the ODBC Refresh Interval, the higher this number is, the lower the chance that the data viewed by the user is current. The lower this number is, the more network traffic is generated. The default for this setting is 60 seconds. The value can range from 1 to 32,766 seconds.

TIP: *Access automatically refreshes the data in a record whenever the user attempts to edit the record. The benefit of a shorter Refresh Interval is that the user sees that the record has been changed or locked by another user before the user attempts to edit it.*

Update Retry Interval

The Update Retry Interval is used to determine how many seconds Access waits before once again attempting to update a locked record. The default for this setting is 250 milliseconds. The value can range from 0 to 1,000 milliseconds.

Refreshing Vs. Requerying Data

It's important that you understand the difference between refreshing and requerying a recordset. The process of refreshing a recordset updates changed data and indicates any deleted records. The refresh process doesn't attempt to bring a new recordset over the network wire. Instead, it *refreshes* the data in the existing recordset. This means that records aren't reordered, new records don't appear, and deleted records aren't removed from the display. The record pointer remains on the same record.

The refresh process is quite different from the requery process. The requery process obtains a new set of records. This means that the query is run again and all of the resulting data is sent over the network wire. The data is reordered, new records appear, and deleted records are no longer displayed. The record pointer is moved to the first record in the recordset.

Form Locking Strategies

Earlier in the chapter, you learned about the locking strategies for forms—No Locks, All Records, and Edited Record. Utilizing the three locking strategies as appropriate, you can develop a multiuser application with little to no multiuser programming. You won't gain the same power, flexibility, and control that you get out of recordsets, but you can quickly and easily implement multiuser techniques.

In this section, you'll see how all three of these strategies impact the bound forms within your application.

Using The No Locks Option

The No Locks option means that the page of data containing the edited record won't be locked until Access attempts to write the changed data to disk. This occurs when there's movement to a different record or the data within the record is explicitly saved. The No Locks locking option is the least restrictive of the three locking options for forms. Multiple users can be editing data within the same 4K page of data at the same time. The conflict occurs when two users attempt to modify the same record. Consider the following example: User 1 attempts to modify data within the record for customer ABCDE. User 2 attempts to modify the *same* record. No error occurs because the No Locks option is specified for the form both users are accessing. User 1 makes a change to the address. User 2 makes a change to the Contact Title. User 1 moves off of the record, saving her changes. No error occurs because Access has no way of knowing that User 2 is modifying the record. Now User 2 attempts to move off of the record. The Write Conflict dialog box will appear. User 2 has the choice of saving his changes, thereby overwriting the changes that User 1 made; copying User 1's changes to the clipboard so that he can make an educated decision as to what to do; or dropping his own changes and accepting the changes that User 1 made.

Using The All Records Option

The All Records locking option is the most restrictive. When All Records is in effect, other users can only view the data in the tables underlying the form. They can't make any changes to the data, regardless of their own locking options. When opening the form, they receive a quick status bar message that the data isn't updatable. If they attempt to modify data within the form, the computer beeps and a message is displayed in the status bar.

Using The Edited Record Option

The Edited Record option is used when you want to prevent the conflicts that occur when the No Locks option is in place. Instead of getting potential conflicts regarding changed data, the users are much more likely to experience locking conflicts because every time a user begins editing a record, the entire 4K page of data surrounding the record will be locked. Consider this scenario: User 1 begins editing a record. User 2 attempts to modify the same record. The computer will beep and a lock symbol will appear in the form's record selector. Now User 2 moves to another record. If the other record is in the same 4K page as the record User 1 has locked, the locking symbol appears and User 2 is unable to edit that record as well until User 1 has saved the record that she was working on, thereby releasing the lock.

When you want to override any of the default locking error dialogs that appear in a form, you must code the Error event of the form. Although you can use this method to replace any error message that appears, you can't trap for the situation with pessimistic locking when another user has the record locked. Users are only cued that the record is locked by viewing the locking symbol and hearing the beep that occurs when they attempt to edit the record. If you want to inform users that the record is locked before they attempt to edit it, you need to place code in the timer event of the form that checks to see whether the record is locked. Checking to see whether a record is locked is covered in the "Testing A Record For Locking Status" section of this chapter.

Recordset Locking

Recordset locking is the process of locking pages of data contained within a recordset. Using recordset locking, you can determine when and for how long the data is locked. This is different from locking data using bound forms, because with bound forms, you have little control over the specifics of the locking process.

When you're traversing through a recordset, editing and updating data, locking occurs regardless of whether you intervene. It's important for you to understand when the locking occurs and whether you need to step in to intercept the default behavior.

If you do nothing, an entire page of records will be locked each time you issue an **Edit** method from within your Visual Basic for Applications (VBA) code. This page is 4,096 bytes (4K) in size and surrounds the record being edited. When an object linking and embedding (OLE) object is contained within the record being edited, it's not locked with the record because it occupies its own space.

Using Pessimistic Locking

VBA enables you to determine when and for how long a page is locked. The default behavior is called pessimistic locking. This means that the page is locked when the **Edit** method is issued. Here is some sample code (using Data Access Objects [DAO]) that illustrates this process:

```
Sub PessimisticLock(strCustID As String)
    Dim db As Database
    Dim rst As Recordset
    Dim strCriteria As String

    Set db = CurrentDb()
    Set rst = db.OpenRecordSet("tblCustomers", dbOpenDynaset)
    rst.LockEdits = True   'Invoke Pessimistic Locking
    strCriteria = "[CustomerID] = '" & strCustID & "'"
```

```
    rst.FindFirst strCriteria
    rst.Edit                         ' Lock Occurs Here
       rst.Fields("City") = "Las Vegas"
    rst.Update                       ' Lock Released Here
End Sub
```

In this scenario, although the lock occurs for a very short period of time, it's actually being issued at the edit. It's then released upon update.

This method of locking is advantageous because you can ensure that no changes are made to the data between the time that the **Edit** method is issued and the time that the **Update** method is invoked. Furthermore, when the **Edit** method succeeds, you're ensured write access to the record. The disadvantage is that the time between the edit and the update might force the lock to persist for a significant period of time, locking other users out of not only that record but the entire page of records within which the edited record is contained. This phenomenon is exacerbated when explicit transaction processing is invoked. Basically, transaction processing ensures that when you make multiple changes to data, all changes complete successfully or no changes occur (you'll learn more about transaction processing later). The "Immediate Solutions" section of this chapter details code that shows how pessimistic record locking affects transaction processing.

Using Optimistic Locking

Optimistic locking delays the time at which the record is locked. The lock is issued upon update rather than edit. The code to use optimistic locking will often look similar to the following:

```
Sub OptimisticLock(strCustID As String)
   Dim db As Database
   Dim rst As Recordset
   Dim strCriteria As String

   Set db = CurrentDb()
   Set rst = db.OpenRecordSet("tblCustomers", dbOpenDynaset)
   rst.Lockedits = False 'Optimistic Locking
   strCriteria = "[CustomerID] = '" & strCustID & "'"
   rst.FindFirst strCriteria
   rst.Edit
      rst.Fields("City") = "Las Vegas"
   rst.Update 'Lock Occurs and is Released Here
End Sub
```

As you can see, in this case, the lock doesn't happen until the **Update** method is issued. The advantage of this method is that the page is locked very briefly. The disadvantage of this method occurs when two users retrieve the record for editing at the same time. When one user attempts to update, no error occurs. When the other user attempts to update, she receives an error indicating that the data has changed since her edit was first issued. The handling of this error message is covered later in this chapter.

Effectively Handling Locking Conflicts

When a user has a page locked and another user tries to view data on that page, no conflict occurs. On the other hand, when other users attempt to edit data on that same page, they experience an error.

You won't always want Access's own error handling to take over when a locking conflict occurs. For example, rather than having Access display its generic error message indicating that a record is locked, you might want to display your own message and attempt to retrieve the record a couple of additional times. To do something like this, it's necessary that you learn to interpret each locking error that's generated by VBA, so you can make a decision about how to respond.

Locking conflicts occur in the following situations:

- A user tries to edit or update a record that's already locked.
- A record has changed or been deleted since the user first started to edit it.

These errors can occur whether you're editing bound data using a form or accessing the records through VBA code.

Errors With Pessimistic Locking

To begin the discussion of locking conflicts, let's take a look at the types of errors that occur when pessimistic locking is in place. With pessimistic locking, you generally need to code for the errors detailed in Table 31.1.

Errors With Optimistic Locking Or New Records

Now that you've seen the errors returned by VBA when a conflict occurs with pessimistic locking, let's see what errors are returned when optimistic locking is

Table 31.1   The errors you should generally trap for with pessimistic locking.

Error Number	Description
3260	This error occurs when the current record is locked by another user. It's generally sufficient to wait a short period of time and try the lock again.
3197	This error occurs when a record has been changed since the user last accessed it. It's best to refresh the data and attempt the **Edit** method again.
3167	This error occurs when the record has been deleted since the user last accessed it. It's best to refresh the data.

Table 31.2   The errors you should generally trap for with optimistic locking.

Error Number	Description
3186	This error occurs when the update method is used to save a record on a locked page. This error generally occurs when a user tries to move off of a record that she is adding onto a locked page. It also can occur when optimistic locking is used and a user tries to update a record on the same page as a record that's locked by another machine. It's generally sufficient to wait a short period of time and try the locked record again.
3197	This error occurs with optimistic locking when User 1 has updated a record in the time since User 2 first started viewing it. It can also occur when User 2 is viewing data that isn't current; the data has changed, but the changes haven't yet been reflected on User 2's screen. You have two options: You can requery the recordset, losing User 2's changes, or you can resume and issue the **Update** method again, overwriting User 1's changes.
3260	This error usually occurs when the **Edit** method is issued and the page containing the current record is locked. It's best to wait a short period of time and try the lock again.

in place or when users are adding new records. The three most common error codes generated by locking conflicts when optimistic locking is in place are detailed in Table 31.2.

Testing A Record For Locking Status

Often, you want to determine the locking status of a record *before* you attempt an operation with it. By setting the **LockEdits** property of the recordset to **True** and attempting to modify the record, you can determine whether the current row is locked. The code looks like this:

```
Sub TestLocking()
    Dim db As Database
    Dim rst As Recordset
    Dim fLocked As Boolean

    Set db = CurrentDb
    Set rst = db.OpenRecordset("tblCustomers", dbOpenDynaset)
    fLocked = IsItLocked(rst)
    MsgBox fLocked
End Sub

Function IsItLocked(rstAny As Recordset) As Boolean
    On Error GoTo IsItLocked_Err
    IsItLocked = False
    With rstAny
```

```
      .LockEdits = True
      .Edit
      .MoveNext
      .MovePrevious
    End With
    Exit Function
IsItLocked_Err:
  If Err = 3260 Then
    IsItLocked = True
    Exit Function
  End If
End Function
```

The **TestLocking** routine sends its recordset to the **IsItLocked** function. The **IsItLocked** function receives the recordset as a parameter and sets its **LockEdits** property to **True**. It then issues an **Edit** method on the recordset. When an error occurs, the record is locked. The error handler sets the return value for the function to **True**.

Using Code To Refresh Or Requery

Throughout the chapter, references have been made to the need to requery a recordset. In this section, you'll see how to accomplish the requery process using code.

The **Requery** method ensures that the user gets to see any changes to existing records, as well as any records that have been added. It also ensures that deleted records are removed from the recordset. It's easiest to understand the requery process by looking at the data underlying a form.

```
Private Sub cmdRequery_Click()
  If Me.RecordsetClone.Restartable Then
    Me.RecordsetClone.Requery
  Else
    MsgBox "Requery Method Not Supported on this Recordset"
  End If
End Sub
```

This code first tests the **Restartable** property of the recordset underlying the form. When the **Restartable** property is **True**, the recordset supports the **Requery** method. The **Requery** method is performed on the form's recordset. Of course, the **Restartable** property and **Requery** method work on any recordset, not just the recordset underlying a form. The only reason that a recordset might not be restartable is because some back-end queries can't be restarted.

Before the running of this code, new records don't appear in the recordset and deleted records appear with **#Deleted**. After the **Requery** method is issued, all new records appear, and deleted records are removed.

Understanding The LDB File

Every database that's opened for shared use has a corresponding LDB file. This is a locking file that's created to store computer and security names and to place byte range locks on the recordset. The LDB file always has the same name and location as the databases whose locks it's tracking, and it's automatically deleted when the last user exits the database file. There are two times when the LDB file isn't deleted:

- The database is marked as damaged.

- The last user out doesn't have delete rights in the folder containing the database and LDB files.

The Jet database engine writes an entry to the LDB file for every user who opens the database. The size of the entry is 64 bytes. The first 32 bytes contain the user's computer name, and the last 32 bytes contain the user's security name. Because the maximum number of users for an Access database is 255, the LDB file can get only as large as 16K. The LDB file information is used to prevent users from writing data to pages that other users have locked and to determine who has the pages locked.

When a user exits an Access database, the user's entry in the LDB file isn't removed. Instead, the entry is overwritten by the next person accessing the database. For this reason, the LDB file doesn't provide an accurate picture of who is currently accessing the database.

Creating Custom Counters

Access provides an **AutoNumber** field type. The **AutoNumber** field can be set to automatically generate sequential or random values. Although the **AutoNumber** field type is sufficient for most situations, you might want to home-grow your own **AutoNumber** fields for any of the following reasons:

- You want an increment value other than 1.

- You don't like the fact that the **AutoNumber** field discards values from canceled records.

- The primary key value needs to be some algorithm of the other fields in the table (for example, the first few characters from a couple of fields).

- The primary key value needs to contain an alphanumeric string.

To generate your own automatically numbered sequential value, you should probably build a system table. This table contains the next available value for your custom autonumber field. It's important that you lock this table while a user is grabbing the next available sequential value. Otherwise, it's possible that two users will be assigned the same value.

Unbound Forms

One solution to locking conflicts is to use unbound forms. They allow you to greatly limit the amount of time that a record is locked, and you can fully control when Access attempts to secure the lock. Unbound forms require significantly more coding than bound forms, so make sure that the benefits you receive from using unbound forms outweigh the coding and maintenance involved. With improvements to both forms and the Jet engine, the reasons to use unbound forms with Access data are less compelling. Unbound forms are covered in more detail later in this chapter.

Using Replication To Improve Performance

Replication, covered later, can be used to improve performance in a multiuser application. You can place multiple copies of the database containing the tables out on the network, each on a different file server. Different users can be set up to access data from the different file servers, thereby better distributing network traffic. Using the Replication Manager, the databases can be synchronized at regular intervals. Although this isn't a viable solution when the data that users are viewing needs to be fully current, there are many situations in which this type of solution might be adequate. It's often the only solution when limited resources don't allow the migration of an application's data to a client-server database.

Using External Data

Microsoft Access is very capable of interfacing with data from other sources. It can utilize data from any ODBC data source, as well as data from FoxPro, dBASE, Paradox, Lotus, Excel, and many other sources. In this chapter, you'll learn how to interface with external data sources both with the user interface and using code.

External data is data stored outside the current database. It can refer to data stored in another Microsoft Access database as well as to data stored in a multitude of other file formats including ODBC, ISAM, spreadsheet, ASCII, and more. This section focuses on accessing data sources other than ODBC data sources. ODBC data sources are covered extensively later in this chapter.

Access is an excellent front-end product, which means that it provides a powerful and effective means of presenting data—even data from external sources. Data is stored in places beside Access for many reasons. For instance, large databases can be more effectively managed on a back-end database server such as Microsoft SQL Server. Data is often stored in a FoxPro, dBASE, or Paradox file format because the data is being used by a legacy application written in one of these environments. Text data has often been downloaded from a mainframe. Regardless of the reason why data is stored in another format, it's necessary that you understand how to manipulate this external data within your VBA modules. When you're able to access data from other sources, you can create queries, forms, and reports, utilizing the data.

In accessing external data, you have three choices. You can import the data into an Access database, access the data by linking to it from within your Access database, or open a data source directly. As you'll learn in the next section, importing the data is optimal (except with ODBC data sources) but not always possible. Short of importing external data, you should link to external files because Microsoft Access maintains a lot of information about these linked files. This optimizes performance when manipulating the external files. Sometimes a particular situation warrants accessing the data directly. It is therefore necessary to know how to work with linked files, as well as how to open and manipulate files directly.

TIP: *Many of the examples in this chapter use data stored in the ISAM file format, which includes files created in FoxPro, dBASE, and Paradox. If you performed a standard installation of Access 2000, you probably didn't install the drivers necessary to communicate with an ISAM file. You need to rerun setup and select the ISAM's check box if you want to perform many of the exercises covered in this chapter.*

When And Why To Use Importing, Linking, And Opening

The process of importing data into an Access table makes a copy of the data, placing the copy within an Access table. After data is imported, it's treated like any other native Access table. In fact, neither you nor Access has any way of knowing where the data came from. As a result, imported data offers the same performance and flexibility as any other Access table.

The process of linking to external data is quite different from the process of importing data. Linked data remains in its native format. By establishing a link to the external data, you're able to build queries, forms, and reports that use or display the data. After you've created a link to external data, the link remains permanently established unless you explicitly remove it. The linked table appears in the database window just like any other Access table. The only difference is you can't modify its structure from within Access. In fact, if the data source permits multiuser access, the users of your application can be modifying the data along with users of the applications written in its native database format (such as FoxPro, dBASE, or Paradox).

The process of opening an external table is similar to linking to the table, except that a permanent relationship isn't created. When you link to an external table, connection information is maintained from session to session. When you open the table, you create a recordset from the table, and no permanent link is established.

Knowing Which Option To Select

It's important that you understand when to import external data, when to link to external data, and when to open an external table directly. Import external data under the following circumstances:

- When you're migrating an existing system into Access.
- When you want to take advantage of and access external data that you will then use to run a large volume of queries and reports, but you won't be updating the data. In such cases, you will often want the added performance that native Access data provides without converting the data between formats.

When you're migrating an existing system to Access and you're ready to permanently migrate either test or production data into your application, you should then import the tables into Access. Another good reason to import external data is because data is downloaded from a mainframe into ASCII format on a regular basis, and you want to utilize the data for reports. Rather than attempting to link to the data and suffer the performance hits associated with such a link, you can import the data each time it's downloaded from the mainframe. You should link to external data under the following circumstances:

- The data is used by a legacy application requiring the native file format.
- The data resides on an ODBC-compliant database server.
- You'll access the data on a regular basis.

Often, you won't have the time or resources to rewrite an application in FoxPro, Paradox, or some other language. You might be developing additional applications that will share data with the legacy application, or you might want to utilize the strong querying and reporting capabilities of Access rather than developing queries and reports in the native environment. By linking to the external data, users of existing applications can continue to work with the applications and their data. Your Access applications can retrieve and modify data without concern for corrupting, or in any other way harming, the data.

When the data resides in an ODBC database such as Microsoft SQL Server, you want to reap the data-retrieval benefits provided by a database server. By linking to the ODBC data source, you can take advantage of Access's ease of use as a front-end tool, while taking advantage of client-server technology at the same time. Finally, if you intend to access data on a regular basis, linking to the external table, rather than temporarily opening the table directly, provides you with ease of use and performance benefits. When you've created the link, Access treats the table just like any other Access table.

WARNING!   Access can corrupt linked data when it rewrites data to the linked file.

Open an external table directly under the following circumstances:

- When you rarely need to establish a connection to the external data source.
- When you've determined that performance actually improves by opening the data source directly.

If you rarely need to access the external data, it might be appropriate to open it directly. Links increase the size of your MDB file. This size increase isn't necessary if you'll rarely access the data. Furthermore, in certain situations, when accessing ISAM data, you might find that opening the table directly provides better performance than linking to it.

Although this chapter covers the process of importing external data, it focuses on linking to or directly opening external data tables rather than importing them. We focus on linking to external data because the import process is a one-time process. When data is imported into an Access table, it's no longer accessed by the application in its native format.

Microsoft Access enables you to import, link to, and open files in the following formats:

- Microsoft Jet databases (including previous versions of Jet)
- Microsoft FoxPro versions 2, 2.5, 2.6, 3, and DBC (Visual FoxPro)
- dBASE III, dBASE IV, and dBASE 5
- Paradox versions 3.x, 4.x, and 5.x
- Microsoft Excel spreadsheets versions 3, 4, 5, 6, 7, Excel 97, and Excel 2000
- Lotus WKS, WK1, WK3, and WK4 spreadsheets
- ASCII text files stored in a tabular format

Importing External Data

The process of importing external data is quite simple. You can import external data using the user interface or by using VBA code. When you're planning to import the data only once or twice, utilize the user interface. When you're importing data on a regular basis—for example, from a downloaded mainframe file—write code that accomplishes the task transparently to the user.

Importing External Data Using Code

The **DoCmd** object has three methods that assist you with importing external data. They are **TransferDatabase**, **TransferText**, and **TransferSpreadsheet**. You'll see implementations of each of these methods in the "Immediate Solutions" section of this chapter.

Creating A Link To External Data

When you need to keep the data in its original format but want to treat the data just like any other Access table, linking is the best solution. All of the information required to establish and maintain the connection to the remote data source is stored within the linked table definition. Links can be created through the user interface and by using code. Both alternatives are covered in this section.

Probably one of the most common types of links is a link to another Access table. This type of link is created so the application objects (queries, forms, reports, macros, and modules) can be placed in a local database and the tables can be stored in another database on a file server. Numerous benefits are associated with such a configuration, as you saw earlier in this chapter.

Creating A Link Using The User Interface

It's very common to create a link using the user interface. When you know what links you want to establish at design time, this is probably the easiest way to establish links to external data. You can establish links using the Database Splitter or manually. You learned about the Database Splitter previously in this chapter, and the "Immediate Solutions" section details how to create links with the Database Splitter. The "Immediate Solutions" section also details other methods you can use to create links.

Creating A Link Using Code

Creating a link to an external table using DAO code is a five-step process. Here are the steps involved in establishing the link:

1. Open the Microsoft Access database that will contain the link to the external file.

2. Create a new table definition using the external data source.

3. Set connection information for the external database and table.

4. Provide a name for the new table.

5. Link the table by appending the table definition to the database.

The code to do so looks similar to the following:

```
Sub LinkToAccessTableProps()
  Dim db As DATABASE
  Dim tdf As TableDef

  Set db = CurrentDb
  Set tdf = db.CreateTableDef("tblLinkedTable")
  tdf.Connect = ";Database=c:\Databases\Chap31Data.mdb"
  tdf.SourceTableName = "tblClients"
  db.TableDefs.Append tdf
End Sub
```

Following the preceding steps, the database does not need to be opened because you're adding a table definition to the current database. The **CreateTableDef** method is used to create the new table definition. The **Connect** property is set and the **SourceTableName** is defined. Finally, the table definition is appended to the **TableDefs** collection of the database. All of this is discussed in further detail in the following sections.

Providing Connection Information

When you link to an external table, you must provide information about the type, name, and location of the external database. This can be accomplished in one of two ways:

- Set the **SourceTableName** and **Connect** properties of the **TableDef** object.
- Include the **Source** and **Connect** values as arguments to the **CreateTableDef** method.

The process of setting the **SourceTableName** and **Connect** properties is illustrated by the following three lines of code:

```
Set tdf = db.CreateTableDef("tblLinkedTable")
tdf.Connect = ";Database=c:\Databases\Chap31Data.MDB"
tdf.SourceTableName = "tblClients"
```

Including the **Source** and **Connect** values as arguments to the **CreateTableDef** method looks like this:

```
Set tdf = db.CreateTableDef("tblLinkedTable", _
    0, "tblClients", _
    ";Database=c:\Databases\Chap31Data")
```

As you can see from the example, both the **Source** (**tblClients**) and the **Connect** value are included as arguments to the **CreateTableDef** method.

The connect string is actually composed of several pieces. These include the source database type, database name, password, and Data Source Name (DSN). The database name is used for tables that aren't ODBC-compliant, and the DSN is used for ODBC tables.

The source database type is the ISAM format that'll be used for the link. Each source database type is a different key in the Windows Registry. The source database type must be entered exactly as it appears in the Registry. Valid source database types include the following:

- dBASE: dBASE III, dBASE IV, dBASE 5, dBASE 6, and dBASE 7, as well as Visual dBASE databases and subsequent InterBase products, up to and including InterBase 5.5

- Excel: Excel 3, Excel 4, Excel 5, Excel 7, Excel 8/97, Excel 9/2000

- FoxPro: FoxPro 2, FoxPro 2.5, FoxPro 2.6, FoxPro 3, FoxPro DBC

- Lotus: Lotus WK1, Lotus WK3, Lotus WK4

- ODBC: ODBC

- Paradox: Paradox 3.x, Paradox 4.x, Paradox 5.x

- Text

WARNING! *If you don't use the exact spaces and punctuation, Access will be unable to communicate with the database engine to correctly convert or link to the file.*

The database name must include a fully qualified path to the file. The path can be specified with a drive letter and directory path or by using Uniform Naming Conventions (UNC). For a local database, the path must be specified in this fashion:

```
Database=c:\Databases\Chap31Data
```

For a file server, either the UNC path or the drive letter path (if you've mapped a drive to the directory) can be specified. The UNC path looks like this:

```
\\FILESERVERNAME\\Databases\\Chap31Data
```

In this case, the database called Chap31Data is stored on the Databases share of a particular file server.

Password is used to supply a password to a database (Access or other) that has been secured. It's best to fill in this part of the connection string from a variable at runtime rather than hard coding it into the VBA code. Sending a password is covered in further detail in the "Working With Passwords" section of this chapter.

The completed connection string is shown at the top of the next page.

```
tdf.Connect = "FoxPro 2.6;Database=c:\clients\database;PWD="
```

In this example, the connect string is set up to link to a FoxPro 2.6 database in the c:\clients\database directory. No password is specified.

Creating The Link

So, after all that, here's how you put it all together to establish a link to an external table:

```
Sub LinkToFox26(strDirName As String, strTableName As String, _
    strAccessTable)
  Dim db As DATABASE
  Dim tdf As TableDef

  Set db = CurrentDb
  Set tdf = db.CreateTableDef(strAccessTable)
  tdf.Connect = "FoxPro 2.6;Database=" & strDirName
  tdf.SourceTableName = strTableName
  db.TableDefs.Append tdf
End Sub
```

Here is an example of how this subroutine would be called:

```
Call LinkToFox26("c:\customer\data","customer","tblCustomers")
```

The **LinkToFox26** subroutine receives three parameters. The first parameter is the name of the directory in which the FoxPro file is stored. The second parameter is the name of the file (name of the table, without the .DBF extension) to which you want to connect. The third parameter is the name of the Access table that you're creating. The subroutine creates two object variables: a database object variable and a table definition object variable. It points the database object variable at the current database. Next, it creates a table definition called **tblCustomers**. It establishes a connection string for that table definition. The connection string specified in the subroutine indicates that you'll link to a FoxPro 2.6 table. The directory name acts as the database to which you're linked. After you've set the **Connect** property of the table definition, you're ready to indicate the name of the table with which you're establishing the link. This is the name of the FoxPro file. Finally, you're ready to append the table definition to the database.

TIP: *Alternately, you could pass all the information into the function and use the values as parameters to the* ***CreateTableDef*** *method.*

You've seen how you can link to a FoxPro table. Putting everything that you've learned together, let's review how you can create a link to an Access table stored in another database. The following code shows an example:

```
Sub LinkToAccess(strDBName As String, strTableName As String, _
    strAccessTable)
  Dim db As DATABASE
  Dim tdf As TableDef

  Set db = CurrentDb
  Set tdf = db.CreateTableDef(strAccessTable)
  tdf.Connect = ";DATABASE=" & strDBName
  tdf.SourceTableName = strTableName
  db.TableDefs.Append tdf
End Sub
```

Notice that the connection string no longer specifies the type of database to which you're connecting. Everything else in this routine is the same as the routine that connected to FoxPro. Also, looking at the parameters passed to the routine (listed next), the database passed to the routine is an actual Access database (as opposed to a directory), and the table name is the name of the Access table in the other database (rather than the DBF file name).

```
Call LinkToAccess("C:\databases\northwind","Customers","tblCustomers")
```

Opening An External Table

As mentioned earlier in the chapter, it's generally preferable to link to, rather than open, an external table because of the additional performance that linking provides and the ease of use in dealing with a linked table. After you link to a table, it's treated just like any other Access table. But there are occasions when it's necessary to open an external table without creating a link to it. Opening an external table is a two-step process.

1. Open the database using the **OpenDatabase** method.

2. Create a recordset object based upon the external table.

Providing Connection Information

The connection information you provide when you open an external table is similar to the information you provide when you link to the table. The connection information is provided as arguments of the **OpenDatabase** method. An example is shown at the top of the next page.

```
OpenDatabase("c:\customer\data", False, False, "FoxPro 2.6")
```

Here, the connection string is to the c:\customer\data database using the FoxPro 2.6 ISAM.

Opening the Table

The **OpenDatabase** method receives the following arguments:

```
OpenDatabase(DBname, Exclusive, Read-Only, Source)
```

The **DBname** is the name of the database you're opening. The **Exclusive** and **Read-Only** parameters are used to specify whether you're opening the database exclusively or as read-only. The **Source** argument is used to specify the database type and connection string. When you put it all together, it'll look similar to the following code:

```
Sub OpenExternalFox(strDBName As String, strTableName As String)
  Dim db As DATABASE
  Dim rst As Recordset

  Set db = DBEngine.Workspaces(0).OpenDatabase(strDBName, False, _
      False, "FoxPro 2.6")
  Set rst = db.OpenRecordset(strTableName)
  Do While Not rst.EOF
    Debug.Print rst.Fields(0).Value
    rst.MoveNext
  Loop
End Sub
```

This code is called as follows:

```
Call OpenExternalFox("c:\customer\data","Customer")
```

Notice that here, you aren't appending a table definition. Instead, you're creating a temporary recordset that refers to the external data. After the external table is opened as a recordset, the code traverses through each record of the table, printing out the value of the first field. Of course, after the recordset is opened, you can manipulate it in any way you like. The table won't show up as a linked table in the database window. In fact, when the routine has completed and the local variable has gone out of scope, the recordset no longer exists.

Now that you've seen how you can link to external tables as well as open them, you're ready to take a look at how you can refine both of these processes. This involves learning the Windows Registry settings that affect the linking process, learning more about the parameters that are available to you in specifying connection information, learning how to specify passwords, learning how to refresh and remove links, and learning how to create an external table using VBA code.

Understanding Windows Registry Settings

Each ISAM driver has a separate key in the Windows Registry. These keys are used to configure the driver upon initialization. As you can see in Figure 31.3, the setup program for Access 2000 has created entries for each of the available data sources. Looking at a specific data source (in this case Paradox 7.X), you can see all of the settings that exist for the Paradox 7.X driver. For example, the **ExportFilter** is set to Paradox 7 (*.db). At times, you'll need to modify one of the registry settings to customize the behavior of the ISAM driver. This is covered in the section titled "Special Considerations." You can find this entry under **HKEY_LOCAL_MACHINE\Software\Microsoft\Jet\4.0\ISAM Formats**.

Further Considerations On The Connection String

The connection string comprises the source database type, database name, user ID, password, and DSN. Each part of the connection string must be separated by a semicolon.

Each source database type has a valid name. This is the name that must be used when accessing that type of data. These database types are listed in Help under the Connect Property item. They can also be found in the Windows Registry under:

```
HKEY_LOCAL_MACHINE\Software\Microsoft\Jet\4.0\ISAM Formats
```

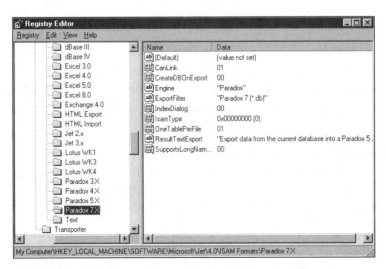

Figure 31.3 The Windows Registry with keys for ISAM drivers.

(Sidebar, right margin: 31. Client-Server Programming With Access 2000)

The source database type must be specified accurately, or you won't be able to access the external data.

The source database name is the name of the database to which you're linking. In the case of ISAM files, this is the name of the directory in which the file is contained. The Database keyword is used to specify the database name.

The user ID is used whenever a user name must be specified to successfully log onto the data source. This is most common when dealing with back-end databases such as Oracle, Sybase, or Microsoft SQL Server. This part of the parameter string can be required to successfully log the user onto the system where the source data resides. The UID keyword is used to refer to the user ID.

As with the user ID, the password is most often included in dealing with back-end data. It can also be used on other database types that support passwords, such as Paradox, or when linking to an external Access table. The PWD keyword is used when specifying the password.

Finally, the data set name is used to refer to a defined ODBC data source. Communicating with an ODBC data source is covered in detail later in this chapter. The DSN keyword is used when referring to the data set name in the connection string.

TIP: *ActiveX Data Objects (ADOs) let you connect to databases without DSNs.*

Refreshing And Removing Links

Refreshing links refers to the updating of the link to an external table. It's done when the location of an external table has changed. Removing links refers to the process of permanently removing a link to an external table.

Access can't find external tables if their location has been moved. You need to accommodate for this in your VBA code. Furthermore, there might be times when you want to remove a link to external data. This occurs when it's no longer necessary to use the data or when the data has been permanently imported into Access.

Creating An External Table

Not only can you link to existing tables, you can even create new external tables. This means you can actually design a FoxPro, Paradox, or other type of table using VBA code. The table will reside on disk as an independent entity and can be used by the application for which it was created.

It's sometimes necessary for your application to provide a data file to another application. That other application might not be capable of reading an Access table. In such cases, it's necessary for you to create the file in a format native to the application that needs to read it.

Creating a "foreign" table isn't as difficult as you might think. It's actually not very different from creating an Access table using VBA code. The "Immediate Solutions" section details how to create a foreign table with VBA code.

Special Considerations

When you are dealing with different types of external files, different problems and issues arise. If you understand these stumbling blocks before they affect you, you'll get a great head start in dealing with these potential obstacles.

Considerations With dBASE

The major concerns you'll have in dealing with dBASE files surround deleted records, indexes, data types, and memo fields. When you delete a record from a dBASE table, it's not actually removed from the table. Instead, it's just marked for deletion. A **Pack** process must be completed for the records to actually be removed from the table. When records are deleted from a dBASE table using an Access application, the records aren't removed. Because you can't pack a dBASE database from within an Access application, the records still remain in the table. In fact, they aren't automatically filtered from the Access table. To filter deleted records so they can't be seen within the Access application, the **Deleted** value in the **\Jet\4.0\Engines\Xbase** section of the Registry must be set to 01 (true).

The dBASE indexes can be utilized by Access to improve performance. When you link to a dBASE table and select an index, an INF file is created. This file has the same name as your dBASE database with an .INF extension. It contains information about all of the indexes being used. Here's an example of an INF:

```
[dBASE IV]
NDX1=CUSTID.NDX
UNDX1=CUSTID.NDX
```

dBASE IV is the database type identifier. NDX1 is an index number for the first index. The UNDX1 entry is used to specify a unique index.

The data types available in dBASE files are different than those available in Access files. It's important to understand how the field types map. Table 31.3 shows how each dBASE data type is mapped to a Jet data type.

Finally, it's important to ensure that the dBASE memo files are stored in the same directory as the table. Otherwise, Access is unable to read the data in the memo file.

Table 31.3 Mapping of dBASE types to Jet data types.

dBASE Data Type	Jet Data Type
Character	Text
Numeric, Float	Double
Logical	Boolean
Date	Date/Time
Memo	Memo
OLE	OLE Object

FoxPro Considerations

Like dBASE files, the major concerns you'll have in dealing with FoxPro files surround deleted records, indexes, data types, and memo fields. Deleted records are handled in the same way as with dBASE files. By setting the Deleted value in the **\Jet\4.0\Engines\Xbase** section of the Registry to 01, you filter deleted records.

As with dBASE indexes, the Access Jet engine can take advantage of FoxPro indexes. The format of an INF file for a FoxPro file is identical to that of a dBASE file.

FoxPro field types are mapped to Jet field types in the same way that dBASE fields are mapped. The only difference is that FoxPro 3.0 supports **Double**, **Currency**, **Integer**, and **DateTime** field types. These map to the corresponding Jet field types. As with dBASE, make sure the Memo files are stored in the same directory as the data tables.

Text Data Considerations

When linking to an ASCII Text file, Jet can determine the format of the file directly, or it can use a Schema Information file. The Schema Information file resides in the same directory as the Text file. It's always named SCHEMA.INI and contains information about the format of the file, column names, and data types. The Schema Information file is optional for delimited files, but it's required for fixed-length files. It's important to understand that ASCII files can never be opened for shared use.

Troubleshooting With External Data

Unfortunately, the process of working with external data isn't always a smooth one. Many things can go wrong, including connection problems and a lack of temporary disk space. Both of these are discussed in this section.

Connection Problems

Difficulties with accessing external data can be caused by any of the following:

- The server on which the external data is stored is down.
- The user doesn't have rights to the directory in which the external data is stored.
- The user doesn't have rights to the external data source.
- The external data source was moved.
- The UNC path or network share name was modified.
- The Connection string is incorrect.
- The installable ISAM driver has not been installed.

Temporary Disk Space

Access requires a significant amount of disk space to run complex queries on large tables. This disk space is required whether the tables are linked tables stored remotely in another format or whether they reside on the local machine. When enough disk space isn't available to run a query, the application will behave unpredictably. Therefore, it is necessary to ensure that all users have enough disk space to meet the requirements of the queries that are run.

Links And Performance Considerations

Because your application has to go through an extra translation layer, the installable ISAM, performance is nowhere near as good with ISAM files as it is with native Jet data. It's always best to import ISAM data whenever possible. When it's not possible to import the data, you need to either accept the performance linking offers or consider linking the best solution to an otherwise unsolvable problem. Opening the recordset using the **OpenDatabase** method might alleviate the problem, but remember that this option can't be used with bound forms.

Moving On To Specific Client-Server Techniques

Client-server refers to distributed processing of information. It involves the storage of data on database servers that are dedicated to the tasks of processing data as well as storing it. These database servers are referred to as back ends. The presentation of the data is accomplished by a front-end tool such as Microsoft Access. Microsoft Access, with its tools that assist in the rapid development of queries, forms, and reports, provides an excellent front end for the presentation of back-end data. As more and more applications are downsized from mainframes and upsized from personal computers, it's becoming necessary for more of us to understand the details of client-server technology.

For years, most information professionals have worked with traditional programming languages. These languages are responsible for both processing and maintaining data integrity within the application. This means that data-validation rules must be embedded within the programming code. Furthermore, these types of applications are record-oriented. All records are read into memory and processed. This scenario has several drawbacks:

- If the underlying data structure changes, every application that uses the data structure has to be changed.

- Data-validation rules must be placed in *every* application that accesses a data table.

- Presentation, processing, and storage are all handled by one program.

- Record-oriented processing results in an extraordinary amount of unnecessary network traffic.

The client-server model introduces a separation of functionality. The client, or front end, is responsible for presenting the data and doing some processing. The server, or back end, is responsible for storing, protecting, and performing the bulk of the processing on the data.

Determining When Client-Server Is Appropriate

Client-server was not as necessary when there was a clear delineation between mainframe applications and personal computer applications. Today, the line of demarcation has become blurry. Personal computer applications are beginning to take over many applications that had been relegated to mainframe computers in the past. The problem is that we're still very limited by the bandwidth of network communications. This is one place where client-server can really help.

Many developers are confused about what client-server really is. Access is a front-end application that can process data stored on a back end. In this scenario, the Access application runs on the client machine accessing data stored on a database server running software such as Microsoft SQL Server. Access does an excellent job acting as the client-side, front-end software in this scenario. The confusion lies in Access's capability to act as a database server.

Many people mistakenly believe that an Access MDB database file stored on a file server acts as a database server. This isn't the case. The difference lies in the way in which data is retrieved when Access is acting as the front end to a database server versus when the data is stored in an Access MDB file. Imagine the following scenario:

You have a table with 500,000 records. A user runs a query that's based on the 500,000-record table stored in an Access database on a file server. The user wants to see a list of all the Californians who make over $75,000 per year. With the data stored on the file server in the Access MDB file format, all records are sent over the network to the workstation, and the query is performed on the workstation. This results in significant network traffic, as shown in Figure 31.4.

On the other hand, assume that these 500,000 records are stored on a database server such as Microsoft SQL Server. The user runs the same query. In this case, only the names of the Californians who make more than $75,000 per year are sent over the network. In fact, if you request only specific fields, only the fields you request are retrieved, as shown in Figure 31.5.

Considering the implications of this for your development, why you should become concerned with client-server technology, and what doing so can offer you are difficult—but important—questions. The following sections are meant to be guidelines for why you might want to upsize.

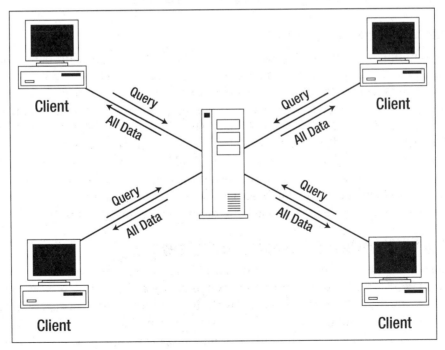

Figure 31.4   Network traffic resulting from Access running on a file server.

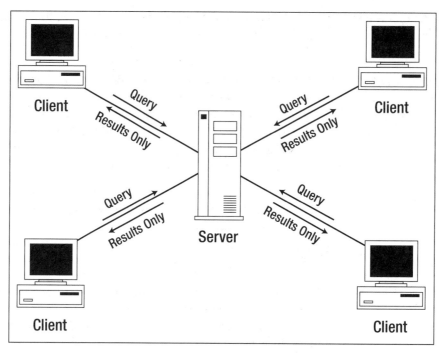

Figure 31.5   Access as a front end using a true server back end.

Large Volume Of Data

As the volume of data within an Access database increases, you'll probably notice a degradation in performance. Many people say that 100MB is the magical number for the maximum size of an Access database, whereas many back-end database servers can handle databases containing multiple gigabytes of data. Although a maximum size of 100MB for an Access database is a good general guideline, it's *not* a hard-and-fast rule. You might find that the need to upsize occurs when your database is significantly larger or smaller than 100MB. The magic number for you depends on all the factors discussed in the following sections, as well as on how many tables are included in the database. Generally, Access performs better with large volumes of data stored in a single table rather than in multiple tables.

Large Number Of Concurrent Users

Just as a large volume of data can be a problem, so can a large number of concurrent users. In fact, more than 10 users concurrently accessing an Access database can really degrade performance. As with the amount of data, this isn't a magical number. As a developer, you may have seen applications with fewer than 10 users where performance is awful, and you may have seen applications with significantly more than 10 users where performance is acceptable. It often depends on how the application is designed, as well as what tasks the users are performing.

Demand For Faster Performance

Certain applications, by nature, demand better performance than other applications. An online transaction processing system (OLTP) generally requires significantly better performance than a decision support system (DSS). Imagine 100 users simultaneously taking phone orders. It would not be appropriate for the users of the system to ask their customers to wait 15 seconds between entering each item that's ordered. On the other hand, asking a user to wait 60 seconds to process a management report the user runs once each month isn't a lot to ask (although many will still complain about the minute). Not only does the client-server architecture itself lead to better performance, but most back-end database servers can take full advantage of multithreaded operating systems with multiple processors. Access, on the other hand, can't.

Problems With Increased Network Traffic

As a file server within an organization experiences increasing demands, the Access application might simply exacerbate an already growing problem. By moving the application data to a database server, the reduced demands on the network overall might provide all users on the network with better performance regardless of whether or not they're utilizing the Access application.

Probably one of the most exaggerated situations where this might be true is one in which all the workstations were diskless. Windows and all application software would be installed on a file server. The users might all concurrently load Microsoft Word, Microsoft Excel, and Microsoft PowerPoint over the network. In addition, they might have large Access applications with many database objects and large volumes of data, which would all be stored on the file server as well. In such a situation, needless to say, performance would be terrible. You can't expect an already overloaded file server to be able to handle sending large volumes of data over a small bandwidth. The benefits offered by client-server technology can help alleviate this problem.

Importance Of Backup And Recovery

The backup and recovery options offered with an Access MDB database stored on a file server simply don't rival the options for backup and recovery on a database server. Any database server worth its salt sports very powerful uninterruptable power supplies (UPSs). Many have hot swapping disk drives with disk mirroring, disk duplexing, or disk striping with parity (redundant array of independent disks [RAID] Level 5 protection). Disk mirroring and duplexing mean that data can be written to multiple drives at one time, providing instantaneous backups.

Furthermore, some database server tape backup software enables backups to be completed while users are accessing the system. Many offer automatic transaction logging. All these mean that there is less chance of data loss or application down-time. With certain applications, this type of backup and recovery is overkill. With other applications, it's imperative.

TIP: *Some of what back ends have to offer in terms of backup and recovery can be mimicked by using code and replication. However, it's nearly impossible to get the same level of protection from an Access database stored on a file server that you can get from a true back-end database stored on a database server.*

Importance Of Security

Access offers what can be considered the best security for a desktop database. Although this is the case, the security offered by an Access database can't compare with that provided by most database servers. Database server security often works in conjunction with the network operating system. This is the case, for example, with Microsoft SQL Server and Windows NT Server. Remember that no matter how much security you place on an Access database, this doesn't prevent a user from deleting the entire MDB file from the network disk. It's very easy to offer protection from this potential problem, and others on a database server. Furthermore, many back-end application database server products offer field-level security not offered within an Access MDB file. Finally, many back ends offer integrated security with one logon for both the network and the database.

Need To Share Data Among Multiple Front-End Tools

The Access MDB file format is proprietary. Many other products can't read data stored in the Access database format. With a back-end database server that supports ODBC, front-end applications can be written in a variety of front-end application software, all concurrently utilizing the same back-end data.

Applying The Guidelines

Well, everything in the previous sections is important and useful. Nevertheless, you need to make a determination for your application in your environment. To do so, you need to evaluate the specific environment in which your application will run, including the following considerations:

- How many users are there?
- How much data is there?
- What is the network traffic like already?
- What type of performance is required?
- How disastrous is downtime?
- How sensitive is the data?
- What other applications will utilize the data?

After you answer all these questions, and additional ones, you can begin to make decisions as to whether the benefits of the client-server architecture outweigh the costs involved. The good news is that it's not an all-or-none decision. Various options are available for client-server applications utilizing Access as a front end. Furthermore, when you design your application with upsizing in mind, moving to client-server won't require you to throw out what you've done and start again.

Roles That Access Can Play In The Application Design Model

Before you move on to learn more about client-server technology, let's take a look at the different roles that Access can take in an application design. Several options are available.

Access As The Front End And Back End

In previous chapters of this book, you've learned about using Access as both the front end and the back end. However, in such situations, the Access database isn't acting as a true back end in that it's not doing any processing. The architecture in this scenario is shown in Figure 31.6. The Access application resides on the workstation. Utilizing the Microsoft Jet engine, it communicates with data stored in an Access MDB database file stored on the file server.

Access As The Front End Using Links To Communicate To A Back End

In the second scenario, back-end tables can be linked to the front-end application database. The process of linking to back-end tables is almost identical to that of

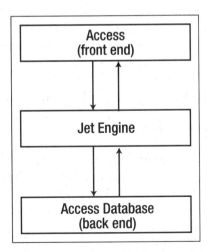

Figure 31.6   Access as a front end using an MDB file for data storage.

linking to tables in other Access databases or to external tables stored in FoxPro, Paradox, or dBASE. After the back-end tables have been linked to the front-end application database, they can be treated like any other linked tables. Access uses ODBC to communicate with the back-end tables.

In use, your application sends an Access SQL statement to the Access Jet engine. Jet translates the Access SQL statement into ODBC SQL. The ODBC SQL statement is then sent to the ODBC manager. The ODBC manager locates the correct ODBC driver and passes it the ODBC SQL statement. The ODBC driver, supplied by the back-end vendor, translates the ODBC SQL statement into the back end's specific dialect. The back-end specific query is sent to the SQL server and to the appropriate database. As you might imagine, all this translation takes quite a bit of time. That's why one of the two alternatives that follow might be a better solution.

Access As The Front End Using SQL Pass-Through To Communicate To A Back End

One of the bottlenecks of linked tables is the translation of the Access SQL statement by Jet to ODBC SQL, which is translated by the ODBC driver to a generic SQL statement. Not only is the translation slow, but there might be other reasons why you'd want to bypass the translation process:

- Access SQL might not support some operation that's supported by the native query language of the back end.

- Either the Jet engine or the ODBC driver produces a SQL statement that isn't optimized for the back end.

- You want a process performed in its entirety on the back end.

Pass-through queries are covered in more detail in the "Pass-Through Queries" section of this chapter. For now, let's look at what happens when a pass-through query is executed. The pass-through query is written in the syntax specific to the back-end database server. Although the query does pass through the Jet engine, Jet does not perform any translation on the query. Neither does ODBC. The ODBC manager sends the query to the ODBC driver. The ODBC driver passes the query on to the back end without performing any translation. In other words, exactly what was sent from Access is what is received by the SQL database. This scenario is shown in Figure 31.7.

Notice that the Jet engine, the ODBC manager, and the ODBC driver aren't eliminated entirely. They're still there, but they have much less impact on the process than they do with attached tables. As you'll see in the section on pass-through queries, pass-through queries aren't a complete solution, although they're very useful. For example, the results of a pass-through query aren't updatable. Furthermore, because pass-through queries are written in the back end's specific

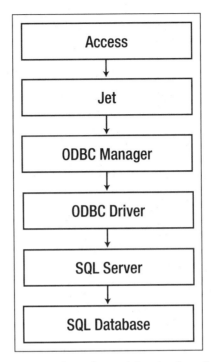

Figure 31.7   Access sending a pass-through query to a back-end database.

SQL dialect, you need to rewrite them if you swap out your back end. For these reasons, and others, pass-through queries are usually used in combination with other solutions.

Access As The Front End Using ActiveX Data Objects To Communicate To A Back End

One additional scenario is available when working with a back-end database server. This involves using ADO, which you've learned about in previous chapter. Using ADO, you bypass the Jet engine entirely. SQL statements are written in ODBC SQL. Figure 31.8 illustrates this scenario.

As you've learned previously, ADO is a very thin wrapper on the OLE DB com interfaces—which are themselves a wrapper of the ODBC application programming interface (API) calls. The SQL statement travels quickly through all the layers to the back-end database. From a performance standpoint, this solution puts Jet to shame. The major advantage of ADO over pass-through queries is you write the SQL statements in ODBC SQL rather than the back-end–specific SQL. This means your application is easily portable to other back-end database servers. You can swap out your back end with little modification to your application.

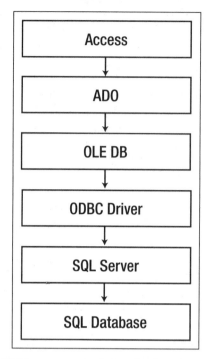

Figure 31.8   Access using ADO to communicate to a back end.

The major disadvantage of ADO is that it can't be used with bound forms or re-ports—meaning a lot more coding for you. As with pass-through queries, this option can be used in combination with the other solutions to gain required per-formance benefits in mission-critical parts of the application.

Upsizing: What To Worry About

Suppose your database is using Microsoft Access as both the front end and back end. Although an Access database on a file server might have been sufficient for awhile, the need for better performance, enhanced security, or one of the other benefits that a back-end database provides is compelling your company (or your client's company) to upsize to a client-server architecture. The Access tables have already been created and even contain volumes of data. In this scenario, it might make sense to upsize.

Because all the tables have been designed as Access tables, they need to be upsized to the back-end database server. Upsizing means moving tables from a local Access database (or from any PC database) to a back-end database server that usually runs on Unix, Windows NT Server, OS/2 LAN Server, or as a Novell NetWare NLM.

Another reason that tables are upsized from Access to a back-end server is that many developers prefer to design their tables from within the Access environment. Access offers a more user-friendly environment for table creation than do most server applications—an issue less important with the introduction of ADPs.

Regardless of your reasons for upsizing, you need to understand several issues regarding the movement, or upsizing, of Access tables to a database server. Indeed, because of the many caveats in moving tables from Access to a back end, many people opt to design the tables directly on the back end. If you do design your tables in Access, you should export them to the back end, then link them to your local database. As you export your tables to the database server, you need to be aware of the issues covered in the sections that follow.

Index Considerations

When exporting a table to a server, no indexes are created. All indexes need to be re-created on the back-end database server—unless you use the SQL Server Upsizing Wizard.

Exporting AutoNumber Fields

AutoNumber fields are exported as **Long** integers. Because most database servers don't support autonumbering, you have to create an insert trigger on the server that provides the next key value. Autonumbering can also be achieved using form-level events, but this isn't desirable because the numbering won't be enforced when other applications access the data.

Using Default Values

Default values aren't automatically moved to the server, even when the server supports default values. You can set up default values directly on the server, but these values do *not* automatically appear when new records are added to the table unless the record is saved without data being added to the field containing the default value. As with autonumbering, default values can be implemented at the form level, with the same drawbacks.

Exporting Validation Rules

Validation rules aren't exported to the server. They must be re-created using triggers on the server. No Access-defined error messages are displayed when a server validation rule is violated. Your application should be coded to provide the appropriate error messages. Validation rules can also be performed at the form level, but they're enforced if the data is accessed by other means.

Exporting Relationships

Relationships need to be enforced using server-based triggers. Access's default error messages don't appear when referential integrity is violated. You need to respond to, and code for, these error messages within your application. Relationships can be enforced at the form level, but as with other form-level validations, this method of validation doesn't adequately protect your data.

Applying Security To The New Database

Security features that you've set up in Access don't carry forward to the server. You need to reestablish table security on the server. When security has been set up on the server, Access becomes unaware that the security exists until the Access application attempts to violate the server's security. Then, error codes are returned to the application. You must handle these errors by using code and display the appropriate error message to the user.

Exporting Table And Field Names

Servers often have much more stringent rules regarding the naming of fields than Access does. When you export a table, all characters that aren't alphanumeric are converted to underscores. Most back ends don't allow spaces in field names. Furthermore, most back ends limit the length of object names to 30 characters or less. If you've already created queries, forms, reports, macros, and modules that utilize spaces and very long field and table names, these database objects might become unusable when you move your tables to a back-end database server.

Considerations With Reserved Words

Most back ends have many reserved words. It's important that you're aware of the reserved words of your specific back end. It's quite shocking when you upsize a table to find that field names that you've been using are reserved words on your database server. When this is the case, you need to rename all the fields in which a conflict occurs. Once again, this means modifying all the queries, forms, reports, macros, and modules that reference the original field names.

Understanding Case Sensitivity

Many back-end databases are case sensitive. When this is the case with your back end, you might find that your queries and application code don't process as expected. Queries or code that refer to the field or table name by using the wrong case aren't recognized by the back-end database and don't process correctly.

Using Properties With Remote Tables

Most properties can't be modified on remote tables. Any properties that can be modified are lost upon export, so you need to set them up again when the table is exported.

Proactively Preparing For Upsizing

When you set up your tables and code modules with upsizing in mind, you can eliminate many of the preceding pitfalls. Despite any of the problems that upsizing can bring, the scalability of Access is one of its stronger points. Sometimes resources aren't available to implement client-server technology in the early stages of an application. If you think through the design of the project with the possibility of upsizing in mind, you'll be pleased at how relatively easy it is to move to client-server when the time is right.

In fact, Microsoft provides an Access upsizing tool, specifically designed to take an Access application and upsize it to Microsoft SQL Server. The Access 2000 version of this tool ships with the Microsoft Office CD-ROM.

Defining An ODBC Data Source

Before you can use Microsoft Access with a database server, you need to load the ODBC drivers. These drivers come with Access, but—depending on which version of Office you are using—they may not be installed automatically when you select the standard installation of the product. Depending on how you ran the setup, if you need to subsequently install the ODBC drivers, the Windows Installer may prompt you for a CD-ROM, or you may need to rerun Setup and choose the Custom installation option.

In addition to installing the ODBC Driver manager and the default drivers, you will also need to load drivers for the specific back-end database servers to which you want to connect. These drivers are usually purchased from the back-end database vendor and often come with a per-seat charge. This means you must purchase a client license for each user who will connect to the remote data.

An ODBC data source is a user-defined name that points to a remote source of data. It contains all the properties of the data source necessary to communicate to data stored on a database server.

Before you can access a remote table from Access, you must define it using the ODBC administrator. If you don't define that data source, or if it's not defined correctly, you'll be unable to obtain access to the data.

ODBC data sources are set up in the ODBC administrator. Depending on your installation, the ODBC administrator could be a standalone application, or it could appear as a control-panel icon. It enables you to create, modify, and delete data sources, and to obtain information about existing drivers. Remember that a data source is simply a user-definable name that stores settings that can be used to access a back end located on a particular server using a specified driver. Figure 31.9 shows the User DSN tab within the ODBC administrator.

When you've entered the ODBC administrator, you should probably set up a new data source. To define a new data source, click on the Add button in the ODBC Administrator dialog. The Create New Data Source dialog box, where you must select the name of the driver that the data source will use, will appear, as shown in Figure 31.10.

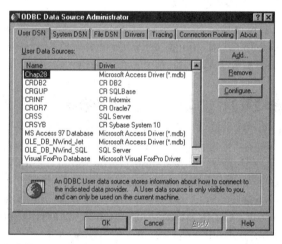

Figure 31.9   The User DSN tab within the ODBC administrator.

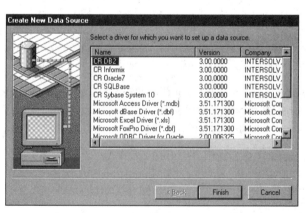

Figure 31.10   The Create New Data Source dialog box.

The list of available drivers varies depending on which client drivers have been installed on the machine. After you select a data source and click OK, you're shown another dialog, which varies depending on which driver you've selected. It enables you to define specific information about the data source you're creating. An example is the ODBC Create New Data Source to SQL Server dialog box shown in Figure 31.11.

As you can see, the ODBC SQL Server Setup dialog enables you to specify database-specific information, such as the data source name, a description of the data source, and the network name of the SQL Server to connect to.

TIP: *You might be wondering how you can possibly go through the process of defining data sources on thousands of user machines in a large installation. Fortunately, you can automate the process of defining data sources by using dynamic-linked library functions. It's a matter of using the ODBC Administrator DLL function calls to set up the data source by using code. However, explaining the process is beyond the scope of this work.*

Connecting To A Database Server

After you define a data source, you're ready to connect to it. Use one of four methods to access server data:

- Link to tables residing on the server.
- Link to views residing on the server.
- Use pass-through queries to send SQL statements directly to the server.
- Use VBA code to open the server tables directly.

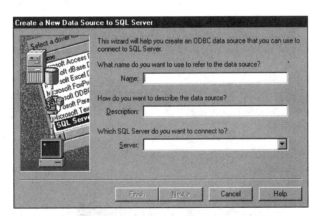

Figure 31.11   The Create New Data Source to SQL Server dialog box.

Working With Linked Tables

The easiest method of accessing data on the server is to link to the external tables. These linked tables act almost exactly like native Access tables. When you link to remote tables, Access analyzes the fields and indexes contained within the tables so it can achieve optimal performance. It's important to relink the tables when the structures of the remote tables change. The following sections discuss how you can link to remote tables both through the user interface and through code.

Linking To External Tables Using The User Interface

To link to a remote table through the user interface, right-click your mouse on the Tables tab of the Database window. Select Link Tables. Select ODBC Databases from the Files Of Type drop-down list. The Select Data Source dialog box shown in Figure 31.12 will appear.

You can select an existing data source or define a new data source directly from the Select Data Source dialog. After selecting a data source, you're prompted for a password. You can't obtain access to the server data unless you have a valid login ID and password.

When you successfully log onto the server, you're presented with a list of tables contained within the database that the data source is referencing. Here, you must select the table to which you want to link.

After you select one or more tables and click OK, you might be prompted with the Select Unique Record Identifier dialog box. Selecting a unique identifier for the table enables you to update records on the back-end data source. Select a unique

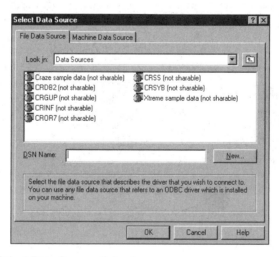

Figure 31.12   The Select Data Source dialog box.

identifier and click OK. The linked tables will appear in the Database window. You can treat these linked tables just as you would any other table (with a few exceptions covered later in the chapter).

Linking To External Tables Using Program Code

You've just learned how you can link to a remote table by using Access's user interface. Now let's take a look at how you can link to the same table by using code. The following subroutine accepts six parameters. They're the names for the Access table, the server database, the server table, the dataset, the user ID, and the password:

```
Sub LinkToSQL(strAccessTable, strDBName, strTableName, _
    strDataSetName, strUserID, strPassWord)
  Dim db As DATABASE
  Dim tdf As TableDef

  Set db = CurrentDb
  Set tdf = db.CreateTableDef(strAccessTable)
  tdf.Connect = "ODBC;Database=" & strDBName _
      & ";DSN=" & strDataSetName & ";UID=" & strUserID _
      & ";PWD=" & strPassWord
  tdf.SourceTableName = strTableName
  db.TableDefs.Append tdf
End Sub
```

So, presume for the moment that the Access table you're creating is called **tblStores**. The database name on the server is **Pubs**. The table to which you're linking is called **dbo.Stores**, and the dataset name is **PublisherData**. You're logging in as database system administrator (SA) without a password. The user ID and password could have been supplied as the user logged into your application and could have been stored in variables until needed for logging into the server. The following call will do just that from the program code:

```
Call LinkToSQL("tblStores", "Pubs", "dbo.Stores", _
    "PublisherData", "SA", "")
```

Linking To Views Rather Than To Tables

Views on a database server are like Access queries. They provide a form of security by limiting what rows and columns a user can see. Access is granted to the user for the view rather than directly to the underlying table. By default, views aren't updatable. You can make a view updatable by including all the fields that comprise the primary key in the view and building a unique index on the primary key. Views can be created in one of two ways:

- Using the SQL Server Enterprise Manager for SQL Server 7.0 (or the equivalent option for your back-end database server or ADP project).

- Using the Create View statement in Access.

The "Immediate Solutions" section of this chapter details how to create a remote view from Access.

Pass-Through Queries

Ordinarily, when you store and execute a query in Access, even if it's running on remote data, Access compiles and optimizes the query. In many cases, this is exactly what you want. On certain other occasions, however, it might be preferable for you to execute a pass-through query because they aren't analyzed by Access's Jet engine. They're passed directly to the server, and this reduces the time Jet analyzes the query and enables you to pass server-specific syntax to the back end. Furthermore, pass-through queries can log informational messages returned by the server. Finally, bulk update, delete, and append queries are faster using pass-through queries than they are using Access action queries based on remote tables.

Pass-through queries do have their downside. They always return a snapshot, rendering them not updatable. You also must know the exact syntax that the server requires, and you must type the statement into the query window rather than painting it graphically. Finally, you can't easily parameterize a query so it prompts the user for a value.

Creating A Pass-Through Query Using The User Interface

To create a pass-through query, you can build the query in the Access query builder. To do this, select the Query menu SQL Specific submenu Pass-Through option. Access will present you with a text-editing window in which you can enter the query statement. The SQL statement that you enter must be in the SQL flavor specific to your back end.

Executing A Pass-Through Query Using Code

You can also perform a pass-through query using VBA code. In fact, you must create the pass-through query by using VBA code if you want the query to contain parameters that you'll pass to the server. Here's one way you can create a pass-through query using VBA code:

1. Use the **OpenDatabase** method of the workspace object to open the SQL server database. You must supply the connect string as the fourth parameter to the **OpenDatabase** function.

2. Use the **Execute** method to execute the SQL statement on the back-end database server. As with a SQL statement created by using the Query menu, the statement you create must be in the syntax specific to your particular back end. The code to perform such processing looks similar to the following:

```
Sub PassThroughQuery(strDBName As String, strDataSetName As String, _
    strUserID As String, strPassWord As String)
  Dim ws As Workspace
  Dim db As DATABASE
  Dim strConnectString As String

  strConnectString = "ODBC;DATABASE=" & strDBName & _
      ";DSN=" & strDataSetName & ";UID=" & strUserID & _
      ";PWD=" & strPassWord
  Set ws = DBEngine(0)
  Set db = ws.OpenDatabase( "", False, False, strConnectString)
  db.Execute "Update dbo.Sales Set Qty = Qty + 1", _
  dbSQLPassThrough
End Sub
```

You would then call this routine from elsewhere in your program with the following statement:

```
Call PassThroughQuery("Pubs", "PublisherData", "SA","" )
```

This subroutine uses a connect string that connects to a database called **Pubs**, with a datasource named **PublisherData**, a user ID of **SA**, and no password. It then executes a pass-through query that updates the **Qty** field of each record to **Qty+1**.

As you saw, one method of executing a pass-through query is to open the database using the **OpenDatabase** method and execute the query using the **Execute** method on the database object. The limitation of this method is that the **Execute** method doesn't enable you to execute queries that return data. There's another method of executing a pass-through query you can use when you want to return records. It involves creating a query definition within the local database and opening a recordset using a pass-through query or a stored procedure as the SQL property for the query definition. This method is covered in the next section.

Executing A Stored Procedure

You can also execute a stored procedure on a back-end database server. A stored procedure is like a query or program stored on the back end, and it performs some action. An example is the SQL Server 7 stored procedure called **sp_columns**.

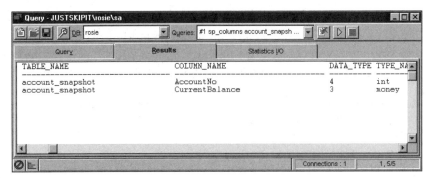

Figure 31.13   Executing the **sp_columns** stored procedure from the Query Design window.

This stored procedure returns information on the fields in a particular table. Figure 31.13 illustrates how you would execute the **sp_columns** stored procedure from the Query Design window.

As you can see from the figure, you simply type the name of the stored procedure and any parameters that it must receive. Take a good look at the Query Properties window shown in Figure 31.13. If you enter a valid ODBC connect string, the user won't be prompted to log in at runtime. The Return Records property is another important property. In this case, you want to set the value of the property to Yes so that you can see the results of the stored procedure. When the stored procedure doesn't return records, as is the case with the Create View pass-through query created in the section titled Linking to Views Rather than Tables, it's important to set this property to No. Otherwise, you receive an error message indicating that no rows were returned.

Opening A Server Table Directly

As you saw, the **OpenDatabase** method of the **Workspace** object can be used to execute pass-through queries. This is a valid use of the **OpenDatabase** method. This method can also be used in place of linking to tables to access server data directly. This is generally extremely inefficient because the data structure isn't analyzed and maintained in the Access database engine. With linked tables, the fields, indexes, and server capabilities are all cached in memory so they'll be readily available when needed.

Regardless, there are times when you might want to open a database directly. One reason is to preconnect to a server so you'll be connected when you need access to the data. The "Immediate Solutions" section of this chapter details how you can use the **OpenDatabase** function to connect to a remote server database.

Client-Server Strategies

As you might have inferred from the previous sections, it's very easy to implement client-server ineffectively. This can result in worse rather than better performance. The developer's task is to intelligently apply appropriate techniques that deploy client-server systems effectively. The following sections discuss strategies to help you develop smart client-server applications.

Selecting The Best Recordset Type

Sometimes it's best to create a dynaset, and at other times it's more efficient to create a snapshot. It's very important that you understand under what circumstances each choice is the most appropriate.

In essence, a *dynaset* is a collection of bookmarks that enables each record on the server to be identified uniquely. Each bookmark corresponds to one record on the server and is generally equivalent to the primary key of the record. Because the bookmark is a direct pointer back to the original data, a dynaset is an updatable set of records. When you create a dynaset, you create a set of bookmarks of all rows that meet the query criteria. When you open a recordset using code, only the first bookmark is returned to the user's PC's memory. The remaining columns from the record are brought into memory only when they're directly referenced using code. This means that large fields, such as OLE and Memo, aren't retrieved from the server unless they're explicitly accessed using code. Access uses the primary key to fetch the remainder of the columns. As the code moves from record to record in the dynaset, additional bookmarks and columns are retrieved from the server.

> **WARNING!** *All the bookmarks aren't retrieved unless a MoveLast method is issued or each record in the recordset is visited using code.*

Although this keyset method of data retrieval is relatively efficient, dynasets carry significant overhead associated with their ability to be edited. This is why snapshots are often more efficient.

When you open a snapshot type of recordset, all columns from the first row are retrieved into memory. As you move to each row, all columns within the row are retrieved. When a **MoveLast** method is issued, all rows and all columns meeting the query criteria are immediately retrieved into the client machine's memory. Because a snapshot isn't editable and maintains no link back to the server, it can be more efficient. This is generally true only for relatively small recordsets. The caveat lies in the fact that all rows and all columns in the result set are returned to the user's computer memory whether they're accessed or not. With a result set containing over 500 records, the fact that all columns are returned to the user's computer memory outweighs the benefits provided by a snapshot. In these cases, you may want to create a Read Only dynaset.

Forward-Scrolling Snapshots

When your data doesn't need to be updated and it's sufficient to move forward through a recordset, you may want to use a forward-scrolling snapshot. Forward-scrolling snapshots are extremely fast and efficient. You create a forward-scrolling snapshot using the **dbForwardOnly** option of the **OpenRecordset** method. This renders the recordset forward-scrolling only. This means that you can't issue a **MovePrevious** or **MoveFirst** method. You also can't use a **MoveLast**. This is because only one record is retrieved at a time. There is no concept of a set of records, so Access can't move to the last record. This method of data retrieval provides significantly better performance than regular snapshots with large recordsets.

Keyset Fetching

The fact that dynasets return a set of primary keys causes problems with forms. With a very large set of records and a large primary key, sending just the primary keys over the network wire can generate a huge volume of network traffic. When you open a form, Access retrieves just enough data to display on the form. It then continues to fetch the remainder of the primary keys satisfying the query criteria. Whenever keyboard input is sensed, the fetching process stops until idle time is available. It then continues to fetch the remainder of the primary keys. To prevent the huge volume of network traffic associated with this process, you must carefully limit the size of the dynasets that are returned. Methods of accomplishing this are covered in the section titled "Optimizing Forms."

Connecting Using Pass-Through Queries And Stored Procedures

It's important to remember that executing pass-through queries and stored procedures is much more efficient than returning a recordset to be processed by Access. The difference lies in where the processing occurs. With pass-through queries and stored procedures, all the processing is completed on the server. When operations are performed using VBA code, all the records that will be affected by the process must be returned to the user's memory, modified, then returned to the server. This generates a significant amount of network traffic and slows down processing immensely.

Preconnecting To ODBC Databases

In dealing with ODBC databases, connections to the server are transparently handled by Jet. When you issue a command, a connection is established with the server. When you finish an operation, Jet keeps the connection open in anticipation of the next operation. The amount of time that the connection is cached is determined by the **ConnectionTimeout** setting in the Windows Registry. You may want to take advantage of the fact that a connection is cached to connect to the back end when your application first loads, before the first form or report even opens. The connection and authentication information will be cached and used when needed.

As seen in the **LinkToSQL** routine in the "Immediate Solutions" section of this chapter, you can send password information stored in variables as parameters when creating a link to a server. These values could easily have come from a login form. You could generally preconnect to a database from the login form. The "Immediate Solutions" section details how to perform this task from VBA code.

Reducing The Number Of Connections

Some database servers are capable of running multiple queries on one connection. Other servers, such as Microsoft SQL Server, are capable of processing only one query per connection. You should try to limit the number of connections required by your application. The following paragraphs discuss some ways that you can reduce the number of connections your application requires.

Dynasets containing more than 100 records require two connections, one to fetch the key values from the server, and the other to fetch the data associated with the first 100 records. Therefore, try to limit query results to under 100 records wherever possible.

When connections are at a premium, close connections that you're no longer using. This can be accomplished by moving to the last record in the result set or by running a Top 100 Percent query. Both of these techniques have dramatic negative effects on performance because all the records in the result set are fetched. Therefore, these techniques should be used only when reducing connections is more important that optimizing performance.

Finally, you might want to set a connection time-out. This means that if no action has been taken for a specified period of time, the connection will be closed. The default value for the connection time-out is 10 minutes. This value can be modified in the **HKEY_LOCAL_MACHINE\SOFTWARE\Microsoft\Jet\4.0\Engines\ODBC** key of the Windows Registry by changing the **ConnectionTimeout** setting. The time-out occurs even if a form is open. Fortunately, Access automatically reestablishes the connection when it's needed.

Optimizing Data Handling

One of the best things that you can do to optimize data handling—such as edits, inserts, and deletes—is to add a version field (time stamp) to each remote table. This version field is used when users update the data on the remote table to avoid overwrite conflicts. When this field doesn't exist, the server compares every field to see whether you've changed its value since the user first began editing the record. This is quite inefficient and is much slower than evaluating a time stamp.

The use of transactions is another way to improve performance significantly, because transactions enable multiple updates to be written as a single batch. As an added benefit, they protect your data by ensuring that everything has executed successfully before changes are committed to disk.

Optimizing Queries And Forms

On the whole, the movement to client-server improves performance. Howerver, if you aren't careful when designing your queries, forms, and reports, the movement to client-server can actually degrade performance. You can do several things to ensure that the movement to client-server is beneficial. These techniques are broken down into query techniques, form techniques, and report techniques.

Optimizing Queries

Servers can't perform many of the functions offered by the Access query builder. The functions that can't be processed on the server are performed on the workstation. This often results in a large amount of data being sent over the network wire. This extra traffic can be eliminated if your queries are designed so they can be processed solely by the server.

The following are examples of problem queries that can't be performed on the server:

- Top N percent queries.
- Queries containing user-defined or Access functions.
- Queries that involve tables from two different data sources—for example, a query that joins tables from two different servers or from an Access table and a server table.

Optimizing Forms

The following techniques can help you design forms that capitalize on the benefits of the client-server architecture. The idea is to design your forms so they request the minimal amount of data from the server and they obtain additional data only when requested by the user. This means that you request as few records and fields as possible from the server. This can be accomplished by basing forms on queries rather than directly on the tables. It can be further refined by design-ing your forms specifically with data retrieval in mind. For example, a form can initially be opened with no **RecordSource**. The form can require that users limit the criteria before any records are displayed.

You should store static tables, such as a **State** table, locally. This reduces net-work traffic and requests to the server. Furthermore, combo boxes and list boxes shouldn't be based on server data. Whenever possible, the row source for combo boxes and list boxes should be based on local static tables. If this isn't possible, you can use a text box in conjunction with a combo box. The **Row Source** prop-erty of the combo box is initially left blank. The user must enter the first few characters into the text box. The **Row Source** of the combo box is based on a SQL **Select** statement using the characters entered into the text box.

Furthermore, OLE Object and Memo fields are large and, therefore, significantly increase network traffic. It's best not to display the contents of these fields unless they're specifically requested by the user. This can be accomplished by setting the **Visible** property of OLE and Memo fields to **False**, or by placing these fields on another page of the form. You can add a command button that enables the user to display the additional data when required.

Finally, you may want to use unbound forms. This involves creating a form and removing its **RecordSource**. Users are provided with a combo box that enables them to select one record. A recordset is built from the client-server data with the one row the user selected. With this method of form design, everything needs to be coded. Your form code needs to handle all adds, edits, and deletes. None of the controls on the form should have their **Control Source** property filled in. The name of each control will then correspond with a field in the database server table. The **Open** event of such a form might look similar to the following:

```
Private Sub Form_Open(Cancel As Integer)
  Set mdb = CurrentDb
  Me.txtTitle.SetFocus
End Sub
```

The event code sets a module-level database variable to the current database and sets the focus to the **txtTitle** text box. The **AfterUpdate** event of the text box would then look similar to the following:

```
Private Sub txtTitle_AfterUpdate()
  Me!cboTitle.RowSource = "SELECT DISTINCTROW " _
      & " [dbo_titles].[title_id] FROM [dbo_titles] " _
      & "WHERE [dbo_titles].[title_id] Like '" & Me!txtTitle.Text & "*';"
End Sub
```

The code in the **AfterUpdate** event sets the **RowSource** property of the combo box to a SQL **Select** statement that selects all records from the **Titles** table where the **title_id** field begins with the first few characters that the user typed. In this way, the combo box isn't populated with all the titles from the server. The **AfterUpdate** event of the combo box would look similar to the following:

```
Private Sub cboTitle_AfterUpdate()
  Dim fSuccess As Boolean

  Set mrst = mdb.OpenRecordset("Select * From dbo_Titles " _
      & "Where Title_ID = '" & Me!cboTitle.Value & "';")
  fSuccess = PopulateForm(Me, mrst)
  If Not fSuccess Then
    MsgBox "Record Not Found"
  End If
End Sub
```

The **OpenRecordset** method is used to open a recordset based on the linked table called **dbo_Titles**. Notice that only the records with the matching **Title_ID** are retrieved. Because the **Title_ID** is the primary key, only one record is returned. The **PopulateForm** function is then called, which you might implement as shown here:

```
Function PopulateForm(frmAny As Form, rstAny As Recordset)
  If rstAny.EOF Then
    PopulateForm = False
  Else
    Dim fld As Field
    For Each fld In rstAny.Fields
      frmAny(fld.Name) = fld
    Next fld
    PopulateForm = True
  End If
End Function
```

The **PopulateForm** function checks to ensure that the recordset that it received has records. It then loops through each field on the form, matching field names with controls on the form. It sets the value of each control on the form to the value of the field in the recordset with the same name as the control name.

Note that these changes to the data within the form don't update the data on the database server. Furthermore, the form doesn't provide for inserts or deletes. You need to write code to issue updates, inserts, and deletes, and you have to provide command buttons to give your users access to that functionality.

Immediate Solutions

Using The Database Splitter Wizard

To use the Database Splitter Wizard to split the objects within a database into two separate MDB files, perform the following steps:

1. Open the database whose objects you want to split.

2. Select the Tools menu Database Utilities submenu Database Splitter option. The Database Splitter dialog box appears, as shown in Figure 31.14.

3. Click Split Database. The Create Back-End Database dialog box will appear.

4. Enter the name for the database that will contain all of the tables and click Split. The Database Splitter Wizard creates a new database that contains all of the tables. Links are created between the current database and the database containing the tables. When it finishes, the wizard will display a message indicating that the split was successful and then return you to the Database window.

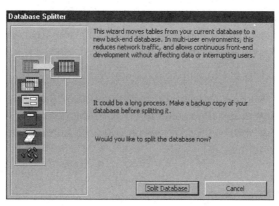

Figure 31.14   The Database Splitter dialog box.

Creating Links To Access Tables

To create a link to an Access table, perform the following steps:

1. Click with the right mouse button on any tab of the Database window.

2. Select Link Tables. The Link dialog box will appear.

3. Within the Link dialog box, select the name of the database containing the table you want to link to.

4. Click Link. The Link Tables dialog box will appear.

5. Within the Link Tables dialog box, select the tables to which you want to establish a link.

6. Click OK. The link process finishes. Notice the arrow indicating that the tables are linked tables rather than tables whose data is stored within the current database.

Creating Links To Other Types Of Tables

The process of creating links to other types of database files is a little different. To create a link to another type of database file, perform the following steps:

1. Click with the right mouse button on any tab of the Database window.

2. Select Link Tables. The Link dialog box will appear.

3. Within the Link dialog box, use the Files Of Type drop-down to indicate the type of table you're linking to.

4. Select the external file whose data you'll be linking to.

5. Click Link. The Select Index Files dialog box will appear. It's important that you select any index files associated with the data file. These indexes are automatically updated by Access as you add, change, and delete table data from within Access.

6. You'll receive a message indicating that the index was added successfully and that you can add other indexes if you choose. Click OK.

7. Add any additional indexes and click Close when done.

8. Access will display the Select Unique Record Identifier dialog box. This dialog box enables you to select a unique identifier for each record in the table. Select a unique field and click OK.

Notice the icon indicating the type of file you linked to. This is particularly important if your front ends link to multiple back-end data sources.

Using Pessimistic Code With Transaction Processing

The following code provides an example of how to perform transaction processing from code with pessimistic record locking:

```
Sub PessimisticTrans(strOldCity As String, strNewCity As String)
  Dim wrk As Workspace
  Dim db As Database
  Dim rst As Recordset
  Dim strCriteria As String

  Set wrk = DBEngine(0)
  Set db = CurrentDb()
  Set rst = db.OpenRecordSet("tblCustomers", dbOpenDynaset)
  rst.Lockedits = True    'Pessimistic Locking
  strCriteria = "[City] = '" & strOldCity & "'"
  rst.FindFirst strCriteria
  wrk.BeginTrans
  Do Until rst.NoMatch
    rst.Edit                          ' Lock occurs Here
    rst.Fields("City") = strNewCity
    rst.Update
    rst.FindNext strCriteria
  Loop
  wrk.CommitTrans                      ' Lock released here
End Sub
```

Here you can see that the lock is in place from the very first edit that occurs until
the **CommitTrans** is issued. This means no one can update any pages of data
involving the edited records until the **CommitTrans** is issued. This can be prohibitive during a long process.

Using Optimistic Locking With Transaction Processing

Optimistic locking with transaction handling isn't much different from pessimistic locking. As the code reaches the **Update** method for each record, that record
is locked. The code appears as follows:

```
Sub OptimisticTrans(strOldCity As String, strNewCity As String)
  Dim wrk As Workspace
  Dim db As Database
  Dim rst As Recordset
  Dim strCriteria As String
```

```
        Set wrk = DBEngine(0)
        Set db = CurrentDb()
        Set rst = db.OpenRecordSet("tblCustomers", dbOpenDynaset)
        rst.Lockedits = False  'Optimistic Locking
        strCriteria = "[City] = '" & strOldCity & "'"
        rst.FindFirst strCriteria
        wrk.BeginTrans
        Do Until rst.NoMatch
          rst.Edit
          rst.Fields("City") = strNewCity
          rst.Update                          ' Lock occurs
          rst.FindNext strCriteria
        Loop
        wrk.CommitTrans                       ' Locks are released here
      End Sub
```

Coding Around Pessimistic Locking Conflicts

It's fairly simple to write code to handle pessimistic locking conflicts. Here is an example of what your code should look like:

```
Sub PessimisticRS(strCustID As String)
  Dim db As Database
  Dim rst As Recordset
  Dim strCriteria As String
  Dim intChoice As Integer

  On Error GoTo PessimisticRS_Err
  Set db = CurrentDb()
  Set rst = db.OpenRecordSet("tblCustomers", dbOpenDynaset)
  rst.LockEdits = True  'Invoke Pessimistic Locking
  strCriteria = "[CustomerID] = '" & strCustID & "'"
  rst.FindFirst strCriteria
  rst.Edit                          ' Lock occurs here
  rst.Fields("City") = "Las Vegas"
  rst.Update                        ' Lock released here
  Exit Sub

PessimisticRS_Err:
  Select Case Err.Number
    Case 3197
      rst.Move 0
      Resume
    Case 3260
```

```
        intChoice = MsgBox(Err.Description, vbRetryCancel + vbCritical)
        Select Case intChoice
          Case vbRetry
            Resume
          Case Else
            MsgBox "Couldn't Lock"
        End Select
      Case 3167
        MsgBox "Record Has Been Deleted"
      Case Else
        MsgBox Err.Number & ": " & Err.Decription
      End Select
End Sub
```

The error-handling code for this routine handles all of the errors that can occur with pessimistic locking. If a Data Has Changed error occurs, the data is refreshed by the **rs.Move 0** invocation, and the code resumes on the line causing the error, forcing the **Edit** to be reissued. If a 3260 error occurs, the user is asked whether he or she wants to try again. If he or she responds affirmatively, the **Edit** is reissued; otherwise, the user is informed that the lock failed. If the record being edited has been deleted, an error 3167 occurs. The user is informed that the record has been deleted. Here's what your code should look like when transaction processing is involved:

```
Sub PessimisticRSTrans()
  Dim wrk As Workspace
  Dim db As Database
  Dim rst As Recordset
  Dim intCounter As Integer
  Dim intTry As Integer
  Dim intChoice As Integer

  On Error GoTo PessimisticRSTrans_Err
  Set wrk = DBEngine(0)
  Set db = CurrentDb
  Set rst = db.OpenRecordSet("tblCustomers", dbOpenDynaset)
  rst.LockEdits = True
  wrk.BeginTrans
  Do While Not rst.EOF
    rst.Edit
    rst.Fields("CompanyName") = rst.Fields("CompanyName") & "1"
    rst.Update
    rst.MoveNext
  Loop
  wrk.CommitTrans
  Exit Sub
```

```
PessimisticRSTrans_Err:
  Select Case Err.Number
    Case 3197
      rst.Move 0
      Resume
    Case 3260
      intCounter = intCounter + 1
      If intCounter > 2 Then
        intChoice = MsgBox(Err.Description, vbRetryCancel + vbCritical)
        Select Case intChoice
          Case vbRetry
            intCounter = 1
          Case vbCancel
            Resume CantLock
        End Select
      End If
      DoEvents
      For intTry = 1 To 100: Next intTry
      Resume
    Case Else
      MsgBox "Error: " & Err.Number & ": " & Err.Description
  End Select
CantLock:
  wrk.Rollback
  Exit Sub
End Sub
```

This code attempts to lock the record. If it's unsuccessful (that is, an error 3260 is generated), it tries three times before prompting the user for a response. When the user selects Retry, the process repeats. Otherwise, a rollback occurs and the subroutine is exited. When a Data Has Changed error occurs, the subroutine refreshes the data and tries again. When any other error occurs, the **Rollback** is issued and none of the updates are accepted.

Coding Around Optimistic Locking Conflicts

Remember that with optimistic locking, VBA attempts to lock the page when the Update method is issued. A strong chance exists that a 3197 (Data Has Changed) error could occur. This needs to be handled within your code. Let's modify the preceding subroutine for optimistic locking:

```
Sub OptimisticRS(strCustID)
  Dim db As Database
  Dim rst As Recordset
```

```
    Dim strCriteria As String
    Dim intChoice As Integer
    Set db = CurrentDb()

    On Error GoTo OptimisticRS_Err
    Set rst = db.OpenRecordSet("tblCustomers", dbOpenDynaset)
    rst.Lockedits = False 'Optimistic Locking
    strCriteria = "[CustomerID] = '" & strCustID & "'"
    rst.FindFirst strCriteria
    rst.Edit
    rst.Fields("City") = "Las Vegas"
    rst.Update                          ' Lock occurs and is released here
    Exit Sub

OptimisticRS_Err:
  Select Case Err.Number
    Case 3197
      If rst.EditMode = dbEditInProgress Then
        intChoice = MsgBox("Overwrite Other User's Changes?", _
        vbYesNoCancel + vbQuestion)
        Select Case intChoice
          Case vbCancel, vbNo
            MsgBox "Update Cancelled"
          Case vbYes
            rst.Update
            Resume
        End Select
      End If
    Case 3186, 3260   'Locked or Can't Be Saved
      intChoice = MsgBox(Err.Description, vbRetryCancel + vbCritical)
        Select Case intChoice
          Case vbRetry
            Resume
          Case vbCancel
            MsgBox "Udate Cancelled"
        End Select
    Case Else
      MsgBox "Error: " & Err.Number & ": " & Err.Description
    End Select
End Sub
```

As with the pessimistic error handling, this routine traps for all potential errors that can occur with optimistic locking. In the case of a Data Has Changed conflict, the user is warned of the problem and asked whether she wants to overwrite the other user's changes or cancel her own changes. In the case of a locking conflict, the user is asked whether he wants to try again. Here's what it looks like with transaction processing involved:

```
Sub OptimisticRSTrans()
  Dim db As Database
  Dim rs As Recordset
  Dim iCounter As Integer
  Dim iTry As Integer
  Dim iChoice As Integer

  On Error GoTo OptimisticRSTrans_Err
  Set db = CurrentDb
  Set rs = db.OpenRecordSet("tblCustBackup", dbOpenDynaset)
  rs.Lockedits = False
  BeginTrans
  Do While Not rs.EOF
    rs.Edit
    rs.Fields("CompanyName") = rs.Fields("CompanyName") & "1"
    rs.Update
    rs.MoveNext
  Loop
  CommitTrans
  Exit Sub

OptimisticRSTrans_Err:
  Select Case Err.Number
    Case 3197
      If rs.EditMode = dbEditInProgress Then
        iChoice = MsgBox("Overwrite Other User's Changes?", _
        vbYesNoCancel + vbQuestion)
        Select Case iChoice
          Case vbCancel, vbNo
            Resume RollItBack
          Case vbYes
            'rs.Update
            Resume
        End Select
      End If
    Case 3186, 3260   'Locked or Can't Be Saved
      iCounter = iCounter + 1
      If iCounter > 2 Then
        iChoice = MsgBox(Err.Description, vbRetryCancel + vbCritical)
        Select Case iChoice
          Case vbRetry
            iCounter = 1
          Case vbCancel
            Resume RollItBack
        End Select
      End If
      DoEvents
```

```
      For iTry = 1 To 100: Next iTry
      Resume
    Case Else
      MsgBox "Error: " & Err.Number & ": " & Err.Description
    End Select

RollItBack:
  Rollback
  Exit Sub
End Sub
```

When a Data Has Changed conflict occurs and the user opts not to overwrite the other user's changes, the entire processing loop is canceled (a rollback occurs). When a locking error occurs, the lock is retried several times. If it's still unsuccessful, the entire transaction is rolled back.

Testing To See Who Has A Record Locked

Regardless of what type of error occurs with record locking, it's often useful to find out who has locked a particular record. This can be easily accomplished using VBA code. It's simply a matter of parsing the **Description** property of the **Err** object, as shown in the following code:

```
Sub WhoLockedIt()
  Dim db As Database
  Dim rst As Recordset

  On Error GoTo WhoLockedIt_Err
  Set db = CurrentDb
  Set rst = db.OpenRecordset("tblCustomers", dbOpenDynaset)
  rst.Edit
    rst.Fields("CompanyName") = "Hello"
  rst.Update
  Exit Sub

WhoLockedIt_Err:
  Dim strName As String
  Dim strMachine As String
  Dim intMachineStart As Integer

  intMachineStart = InStr(43, Err.Description, " on machine ") + 13
  If Err = 3260 Then
    strName = Mid(Err.Description, 44, _
      InStr(44, Err.Description, "'") - 44)
```

```
      strMachine = Mid(Err.Description, intMachineStart, _
          Len(Err.Description) - intMachineStart - 1)
  End If
  MsgBox strName & " on " & strMachine & " is the culprit!"
End Sub
```

The preceding routine simply parses the standard error description, pulling out the user name and machine name, and displays the information within a custom error message box.

Importing External Data Using The User Interface

To import an external data file using the user interface, perform the following steps:

1. Click with the right mouse button on any tab of the database window.

2. Within the pop-up menu, select the Import option. The Import dialog box will appear.

3. Use the Files Of Type drop-down to select the type of file you're importing.

4. Select the file you want to import and click Import.

Depending on the type of file you select, the import process might finish, or you might be provided with additional dialogs. For example, when you select Excel Spreadsheet, Access will invoke the Import Spreadsheet Wizard, as shown in Figure 31.15. The Import Spreadsheet Wizard will walk you through the process of importing spreadsheet data.

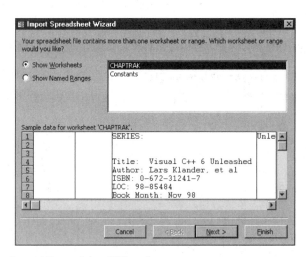

Figure 31.15   The Import Spreadsheet Wizard.

TIP: Although this procedure is correct, if you find that you can't bring a text file directly into a large (4MB to 5MB) Access database, change the text file into an Excel spreadsheet first, then import that file.

Importing Database Data Using Code

The **TransferDatabase** method of the **DoCmd** object is used to import data from a database such as FoxPro, dBASE, Paradox, or another Access database. The code to do so looks similar to the following:

```
Sub ImportDatabase()
  DoCmd.TransferDatabase _
      TransferType:=acImport, _
      DatabaseType:="FoxPro 2.6", _
      DatabaseName:="c:\Databases",
      ObjectType:=acTable, _
      Source:="Customers", _
      Destination:="tblCustomers", _
      StructureOnly:=False
End Sub
```

Table 31.4 details the arguments to the **TransferDatabase** method.

*Table 31.4   The arguments for the **TransferDatabase** method.*

Argument	Description
TransferType	Type of transfer being performed.
DatabaseType	Type of database being imported.
DataBaseName	Name of the database. When the table is a separate file—as is the case with dBASE, Paradox, and earlier versions of FoxPro—the database name is the name of the directory containing the table file. Do *not* include a backslash after the name of the directory.
ObjectType	Type of object you want to import. This argument is ignored for all but Access objects.
Source	Name of the object you're importing. Do *not* include the file extension.
Destination	Name of the imported object.
StructureOnly	Specification for whether you want the structure of the table only or the structure and data.

Importing Text Data Using Code

The **TransferText** method of the **DoCmd** object is used to import text from a text file. The following code is an example of how you might use this method:

```
Sub ImportText()
  DoCmd.TransferText _
      TransferType:=acImportDelim, _
      TableName:="tblCustomerText", _
      FileName:="c:\Databases\Customer.txt"
End Sub
```

Table 31.5 lists the arguments for the **TransferText** method.

Table 31.5   The arguments for the *TransferText* method.

Argument	Description
TransferType	Type of transfer you want to make.
SpecificationName	Specification name for the set of options that determines how the file is imported.
TableName	Name of the Access table that will receive the imported data.
FileName	Name of the text file to import from.
HasFieldHeadings	Specifies whether the first row of the text file contains field headings.

Importing Spreadsheet Data Using Code

The **TransferSpreadsheet** method of the **DoCmd** object is used to import data from a spreadsheet file. The following code provides an example:

```
Sub ImportSpreadsheet()
  DoCmd.TransferSpreadsheet _
      TransferType:=acImport, _
      SpreadsheetType:=5, _
      TableName:="tblCustomerSpread", _
      FileName:="c:\Databases\Customer.xls", _
      HasFieldNames:=True
End Sub
```

Table 31.6 explains the arguments to the **TransferSpreadsheet** method.

*Table 31.6   The arguments for the **TransferSpreadsheet** method.*

Argument	Description
TransferType	Type of transfer you want to make.
SpreadsheetType	Type of spreadsheet to import from. The default is Excel 2000.
TableName	Name of the Access table that will receive the imported data.
FileName	Name of the spreadsheet file to import from.
HasFieldNames	Specification for whether the first row of the spreadsheet contains field headings.
Range	The range of cells to import.

> **WARNING!**   *You can import from and link (read-only) to Lotus WK4 files, but you can't export Access data to this spreadsheet format. Access also no longer supports importing, exporting, or linking data from Lotus WKS or Excel version 2.0 spreadsheets with this action. If you want to import from or link to spreadsheet data in Excel version 2.0 or Lotus WKS format, convert the spreadsheet data to a later version of Excel or Lotus 1-2-3 before importing or linking the data into Access.*

Updating Links That Have Moved

To refresh a link using VBA code, perform the following steps:

1. Redefine the connection string.

2. Perform a **RefreshLink** method on the table definition.

The code looks like this:

```
Sub RefreshLink()
  Dim db As Database

  Set db = CurrentDb
  db.TableDefs!FoxCusts.Connect = "FoxPro 2.6;DATABASE=d:\newdir"
  db.TableDefs!FoxCusts.RefreshLink
End Sub
```

This routine can be modified to prompt the user for the directory containing the data tables. The modified routine looks like this:

```
Sub RefreshLink()
  Dim db As DATABASE
  Dim tdf As TableDef
  Dim strNewLocation As String
```

```
On Error GoTo RefreshLink_Err
Set db = CurrentDb
Set tdf = db.TableDefs("tblClients")
tdf.RefreshLink
Exit Sub

RefreshLink_Err:
  strNewLocation = InputBox("Please Enter Database Path and Name")
  db.TableDefs!tblClients.Connect = ";DATABASE=" & strNewLocation
  Resume
End Sub
```

This routine points a **TableDef** object to the **tblClients** table. It then issues a **RefreshLink** method on the table definition object. The **RefreshLink** method attempts to refresh the link for the table. When an error occurs, an input box prompts the user for the new location of the database. The **Connect** property for the database is modified to incorporate the new location. The code then resumes on the offending line of code (the **RefreshLink**). This routine should be modified to allow the user a way out because the **Resume** routine in this code throws the user into an endless loop when the database isn't available. Modifying the code is left as an exercise for you.

Deleting Links From Code

To remove a link using VBA code, simply execute a **Delete** method on the table definition collection of the database, as shown here:

```
Sub RemoveLink()
  Dim db As Database

  Set db = CurrentDb
  db.TableDefs.Delete "SAMPLES"
End Sub
```

Creating A Foreign Table From Code

Creating a foreign table from code isn't particularly difficult. Here's how it works:

```
Sub CreateFoxTable()
  Dim db As Database
  Dim rst As Recordset
```

```
   Dim fld As Field
   Dim dbFox As Database
   Dim tdfFox As TableDef

   Set dbFox = DBEngine.Workspaces(0).OpenDatabase_
       ("c:\databases", False, False, "FoxPro 2.6")
   Set tdfFox = dbFox.CreateTableDef("PayMeth")
   Set db = CurrentDb
   Set rst = db.OpenRecordset("tblPaymentMethods", dbOpenSnapshot)
   For Each fld In rst.Fields
     Set fld = tdfFox.CreateField(fld.Name, fld.Type, fld.Size)
     tdfFox.Fields.Append fld
   Next fld
   dbFox.TableDefs.Append tdfFox
End Sub
```

This example reads an Access table and writes its structure out to a FoxPro table. It utilizes two database object variables, one recordset object variable, a table definition object variable, and a field object variable. It opens up a table called **tblPaymentMethods** as a snapshot. This is the table whose structure you'll send out to FoxPro. Looking at each field in the table, it grabs that field's name, type, and size properties. It uses these properties as parameters to the **CreateField** method of the FoxPro table definition, appends each FoxPro field as it loops through each field in the Access table definition, and appends the table definition to create the FoxPro table.

Creating A Remote View From Access

To create a remote view from Access, perform the following steps:

1. Create a new query.
2. When you're prompted with the Show Table dialog box, click on Close *without* selecting a table.
3. Select the Query menu SQL Specific submenu Pass-Through option.
4. Type the Create View statement.
5. Click on Run.
6. Select a SQL Data Source. Click OK.
7. Supply the Login Information and click OK.

Once you create a remote view, you can link to it like any other table. When you link to the view, you're prompted with the Select Unique Record Identifier dialog box. It's very important to supply Access with a unique index. Otherwise, the results of the view won't be updatable. The view can then be treated as if it were a link to a table.

Executing A Stored Procedure With VBA Code

The following procedure executes the **sp_columns** stored procedure using code:

```
Sub StoredProcedure()
  Dim ws As Workspace
  Dim db As Database
  Dim dbAccess As Database
  Dim qdf As QueryDef
  Dim rst As Recordset

  Set dbAccess = CurrentDb
  Set ws = DBEngine(0)
  Set db = ws.OpenDatabase("", False, False, _
      "ODBC;DATABASE=Pubs;DSN=PublisherData;UID=SA;PWD=")
  Set qdf = dbAccess.CreateQueryDef("")
  qdf.Connect = "ODBC;DATABASE=Pubs;DSN=PublisherData;UID=SA;PWD="
  qdf.SQL = "sp_columns 'sales'"
  qdf.ReturnsRecords = True
  Set rst = qdf.OpenRecordset(dbOpenSnapshot)
  Do While Not rst.EOF
    Debug.Print rst.Fields("Column_Name")
    rst.MoveNext
  Loop
End Sub
```

Here's how it works. Because you want to return records, you can't use the **Execute** method. Another way to execute a pass-through query is to first create a DAO **QueryDef** object. In this case, the **QueryDef** object is temporary (notice the quotation marks). The **Connect** property is set for the **QueryDef** object. Rather than specifying a back-end–specific SQL statement, the SQL property of the **QueryDef** object is set to the name of the stored procedure and any parameters it expects to receive. The **ReturnsRecords** property of the **QueryDef** object is set to **True**. The **OpenRecordset** method is then issued on the **QueryDef** object. This returns the snapshot from the stored procedure. The **Do While** loop loops through the resulting recordset, printing the **Column_Name** column of each row returned from the **sp_columns** stored procedure.

Using **OpenDatabase** To Connect To A Remote Server Database

The following subroutine shows how you can use the **OpenDatabase** function to connect to a remote server database:

```
Sub OpenRemoteDB(strDBName As String, strDataSetName As String, _
    strUserID As String, strPassWord As String)
  Dim ws As Workspace
  Dim db As Database
  Dim tdf As TableDef
  Dim intCounter As Integer
  Dim strConnectString As String

  Set ws = DBEngine(0)
  strConnectString = "ODBC;DATABASE=" & strDBName & _
      ";DSN=" & strDataSetName & ";UID=" & strUserID & _
      ";PWD=" & strPassWord
  Set db = ws.OpenDatabase( "", False, False, strConnectString)
  For Each tdf In db.TableDefs
    Debug.Print tdf.Name
  Next tdf
End Sub
```

The routine is called like this:

```
Call OpenRemoteDB("Pubs", "PublisherData", "SA", "")
```

The routine uses the **OpenDatabase** method of the **Workspace** object to open the database called **Pubs** with the connect string specified. It then loops through the collection of table definitions, listing all the tables found within the remote server database.

Preconnecting To A Server

The following code preconnects to the server. It would generally be placed in the startup form for your application:

```
Sub PreConnect(strDBName As String, strDataSetName As String, _
    strUserID As String, strPassWord As String)
  Dim db As Database
  Dim strConnectString As String
```

```
    strConnectString = "ODBC;DATABASE=" & strDBName & _
        ";DSN=" & strDataSetName & ";UID=" & strUserID & _
        ";PWD=" & strPassWord
    Set db = OpenDatabase("", False, False, strConnectString)
    db.Close    ' Closes the database but maintains the connection
End Sub
```

The trick here is that the connection and authentication information will be maintained even when the database is closed.

Chapter 32

Using Oracle And Access
For Client-Server

In Depth

In Chapter 31, you learned more about using Access to build front ends for the client-server architecture. In that chapter, we focused specifically on implementing Access with SQL Server back ends. However, Oracle is another very common back-end architecture. In this chapter, you'll learn more about using Access for client-server, specifically in the context of the Oracle architecture. We'll begin by examining Oracle, specifically with an eye toward some of the differences between Oracle and Access, as well as differences between Oracle and SQL Server. Next, we'll address some of the issues surrounding conversion of existing Access databases to Oracle databases. Finally, we'll look at using open database connectivity (ODBC) and ActiveX Data Objects (ADO) to attach to Oracle database back ends and we'll consider some issues to keep in mind when working with Oracle back ends.

TIP: *The work in this chapter requires that you have Oracle8 installed on a Windows NT or Unix server on your network. If you don't use Oracle within your environment, you may wish to skip this chapter entirely. Many of the techniques for client-server presented herein are similar to those you saw in Chapter 31 when working with SQL Server databases.*

Before considering Access-specific issues, we'll take some time to describe most of Oracle database software. These components are present (in one form or another) on all machines on which the Oracle database can run. Although we'll only briefly touch on some of the various components (such as memory, process, hardware, and network components) and discuss the interaction between them, we'll spend more time discussing some of the internal objects (such as rollback segments) of Oracle databases.

Global View Of The Oracle Architecture

The Oracle architecture described in this section is the generic architecture that applies to all platforms on which Oracle runs. There might be differences in the architecture between various platforms, but the fundamentals are the same.

Understanding Oracle Databases

As you've learned in previous chapters, a database is a collection of related data that's used and retrieved together for one or more application systems. The physical location and implementation of the database is transparent to the application programs, and in fact, you could move and restructure the physical database without affecting the programs.

Physically, in its simplest form, an Oracle database is nothing more than a set of files somewhere on disk. The physical location of these files is irrelevant to the function (although important for the performance) of the database. The files are binary files that you can only access using the Oracle kernel software. Querying data in the database files is typically done with one of the Oracle tools (such as SQL*Plus) using structured query language (SQL). The first, major difference between Oracle databases and Access 2000 databases occurs here at the physical layer.

The Access database, together with all the information associated with it (with the notable exception of the entries within the system.mdw file) is all stored within a single file. The Oracle database, on the other hand, stores each table within its own physical file—a structure more in line with what you learned about relational databases in Chapter 5.

Logically, the database is divided into a set of Oracle user accounts (schemas), each of which is identified by a username and password unique to that database. Tables and other objects are owned by one of these Oracle users, and access to the data is only available by logging in to the database using an Oracle username and password. Without a valid username and password for the database, you're denied access to anything on the database.

It's important to note that the Oracle username and password are different from the operating system username and password. For example, a database residing on a Windows NT server requires that the user log in to the system with his or her system-defined login. If the user then wants to connect to the Oracle database, he or she has to log in to Oracle as well, using another ID and password set. This process of logging in, or connecting to, the database is required whether you're using an Oracle or non-Oracle tool to access the database.

The differences between the Oracle construction and the Access construction are obvious at the logical layer. In general, you can visualize the difference between the two by recognizing that Oracle's construction is designed to manage a much larger number of users and amount of data than the Access construction and also to be more secure from unauthorized access to the data.

The same table name can coexist in two separate Oracle user accounts. Even though the tables might have the same name, they're different tables. Sometimes, the same database (same set of physical database files) is used for holding different versions of tables (in separate Oracle accounts) for the developers, system testing, or user testing. Alternately, different applications systems may use the same table name for different purposes within a single database.

Often, people refer to an Oracle user account as a database, but this isn't strictly correct. You could use two Oracle user accounts to hold data for two entirely different application systems. In such a construction, you would have two logical databases implemented in the same physical database using two Oracle user accounts.

In addition to physical files, Oracle processes and memory structures must also be present before you can use the database. Figure 32 1.1 shows the basic Oracle architecture that you'll review throughout this chapter.

While the architecture consists of many components, the root of what comprises a database are the Oracle database files. The next section discusses the files that make up a database in Oracle.

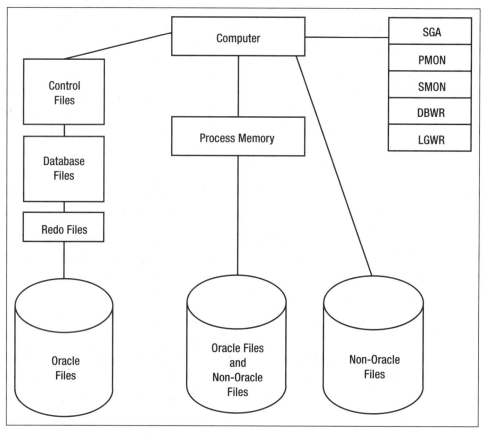

Figure 32.1   The basic Oracle architecture.

Understanding The Oracle Files That Comprise A Database

As you've learned, Oracle implements databases in a manner significantly different from what you're used to with Access. Each database consists of a series of files, each of which corresponds loosely to one or more database objects. Three major sets of files on disk compose a database:

- Database files
- Control files
- Redo logs

The most important of these files are the database files because they contain the actual data itself. The control files and the redo logs support the functioning of the architecture. In the event of an operating system failure or other problem, however, the control files and the redo files can be mostly reconstructed.

However, all three sets of files must be present, open, and available to Oracle for any data on the database to be useable. Without these files, you can't access the database, and the database administrator (DBA) might have to recover some or all of the database using a backup. All the files are binary—meaning that users can't, for all intents and purposes, access the information that the files contain without going through the Oracle kernel to do so.

System And User Processes

For database files to be useable, you must have the Oracle system processes and one or more user processes running on the machine. The Oracle system processes, also known as Oracle background processes, provide functions for the user processes—functions that would otherwise be done by the user processes themselves. You can initiate many background processes, but at a minimum, only the **PMON**, **SMON**, **DBWR**, and **LGWR** processes (all described later in this chapter) must be up and running for the database to be useable. Other background processes support optional additions to the way the database runs.

In addition to the Oracle background processes, there is one user process per connection to the database in its simplest setup. The user must make a connection to the database before he can access any of the objects. If one user logs into Oracle using SQL*Plus, if another user chooses Oracle Designer/2000, and if yet another user employs an Access front end that gets its data from Oracle, then you have three user processes against the database—one for each connection. Like other operating system processes, Oracle runs within the computer's memory. Oracle divides the memory that it uses into several different categories, as detailed in the following section.

Understanding Oracle System Memory

Oracle database-wide system memory is known as the *system global area* or *shared global area* (SGA). The data and control structures in the SGA are shareable, and all the Oracle background and user processes can use them.

TIP: *The combination of the SGA and the Oracle background processes is known as an Oracle instance, a term that you'll encounter often with Oracle. Although there's typically at least one instance for each database, it's common to find many instances (running on different processors or even on different machines) all running against the same set of database files.*

User Process Memory

For each connection to the database, Oracle allocates a *process global area* or *program global area* (PGA) in the machine's memory. Oracle also allocates a PGA for the background processes. This memory area contains data and control information for one process and isn't shareable between processes.

As you saw earlier in this chapter, the Oracle architecture in and of itself does not include network support. In fact, you must use the SQL*Net process and stubs that talk to network protocols to support network connections to your Oracle database. The next section discusses network considerations in more detail.

Network Software And SQL*Net

A simple configuration for an Oracle database has the database files, memory structures, and Oracle background and user processes all running on the same machine, without any networking involved. However, a much more common configuration is one that implements the database on a server machine and the Oracle tools or a database front end on a different machine (such as a PC with Microsoft Windows). For this type of client-server configuration, the machines are connected with some non-Oracle networking software that enables the two machines to communicate. Also, you might want two databases running on different machines to talk to each other—perhaps you're accessing tables from both databases in the same transaction or even in the same SQL statements. Again, the two machines need some non-Oracle networking software to communicate.

> **WARNING!** *Oracle can support many different types of networks and protocols. However, if you require communication between machines running Oracle software, you must install the Oracle SQL*Net software on all machines requiring network access.*

Whatever type of networking software and protocols you use to connect the machines (such as Transmission Control Protocol/Internet Protocol [TCP/IP]) for either the client-server or server-server setup mentioned previously, you must have the Oracle SQL*Net product to enable Oracle to interface with the networking protocol. SQL*Net supports most of the major networking protocols for both

PC local area networks (LANs) (such as Internetwork Packet Exchange/Sequenced Packet Exchange [IPX/SPX]) and the largest mainframes (such as Systems Network Architecture [SNA]). Essentially, SQL*Net provides the software layer between Oracle and the networking software, providing seamless communication between an Oracle client machine (running SQL*Plus) and the database server or between one database server and another.

You must install the SQL*Net software on both machines on top of the underlying networking software for both sides to talk to each other. SQL*Net software options enable a client machine supporting one networking protocol to communicate with another supporting a different protocol.

You don't need to change the application system software itself if the networking protocols or underlying networking software changes. You can make the changes transparently with the DBA, installing a different version of SQL*Net for the new network protocol.

Figure 32.2 shows the role of SQL*Net in a client-server environment with two server database machines.

Now that you have learned about the generalities of the Oracle architecture, let's take some time to consider the specifics of the different types of files that Oracle uses to perform its processing. The following section discusses Oracle file types.

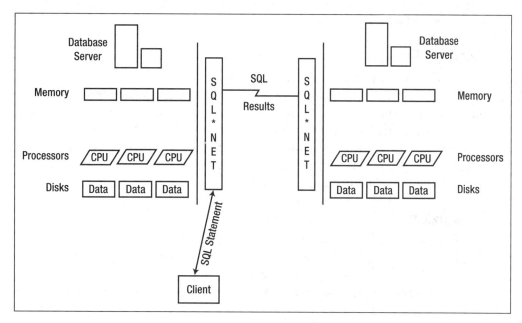

Figure 32.2   SQL*Net diagram in a client-server environment.

Considering Oracle's File Types

As you saw earlier in this chapter, Oracle uses three general types of files to construct and administer the database. The following sections discuss each of the different file types in greater detail.

Database Files

The database files hold the actual data and are typically the largest in size (from a few megabytes to many gigabytes). The other files (control files and redo logs) support the rest of the architecture. Depending on their sizes, the tables (and other objects) for all the user accounts can obviously go in one database file. However, such a construction isn't ideal because it doesn't make the database structure very flexible. Such issues as controlling access to storage for different Oracle users, putting the database on different disk drives, or backing up and restoring just part of the database become significantly more complex when all the information is within a single database file.

You must have at least one database file (adequate for a small or testing database), but usually, you'll have many more than one. In terms of accessing and using the data in the tables and other objects, the number (or location) of the files is immaterial. The database files are fixed in size and never grow bigger than the size at which they were created. As with a SQL Server, this is an important issue because you must make sure that you create the files big enough initially to handle whatever you fill the files with.

Control Files

Any Oracle database must have at least one control file, although you typically have more than one to guard against loss. The control file records the name of the database, the date and time it was created, the location of the database and redo logs, and the synchronization information for the database. Oracle uses the synchronization information to ensure that all three sets of files are always in step. Every time you add a new database file or redo log file to the database, the information is recorded in the control files.

Redo Logs

Any database must have at least two redo logs. These are the journals for the database, recording all changes to the user objects or system objects. If any type of failure occurs, such as loss of one or more database files, you can use the changes recorded in the redo logs to bring the database to a consistent state without losing any committed transactions. Were a machine to crash or fail without losing data, Oracle could then apply the information in the redo logs automatically without intervention from the DBA. The **SMON** background process automatically reapplies the committed changes in the redo logs to the database files. Like the other files used by Oracle, the redo log files are fixed in size and never grow dynamically from the size at which they were created.

Online Redo Logs

The online redo logs are the two or more redo log files always in use while the Oracle instance is up and running. Changes you make are recorded to each of the redo logs in turn. When one is full, the other is written to. When the second one becomes full, the first is overwritten, and the cycle continues.

Offline/Archived Redo Logs

The offline or archived redo logs are exact copies of the online redo logs that have been filled. It's optional to ask Oracle to create these. Oracle only creates them when the database is running in **ARCHIVELOG** mode. If the database is running in **ARCHIVELOG** mode, the **ARCH** background process wakes up and copies the online redo log to the offline destination (typically another disk drive) once it becomes full. While this copying is in progress, Oracle uses the other online redo log. If you have a complete set of offline redo logs since the database was last backed up, you have a complete record of changes that have been made. You could then use this record to reapply the changes to the backup copy of the database files if one or more online database files are lost.

In general, particularly for critical business processes, it's a good idea to use Oracle's archiving features. If you use them together with Oracle's built-in backup support, the system will automatically retain what actions occurred before and after the backup, which can radically speed restorations in the event of a failure.

Other Supporting Files

When you start an Oracle instance (in other words, when the Oracle background processes are initiated and the memory structures allocated), the instance parameter file determines the sizes and modes of the database. This parameter file is known as the INIT.ORA file (the actual name of the file has the Oracle instance identifier appended to the filename). This is an ordinary text file containing parameters for which you can override the default settings. The DBA is responsible for creating and modifying the contents of this parameter file.

On some Oracle platforms, a SGAPAD file is also created, which contains the starting memory address of the Oracle SGA. All these files are important for the long-term usability of processing of the Oracle database. However, the actual processing occurs within the Oracle system and user processes, which the following sections discuss in detail.

TIP: *A sample INIT.ORA file can be found on the companion CD-ROM.*

System And User Processes

The following sections discuss some of the Oracle system processes that must be running for the database to be useable, including the optional processes and the processes created for users connecting to the Oracle database. These sections are not, by any means, a definitive treatment of all the system processes in Oracle; rather, they explain the most important processes that *must* run for Oracle to work correctly.

Mandatory System Processes

The four Oracle system processes that must always be up and running for the database to be useable include database writer (**DBWR**), log writer (**LGWR**), system monitor (**SMON**), and process monitor (**PMON**).

The Database Writer (DBWR)

The database writer background process writes modified database blocks in the SGA to the database files. It reads only the blocks that have changed (for example, if the block contains a new record, a deleted record, or a changed record). These blocks are also called *dirty* blocks. The database writer writes out the least recently used blocks first. These blocks aren't necessarily written to the database when the transaction commits; the only thing that always happens on a commit is that the changes are recorded and written to the online redo log files. The database blocks will be written out later when there aren't enough buffers free in the SGA to read in a new block—that is, when the SGA's buffers fill, the Oracle processes will write out blocks to create space for the new, incoming blocks.

The Log Writer (LGWR)

The log writer process writes the entries in the SGA's redo buffer for one or more transactions to the online redo log files. For example, when a transaction commits, the log writer must write out the entries in the redo log buffer to the redo log files on disk before the process receives a message indicating that the commit was successful. Once committed, the changes are safe on disk even though the modified database blocks are still in the SGA's database buffer area waiting to be written out by **DBWR**. The **SMON** can always reapply the changes from the redo logs if the memory's most up-to-date copy of the database blocks is lost.

The System Monitor (SMON)

The system monitor process looks after the instance. If two transactions are both waiting for each other to release locks and neither of them can continue (known as a *deadlock* or *deadly embrace*), **SMON** detects the situation and sends one of the processes an error message indicating that a deadlock has occurred. **SMON** also releases temporary segments no longer in use by the user processes that caused them to be created.

During idle periods, **SMON** compacts the free-space fragments in the database files, making it easier and simpler for Oracle to allocate storage for new database objects or for existing database objects to grow.

In addition, **SMON** automatically performs recovery when the Oracle instance is first started up (if none of the files have been lost). You won't see a message indicating that instance recovery is occurring, but the instance might take longer to come up.

The Process Monitor

The process monitor monitors the user processes. If any failure occurs with the user processes (for example, if the process is killed in the middle of a transaction), **PMON** automatically rolls back the work of the user process since the transaction started (anything since the last **Commit** or **Rollback**). It releases any locks taken out and other system resources taken up by the failed process. **PMON** also monitors the dispatcher and shared server processes, which are part of the multithreaded server setup, and restarts them if they have died.

Optional System Processes

Beside the four mandatory system processes, you can initiate a number of optional system processes. The following sections describe the most common of these.

The Archiver Process (ARCH)

When the database is running in **ARCHIVELOG** mode and you've started the Archiver background process, it makes a copy of one of the online redo log files to the archive destination (the exact location is specified in an **INIT.ORA** parameter). In this way, you can have a complete history of changes made to the database files recorded in the offline and the online redo logs. Just remember, there's no point in keeping the Archiver background process running if the database isn't running in **ARCHIVELOG** mode.

The Checkpoint Process (CKPT)

A checkpoint occurs when one of the online redo log files fills. Oracle will overwrite the checkpoint when one of the other online redo logs fills. If the redo log file is overwritten, the changes recorded in that file aren't available for reapplying in case of system failure. At a checkpoint, the modified database buffer blocks are written down to the relative safety of the database files on disk by the database writer background process. In effect, this means that you won't need the record of changes in the event of system failure with lost memory areas. After a checkpoint occurs, the redo log can be reused.

At a checkpoint, all the database file headers and redo log file headers are updated to record the fact that a checkpoint has occurred. The **LGWR** background process performs the actual updating task, which could be significant if a large number of database and redo log files exist. The entire database might have to wait for the checkpoint to complete before the redo logs can record further database changes. To reduce the time it takes for **LGWR** to update the database and redo log file headers, you can initiate the checkpoint process.

A checkpoint can occur at other times, such as when the entries in the redo log files reach a limit defined by the DBA. Such a construction is generally sensible in environments where most processing occurs during a specified block of time, and the database has time for other tasks at other times. In other words, the administrator might want to initiate a checkpoint during the nighttime, such as around early morning, rather than letting the database reach a natural checkpoint during the day, when most database access is occurring.

TIP: *Whether or not the **CKPT** background process is initiated, checkpointing still occurs when one of the redo log files fills.*

The Recoverer Process (RECO)

You use the Recoverer background process when a failure in a distributed transaction has occurred (a transaction where two or more databases are updated) and one or more of the databases involved needs to either commit or roll back their changes. If initiated, the Recoverer attempts to automatically commit or roll back the transaction on the local database at timed intervals in synchronization with the Recoverer processes on the other Oracle databases. And as a reminder, there's no point in keeping the Recoverer background process running if you're not using distributed transactions on the database.

The Lock Process (LCK)

Use the Lock background process in the parallel server setup of Oracle in which more than one instance is running against the same set of database files. The **LCK** processes running on all instances will synchronize locking between the instances. If a user connects to one instance and locks a row, the row remains locked for a user attempting to make a change on another instance. Other users can always query the rows regardless of how the rows are locked by other users.

You can initiate up to 10 **LCK** background processes to reduce the bottleneck of synchronizing locking, but one is usually more than enough. However, you shouldn't initiate the **LCK** background processes unless you're implementing a parallel server (multi-instance) setup of Oracle.

SQL*Net Listener

The SQL*Net listener is a process running on the machine that routes requests coming in from client machines through to the correct Oracle instance. It communicates with the underlying networking software to route requests to and from the database server and the client machine (whether that client machine is a machine running an Oracle tool or even another database server).

For example, the communications between a client machine running an Access front end on a PC with Windows 98 and a database server on a Unix machine with TCP/IP as the networking protocol would involve the following major steps:

1. The client machine sends the SQL statement execution request to the Unix database server machine.

2. The non-Oracle TCP/IP listener process picks up the request and recognizes it as a request for Oracle.

3. The request is sent to the Oracle SQL*Net listener, which routes the request to the correct Oracle instance on the machine. (The machine might be running many instances for many different databases.)

4. A process on the instance executes the statement.

5. The results are then sent back up the communications link to the client machine, using a similar process.

The SQL*Net listener isn't related to the Oracle instance itself, but rather is related systemwide and will process requests for all instances running on the machine. You can initiate more than one SQL*Net listener, but this is uncommon.

Considering User Processes

User processes logically consist of two halves: the Oracle server code, which translates and executes SQL statements and reads the database files and memory areas, and the tool-specific code, which is the executable code for the tool that's used. The server code is the same regardless of the tool that's executing the SQL statement—that is, the same steps are involved. The server code is sometimes known as the Oracle *kernel code*.

You can configure the user processes in Oracle three different ways, all of which could coexist for the same instance. These three configurations are single task, dedicated server, or multithreaded server.

Single-Task Configuration

In the single-task configuration, the tool-specific code and database server code are both configured into one process running on the machine. Each connection to the database has one user process running on the machine. This is common on the virtual address extension (VAX) Virtual Memory System (VMS) platforms without a client-server environment. It isn't a typical configuration that you'll encounter when writing Access front ends for Oracle back ends because the tool-specific code will run in its own process (the Access process) on the client machine.

Dedicated Server Processes

In the dedicated server configuration (also known as *two-task* or running with *shadow* processes), the two parts of a user process are implemented as two separate processes running on the machine. They communicate with each other using the machine's interprocess communication mechanisms. Each connection to the database has two processes running on the machine. The Oracle kernel software in one process is sometimes called the shadow process.

This configuration is common for Unix platforms because the operating system can't (in some implementations of Unix) protect the Oracle code and memory areas from the application code. It's also common for client-server configurations in which the server code resides on the server machine and the tool-specific code runs on the client machine with communication over a network. This, of course, is the way that the vast majority of your Windows applications will interact with the Oracle database. The way the two component parts of one logical process communicate is fundamentally the same as if one process were implemented on the same machine. However, the two halves of the logical process happen to reside on two different machines and communicate over the network using SQL*Net rather than the interprocess communication mechanisms of the operating system.

The dedicated server configuration can be wasteful because memory is allocated to the shadow process and the number of processes that must be serviced on the machine increases, even when the user isn't making any database requests. The dedicated server (shadow process) will only process requests from one associated client process.

Multithreaded Server Configuration

The multithreaded server configuration enables one Oracle server process to perform work for many user processes. This overcomes the drawbacks of the dedicated server configuration. It reduces the number of processes running and the amount of memory used on the machine and can improve system performance. The multithreaded server introduces two new types of system processes that support this part of the architecture.

Using one of the shared server processes that comes as part of the multithreaded server configuration isn't appropriate when a user process is making many database requests (such as an export backup of the database); for that process, you could use a dedicated server. A mixture of both configurations can coexist.

Dispatchers

One or more dispatcher processes retrieves requests for the client processes from the SQL*Net listener and routes the request to one of the shared server processes. The SQL*Net listener is required for the multithreaded server configuration even if no networking is involved.

You must configure at least one dispatcher for each network protocol that's used to route requests to the instance. The number of dispatchers configured doesn't increase if the system load increases because the dispatchers are only providing the routing. The actual work is done by the shared servers.

TIP: *The multithreaded server requires SQL*Net 2 or newer even if both the dispatcher and the user process are running on the same machine.*

Shared Servers

The shared servers provide the same functionality as the dedicated server processes and contain the Oracle server code that performs the work for the client. They can service requests from many different user processes. The actual shared server used might differ from one call to another so no user process can monopolize any one particular shared server process. Oracle uses an area in the SGA for messaging between the different processes involved.

The number of shared server processes is automatically increased (or decreased to an initial number defined by the DBA) according to the system activity. Note, however, that although the number of shared servers is increased or decreased automatically, the number of dispatchers isn't. Just as Oracle performs certain actions in its management of server processes, its also manages memory in specific fashions. The following sections discuss in detail how Oracle uses memory.

Understanding How Oracle Uses Memory

In this part, you'll learn a little about how Oracle uses the computer's memory. Generally, the greater the real memory available to Oracle, the quicker the system runs. Although these issues are significant for Oracle development, we'll really only touch on them here, with the presumption that you have other Oracle knowledge with which to flesh out these broad strokes. If you're using Oracle for your back end, it's likely that your company has an Oracle DBA whose job it is to manage the Oracle server process—if you run into trouble, you may wish to consult that person or persons for assistance in connecting. However, understanding the memory usage of Oracle is important in either situation. The most important area of memory for Oracle is the system global area (SGA), discussed in the next section.

System Global Area

The system global area, sometimes known as the shared global area, is for data and control structures in memory that can be shared by all the Oracle background and user processes running on that instance. Each Oracle instance has its own SGA. In fact, the SGA and affiliated background processes are what defines an instance. The SGA memory area is allocated when the instance is started, and Oracle flushes and deallocates the memory when it shuts the instance down.

The contents of the SGA are divided into three main areas: the database buffer cache, the shared pool area, and the redo cache. The size of each is controlled by parameters in the INIT.ORA file. The bigger you can make the SGA and the more of it that can fit into the machine's real memory (as opposed to virtual memory), the quicker your instance will run. Figure 32.3 shows the Oracle SGA in memory.

Database Buffer Cache

The SGA's database buffer cache holds Oracle blocks that have been read in from the database files. When one process reads the blocks for a table into memory, all the processes for that instance can access those blocks.

If a process needs to access some data, Oracle checks to see if the block is already in this cache (thereby avoiding a disk read). If the Oracle block isn't in the buffer, it must be read from the database files into the buffer cache. The buffer cache must have a free block available before the data block can be read from the database files.

The Oracle blocks in the database buffer cache in memory are arranged with the most recently used at one end and the least recently used at the other. This list is constantly changing as the database is used. If data must be read from the database files into memory, the blocks at the least recently used end are written back to the database files first (if they've been modified). The **DBWR** process is the only process that writes the blocks from the database buffer cache to the database files.

As you might expect, the more database blocks your instance can hold in real memory, the quicker it will run.

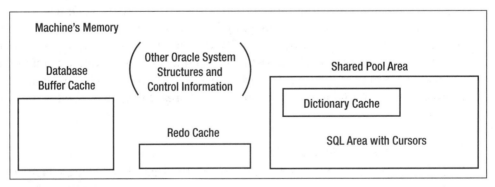

Figure 32.3   The Oracle SGA in the computer's memory.

Redo Cache

The online redo log files record all the changes made to user objects and system objects. Before the changes are written out to the redo logs, Oracle stores them in the redo cache memory area. For example, the entries in the redo log cache are written down to the online redo logs when the cache becomes full or when a transaction issues a commit.

The entries for more than one transaction can be included together in the same data writing to the disk as the redo log files. The **LGWR** background process is the only process that writes out entries from this redo cache to the online redo log files.

Shared Pool Area

The shared pool area of the SGA has two main components: the SQL area and the dictionary cache. You can alter the size of these two components only by changing the size of the entire shared pool area.

A SQL statement sent for execution to the database server must be parsed before it can execute. The SQL area of the SGA contains the binding information, run-time buffers, parse tree, and execution plan for all the SQL statements sent to the database server. Because the shared pool area is a fixed size, you might not see the entire set of statements that have been executed since the instance first came up; Oracle might have flushed out some statements to make room for others.

If a user executes a SQL statement, that statement takes up memory in the SQL area. If another user executes exactly the same statement on the same objects, Oracle doesn't need to reparse the second statement because the parse tree and execution plan is already in the SQL area. This part of the architecture saves on reparsing overhead. The SQL area is also used to hold the parsed, compiled form of programming language/structured query language (PL/SQL) blocks, which can also be shared between user processes on the same instance.

TIP: *Make SQL statements exactly the same in application code (using procedures) to avoid reparsing overhead.*

The dictionary cache in the shared pool area holds entries retrieved from the Oracle system tables, otherwise known as the Oracle data dictionary. The data dictionary is a set of tables located in the database files, and because Oracle accesses these files often, it sets aside a separate area of memory to avoid disk input/output (I/O).

The cache itself holds a subset of the data from the data dictionary. It's loaded with an initial set of entries when the instance is first started then populated from the database data dictionary as further information is required. The cache holds information about all the users, tables and other objects, structure, security, storage, and so on. The data dictionary cache grows to occupy a larger proportion of memory within the shared pool area as needed, but the size of the shared pool area remains fixed.

In addition to the system global area, Oracle manages separate areas of memory for each user or server process. These areas, called process global areas, are discussed in the following section.

Process Global Area

The process global area, sometimes called the program global area or PGA, contains data and control structures for one user or server process. One PGA is allocated for each user process (connection) to the database.

The actual contents of the PGA depend on whether the multithreaded server configuration is implemented, but it typically contains memory to hold the session's variables, arrays, some rows results, and other information. If you're using the multithreaded server, some of the information that's usually held in the PGA is instead held in the common SGA.

The size of the PGA depends on the operating system used to run the Oracle instance, and once allocated, it remains the same. Memory used in the PGA doesn't increase according to the amount of processing performed in the user process. The DBA can control the size of the PGA by modifying some of the parameters in the instance parameter file **INIT.ORA**. For example, one of the parameters that DBAs most often change is the **SORT_AREA_SIZE** parameter.

The Oracle Programs

The Oracle server code mentioned previously is code that performs the same function regardless of which tool the front-end programs are using (such as SQL*Plus, Oracle Designer/2000, Reports, Excel, and so on). On some platforms, the server code is loaded only once into the machine's memory, and all the processes using the instance can share it—even across instances (as long as you are running the same version of Oracle for both instances). This Kernel code, also known as *reentrant code*, saves memory because it requires that only one copy of the code be loaded into memory.

Understanding Oracle Data Storage

You've already learned that the database files are binary, fixed-size files on disk. However, it's worthwhile, if you're going to be working closely with Oracle databases, to understand a little more detail about the construction of the binary files themselves. In the following sections, you'll learn more about these constructions.

Understanding The Relations Between Tablespaces And Database Files

For management, security, and performance reasons, the database is logically divided into one or more *tablespaces* that each contain one or more database files. A database file is always associated with only one tablespace. A tablespace is a logical division of a database that contains one or more physical database files.

Every Oracle database has a tablespace named **SYSTEM** to which Oracle allocates the very first file of the database. The **SYSTEM** tablespace is the default location of all objects when a database is first created. The simplest database setup is one database file in the **SYSTEM** tablespace (simple, but not recommended).

Typically, you create many tablespaces to partition the different parts of the database. For example, you might have one tablespace for tables, another to hold indexes, and so on, and each of these tablespaces would have one or more database files associated to them.

When you create objects that use storage in the database (such as tables), you should specify the tablespace location of the object as part of the **CREATE** statement for the object. Only system tables should occupy storage in the **SYSTEM** tablespace. The system tables are tables such as **tab$, col$, ind$, fet$**, and other internal tables. Objects, such as synonyms and views, don't take up storage within the database other than the storage in the data dictionary table for their definitions, along with the definitions for all other types of objects.

Tablespaces can be added, dropped, taken offline and online, and associated with additional database files. By adding another file to a tablespace, you increase the size of the tablespace and, therefore, the database itself. However, you can't drop the **SYSTEM** tablespace; doing so would destroy the database because it contains the system tables. You also can't take the **SYSTEM** tablespace offline.

Tablespaces, along with other storage objects, are all placed within *segments*. The following section explains segments in detail.

Understanding Segments

A segment is a generic name given to any object that occupies storage in the database files. Some examples of segments are table segments (data segments), index segments, rollback segments, temporary segments, and the cache (bootstrap) segments. A segment uses a number of Oracle blocks in the same tablespace (although the blocks themselves can be in different files that make up the tablespace).

Extents And Their Composition

The storage for any object on the database is allocated in a number of blocks that must be contiguous in the database files. These contiguous blocks are known as *extents*. For example, when a table is first created using default settings, five Oracle blocks are allocated to the table for the very first extent (otherwise known as the initial extent). As rows are inserted and updated into the table, the five blocks fill with data. When the last block has filled and new rows are inserted, the database automatically allocates another set of five blocks for the table, and the new rows are inserted into the new set of blocks. This allocating of additional storage (additional extents) continues until no more free space is available in the tablespace. The table starts with the one initial extent and is then allocated other secondary (or next) extents. The blocks for an extent must be contiguous within the database files.

Once an extent is allocated to a segment (table), these blocks can't be used by any other database object, even if all the rows in the table are deleted. The table must be dropped or truncated to release the storage allocated to the table. The exception to this is *rollback segments*, which can dynamically release storage that was allocated to them.

The Lowest Level Of Construction: Oracle Blocks

Oracle "formats" the database files into a number of Oracle blocks when they're first created—making it easier for the relational database management system (RDBMS) software to manage the files and easier to read data into the memory areas.

These blocks are usually 1K (the default for Windows NT systems), 2K (the default for most Unix machines and VAX VMS), 4K (the default for IBM mainframes), or larger. For a 50MB database file, there would be 25,600 Oracle blocks, assuming a block size of 2K (50MB/2K). The block size should be a multiple of the operating system block size (a figure which represents how the operating system stores data onto disk media). Regardless of the block size, not all of the block is available for holding data because Oracle takes up some space to manage the contents of the block. This block header has a minimum size, but it can grow.

These Oracle blocks are the smallest unit of storage in the Oracle environment. Increasing the Oracle block size can improve performance, but you should do this only when the database is first created because changing block size later can corrupt or even destroy the database. In fact, some installations of Oracle don't even provide you with the opportunity to increase block size after the database is created.

When you first create a database, it uses some of the blocks within the first file, and the rest of the blocks are free. In the data dictionary, Oracle maintains a list of the free blocks for each data file in each tablespace.

Each Oracle block is numbered sequentially for each database file starting at 1. Two blocks can have the same block address if they're in different database files.

> **WARNING!** *Again, as just noted in the previous text, it's a very bad idea to modify the Oracle block size once you've created the database. Doing so can corrupt or destroy the data within your database.*

Understanding ROWIDs

The **ROWID** is a unique database-wide physical address for every row on every table. Once assigned (when the row is first inserted into the database), it never changes until the row is deleted or the table is dropped.

The **ROWID** consists of the following three components, the combination of which uniquely identifies the physical storage location of the row.

- Oracle database file number, which contains the block with the row
- Oracle block address, which contains the row
- The row within the block (because each block can hold many rows)

The **ROWID** is used internally in indexes as a quick means of retrieving rows with a particular key value. Application developers also use it in SQL statements as a quick way to access a row once they know the **ROWID**.

Free Space And Automatic Compaction

When a database file is first created or added to a tablespace, all the blocks within that file are empty blocks that have never been used. As time goes by, the blocks within a database file are used by a segment (table), or they remain free blocks. Oracle tracks the file's free blocks in a list in the data dictionary. As you create and drop tables, the free space becomes fragmented, with free space in different parts of the database file. When the free blocks are scattered in this way, Oracle has no way to automatically bring the free storage together.

When two fragments of free space are physically next to each other in the database file, the two smaller fragments can be compacted together into one larger fragment, which is recorded in the free space list. This compacting reduces the overhead when Oracle actually needs the free space (when a table wants to allocate another extent of a certain size, for example). The **SMON** background process performs this automatic compaction.

Understanding Some Of The System Database Objects

Now that you've learned how Oracle constructs the database and its components, it's worthwhile to learn more about some of the system objects that Oracle uses to implement the construction. The following sections discuss some of the system objects that support the workings of the architecture and, in turn, provide the user or administrator with information about the structure of the database.

The Data Dictionary

The first tables created on any database are the system tables, also known as the Oracle data dictionary. These tables are owned by the first Oracle user account that's created automatically—that is, by the user **SYS**. The system tables record information about the structure of the database and the objects within it, and Oracle accesses them when it needs information about the database or every time it executes a data definition language (DDL) statement or data manipulation language (DML) statement. It's important to note that these tables are never directly updated. However, updates to them occur in the background whenever a DDL statement is executed.

The core data dictionary tables hold normalized information that's cryptic to understand, so Oracle provides a set of views to make the information in the core system tables more meaningful. You can access the names of over 170 of the views in the data dictionary with the following command:

```
SELECT * FROM DICT;
```

Oracle requires the information in the data dictionary tables to parse any SQL statement. The information is cached in the data dictionary area of the shared pool in the SGA. Because the very first tablespace created is the **SYSTEM** tablespace, the data dictionary tables use storage in the database files associated with the **SYSTEM** tablespaces.

Rollback Segments

Whenever you change data in Oracle, the change must be either committed or reversed. If a change is reversed or *rolled back*, the contents of the data block are restored back to the original state before the change. Rollback segments are system-type objects that support this reversing process. Whenever you make any kind of change to either application tables or system tables, a rollback segment automatically holds the previous version of the data that's being modified, so the old version of the data is available if a rollback is required.

If other users want to see the data while the change is pending, they always have access to the previous version from the rollback segment. They're provided with a *read-consistent* version of the data. Once the change is committed, the modified version of the data is available. Keep a few important things in mind when considering rollback segments:

- Rollback segments are always owned by the user **SYS**, and no Oracle user can access them for viewing.

- Rollback segments use storage in the same way as other segments in terms of extents. With a rollback segment, however, you must initially allocate a minimum of two extents instead of only one.

- The first rollback segment is created automatically when the database is first created and has a name of **SYSTEM**, and it uses storage in the first tablespace, which also has a name of **SYSTEM**.

WARNING! That Oracle uses the same name for three different types of objects can get confusing; the first tablespace is called **SYSTEM**, the first rollback segment is called **SYSTEM**, and one of the first Oracle accounts created is called **SYSTEM**. They're different types of objects, so don't confuse them.

Temporary Segments

Temporary segments use storage in the database files to provide a temporary work area for intermediate stages of SQL processing and for large sort operations.

Oracle creates temporary segments on the fly, and they are automatically deleted when the **SMON** background process no longer needs them. If only a small working area is required, Oracle doesn't create a temporary segment but instead uses a part of the PGA memory as a temporary work area.

The following operations might cause Oracle to create a temporary segment:

- Creating an index

- Using the **ORDER BY**, **DISTINCT**, or **GROUP BY** clauses in a **SELECT** statement

- Using the set operators **UNION**, **INTERSECT**, **MINUS**

- Creating joins between tables

- Using some subqueries

The DBA can control which tablespaces contain the temporary segments on a user-by-user basis. However, Oracle automatically allocates and manages certain types of segments on its own. One of these segments is the bootstrap segment, discussed in the following section.

Bootstrap/Cache Segment

A bootstrap or cache segment is a special type of object on the database that's used to perform an initial load of the data dictionary cache in the shared pool area of the SGA. Oracle uses the cache segment only when the instance first starts and doesn't use it again until the instance restarts. Once the segment is used to perform the initial load of the data dictionary cache, the remainder of the cache in memory is steadily populated as statements are executed against the database.

Now that you have learned some of the fundamentals of Oracle databases and some of the issues you must consider when creating those databases, its time to move on to working with the actual data within the database. The following sections discuss some of the specific issues that you must keep in mind when working with Oracle back ends from your Access front end.

Oracle Data Management Considerations

Although you've spent quite a bit of time in recent chapters learning how to manage data in your Access databases and even learned a little bit about how to manage data in SQL Server databases in the preceding chapter, some differences occur when dealing with Oracle. The following sections will discuss some of these considerations in the Oracle environment to help you better manage your development.

Transactions And Using The Commit And Rollback Actions

Database changes aren't saved until the user explicitly decides that the insert, update, and delete statements should be made permanent. Up until that point, the changes are in a pending status, and any failures, such as a machine crash, will reverse the changes.

A *transaction* is an atomic unit of work comprising one or more SQL statements; it begins when the user first connects to the database and ends when a **COMMIT** or **ROLLBACK** statement is issued. Upon a **COMMIT** or **ROLLBACK**, the next transaction automatically begins. All the statements within a transaction are either all saved (committed) or all reversed (rolled back).

Committing a transaction makes changes permanent in the entire transaction to the database, and once committed, the changes can't then be reversed. Rolling back reverses all the inserts, updates, deletes in the transaction; again, once rolled back, these changes can't then be committed. Internally, the process of committing means writing out the changes recorded in the SGA's redo log buffer cache to the online redo log files on disk. If this disk I/O succeeds, the application receives a message indicating a successful commit. (The text of the message changes from one tool to another.) The **DBWR** background process can write out the actual Oracle data blocks in the SGA's database buffer cache at a later time. If the system should crash, Oracle can automatically reapply the changes from the redo logs files even if the Oracle data blocks weren't written back to the database files before the failure.

TIP: *DDL statements such as **CREATE TABLE** will automatically issue a **COMMIT**, even if the DDL statement itself fails.*

Oracle also implements the idea of statement-level rollback. If a single statement fails during a transaction, the entire statement will fail. In other words, an **IN-SERT** statement for 1,000 rows will insert either all 1,000 rows or none at all. That is, the entire statement works, or nothing happens. If a statement does fail within a transaction, the rest of the statements in the transaction are still in a pending state and must be committed or rolled back.

If a user process terminates abnormally (the process is killed, for example), the **PMON** background process automatically rolls back changes. Any changes that the process had committed up to the point of failure remain committed, and only the changes for the current transaction are rolled back.

All locks held by the transaction are automatically released when the transaction commits or rolls back or when the **PMON** background process rolls back the transaction. In addition, other system resources (such as rollback segments) are released for other transactions to use.

Savepoints enable you to set up markers within a transaction so that you have the option of rolling back just part of the work performed in the transaction. You can use savepoints in long and complex transactions to provide the reversing option for certain statements. However, this causes extra overhead on the system to perform the work for a statement and then reverse the changes; usually, changes in the logic can produce a more optimal solution. When Oracle performs a rollback to a savepoint, the rest of the statements in the transaction remain in a pending state and must be committed or rolled back. Oracle releases the locks taken by these statements that were rolled back.

Data Integrity

As you've learned, data integrity is about enforcing data validation rules—such as checking that a percentage amount is between 0 and 100—to ensure that invalid data doesn't get into your tables. Historically, these rules were enforced by the application programs themselves (and the same rules were checked repeatedly in different programs). In many cases, this will still be the most efficient way to enforce rules—it makes no sense, for example, to generate network traffic if the application itself can determine the invalidity of the data.

However, Oracle enables you to define and store data validation rules against the database objects to which they relate. The major benefit of such a construction is that you need to code them only once—which ensures that they're enforced whenever any kind of change is made to the table, regardless of which tool issues the insert, update, or delete statement. This checking takes the form of *integrity constraints* and *database triggers*.

Understanding Integrity Constraints

Integrity constraints enforce business rules at the database level by defining a set of checks for the tables in your system. These checks are automatically enforced whenever you issue an insert, update, or delete statement against the table. If any of the constraints are violated, the insert, update, or delete statement is rolled back. The other statements within the transaction remain in a pending state and can be committed or rolled back according to application logic.

Because integrity constraints are checked at the database level, they're performed regardless of where the insert, update, or delete statement originated—whether it was an Oracle or a non-Oracle tool. Defining checks using these constraints is also quicker than performing the same checks using SQL. In addition, the information provided by declaring constraints is used by the Oracle optimizer to make better decisions about how to run a statement against the table. The Oracle Designer/2000 product can also use constraints to automatically generate code in the front-end programs to provide an early warning to the user of any errors.

The types of integrity constraints that you can set up on a table are **NOT NULL**, **PRIMARY KEY**, **UNIQUE**, **FOREIGN KEY**, **CHECK**, and indexes. Most of these are consistent with their similar definitions in the Access 2000 product. However, it's worthwhile to take a moment to consider each of the integrity constraints individually:

- You set the **NOT NULL** constraint against a column to specify that the column must always have a value on every row; it can never be **NULL**. By default, all the columns in a table are nullable. For example, by using a **NOT NULL** constraint on an **Orders** table, you can specify that there must always be an order amount.

- The **PRIMARY KEY** constraint defines a column or a set of columns that you can use to uniquely identify a single row. No two rows in the table can have the same values for the primary key columns. In addition, the columns for **PRIMARY KEY** constraint must always have a value—in other words, they're **NOT NULL**. If you add a constraint to a table after it has been created, any columns that make up the **PRIMARY KEY** constraint are modified to **NOT NULL**. Only one **PRIMARY KEY** constraint can exist for any table. For example, by using a **PRIMARY KEY** constraint on an **Orders** table, you can specify that a table can't have two records with the same order number. The

Oracle **PRIMARY KEY** constraint performs identically to the creation of primary keys in Access.

- The **UNIQUE** constraint defines a secondary key for the table. This is a column or set of columns that you can use as another way of uniquely identifying a row. No two rows can have the same values for the **UNIQUE** key column or columns. Although it isn't possible for a table to have more than one primary key, a table can have more than one **UNIQUE** constraint. The columns for a **UNIQUE** constraint don't have to be identified as **NOT NULL** (although they usually are—and, in any event, the table could have only a single **NULL** value in that column). If the values for any of the columns that form the unique constraint are **NULL**, the constraint isn't checked. For example, by using a **PRIMARY KEY** and **UNIQUE** constraint on a **Customers** table, you can specify that the **Customer Number** field is a primary key. Additionally, you can specify that the **Customer Name** is a unique key (which would mean that you couldn't have two customers with the same name on your table—a rare situation). The **UNIQUE** constraint isn't checked if the values in the column are **NULL**. Using the **UNIQUE** constraint is similar to specifying the **Indexed: Yes (No Duplicates)** property for a field in an Access table.

- The **FOREIGN KEY** or referential integrity constraint enforces relationship integrity between tables. It dictates that a column or set of columns on the table match a **PRIMARY KEY** or **UNIQUE** constraint on a different table. For example, you could set up a **FOREIGN KEY** constraint on the **Orders** table to specify that whenever an order record is inserted or updated, the **Customer Number** must also exist in the **Customers** table. This ensures that you don't get orders for nonexistent customers. You use **FOREIGN KEY** constraints to enforce parent/child relationships between tables. You can even use them to enforce self-referential constraints, usually in situations where a hierarchical structure is set up with all the rows held in the same table. If any of the columns of the foreign key are **NULL**, the constraint isn't checked at all. Foreign key columns are usually declared as **NOT NULL**. Again, **FOREIGN KEY** constraints are similar to Access foreign keys or referential integrity relationships.

TIP: *It's possible to specify that when the parent row is deleted, the delete should automatically cascade and delete the child rows—a dangerous situation. The user is informed only about the master rows that were removed, and he or she might not be aware of the additional rows that were deleted automatically in the background because he or she isn't told that this cascading deletion has happened.*

*Only this automatic deletion of child rows is supported by specifying the **ON DELETE CASCADE** clause at the end of the foreign key creation statement. If you change the master table's key value, however, the child rows aren't updated automatically to reflect the new key; you can implement this update cascade requirement using database triggers.* ***FOREIGN KEY*** *constraints aren't checked at all if any of the columns in the foreign key are **NULL**.*

- A **CHECK** constraint specifies additional logic that must be true for the insert, update, or delete statement to work on the table. The additional logic returns a **Boolean** result, and in the check constraint, you ensure the values in the row being modified satisfy a set of validation checks that you specify. The syntax of a **CHECK** constraint is very similar to the syntax found in the **WHERE** clause of a **SELECT** statement. However, you can't use subqueries or other columns that vary over time (such as **SYSDATE**). You can use database triggers to perform this additional processing that you can't put into constraints. For example, using a **CHECK** constraint on the **Orders** table, you can specify that the order amount must be greater than zero and the salesman's commission can't be greater than 10 percent of the order total. The **CHECK** constraint is similar to the **Validation Rule** property in Access.

- **PRIMARY KEY** and **UNIQUE** constraints automatically create an index on the columns they're defined against if the constraint is enabled upon creation. If an index already exists on the columns that form the **PRIMARY KEY** or **UNIQUE** constraint, that index is used, and Oracle can't create a new one. Oracle creates indexes when the constraint is enabled (which is the default when the constraint is first added to the table). Oracle drops the indexes from the table when the constraint is disabled. Enabling and disabling constraints can take significant time and system overhead due to the index creation and removal.

TIP: When you set up a *FOREIGN KEY* constraint, the columns aren't indexed automatically. Because the foreign key columns are usually involved in joining tables together, you manually create indexes on these columns. Disabling a *PRIMARY KEY* or *UNIQUE* constraint drops the index for the constraint.

Database Triggers

A database trigger is a PL/SQL block that you can define to automatically execute for insert, update, and delete statements against a table. You can define the trigger to execute once for the entire statement or once for every row that's inserted, updated, or deleted. For any one table, you can define database triggers for 12 events. For each of the 12 events, you can define many database triggers for the same event.

A database trigger can call database procedures that are also written in PL/SQL. Unlike database triggers, procedures on the database are stored in a compiled form. For this reason, you should put the longer code segments into a procedure then call the procedure from the database trigger.

In addition to implementing complex business rules, checking, and defaulting, you can use database triggers to insert, update, and delete other tables. An example of this use is providing an auditing facility where an audit trail is automatically created in an audit table whenever a row is changed on another table. Without database triggers, this function would be implemented in the front-end programs that make the change to the database; however, someone bypassing the code in the front-end programs (using SQL*Plus, for example) wouldn't go through the checks and processing defined.

Database triggers differ from constraints in that they enable you to embed SQL statements within them, whereas constraints don't. If possible, use constraints for checking; they're quicker than using database triggers.

System-Level Privileges

Each Oracle user defined on the database can have one or more of over 80 system-level privileges. These privileges control on a very fine level the right to execute SQL commands. The DBA assigns system privileges either directly to Oracle user accounts or to roles. The roles are then assigned to the Oracle user accounts.

For example, before you can create a trigger on a table (even if you own the table as an Oracle user), you must have the system privilege called **CREATE TRIGGER** either assigned to your Oracle user account or assigned to a role given to the user account.

The **CREATE SESSION** privilege is another frequently used system-level privilege. To make a connection to the database, an Oracle account must have the **CREATE SESSION** system-level privilege assigned to it. This gives the account the privilege to make connections to the database.

Object-Level Privileges

Object-level privileges provide the capability to perform a particular type of action (select, insert, update, delete, and so on) on a specific object. The owner of the object has full control over the object and can perform any action on it; he doesn't need to have object-level privileges assigned to him. In fact, the owner of the object is the Oracle user who grants object-level privileges to others.

For example, if the user who owns a table wants another user to select and insert rows from his table (but not update or delete), he grants the **SELECT** and **INSERT** object-level privileges on that table to the other user. You can assign object-level privileges either directly to users or to roles that are then assigned to one or more Oracle user accounts.

However, in general you should administer privileges through a level of indirection. Rather than assigning them directly to users, you should use *roles* to specify privileges. Roles are conceptually similar to Access groups. The following section discusses roles in detail.

Users And Roles

A role is a type of object that you can use to simplify the administration of system and object-level privileges. Instead of assigning privileges directly to user accounts, you can assign the privileges to roles that are then assigned to users. (The metaphor of roles and users is similar to Windows NT Groups and Users.)

Roles are essentially groupings of system and object-level privileges. They make the administration of privileges much easier because you can configure the privileges for a particular type of user once and assign these privileges to a role. When a user needs that set of privileges, you can use a single role assignment command to set that user up. Without the use of roles, you'd need to issue many commands for each of the different privileges required.

In addition, you can set up different roles with the correct privileges even though you don't yet have Oracle user accounts that require these assignments. You can assign a role to another role, building hierarchies of roles. Also, you can protect a role with a password that the user must supply when he wants to enable the role.

As already discussed, a physical database could contain many Oracle user accounts that are protected by passwords. You must supply the username and password regardless of which tool you use to gain access to the database. By the way, roles aren't the same as Oracle users; you can't connect to the database by supplying a role name and password.

Auditing

Oracle's auditing mechanism provides three types of audit trails. One audit trail tracks which system privileges are used. Statement auditing keeps track of which SQL statements are used without regard to specific objects. Object-level auditing audits access to specific objects. You can initiate these audit trails to track when statements succeed, when they fail, or both, so all accesses are audited. You can use auditing to keep track of anyone attempting to break into the system.

In addition, you can set up how all the different types of auditing record the entries. The audit trail can record one entry per operation regardless of how many attempts are made on the operation during the connection session. Alternatively, request one entry in the audit trail for every attempt (successful or not) on the operation during the session.

If it's set up and enabled, the audit trail keeps the audit information in a data dictionary table owned by the user **SYS**. This table indicates the operation being audited, the user performing the operation, and the date and time of the operation. Oracle provides a set of data dictionary views to make the information in the dictionary audit table more meaningful. Although the audit trail is implemented in a data dictionary table, it keeps the insertion of rows in the audit trail even if the user rolls back his transaction. The DBA can clear out or archive the audit trail periodically.

One of the most important tasks in data management is protecting not only the integrity, but the existence of the data within your systems. In the event of a hard drive crash or other anomaly, your data can be lost entirely without the use of backup systems. The following sections discuss the backup and recovery of Oracle database information in detail.

Backup And Recovery

As you've seen in previous chapters, one of the most important considerations in any real-world database implementation is the ability to backup and restore the information within the database. The following sections take some time to discuss some of the options that the Oracle architecture gives you when it comes to backing up and recovering your database. The list and discussion are by no means comprehensive; again, you should refer to an Oracle-specific text if you need further information.

This section outlines at a high level some of the options available for backing up and restoring your database. Additionally, the sections discuss the types of failure that can occur and the actions to take. The major part of this section describes preventive action to guard against loss of your database files.

Different Types Of Failure

The major types of failure that can occur are statement failure, user process failure, machine failure, distributed transaction failure, instance failure, and disk failure/file loss.

Statement Failure

In Oracle, a DML statement, such as **UPDATE,** operates on either all the rows satisfying its **WHERE** clause or none at all. Failure within such a statement occurs for a myriad of reasons. For example, when you insert rows into a table, the table might require more storage. If the database software discovers, in turn, that no more free storage is available, it returns an error message to the user. Oracle doesn't leave only half the rows updated. Even if the failure occurs halfway through the statement, the rows already modified are "unmodified." This is known as statement-level rollback. Note that other DML statements in the transaction remain in a pending state ready for a commit or rollback.

User Process Failure

A user process failure occurs when the user process making the connection to the database terminates abnormally during execution. For example, the system administrator could have killed the user process. If this does occur, the Oracle background process **PMON** automatically rolls back any changes for the current transaction. All changes already committed by the user process are saved, but inserts, updates, and deletes since the last commit or rollback are reversed.

Also, the **PMON** background process releases any locks, rollback segments, and other system resources acquired by the user process when it was alive. No DBA involvement is necessary. The database continues to function as usual, and the tables are accessible to other users. (A slight delay could occur before the locks are released.)

Machine Failure

When the machine on which the database server is running fails and shuts down (the power is turned off, for example), the Oracle instance stops running. As long as no database files are lost, the only action required of the DBA is restarting the Oracle instance. When you do this, the **SMON** background process reads the online redo log files and reapplies any changes for committed transactions. Any changes that hadn't been committed are rolled back.

Remember that a **COMMIT** statement writes only the changes to the redo log files; it doesn't write the database blocks back to disk at the point at which the commit was issued. If the database blocks with committed changes were written to the database files before the machine failure, the **SMON** background process obviously doesn't need to reapply the changes for these blocks.

Instance Failure

Instance failure occurs when the machine is still up and running but the Oracle instance itself fails (perhaps one of the background processes was killed). This situation is very similar to machine failure in that the DBA needs only to restart the instance; the **SMON** process reapplies any changes. When restarting the instance after this kind of failure, you'll notice no difference from the point at which the instance is started after a normal shutdown.

Distributed Transaction Failure

A distributed transaction is one that involves changes to more than one database. If a failure occurs during a distributed transaction, the **RECO** background process (if it's running) automatically synchronizes the rollbacks of the transaction's changes across all the databases involved. Again, no manual intervention is required in all but the most serious cases. The DBAs of the instances involved in the distributed transaction can manually force the commit or rollback of the changes on their databases. However, most professionals recommend that you leave the recovery to the **RECO** background process if possible. This might not be possible if the links between the databases aren't available for the **RECO** processes on all the instances to communicate.

Disk Failure/File Loss

The only time you really need to concern yourself with recovery is when you lose one or more of the files making up the database—the database files themselves, the control file, and the redo logs. In such a case, some type of manual recovery is then necessary.

If you lose one or more of the files (database, redo, control), you have available the options highlighted in the following sections. In every situation, you must work with a previous backup of the database.

Cold Backup

A cold backup is a copy of the three sets of files (database files, redo logs, and control file) when the instance is shut down. This is a straight file copy, usually from the disk directly to tape. You must shut down the instance to guarantee a consistent copy. (It's possible to back up the files without shutting down the instance. Such an event is known as a *hot backup* and is discussed later in this chapter.)

If you only perform a cold backup, the only option available in the event of data file loss is restoring all the files from the latest backup. All work performed on the database since the last backup is lost.

Archiving

If you've set up the database to run in **ARCHIVELOG** mode (easily done by the DBA), the database changes recorded in the redo logs are archived to an archive destination whenever the redo logs fill. Using this option, you have a complete record of changes made to the database files in the offline and online redo log files.

If you lose one or more of the database files, you could restore them from the last backup and reapply the changes since the last backup from the online and offline redo log files. You must have some kind of backup of the files and the complete set of online and offline redo logs from which to reapply all the changes made to the database.

With the archiving option, you lose no changes in the database if the complete set of redo logs is available. All the changes committed before the file was lost are reapplied. It's also possible to perform recovery if the control or redo log files are lost.

Hot Backups

Some sites (such as worldwide airline reservations systems) can't shut down the database while making a backup copy of the files. The cold backup isn't an available option.

You can use a different means of backing up your database—the hot backup. To perform a hot backup, you issue a SQL command to indicate to Oracle, on a tablespace-by-tablespace basis, that you want to back up the files of the tablespace. The users can continue to make full use of the files, including making changes to the data. Once you've indicated that you want to back up the tablespace files, you can use your operating system to copy these files to your backup destination.

If a data loss failure does occur, you can restore the lost database files using the hot backup and the online and offline redo logs created since the backup was done. The database is restored to the most consistent state without any loss of committed transactions.

> **WARNING!**   The database must be running in ARCHIVELOG mode for you to have the hot backup option.

Export And Import

Along with the RDBMS software, Oracle provides two utilities that you can use to back up and restore the database. These utilities are useful to DBAs for system-wide backups and recoveries and also to application developers for temporary backups of their own data and object recovery into their own user accounts. Both these utilities can be found within the Backup Manager.

The Export utility dumps the definitions and data for the specified part of the database to an operating system binary file. The Import utility reads the file produced by an Export, re-creates the definitions of objects, and inserts the data.

> **WARNING!**   For a full database import, you must have an existing template database already created.

If you use Export and Import as a means of backing up and recovering the database, you can't recover all the changes made to the database since the export was performed. This is similar to the situation with the cold backup. The best you can do is recover the database to the time when the export was last performed.

On large, data-filled databases, the Export and Import utilities can take a long time to run—in fact, many hours isn't unusual. However, the utilities do provide an option to selectively export and import different user accounts and even objects within an Oracle user account.

Understanding Multiplexing

Despite the usefulness of tape backups and other backup methods, it probably seems to you as if there is still significant risk to manage for Oracle databases. However, Oracle does provide other options to duplicate data. These options provide an extra level of protection in the event of data loss. The following sections discuss some of the more important additional options.

Control Files

To protect against control file loss, the Oracle RDBMS software can maintain more than one copy of the control file. You do this by making a consistent copy of the existing control file and modifying an **INIT.ORA** parameter. This doesn't significantly impact the performance of the database. If all copies of the control file are lost, you can manually re-create them using the **CREATE CONTROLFILE** command.

Redo Logs

Redo logs record all the changes made to data blocks on the database. If the database is running in **ARCHIVELOG** mode and only the offline redo logs are lost, you should shut down the database and make another backup of the three sets of files for the database.

If the online redo logs are lost, however, you could lose some work because some of the information required to reapply changes to the database files is in the online redo log files. To guard against this, you can multiplex (mirror) the online redo log files in the same way as the control files. When the RDBMS software writes changes to one redo log, the exact same information is written to an exact copy of the redo log.

In today's enterprise environment, ensuring that you maintain backups of your data is a crucial consideration. However, many enterprises will nevertheless find that they need to split their databases up into multiple physical components—for security, for protection from failure, or for enterprise-specific concerns. Oracle supports *distributed databases* to help address this issue. The following section addresses distributed databases in detail.

Distributed Databases

A distributed database is one logical database that's implemented as two or more physical databases on either the same machine or separate machines. In some cases, the separate machines could be right next to each other—in other cases, they could be thousands of miles away. The system's designers decide where the tables should physically reside.

Each physical database has its own instance and sets of files, and the machines on which the databases reside are connected over a network. The location of tables can be made transparent to the application using database links and synonyms.

Oracle enables a transaction and even a single statement to access tables on two or more distributed databases. This doesn't necessitate any more coding by the application developers.

A distributed transaction is a transaction that modifies tables on more than one database then expects all the changes to be committed. With any kind of failure, all the changes on all the databases are rolled back. A distributed transaction can involve many Oracle databases and only one non-Oracle database. The Oracle two-phase commit mechanism controls the synchronization of commits across all databases and can automatically roll back changes on all the databases were any kind of failure to occur. The **RECO** background process synchronizes this operation.

In addition to this functionality, Oracle also provides the capability to replicate tables from one database to others. This is called *creating a snapshot* of the table.

You create a snapshot with the **CREATE SNAPSHOT** command on the database where you want to have the copy of the data. The Oracle RDBMS software automatically sends down any changes made to the master copy of the table to each of the snapshot copies at user-defined intervals without any manual intervention. The snapshot mechanism enables you to make updates to the snapshot copy of the table, in which case the changes are sent from the copy table back to the master table.

Needless to say, the Oracle architecture is significantly more complex than the Access architecture—as you would expect it to be to support the number and volume of transactions it is intended for. Understanding the steps a SQL statement proceeds through in this more complex environment is therefore useful. The following section describes those steps in detail.

Following A SQL Statement Through The Architecture

Before we move on to a consideration of the Access connection to the Oracle back end, it's worthwhile to consider the steps a typical SQL statement might go through to be executed on the Oracle machine. The discussion uses a simple scenario with both the client and the Oracle database server machine on Windows NT Server without any networking involved. Using a single-task configuration makes tracking the steps a little more simple. However, the knowledge that you've put together in previous chapters should help you recognize some of the places where network communications would be appropriate.

The following shows some of the steps involved in executing SQL statements.

1. The user executes the client and enters the Oracle username and password.

2. Oracle validates the username and password against the data dictionary and sends a response to the user process to indicate connection.

3. The user enters a **SELECT** statement.

4. Oracle must translate the **SELECT** before it executes it, so the Oracle parser and optimizer are called. If any user has issued *exactly* the same statement before, the parsed version might be in the shared pool area in memory. In such a case, Oracle uses the parsed version, so no extra parsing is done for this statement.

5. To translate the **SELECT** statement, Oracle must obtain the names of the objects, privileges, and other information from the data dictionary. The data dictionary cache area in the shared pool in the **SGA** doesn't have the information on the tables, so parsing of the **SELECT** statement is suspended while the information is read in.

6. Oracle runs a recursive SQL statement (a system-generated statement) to load information about the objects from the data dictionary tables in the database files into the data dictionary cache in memory.

7. Parsing of the original user **SELECT** statement resumes, and Oracle constructs an optimization plan to control the way the statement runs.

8. The statement accesses a table. If you assume the Oracle blocks for the table aren't in the database buffer cache in the **SGA**, the required Oracle blocks are then read in from the database files and held in the cache area of the SGA. (If they're already in the cache, Oracle simply moves on to Step 9.)

9. Oracle runs the statement and returns the results to the user.

Now, let's consider what happens when the user then issues an **UPDATE** statement to modify some of the fields on the rows he's just selected. Oracle will, in such a case, perform the following steps:

1. Because the data dictionary cache already has the information about the table in memory, no more recursive SQL is generated (assuming that the information hasn't been flushed out by another process requiring space in the cache area). Also, the Oracle blocks for the table are in the database buffer cache, so you won't do another disk I/O to read these blocks in.

2. Oracle locks the rows to be updated.

3. Before Oracle makes the **UPDATE**, information about the old state of the blocks is recorded in a rollback segment, and the original version of the values is also recorded in the redo buffers cache.

4. Oracle updates the rows and records the new version of the values in the redo buffer cache in the SGA.

5. The user issues the **COMMIT** command to make the change permanent to the database.

6. Oracle records an entry indicating a commit in the redo buffer cache, and the old, new, and commit entry are all flushed down to the online redo log (whichever one is the current one in use).

7. The rollback segment is released (but not overwritten) for other processes to use.

8. Oracle releases the locks on the table.

9. The user receives a commit successful message (the exact wording of this message varies from tool to tool).

10. If the user issues a **ROLLBACK** instead of a **COMMIT**, the old versions of the values changed are restored back to the Oracle data blocks from the rollback segment. Oracle also writes to the redo buffer cache an entry indicating that a rollback was performed.

Immediate Solutions

Creating A Data Source Name (DSN)

As you know, the first step before you can connect to any data source that isn't an Access data source is to locate it and make sure drivers for connection are present on the client machine. Although ActiveX Data Objects let you connect to a data source without defining a DSN (as you saw in previous chapters), it's still worthwhile to create the data source in the ODBC administrator.

As you saw in Chapter 31, ODBC data sources are set up in the ODBC administrator. Depending on your installation, the ODBC administrator could be a standalone application, or it could appear as a control-panel icon. It enables you to create, modify, and delete data sources and to obtain information about existing drivers. Remember that a data source is simply a user-definable name that stores settings that can be used to access a back end located on a particular server using a specified driver. Figure 32.4 shows the Drivers tab within the ODBC administrator. Note the existence of two Microsoft-designed Oracle drivers in the figure. Your installation may differ.

To define a new data source, change back to the User DSN tab and click on the Add button in the ODBC Administrator dialog. The Create New Data Source dialog box, where you must select the name of the driver that the data source will

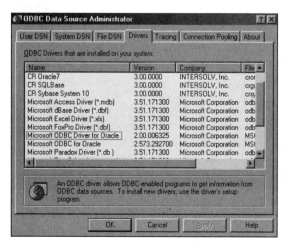

Figure 32.4 The Drivers tab within the ODBC administrator showing the Oracle drivers.

use, will appear. In this case, we're opting to the use the Oracle8 drivers provided by Oracle, as shown in Figure 32.5.

After you select a data source and click OK , you're shown another dialog, which varies depending on which driver you've selected. It enables you to define specific information about the data source that you're creating. An example is the Oracle8 ODBC Driver Setup dialog box shown in Figure 32.6.

As you can see, the Oracle8 ODBC Driver Setup dialog box enables you to specify information, such as the data source name, a description of the data source, and the network name of the Oracle database to connect to.

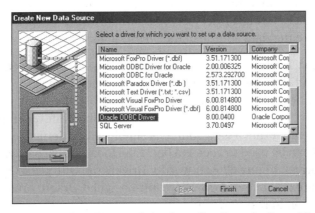

Figure 32.5   The Create New Data Source dialog box after the selection of the Oracle drivers.

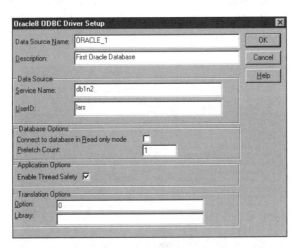

Figure 32.6   The Oracle8 ODBC Driver Setup dialog box.

Connecting To The Database

No additional configuration is required to connect to an ODBC data source from Visual Basic for Applications (VBA) (except through the ODBC administrator). Any drivers and data sources installed and configured using the ODBC administration program are accessible. If you're using Data Access Objects (DAO), the **Database** object is used to establish connections through its **OpenDatabase** method. As you've learned, the **OpenDatabase** method takes four arguments, three of which apply only to local desktop databases:

- *Database name parameter*—An empty string for ODBC data sources.
- *Open exclusive **Boolean** parameter*—Always set to False for ODBC data sources.
- *Read only **Boolean** parameter*—Always set to False for ODBC data sources.
- *Connect string parameter*—Contains the ODBC connect string. The string includes the word "ODBC;", the data source name, user ID, password, and any additional database specific parameters.

To connect to Oracle, the connect string requires no special parameters. The code fragment shown here uses values from a generic ODBC login form to build a connect string:

```
Dim dbOracle As Database
Dim szConnect As String

szConnect = "ODBC;DSN=" & lstDSNs.Text & ";" & "UID=" & _
    txtID.Text & ";" & "PWD=" & txtPassword.Text & ";"
Set dbOracle = OpenDatabase("", False, False, szConnect)
```

The connect string might look something like the following in such an example:

```
"ODBC;DSN=ORACLE_1;UID=lars;PWD=kimba;"
```

Creating A Snapshot-Type Recordset With Oracle

The primary means of retrieving results from an ODBC data source is the Snapshot-type **Recordset** object. This **Recordset** object is created using the **OpenRecordset** method of the **Database** object. As you've learned previously, the **OpenRecordset** method takes a series of arguments, one of which lets you specify the **Recordset** type—in this case, **dbOpenSnapshot** is the constant to pass. Additionally, you can pass a SQL **SELECT** statement or other query definition, and a numeric constant used to control processing of the SQL. Unless the application needs to be portable to different RDBMSs, this numeric constant should be set to **dbSQLPassThrough**, which sends the statement directly to the server for processing. This mode allows the developer to use the native syntax of the RDBMS, and it prevents the local Microsoft Access engine from attempting to parse and process the SQL (as you've seen in previous chapters, this is known as the ODBC Direct model). The following code fragment provides a simple example of the use of the **OpenRecordset** method to create a snapshot against an Oracle database:

```
'  Other code to open the workspace and connect to the database
'  must come first

Dim dsContacts As Recordset
Dim rsString as String

rsString = "SELECT a.last_name, a.first_name, b.phone_nbr " & _
    "FROM individual a, phone b " & _
    "WHERE a.ID = b.IndividualID(+) " & _
    "ORDER BY 1, 2"
Set dsContacts = dbOracle.OpenRecordset(rsString, dbOpenSnapshot, _
    dbSQLPassThrough)
```

The example assumes that the **Database** object has already connected to the data source. Note that if **dbSQLPassThrough** isn't specified, a syntax error results because the local Access engine attempts to parse the SQL and doesn't recognize the Oracle-specific outer join syntax.

After applying the SQL and creating the result set, numerous methods can be applied to position the record pointer in the cursor. The **MoveFirst**, **MoveLast**, **MoveNext**, and **MovePrevious** methods are the most commonly used—you've learned about them previously.

Using The ODBC Application Programming Interface (API) From VBA With Oracle

When working with Oracle data sources, it's possible that you may want to use the ODBC API directly (although you're generally better served using ADO). Doing so opens numerous possibilities, including the creation of a truly portable client application.

A small subset of the ODBC API can be used to provide transaction control in Access applications accessing ODBC data sources. The ODBC API functions shown in Table 32.1 provide access to all functions needed to connect, apply transactions through embedded SQL, and rollback or commit them, as needed. Table 32.1 lists some of the ODBC API functions and their usages.

The companion CD-ROM contains the ODBCAPI.bas module, which includes the definitions for these functions and the constants they use for execution.

Using The ODBC API Calls

Assume for the moment that you wanted to disable the SQL **Autocommit** function. After establishing a connection for retrieving results with the **OpenDatabase**

Table 32.1   ODBC API declarations for Visual Basic.

Function	Description
SQLAllocConnect	Allocates memory for a connection handle within the environment returned from **SQLAllocEnv**.
SQLAllocEnv	Allocates memory for an environment handle and initializes the ODBC call-level interface for use by an application. An application must call **SQLAllocEnv** before calling any other ODBC function.
SQLAllocStmt	Allocates memory for a statement handle and associates the statement handle with the connection returned from **SQLAllocConnect**. An application must call **SQLAllocStmt** before submitting SQL statements
SQLDisconnect	Closes the connection associated with a specific connection handle.
SQLDriverConnect	An alternative to the **SQLConnect** function. It supports data sources that require more connection information than the three arguments in **SQLConnect** dialog boxes to prompt the user for all connection information and data sources that aren't defined in the **ODBC.INI** file or registry.
SQLExecDirect	Executes a preparable statement using the current values of the parameter marker variables if any parameters exist in the statement. **SQLExecDirect** is the fastest way to submit a SQL statement for one-time execution.
SQLFreeConnect	Releases a connection handle and frees all memory associated with that handle.
SQLFreeEnv	Releases an environment handle and frees all memory associated with that handle.
SQLFreeStmt	Releases a statement handle and frees all memory associated with that handle.
SQLSetConnectOption	Sets options that govern aspects of connections. For example, the **SQLAutocommit** option can be set with this function.
SQLTransact	Requests a **COMMIT** or **ROLLBACK** operation for all active operations on all statements associated with a connection. **SQLTransact** can also request that a **COMMIT** or **ROLLBACK** operation be performed for all connections associated with an environment.

method, the application should establish a second connection to the database using the API functions—for applying transactions. After establishing this connection, **SQLSetConnectOption** should be used to disable **AutoCommit**. The following listing shows how all this might be accomplished.

```
Dim hEnv As Long
Dim hDBc As Long
Dim szConnectString As String
Dim iError As Integer
Dim hWnd As Integer
Dim iLenCSOut As Integer
Dim szCSOut As String * 254

szConnectString = "ODBC;DSN=ORACLE_1;UID=lars;PWD=kimba;"
hWnd = frmMDIChild.hWnd
iError = SQLAllocEnv(hEnv)                  ' Allocate environment
iError = SQLAllocConnect(hEnv, hDBc)     ' Allocate connection

' Load driver & connect to ODBC data source
iError = SQLDriverConnect(hDBc, hWnd, szConnectString, SQL_NTS, _
    szCSOut, 254, iLenCSOut, SQL_DRIVER_NOPROMPT)

' Disable autocommit
iError = SQLSetConnectOption(hDBc, SQL_AUTOCOMMIT, 0)
```

In practice, the connect string wouldn't be hard-coded and the return value of each function should be checked.

Applying A Transaction Using Embedded SQL

Once a connection has been established, the application can apply transactions using **SQLExecDirect** after allocating a statement handle with **SQLAllocStmt**. **SQLTransact** can then be used to commit or roll back a transaction based on the return value of **SQLExecDirect**. After applying the transaction, the application should call **SQLFreeStmt** to free the resources allocated to the statement handle. The following code shows an example of the calls to these functions.

```
Dim hStmt As Long

iError = SQLAllocStmt(hDBc, hStmt)       ' Allocate a statement handle
For i = 0 To iStmts
  iError = SQLExecDirect(hStmt, szSQL(i), SQL_NTS)      ' Apply SQL
  If iError Then                              ' Rollback transaction
    iNextErr = SQLTransact(hEnv, hDBc, SQL_ROLLBACK)
    Exit For
```

```
   End If
Next i
If (iError = 0) Then                        ' Commit transaction
   iError = SQLTransact(hEnv, hDBc, SQL_COMMIT)
End If
iError = SQLFreeStmt(hStmt, SQL_DROP)
```

The sample code assumes that the environment and connection handles, **hEnv** and **hDBc**, are valid and connected to the data source, and that **szSQL** is an array of **iStmts** SQL statements. If any statement in the transaction fails, a rollback is issued and processing of the transaction is discontinued. If all statements are processed without errors, the entire transaction is committed. Regardless of whether the transaction is committed or rolled back, the application frees the statement handle.

When the application exits, it needs to disconnect from the data source and free all resources allocated to the environment and connection handles. This can be accomplished with three functions calls, as illustrated in the following lines:

```
iError = SQLDisconnect(hDBc)
iError = SQLFreeConnect(hDBc)
iError = SQLFreeEnv(hEnv)
```

The full capabilities of ODBC are far beyond the scope of this discussion, but many additional capabilities can be provided, and an application can be constructed in a manner that's completely database-independent using embedded SQL. However, if an application doesn't need to be portable to other database platforms, it may be easier to use stored procedures or a third-party product to apply transactions from VBA/Access.

Using ADO Objects With Oracle

Not surprisingly, the way that you manipulate Oracle databases with ADO is almost identical to the way you manipulate SQL Server databases with ADO—that, of course, is ADO's intention. For example, the following code connects to an Oracle database and iterates through every record that meets certain criteria, adjusting these record values accordingly. By making a change to the connection string, the code could just as easily connect to a SQL Server database.

Because most databases don't support the Jet engine **Find** methods, when working with ADO, you must create the recordset to update with a SQL **SELECT** statement, then move through the records in order, as shown here:

```
Sub IncreaseBaseCharges()
  Dim cnnLocal As ADODB.Connection
  Dim cmdLocal As ADODB.Command
  Dim rstLocal As ADODB.Recordset
  Dim intUpdated As Integer

  ' Create Connection Object and open it on the Oracle database
  Set cnnLocal = New ADODB.Connection

  cnnLocal.ConnectionString = "dsn=ORACLE_1;UID=lars;PWD=kimba;"
  cnnLocal.Open

  Set cmdLocal = New ADODB.Command
  Set cmdLocal.ActiveConnection = cnnLocal
  cmdLocal.CommandText = "SELECT * FROM tblCustomerQuotations " _
      & "WHERE BaseEstimate < 10000"
  rstLocal.CursorType = adOpenForwardOnly
  Set rstLocal = cmdLocal.Execute()

  intUpdated = 0
  Do While Not rstLocal.EOF
    intUpdated = intUpdated + 1
    rstLocal.Fields("BaseEstimate") = 10000
    rstLocal.Update
    rstLocal.MoveNext
  Loop
  Debug.Print intUpdated & " Records Updated"
  rstLocal.Close
End Sub
```

Of course, in the case of this particular example, you would probably be just as well served to simply run an **UPDATE** query against the Oracle table. However, the example's intention is simply to show how to use ADO with Oracle tables.

TIP: *Changing the line **cnnLocal.ConnectionString** to point to a SQL Server database definition is the only change that you would have to make to use the code against a different data source (assuming, or course, that the SQL Server contains the same tables and field definitions).*

Chapter 33

Advanced Client-Server Techniques

In Depth

Throughout the previous chapters you've been exposed to a brief overview of the techniques that you can use with Access to connect to a server-side database. You've explored how to work with both SQL Server and Oracle (the two most commonly used server-side databases for the Windows environment). In the last two chapters of the book, you'll explore some of the issues surrounding the development of Web-based front ends for your applications.

Client-server database design is, needless to say, a complex enough topic that you could write entire books on it. In fact, in today's IS department, whole books on singular topics such as transactions, rules, stored procedures, and triggers could often be useful. Unfortunately, we don't have that much space available to us. However, these concepts are crucial to effective client-server management. Therefore, in this chapter we'll discuss these crucial topics and consider how they work and how they impact your application design. Arguably the most important concept for working in distributed processing is the concept of a *transaction*—an atomic group of actions against a database that either all succeed or all fail. In the following sections, we'll begin our exploration of some of the other client-server processing issues with a discussion of transaction processing.

Understanding Transaction Processing

Transaction processing refers to the grouping of a series of changes into a single batch. The entire batch of changes is either accepted or rejected as a group. One of the most common implementations of transaction processing is a bank automated teller machine (ATM) transaction. Imagine that you go to the ATM machine to *deposit* your paycheck. In the middle of processing, a power outage occurs. Unfortunately, the bank recorded the incoming funds before the outage, but the funds hadn't yet been credited to *your* account when the power outage occurred. In other words, the bank had your money, so you couldn't redeposit the check, but they didn't credit the money to your account, so you couldn't access the money either.

Needless to say, you'd likely be pretty unhappy with this particular outcome. Transaction processing would prevent this scenario from occurring. With transaction processing, the whole process either succeeds or fails as a unit. A group of operations is considered a transaction if it meets the following criteria (the so-called ACID test):

- *It's Atomic*—This means the group of operations should complete as a unit or not complete at all.

- *It's Consistent*—This means the group of operations, when completed as a unit, retains the consistency of the application.

- *It's Isolated*—This means the group of operations is independent of anything else going on in the system.

- *It's Durable*—This means that after the group of operations is committed, the changes persist, even if the system crashes.

If your application contains a group of operations that are atomic and isolated, and if to maintain the consistency of your application all changes must persist even if the system crashes, you should place the group of operations in a transaction loop. With Access 2000, the primary benefit of transaction processing is data integrity. As you'll see in the following section, "Understanding The Benefits Of Transaction Processing," with prior versions of Access, transaction processing also provided significant performance benefits. Transaction processing still provides performance benefits in Access 2000, but they're minor and generally aren't the primary reason why you'll use transaction processing in your development.

Understanding The Benefits Of Transaction Processing

In Access 2, the benefits of transaction processing were many, above and beyond simple integrity issues. In general, these benefits were so much more significant because Access 2 did no implicit transaction processing. With the following code run in Access 2, each time the **Update** method occurs within the loop, the data is written to disk. These disk writes are costly in terms of performance, especially if the tables aren't located on a local machine.

```
Sub IncreaseQuantity()
  On Error GoTo IncreaseQuantity_Err
  Dim db As Database
  Dim rst As Recordset

  Set db = CurrentDb
  Set rst = db.OpenRecordset("Select OrderId, _
      Quantity From tblOrderDetails", dbOpenDynaset)
  'Loop through recordset increasing Quantity field by 1
  Do Until rst.EOF
    rst.Edit
      rst!Quantity = rst!Quantity + 1
    rst.Update
    rst.MoveNext
  Loop
```

```
IncreaseQuantity_Exit:
  Set db = Nothing
  Set rst = Nothing
  Exit Sub

IncreaseQuantity_Err:
  MsgBox "Error # " & Err.Number & ": " & Error.Description
  Resume IncreaseQuantity_Exit
End Sub
```

This code, and all of the Access-specific code in this chapter, can be found in the Chap33.mdb database on the sample code CD-ROM. This particular code fragment can be found in the module called **basTransactionRoutines**.

This same code, when run in Access 2000, performs much differently. In addition to any *explicit* transaction processing you might implement for data-integrity reasons, Access 2000 does its own, behind-the-scenes transaction processing. This *implicit transaction processing* is done solely to improve the performance of your application. As the processing loop in the **IncreaseQuantity** routine executes, Access buffers periodically write the data to disk. In a multiuser environment, by default, Jet automatically (implicitly) commits transactions every 50 milliseconds. This period of time is optimized for concurrency rather than performance. If you think it's necessary to sacrifice concurrency for performance, a few Windows Registry settings can be modified to achieve the specific outcome you want. These settings are covered in the next section, "Modifying The Default Behavior Of Transaction Processing."

In general, implicit transaction processing, along with the modifiable Windows Registry settings, afford you better performance than explicit transaction processing; however, it's not a cut-and-dried situation. Many factors, including these in the following list, impact the performance benefits gained by *both* implicit and explicit transaction processing:

• The amount of free memory

• The number of columns and rows being updated

• The size of the rows being updated

• Network traffic

If you plan to implement explicit transaction processing solely for the purpose of improving performance, you should make sure you benchmark your application's performance using both implicit and explicit transactions. It's critical that your application-testing environment be as similar as possible to the production environment within which the application will run—otherwise, your benchmarking is relatively useless.

However, the likelihood is that you will implement explicit transaction processing for reasons pertaining to the way in which you manage the data. In such cases, you will have several different options of how to implement the transaction processing. The following section discusses how to modify the default behaviors of transaction processing in Access.

Modifying The Default Behavior Of Transaction Processing

Before you learn how to implement transaction processing, let's see what you can do to modify the default behavior of the transaction processing built into Access 2000. Three Registry settings affect *implicit* transactions within Access 2000. They're **ImplicitCommitSync**, **ExclusiveAsyncDelay**, and **SharedAsyncDelay**. These keys aren't automatically found in the System Registry. Instead, you must add them to the Registry using the Registry Editor if you determine that you want to control the implicit settings.

The **ImplicitCommitSync** setting determines whether or not implicit transactions are used. The default is No, which might seem to imply that no implicit transactions occur. Actually, because of a documented Jet 3.x bug that seems to have carried over to Jet 4, the value of No means that implicit transactions *are* used. You generally won't want to change this setting because implicit transactions are typically very beneficial to application performance. Furthermore, by placing a series of commands within an *explicit* transaction loop, any *implicit* transaction processing is disabled for that loop.

The **ExclusiveAsyncDelay** setting specifies the maximum number of milliseconds that elapse before Jet commits an implicit transaction when a database is opened for exclusive use. The default value for this setting is 2,000 milliseconds. This setting doesn't in any way affect databases that are open for shared use.

The **SharedAsyncDelay** setting is similar to the **ExclusiveAsyncDelay** setting. It determines the maximum number of milliseconds that elapse before Jet commits an implicit transaction when a database is opened for shared use. The default value for this setting is 50 milliseconds. The higher this value, the greater the performance benefits reaped from implicit transactions, but the higher the chances that concurrency problems will result. These concurrency issues are discussed in detail in the section entitled "Transaction Processing In A Multiuser Environment."

Besides the settings that affect implicit transaction processing in Access 2000, an additional Registry setting affects explicit transaction processing. The **UserCommitSync** setting controls whether explicit transactions are completed synchronously or asynchronously. With the default setting of Yes, control doesn't return from a **CommitTrans** statement until the transactions are actually written to disk. When this value is changed to No, a series of changes are queued, and control returns before the changes are complete.

However, despite the simple model of transaction processing, when you use explicit processing there are certain issues that you need to consider to ensure that the processing occurs correctly. Issues such as record locks, field locks, and more all carry over with special significance during transaction processing. The next section begins the discussion of how to properly implement transaction processing.

Properly Implementing Explicit Transaction Processing

Now that you're aware of the settings that affect transaction processing, you're ready to see how transaction processing is implemented. From Data Access Objects (DAO), three methods of the **Workspace** object control transaction processing:

- **BeginTrans**
- **CommitTrans**
- **Rollback**

The **BeginTrans** method of the **Workspace** object begins the transaction loop. The moment **BeginTrans** is encountered, Access begins writing all changes to a log file in memory. Unless the **CommitTrans** method is issued on the **Workspace** object, the changes are never actually written to the database file. After the **CommitTrans** method is issued, the updates are permanently written to the database object. If a **Rollback** method of the **Workspace** object is encountered, the login memory is released. Here's an example of simple transaction processing using DAOs:

```
Sub IncreaseQuantityTrans()
  On Error GoTo IncreaseQuantityTrans_Err
  Dim wrk As Workspace
  Dim db As Database
  Dim rst As Recordset

  Set wrk = DBEngine(0)
  Set db = CurrentDb
  Set rst = db.OpenRecordset("Select OrderId, _
      Quantity From tblOrderDetails", dbOpenDynaset)
  'Begin the Transaction Loop
  wrk.BeginTrans
    'Loop through recordset increasing Quantity field by 1
    Do Until rst.EOF
      rst.Edit
        rst!Quantity = rst!Quantity + 1
```

```
        rst.Update
        rst.MoveNext
      Loop
    'Commit the Transaction; Everything went as Planned
    wrk.CommitTrans

IncreaseQuantityTrans_Exit:
    Set wrk = Nothing
    Set db = Nothing
    Set rst = Nothing
    Exit Sub

IncreaseQuantityTrans_Err:
    MsgBox "Error # " & Err.Number & ": " & Error.Description
    'Rollback the Transaction; An Error Occurred
    wrk.Rollback
    Resume IncreaseQuantityTrans_Exit
End Sub
```

This code uses a transaction loop to ensure that everything completes as planned or not at all. Notice that the loop that moves through the recordset, increasing the quantity field within each record by one, is placed within a transaction loop. If all processing within the loop completes successfully, the **CommitTrans** method is executed. If the routine invokes the error-handling code for any reason, the error-handler issues the **Rollback** method, ensuring that none of the changes are written to disk.

When working with ActiveX Data Objects (ADOs), you'll generally use the **BeginTrans**, **CommitTrans**, and **RollbackTrans** methods of the **Connection** object to perform your transaction processing. The following program code shows, briefly, how you can use ADOs to perform the same processing shown previously using DAOs:

```
Sub ADOIncreaseQuantityTrans()
  On Error GoTo ADOIncreaseQuantityTrans_Err
  Dim cnnLocal As ADODB.Connection
  Dim cmdLocal As ADODB.Command
  Dim rstLocal As ADODB.Recordset

  ' Create Connection Object and open it on CHAP33.MDB
  Set cnnLocal = New ADODB.Connection
  cnnLocal.ConnectionString = "dsn=Chap33;UID=admin;PWD=;"
  cnnLocal.Open

  Set cmdLocal = New ADODB.Command
  Set cmdLocal.ActiveConnection = cnnLocal
```

```
cmdLocal.CommandText = "Select OrderId, Quantity From tblOrderDetails"
rstLocal.CursorType = adOpenForwardOnly
Set rstLocal = cmdLocal.Execute()

'Begin the Transaction Loop
cnnLocal.BeginTrans
  'Loop through recordset increasing Quantity field by 1
  Do Until rstLocal.EOF
    rstLocal.Fields("Quantity") = rstLocal.Fields("Quantity") + 1
    rstLocal.MoveNext
  Loop
'Commit the Transaction; Everything went as Planned
cnnLocal.CommitTrans

ADOIncreaseQuantityTrans_Exit:
  Set cnnLocal = Nothing
  Set cmdLocal = Nothing
  Set rstLocal = Nothing
  Exit Sub

ADOIncreaseQuantityTrans_Err:
  MsgBox "Error # " & Err.Number & ": " & Error.Description
  'Rollback the Transaction; An Error Occurred
  cnnLocal.Rollback
  Resume ADOIncreaseQuantityTrans_Exit
End Sub
```

Needless to say, while transaction processing is still a relatively straightforward activity (as are most things from within VBA), the basic nature of it nevertheless introduces certain issues. The following sections discuss some of the issues that you might encounter when you are performing transaction processing.

Potential Issues With Transaction Processing

Before you decide that transaction processing is the greatest thing in the history of database design, you should keep several issues in mind concerning transaction processing. These issues are outlined within this section.

Making Sure The Datasource Supports Transactions

Not all recordsets support transaction processing. For example, older FoxPro and dBASE files don't support transaction processing. Neither do certain back-end, open database connectivity (ODBC) database servers. To make matters worse, no errors are encountered when using the transaction processing methods on FoxPro or dBASE tables. It'll appear as if everything processed as planned, but actually, all references to transactions are ignored. When in doubt, you can use the **Transactions** property of the DAO **Database** or **Recordset** object to determine whether the data source supports transaction processing. The **Transactions** property is equal to True if the data source supports transaction processing and equal to False if the data source doesn't support transaction processing. The "Immediate Solutions" section of this chapter contains an example of how to perform this checking with both DAO and ADO code.

Nesting Transactions

Another issue to be aware of with transactions is that you can nest transactions up to five levels deep. The inner transactions must always be committed or rolled back before the outer transactions. Furthermore, nested transactions aren't supported at all for ODBC datasources. This is covered in the section of this chapter entitled "Transaction Processing In A Client-Server Environment."

Neglecting To Explicitly Commit Transactions

When a transaction loop is executing, all updates are written to a log file in memory. If a **CommitTrans** is never executed, the changes are, in effect, rolled back. In other words, a **Rollback** is the default behavior if the changes are never explicitly written to disk with the **CommitTrans** method. This generally works to your advantage. If the power is interrupted or the machine "hangs" before the **CommitTrans** is executed, all changes are, in effect, rolled back. But this behavior can get you into trouble if you forget the **CommitTrans** method. If the workspace is closed without the **CommitTrans** method being executed, the memory log is flushed and the transaction is implicitly rolled back.

Available Memory And Transactions

Another problem to watch out for with transactions occurs when the computer's physical memory is exhausted (or filled) by the transaction log. In such a situation, Access first attempts to use virtual memory. The transaction log is written to the temporary directory specified by the **TEMP** environment variable of the user's machine. This has the effect of dramatically slowing down the transaction process. However, if the transaction process exhausts both physical and virtual memory, an error 2004 results from DAO processing. The error number returned from ADO may vary. You must issue a **Rollback** at this point. Otherwise, you're in danger of violating the consistency of the database.

> **WARNING!** *If your DAO code attempts to commit the transaction after a 2004 error has occurred, the Jet engine commits as many changes as possible, leaving the database in an inconsistent state. In general, ADO won't let you commit transactions after this type of error occurs.*

Transactions And Forms

Access handles its own transaction processing on bound forms—unless you have used the new support within Access for thin-form binding to SQL Server databases. In such cases, you'll have some control of the transaction processing Access performs.

Except as noted, you can't control the transaction processing Access performs on bound forms in any way. If you want to utilize transaction processing with forms, you must create unbound forms.

Transaction Processing In A Multiuser Environment

In a multiuser environment, transaction processing has implications beyond the protection of data. By wrapping a process in a transaction loop, you ensure that you're in control of all records involved in the process. The cost of this additional control is reduced concurrency for the rest of the users of the application. The following code illustrates this scenario:

```
Sub MultiPessimistic()
  On Error GoTo MultiPessimistic_Err
  Dim wrk As Workspace
  Dim db As Database
  Dim rst As Recordset
  Dim intCounter As Integer, intChoice As Integer
  Dim intTry As Integer

  Set wrk = DBEngine(0)
  Set db = CurrentDb
  Set rst = db.OpenRecordset("Select OrderId, ProductID, UnitPrice " & _
      "From tblOrderDetails Where ProductID > 50", dbOpenDynaset)
  rst.LockEdits = True
  'Begin the Transaction Loop
  wrk.BeginTrans
    'Loop through recordset increasing UnitPrice
    Do Until rst.EOF
      'Lock Occurs Here for Each Record in the Loop
      rst.Edit
        rst!UnitPrice = rst!UnitPrice * 1.1
      rst.Update
      rst.MoveNext
    Loop
  'Commit the Transaction; Everything went as Planned
  'All locks released for ALL records involved in the Process
  wrk.CommitTrans
  Set wrk = Nothing
  Set db = Nothing
  Set rst = Nothing
  Exit Sub

MultiPessimistic_Err:
  Select Case Err.Number
    Case 3260
```

```
        intCounter = intCounter + 1
        If intCounter > 2 Then
          intChoice = MsgBox(Err.Description, vbRetryCancel + vbCritical)
          Select Case intChoice
            Case vbRetry
              intCounter = 1
            Case vbCancel
              'User Selected Cancel, Roll Back
              Resume TransUnsuccessful
          End Select
        End If
        DoEvents
        For intTry = 1 To 100
        Next intTry
        Resume
      Case Else
        MsgBox "Error # " & Err.Number & ": " & Err.Description
    End Select

TransUnsuccessful:
  wrk.Rollback
  MsgBox "Warning: Entire Process Rolled Back"
  Set wrk = Nothing
  Set db = Nothing
  Set rst = Nothing
  Exit Sub
End Sub
```

The **MultiPessimistic** routine employs pessimistic locking. This means that each time the **Edit** method is issued, the record on which the edit is issued is locked. If all goes well and no error occurs, the lock is released when the **CommitTrans** is reached. The error-handling code traps for a 3260 error (you should, of course, trap for all possible errors in your code). This error means that the record is locked by another user. The user running the transaction processing is given the opportunity to retry or cancel. If the user selects retry, the code once again tries to issue the **Edit** method on the record. If the user selects cancel, a **Rollback** occurs. This causes the changes made to any of the records involved in the process to be canceled.

You should recognize and understand two key points about the **MultiPessimistic** routine. The first point is that, as this routine executes, each record involved in the process is locked. This potentially means that all other users will be unable to edit a large percentage, or even any, of the records until the transaction process is complete. This is wonderful from a data-integrity standpoint, but it might not be practical within an environment in which users must update data on a frequent basis. For this reason, it's a good idea to keep transaction loops as short in duration as possible. The second point is if any of the lock attempts are unsuccessful, the entire transaction must be canceled. Once again, this might be what you want or need from a data-integrity standpoint, but it might require that all users refrain from editing data while an important process completes.

With optimistic locking, the lock attempt occurs when the **Update** method is issued rather than when the **Edit** method is issued. In general, this doesn't make too much of a difference—all of the records involved in the transaction remain locked until the **CommitTrans** or **Rollback** occurs. An additional difference is in the errors that you must trap for. The DAO code looks like this:

```
Sub MultiOptimistic()
  On Error GoTo MultiOptimistic_Err
  Dim wrk As Workspace
  Dim db As Database
  Dim rst As Recordset
  Dim intCounter As Integer, intChoice As Integer
  Dim intTry As Integer

  Set wrk = DBEngine(0)
  Set db = CurrentDb
  Set rst = db.OpenRecordset("Select OrderId, ProductID, UnitPrice " & _
      "From tblOrderDetails Where ProductID > 50", dbOpenDynaset)
  rst.LockEdits = False
  'Begin the Transaction Loop
  wrk.BeginTrans
    'Loop through recordset increasing UnitPrice
    Do Until rst.EOF
      rst.Edit
        rst!UnitPrice = rst!UnitPrice * 1.1
        'Lock Occurs Here for Each Record in the Loop
      rst.Update
      rst.MoveNext
    Loop
  'Commit the Transaction; Everything went as Planned
  'All locks released for ALL records involved in the Process
  wrk.CommitTrans
  Set wrk = Nothing
  Set db = Nothing
  Set rst = Nothing
  Exit Sub

MultiOptimistic_Err:
  Select Case Err.Number
    Case 3197  'Data Has Changed Error
```

```
        If rst.EditMode = dbEditInProgress Then
          intChoice = MsgBox("Overwrite Other User's Changes?", _
              vbYesNoCancel + vbQuestion)
          Select Case intChoice
            Case vbCancel, vbNo
              MsgBox "Update Canceled"
              Resume TransNotSuccessful
            Case vbYes
              rst.Update
              Resume
          End Select
        End If
      Case 3186, 3260  'Locked or Can't be Saved
        intCounter = intCounter + 1
        If intCounter > 2 Then
          intChoice = MsgBox(Err.Description, vbRetryCancel + vbCritical)
          Select Case intChoice
            Case vbRetry
              intCounter = 1
            Case vbCancel
              'User Selected Cancel, Roll Back
              Resume TransNotSuccessful
          End Select
        End If
        DoEvents
        For intTry = 1 To 100
        Next intTry
        Resume
      Case Else
        MsgBox "Error # " & Err.Number & ": " & Err.Description
    End Select

TransNotSuccessful:
  wrk.Rollback
  MsgBox "Warning: Entire Process Rolled Back"
  Set wrk = Nothing
  Set db = Nothing
  Set rst = Nothing
  Exit Sub
End Sub
```

Notice that in the **MultiOptimistic** routine the lock occurs each time the **Update** method is issued. All of the locks are released when the **CommitTrans** is executed. Furthermore, the error handling checks for a 3197 (data has changed) error. The 3197 occurs when the data is changed by another user between the time that the **Edit** method is issued and just before the **Update** method is issued.

33. Advanced Client-Server Techniques

TIP: *The Chap33.mdb file on the companion CD-ROM contains example code in the routines **ADOMultiPessimistic** and **ADOMultiOptimistic** that shows how to perform this type of processing and locking with ADO objects rather than with DAO objects.*

Transaction processing, then, clearly has its own set of issues in any environment. However, in a client-server environment, some issues are different, some are more serious, and some are less serious. The following sections discuss some of the issues surrounding transaction processing in a client-server environment.

Transaction Processing In A Client-Server Environment

When utilizing transactions in a client-server environment, several additional issues must be considered. These issues concern when and how transactions occur, what types of transactions are supported, and what potential problems can occur.

Implicit Transactions And The Client-Server Environment

When explicit transactions aren't used, the way that transactions are committed on the database server depends upon what types of commands are being executed. In general, each and every line of code has an implicit transaction around it. This means that there isn't a way to roll back an action because it's immediately committed on the database server. The exceptions to this rule are any SQL statements issued that modify data. These SQL statements (**UPDATE**, **INSERT**, and **APPEND**) are executed in batches. This means a transaction loop is implicitly placed around the entire statement. If any records involved in the SQL statement can't be updated successfully, the entire **UPDATE**, **INSERT**, or **APPEND** is rolled back.

Explicit Transactions And The Client-Server Environment

When explicit transactions are used, ODBC or OLE DB (depending on which object set you're using) translates the **BeginTrans**, **CommitTrans**, and **Rollback** methods to the appropriate syntax of the back-end server and the transaction processes as expected. The main exception to this rule is when transactions aren't supported by the specific back end that you're using. An example of transaction processing with a SQL Server back end is shown in the following code:

```
Sub TransSQLServer()
  Dim wrk As Workspace
  Dim db As Database
  Dim qdf As QueryDef

  Set wrk = DBEngine(0)
  Set db = CurrentDb
  wrk.BeginTrans
```

```
    Set qdf = db.CreateQueryDef("")
    qdf.Connect = ("ODBC;Database=Pubs" & _
        ";DSN=PublisherData;UID=SA;PWD=")
    qdf.ReturnsRecords = False
    qdf.SQL = "UPDATE sales Set qty = qty + 1 " & _
        "Where Stor_ID = '7067';"
    qdf.Execute
    qdf.SQL = "Update titles Set price = price + 1 " & _
        "Where Type = 'Business'"
    qdf.Execute
  wrk.CommitTrans

TransSQLServer_Exit:
  Set wrk = Nothing
  Set db = Nothing
  Set qdf = Nothing
  Exit Sub

TransSQLServer_Err:
  MsgBox "Error # " & Err.Number & ": " & Err.Description
  wrk.Rollback
  Resume TransSQLServer_Exit
End Sub
```

The **TransSQLServer** routine begins by creating both **Workspace** and **Database** object variables. Next, it executes the **BeginTrans** method on the workspace. It then creates a temporary query definition and sets several properties for the query definition. These include the **Connect** property, the **ReturnsRecords** property, and the **SQL** property. When these properties have been set, the temporary query is executed. The **SQL** property of the query definition is modified and the query is executed again. If both **Execute** methods complete successfully, the **CommitTrans** method is issued on the **Workspace** object. If any error occurs during processing, the **Rollback** method is issued. The "Immediate Solutions" section shows how to perform this explicit-style processing with ADO.

Nested Transactions In A Client-Server Environment

One occasion in which transactions might not perform as expected is when your code employs nested transactions. ODBC doesn't support them. If your code includes nested transactions, all but the outermost transaction loop will be ignored.

Lock Limits In A Client-Server Environment

A potential pitfall when dealing with client-server databases involves lock limits. Many database servers impose strict limits upon how many records can be concurrently locked. As you saw in the code examples within the "Properly Implementing Explicit Transaction Processing" section of this chapter, a transaction loop can potentially lock a significant number of records. It's important to consider the maximum number of locks supported by your back end when employing the use of transaction loops in your VBA code.

Negative Interactions With Server-Specific Transaction Commands

You should never utilize the server-specific transaction commands when building pass-through queries. These server-specific commands can conflict with the **BeginTrans**, **CommitTrans**, and **Rollback** methods, causing confusion and potential data corruption.

All the discussions that we've had so far of what to do to improve your application's client-server processing have focused, for the most part, on what to do from the client side of the communication. However, you can use some important techniques at the server to improve processing. The following sections discuss some of these techniques, with a specific eye toward SQL Server because of Access 2000's close integration with SQL Server 7. Although the techniques discussed in the remainder of this chapter may have different names or specific implementations within other database server products, the logic is the same. Check your server product for specifics.

Now that we have briefly considered some of the issues surrounding transaction processing, both at the local level and in the client-server environment, let's move on to more specific considerations of some of the issues surrounding the use of client-server database products. One of the biggest differences between programming for Access and programming for client-server is the use of stored procedures and extended SQL code in the client-server environment. The following sections continue our discussion of client-server issues with consideration of stored procedures.

Managing Stored Procedures And Using Flow-Control Statements

As your systems become more complex, you'll need to spend more time carefully integrating SQL code with your host application code. In the following sections, you'll review some of the logic and flow control statements that you have available to you in your SQL code.

At a high level, stored procedures are a way you can create routines and procedures that are run on the server, by server processes. These routines can be started when called by an application or by data integrity rules or triggers (triggers are explained in detail later in this chapter).

The benefit of stored procedures comes from the fact that they run within the server environment on the server. Although this might not seem to be an obvious advantage at first, it goes to the heart of the client-server model. Because the server environment is the manager of any databases in your system once you fully transition to the client-server model, it makes sense that it would be the best place to run the stored procedures against that data. Stored procedures can return values, modify values, and be used to compare a user-supplied value against the prerequisites for information in the system. They run quickly, with the added horsepower of the average server hardware, and they're database-aware and able to take advantage of most servers' optimizers for best performance at runtime. In general, you can think of a stored procedure as being similar to a query definition in Access 2000.

You can also pass values to a stored procedure, and it can return values that aren't necessarily part of an underlying table but are, instead, calculated during the running of the stored procedure. The benefits of stored procedures in a client-server implementation, from a high-level perspective, include the following:

- *Performance*—Because stored procedures run on the server, typically a more powerful machine, the execution time is generally much less than at the workstation. In addition, because the database information is readily at hand and on the same system physically, there's no wait for records to pass over the network for processing. Instead, the stored procedure has immediate, ready access to the database, which makes working with the information extremely fast.

- *Client-server development benefits*—By breaking apart the client and server development tasks, you can sometimes help to decrease the time needed to bring your projects to completion. You can develop the server-side pieces separately from the client-side pieces, and you can reuse the server-side components between client-side applications.

- *Security*—You can use stored procedures as a tool to apply some serious security to your server-side databases. You can create stored procedures for all add, change, delete, and list operations and make it so you can programmatically control each of these aspects of information access.

- *Server-side enforcement of data-oriented rules*—This is ultimately one of the most important reasons for using an intelligent database engine. The stored procedures let you put into place the rules and other logic that help control the information put into your system.

WARNING! *When you design for the client-server model, it's critical that you keep the model in mind when you're building your systems. Remember, data management belongs on the server, and data presentation and display manipulation for reports and inquiries should reside on the client in the ideal model. As you build systems, be on the lookout for those items that can be moved to the different ends of the model to optimize the user's experience with your application.*

Although SQL is defined as a nonprocedural language, SQL Server permits the use of flow-control keywords. You use the flow-control keywords to create a procedure you can store for subsequent execution. You can use these stored procedures to perform operations with a SQL Server database and its tables instead of writing programs using VBA to perform these operations.

Stored procedures are compiled the first time that they're run and are stored in a system table of the current database. When they're compiled, they're optimized to select the best path to access information in the tables. This optimization takes into account the actual data patterns in the table, indexes that are available, table loading, and more. These compiled stored procedures can greatly enhance the performance of your system.

Another benefit of stored procedures is that you can execute a stored procedure on either a local or remote SQL Server. This enables you to run processes on other machines and work with information across servers, not just local databases.

An application program written in Access can also execute stored procedures, providing an optimum solution between the client-side software and SQL Server.

Although an in-depth exploration of stored procedures is beyond the scope of this chapter, it's worthwhile to take a brief look at how to define stored procedures—a process you can actually perform by sending SQL statements to the server from your programs. In the following sections, we consider how to define and manage stored procedures. We begin with a discussion of how to create a stored procedure.

Defining Stored Procedures

You use the **CREATE PROCEDURE** statement to create a stored procedure. Permission to execute the procedure you create is set by default to the owner of the database. An owner of the database can change the permissions to allow other users to execute the procedure. The maximum stored procedure name length is 30 characters. The SQL syntax that you use to define a new procedure is as follows:

```
CREATE PROCEDURE [owner,] procedure_name [;number]
[@parameter_name datatype [=default] [OUTput]
...
[@parameter_name datatype [=default] [OUTput]
[FOR REPLICATION] | [WITH RECOMPILE] , ENCRYPTION
AS sql_statements
```

The following code fragment (which you can execute from the SQL Enterprise Manager [ISQL/W] tool or from the SQL Enterprise Manager's Query tool) creates a simple procedure that contains a **SELECT** statement to display all rows of a table. After the procedure is created, its name is entered on a line to execute the procedure. If you precede the name of a stored procedure with other statements, you use the **EXEC[UTE]** procedure name statement to execute the procedure.

```
CREATE PROCEDURE all_employees
AS SELECT * FROM employees
EXEC all_employees
```

As you can see, the code simply creates the **all_employees** stored procedure, with the definition "**SELECT * FROM employees**." It then executes the stored procedure, which might return values similar to the following in the Query tab of the Query tool you're using:

```
Name                    Department              Badge
--------------------    --------------------    ----------
Lars Klander            Tech Support            1234
Dave Mercer             MIS Admin               4321
(2 row(s) affected)
```

You can create a new procedure in the current database only. If you're working in ISQL or ISQL/W, you can execute the **USE** statement followed by the name of the database to set the current database to the database in which the procedure should be created. You can use any Transact-SQL statement in a stored procedure with the exception of **CREATE** statements.

33. Advanced Client-Server Techniques

When you submit a stored procedure to the system, SQL Server compiles and verifies the routines within it. If any problems are found, the procedure is rejected and you'll need to determine what the problem is before resubmitting the routine. If your stored procedure references another as yet unimplemented stored procedure, you'll receive a warning message, but the routine will still be installed. If you leave the system with the stored procedure that you previously referred to uninstalled, the user will receive an error message at runtime.

Although stored procedures—like Access queries—are obviously powerful and important tools, by themselves they are rather generic. However, adding parameters to stored procedures makes them extremely useful and powerful. The following section discusses how to create parameterized procedures.

Using Parameters With Procedures

Stored procedures are very powerful, but to be most effective, the procedure must be somewhat dynamic, which enables you, the developer, to pass in values to be considered during the functioning of the stored procedure. Here are some general guidelines for using parameters with stored procedures:

- You can define one or more parameters in a procedure.

- You use parameters as named storage locations just like you would use the parameters as variables in VBA.

- You precede the name of a parameter with an at symbol (@) to designate it as a parameter.

- Parameter names are local to the procedure in which they're defined.

- You can use parameters to pass information into a procedure from the line that executes the parameter. You place the parameters after the name of the procedure on a command line, with commas to separate the list of parameters if there is more than one. You use system data types to define the type of information to be expected as a parameter.

In the following SQL code fragment, the procedure is defined with three input parameters. The defined input parameters appear within the procedure in the position of values in the **VALUE** clause of an **INSERT** statement. When the procedure is executed, three literal values are passed into the **INSERT** statement within the procedure as a parameter list. A **SELECT** statement is executed after the stored procedure is executed to verify that a new row was added through the procedure.

```
CREATE PROCEDURE sampproc (@p1 char(15), @p2 char(20), @p3 int) as
INSERT INTO Workers
VALUES (@p1, @p2, @p3)

sampproc 'Dave Mercer','MIS Management',4321
```

After the creation of the procedure and the insertion of the worker using the stored procedure, you can check the insertion using the following code:

```
SELECT * FROM Workers
WHERE Badge=4321
```

This code would then return values similar to the following in the Results tab of the Query window:

```
Name                            Department        Badge
------------------------------- ---------------- ----------
Dave Mercer                     MIS Management   4321
(1 row(s) affected)
```

Clearly, using stored procedures from the ISQL or ISQL/W or utility is a simple matter. Similarly, invoking a procedure from your application can be accomplished with only a single statement. The following section discusses how your application can call stored procedures from code.

Calling Stored Procedures From Your Application

Before you call stored procedures from the Access and VBA application environments, you should know about a few useful tricks. For starters, when your stored procedures take parameters, you have a couple of different options.

First, you can always provide all parameters in the order in which they're declared. Although this is easy to develop for, consider carefully whether this makes sense in the long run. There'll probably be cases in which you want to make a multipurpose stored procedure that calls for more parameters than would be required, on the whole, for any given call. In these cases, you're *expecting* to have some parameters that aren't specified in each call.

You use a test for **Null** on a parameter to determine whether it was provided. This means you can test directly against **Null**, or you can use the **IsNull** comparison operator.

On the application side, it can be quite cumbersome to have to specify each value on every call to the stored procedure, even in cases in which the value is **Null**. In these cases, the calling application can use *named arguments* to pass information to SQL Server and the stored procedure. For example, if your stored procedure allows up to three different arguments—name, address, and phone—you can call the routine as follows:

```
Exec sp_routine @name="Dave Mercer"
```

When you provide the name of the argument being passed, SQL Server can map it to its corresponding parameter. This is, typically, the best way to pass information to SQL Server, and it also helps make the code more readable because you can tell which parameters are being passed.

In general, you'll use the ADO **Command** object and its **Execute** method to send commands down the wire to the SQL Server. Code to execute a stored procedure named **sp_routine** might look similar to the following:

```
cmdLocal.CommandText = "Exec sp_routine @name=""" & strNameParam & """"
Set rstLocal = cmdLocal.Execute()
```

Inevitably, whenever you create a stored procedure, there will come a time when you need to either change the procedure or drop it entirely from the database. The next section discusses how to modify or delete procedures after their creation.

Making Changes And Dropping Stored Procedures

Two closely related tasks that you'll no doubt have to perform are making changes to existing stored procedures and removing stored procedures that are no longer used. In the next two sections, you see exactly how you accomplish both of these tasks and understand why they're so closely related.

Changing An Existing Stored Procedure

Stored procedures can't be modified in place, so you're forced to drop the procedure first, then create it again. Unfortunately, there's no **ALTER** statement that can be used to modify the contents of an existing procedure. This stems largely from the query plan that's created and from the fact that stored procedures are compiled after they're initiated. Because the routines are compiled, and the query plan relies on the compiled information, SQL Server uses a binary version of the stored procedure when it's executed. It would be difficult or impossible to convert from the binary representation of the stored procedure back to English to allow for edits. For this reason, it's imperative that you maintain a copy of your stored procedures in a location other than SQL Server. Although SQL Server can produce the code that was used to create the stored procedure, you should always maintain a backup copy.

TIP: *You can pull the text associated with a stored procedure by using the **sp_helptext** system stored procedure. The syntax of **sp_helptext** is as follows:*

```
sp_helptext procedure name
```

Alternatively, if you want to review the stored procedure in the Enterprise Manager, you can do so by selecting the Database menu, Objects submenu, Stored

Procedures option, then double-clicking the stored procedure you want to view. The result isn't just a listing of the stored procedure, but also the proper statement to drop it and insert a new copy, should you so desire.

Removing Existing Stored Procedures

You should use the **DROP PROCEDURE** statement to drop a stored procedure that you've created. Multiple procedures can be dropped with a single **DROP PROCEDURE** statement by listing multiple procedures separated by commas after the keywords **DROP PROCEDURE** in the syntax:

```
DROP PROCEDURE procedure_name_1, ...,procedure_name_n
```

Multiple versions of a procedure can't be selectively dropped. All versions of a procedure with the same name must be dropped at the same time by using the **DROP PROCEDURE** statement that specifies the procedure without a version number.

Although it is not crucial to understand how the server manages procedures, it is useful. The following section discusses the methods used by the server to resolve and compile stored procedures.

Understanding Procedure Resolution And Compilation

The benefit of using a stored procedure for the execution of a set of Transact-SQL statements is that it's compiled the first time that it's run. During compilation, the Transact-SQL statements in the procedure are converted from their original character representation into an executable form. During compilation, any objects that are referenced in procedures are also converted to alternate representations. For example, table names are converted to their object IDs and column names to their column IDs.

An execution plan is also created just as it would be for the execution of even a single Transact-SQL statement. The execution plan contains, for example, the indexes to be used to retrieve rows from tables that are referenced by the procedure. The execution plan is kept in a cache and is used to perform the queries of the procedure each time it's subsequently executed. In general, the procedure will always execute from the cache, unless certain conditions occur that result in recompilation of the procedure. The following section discusses automatic recompilation of procedures.

Automatic Recompilation

Normally, the procedure's execution plan is run from the memory cache of procedures—a process that helps the procedure to execute rapidly. A procedure, however, is automatically recompiled under the circumstances listed on the next page.

- A procedure is always recompiled when SQL Server is started, usually after a reboot of the underlying operating system, and when the procedure is first executed after it has been created.

- A procedure's execution plan is also automatically recompiled whenever an index on a table referenced in the procedure is dropped. A new execution plan must be compiled because the current one references an object, the index, for the retrieval of the rows of a table that doesn't exist. The execution plan must be redone to permit the queries of the procedure to be performed.

- Compilation of the execution plan is also reinitialized if the execution plan in the cache is currently in use by another user. A second copy of the execution plan is created for the second user. If the first copy of the execution plan weren't in use, it could have been used rather than a new execution plan being created. When a user finishes executing a procedure, the execution plan is available in the cache for reuse by another user with appropriate permissions.

- A procedure is also automatically recompiled if the procedure is dropped and re-created. All copies of the execution plan in the cache are removed because the new procedure may be substantially different from the older version, and a new execution plan is necessary.

Note that because SQL Server attempts to optimize stored procedures by caching the most recently used routines, it's still possible that an older execution plan, one previously loaded in the cache, may be used in place of the new execution plan.

To prevent this problem, you must both drop and re-create the procedure or stop and restart SQL Server to flush the procedure cache and ensure that the new procedure is the only one that will be used when the procedure is executed.

You can also create the procedure using a **WITH RECOMPILE** option so the procedure is automatically recompiled each time it's executed. You should do this if the tables accessed by the queries in a procedure are very dynamic. Dynamic tables have rows added, deleted, and updated frequently, which results in frequent changes to the indexes that are defined for the tables.

In other cases, you may want to force a recompilation of a procedure when it wouldn't be done automatically. For example, if the statistics used to determine whether an index should be used for a query are updated, or an entire index is created for a table, recompilation isn't automatic. You can use the **WITH RECOMPILE** clause on the **EXECUTE** statement when you execute the procedure to do a recompilation. The syntax of the **EXECUTE** statement with a recompile clause is as follows:

```
EXECUTE procedure_name AS
    Transact-SQL statement(s)
WITH RECOMPILE
```

If the procedure you're working with uses parameters and these parameters control the functionality of the routine, you may want to use the **WITH RECOMPILE** option. This is because within the stored procedure, if the routine's parameters may determine the best execution path, it may be beneficial to have the execution plan determined at runtime, rather than determining it once. Then, the server will use the plan determined at runtime for all accesses to the stored procedure during that execution and will compute a new execution plan the next time the program is executed.

TIP: *It may be difficult to determine whether a procedure should be created with the **WITH RECOMPILE** option. If in doubt, you'll probably be better served by not creating the procedure with the **WITH RECOMPILE** option. This is because, if you create a procedure with the **WITH RECOMPILE** option, the procedure is recompiled each time the procedure is executed, and you may waste valuable CPU time to perform these compiles. You can still add the **WITH RECOMPILE** clause to force a recompilation when you execute the procedure.*

WARNING! *You can't use the WITH RECOMPILE option in a CREATE PROCEDURE statement that contains the FOR REPLICATION option. You use the FOR REPLICATION option to create a procedure that's executed during replication.*

You can add the **ENCRYPTION** option to a **CREATE PROCEDURE** statement to encrypt the definition of the stored procedure that's added to the system table **syscomments**. You use the **ENCRYPTION** option to prevent other users from displaying the definition of your procedure and learning what objects it references and what Transact-SQL statements it contains.

WARNING! *Unless you absolutely must encrypt procedures for security reasons, you should leave procedures unencrypted. When you upgrade your database for a version change or to rebuild it, your procedures can only be re-created if the entries in the syscomments table aren't encrypted.*

Stored procedures, together with flow-control statements, are two of the biggest benefits of using a server-side database engine. We have already discussed procedures in detail; the following section moves on to a discussion of flow-control statements.

Using Flow-Control Statements

Transact-SQL contains several statements that are used to change the order of execution of statements within a set of statements, such as a stored procedure. The use of such flow-control statements permits you to organize statements in stored procedures to provide the capabilities of a conventional programming language, such as VBA. You may find that some of the retrieval, update, deletion, addition, and manipulation of the rows of database tables can more easily be performed through the use of flow-control statements in objects, such as stored procedures.

In general, your analysis should focus on the reduction of network traffic. If the decision making (for the flow control) can be effectively made at the server, meaning that the decision is solely dependent on the data within the database itself, you may be better served to place the decision making at the server. If the decision making requires information from the client (front-end), then you're generally better off with the flow control at the front end. As you work more with the client-server environment, you'll become more comfortable with the decision about where to put flow-control code. The most commonly used type of flow-control statement set is the **IF...ELSE** combination. The following section discusses this construction.

Using IF...ELSE With SQL Server

You can use the keywords **IF** and **ELSE** to control conditional execution within a batch, such as a stored procedure. The **IF** and **ELSE** keywords enable you to test a condition and execute either the statements that are part of the **IF** branch or the statements that are part of the **ELSE** branch. You define the condition for testing as an expression following the keyword **IF**. The syntax of an **IF...ELSE** statement is as follows:

```
IF expression
     statement
[ELSE]
     [IF expression]
     statement
```

The keyword **EXISTS** is usually followed by a statement within parentheses when used in an **IF** statement. The **EXISTS** statement is evaluated to either True or False, depending on whether the statement within the parentheses returns one or more rows, or no rows, respectively.

You needn't use an **ELSE** clause as part of an **IF** statement. The simplest form of an **IF** statement is constructed without an **ELSE** clause. In the following example, a **PRINT** statement is used to display a confirmation message that a row exists in a database table. If the row doesn't exist in the table, the message "No entry" is displayed. Unfortunately, the message is also displayed after the verification message is displayed because the code doesn't use the **ELSE** option:

```
IF EXISTS (SELECT * FROM Workers WHERE Badge=1234)
  PRINT 'entry available'
PRINT 'No entry'
```

In the following example, the row isn't found in the table so only the **PRINT** statement that follows the **IF** statement is executed:

```
IF EXISTS (SELECT * FROM Workers WHERE Badge=1235)
  PRINT 'entry available'
PRINT 'No entry'
```

The previous two examples show the problem of using an **IF** statement that doesn't contain an **ELSE** clause. In the examples, it's impossible to prevent the message, "No entry", from appearing. You should add an **ELSE** clause to the **IF** statement to print the **No entry** message if a row isn't found and the condition after the **IF** isn't **True**.

In the following example, the previous examples are rewritten to use **IF** and **ELSE** clauses. If a row that's tested for in the **IF** clause is in the table, only the message "employee present" is displayed. If the row isn't found in the table, only the message "employee not found" is displayed:

```
IF EXISTS (SELECT * FROM employees WHERE name='Bob Smith')
  PRINT 'employee present'
ELSE
  PRINT 'employee not found'
```

WARNING!   Unlike VBA, when used alone, the Transact-SQL IF statement can have only one statement associated with it. As a result, there's no need for a keyword, such as END IF, to define the end of the IF statement. See "Using BEGIN...END" in the next section for information on grouping statements and associating them with an IF...ELSE condition.

In addition to the common **IF...ELSE** construction, you will also frequently use **BEGIN...END** blocks. These blocks allow you to group sets of statements together and are explained in detail in the next section.

Using BEGIN...END

You use the keywords **BEGIN** and **END** to designate a set of Transact-SQL statements to be executed as a unit. You use the keyword **BEGIN** to define the start of a block of Transact-SQL statements. You use the keyword **END** after the last Transact-SQL statement that's part of the same block of statements. **BEGIN...END** uses the following syntax:

```
BEGIN
  statements
END
```

You often use **BEGIN** and **END** with a conditional statement such as an **IF** statement. **BEGIN** and **END** are used in an **IF** or **ELSE** clause to permit multiple Transact-SQL statements to be executed if the expression following the **IF** or **ELSE** clause is **True**. As mentioned earlier, without a **BEGIN** and **END** block enclosing multiple statements, only a single Transact-SQL statement can be executed if the expression in the **IF** or **ELSE** clause is **True**.

The following code shows how to use **BEGIN** and **END** statements with an **IF** statement to define the execution of multiple statements if the condition tested is **True**. The **IF** statement contains only an **IF** clause; no **ELSE** clause is part of the statement.

```
IF EXISTS (SELECT * FROM employees WHERE badge=1234)
  BEGIN
    PRINT 'entry available'
    SELECT name,department FROM employees
        WHERE badge=1234
  END
```

This code will display the text "entry available", then output the information associated with badge 1234. The following code listing adds an **ELSE** clause to the **IF** statement to display a message if the row isn't found:

```
IF EXISTS (SELECT * FROM employees WHERE department='Sales')
  BEGIN
    PRINT 'row(s) found'
    SELECT name, department FROM employees
        WHERE department='Sales'
  END
ELSE
  PRINT 'No entry'
```

As your procedures become more complex, it is likely that you will need to use looping constructs within them to handle specific types of processing. In general, you can use the **WHILE** keyword to indicate a loop, which will iterate until a certain condition is met. The following section explains the use of the **WHILE** keyword.

Using WHILE

You can use the keyword **WHILE** to define a condition that executes one or more Transact-SQL statements when the condition tested evaluates to **True**. The statement that follows the expression of the **WHILE** statement continues to execute as long as the condition tested is **True**. The syntax of the **WHILE** statement is as follows:

```
WHILE
  <boolean_expression>
  <sql_statement>
```

TIP: As with the **IF...ELSE** statements, you can only execute a single SQL statement within the **WHILE** clause. If you need to include more than one statement in the routine, use the **BEGIN...END** construct as described previously.

In the following code fragment, a **WHILE** statement is used to execute a **SELECT** statement that displays a numeric value until the value reaches a limit of five:

```
DECLARE @x int
SELECT @x=1
WHILE @x<5
  BEGIN
    PRINT 'x still less than 5'
    SELECT @x=@x+1
  END
```

You define the datatype of a variable using a **DECLARE** statement to control the way information is represented in the variable. A variable is always preceded by an at sign (@), like a SQL Server parameter. In the example, the value stored in the variable is initialized to one and subsequently incremented. The statements associated with the **WHILE** execute until the variable *x* reaches a value of five.

A more meaningful example of the use of a **WHILE** statement can be shown after two additional Transact-SQL keywords are introduced and explained. An example using **WHILE** along with the keywords **BREAK** and **CONTINUE** will be shown a little later in this chapter. The next section discusses the use of **BREAK** together with **WHILE**.

Using BREAK

You use the keyword **BREAK** inside a block of Transact-SQL statements that's within a conditional **WHILE** statement to end the execution of the statements. The execution of a **BREAK** results in the first statement following the end of block to begin executing. The syntax of a **BREAK** clause is as follows:

```
WHILE
  <boolean_expression>
  <sql_statement>
BREAK
  <sql_statement>
```

In the following code fragment, the **BREAK** within the **WHILE** statement causes the statement within the **WHILE** to terminate. The **PRINT** statement executes once because the **PRINT** statement is located before the **BREAK**. After the **BREAK** is encountered, the statements in the **WHILE** clause aren't executed again:

```
DECLARE @x int
SELECT @x=1
WHILE @x<5
  BEGIN
    PRINT 'x still less than 5'
    SELECT @x=@x+1
    BREAK
  END
```

In general, a **WHILE** loop will iterate until it encounters either the ending condition or a **BREAK** statement. However, there may be situations within a **WHILE** loop when you want the loop to iterate immediately, rather than executing the remaining code within the loop. In such cases, you can use the **CONTINUE** keyword, explained in the next section.

Using CONTINUE

You use a **CONTINUE** keyword to form a clause within a conditional statement, such as a **WHILE** statement, to explicitly continue the set of statements that are contained within the conditional statement. The syntax of the **CONTINUE** clause is as follows:

```
WHILE
  <boolean_expression>
  <statement>
BREAK
  <statement>
CONTINUE
```

In the following code fragment, a **CONTINUE** is used within a **WHILE** statement to explicitly define that execution of the statements within the **WHILE** statement should continue as long as the condition specified in the expression that follows **WHILE** is **True**. The use of **CONTINUE** in the following example skips the final **PRINT** statement:

```
DECLARE @x int
SELECT @x = 1
WHILE @x < 5
  BEGIN
    PRINT 'x still less than 5'
```

```
    SELECT @x = @x + 1
    CONTINUE
    PRINT 'this statement will not execute'
END
```

Needless to say, you should generally avoid using **BREAK** and **CONTINUE** whenever you can. They are not only bad programming style, but they tend to be confusing to anyone who reads your procedures subsequently. Instead, you should carefully construct your loops so that your ending conditions are correctly met during the loop's normal execution. However, there will occasionally be times when using either of these statements will be necessary for your programming, so don't discard their use entirely.

In addition to the conditional-construct keywords that you have seen in this section, there are also a large number of additional procedure and batch keywords. In the following section, we will discuss the use of some of these keywords.

Using Additional Procedure And Batch Keywords

Several additional keywords can be used within stored procedures or batches of Transact-SQL commands. These additional keywords don't fall into a single descriptive category of similar function. Some of these keywords include **GOTO**, **RETURN**, **RAISERROR**, **WAITFOR**, and **CASE**.

Using GOTO

You use a **GOTO** to perform a transfer from a statement to another statement that contains a user-defined label. A **GOTO** statement used alone is unconditional. The statement that contains the destination label name follows rules for identifiers and is followed by a colon (:).

You only use the label name without the colon on the **GOTO** line. The syntax of the **GOTO** statement is as follows:

```
label:
GOTO label
```

The following code fragment shows the use of the **GOTO** statement that transfers control to a statement displaying the word *yes* until the value of a variable reaches a specified value. The **COUNT** was turned off before execution of the statements in the example:

```
DECLARE @count smallint
SELECT @count =1
```

```
RESTART:
  PRINT 'yes'
  SELECT @count =@count + 1
  WHILE @count <= 4
    GOTO RESTART
```

As you have seen, a **GOTO** statement transfers execution within the stored procedure. However, when the procedure finishes its execution—as all procedures eventually should—you should explicitly exit the procedure. There may also be times when you need to return a value to the calling program. The **RETURN** statement exits the procedure and lets you return a value, as described in the following section.

Using RETURN

You use the **RETURN** statement to formally exit from a query or procedure and optionally provide a value to the calling routine. A **RETURN** is often used when one procedure is executed from within another. The **RETURN** statement, when used alone, is unconditional, though you can use the **RETURN** within a conditional **IF** or **WHILE** statement. The syntax of the **RETURN** statement is as follows:

```
RETURN [integer]
```

You can use a **RETURN** statement at any point in a batch or procedure. Any statements that follow the **RETURN** aren't executed. A **RETURN** is similar to a **BREAK** with one difference: A **RETURN**, unlike a **BREAK**, can be used to return an integer value to the procedure that invoked the procedure containing the **RETURN**. Execution of statements continues at the statement following the statement that executed the procedure originally.

To understand the use of the **RETURN** statement, you must first understand the action performed by SQL Server when a procedure completes execution. SQL Server always makes an integer value available when a procedure ends. A value of zero indicates that the procedure executed successfully. Negative values from –1 to –99 indicate reasons for the failure of statements within the procedure. These integer values are always returned at the termination of a procedure even if a **RETURN** statement isn't present in a procedure.

You can optionally use an integer value that follows the **RETURN** statement to replace the SQL Server value with your own user-defined value. You should use nonzero integer values so your return status values don't conflict with the SQL Server status values. If no user-defined return value is provided, the SQL Server value is used. If more than one error occurs, the status with the highest absolute value is returned. You can't return a **NULL** value with a **RETURN** statement. Table 33.1 shows several of the return status values that are reserved by SQL Server.

Table 33.1   Selected Microsoft SQL Server status values.

Return Value	Meaning
0	Successful execution
-1	Missing object
-2	Datatype error
-3	Process was chosen as a deadlock victim
-4	Permission error
-5	Syntax error
-6	Miscellaneous user error
-7	Resource error, such as out of space
-8	Nonfatal internal problem
-9	System limit was reached
-10	Fatal internal inconsistency
-11	Fatal internal inconsistency
-12	Table or index is corrupt
-13	Database is corrupt
-14	Hardware error

You must provide a local variable that receives the returned status in the **EXECUTE** statement, which invokes the procedure that returns status. The syntax to specify a local variable for the returned status value is the following:

```
EXEC[ute] @return_status=procedure_name
```

You can, therefore, pass in a variable from the ADO **Command** object and use the return value from the stored procedure with the variable to perform client-side processing in the case of a return from a server-side procedure. The most commonly returned value from a procedure, however, is one that you send back in response to an error in processing. In such cases, you should use the **RAISERROR** statement to let the user know of the problem. The following section discusses the **RAISERROR** statement.

Using RAISERROR

You use the **RAISERROR** statement to return a user-specified message in the same form that SQL Server returns errors. The **RAISERROR** also sets a system flag to record that an error has occurred. The syntax of the **RAISERROR** statement is shown on the top of the next page.

```
RAISERROR (<integer_expression>|<'text of message'>,
    [severity] [, state]
    [, argument1] [, argument2] )
[WITH LOG]
```

The **integer_expression** is a user-specified error or message number and must be in the range 50,000 to 2,147,483,647. The **integer_expression** is placed in the global variable, **@@ERROR**, which stores the last error number returned. An error message can be specified as a string literal or specified through a local variable. The text of the message can be up to 255 characters and is used to indicate a user-specified error message. A local variable that contains an error message can be used in place of the text of the message. **RAISERROR** always sets a default severity level of 16 for the returned error message.

You can also add your message text and an associated message number to the system table **sysmessages**. You use the system stored procedure, **sp_addmessage**, to add a message with a message identification number within the range 50,001 and 2,147,483,647. The syntax of the **sp_addmessage** system procedure is as follows:

```
sp_addmessage message_id, severity,
    'message text' [, language [, {true | false}
    [, REPLACE]]]
```

> **WARNING!** *If you enter a user-specified error number that hasn't been added to the sysmessages table and don't explicitly specify the message text, you'll receive an error that the message can't be located in the system table, as shown here:*
>
> *"RAISERROR could not locate entry for error 99999 in Sysmessages"*

User-defined error messages generated with a **RAISERROR** statement, but without a number in the **sysmessages** table, return a message identification number of 50,000.

The severity level is used to indicate the degree or extent of the error condition encountered. Although severity levels can be assigned in the range of one through 25, you should usually assign your system message a severity level value from 11 to 16.

Severity levels of 11 through 16 are designed to be assigned through the **sp_addmessage** statement, and you can't assign a severity level from 19 to 25 unless you're logged in as the administrator. Severity levels 17 through 19 are more severe software or hardware errors, which may not permit your subsequent statements to execute correctly.

Severity levels of 20 through 25 are severe errors and won't permit subsequent Transact-SQL statements to execute. System messages that have severity levels over 19 can be problems, such as connection problems between a client system and the database server system or corrupted data in the database.

TIP: *Microsoft suggests that severe errors (that is, those that have a severity level of 19 or higher) should also notify the database administrator in addition to the user. The database administrator needs to know of these problems because such problems are likely to impact many different users and should be attended to as soon as possible.*

When specifying messages, you enter an error message of up to 255 characters within single quotes. The remaining parameters of the **sp_addmessage** procedure are optional. The language parameter specifies one of the languages SQL Server was installed with. U.S. English is the default language if the parameter is omitted.

The next parameter, either **True** or **False**, controls whether the system message is automatically written to the Windows NT application event log. Use **True** to have the system message written to the event log. In addition, **True** results in the message being written to the SQL Server error log file.

The last parameter, **REPLACE**, is used to specify that you want to replace an existing user-defined message in the **sysmessages** table with a new entry.

You can use the system-stored procedure, **sp_dropmessage**, to remove a user-defined message from the system table **sysmessages** when it's no longer needed. The syntax of the **sp_dropmessage** is as follows:

```
sp_dropmessage [message_id [, language | 'all']]
```

You're only required to enter the message number to drop the message. The two additional optional parameters permit you to specify the language from which the message should be dropped. You can use the keyword **all** to drop the user-defined message from all languages.

Using WAITFOR

You use a **WAITFOR** statement to specify a time, a time interval, or an event for executing a statement, statement block, stored procedure, or transaction. The syntax of the **WAITFOR** statement is as follows:

```
WAITFOR {DELAY <'time'> | TIME <'time'> | ERROREXIT | PROCESSEXIT |
    MIRROREXIT}
```

The meaning of each of the keywords that follow the **WAITFOR** keyword is shown in Table 33.2.

*Table 33.2   Descriptions of the keywords for the **WAITFOR** statement.*

Keyword	Description
DELAY	Specifies an interval or time to elapse
TIME	A specified time, no date portion, of up to 24 hours
ERROREXIT	Until a process terminates abnormally
PROCESSEXIT	Until a process terminates normally or abnormally
MIRROREXIT	Until a mirrored device fails

In the following example of a **WAITFOR** statement, a **DELAY** is used to specify that a pause of 40 seconds is taken before the subsequent **SELECT** statement is executed:

```
WAITFOR DELAY '00:00:40'
SELECT * FROM employees
```

In the following code, a **TIME** is used to wait until 3:10:51 P.M. of the current day until the subsequent **SELECT** statement is executed.

```
WAITFOR TIME '15:10:51'
SELECT * FROM employees
```

Earlier in this chapter, you saw the use of the **IF...THEN** construct. As you saw, it allowed you to perform conditional processing within your procedures based on the result of a specific condition. However, you will often need to make conditional processing decisions based on where a variable falls within a series of values. To meet such requirements, SQL provides the **CASE** keyword, explained within the next section.

Using CASE Expressions

You can use a **CASE** expression to make an execution decision based on multiple options. Using the **CASE** construct, you can create a table that'll be used to look up the results you're testing and apply them to determine what action should be taken. The syntax of the **CASE** expression is as follows:

```
CASE [expression]
WHEN simple expression1|Boolean expression1 THEN expression1
[[WHEN simple expression2|Boolean expression2 THEN expression2] [...]]
     [ELSE expressionN]
END
```

If you use a comparison operator in an expression directly after the **CASE** keyword, the **CASE** expression is called a *searched expression* rather than a *simple*

CASE expression. You can also use a Boolean operator in a searched **CASE** expression.

In a simple **CASE** expression, the expression directly after the **CASE** keyword always exactly matches a value after the **WHEN** keyword. In the following example, a **CASE** expression is used to return a corresponding set of alternate values for three department values of a table company.

```
SELECT name,division=
CASE department
  WHEN "Sales" THEN "Sales & Marketing"
  WHEN "Field Service" THEN "Support Group"
  WHEN "Logistics" THEN "Parts"
  ELSE "Other department"
END,
badge
FROM company
```

If you don't use an **ELSE** as part of the **CASE** expression, a **NULL** is returned for each nonmatching entry.

You'll recall that a searched **CASE** expression can include comparison operators and the use of **AND** as well as **OR** between each Boolean expression to permit an alternate value to be returned for multiple values of the column of a table. Unlike a simple **CASE** expression, each **WHEN** clause isn't restricted to exact matches of the values contained in the table column.

In the following code fragment, comparison values are used in each **WHEN** clause to specify a range of values that are substituted by a single alternative value:

```
SELECT "Hours Worked" =
CASE
  WHEN hours_worked < 40 THEN "Worked Insufficient Hours"
  WHEN hours_worked = 40 THEN "Worked Sufficient Hours"
  WHEN hours_worked > 60 THEN "Overworked"
  ELSE "Outside Range of Permissible Work"
END
FROM pays
```

> **WARNING!**   *You must use compatible data types for the replacement expression of the THEN clause. If the replacement expression of a THEN clause is a data type that's incompatible with the original expression, an error message is returned. For example, a combination of original and replacement data types is compatible if the one is a variable length character data type (VARCHAR) with a maximum length equal to the length of a fixed length character data type (CHAR). In addition, if the two data types in the WHEN and THEN clauses are integer and decimal, the resultant data type returned will be decimal to accommodate the whole and fractional portion of the numeric value.*

You can also use both the **COALESCE** and **NULLIF** functions in a **CASE** expression. You use the **COALESCE** function to return a replacement value for any **NULL** or **NOT NULL** values that are present in, for example, the column of a database table. The syntax of one form of the **COALESCE** function is:

```
COALESCE (expression1, expression2)
```

You can also use a **NULLIF** function with or in place of a **CASE** expression. The **NULLIF** function uses the following syntax:

```
NULLIF (expression1, expression2)
```

Throughout the previous sections, you've studied stored procedures and constructs that you can use to make your procedures more effective. You've also seen how using stored procedures can result in more efficient performance on the part of your applications.

As you've seen time and again, enforcing referential integrity is a crucial concern in any real-world database design. SQL Server provides specific tools, called *triggers*, for providing fine-grained control of referential integrity. In the following sections, you'll learn about triggers and their effective use in a client-server environment.

Understanding SQL Server Triggers

Triggers are methods that SQL Server provides to the application programmer and database analyst to ensure data integrity. These methods are quite useful for those databases that will be accessed from a multitude of different applications because they enable the database to enforce business rules instead of relying on the application software.

SQL Server's capability to manage your information effectively stems from its ability to help you control the data in your system as it flows through the tables and application logic that you build into your application. You've seen how stored procedures enable you to execute logic on the server, and you've seen how you can implement rules and defaults to help further manage the information in the database.

SQL Server considers rules and defaults *before* information is written to the database. They're a sort of "prefilter" for information and can prevent an action against the data item based on their role in controlling the database activity. Triggers, on the other hand, are "postfilters" that execute after the data update passes and SQL Server has considered the rules, defaults, and so on.

A trigger is a special type of stored procedure that SQL Server executes when an insert, modify, or delete operation is performed against a given table. Because triggers run after the operation would take effect, they represent the "final word" on the modification. If the trigger causes a request to fail, SQL Server refuses the information update and returns an error message to the application attempting the transaction.

The most common use of a trigger is to enforce business rules in the database. Triggers are used when the standard constraints or table-based Declarative Referential Integrity (DRI) are inadequate.

TIP: *Triggers run after the application of rules and other referential integrity checks. Therefore, if an operation fails these other checks, the trigger doesn't run. An operation must have otherwise succeeded before SQL Server will consider or execute a trigger's conditions or operations.*

Triggers don't affect the server's performance significantly and are often used to enhance applications that must perform many cascading operations on other tables and rows.

In SQL Server 6.x, Microsoft added American National Standard Institute (ANSI)–compliant DRI statements you can use in the **CREATE TABLE** statement. The types of rules these DRI statements can enforce are relatively complex. When these DRI statements are used in a **CREATE TABLE** statement, understanding exactly how SQL Server created the table can be quite difficult.

Besides the inability to perform complex business rule analysis based on values supplied when a trigger executes, DRI has one important limitation: The current implementation doesn't permit referencing values in other databases. Although this problem might seem relatively insignificant, it has a substantial impact on programmers attempting to write distributed applications that might need to check data constraints or values on other databases and servers. In general, however, when you are performing data integrity checks—either for distributed environments or most other processing environments—triggers are your most value asset. Modifiable, and with a high degree of programmer control, triggers are an important addition to your client-server tool chest. The following sections discuss triggers in detail.

Creating Triggers

When you create a trigger, you must be the database's owner. This requirement might seem odd at first, but if you consider what's happening, it really makes a lot of sense. When you add a trigger to a column, row, or table, you're changing how the table can be accessed, how other objects can relate to it, and so on. Therefore, you're actually changing the database schema. Of course, this type of operation is reserved for the database owner, protecting against someone inadvertently modifying your system's layout.

Creating a trigger is much like declaring a stored procedure, and it has a similar syntax, as shown here:

```
CREATE TRIGGER [owner.]trigger_name
ON [owner.]table_name
FOR {INSERT, UPDATE, DELETE}
[WITH ENCRYPTION]
AS sql_statements
```

The **trigger_name** must conform to standard SQL Server naming conventions. The **INSERT**, **UPDATE**, and **DELETE** keywords define the trigger's scope, determining the actions that initiate the trigger.

The **WITH ENCRYPTION** option enables developers to prevent users in their environment from reading the trigger's text after it has been loaded onto the server. The option is convenient for third-party application developers who embed SQL Server into their products and don't want to enable their customers to disassemble and modify the code. SQL Server stores the text of a trigger in the system catalog table **syscomments**. Use the **WITH ENCRYPTION** option carefully because if the original trigger text is lost, you can't restore the encrypted text from **syscomments**.

> **WARNING!**   As with stored procedures, SQL Server uses the unencrypted text of a trigger stored in syscomments when a database is upgraded to a newer version. If the text is encrypted, you can't update and restore the trigger to the new database. Make sure that the original text is available to upgrade the database when necessary.

A trigger can contain any number of SQL statements in Transact-SQL if you enclose them in valid **BEGIN** and **END** delimiters. The next section describes limitations on the SQL permitted in a trigger.

> **TIP:**   When a trigger executes, SQL Server creates a special table into which it places the data that caused the trigger to execute. The table is either **inserted** for insert and update operations or **deleted** for delete and update operations. Because triggers execute after an operation, the rows in the **inserted** table always duplicate one or more records in the trigger's base table. Make sure that a correct join identifies all the record's characteristics being affected in the trigger table so that the trigger doesn't accidentally modify the data itself.

Clearly, triggers are useful and powerful tools at your disposal. However, they do have limitations—just like any other programming tool. The following section discusses some of the limitations of triggers that you should be aware of during your design process.

Examining Limitations Of Triggers

SQL Server limits the types of SQL statements you can execute while performing a trigger's actions. Most of these limitations derive from the fact that you can't roll back the trigger's SQL, which you might need to do if the update, insert, or delete causing the trigger to execute in the first place is also rolled back.

The following is a list of Transact-SQL statements that you can't use in a trigger's body text. SQL Server rejects the compilation and storing of a trigger with these statements:

- All database- and object-creation statements, including **CREATE DATA-BASE, TABLE, INDEX, PROCEDURE, DEFAULT, RULE, TRIGGER**, and **VIEW**

- All **DROP** statements

- Database object modification statements, including **ALTER TABLE** and **ALTER DATABASE**

- **TRUNCATE TABLE**

- Object permissions, including **GRANT** and **REVOKE**

- **UPDATE STATISTICS**

- **RECONFIGURE**

- Database load operations, including **LOAD DATABASE** and **LOAD TRANS-ACTION**

- All physical disk modification statements, including anything starting with the **DISK** keyword

- Temporary table creation, either implicit through **CREATE TABLE** or explicit through **SELECT INTO**

Additionally, you need to understand the following limitations clearly:

- You can't create a trigger on a view but only on the base table or tables in which you created the view.

- Any **SET** operations that change the environment, although valid, are in effect only for the life of the trigger. All values return to their previous states after the trigger finishes executing.

- You can't execute a trigger by manipulating binary large object (BLOB) columns of data type **Text** or **Image**, whether logged or not by the database.

- You shouldn't use **SELECT** operations that return result sets from a trigger because of the special handling of result sets required by the client application code, whether in a stored procedure or not. Carefully ensure that all **SELECT** operations read their values into locally defined variables available in the trigger.

Now that you understand a little more about the creation and limitations of triggers, let's consider how you can actually use them within your environment. The following sections discuss the use of triggers with a client-server database.

Using Triggers

Triggers *fire* or *execute* whenever a particular event occurs. The following subsections demonstrate the different events that can cause a trigger to execute and should give you some ideas of what you might have your trigger do when such events occur.

Using INSERT And UPDATE Triggers

INSERT and **UPDATE** triggers are particularly useful because they can enforce referential integrity constraints and ensure that your data is valid before it enters the table. Typically, **INSERT** and **UPDATE** triggers are used to update time stamp columns or to verify that the data on the columns that the trigger is monitoring meets the criteria required. Use **INSERT** and **UPDATE** triggers when the criteria for verification are more complex than a declarative referential integrity constraint can represent.

In the following code, the trigger executes whenever a record is modified or inserted into the **SALES** table. If the order date isn't during the first 15 days of the month, the record is rejected.

```
CREATE TRIGGER Trig_Ins_Sales
ON SALES
FOR INSERT, UPDATE
AS
  /* declare local variables needed */
  DECLARE @nDayOfMonth tinyint

  /* Find the information about the record inserted */
  SELECT @nDayOfMonth = DatePart( Day, INS.ORD_DATE )
  FROM SALES S, INSERTED INS
  WHERE S.STOR_ID = INS.STOR_ID
  AND S.ORD_NUM = INS.ORD_NUM
  AND S.TITLE_ID = INS.TITLE_ID

  /* Now test rejection criteria and return an error if necessary */
  IF @nDayOfMonth > 15
    BEGIN
      /* Note: Always Rollback first. You can never be sure what
      kind of error processing a client may do that may force locks
      to be held for unnecessary amounts of time */
      ROLLBACK TRAN
```

```
RAISERROR ('Orders must be placed before the 15th of the month',
     16, 10)
End
```

TIP: *Notice how the previous join refers to the inserted table. SQL Server specially creates this logical table to enable you to reference information in the record you're modifying. By using the alias **INS** as shown, you can easily reference the table in the join criteria specified in the **WHERE** clause.*

Notice that the code segment references a new table. If you review the list of tables, you'll notice that the database doesn't include the table. In this case, the inserted table contains a copy of every row that would be added if the transaction is allowed to complete. You use the inserted table's values to feed the information to any comparisons that you want to make to validate the transaction.

The columns in the inserted table exactly match those in the table with which you're working. You can perform comparisons on the columns, as in the example, which compares the columns against the sales database to verify that the sales date is valid.

You can also create triggers that can do their work only if a given column is updated. You can use the **IF UPDATE** statement in your trigger to determine whether the trigger processing should continue:

```
IF UPDATE(au_lname) AND (@@rowcount=1)
  BEGIN
    ...
  END
```

In this case, the only time that the code within the segment executes is when the specific column, **au_lname**, is updated. Keep in mind that although a column is being updated, it isn't necessarily being *changed*. Many applications, including most proprietary systems, simply update the entire record if any change is made.

Before taking further action in the trigger, you might find it helpful to compare the new value against the old value (with the inserted table stores) to see whether the value has indeed changed.

In addition to performing update actions with a trigger, you can also use triggers to perform deletions automatically or stop deletions automatically. The following section discusses the use of **DELETE** triggers in more detail.

Using DELETE Triggers

DELETE triggers are typically used for two reasons. The first reason is to prevent deletion of records that will cause data integrity problems if they, indeed, are deleted. An example of such records are those used as foreign keys to other tables.

The second reason for using a **DELETE** trigger is to perform a cascading delete operation that deletes children records of a master record. You might use such a trigger to delete all the order items from a master sales record.

TIP: *When you create a trigger, remember that it can affect more than one row. You must consider this possibility in any procedure the trigger runs. Be sure you check the* **@@rowcount** *global variable to see exactly what is happening before you begin working with the information.*

Triggers take into account the sum total of all rows the requested operation affects, so they must be capable of considering the different combinations of information in the table and respond according to what you need. For example, if you issue a **DELETE * FROM AUTHORS** *statement, the trigger must accommodate the fact that the statement will delete all records from the* **AUTHORS** *table.*

As you might have guessed already, triggers play an important role in the server's processing at all times, but can play a particularly important role when working with transactions. The following section discusses the use of rollback triggers with transactions.

Performing Special Transaction Management With Rollback Triggers

If you're working with triggers and transactions, you might want to consider working with a special trigger option, the *rollback trigger*:

```
ROLLBACK TRIGGER [with raiserror errornumber [message]]
```

The rollback trigger option is, in essence, an abort-all statement. When a rollback is encountered, the trigger's processing stops and the data modification that caused the trigger to execute in the first place is allowed.

When you use the rollback trigger statement, you have the option—even the responsibility—to indicate an error number and optional message. Except in very rare situations, you should use the **RAISERROR** option because it tells the calling routines you've stopped the action from occurring. The rollback trigger statement doesn't stop processing for a batch of updates; instead, the trigger fails only the current item. Therefore, the code you develop to update the database must check the return state of the update to ensure it succeeded.

When the routine returns from the update operation, always check the **@@ERROR** global variable to ensure that the updates happened as planned.

In addition to such crucial processing as that performed by **DELETE** and **ROLLBACK** triggers, you can also use triggers to assist you in other areas of database management. A useful tool provided to you by triggers is the ability to construct a trigger that sends email. The following section discusses triggers that email in detail.

Using Triggers That Send Email

One of the better features of SQL Server is its capability to invoke behavior directly from the operating system. You must predefine such behavior through SQL Server's extended procedures, but they enable you to create incredibly powerful trigger operations. SQL Server is relatively unique in its capability to support features specific to the operating system. SQL Server can offer this support because it runs only on Windows NT, which has a very standardized programming interface across all its supported hardware platforms.

Triggers can call any of the extended procedures (**xp_***) available to the server and any external procedures you add to the server with the **sp_addextendedproc** system-level stored procedure. In the following code fragment, the trigger demonstrates how to send email when a record is deleted from the underlying **AUTHORS** table.

```
CREATE TRIGGER Trig_Del_Authors_Mail
ON AUTHORS
FOR DELETE
AS
  /* declare some variables to store the author's name */
  DECLARE @sLName varchar(40), @sFName varchar(20),
    @sAuthor varchar(60)

  /* now get the value of the author being removed */
  SELECT @sLName = D.AU_LNAME, @sFName = D.AU_FNAME
    FROM AUTHORS A, DELETED D
    WHERE A.AU_ID = D.AU_ID

  /* Send mail message */
  SELECT @sAuthor = @sLName + ', '' + @sFName
  EXEC master.dbo.xp_sendmail @recipient = ''Acquisitions Editor'',
    @message = ''deleted '' + @sAuthor
GO
```

Although triggers in and of themselves are very useful, and generally not too complex, you can build layers of triggers to create more complexity in your data validation and to perform a variety of tasks in response to a single event. Such constructs are known as *nested triggers* and are explained in the next section.

Using Nested Triggers

You can nest triggers up to 16 layers deep. If nested trigger operations aren't desirable, however, you can configure SQL Server to disallow them. To toggle this option, use the nested trigger option in the **sp_configure** system stored procedure.

Triggers become nested when the execution of one trigger modifies another table that includes another trigger, which, therefore, executes.

TIP: *You can check your nesting level at any time by inspecting the value in **@@NestLevel**. The value is between 0 and 16.*

SQL Server can't detect nesting that causes an infinite loop during the creation of a trigger until the situation occurs at execution time. A trigger can cause an infinite loop. For example, suppose that **TABLE1** includes **TRIG1**, which executes when **TABLE1** is updated. When executed, **TRIG1** causes an update on **TABLE2**. **TABLE2** has a similar trigger, **TRIG2**, that executes when **TABLE2** is updated and causes an update of **TABLE1**. Thus, if a user updates either table, the two triggers continue executing each other indefinitely. On detecting such an occurrence, SQL Server shuts down or cancels the trigger.

If a trigger causes an additional modification of the table from which it executes, the trigger doesn't cause itself to execute recursively. The current version of SQL Server has no support for *reentrant* or *recursive* stored procedures or triggers.

> **WARNING!**   **Triggers and DRI usually don't work well together. Wherever possible, you should implement either triggers or DRI for integrity constraints, but not both.**

Dropping Triggers

You might want to remove triggers from a table or tables for several reasons. You might, for example, be moving into a production environment and want to remove any triggers you put in place to ensure good quality but which were hurting performance. You might also want to drop a trigger simply to replace it with a newer version.

To drop a trigger, use the following syntax:

```
DROP TRIGGER [owner.]trigger_name[,[owner.]trigger_name...]
```

Dropping a trigger isn't necessary if a new trigger is to be created to replace the existing one. When you drop a table, you also drop all its child-related objects, including triggers.

Access Data Projects

With the addition of new Access Data Projects (ADPs), the new Access 2000 supports client-server design at a level never before possible in Access. Access projects let you actually design client-server databases directly against an SQL Server back end and maintain them from within Access. Moreover, the project is essentially a very thin client against the back end database.

The support within Access for new Data Access Pages (DAPs) makes designing Web pages that work against an SQL Server database easier than ever before. The Access Database window even supports new objects to help you work with SQL Server databases when you create an ADP.

When you are working with an ADP, the Database window adds support for views, database diagrams, and stored procedures and removes queries from the accessible objects. The following sections briefly discuss these new objects, and we'll also look briefly at database diagrams.

Views allow you to specify exactly how a user will see data. They can be thought of as stored queries. Stored procedures are precompiled SQL statements. Because stored procedures are precompiled, they run much more quickly than straight SQL queries do—they are, functionally, equivalent to Jet query objects created in Access. Triggers can be very complex, and they have several rules about how and when they should be created. Triggers allow you to ensure data integrity, domain integrity, and referential integrity within your database. All of these objects can be defined within ADPs using the guidelines that have been laid out earlier in this chapter.

ADPs are a powerful and useful tool for front-end client-server development; in the event you want to develop SQL Server applications directly from Access, you can use ADPs. In addition to all the SQL Server tools discussed earlier in this chapter, you can also use database diagrams to create databases and specify specifics about the database on an SQL Server.

Using Database Diagrams To Create Databases

You can use Database Diagrams to create, edit, or delete database objects for SQL Server or MSDE databases while you're directly connected to the database in which those objects are stored. Database diagrams graphically represent tables, the columns they contain, and the relationships between them. You can use database diagrams to do the following:

- Simply view the tables in your database and their relationships.
- Perform complex operations to alter the physical structure of your database.

When you modify a database object through a database diagram, the modifications you make are not saved in the database until you save the table or the database diagram. Thus, you can experiment with "what if" scenarios on a database's design without permanently affecting its existing design or data.

In any event, when you finish working with a database diagram, you have the following options:

- Discard your changes.

- Save the changes to selected tables in the diagram or the entire database diagram and have the changes modify the server database.

- Save the Transact-SQL code that your changes to the diagram would invoke against the database in a change script. If you save a change script instead of saving your changes to the database, you then have more options as to its application. You can either apply the change script to the database at another time using a tool such as Microsoft SQL Server's ISQL command-line utility, or further edit the change script in a text editor and then apply the modified script to the database.

You control the timing, type, and extent of the changes to your database by choosing how changes to the database diagram affect the server database.

Creating And Modifying Database Objects

As noted previously, you can use a Database Diagram to create and modify database objects, including the following objects:

- Tables

- Table columns and their properties

- Indexes

- Constraints

- Table relationships

You can modify tables and their columns directly in a database diagram. You modify indexes, constraints, and relationships through the Properties window for a table in your diagram.

Creating And Managing Database Diagrams

Needless to say, database diagrams duplicate functionality available to you elsewhere from the Access Database window. However, database diagrams simplify your interaction with the SQL Server by letting you view both abstract and detail information simultaneously in a somewhat more intuitive interface. In general, you can use database diagrams to do the following:

- Manipulate database objects without having to write Transact-SQL code.

- Visualize the structure of your database tables and their relationships.

- Provide different views of complex databases.
- Experiment with database changes without modifying the underlying database.
- Create new objects and relationships.
- Alter the structure of your database.

Using Database Diagrams To Perform Database Operations

You can create database diagrams of varying complexity, from diagrams that contain just one table to diagrams that contain hundreds of tables. When you first create a diagram, you are presented with a blank diagram surface to which you can add tables. In the diagram, you can do the following:

- Add tables by dragging them from the Show Table window, other open diagrams, or the view designer.
- Create new tables that have not yet been defined in the database.
- Edit the tables you have added to or created within the diagram and their properties.
- Edit the database objects, such as constraints and indexes, that are attached to the tables in the diagram.
- Create relationships between tables.
- Delete tables or relationships from the diagram.
- As mentioned previously, save an SQL change script, which places the Transact-SQL code for your changes in a file so that you can later apply them to the database or perform further editing upon them.
- Save your diagram to update the database with your changes.

It is important to note that changes that you make outside of the database diagram will pass through to the diagram. For example, if you add a table to the diagram, then proceed to add additional fields (columns) to the table from the Table designer, when you return to the diagram, that table will indicate your new fields (columns) within the designer.

Using Database Diagrams To Graphically Lay Out Your Tables

You can perform a variety of diagramming operations in a database diagram without affecting the object definitions in your database. You can customize the appearance of your diagram to meet your development needs in the following ways:

- Use the keyboard or mouse to move around in a diagram.
- Select and move tables and relationship lines.
- Change the size and shape of tables.
- Remove tables from the diagram without deleting them from the database.

- Change the magnification of a diagram.

- Open the Properties window to view properties for the objects in your diagram.

These operations affect the appearance of your diagram, but they do not affect the structure of your database.

Immediate Solutions

Needless to say, there are many issues involved in client-server programming. Most of the issues are simply logical extensions of the battles you have fought when developing for local applications, but some are unique to the client-server environment. In addition to all the examples spread throughout this chapter, there are few specific issues worthy of consideration.

Checking A Database Object For Transaction Support

As you've learned, some databases won't support transactions. Ensuring that a database does before your code tries to send transaction-processing code to the object is an important task. You can check these capabilities from both DAO and ADO. To do so from DAO, you'll use code similar to the following:

```
Sub SupportsTrans(strTableName)
  On Error GoTo SupportsTrans_Err
  Dim wrk As Workspace
  Dim db As Database
  Dim rst As Recordset
  Dim fSupportsTrans As Boolean

  fSupportsTrans = False
  Set wrk = DBEngine(0)
  Set db = CurrentDb
  Set rst = db.OpenRecordset(strTableName, _
      dbOpenDynaset)
  'Begin the Transaction Loop Only if Recordset Supports Transaction
  If rst.Transactions Then
    fSupportsTrans = True
    wrk.BeginTrans
  End If
  'Loop through recordset decreasing Quantity field by 1
  Do Until rst.EOF
    rst.Edit
      rst!Quantity = rst!Quantity - 1
    rst.Update
    rst.MoveNext
```

```
        Loop
        'Issue the CommitTrans if Everything went as Planned
        'and Recordset Supports Transactions
        If fSupportsTrans Then
          wrk.CommitTrans
        End If

SupportsTrans_Exit:
  Set wrk = Nothing
  Set db = Nothing
  Set rst = Nothing
  Exit Sub

SupportsTrans_Err:
  MsgBox "Error # " & Err.Number & ": " & Error.Description
  'Rollback the Transaction if An Error Occurred
  'and Recordset Supports Transactions
  If fSupportsTrans Then
    wrk.Rollback
  End If
  Resume SupportsTrans_Exit
End Sub
```

Notice that this code uses a Boolean variable called **fSupportsTrans** to track whether or not the recordset supports transactions. The code tests the recordset to see whether the **SupportsTrans** property evaluates to **True**. If so, the **BeginTrans** is issued and the **fSupportsTrans** variable is set equal to **True**. The **fSupportsTrans** variable is evaluated two different times in the remainder of the routine. The **CommitTrans** method is issued only if **fSupportsTrans** evaluates to **True**. Within the error handling routine, the **Rollback** method is issued only if the **fSupportTrans** variable is equal to **True**.

Using **WHILE, BREAK,** And **CONTINUE**

Although the examples earlier in this chapter use **BREAK** and **CONTINUE** alone, you don't typically use either **CONTINUE** or **BREAK** within a **WHILE** statement alone. Both **BREAK** and **CONTINUE** are often used following an **IF** or **ELSE** that are defined within a **WHILE** statement, so an additional condition can be used to break out of the **WHILE** loop. If two or more loops are nested, **BREAK** exits to the next outermost loop.

In the following code, a **BREAK** is used with an **IF** statement, both of which are within a **WHILE** statement. The **BREAK** is used to terminate the statements associated with the **WHILE** if the condition specified by the **IF** statement is **True**. The **IF** condition is **True** if the value of the local variable, **@y**, is **True**:

```
DECLARE @x int
DECLARE @y tinyint
SELECT @x=1, @y=1
WHILE @x<5
  BEGIN
    PRINT 'x still less than 5'
    SELECT @x=@x+1
    SELECT @y=@y+1
    IF @y=2
      BEGIN
        PRINT 'y is 2 so break out of loop'
        BREAK
      END
  END
PRINT 'out of while loop'
```

In the following code, a **WHILE** statement is used to permit only the rows of a table that match the criteria defined within the expression of the **WHILE** statement to have their values changed:

```
BEGIN tran
  WHILE (SELECT avg(price)FROM titles) < $30
    BEGIN
      SELECT title_id, price
      FROM titles
      WHERE price >$20
      UPDATE titles SET price=price * 2
    END
```

You must be careful when defining the **WHILE** statement and its associated statements. As shown in the following example, if the condition specified with the **WHILE** expression continues to be **True**, the **WHILE** loop executes indefinitely.

```
WHILE EXISTS (SELECT hours_worked FROM pays)
  PRINT 'hours worked is less than 55'
```

If the evaluation of the expression following the **WHILE** returns multiple values, you should use an **EXISTS** instead of any comparison operators.

Chapter 34

Web Front-End Development

In Depth

Thus far, throughout this book we've concerned ourselves with two specific types of design implementations—designing for use on a single machine and designing for use in a client-server environment. Although not specifically stated, we've generally assumed that the client-server environment that you might develop for exists within the physical boundaries of your organization—that is, either on a local area network (LAN) or wide area network (WAN).

However, there's another kind of client-server design that's become vastly more common in today's world—design for the Internet. As corporate intranets and extranets apply the browser-based model more and more, designing pages that work efficiently with the Internet will continue to become an ever-more important consideration. In this chapter, we'll consider some of the historical tools that Access provides for your use in creating Web-based applications. We'll also consider some of the other solutions at your disposal for creating Web-based applications—such as Visual Basic Active Documents and Web Objects and the SQL Server Web Assistant. In Chapter 35, we'll consider the new technology unique to Access 2000 for Web page design—Data Access Pages (DAP).

Needless to say, the Internet, and the design of Web-based front ends for databases, is an incredibly large topic. Despite some of the other large chapters in this book, we'll try not to run on for too long about designing for the Web. In fact, the discussion in this chapter will focus on a series of specific issues:

- Web basics, wherein you'll learn a little more about the construction of Web pages and addresses and their implications for Access front-end design.
- The **Hyperlink** data type, in which you'll learn about the uses for this relatively new data type, first introduced with Access 97.
- Using the Microsoft WebBrowser control with your Access applications.
- Using Microsoft Visual Basic Active Documents to create database-supporting applications.
- Using Microsoft Visual Basic's Web Objects to create database-supporting applications.
- Using SQL Server's Web Assistant to create database front ends.

The easiest way to put HTML pages representing Access data directly onto the Internet or onto a corporate intranet is to use the DAP wizard. We'll consider both of these cases in the next chapter.

However, simply covering the topics laid out earlier should be more than enough for this chapter. Before we launch into some of the specific uses of Access technology, its worthwhile to consider some of the basics of HTML and the use and importance of hyperlinks. The next several sections consider some of these issues and their implications to Access. After the discussion of some of the issues surrounding HTML and HTTP, we'll move on to more specific considerations of how these protocols apply to Access. If you're already comfortable with HTML and HTTP, you may want to skip the following sections and go directly to the discussion of the hyperlink data type.

Considering The Modern-Day Internet Model

In the mainframe era, the computing model began as a host-based model within which users working at terminals ran programs that resided on the mainframe computer. With the advent of PC workstations and computer networks, the client-server model emerged. In the client-server model, users run programs that reside on their own PCs. These client-side programs, in turn, request information across the network from a server computer. In two-tier client-server architecture, the client program handles the user interface and user-input validation while the server program processes client requests. The client and server communicate over a network.

One of the best ways to understand the traditional two-tier client-server model and how it applies to the Internet is to consider *Hypertext Transfer Protocol (HTTP)* transactions over the Internet between a client and a server. Because of widespread Internet use, the HTTP model has continued to evolve client-server processing. Within the HTTP-based model, a client (normally a browser) interacts with a server. Typically, the client-server interaction involves client requests to the server to provide specific Web pages. Because Web pages consist of HTML documents, the model is sometimes called the HTTP-HTML client-server model. As you probably know, the World Wide Web is based on this HTTP-based model, as Figure 34.1 shows.

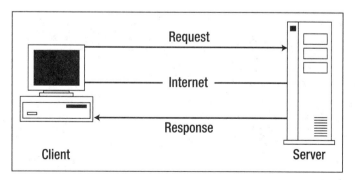

Figure 34.1   The HTTP-based Web model.

From the user's perspective, the HTTP model is inactive, offering little or no interaction. In short, the user could simply view a Web page's contents without interacting with elements on the page. Therefore, an interactive model was the natural next step for the Web's evolution. The Web gained such interactivity through the use of interactive forms programmers created with the Common Gateway Interface (CGI), Perl, and other programming languages. Using HTML entries, a Web designer can create a form with which users (via their browser) can interact with the server. When a user clicks on a form's Submit button, the browser sends the form to the server that, in turn, runs a program (normally written in Perl, C/C++, or some other Web language) that processes the form's entries. Depending on the server program's purpose, the program may generate an HTML-based response the server sends back to the browser.

The drawback to CGI-based forms processing is that the server must spawn (create) a new process every time the browser invokes a CGI script. As the number of server processes increases, the server's processing power decreases. Figure 34.2 shows a client-server model that uses CGI.

About two years ago, Microsoft introduced the Active Platform—a computing model Microsoft designed specifically for the Internet. The Active Desktop and Server are functionally symmetric, which means you can use ActiveX controls and scripting on both. In other words, both the client and the server can take advantage of ActiveX controls. As Figure 34.3 shows, the Active Platform includes the Active Desktop (the client) and Active Server (the server).

After the introduction of the ActiveX Internet model, the development of Web pages—specifically Web front ends for databases—became much, much easier. Microsoft introduced a handful of supporting technologies to go along with the new model, as well as upgrading and renaming some existing technologies. The release of new versions of development platforms like Visual Basic has also had important implications. Specifically, early iterations of the ActiveX Internet model

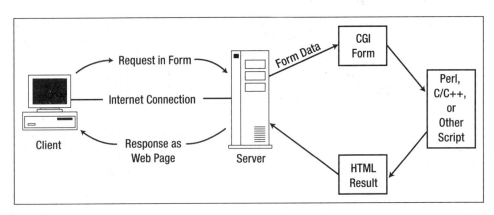

Figure 34.2 A client–server model that uses CGI.

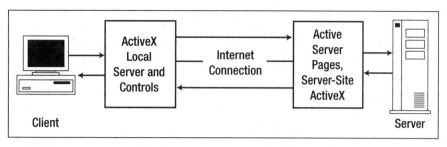

Figure 34.3   The Microsoft ActiveX Internet model.

required that the server be Windows NT running Internet Information Server (IIS), which would then serve up Web pages that only Internet Explorer (IE) could read. Figure 34.4 shows an abstraction of how the model was constructed.

Many developers pushed back hard against Microsoft on the Active Platform. When you design pages that are meant to be seen by thousands, hundreds of thousands, or millions of viewers, there's no way to control what browser they're using. Developers became forced to develop two sets of Web sites—one that ran on IE and one that ran on other platforms. Needless to say, it was a logistical nightmare. So, Microsoft introduced some new server-side technologies that, when used in conjunction with the new HTML 4 standard, simplified the design of browser-independent Web sites. Such technologies included the expansion of the Internet Server API (ISAPI) model and the creation of the new Visual Basic (VB) Web Objects technology. Figure 34.5 shows how these technologies differ from some of the other Active Platform technologies.

There are still specific features—namely ActiveX controls—you can use within Active Web pages that can make them browser specific. However, the growth of technologies like persistent client-side Java applets have made this problem less

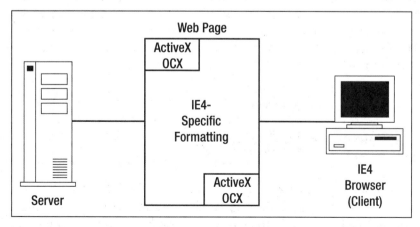

Figure 34.4   The ActiveX Internet model fully worked with Microsoft products on both ends.

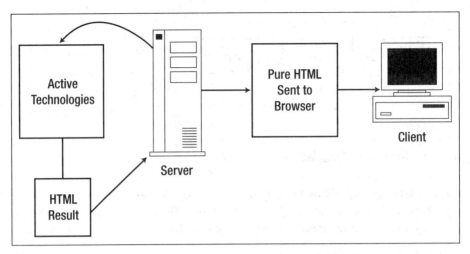

Figure 34.5   New technologies make the Active model more browser independent.

significant—and the power of the server-side tools has gone a long way toward simplifying development.

No matter what additional tools you use in your development, all Web-based objects use the underlying HTTP protocol for transmissions. The following sections discuss the HTTP protocol in more depth.

More On HTTP

As you probably know, the Internet supports more than one protocol, including the File Transfer Protocol (FTP) and HTTP protocols. The FTP protocol will provide you with a continuous Internet connection until an error occurs or until you break the connection. Because the FTP connection is continuous, it's a *state-maintaining connection*. However, the HTTP protocol is *stateless*. Stateless means that a browser and server combine to make a network connection, and both later break the connection. For example, when you connect to a Web site, your browser and the server create a connection that lets the server download the site's HTML file to the browser.

TIP: *Web authors generally name files they write in HTML as "FileName.HTML" or "FileName.HTM". Either way is acceptable to HTTP, which doesn't care about file names, their length, or their format. However, you should name your files consistently throughout your Web site. Moreover, some of the tools that you might use to create your Web front end might name files differently—with .ASP or other extensions.*

After the browser receives the file, the server breaks the connection. As your browser parses the HTML file (that is, breaks the file down into its component parts), it may encounter HTML references to images, Java applets, or other objects it must then download from the server. Each time the browser must download a file, it must establish a new connection to the server. A primary reason for developing some of the new HTML standards (such as dynamic HTML) is that stateless transmissions are, by their nature, very slow.

On one hand, because the server and your browser must establish a new connection for each file the Web server downloads to the browser (which causes delays in delivering content to users), much of the Web's promise remains unrealized. On the other hand, stateless HTML is much more efficient from the server perspective than the new proposed standards. To illustrate the differences, Figure 34.6 compares the way servers handle stateless HTML with the way servers might handle some of the proposed, state-maintaining HTML.

However, for now, the Web is built around stateless communications. Understanding the efficiency of stateless communications is important for Web development, and so the next section considers its benefits in some detail.

Better Understanding The Efficiency Of Stateless Communications

A single HTTP request and response pair is a *transaction*. HTTP uses a Transmission Control Protocol/Internet Protocol (TCP/IP) connection that it maintains only for the single transaction's duration. The TCP/IP describes the set of protocols that determines the form and transport of communications on the Internet.

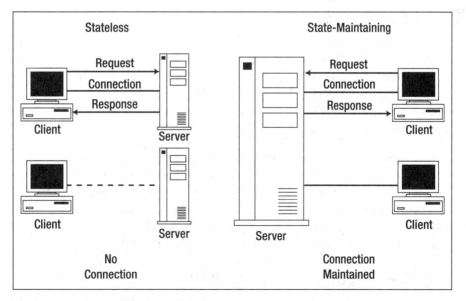

Figure 34.6   Stateless HTML transmissions versus the proposed, state-maintaining HTML transmissions.

34. Web Front-End Development

Neither the client (which usually runs a Web browser program) nor the server remembers a connection's last state. When you think about how you browse a Web site, the HTTP transactions will make sense.

When you click on a hypertext link, or *hyperlink*, your browser will move you from one site to another. Knowing that you may use a hyperlink to leave a Web site at any time, it's easier for the server to assume you're going to leave and break the connection first. If you stay, the server simply creates a new connection. If you leave, the server doesn't have to do anything else—it has already broken the connection. Releasing connections in this way lets a server respond to other clients and, thereby, improves the server's efficiency.

Recently, however, server programmers have experimented with *connection caching*, in which a server doesn't immediately close a connection after providing a response. By caching the connection, the server can respond quickly to a client should the client "revisit" the site. As Web sites become more complex and offer users more local links, connection caching (for known local links) will improve performance. However, connection caching is not currently widespread.

To really understand how stateless communications work, however, you need to understand the four steps to the HTTP transaction. The following sections explain the HTTP transaction model in detail.

Understanding The Four-Step HTTP Transaction

Before a client and server can exchange data on a local network, they must first establish a connection. Clients and servers on the Internet must also establish connections before they can communicate. On the Internet, clients and servers use TCP/IP to establish the connection. Just as with the local area network model, in the Internet model, clients request data from servers and servers respond to client requests to provide the data the client requests.

In the Internet (and Internet-based) model, clients and servers use HTTP for their requests and responses. In addition, you know that servers and clients only maintain their TCP/IP connection for one transaction (HTTP is stateless), and that servers usually close the connection after the transaction is complete. Therefore, when you put this information together, you can visualize the four-step HTTP transaction process, which the following sections describe in detail.

Step 1—Establish A Connection

Before a client and a server can exchange information, they must first establish a TCP/IP connection. As you saw earlier in this chapter, the Internet uses the TCP/IP protocol suite to let computers communicate. To distinguish protocols, applications use a unique number, called a *port number*, for each protocol. Common protocols, such as FTP and HTTP, have *well-known* port numbers that client and server programs use. Developers refer to ports as "well-known" because programmers commonly use the ports for certain protocols, even though no standards body has specified them as the "correct" ports for these protocols. The usual port assignment for HTTP is port 80, but HTTP can use other ports—provided the client and the server agree to use a different port number. Table 34.1 lists the well-known port assignments for commonly used Web and Internet protocol ports.

TIP: *TCP/IP treats all ports below 1024 as privileged ports (that is, TCP/IP reserves the ports for protocols), and all well-known port assignments fall under the privileged port category. You should never designate your own port numbers to be less than 1024.*

Step 2—Client Issues A Request

Each HTTP request a client issues to a Web server begins with a *request method*, followed by an object's URL. The client appends to the method and the URL the HTTP protocol version the client uses, followed by a Carriage Return/ Line Feed (CR/LF) character pair. The browser, depending on the request, may follow the CR/LF with information the browser encodes in a particular header style. After it completes the preceding information, the browser appends a CR/LF to the request. Again, depending on the request's nature, the browser may follow the entire request with an entity body (a Multipurpose Internet Mail Extensions [MIME]–encoded document).

An HTTP *method* is a command the client uses to specify the purpose of its server request. All HTTP methods correspond to a resource (which its URL identifies). The client also specifies the HTTP version it's using (such as HTTP 1.1). Together, the method, the URL, and the HTTP protocol version comprise the *Request-Line*. The Request-Line is a section within the *Request-Header* field. For example, a client may use the HTTP **GET** method to request a Web-page graphic from a server.

Table 34.1   Well-known port assignments on the Internet.

Protocol	Port Number
File Transfer Protocol	21
Telnet Protocol	23
Simple Mail Transfer Protocol	25
Trivial File Transfer Protocol	69
Gopher Protocol	70
Finger Protocol	79
Hypertext Transfer Protocol	80

The client uses a Request-Header field to provide information to the server about the request itself and about the client making the request. In a request, the entity body simply contains supporting data for the request. The client generally uses the name of the data the server is to transfer to compose the entity body. Figure 34.7 shows the process the client and the server perform when they make a connection and the client sends a request.

Step 3—Server Issues A Response

After a Web server receives and interprets a request message, the server responds to the client with an HTTP *response message*. The response message always be-gins with the HTTP protocol version, followed by a three-digit status code and a reason phrase. Next, the response message includes a CR/LF, and depending on the client's request, information the client requested, which the server encodes in a particular header style. Finally, the server appends a CR/LF to the preceding information, optionally following it with an entity body.

The *status code* is a three-digit number that describes the server's ability to un-derstand and satisfy the client's request. The *reason phrase* is a short text de-scription of the status code. A great number of books out there can provide you with more information on understanding the HTTP Response-Code Classes, as well as a list of the HTTP three-digit status codes and their corresponding reason phrases. However, such a discussion is beyond the scope of our work here. The HTTP protocol version, status code, and reason phrase, when combined, com-prise the *status line*.

A Response-Header may contain specific information relating to the requested resource, plus whichever MIME declarations the server may require to deliver the response. When a Web server sends a Response-Header to a client, the Web server usually includes the same information the client's Request-Header sup-plies. The entity body (which the server composes in bytes) within the response contains the data the server is transferring to the client. Figure 34.8 depicts the server's response to the client.

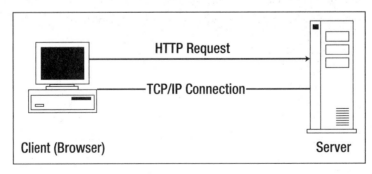

Figure 34.7   The communication between the client (browser) and the server on a client request.

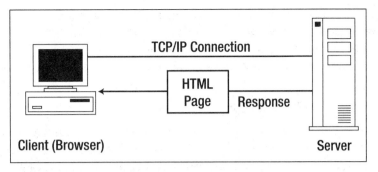

Figure 34.8   The server's response to the client (browser).

Step 4—Server Terminates The Connection

The server is responsible for terminating a TCP/IP connection with a client after it performs the client's request. However, both the client and the server must manage a connection's unexpected closing. That is, when you click your mouse on your browser's Stop button, the browser must close the connection. Therefore, the surviving computer must recognize the other connected computer's crash. The surviving computer, in turn, will close the connection. In any case, when either one or both parties close a connection, the current transaction always terminates, regardless of the transaction's status. Figure 34.9 shows a complete HTTP transaction.

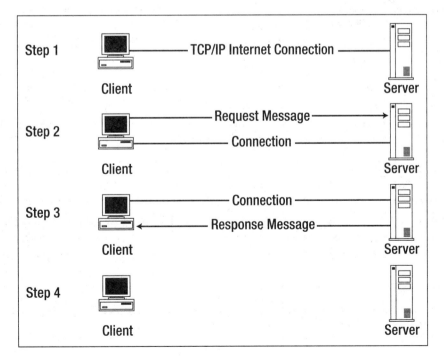

Figure 34.9   The complete, four-step HTTP transaction.

Now that you understand the underlying steps that occur during all Web-based communications, its time to consider some of the implementation issues with such development. Arguably the most important concept to understand is how the client computer knows what document or file to retrieve from the server.

A Closer Look At URIs

As you read Web literature, you may encounter the term Uniform Resource Identifier (URI). Most texts refer to URIs as Web addresses, Uniform Document Identifiers, Uniform Resource Locators (URLs), and Uniform Resource Names (URNs) combined. HTTP defines a URI as a formatted string that uses names, locations, or other characteristics to identify a network resource. In other words, a URI is a simple text string that addresses an object on the Web.

The most commonly used type of URI is a URL. To most of us, having worked with a Web browser at least minimally, URLs are a well-known concept. The following sections consider URLs in more detail.

Reviewing URLs

To locate a document on the Web, you must know the document's Internet address. A Web document's Internet address is called a URL. You can compare the relationship between a URL and a resource to the relationship between a book and its index. To find information in a book, you look in the book's index. To find a Web resource, you must use its address (URL). Web browsers use URLs to locate Web resources.

The basic syntax for a URL is simple. A URL contains two parts, the scheme and the scheme-specific-part, in the format **<scheme>:<scheme-specific-part>**. Using this structural model, you would then construct an HTTP URL using the form at **http://<host>:<port>/<path>?<search part>**.

As you can see, the URL's **<scheme>** portion is "**http**", and the **<scheme-specific-part>** identifies a **host**, an optional **port**, an optional **path**, and an optional **search_part**. If you omit the **port** element in the URL, the URL will default to the protocol port 80 (the well-known port for HTTP). Don't include the **search_part** within your URLs because HTTP doesn't currently implement the URL's **search_part**, though you'll often see it in combination with scripted pages to pass queries.

TIP: *URLs aren't unique to the Web. In fact, several other protocols use URLs, such as FTP, Gopher, and Telnet. However, all URLs have the same purpose: to identify an object's address on the Internet.*

So, clearly, the URL plays an important role in the client's conversation with the server. In the following section, you will consider further what information the URL provides to both ends of the communication about how the communication will proceed.

Relating URLs, Protocols, And File Types

A URL not only provides an address for an Internet object, it also describes the protocol the application must use to access that object. For example, the HTTP URL scheme indicates a Web space (area), while an FTP scheme indicates an FTP space. You can think of a space on the Internet as an area reserved for information of a particular type. For example, all Internet FTP documents reside in FTP space. Figure 34.10 shows the difference between an HTTP document within a Web space and a directory within an FTP space.

A URL can also include a *document-resource identifier*. The document-resource identifier specifies the file's format—provided the file's creator followed the correct naming conventions for the resource. For example, file names with an .HTML file extension should contain text in the HTML format, and a file with an .AU extension should contain audio.

Understanding URL Pieces

As you examine a URL, you may find it easier to identify the URL's exact reference if you break the URL into pieces. To better understand this, consider the URL **http://www.klander.com/books/accessbb/2000.htm**. The URL's scheme specifies the HTTP protocol. The double slashes that follow the colon indicate that the object is an Internet object. Following the slashes, you'll find the server's address, which in this case is **www.klander.com**. Next, the slash separator specifies a directory path, **books/accessbb**. Finally, the last (rightmost) slash specifies the name (**2000**) and, optionally, the document-resource identifier extension

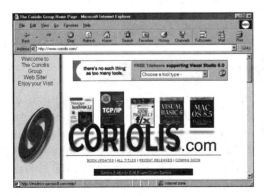

Figure 34.10   The difference in the appearance of HTTP and FTP documents.

that corresponds to the desired object (**htm**). Breaking a URL into pieces is important when you create *relative URLs*. You'll learn more about relative URLs later in this chapter. However, in the next section, you will consider in more detail the relationship of HTML files to URLs.

Looking At URLs And HTML

Explaining HTML in detail is beyond this book's scope. For this book's purposes, you can view HTML as a language designers use to structure Web documents. Hyperlinks are a significant portion of this structure. When a browser renders a Web document for display, the browser typically highlights the document's hyperlink portions to differentiate them from the normal text. When you create a Web document, HTML lets you control the creation of each hyperlink you add to the document.

Within an HTML document, you use a special HTML element, called an anchor, to represent a link in a Web document. An HTML anchor is a tag the developer inserts into a Web document to specify a link (a corresponding URL) that the browser should associate with specific text or a graphic image. Developers specify a URL within an anchor element to inform the browser of the linked resource's address. The following example contains a reference to the access2000.htm file, which is up two levels in the directory tree from the current page (as the next section, "Considering Absolute And Relative URLs," explains). The example also references a GIF image file, as shown here:

```
<A target="main" href="../../access2000.htm">
    <img align=bottom src="../../access2000.gif"></a>
```

In other words, the anchor contains the URL of the resource attached to your hypertext or, as in this example, a graphic image. The URL of the resource, which is constructed slightly differently from the absolute URLs you have seen so far, is a relative URL. The following sections discuss the differences between absolute and relative URLs in detail.

Considering Absolute And Relative URLs

A *hypertext* document is a document that contains many *links*, often known as *hyperlinks*. The Web is a maze of hyperlinked documents. When designers create a Web document, they typically link their document to other documents they or someone else created, though they may also link it to video files, graphics, and other interactive content. Each link requires a URL address to identify the corresponding object. As you've learned, browsers use URLs to locate Web documents. As designers specify URLs, they can use two address types: *absolute URLs* and *relative URLs*.

Defining Absolute URLs

An absolute URL specifies an object's complete address and protocol. In other words, when the URL's scheme (such as **http**) is present, the URL is an absolute URL. The URL **http://www.klander.com/books/accessbb/2000.htm**, then, is an absolute URL.

Defining Relative URLs

A relative URL, on the other hand, uses the URL associated with the document currently open in your browser. Using the same scheme, server address, and directory tree (if present) as the open document, the browser reconstructs the URL by replacing the file name and extension with those of the relative URL. For example, consider the URL **http://www.klander.com/books/default.htm**, an absolute URL. If a hyperlink within the **default.htm** document specifies a reference to the relative URL **accessbb/2000.htm**, as shown in the following code, the browser will reconstruct the URL as **http://www.klander.com/books/accessbb/2000.htm**:

```
<A HREF="/accessbb/2000.htm"> Access 2000 Developer's Black Book
    Information</A>
```

TIP: *When you use the single dot (.) in front of the relative URL (for example, .accessbb/2000.htm), it has the same result as entering accessbb/2000.htm.*

Where You Might Find The Links

You'll generally find hyperlinks within Access in three places:

- In tables in fields of the **Hyperlink** data type
- Embedded in special properties of command button, label, and image controls of forms and printed reports
- In Visual Basic for Applications (VBA) code

Field-Based Hyperlinks

In Access 97, Microsoft added the special **Hyperlink** data type to Jet tables, so you could store hyperlinks in a table just like normal text. The difference is when Access displays the hyperlink—on a datasheet or in a bound control on a form—you can simply click on the hyperlink with the mouse to follow the link.

The Chap34.mdb database contains a form called **frmHyperlinks** that shows several different ways you can use hyperlinks on a form. If you click on the Field Links tab of this form, you'll bring up an embedded subform bound to the

tblHyperlinkOne table in the database. Figure 34.11 shows the Field Links tab with some of the database's default entries displayed.

If you then click on one of the Web-based hyperlinks—for example, the one labeled "Coriolis Front Page," Access will launch your default browser and bring up the page, as shown in Figure 34.12.

You can enter a hyperlink into a **Hyperlink**-type field either by typing it in directly or by using the Edit Hyperlink dialog box. The "Immediate Solutions" section of this chapter details how to use the Edit Hyperlink dialog box.

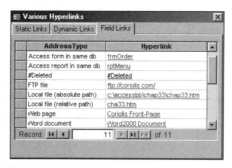

Figure 34.11 The Field Links tab shows some of the different types of hyperlinks you can reference within your tables.

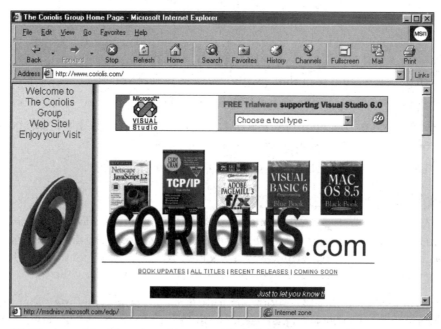

Figure 34.12 Launching the external browser after clicking on a hyperlink.

Control-Based Hyperlinks

Access forms support hyperlinks in several places. First, you can use text box, combo box, and list box controls bound to fields with a **Hyperlink** data type. You can also associate hyperlinks with the following types of unbound controls:

- Labels
- Command buttons
- Image controls

For example, the Static Links tab on the **frmHyperlinks** form contains the three types of unbound controls that can contain hyperlinks, as shown in Figure 34.13.

You create control-based hyperlinks by entering each of the hyperlink parts into three different properties of the control, as detailed in Table 34.2.

The image control doesn't have a **Caption** property, simply because the image itself is intended to be the caption for the hyperlink. You should make sure that graphics you use in such cases clearly indicate the hyperlink's purpose.

As with field-based links in tables, you can use the Edit Hyperlink dialog box to help create the hyperlink. You can click on the Build button to the right of either the **HyperlinkAddress** or **HyperlinkSubAddress** property on the control's property sheet to bring up this dialog box, as shown in Figure 34.14.

Table 34.2 *The important property settings when working with control-based hyperlinks.*

Hyperlink Part	Control Property
Address	**HyperlinkAddress**
Subaddress	**HyperlinkSubAddress**
DisplayText	**Caption**

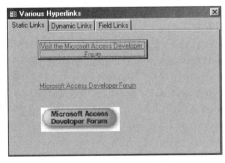

Figure 34.13   Static hyperlinks inside of a command button, a label, and an image control.

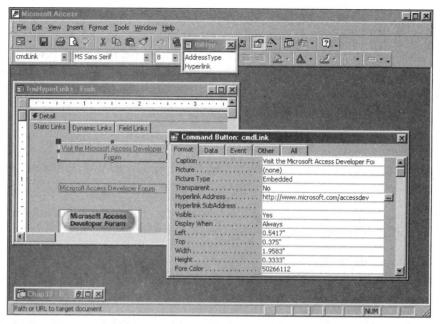

Figure 34.14   Using the property sheet to set hyperlink properties.

You can also set the **HyperlinkAddress** and **HyperlinkSubAddress** properties of a control at runtime to create dynamically-linked controls. The dynamic links tab of **frmHyperlinks** displays this feature. When you choose a hyperlink from the combo box list, code attached to the combo box control's **AfterUpdate** event sets the command button's **HyperlinkAddress**, **HyperlinkSubAddress**, and **Caption** properties. The following code shows how it's done:

```
Private Sub cboLinks_AfterUpdate()
  Dim ctlLinks As ComboBox
  Set ctlLinks = Me!cboLinks

  If Not IsNull(ctlLinks) Then
    Me!txtAddress = ctlLinks.Column(1)
    Me!cmdGo.HyperlinkAddress = ctlLinks.Column(1)
    Me!txtSubAddress = ctlLinks.Column(2)
    Me!cmdGo.HyperlinkSubAddress = ctlLinks.Column(2)
    Me!cmdGo.Caption = ctlLinks
  End If
End Sub
```

The row source for the **cboLinks** control is the **tblHyperlinksTwo** table. The code also sets the values of the two text boxes (just for further helpful information).

Hyperlinks On Reports

Hyperlinks operate differently on reports than they do on forms. Hyperlinks on a report are operational only when the report is exported to an HTML document. You can export a report to an HTML document using the File menu Export option when the report is displayed in print preview. Be sure to set the file type to HTML. Access will automatically generate the necessary HTML for the report. Hyperlinks are visible, but don't function, in the print preview view.

In reports, you should use unbound label or bound text box controls to store hyperlinks. When exported as HTML documents, the reports can be published on a Web server, or the files can be directly loaded using your Web browser. This latter version may be useful because it lets you distribute HTML versions of your reports without having a runtime version of Access on each user's desktop.

For example, Figure 34.15 shows the **rptCustomerOrders** report as it looks in Internet Explorer. Note that the report looks much the same as it does in the normal, print preview environment—we're simply exposing it through the browser.

Clearly, you can use hyperlinks to expose semi-fixed data—such as that within a report—on the Internet. However, you can also use hyperlinks to perform navigation within your database. The following section discusses how to do so.

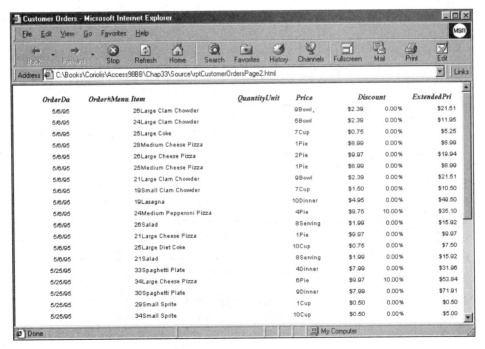

Figure 34.15   The **rptCustomerOrders** report as viewed inside a browser.

Using Hyperlinks For Intradatabase Navigation

Although you may not want to move your workgroup's entire reporting system to the Web (or even to your intranet), there'll likely be situations in which you want to make it easy for users to navigate within a database. Hyperlinks are well understood by most users, making them a good choice for such activities. By using only the subaddress portion of a hyperlink, you can jump from one database form or report to another.

By combining this technique with lightweight forms, you can create user interfaces without any code or macros. *Lightweight forms* are forms with no VBA class module associated with them. Because Access doesn't need to load VBA when opening the form, it opens the form more quickly than it does a form with VBA code behind it. Hyperlinks don't need VBA and, thus, are excellent for use with lightweight forms.

All Access forms start out as lightweight forms. Access adds a class module to the form only if you try to insert VBA code behind the form. You can make a "heavyweight" form lightweight by setting its **HasModule** property to No in design view. Doing so will, however, destroy any existing VBA code behind the form.

Although using hyperlinks for database navigation can be useful, it does have its drawbacks. First and probably most visibly, Access displays the text of the command button that contains the hyperlink just as it does other hyperlink text. In other words, the text is displayed as colored, underlined text. After the user follows the hyperlink, it changes color—a look that's useful on a page-based program but rather irritating in a switchboard or other navigation tool.

You can control Access's formatting of hyperlinks by setting properties on the Web Options dialog box that you can reach from the Options dialog box General tab. However, changing this setting will affect all hyperlinks in the database. A better alternative is to change the formatting properties of the control (such as **ForeColor** and **FontUnderline**) after you've inserted the hyperlink address. Doing so will override the settings that Access made when you added the hyperlink to the control. Access will also change the mouse cursor to the hyperlink hand automatically when you move it over control—which is, however, a small price to pay for the ease of navigation that hyperlinks offer.

Taking advantage of the power of hyperlinks only gets easier when you add VBA code to the mix. The following section discusses some of the ways that you can use VBA code with hyperlinks to Web-enable your applications.

Controlling Hyperlinks With VBA

As mentioned earlier in this chapter, you can set the **HyperlinkAddress** and **HyperlinkSubAddress** properties of a control using VBA code. In addition, you can manipulate hyperlinks as objects. Hyperlink-based controls (including unbound label, command button, and image controls, as well as bound text box, combo box, and list box controls) have an additional property, **HyperLink**, that doesn't appear on the control's property sheet. You can use this property to establish a reference to a VBA **Hyperlink** object. Table 34.3 shows a summary of the properties and methods for the **Hyperlink** object.

Considering The Address And SubAddress Properties

The **Address** and **SubAddress** properties perform pretty much as you might expect. The following code fragment prints the hyperlink information for a text box named **txtHyper** to the Immediate window using the **Hyperlink** object properties:

```
With Me!txtHyper.Hyperlink
  Debug.Print .Address
  Debug.Print .SubAddress
End With
```

Considering The AddToFavorites Method

As you might expect, the **AddToFavorites** method adds the hyperlink to your browser's list of favorite sites. Its syntax is simple—it supports no parameters (meaning it'll also add the hyperlink to the root tree of your favorites). The invocation looks like this:

```
Hyperlink.AddToFavorites
```

The following code, then, adds the hyperlink stored within the **txtHyper** control to the browser's favorites list:

```
Me!txtHyper.Hyperlink.AddToFavorites
```

Table 34.3 The Hyperlink object has limited methods and properties.

Type	Name	Description
Property	**Address**	Address component of the hyperlink
	SubAddress	Subaddress component of the hyperlink
Method	**AddToFavorites**	Adds the hyperlink to the browser's favorites list
	Follow	Jumps to the hyperlink using the default browser

Using The Follow And FollowHyperlink Methods

The **Follow** method links directly to a specified hyperlink. It takes several parameters, as shown in the following prototype:

```
Hyperlink.Follow [( [newwindow], [addhistory], [extrainfo],
    [method], [headerinfo] )]
```

Table 34.4 explains the parameters for the method in more detail.

The **FollowHyperlink** method of the **Application** object is very similar to the **Follow** method of the **Hyperlink** object. With the **FollowHyperlink** method, however, you don't need to establish a reference to a **Hyperlink** object. Instead you can simply use **FollowHyperlink** to jump to any arbitrary address.

VBA, then, adds functionality for the management of databases and information across the Internet. Microsoft has also provided their WebBrowser control to developers to help them more easily build Web-enabled applications. The following section discusses the WebBrowser control in detail.

Using The Microsoft WebBrowser Control

As you've learned, in general, when you click on a hyperlink that refers to an HTML page, Access will spawn an instance of your default browser to use when viewing the page. Often, however, you may want to provide your users with certain Web browser-based functionality within your applications. You can browse Web pages within an Access form using a Web ActiveX control such as Microsoft's WebBrowser control. This control automatically installs with Access 2000.

Table 34.4   The parameters for the Follow method of the Hyperlink object.

Parameter	Description
newwindow	Boolean value that, when set to **True**, opens the document in a new window. Default is **False**.
addhistory	Boolean value that, when set to **True**, adds the hyperlink to the History folder. Default is **True**.
extrainfo	String or byte array that specifies additional information about the hyperlink. You can use this to specify a search parameter for an Internet Database Connector (IDC) or Active Server Page (ASP) file. Default value is **Null**.
method	Integer that specifies the format of the **extrainfo** argument. Can be **msoMethodGet**, for a string argument that's appended to the address (that is, it appears at the end of the address with a question mark separating the string from the rest of the address). Alternately, it can be **msoMethodPost**, indicating that it's a string or byte array that's posted to the page.
headerinfo	String that specifies additional HTTP header text that's passed to the browser. Default is a zero-length string.

The WebBrowser ActiveX control has a couple of idiosyncrasies that are important to point out. These include the following:

- Unlike most other ActiveX controls, its properties (except for the **TopLevelContainer** and **Busy** properties) aren't merged with the Access property sheet or exposed via a custom property sheet

- Help for the control doesn't come with Internet Explorer

The Chap34.mdb file includes several forms that have support for the WebBrowser control. In addition, the "Immediate Solutions" section of this chapter details some of the navigation methods you can use with the control.

In addition to ActiveX controls, Microsoft provides a battery of Active technologies to help with your Web development. One of the most important of these is the ActiveX document, discussed in detail in the following section.

Working With ActiveX Documents

One of the most interesting, and useful, types of ActiveX components is the *ActiveX document*. An ActiveX document is a special file that you can download from a Web server. When the browser sees an ActiveX document file, it automatically loads the corresponding ActiveX document server program to your hard disk, and that program takes over the whole browser window to display the contents of the document.

The Microsoft Internet Explorer browser isn't the only ActiveX document container, however. The Microsoft Office Binder program also runs ActiveX document server programs, storing the several ActiveX documents in a single disk file. Working with ActiveX documents is a little more complex than working simply with controls; the following section covers some of the underlying issues of working with ActiveX documents.

Understanding ActiveX Document Theory

Before you start working with them, it's helpful to discuss ActiveX documents within the context of Component Object Model (COM) and object linking and embedding (OLE). An OLE embedded server program runs in a child window of an OLE container application and occupies a rectangular area in a page of the container's document, as shown in Figure 34.16.

Unless an embedded server program is classified as a miniserver, it can also run alone. In embedded mode, the server program's data is held in a storage inside the container application's file. The embedded server program takes over the container program's menu and toolbar when the user activates it by double-clicking on its editable area.

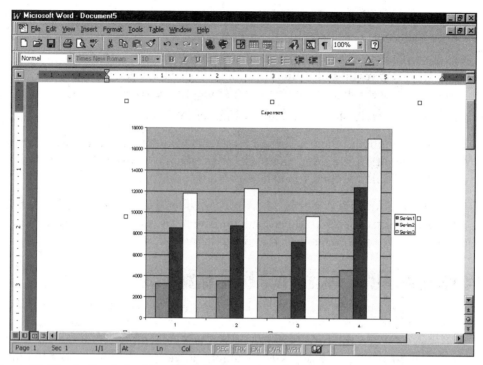

Figure 34.16   An Excel chart in a Word document is a common embedded server example.

In contrast to an embedded server, an ActiveX document server takes over a whole frame window in its container application, and the document is always active. An ActiveX server application, running inside a container's frame window, runs in about the same way it would in standalone mode. You can see this for yourself. Office includes an ActiveX container program called Binder. Moreover, all the Office applications have ActiveX server capability. Figure 34.17, then, shows two Word documents and an Excel spreadsheet within a single binder.

Like an embedded server, the ActiveX document server saves its data in a storage location inside the ActiveX container's file. When the Office user saves the Binder program's contents from the File menu, Binder will write a single Office Binder Document (OBD) file to disk. The file contains one storage area for the Word document and another for the Excel spreadsheet.

Running An ActiveX Document Server From Internet Exchange 4

Despite the Binder's usefulness in responding to certain specific business requirements, it's both more fun and (generally) more useful to run an ActiveX document server from within Internet Explorer than it is from within Binder. Rather

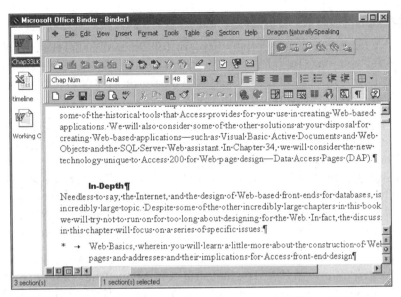

Figure 34.17 An Excel spreadsheet and two Word documents inside a binder.

than load a stored item only from an OBD file, the server program can load its storage from the other side of the world. You simply enter a URL in the browser, such as **http://www.anycompany.com/accessbb/chap34.doc**, and a Microsoft Word document will open inside the browser window, taking over the browser's menu and toolbar. That does, of course, assume that you've installed the Microsoft Word program. If not, a Word document viewer is available, but you must install it to your hard drive before you download the file.

An ActiveX document server won't let you save your changes back to the Internet host, but it'll let you save them on your own hard drive. (In other words, the server disables File Save but enables File Save As.)

TIP: *Internet Explorer recognizes documents, worksheets, presentations, and so on not by their file extensions but, instead, by the object's globally-unique class identifier (CLSID) inside the files. In fact, if you rename a Word document with an .XLS or .XLW extension, Internet Explorer will still load the file as a Word document (and will load the Word container, as well).*

The companion CD-ROM that accompanies this book includes a simple ActiveX document program written in Visual Basic that accesses the Chap34.mdb database. To run it, load the Chap34Doc.Htm file into Internet Explorer.

In addition to ActiveX documents, which you can create from Visual Basic, Visual C++, or other development platforms, Visual Basic 6 adds support for WebObjects. The next section discusses WebObjects in detail.

Understanding Visual Basic WebObjects

As you've learned in several other chapters, full-fledged Visual Basic projects will often offer you more functionality in some ways than VBA-enabled Access databases will. One of the features of VB that VBA doesn't natively support is the new **WebClass** object set (supported in VB6).

The ASP API was exposed to VB5 through a simple but restrictive interface. You had to do everything by hand; simply getting to the "Hello World" stage was difficult. The VB6 Web classes make it easy to write a DLL that takes over the server, managing all aspects of interaction with the browser. You can control as much—or as little—of the data as you need to manage, in both directions. Because you work at a higher level of abstraction than you do when dealing with the API, you can focus on the tasks at hand rather than the details of implementing them.

The IIS projects are browser independent because all the logic is performed on the server side through IIS4. You have full control over the content your applications send, so you can tailor your projects for Internet Explorer clients. However, you don't have to limit your user base because your apps run on the server— meaning, the pages can serve Navigator clients just as easily. WebObjects are pretty straightforward if you are an experienced VB programmer; the following section provides you with a brief overview of the technology.

WebClass Essentials

HTML templates, which are HTML files included in a **WebClass** project, can be sent to the browser by VB code. You need to create your template initially outside the VB Interactive Development Environment (IDE). But once you create and import it into the project, you can maintain it by bringing up the editor of your choice—such as Notepad or FrontPage—from within the IDE.

To change editors in the IDE, select the Options entry from the Tools menu, then click on the Advanced tab. Enter the path to your editor in "External HTML Editor." The default editor is Windows Notepad. You can use whatever HTML designer you're comfortable with.

HTML templates can be as simple or as complex as necessary. Once you import them into the project, you can link their elements to VB event code.

The **WebClass_Start** event fires when a user requests the URL for your application. A simple application (Simple.vbp on the CD-ROM) needs only one line of code to serve up a template file from its **WebClass_Start** event, as shown here:

```
Private Sub WebClass_Start()
  Template1.WriteTemplate
End Sub
```

Before you write that code, you should create the **WebClass** project in the designer. In the Project tree for Simple.vbp, double-click on WebClass1 (WebClass1.Dsr) to bring up the designer.

The first step: Import your HTML template file. If you don't have an HTML template file, create one using Notepad or any other editor. For the Simple.vbp example, the simple HTML file looks like:

```
<html>
<body>
Chapter34--WebClass Example
</body>
</html>
```

Then name the file Simple.htm and import it into the designer. To import a file, either right-click on the designer's tree panel and select "Edit HTML Template," or click on the toolbar button with the IE Globe icon.

When you import a template, the designer creates a copy of it to protect your original file. So in this project, the actual project file is "Simple1.htm." This distinction is important if you ever decide to edit an existing imported template from outside the designer.

The **WebClass_Start** event is a counterpart to the **Form_Load** event in a traditional VB application. The **WebClass** object also has other events, including **Initialize** and **Terminate**, similar to their traditional VB counterparts.

The **WriteTemplate** method sends the specified template to the browser. If your project has more than one template, you can use the **NextItem** property to tell the project which template to start with, as shown here:

```
Private Sub WebClass_Start()
  Set NextItem = Template1
End Sub
```

When you use this technique, you should place the **WriteTemplate** call in the appropriate template's **Respond** event, as shown here:

```
Private Sub Template1_Respond()
  Template1.WriteTemplate
End Sub
```

NextItem is also useful whenever you want to force a specific item to be processed under program control. You can write logic that sends pages to users based on data they supply, without being limited to a hard-coded order of presentation.

Selecting an item—by setting the **NextItem** property from the server side—fires its **Respond** event. A client-side request for an event that doesn't exist also fires the event.

You can also create HTML on the fly in VB code, whether or not you're using templates. To do so, use the **Response** object's **Write** method to send string data to the browser. Because you're using the **Write** method to write actual HTML, you must include any formatting instructions within the text you send. For example, don't use **vbCrLf** if you want to insert a line break. Instead, you should place **<p>** where you want to break the line.

While WebObjects provide you with an effective tool for publishing information to the Internet or a corporate intranet, like ActiveX documents they do require knowledge of another programming environment. However, SQL Server provides you with tools that you can use to publish to the Internet directly against an SQL Server database, as discussed in the next section.

Using SQL Server To Publish To The Internet

Database access with the IIS system is provided by giving you open database connectivity (ODBC) to the HTML pages that execute on the server when the user makes a request of the system. In this section, you'll see how to set up pages, what types of information you can provide, and how you can enhance the presentation of the information to make it the most meaningful to the people who request it.

TIP: Be aware that the database connector files are likely to contain and convey sensitive and sometimes very confidential information. For example, they'll contain query information that calls out column names, table names, and database sources that map to your ODBC configurations on the server.

In addition, when users click a link to a database connector file, they'll be able to see where you're keeping your scripts and other programs, because it'll show up in the URL that's displayed to them.

It's extremely important that your programs, scripts, and supporting files reside in the scripts subdirectory structure and that you provide **Execute Only** privileges on that directory. Be sure you don't provide **Read** privileges. This will open your system to unneeded possibilities for trouble because people would be able to browse and review the applications that are the core of your system.

When working with SQL Server to publish to the Internet, you will generally need to set up certain features of IIS before you begin. The following section discusses how to set up the Internet Database Connector, the first step in this process.

Setting Up The Internet Database Connector

The IIS provides access to the ODBC layer with the use of the Internet Database Connector, or IDC. The IDC acts as a go-between for your system, providing the interaction between what is seen in the viewer in terms of HTML and how the information is queried at the database level.

When users specify the IDC file in the URL from the browser, they're asking the IIS system to use the IDC file and its statements to query the database and return the results. The IDC is specified in the URL, but the HTX file, or HTML Extension file, is what is actually returned to the user. The HTX file, still a standard HTML file, indicates how the resulting data is displayed, what lines constitute the detail lines of information, and more.

The engine that's doing the database work with ODBC is HTTPODBC.DLL. This DLL, included when you install the IIS system, is an ISAPI application that runs as an extension to the server software. This extension is database aware and is able to use the two source files, the IDC and HTX files, required to give the information back to the user.

TIP: *If you didn't install the ODBC component of IIS, you'll need to do so to use the IDC. This not only installs the ODBC portions of the environment, but also configures the server to be aware of the IDC files you'll be using. If you don't install the ODBC components, when users click the IDC link on their Web page, they'll see a prompt to download the IDC file, rather than view the results of the query.*

When you install IIS, the ODBC option must be selected. Though it may not indicate disk space requirements if you've already installed ODBC from other applications, it'll still be necessary to install it to activate the IDC capabilities.

The following code shows a sample IDC file taken from the samples included with the server. The sample installs into the \scripts\samples subdirectory on your system in the IIS directory structure.

```
Data source: web sql
Username: sa
Template: sample.htx
SQLStatement:
+SELECT au_lname, ytd_sales from pubs.dbo.titleview
    where ytd_sales>5000
```

TIP: *Depending on your installation, the IIS directory structure may vary from machine to machine.*

You can indicate more than one SQL statement by using the IDC parameter more than once in the IDC file. Start each SQL statement with the **SqlStatement:** heading. You'll be able to access both results sets in the HTX file.

When this file is loaded by IIS, IIS examines the extension and determines what application should be used for the source file. For certain items, including the IDC extension, the server comes preinstalled, knowing what to do with the source when it's requested. One of the very powerful capabilities and features of IIS is that it's able to use the same Windows-based extension resolution to determine what to do with a given request. Files with a .GIF extension, for example, are known to be graphic images, and files with an .IDC extension are database connector "applets." You set up custom keys in the Registry. Associations are set up in the tree location shown here:

```
location:HKEY_LOCAL_MACHINE
SYSTEM
  CurrentControlSet
    Services
      W3SVC
        Parameters
          ScriptMap
```

If you add a new entry, make it of the type **REG_SZ** and indicate the extension to associate. You'll need to include the period before the extension—for example, .IDC—to correctly map the association. For the value, indicate the path and file name that should be executed when the specified extension is loaded. Remember to provide the path from the root, and start the path with a backslash because this will ensure that IIS will be able to locate the application, regardless of the current working directory.

If you're indicating parameters to the call, you can use **%s** on the key value where you indicate the application to run. For example, suppose that you have a DLL that you want to run whenever a request is received to open a file with a .FUN extension. Your entry would be as follows:

```
.test = c:\inetsrv\scripts\test\testdll.dll %s %s
```

When you use this option, the first time you use **%s**, you'll receive the application to run that was passed in the URL. For example, if your TESTDLL is an application that processes a text file and searches it for a given value, you would expect the user to be passing in the text file and the value to search for. When you provide the URL at the browser level, you first indicate the location of the file you want to run. A question mark is next, followed by any applicable parameters to the call.

For the examples here, the URL that would be used would be something like **http://serv1/scripts/search.text?text+to+find**. The resulting command line would then be **c:\inetsrv\scripts\test\testdll.dll search.test text+to+find**. As you can see, each of the two items specified—the source file and search text—is passed as a command-line parameter.

TIP: *Because parameters are passed as a single string to your application, as shown here with the **text+to+find** string, your application must be able to parse out the plus signs and rebuild the string. In general, you'll do so within a buffer that can be used by your application to search the database or text file, as needed.*

The results-formatting file, or HTX file, is where things can get a little tricky. As you'll see later in this chapter, the real power and capability of your system is exposed with the HTX file. Until the information is provided to the template, it's of no use to the requester as he or she won't yet have seen the information. You can have one of the best, most comprehensive databases around, but if the presentation of the data isn't what your audience needs, the information might as well be under lock and key.

As mentioned earlier, the IDC source file indicates the ODBC data source that's used to access the database on your system. From the IDC file listing, notice the data source item. This item indicates that the Web **sql** data source will be used. Before this sample will work on your system, you must have installed and configured the data source for that name using the ODBC control panel applet.

In the next couple of sections, you'll see how to set up the ODBC data sources for both SQL Server and Microsoft Access. You can use any 32-bit ODBC data source with your IIS application, and changes between setting up other data sources should be minimal; therefore, if you use the information presented here, you'll find that the IDC can work with nearly any database installation you may need to use.

Building ODBC Data Sources For SQL Server Databases

One of the most common reasons for problems with the database connector is the setup of the ODBC data source. This is true across database sources not specific to the SQL Server, so it's important to understand the details of the driver setup for access to the data by IIS.

You may recall that IIS is running as a service. This means that while it's running, it's not logged in as you, the administrator; instead, it's running in the background, logging in when needed as either the anonymous user you've created or as a validated user that's been authenticated by the NT security subsystem. Because you want to give this service access to a database and because you don't know whom the service will be logging in as, you need to configure the database source a bit differently than you may be accustomed to.

Microsoft includes an option in the ODBC configurations to support a System Data Source Name (DSN). These special data sources give you a way to implement a globally available data source. Because users who log on may have different levels of access to your system and resources, you need to use the System DSN to make sure they have access to the right databases, regardless of where they log in or who they log in as.

TIP: *If you find that you receive errors trying to access an ODBC data source from your Web pages, one of the first things you should check is whether the data source you're referencing is set up as a system data source.*

When you start the ODBC manager utility, if the data source is listed in the initial dialog box, it's defined as a user-based data source, not a System DSN. Remove the user-based DSN and redefine it as a System DSN, and you'll be able to see the database.

Remember that the only data sources that the Database Connector can use are System-level data sources.

After you select System DSN, you'll be able to use essentially the same options to configure the drivers. Note, too, that you can have more than one driver at the system level. This allows you to arrange drivers for the different applications you'll be running on the Web. The Data Source Name you provide is what you'll be using in the IDC file as the data source, so be sure to make note of the database configuration names you select.

In most cases, you'll want the configuration to be as specific as possible. If it's possible to indicate a default database or table, be sure to do so. It'll take some of the variables out of the Web page design you'll be doing. By specifying as much information as possible, you'll help ensure that the information is accessible. Working with Access databases is similar, as you will see in the following section.

Building ODBC Database Sources For Access Databases

Microsoft Access database data sources are established the same way as they are for the SQL Server. You must configure each data source as a System DSN, making it available to the IDC as it logs in to NT's security subsystem.

Of course, there'll likely be changes in the **SQLStatement** options you indicate in the IDC file. These differences relate to how Access interprets the SQL elements. However, the statements should be nearly identical, especially in those cases where you're issuing SQL statements that are basically **SELECT** statements, rather than calling stored procedures (which, as you know, aren't supported by Access databases).

When you create the DSN, you'll be prompted to select the database with which ODBC should connect. Be sure to provide this information because, even though you can indicate it in code, you can make the connection to the database far more bulletproof with this option turned on. The system won't have to guess where to go to get the information.

Building DSNs and using Web pages to access them is generally pretty straightforward, in terms of initial design. However, IDC has some general limitations that you should be aware of—most importantly, in the security model's implementation. The following section discusses security concerns in more detail.

User Rights And Security Concerns

Database access using the IDC provides a wide-open query system to your database. You shouldn't allow users to have system-administrator-level access to your databases just because it provides a way for someone to gain unwanted administrative access to your system. Instead, consider one of two options. First, if you're allowing anonymous connections to your site, be sure the user you've indicated as the anonymous user (usually **IUSR_<machine name>**) has appropriate rights to the databases that'll be needed.

The way the login process works is to first validate the user using the anonymous login if it's enabled. If it is enabled and the user indicated as the anonymous user doesn't have sufficient rights, he or she will receive an error message that indicates he or she may not have rights to the object(s) requested.

If anonymous login is disabled, the IDC will use the current user's name and password to log on to the database. If this login fails to gain access, the request is denied, and the user is prevented from accessing the database requested.

In short, if you want anonymous users gaining access to your system, you'll need to create the user account you want to access the information. Next, assign the user to the database and objects, allowing access to the systems needed.

The second option you have is to use NT's integrated security with SQL Server. Using this method, the currently logged-in user will be logged on to SQL Server, and the same rights will be in force.

All of the considerations that you have addressed so far, including security and connection concerns, have been focused on static Web pages. However, one of the most important uses of these technologies is the creation of dynamic Web pages, as discussed in the next section.

Building Dynamic Web Pages

Dynamic Web pages, those that build themselves on the fly to provide up-to-date information, are going to quickly become the mainstay of the intranet and Internet. This is because, with a dynamic Web page, you can always count on getting the latest and greatest information. With the IDC, you can create these dynamic Web pages and have them work against a database to retrieve the information you need to let the user review.

Three components form this type of page:

- Initial source HTML document often containing form fields or other options
- The IDC file for making and carrying out the database commands and data acquisition
- The HTX file for presenting the information returned

You'll need to take these samples and adapt them to your organization's way of doing business on the Internet. In short, the HTML code that may be required consists of the field, list box, and check box options provided by HTML. By using these options and ODBC connectivity, you enable the user to search the possibilities for making a meaningful interface for the user.

When you create a form that you'll be using to prompt the user for information, you create fields and other controls much as you do when creating an application. You'll name the fields, then pass the name and its value to the IDC to be used in your database query, if you desire. In the next sections, you'll see how to create these files and what makes them drive the output pages with the information from the database.

Building Initial Forms To Prompt For Values

Generally speaking, you'll start the process of working with a database by presenting the users with a form, allowing them to select what information they need. As will often be the case, you have the ability to create forms that allow input that can be used to form the SQL statements you'll be passing to the data source. In the cases where you're creating a form, you'll see two basic HTML tags—the **<INPUT>** and **<FORM>** tags—that allow you to designate actions to take and information to accept on behalf of the user. The following code shows a simple form that prompts for an author name to be searched for in the author's table:

```
<HTML>
<HEAD>
<TITLE>
Chapter 34's Very Simple Demonstration Form
</TITLE>
</HEAD>
<h1>Sample Form for Database Access</h1>
<FORM METHOD="POST" ACTION="/scripts/accessbb/chap34.idc">
Enter Name to Find in the Pubs Database: <INPUT NAME="au_name">
<p>
<INPUT TYPE="SUBMIT" VALUE="Run Query">
```

```
</FORM>
</BODY>
</HTML>
```

The key elements are the **POST** instructions and the text box presented to the user. The **<FORM>** tag indicates what should happen when the form is executed. In this case, the form will send information to the server, hence the **POST** method. The **<ACTION>** tag calls out the program or procedure that's run on the server to work with the information sent in. In the example, the chap34.idc file is called and passed the parameters.

It's not immediately apparent what these parameters might be, but if you examine the one or more **INPUT** fields, you can see that they're named. The following syntax is the basic, required element if you need to pass information back to the host in a forms-based environment:

```
<INPUT NAME="<variable name>">
```

The **<variable name>** is the name you'll use to reference the value provided by the user. Much as you define a variable in VBA by dimensioning it, you must define and declare the different variables and other controls used by your HTML. Other attributes can be used with the **<INPUT>** tag, including **VALUE**, which allows you to set the initial value of the item you're declaring. For example, the following line declares a new variable, **MyName**, and assigns an initial value of **Klander** to it:

```
<INPUT NAME="MyName" VALUE="Klander">
```

For the preceding example, the intention is to create a very simple form that allows the user to type in a name, or portion of the name, that can be used to search the **Author** table in the **Pubs** database. Creating forms, then, is pretty easy once you know the basic tools. Retrieving data—specifically, data from a stored query—is slightly more difficult. Doing so is discussed in the following section.

Building Server Query Source Files

The query source files reside in files in your **SCRIPTS** area and have a file name extension of .IDC by convention. When the URL is accessed, the server will run the indicated IDC file. As mentioned earlier in this chapter, the IDC file contains the SQL statements and directives necessary to carry out the commands as needed.

> **WARNING!** To reiterate the note earlier about security, be sure you place your IDC files in directories that have been configured with Execute, but not Read, privileges. This is important because if users can review your source files, they can see column names, table names, SQL login names and passwords, and so on. This is information you want to make sure is private.

TIP: *You can call SQL Server's stored procedures from an IDC file if you want to specify them in the SQL statement portion of the file. To do so, use the following syntax:*

```
EXEC MySP_Name Param1[, Param2...]
```

*Include the name of your stored procedure in place of **MySP_Name**. In the stored procedure, be sure you're returning result sets, even if they represent only a status value indicating success or failure on the operation. Remember, as with other ODBC data sources, the stored procedure will be passed to the server, and the client will await the response. If your stored procedure doesn't return a value to the calling routine, you may give the user the impression that you've caused the browser to become frozen.*

After you've retrieved the values you want to display, you can move on to the results set source files. These files do the work of formatting and displaying information to the user and are explained next. The following section discusses results set source files in detail.

Building Results Source Files

The results files are where the fun begins in working with the data that comes back from the query. The HTML extension files, with file name extensions of .HTX, are referenced in the Template entry in the IDC. These files dictate how the information is presented, what the user will see, whether items that are returned actually represent links to other items, and so on.

When the URL is accessed, the server is going to run the indicated IDC file. As mentioned earlier in this chapter, the IDC file contains the SQL statements and directives necessary to carry out the commands as needed.

When you design data-oriented pages, you'll want to make sure you take advantage of HTML's start- and end-tag metaphor. To put it simply, for many of the different items in HTML, when you establish a tag, for instance **<HEAD>**, until the reciprocal argument, **</HEAD>**, is encountered, the feature you enabled with the first instance of the keyword is in force.

Needless to say, all this creation makes for some complex steps in creating frontends. SQL Server includes an additional feature—the Web Page Wizard—to simplify the creation of Web pages, and to save you time in deploying applications to the Web.

Using SQL Server's Web Page Wizard

As you're sure to have noticed, the race to bring content to your Internet site and make all different types of information available to the user base has been fast and furious. One of the recent advances is the capability to have the database engine automatically generate Web pages for you based on content in the database.

With SQL Server 6.5 (and 7.0), you have the ability to schedule a task in the system to automatically create these HTML documents at time intervals ranging from a one-time run to many times per day. You can use this capability for a number of things, including reporting on your server's activity levels to you as an administrator.

In the following sections, you'll see how to set up these automatically generating pages and what the results of the process are. It's not possible to go into great detail on how to use SQL Server, form good database table design, and other administrative issues regarding SQL Server because they warrant a much more comprehensive discussion than the single group of sections here.

Prerequisites For SQL Server

Before you can successfully use the Web Page Wizard and the processes it'll create, you'll have to have set up your server to allow for this type of access. Specifically, the Web Page Wizard relies on the task manager and **SQLExecutive** service. You must have the **SQLExecutive** service established to automatically begin on startup of your server.

To confirm that the service is set to automatically start, select Services from the Control Panel. Scroll down through the list of services installed until you see the **SQLExecutive** service.

If the service isn't already started, click the service and select Startup. You'll be able to set the options that govern when the service is active and, most importantly, when it'll be started by the operating system. You'll want to make sure you indicate a valid user account that'll be used to log in to SQL Server. This account must exist in both SQL Server and the User database for your domain if you aren't using integrated security, and the user name and password must be the same in both SQL Server and the domain.

If you're using integrated security, selecting a user from the domain user's list will also provide the name to be logged in to the SQL Server.

TIP: It's a requirement that the information you provide as it relates to the user and password is valid in SQL Server. You'll also need to ensure that the account you indicate has access to the database you're reporting against and the MSDB database because these are key to the creation of the page.

If you don't set the **SQLExecutive** to start automatically, the services required to generate the Web content you're arranging won't be available, and the page won't be generated.

If this is the first time you're setting these options, and the **SQLExecutive** wasn't previously started, when you select OK to save the user ID and startup option changes, you'll need to reselect the **SQLExecutive** service, then select Start.

Once you have ensured that your environment meets the prerequisites for SQL Server, you can proceed to use the wizard. The following section explains how to use the wizard to build Web pages.

Using The Wizard

The SQL Web Page Wizard is located in the SQL Server program group on your system. You can run the wizard from a workstation or from the server. In either case, it'll generate the pages for you in a directory you'll specify later in the process.

From the initial SQL Server log in dialog box you're presented with from the wizard, you'll need to provide an appropriate login that'll allow you access to all tables and databases you want to use in providing content for your page.

The option to use Windows NT Security to log on assumes you're using integrated security. If you are, selecting this item means that you don't have to provide separate login account and password information prompted for earlier in the dialog box and that the users will be logged on with their own security rights intact for SQL Server. Their NT logon name is used as their SQL Server logon name.

Selecting The Content For The Page

When you select Next, you'll have three initial options. The first option, Build A Query From A Database Hierarchy, allows you to use the point-and-click interface and indicate the tables and other items you want to include in your query that'll be used to generate the page.

If you select the Free Form Query option, you'll be able to create any SQL statement you need to fulfill the requirements for your software. Be sure to select the database you need to work against from the "Which database do you want to query?" list box, or you may end up querying the wrong table, and you'll need to come back and rewrite the query or queries on which you based the page.

Using this option also means that you're taking all responsibility for the formation of SQL Server–specific calls. The query you enter will be passed along and executed by the server.

The final option you have in setting up the source of information for your page is to call a stored procedure. When you select the Use A Query In A Stored Procedure button, you'll be able to provide information on the database and stored procedure you want to use. You'll also notice that the text of the stored procedure is shown in the dialog box. You can use this information to verify that you've selected the correct stored procedure.

Stored procedures are a powerful mechanism for optimizing your server and providing good database query tuning. You can also take advantage of the fact that if you have another system based on SQL Server and if you're using a stored procedure to produce the results for a printed report, you may be able to reference the same stored procedure in the dialog box and create the report in HTML, making it available at any time.

The text box showing your stored procedure is provided as reference only; you can't make changes to the code here. If you need to make changes to the code, you'll need to do so by updating the stored procedure in SQL Server. This can be done with ISQL/W, the SQL Enterprise Manager, or any other utility you may be using to manage your stored procedures.

Setting The Update Interval

The next dialog box will prompt you for the frequency at which you'd like to have the page rebuilt. Because the database is the source of information for the page, this item may take some work. The reason is you'll need to talk with all of the users of the application that creates the data in the database and determine how frequently it's changed. A frequency set too small will cause additional overhead on the server as it handles the request. The impact on performance should be minimal, but if many, many requests come in for data pages such as this, it may begin to show on the access times to the server.

Your time-frame options and their associated parameters are as follows:

- *Now*—No parameters.
- *Later*—Specify date and time that the page should be created (once only).
- *When Data Changes*—Select data tables and indicate anticipated change that should be monitored as a trigger to update the HTML code.
- *On Certain Days Of The Week*—Indicate day of week and time of day.
- *On A Regular Basis*—Specify number of hours, days, or weeks that should pass before the item is regenerated.

Setting Page Options

Two different dialog boxes contain information about final formatting. Formatting options include headings for the page, column names on the resulting document, or changing the title or output location of the resulting HTML code. These are the steps you'll be using to create the database-related HTML you establish.

After you've made any changes you need, you can select Finish to generate the code that'll be used to execute the different operations that manage the wizard and its pages. Now, whenever the page is referenced by a browser, the HTML generated by the wizard will be the results. The user will be able to see the new view you've constructed and will be assured of up-to-date information.

TIP: One thing you'll want to consider including on every page you generate is a link to another page on your site. For example, you may always want to include a link with the following attributes:

Description: Return to Home Page

URL: **http://www.klander.com/default.htm**

It's a good idea to come up with a set of links that you include on each page on your site. These may be back to the home page, back to a search page, and back to a copyright page, for example. Consistency across your site will make it much easier for users to navigate and to understand.

Once you fulfill all the steps described in these sections, the wizard will create the page for you. Understanding what the wizard actually does to your database is important, however, so we will consider it further in the next section.

Seeing The Results In SQL Server

It's helpful to review your SQL Server installation to understand what's happening when you implement a wizard-generated Web page. A couple of things have happened when you create a page in this manner:

- A master stored procedure is inserted into your database.

- A page-specific stored procedure is inserted into your database.

- A new task is created to be run by the SQL Executive at the intervals you requested.

The master stored procedure, **sp_makewebpage**, is created in the database you're setting up. This is used by the wizard to create the code necessary to generate the page. You won't be making changes to this or the other stored procedures, and if you ever want to re-create it, you can run the wizard again and create another page in the same database. This will create the stored procedure for you.

The page-specific stored procedure is created with a name that begins with **Web_** and includes a unique numeric name that contains the date it was created. If you review the stored procedures, you'll see that they're encrypted, so you won't be able to make any changes to them directly. Of course, the easiest way to make any changes you need is to remove the stored procedures and their associated tasks from SQL Server and re-create them using the Web Page Wizard.

By selecting the Server menu Tasks option, you can review the tasks created to run the page at the intervals you indicated. You can quickly determine that the Web pages are queued up and ready to go.

You can also check to make sure a Web page generation process is occurring as you'd expect by clicking the History button from the Task Scheduling dialog box. When you do, you'll see a dialog box that indicates the times the procedure has run and whether it was successful. It's a good idea to start with the history review process in any diagnostics you need to run in the future should you encounter problems. In most cases, you can quickly determine exactly what's wrong by just doing some quick investigation with the Task Scheduler.

Keep in mind that you can also change the frequency at which your page is generated by modifying the task scheduling options. If you double-click the page you want to modify, you can set all the different options that control how often the page is generated. This might be helpful if you find that, after installing several pages and your site traffic picks up, you need to lessen server load a bit to provide better throughput at peak times. Simply change the times at which the pages are generated, and you'll be set.

Immediate Solutions

Using The Edit Hyperlink Dialog Box To Enter Hyperlinks Into A Field

As you learned earlier in this chapter, you can enter hyperlinks into database fields easily, either by typing the hyperlink in directly or by using the Edit Hyperlink dialog box. To open the Edit Hyperlink dialog box, right-click within a **Hyperlink** field and select the Hyperlink menu Edit Hyperlink option from the pop-up menu. Figure 34.18 shows the Edit Hyperlink dialog box.

The Edit Hyperlink dialog box provides you with all the tools you need to insert hyperlinks into your database. The Text To Display field lets you specify what text the hyperlink should display—as you saw earlier in the chapter, a hyperlink doesn't necessarily have to display its actual address, but should display meaningful text about the address.

You should then enter the file information in the Type The File Or Web Page Name text box. Note that you can browse for the file or Web page to insert by clicking on either of the buttons to the right. Alternately, you can display a list of recent files, browsed pages, and inserted links.

Down the left-hand side of the dialog box are a series of options you can use to control what the hyperlink links to or does. You can link to another object in the

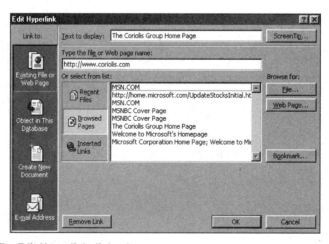

Figure 34.18   The Edit Hyperlink dialog box.

same database, or you can use the hyperlink to create a new document. Finally, your hyperlink can point to an email address.

Using Relative Addresses Within Your Database

You can use relative addresses within your database for hyperlinks, as shown by some of the examples in Figure 34.11. You can then set the base URL for your database in one of two places. The easiest place to do so is within the Database Properties dialog box, as shown in Figure 34.19.

Alternately, you can use code to set the base address, using an assignment statement that looks similar to the following:

```
Currentdb.Containers!Databases. _
    Documents!SummaryInfo. _
    Properties![Hyperlink Base] = http://www.coriolis.com/
```

TIP: *Jet stores hyperlink data internally as a **Memo** field with a special bit mask (**dbHyperlinkField**) set on the field's **Attributes** property. Hyperlinks are really a function of how Access interprets these special **Memo** fields. In fact, if you access **Hyperlink** fields from outside of Access—for example, from a Visual Basic program—you'll get memo data with no special hyperlinking capabilities.*

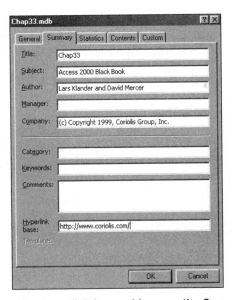

Figure 34.19   You can specify a hyperlink base address on the Summary tab of the Database Properties dialog box.

Navigating With The WebBrowser Control

Navigating with the WebBrowser control is fairly intuitive. In the Chap34.mdb database, the form **frmBrowse** embeds a WebBrowser control in a page that also contains command buttons for navigation. The code to manage the navigation is behind the buttons. For example, if the user clicks on the Back button, the program invokes the following code:

```
Private Sub cmdBack_Click()
  On Error Resume Next
  Me!webBrowse1.GoBack
End Sub
```

The code simply invokes the **GoBack** method against the control (and uses error trapping in the event there is no back information). Similarly, the **GoForward** method navigates forward through the history list, as shown here:

```
Private Sub cmdForward_Click()
    On Error Resume Next
    Me!webBrowse1.GoForward
End Sub
```

Finally, you can use the browser's built-in home setting to display the user's default home page, as shown here:

```
Private Sub cmdHome_Click()
    On Error Resume Next
    Me!webBrowse1.GoHome
End Sub
```

Chapter 35

Using Data Access Pages For Web Front Ends

In Depth

As you saw in Chapter 34, a wide variety of tools and techniques are at your disposal for placing front ends for your databases on the Web or on your corporate intranet. In addition to the many means not discussed in that chapter—such as Cold Fusion or other server products—Access 2000 provides a very convenient method for converting your applications into Web pages that your users can easily access using a simple front end.

Understanding Data Access Pages

Access 2000's primary development tool for this type of publishing is called a *Data Access Page (DAP)*. Microsoft has integrated DAPs so closely into the Access Interactive Development Environment (IDE) that they've actually added them onto the Database window. Figure 35.1 shows the new DAP tab (called Pages) in the Database window.

As you can see, the tab offers you three options for working with DAPs—creating with a wizard, creating from Design view, and editing a currently existing page. In the following sections we'll consider each of these options, as well as the Save As option that you can use to convert forms. We'll also consider some differences between DAPs and forms.

Probably the most common uses of a DAP will be as a vehicle for displaying and editing existing data, as a means for adding new data, or as a method of display-

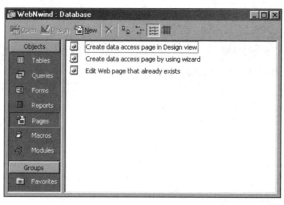

Figure 35.1   The new DAP tab (called Pages) in the Database window.

ing output only, using a report-style DAP page. Fortunately, Access provides numerous features that enable you to build DAPs that greatly ease the data-entry process for your users. Access also makes it easy for you to design DAPs that allow your users to view data but not modify it, view and modify data, or add new records only.

Strategies For Creating Data Access Pages

Needless to say, DAPs open up a whole new world of possibilities for database front-end design. Although they aren't necessarily the greatest thing ever, they're useful tools in responding to four specific needs: analyzing data, entering and editing data, making projections, and reviewing data. The following sections discuss how you can use DAPs to perform such tasks.

Analyzing Data

Arguably, the best way to analyze data from a Data Access Page is to use an Office PivotTable list control. The PivotTable control lets you reorganize data in different ways, but it downloads the necessary data only once (unless a change results in a change to recordset organization). The control's ability to provide data rapidly and in an interactive manner makes it very useful in DAP design. You can bind a PivotTable list to data in the database or use data from a Microsoft Excel spreadsheet. You can use the PivotTable list as the only control on a page or use it in combination with other controls. However, keep some important considerations in mind when working with PivotTable list controls:

- When using a PivotTable list on an ungrouped page, place the PivotTable list control and other controls either in the body or in the data section.

- When using a PivotTable list on a grouped page, place the PivotTable list and any other bound controls in the data section.

- When using a PivotTable list on a grouped page, make sure the PivotTable list is in the innermost group level.

- When using a PivotTable list on a grouped page, if the PivotTable list is the only control in a section, delete or hide the navigation section for the group level that the PivotTable list is in.

- Finally, when using a PivotTable list on a grouped page, make sure the **DataPageSize** property in the Sorting And Grouping box is set to 1.

Modifying Or Entering Data

Perhaps the most common implementation of a DAP is as a Web-based form that users can employ to enter, edit, and delete data in the database. Although most of the design rules for forms still hold, keep in mind the additional considerations listed on the next page.

- You can place controls either in the body or in the section. If you aren't binding the page to a data source, you can delete the section.

- Create only one group level for the page. The Sorting And Grouping box will list only one group record source. Note that, if you do grouping for the page from within the Page Wizard, the wizard will automatically make the page read-only if you place grouping levels on the page.

- Make sure the **DataPageSize** property in the Sorting And Grouping box is set to 1.

- You should use the Office spreadsheet control (explained later) to perform calculations on the fields in a record. After you perform the calculations, you can either display the calculated values in the spreadsheet control or hide the control and display the calculated values in bound HTML controls.

- If you want to edit data from tables that have a one-to-many relationship, create one page that's bound to the table on the one side of the relationship and another page that's bound to the many side. Then you can use the Insert Hyperlink dialog box to create a link between the two pages. To display the data from both pages on a single browser page, you can use an HTML editor to create frames within the browser—specifying the one page as the left frame and the many page as the right frame.

Creating A DAP For Making Projections

You can use the Office chart control to analyze trends, show patterns, and make comparisons on the data in your database. If you need to perform calculations on data, you can provide users with an enabled Office spreadsheet control in which they can do so. If you use a spreadsheet control in this fashion, be sure to keep in mind the following design considerations:

- When using an Office spreadsheet control on an ungrouped page, you can place the spreadsheet control and other controls either in the body or in the section. Again, you can delete the section if you don't need it.

- When using a spreadsheet control on a grouped page, place the spreadsheet control and other controls bound to fields in the database in the section. You can use a spreadsheet control in any group level.

- Make sure the **DataPageSize** property in the Sorting And Grouping box is set to 1 for the section that contains the spreadsheet control.

Using Pages For Data Review

Pages give you a way to let your users interact with large amounts of data across the Internet or a corporate intranet in a selective way. By expanding and collapsing groups of records, users can focus on just the data they want to see. Keep the following points in mind when you create a group page and want to make it load faster into Internet Explorer:

- Use Bound HTML controls instead of text boxes.
- Make sure the **ExpandedByDefault** property is set to No for all group levels. Users will use the Expand control to expand the information they need.
- Make sure the **DataPageSize** property in the Sorting And Grouping box, which determines the number of records displayed in a group on a page, is set to a lower number rather than a higher number or to All. The lower the number, the faster the records are displayed

Describing The Data Access Page's Components

Like Access forms, DAPs contain a few sections, each of which has its own function and behavior. An Access DAP has three sections:

- Caption
- Group Header
- NavigationSection

Unlike forms, the Group Header section of a DAP is the main section—at least for the display of data (rather than the Detail section). It's the section that's used to display the data of the table or query underlying the DAP. As you'll see, the Group Header section can take on many different looks; it's very flexible and robust.

The Caption section is used to display information that doesn't change from record to record (such as a page title). The NavigationSection is used to display navigation information about the record being viewed, as well as letting the user perform tasks such as setting filters (unless you disable these features, as discussed later). Command buttons that control the DAP are often placed in the Group Header or NavigationSection of the DAP. An example would be a command button that allows the user to view all the projects associated with a particular client. Controls can also be used to help the user navigate around the records associated with the DAP.

Selecting The Correct Control For The Job

Windows programming in general, and Access programming in particular, isn't limited to just writing code. Your ability to design a user-friendly interface will often determine the success of your application. Access and the Windows programming environment offer a variety of controls; each is appropriate in different situations. The next sections discuss each control that the DAP structure supports, outlining when and how you should use each one.

Labels

Labels are used to display information to your users. Attached labels are automatically added to your DAP as you add other controls such as text boxes, drop-down list boxes, and so on. They can be deleted or modified as necessary. Their default captions are based on the **Caption** property of the field that underlies the control to which they are attached. If nothing has been entered into the **Caption** property of the field, the field name is used for the caption of the label.

The Label tool, found in the toolbox, can be used to add any text to the DAP. Click the Label tool, and click and drag the label to place it on the DAP. Labels are often used to provide a description of the DAP or to supply instructions to users. Labels can be customized by modifying their font, size, color, and so on. They can't be modified by the user at runtime, but they can be modified at runtime using VBScript code.

Text Boxes

Text boxes are used to obtain information from the user. Bound text boxes display and retrieve field information, whereas unbound text boxes gather information from the user that's not related to a specific field in a specific record. For example, a text box can be used to gather information from a user regarding report criteria.

Text boxes are automatically added to a DAP when you click and drag a field from the field list to the DAP and the Display Control property for the field is set to Text Box. Another way to add a text box to a DAP is to select the Text Box tool from the toolbox. Click to select the Text Box tool, then click and drag to place the text box on the DAP. This process adds an unbound text box to the DAP. If you want to bind the text box to data, you must set its **Control Source** property.

Combo Boxes

Access offers several easy ways to add a combo box to a DAP. If the **Display Control** property of a field has been set to Combo Box, a combo box is automatically added to a DAP when the field is added to the DAP. The combo box automatically knows the source of its data as well as all its other important properties.

If the **Display Control** property of a field hasn't been set to Combo Box, the easiest way to add a combo box to a DAP is to use the Control Wizard. The Control Wizard, when selected, helps you to add combo boxes and list boxes to your DAPs. Although all the properties set by the Combo Box Wizard can be set manually, using the wizard saves both time and energy. If you want the Combo Box Wizard to be launched when you add a combo box to the DAP, make sure the Control Wizard tool in the toolbox has been pressed (switched on) before you add the combo box. You'll learn more about adding combo boxes to your DAPs in the "Immediate Solutions" section of this chapter.

Combo boxes are extremely powerful controls. Though covering them in much detail is beyond the scope of this book, you'll use and analyze them in several different implementation environments over the course of the examples and solutions.

List Boxes

List boxes are very similar to combo boxes but differ from them in three major ways:

- They consume more screen space.

- They let the user select only from the list that's displayed. This means that you can't type new values into a list box (as you can with a combo box).

- They can be configured to allow you to select multiple items.

As with a combo box, the **Display Control** property of a field can be set to List Box. If the **Display Control** property has been set to List Box, a list box is added to the DAP when the field is clicked and dragged from the field list to the DAP.

The List Box Wizard is almost identical to the Combo Box Wizard. (You'll learn about both wizards in the "Immediate Solutions" section of this chapter.) After running the List Box Wizard, the List Box properties affected by the wizard are the same as the Combo Box properties.

Check Boxes

Check boxes are used when you want to limit your user to entering one of two values. The values entered can be limited to Yes/No, True/False, or On/Off. You can add a check box to a DAP in several ways:

- Set the Display control of the underlying field to Check Box, then click and drag the field from the field list to the DAP.

- Click the Check Box tool in the toolbox, then click and drag a field from the field list to the DAP. This method adds a check box to the DAP even if the Display control of the underlying field isn't a check box.

- Click the Check Box tool in the toolbox, then click and drag to add a check box to the DAP. The check box you've added is unbound. To bind the check box to data, you must set the **Control Source** property of the control.

Bound HTML Control

The Bound HTML control is, essentially, a "thin" text box control. You can use it within your DAPs to display information from a record source. In general, HTML controls will load faster through the browser than text box controls will. This is especially helpful in large, banded DAPs. Bound HTML controls are windowless controls, while the text boxes used in Internet Explorer are windowed controls. Thus, each text box requires a certain amount of overhead to be drawn on the screen.

If the controls wrap text in a way that you don't like, select the Bound HTML control, open the property sheet to the Format tab and set the **Overflow** property to "Hidden."

Note, however, the limitations of Bound HTML controls: You can't use them with updateable fields, and you can't index or filter based on the contents of a Bound HTML control.

Scrolling Text Control

The Scrolling Text control, which the DAP toolbox includes, is the same as the Microsoft Marquee ActiveX control. This control lets you place text within a rectangular area on a DAP, which will then scroll around the control based on the properties you specify. You might use this control to provide update information, advertising, or similar marquee-style displays on your DAPs.

Although the control can be bound to a data source, you're probably more likely to set the text the control displays within the Design view. Alternately, you might use VBScript that you attach to the page to change the control's scrolling value based on actions that the user performs on the page (such as moving the mouse over a specific field, and so on).

Hyperlinks And Bound Hyperlinks

The Hyperlink control lets you place hyperlinks on your DAPs—a necessary tool for helping users navigate around the DAPs that comprise the Web front end. When you insert a Hyperlink control onto a DAP, Access will display the Insert Hyperlink dialog box, as shown in Figure 35.2.

As you can see, the dialog box lets you insert a hyperlink to an existing file or Web page, a hyperlink to another DAP, or a hyperlink to an email address. It also lets you create a new page and insert a hyperlink to that new page on the current page.

You can also use the Bound Hyperlink control, which lets you specify the hyperlink that appears within the page by binding the control to a **Hyperlink** field in a

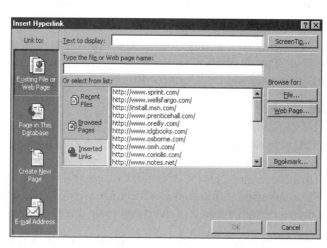

Figure 35.2   The Insert Hyperlink dialog box.

database. For example, if you have an Employees database, you might associate a **Hyperlink** field with each employee, which corresponds to that employee's email address. You can then use a **Bound Hyperlink** field on the DAP to display that email address with the employee information. The user could then click on the email address to send email to the employee in question. As the user navigated the database, going from employee to employee, the value in the **Bound Hyperlink** field will also change to reflect the value stored for each new record.

Other Controls You Can Use With DAPs

In addition to the standard controls detailed in the previous sections, you can use a large number of other controls with DAPs. In fact, you can insert any ActiveX control that supports Web downloading into a DAP. Table 35.1 lists some of these controls and their uses.

Each of the controls listed in Table 35.1 is included with the Access 2000 installation; however, a great number of third-party controls are available that you can also use when designing DAP pages.

Changing The Format Of A Control

When you first build a DAP, you might not always make the best choice for the type of control to display each field on the DAP. Alternately, you might make what you think is the best choice for the control only to find out later that it wasn't exactly what your user had in mind. Unfortunately, though you can easily convert a control type when working with forms, the DAP designer doesn't let you change the type of a control once it's placed. You must, instead, delete the existing control, and replace it with the new control.

Understanding And Using DAP Properties

DAPs have many properties that can be used to affect the look and behavior of the DAP. The properties are broken down into three categories—Format, Data, and Other. To view a DAP's properties, you must select the DAP in one of two ways:

- Click the DAP Selector—the blue bar across the top of the DAP designer window

- Select the Edit menu Select Page (Ctrl+R) option.

After you select the DAP, you should choose the View menu Properties option to display the DAP's properties. Alternately, you can right-click on the DAP and select the Properties option from the pop-up menu.

Table 35.1   Other ActiveX controls that you can use with DAPs.

Control Name	Description
Expand	When you use grouping levels or other ordering controls in your DAPs, you may want to provide users with the ability to expand the detail information or hide the detail information and view only summary information. The Expand control lets you do just that.
Hotspot Image	The Hotspot Image control lets you place an image onto a DAP and associate that image with a hyperlink. If the user clicks on the image, the browser will navigate to the hyperlink associated with the image inside the control.
Image	The Image control lets you embed an image onto your DAP page.
Line	The Line control lets you draw lines on your DAP page. You'll generally use this control either for decoration or to clarify the flow of a page for your users.
Movie	The Movie control lets you embed MPG, AVI, QuickTime, and other video files within your DAPs. In general, you'll likely provide additional scripting on the page to let the user invoke this control. For example, your Employees database might include a link to a movie file that contains an introduction for each employee in the database. Users could then click on a button on the DAP which had VBScript behind it to load and play the movie file within the control.
Office Chart	The Office Chart control lets you display charts and graphs within your DAPs. You can use the properties of the control to specify where the chart obtains its data, the appearance of the chart, and so on.
Office Pivot Table	A PivotTable is a table that summarizes, or cross-tabulates, large amounts of data. PivotTables are very interactive because the user can rotate the data, changing the way it's displayed. PivotTables are in widespread use in Excel, and the control lets you display them within your DAP using Access table data.
Office Spreadsheet	The Office Spreadsheet control is a thin-client control that lets you display data from Access within a DAP in a spreadsheet-style format.
Record Navigation	The Record Navigation control lets you provide a navigation bar to the user. If you use the Page Wizard to design your DAP, the wizard will always insert the Record Navigation bar at the bottom of the DAP. If you design your DAP from scratch, you'll need to insert this control manually (alternately, you can design your own record navigation interface).
Rectangle	The Rectangle control lets you draw rectangles onto a form. You'll generally use this control either for decoration or to clarify the flow of a page for your users.

Working With The Properties Window

After a DAP has been selected for design work, setting DAP properties (and the properties of any DAP components) is a simple task. Determining what DAP properties to set isn't quite so simple; many people have suggested that DAP design is more of an art than a science, requiring nothing so much as experience to develop quality interfaces. To view the properties for a DAP, click the Properties button on the toolbar to view its properties. Access will display the Properties window.

Notice that the Properties window consists of four tabs: Format, Data, Other, and All. Many developers prefer to view all the DAP's properties at once (in which case you can select the All tab), but a DAP has a total of over 50 properties. Rather than viewing all the properties at once, try viewing the properties by category. The Format category includes all the physical attributes of the DAP. These attributes affect the DAP's appearance. An example is the DAP's background color. The Data category includes all the properties that relate to the data to which the DAP is bound. An example is the DAP's underlying record source. The Other category contains a small number of properties that don't fit into either of the other two categories.

Working With The Important DAP Properties

As mentioned, DAPs have over 50 properties. This section covers many of the Format, Data, and Other properties of DAPs.

Format Properties Of A DAP

The Format properties of a DAP affect its physical appearance. DAPs have 25 Format properties, as detailed in the following list:

- *Background*—The **Background** property lets you specify a file name for a background to use with the page (which might be a corporate logo or a similar graphic).

- *Background Color*—The **Background Color** property lets you set the background color for the DAP. This property always defaults to *#FFFFFF* (white), but can be set to any color in the color table. If you use a background that fills the page, this property has no effect.

- *BackgroundPositionX*—This property lets you specify where to place the background horizontally on the page—at the left side, centered, or at the right side. You can also specify a distance from the left edge of the page as a percentage of the page's total size.

- *BackgroundPositionY*—This property lets you specify where to place the background vertically on the page—at the top, centered, or at the bottom. You can also specify a distance from the top edge of the page as a percentage of the page's total size.

- *BackgroundRepeat*—This property lets you specify whether to repeat the background image (tiling) or simply place one copy on the page. You can control the nature of the repeating as well—multiple copies across, multiple copies down, and so on.

- *BorderColor*—The **BorderColor** property lets you specify the color of the page border.

- *BorderStyle*—The **BorderStyle** property lets you specify the style of the border. The default is *inset*.

- *BorderWidth*—The **BorderWidth** property lets you specify the size of the border. The default is *medium*; additional values are *small* and *large*.

- *Display*—The **Display** property lets you specify how the page will be displayed. It allows you to select from seven options; whichever option you select will become the default view for the DAP. These options define how the page's contents appear, and are important considerations when using a PivotTable or other Web component.

- *FgColor*—The **FgColor** property lets you specify the default foreground color for all controls on the sheet. You can override this setting for individual controls by setting the control's **Color** property.

- *FontFamily*—The **FontFamily** property lets you specify what font family to use for the fonts on a DAP. The default is *Tahoma*.

- *FontSize*—The **FontSize** property lets you specify the default font size for the page.

- *FontStyle*—The **FontStyle** property lets you specify additional characteristics about the default font, including whether or not it's italicized, and so on.

- *FontVariant*—The **FontVariant** property lets you specify variant characteristics about the default font. Other than *normal*, the other option for this property is *small-caps*.

- *FontWeight*—The **FontWeight** property lets you specify characteristics about the font's display, including *bold, bolder, lighter*, and various intensity values. The default is *normal*.

- *Grid X, Grid Y*—The **Grid X** and **Grid Y** properties can be used to modify the spacing of the horizontal and vertical lines that appear in the DAP when in Design view. By setting these properties, you can affect the precision of the placement of objects on the DAP when the Snap to Grid option is active.

- *Height*—The **Height** property lets you specify the height of the page. The default is *auto*, which determines the page's height based on its contents.

- *Left*—The **Left** property lets you specify the leftmost position of the page. Again, this is generally automatically determined by the page's contents.

- *Overflow*—The **Overflow** property lets you specify how the page will display contents that exceed the size of the containing controls. The default is *visible*. You can also choose *hidden* or *scroll*, which forces the control to scroll data from right to left inside the control.

- *Position*—The **Position** property provides you with further control over how the page appears within the Web browser. If you use frames, Active Server Pages, JScript menus, or similar additional objects within the browser, and embed the DAP within them, or when you are inheriting style sheets, you will want to set the position to *relative*. The default is *static*.

- *TextAlign*—The **TextAlign** property lets you specify the default alignment for text on the page, whether within Label, Text Box, or other controls. You can override this property for each control on the DAP.

- *Top*—The **Top** property is used to specify the top of the DAP. This option defaults to *auto* and generally won't be changed unless you have a specific requirement to do so. You might want to set this property manually when you're inheriting style sheets from elsewhere on the Web site and have display specifics within the style sheet that appears at the top of the page.

- *Visibility*—The **Visibility** property specifies whether the page is visible or hidden. It defaults to *inherit*, which means its visibility will be set by the controlling page that opens the page.

- *Width*—The **Width** property is used to specify the width of the DAP. This option is most often set graphically by clicking and dragging to select an appropriate size for the DAP. You might want to set this property manually when you want more than one DAP to be exactly the same size.

- *ZIndex*—The **ZIndex** of the page specifies where it will appear when displayed. In general, the **ZIndex** is automatically determined based on what is open already in the application. However, if a page must always appear in front, setting the **ZIndex** will let you force where the computer displays the page.

Data Properties Of A DAP

You'll use the Data properties of a DAP to control the source for the DAP's data, to specify what actions the user can take on the data within the DAP, and to determine how the data within the DAP is locked in a multiuser environment. A DAP contains seven Data properties detailed within the following list:

- *ConnectionString*—The **ConnectionString** is the ActiveX Data Object (ADO) connect string to the data source for the page. It includes such values as the provider name, the nature of the connection, who the user logs in as, and the actual name of the data source itself. Without a **ConnectionString**, a DAP is treated as unbound.

- *Data Entry*—The **Data Entry** property is used to determine whether your users can only add records within a DAP. Set this property to *Yes* if you don't want your users to be able to view or modify existing records but do want them to be able to add new records.

- *DefaultControlType*—The **DefaultControlType** property specifies the default control type for the page. Valid values are *Text Box* or *Bound HTML*.

- *DisplayAlerts*—The **DisplayAlerts** property controls whether the page will display database alerts to the user. The default is *True*.

- *MaxRecords*—The **MaxRecords** property controls the maximum number of records displayable within a single page. Although not important for data-entry–style pages, this value can be important if you're using DAPs as report pages and returning large sets of records. The default value is *10,000*.

- *RecordsetType*—The **RecordsetType** property is used to specify whether the recordset for the DAP is a read-only snapshot or an updateable snapshot. DAPs support ONLY snapshot-type recordsets—you can't, for example, set this value to "dynaset."

- *UseRemoteProvider*—The **UseRemoteProvider** property lets you specify whether the user should use a provider on the local machine (preferable) or a provider on the remote machine (the database server) to get the data to fill the page.

Other Properties Of A DAP

In addition to the DAP properties detailed in the previous sections, some DAP properties appear only under the Other tab (and under the All tab). These properties control a variety of different features, as shown in the following list:

- *BaseURL*—The **BaseURL** property specifies the HTML **BaseURL** property for the page. This consideration is important if, for example, you place certain types of relative hyperlinks (as opposed to absolute hyperlinks) onto the page. In such cases, the browser will resolve the relative hyperlink from the **BaseURL** value. Using **BaseURL**s often simplifies Web site administration—making it easier to relocate pages without breaking links.

- *Dir*—The **Dir** property allows you to specify how the contents of the page are placed within the designer. The default is *not set*, which lets you place them as you desire. The other two settings are *ltr*, which left-justifies all the contents of the page, and the *rtl*, which right-justifies all the contents of the page. Again, you can overload this setting for specific controls with the control's **Dir** property.

- *InheritStyleSheets*—The **InheritStyleSheets** property controls whether or not the page inherits style sheets used on your Web site. This property is particularly important in intranet applications, where most pages on the site share a common style sheet. Telling the page to inherit the style sheet results in the style sheet being applied to the page, just as it would if the page was a standard HTML document.

- *LinkColor*—The **LinkColor** property is used to specify the default color for hyperlinks on the page. You'll generally use it in conjunction with the **AlinkColor** and **VlinkColor** properties, which also control the appearance of hyperlinks.

- *NodeValue*—This property is not implemented in Access 2000, but is reserved for further development by Microsoft.

- *Title*—The **Title** property specifies the title to display in the browser's window bar when the user accesses the page.

Considering The Available Control Properties

Although many different properties are available for DAPs, these properties will be consistent from DAP to DAP. Control properties, on the other hand, will vary significantly, depending on the type of control you're working with. The more common properties are covered in this section. More individualized properties are covered throughout the book as they apply to a specific topic, and you can find more about any property from within the Access online help file.

Format Properties Of A Control

Though control properties differ, Access will group them into the same three categories that it groups DAP properties into: Format, Data, and Other. The first of the property sets is the Format category. The Format category's values will vary. Most of the Format properties are consistent with the Page Format properties. However, some of the most common properties are shown in the following list:

- *Left*, *Top*, *Width*, *Height*—These properties are used to set the position and size of the control. They're generally reflected in fractions of an inch.

- *BackgroundColor*, *BackgroundImage*, *BackgroundPositionX*, *BackgroundPositionY*, *BackgroundRepeat*—The Background properties control the background of the control. Their values are consistent with property sets for the page; however, you can specify an individual image as a background for each control on the page.

- *Position*—The **Position** property lets you modify how the control is placed on the form. The default is *absolute*; however, if you set specific values for the page's **Top** or **Left** properties, you can set the control's position as being relative to these values.

Data Properties Of A Control

Just as you'll typically affiliate a DAP with a data source—a database that you connect it to with the **ConnectionString** property—you'll typically create sections on that DAP that correspond to specific data sources, such as recordsets. You'll then affiliate the controls on your DAP with specific items within that data source. Generally, each field in the record source will correspond to one control in the DAP's area for that record source. The following list describes the common control data properties to help you format the control's output correctly:

- *AlternateDataSource*—This property lets you instruct the control to get data from a different source other than the default data source for the section on the page. For example, a drop-down list box might use a query as an alternate record source.

- *Control Source*—The **Control Source** property is used to specify the field from the record source that's associated with that particular control. A control source can also be any valid Access expression.

- *DataFormatAs*—This property allows you to specify a format string or other format information to control how data in the control (returned from the data source) is displayed within the page.

- *Default Value*—The **Default Value** property of a control determines the value that's assigned to new records entered within the DAP. This property can be set within the field properties. A default value set at the field level is automatically inherited into the DAP. The default value set for the control overrides the default value set at the field level.

- *TotalType*—The **TotalType** property lets you specify summary information to place within the control. You'll generally use this property when you're creating a report-type DAP.

Other Properties Of A Control

Just as with DAPs, in addition to the Format and Data properties, most controls will have other miscellaneous properties, which Access groups together under the Other tab in the Properties window. The following list describes some of the most commonly listed properties:

- *ID*—Employ the **ID** property to name the control. This name is used when you refer to the control in code. It's also displayed in various drop-downs that show all the controls on a DAP. It's very important to name your controls because named controls improve the readability of your code and facilitate the process of working with Access DAPs and other objects (and naming doesn't mean **Text1**, **Text2**; it means meaningful names for Access objects).

- *Disabled*—Similar to the form control's **Enabled** property, this property lets you specify whether a control is enabled or disabled.

- *ReadOnly*—The **ReadOnly** property specifies whether the user can change the value displayed within a bound control. Typically, this property inherits from the data source for the control.

- *Tab Index*—The **Tab Index** property is used to set the tab order for the control. Most developers generally set the **Tab Index** property using the View menu **Tab Order** property, rather than by setting the value directly within the **Tab Index** property of the control.

- *Wrap*—When the user reaches the "end" of a control, some controls will automatically "wrap" text to the next line. This property lets you control whether the page inserts a hard return (*hard* setting) or a soft return (*soft* setting) when the control wraps the text.

Bound, Unbound, And Calculated Controls

Important differences exist between bound and unbound controls. Unbound controls are used to display information to the user or gather information from the user that isn't going to be stored within your database. Examples of unbound controls include the following:

- A label providing instructions to the user

- A logo placed on a DAP

- A combo or text box placed on a DAP so the user can enter report criteria

- A rectangle placed on the DAP to logically group several controls

Bound controls are used to display and modify information stored in a database table. A bound control automatically appears in the DAP specified in its **Display Control** property. The control automatically inherits many of the attributes that were assigned to the field to which the control is bound.

A Calculated control is a special type of control that displays the results of an expression. The data within a Calculated control can't be modified by the user. The control's value automatically changes as the values within its expression are changed. For instance, the Sales Total within an invoice DAP would change as the Price or Quantity of different objects is changed.

Scripting With Data Access Pages

As you've seen in previous chapters, most Access objects are exposed to the Visual Basic for Applications object model, which lets you apply program control to the user's actions. As you might expect, because they're designed for distribution through a browser, Data Access Pages are a bit different.

DAPs expose their functionality through VBScript, a subset and derivative of the Visual Basic programming language. Like VB, VBScript is event-oriented; most of your code with DAPs will manipulate VBScript in the background to accomplish responses to events. Moreover, most of the code in VBScript is very similar to VBA code. For example, the following script sequence might be evoked whenever the user moves the mouse over the AssetDescription control:

```
<SCRIPT event=onmouseover for=AssetDescription language=vbscript>
<!--
EmployeeID_Label.innerText = "Changed!"
-->
</SCRIPT>
```

As you can see, the event is called **onmouseover** and is the Internet Explorer equivalent to the VBA **MouseOver** event. The code within the event changes the caption of the **EmployeeID_Label** control to "**Changed!**" Presumably, there's other code elsewhere (like the **onmouseover** event for the entire page) that changes the caption back to its normal value.

In general, event scripting in DAPs takes the place of event code in Access forms and reports. The "Immediate Solutions" section details how you enter a script that's associated with a given control on a DAP, in the section entitled "Calculating A Total On A Grouped DAP."

TIP: As a side note, the scripting environment for Access is based on Microsoft Developer Studio and Visual InterDev. Although there are some changes in appearance from the VBA environment that you're used to, getting comfortable with the scripting environment won't take long.

Understanding Themes

A theme is a set of unified design elements and color schemes for bullets, fonts, horizontal lines, background images, and other DAP elements. A theme helps you easily create professional and well-designed DAPs. Microsoft provides you with a large number of themes that are installed with the Access product.

When you apply a theme to a DAP, the following elements are customized in your Data Access Page:

- Body and heading styles
- Background color or graphic
- Table border color
- Horizontal lines
- Bullets
- Hyperlink colors
- Controls

You can apply a theme for the first time, apply a different theme, or remove a theme using the Format menu's Theme option. When you select the option, Access will display the Theme dialog box, as shown in Figure 35.3.

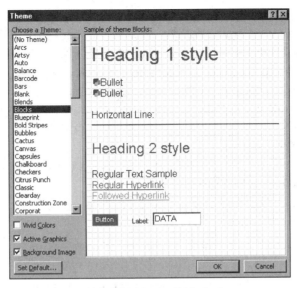

Figure 35.3   The Theme dialog box from within the DAP designer.

You can preview a theme before applying it by selecting it from the list of available themes and viewing the display of sample DAP elements in the Sample Of Theme Blocks box. Before applying a theme to the page, you can also select options to apply brighter colors to text and graphics, animate certain theme graphics, and apply a background to your DAP. Theme graphics are animated only when you view the DAP in a Web browser, not while you view the DAP in Microsoft Access.

TIP: *If you have Microsoft FrontPage 4, 98, or 2000 installed, you can use the FrontPage themes as well. Additional themes are available from the Microsoft Web site.*

Optimizing Data Access Page Performance

Because Data Access Pages are a relatively new technology, there aren't quite as many known ways to optimize their performance as there are with forms and other historical Access objects. However, you can use several known optimization techniques to make your DAPs load faster in Page view or in Internet Explorer 5. Although many of these were discussed earlier, they're worth restating and expanding here (in addition to these, typical rules for Web page design also apply):

- Avoid overlapping controls on a page.

- Make sure the **ExpandedByDefault** property in the Sorting And Grouping box is set to *No* for the highest group level. Doing so ensures that the page opens faster because it doesn't need to display all the entries at once. Setting it to *No* for lower group levels will speed up other interactions once the page is opened.

- Make sure the **DataPageSize** property in the Sorting And Grouping box is set to a lower number rather than a higher number or to *All*. The lower the number, the faster the records are displayed.

- Use Bound HTML controls instead of text boxes to display any data that isn't updateable. Common examples of appropriate places to use Bound HTML controls include autonumber values, values derived from expressions, and hyperlinks. Note, however, that you can't sort or filter the values in a Bound HTML control.

- On grouped pages (that is, where the data is read-only), use Bound HTML controls, instead of text boxes, to display data.

- On pages used for data entry, set the **DataEntry** property of the page to **True**, so the page opens to a blank record.

- On grouped pages that contain records with a one-to-many relationship, group records by table rather than by a field or expression.

- On grouped pages based on tables with a one-to-many relationship, bind each section to a table rather than to a query. Access retrieves the records from a table only as it needs to display them on the page. With a query, Access retrieves all the records before it displays any records on the page. Use a query only when you want to limit the data used on the page, calculate aggregate values, or perform a task that's possible only in a query.

This list is by no means exhaustive—it just points out some of the issues to watch for in your design.

Immediate Solutions

Creating A New DAP

You can create a new DAP in several ways. The most common is to select the DAP tab of the Database window and click New. The New Data Access Page dialog box will appear, as shown in Figure 35.4.

This dialog box lets you select from the multitude of options available for creating a new DAP. DAPs can be created from scratch using Design view or with the help of six wizards. The wizards are covered briefly before you move on to the process of creating a DAP from scratch. Even the most experienced of developers will employ the DAP Wizard to complete certain tasks.

Creating A DAP Using The Wizard

The easiest way to get started with DAPs is to use the wizard to create your first page. The steps to creating the DAP are as follows:

1. Double-click on the Create A New Data Access Page By Using Wizard option. Access will display the Page Wizard dialog box, as shown in Figure 35.5.

2. Select the table to work from to create the page. Using the Chap35.mdb database, select the Employees table. Next, click on the >> button to copy all the fields to the page. Click Next to move to the next dialog box in the wizard.

3. The next dialog box asks if you want to add any grouping levels to the page (much as the Report Wizard does). In this case, select Group By Title. When you finish, the dialog box will look similar to Figure 35.6.

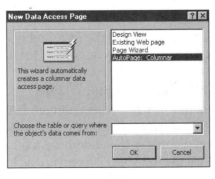

Figure 35.4   The New Data Access Page dialog box.

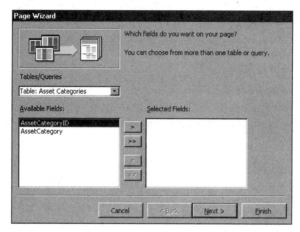

Figure 35.5   The Page Wizard dialog box.

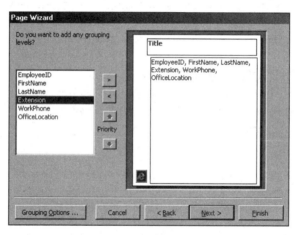

Figure 35.6   The Page Wizard with Grouping By Title selected.

4. The next dialog box tells you to select sorting levels to use with the DAP. For this example, select **LastName** and **FirstName** as your sorting fields. Click Next to move to the last dialog box.

5. The last dialog box lets you name the page and open it for viewing or additional design. Click the Finish button to exit the wizard.

Creating A DAP Using The AutoPage Wizard

The second most common way to create a simple DAP is to use the AutoPage Wizard. The AutoPage Wizard creates a DAP that contains all fields (except fields that store pictures) and records in the underlying table, query, or view. The steps to creating the DAP with the AutoPage Wizard are as follows:

1. Within the Database window, make sure the display is set to Pages. Then, click on the New Page icon at the top of the window. Access will display the New Data Access Page dialog box.

2. Select the AutoPage: Columnar option, then choose the table or query to work from to create the page within the drop-down. Using the Chap35.mdb database, select the Employees table. Next, click on the Okay button.

The AutoPage Wizard will generate a simple DAP with all the fields in the underlying table and a navigation bar across the bottom. Figure 35.7 shows the simple page created by the wizard.

Note that Access applies the default theme to the page. If you haven't set a default theme, it uses the Straight Edge theme. Additionally, when you create a page using the AutoPage Wizard, Access automatically saves the page as an HTML file in the current folder and adds a shortcut to the page in the Database window.

Creating A DAP From Design View

Although the DAP wizards are extremely powerful and useful, in many cases it's better to build a DAP from scratch, especially if you're building a DAP that's not bound to data. To create a DAP without the use of a wizard, click the Pages tab, then click New. The New DAP dialog appears. Select Design view (the default choice). If your DAP will be bound to data, use the drop-down included in the New DAP dialog to select the table or query that will serve as the foundation for the DAP. Click OK. The DAP Design window will appear as shown in Figure 35.8.

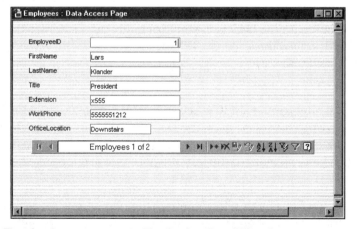

Figure 35.7 The simple page generated by the AutoPage Wizard.

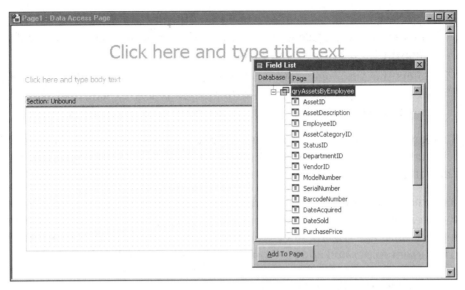

Figure 35.8   The DAP Design window.

Adding Fields To The DAP

Fields can easily be added to a DAP using the Field List window because the Field List window contains all the fields that are part of the record source for the DAP. For example, in Figure 35.7 the record source of the DAP is **qryAssetsByEmployee**. The fields listed in the Field List window are the fields that are part of the query. The record source for the DAP is the table or query that underlies the DAP. To add fields to a DAP, follow these steps:

1. Make sure the Field List window is visible. If it's not, click on the Field List button on the toolbar.

2. Locate the field you want to add to the DAP. Click and drag the field from the field list to the location on the DAP where you want the field to appear. The location you select becomes the upper-left corner of the text box. The attached label appears to the left of where you dropped the control.

To add multiple fields to a DAP at the same time, select several fields from the field list. Use the Ctrl key to select multiple noncontiguous fields or the Shift key to select multiple contiguous fields. Click and drag any of the selected fields to the DAP. All selected fields are added to the DAP at once. Although Microsoft has indicated that multiple-field selection functionality will be supported in the release of the Office 2000 product, it was *not* supported within the Beta.

Selecting DAP Objects

The easiest way to select a single object on a DAP is to click on it. When the object is selected, you can move it, size it, or change any of its properties. Selecting multiple objects is a bit trickier and can be done in several ways. Different methods are more efficient in different situations. To select multiple objects, you can hold down the Shift key and click on each object that you want to select. Each selected object is surrounded by selection handles, indicating that it's selected.

You can also select objects by lassoing them. To lasso objects, the objects must be located close to one another on the DAP. Place your mouse pointer on a blank area of the DAP (not over any objects), then click and drag. You'll see that a thin line appears around the objects that your mouse pointer is encircling. When you let go, any objects that were anywhere within the lasso, including those that were only partially surrounded, are selected. If you want to deselect any of the selected objects to exclude them from the selection, hold down your Shift key and click on the object you want to deselect. Again, as noted previously, although Microsoft has indicated that multiple-field selection functionality will be supported in the release of the Office 2000 product, it was *not* supported within the Beta— using either the Shift-click method or the lassoing method.

One other useful way to select multiple objects is to use the horizontal and vertical rulers that appear at the edges of the DAP Design window. Click and drag within the ruler. Notice that as you click and drag on the vertical ruler, two horizontal lines appear, indicating which objects will be selected. As you click and drag across the horizontal ruler, two vertical lines appear, indicating the selection area. When you let go of your mouse, any objects that are anywhere within the lines are selected. As with the process of lassoing, to remove any objects from the selection, hold down your Shift key and click on the object you want to deselect.

Moving Things Around On The DAP

To move a control along with its attached label, you don't need to select it first. Place your mouse over the object and click and drag. An outline appears, indicating the new location of the object. When the object reaches the desired position, release the mouse. An attached label automatically moves with its corresponding control.

To move more than one object at a time, you must first select the objects you want to move. Select the objects using any of the methods outlined in the previous section. Place your mouse over any of the selected objects and click and drag. An outline appears, indicating the proposed new position for the objects. Release the mouse when you've reached the desired position.

Sometimes, you want to move a control independent of its attached label, which requires a special technique. If you click on a control, such as a text box, you see that as you move your mouse over the border of the control, a hand appears with five fingers pointing upward. If you click and drag, both the control and the attached label move as a unit. The relationship between them is maintained. Placing your mouse pointer over the larger handle in the upper-left corner of the object makes the mouse pointer appear as a hand with only the index finger pointing upward. If you click and drag here, the control moves independently of its attached label. The relationship between the objects changes.

Aligning Objects To One Another

Access makes it easy to align objects within a DAP. Notice that the attached labels of both the objects are selected. To align any objects (even objects of different types), select the Format menu Alignment and Sizing option. Access will display the Alignment and Sizing dialog box, as shown in Figure 35.9.

You can align the left, right, top, or bottom edges of any objects on a DAP.

Don't confuse the Alignment and Sizing toolbar with the Align tools on the Formatting toolbar. The Alignment and Sizing toolbar aligns objects one to the other, whereas the Align tools on the Formatting toolbar align the text of an object within its borders.

Figure 35.9   The Alignment and Sizing dialog box.

Using The Snap To Grid Feature

The Snap to Grid feature determines whether the objects snap to the gridlines on the DAP as you move and size them. This feature is found under the Format menu. If you turn this feature off (it's a toggle), objects can be moved and sized without regard for the gridlines.

Most developers leave the Snap to Grid feature on all the time. However, you can use a special trick to temporarily deactivate the feature when needed. To do this, hold down your Ctrl key as you click and drag to move objects. The Snap to Grid setting is ignored.

DAP Control Sizing Techniques

Just as there are several ways to move objects, there are several ways to size objects. When an object is selected, each handle (except for the handle in the upper-left corner of the object) can be used to size the object. The handles at the top and bottom of the object allow you to change the height of the object. Those at the left and right of the object allow you to change the width of the object. The handles in the upper-right, lower-right, and lower-left corners of the object allow you to change the width and height of the object simultaneously. To size an object, place your mouse pointer over a sizing handle and click and drag. You can select multiple objects and size them at the same time. Each of the selected objects increases or decreases in size by the same amount. The relative sizes of the objects remain intact.

Access provides several powerful methods of sizing multiple objects, found on the Alignment and Sizing toolbar:

- *Size Height*—Sizes the selected objects to the height of the tallest object within the selection.

- *Size Width*—Sizes the selected objects to the width of the widest object within the selection.

- *Size Height/Width*—Sizes the selected objects to the width of the narrowest object within the selection.

Modifying Object Tab Order

The tab order for the objects on a DAP is determined by the order in which you add the objects to the DAP. This order isn't necessarily appropriate for the user. It might become necessary to modify the tab order of the objects on the DAP. Unfortunately, DAPs don't provide the Tab Order dialog box, unlike forms. Instead, you have to manually set the **TabIndex** property of the controls on the DAP to ensure that they're in the order you desire.

Adding A Combo Box To A DAP

To add a combo box to a DAP, select the Dropdown List tool in the toolbox. Click and drag to place the Dropdown List control on the DAP. The Combo Box Wizard is launched. In the first dialog box of the Wizard, you're asked whether you want the combo box to look up the values in a table or query or whether you prefer to type the values yourself. The first option should be used if your combo box is going to be used to select the data that's stored in a field. An example would be the state associated with a particular client.

Most developers rarely, if ever, use the second option, which requires that you type the values for the combo box. Populating a combo box this way makes it difficult to maintain. Every time you want to add an entry to the combo box, your application must be modified.

The second step of the Combo Box Wizard lets you select a table or query to populate the combo box. For optimal performance, you should select a query. The third step of the Combo Box Wizard allows you to select the fields that appear in your combo box.

The fourth step of the Combo Box Wizard lets you specify the width of each field in the combo box. Access will recommend that the key column for the table or query be hidden. The idea is that the user will see the meaningful English description while Access worries about storing the appropriate key value into the record.

The fifth and final step of the Combo Box Wizard prompts for the text that becomes the attached label for the combo box. The Finish button completes the process, building the combo box and filling in all its properties with the appropriate values.

Adding A PivotTable List Control To A DAP

As you saw earlier in this chapter, the PivotTable list control is one of the most useful controls for interactive page design with Access. It does have its limitations, however; although you can rearrange the layout in a PivotTable list and set properties to affect its look and behavior, you can't ever add, delete, or change the stored values in the control in a DAP. To add a PivotTable list control to a DAP, perform the following steps:

1. From the Design view, make sure that the toolbox is displayed.

2. Within the toolbox, select the Office PivotTable component. Click on the page and drag until the control is the size you want and until it displays the entire toolbar.

What you do next with the PivotTable depends on what kind of data you want to display within the control. To use the current Access or SQL Server database as the data source for the PivotTable list (that is, the database that the page is bound to), perform the following steps:

1. Display the page's Field List dialog box (select the View menu Field List option).

2. Drag from the Field List dialog box the table or query for the DAP to use with the PivotTable. Alternately, you can drag individual fields from a single record source or multiple record sources, one field at a time.

When you create a PivotTable list by dragging fields from the field list, Microsoft Access automatically sets the Data Source control option in the PivotTable properties to MSODSC, an acronym for Microsoft Online Data Source Control. This predefined system value specifies that Access will use the same data source for the PivotTable list as it does for the page itself.

The steps are a little bit different to use an external data source for the PivotTable list. To use an external data source, perform the following steps:

1. Right-click on the control and select Property Toolbox from the pop-up menu to display the PivotTable Property Toolbox.

2. Within the Property Toolbox, click the Data Source bar. The Property Toolbox will look similar to Figure 35.10.

3. Next, click on the Connection option. The dialog box will enable the button labeled Connection Editor. Click the Connection Editor button, and Access will display the Data Link Properties dialog box, as shown in Figure 35.11.

Figure 35.10   The Property Toolbox for the PivotTable control.

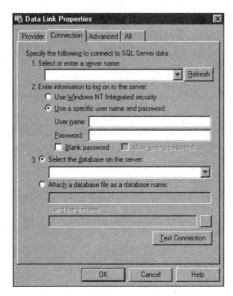

Figure 35.11   The Data Link Properties dialog box.

4. Within the Data Link Properties dialog box, click the Provider tab. The dialog box will display a list of installed object linking and embedding (OLE) DB providers. Select the OLE DB provider you want to use to retrieve the data from the list.

5. Next, click the Connection tab, then provide the necessary connection information to the data you want to use for the PivotTable list. The connection string will be similar to the ADO connection string you would use to connect to the database. If you need assistance with the dialog box, you can click on the Help button for more information about establishing the connection. You can also click on the Test Connection button to ensure that the program is able to successfully connect to the data source. After you finish the connection, click Okay to exit the dialog box.

WARNING!   *Once you set a connection, you should not move the source database; if you do, you will need to update the connection information in all the DAPs that access that database. Similarly, you should be careful about moving DAP HTML pages, as the database may not be able to locate them either, and doing so could cause your program's execution to halt.*

After selecting a connection, do one of the following steps within the Use Data From section of the PivotTable Property Toolbox:

1. To use the data from a specific record source within the database, click on the Data member option button under the Data Source option, then select the element you want from the drop-down list.

2. To use a query or command, such as a SQL statement, to select the data, click on the Command text option button, then type the query or command in the box. Make sure your query syntax conforms to the specifications for the external data source.

Finish the PivotTable list by arranging the layout and using the toolbar in the PivotTable list and the PivotTable Property Toolbox to add totals, set properties, and so on until the control looks and behaves the way you want.

You should keep a few important considerations in mind when working with the PivotTable control within your Data Access Pages. These include the following:

• To create a PivotTable list that uses data from an Excel worksheet, you have to publish the data to a Web page from Excel. If you then want to turn the exported Web page into a DAP, you should open it in Access, and then add controls bound to Access or SQL Server database data.

• When you have a Web Component control bound to an external data source on the same page with controls bound to an Access database or a SQL Server database, the component control will use a *different data source control* than the rest of the page. This may result in somewhat slower loading of the page.

• When you add a PivotTable list to a grouped page, a PivotTable list appears for each unique group and contains only records for that group. For example, on a page grouped by month with a PivotTable list containing sales information, there will be a PivotTable list for each month, which contains only the sales data for that month.

WARNING!   *You can't display the PivotTable for more than one group at a time within a single page.*

Adding An Office Spreadsheet Control To A DAP

As you've learned, you can add a spreadsheet control to a DAP to provide some of the same capabilities you have in a Microsoft Excel worksheet. You can enter values, add formulas, apply filters, and so on. You can enter raw data in the spreadsheet, import data from an external source (a Web page or a text file), or use data from other controls on the business. To add the Office Spreadsheet control, perform the following steps:

1. Within the toolbox, click the Office Spreadsheet tool.
2. Click the DAP, then drag until the control is the size you want.

3. Within the resulting control, enter the data and formulas you want to use or right-click on the control to display the Property Toolbox. Within the Property Toolbox, enter the address from which the control should import the data. You can even tell the control to update the data it displays every time it loads within the page.

You can also use the scripting model for DAPs to control the performance of the spreadsheet control at runtime.

Setting Document Properties For The DAP

There may be times when you want to set properties that apply to the entire DAP. To do so is a relatively simple process. First, open the DAP in Design view. Next, select the File menu Page Properties option (you may have to expand the menu). Access will display the Page Properties dialog box, as shown in Figure 35.12.

The Page Properties dialog box lets you set the following page properties:

- *General*—This is the same information that's displayed when you right-click the name of a file in Windows Explorer, then click Properties on the shortcut menu. The only difference is that when you view these properties in Access, the Attributes settings are read-only. You can't make changes to this tab.

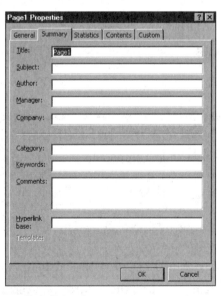

Figure 35.12   The Page Properties dialog box.

- *Summary*—The information you enter on this tab is added to the **SummaryInfo Document** object in the **Documents** collection. Summary information allows you to better identify a page both from within Access and from other programs, such as the Windows Find Files program. The Hyperlink Base setting on the Summary tab is used to create the base hyperlink path that's appended to the beginning of relative **HyperlinkAddress** property settings. Additionally, information you insert in this tab will appear when you document pages.

- *Statistics*—This information includes the date and time the active page was created, the last date and time it was modified, who modified it, the number of times it's been revised, and total editing time. Again, you can't modify the entries on this tab.

- *Contents*—This tab displays the page's title and the connection string it uses to connect to its data source. This information is read-only.

- *Custom*—The custom properties you enter become properties of the **UserDefined Document** object in the **Documents** collection. The tab provides you with a list of predefined custom properties and also lets you enter your own custom properties. You'll typically use these properties to simplify site management.

Calculating A Total On A Grouped DAP

As you've learned, you can use certain fields within your DAPs to represent totals or other summary information. To create a field that calculates a total, perform the following steps:

1. Open the DAP in Design view.

2. Add the controls that are bound to fields you'll use in the expression to the page.

3. Click the Bound HTML tool in the toolbox, and draw the control onto the page where you want the control's upper-left corner to be on the page.

4. Display the Properties sheet for the newly-placed Bound HTML control.

5. In the **ControlSource** property for the control, enter an alias and an appropriate expression. For example, if you want to compute the salary for an employee and format it as currency, with the two component fields having the names **HourlyWage** and **AnnualHours**, enter the following expression in the **ControlSource** property for the Bound HTML control:

```
Salary: Format(HourlyWage * AnnualHours, "$###,##0.00")
```

If you don't want to display the values in the fields used in the expression when the user views the page, you can hide or delete the controls. To hide the controls, set their **Visibility** property to Hidden. If a page is based on a query, you can put the expression in the page's underlying query. If you're going to calculate totals for groups of records, it's easier to use the name of a calculated field.

Note that you should really only apply this method to simple calculations involving straightforward math. If, instead, you need to do complex calculations, which may or may not use spreadsheet functions, you should probably use the Office Spreadsheet control.

Choosing A Default Theme For New DAPs

When you're designing a series of DAPs, particularly for a corporate intranet, you'll generally want to have all the pages display the same background. To set a default theme for your pages, perform the following steps:

1. Open any DAP in Design view.

2. Select the Format menu Theme option. Access will display the Theme dialog box.

3. In the Choose A Theme list, click the theme you want to be the new default theme.

4. Click on the Set Default button. Access will set the theme as your new default theme.

5. Click Yes and then click OK to exit the dialog box.

Appendix

Additional Resources

Books

The following books were used as resources for the production of this book and contain valuable additional information about the topics discussed:

Berson, Alex. *Data Warehousing, Data Mining, and OLAP*. New York: McGraw-Hill, 1997. ISBN: 0-07-006272-2. This is a data warehousing text that provides a solid introduction and overview to data warehousing, including historical background, architecture, characteristics, related hardware and software, design, implementation, and online analytical processing (OLAP).

Elmasri, Ramez A. and Shamkant B. Navathe. *Fundamentals of Database Systems*. New York: McGraw-Hill, 1997. ISBN: 0-8053-1748-1. This is a database text containing basic database concepts, relational models, data models, design techniques, structured query language (SQL), transaction processing and security, and emerging database technologies.

Haas, Robert W. and Thomas R. Wotruba. *Marketing Management: Concepts, Practice and Cases*. Business Publications, Inc., 1983. ISBN: 0-256-02956-3. This is a hardbound text covering marketing concepts, including management, organization, measurement, market segmentation, demographics, target marketing, planning and strategy, and implementation.

Modell, Martin E. *A Professional's Guide to Systems Analysis*. 2nd ed. New York: McGraw-Hill, 1996. ISBN: 0-07-042948-0. This is a hardbound primer to systems analysis covering systems analysis basics, life cycle methodology, project planning, data gathering, entity relationship diagramming approach, process and task analysis, and validation.

Siyan, Karanjit S. *Windows NT Server 4 Professional Reference*. Indianapolis, IN: New Riders Publishing, 1996. ISBN: 1562058053. This is a hardbound reference covering Windows NT Server 4 from the basics to the most advanced aspects, including installation, domains, Registry, security, Transmission Control Protocol/Internet Protocol (TCP/IP), remote access server (RAS), and a very nice primer on networking concepts.

Tenner, Arthur R. and Irving J. DeToro. *Process Redesign: The Implementation Guide for Managers.* Reading, MA: Addison Wesley Longman, Inc., 1996. ISBN: 0-201-63391-4. This is a hardbound primer about business process redesign, including process analysis, process improvement, process management, leadership, process measurement, benchmarking, and reengineering

Web Sites

Web sites, of course, come and go. Although the authors have made every effort to find and utilize current Web sites, some of these links may have changed or disappeared by this time. However, if you can't find this information, please drop us an email and we'll try to help you locate it.

The following Web sites were referenced during the production of this book and contain valuable additional information on a variety of topics:

Babcock, Charles. "Middleware Market Mushrooms." *Inter@ctive Week* (Nov. 21, 1997): no page number. Available from **http://www4.zdnet.com/intweek/ printhigh/111797/nt1117.html**. An article concerning the growing middleware market.

Cognos Corporate Web Site. Available from **http://www.cognos.com**. Home of Cognos Corporation, makers of a fine data analysis tool.

Demarest, Marc. "Building the Data Mart." *DBMS Magazine* 7, no. 8 (July 1994): 44. Available from **http://vista.hevanet.com/demarest/marc/marts.html**. An article about building data marts and data warehousing concepts.

Derbyshire, A., and K.C. Rajh. "Video Transmission Over Broadband Networks." Surprise 96 Journal, Volume 4 (Dec. 1996). Available from **http://www-dse.doc.ic.ac.uk/~nd/surprise_96/journal/vol4/arad/report.html**. An overview of video transmission techniques.

Holland and Davis, Inc. "The Change Management Toolkit." Houston, TX: Worthing Brighton Press, 1995. Available from **http://www.utsi.com/wbp/reengineering/ overview.html**. A primer concerning change management and process reengineering.

Legacy Systems Research Products/Services. Available from **http://www. costbenefit.com/product.htm**. Home of Legacy Systems, makers of a Cost$Benefit Analysis Tool (CBATool).

Malhotra, Yogesh. "Business Process Redesign: An Overview." *IEEE Engineering Management Review* 26, no. 3 (fall 1998). Available from **http://www.brint.com/papers/bpr.htm**. A primer to business process redesign.

"Competitive Intelligence Programs: An Overview." Available from **http://www.brint.com/papers/ciover.htm**. A primer to competitive intelligence.

"One Hundred Rules for NASA Project Managers." Available from **http://pscinfo.pscni.nasa.gov/online/msfc/project_mgmt/100_Rules.html**. Contains some excellent pointers about implementing project management successfully.

Palisade Corporation. Available from **http://www.palisade.com/index3.html**. Home of Palisade Corporation, makers of very good risk analysis tools.

Rauch, Stephen. "Manage Data from Myriad Sources with the Universal Data Access Interfaces." *Microsoft Systems Journal* (Sept. 1997). Available from **http://www.microsoft.com/msj/0997/universaldata.htm**. An overview and commentary on using Microsoft's Data Access Objects (DAO).

Rodrigue, Jean-Paul and Phil Croucher, eds. *The BIOS Survival Guide.* Available from **http://www.lemig.umontreal.ca/bios/bios_sg.htm**. A comprehensive guide to basic input/output systems (BIOSs).

Sikora, Thomas. "The MPEG-4 Video Standard Verification Model." IEEE Trans. *CSVT* 7, no. 1 (Feb. 1997). Available from **http://wwwam.HHI.DE/mpeg-video/papers/sikora/final.htm**. Technical paper concerning the development and specs of Moving Pictures Experts Group-4 (MPEG-4).

Strom, David. "Creating Private Intranets: Challenges and Prospects for IS." Available from **http://www.strom.com/pubwork/intrnetp.html**. A short white paper about intranet development.

WWW Virtual Library on Knowledge Management. Available from **http://www.brint.com/km**. A nice set of links to knowledge management resources and articles.

Index

Q

R

Y

Z